STATISTICAL METHODS
OF ECONOMETRICS

STUDIES
IN MATHEMATICAL AND
MANAGERIAL ECONOMICS

Editors

HENRI THEIL

HERBERT GLEJSER

VOLUME 6

1980

NORTH-HOLLAND PUBLISHING COMPANY
AMSTERDAM – NEW YORK – OXFORD

STATISTICAL METHODS
OF ECONOMETRICS

Third revised edition

E. MALINVAUD

*Institut National de la Statistique
et des Études Économiques
Paris*

Translation by MRS. A. SILVEY

1980

NORTH-HOLLAND PUBLISHING COMPANY
AMSTERDAM – NEW YORK – OXFORD

This book was originally published by Dunod, Paris, 1964, under the title Méthodes statistiques de l'économétrie. Revised French edition published 1969.

Library of Congress Catalog Card Number 80-11268
North-Holland ISBN 0 444 85473 8

Publishers:
NORTH-HOLLAND PUBLISHING COMPANY
AMSTERDAM · NEW YORK · OXFORD

Sole distributors for the U.S.A. and Canada:
ELSEVIER NORTH-HOLLAND, INC.
52 VANDERBILT AVENUE,
NEW YORK, N.Y. 10017

First edition 1966
Second edition 1970
2nd printing 1972
3rd printing 1975
4th printing 1978
Third edition 1980

局版臺業字第〇八五二號

發行人：張　澤　雲

住址：台北市羅斯福路四段六號

發行所：雙　葉　書　店

總經銷：雙葉書廊有限公司

地址：台北市羅斯福路四段六號

電話：三四一一四一九八號

郵政劃撥：七一一二六號

中華民國七十三年　月　日

Introduction to the series

This is a series of books concerned with the quantitative approach to problems in the behavioural science field. The studies are in particular in the overlapping areas of mathematical economics, econometrics, operational research, and management science. Also, the mathematical and statistical techniques which belong to the apparatus of modern behavioural science have their place in this series. A well-balanced mixture of pure theory and practical applications is envisaged, which ought to be useful for Universities and for research workers in business and government.

The Editors hope that the volumes of this series, all of which relate to such a young and vigorous field of research activity, will contribute to the exchange of scientific information at a truly international level.

THE EDITORS

Preface to the French edition

Econometrics may be broadly interpreted to include every application of mathematics or of statistical methods to the study of economic phenomena. From this point of view it is not a separate discipline, since every branch of political economy becomes econometric as soon as mathematics or statistics is applied to it.

In this book we shall adopt a narrower interpretation and define the aim of econometrics to be the empirical determination of economic laws. Econometrics rounds off theory by using numerical data to verify the existence of postulated relationships and to define their precise forms. It is therefore a branch of economic science.

Just as it is indispensable to theoreticians who could not otherwise assess the validity of their assumptions, econometrics must be of service to economists in government and business. In order that reliable predictions should be made as to the course of saving, investment or imports, the permanent characteristics of the behavior of savers, investors and importers must first have been analyzed and measured. In order to know what the future output of some product is likely to be, one must first have determined how demand varies as a function of price and consumer income.

In its methodology econometrics borrows from mathematical statistics. The latter is concerned with inductive procedures which, when applied to a set of data, allow hypotheses to be tested or the parameters of a relationship to be estimated. The fact that data, hypotheses or parameters relate to economic phenomena does not affect the logic underlying the procedures adopted.

However, to meet their own particular needs, econometricians have developed some methods which are rarely discussed in general textbooks of mathematical statistics. Classical methods certainly apply to the simplest problems. But often the nature of the hypotheses to be tested, or the structure of theoretical relationships to be estimated, imposes the adoption of more complex methods. Moreover, economic data do not satisfy the conditions required in general textbooks, and need special treatment. The statistical methods used in econometrics have a common basis in principle with those used in other fields, but they have special characteristics relating to the particular features of problems arising in economic science.

Many different inference procedures, each relevant to a particular situation, have of course been developed by econometricians to meet the needs of practical research. There is now some danger that the researcher may find himself lost in the abundance and complexity of available methods. He may see in them only so many peculiar techniques, and may well make a bad choice through failure to understand the spirit in which they were conceived and the particular problem for which each is valid.

The aim of this book is to help toward a clear understanding of the statistical methods used in econometrics. It is not confined to simple description of available techniques, but tries to provide the best possible justification for them, and to study their properties. Thus the reader should be in a position to interpret correctly the results given by these techniques in the practical situations which confront him.

Proofs will usually be given in the text, as they often help toward an exact understanding of the properties stated. However, for certain results which are particularly laborious to establish, the reader must refer to the original papers. Moreover, general theories of estimation and testing will not be given here, since they appear in general textbooks on mathematical statistics.

The text will naturally include detailed guidance on the practical application of the methods described. Some readers may regret the scarcity of examples. But this book, already of considerable size, would have been much extended, and its publication delayed, by the inclusion of a separate example for each method.

Systematic description of the foundations and general concepts of mathematical statistics will not be given. The principles of inference currently in use will be applied to economic problems.

These principles are known to be subject to criticism, and this will perhaps lead to a general revision of statistical methods. But even if this happens, time will be needed for the development of new conceptual systems, and the theories described here will certainly retain some validity.

The learned reader will note that the introduction of stochastic models is justified on the basis of subjective probabilities. Indeed it is clear, that, in economics, irregularities of the data do not in general arise in a purely random way. The establishment of a subjective theory of statistics based on the Bayesian principle would, therefore, be of great interest. But research on this line is not yet sufficiently advanced to allow the systematic application of this principle.

The book is divided into five parts. The first is introductory; it presents and discusses the principles involved in the statistical treatment of economic data. The second is devoted to linear estimation, which has a major role in econometrics as in other fields of applied statistics, and which must be given here in sufficient generality for our purposes. The third deals successively with non-linear regressions and models with errors on the variables. The fourth considers the particular problems raised by the use of time series. The fifth is concerned with estimation in simultaneous equation models.

A thorough reading of the book demands a good mathematical background and knowledge of general theories of probability calculus and mathematical statistics. Some chapters are particularly difficult, requiring sustained effort from the reader who seeks complete mastery of the proofs.

However, the book ought to be equally useful to those who wish to understand the general nature of econometric methods, but have neither time nor means for an exhaustive study of their properties. Some whole chapters and many sections are relatively simple in exposition and contain only elementary proofs. Readers wishing to avoid the most difficult parts of the book are advised to read the following[†] chapters and sections: 1.1 to 1.5, 2.1 to 2.10, 2.15, 2.16, 3.1 to 3.4, 3.7, 3.9, 4, 5.1 and 5.2, 6.1 to 6.6, 6.9(i), 10.1 to 10.3, 11.1 to 11.4, 12.1, 12.2, 12.5, 13.1, 13.2, 14.1 to 14.3, 15 and 16.

So many people have helped in the preparation of this book that it would be impossible to name them all. But I cannot omit mention of Professor Eugène Morice who gave me a rigorous and sound introduction to statistical reasoning; Professor René Roy and Professor Maurice Allais who awakened my interest in quantitative economics; the late Georges Darmois, a teacher whom I held in the highest esteem, and who encouraged me to produce a book on econometrics; G. Calot, R. Fortet, C. Fourgeaud, E. Morice, R. Rottier and L. J. Savage who took the trouble to read all or part of an earlier version of the book, and whose advise was very helpful; students at the 'Ecole d'Application' of the I.N.S.E.E. who had to learn econometric methods in spite of very imperfect teaching and made the difficulties of the subject clear to me; and finally the publishing house of Dunod who were willing to undertake the financial risk of publication.

E. MALINVAUD

[†] First numbers denote chapters, second numbers sections. When only one number is given, the whole chapter can be read without difficulty.

Preface to the English Edition

This book was written for French students or research workers who specialize in econometrics. The typical French reader whom I had in mind has a good mathematical training and can even follow an elaborate deduction, but his knowledge of economics is often weak. Readers from other countries, who have a different background, may find the book at places mathematically difficult and too pedantic in the exposition of economic ideas. I hope they may, however, learn from it the essentials of present-day econometric methods.

In the process of writing I found it useful to do some additional work on the basic statistical theory. Thus I was led to expand some sections dealing with aspects of mathematical statistics for which I did not find the available literature sufficient to my purpose. This is particularly clear in chapters 5 and 9 where the foundations of linear estimation and non-linear regressions are established with the generality required for other chapters. As a consequence, the book is a little unbalanced. The teacher who will use it as a reference may wish to provide his students with a less general but simpler presentation of some main results of mathematical statistics.

This edition has benefited from a number of minor improvements, which are scattered through the book and sometimes result from suggestions made to me by readers and students. I cannot here acknowledge individually the contributions made by each of them.

The English text owes its stylistic quality to Mrs. Anne Silvey who translated from the French edition with such a good understanding of the subject that she succeeded in maintaining the logic of the argument while escaping the idiomatic features of the French sentences. My thanks are also due to Professor J. Johnston who checked the entire translation and made a number of useful suggestions.

Paris, April 1966

Preface to the Third English Edition

During the past ten years the statistical methods of econometrics have been the object of intensive research so that a revision was necessary to make this book roughly up to date. Most of the recent publications, among those that should interest students to which the book is addressed, concerned consolidation or improvement of previously known methods. Hence, appropriate references and quick presentation of the results achieved was feasible without major reorganization of the chapters or paragraphs.

There were, of course, a few exceptions, two of them being particularly worth mentioning. In an advanced econometrics course, a full discussion is now required of the linear model with a partially unknown covariance matrix, a model that covers many situations of interest; this is done in chapter 8, which is completely rearranged. Courses in methodology no longer have to neglect, as was previously the case, the treatment of models that are non linear in the endogenous variables; a new chapter is added to this effect at the end of part 5.

Due to many more or less minor additions the book would have become excessively lengthy if no material had been deleted. Confronted with this fact, I decided to eliminate the purely mathematical parts, that is, appendices to chapters 5, 6 and 9, as well as chapter 11, which in the previous editions was intended to introduce the theory of stochastic processes. For these parts the reader may find many alternative sources and, if he wishes, refer to the second edition, or better to the third French edition in which minor revisions are made. The length of the book may also offer a justification for the fact that it was not extended in a few directions which interest applied econometricians. This could have been done in the less formalized chapters and would have then concerned, for instance, the analysis of qualitative data, the risk of a selection bias, the tests of causality among time series, or a discussion of exogeneity.

For the second and third editions of this book I benefited not only from my reading of an extensive literature but also from recommendations that were given directly to me by many colleagues. I cannot quote all of them, but I must make special mention of T. Amemiya, D. Brillinger, C. Fourgeaud, E. J. Hannan, B. Lenclud, W. L. L'Espérance, E. Lyttkens, W. J. Keller, P. Mazodier, M. Nerlove, P. C. B. Phillips, T. Rothenberg, P. Schönfeld, C. A. Sims, L. D. Taylor and K. F. Wallis.

Paris, October 1978

Contents

PART 2

LINEAR ESTIMATION

PART 3

TWO IMPORTANT STOCHASTIC MODELS

PART 5

SIMULTANEOUS EQUATION MODELS

Part 1

INTRODUCTION

CHAPTER 1

Econometrics without stochastic models

1 Introduction

According to our conception of the subject, all econometric research is based on a set of numerical data relating to certain economic quantities, and makes inferences from the data about the ways in which these quantities are related.

If there are n quantities under study, each is denoted by an index i, $(i = 1, 2, .., n)$. If we have T observations, each has an index t, $(t = 1, 2, ..., T)$. We denote by x_{it} the tth observation on x_i. The set of data consists of the nT numbers x_{it}, which will be analyzed in order to ascertain the relationships among the x_i.

We shall suppose also that there exists a model, given a priori, which specifies certain general assumptions about the nature of the relationships among the x_i. This model, that is to say the set of assumptions which it contains, will always be accepted without question. It will be considered to be perfectly applicable to the data on the one hand, and on the other hand to the situations in which the results of econometric analysis will be used. In short, this book deals with the problem of determining procedures which allow the set of the x_{it} to be used in order to ascertain certain elements of a model relating to the x_i, the general form of this model being given a priori.

This point of view will be discussed in greater detail in the following chapter. It should not seem unusual, since it is now adopted throughout mathematical statistics. However, it was not in force in the initial stages of econometrics, and only appeared clearly formulated by HAAVELMO [1944][†].

In this first chapter, we propose to study the set of data without introducing any model. We will encounter certain logical difficulties which will demonstrate the necessity for the attitude adopted subsequently. We shall also introduce some important questions and some formulae for calculation which will be justified in other chapters[††].

Several parts of this chapter appear in the literature of mathematical statistics. However, it seemed convenient to reproduce them briefly in order to give a better introduction to the techniques with which we shall be concerned, and also in order not to evade some general logical problems which arise when these techniques are applied to economic data.

[†] Bibliographical references are listed at the end of the book.

[††] In a series of lectures delivered in 1951–1952 and recently published GUILBAUD [1968] showed how useful can sometimes be in econometrics a good understanding of various questions which do not call for the introduction of a stochastic model. The present chapter is inspired by his line of reasoning.

2   *Fitting by graph*

Let us suppose first that the data relate to only two quantities, x_1 and x_2. It is easy to draw a graph representing these data. On a plane with values of x_1 as abscissa and values of x_2 as ordinate, each observation t is clearly represented by the point with coordinates (x_{1t}, x_{2t}). The T points so determined represent the set of data.

Thus fig. 1 represents 25 observations relating to the price x_2 of a car aged x_1. The graph clearly shows that x_1 and x_2 are associated, and the nature of their relationship is easily determined. Indeed we know a priori that there must be

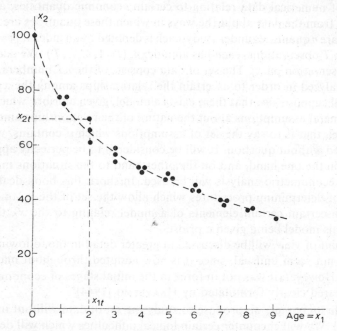

Fig. 1. Coefficients of depreciation of the 11 CV Citroën[†].

continuous dependence between the two variables. As the observations may have been affected by errors in measurement, or by chance factors which are in no respect permanent, a simple continuous curve is drawn to pass as closely as possible to the points but not necessarily through them.

Such a curve has been drawn by eye in fig. 1. In this case at least, this method of fitting is adequate, since the points all lie very near the curve. It might well be interesting to find an analytic expression for this curve in order to understand

---

[†] This diagram is borrowed from a study by Boiteux [1956]. Let $V(\theta,s)$ be the value in year θ of an 11 CV Citroën car manufactured in year s. The age of the car is by definition $x_1 = \theta - s$; the coefficient of depreciation is $x_2 = V(\theta,s)/(V(\theta,\theta)$. The prices studied relate to the years 1946 to 1952.

more clearly the dependence between x_1 and x_2. But that raises no statistical problem of any real importance, since nothing is known a priori about the analytic nature of the relationship. In short, a simple inspection of the graph is sufficient to demonstrate its existence and nature.

Situations like that illustrated by fig. 1 are often encountered in the study of physical phenomena. They are exceptional in the field of economics, where the data are more often represented by a scatter of points, as in fig. 2. Such scatters generally show that dependence exists, but that its form is not clear-cut.

The reasons for this are easily understood. The fact that economic statistics lack precision is well known and often even exaggerated. The following consideration is certainly more important. Economic phenomena are generally influenced by many different factors and the effect of a single factor can rarely be observed independently. In the physical sciences it is often possible to devise experiments where one factor can be isolated and its effect separately assessed. Such experimentation is generally impossible in economic science. We must be content to observe economic life as it actually happens, with all its inter-dependencies.

For the study of a particular phenomenon, we must first draw up a list of the variables to be taken into account, and then it is often clear that the phenomenon cannot be isolated completely. To describe it adequately we would need to take account of many factors, some of which are even non-quantitative, such as social cohesion, psychological climate, etc. We must, therefore, make do with a set of data which we know a priori are not adequate for a complete characterization of the phenomenon. It is not therefore surprising that the dependence between the variables appears to be rather loose.

In the situation where the best fit is not immediately obvious from the diagrammatic representation of the data, the selection of the method used to determine it becomes important. It is just because of this lack of precision of observed relationships in the economic field that econometricians must frequently resort to the methods of mathematical statistics. The less strict the relationships, the more important it becomes to use rigorous methods in their determination.

3 Simple regression

Figure 2 represents the values observed in 1951 for expenditure on clothing and for total expenditure in 112 households of minor officials living in provincial towns in France. Each type of expenditure is expressed in thousands of francs per week. These results are taken from an inquiry into family budgets in provincial towns. In order to make the diagram legible, a fairly limited group of households has been chosen. The households concerned were selected at random. Some refused to give information; others gave obviously incomplete information and were discarded.

The diagram shows that a clear dependence exists between x_1 and x_2 (here x_1

and x_2 denote respectively the logarithms of total expenditure and expenditure on clothing). But how can this dependence be expressed? The problem was easily solved in the preceding example. We only had to fit a curve to the points,

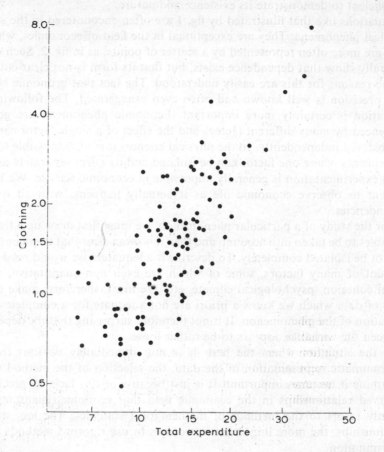

Fig. 2. Expenditure on clothing and total expenditure in a group of households.

that is, we found a functional relationship between x_1 and x_2; and the choice of curve presented no difficulty. Now, on the other hand, a functional relationship between x_1 and x_2 is no longer sufficient to describe the exact nature of the observed dependence. We must also take account of the dispersion of observations about their general trend, and, even when the necessity for this has been recognized, the average functional relationship cannot be determined in such an obvious way.

How can we define an equation relating x_1 and x_2 which describes the general trend of their relationship? Since in any case they are loosely related, the equation chosen must have the simplest possible analytic structure. Here and in many similar cases a linear equation is good enough. In fig. 2 this equation will be represented by a line passing through the set of points.

It is obviously desirable that the average distance between the points and the line should be minimized. But this common sense criterion is completely defined only when we have shown how to measure the distance between a point and the line, and how to calculate the average of the distances for different points

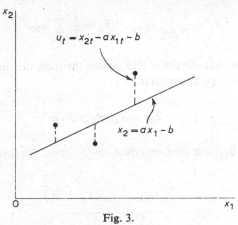

$$u_t = x_{2t} - a x_{1t} - b$$

$$x_2 = a x_1 - b$$

Fig. 3.

A quadratic mean is generally chosen, since such a formula involves the simplest calculations[†]. So we look for a line such that the sum of squares of the distance from the points to the line should be as small as possible. But several different measures of this distance can be, and are in fact, used. Let us consider first the most common measure, which consists in taking the distance parallel to the x_2-axis (cf. fig. 3).

Let us determine a line:

$$x_2 = ax_1 + b \tag{1}$$

such that:

$$U = \sum_{t=1}^{T} (x_{2t} - a x_{1t} - b)^2 \tag{2}$$

is minimized.

We know that the values a_{21} and b_{21} of a and b which satisfy this condition are obtained by equating to zero the derivatives of U with respect to a and b. They are found by solving the equations:

$$\sum x_{1t} x_{2t} - a_{21} \sum x_{1t}^2 - b_{21} \sum x_{1t} = 0$$
$$\sum x_{2t} \quad - a_{21} \sum x_{1t} - T b_{21} \quad = 0, \tag{3}$$

where the summation index t has been omitted to simplify the notation.

---

† Note also that the use of the quadratic mean is justified in the statistical theory presented in subsequent chapters. However, this justification presupposes the existence of stochastic models (that of ch. 2, or of ch. 10, for example).

The second equation can be written:

$$b_{21} = \bar{x}_2 - a_{21}\bar{x}_1, \tag{4}$$

where $\bar{x}_2$ and $\bar{x}_1$ are the means of observations on x_2 and x_1:

$$\bar{x}_1 = \frac{1}{T}\sum_{t=1}^{T} x_{1t}, \qquad \bar{x}_2 = \frac{1}{T}\sum_{t=1}^{T} x_{2t}. \tag{5}$$

Expression (4) shows that the fitted line passes through the mean point $(\bar{x}_1, \bar{x}_2)$. Its equation can therefore be written:

$$(x_2 - \bar{x}_2) = a_{21}(x_1 - \bar{x}_1). \tag{6}$$

After eliminating b_{21}, the first equation of (3) gives the following expression for a_{21}:

$$a_{21} = \frac{\sum_{t=1}^{T} (x_{2t} - \bar{x}_2)(x_{1t} - \bar{x}_1)}{\sum_{t=1}^{T} (x_{1t} - \bar{x}_1)^2}. \tag{7}$$

Formulae (7) and (4) allow us to determine the fitted line from the data. This line is called the *linear regression of x_2 on x_1*.

The dispersion of points about this line can be characterized by the value of U when a and b are replaced by a_{21} and b_{21}, say:

$$U = \sum (x_{2t} - \bar{x}_2)^2 - \frac{[\sum (x_{2t} - \bar{x}_2)(x_{1t} - \bar{x}_1)]^2}{\sum (x_{1t} - \bar{x}_1)^2}.$$

Actually, it is customary to give the value taken by the scale invariant measure:

$$R^2 = 1 - \frac{U}{\sum (x_{2t} - \bar{x}_2)^2}$$

which is equal to the square of the linear correlation coefficient between the x_{2t} and the x_{1t}.

Clearly we might equally well measure distances parallel to the x_1-axis, and obtain in the same way the linear regression of x_1 on x_2:

$$(x_1 - \bar{x}_1) = a_{12}(x_2 - \bar{x}_2) \tag{8}$$

where:

$$a_{12} = \frac{\sum (x_{1t} - \bar{x}_1)(x_{2t} - \bar{x}_2)}{\sum (x_{2t} - \bar{x}_2)^2} \tag{9}$$

This second line passes through the mean point, like the first line, but has a different gradient $1/a_{12}$. Formulae (7) and (9) show directly that the *ratio of the gradients of the two simple regression lines is the square of the linear correlation coefficient* R^2.

The following results were calculated for the example of fig. 2:

$$\bar{x}_1 = 4.1129, \qquad \bar{x}_2 = 3.1622,$$

$$\frac{1}{T}\sum (x_{1t} - \bar{x}_1)^2 = 0.019934, \qquad \frac{1}{T}\sum (x_{2t} - \bar{x}_2)^2 = 0.048918,$$

$$\frac{1}{T}\sum (x_{1t} - \bar{x}_1)(x_{2t} - \bar{x}_2) = 0.023932.$$

The linear regression of x_2 on x_1 is:

$$x_2 = 1.20 x_1 - 1.78;$$

that of x_1 on x_2 is:

$$x_1 = 0.49 x_2 + 2.57,$$

or equivalently:

$$x_2 = 2.04 x_1 - 5.25.$$

The coefficient R^2 has the value 0.59.

4 Orthogonal regression

Rather than measure distances parallel to one of the axes, it might seem natural to keep to the usual idea of distance, that is, to measure the perpendicular deviations of the points from the fitted line (cf. fig. 4). By minimizing the mean square of these deviations, we obtain the *orthogonal regression*. For ease of calculation let us write the equation of the line in the form:

$$a_1 x_1 + a_2 x_2 = b \tag{10}$$

and subject a_1 and a_2 to the condition:

$$a_1^2 + a_2^2 = 1. \tag{11}$$

a_1 and a_2 are then the cosine and sine of the angle which the normal to the line makes with $0x_1$; b is the distance from the origin to the line.

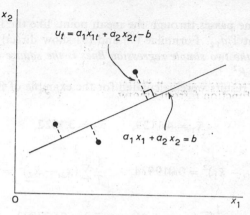

Fig. 4.

The sum of squares of the distances is:

$$U = \sum_{t=1}^{T} (a_1 x_{1t} + a_2 x_{2t} - b)^2. \tag{12}$$

To find the values $\tilde{a}_1$, $\tilde{a}_2$ and $\tilde{b}$ of the coefficients of the fitted line, we must equate to zero the derivatives with respect to a_1, a_2 and b of:

$$\sum (a_1 x_{1t} + a_2 x_{2t} - b)^2 - \lambda(a_1^2 + a_2^2 - 1),$$

where λ is a Lagrange multiplier.

Differentiation with respect to b gives:

$$\tilde{b} = \tilde{a}_1 \bar{x}_1 + \tilde{a}_2 \bar{x}_2 \tag{13}$$

which shows that the fitted line passes through the mean point $(\bar{x}_1, \bar{x}_2)$ and that its equation can be written:

$$\tilde{a}_1 (x_1 - \bar{x}_1) + \tilde{a}_2 (x_2 - \bar{x}_2) = 0. \tag{14}$$

Differentiation with respect to a_1 and a_2 yields, after elimination of b, the system:

$$\tilde{a}_1 \left[\sum (x_{1t} - \bar{x}_1)^2 - \lambda \right] + \tilde{a}_2 \sum (x_{1t} - \bar{x}_1)(x_{2t} - \bar{x}_2) = 0,$$
$$\tilde{a}_1 \sum (x_{1t} - \bar{x}_1)(x_{2t} - \bar{x}_2) + \tilde{a}_2 \left[\sum (x_{2t} - \bar{x}_2)^2 - \lambda \right] = 0, \tag{15}$$

which we can write:

$$\tilde{a}_1(m_{11} - \lambda/T) + \tilde{a}_2 m_{12} = 0,$$
$$\tilde{a}_1 m_{12} + \tilde{a}_2(m_{22} - \lambda/T) = 0, \tag{15'}$$

where m_{11}, m_{12} and m_{22} denote the second order moments about the mean of the x_{1t} and x_{2t}.

The homogeneous linear system (15) has a non-zero solution only if its determinant is zero. Moreover, for a non-zero solution $\tilde{a}_1, \tilde{a}_2$, the quantity U to be minimized takes the value λ, as is shown by:

$$U = T[\tilde{a}_1^2 m_{11} + \tilde{a}_2^2 m_{22} + 2\tilde{a}_1 \tilde{a}_2 m_{12}] = \lambda(\tilde{a}_1^2 + \tilde{a}_2^2) = \lambda.$$

To minimize U we must solve (15) with condition (11), giving λ the value of the smaller root of:

$$\begin{vmatrix} m_{11} - \lambda/T & m_{12} \\ m_{12} & m_{22} - \lambda/T \end{vmatrix} = 0. \tag{16}$$

This smaller root λ_1 is given by:

$$2\lambda_1/T = m_{11} + m_{22} - \sqrt{(m_{11} - m_{22})^2 + 4m_{12}^2}$$

and then

$$-\tilde{a}_1/\tilde{a}_2 = \frac{m_{22} - m_{11} + \sqrt{(m_{11} - m_{22})^2 + 4m_{12}^2}}{2m_{12}}. \tag{17}$$

Thus for the example of fig. 2, we have:

$$-\tilde{a}_1/\tilde{a}_2 = 1.77$$

whence, by using formula (14), we obtain the orthogonal regression:

$$x_2 = 1.77 x_1 - 4.13.$$

In general we can see from these formulae that *the orthogonal regression line lies between the regression line of x_2 on x_1, and that of x_1 on x_2.*
More precisely:

$$|a_{21}| \leqq \left| -\frac{\tilde{a}_1}{\tilde{a}_2} \right| \leqq \left| \frac{1}{a_{12}} \right|, \tag{18}$$

the equalities holding only in the case of strict linear dependence ($R^2 = 1$).

Let us suppose, for example, $m_{12} > 0$, and let us verify the second inequality of (18), namely:

$$\frac{m_{22} - m_{11} + \sqrt{(m_{11} - m_{22})^2 + 4m_{12}^2}}{2m_{12}} \leqq \frac{m_{22}}{m_{12}}$$

or:

$$\sqrt{(m_{11} - m_{22})^2 + 4m_{12}^2} \leqq m_{11} + m_{22}$$

or

$$m_{12}^2 \leqq m_{11} m_{22}.$$

This may be written $R^2 \leqq 1$, and is the well-known Schwarz inequality.

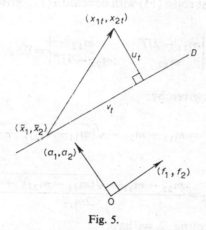

Fig. 5.

It is easy to see that the orthogonal regression corresponds to the 'principal component' of the scatter of points. Indeed by definition the *principal component* of a set of observations on two variables x_1 and x_2 is, of all the linear forms:

$$v = f_1(x_1 - \bar{x}_1) + f_2(x_2 - \bar{x}_2) \tag{19}$$

satisfying:

$$f_1^2 + f_2^2 = 1, \tag{20}$$

that which has the greatest quadratic mean over the set of observations.

To find the principal component we must find the line D passing through the mean point $(\bar{x}_1, \bar{x}_2)$ and maximizing the sum V of the squares of the projections v_t on D of the vectors with components $(x_{1t} - \bar{x}_1)$ and $(x_{1t} - \bar{x}_1)$. If u_t measures the perpendicular distance from (x_{1t}, x_{2t}) to the line D, the sum $u^2 + v^2$, equal to:

$$(x_{1t} - \bar{x}_1)^2 + (x_{2t} - \bar{x}_2)^2,$$

is independent of the position of D. The line D which maximizes V is therefore the same line which minimizes the sum U of the squares of the distances u_t; it is in fact the orthogonal regression line. The coefficients f_1 and f_2 of the linear form required are then:

$$f_1 = \tilde{a}_2, \qquad f_2 = - \tilde{a}_1. \tag{21}$$

If λ_1 and λ_2 denote the two roots of equation (16),

$$\lambda_1 + \lambda_2 = \sum (x_{1t} - \bar{x}_1)^2 + \sum (x_{2t} - \bar{x}_2)^2 = U + V.$$

As the smaller value of U is equal to λ_1, the greater value of V is equal to λ_2.

The value λ_1 of the smaller root of (16) measures the dispersion of the points about the orthogonal regression line. As a scale invariant measure is of more direct use, we shall prefer to calculate:

$$\phi^2 = 1 - \frac{\lambda_1}{\sum (x_{1t} - \bar{x}_1)^2 + \sum (x_{2t} - \bar{x}_2)^2} = \frac{\lambda_2}{\lambda_1 + \lambda_2} \tag{22}$$

which takes the value 1 when the points representing the observations all lie on a straight line.

In the example of fig. 2 we have:

$$\phi^2 = 0.94.$$

Finally we must take note of *an important difference between the regression of x_2 on x_1 and the orthogonal regression; the former is independent of the units of measurement of the variables x_1 and x_2, but the latter is not.*

For example, suppose the unit of measurement of the x_2 be divided by a number r. The x_{2t} will all be multiplied by this number, the x_{1t} remaining unchanged. The whole diagram will undergo an affine transformation relative to the x_1-axis. Obviously the regression lines of x_2 on x_1 and x_1 on x_2 will be transformed along with the collection of points. Besides we can verify from formulae (7) and (9) that a_{21} will be multiplied by r, and a_{12} divided by r, so that the regression equations (6) and (8) will have no change other than that resulting from the change of units.

On the other hand, since the affine transformation applied to fig. 4 does not preserve angles, the perpendicular distances to a given line will be multiplied by a factor which depends on the direction of the line; the orthogonal regression line will undergo a more complex change than the simple regression lines. Formula (17) shows moreover that its gradient will be multiplied by a number other than r (except when $m_{12} = 0$).

5   *Deficiencies of deterministic methods*

The line of research described in the preceding sections can be developed in two ways.

On the one hand, we can envisage different characterizations for the general trend of the relationship between x_1 and x_2. For example we can adopt other definitions of the distance between a point and the line of trend, or we might well use different formulae for calculating the average distance. Fitting procedures which are not based on minimization of an average distance have also been proposed. Again we may try to define a line of trend which would lie between the two simple regression lines of x_2 on x_1 and x_1 on x_2, but which would be independent of the units of measurement, unlike the orthogonal regression line. Thus Ragnar Frisch has proposed the *diagonal regression line* which by definition satisfies equation:

$$(x_2 - \bar{x}_2) = \sqrt{\frac{a_{21}}{a_{12}}}(x_1 - \bar{x}_1) \tag{23}$$

and whose gradient is therefore the geometric mean of the gradients of the two simple regression lines.

We shall not follow up this line of research. Simple and orthogonal regressions are by far the most commonly used in practice. As we shall make a very full study of them in the course of this book, it seemed convenient to introduce them right at the beginning. The description of other fitting procedures seems simply gratuitous, and at this stage would be of only incidental interest. After studying some stochastic models, we shall be in a better position to see why some other formulae are sometimes useful in defining the dependence between two variables.

On the other hand, we must generalize the concepts so far introduced so that they apply to sets of observations on more than two variables. For the reasons previously indicated, econometric analysis is often concerned with several variables. Determination of the characteristics of observed sets of data becomes the more important as graphical representation becomes impossible. We shall therefore devote the last sections of this chapter to generalization of simple and orthogonal regressions.

But, after the preceding paragraph, we can already see how uncertain our interpretation of the results of econometric analysis must be when we do not use a stochastic model. We are now therefore in a position to understand the methodological necessity for the introduction of models.

Determination of the characteristics of a set of data is obviously not an end in itself. The data are not considered to have arisen accidentally, but to have some relevance in a general context. Their characteristics must therefore reflect certain permanent features of the phenomenon under study. They must lend themselves to interpretation and prediction, which alone matter in the end.

We must therefore understand the general significance of the data and of the regressions which we calculate from them.

For a better understanding of the nature of the problem we first consider again the example of fig. 1, which exhibits a functional relationship between x_1 and x_2. The existence of this relationship might be assumed a priori, and in that case it receives some empirical confirmation. If it seems reasonable to assume that this functional relationship is generally valid, we can 'predict' values of x_2 from those of x_1. This can be done by referring to the broken curve drawn on fig. 1.

The process of using the data may be formally described as follows. We have assumed that a permanent functional relationship $x_2 = f(x_1)$ exists between the variables x_1 and x_2. The set of data relating to these variables has not given us grounds for rejecting this hypothesis, and has allowed us to determine the function f. We believe that a different set of data would have suggested virtually the same function. We are now in a position to say what value of x_2 will correspond to each possible value of x_1.

The part played by the initial hypothesis is obvious. It is the 'model' in the light of which we have made use of the data. In this case the model is so simple and so natural that there is no profit in discussing it. The situation is different for the example of fig. 2.

To make use of the collection of observed points, we must assume that the relationship between x_1 and x_2 has some kind of permanence. But various hypotheses are then possible. Here are three examples chosen from the hypotheses frequently used.

(i) We may assume that pairs of values of the variables x_1 and x_2 will always be distributed in the same way as in the observed sample. In other words, we suppose that any pair of values results from random selection from a two-dimensional probability distribution $F(x_1, x_2)$ which applies permanently.

(ii) We may also assume that, for every given value of x_1, the value of x_2 will be distributed similarly to the x_{2t} observed for the same value of x_1. We will suppose then that the value of x_2 results from random selection from a one-dimensional probability distribution $G(x_2/x_1)$ which varies according to the value of x_1.

(iii) Again we may consider that, in the absence of disturbances or errors of measurement, the values of x_1 and x_2 obey a strict functional relationship. Then let y_1 and y_2 be the true (and unobservable) values of x_1 and x_2. We assume in this case the existence of y_1 and y_2, a function $y_2 = f(y_1)$ and unobservable errors:

$$\varepsilon_1 = x_1 - y_1, \qquad \varepsilon_2 = x_2 - y_2.$$

We assume also that the errors are always distributed in the same way, that is, that they result from random selection from some two-dimensional probability distribution $H(\varepsilon_1, \varepsilon_2)$.

The hypotheses adopted in (i), in (ii) or in (iii) define the sense in which the relationship observed between x_1 and x_2 can be generalized.

They play the same part as that of the assumption in the first example of the existence of a functional relationship, since they constitute the model in the light of which we can make use of the observations.

The object of econometric analysis is in the first place to test this model and then to give it a specific form. We have to choose a distribution F, or a distribution G for each value of x_1, or a distribution H and a function f, from among those which seemed legitimate a priori. Analysis of the set of data is then seen as a necessary intermediate step toward finding the distributions or the functions of the model.

We note also that a complete specification of the model is not generally indispensable. A knowledge of some particular characteristics of the distributions will often be sufficient for the interpretation or prediction which we have in mind. The empirical characteristics calculated from the data can then give direct information about the relevant characteristics of the distributions.

We do not carry out econometric analysis in the framework of models only for the sake of rigor. The use of models is indispensable to a proper appreciation of the applicability and the worth of the different methods available. There are three important reasons for this.

In the first place, *how could we decide which empirical characteristics to calculate, if we made no assumption about the phenomenon under study?* We have already seen that there are many possible formulae for defining, for example, a regression between two variables. Which must we choose? This question becomes meaningful when we use a model, for, relative to this model, one particular regression will be especially interesting.

We shall give numerous illustrations of this remark. Thus, in ch. 3 we shall introduce a model which is often applicable and for which it is preferable to calculate the regression of x_2 on x_1. On the other hand, in ch. 10 we shall justify the use of orthogonal regression, in the context of a different model, of course.

In the second place, where the data do not obey a strict functional relationship, we cannot wait for two separate sets of data to give exactly the same values for the calculated characteristics. The observations are to some extent random, and therefore there is also a random element in results calculated from them. It is then important to assess the variability of the calculated characteristics. But how could we do so without making some assumption about the variability of the observations themselves? *For example, how imprecise is the regression of x_2 on x_1?*

General assumptions about the random nature of the variables provide the basis for determining in practice the distribution of every measure calculated from the data. It is the fact that they are based on models which enables econometric methods to provide a proper assessment of the precision finally obtained. Besides, as we can easily imagine, for the same quantity and the same set of data, this assessment varies according to the model adopted. We will have many occasions to show that this is true.

Finally, since the calculated characteristics must serve as the basis for certain predictions, it is important that we should know how these predictions must be made. *But how could we set up formulae for calculating predicted values if we were ignorant of the permanent characteristics of the phenomenon?* Here again only a model leads to a correct solution of the problem.

To sum up, models must be introduced for the justification and thorough understanding of econometric methods. This is a logical necessity which cannot be dispensed with in a discussion of these methods.

However, for reasons to be developed in the next chapter, it is sometimes difficult to decide a priori which model is relevant to this or that practical situation. An open-minded examination of the data can help to avoid some gross mistakes.

The need to examine a set of data efficiently without reference to a stochastic model has inspired much recent research grouped under the general heading of *data analysis.* BENZÉCRI and others [1973] give a very informative account of this research. In the main, it deals with qualitative variables which allow classi-fication of the different observations, rather than with quantitative variables, with which we are concerned in this book.

In this chapter we now turn to the generalization of regression to observations on several variables, and we shall do so still without introducing a model. We are simply concerned here to describe the principal characteristics of a set of data with too many variables to be represented by a two-dimensional graph. We shall see that the techniques described are of more general interest[†].

The following sections will involve fairly heavy mathematics. Chapters 2, 3 and 4 can be read independently, and the reader may therefore go straight on to the next chapter[††].

6 Notation

We shall give an example to provide a practical basis for the discussion which follows. From French national accounts for the years 1949 to 1966 we extract figures for certain global quantities, namely imports, gross domestic production, stock formation and consumption. These quantities are expressed in milliards of new francs at 1959 prices, and the results are shown in table 1 and fig. 6.

A priori it is plausible that the four quantities chosen are related. In particular, imports are composed on the one hand of raw materials and semi-finished

[†] The methods of analysis of economic data relating to several variables have been discussed in detail by FRISCH [1928]. The discussion which follows is in many respects close to his.
[††] Proofs given in this and the following chapters will often involve matrix theory. The basic principles of matrix algebra have been described by numerous authors, for example by BASS [1956], AITKEN [1939] or LENTIN and RIVAUD [1958].

products, and on the other hand of foodstuffs and finished products. They must depend partly on the needs of domestic production and fluctuations in stock formation, and partly on consumer demand[†]. We shall examine the relationships suggested by the experience of the period 1949–66.

At this point we must define the notation to be used here and throughout the book.

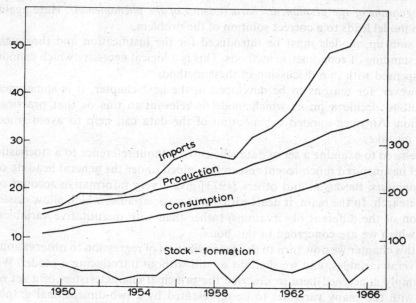

Fig. 6. The behavior of quantities relating to French economic activity[††].

As before, x_{it} denotes the tth observation on x_i. In this example we have 4 variables $(n = 4)$ and 18 observations $(T = 18)$. Thus $x_{3,6} = 2.2$, which is the value of stock formation $(i = 3)$ in 1954 $(t = 6)$. We shall denote by x_t the n-dimensional vector with components x_{it} $(i = 1, ., 3, 4)$. Similarly $\bar{x}$ will be the vector whose components are the means $\bar{x}_i$:

$$\bar{x}_i = \frac{1}{T} \sum_{t=1}^{T} x_{it}. \qquad (24)$$

We shall also denote by x_t and $\bar{x}$ the matrices of order $n \times 1$ whose elements are respectively the x_{it} and the $\bar{x}_i$. The transpose of a matrix A will be denoted as usual by A'. So $\bar{x}'\bar{x}$ is the sum of squares of the means $\bar{x}_i$, while $\bar{x}\bar{x}'$ is the

---

[†]   As this example shows, selection of the quantities to be studied depends on some idea which is held a priori. Although no model is formulated, it is neither possible nor desirable to ignore previously existing notions about the phenomenon to be analyzed.
[††] Results are expressed in milliards of new francs at 1959 prices. The lefthand scale refers to imports and stock-formation, the right hand scale to gross domestic production and consumption. The data are given in table 1.

TABLE 1

Imports, production, stock-formation and consumption in France
(in milliards of new francs at 1959 prices).

Year	t	x_1 Imports	x_2 Gross domestic production	x_3 Stock-formation	x_4 Consumption
1949	1	15.9	149.3	4.2	108.1
1950	2	16.4	161.2	4.1	114.8
1951	3	19.0	171.5	3.1	123.2
1952	4	19.1	175.5	3.1	126.9
1953	5	18.8	180.8	1.1	132.1
1954	6	20.4	190.7	2.2	137.7
1955	7	22.7	202.1	2.1	146.0
1956	8	26.5	212.4	5.6	154.1
1957	9	28.1	226.1	5.0	162.3
1958	10	27.6	231.9	5.1	164.3
1959	11	26.3	239.0	0.7	167.6
1960	12	31.1	258.0	5.6	176.8
1961	13	33.3	269.8	3.9	186.6
1962	14	37.0	288.4	3.1	199.7
1963	15	43.3	304.5	4.6	213.9
1964	16	49.0	323.4	7.0	223.8
1965	17	50.3	336.8	1.2	232.0
1966	18	56.6	353.9	4.5	242.9

square matrix of order n whose (i, j)th element is $\bar{x}_i \bar{x}_j$ the product of the means
of the variables i and j.

We shall denote by m_{ij} the second order moments about the mean:

$$m_{ij} = \frac{1}{T} \sum_{t=1}^{T} (x_{it} - \bar{x}_i)(x_{jt} - \bar{x}_j) \qquad (25)$$

and by M the square matrix of order n of the m_{ij}, so that:

$$M = \frac{1}{T} \sum_{t=1}^{T} (x_t - \bar{x})(x_t - \bar{x})'. \qquad (26)$$

Subsequently it will be necessary to introduce similar matrices for different
sets of variables, for example, the x_i and the z_k, $(i=1, 2,\ldots,n; \ k=1, 2,\ldots,m)$.
Matrix (26) will then be denoted by M_{xx}, while M_{zz} will be the square matrix
of order m which has as elements the second order moments[†] about the mean
of the z_k. Again M_{xz} will denote the $n \times m$ matrix:

$$M_{xz} = \frac{1}{T} \sum_{t=1}^{T} (x_t - \bar{x})(z_t - \bar{z})'. \qquad (27)$$

[†] In ch. 6 and subsequently, M_{xx}, M_{xz} and M_{zz} will be matrices of moments not taken about
the mean, and this will simplify the theory. (See especially ch. 6, § 5 in this connection.)

Some authors use a different notation with which the reader should acquaint himself. They denote by X the $T \times n$ matrix whose (t,i)th element is $x_{it} - \bar{x}_i$. This matrix represents the deviations of the given values from their means. The (i,j)th element of $X'X$ is then the product by T of the moment about the mean m_{ij}, calculated as in formula (25). In this notation TM_{xx} is replaced by $X'X$ and similarly TM_{zz} by $Z'Z$ and TM_{xz} by $X'Z$.

7 Multiple regression

When studying data for two variables, we tried to find a functional relationship describing the general trend of the observed association between them, and a measure of the dispersion about this trend. For the sake of simplicity we chose a linear relationship, and this is often satisfactory. We chose a line in such a way that an average distance between the observed points and this line should be minimized. The same principles may be adopted for sets of observations on several variables.

The general trend will in this case be represented by a linear equation of the type:

$$x_1 = a_{12}x_2 + a_{13}x_3 + \cdots + a_{1n}x_n + b_1. \tag{28}$$

In n-dimensional space where the coordinates of a point are the values of the n variables x_i, the above equation defines an $(n-1)$-dimensional hyperplane, P say. The tth observation is represented by the end point of the vector x_t with coordinates x_{it}.

The position of P, that is the value of the coefficients a_{1i} and b_1, will be determined in such a way that the square U of the mean distance between the points x_t and P is minimized. If the distances are taken parallel to the x_1-axis, U is expressed by:

$$U = \frac{1}{T} \sum_{t=1}^{T} [x_{1t} - a_{12}x_{2t} - a_{13}x_{3t} - \cdots - a_{1n}x_{nt} - b_1]^2. \tag{29}$$

We calculate the values of the coefficients by equating to zero the derivatives of U with respect to a_{1i} and b_1. In particular, differentiation with respect to b_1 yields:

$$\bar{x}_1 = a_{12}\bar{x}_2 + a_{13}\bar{x}_3 + \cdots + a_{1n}\bar{x}_n + b_1, \tag{30}$$

which is the condition that P should contain $\bar{x}$. Its equation can therefore be written:

$$(x_1 - \bar{x}_1) = a_{12}(x_2 - \bar{x}_2) + a_{13}(x_3 - \bar{x}_3) + \cdots + a_{1n}(x_n - \bar{x}_n) \tag{31}$$

and the expression for U becomes:

$$U = \frac{1}{T} \sum_{t=1}^{T} [(x_{1t} - \bar{x}_1) - a_{12}(x_{2t} - \bar{x}_2) - \cdots - a_{1n}(x_{nt} - \bar{x}_n)]^2. \tag{32}$$

Differentiations with respect to the a_{1i} yield the 'normal equations':

$$m_{21} - m_{22}a_{12} - m_{23}a_{13} - \cdots - m_{2n}a_{1n} = 0$$

$$m_{31} - m_{22}a_{12} - m_{33}a_{13} - \cdots - m_{3n}a_{1n} = 0 \tag{33}$$

$$\cdots\cdots\cdots\cdots\cdots\cdots\cdots\cdots\cdots\cdots\cdots\cdots$$

$$m_{n1} - m_{n2}a_{12} - m_{n3}a_{13} - \cdots - m_{nn}a_{1n} = 0.$$

Matrix notation is more concise.

Let a^1 be the $(n-1)$-dimensional vector with components a_{1i}, $(i=2,\ldots,n)$, of the $(n-1) \times 1$ matrix with elements a_{1i}. Similarly let x^1 be the $(n-1)$-dimensional vector with components x_i, $(i=2,\ldots,n)$; let m^1 be the vector with components m_{1i}, $(i=2,\ldots,n)$. Finally let M^1 be the square matrix of order $n-1$ with elements m_{ij} $(i=2,\ldots,n; j=2,\ldots,n)$. Then M can be partitioned as follows:

$$M = \begin{bmatrix} m_{11} & m^1 \\ m^1 & M^1 \end{bmatrix}. \tag{34}$$

The equation of P is:

$$(x_1 - \bar{x}_1) = a^{1'}(x^1 - \bar{x}^1) \tag{31'}$$

and the normal equations are:

$$m^1 - M^1 a^1 = 0. \tag{33'}$$

System (33) will have a unique solution if the determinant of the coefficients of the a_{1i} is not zero, that is if M^1 is non-singular. In this case, the a_{1i} can be calculated from:

$$a^1 = (M^1)^{-1} m^1, \tag{35}$$

where $(M^1)^{-1}$ is of course the inverse of M^1.

When M^1 is singular, $x_2, x_3, \ldots, x_n$ are said to be *collinear*. We shall shortly see why. This is an exceptional case not found in practice. But it often happens that the determinant of M^1 is very near zero and this makes for a complicated situation to which we shall refer on several occasions.

The minimum value of U is obtained by substituting in (32) the solution (35). Indeed U can be written:

$$U = m_{11} - 2a^{1'}m^1 + a^{1'}M^1 a^1,$$

whence, from (35):

$$U = m_{11} - m^{1'}(M^1)^{-1}m^1. \tag{36}$$

The dispersion about P of the observed points is usually measured by the coefficient

$$R^2 = 1 - U/m_{11}$$

similar to that used in the case of simple regression. Here:

$$R^2 = \frac{m^{1'}(M^1)^{-1}m^1}{m_{11}}. \tag{37}$$

The square root R of this expression is called the 'multiple correlation coefficient' of x_1 on $x_2, x_3, \ldots, x_n$.

Consider, for example, the data in table 1. They yield the following values for the first and second order moments:

$$\bar{x} = \begin{bmatrix} 30.08 \\ 237.52 \\ 3.68 \\ 167.38 \end{bmatrix}, \quad M = \begin{bmatrix} 147.13 & 736.88 & 5.46 & 482.69 \\ 736.88 & 3810.20 & 22.51 & 2491.70 \\ 5.46 & 22.51 & 2.86 & 14.61 \\ 482.69 & 2491.70 & 14.61 & 1632.90 \end{bmatrix}, \tag{38}$$

whence

$$m^1 = \begin{bmatrix} 736.88 \\ 5.46 \\ 482.69 \end{bmatrix} \quad (M^1)^{-1} = \begin{bmatrix} 0.1233 & -0.0093 & -0.1880 \\ -0.0093 & 0.3666 & 0.0110 \\ -0.1880 & 0.0110 & 0.2874 \end{bmatrix}$$

and, applying formulae (35), (30) and (37):

$$a^1 = \begin{bmatrix} 0.032 \\ 0.414 \\ 0.243 \end{bmatrix}, \quad b_1 = -19.72, \quad R^2 = 0.97.$$

The 'regression of x_1 on x_2, x_3, x_4' can therefore be given as follows:

$$x_1 = 0.032\,x_2 + 0.414\,x_3 + 0.243\,x_4 - 19.72, \quad R^2 = 0.97. \tag{39}$$

The problems arising in multiple regression can often be more easily understood with the help of a different geometric representation from the one we have been using. We now consider a T-dimensional rather than an n-dimensional space. Each variable x_i is represented by a vector X_i whose T components are the observed values $x_{it} - \bar{x}_i$ where $t = 1, 2, \ldots, T$.

The regression of x_1 on $x_2, x_3, \ldots, x_n$ is now determined by finding a vector X_1^* which is a linear combination of $X_2, X_3, \ldots, X_n$ and is as near as possible to X_1. Indeed we set

$$x_{1t}^* - \bar{x}_1 = a_{12}(x_{2t} - \bar{x}_2) + \cdots + a_{1n}(x_{nt} - \bar{x}_n).$$

Expression (32) becomes:

$$U = \frac{1}{T} \sum_{t=1}^{T} [(x_{1t} - \bar{x}_1) - (x_{1t}^* - \bar{x}_1)]^2.$$

The vector X_1^* with components $x_{1t}^* - \bar{x}_1$ is therefore the linear combination of $X_2, X_3, \ldots, X_n$ which is nearest X_1, distances being reckoned according to the usual Euclidean definition.

Let the linear manifold (or vector subspace) L be defined as the set of all linear combinations of $X_2, X_3, \ldots, X_n$. The vector X_1^* is the orthogonal projection of X_1 on L. The coefficient R^2 is the square of the cosine of the angle which X_1 makes with L.

The vector X_1^* is always uniquely determined. In order that the a_{1i} also should be uniquely determined, the expression or each vector of L as a linear combination of $X_2, X_3, \ldots, X_n$ *should be unique*. That is, L should be of dimension $n-1$, or the vectors $X_2, X_3, \ldots, X_n$ should be linearly independent.

If there exists a linear relationship among the $X_2, X_3, \ldots, X_n$, then these vectors, and the variables $x_2, x_3, \ldots, x_n$, are said to be *collinear*. This is the case if and only if M^1 is singular[†].

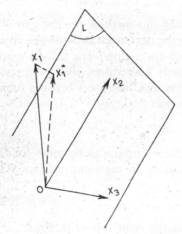

Fig. 7.

Geometric and analytic methods therefore lead to the same result; the regression of x_1 on $x_2, x_3, \ldots, x_n$ is uniquely determined if and only if M^1 is non-singular.

---

† This is easily proved:

Proposition. The matrix M defined by equation (26) is singular if and only if there exists a non-zero vector λ such that $\lambda'(x_t - \bar{x}) = 0$ for $t = 1, 2, \ldots, T$, that is, if the variables x_t are linearly dependent.

If such a vector exists, it is immediately obvious from the definition of M that $\lambda'M = 0$, and M is therefore singular.

Conversely, if M is singular, a non-zero vector λ exists such that $\lambda'M = 0$; therefore also $\lambda'M\lambda = 0$ and this can be written:

$$\sum_{t=1}^{T} [\lambda'(x_t - \bar{x})]^2 = 0.$$

This implies:

$$\lambda'(x_t - \bar{x}) = 0 \qquad \text{for} \qquad t = 1, 2, \ldots, T.$$

8   Regression on two sets of variables[†]

In studying the empirical relationships among three variables, one sometimes uses a graphical method whose efficiency must be thoroughly understood. We can apply it to values of x_1, x_2 and x_3 given in table 1.

The first part of fig. 8 is a scatter diagram for production and imports. We see from this diagram that there exists a fairly strict dependence which may be adequately described by a linear equation. We can draw on the graph the regression line of x_1 on x_2, which has equation:

$$x_1 = 0.193 \, x_2 - 15.86. \tag{40}$$

(In using this method, the line can often be well enough drawn by eye.)

Are the deviations between the points and this line connected with variations in stock-formation? The second graph in fig. 8 is relevant here. As abscissae the points have values of stock formation (x_3) and as ordinates the 'residuals' δ, that is, the differences between imports (x_1) and the regression of imports on production (x_2), say:

$$\delta_t = x_{1t} - 0.193 \, x_{2t} + 15.86.$$

As there appears to be some connection between δ and x_3, it seems natural to calculate the regression of δ on x_3, which gives

$$\delta = 0.406 \, x_3 - 1.47.$$

Adding the right side of this equation to the regression of x_1 on x_2, we have:

$$x_1 = 0.193 \, x_2 + 0.406 \, x_3 - 17.33. \tag{41}$$

which may be considered to describe the relationship of x_1, x_2 and x_3.

This procedure would be completely justified if the three variables were connected by a strict linear relationship. In this example the equation found is quite acceptable, and very close to the regression of x_1 on x_2 and x_3, namely:

$$x_1 = 0.191 \, x_2 + 0.405 \, x_3 - 16.78. \tag{42}$$

But this method is not always valid.

Consider again a geometric representation in T-dimensional space. Figure 9 shows a set of vectors in the space L spanned by X_2 and X_3. The regression of x_1 on x_2 and x_3 is represented, as in fig. 7, by the vector X_1^*. The regression of x_1 on x_2 is represented by the projection of X_1 on X_2, that is by the projection of X_1^* on X_2, or OH. The projection of the vector of the residuals δ_t on L is the vector $\varDelta$ which is equal to HX_1^*. The regression of δ on x_3 is represented by

---

[†] On this question the reader may refer to GOLDBERGER [1961].

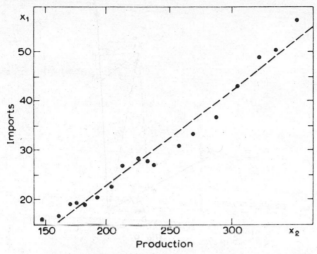

Simple regression between imports and production.

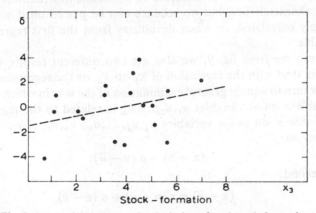

Fig. 8. Regression between the deviations δ and stock-formation.

the projection OK of Δ on X_3. In equation (41) the coefficient of x_2 is therefore the ratio of the lengths of OH and X_2, and the coefficient of x_3 is the ratio of the lengths of OK and X_3. In the multiple regression equation (42) the coefficient of x_2 is the ratio of the lengths of OM and X_2 and the coefficient of x_3 is the ratio of the lengths of ON and X_3 (where OM and ON are the components of X_1^* on X_2 and X_3).

In the example considered, the results are very similar because of two favorable circumstances. On the one hand, the residuals δ_t are small relative to the values of $x_{it} - \bar{x}_i$. On the other hand, there is almost a right angle between the vectors X_2 and X_3. (Indeed the cosine of this angle, which is the value of the correlation coefficient between x_2 and x_3, is 0.21 according to the data in table 1.)

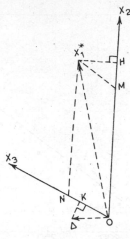

Fig. 9.

The graphical method will therefore be profitable in situations with the same favorable characteristics, but no reliance can be placed on it when x_2 and x_3 are strongly correlated, or when deviations from the first regression line are considerable.

As we can see from fig. 9, we also get two different results, depending on whether we start with the regression of x_1 on x_2, or the regression of x_1 on x_3.

We now turn to a more general examination of the way in which the regression of a variable x on m variables $u_1, u_2, \ldots, u_m$ is related to the regression of the same variable x on $m+n$ variables $u_1, u_2, \ldots, u_m; v_1, v_2, \ldots, v_n$. We write the first regression:

$$(x - \bar{x}) = a'(u - \bar{u});$$

and the second:

$$(x - \bar{x}) = c'(u - \bar{u}) + d'(v - \bar{v}).$$

With this notation, formula (35) gives the following values[†] for the vectors

---

† We can calculate c and d separately by:

$$c = \left(M_{uu} - M_{uv}M_{vv}^{-1}M_{vu}\right)^{-1}\left(M_{ux} - M_{uv}M_{vv}^{-1}M_{vx}\right)$$

$$d = \left(M_{vv} - M_{vu}M_{uu}^{-1}M_{uv}\right)^{-1}\left(M_{vx} - M_{vu}M_{uu}^{-1}M_{ux}\right)$$

these expressions being directly obtainable from (43) by applying the following useful remark:
Remark. If A and B are two non-singular square matrices the inverse of the non-singular matrix $\begin{bmatrix} A & C \\ C' & B \end{bmatrix}$ is:

$$\begin{bmatrix} A & C \\ C' & B \end{bmatrix}^{-1} = \begin{bmatrix} (A - CB^{-1}C')^{-1} & -(A - CB^{-1}C')^{-1}CB^{-1} \\ -(B - C'A^{-1}C)^{-1}C'A^{-1} & (B - C'A^{-1}C)^{-1} \end{bmatrix}.$$

a, c and d:

$$a = M_{uu}^{-1}M_{ux} \qquad \begin{bmatrix} c \\ d \end{bmatrix} = \begin{bmatrix} M_{uu} & M_{uv} \\ M_{vu} & M_{vv} \end{bmatrix}^{-1} \begin{bmatrix} M_{ux} \\ M_{vx} \end{bmatrix} \qquad (43)$$

It is clear that a exactly equals c if $M_{uv}=0$, that is, if:

$$\frac{1}{T}\sum_{t=1}^{T}(u_{jt} - \bar{u}_j)(v_{kt} - \bar{v}_k) = 0 \qquad (44)$$

for every pair u_j and v_k ($j=1,2,\ldots,n$; $k=1,2,\ldots,n$), whence we obtain the following definition and proposition:

Definition. Two groups of variables $u_1,u_2,\ldots,u_m$ and $v_1,v_2,\ldots,v_n$ are said to be *orthogonal* over a set of observations if condition (44) is satisfied.

Proposition. If the two groups of variables $u_1,u_2,\ldots,u_m$ and $v_1,v_2,\ldots,v_n$ are orthogonal, the regression coefficients of any variable x on $u_1,u_2,\ldots,u_m$; $v_1,v_2,\ldots,v_n$ are respectively equal to the regression coefficients of x on $u_1,u_2,\ldots,u_m$ and x on $v_1,v_2,\ldots,v_n$.

Calculation of regression is thus much simpler when orthogonality is present among the variables. This is rarely so with economic data. However, we shall encounter an example when dealing with the analysis of time series (cf. ch. 12 § 2(iii).

9   Comparison of different multiple regressions

Until now we have been interested only in formulae for calculating multiple regressions. We have still to show that the examination of such regressions can help us to grasp the nature of the relationships among observed variables, or to put it another way, to determine the shape of the collections of points which would represent the set of data in n-dimensional space.

Two types of comparison will be of interest. On the one hand, we will compare the linear relationship found in the regression of x_1 on $x_2,x_3,\ldots,x_n$ with those found in other regressions among the same variables, for example, the regression of x_2 on $x_1,x_3,\ldots,x_n$. On the other hand, regressions relating to $x_1,x_2,x_3,\ldots,x_n$ will be compared with regressions relating to more restricted sets of variables, for example $x_1,x_2,x_3,\ldots,x_{n-1}$.

We start by discussing two different situations that occur with the data in table 1.

(i)   Linear relationship among x_1, x_2 and x_3

The first comparison is made of the three multiple regressions among the variables x_1, x_2 and x_3 (imports, production and stock formation). The three regressions are:

$$x_1 = 0.191 \, x_2 + 0.405 \, x_3 - 16.78; \qquad R^2 = 0.972.$$

$$x_2 = 5.08 \, x_1 - 1.82 \, x_3 + 91.53; \qquad R^2 = 0.971, \qquad (45)$$

$$x_3 = 0.239 \, x_1 - 0.040 \, x_2 + 6.07; \qquad R^2 = 0.139.$$

Solving with respect to x_1, we have:

$$x_1 = 0.191 \, x_2 + 0.405 \, x_3 - 16.78;$$

$$x_1 = 0.197 \, x_2 + 0.359 \, x_3 - 18.05; \qquad (46)$$

$$x_1 = 0.169 \, x_2 + 4.184 \, x_3 - 25.35.$$

The first two equations are very similar, and while the third is quite different, it gives a coefficient of the same magnitude for x_2. The values of R^2 show that in three-dimensional space points representing the data are all near a plane. We can now see that this plane is fairly well determined.

Again the regression equations (46) can be compared with the two regressions relating to x_1 and x_2 (imports and production):

$$x_1 = 0.193 \, x_2 - 15.86; \qquad R^2 = 0.969,$$
$$x_2 = 5.008 \, x_1 + 86.87; \qquad R^2 = 0.969, \qquad (47)$$

which, when solved for x_1, give:

$$x_1 = 0.193 \, x_2 - 15.86;$$
$$x_1 = 0.199 \, x_2 - 17.32. \qquad (48)$$

We see that the coefficients of x_2 in these two equations are near the corresponding coefficients of the first two equations of (46), although they differ more markedly from each other. Similarly the values of R^2 remain high although slightly reduced.

The result is that, when projected on the (x_1, x_2)-plane, the representative points are again grouped near a line which is parallel to the intersection of x_1Ox_2 with the previously determined plane. We have already observed this approximate alignment in the first part of fig. 8. It is explained solely by the slight dispersion of the values of x_3, since in equations (46) the coefficients of this variable are considerably different from zero.

We consider now the regressions involving x_1 and x_3 (imports and stock-formation):

$$x_1 = 1.91 \ x_3 + 23.07; \qquad R^2 = 0.071,$$
$$x_3 = 0.037 \ x_1 + 2.56; \qquad R^2 = 0.071, \tag{49}$$

or again:

$$x_1 = \ 1.91 \ x_3 + 23.07;$$
$$x_1 = 26.9 \ \ x_3 - 69.0. \tag{50}$$

The difference between the two coefficients of x_3 and the low value of R^2 show that projections of the representative points on the plane (x_1, x_3) are not concentrated near a line. To disclose dependence between imports and stock-formation, we must introduce another variable, for example production.

(ii)   Linear relationship among x_1, x_2 and x_4

Let us make similar comparisons involving the regressions among x_1, x_2 and x_4 (imports, production and consumption):

$$x_1 = 0.043 \ x_2 + 0.230 \ x_4 - 18.63; \qquad R^2 = 0.970,$$
$$x_2 = 0.078 \ x_1 + 1.503 \ x_4 - 16.37; \qquad R^2 = 0.998, \tag{51}$$
$$x_4 = 0.174 \ x_1 + 0.620 \ x_2 + 14.81; \qquad R^2 = 0.998,$$

or again:

$$x_1 = \ \ \ 0.043 \ x_2 + \ 0.230 \ x_4 - \ 18.63;$$
$$x_1 = \ 12.81 \ \ x_2 - 19.28 \ \ x_4 + 209; \tag{52}$$
$$x_1 = -3.56 \ \ x_2 + \ 5.75 \ \ x_4 - \ 85.2.$$

The values of R^2 show that each fit is fairly good. But the three are very different. In this case, the representative points in three-dimensional space are near the same line and therefore near all planes containing this line.

We note also that the correlation coefficients between these variables, taken in pairs, are all high. In fact $r_{12} = 0.984$, $r_{14} = 0.985$ and $r_{24} = 0.999$. We could also verify, as we did for x_1 and x_2, that the two simple regressions between x_1 and x_4 (or between x_2 and x_4) are very near each other.

Moreover, the effect of the strong correlation between x_4 and x_2 is that the coefficient of x_2 in the regression of x_1 on x_2 and x_4 (0.043) is radically different from the coefficient in the regression of x_1 on x_2 (0.193). Here is an example in which the graphical method of section 8 would lead to a very different result from the multiple regression.

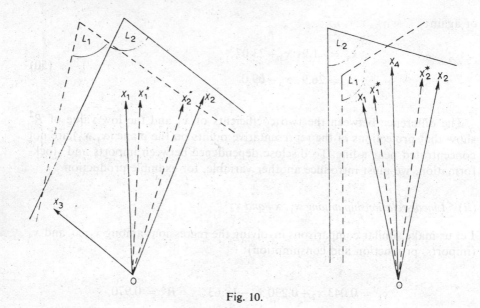

Fig. 10.

The difference between the two situations discussed above can be illustrated by a geometric picture in T-dimensional space. On the left side of fig. 10 we see how the regression of x_1 on x_2 and x_3 is determined, and also that of x_2 on x_1 and x_3. The former expresses X_1^* (a vector in the linear space L_2 spanned by X_2 and X_3) as a linear combination of X_2 and X_3. When solved for x_1 the latter regression expresses X_1 as a linear combination of X_2^* and X_3 (which is possible since X_2^* lies in the linear space L_1 spanned by X_1 and X_3). The linear spaces L_1 and L_2 are near each other; so also are these two expressions.

On the right side of fig. 10 the two regressions of x_1 on x_2 and x_4, and x_2 on x_1 and x_4, are established in the same way. But in this case the three vectors X_1, X_2 and X_4 are almost collinear; the linear spaces L_2, spanned by X_2 and X_4, and L_1, spanned by X_1 and X_4, can be very different; and the expression of X_1^* in terms of X_2 and X_4 may be very different from that of X_1 in terms of X_2^* and X_4. This explains the disparity in the first two equations of (52).

R. FRISCH [1934] devised a method which allows comparisons of the above type to be made systematically. This method depends on the construction of graphs which are called 'bunch maps'. However, it suffers from the serious drawback that it demands very heavy computation, and so could not be used in the preparatory stages of econometric study. The burden of computation, together with the confidence now placed in stochastic models, explains why the method of bunch maps has fallen into disuse[†].

10 Principal components

We can generalize orthogonal regression to the case of several variables, as we have done for the regression of x_1 on x_2. We saw that, in the case of two variables, determination of the orthogonal regression is equivalent to finding the principal component. Similarly in the case of n variables, determination of the orthogonal regressions is equivalent to finding the successive principal components. In this section, principal components will be examined. We shall show, in the next section, how orthogonal regressions are deduced from them.

The principal component of a set of observations on two variables x_1 and x_2 is, of all the linear forms

$$v = f_1(x_1 - \bar{x}_1) + f_2(x_2 - \bar{x}_2)$$

satisfying

$$f_1^2 + f_2^2 = 1,$$

that which has the greatest quadratic mean.

Similarly the *first principal component* of a set of observations on n variables $x_1, x_2, \ldots, x_n$, is, of all linear forms

$$v = f'(x - \bar{x}) = \sum_{i=1}^{n} f_i(x_i - \bar{x}_i) \tag{53}$$

satisfying

$$f'f = 1, \tag{54}$$

that which maximizes:

$$V = \frac{1}{T} \sum_{t=1}^{T} v_t^2 = f'M_{xx}f. \tag{55}$$

[†] The method was described in the first edition of this book.

In order that f should maximize (55) subject to condition (54), it is necessary that

$$(M_{xx} - \lambda I)f = 0. \tag{56}$$

This homogeneous system is obtained by equating to zero the first derivatives of

$$f'M_{xx}f - \lambda f'f,$$

λ being a Lagrange multiplier. When f satisfies (56), V takes the value λ because of (54). Expression (55) is therefore maximized by any vector f satisfying equation (54) and system (56) with λ replaced by the largest root λ_1 of:

$$|M_{xx} - \lambda I| = 0. \tag{57}$$

Since M_{xx} is positive definite, we know that all the roots of (57) are real[†]. They are called the characteristic roots of M_{xx}.

If λ_1 is a simple root, $M_{xx} - \lambda_1 I$ has rank $n-1$ and the solution f_1 of (54) and (56) is therefore uniquely determined, apart from a possible arbitrary multiplication of all its components by -1. If λ_1 is a multiple root, the number of solutions is infinite. We shall choose some solution from among them as the first principal component, and denote it by f_1. In every case f_1 is a characteristic vector of M_{xx}, associated with the greatest characteristic root.

The linear form (of type (53)–(54)) which has the greatest length among all linear forms orthogonal to the first principal component, is called the *second principal component*. In other words, the second principal component is defined by the vector f_2 which maximizes (55) subject to conditions (54) and

$$\frac{1}{T} \sum_{t=1}^{T} v_t v_{1t} = f'M_{xx}f_1 = 0. \tag{58}$$

Since (56) has solution f_1, the above condition can be written:

$$f'f_1 = 0. \tag{59}$$

If λ and 2μ are two Lagrange multipliers, f_2 must satisfy:

$$(M_{xx} - \lambda I)f - \mu f_1 = 0. \tag{60}$$

---

† See, for example, BASS [1956], ch. III.

Premultiplying this equation by f_1', we see that μ must be zero. The vector f_2 must therefore be, like f_1, a characteristic vector of M_{xx}, that is, it must satisfy (56). It gives a value for V which is the value of the characteristic root with which it is associated. If λ_1 is a simple root, there is only one corresponding characteristic vector f_1; in this case f_2 is a characteristic vector associated with the second root λ_2. If λ_1 is a multiple root, f_2 is any characteristic vector associated with λ_1 and orthogonal to f_1 (that is, it satisfies (59), and of course (54)). We shall then write $\lambda_2 = \lambda_1$.

The preceding equations can be expressed more concisely by introducing two matrices. These are the diagonal matrix of order 2 whose non-zero elements are the characteristic roots associated with f_1 and f_2, and the $n \times 2$ matrix F which by definition is $[f_1, f_2]$. Equations (54), (59) and (56) can now be written:

$$F'F = I, \tag{61}$$

$$M_{xx}F = F\Lambda. \tag{62}$$

The third component is the linear form of greatest length among all linear forms orthogonal to the first two principal components. We find it from a characteristic vector of M_{xx}, associated with the third characteristic root if λ_1 and λ_2 are simple.

By extending this process, n principal components corresponding to n orthogonal characteristic vectors of M_{xx} may be defined. The matrix F thus obtained is orthonormal, and (62) then implies $M_{xx} = F\Lambda F'$. This is called the *canonical reduction* of the matrix M_{xx}. In n-dimensional space, λ_i will measure the quadratic mean of the ith principal component, the mean being taken over the set of observations. The greater the value of λ_i, the more the points will tend to be distributed in the direction of the ith principal component.

Thus the set of principal components and the set of corresponding roots λ give us information about the directions in which the points are mainly distributed, and of the relative importance of the dispersion in different directions. It is therefore a useful way of investigating the shape taken by the collection of points. Unfortunately, when n is greater than 4, the determination of the vectors and characteristic roots of M_{xx} is often laborious. However, the use of computers may make this method more useful.

The principal components can be calculated from the observations themselves or from the corresponding standardized variables y_{it} defined by

$$y_{it} = \frac{x_{it} - \bar{x}_i}{\left[\dfrac{1}{T}\sum_{t=1}^{T}(x_{it} - \bar{x}_i)^2\right]^{\frac{1}{2}}}. \tag{63}$$

The two results are not equivalent, since we have already seen, in the case where $n = 2$, that the result depends on the units of measurement. The two systems of principal components will correspond the more closely (after changing the units of measurement), the nearer are the dispersions of the different variables and the more disparate are the characteristic roots of M_{yy}.

The principal components of the variables x_1, x_2, x_3 and x_4 of table 1 have been calculated, giving the following results:

$$\lambda_1 = 558.36; \qquad \lambda_2 = 4.98; \qquad \lambda_3 = 2.58; \qquad \lambda_4 = 2.01.$$

$$f_1 = \begin{bmatrix} 0.160 \\ 0.826 \\ 0.005 \\ 0.541 \end{bmatrix}, \quad f_2 = \begin{bmatrix} 0.882 \\ -0.191 \\ 0.431 \\ -0.027 \end{bmatrix}, \quad f_3 = \begin{bmatrix} 0.147 \\ -0.467 \\ -0.551 \\ 0.676 \end{bmatrix}, \quad f_4 = \begin{bmatrix} -0.419 \\ -0.251 \\ 0.715 \\ 0.501 \end{bmatrix}. \tag{64}$$

The principal components of the standardized variables y_1, y_2, y_3 and y_4, are:

$$\mu_1 = 3.057; \qquad \mu_2 = 0.924; \qquad \mu_3 = 0.018; \qquad \mu_4 = 0.001.$$

$$g_1 = \begin{bmatrix} 0.567 \\ 0.566 \\ 0.191 \\ 0.566 \end{bmatrix}, \quad g_2 = \begin{bmatrix} -0.072 \\ -0.129 \\ 0.980 \\ -0.131 \end{bmatrix}, \quad g_3 = \begin{bmatrix} -0.820 \\ 0.419 \\ 0.046 \\ 0.387 \end{bmatrix}, \quad g_4 = \begin{bmatrix} -0.019 \\ -0.698 \\ 0.002 \\ 0.716 \end{bmatrix}. \tag{65}$$

To simplify comparison of the two systems of principal components, we express the vector g_k in the same units as the vector f_k; that is, we multiply each component g_{ki} by the standard deviations s_i of x_i; then we normalize the resulting vector so that the sum of its components is 1 (cf. condition (54)). The ith component of the new vector h_k is then:

$$h_{ki} = \frac{s_i g_{ki}}{\left[\sum_{j=1}^{4} s_j^2 g_{kj}^2 \right]^{\frac{1}{2}}}.$$

In the present example we obtain:

$$h_1 = \begin{bmatrix} 0.162 \\ 0.823 \\ 0.008 \\ 0.540 \end{bmatrix}, \quad h_2 = \begin{bmatrix} -0.093 \\ -0.777 \\ 0.178 \\ -0.566 \end{bmatrix}, \quad h_3 = \begin{bmatrix} -0.313 \\ 0.812 \\ 0.003 \\ 0.494 \end{bmatrix}, \quad h_4 = \begin{bmatrix} -0.004 \\ -0.826 \\ 0.000 \\ 0.553 \end{bmatrix}. \tag{66}$$

These results show that, in the four-dimensional space of the x_i, the shape of the collection of representative points is much elongated in the direction of f_1.

Indeed the first characteristic root λ_1 of M_{xx} is much greater than the subsequent roots λ_2, λ_3 and λ_4. Moreover, we establish that h_1 is very near f_1 so that the major axis of the collection of points in the space of the standardized variables corresponds almost exactly to the direction f_1, after changing the units of measurement, and this is so even though the standard deviations s_i differ widely from each other. On the other hand, the vectors h_2, h_3 and h_4 are very different from f_2, f_3 and f_4.

For a clear understanding of the data, it is generally helpful to try also to interpret the meaning of the few first principal components. If, in the present example, we consider the standardized variables then the first two components defined by the vectors g_1 and g_2 obviously characterize respectively the general volume of activity, which acts on the four quantities simultaneously, and fluctuations in stock formation in so far as they exceed those fluctuations resulting from movements in production and consumption. If we consider the directly observed variables, then again f_1 represents the volume of activity; we have just seen that the role of f_1 is virtually the same as that of g_1. The second component, with vector f_2, represents variations in imports and stocks relative to the level of production.

With the development of computational aids and methods of data analysis it has also become usual practice to look at the position of each observation in the plane of the first two principal components. Thus, on fig. 11 each annual observation is represented by a point whose abscissa and ordinate are the values of the first two principal components v_1 and v_2. For ease of inspection, a line is drawn joining the points in order of time. We note the almost regular increase in v_1 and the large fluctuations in v_2 (with high values relative to adjacent years in 1949, 1956 and 1964, and low values in 1955, 1959 and 1962). We note also that v_2 tends to decrease in the decade 1950–59; this suggests that imports and stocks grew less quickly than the increase in production could lead one to expect.

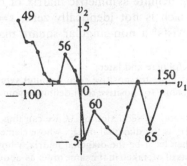

FIG. 11.

11   Orthogonal regression

When discussing linear equations which characterize the dependence between two variables, we defined the orthogonal regression as the line $a_1x_1 + a_2x_2 = b$, satisfying $a_1^2 + a_2^2 = 1$ and passing as closely as possible to the observed points, distances being measured perpendicularly. The coefficients a_1, a_2 and b minimized:

$$U = \sum_{t=1}^{T}(a_1x_{1t} + a_2x_{2t} - b)^2,$$

subject to the condition

$$a_1^2 + a_2^2 = 1.$$

In econometric studies involving n variables we can similarly define the orthogonal regression of order m to be the $(n-m)$-dimensional hyperplane which in n-dimensional space passes as closely as possible to the observed points, distances being measured perpendicularly.

An $(n-m)$-dimensional hyperplane in n-dimensional space consists of the set of vectors x whose components $x_1, x_2,\ldots,x_n$ satisfy m independent linear equations. These m equations can be written:

$$Ax = b, \tag{67}$$

where A is an $(m \times n)$ matrix of rank m and b is a vector with m components.

If C is a non-singular square matrix of order m, the same hyperplane is defined by (67) and by

$$CAx = Cb.$$

In particular, we can choose C so that

$$(CA)(CA)' = I.$$

In fact, AA' is a positive definite symmetric matrix of order m, since for any m-dimensional vector which is not identically zero, $s = A'r \neq 0$ and $r'AA'r = s's > 0$. Therefore there exists[†] a non-singular square matrix of order m, such

---

[†] The following lemma is useful here and later:

LEMMA. If M is a positive definite (or positive semi-definite) symmetric matrix of order m, then there exists a positive definite (or positive semi-definite) symmetric matrix N of order m, such that $M = N'N = N^2$.

For, by carrying out the canonical reduction of M, we can find an orthonormal (real unitary) matrix P such that PMP' is the diagonal matrix whose elements are the m positive real characteristic roots of M. Then let Δ be the diagonal matrix, whose elements are the square roots of the characteristic roots of M, taken in the same order as above. Obviously $PMP' = \Delta'\Delta$ and therefore also

$$M = P'\Delta'PP'\Delta P.$$

The above lemma is thus proved where $N = P'\Delta P$.

that $B'B = AA'$; and it follows that $(B')^{-1}AA'B^{-1} = I$. By choosing $C = (B')^{-1}$ we have $(CA)(CA)' = I$.

We therefore lose no generality by imposing on A in system (67) the restriction that:

$$AA' = I, \tag{68}$$

which we impose for convenience in calculation.

We find, first of all, the expression for the square of the distance between the point x_t in n-dimensional space and the hyperplane $Ax = b$. This is equivalent to finding the minimum of

$$u_t = (x_t - y_t)'(x_t - y_t), \tag{69}$$

where y_t is restricted to lie in the hyperplane:

$$Ay_t = b. \tag{70}$$

To find the minimum of (69) subject to the m linear restrictions, we must differentiate the following expression with respect to the unknown components of y_t:

$$(x_t - y_t)'(x_t - y_t) + 2w_t'(Ay_t - b), \tag{71}$$

where $2w_t$ is a vector of m Lagrange multipliers. We then obtain:

$$(x_t - y_t)' = w_t'A.$$

Multiplying this equation by A', taking account of the fact that $AA' = I$, and transposing, we have $w_t = A(x_t - y_t)$; or again, from (70), $w_t = Ax_t - b$. Hence we obtain the square of the minimum distance:

$$u_t = w_t'AA'w_t = w_t'w_t = (Ax_t - b)'(Ax_t - b). \tag{72}$$

Thus the orthogonal regression of order m will be defined by the matrix A and the vector b which minimize:

$$U = \sum_{t=1}^{T} (Ax_t - b)'(Ax_t - b). \tag{73}$$

subject to the condition $AA' = I$.

The quantity to be minimized can also be written:

$$U = \sum_{t=1}^{T} (x_t - \bar{x})'A'A(x_t - \bar{x}) + T(A\bar{x} - b)'(A\bar{x} - b).$$

As b occurs only in the last term, which is never negative and becomes zero for $b = A\bar{x}$, the orthogonal regression must pass through the mean point $\bar{x}$ of the collection. The condition

$$A\bar{x} = b \tag{74}$$

is sufficient to determine b when A is known.

We have still to minimize:

$$U = \sum_{t=1}^{T} (x_t - \bar{x})'A'A(x_t - \bar{x}), \tag{75}$$

subject to the condition $AA' = I$.

It is convenient to denote by a'_j the row-vector of the elements of the jth row of $A(j = 1, 2, \ldots, m)$. Obviously (75) can also be written

$$U = T \sum_{j=1}^{m} a'_j M_{xx} a_j \tag{76}$$

and the condition $AA' = I$ can be written:

$$a'_j a_k = \delta_{jk}, \qquad j, k = 1, 2, \ldots, m, \tag{77}$$

where $\delta_{jk} = 1$ if $j = k$, and $\delta_{jk} = 0$ if $j \neq k$. The vectors a_j must have unit length and be mutually orthogonal.

For minimization, these vectors must satisfy the conditions obtained by differentiating:

$$\sum_{j=1}^{m} a'_j M_{xx} a_j - \sum_{j=1}^{m} \mu_j a'_j a_j - \sum_{k \neq j} v_{jk} a'_j a_k, \tag{78}$$

where μ_j and $v_{jk} = v_{kj}$ are $m(m+1)/2$ Lagrange multipliers corresponding to conditions (77). Differentiation with respect to the components of a_j yields:

$$(M_{xx} - \mu_j I)a_j - \sum_{k \neq j} v_{jk} a_k = 0 \qquad j = 1, 2, \ldots, m. \tag{79}$$

This system has solution $v_{jk} = 0$, for every pair (j, k), provided that the a_j satisfy (77) and

$$(M_{xx} - \mu_j I)a_j = 0, \qquad j = 1, 2, \ldots, m. \tag{80}$$

Conversely, we can show that[†], to each solution A of (77) and (79) for given

† Let us denote by N the symmetric square matrix of order m whose diagonal elements are the μ_j and non-diagonal elements the v_{jk}. Let μ_j^* and c_j be the m characteristic roots of N and m characteristic vectors satisfying

$$(N - \mu_j^* I)c_j = 0 \quad \text{and} \quad c'_k c_j = \delta_{kj}.$$

Consider the m vectors

$$a_j^* = \sum_{k=1}^{m} c_{jk} a_k.$$

It can be verified that the a_j^* and the μ_j^* satisfy equations (77) and (80).

values of μ_j and v_{jk}, there corresponds a solution $A^* = CA$ of (77) and (80) for some numbers μ_j^* and some square matrix C. To determine the orthogonal regression, we can therefore confine ourselves to the matrices A which satisfy (77) and (80) with suitably chosen μ_j. Moreover (77) and (80) imply:

$$a_j' M_{xx} a_j = \mu_j,$$

whence

$$U = T \sum_{j=1}^{m} \mu_j. \tag{81}$$

To minimize U, one must choose for the μ_j the m smallest characteristic roots of M_{xx}, multiple roots being repeated according to their multiplicities.

Systems (77) and (80) are equivalent. The vectors a_j which we are trying to find correspond therefore to the m last principal components of the collection of points (that is, to the directions in which the dispersions of the points are smallest).

To sum up, *the orthogonal regression of order m is the $(n-m)$-dimensional hyperplane passing through the mean point $\bar{x}$ and orthogonal to the m last principal components.*

Thus for the example of table 1, the orthogonal regression of order 2 is defined by the two linear equations:

$$f_3'(x - \bar{x}) = 0, \qquad f_4'(x - \bar{x}) = 0,$$

say, which are in this case:

$$0.147(x_1 - \bar{x}_1) - 0.467(x_2 - \bar{x}_2) - 0.551(x_3 - \bar{x}_3) + 0.676(x_4 - \bar{x}_4) = 0,$$

$$-0.419(x_1 - \bar{x}_1) - 0.251(x_2 - \bar{x}_2) + 0.715(x_3 - \bar{x}_3) + 0.501(x_4 - \bar{x}_4) = 0.$$

They can be written:

$$x_1 = 0.179x_2 + 2.133x_3 - 20.27,$$
$$x_1 = 2.030x_3 + 0.278x_4 - 23.99. \tag{82}$$

We see that the first of the equations (82) is intermediary between the equations (46) obtained by multiple regression.

12   Change of variables

When dealing with regressions between two variables, we saw that changes of units do not affect the determination of simple regressions, but that on the other hand they do cause a change in the principal component and the orthogonal regression. We return now to this question and discuss changes of units of n variables, or more generally, linear transformations of these variables.

Let C be a non-singular square matrix of order n. The n-dimensional vector x of the variables x_i can be replaced by the vector

$$y = Cx, \tag{83}$$

the y_i being called 'transformed variables'.

The means $\bar{y}_i$ of the y_{it} will form the vector $\bar{y} = C\bar{x}$. Similarly the matrix M_{yy} of second order moments will be:

$$M_{yy} = CM_{xx}C'. \tag{84}$$

We consider first the multiple regression of a variable, say x_1, on the other variables $x_2, x_3, \ldots, x_n$. How is this regression affected by the change of variables? The variable x_1 has a privileged position and we therefore confine ourselves to changes in variables which do not affect x_1. More precisely, we can prove the following result.

PROPOSITION. *If y_1 differs from x_1 only by a constant factor, and if $y_2, y_3, \ldots, y_n$ are independent linear combinations of $x_2, x_3, \ldots, x_n$, then the regression of y_1 on $y_2, y_3, \ldots, y_n$ is the transformation of the regression of x_1 on $x_2, x_3, \ldots, x_n$.*

In fact the matrix of the linear transformation can be partitioned as follows

$$C = \begin{bmatrix} c & 0 \\ 0 & C^1 \end{bmatrix},$$

where c is a non-zero number, 0 a zero row-vector and a zero column-vector and C^1 a non-singular square matrix of order $n-1$. If, as in section 7, x^1 and y^1 denote the vectors of the $n-1$ last components of x and y, then:

$$y_1 = cx_1, \qquad y^1 = C^1 x^1.$$

The regression of x_1 on $x_2, x_3, \ldots, x_n$ was

$$(x_1 - \bar{x}_1) = a^{1'}(x^1 - \bar{x}^1),$$

where a^1 is an $(n-1)$-dimensional vector (cf. eq. 31'). The transform of this regression is obviously:

$$\frac{1}{c}(y_1 - \bar{y}_1) = a^{1'}(C^1)^{-1}(y^1 - \bar{y}^1).$$

It is therefore sufficient to verify that the vector of the regression coefficients of y_1 on $y_2, y_3, \ldots, y_n$ is $ca^{1'}(C^1)^{-1}$.

This vector is determined by formula (35) in section 7, the formula being applied to a partition of M_{yy} similar to (34). In view of expression (84) for M_{yy}, this partition can be expressed:

$$M_{yy} = \begin{bmatrix} c^2 m_{11} & cm^{1'}C^{1'} \\ cC^1 m^1 & C^1 M^1 C^{1'} \end{bmatrix}$$

whence we obtain, for the column-vector of the regression coefficients:

$$c[C^1 M^1 C^{1'}]^{-1} C^1 m^1 = c[C^{1'}]^{-1}(M^1)^{-1} m^1 = c[C^{1'}]^{-1} a^1,$$

and this is identical to the expression obtained above.

In the case where $n = 2$ we have already seen that a change of variables affects the orthogonal regressions and the principal components. The transform of the jth principal component of the x's is not the same as the jth principal component of the y's. Similarly the transform of the orthogonal regression of order m of the x's is not identical to the orthogonal regression of order m of the y's.

We now state the two following problems. How can we determine in x-space the vector which, when transformed, will coincide with the jth principal component of the y's? How can we determine in x-space the $(n-m)$-dimensional hyperplane which, when transformed, will coincide with the orthogonal regression of order m of the y's?

The n principal components of the y's are, by definition, n vectors g_j ($j = 1, 2, \ldots, m$) which satisfy:

$$(M_{yy} - \mu_j I)g_j = 0,$$
$$g_j' g_k = \delta_{jk},$$
(85)

where the μ_j are the values of the characteristic roots of M_{yy}, in decreasing order of magnitude, and where the usual Kronecker symbol is used: $\delta_{jj} = 1$, $\delta_{jk} = 0$ if $j \neq k$. The vectors g_j are the transforms of certain vectors h_j and therefore $g_j = Ch_j$. In view of (84) we see that the h_j satisfy:

$$[CM_{xx}C' - \mu_j I]Ch_j = 0,$$
$$h_j' C'Ch_k = \delta_{jk}.$$

$C'C$ is obviously a positive definite symmetric matrix. Setting $C'C = \Omega^{-1}$ and multiplying the first of the above equations by C^{-1}, we obtain:

$$(M_{xx}\Omega^{-1} - \mu_j I)h_j = 0,$$
$$h_j' \Omega^{-1} h_k = \delta_{jk},$$
(86)

from which we can determine the h_j directly.

Similarly, the orthogonal regression of order m of the y's is the $(n-m)$-dimensional hyperplane which satisfies:

$$g_j'(y - \bar{y}) = 0 \quad \text{for} \quad j = n - m + 1, n - m + 2, \ldots, n. \tag{87}$$

It is the transform of the hyperplane

$$l_j'(x - \bar{x}) = 0 \quad \text{for} \quad j = n - m + 1, n - m + 2, \ldots, n, \tag{88}$$

where $l_j = C'g_j$. Transformations similar to those applied above show that system (85) can be written:

$$\begin{aligned} (M_{xx} - \mu_j\Omega)l_j &= 0, \\ l_j'\Omega l_k &= \delta_{jk}. \end{aligned} \tag{89}$$

Minimization of the sum of squares of the Euclidean distances between the observed points and the hyperplane which we are looking for in the y-space, is therefore equivalent in the x-space to the minimization of:

$$U = \sum_{t=1}^{T} (x_t - z_t)'\Omega^{-1}(x_t - z_t), \tag{90}$$

where z_t is restricted to lie in an $(n-m)$-dimensional hyperplane. For this reason the hyperplane defined by equations (88) and (89) is sometimes called the 'regression of order m in the metric Ω^{-1}'. An orthogonal regression is therefore a regression in the metric I.

By virtue of the lemma given in the footnote to page 36, provided Ω is positive definite, it is always possible to find a change of variables which allows us to convert a regression in the metric Ω^{-1} to an orthogonal regression.

Moreover, we can verify from (89) that, if M_{xx} is a singular matrix, then the regression of order 1 is independent of the chosen metric; the smallest characteristic root is then zero and l is a corresponding characteristic vector of M_{xx}.

13   Relationships between different regressions

We have defined different types of regression while generalizing the methods previously introduced for sets of observations on two variables. We could go on to study the relationships between these regressions, but shall confine ourselves here to two remarks.

In the first place, we note that the multiple regression of x_1 on $x_2, x_3, \ldots, x_n$ is related in a certain way to regressions in well-defined metrics.

Let us consider the regression of order 1 in the metric Ω^{-1}. We make a slight change in system (89) by ignoring the second equation, which imposes the condition that the vector l should have unit length; instead we choose this vector so that its first component is equal to -1. Obviously this change in the normalizing rule does not affect the regression.

It is clear that, when system (89) is changed in this way, the vector l varies continuously with Ω, at least if the smallest root of $|M_{xx} - \mu\Omega| = 0$ is simple. Let us suppose then that Ω tends to the singular matrix Q whose first element $q_{11} = 1$, all the others being zero. The smallest root of $|M_{xx} - \mu\Omega| = 0$ remains finite, the other $n-1$ roots tending to infinity. The vector l tends to the solution of the system:

$$(M_{xx} - \mu Q)l = 0. \tag{91}$$

Now this solution is just the vector of the multiple regression of x_1 on $x_2, x_3, \ldots, x_n$. In fact, when we introduce the partition of M_{xx}, as in section 7, the above equation can be written:

$$\begin{bmatrix} m_{11} - \mu & m^{1'} \\ m^1 & M^1 \end{bmatrix} \begin{bmatrix} -1 \\ l^1 \end{bmatrix} = 0 \tag{92}$$

which has the solution

$$l^1 = (M^1)^{-1} m^1 = a^1.$$

The matrix Q does not define a true metric since it is singular. *However, the multiple regression can be interpreted as the limit of regressions in metrics which give less and less importance to one coordinate relative to the others* (in this case, the first coordinate).

In the second place, the orthogonal regression of order 1 appears to be located in between the n multiple regressions. More precisely, let us denote by p_j an n-dimensional vector orthogonal to the hyperplane of the regression of x_j on $x_1, x_2, \ldots, x_{j-1}, x_{j+1}, \ldots, x_n$. Suppose that there exists a definition of the p_j (for $j = 1, 2, \ldots, n$), such that these n vectors belong to the same quadrant, that is, that their ith components have the same sign, whatever the value of i. Then the vector f of the orthogonal regression is contained in the solid angle

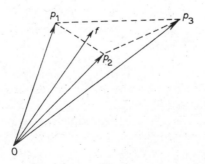

Fig. 12.

formed by the p_j. In other words, there exist n positive numbers $\alpha_1, \alpha_2, \ldots, \alpha_n$, such that:

$$f = \sum_{j=1}^{n} \alpha_j p_j. \tag{93}$$

For the proof of this property[†] we can discuss directly the case where f is the vector of the regression of order 1 in the metric Ω^{-1}, *where Ω is a diagonal matrix*. (When Ω is not diagonal, the property no longer necessarily holds, as can be verified for the case where $n = 2$.)

Let us assume that the range of the p_j is the set of vectors with no negative component (we can always revert to this case by changing the sign of some variables x_i). Equation (92) shows that, apart from a positive multiplicative coefficient, the vector p_1 is equal to the first column of M_{xx}^{-1} (the case where M_{xx} is singular has already been discussed at the end of the previous section). Similarly p_j is positively proportional to the jth column of M_{xx}^{-1}. So the assumption adopted is equivalent to assuming that M_{xx}^{-1} has no negative component.

Now, the equation defining the regression of order 1 in the metric Ω^{-1} can be written

$$\left(\Omega M_{xx}^{-1} - \frac{1}{\mu} I \right) M_{xx} f = 0 \tag{94}$$

where $1/\mu$ is the largest characteristic root of the non-negative matrix ΩM_{xx}^{-1}. It follows that the corresponding characteristic vector $w = M_{xx} f$ has no negative component (see, for example, DEBREU and HERSTEIN [1953]). So from $f = M_{xx}^{-1} w$ we can go directly to (93) with non-negative numbers α_j.

---

† This proof was given to me by Ir. W. L. KELLER in a note dated 6th June, 1973.

CHAPTER 2

Economic models and statistical inference

1 *Representation of economic phenomena*

After this chapter we shall be studying the different econometric methods applicable within the framework of well-defined models, and so it seems opportune to make a preliminary study of the general nature of economic models and of the principles of statistical inference. This is our present aim.

A model is the formal representation of the notions that we have about a phenomenon. These notions, often called the 'theory of the phenomenon', are expressed by a set of assumptions about the essential elements of the phenomenon and the laws which regulate it. They are generally expressed in terms of a mathematical system, and this system is then called 'the model'.

By basing our reasoning on the model we can investigate the logical consequences of the assumptions we have made, compare them with observations and thus find ourselves better equipped to understand the real world and to act efficiently on it.

All the sciences make use of models. Each isolates certain phenomena and studies their basic laws. The aim then is to simplify complex real situations so that the two or three relations which seem most important for the particular problem can be applied to them. The isolation of phenomena and the establishment of abstract representations of them is therefore the point of departure of all scientific method.

In the physical sciences faithful and exact representations can generally be made. The permanent nature of the underlying laws and the practical possibilities of experimentation facilitate the study of the different aspects of reality. By constructing artificial situations or by combining long series of observations, scholars in each field can study how some particular cause affects a gas pressure, the motion of a star or the signs of a physiological equilibrium. They are thus able to determine how two quantities vary simultaneously when the others are held constant and the general environment is unchanged.

The situation is very different in the social sciences and particularly in economics. The phenomena which they study are bound up with the essentially moving organization of human communities. Experiment is often impossible, and great care must be taken in simply observing phenomena, as this can rarely be done under invariable conditions. The separate study of social and economic laws is therefore much more difficult than that of physical laws. The economist is forced to make simplified representations much more often than the physicist or the biologist. He must simplify not only when he is trying to make practical

use of accumulated theoretical knowledge, but also when collecting or interpreting observations, and even when trying to formulate new theoretical
relations.

We note also that the introduction and spread of the word 'model' in the
social sciences has been accompanied by a growth in rigor. It reflects a conscious-
ness of imperfection in these sciences and expresses a certain humility.

The logic of reasoning with models is thus the chief basis of scientific method
in economics. It has had a most important part in the building up of economic
theory, and has been of even more obvious importance in the different
techniques of applied economics.

To discover the chief characteristics of economic models, we start by examining three examples to which we shall also make occasional reference in
other chapters.

2   First example: supply and demand in a competitive market

The division of labor in modern societies involves many exchanges in the course
of which the goods produced are distributed among their different uses. Each
exchange is the result of a contract freely entered into by the seller and the buyer
of the good, at a price chosen by them. How is equilibrium reached in operations
of this kind? Why is there no lasting surplus or deficiency in supply relative
to demand?

Since the days of the first classical economists it has been known that
equilibrium in a competitive market is reached after confronting all demands
with all supplies. Sales of the same product are all concluded at the same price
which must be exactly that price which leaves no unsatisfied demand nor surplus
supply. We do not propose to present this theory in detail, but simply to
examine the model which expresses it.

Let q_1 and q_2 be the quantities demanded and supplied of a certain product,
on a certain day and in a certain market. Let p be the price at which exchanges
take place. The quantities q_1 and q_2 depend on p, because the buyers and sellers
can decide not to buy or not to sell if the price is unsatisfactory. To express
this, we say that there exist two functions, a demand function $q_1 = f(p)$ and a
supply function $q_2 = g(p)$, which determine q_1 and q_2 respectively from p. This
is the same as saying that, once the price of the product is known, q_1 and q_2
are also known. The condition of equilibrium in the market is that $q_1 = q_2$.

*Formally, the model of the market establishes, among three real, non-negative
variables q_1, q_2 and p, two equations, $q_1 = f(p)$, $q_2 = g(p)$, where f and g are given
functions. Equilibrium exists if $q_1 = q_2$. Or:*

$$q_1 = f(p),$$
$$q_2 = g(p), \tag{1}$$
$$q_1 = q_2.$$

This model takes account only of the dependence of supply and demand on the price of the commodity in question, whereas they depend to varying degrees on the whole set of prices and supplies in the economy in question. Thus the demand for beer very probably depends not only on the price of beer but also on the price of wine, family income and the temperature. These complications have been ignored in the system chosen. We must always ask ourselves in every practical situation if such simplification is legitimate.

It is often preferable to make explicit allowance for the dependence of supply and demand on variables other than price, by stating precisely those variables which influence them most strongly. In the case of the demand for beer, the function f_1 would then be $f_1(p, z_1, z_2, z_3)$, where z_1, z_2 and z_3 respectively denote the price of wine, family income and the temperature.

More generally, model (1) could be replaced by:

$$q_1 = f(p, z_1, z_2, \ldots, z_m),$$
$$q_2 = g(p, z_1, z_2, \ldots, z_m), \tag{2}$$
$$q_1 = q_2,$$

where $z_1, z_2, \ldots, z_m$ are as many variables as are needed to give an adequate picture of the factors influencing supply and demand.

These models assume that demand and supply react instantly to variations in price, since no explicit account has been taken of time. In some cases this will be an oversimplification. Thus the supply of many agricultural products depends very little on the price at which they will sell, but to a much greater extent on prices in the preceding year. If q_{1t}, q_{2t} and p_t denote supply, demand and price during year t, model (1) is superseded by the following model[†]:

$$q_{1t} = f(p_t),$$
$$q_{2t} = g(p_{t-1}), \tag{3}$$
$$q_{1t} = q_{2t}.$$

Price p_{t-1} in year $t-1$ determines supply q_{2t} in year t; price p_t in year t is determined by the necessity for equilibrium and by conditions of demand; price p_t in year t determines supply $q_{2,t+1}$ in year $t+1$, and so on.

In the literature of economics this model is known as the 'cobweb model'. On a graph with price as abscissa and quantity as ordinate, we can draw the demand curve D and the supply curve O representing the two functions f and g. Starting from price p_{t-1}, the point A on the supply curve determines q_{2t} and therefore q_{1t}, the point B on the demand curve determines p_t, the point C on

---

[†] The index t in this case denotes a period of time, whereas we use it elsewhere to denote an observation. This notation is convenient when the observations relate to successive periods of time and should not lead to any confusion.

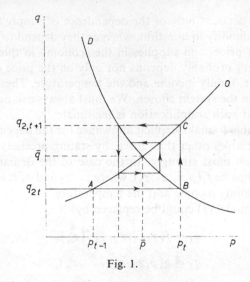

Fig. 1.

the supply curve determines $q_{2,t+1}$, and so on. The path traced out by A, B, C, etc. looks like a cobweb (cf. fig. 1). The shape of the curves D and O determines whether or not it will converge to the equilibrium point $(\bar{p}, \bar{q})$ of model (1).

3   Second example: elementary Keynesian model

The object of Keynesian theory was to explain the *level of production in a period of underemployment* of labor and capital. Classical theory was not particularly concerned with phases of underemployment which were considered as temporary accidents. It was more interested in problems of equilibrium and long-term growth than in fluctuations in the short period. However, from 1930 to 1940, most industrial countries experienced a prolonged spell of underemployment. To allow prediction of the spontaneous behavior of the economy and assessment of the different measures proposed for its guidance, it was essential to know how the level of production at any one time was determined, and why it was neither higher nor lower.

In his best-known book KEYNES [1936] was mainly concerned with the solution of this problem. Many other economists have followed him in research directed towards clarification of some obscure points in the Keynesian theory or towards their own solutions of the problem. Their work leads to the conclusion that investment is of fundamental importance in the development of the general economic system. There are two reasons for this.

In the first place, decisions on investment are largely autonomous. Some large-scale projects need the assent of public authority and can only be undertaken after a political decision. In industry itself, it is generally possible either to defer or to bring forward the installation of new capital equipment. It is true that investment is partly stimulated by the development of production. But it is easier to understand equilibrium in underemployment if we focus attention on investment as autonomous rather than as induced behavior.

Moreover the decision to invest directly stimulates a growth in production in the sectors of industry which manufacture capital equipment. Indirectly, this increased production is accompanied by a distribution of income (wages and dividends) in these sectors. This new income leads to an increase in private spending and therefore to an increase in production in industries producing consumer goods. There follow further distributions of income, further spending, and a further increase in production.

The level of production can be summarily explained on the basis of these ideas:

(i) investment is autonomous;
(ii) production is divided into two sectors, namely, production of consumer goods and production of capital goods;
(iii) production of consumer goods depends on disposable income;
(iv) disposable income depends on the level of production.

Formally we define P as total production, C as production of consumer goods, I as production of capital goods (investment) and Y as disposable income. The four propositions stated above can be expressed as follows:

$$I \quad \text{autonomous},$$

$$P = C + I,$$

$$C = F(Y),$$

$$Y = P,$$

$$\tag{4}$$

where F is the function defining the relationship between disposable income and consumption.

The model–system (4)–which we have just described is very naive, and does justice neither to the thoughts of the Keynesian school nor to the complexities of real life. However, it can often be useful for posing certain questions in a very illuminating way. It does provide an explanation of the level of production, as we can deduce from its three equations:

$$P - F(P) = I. \tag{5}$$

Solved for P, this equation defines the level of production associated with each level of investment.

If, for example, $F(Y)$ is a linear function of the form:

$$C = F(Y) = \alpha Y + \beta, \tag{6}$$

equation (5) can be written:

$$(1 - \alpha)P - \beta = I.$$

whence:

$$P = \frac{I}{1-\alpha} + \frac{\beta}{1-\alpha}. \tag{7}$$

This last equation defines P on the basis of I, which we have assumed to be determined autonomously. We have therefore found an explanation of the type sought. The coefficients α and β depend on the 'consumption function' (6), that is, on the relationship between Y and C. In particular, α measures the increase in consumption associated with a unit increase in income. It has been called the 'marginal propensity to consume'[†]. It is generally less than 1, say of the order of 0.6. Equation (7) shows then that a unit increase in I causes a rise of $1/(1-\alpha)$ in P, and this coefficient is always greater than 1. (If $\alpha = 0.6$ it is in fact 2.5.) This coefficient is the factor by which an autonomous increase in investment has to be multiplied to obtain the increase in production which it causes. It is called the *multiplier*.

Model (4) gives formal expression to the simplest Keynesian theory. Its interest goes beyond this, since it allows the examination of certain practical questions about the general economic system in a country for which the exact form of the function $F(Y)$ has been 'estimated'. However, to obtain reliable answers to these questions, the model would have to correspond closely with the real situation, and this would not be possible for a model involving such a high degree of abstraction. Macromodels of an actual economy used in short term prediction take account of a much greater number of variables and relationships. But their logic is fairly near that of model (4). We shall make further reference to it.

4   Third example: a law of demand

The two preceding examples have been taken from economic theory and are enough to reveal some general characteristics of models, as we shall see below. In particular they allow us to examine the logical problems which arise when we are faced with observed data. The essential difficulty is that theoretical models do not lend themselves directly to econometric investigations. For a fuller explanation of this remark, we consider one last example which is even simpler than those given above.

The object of *empirical demand studies* is to find the conditions governing variation in the consumption of a good, or of a group of goods, in relation to price, income and all other important variables. To this end they use observed results in order to determine general laws. For example, by means of an examination of family budgets during a certain period, they try to determine how the consumption of a particular good will change following a general rise in income.

[†] We shall also see later on that function (6) is in fact only a fair representation of the real connection between disposable income and consumption.

Such research implies certain assumptions about the permanence of the relationships between consumption and the factors which determine it. We must be able to interpret a correlation observed on a restricted sample as proof of a more general dependence. Assumptions which are thus basic to the study of demand can be formally represented by a model. For the sake of clarity we shall confine ourselves here to a particularly simple scheme.

Let c_i be the consumption of a certain product by household i whose income is y_i. Suppose that we know, for a given period, the values of c_i and y_i for a limited number of individual households. How can we deduce a law which allows us to determine the consumption of this product by any household at any time?

The simplest approach would be to suppose that there exists a strict functional relationship between y_i and c_i, this relationship being independent of time or of the particular characteristics of each household. The model could then be written:

$$c_i = f(y_i). \tag{8}$$

However, it would not be difficult to demonstrate the inadequacy of this assumption and this model. Indeed the latter would imply that two households with the same income would consume the same amount. The observations themselves generally contradict this.

Model (8) must therefore be discarded since it is too rigid and simple. We might first modify it by the inclusion of explanatory variables other than income, such as price, composition of household, liquid assets, etc. In this way we could give a more complete description of consumption. But it is to be feared that a purely functional relationship is still unsatisfactory, even when four or five explanatory variables are included. Two households with exactly the same income, composition, liquid assets, etc. will generally behave differently. The most reasonable solution is therefore *to take account in our assumptions of the fact that the factors determining consumption are partly unknown to us.* They seem to some extent random and we can only hope to estimate their probable influence. We must therefore modify the model by the introduction of random elements. With a single explanatory variable, we could, for example, set:

$$c_i = f(y_i) + \varepsilon_i, \tag{9}$$

where ε_i is a real value obtained by random selection from a distribution whose characteristics are more or less precisely known. This random element ε_i will be called the 'error', and this terminology will be systematically maintained.

The assumption expressed in eq. (9) results from the fact that the difference between the quantities consumed by two households with the same income appears to have all the characteristics of a random variable. It does not necessarily presuppose the existence of some specific chance mechanism, but is admissible whenever our state of ignorance is well represented by the distribution of the ε_i.

Model (9) involves the function f and the distribution P of the ε_i. But it happens most often that neither f nor P is completely specified, and only their properties are given. Thus we may say that f is a linear function:

$$f(y_i) = ay_i + b,$$

where a and b are two unknown numerical constants. Similarly, we generally allow P to be independent of the value of y_i and to have zero mean, sometimes even to be normal.

Formally, the model is defined by postulating eq. (9) *and by giving the classses to which the function f and the distribution P belong.*

The model therefore provides the logical structure on which the study of demand can be carried out.

We must first see that this structure does not conflict with the results of experience, that is, we must '*test the model*,' by comparing it with available data. If this is satisfactory, the model is accepted as the simplest of all those which agree with the facts. If not, the assumptions must be changed, other explanatory variables must be introduced, another class of functions must be chosen for f, a less restrictive specification of P must be adopted, etc.

Once the model has been chosen we have still to '*estimate*' the law of consumption, that is we must find the exact form of the function f and the distribution P, making use here of available data. This estimate will define the distribution of c_i for every y_i. It will only remain to decide on a '*prediction*' rule, that is to decide how c_i can be deduced when y_i is known.

Each sentence of the two preceding paragraphs obviously implies a whole series of studies which we shall examine later. For the moment we emphasize only the fundamental part played, at each stage of the reasoning, by precise formulation of the model and the assumptions contained in it. Without this, the determination and application of laws would remain very vague and unsatisfactory.

5   Endogenous and exogenous variables

These examples leave us in a position to examine in more detail the general characteristics of models and some problems of principle which arise when they are used in econometric investigations.

Every model specifies relationships among certain quantities, these relationships being assumed to be true for all values of the quantities, at least within a certain range. Each quantity is represented by a '*variable*', which can take any value contained in a fixed range. Thus the first model represents quantity demanded, quantity supplied and price by three real variables q_1, q_2 and p, which can take a priori any non-negative values.

The model tries to explain how certain of the quantities considered are determined. The quantities, and the variables which represent them, can be arranged in two distinct groups according to whether they are or are not to be explained by the model. The former, called *endogenous*, are considered to be determined by the phenomenon expressed in the model. The latter, called *exogenous*, occur in the equations but are considered to be determined independently.

In the first model of the competitive market described by system (1), the three variables are endogenous. There is no exogenous variable. Specification of the demand and supply functions is sufficient to determine completely the values of q_1, q_2 and p. We say that such a model with no exogenous variable is 'closed'. In model (2) we introduced exogenous variables $z_1, z_2, \ldots, z_m$, representing the factors other than price of the product which influence supply or demand.

The elementary Keynesian model has three endogenous variables, production P, income Y and consumption C, and an exogenous variable, investment I.

The demand law establishes a relationship between the income of a household and its demand for the product under consideration. Obviously in this case income is an exogenous variable and quantity consumed an endogenous variable.

In a general way we can say that *a model represents the determination of endogenous variables on the basis of exogenous variables*. For a definition of the model, it is not enough to state the assumed relationships; we must also spell out which of the variables are considered to be endogenous. The importance of the assumption that the exogenous variables are determined independently of the phenomenon represented must be emphasized. We shall generally retain this assumption in our theoretical studies, and shall·then give it more precise formulation. In practical applications we must always ask ourselves if the assumption is admissible. It will often be allowed only as a first approximation. Thus, when discussing the elementary Keynesian model, we pointed out that in fact investment was not independent of the level of production, except in the very short term. We shall return to this question in ch. 16 and for the moment we note it only in passing.

Let x denote the set of endogenous variables and z the set of exogenous variables. With this convention, if there exists a single real endogenous variable and a single real exogenous variable, x and z represent them respectively and are themselves real variables. This is the case, for example, with the demand law (9). But generally x and z each represents a set of real variables. Thus in the elementary Keynesian model, x corresponds to the three variables P, C and Y.

The model represents the determination of x on the basis of z. We can say in most cases that x (the set of endogenous variables) is a function of z (the set of exogenous variables) and we can write:

$$x = f(z). \tag{10}$$

If x and z are two real variables (that is, if there is a single endogenous variable and a single exogenous variable) expression (10) corresponds to the usual form of the functions studied in classical analysis. Similarly, when the model contains n endogenous variables $x_1, x_2, \ldots, x_n$ and m exogenous variables $z_1, z_2, \ldots, z_m$, formula (10) is only a convenient way of writing a system of n independent functions:

$$x_1 = f_1(z_1, z_2, \ldots, z_m),$$

$$x_2 = f_2(z_1, z_2, \ldots, z_m),$$

$$\cdots\cdots\cdots\cdots\cdots\cdots \tag{11}$$

$$x_n = f_n(z_1, z_2, \ldots, z_m).$$

The expression:

$$f : Z \to X \tag{12}$$

states still more clearly, though in a form less usual in classical mathematics, that, to each value of z in Z, f associates a value of x in X.

For example, in the case of the elementary Keynesian model with the consumption function (6), formula (10) or (12) corresponds to one or other of the two equivalent systems:

$$
\begin{cases}
P = C + I, \\[2mm]
C = \alpha Y + \beta, \\[2mm]
Y = P,
\end{cases}
\qquad
\begin{cases}
P = \dfrac{I}{1-\alpha} + \dfrac{\beta}{1-\alpha}, \\[3mm]
C = \dfrac{\alpha I}{1-\alpha} + \dfrac{\beta}{1-\alpha}, \\[3mm]
Y = \dfrac{I}{1-\alpha} + \dfrac{\beta}{1-\alpha},
\end{cases}
\tag{13}
$$

the second being solved for the endogenous variables as in system (11).

Thus f represents the set of operations which allow us to derive the endogenous variables x from the exogenous variables z. These operations may be more or less complex according to the model considered. Formulae (10) and (12) therefore provide a general representation of models, subject to two reservations.

We note first that the proposed formulation takes no account of difficulties in *calculation* of the values of x associated with a given value of z. Sometimes the model is stated in such a form that such calculation presents a real problem. Actually we shall later come to distinguish between the initial form of the model, called the 'structural form', and the form in which the endogenous variables are expressed as a function of the exogenous variables, called the 'reduced form' (cf. ch. 16).

Moreover, formulae (10) and (12) imply that to a set of values of the exogenous variables there corresponds a well-defined set of values of the endogenous variables, so that the latter are completely determined by the former. This property is lost in the stochastic models which will be discussed in section 7. Thus model (9) could only be expressed in the form (10) if ε_i were considered to be an exogenous variable. This approach is hardly helpful since ε_i cannot be observed.

6   Causality and recursive models

Formulae (10) and (12) can be considered to represent the dependence of the set of endogenous variables on the set of exogenous variables. However, we must note that *causal relationships are not always made completely explicit in models*.

Thus, the elementary Keynesian model represents a theory which states that the demand for consumption goods depends on disposable income, production depends on the demand for consumption goods and the demand for capital goods (the latter being exogenous), and disposable income depends on production. The causal relationships are represented by the arrows in the following diagram:

$$Y \leftarrow P \leftarrow I \quad \overset{\nearrow C_{\searrow}}{}$$

They are not clearly shown in the system of eqs. (4), and in any case they disappear when the system is solved, as in eqs. (13).

Is our diagram itself appropriate for describing causal relationships? It contains a cycle in the three endogenous variables Y, P and C, so that Y, for example, appears in it as both cause and effect of P.

This paradox obviously arises because we have disregarded time lags. There is an interval between the distribution of income and the emergence of demand, another while production is adjusted to meet demand, and another between production and the distribution of income. If we had related the variables to time, the diagram would have taken the form of a directed chain of the following type:

$$Y_{t-1} \rightarrow C_t \rightarrow P_{t+1} \rightarrow Y_{t+2}$$
$$I_t \nearrow$$

It would now have been clear that Y_t is caused by P_{t-1} and causes P_{t+2}.

The cobweb model of the market for an agricultural product (cf. system (3)) leads straight to the directed chain:

$$\begin{array}{ccc} P_{t-1} & P_t & P_{t+1} \\ & \uparrow & \uparrow \\ & q_{1t} & q_{1,t+1} \\ \searrow & \searrow \\ & q_{2t} & q_{2,t+1} \end{array}$$

Supply q_{2t} depends on price p_{t-1}, effective demand q_{1t} must equal supply q_{2t} and price p_t results.

Before proceeding further, we note that the expression '*lagged endogenous variable*' is often used, in equations relating to a period t, to denote those endogenous variables which relate to periods previous to t. Thus system (3) contains the lagged endogenous variable p_{t-1}. We can say in a general way that every model represents the determination of endogenous variables of period t by lagged endogenous variables and by exogenous variables (which may or may not be lagged). Hence the expression '*predetermined variables*' denotes both lagged endogenous variables and exogenous variables.

As the examples of this chapter show, certain economic models, but not all, correspond to directed chains. This allows us to state the following definition. *A model is said to be 'recursive' if there exists an ordering of the endogenous variables and an ordering of the equations such that the ith equation can be considered to describe the determination of the value of the ith endogenous variable during period t as a function of the predetermined variables and of the endogenous variables of index less than i. A model is said to be 'interdependent' if it is not recursive*[†].

Thus the relationships established by a recursive model can be represented by a directed chain.

Every model comprising only one endogenous variable is obviously recursive, notably the model of demand (9). Among our examples the cobweb model (3) is the only recursive model of those containing several endogenous variables. The ordering of these variables is: q_{1t}, q_{2t}, p_t; the ordering of equations is: supply law, equilibrium equation, demand law.

In several publications which appeared around 1955, Herman Wold supported the thesis that a model has explanatory power only if it describes causal chains, and therefore if it is recursive, since in reality one quantity cannot be at the same time cause and effect of another (see particularly WOLD [1954, 1955]). Why do we so often encounter interdependent models in economic theory?

Let us consider the first model of the competitive market defined by system (1). How was it justified by classical economists? WALRAS [1874] is particularly clear on this point as on so many others, and suggests the following systematic description of the process of exchange in a competitive market. When buyers and sellers have met, a first price is suggested and offers to buy and sell are then made. If the total supply exceeds the total demand, the price is lowered; if the total demand exceeds the total supply, the price is raised. In either case no transaction takes place. At the new price new offers to buy and sell are made, and the price is altered according to the over-all discrepancy between them. The process continues until the total supply exactly balances the total demand. All exchanges then take place at the price finally arrived at. Thus effective supply, effective demand and price are finally determined at the same time. This is expressed by the interdependent system.

However, it is true that the model does not describe the actual process of

[†] This definition applies only to deterministic models. It will be generalized in ch. 16 § 4. Its use in econometrics has been propagated by H. Wold.

reaching equilibrium, and therefore it obscures the elementary relationships of cause and effect. A different model would give a better description of the tentative movements towards equilibrium. Indeed let $...p_{t-1}, p_t, p_{t+1},...$ denote the sequence of suggested prices, and q_{1t} and q_{2t} demand and supply at price p_t. Walras' system will clearly be represented by:

$$p_t - p_{t-1} = h(q_{1,t-1} - q_{2,t-1}),$$
$$q_{1t} = f(p_t), \qquad\qquad (14)$$
$$q_{2t} = g(p_t),$$

where h is a continuous function that takes the same sign as its argument. This system is indeed recursive with the ordering in which the variables and the equations have been written. There corresponds to it a non-cyclical causal chain:

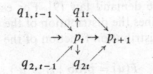

So this example does not in the end cast doubt on the thesis that a detailed description of the facts should lead to a recursive system[†]. But it also shows why we must often make do with interdependent models in econometric investigations. For it is impossible for us to observe the process of reaching equilibrium at every moment of time. We must be content to record from actual transactions the prices which hold and the quantities which are exchanged. Only the interdependent models (1) and (2) will interpret such statistics correctly.

More generally, available statistics often relate to relatively long periods, for example to periods of a year, in which time lags are much less significant. Thus, for a study of the short run fluctuations of an economy, a model based on periods of a month would no doubt reveal a causal chain among income, consumption and production. But this model could not be used directly to interpret annual data. It is then better to keep to an interdependent system like the elementary Keynesian model, than to introduce the blatantly false assumption that consumption in year t depends solely on disposable income in year $t-1$, which depends solely on production during year $t-2$.

We must add here that in most cases the available data refer to broad aggregates and not to detailed economic quantities. The aggregation of basic units can obscure causal relationships among units belonging to the same aggregate, and can also indicate apparent interdependence among different aggregates even where relationships among the basic units might be represented by a causal chain.

† Of course Walras' system itself gives an idealized picture of the actual process of reaching equilibrium. But more literal description would not lead to different conclusions in the aspect which interests us.

These remarks have been discussed fully and incisively by BENTZEL and HANSEN [1954].

Whatever conclusions are drawn on this matter, precise statement of the causal relationships embodied in the model is always of great importance. An arrowed diagram like those we have been discussing will often be found useful, as we shall see when we study the statistical procedures devised for models involving several equations (cf. part 5).

7 Stochastic models

In the two preceding sections we ignored random elements which may be contained in the model, and therefore found simple functional dependence between the exogenous and endogenous variables.

The transition to stochastic models presents hardly any difficulty. For example, we consider the demand law (9). For each value of the exogenous variable y_i the model defines the distribution of the endogenous variable c_i. Let $F(u)$ be the cumulative distribution function of the ε_i:

$$F(u) = \text{prob} \{ \varepsilon_i \leq u \}.$$

When y_i is known, the probability that c_i is less than a given number v is:

$$G(v) = F[v - f(y_i)],$$

and this function defines the distribution of c_i.

More generally, *for every set of values of the exogenous variables, a stochastic model defines the corresponding distribution of the endogenous variables.* For a formal representation of the dependences established by a stochastic model, we could resort to a general equation of type (10) in which the distribution of the endogenous variables would be determined as a function of the exogenous variables.

When discussing the demand law, we saw that there is a need for the introduction of random elements to the model, since the statistics to be interpreted are not governed exactly by a simple functional relationship. This is generally the case with economic data, and the methods considered in this book have therefore been devised in the context of stochastic models.

To be strictly logical, we should insist that economic theory provides stochastic models which would apply directly to observed data. Statistical inferences could then be made in the context of these models. In fact the theoretical models set up by economic science almost always establish functional relationships. In their different spheres the model of the competitive market and the elementary Keynesian model illustrate the fairly general point that theoretical representations disregard random fluctuations which cannot be ignored in empirical investigations.

This situation is not unique to economic science. Science generally has developed mainly by way of functional representation. The fitting of observations was the aim of what was originally called the 'theory of errors', a very significant name.

However, in economics the gap between theoretical picture and observed facts is much wider than in the 'exact' sciences, and the problems which arise in going from one to the other become much more important.

Thus the econometrician must substitute to the functional model given by economic theory a stochastic model that allows him to assess the statistical methods which he uses, and to interpret their results correctly. This formulation of a stochastic model is often called '*specification*', and is of great importance since it is basic to every study in econometrics. However, there is no point in elaborating this topic at present, since we shall discuss it thoroughly in ch. 4 when we are considering the empirical determination of factors affecting household savings.

8   Models and structures

The model does not generally specify completely the functional or stochastic dependence between the exogenous and the endogenous variables.

Thus system (1), relating to equilibrium in a competitive market, contains two functions of demand and supply, and only some of their general properties are specified a priori; for example, f and g are defined for every non-negative value of p; they are continuous and never negative; the demand function f is never increasing, etc.

The elementary Keynesian model introduces a consumption function $C = F(Y)$ about which only fairly general assumptions can be made a priori. Keynes states that F is positive; that its derivative F' (the 'marginal propensity to consume') is less than 1, that is, that an increase in income dY causes an increase in consumption $dC = F'dY < dY$; that its second derivative F'' is negative, that is, that the marginal propensity to consume decreases as income increases. In certain simple cases F is given a linear expression of form (6) where α and β are two parameters about which it is assumed only that $\alpha < 1$, $\beta > 0$.

As we have seen, the model of the demand law contains a function f and a distribution P, neither of which is completely specified.

To avoid confusion, we use the word *structure* to denote the form in which a model is expressed when all its characteristics are specified, including those which were not given a priori. A structure therefore defines completely the functional or stochastic relationship between the exogenous variables and the endogenous variables.

In the context of the model of the competitive market, a structure is obtained by choosing two specific functions f and g, for example:

$$f(p) = 4/p, \qquad g(p) = 1 + p/2.$$

Similarly, a structure of the elementary Keynesian model is defined by giving a function F, for example:

$$F(R) = 0.6\, Y + 60.$$

Finally, in the case of the demand law, a structure comprises a function F and a completely specified distribution P; it can be written, for example:

$$c_i = 0.4\, y_i + 20 + \varepsilon_i,$$

where ε_i is normally distributed with zero mean and standard deviation 3.

A model can therefore be regarded as a set of structures. Alternatively, we may say that, to set up a model, we must:

define the exogenous variables and their ranges,

define a set of structures which establish a functional or stochastic relationship between exogenous and endogenous variables.

9   The problem of statistical inference

The aim of statistical inference is to narrow the scope of the model in the light of observed values of the exogenous and endogenous variables. Certain structures which seemed plausible a priori may now appear to be improbable and must be eliminated, at least provisionally. Or perhaps some practical question may force a choice from the set of structures; in that case one structure is selected as best in view of the available data and the applications which we have in mind. Or else our views as to the respective likelihood of various structures are revised more or less thoroughly.

In statistical inference proper, the model is never questioned. In other words, *we always assume that one of the structures of the model exactly represents the actual process* by which the values of the observed quantities have been determined. The methods of mathematical statistics do not provide us with a means of specifying the model. They guide us in choosing between two possible models only when the latter are embodied in a more general model containing all the structures of each.

This basic limitation on the scope of statistical inference is of no serious importance for models whose assumptions are not very restrictive. But in econometrics the complexity of phenomena, the impossibility of experimentation and the scarcity of data impose the choice of fairly restrictive models.

In practice, however, we can find out the form of economic laws by making statistical inferences from many different sets of data and by eliminating at each stage those theoretical pictures which do not agree sufficiently with the facts. We shall see this in more detail in the course of ch. 4 when we shall examine econometric investigations on household savings.

We must now recall to mind the essential operations in statistical inference and find, in general terms, how they can be applied in the theoretical context introduced above.

The problems of methodology examined in this book arise only with stochastic models, and therefore endogenous variables will always be considered to result from a generating process comparable to a chance mechanism. A structure of the model will specify for the endogenous variables a probability distribution which depends on the values of the exogenous variables.

The use of probability calculus in the analysis of statistical data is justified on one or other of the two following bases. On the one hand, the phenomenon to be studied may be considered to resemble a process entailing random determination of certain quantities which are in this case assumed to be random in the universe as well as in the observed sample. On the other hand, the individual observations may be selected at random in which case the sample is random in composition and therefore the data are also random even if they refer to non-random quantities.

We shall always adopt the first position. The stochastic model will be supposed to represent the process which generates the quantities studied. This attitude is necessary when the individual statistics do not arise from random selection, for example when the same group is observed during different successive years. It is also generally necessary in the analysis of the results of inquiries based on random sampling; for in that case the econometrician is not interested in evaluating characteristics of the population from which the samples were drawn, but rather in distinguishing laws which have more general validity. He wishes to make inferences, not about the value of some quantity in the observed population, but rather on the permanent characteristics of the laws which he studies, and must therefore avail himself of a stochastic model in order to make his inferences meaningful.

We can conveniently regard the set of observations on the endogenous variables as a point in a suitable space, called *the sample space*, denoted by E. In practice the endogenous variables are usually n numerical observations on T individuals, or taken on T occasions. E is therefore an nT-dimensional Euclidean space. We associate with the sample a point x whose coordinate x_{it} is the value of the tth observation on x_i.

If *the values of the exogenous variables are assumed to be fixed and known*, a structure of the model defines a probability distribution on the sample space. In particular, the true structure, which by hypothesis is part of the model, defines the probability distribution that would be found if numerous samples were taken with the same set of values of the exogenous variables.

In the general terms used when studying the methods of mathematical statistics, a structure is considered as a point ω in a suitable space Ω, called the '*structure space*', or the 'parameter space' if a structure is defined by a certain number of parameters. Suppose for example that the model of the demand law specifies that the function f is linear and that the ε_i are independent, identically normally distributed with zero means. To obtain a structure, it will be sufficient to specify the values of the parameters a and b of $f(y_i) = ay_i + b$, and the standard deviation σ of the ε_i. The structure will then be represented by the point with coordinates (a, b, σ) in three-dimensional Euclidean space. The structure space is often much more complex, but that is not important for the summary exposition given in this section.

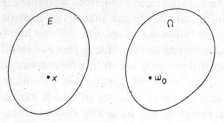

Fig. 2.

In this general system of representation[†] each structure ω of Ω defines a distribution of x in E; in particular the true structure ω_0 does so. The problem of statistical inference can then be expressed in the following terms: when an observed value x is known, how can we make an inference about the position of ω_0 in Ω?

10 Identifiability[††]

Every structure determines one, and only one, distribution of the observed variables. But the converse is not always true. It may happen that two different structures lead to the same distribution. This can be demonstrated by a fresh example which we shall not for the moment interpret in terms of economics[†††].

We suppose that the two observed variables x_1 and x_2 arise from the model:

$$
\begin{aligned}
x_1 &= v + \varepsilon_1, \\
x_2 &= v \operatorname{tg} \theta + \varepsilon_2,
\end{aligned}
\tag{15}
$$

where θ is a parameter and v is an unobservable random characteristic, normally

---

[†] It may happen that the exogenous variables cannot be observed. There are then two distinct situations according to whether they are assumed to be random, or to be fixed but unknown. In the former case, a structure must be defined by specifying not only the parameters, or laws, of the relationship between the exogenous variables and the endogenous variables, but also the probability distribution of the exogenous variables. Similarly, in the latter case, specific values must be chosen for exogenous variables. Under these conditions every structure will still define a distribution of the endogenous variables, and the general method of representation which we have proposed will still hold.

[††] On this section, see KOOPMANS and REIERSØL [1950].

[†††] For this see chapter 10.

distributed with zero mean and variance S^2; ε_1 and ε_2 are two unobservable random errors, independent of v and having a bivariate normal distribution with zero means and covariance matrix:

$$\begin{bmatrix} \sigma_1^2 & \varrho\sigma_1\sigma_2 \\ \varrho\sigma_1\sigma_2 & \sigma_2^2 \end{bmatrix}$$

The parameters S^2, σ_1 and σ_2 can take any positive values, θ can take any value between $-\tfrac{1}{2}\pi$ and $\tfrac{1}{2}\pi$ and ϱ any value between -1 and $+1$.

With this model it is immediately obvious that the pair of observed variables (x_1, x_2) is normally distributed with zero means and covariance matrix:

$$S^2 \begin{bmatrix} 1 & \operatorname{tg}\theta \\ \operatorname{tg}\theta & \operatorname{tg}^2\theta \end{bmatrix} + \begin{bmatrix} \sigma_1^2 & \varrho\sigma_1\sigma_2 \\ \varrho\sigma_1\sigma_2 & \sigma_2^2 \end{bmatrix}. \tag{16}$$

A structure of the model is defined by particular values given to the five parameters θ, S^2, σ_1, σ_2 and ϱ which are sufficient to determine the matrix (16) and therefore also the distribution of (x_1, x_2). The matrix (16) has only three independent elements (since it is always symmetric). It is clear, therefore, that several structures will lead to the same distribution of (x_1, x_2). Thus:

$$\theta = 0, \qquad S^2 = 2, \qquad \sigma_1^2 = 1, \qquad \sigma_2^2 = 2, \qquad \varrho = 0$$

and

$$\theta = \tfrac{1}{4}\pi, \qquad S^2 = 1, \qquad \sigma_1^2 = 2, \qquad \sigma_2^2 = 1, \qquad \varrho = -\tfrac{1}{2}\sqrt{2}.$$

both yield:

$$\operatorname{var}(x_1) = 3, \qquad \operatorname{var}(x_2) = 2, \qquad \operatorname{cov}(x_1 x_2) = 0.$$

When two or more different structures imply the same distribution of the observed variables, we say that they are not *identifiable*. Statistical inference always provides information only about the characteristics of the distribution of the observed variables. Its limit, which is complete detailed knowledge of the distribution, can hardly ever be attained but can be closely approached if large samples are available. Thus a non-identifiable structure can never be determined from the data, however numerous they may be.

Of course, certain characteristics of a non-identifiable structure can sometimes be determined completely. More precisely, we say that two structures are 'equivalent' if they give the same distribution of the observed variables. A parameter of a structure S will be said to be identifiable if it takes the same value in all structures equivalent to S.

When we set up a model to represent a specific economic phenomenon, we necessarily introduce equations and parameters describing the effect of the different factors which take part in it. We take account then of the different economic laws whose existence is assumed. The structures of the model so defined are not always identifiable, as we shall see in later examples.

When the structures are not identifiable it is impossible to determine from the observations all the parameters included in the representation of the phenomenon. The internal characteristics of the process generating the data will not be known completely, as only its final results will appear. In certain situations it will be sufficient to know the distribution of the endogenous variables, so that statistical inference will still be useful. But there will be no hope of singling out a true structure from the original model.

It may be asked why we should be preoccupied with characteristics which do not affect the observable manifestations of the phenomenon studied. Is it not always sufficient to know the distribution of the endogenous variables for each set of values of the exogenous variables? Is not the problem of identifiability spurious?

These doubts would be completely justified if the model represented the phenomenon with complete and universal validity for the purposes of the statistical inferences in mind as well as for the practical applications to which their results will serve. But it often happens that the model chosen as the basis for econometric investigation relative to one group or during one period of time may not be suitable, just at it is, for another group or another period of time. Certain of the model's laws will still apply but others will have to be modified. Only an exact knowledge of the structures can provide the basis for the necessary revision. This point has been elaborated with great force by MARSCHAK [1953].

We shall return to this question in the particular context of ch. 16 but some general reference had to be made to it here. In short, if it is not enough to know the distribution of the observed variables, if we wish to determine all the parameters occurring in the original formulation of the model, then we are really considering these parameters, taken individually, to be more stable, less often subject to revision, more 'autonomous' than the directly observable distributions.

11   Bayesian principles of inference

Statistical inference, as carried out in the context of economic models, obviously depends on general principles of mathematical statistics which are not the proper concern of the present book. There would be no need to linger over them if there were unanimous agreement on the foundations of statistical procedures. But this is not the case. Different schools of thought give differing justifications for the same procedures, or propose different methods for dealing with the same problems. Econometric literature shows traces of such disagreements, which we shall now discuss briefly. Essentially, we find a 'Bayesian school' opposed to a 'classical school', each putting forward a group of principles which we shall examine in succession.

The aim of statistical inference is to make the model more precise, using available observations. The Bayesian school lays down the following approach.

Knowledge of the phenomenon under analysis stipulates not only that the true structure ω_0 must belong to a space Ω, but also implies that a distribution P over Ω defines the probability that ω_0 lies in such or such a probabilisable subset of Ω.

Most frequently, this probability does not result from a true random process; rather, it expresses certain a priori ideas about the likelihood of the different ω in Ω. The object of statistical inference is then to determine how the available observations modify the (probability) distribution P which represents accumulated knowledge on the structure of the phenomenon under study. Suppose P^1 is the distribution accepted before consideration of the observations, that is, the *prior distribution*: let P^2 be the distribution accepted after consideration of the observations, that is, the *posterior distribution*. Statistical inference is concerned with the transformation of P^1 into P^2. Now, *Bayes' theorem* gives a simple rule for this transformation.

Suppose that the sample space E and the structure space Ω are both finite-dimensional vector spaces, or subsets of these. Let us assume that the distribution defined by the model has density $p(x/\omega)$ on E, and similarly that the prior distribution has density $p(\omega)$ on Ω. These assumptions, which are not essential, conform in most cases to the problems encountered in econometrics[†]. It follows that the posterior distribution also has density $p(\omega/x)$ defined by

$$p(\omega/x) = \frac{p(x/\omega)p(\omega)}{\int_\Omega p(x/\omega)p(\omega)\,d\omega}.$$ (17)

For, on the product space $E \times \Omega$, the distribution of the pair (x, ω) has density $p(x,\omega)=p(x/\omega)p(\omega)$. So the denominator of the right-hand side of (17) defines the density of the marginal distribution $p(x)$ on E. Moreover, the conditional distribution for given x on Ω then has density $p(\omega/x)$ which must be such that $p(x,\omega) = p(\omega/x)p(x)$. The equality (17) follows from this.

Bayes' theorem states that knowledge of x affects the probabilities of the different probabilisable sets of Ω. Determination of $p(\omega/x)$ could be the ultimate aim of inference, particularly in econometrics. But on the one hand, the econometrician often wishes to answer a simple question, or to fix attention on a few numbers rather than on an entire function (the posterior density $p(\omega/x)$ is a function on Ω); on the other hand, it is only rarely that the statistician has objective knowledge of the prior probability relating to the question under discussion. Let us examine each of these aspects in turn.

A natural way of characterizing the posterior distribution is to associate with it measures of central tendency and dispersion, for example the expected

---

[†] For a more systematic discussion of this, see WALD [1950a].

value ω^* of ω and its covariance matrix, when they exist, as is the case in most of the current problems in econometrics. The expected value is defined in particular by[†]

$$\omega^* = E(\omega) = \int_\Omega \omega p(\omega/x)\,d\omega. \tag{18}$$

Knowledge of ω^*· is sufficient for the user if the error he incurs by fixing attention on a particular value $\hat\omega$ implies losses proportional to a positive definite quadratic form of the error $\hat\omega - \omega_0$ and if he seeks to minimise the expected value of these losses[††]. (In the error $\hat\omega - \omega_0$, the random element is then the true value ω_0 of which only the posterior distribution is known. To stress this, we shall write ω in place of ω_0.) For, if we let

$$\mathfrak{P} = (\hat\omega - \omega)' W(\hat\omega - \omega) \tag{19}$$

be the quadratic form in question, and substitute for $(\hat\omega - \omega)$ in $\mathfrak{P}$ the sum

$$(\hat\omega - \omega^*) + (\omega^* - \omega),$$

we obtain

$$E\mathfrak{P} = (\hat\omega - \omega^*)' W(\hat\omega - \omega^*) + E[(\omega^* - \omega)' W(\omega^* - \omega)] \tag{20}$$

since $(\hat\omega - \omega^*)' W(\omega^* - \omega)$ is random only because of $\omega^* - \omega$ whose expectation is zero in view of the definition (18) of ω^*. In the right hand side of (20), the second term does not depend on $\hat\omega$ and so the value of $\hat\omega$ which minimises $E\mathfrak{P}$ is that value which minimises the quadratic form $(\hat\omega - \omega^*)' W(\hat\omega - \omega^*)$; this is $\hat\omega = \omega^*$, since this quadratic form is positive for any other value of $\hat\omega$. In short, in this case ω^* appears as a good *estimator* of the vector ω of the parameters characterising the structure of the model.

More generally, in any situation where a loss function $\mathfrak{P}(\hat\omega, \omega)$ has been defined, we can take as *Bayesian estimator* the vector $\hat\omega$ which minimises the expected value of $\mathfrak{P}$ when ω is distributed according to the posterior distribution resulting from Bayes' theorem.

In certain favourable cases, the posterior distribution belongs to a classical family of distributions; it may, for example, be a normal distribution. Here knowledge of the expected value of ω and its covariance matrix may be sufficient fully to characterize the posterior distribution within the family in question. When this is not the case, the covariance matrix may be difficult to interpret as a measure of dispersion. It may be preferable to define a *confidence region* Ω_0,

---

[†] For the definition of the covariance matrix, see page 158.

[††] This rule is justified by decision theory which is not unrelated to the questions under discussion. See in particular SAVAGE [1954].

that is, a subset Ω_0 of Ω, which has a given posterior probability $1 - \alpha$ of containing ω_0:

$$\int_{\Omega_0} p(\omega/x)\, d\omega = 1 - \alpha. \tag{21}$$

(We know that the custom is generally to define such confidence regions for a probability level of 5%, or sometimes 10% or 1%.) Condition (21) leaves great latitude for the choice of Ω_0. But it is customary to demand that this region be as concentrated as possible, for example that it has minimum volume in Ω considered as a Euclidean space.

Finally, it often happens that the aim of statistical inference is to decide if some hypothesis about the true structure ω_0 is to be accepted or rejected on the basis of the available observations. Such a hypothesis is expressed by the fact that ω_0 belongs to a particular subset Ω_1 of Ω. It is to be rejected if the posterior probability that ω belongs to Ω_1 is too small, that is, if it is smaller than a previously chosen number α:

$$\int_{\Omega_1} p(\omega/x)\, d\omega < \alpha. \tag{22}$$

This is called *testing* the hypothesis.

The three procedures concerning estimation, tests and the establishment of confidence regions may give rise to many variants which will not be discussed here. For example, in many cases we are interested only in some, not all, of the components of the vector ω of the parameters, and we wish to establish a confidence region for the vector of these components. In this case the density of the marginal distribution relating to the vector in question should be substituted for $p(\omega/x)$.

We have just discussed these procedures in the context of Bayesian theory. In the so-called 'classical' theory, there are corresponding procedures which have the same objects but which are not generally of the same form as Bayesian procedures. Bayesian and classical procedures are not equivalent from the point of view of applications. However, it will be shown subsequently that in most of the major problems of econometrics, there is little difference between the practical recommendations of the two theories.

12   Prior probability and the likelihood function

The posterior probability P_2 which serves as a basis for the various Bayesian procedures was determined by applying formula (17), which implies the prior probability represented by its density $p(\omega)$. How is this prior probability defined? At the beginning of the previous section we assumed that it formed part of the specification of the model. The knowledge synthesized by the model fixed not only the nature of the stochastic dependence between the exogenous and endogenous variables, but also a probability distribution assigned a priori to the values of the unknown parameters.

Let us consider in this light the model relating to the demand law, $c_i = ar_i + b + \varepsilon_i$, where the ε_i are assumed to be normal, independent, with zero mean and standard deviation σ. The specification should also include a distribution for the vector $\omega = (a, b, \sigma)$ of the parameters. We ought to be able to express in this way what we already know about the demand for the product in question.

For example, the model might specify that a, b, and σ are mutually independent, a being normally distributed with mean μ_a and standard deviation σ_a, b being normally distributed with zero mean and standard deviation σ_b, and finally σ having a Gamma[†] distribution with coefficient $v/2$. The density $p(\omega)$ would then be[††]

$$p(a,b,\sigma) = \frac{\sigma^{v/2-1}}{2\pi\Gamma\left(\dfrac{v}{2}\right)\sigma_a\sigma_b} \exp\left\{-\sigma - \frac{(a-\mu_a)^2}{2\sigma_a^2} - \frac{b^2}{2\sigma_b^2}\right\}. \tag{23}$$

Many econometricians find it difficult to allow that the specification of the model can go so far. Some refuse to consider the parameters as random. According to them, determination of the true structure ω_0 does not result from a random process, and we cannot talk of the probability that ω_0 belongs to such and such a subset Ω_0 of Ω. It is true or false that ω_0 belongs to Ω_0; no probability is really involved. The whole Bayesian approach must be rejected, since it starts off from an incorrect analysis of the problem.

Other econometricians are prepared, with the Bayesians, to find meaning in the prior and posterior probabilities that ω_0 belongs to Ω_0. For them, this is a measure of the likelihood we attribute to such a possibility, when we do not know if it is true or false. This measure completes the model's representation of the phenomenon under study. In particular, it synthesizes the result of past observation. But, as opposed to the Bayesians, they consider any prior probability as too subjective to have a valid role in econometric analysis, which should aim at objective inference on the basis of the data considered[†††].

According to this second point of view, the choice of prior distribution introduces too much arbitrariness into statistical procedures. The econometrician should analyze a sample considered pertinent to the phenomenon under study, and then pass on the results of his analysis in a form which is independent of all presuppositions other than those which specify the stochastic dependences expressed by the model. Thus every possible user of his work would be free to take account of his results, combining them as he wishes with

[†] For the definition of Gamma distributions, see CALOT [1967a], ch. 13, § 2, or RAIFFA and SCHLAIFER [1961], ch. 7, § 6.

[††] The expression exp $\{x\}$ is used in this book to denote the exponential function e^x.

[†††] Some Bayesian statisticians propose that the prior distribution should be chosen so as to represent a state of complete ignorance about the vector ω of the parameters. But, in the first place, this is equivalent to restricting the scope of the procedures to situations of this kind; in the second place, the very definition of complete ignorance is arbitrary and cannot be objectively based.

any others which he considers equally relevant, and with his own a priori ideas.

This second outlook does not imply the complete abandonment of the entire Bayesian approach. Let us consider formula (17), which expresses Bayes' theorem. It shows clearly how the posterior probability $p(\omega/x)$ is calculated from the prior probability $p(\omega)$ and from $p(x/\omega)$ *considered as a function of ω*. By determining and presenting this function, the econometrician provides for a user who already has $p(\omega)$, all he needs to find $p(\omega/x)$. This is expressed as the *likelihood principle* according to which all the information about ω which the sample x contains is expressed by the *likelihood function*, that is, by $p(x/\omega)$ considered as a function of ω for the value of x taken from the given sample.

In short, if while accepting the logical foundations of the Bayesian theory we consider that the econometrician should not choose a prior distribution since this would introduce an arbitrary element, then his task must be to determine and communicate the likelihood function.

However, such an aim is generally insufficient since the expression for the likelihood function is too complex in the parameters. Since $p(x/\omega)$, considered as a function of x and ω, is defined by the specification of the model, to report the sample x is also to report the likelihood function. But in fact, what we demand of the econometrician is just that he should reduce the complexity of the sample, calculate a few characteristics which, together with the prior probability $p(\omega)$, allow the determination of estimators, confidence regions or tests. In practice there are three ways of solving this dilemma.

1. In the first place, we can restrict the choice of $p(\omega)$ and define not only the likelihood function, but also what would be the posterior probability for each of the prior distributions $p(\omega)$ of a family $\mathfrak{F}$. This family must be sufficiently rich to cover situations which differ widely in respect of previous knowledge about ω, but it must depend on only a small number of parameters so that the econometrician can define simply the posterior distribution considered as a function of these parameters. In some models which we shall discuss, a particular family $\mathfrak{F}$, the family of so-called 'conjugate' distributions, lends itself to convenient analysis and so is often preferred.

2. In the second place, some important problems of mathematical statistics characteristically involve simple *sufficient statistics*. In these cases the function $p(x/\omega)$ is given as the product of two factors

$$p(x/\omega) = p[t(x)/\omega] \cdot q(x), \tag{24}$$

the first depending on x through the usually vector-valued function $t(x)$, and the second not being dependent on ω. The function $t(x)$ is called a sufficient statistic. The function $p[t(x)/\omega]$ can be chosen in such a way that it is the probability density of $t(x)$. In formula (17), which expresses Bayes' theorem, this function can be substituted for $p(x/\omega)$ since $q(x)$ occurs as a factor in the numerator and in the denominator. Now, $p[t(x)/\omega]$ is often much simpler than $p(x/\omega)$.

In such cases the econometrician may be content to calculate the value of the sufficient statistic $t(x)$ and to define its distribution as a function of ω, this giving the user the equivalent of a likelihood function.

3. Finally, in situations where a simple sufficient statistic does not exist, and the econometrician is obliged to reduce the complexity of the situation, he may decide to replace his complete sample by a small number of characteristics calculated from it, that is, by a vector function $t(x)$; he proceeds from there as if only $t(x)$ had been observed. By finding the value of $t(x)$ and its distribution as a function of ω, he provides for any user who already has his own prior probability $p(\omega)$, what is required for determining the posterior probability $p[\omega/t(x)]$ resulting from knowledge of $t(x)$. Since $t(x)$ is not a sufficient statistic, this last distribution is different from $p(\omega/x)$; the substitution of $t(x)$ for x results in some loss of information[†], the reflection of the simplification carried out. The choice of $t(x)$ must therefore be guided by the need to limit this loss of information.

This third method whose principle has just been presented results from a compromise which does not appear to be very rigorous. However, many of the usual procedures in econometrics are meaningful in the light of Bayesian theory if they are interpreted in this way. But in the present state of development of statistical methodology, rigorous application of Bayes' theorem is impossible in one case which is of great importance for econometrics. This will be discussed briefly in section 14.

13   Classical principles of inference

Statisticians of the so-called 'classical' school, refusing to allow the existence of distributions in the structure space Ω have tried rigorously to establish principles of inference which are completely independent of Bayesian ideas[††]. Their reasoning starts from the concept of sample distribution and adopts the following point of view.

The observed sample x results from a random process. To assess a procedure, we must find the properties which it would have if it had been applied systematically to the result of this process: it must be considered as if defined for the whole space E and not as if applying only to the particular observed sample x. *A procedure will be approved to the extent that it would give good results if applied repeatedly to independent samples arising from the same process.*

The methodological study is concerned therefore with the random properties of procedures, random properties which result from those of the sample.

The distribution of x, also called the *sampling distribution*, will, for example, be characterized by its density $p(x/\omega)$; it implies a distribution for some quantity fixed by the procedure. These distributions depend on the unknown structure ω. However, conclusions arising from them may be independent, that is,

[†] See RAIFFA and SCHLAIFER [1961], § 2.2.1 to 2.2.3.

[††] The classical school was inspired by J. Neyman and E. S. Pearson. A detailed discussion of its approach can be found, for example, in KENDALL [1948].

may be true for every ω in Ω. Let us consider the effect of this point of view on the various modalities of statistical inference.

1. Given the sample x, to *estimate* the structure ω is to choose a structure $\hat\omega$ on which we fix attention as if it were the true structure. An *estimator*, that is, an estimation rule, is a function $t(x)$ which associates an element $\hat\omega$ of Ω with each element x of E.

To study the qualities of the estimator $t(x)$, we consider its distribution and, for example, the density $p[t(x)/\omega]$; we should like this distribution to be concentrated in the neighbourhood of the true structure ω. To choose between two estimators $t(x)$ and $s(x)$ we also consider their respective distributions.

Suppose then that Ω is a vector space of finite dimension. It is natural to consider the first and second-order moments of the distribution of $t(x)$. Its expected value is

$$E_\omega t = \int_\Omega t \cdot p(t/\omega)\, dt = \int_E t(x) \cdot p(x/\omega)\, dx. \tag{25}$$

The estimator $t(x)$ is said to be *unbiased* if

$$E_\omega t = \omega. \tag{26}$$

When no more detail is given, we understand that this equality is an identity in ω, that is, it holds whatever the true structure in Ω may be. Similarly, the covariance between the components $t_i(x)$ and $t_h(x)$ of $t(x)$ is defined by

$$v_{ih} = E_\omega[(t_i - E_\omega t_i)(t_h - E_\omega t_h)]. \tag{27}$$

Generally this is a determinable function of ω.

An important result of classical mathematical statistics states that the matrix V with elements v_{ih} has a lower bound. More precisely, there exists a matrix V^* such that

$$\lambda' V \lambda \geq \lambda' V^* \lambda \tag{28}$$

for any vector λ and estimator $t(x)$ whenever the latter is unbiased and satisfies certain general regularity conditions[†]. (We note that $\lambda' V \lambda$ is the variance of the linear form $\lambda' t(x)$ of the coordinates of the estimator t.) This result can be considered to provide justification for an unbiased estimator $t(x)$ whose covariance matrix V is near V^*.

Suppose also that the error involved in estimating ω by $\hat\omega$ incurs losses proportional to the positive definite quadratic form

$$\mathfrak{P} = (\hat\omega - \omega)' W(\hat\omega - \omega). \tag{29}$$

When the estimator $t(x)$ is applied to the sample x, the resultant losses are given by

$$\mathfrak{P}_t(x, \omega) = [t(x) - \omega]' W[t(x) - \omega]. \tag{30}$$

---

† See, for example, CRAMER [1946], ch. 32, § 3.

They are given by a similar expression $\mathfrak{P}_s(x,\omega)$ when the estimator $s(x)$ is used. These losses depend on the sample. In order to assess the qualities of the estimators, which we assume to have been applied repeatedly to independent samples arising from the same process, we must consider the sampling distributions of $\mathfrak{P}_t(x,\omega)$ and $\mathfrak{P}_s(x,\omega)$. If, as is often assumed, only the expected value of the losses is important, we need only examine the *risks* $\mathfrak{R}_t(\omega)$ and $\mathfrak{R}_s(\omega)$ defined by[†]

$$\mathfrak{R}_t(\omega) = E\mathfrak{P}_t = \int_\Omega [t-\omega]' W[t-\omega] \cdot p[t/\omega]\, \mathrm{d}t$$

$$= \int_E [t(x)-\omega]' W[t(x)-\omega] \cdot p[x/\omega]\, \mathrm{d}t. \tag{31}$$

In particular, $t(x)$ will appear preferable to $s(x)$ if

$$\mathfrak{R}_t(\omega) \le \mathfrak{R}_s(\omega) \qquad \text{for all} \qquad \omega \in \Omega \tag{32}$$

(the sign of equality being strict for at least some values of ω).

In those cases where $\mathfrak{R}_t(\omega)$ is greater than $\mathfrak{R}_s(\omega)$ over a subset Ω_1 of Ω and is smaller than $\mathfrak{R}_s(\omega)$ over a subset Ω_2, then under strict classical logic no conclusion can be drawn. Any preference given to one of the two estimators over the other is equivalent to an implicit assessment of the probabilities that the true structure ω lies in Ω_1 and Ω_2 respectively. At this point some eclectic spirits, otherwise faithful to classical thinking, recommend the explicit introduction of a subjective probability on Ω, and the choice of that estimator which has the smallest average risk:

$$\overline{\mathfrak{R}}_t = \int_\Omega R_t(\omega)p(\omega)\, \mathrm{d}\omega. \tag{33}$$

We note that (31) and (33) imply

$$\overline{\mathfrak{R}}_t = \int_\Omega \int_E \mathfrak{P}_t(x,\omega)p(x/\omega)p(\omega)\, \mathrm{d}x\, \mathrm{d}\omega \tag{34}$$

or again, if $p(x)$ denotes the denominator of (17) which expresses Bayes' theorem, then

$$\overline{\mathfrak{R}}_t = \int_\Omega \int_E \mathfrak{P}_t(x,\omega)p(\omega/x)p(x)\, \mathrm{d}x\, \mathrm{d}\omega. \tag{35}$$

If the integration signs can be interchanged, then (35) can also be written

$$\overline{\mathfrak{R}}_t = \int_E \left[\int_\Omega \mathfrak{P}_t(x,\omega)p(\omega/x)\, \mathrm{d}\omega \right] p(x)\, \mathrm{d}x, \tag{36}$$

which shows that the mean risk will be minimized by the Bayesian estimator $t(x)$ which gives the smallest possible value for the expected posterior loss.

[†] The expected value $E\mathfrak{P}_t$ now introduced should not be confused with the expectation $E\mathfrak{P}$ defined by formula (20) in section 11, where ω was taken as random while x was fixed, in accordance with Bayesian logic. Here classical logic stipulates that x is random, and ω is not.

Later on, when we consider the general problems to which are related the different situations encountered in econometrics, we shall see that in certain important cases the risk function $\mathfrak{R}_t(\omega)$ is sufficient for the choice of an estimator $t(x)$ which appears optimal within a class of estimators, and is so uniformly with respect to ω.

2. To define a *confidence region* for ω is to choose a subset Ω_0 of Ω on which attention is fixed, since it is held to be highly likely that Ω_0 contains the true structure. A rule for the determination of a confidence region associates a subset Ω_0 with each possible value of the sample x in E; so it is expressed by a function $\Omega_0(x)$ of E in the set of subsets of Ω.

For a given significance level α classical statistical theory chooses confidence regions such that there is probability $1 - \alpha$ that $\Omega_0(x)$ contains the true structure ω, this probability to be interpreted in relation to a population of independent samples x all with the same distribution $p(x/\omega)$. We express this chosen condition in the form

$$\text{Prob } \{\Omega_0(x) \ni \omega/\omega\} = 1 - \alpha \tag{37}$$

to emphasize the fact that the event $\omega \in \Omega_0(x)$ is random because of x and not because of ω. This constitutes the essential difference from (21), which applies to Bayesian confidence regions.

Clearly condition (37) is compatible with many definition rules for confidence regions. The most useful are those which lead to the most precise conclusions, that is, to regions $\Omega_0(x)$ which are smallest on average.

In practical econometrics a choice of confidence region is always associated with a choice of estimate; the user fixes attention both on a value $t(x)$ considered to be near the true structure ω and on a region $\Omega_0(x)$ containing $t(x)$ and measuring in some way the precision with which $t(x)$ probably approximates to ω. Rather than investigate directly the choice of optimal rules for the construction of confidence regions, in this book our general approach will be first to study an estimator $t(x)$ and then to associate with it a region suggested by the sampling distribution of $t(x)$.

3. To *test* the hypothesis that the true structure belongs to a given subset Ω_1 of Ω is to decide if this hypothesis is to be rejected on the grounds that it appears improbable in the light of the sample. A decision rule is then a partition of the sample space E into two regions R_1 and R_2, such that the hypothesis is to be rejected if x belongs to R_2, and accepted in the other case; R_2 is called a *critical region*. So the choice of test is reduced to the choice of critical region.

Classical statistics characterizes a test by its probabilities of error, these probabilities being derived from the sampling distribution of x. The name *type 1 error* is given to the probability that the hypothesis is rejected when it is true:

$$r_1(\omega) = \int_{R_2} p(x/\omega) \, dx \qquad \omega \in \Omega_1; \tag{38}$$

this is a function defined on Ω_1. Similarly a *type 2 error* is the probability that the hypothesis is accepted when it is not true:

$$r_2(\omega) = \int_{R_1} p(x/\omega)\,dx \qquad \omega \in \Omega_2; \tag{39}$$

this is a function defined on $\Omega_2 = \Omega - \Omega_1$.

The choice of a test must be guided by the desire to minimize both $r_1(\omega)$ and $r_2(\omega)$. The generally adopted procedure is to fix the type 1 error at a low level chosen in advance, then to find a test for which the type 2 error is also small. Thus we demand

$$r_1(\omega) = \alpha \qquad \text{for all } \omega \in \Omega_1, \tag{40}$$

α being called the 'significance level' of the test. On the other hand, the type 2 error remains variable as a function of ω. This is why we also talk of the *power of the test against the alternative* ω belonging to Ω_2, to denote the value of $1 - r_2(\omega)$, that is, the probability of rejecting the hypothesis when the true structure is ω, the hypothesis under test then not being true.

Two different tests which have the same significance level generally have different powers. If one of them is found to be uniformly more powerful for every ω in Ω_2, it will naturally be preferred. Unfortunately this principle does not turn out to be selective enough in many problems of mathematical statistics. In ch. 5, when we discuss testing the 'linear hypothesis', we shall see that a similar principle can be devised to justify the choice of certain commonly used tests.

The significance level α often appears as a parameter which is left to the discretion of the user of the test. In applied econometrics it is customary to choose a value of 5%, and occasionally 1% or 10%, without considering the power of the test. This is a very questionable habit, since it implies neglect of the comparison of type 1 and type 2 errors.

For a given test and a variable significance level the critical region depends on α. Let the region be $R_2(\alpha)$. Currently used tests all have the property that $\alpha_1 < \alpha_2$ implies that $R_2(\alpha_1)$ contains $R_2(\alpha_2)$ and that consequently $r_2(\omega,\alpha_1)$ is less than $r_2(\omega,\alpha_2)$ for every ω in Ω_2. The value $\alpha = 5\%$ will generally be too small when the corresponding error r_2 reaches 50% for alternative ω's which are not near Ω_1. On the other hand, this value will in most cases be too high when the error r_2 is less than 1% for all alternative ω's with the exception of those which are near Ω_1. In short, the significance level should be established at a value which is correspondingly lower, the more powerful the test[†].

[†] On this topic, see ARROW [1960] or the recent and provocative book by LEAMER [1978]. We note also that many practical problems involve rather less simple decisions than that formalized by classical tests of hypothesis. For example, suppose the space Ω is partitioned into three regions, Ω_1 in which the hypothesis under consideration applies closely, Ω_2 in which it does not hold at all and Ω_3 in which it gives only a mediocre approximation. In this situation we wish to accept or to reject the hypothesis in such a way that there is a small chance of acceptance when ω belongs to Ω_2 or of rejection when ω belongs to Ω_1. This situation is investigated by CALOT [1967b].

14 Non-parametric models

Up till now we have assumed that the econometrician is trying to determine all the characteristics of the unknown structure ω. In fact he is often concerned with only some of them. This does not raise much difficulty so long as the space Ω is of finite dimension.

Let θ denote the sub-vector of the components of ω in which the econometrician is interested, and ξ the sub-vector of its other components: $\omega = (\theta, \xi)$. The latter are said to be 'nuisance parameters'. To avoid some rare complications, we assume that Ω is the Cartesian product of the two sets Θ and Ξ to which θ and ξ belong respectively. It is easy to see how the principles just discussed must be adapted for this new situation.

Bayesian theory concentrates attention on the posterior probability of θ, that is, on the marginal distribution of θ derived from the posterior distribution of ω. Its density is given by

$$p(\theta/x) = \int_{\Xi} p(\theta, \xi/x) \, \mathrm{d}\xi. \tag{41}$$

Similarly according to classical theory an estimator of θ is a function $t(x)$ taking its values in Θ. This estimator is unbiased if

$$E_\omega t = \theta \tag{42}$$

identically in ω, that is, in θ and ξ. Equation (27) applies unchanged to the definition of the covariance matrix of $t(x)$. The discussion of choice of estimator can be transposed with no difficulty on the basis of that given in section 13.1.

But, in many econometric applications we do not wish to be restricted to choosing a specification which strictly lays down the nature of the distribution of the random elements. We prefer to have a model compatible with widely varying distributions. The most natural formulation of the problem leads to a space Ω in which an element ω is no longer characterized by a finite number of parameters. For this reason the model is said to be 'non-parametric'. In most cases, Ω is still taken as the Cartesian product of a space Θ of finite dimension containing the vector θ of the parameters of particular interest, and of a space Ξ of which an element ξ defines the other characteristics of the structure; but Ξ is of infinite dimension.

For example, consider the model relating to the demand law $c_i = ar_i + b + \varepsilon_i$ in which the ε_i are independent and have the same distribution with expected value zero. We are often reluctant to assume in addition that ε_i has a specified, for example a normal, distribution. Such an assumption would have no basis in real knowledge of the distribution of the ε_i and would be motivated only by reasons of convenience. So it is preferable to define θ as the pair (a,b) and

Ξ as the space of all distributions with zero expectation and, possibly, satisfying some other general condition (for example, that they should have finite variance).

The statistical treatment of non-parametric models clearly raises new difficulties. The sample probability density, $p(x/\omega)$ takes forms which vary widely as ω varies. The likelihood function, $p(x/\omega)$ considered as a function of ω, is extremely complex.

In the present stage of development of Bayesian theory there exists no operating procedure for non-parametric models. This seriously limits the usefulness of Bayesian methods in econometrics, since they start necessarily from precise specification of the type of distribution of the random elements.

Serious difficulties are also present for classical theory. Yet in the most frequent econometric problems they can be at least partially solved, since some questions are discussed directly in a non-parametric theory. In this book we shall see this in two connections.

In the first place, when we discuss the general linear estimation model on which many econometric procedures are based, the problem of choice of estimator will be dealt with without strict specification of the distribution of the errors. In the second place, on various occasions we shall be able to determine approximations to the sampling distributions affecting many estimators and tests. These approximations will be valid for non-parametric classes of distributions of the errors, and yet will depend only on a finite number of parameters. For example, the distribution $p(t/\omega)$ of an estimator $t(x)$ will be approximated by a distribution $\tilde{p}(t/\theta)$ which is dependent on the structure ω only through a vector θ with a small number of components.

Before examining briefly the nature of such approximations, we note that they provide a means for partial application of Bayesian principles. As outlined in section 12 (cf. the conclusion of 3), we can treat $\tilde{p}(t/\theta)$ as corresponding approximately to the likelihood function which would apply if only $t(x)$, and not x, had been observed. Combined with a prior distribution $p(\theta)$ for θ according to a formula like (17) for Bayes' theorem, this function allows us to determine $p[\theta/t(x)]$, which provides an approximation to the posterior distribution of θ when only $t(x)$ has been observed. For want of something better, $\tilde{p}[\theta/t(x)]$ can be used as a basis for inference instead of the true posterior probability $p(\omega/x)$.

What is the logic behind approximate sampling distributions? This will be clearer when we have discussed it in the context of the multiple regression model (cf. ch. 6, § 8). It is based on an *asymptotic theory* which would be rigorously applicable in the imaginary situation where the number of observations tends to infinity.

The sample x consists of T observations. Let us call the sample x_T. Then let us consider a family of samples $\{x_T\}$ all obtained from the same model but containing an increasing number of observations ($T = 1,2,\ldots$). To investigate $t(x)$, we associate with it a family of estimators $t_T(x_T)$ and consider the

family of sampling distributions $p_T(t_T/\omega)$ of the $t_T(x_T)$. The asymptotic behaviour of this last family often suggests a simple approximation $\tilde{p}_T(t_T/\theta)$ for
each of the $p_T(t_T/\omega)$, the approximation being justified by the fact that $\tilde{p}_T(t_T/\theta)$
and $p_T(t_T/\omega)$ are asymptotically equivalent (at this level of generality the notion
of equivalence is purposely left vague)[†].

Asymptotic theories, like all other theories seeking to justify approximations,
have rather ambiguous implications for practice, which is always concerned
only with a given sample. The assessment of the quality of the approximation
in each particular case is a question of fact. However, asymptotic theories have
long been referred to in mathematical statistics. The study of many examples
has given us some awareness of the differences between the approximate and
the true distributions (see, for example, ch. 8, § 4). In particular, we know that
in many c   s the approximations have been found to be very close.

15   Prediction

The use of statistical procedures enables us to state in precise numerical terms
the description of the phenomenon provided by the model and thus to improve
our understanding of the economic facts. But description is not an end in itself.
Directly or indirectly it must help us in reaching decisions. A better knowledge
of economic laws is necessary if we are to improve social organization or the
development of the general economy, or if we are to better able to direct the
activity of some individual or some enterprise.

We are not concerned in this book with decision problems pure and simple,
but must give some space to the study of prediction. For the econometrician
can make a contribution when the models which he has estimated are to be
used; he must know how the results of his calculations will be taken into
account.

Before a final decision is reached, some *conditional predictions* are generally
made. We ask how certain interesting quantities will behave after some particular event or some particular decision. It is at this stage that models are
useful, since they describe exactly how the quantities in question are determined.

In conditional prediction the values of the endogenous variables are predicted
according to assumptions about the values which will be taken by the exogenous
variables following either some deliberate decisions or some events over which
we have no control. The model is thus directly useful, and allows the results of
statistical inference to be transposed with ease.

We note that the logical operation which we have here called 'prediction'
does not necessarily relate to future events. It aims to find the value of any

---

[†] J. B. Kadane, a young econometrician at Yale, has recently proposed another approach.
The model under study is considered as an element in a sequence of models, all identical
save for the dispersion of the random elements. The values of a number σ proportional to this
dispersion are diminishing in the sequence of models. So to find approximations, we should
place ourselves in the neighbourhood of $\sigma = 0$.

unobserved quantity. Thus, in the context of model (9) for the demand law, we can try to predict the level of demand of a household which was not included in the observed sample, when only the income of this particular household is known.

As we saw at the end of the preceding section, it sometimes happens that the phenomenon does not obey exactly the same laws in the statistical sample analyzed and in the range to which predictions relate. We must in that case change some coefficients of the model and even some equations. This will be possible if we have been able to identify the chosen structure and if the changes to be introduced are well defined.

In principle, *we could content ourselves with predicting only the conditional distribution of endogenous variables* for particular values assumed by the exogenous variables. *But it is more convenient to predict a definite value for each endogenous variable*, making the reservation that there is some degree of uncertainty associated with it.

The problem therefore presents a double difficulty. On the one hand, in most cases the distribution of the endogenous variables is not completely known, but only 'estimated' in the light of more or less numerous observations. The selected estimates still include a greater or lesser degree of uncertainty. On the other hand, even if we have complete knowledge of the conditional distribution of the endogenous variables, we still have to know what principle to follow in substituting for this distribution a set of n values for the n endogenous variables.

In the next chapter we shall have occasion to examine these questions and they will recur in different places in the course of other chapters. We confine ourselves here to a general comment.

Logically, we really should study the determination of inference procedures and of rules for calculating predicted values simultaneously. In other words, we ought to find the best formulae allowing direct transition from the observed sample to what we want to predict. Estimation of the parameters of the model might well even be a waste of time.

In fact we always work in two stages. We start by estimating a structure of the model, and go on to use this structure as the basis for prediction, acting in this case almost as if it were the true structure.

This procedure can be explained on two counts. In the first place, statistical theory has not yet solved in general the problem of direct prediction, where no intermediate estimate is made. In the second place estimation itself is of interest for our knowledge of economic laws, essentially because it lends itself to many predictions which can be made as required in different contexts.

We note again that, since prediction is rarely an end in itself, it would be better in most cases to state the decision problem in its entirety: In a given situation what decision must be taken when a specific model is accepted and there is a known sample on the quantities of this model? As FISHER [1962] has shown, the consideration of conditional predictions does not generally lead to the best decisions.

16 Errors of specification

The model offers a simplified picture which cannot be perfectly exact. Even a stochastic model contains assumptions which are not completely satisfied in practice. The general name of errors of specification is given to the differences between the assumptions of the model and the real properties of the phenomenon which it purports to represent.

Errors of specification affect econometric work in two different ways, for statistical inference proper and for predictions made on the basis of the model.

Statistical inference is known to imply the choice of estimators or tests whose properties have previously been studied in the context of the model in question. The distribution of the estimate, the significance level and the power of the test will have been determined and compared with the properties of other estimators or other tests. Such a study will have taken account of all the characteristics of the model, and itself will often have imposed the introduction of quite specific assumptions. For example, we assumed that certain random elements were mutually independent or were normally distributed. These assumptions were not imposed a priori but were chosen because they were convenient and seemed admissible as a first approximation.

Actually, since certain of the assumptions of the model, and in particular those relating to random errors, are not exactly verifiable, the real properties of the estimators or the tests can differ to a greater or lesser extent from the 'theoretical' properties on which the choice of a statistical procedure has been based. The importance of these differences obviously depends on the importance of the errors of specification, but also perhaps on the nature of the estimators and tests considered. The properties of some procedures can be greatly affected by changes in the assumptions of the model, while other procedures show very little sensitivity to such changes.

In the methodological study of the estimators and tests appropriate to a model, *we must investigate the sensitivity of their theoretical properties to changes in the assumptions of the model*, and above all with reference to those assumptions which have been adopted especially for reasons of convenience. We must use *robust* tests or estimators, that is, those whose properties are not dependent on the more debatable assumptions of the model.

The best way of avoiding the consequences of errors of specification would obviously be to find statistical procedures which could be studied directly in the context of models that are not very restrictive, and which could then be shown to be good. Indeed it is this point of view which causes non-parametric methods to be preferred nowadays in mathematical statistics, since these methods involve estimators or tests whose distributions can be established without any assumption about the analytic form of the distributions of random elements. (The set of structures of the model can therefore no longer be characterized by parameters, since it contains as many structures as there are possible analytic forms for these distributions.) Unfortunately such methods still have only limited relevance to the solution of statistical problems encountered in econometrics.

In most cases, therefore, we shall have to formulate fairly restrictive models. Very fortunately we shall be able to show that the most common procedures are 'robust', at least for some of the assumptions made.

It is often forgotten that *predictions can be greatly affected by errors of specification*, although this seems obvious. It can happen that the boldest predictions are made on the basis of a model with no strong theoretical foundation, and which has been estimated from very few observations. We should therefore always bear in mind the fact that the prediction is only as valid as the model. In ch. 4 we shall recall a notorious example in which an error of specification led to wrong predictions. There would be no difficulty in citing many other examples. Thus predictions for market research have sometimes been made by rudimentary extrapolation from the trends observed in five or six successive years. It was not surprising that the facts did not subsequently tally with these alleged 'laws'.

The uncertainty implied by errors of specification cannot easily be measured numerically, and this is one reason why they are often undetected. On the contrary, as we shall show later, the econometrician can give a measure of the errors of predictions made from a model. More precisely, he can determine the variance of a predicted value, taking into account both the random elements in the model and the random nature of the estimates which were used in specifying the unknown parameters of the model. But calculation of the variance in this way assumes that the model is a perfect representation of the facts. It measures only part of the uncertainty affecting prediction[†].

If it is impossible to make an exact comparison of the errors of specification and the errors of which the model takes account, we can nevertheless assert that the former will be all the more important for predictions as the sample used in estimation will be smaller in size, will cover a shorter period of time, or will arise from a more limited geographical or sociological domain. For it often happens then that some relevant factors have a virtually identical effect on all the individual observations, that their importance is not revealed and that they are ignored in the formulation of the model.

Of course the existence of errors of specification expresses the inevitable difficulty of all scientific inference, but is not sufficient cause for abandoning it. Prediction is indispensable to action; and, as we saw in the first chapter, we cannot make any prediction simply on the basis of the straight facts. To be useful, they must be interpreted in the context of a set of assumptions, that is, of a model.

[†] Instead of saying that an error of specification affects a prediction, we might say that the phenomenon under study has undergone a structural change; the true structure was represented correctly by the model during the period of observation; but it has changed. In this new terminology we must say that the uncertainty of a prediction is composed of two parts, one well evaluated by the usual econometric methods and the other due to structural modifications. On this question the reader may usefully consult HOLTE [1962].

CHAPTER 3

Linear model of simple regression

This chapter is devoted to the statistical treatment of the simplest possible model, in which a single endogenous variable is linearly dependent on a single exogenous variable and an unobservable random disturbance. The method of least squares which was introduced in the first chapter will be shown to be the appropriate method for estimating the parameters of this model.

We shall return later to a much more general discussion of this first example of a statistical analysis made within the framework of a model, but it seems useful to start with a preliminary study which will describe in a simple context a logical approach and also procedures and results which are of great importance for econometric studies. Moreover, some readers will no doubt prefer the analytic treatment which is used here to the more general but more abstract mathematical reasoning of chs. 5 and 6, since it will help them to a better understanding of the full significance of important properties.

1 The model

A certain quantity x is considered to be determined by another quantity z. The assumed dependence can be represented by a linear equation of the type:

$$x = az + b + \varepsilon, \tag{1}$$

where a and b are unknown coefficients, and ε an unobservable random term.

There are T observations on the values of the pair of quantities x and z. Let (x_t, z_t) be an observation, where $t = 1, 2, \ldots, T$. The data consist of the $2T$ numbers:

$$x_1, x_2, \ldots, x_t, \ldots, x_T,$$

$$z_1, z_2, \ldots, z_t, \ldots, z_T.$$

We wish to estimate from these data the coefficients a and b and certain characteristics of the distribution of ε.

We have already met this model in the previous chapter when discussing the demand law (cf. § 4). Similarly for the example in ch. 1 § 3, x may be taken as the logarithm of expenditure on clothing by a household, and z the logarithm of its total expenditure in the same year. The model specifies in this case that x is determined by z and by other unobservable elements, according to a linear formula which holds for all households.

Some reasons for introducing this model were given in the previous chapter, and we recall here only that the observable quantity z and the unobservable quantity ε are considered to be the 'causes' which determine the value of the quantity x. A linear formula of type (1) is often chosen for its simplicity, and for want of precise theoretical knowledge of the nature of the dependence between z and x. The term ε represents the effect of all those factors which we cannot identify for one reason or another. It is considered random since our lack of knowledge about the process generating it gives it the nature of a random variable.

It follows from eq. (1) that, since ε is random, so also is x. There is a distribution of x for every fixed value of z. Each x_t is an observation on the random variable x, that is, it can be considered to have been selected according to the probability distribution of x for the corresponding value of z, say z_t. Similarly the set of values $x_1, x_2, \ldots, x_T$ is treated as a sample from the distributions corresponding respectively to $z_1, z_2, \ldots, z_T$.

The sample space is therefore the T-dimensional Euclidean space in which the observed point[†] has coordinates $x_1, x_2, \ldots x_T$. The probability distribution of this point can be deduced directly from that of x for the T values $z_1, z_2, \ldots, z_T$ of z. It depends on the unknown parameters: a, b and certain characteristics of the distribution of ε. The statistical problem lies in the estimation of these parameters from the sample.

We can describe the model in another way which sometimes seems more fruitful, and say that *the model specifies the conditional distribution of the endogenous variable x for each fixed value of the exogenous variable z.* The sample allows us to estimate characteristics of the conditional distribution of $x_1, x_2, \ldots, x_T$ for the values $z_1, z_2, \ldots, z_T$ of z.

This formulation may suggest that the exogenous variable z is considered random and that there is a distribution of the pair (x, z). In fact, the methods and properties which we shall consider are equally applicable whether the exogenous variable is fixed or random. They always involve only the conditional distribution of x for fixed values of z.

Moreover, we shall encounter many cases where certain exogenous variables cannot be considered as random. Thus z_t will sometimes denote the time, month or year, of the observation x_t. When z represents an economic quantity, we can often assume that its value results from a partly random phenomenon. But this phenomenon itself involves other quantities in the role of exogenous variables. So, even when it could be considered as random, the variable z would not generally have a simple distribution, and similarly the distribution of the pair (x, z) would be complex. It would be an unnecessary complication to include it in the specification of the model.

---

† The symbol x is used in this book to denote both the random variable and the set of observations on it. This should not cause any confusion.

2 Basic assumption

We must now give a precise statement of the model by formulating the assumptions which we shall adopt in the rest of this chapter. For the sake of clarity these assumptions have been given in the greatest possible detail, and a complete list of them is given below, although most results depend on only some of them. These assumptions are mainly concerned with the distribution of ε; the last two relate to the values of exogenous variables and to parameters.

Assumption 1. The variables x_t and z_t (where $t = 1, 2, \ldots, T$) represent numerical quantities observed without error. The variable x_t is random and satisfies:

$$x_t = az_t + b + \varepsilon_t \qquad \text{for} \qquad t = 1, 2, \ldots, T, \tag{2}$$

where a and b are two numerical coefficients, and ε_t is an unobservable random variable whose expected value is zero for all $z_1, z_2, \ldots, z_T$.

This assumption repeats the general information about the model that was given in the preceding section, but with two additions.

In the first place, it lays down that *the variables x and z are observed without error*. If there were appreciable differences between the observed values and the true values which satisfy the model, we would have to resort to different statistical methods and to a different theoretical analysis, as we shall see in ch. 10. Although economic data are undoubtedly subject to some degree of error in measurement, we often consider that these errors are negligible in comparison with the unobservable elements which take part in the determination of the endogenous variables (the ε in the present model).

Thus the results for expenditure on clothing and total expenditure in a group of households (ch. 1 § 3) are the outcome of an inquiry which could not claim complete precision in spite of the care with which it was carried out. The expenditures recorded for each household differ to some extent from the quantities which were the object of measurement. But in most cases the differences are very slight relative to the term ε which in model (1) represents the effect on expenditure on clothing of all elements other than annual total expenditure. This is why we can agree to ignore errors of measurement in the econometric analysis of these data.

In the second place, assumption 1 specifies that the expected value of ε is zero whatever the values of the z. Without an assumption of this kind, the parameters a and b of the model would not be identifiable. For example, a structure in which $a = 1$, $b = 0$, $E(\varepsilon) = 0$ would lead to the same conditional distribution of the x's as another structure in which $a = 0$, $b = 1$, $E(\varepsilon) = z - 1$, the ε's in the two cases being similarly distributed about their respective means. In short, the expected value of ε must be zero if the model is to provide the basis for econometric analysis. This condition was therefore imposed right from the start in assumption 1.

In practice this condition means that the additive term ε of the model takes values which are sometimes positive and sometimes negative for any value of the exogenous variable. *It is not satisfied if the effect of unobservable or unidentified factors is correlated with the effect of the explanatory variable z.* In every practical application we must therefore bear in mind that this condition may be restrictive. We shall see on several occasions that there are important cases in which it does not hold, and we shall then consider statistical methods which differ from those of the present chapter.

We could formulate assumption 1 in such a way as to avoid the difficulty of identifiability which we have pointed out. It would be sufficient to state directly that the conditional distribution of x_t for fixed values of $z_1, z_2, \ldots, z_T$ has expected value $\alpha z_t + \beta$, say[†]

$$E(x_t / z_1, z_2, \ldots, z_T) = \alpha z_t + \beta. \tag{3}$$

The parameters α and β would then be characteristics of the conditional distribution of the x's. If the values of these parameters and of z_t are known, we can directly obtain the expected value of x_t as $\alpha z_t + \beta$. It is of little account whether αz_t actually is the effect of the exogenous variable (as in the structure $a = 1$, $b = 0$, $E(\varepsilon) = 0$) or of other unobservable or unidentified factors (as in the structure $a = 0$, $b = 1$, $E(\varepsilon) = z - 1$). It is sufficient in each case, for finding the conditional mean of x_t, that z_t and the parameters α and β are known.

WOLD [1960b] has advocated this point of view which is more general than that adopted in the statement of assumption 1, since it does not exclude structures of the type $a = 0$, $b = 1$, $E(\varepsilon) = z - 1$. It shows that the results established below can have a rather different interpretation from that which we shall make.

In fact we may repeat here the conclusions reached in the preceding chapter on the subject of identifiability. We saw then that knowledge of the conditional distribution of the endogenous variables is sufficient for prediction, at least so long as the model undergoes no change. The difficulties connected with identifiability emerge only when we try to go from the distribution of the endogenous variables to the structure which explains it. But we also saw that such identification was sometimes necessary.

Moreover the basic assumptions must be formulated in such a way that they apply as directly as possible to the models worked out by economic theory, and that they lend themselves to a discussion based on the direct examination of the phenomena which they represent. This explains the particular statement which we have given for assumption 1.

3   Other assumptions

We consider now stricter limitations on the distribution of the unobservable terms ε, which we shall call 'errors' when there is no possibility of confusion.

[†] In the case where assumption 1, as first formulated, is satisfied, the parameters a and b obviously equal α and β.

Assumption 2 (homoscedasticity).   The error ε_t is distributed independently of t and of the z_θ (where $\theta = 1, 2, \ldots, T$); it has a variance σ^2.

This assumption reinforces the condition already included in assumption 1, that the mean of ε_t is zero whatever the values of the z_θ. Here we suppose ε_t to be independent of the z_θ; that is, its whole distribution is unchanged whatever the values of the z_θ. The remarks made above therefore apply with greater force.

It was implicit in assumption 1 that the distribution of ε_t had a mean. Assumption 2 imposes the additional condition that the distribution has a variance. We shall return later to the discussion of this condition (ch. 8, § 5 (iv)). It is considered to be satisfied in the great majority of practical cases.

Finally assumption 2 stipulates further that all the errors ε_t have the same distribution. These errors are said to be homoscedastic when their distribution is independent of t and of the z_θ. They may lack homoscedasticity for various reasons, and are then said to be heteroscedastic. In many cases simple transformations on the variables allow us to eliminate the most important effects of heteroscedasticity (see ch. 8, § 5 (ii)).

Assumption 3 (independence of the different observations).   The errors ε_t and ε_θ relating to any two different observations t and θ are mutually independent.

This assumption is particularly important when the observations are successive in time with the order $1, 2, \ldots, T$. In this case there is often a positive correlation between ε_t and the next error ε_{t+1}, since the unidentified factors in the phenomenon behave with some degree of continuity and often have a similar effect on two successive values of the endogenous variable. Independence of the errors is also suspect if, as often happens, the observations have different sources and if there is reason to think that observations from the same source are affected by certain unobservable common factors.

Assumption 4 (normality).   The errors ε_t have a normal or Laplace–Gauss distribution.

Contrary to the belief sometimes held, the assumption of normality of the ε_t is not of basic importance for the present theory. Homoscedasticity, or even only the existence of the variance (cf. assumption 2) is sufficient for many results. However, normality is necessary for the complete justification of some of the proposed procedures.

Assumption 5 (exogenous variables).   When T tends to infinity, the sequence of values of the exogenous variable z_t (where $t = 1, 2, \ldots, t, \ldots$) is such that its mean

$$\bar{z} = \frac{1}{T} \sum_{t=1}^{T} z_t$$

and its mean square deviation

$$\frac{1}{T} \sum_{t=1}^{T} (z_t - \bar{z})^2$$

tend to the finite limits z_0 and S^2 respectively. The limit S^2 is positive.

This assumption obviously comes into play only in the study of the asymptotic properties of the proposed methods, when we suppose that the number T of observations tends to infinity. It is not always satisfied, notably if z_t is a continuously increasing function, or a damped sinusoidal function. The asymptotic results quoted here could be established on the basis of rather less restrictive assumptions. But they are not of great importance for the validity of the methods studied and it seemed better to keep to a simple assumption.

We note also that we always suppose, without its being explicitly stated, that the T values of z_t are not all the same and equal to z_0, say. If this were the case we could not identify the two parameters a and b of the model, since all the x_t would have the same distribution in which only the mean $az_0 + b$ would depend on the two parameters in question. Even complete knowledge of this distribution and its mean would only allow us to determine $az_0 + b$, and not a and b individually.

Assumption 6. Except for the sample, there is no information available about the numerical coefficients a and b, which can take a priori any values, positive, negative or zero.

The very formulation of the model, that is assumption 1, could be considered to imply this new assumption automatically. We state it separately here because it is not satisfied in certain cases. Theoretical study of the model sometimes reveals that the coefficients are subject to certain constraints which are expressed in the form of equalities or inequalities. It may be, for example, that a and b must satisfy $a + b = 1$, or $a \geqslant 0$. For the present we exclude such cases, which will be discussed in chapter 9.

4   *The method of least squares*

In the context of our model the best estimates of a and b are the simple regression coefficients of x on z. We shall now demonstrate this by studying the properties of these estimates. In ch. 1 the usual regressions were defined independently of any stochastic model. In contrast the properties which we shall establish will show why neither the regression of z on x nor the orthogonal regression is suitable for the statistical treatment of the present model.

The regression of x on z is defined as the linear equation $x^* = a^* z + b^*$, where a^* and b^* are the values of a and b which minimize

$$U = \sum_{t=1}^{T} (x_t - az_t - b)^2. \tag{4}$$

The calculations shown in ch. 1 § 3 yield the following expressions for a^* and b^*:

$$a^* = \frac{\sum_{t=1}^{T} (x_t - \bar{x})(z_t - \bar{z})}{\sum_{t=1}^{T} (z_t - \bar{z})^2}, \tag{5}$$

$$b^* = \bar{x} - a^* \bar{z}, \tag{6}$$

where

$$\bar{x} = \frac{1}{T} \sum_{t=1}^{T} x_t, \qquad \bar{z} = \frac{1}{T} \sum_{t=1}^{T} z_t.$$

These expressions are linear in the values x_t of the endogenous variable. Let us denote by x^1, x^2, x^3 and x^4 four samples taken with the same true structure and the same values $z_1, z_2, \ldots, z_T$, in conformity with the general principles laid down above. Let x_t^1, x_t^2, x_t^3 and x_t^4 be the values of x_t in x^1, x^2, x^3 and x^4, and also a^{*1}, b^{*1}, a^{*2}, b^{*2}, a^{*3}, b^{*3}, a^{*4}, b^{*4} be the values of the estimates (5) and (6). The fact that a^* and b^* are linear results from the two following remarks:

If $x_t^3 = kx_t^1$ for every t with the same suitable number k, then also $a^{*3} = ka^{*1}$ and $b^{*3} = kb^{*1}$;

If $x_t^4 = x_t^1 + x_t^2$ for every t, then also $a^{*4} = a^{*1} + a^{*2}$ and $b^{*4} = b^{*1} + b^{*2}$.

Because of eq. (2) we can express a^* and b^* as a function of the true coefficients a and b, the values of z_t and the errors ε_t. We obtain directly from (2):

$$x_t - \bar{x} = a(z_t - \bar{z}) + (\varepsilon_t - \bar{\varepsilon}),$$

whence, by substituting in (5):

$$a^* = a + \frac{\sum_{t=1}^{T} (\varepsilon_t - \bar{\varepsilon})(z_t - \bar{z})}{\sum_{t=1}^{T} (z_t - \bar{z})^2} = a + \frac{\sum_{t=1}^{T} \varepsilon_t (z_t - \bar{z})}{\sum_{t=1}^{T} (z_t - \bar{z})^2}, \tag{7}$$

or again:

$$a^* = a + \sum_{t=1}^{T} w_t \varepsilon_t, \tag{8}$$

$$b^* = b + \bar{\varepsilon} - (a^* - a)\bar{z}, \tag{9}$$

where:

$$w_t = \frac{z_t - \bar{z}}{\sum\limits_{t=1}^{T} (z_t - \bar{z})^2}. \tag{10}$$

By taking expectations with respect to the distribution of $\varepsilon_1, \varepsilon_2, \ldots, \varepsilon_T$ for the given values of $z_1, z_2, \ldots, z_T$, in (8) and (9), we obtain directly the following property:

Proposition 1. If assumption 1 is satisfied, the estimates a^* and b^* are *'unbiased'* since their expected values are the true values a and b.

Similarly from expression (8):

$$E(a^* - a)^2 = \sum_{t,\theta} w_t w_\theta E(\varepsilon_t \varepsilon_\theta).$$

If assumptions 2 and 3 are satisfied (homoscedasticity and independence of the observations), $E(\varepsilon_t \varepsilon_\theta) = 0$ when $t \neq \theta$ and $E(\varepsilon_t \varepsilon_\theta) = \sigma^2$ when $t = \theta$. Therefore:

$$E(a^* - a)^2 = \sigma^2 \sum_t w_t^2 = \frac{\sigma^2}{\sum\limits_{t=1}^{T} (z_t - \bar{z})^2}.$$

This expression could be written σ_{a*}^2. We shall denote it more simply by σ_a^2, which should lead to no confusion.

Similar calculations apply for

$$E(b^* - b)^2 = \sigma_b^2 \quad \text{and} \quad E[(a^* - a)(b^* - b)] = \text{cov}(a^*, b^*).$$

Hence:

Proposition 2. Under assumptions 1, 2 and 3, the second order moments of a^* and b^* are:

$$\sigma_a^2 = \frac{\sigma^2}{\sum\limits_{t=1}^{T} (z_t - \bar{z})^2}, \qquad \sigma_b^2 = \frac{\sigma^2}{T} \left[1 + \frac{T\bar{z}^2}{\sum\limits_{t=1}^{T} (z_t - \bar{z})^2} \right], \tag{11}$$

$$\text{cov}(a^*, b^*) = -\bar{z}\sigma_a^2. \tag{12}$$

Now we consider the behavior of $a^* - a$ and $b^* - b$ when the number of observations tends to infinity and where the z_t make a sequence satisfying assumption 5. Formulae (11) show that in this case the variances of a^* and b^* tend to zero. These estimates tend to the true values a and b, in mean square, and therefore also in probability. Hence:

Proposition 3. If assumptions 1, 2, 3 and 5 hold, the estimates a^* and b^* are *'consistent'*[†].

† We shall see in ch. 6 that this property is still true under less restrictive assumptions.

The difference between the observed value x_t and the value deduced from the regression $a^*z_t + b^*$ is called the '*residual*' and is denoted by ε_t^*. Let:

$$\varepsilon_t^* = x_t - a^*z_t - b^* = (a - a^*)z_t + (b - b^*) + \varepsilon_t. \qquad (13)$$

This residual differs from ε_t by a term depending on the 'errors of estimation' $a^* - a$ and $b^* - b$. Its mean becomes zero whenever assumption 1 is satisfied. It tends in probability to ε_t if assumptions 2, 3 and 5 are also satisfied. The empirical distribution of the ε_t^* then tends in probability to the probability distribution of the ε_t; and the empirical moments of the ε_t^* to the theoretical moments of the ε_t.

In practice the variance σ^2 of the errors is generally unknown and so are most of the characteristics of their distribution. We might consider estimating σ^2 from the empirical variance of the ε_t^* ,since the latter tends to σ^2 in large samples.

For the study of small samples we can write, from (13) and (9):

$$\varepsilon_t^* = (a - a^*)(z_t - \bar{z}) + (\varepsilon_t - \bar{\varepsilon}).$$

The sum of squares of the residuals is therefore

$$\sum_{t=1}^{T} \varepsilon_t^{*2} = \sum_{t=1}^{T} (\varepsilon_t - \bar{\varepsilon})^2 + (a - a^*)^2 \sum_{t=1}^{T} (z_t - \bar{z})^2 + 2(a - a^*) \sum_{t=1}^{T} (z_t - \bar{z})(\varepsilon_t - \bar{\varepsilon})$$

or, from (7):

$$\sum_{t=1}^{T} \varepsilon_t^{*2} = \sum_{t=1}^{T} (\varepsilon_t - \bar{\varepsilon})^2 - (a - a^*)^2 \sum_{t=1}^{T} (z_t - \bar{z})^2. \qquad (14)$$

The first term on the right hand side has expected value $(T-1)\sigma^2$ whenever assumptions 2 and 3 hold; proposition 1 above establishes that the expected value of the second term is $-\sigma^2$.

Thus:

Proposition 4. If assumptions 1, 2 and 3 are satisfied the expected value of the sum of squares of the residuals is $(T-2)\sigma^2$. If assumption 5 is also satisfied the residuals ε_t^* tend in probability to the true values ε_t of the errors.

Proposition 4 shows that an unbiased estimator of σ^2 will be given by the '*residual variance*' which is by definition:

$$\sigma_\varepsilon^{*2} = \frac{1}{T-2} \sum_{t=1}^{T} \varepsilon_t^{*2}. \qquad (15)$$

To find the value of this estimate we do not have to calculate the ε_t^* individually.

Equation (6) shows that ε_t^* can be written:

$$\varepsilon_t^* = (x_t - \bar{x}) - a^*(z_t - \bar{z}). \tag{16}$$

Equation (5) shows that the sum of squares of this expression is:

$$(T - 2)\sigma_\varepsilon^{*2} = \sum_{t=1}^{T}(x_t - \bar{x})^2 - a^{*2}\sum_{t=1}^{T}(z_t - \bar{z})^2, \tag{17}$$

this formula being generally used to calculate σ_ε^*.

Subject to the assumptions for proposition 4, unbiased estimators σ_a^{*2} and σ_b^{*2} of σ_a^2 and σ_b^2 are found simply by substituting σ_ε^{*2} for σ^2 in formulae (11). For example:

$$\sigma_a^{*2} = \frac{\sigma_\varepsilon^{*2}}{\sum_{t=1}^{T}(z_t - \bar{z})^2}. \tag{18}$$

The preceding propositions justify the usual ways of calculating estimates of a and b. Thus, applying the data in ch. 1 § 3 to the model which represents the determination of expenditure on clothing as a function of total expenditure, we find

$$\bar{x} = 3.1622, \qquad \bar{z} = 4.1129,$$

$$\frac{1}{T}\sum(x_t - \bar{x})^2 = 0.048918, \qquad \frac{1}{T}\sum(z_t - \bar{z})^2 = 0.019934,$$

$$\frac{1}{T}\sum(x_t - \bar{x})(z_t - \bar{z}) = 0.023932;$$

whence, from formulae (5) and (6):

$$a^* = 1.20, \qquad b^* = -1.78.$$

From formula (17):

$$(T - 2)\sigma_\varepsilon^{*2} = T \cdot 0.0202.$$

and so:

$$\sigma_\varepsilon^{*2} = 0.0206.$$

From formula (18) and a similar formula deduced from (11) for σ_b^{*2}, we have finally

$$\sigma_a^{*2} = 0.0092, \qquad \sigma_b^{*2} = 0.1563,$$

$$\sigma_a^* = 0.10, \qquad \sigma_b^* = 0.40.$$

These results are generally presented as follows:

$$x_t = 1.20\,z_t - 1.78, \qquad (19)$$
$$(0.10) \quad (0.40),$$

the estimated standard errors of a^* and b^* being given in brackets below the corresponding regression coefficients.

Of course these results can hardly be valid if the assumptions of the model are too far removed from reality. In particular, if assumption 3 is inadmissible, σ_a^* and σ_b^* are bad estimators of the standard errors of a^* and b^*. We shall return to this question in chs. 8 and 13.

The value of the coefficient R^2 is often given on the right of the regression. With the notation used in this chapter this coefficient, already defined in chapter 1, can be written:

$$R^2 = \frac{[\sum (x_t - \bar{x})(z_t - z)]^2}{\sum (x_t - \bar{x})^2 \cdot \sum (z_t - \bar{z})^2},$$

or

$$R^2 = 1 - \frac{(T - 2)\sigma_\varepsilon^{*2}}{\sum\limits_{t=1}^{T} (x_t - \bar{x})^2}. \qquad (20)$$

This formula will be generalized in ch. 6.

However, we must point out that in the present context this coefficient is not particularly interesting. It gives no information about the goodness of the fit, but only about the shape of the collection of points. For the small samples which are often used in econometric analysis, R^2 can be high although σ_a^* and σ_b^* are not trivial. On the other hand, an extensive sample sometimes yields an exact estimate of a and b although R^2 remains fairly low. (However, we shall see in § 6 below that there is a connection between R^2 and an important test.)

Thus in the regression equation (19), R^2 is only 0.59. On the other hand, it is 0.97 in the regression between imports and gross domestic production, based on the data of table 1, ch. 1, which was:

$$x_t = 0.155\,z_t - 6.20. \qquad (21)$$
$$(0.012) \quad (1.88)$$

However, the standard errors given in parentheses show that the ratios of the errors to the estimated coefficients are almost the same in each case. This results from the fact that regression (19) was calculated from 112 observations and regression (21) from only 18.

Formula (8) also allows us to calculate *moments of order higher than 2*. For, let

$$\mu_k(a^*) = E(a^* - a)^k \qquad \mu_k(\varepsilon) = E\varepsilon_t^k$$

$$\mu_k(z) = \frac{1}{T}\sum_{t=1}^{T}(z_t - \bar{z})^k$$

and, in view of (10), note that

$$\sum_t w_t^k = \frac{\mu_k(z)}{T^{k-1}\mu_2^k(z)}.$$

Assuming that the ε_t are independent and identically distributed (assumptions 2 and 3), we see immediately that

$$\mu_3(a^*) = \sum_t w_t^3 E\varepsilon_t^3.$$

Hence, by the previous formulae,

$$\mu_3(a^*) = \frac{\mu_3(z)\mu_3(\varepsilon)}{T^2\mu_2^3(z)}.$$

Introducing the classic quantity

$$\beta_1 = \frac{\mu_3}{\mu_2^{\frac{3}{2}}}$$

we can also write

$$\beta_1(a^*) = \frac{1}{T}\beta_1(z)\cdot\beta_1(\varepsilon). \qquad (22)$$

The sample moments $\mu_k(z)$ of the distribution of z obviously depend on T; but, as in assumption 5, we can assume that they tend to finite limits as T tends to infinity. It then follows from (22) that $\beta_1(a^*)$ tends to zero.

It is almost as straightforward to calculate $\mu_4(a^*)$. Still under assumptions 2 and 3, we find that

$$\mu_4(a^*) = \sum_t w_t^4 E\varepsilon_t^4 + 3 \sum_{t,\theta \neq t} w_t^2 w_\theta^2 E\varepsilon_t^2 E\varepsilon_\theta^2$$

$$= \sum_t w_t^4[\mu_4(\varepsilon) - 3\sigma^4] + [3\sum_t w_t^2\sigma^2]^2$$

$$= \frac{\mu_4(z)[\mu_4(\varepsilon) - 3\sigma^4]}{T^3\mu_2^4(z)} + \frac{3\sigma^4}{T^2\mu_2^2(z)}.$$

Introducing the coefficient

$$\beta_2 = \frac{\mu_4}{\mu_2^2},$$

we obtain

$$\beta_2(a^*) - 3 = \frac{1}{T}\beta_2(z) \cdot [\beta_2(\varepsilon) - 3]. \tag{23}$$

This equation shows that $\beta_2(a^*)$ tends to 3 as T tends to infinity. This limiting value and that of $\beta_1(a^*)$ can also be obtained from a more general property, namely that $\sqrt{T}(a^*-a)$ has a limiting normal distribution (we shall discuss this in ch. 6).

But (22) and (23) also show exactly how the first moments of the distribution of a^* depend on the distributions of the ε_t and the z_t. The same method can obviously be used to find higher order moments, whether in the case of simple regression or of multiple regression. For this, see MISRA [1972].

5 An important property of the method of least squares

We have described the method of least squares and certain important properties of the estimates to which it leads, but we have not shown why this method should be preferred to some others which might also be suggested. Propositions 1 and 3 clearly establish that a^* and b^* are unbiased and consistent, but other estimators would have the same properties. We must now examine stronger properties of the method.

We denote by $\hat{a} = f(x)$ some estimator of a, where x is the vector of the T observed values of the endogenous variable x_t, and f is a real function of the T variables x_t. The function f may depend on the observable exogenous variables z_t, but must be independent of the true values of the parameters a and b since they are assumed to be unknown. We shall say that the estimator is linear if:

$$f(kx) = kf(x) \quad \text{and} \quad f(x^1 + x^2) = f(x^1) + f(x^2),$$

whatever the samples x, x^1, x^2 and the number k. We have already seen that a^* and b^* were unbiased linear estimators. We shall now prove that they have the smallest variances among all unbiased linear estimators of a and b.

Proposition 5[†]. If assumptions 1, 2, 3 and 6 are satisfied, the estimators a^* and b^* have minimum variances among all unbiased linear estimators of a and b.

---

† We could also establish here the rather stronger property which we shall prove in ch. 5:

Proposition 5′. If assumptions 1, 2, 3 and 6 are satisfied the linear form $\lambda a^* - \mu b^*$ has minimum variance in the class of linear estimators whose expected value is $\lambda a + \mu b$.

We shall prove this by determining directly the unbiased linear estimators with minimum variances and by verifying that these are in fact a^* and b^*. The most general form of linear estimators is:

$$\hat{a} = \sum_{t=1}^{T} r_t x_t, \qquad \hat{b} = \sum_{t=1}^{T} s_t x_t, \tag{24}$$

in which the r_t and s_t may depend on the values of the exogenous variables $z_1, z_2, \ldots, z_T$, but not on the values of the x_t.

The mean of x_t is $az_t + b$. Therefore:

$$E(\hat{a}) = a \sum_{t=1}^{T} r_t z_t + b \sum_{t=1}^{T} r_t, \qquad E(\hat{b}) = a \sum_{t=1}^{T} s_t z_t + b \sum_{t=1}^{T} s_t.$$

In order that $\hat{a}$ and $\hat{b}$ should be unbiased estimators, these two expressions must equal a and b respectively and these equalities must be satisfied identically for all real a and b (cf. assumption 6).

As r_t and s_t are not dependent on a and b, obviously we must have:

$$\sum_{t=1}^{T} r_t z_t = 1, \qquad \sum_{t=1}^{T} s_t z_t = 0,$$

$$\sum_{t=1}^{T} r_t = 0, \qquad \sum_{t=1}^{T} s_t = 1. \tag{25}$$

If we substitute for x_t the expression given in eq. (2) and take account of eqs. (25), eqs. (24) become

$$\hat{a} - a = \sum_{t=1}^{T} r_t \varepsilon_t, \qquad \hat{b} - b = \sum_{t=1}^{T} s_t \varepsilon_t.$$

Therefore, in view of assumptions 2 and 3:

$$E(\hat{a} - a)^2 = \sigma^2 \sum_{t=1}^{T} r_t^2, \qquad E(\hat{b} - b)^2 = \sigma^2 \sum_{t=1}^{T} s_t^2.$$

The minimum variance estimators $\hat{a}$ and $\hat{b}$ are therefore obtained by using the coefficients r_t and s_t which minimize[†] $\sum_{t=1}^{T} r_t^2$ and $\sum_{t=1}^{T} s_t^2$ subject to conditions (25).

Since the form to be minimized is the sum of squares of the r_t (or the s_t) and the side conditions are linear in r_t (or in s_t), we find the unique minimum by

---

[†] It is worth noting that the quantities to be minimized do not depend on the unknown parameters a and b, so that the analytic expressions for the minimum variance estimators will not involve these parameters either. It is precisely this circumstance which is the basis of proposition 5.

equating to zero the derivatives with respect to r_t (or s_t) of the form

$$\sum_{t=1}^{T} r_t^2 - 2\alpha \sum_{t=1}^{T} r_t z_t - 2\beta \sum_{t=1}^{T} r_t$$

(or of the following):

$$\sum_{t=1}^{T} s_t^2 - 2\gamma \sum_{t=1}^{T} s_t z_t - 2\delta \sum_{t=1}^{T} s_t,$$

where α, β, γ and δ are obviously Lagrange multipliers.

Differentiation gives:

$$r_t = \alpha z_t + \beta, \qquad s_t = \gamma z_t + \delta$$

and conditions (25) imply that α, β, γ and δ satisfy:

$$\alpha \sum_{t=1}^{T} z_t^2 + \beta \sum_{t=1}^{T} z_t = 1, \qquad \gamma \sum_{t=1}^{T} z_t^2 + \delta \sum_{t=1}^{T} z_t = 0,$$

$$\alpha \sum_{t=1}^{T} z_t + \beta T = 0, \qquad \gamma \sum_{t=1}^{T} z_t + \delta T = 1.$$

Therefore:

$$\alpha = \frac{1}{\sum_{t=1}^{T} (z_t - \bar{z})^2}, \qquad \gamma = \frac{-\bar{z}}{\sum_{t=1}^{T} (z_t - \bar{z})^2},$$

$$\beta = -\alpha \bar{z}, \qquad \delta = -\gamma \bar{z} + \frac{1}{T},$$

$$r_t = \frac{z_t - \bar{z}}{\sum_{t=1}^{T} (z_t - \bar{z})^2}, \qquad s_t = \frac{1}{T} - r_t \bar{z},$$

$$\hat{a} = \frac{\sum_{t=1}^{T} (z_t - \bar{z})(x_t - \bar{x})}{\sum_{t=1}^{T} (z_t - \bar{z})^2}, \qquad \hat{b} = \bar{x} - \hat{a}\bar{z}.$$

These last two expressions establish that the estimators we have found are in fact a^* and b^* respectively, and therefore proposition 5 is proved.

This proposition shows that, if the ε_t are homoscedastic and mutually independent, the method of least squares yields estimates whose dispersion is as small as possible, at least so long as we consider only unbiased linear estimators. It is of particular interest since it assumes nothing about the distribution of ε_t except the existence of a variance σ^2, and is therefore of great value in applied econometric studies where it would generally be difficult to describe the distributions in detail.

We shall later examine the significance of proposition 5 in a more general context (cf. ch. 5), and shall then ask if only unbiased linear estimators should be considered. Non-linear or biased estimators would be preferable to a^* and b^* if they yielded errors which would be smaller than $a^* - a$ and $b^* - b$. We shall see that least squares estimators enjoy optimal properties not only in the class of linear estimators, but also in the class of all possible estimators.

Be that as it may, the reader can see for himself that it is wrong to state, as it often is stated, that least squares estimation assumes that the errors ε_t are normally distributed. In fact normality is necessary to justify only certain tests associated with the method of least squares and not the estimation formulae (5) and (6).

6   Role of the assumption of normality

Subject to assumptions 1 to 4, the distribution of the T errors ε_t (for $t = 1, 2, \ldots, T$) has density[†]:

$$\frac{1}{(2\pi)^{T/2}\sigma^T} \exp\left\{-\frac{1}{2\sigma^2} \sum_{t=1}^{T} \varepsilon_t^2\right\}.$$

The distribution of the sample values of the x_t therefore has density:

$$C\sigma^{-T} \exp\left\{-\frac{1}{2\sigma^2} \sum_{t=1}^{T} (x_t - az_t - b)^2\right\}, \tag{26}$$

where C denotes the constant $(2\pi)^{T/2}$.

We can write:

$$(x_t - az_t - b)^2 = (x_t - a^*z_t - b^*)^2 + [(a^* - a)z_t + (b^* - b)]^2$$
$$+ 2(x_t - a^*z_t - b^*)[(a^* - a)z_t + (b^* - b)],$$

whose last term can also be written:

$$2[(x_t - \bar{x}) - a^*(z_t - \bar{z})][(a^* - a)(z_t - \bar{z}) + (b^* - b) + (a^* - a)\bar{z}].$$

The sum over t of this latter expression is zero, according to the formulae defining $\bar{x}$, $\bar{z}$ and a^*. After substituting in (26) we see that the probability

[†] The exponential function e^x is denoted by $\exp\{x\}$.

density of the x_t is also expressed by:

$$C\sigma^{-T} \exp\left\{-\frac{1}{2\sigma^2} \sum_{t=1}^{T} (x_t - a^* z_t - b^*)^2\right\}$$

$$\times \exp\left\{-\frac{1}{2\sigma^2}\left[(a^* - a)^2 \sum_{t=1}^{T} z_t^2 + 2T\bar{z}(a^* - a)(b^* - b) + T(b^* - b)^2\right]\right\}. \quad (27)$$

In view of (13) and (15), the expression in the first exponential is equal to $-(T-2)\sigma_\varepsilon^{*2}/\sigma^2$. So we can write the probability density of the x_t in the form

$$C\sigma^{-T} \exp\left\{-\frac{1}{2\sigma^2}\left[(T-2)\sigma_\varepsilon^{*2} + (a^* - a)^2 \sum_{t=1}^{T} z_t^2\right.\right.$$

$$\left.\left. + 2T\bar{z}(a^* - a)(b^* - b) + T(b^* - b)^2\right]\right\}. \quad (28)$$

This last expression has the feature that it involves the x_t only through the three functions a^*, b^* and σ_ε^*. *This shows that the three estimators in question constitute a sufficient statistic* of the sample for estimation of (a, b, σ); given the values of a^*, b^* and σ_ε^*, the (conditional) distribution of the sample no longer depends on (a, b, σ); so knowledge of the values of other characteristics of the sample gives no additional information about the values of the unknown parameters[†].

Thus the simple regression calculations which give a^*, b^* and σ_ε^* make complete use of the sample. This leads to the intuitive conclusion that the corresponding estimators are efficient. In fact we could refer to the general theory of sufficient estimators in order to establish certain useful results (see in particular CRAMER [1946], ch. 32, § 3 and 6, especially exercise 1). But a still more powerful property has been established directly by RAO [1965] (see pp. 257–8) which proves that all unbiased estimators $\hat{a}$ and $\hat{b}$ (that is, such that $E(\hat{a}) = a$ and $E(\hat{b}) = b$ identically in a and b) have variances at least equal to those of a^* and b^* respectively.

In order to determine the distribution of a^*, b^* and σ_ε^* completely, let us carry out a change of coordinates in the sample space by rotating the axes so that, under the old system, the unit vectors of the first two axes have the following coordinates:

$$\frac{1}{\sqrt{T}}\begin{bmatrix} 1 \\ 1 \\ \vdots \\ 1 \end{bmatrix}, \quad \frac{1}{[\sum(z_t - \bar{z})^2]^{\frac{1}{2}}}\begin{bmatrix} z_1 - \bar{z} \\ z_2 - \bar{z} \\ \vdots \\ z_T - \bar{z} \end{bmatrix}.$$

(It can be verified that the two vectors are orthogonal.)

---

† The concept of 'sufficient statistic' was introduced and discussed by DARMOIS [1937]. To deduce from (28) the fact that $(a^*, b^*, \sigma_\varepsilon^*)$ constitutes a sufficient statistic, the factorization theorem stated in ch. 2, § 12 must be applied.

Let $y_1, y_2, \ldots, y_T$ be the new coordinates of the sample point. We can verify immediately that:

$$y_1 = \bar{x}\sqrt{T} = (a^*\bar{z} + b^*)\sqrt{T},$$
$$y_2 = a^*\left[\sum(z_t - \bar{z})^2\right]^{\frac{1}{2}}.$$

The sample point can therefore be considered as the end point of the sum of two orthogonal vectors, x^* with coordinates $(y_1, y_2, 0, \ldots, 0)$ in the new system or the $a^*z_t + b^*$ $(t = 1, 2, \ldots, T)$ in the old, and ε^* with coordinates $(0, 0, y_3, \ldots, y_T)$ in the new system or the $\varepsilon_t^* = x_t - a^*z_t - b^*$ in the old.

Now the jacobian of the transformation of the $(x_1, x_2, \ldots, x_T)$ into $(y_1, y_2, \ldots, y_T)$ is $+1$, since a rotation is a linear transformation defined by an orthogonal matrix (see LENTIN and RIVAUD [1958], pp. 241, 242). Expression (27) gives the probability density of the $y_1, y_2, \ldots, y_T$ as well as that of the $x_1, x_2, \ldots, x_T$. The first factor in (27) involves only the ε_t^*, that is the $y_3, y_4, \ldots, y_T$; the second factor involves only a^* and b^*, that is, after the change in coordinates, y_1 and y_2 (since the z_t are in this case non-random elements). Thus the probability density of the sample point is the product of two factors, one of which depends only on ε^* and the other only on x^*.

We see that ε^* and x^* are independent and that each is normally distributed, the former in a $(T-2)$-dimensional space and the latter in a two-dimensional space. Since in T-dimensional space the vector x has a spherical normal distribution, this result could have been deduced directly from the remark that x^* and ε^* are the orthogonal projections of x on two mutually orthogonal subspaces[†] which are the subspace L spanned by the two vectors e and $z - \bar{z}$

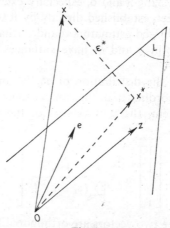

Fig. 1.

[†] The reader will note that the geometric representation introduced here is very similar to that used for multiple regression in chapter 1.

with coordinates $e_t = 1$ and $z_t - \bar{z}$ respectively (and therefore also the subspace spanned by e and z), and its orthogonal complement K. The subspace L contains the vector $E(x)$, which is the expected value of the vector x and has coordinates $az_t + b$.

The two factors of (27) define the probability densities of ε^* and x^*. Thus we see that, in the new system, the $T - 2$ non-zero coordinates of ε^* $(y_3, y_4, \ldots, y_T)$ are independent and normally distributed, each with zero mean and standard deviation σ. The quantity

$$\frac{1}{\sigma^2} \sum_{t=1}^{T} \varepsilon_t^{*2},$$

which is the sum of squares of the residuals divided by σ^2 is therefore distributed as χ^2 with $T - 2$ degrees of freedom.

Similarly the expression for the second factor shows that the true values a and b are the means of a^* and b^* whose covariance matrix is the inverse of:

$$\frac{1}{\sigma^2} \begin{bmatrix} \sum_{t=1}^{T} z_t^2 & T\bar{z} \\ T\bar{z} & T \end{bmatrix}, \tag{29}$$

the elements of this inverse being precisely the expressions given by formulae (11) and (12).

We can therefore state:

Proposition 6. If assumptions 1–4 and 6 are satisfied, the unbiased estimators a^*, b^* and σ_ε^{*2} obtained by least squares regression constitute a sufficient statistic. The estimators a^* and b^* have minimum variance in the class of unbiased estimators. They have a normal distribution independent of the distribution of the residuals. The sum of squares of the residuals, divided by σ^2, is distributed as χ^2 with $T - 2$ degrees of freedom.

This proposition, which defines completely the distribution of the estimators a^* and b^*, provides the justification for tests and confidence intervals which are frequently used.

In particular it shows that $(a^* - a)/\sigma_a$ has a standard normal distribution and that

$$(T - 2) \frac{\sigma_a^{*2}}{\sigma_a^2} = (T - 2) \frac{\sigma_\varepsilon^{*2}}{\sigma^2}$$

is distributed as χ^2 with $T - 2$ degrees of freedom, independently of the distribution of $(a^* - a)/\sigma_a$. Therefore $(a^* - a)/\sigma_a^*$ has a Student distribution with $T - 2$ degrees of freedom. To test whether the true value a is equal to a given value

a_0, we can therefore compare $(a^* - a_0)/\sigma_a^*$ with the value t_α given in the Student table for $T-2$ degrees of freedom and level of significance α.

Similarly a 90% confidence interval[†] is given by the set of values of a which satisfy:

$$|a - a^*| \leq t_{0.05}\sigma_a^*, \tag{30}$$

where $t_{0.05}$ is the value given by the Student table for the 5% level of significance.

The same procedures could be applied in the construction of tests or confidence regions relating to the true value of the coefficient b independently of the value of a. It is also possible to test the two coefficients a and b simultaneously. Indeed, since the pair (a^*, b^*) has a bivariate normal distribution with mean (a, b) we know that:

$$\delta = \begin{bmatrix} a^* - a \\ b^* - b \end{bmatrix} \begin{bmatrix} \sigma_a^2 & \mathrm{cov}(a^*, b^*) \\ \mathrm{cov}(a^*, b^*) & \sigma_b^2 \end{bmatrix}^{-1} \begin{bmatrix} a^* - a \\ b^* - b \end{bmatrix}$$

is distributed as χ^2 with two degrees of freedom[††]. The inverse of the covariance matrix is given here by the matrix (29) so that δ takes the form:

$$\delta = \frac{1}{\sigma^2} \left[\sum_{t=1}^{T} z_t^2 (a^* - a)^2 + 2T\bar{z}(a^* - a)(b^* - b) + T(b^* - b)^2 \right]. \tag{31}$$

Proposition 6 shows that $(T-2)\sigma_\varepsilon^{*2}/\sigma^2$ is distributed as χ^2 with $T-2$ degrees of freedom, independently of the distribution of δ. Thus:

$$F = \frac{\delta}{2} \bigg/ \frac{T-2}{T-2} \cdot \frac{\sigma_\varepsilon^{*2}}{\sigma^2} = \frac{1}{2} \cdot \frac{\sigma^2 \delta}{\sigma_\varepsilon^{*2}} \tag{32}$$

has an F-distribution with 2 and $T-2$ degrees of freedom.

To test if a and b are equal to two given values a_0 and b_0 we can calculate the value of F when a_0 and b_0 are substituted for a and b in δ; we can then compare this value with the value F_α given in tables of the F-distribution for significance level α and degrees of freedom 2 and $T-2$. Similarly, on a two-dimensional graph with a as abscissa and b as ordinate, a confidence region of level α for the pair (a, b) consists of the region bounded by the ellipse E whose equation is $F = F_\alpha$.

[†] By definition, a *confidence interval* of level α for the unknown parameter a is an interval which covers the true value a^0 of a with probability α. Similarly, a *confidence region* of level α for the vector θ of the p parameters θ_k, $(k=1, 2, \ldots, p)$ is, in p-dimensional space, a region which covers the true value θ^0 of θ with probability α.

[††] This result will be established later in a more general context (cf. ch. 5, proposition 5).

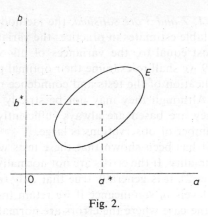

Fig. 2.

We must note that these tests and confidence regions do not involve the value found for the coefficient R^2. As we have already said, this coefficient is of no great interest in the context of the present model[†].

7 Properties of the method of least squares

We shall now give a résumé of the results just established and round them off by some observations which will be more fully discussed in other chapters. In this way we shall show more clearly the advantages and limitations offered by least squares estimates for the statistical treatment of the linear model.

If assumptions 1 to 4 are satisfied, all the statistical procedures usually associated with the method of least squares are completely justified.

The estimators a^* and b^* appear as sufficient for estimation of the parameters a and b. Their variance is the smallest possible for regular unbiased estimators. The 'residual variance' σ_ε^{*2} is an unbiased estimator of the variance σ^2 of the errors.

In this case the distribution of the estimators is sufficiently well known to allow the application of rigorous tests or the construction of exact confidence regions. The pair (a^*, b^*) is normally distributed with mean (a, b) and a covariance matrix which can be estimated without bias, (formula (18) for example). Expressions like $(a^* - a)/\sigma_a^*$ have Student distributions and allow the application of classical tests.

However, we can verify that

$$\frac{a^{*2}}{\sigma_a^{*2}} = (T - 2)\frac{R^2}{1 - R^2}$$

so that we can calculate directly from R^2 the value of Student's t-statistic for testing that the true value of a is zero.

If only assumptions 1, 2 and 3 are satisfied, the method of least squares still provides the best available estimates in practice; the variances of a^* and b^* are smaller than, or at most equal to, the variances of all other unbiased linear estimators. In ch. 5 § 9 we shall re-examine their optimal properties.

In practice the application of the tests and confidence regions defined above can still be justified. Although they may not be strictly correct, the approximations on which they are based are always sufficiently good and are even excellent when the number of observations is large.

On the one hand, it has been shown that these tests were not very sensitive to departure from normality. If the errors are not normally distributed but have a variance (assumption 2), it is generally true that only trivial errors are made in the powers or the levels of significance if we retain the formulae which are strictly applicable in the case where the errors are normal. In short, these tests and confidence regions are 'robust' with respect to assumption 4 (see ch. 8 § 5).

On the other hand, we shall prove that, subject to the addition of assumption 5, the asymptotic distribution of $\sqrt{T}(a^*-a)$ and $\sqrt{T}(b^*-b)$ are normal (cf. ch. 6). When the number of observations tends to infinity, the tests and confidence regions tend to become exact, even if the errors are not normally distributed.

If only assumption 1 is satisfied, and if in addition the distribution of the errors has second order moments, the means of a^* and b^* are still the true values a and b; but none of the other properties generally applies. It may happen that we know the covariance matrix of the set of T errors $\varepsilon_1, \varepsilon_2, \ldots, \varepsilon_T$ (a square matrix of order T). In such a case we can find a method of linear estimation which is generally different from the method of least squares but which possesses the interesting properties examined above and lends itself to similar tests (ch. 5). Again it may happen that the covariance matrix of the $\varepsilon_1, \ldots, \varepsilon_T$ is not completely known, but that it may be possible to make assumptions about it which allow estimation of the unknown characteristics and better determination of a and b. We shall encounter situations where this idea is applied.

In particular, assumption 3 is not satisfied when the ε_t arise from a stochastic process involving time dependence, that is, when the error at time t is associated with the error at time $t-1$. This case will be studied in ch. 13 after we have recalled to mind the principal foundations of the theory of stochastic processes.

Assumption 1 obviously maintains its basic importance for the application of the method of least squares. We shall see, as early as in the next chapter, some examples where it does not hold, and where we shall introduce models which will be discussed in other chapters.

These properties enable us to assess the method of least squares. Its main advantage in econometrics lies in the fact that it gives good results without imposing too restrictive assumptions about the distribution of the variables, and therefore has a fairly wide field of application. The econometrician, who rarely has detailed information available about the distributions, can generally resort to this method without the risk of making too serious errors.

8   Regressions in bivariate distributions

The properties of simple regression have just been studied in the context of the linear model defined at the beginning of the chapter. Naturally it would be possible to make a similar analysis with other models. In particular we shall have occasion to ask what happens to certain of these properties when assumption 1 is no longer wholly satisfied.

In mathematical statistics simple regression is often considered and justified in a different way from that which we have chosen, but on the basis of fairly similar models or assumptions. To avoid confusion we shall give a little space to these other approaches.

The variable z is now considered to be random as well as the variable x. More precisely, the pair (x, z) has a bivariate distribution. The data (x_1, z_1), $(x_2, z_2), \ldots, (x_T, z_T)$ appear as T independent observations on the random vector (x, z).

We have already indicated that this attitude does not necessarily conflict with that adopted in our model. It matters little whether z is random if our assumptions apply to the conditional probability of the x_t for the given values of the z_t, and if we are only interested in the conditional distribution of a^* and b^* for these values of the z_t.

But, with models in which the pair (x, z) has the same distribution for all the observations, we are always interested in the unconditional distribution of the regression coefficients a^* and b^*.

This is a very natural attitude, but it is an additional cause of divergence from the theory described above.

Let us therefore consider three increasingly restrictive models and examine the properties of a^* and b^* in each.

(i) The data (x_t, z_t) are T independent observations on the same random pair (x, z) possessing second order moments[†].

On the basis of the bivariate distribution of the pair (x, z) we can define the 'theoretical linear regression of x on z' as the line $x = az + b$ whose coefficients a and b minimize the expression:

$$E(x - az - b)^2. \tag{33}$$

This linear regression must be carefully distinguished from the 'theoretical regression of x on z' which is defined as:

$$x = E(x/z). \tag{34}$$

There is obviously no reason a priori for this to be linear.

[†] WOLD [1952] has proposed the use of the terms 'Galton–Yule specification' and 'Gauss–Fisher specification' to denote on the one hand the model defined in (i) and on the other hand the linear model studied in the rest of this chapter.

If ξ and ζ denote the expected values of x and z, the coefficients a and b of the theoretical linear regression satisfy:

$$a = \frac{E[(x - \xi)(z - \zeta)]}{E[(z - \zeta)^2]}, \qquad b = \xi - a\zeta \qquad (35)$$

these equations being easily established.

If the number T of observations tends to infinity, the means $\bar{x}$ and $\bar{z}$ generally tend in probability to the expected values ξ and ζ, and the empirical moments:

$$\frac{1}{T} \sum_{t=1}^{T} (x_t - \bar{x})(z_t - \bar{z}) \qquad \text{and} \qquad \frac{1}{T} \sum_{t=1}^{T} (z_t - \bar{z})^2$$

to the theoretical moments:

$$E[(x - \xi)(z - \zeta)] \qquad \text{and} \qquad E[(z - \zeta)^2].$$

Therefore the coefficients a^* and b^* of the empirical regression tend in probability to the coefficients a and b of the theoretical linear regression.

(ii) *Conditions* (i) *are satisfied, and moreover the theoretical regression of* x *on* z *is linear.*

Let us write this theoretical regression:

$$x = E(x/z) = az + b \qquad (36)$$

and verify that the coefficients a and b do in fact minimize expression (33). Indeed let α and β be any other two numbers. We can write:

$$E(x - \alpha z - \beta)^2 = E(x - az - b)^2 + E[(\alpha - a)z + (\beta - b)]^2 + E(H),$$

where:

$$H = 2(x - az - b)[(a - \alpha)z + (b - \beta)].$$

Now from (36), $E(H/z)=0$, therefore also $E(H)=0$. The minimum of $E(x - \alpha z - \beta)^2$ is in fact obtained when $\alpha = a$ and $\beta = b$.

In dealing with this case we can use the results established for the linear model $x = az + b + \varepsilon$. Assumptions 1 and 3 are automatically satisfied, and assumption 2 would also be satisfied if we imposed that the conditional distribution of $x - E(x/z)$ for fixed z be independent of z.

In particular we know that a^* and b^* are unbiased estimators of a and b for the fixed values of $z_1, z_2, \ldots, z_T$, therefore also unconditionally:

$$E(a^*) = E[E(a^*/z_1, z_2, \ldots, z_T)] = E(a) = a.$$

When assumption 2 is satisfied, a^* and b^* have smaller variances than all other unbiased linear estimators, $\hat{a}$ and $\hat{b}$ say. In fact we know that:

$$\mathrm{var}\,(a^*/z_1,\ldots,z_T) \leqq \mathrm{var}\,(\hat{a}/z_1,\ldots,z_T)$$

for any $z_1, z_2, \ldots, z_T$. Therefore:

$$\mathrm{var}\,(a^*) = E[\mathrm{var}\,(a^*/z_1,\ldots,z_T)] \leqq E[\mathrm{var}\,(\hat{a}/z_1,\ldots,z_T)] = \mathrm{var}\,(\hat{a})$$

and similarly for b^* and $\hat{b}$.

(iii) *Conditions* (i) *are satisfied and moreover* (x,z) *is normally distributed.*

We know that in this case the theoretical regression of x on z is linear, so that (36) still applies. In addition, the distribution of (x,z) depends only on five parameters, which are the two expected values ξ and ζ and the three theoretical second order moments. We can prove that, for the estimation of these parameters and therefore also of the coefficients of the theoretical regression, the two means and the three empirical second-order moments constitute a sufficient statistic.

The estimators a^* and b^* are therefore justified in the same way as that described in the context of the linear model (cf. § 7 above). We can even deduce their properties from those obtained in that case. Indeed it is easy to verify[†] that assumptions 1 to 4 are satisfied subject to (iii).

Thus the conditional distribution of $(a^* - a)/\sigma_a^*$ is Student's distribution with $T-2$ degrees of freedom. As this distribution does not depend on the values of the $z_1, z_2, \ldots, z_T$, it is also the marginal distribution of $(a^* - a)/\sigma_a^*$. Therefore in this case tests and confidence regions for a are established exactly as if we were adopting the attitude of section 7.

The second order moments of a^* and b^* can easily be deduced in a similar way. Thus:

$$\mathrm{var}\,(a^*) = E\{\mathrm{var}[(a^*/z_1, z_2, \ldots, z_T)]\},$$

$$\mathrm{var}\,(a^*/z_1, z_2, \ldots, z_T) = \frac{\sigma^2}{\sum\limits_t (z_t - \bar{z})^2}.$$

In addition $\sigma^2 = E(\varepsilon^2/z)$ does not depend on z (cf. footnote on this page).

---

† Consider the pair (ε, z) where $\varepsilon = x - az - b$. It is normally distributed. There is zero correlation between ε and z because

$$E[\varepsilon(z - \zeta)] = E[(x - \xi)(z - \zeta)] - aE[z - \zeta]^2 = 0.$$

The normal random variable ε is therefore independent of z. The T values $\varepsilon_1, \varepsilon_2, \ldots, \varepsilon_T$ are obviously mutually independent.

Therefore:

$$\text{var}(a^*) = \sigma^2 E\left[\frac{1}{\sum_t (z_t - \bar{z})^2}\right]$$

and, as a first approximation:

$$\text{var}(a^*) \sim \sigma^2 / T\sigma_z^2,$$

where σ_z^2 obviously denotes the variance of z.

In fact, the exact distribution of the pair (a^*, b^*) is a student distribution in two dimensions. This result was proved by WEGGE [1971], who also discusses more general specifications.

Finally we note that this approach is of little interest for econometric analysis, since the observations (x_t, z_t) can rarely be considered as independently selected from the same bivariate distribution. We shall say no more about this approach but the interested reader can refer for example to FÉRON [1956].

9   Prediction

At the end of ch. 2 we defined the problem of prediction in general terms. For the model of this chapter the problem can be posed as follows: Given the value z_θ of the exogenous variable during a future period θ, or for an unobserved individual θ, how can we determine the corresponding value x_θ of the endogenous variable? It is possible that in fact z_θ is not completely known, but is itself a predicted result. However, we shall now proceed under the assumption that z_θ does not involve any error, or more precisely, we shall be interested in the conditional prediction of the values of the endogenous variable for given values of the exogenous variable.

We shall retain the model defined in the first sections of the present chapter, and assume that the parameters a and b have been estimated from a sample of T observations $(t = 1, 2, \ldots, T)$ which obviously does not contain θ. We shall distinguish between the predicted value x_θ^P and the value x_θ which will actually be obtained, and shall analyze the properties of the prediction error $x_\theta^P - x_\theta$.

This error is obviously random since x_θ is random according to the formulation of the model, and since x_θ^P depends on random estimates of the parameters a and b. The distribution of the prediction error will be considered to be conditional with respect both to z_θ and to $z_1, z_2, \ldots, z_T$.

We could also study prediction from the point of view described in the previous section. We should then have to find for $x_\theta^P - x_\theta$ a distribution which would now be conditional only with respect to z_θ. But, as we have seen, economic phenomena rarely conform to the models which would have to be used in this case.

The simplest and most usual formula for calculating the prediction x_θ^P is based on direct application of the regression. It gives:

$$x_\theta^P = a^* z_\theta + b^*. \tag{37}$$

The prediction error can therefore be expressed as:

$$x_\theta^P - x_\theta = (a^* - a)z_\theta + (b^* - b) - \varepsilon_\theta. \tag{38}$$

The formulation of the model (assumption 1) and the fact that $E(a^*)=a$, $E(b^*)=b$ (proposition 1) yield:

$$E(x_\theta^P - x_\theta) = 0. \tag{39}$$

The prediction error has therefore zero mean.

If in addition the errors ε_t are homoscedastic and mutually independent (assumptions 2 and 3), the variance of $x_\theta^P - x_\theta$ is:

$$E(x_\theta^P - x_\theta)^2 = z_\theta^2 \operatorname{var}(a^*) + 2z_\theta \operatorname{cov}(a^*, b^*) + \operatorname{var}(b^*) + \sigma^2,$$

and formulae (11) and (12) for the second order moments of a^* and b^* therefore give:

$$E(x_\theta^P - x_\theta)^2 = (z_\theta - \bar{z})^2 \operatorname{var}(a^*) + (1 + 1/T)\sigma^2, \tag{40}$$

or

$$E(x_\theta^P - x_\theta)^2 = \sigma^2 \left[1 + \frac{1}{T} + \frac{(z_\theta - \bar{z})^2}{\sum\limits_{t=1}^{T} (z_t - \bar{z})^2} \right]. \tag{41}$$

If the errors ε_t are normally distributed (assumption 4), then a^* and b^* are normally distributed and formula (38) shows that so also is $x_\theta^P - x_\theta$. The same formula allows us to state that $x_\theta^P - x_\theta$ is independent of σ_ε^{*2} since a^*, b^* and ε_θ are independent of σ_ε^{*2}.

We can therefore state:

Proposition 7. If assumptions 1, 2 and 3 are satisfied, a prediction calculated from formula (37) implies an error whose mean is zero and whose variance is given by (41). In addition when the ε_t are normally distributed, the prediction error is independent of σ_ε^{*2} and normally distributed

The variance of the prediction error contains a first irreducible term σ^2 which expresses the existence of the unobservable error ε_θ relating to the period or to the individual to which the prediction refers. The two following terms become smaller as the number T of observations used to estimate a and b increases. Finally the last term depends on the value of z_θ. It is zero when z_θ is equal to the sample mean $\bar{z}$, and increases as z_θ departs from this mean.

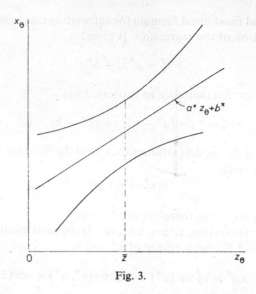

Fig. 3.

For example the variance of the prediction error made on the basis of the regression between expenditure on clothing and total expenditure (cf. § 4 above) can be estimated as:

$$0.0206\,[1.009 + 0.448\,(z_\theta - 4.1129)^2]$$

by substituting σ_ε^{*2} for σ^2 in (41).

In general we can show on a graph, on both sides of the regression line, two curves whose respective vertical distance above and below the line will be k times the standard deviation of the prediction error. This clearly shows the importance of this error for the different values of z_θ (cf. fig. 3).

These two curves can also be used to give an *interval prediction,* that is a 'tolerance interval' which will cover a fraction of the value to be predicted. Such *prediction* takes account of the risks involved in estimating a and b as well as those affecting the determination of the endogenous variable during the prediction period.

Generally σ^2 is not known and therefore σ_ε^{*2} is substituted for σ^2 in (41). Consequently the factor k by which ought to multiply the estimated standard deviation of the prediction errors is obtained from the special tables to this effect[†].

Now we ask how the simple formula (37) can be justified. Obviously the prediction method must give the smallest possible errors, that is, errors which will have on average the least damaging consequences.

[†] See WEISSBERG and BEATTY [1960] for these tables and for an exact definition of tolerance intervals. (T.N. Srinivasan pointed out that the first two editions of this book were not correct on interval prediction.)

For many problems, the loss or the unrealized gain resulting from incorrect prediction is approximately proportional to the square of the error involved. It is therefore natural *to find a formula which minimizes the expected value of the square of the prediction error.*

This criterion would not be suitable if the losses resulting from errors of the same magnitude but with different signs differed considerably from each other, for example where too high a prediction did not have very damaging results and too low a prediction had serious consequences. The minimum average loss in such a case would be expressed by very different formulae from those we consider here.

The criterion of the mean square error has the advantage of simplicity. We shall see that it can be applied when the distribution of the ε_t is not completely known. Other criteria generally demand much more exact knowledge of this distribution.

The prediction error can be written:

$$x_\theta^P - x_\theta = x_\theta^P - az_\theta - b - \varepsilon_\theta.$$

Since ε_θ is unknown and independent of the x_t for $t = 1, 2, \ldots, T$, it is also independent of x_θ^P. Thus:

$$E(x_\theta^P - x_\theta)^2 = \sigma^2 + E(x_\theta^P - az_\theta - b)^2. \tag{42}$$

Minimizing the mean square error is therefore equivalent to minimizing:

$$W = E(x_\theta^P - az_\theta - b)^2. \tag{43}$$

If the coefficients a and b were known exactly, the best prediction formula would obviously be:

$$x_\theta^P = az_\theta + b \tag{44}$$

which would make W zero. By analogy, it is natural to choose the general formula:

$$x_\theta^P = a(x)z_\theta + b(x) \tag{45}$$

where $a(x)$ and $b(x)$ denote functions of the observed sample. (We could also write $a(x_1, x_2, \ldots, x_T)$ and $b(x_1, x_2, \ldots, x_T)$, but this notation would be too complicated.) The quantity W then becomes:

$$W = E\{[a(x) - a]z_\theta + [b(x) - b]\}^2. \tag{46}$$

Thus determining the best prediction is equivalent to determining the estimators $a(x)$ and $b(x)$ which minimize expression (46). Consideration of the losses or unrealized gain associated with a prediction leads to the search for estimators giving rise to statistical decisions which are optimal relative to the 'risk function' W. To complete this chapter we ought therefore to discuss the properties of the estimators a^* and b^* in the context of statistical decision theory. However, it is preferable to do this in ch. 5, when we shall re-examine the same problems in the context of a more general model. For the present we make only two observations.

If assumptions 1 to 4 and 6 are satisfied, and if we confine ourselves a priori to regular unbiased estimators, a^* and b^* appear as optimal with the risk function (46). This follows from proposition 6 and in particular from the footnote which relates to it. If the ε_t are not normally distributed but we confine ourselves a priori to linear unbiased estimators, a^* and b^* are still optimal, as is shown in the footnote to proposition 5. Propositions 5 and 6 are thus shown to be of considerable significance when the model is used for prediction[†].

10   Regression under Bayesian theory[††]

The theory of simple regression was established above by the study of sampling distributions, and so on the basis of classical principles of statistical inference. We must now examine the implications of Bayesian principles. We shall concentrate attention on their aspects in practice rather than on the analytic treatments to which they give rise, and to which we shall return in the more general context of ch. 6.

For ease of exposition, we shall substitute for model (2) the following model:

$$x_t = a z_t + \varepsilon_t, \tag{47}$$

suppressing the unknown constant b. The discussion in ch. 6 will cover (2) and so fill in any gap which might be left by this simplification.

The substitution of (47) for (2) entails little modification in the previous sections. The estimator a^* is then replaced by

$$a^* = \frac{\sum\limits_{t=1}^{T} x_t z_t}{\sum\limits_{t=1}^{T} z_t^2}. \tag{48}$$

The residual becomes

$$\varepsilon_t^* = x_t - a^* z_t. \tag{49}$$

Formula (18) for the variance of a^* becomes

$$\sigma_a^{*2} = \frac{\sigma_\varepsilon^{*2}}{\sum\limits_{t=1}^{T} z_t^2} \tag{50}$$

† W. FISHER [1962] has made a more complete study of the justifications of the estimators a^* and b^* for prediction and for decisions based on the model. The reader will find his paper very rewarding.
†† For an application of the methods discussed in this section, see L'HARDY [1966].

where

$$\sigma_\varepsilon^{*2} = \frac{1}{T-1} \sum_{t=1}^{T} \varepsilon_t^{*2}. \tag{51}$$

The properties of a^* remain unchanged. In the definition of tests and confidence regions, the only change relates to the number of degrees of freedom, now $T-1$.

Application of Bayesian principles assumes determination of the likelihood function and the choice of a prior distribution. In the present state of statistical theory these two operations are practicable only for parametric models, that is, models involving only a finite number of parameters. For this to be so in model (47), the nature of the distribution of the errors ε_t must be specified.

We can conceive of certain cases where the economic theory justifying the model stipulates a particular form for the distribution of the errors, for example a binomial distribution, a rectangular distribution or a gamma distribution. The likelihood function corresponding to such a distribution can then be determined with no particular difficulty. However in most cases, the theory and the knowledge which it formalizes have no precise implication as to the distribution of the errors. This is why the econometrician seeking to apply Bayesian principles is prepared to make the conventional assumption of normality, which has the advantage of leading to well-known methods and calculations.

Let us then adopt this attitude and accept assumptions 1, 2 and 4 already used in this chapter. The model then contains two unknown parameters a and σ. The likelihood function $l(a, \sigma)$ is proportional to

$$\sigma^{-T} \exp \left\{ \frac{-1}{2\sigma^2} \sum_{t=1}^{T} (x_t - az_t)^2 \right\}.$$

Now, it follows from (47) and (49) that

$$x_t - az_t = \varepsilon_t^* + (a^* - a)z_t.$$

Moreover,

$$\sum_{t=1}^{T} (x_t - az_t)^2 = (T-1)\sigma_\varepsilon^{*2} + (a^* - a)^2 \sum_{t=1}^{T} z_t^2$$

since (48) and (49) imply that the sum of $\varepsilon_t^* z_t$ over t is zero. Thus

$$l(a,\sigma) \propto \sigma^{-T} \exp \left\{ \frac{-1}{2\sigma^2} \left[(T-1)\sigma_\varepsilon^{*2} + (a^* - a)^2 \sum_{t=1}^{T} z_t^2 \right] \right\} \tag{52}$$

where the sign $\propto$ denotes proportionality. This formula replaces (27) used for model (2). The likelihood function depends on the sample only through the random quantities σ_ε^* and a^*, to which can be added if desired the non-random quantities $\sum_t z_t^2$ and T. So this set of quantities defines a sufficient statistic, as we have already seen in section 6.

Least squares regression is therefore justified on Bayesian principles, just as much as on classical, when assumptions 1, 2 and 4 apply. Finding $\sum_t z_t^2$, a^* and σ_ε^{*2} is the first operation in the determination of the posterior distribution.

In principle, the likelihood function (52) can be combined with whatever prior density $p(a,\sigma)$ the econometrician or user may wish to consider. However, if $p(a,\sigma)$ is chosen quite freely, there is a risk that the complete calculation of the distribution will be very laborious. In particular, it assumes integration of $p(a,\sigma)l(a,\sigma)$ over the set of possible values of a and σ (this integration determines the proportionality constant between $p(a,\sigma)l(a,\sigma)$ and the posterior density).

It must also be admitted that in most cases, prior ideas are too vague to allow their representation by a density $p(a,\sigma)$ without leaving room for arbitrariness. For example, we may consider a priori that there are 9 chances out of 10 that a belongs to the interval [0.80, 1.20] and yet hesitate to characterize a corresponding distribution more precisely.

Since the prior density is not precisely specified, there is generally no loss of rigour if we choose an expression such that the posterior distribution belongs to a known category on which it is easy to work. Provided that this introduces no notable distortion into the representation of the prior ideas, we try to specify the density $p(a,\sigma)$ in such a way that it combines well with the likelihood function.

For this reason, it is useful to find a family of prior densities which combine easily with functions of the form (52). Such a family is said to be '*conjugate*'.

(i) We note first that, *if σ is known*, the likelihood depends only on a and, in (52), the term in σ_ε^{*2} introduces a simple multiplicative constant. We can then write

$$l(a) \propto \exp\left\{\frac{-(a^*-a)^2}{2\sigma^2} \sum_{t=1}^{T} z_t^2\right\}. \tag{53}$$

This form suggests the type of prior density to be chosen in this case. For it appears that, if the prior distribution is normal, so also is the posterior distribution.

Suppose then that a is normally distributed with prior expected value α. For reasons of convenience we shall write its variance in the form $\sigma^2/\mu M$ (this notation using the two numbers μ and M will facilitate comparison with what follows here and with section 11 of chapter 6). The prior density is

$$p(a) \propto \exp\left\{\frac{-\mu M(a-\alpha)^2}{2\sigma^2}\right\} \tag{54}$$

Similarly, the posterior density is

$$p(a/x) \propto \exp\left\{\frac{-1}{2\sigma^2}\left[(a^*-a)^2 \sum_{t=1}^{T} z_t^2 + \mu M(a-\alpha)^2\right]\right\}. \tag{55}$$

This is the exponential of a quadratic form in a; it is therefore the density of a normal distribution.

For more precise characterization of the posterior distribution we must study the quadratic form appearing in square brackets in (55). To do this, we first set

$$TM_{zz} = \sum_{t=1}^{T} z_t^2. \tag{56}$$

Let us next define the numbers N and β by the equalities

$$(T+\mu)N = TM_{zz} + \mu M \tag{57}$$

$$(T+\mu)N\beta = TM_{zz}a^* + \mu M\alpha. \tag{58}$$

We can then write

$$(a^*-a)^2 \sum_{t=1}^{T} z_t^2 + \mu M(a-\alpha)^2 = (T+\mu)N(a-\beta)^2 +$$

$$+ TM_{zz}(a^{*2}-\beta^2) + \mu M(\alpha^2 - \beta^2). \tag{59}$$

The exponential which appears in (55) is therefore the product of three exponentials constructed from each of the three terms on the right hand side of (59). The last two are constants in a and introduce only proportionality factors. Therefore

$$p(a/x) \propto \exp\left\{\frac{-(T+\mu)N(a-\beta)^2}{2\sigma^2}\right\}. \tag{60}$$

The posterior distribution has expected value β and variance $\sigma^2/(T+\mu)N$.

The above formulae have some interesting consequences. In the first place, the posterior distribution appears to be more concentrated than the prior distribution. Equality (57) and the fact that TM_{zz} is positive show that the variance $\sigma^2/(T+\mu)N$ is smaller than $\sigma^2/\mu M$. More precisely, the denominator of the posterior variance is the sum of the denominator of the prior variance and the denominator of the variance of the sampling distribution of a^* (transposing (11) to the case of the model with no constant term assumes $\bar{z}$ to be replaced by zero).

In the second place, the expectation β of the posterior distribution is a weighted mean of the prior expectation α and the least squares estimator a^*. Formula

(58) shows that the weighting coefficients of α and a^* are inversely proportional to the corresponding variances, the prior variance for α, and the sampling variance for a^*. So the less concentrated the prior distribution, the nearer will β be to a^*.

These very simple results agree well with common sense. However, the fact that σ is not generally known a priori complicates matters.

(ii) When σ is unknown, the likelihood has a more complex expression since (52) does not then take the convenient form (53). However, to determine a conjugate family of prior distributions we can fall back on a principle which has already proved successful; we can adopt a prior density whose analytic expression is similar to that of the likelihood.

So, by analogy with (52), let us consider a probability density defined by

$$p(a,\sigma) \propto \sigma^{-\mu} \exp\left\{\frac{-1}{2\sigma^2}[E + \mu M(a-\alpha)^2]\right\};\tag{61}$$

the four numbers α, M, μ and E must be chosen in such a way that $p(a, \sigma)$ represents a priori ideas about the parameters a and σ as well as possible (M and E must not be negative; we shall investigate the possible values of μ later). Examination of the product of the right hand sides of (53) and (61) reveals that the posterior density has the same form as the prior density. For we can write

$$p(a,\sigma/x) \propto \sigma^{-T-\mu} \exp\left\{\frac{-1}{2\sigma^2}[F + (T+\mu)N(a-\beta)^2]\right\},\tag{62}$$

the numbers N and β being determined by (57) and (58), while F must satisfy

$$F = (T-1)\sigma_\varepsilon^{*2} + E + TM_{zz}(a^{*2} - \beta^2) + \mu M(\alpha^2 - \beta^2)\tag{63}$$

which follows from (59) and the expressions taken by (53) and (61).

For a clear understanding of the corresponding procedure we must study, in the first place, the nature of distributions of the form (61) and (62), and in the second place, the transformation defined by (57), (58), and (63).

For a given value of σ the conditional distribution of a resulting from the distribution (61) clearly coincides with the normal distribution (54) considered previously. It is centred on α and its dispersion decreases as μM increases. For a given value of a the conditional distribution of σ belongs to the family of 'gamma' distributions whose dispersion decreases as μ increases (some notes and references relating to this distribution will be found in ch. 6, § 11). For this reason, distributions of the form (61) or (62) are called 'gamma-normal' distributions. The four numbers α, M, μ and E must be chosen in such a way that α and $E/\mu - 1$ correspond to the values considered to be most probable for a and σ respectively, and μM and μ become smaller according as ideas about a and σ are less precise.

Now we need only investigate the marginal distribution of a. To find it, we must integrate with respect to σ the right hand side of (61). So we set

$$U = E + \mu M (a - \alpha)^2$$

$$h = \frac{U}{2\sigma^2},$$

which gives

$$\frac{d\sigma}{\sigma} = \frac{-1}{2} \cdot \frac{dh}{h} \qquad \sigma = \frac{\sqrt{2}}{2} U^{\frac{1}{2}} h^{-\frac{1}{2}}.$$

We can then write

$$p(a) = \int_0^\infty p(a,\sigma) \, d\sigma \propto U^{-(\mu-1)/2} \int_0^\infty e^{-h} h^{(\mu-1)/2} \, dh.$$

The integral of the right hand side is a number (we know that it is usual to denote this number by $\Gamma[(\mu+1)/2]$, but this is not important). In short,

$$p(a) \propto U^{-(\mu-1)/2},$$

which we can also write

$$p(a) \propto \left[1 + \frac{\mu M}{E} (a - \alpha)^2\right]^{-(\mu-1)/2}. \tag{64}$$

The density just obtained has the form familiar to us through the t-distribution[†]. More precisely, it shows that the variable $(a-\alpha)/\tau$ has a t-distribution with $\mu - 2$ degrees of freedom, the number τ being defined by

$$\tau^2 = \frac{E}{\mu-2} \cdot \frac{1}{\mu M}. \tag{65}$$

(We note in passing that (65) has meaning only if μ is greater than 2; but this is a necessary condition for the right hand sides of (61) and (64) to have convergent integrals, that is, for (61) to define a true probability distribution.)

So the prior marginal distribution of a is the distribution which we have just found. By strictly analogous reasoning we can obtain its posterior marginal distribution. Comparison of (62) and (61) shows that $(a-\beta)/\tau^*$ has a t-distribution with $T + \mu - 2$ degrees of freedom, the number τ^* being defined by

$$\tau^{*2} = \frac{F}{T+\mu-2} \cdot \frac{1}{(T+\mu)N}. \tag{66}$$

[†] See, for example, CRAMER [1946], § 18.2.

We have already seen how the posterior expectation β is a weighted mean of the prior expectation α and the least squares estimator a^*. No change is necessary when σ is known. The prior and posterior dispersions are defined by τ^2 and τ^{*2}. Each of these quantities is the product of two terms on which we can successively bring comparison to bear.

The second term of τ^{*2} is necessarily smaller than that of τ^2 since (57) shows that $(T+\mu)N$ is the sum of the two positive quantities μM and TM_{zz}. The reduction in this second term will be greater as TM_{zz} increases relative to μM, that is, as the concentration of the sampling distribution of a^* is more marked than that of the prior distribution of a for given σ.

Formula (63) also shows that $F/(T+\mu-2)$, the first term of τ^{*2}, is a weighted mean of $((T-1)/T)\sigma_\varepsilon^{*2}$ and $E/(\mu-2)$, the first term of τ^2, to which is added the necessarily positive quantity

$$\frac{TM_{zz}(a^*-\beta)^2+\mu M(\alpha-\beta)^2}{T+\mu-2} \tag{67}$$

(the equality between the numerator of this expression and the sum of the last two terms of (63) follows from (57) and (58), as can easily be verified). So the posterior dispersion will decrease as

1. the prior dispersion decreases;
2. the residuals of the least squares regression decrease;
3. the regression coefficient a^* approaches the prior expectation α.

The effect of (67) is that the posterior distribution of a is less concentrated than the prior distribution if a^* takes a value for which the prior density $p(a)$ is small. If a result a^* with this property appears, then this entails not only a considerable modification of the expectation of a, but also a change in the distribution of σ, since high values of this variable become more probable than before.

The fact that $(a-\beta)/\tau^*$ has a t-distribution implies a certain similarity between the practical procedures based on Bayesian principles and those based on classical principles. In section 6 we constructed a confidence interval using the sampling distribution of $(a^*-a)/\sigma^*$, the parameter a being considered as fixed. With the modification in the number of degrees of freedom due to the disappearance of the constant, this interval is

$$|a-a^*| \leq t_{T-1}(\eta) \cdot \sigma_a^* \tag{68}$$

where $t_{T-1}(\eta)$ denotes the upper 100η per cent value of a t-variable with $T-1$ degrees of freedom. A Bayesian confidence interval established from the posterior distribution of a is given by

$$|a-\beta| \leq t_{T+\mu-2}(\eta) \cdot \tau^*, \tag{69}$$

which is obviously similar to (68).

We can go further and assert that (68) and (69) define intervals for a which are rigorously identical when nothing is known a priori about the parameters of the model. For (68) and (69) to coincide, it is sufficient that $\mu = 1$, $\beta = a^*$ and $\tau^* = \sigma_a^*$. This will be so if the prior distribution is such that $\mu = 1$, $M = 0$ and $E = 0$, since (57) and (58) then imply $(T+\mu)N = TM_{zz}$ and $\beta = a^*$; equation (63) implies $F = (T-1)\sigma_\varepsilon^{*2}$ and hence $\tau^{*2} = \sigma_\varepsilon^{*2}/TM_{zz} = \sigma_a^{*2}$ in view of (66), (50) and (56).

In short, the practical methods based on Bayesian and classical principles are identical if the prior density (61) is replaced by σ^{-1}. We have seen that, the vaguer our ideas about the parameters, the smaller should be μM and μ. The value $M = 0$ in fact gives the minimum possible for μM. On the other hand, $\mu = 1$ is too small for (61) to define a true probability density; the integral of σ^{-1} does not converge on the half-plane of the space (a, σ) for which $\sigma \geq 0$. The function σ^{-1} defines the density of a measure, but not of a probability.

However, Bayesian statisticians suggest that in the case of complete ignorance, the concept of prior probability should be extended to cover measures whose total mass on the parameter space is infinite. They speak of *improper prior distributions*. We shall return to these distributions in ch. 6, and can now conclude our discussion of simple regression[†].

[†] Bayesian principles can clearly be applied to the prediction problem discussed in section 9. See ZELLNER [1969].

CHAPTER 4

The consumption function
Discussion of an econometric problem

1 Introduction

The aim of the three previous chapters was the introduction of the methods to be studied in the rest of the book, and we shall round off this introduction by discussing a particular econometric problem. Indeed to achieve a full understanding of the proposed methods, we must not lose sight of either the type of research in which they are used or the nature of the data to which they are applied. In this chapter we shall discuss both in the context of a practical example and attempt to demonstrate the respective roles of empirical observation and abstract formulation in econometric investigation. We shall take up many questions of statistical methodology, although they can be thoroughly examined only later.

The question we have chosen to investigate is *the determination of an equation which explains variations in consumer saving.* It is of known importance for the sound analysis and prediction of business fluctuations. Consumer demand will increase or decrease with a fall or rise in the proportion of income which is saved, and this will be a factor which is at times stimulating or inflationary, and at other times deflationary or stabilizing.

This question was given particular attention in the economic thinking which followed the great crisis of the 1930's. J. M. Keynes proposed an answer which finds expression in the elementary model described in ch. 2 § 3 and according to which consumption depends mainly on disposable income. We can base our reasoning on the assumption that there is a strict function $C = F(Y)$ relating consumption per head C and disposable income per head Y. This function, called the '*consumption function*', also determines consumer saving, which by definition is the unspent part of disposable income, say, $E = Y - C$ for saving per head.

Keynes also indicates that F should be an increasing function, but should be such that the ratio C/Y decreases as Y increases. In other words, the part of income which is saved should be greater when income is higher.

For this question as for many others, it is the examination of empirical data which provides the final answer, by allowing us to verify the proposed assumption and eventually to determine the exact form of F if the assumption is accepted. If it is not, such an examination of the data suggests other formulations.

Two types of data seem particularly useful in the present case. On the one hand, *time series* relating to national income and similar aggregates allow us to follow year by year variations in the total volume of consumer saving, for many countries and for more or less recent periods. On the other hand, the results of inquiries into family budgets provide *cross-section data* about the saving made by different households during the same period.

By exploiting these two sources we have been able greatly to refine our ideas about the determination of saving. Certain assumptions had to be discarded and others were expressed in numerical terms. The discussion which started in the 1930's has not yet ended, but there is much less difference of opinion. We shall now summarize some of the main developments in this research.

2 Regression and prediction on aggregate time series for the inter-war period

The first studies to be made during the last war seemed to confirm Keynes' assumption, and it was even thought possible to express the consumption function in a precise form. On a graph with Y as abscissa and C as ordinate, the representative curve had to be steadily rising and slightly concave down. The derivative of F, called the 'marginal propensity to consume', seemed to be in the neighborhood of 0.6 for an income equivalent to the average income in the United States, and about 0.7 for the average income level in western Europe.

Thus fig. 1 reproduces the consumption function determined by SAMUELSON [1948] on the basis of a very extensive inquiry into the incomes and consumptions

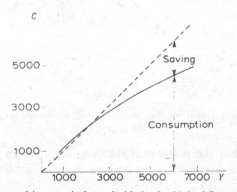

Fig. 1. Consumption and income in households in the United States in 1944 (in dollars).

of households in towns in the United States in 1944. The curve was fitted to a scatter of points each of which represented the income and consumption of a particular household. We shall not make a detailed examination of the statistical procedure which was adopted, and we shall only note that the chosen curve lies in the immediate proximity of the points representing average income and average consumption for households belonging to the same income group.

The curve in fig. 1 is fairly typical of the results obtained when similar fitting procedures are applied to the results of investigations into family budgets. Of course saving was abnormally high in 1944 because of special wartime conditions. The corresponding function for a peacetime period would lie above the present curve and have a slightly steeper gradient, but would look much the same.

The same relationship seemed to be justified by figures relating to the growth in income and consumption in some industrial countries during the interwar period. The points representing results for different years were closely grouped about straight lines whose gradients were roughly 0.6 or 0.7.

Thus the points in fig. 2 represent disposable income per head and consumption per head in the United Kingdom for each of the years 1924 to 1938 (the source is STONE and ROWE [1956][†]). They lie approximately on a straight line, and a similar graph would represent the results for another country during the same period.

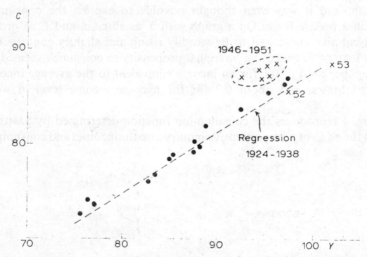

Fig. 2. Consumption and global income in the United Kingdom (in pounds per head, at 1938 prices).

It was thought that the permanent relationship between income and consumption could be determined on the basis of these or similar data referring to

[†] These figures were made available to me in 1955 when I heard R. Stone read a paper which was published subsequently: STONE and ROWE [1956]. K. F. WALLIS has recently drawn my attention to the fact that the series used for figure 2 differ from those which appear in the appendix to the paper in question. Systematic differences appear in the post-war period for disposable income, and in the inter-war period for consumption (total household purchases of durable and non-durable goods, excluding expenditure on housing, called 'Total expenditure' in the article). Somewhat different numerical results from the above are obtained if the Stone and Rowe series are used; but, as in fig. 2, the position of the points relating to 1947–51 remains abnormal.

the United States. In fact the model adopted was:

$$C_t = aY_t + b + \varepsilon_t \tag{1}$$

according to which consumption C_t in year t depends on disposable income Y_t in the same year and on a set of other individually unidentifiable factors represented by the unobservable random variable ε_t. The numbers a and b are obviously the parameters whose values are to be determined.

This model belongs to the category examined in the previous chapter. The assumptions justifying least squares regression (assumptions 1, 2 and 3 in the previous chapter) were more or less explicitly adopted and, for instance, the data for fig. 2 gave the estimate[†]:

$$C_t = 0.65 Y_t + 22.8$$
$$(0.02) \quad (2.12) \tag{2}$$

which seemed all the more satisfactory since R^2, the square of the correlation coefficient, was 0.98. The value 0.65 for the marginal propensity to consume is certainly within the range stated above.

Formulae similar to the regression (2) were used at the end of the last war when the problem arose of reconversion to a peacetime economy. To ensure a satisfactory economic equilibrium it was advisable to predict in particular the spontaneous level of consumption and saving. As we have seen, model (1) allows prediction of the volume of consumption C_θ during a future period θ in which the predicted disposable income is Y_θ. The regression line gives directly what may be considered to be the best prediction. The probable volume of consumption can therefore be found from eq. 2, relating to the interwar period, allowances having been made for income levels.

In fact predictions made in this way turned out to be very poor. Thus in 1948 disposable income per head in the United Kingdom was £ 92.6 at 1938 prices. The regression gives a consumption of £ 83.0 as against an observed £ 87.0. Saving should have been £ 9.6 according to the regression, but in fact came to £ 5.6. Generally, observed results in the immediate post-war period lie clearly above the regression line relating to the interwar period (see the crosses on fig. 2). Such difference would be improbable in the context of the proposed model, for the standard deviation of the predictions would be only about 0.7 (this can be shown by applying formula (40) of ch. 3).

This failure shows that the model which seemed sufficient for the interwar period does not really accord well with the phenomenon studied. Formula (1) contains an 'error of specification' since it offers a picture of the phenomenon which contradicts the most recent data.

[†] We recall here that the figures in parentheses are the estimated standard deviations of the estimates beneath which they appear.

Studies of long-term economic growth have also revealed that the ratio between saving and income is very stable when it is calculated for fairly long periods and on the other hand is liable to fluctuate considerably from one year to the next (see GOLDSMITH [1955]). Thus an increase or decrease in income seems to have a different effect on saving according to whether it occurs suddenly or gradually. Model (1) is incompatible with this situation.

We note in passing that during the whole period 1924–1938 the regression accounted very closely for the values observed. There was a very high correlation between consumption and income, but this was partly accidental. We learn from this experience that *a high empirical correlation can sometimes lead to error and conceal for a time the real complexity of phenomena.*

Since the specification of the model is wrong it must be replaced. Let us see first if we can keep formula (1) with other assumptions about the random term ε_t.

We hardly need to concern ourselves with two of the first three assumptions of ch. 3. Indeed if assumption 1 was satisfied the estimates resulting from the method of least squares would be unbiased even if the errors were neither homoscedastic nor mutually independent (cf. proposition 1 in ch. 3). Their standard deviations might certainly differ from those shown under the regression (2). However, the model would allow us to state that the marginal propensity to consume is near 0.6 or 0.7. Our conclusions would therefore be less precise but little different from conclusions based on assumptions 1, 2 and 3 of ch. 3.

The next section is devoted to the examination of a criticism which was made of assumption 1 in the problem considered. We shall see that this criticism is not enough to resolve the contradiction which was detected above, but is of a methodological interest which goes far beyond the particular example of the consumption function and therefore deserves our attention.

3   A model with simultaneous equations

Determination of the consumption function is viewed as providing the basis for the application of the Keynesian analysis to the practical problems raised by prediction and regulation of economic activity in the short period. Such a function is only meaningful if the Keynesian model describes the facts correctly, and so it is in the context of this model that the statistical problems which concern us now are to be discussed.

Taking the Keynesian theory in its simplest form we saw in ch. 2 that the consumption function is involved in the explanation of the level of production in every period of time. More precisely, four quantities are defined, these being production, income, consumption and investment. Production is considered to equal demand, that is, the sum of consumption and investment. Income is equal to pro   ction since we make the simplifying assumption that all income is distributed to consumers. Finally, investment is considered as a given exogenous quantity in short term equilibrium.

To allow statistical analysis this is expressed by the following system:

$$C_t = aY_t + b + \varepsilon_t$$
$$Y_t = C_t + I_t,$$

(3)

where C_t and Y_t again denote consumption and income while I_t denotes investment[†]. The first equation represents the consumption function for which we keep the linear form (1). The second equation expresses the necessary equality of supply and demand and therefore contains no random terms.

In this model the exogenous elements I_t and ε_t represent respectively the effect of investment decisions by entrepreneurs and the effect of all factors other than income on decisions to consume (expectations about the future course of prices and incomes, market supplies, changes in the weather, etc.). These exogenous elements allow us to determine C_t and Y_t; after solving, model (3) becomes:

$$C_t = (\alpha - 1)I_t + \beta + \alpha\varepsilon_t,$$
$$Y_t = \alpha I_t + \beta + \alpha\varepsilon_t,$$

(4)

where

$$\alpha = \frac{1}{1-a}, \qquad \beta = \frac{b}{1-a}.$$

The parameters α and β can be calculated once the parameters a and b are known. In this sense, estimation of a and b is equivalent to estimation of α and β. Thus the regression of C on Y provides estimates a^* and b^* which allow the model to be used in practice. The point to be decided is just whether these estimates are best for the uses we have in mind.

Applied to eq. (1), assumption 1 of ch. 3 states that ε_t has zero mean for any value of Y_t. Now in this case Y_t is a random variable, since it is determined by the second equation of system (4) which involves the random variable ε_t itself. More precisely Y_t is a linear function of $I_t + \varepsilon_t$. Maintaining Y_t fixed is equivalent to maintaining the sum $I_t + \varepsilon_t$ fixed. The present assumption therefore stipulates that ε_t has zero mean for any value of $I_t + \varepsilon_t$.

Obviously this condition cannot be satisfied if I_t is taken as non-random, since in that case fixing $I_t + \varepsilon_t$ is equivalent to fixing the value of ε_t. It is scarcely more plausible if I_t is assumed to be random. Indeed for the conditional ex-

---

[†] In practical applications I_t should be the difference between disposable income and consumption. It should include besides investment the deficit on current public spending, the surplus in the balance of payments and several other less important quantities. This circumstance is not troublesome to the extent that most of these elements can be considered as exogenous in the short period, like investment.

pected value $E(\varepsilon/I+\varepsilon)$ to be zero, there would have to be negative association between I and ε. Suppose for example that the pair (I, ε) is normally distributed with means $(I_0, 0)$, standard deviations (S, σ) and correlation coefficient ϱ. In order that $E(\varepsilon/I+\varepsilon) = 0$, it is necessary and sufficient that the covariance of ε and $I+\varepsilon$ should be zero, that is, that $\varrho S+\sigma = 0$, and therefore that there should be a certain negative correlation between I and ε.

We saw that I_t and ε_t represent the effects of autonomous factors which influence the decisions taken by entrepreneurs and by consumers. The most natural assumption is therefore that the two exogenous elements are independent or, more precisely, that the *mean of the ε_t is zero for any values of the I_t.*

Having made this new assumption we examine now the estimates obtained from the simple regression of C_t on Y_t. We shall consider the calculated value of a, say:

$$a^* = \frac{\sum_{t=1}^{T}(C_t - \bar{C})(Y_t - \bar{Y})}{\sum_{t=1}^{T}(Y_t - \bar{Y})^2}, \tag{5}$$

where $\bar{C}$ and $\bar{Y}$ denote the means of the C_t and the Y_t over the T observations. More precisely, we suppose that the number T of observations tends to infinity and that the expression

$$\frac{1}{T}\sum_{t=1}^{T}(I_t - \bar{I})^2$$

tends to a positive limit S^2. By applying eqs. (4) we can easily verify that:

$$\frac{1}{T}\sum_{t=1}^{T}(C_t - \bar{C})(Y_t - \bar{Y}) \to \alpha^2\left(\frac{\alpha-1}{\alpha}S^2 + \sigma^2\right),$$

$$\frac{1}{T}\sum_{t=1}^{T}(Y_t - \bar{Y})^2 \to \alpha^2(S^2 + \sigma^2)$$

in probability. Here σ^2 denotes the variance of ε_t, which is assumed to be finite and independent of t.

Thus when the number of observations tends to infinity the limit of a^* is given by:

$$a^* \to \frac{aS^2 + \sigma^2}{S^2 + \sigma^2}, \tag{6}$$

which differs from a whenever σ^2 is positive. The estimate considered therefore contains a bias which increases as the ratio σ/S increases. If a lies between 0 and 1, a^* will tend to exceed the true value a.

This result can usefully be illustrated by a graph with Y_t as abscissa and C_t

as ordinate†. For a given value of I_t the representative point lies on a parallel to the line $C = Y$ near the line D which represents the consumption function. The vertical distance between this point and D is equal to ε. Suppose for example that in the period of observation three successive different values of I_t were observed. The scatter diagram consists of three groups of points lying respectively on the segments Δ_1, Δ_2 and Δ_3 corresponding to the three values of I_t. If the mean of ε_t is zero for a given value of I_t, the points will be distributed in equal proportions on either side of D.

Points which lie above D, those for which ε_t is positive, correspond mostly to high values of Y_t. On the other hand the values of ε_t corresponding to low values of Y_t are mostly negative. The shape of the collection of points shows that the regression line of C_t on Y_t deviates from the line D which it is supposed to represent. It has a steeper gradient and a smaller intercept on the C-axis. The values a^* and b^* are indeed biased estimates of a and b.

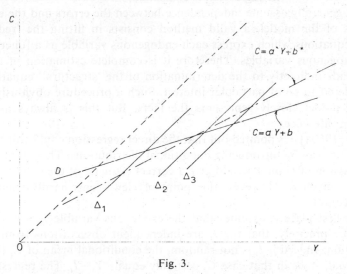

Fig. 3.

These remarks do not cast fresh doubt on the applicability of the method of least squares to the problem in question, but only on the practice which entails consideration of Y_t as an exogenous variable when it is in fact an endogenous quantity determined at the same time as C_t.

In fact the assumption at which we have finally arrived is just assumption 1 of ch. 3, but it is now applied to the exogenous variable I_t and not to Y_t. *The regression of C_t on I_t (or of Y_t on I_t) will give unbiased estimates of $\alpha - 1$ and β.* These estimates will lead to estimates of a and b which will tend in probability to the true values.

The foregoing discussion leads to conclusions whose validity obviously

---

† BENNION [1952] gives a similar presentation.

extends beyond the particular example of the consumption function. We shall meet them again in part 5 of this book, but we can now express them in general terms.

Econometric analysis is applied to behavioral equations which establish associations between certain quantities. It is often the case that we consider several of these quantities to be determined simultaneously by the interplay of a number of relationships. The appropriate model therefore involves several equations, as many as there are quantities considered to be 'endogenous'. We have already discussed the reasons for this in ch. 2 (in particular in § 5 and § 6).

In such a situation a particular behavioral equation typically involves several endogenous variables. The regression of one of these variables on the others no longer seems appropriate for estimating this equation, as it no longer seems tenable that the error in the equation has zero mean for any values of the variables on which the regression is calculated.

As we generally assume independence between the errors and the exogenous variables of the model, a valid method consists in fitting the 'reduced' (or solved) equations which express each endogenous variable as a function of the set of exogenous variables. Therefore it is complete estimation of the model which leads indirectly to the determination of the 'structural' equation which is considered to be of particular interest. Such a procedure obviously assumes that the model closely represents the facts. But this is always assumed in statistical inference.

WOLD [1960a] has pointed out that the direct regression could still be justified in a certain way by introducing conditional distributions. Thus in our example the regression of C on Y would give a correct estimate of the conditional mean of C_t for given I_t. However, this point of view seems hardly fruitful in the present context[†].

In the first place it assumes that the exogenous variable I_t is random; and even more precisely, that the I_t are independent observations from the same distribution. Indeed if I_t is not random, the conditional mean of C_t for a given Y_t is trivial, since in that case C_t certainly equals $Y_t - I_t$. The regression of C_t on Y_t has obviously nothing to do with this mean.

On the other hand, if I is considered to be a normal random variable independent of ε, with mean I_0 and standard deviation σ, if the I_t are considered as T independent values of this random variable and finally if ε is a normal random variable with zero mean, then the conditional mean of C_t for given Y_t (the theoretical regression of C_t on Y_t) is a linear function[††] of Y_t. As we saw in chapter 3 § 8 (ii), the empirical regression provides a consistent estimate of

---

[†] The discussion which follows coincides on many points with that offered by MEYER and MILLER [1954].

[††] Indeed since $C_t = Y_t - I_t$, $E(C_t/Y_t)$ is the difference between Y_t and $E(I_t/Y_t) = E(I_t/I_t + \varepsilon_t)$. Now the pair (I_t, ε_t) has a bivariate normal distribution and therefore so also has the pair $(I_t, I_t + \varepsilon)$. The expected value $E(I_t/I_t + \varepsilon_t)$ is indeed a linear function of $I_t + \varepsilon_t$, that is, also of Y_t.

this conditional expectation [†]. Even if ε and I are not normally distributed, the empirical regression can still be considered as a linear approximation to the theoretical regression.

In this particular problem as in many others in econometrics, such assumptions of randomness of the exogenous variable do not seem easily admissible, as we have already explained in the previous chapter.

Moreover, even when such assumptions might be made about investment, the regression of C_t on Y_t seems inadequate for practical applications involving the consumption function. As a rule we could use this regression if we had available a direct prediction of Y_θ and if we were wanting to predict C_θ, without I_θ. But to state the problem in such a way seems to run counter to the logic of our model.

If we think that Y_θ and C_θ are determined simultaneously by I_θ and ε_θ it is difficult to predict Y_θ correctly without involving I_θ; on the contrary, it is natural to try to predict I_θ independently. The problem is then to predict the values of C_θ and Y_θ which would result from values assumed for I_θ. What we need is not the conditional distribution of C_t given Y_t, but the conditional distribution of C_t given I_t.

Fitting based on reduced equations (solved with respect to the endogenous variables) *is therefore also justified from the point of view of the predictions* which can be made from the model. In a certain sense this is even stronger justification than the fact that the regression coefficients tend asymptotically to α and β, since it applies even if the expected value of ε_t for a given value of I_t is not zero, but is linearly dependent on I_t. (We have shown how this could arise in the model of simple regression. The reader may refer back to ch. 3, the end of § 2.)

For the specification of simultaneous equation models such as (3), MOSBAEK and WOLD [1970] suggest a formulation which, equivalent to that proposed here, appears fairly curious at first sight but suggests a natural estimation method. They propose that the systematic part of each endogenous variable be distinguished from its random part. Laws of behavior are to be considered as affecting the systematic parts of the variables, and as being exact; the random errors are independent of the systematic parts of the variables.

Thus, let $\hat{C}_t$ and $\hat{R}_t$ be the systematic parts of consumption and income where, for example, $C_t = \hat{C}_t + \varepsilon_t$. Model (3) is replaced by

$$\begin{cases} \hat{C}_t = a\hat{R}_t + b \\ \hat{R}_t = \hat{C}_t + I_t. \end{cases}$$

Then we can also write the consumption function

$$C_t = a\hat{R}_t + b + \varepsilon_t$$

[†] It can be verified that the conditional expectation is in fact a linear function of Y whose gradient is exactly equal to the expression of the limit (6).

where $E(\varepsilon_t/\hat{R}_t)$ is zero. Since $\hat{R}_t$ is not strictly observable, its value can be deduced from the previous system as a function of I_t, or $\hat{R}_t = (I_t + b)/(1-a)$. Then to find C_t we revert to the first of equations (4), which justifies the 'indirect regression' which consists of estimating the consumption function by means of the regression of C_t on I_t.

This approach gives great importance to the non-observable variables $\hat{C}_t$ and $\hat{R}_t$, which have little intuitive meaning and whose definition depends on the whole system under consideration. It does not appear to lend itself to critical discussion of the assumptions adopted in each particular case.

Because of their methodological interest, we have discussed at some length the problems raised by estimation of the consumption function in the context of the elementary Keynesian model (3). However, our discussion does not lead to any considerable revision of the estimate given above for the United Kingdom.

The regression of income on investment[†] based on the data for 1924–1938, gives an estimate 2.66 of α, that is, an estimate 0.62 of a. The value found for the marginal propensity to consume is certainly lower than that found from the direct regression of C on Y (0.65), but it does not differ by much.

This new result is therefore just as unsatisfactory as the previous one in explaining the level of consumption in the immediate postwar period. We must look elsewhere for a more suitable model.

4   Short- and long-term effects

The consumption function $C_t = aY_t + b$ which we have been considering assumes that the volume of consumption in period t depends only on disposable income during the same period. Now the previous course of income also seems liable to have a considerable effect on the level of consumption. The same amount of disposable income can lead to very different levels of saving according as it is higher or lower than income in preceding periods.

It seems therefore that the simple function considered above should be replaced by a more complex equation which involves, as explanatory variables, the incomes $Y_t, Y_{t-1}, \ldots, Y_{t-\tau}, \ldots$ extending to a period $t-h$ which is sufficiently remote for Y_{t-h} to have no real influence on behavior in period t. A linear function should give a good enough picture of the phenomenon, since relative variations in income are not very great and the relationship under consideration is necessarily regular. A fairly natural choice of function would be:

$$C_t = a_0 Y_t + a_1 Y_{t-1} + \cdots + a_\tau Y_{t-\tau} + \cdots + a_h Y_{t-h} + b + \varepsilon_t, \qquad (7)$$

where $a_0, a_1, \ldots, a_h$, b are $h+2$ constants and ε_t is an unobservable random term.

According to this formula, the effect of a unit increase in income Y_t, previous

---

† Investment here means the excess of income over consumption (see p. 123, footnote).

incomes remaining the same, will be an increase a_0 in consumption. The coefficient a_0 can therefore be called the 'short-term marginal propensity to consume'. The effect of a unit increase in all incomes Y_t, Y_{t-1} to Y_{t-h} will be an increase $a = a_0 + a_1 + \cdots + a_h$ in consumption. Therefore a is a 'long-term marginal propensity to consume'.

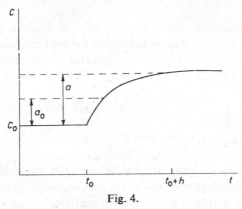

Fig. 4.

More precisely, if income has had a constant value Y_0 during a long series of periods up until t_0 and if its value becomes $Y_0 + 1$ from period $t_0 + 1$, consumption will increase, relative to its level previous to t_0, by a_0 in $t_0 + 1$, by $a_0 + a_1$ in $t_0 + 2$, etc., and by $a = a_0 + a_1 + \cdots + a_h$ from $t_0 + h + 1$ onwards (cf. fig. 4).

Since the coefficients a_τ are obviously positive, the longterm propensity to consume a must exceed the short term propensity a_0.

A model of this type shows clearly that a change in income has different effects according to whether it is sudden or gradual. It seems capable of explaining both figures for long-term growth which reveal particularly the long-term propensity, and data for the interwar period which were subject to sudden and severe fluctuations involving the short-term propensity.

A slightly different formula has also been proposed to accord with the view that consumption must depend on current disposable income and on habits of consumption which were established in the past, that is, on previous levels of consumption. In this case the explanatory variables for C_t should be $Y_t, C_{t-1}, \ldots, C_{t-\tau}, \ldots, C_{t-h}$; and the consumption function would be, for example:

$$C_t = a_0 Y_t + c_1 C_{t-1} + \cdots + c_\tau C_{t-\tau} + \cdots + c_h C_{t-h} + b + \varepsilon_t \qquad (8)$$

Statistical treatment of models of type (7) or (8) raises some methodological problems to which we shall return later. But it is clear that the proposed formulae are still too general for efficient application. They contain too many parameters to allow sound estimation from data for relatively short periods, and therefore we must make some restriction a priori on their generality.

A first restriction consists of choosing a very small maximum time lag h. Thus we can set:

$$C_t = a_0 Y_t + a_1 Y_{t-1} + b + \varepsilon_t, \tag{9}$$

which states that consumption in any one period depends only on income in that period and in the immediately preceding period (or equivalently on income Y_t and the increase $Y_t - Y_{t-1}$ in income relative to the preceding period).

Similarly formula (8) can be reduced to:

$$C_t = a_0 Y_t + c C_{t-1} + b + \varepsilon_t. \tag{10}$$

This often seems sufficient. In this case C_{t-1} is assumed to represent consumption habits as they are at the beginning of period t.

According to formula (10), a_0 would measure the 'short-term marginal propensity to consume', that is, the effect on consumption of a unit increase in income in the same period. The 'long-term marginal propensity to consume' is measured by $a_0/(1-c)$; indeed it can easily be verified that this quantity does in fact correspond to the increase in consumption C_t which follows a unit increase in all previous incomes $Y_t, Y_{t-1}, Y_{t-2}, \ldots$.

DUESENBERRY [1952] suggested a slightly different way of expressing the dependence between C_t and previous values of consumption. Here consumption habits would be represented by the maximum $\bar{C}_t$ reached by C_θ before period t, and we would have:

$$C_t = a_0 Y_t + c \bar{C}_t + b + \varepsilon_t, \tag{11}$$

where

$$\bar{C}_t = \max_{\tau > 0} C_{t-\tau}. \tag{12}$$

This formula is equivalent to (10) when consumption grows from one year to the next and is always above previous levels. It is different from (10) in periods of depression when the volume of consumption decreases. The name 'ratchet effect' is given to the alternation of phases in which eq. (10) applies and phases in which eq. (11) involves a value $\bar{C}_t$ which is constant during several successive periods (but which varies from one phase to another).

Again we might restrict the generality of formula (7) by defining the behavior of the sequence $a_0, a_1, \ldots, a_\tau, \ldots$. It seems obvious a priori that the effect of a variation in income in period t_1 on consumption in period t_2 will decrease when $t_2 - t_1$ increases. Except perhaps for its initial terms, the sequence of a_τ must be positive decreasing. We shall certainly not distort the real situation to any great extent by adopting a particular formula which expresses a_τ as a function of a small number of parameters and which takes account of the decrease defined above. The name *models with distributed lags* is often given to those models which involve a sequence of values of the exogenous variable, where the coefficients are expressed as a function of some independent parameters.

In particular one often assumes that the coefficients a_τ decrease exponentially with τ. They constitute a geometric progression whose first term is a_0 and whose common ratio c lies between 0 and 1:

$$a_\tau = a_0 c^\tau, \qquad 0 < c < 1. \tag{13}$$

Model (7) can then be written:

$$C_t = a_0 \sum_{\tau=0}^{h} c^\tau Y_{t-\tau} + b + \varepsilon_t, \tag{14}$$

and now has only three unknown coefficients a, b and c.

When assumptions (13) is made, one generally assumes that the sequence of the a_τ is infinite, as the model can then be simply expressed. In fact (14) becomes:

$$C_t = a_0 \sum_{\tau=0}^{\infty} c^\tau Y_{t-\tau} + b + \varepsilon_t, \tag{15}$$

and therefore:

$$C_t - cC_{t-1} = a_0 Y_t + b - cb + \varepsilon_t - c\varepsilon_{t-1},$$

or again:

$$C_t = a_0 Y_t + cC_{t-1} + d + \eta_t, \tag{16}$$

where:

$$d = b(1 - c)$$

and

$$\eta_t = \varepsilon_t - c\varepsilon_{t-1}. \tag{17}$$

Formula (16) is similar to (10). The introduction of C_{t-1} into the equation which explains C_t can therefore be justified in two different ways. We may sometimes consider that consumers decide how much they will spend by taking into account both current disposable income and consumption during the preceding period. At other times we may consider that the successive amounts of disposable income which they have had previously do in fact influence their behavior but that this influence decreases exponentially with time.

However, these two points of view are not equivalent as regards the assumptions which seem reasonable for the additional random terms, ε_t in eq. (10) and η_t in eq. (16), since ε_t represents the unobservable random factors which have influenced decisions to consume in period t, while η_t, defined by formula (17), involves both the exogenous factors relating to period t and those relating to period $t-1$. The same assumptions will certainly not be good for both ε_t and η_t; and the statistical procedures which are appropriate for model (10) will probably be different from those for model (16). We shall discuss this question in detail in ch. 15.

Be that as it may, the distinction between short- and long-term effects leads us to replace the simple regression model by more complex models, represented among others by formulae (9), (10) and (15). All these expressions are generalizations of the simple eq. (1) which was used in the first fitting operations. In every case the random term ε_t occurs additively and seems justifiable on the basis of assumptions similar to those we made in the previous chapter when discussing simple regression (assumptions 1 to 4).

However, at this point an important distinction is revealed. In eqs. (9) and (15) the variables on the righthand side are the values of income during the different periods. They can be considered as exogenous and non-random[†] just like Y_t, and thus we can regard these variables in the same way as the explanatory variable z_t in the preceding chapter.

On the other hand, the righthand side of formula (10) contains besides Y_t the explanatory endogenous variable C_{t-1} which must be treated as a random variable since it depends on the random variable ε_{t-1}. In fact model (10) is distinguishable from the simple regression model and from models (9) and (15), because it stipulates that there is direct dependence between successive values of the endogenous variable. It is called *autoregressive*. As we shall see in ch. 14 particular problems are raised by autoregressive models. They cannot be treated by the regression theory which was introduced in ch. 3 and will be developed more fully in later chapters.

Be that as it may, we shall be able to generalize the fitting formula introduced in ch. 3 to models (9), (10) and (15). We shall show that valid estimates of the coefficients of each model can be obtained by determining them in such a way as to minimize the sum of squares of the differences between the observed values of C_t and the values of the expressions other than ε_t which appear on the righthand side of the equation.

What practical results have been obtained from the models which we have just defined? Generally they have revealed a long-term marginal propensity to consume which is clearly higher than the short-term propensity. We cannot give a complete review here of the many empirical studies which have been carried out on this topic, but shall quote only two results.

The following results were obtained by fitting annual data for the United Kingdom in the period 1924–1938 using a model similar to (10) but without a

---

[†] We shall ignore here and in the rest of this chapter the difficulty examined in the last section, that is, the fact that consumption and income are often considered to be determined simultaneously. We have already discussed this sufficiently.

constant term[†]:

$$C_t = 0.18\,Y_t + 0.81\,C_{t-1}.$$
$$(0.09) \quad (0.10)$$
(18)

which shows a short-term propensity of 0.18 and a long-term propensity of $0.18/(1-0.81)=0.95$. However, the accuracy of the results is not outstanding. The standard error shown beneath the estimate of a_0 is as high as 0.09, so that a confidence interval for the short-term propensity would include all positive numbers less than 0.36. Obviously the data for fig. 2 are too few in number for sound estimation of the propensities in which we are interested.

FRIEDMAN [1957] has described the results obtained by fitting annual data for disposable income and consumption per head in the United States, for the period 1905–1951 (excluding the war years), using different models. The use of formula (9) gave[††]:

$$C_t = 0.58\,Y_t + 0.32\,Y_{t-1} + 53.$$
(19)

Here the marginal propensity is 0.58 in the short-term and 0.90 in the long-term.

The use of formula (15) gave a still smaller value, 0.29 for a_0 and a relatively high value, 0.67, for the coefficient c. If the expansion of C_t is limited to its first terms, the consumption function would be:

$$C_t = 0.29\,Y_t + 0.19\,Y_{t-1} + 0.13\,Y_{t-2} + 0.09\,Y_{t-3}$$
$$+ 0.06\,Y_{t-4} + 0.04\,Y_{t-5} + \cdots - 4.$$
(20)

The short-term and long-term propensities are 0.29 and 0.88 respectively. According to these figures, only about a third of an increase in income would be used for additional consumption in the current year and it would be five years before 90% of it was used.

The last eq. (20) may be preferred to the previous eq. (19), both because it was derived from a model which was more satisfactory a priori, and because it has only a very small constant term. Numerous results obtained for different countries during the last ten years confirm this choice, but generally reveal a higher short term propensity to consume[†††]. We must, however, conclude

---

[†] The constant term in (10) is suppressed on the grounds that, if the value of b is markedly different from zero, the ratio C/Y cannot be approximately constant over long periods.

Fitting model (10) itself leads to:

$$C_t = 0.46Y_t + 0.20C_{t-1} + 23.4$$
$$(0.07) \quad (0.12)$$

This is as unsatisfactory as the simple regression (2) for prediction on the postwar period or for explaining long-term growth.

[††] M. Friedman does not give the standard errors of the estimates.

[†††] Sets of estimates have been given for France by VANGREVELINGHE [1966] and by NASSE [1970]. See also ZELLNER and GEISEL [1970], who use quarterly American data to estimate a function of type (16) and carefully investigate the time dependence of the errors η_t, concluding that the dependence is weak.

that it takes longer for consumption to react to a change in income than was thought by Keynes and many other economists.

It is probable that the speed with which consumption reacts to an increase in incomes depends on fairly numerous factors, and in particular on the distribution of such an increase among the different social classes. The incomes received by the poorest people will be quickly spent, while those in more comfortable circumstances will not immediately change their level of consumption. This leads us now to examine the relationship between global saving and the saving in each household, and to discuss the difficult problem of aggregation.

5 Individual consumption functions and aggregate consumption function

The models described above are motivated by the notion that the consumption of a group depends only on the course of its total income. Such an assumption is obviously rather naive and a complete explanation must take account of various other factors.

Thus in discussing the Keynesian theory, PIGOU [1943] made the point that a decrease in consumer saving will result from a growth in accumulated assets. For the same level of income, consumption will vary in accordance with the assets of each household. This is now accepted in most econometric studies which take account of liquid assets in determining the consumption function. Thus ZELLNER [1957] has given the following formula for the volume of consumption[†] in the United States during the quarterly period t:

$$C_t = 0.38\,Y_t + 0.49\,C_{t-1} + 0.22\,L_{t-1} - 19.$$
$$(0.11) \quad (0.16) \quad\quad (0.07)$$

$$(21)$$

In this formula L_{t-1} denotes the liquid assets of households at the start of the quarter t.

Keynes himself emphasized the importance of the distribution of income and proposed measures for redistribution with the aim of stimulating consumer demand. Thus Keynes was thinking not so much of strict dependence between global consumption and global income, but rather between individual consumption and individual income. The consumption function represented at the macro-economic level a relationship which was essentially micro-economic in origin.

If this is really the idea underlying the formulation of aggregate models we must ask under what conditions these models can be used in econometric

---

[†] The data have been corrected for seasonal variation and are expressed at annual rates in billions of dollars at 1947–1949 prices. Fitting was carried out for the period 1947–1955.

studies. This is a very important question from the point of view of methodology and is of much wider reference than the particular problem which is discussed in this chapter. As we shall have no later opportunity to return to it, we shall now give some space to its discussion.

Generally the name *aggregation* is given either to the operation of defining a global quantity to represent a set of simple quantities, or to that of representing a set of relationships among many simple quantities by one or more equations involving global quantities. It would take too long to make a full study of the problems arising in aggregation and this would distract us from our main subject[†]; so we shall only describe, with reference to the consumption function, the difficulties which are liable to affect the interpretation of fitting carried out on the basis of global models.

Let us denote by an index i, $(i=1,...,n)$, each of the n households which make up a group of households. Let y_{it} and c_{it} be the disposable income and consumption respectively of household i during period t, We assume that y_{it} and c_{it} are related. A good model should include explanatory variables other than income in the particular period, especially the previous course of income, and liquid assets. But our further discussion would be much complicated by the introduction of variables other than y_{it} and c_{it}.

Suppose first that the consumption function of each household is linear, say:

$$c_{it} = a_i y_{it} + b_i + \varepsilon_{it}, \tag{22}$$

where a_i and b_i are coefficients peculiar to household i, and ε_{it} is a random term whose expected value is zero for any y_{it}.

Aggregate consumption and aggregate income are clearly:

$$C_t = \sum_{i=1}^{n} c_{it}, \qquad Y_t = \sum_{i=1}^{n} y_{it}. \tag{23}$$

Equation (22) implies:

$$C_t = \sum_{i=1}^{n} a_i y_{it} + b + \varepsilon_t, \tag{24}$$

where:

$$b = \sum_{i=1}^{n} b_i, \qquad \varepsilon_t = \sum_{i=1}^{n} \varepsilon_{it}. \tag{25}$$

Thus aggregate consumption depends on the incomes of the n households. With these explanatory variables the model is linear. It includes an error whose expected value is zero for all y_{it}.

What then is the significance of the coefficients a^* and b^* obtained by simple

---

[†] The reader may refer to MALINVAUD [1957] for a complete methodological study and a list of references.

regression on the aggregate consumption function (1)? How much information do they give concerning the relationship between income and consumption? In what circumstances do they allow valid prediction?

From eqs. (22) to (25), the formulae for calculating a^* and b^* can be expressed in the form:

$$a^* = \sum_{i=1}^{n} a_i \varrho_i^* + \xi, \qquad b^* = b + \sum_{i=1}^{n} a_i \tau_i^* + \eta, \qquad (26)$$

where ϱ^* and τ^* are defined as:

$$\varrho_i^* = \frac{\sum_{t=1}^{T} (y_{it} - \bar{y}_i)(Y_t - \bar{Y})}{\sum_{t=1}^{T} (Y_t - \bar{Y})^2}, \qquad \tau_i^* = \bar{y}_i - \varrho_i^* \bar{Y}, \qquad (27)$$

and ξ and η as:

$$\xi = \frac{\sum_{t=1}^{T} \varepsilon_t (Y_t - \bar{Y})}{\sum_{t=1}^{T} (Y_t - \bar{Y})^2}, \qquad \eta = \bar{\varepsilon} - \xi \bar{Y}. \qquad (28)$$

ξ and η have zero means and are the random components of a^* and b^*, at least so long as the y_{it} are considered to be non-random. We note that the analytic expressions (28) are very similar to those we should have obtained using the aggregate model (1). So the variances of a^* and b^* can be calculated by the usual formulae. Let us consider then only the expected values:

$$E(a^*) = \sum_{i=1}^{n} a_i \varrho_i^*, \qquad E(b^*) = b + \sum_{i=1}^{n} a_i \tau_i^*. \qquad (29)$$

$E(a^*)$ is a weighted mean of the a_i, because formula (27) defining the ϱ^* shows that their sum is 1. The weight ϱ_i^* is equal to the coefficient of a simple regression between y_{it} and Y_t calculated on the period of observation. So the aggregate marginal propensity a^* reflects particularly those a_i referring to households whose incomes have been most sensitive to the changes in aggregate income. The weight carried by these households in formula (29) is more than proportional to their mean income $\bar{y}_i$. For example if, as is usually the case, self-employed people have a smaller marginal propensity to consume a_i than have wage-earners, and if their incomes have varied more during the sample period than those of wage-earners, then a^* will be smaller than the mean of the a_i defined by:

$$\bar{a} = \frac{1}{\bar{Y}} \sum_{i=1}^{n} a_i \bar{y}_i.$$

Similarly $E(b^*)$ differs from b by a sum in which each a_i is multiplied by a coefficient τ_i^* which is equal to the constant term in a simple regression between y_{it} and Y_t. We note that the sum of the τ_i^* for the different households in the group is zero; and that τ_i^* is positive for those households whose incomes have been least sensitive to the changes in aggregate income. So $E(b^*)-b$ will be positive if these households also have the highest propensity to consume, as we assumed in the example described above.

Thus, when there are considerable variations in the distribution of incomes, a^* and b^* can be appreciably biased relative to the directly calculated coefficients $\bar{a}$ and b. The low value of the marginal propensity to consume calculated from the data for the interwar period may be partly explained in this way.

The relationships between micro-economic parameters and global regression coefficients have been systematically studied and discussed by THEIL [1954] who has considered various methods of aggregation in the context of linear models with errors in the equations. The reader can refer to his book to see how the foregoing remarks can be generalized.

Are the differences between a^* and $\bar{a}$ and between b^* and b really as important as we might be led to think on an initial examination? Do they make for serious bias in our statistical procedures? To answer these questions, we must examine the use that is made of estimates. Essentially they are used for conditional prediction. Thus

$$C_\theta^P = a^* Y_\theta + b^* \tag{30}$$

will be taken as the prediction of C_θ on the assumption that global income in period θ will be Y_θ.

This prediction appears satisfactory in two particular cases:

(i) *If all households have the same propensity to consume*, then $a_i = a$. As the sum of the ϱ_i^* is 1, and the sum of the τ_i^* is zero, $E(a^*) = a$ and $E(b^*) = b$. In this case the micro-economic model (22) also implies the validity of the aggregate model (1). The proposed prediction enjoys the properties described at the end of the previous chapter.

(ii) *If the distribution of incomes is described by a stable linear stochastic model*, that is, if the income of each household depends on aggregate income according to:

$$y_{it} = \varrho_i Y_t + \tau_i + \eta_{it}, \tag{31}$$

where ϱ_i and τ_i denote two real parameters and η_{it} is a random term with zero mean. It is obvious from the definition of Y_t that the sum of the ϱ_i is 1, while the sum of the τ_i and that of the η_{it} are zero.

In this case the micro-economic model (22) implies:

$$C_t = \left[\sum_{i=1}^{n} a_i \varrho_i \right] Y_t + \left[b + \sum_{i=1}^{n} a_i \tau_i \right] + \eta_t, \tag{32}$$

where the random term:

$$\eta_t = \varepsilon_t + \sum_{i=1}^{n} a_i \eta_{it}, \tag{33}$$

has expected value zero.

The aggregate model (1) is therefore justified. The regression coefficients a^* and b^* appear as unbiased estimates[†] of the terms in square brackets in model (32). Prediction according to the proposed formula will therefore still be satisfactory in this case.

The conditions just stated are very restrictive. It is unlikely that all individuals have the same propensity to consume. It is also unlikely that the distribution of incomes is described by a rigid system of type (31), which must hold for the period for which the fitting is carried out as well as for the prediction period.

However, we consider often that stable global laws can be obtained by splitting up the population into social groups. We can assume then that at least one of the two conditions given above is satisfied by the set of households belonging to the same group, either because the parameters of behavior differ little from one household to another, or because within each group the distribution of incomes is considered to be stable.

If there are H groups $(h = 1, 2, \ldots, H)$, the consumption C_{ht} of group h is considered to be a stochastic linear function of the group income Y_{ht}:

$$C_{ht} = a_h Y_{ht} + b_h + \varepsilon_{ht}, \tag{34}$$

and the global consumption is described by the model:

$$C_t = \sum_{h=1}^{H} a_h Y_{ht} + b + \varepsilon_t, \tag{35}$$

which includes as exogenous variables the H group incomes.

For reasons of statistical convenience, such *stratification* is often carried out on the basis of the nature of income rather than according to social groups. Thus in their model of the American economy KLEIN and GOLDBERGER [1955] select the following[††] consumption function for year t:

[†] Formula (33) shows that the errors η_t are not independent of the a_i. Nevertheless the estimators a^* and b^* are still efficient in the class of unbiased linear estimators. See WU [1973].
[††] As a general rule, Klein and Goldberger determined the behavioral equations of their model by fitting annual series of figures of American national income for the periods 1929–1941 and 1946–1952. However, the coefficients relating to the three types of income were differently determined on the basis of inquiries into family budgets. In the authors' judgment this method made for greater precision. But straightforward analysis of global time series would have also given different coefficients for the different types of income. Thus, on the basis of annual American data for 1926–1941 and 1946–1949, BROWN [1952] found a marginal propensity to consume of 0.61 for wage income and 0.28 for non-wage income.

$C_t = 0.55\,Y_{st} + 0.41\,Y_{et} + 0.34\,Y_{at} + 0.026\,C_{t-1}$
$\quad\ (0.06)\quad\ \ (0.05)\quad\ \ (0.04)\quad\ \ \ (0.08)$

$$+ 0.072\,L_{t-1} + 0.26\,N_t - 22.26, \qquad (36)$$
$$(0.025)\qquad (0.10)\quad (9.66)$$

where Y_{st} denotes disposable wage income, Y_{at} disposable agricultural income, Y_{et} other classes of disposable income, L_{t-1} liquid assets held by consumers at the start of year t and R_t the population of the United States during year t. (Population is expressed in millions, and all other quantities in billions of dollars at 1939 prices.)

In the case of a function of type (36) a change in the distribution of incomes in favour of wage-earners must cause a growth in consumption since the marginal propensity is higher in their case than in the other categories of income.

Similarly, when discussing the effect of a redistribution, Keynes suggested that a transfer of income to poorer people would stimulate demand, since their propensity to consume is very near 1, while that of the rich must be much lower. In fact Keynes was thinking not nearly so much of the differences between the consumption laws of the different social classes as of a general phenomenon valid for all consumers, namely that the marginal propensity to consume decreases as income increases. He emphasized particularly the non-linear character of the dependence between income y_{it} and consumption c_{it}.

To round off these remarks, let us suppose that the linear model (22) is replaced by:

$$c_{it} = f(y_{it}) + \varepsilon_{it}, \qquad (37)$$

where the non-linear function f is the same for all households. Although behavior is here assumed to be completely uniform, the micro-economic laws (37) no longer imply direct dependence between aggregate consumption C_t and aggregate income Y_t. The level of C_t depends also on the distribution of incomes.

This remark is well illustrated by fig. 5 which shows the curve Γ representing the average consumption function $f(y_{it})$. In accordance with the Keynesian view, this curve is concave down, since the marginal propensity to consume decreases continuously as income increases.

Then let $\bar{y}_t$ be the mean household income at a certain time t $(\bar{y}_t = (1/n)Y_t)$. The mean consumption $(1/n)C_t$ does not differ much from a theoretical mean consumption:

$$\bar{c}_t = \frac{1}{n}\sum_{i=1}^{n} f(y_{it}).$$

The state of the group at time t can be represented by the point P with abscissa $\bar{y}_t$ and ordinate $\bar{c}_t$. This point is the center of gravity of the n points P_i with

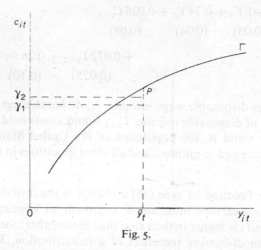

Fig. 5.

abscissa y_{it} and ordinate $f(y_{it})$, all of which lie on the curve Γ. Since the curve is concave, P lies below Γ at a distance which increases with the degree of dispersion of the points P_i.

Therefore to a given value of $\bar{y}_t$, that is also of Y_t, there correspond many possible values for the theoretical mean consumption $\bar{c}_t$. A redistribution of incomes in the direction of greater equality will cause an increase in $\bar{c}_t$ without any change in Y_t; for example $\bar{c}_t$ will go from the level γ_1 to the level γ_2.

However, even in the case of the non-linear model (37), a global equation between C_t and Y_t will be meaningful if the distribution of incomes follows a stable random system, that is, if it is determined, as a first approximation, by global income Y_t. If, for example, the y_{it} satisfy a stable equation of type (31), the global consumption C_t will be a random variable whose distribution will depend on global income. We can accept the linear regression of C_t on Y_i as a means of estimating the expected value of C_t. Similarly a linear regression on the different categories of income (cf. eq. 35) can be chosen if the distribution of incomes within each category follows a stable random system.

We can take this remark further by choosing a particular form for the consumption function (37) and giving a new expression for the stability of the distribution of incomes.

According to Keynes the marginal propensity to consume decreases steadily as income increases, and this seems to agree with the results of inquiries into family budgets. Thus fig. 1 represents the consumption function by a regular curve which is slightly concave down. In these conditions the mean equation $c_{it} = f(y_{it})$ can be expressed fairly exactly by a second-degree function. We shall therefore take as consumption function:

$$c_{it} = \alpha + \beta y_{it} + \gamma y_{it}^2 + \varepsilon_{it}. \tag{38}$$

In addition, we shall say that the distribution of incomes is unchanged if the dispersion of the y_{it} about their mean $\bar{y}_t$ bears a constant ratio to $\bar{y}_t$, more precisely if:

$$\frac{1}{n}\sum_{i=1}^{n}(y_{it}-\bar{y}_t)^2 = \delta^2\bar{y}_t^2, \tag{39}$$

where δ is a constant which characterizes the relative dispersion of incomes. This condition can also be written:

$$\sum_{i=1}^{n} y_{it}^2 = b\bar{y}_t^2(1+\delta^2) = Y_t^2\frac{(1+\delta^2)}{n}. \tag{40}$$

The consumption function (38) then leads to:

$$C_t = n\alpha + \beta Y_t + \frac{\gamma}{n}(1+\delta^2)Y_t^2 + \varepsilon_t, \tag{41}$$

that is, to a second-degree function in Y_t. This function can be determined directly by a regression between C_t and the explanatory variables Y_t and Y_t^2, at least when the coefficient δ is unchanged during the period to which the data refer. The equation obtained will apply so long as the relative dispersion of incomes remains the same. Since the marginal propensity to consume decreases with y_{it}, the coefficient γ is negative. We can verify from (41) that greater equality in incomes (that is a decrease in δ^2) will cause an increase in global consumption C_t.

6   The macro-economic use of micro-economic data

We have been considering the problems which arise when the consumption function is estimated from global data covering the whole group. For a better understanding of the significance of the results obtained, we were led to describe models applying to the different households making up the group. We must also find out how we can make a valid estimate of the law which interests us from direct observation of micro-economic data.

For example let us return to model (38) and suppress the index t so long as we are interested only in quantities for the same period. Then the consumption c_i of household i $(i=1,2,\ldots,n)$ depends on its income y_i as follows:

$$c_i = \alpha + \beta y_i + \gamma y_i^2 + \varepsilon_i, \tag{42}$$

where the coefficients α, β and γ are the same for all households, and ε_i is a random term whose expected value is zero for any y_i. This term ε_i represents the effect of all unobservable factors on the consumption of household i, since we feel justified in representing such an effect by a random variable with zero mean.

If an inquiry into family budgets has provided figures for consumption and income of a certain number of households, we can fit them directly by eq. (42), which includes three unknown coefficients α, β and γ. The estimates α^*, β^* and γ^* of these coefficients can be chosen so as to minimize the sum of squares of the differences between c_i and $\alpha^* + \beta^* y_i + \gamma^* y_i^2$. Since the expected value of ε_i is zero, this random error satisfies assumption 1 of ch. 3, and other assumptions of the same chapter will also be taken as satisfied. The proposed estimates will therefore have certain of the interesting properties previously studied.

It would be premature to examine here all the problems raised by the use of this type of data. We confine ourselves to three general remarks.

In the first place, the random terms have generally greater dispersion in models relating to micro-economic data than in those for macro-economic data. This is quite natural, since random deviations due to differences in behavior largely cancel each other out in aggregate equations. Thus the aggregation of eqs. (38) in formula (41) shows on the one hand the sum Y_t of incomes y_{it} which are all positive, and on the other hand the sum ε_t of errors ε_{it} which are sometimes negative and sometimes positive. The ratio between the standard deviation of ε_t and Y_t is much smaller than the ratio between the standard deviation of ε_{it} and y_{it}. It would obviously be wrong to deduce that the micro-economic model (38) is less well based than the corresponding macro-economic model (41).

But the degree of dispersion of the errors would preclude precise estimation of α, β and γ if micro-economic data were not much more plentiful than macro-economic data. Fortunately, while the time series which we use rarely have more than a few dozen terms, and sometimes only about fifteen, family budget inquiries cover several hundreds or housands of households. It is often the case that the latter source of data gives much greater precision.

In the second place, the values of the explanatory variable are generally much more widely scattered in samples of micro-economic data than in those relating to global quantities. Thus, in the family budget inquiry on which fig. 1 (p. 119) was based, the incomes y_i varied from 1 to about 7. On the other hand, aggregate income in the United Kingdom varied only from 75 to 95 between 1924 and 1938, as can be seen in fig. 2 (p. 120).

As a rule therefore we can determine the structural equations over a wide range of the explanatory variables by studying micro-economic data. However, this advantageous situation gives rise to complications when econometric methods are applied.

In particular the linear equations sufficient for describing the laws relating to aggregate series must often be replaced by more complicated functions. In the present example, consumption c_i has been fitted by a polynomial of second degree in y_i. We must often resort to less simple analytic forms.

Similarly, when the data cover a wide range, we see often that the dispersion of the results about the mean equations varies from one end of the range to the other. Thus the collection of points used for fig. 1 is much more open for high values than for low values of y_i. In this case the dispersion of the ε_i varies with y_i and we can no longer postulate that they are homoscedastic (cf. assumption 2, ch. 3).

In the third place, to assume that a relation such as (42) applies to all the individual data may be unsatisfactory in so far as its coefficients β and γ are the same for all individuals. In the previous section we considered relation (22) in which the a_i may differ from one individual to another. To set up a more realistic model, we could replace β and γ by coefficients such as $\beta + \beta_i$ and $\gamma + \gamma_i$; the additive terms β_i and γ_i, which represent individual deviations from the mean coefficients, are then treated as random.

In ch. 8 we shall find out how to deal with these difficulties, and for the present we go on to another question.

Econometric studies of the consumption function aim at determining laws which can be used to predict consumer demand. We wish to know what increase in consumption will result from a 10% rise in disposable income. Thus the model will be used essentially for macro-economic purposes. *To what extent can equations which hold good for aggregate prediction be determined by analysis of micro-economic data?*

Obviously there is no general answer to this question[†] since everything depends on the phenomenon in question, on its laws and on the kind of micro-economic data available. However, study of the present example may lead to some useful reflection on the problem.

Suppose first that the equation

$$c_{it} = \alpha + \beta y_{it} + \gamma y_{it}^2 + \varepsilon_{it} \tag{38}$$

describes perfectly how the demand of each household i is determined in each period t. This demand depends only on disposable income during the period and on disturbances which are purely random. No other observable factor seems to have any considerable influence on c_{it}. In these circumstances global consumption C_t and global disposable income Y_t are connected by the equation:

$$C_t = n\alpha + \beta Y_t + \frac{\gamma}{n}(1 + \delta^2) Y_t^2 + \varepsilon_t. \tag{41}$$

By analysis of family budgets we can estimate α, β and γ. The number n of households is known. Thus the global equation (41) which allows us to predict C_t on the basis of independent predictions of Y_t and the dispersion of incomes δ, can be obtained directly by transposing the results of micro-economic analysis.

Of course the real-life situation is not as simple as that assumed by eq. (38).

---

† See HOLTE [1962], pp. 75–110, for a general study of this problem.

Factors other than y_{it} have an important influence on the demand of household i during period t.

This does not, as a rule, raise any insurmountable logical difficulty. It is enough to set up a correct micro-economic model which recognizes that all these factors exist, then to find the macro-economic equation which results from it, to analyze the micro-economic data in order to estimate the unknown parameters of the model and finally to deduce the corresponding coefficients of the aggregate equation.

In fact this principle cannot always be applied completely. It demands that all the factors on which consumption depends should have been observed for each household, and that the variations in these factors from one household to another should have been sufficient to allow precise estimation of their respective importance. Now in many cases our inquiries provide information about only some of these factors. Thus we may have observed disposable income for household i, and perhaps also its liquid assets, but not its expectation as to its future resources. It may also happen that certain factors have the same effect in all households so that their influence is not clearly revealed by this particular inquiry. Thus, the observations often relate to a single period in which general expectations have been very much the same for all households.

Some of the consequences of this real situation will certainly be revealed more clearly if we make a fresh examination of simplified models, in order to discuss the significance of a direct regression between the consumptions c_{it} and incomes y_{it}.

Let us suppose first that the true model can be written:

$$c_{it} = a_0 y_{it} + a_1 y_{i, t-1} + b + \varepsilon_{it}, \tag{43}$$

that is, that consumption depends not only on income in the current period, but also on income in the preceding period. We have already discussed the justification for such a model in section 4 above, and note only that the linear micro-economic eq. (43) implies a similar macro-economic equation, that is, eq. (9).

Let us suppose moreover that an inquiry into household consumption and income during period t gives the values of c_{it} and y_{it} for n separate households, but gives no information about $y_{i, t-1}$. By a simple regression on these data the following estimate is found for the 'marginal propensity to consume':

$$a^* = \frac{\sum\limits_{t=1}^{n} (c_{it} - \bar{c}_t)(y_{it} - \bar{y}_t)}{\sum\limits_{i=1}^{n} (y_{it} - \bar{y}_t)^2}. \tag{44}$$

What is the relationship between this estimate and the true parameters of the model, a_0 and a_1?

Substituting in formula (44) the value of c_{it} given by eq. (43), we can write the expected value of a^*:

$$E(a^*) = a_0 + a_1 \frac{\sum_{i=1}^{n} (y_{it} - \bar{y}_t)(y_{i,t-1} - \bar{y}_{t-1})}{\sum_{i=1}^{n} (y_{it} - \bar{y}_t)^2}.$$

The ratio which appears in this formula is near the correlation coefficient between the incomes of the households i during period t, and the incomes of the same households during period $t-1$. Its exact value depends on the changes which have taken place in the distribution of incomes between periods $t-1$ and t. It is likely to be slightly less than 1, at least if the households have very different incomes.

Thus, when model (43) applies, the estimated propensity a^* is near to and generally slightly lower than the long term propensity $a_0 + a_1$. The analysis of family budgets when viewed in this light gives no information about the immediate reaction of consumption to an increase in incomes during the same period[†]. This question has been studied in more general terms by GRUNFELD [1961].

A serious objection has been raised to the macro-economic use of the propensity to consume deduced from analysis of family budgets. The point has been made that the consumption of a household depends not only on its income but also on consumption habits in the group to which it belongs. These habits reflect the group's standard of living and vary as a function of global income. An inquiry based on a given period will not reveal how global consumption adapts itself to a change in global income.

This point of view has sometimes been expressed more precisely. The consumption of a given household would now depend not on its absolute income y_{it} but on its 'relative income' $y_{it}/\bar{y}_t$, which is the ratio between absolute income and the mean income of the group. Hence the name *relative income hypothesis* has been given to this theory, which has received its fullest exposition by DUESENBERRY [1952].

[†] Of course model (43) could be estimated completely if the inquiry gave information both about the incomes y_{it} and about their variations relative to the preceding period:

$$\Delta y_{it} = y_{it} - y_{it-1}.$$

For the equation:

$$c_{it} = (a_0 + a_1)y_{it} - a_1 \Delta y_{it} + b + \varepsilon_{it},$$

equivalent to (43), can be validly estimated by multiple regression.

This notion is expressed by the following simple model:

$$\frac{c_{it}}{\bar{y}_t} = \lambda + \mu \frac{y_{it}}{\bar{y}_t}. \tag{45}$$

Consumption as a ratio of the mean income $c_{it}/\bar{y}_t$ is a linear function of relative income. Therefore c_{it} is a function of both y_{it} and $\bar{y}_t$, say:

$$c_{it} = \lambda \bar{y}_t + \mu y_{it}.$$

By aggregation, this gives the macro-economic equation:

$$C_t = (\lambda + \mu) Y_t. \tag{46}$$

A simple regression between the micro-economic variables c_{it} and y_{it} would yield a propensity to consume in the neighbourhood of μ, and would underestimate the effect of an increase in global income. Sometimes the rather clumsy distinction has been made between μ as the 'static' propensity to consume and $(\lambda + \mu)$ as the 'dynamic' propensity to consume. The latter could be correctly estimated only from time series.

Model (45) and the corresponding macro-economic model (46) are obviously too simple to give a complete picture of reality. The relative income hypothesis can be much less rigidly expressed, but further discussion of this subject is beside the point. We note only that Modigliani proposed the following macro-economic formulation:

$$C_t = a_0 Y_t + a_1 \bar{Y}_t + b + \varepsilon_t, \tag{47}$$

where $\bar{Y}_t$ denotes the maximum value of Y_θ previous to period t, and thus represents an important factor conditioning consumption habits in that period. Equation (47) reminds us of the eq. (11) which we encountered in the study of short and long-term effects; it is coupled with the same 'ratchet effect'.

7   Observed income and permanent income

According to the relative income hypothesis, the absolute value of observed income during a period would not provide a perfect indicator of disposable resources for the study of consumption. The same idea lies behind another assumption which we shall now examine[†].

The 'permanent income hypothesis' proposed by FRIEDMAN [1957] is not only interesting in itself, but also reveals an important limitation of the simple

---

[†] Besides the 'relative income hypothesis' and 'permanent income hypothesis', we must also mention the 'life-cycle plan hypothesis' due to MODIGLIANI and BRUMBERG [1955]. However, the latter has not inspired much econometric research.

regression model and suggests a model of a different kind. As in the previous sections, we shall therefore concentrate here on questions of methodology whose significance extends far beyond the study of the consumption function.

It is clear that consumption is not continually being adapted to casual changes in income. Each household fixes its expenditure according to the level which it considers normal for its income. An exceptionally high level of income in any one period will lead to saving against future needs, and conversely a temporary decrease in income will be compensated by the use of previously accumulated savings.

The level of income which is considered to be normal is therefore more significant than the amount actually received. This distinction is very important if the amount of income received is known for only a short period, say a month. According to Friedman it is also essential for sound interpretation of data for annual income and annual consumption. There is then less difference between the two notions of income, since casual changes will to some extent cancel each other out, but the distinction still should not be ignored.

We shall first give a brief description of Friedman's model, and then examine its consequences for the usual statistical procedures. We shall see that certain particular features of empirical results can be explained, and finally we shall study the consequences of this hypothesis for macro-economic analysis.

We must distinguish, for every household i, two ideas of income. These are the observed income y_i and the 'permanent income' y_i^p, which is defined as the income considered to be normal when the household decides on its consumption for the period of observation. The amount by which observed income exceeds permanent income, which Friedman calls 'transitory income' and which we denote here by y_i^t, can take positive or negative values, since it results from more or less accidental irregularities in the course of income.

The permanent income hypothesis states that the consumption c_i of household i during the period of observation depends on its permanent income and not on its transitory income[†]. To investigate its consequences, we can confine ourselves to a linear dependence of the following type:

$$c_i = ay_i^p + b + \varepsilon_i, \qquad (48)$$

where a and b are two coefficients and ε_i an unobservable random variable with zero mean.

Equation (48) has an essential difference from the simple regression model which we have been studying. The explanatory variable y_i^p cannot be observed exactly, and only income y_i is known. To make the model complete, we must

---

[†] In fact the permanent income hypothesis has been stated in many ways, some of which are less categorical than the statement we have given. In this as in preceding sections, we do not attempt to give an up-to-date survey of existing research, but only to describe an important approach together with its implications for econometric methodology.

state precisely how the true explanatory variable y_i^p and the observed variable y_i are related; that is, we must formulate some general assumption about the transitory income y_i^t, for:

$$y_i = y_i^p + y_i^t. \tag{49}$$

Since y_i^t represents chance variations in the course of income, it is natural to think of it as a random variable with zero mean for any value y_i^p:

$$E(y_i^t/y_i^p) = 0. \tag{50}$$

Thus the transitory income y_i^t appears as an 'error' affecting observation of the true explanatory variable.

If such a model describes consumption, what significance can be attributed to the coefficients a^* and b^* of a direct regression between the values c_i and y_i observed in a sample of n households? This question lies behind Friedman's investigations.

To find an answer, we note that (48) and (49) imply:

$$c_i = ay_i + b + \eta_i, \tag{51}$$

where the random term η_i is:

$$\eta_i = \varepsilon_i - ay_i^t. \tag{52}$$

It might seem that the simple regression model could be applied here, given an adequate definition of the error, but in fact its essential assumption is not satisfied. The expected value of η_i for a given value of y_i is not zero. The two errors ε_i and y_i^t have zero expectations for a given permanent income. Therefore:

$$E(\eta_i/y_i^p) = 0. \tag{53}$$

A high value of y_i corresponds often therefore to a high value of y_i^t, and also to a high value of η_i, at least when ε_i and y_i^t are independent.

As in the simultaneous equations model, but for a different reason, the simple regression leads to biased estimates of the structural coefficients a and b. To find out the nature of this bias, we suppose that ε_i and y_i^t are independent, that y_i^t has a constant variance σ^2 and that the sample mean and variance of the permanent incomes tend to finite limits when the number of households tends to infinity. That is:

$$E(\varepsilon_i y_i^t) = 0, \qquad E(y_i^t)^2 = \sigma^2,$$

$$\lim_{n \to \infty} \frac{1}{n} \sum_{i=1}^{n} (y_i^p - \bar{y}^p)^2 = S^2 > 0.$$

The simple regression leads to the following estimate of a:

$$a^* = \sum \frac{(y_i - \bar{y})(c_i - \bar{c})}{\sum (y_i - \bar{y})^2} = a + \frac{\sum \eta_i (y_i - \bar{y})}{\sum (y_i - \bar{y})^2}. \tag{54}$$

We can easily establish the following probability limits[†]:

$$\frac{1}{n} \sum_{i=1}^{n} \eta_i (y_i - \bar{y}) \to E(\eta_i y_i^t) = - a\sigma^2,$$

$$\frac{1}{n} \sum_{i=1}^{n} (y_i - \bar{y})^2 \to E(y_i^t)^2 + \lim \frac{1}{n} \sum_{i=1}^{n} (y_i^p - \bar{y}^p)^2 = \sigma^2 + S^2.$$

It follows from (54) that:

$$a^* \to a - \frac{a\sigma^2}{\sigma^2 + S^2} = aP_r. \tag{55}$$

The estimated coefficient a^* tends therefore to a limit proportional to the true coefficient a, the proportionality coefficient P_r being the ratio between the variance of permanent income and the variance of observed income.

$$P_r = \frac{S^2}{S^2 + \sigma^2}. \tag{56}$$

Similarly the estimated coefficient b^*, equal to:

$$\bar{c} - a^* \bar{y} = (a - a^*)\bar{y} + b + \bar{\eta},$$

tends to the limit:

$$b \to b + a(1 - P_r)\bar{y}. \tag{57}$$

As P_r is less than 1, the estimated regression line will tend to have a lower gradient than the line which represents the true relationship between c_i and y_i^p, and to have a greater intercept on the c-axis. The marginal propensity to consume will be underestimated, to a degree which will increase as P_r decreases, or as the variance of transitory income increases relative to the variance of permanent income.

This analysis has an effect on the interpretation of the results of inquiries into family budgets. The regression lines obtained directly for different groups of households may have different gradients, even if the behavior of these groups is identical, since all that is required is that their coefficients P_r should differ. Thus we may expect that the transitory income in agriculture will be higher

---

[†] See ch. 10, § 3 for additional remarks on the establishments of these limits.

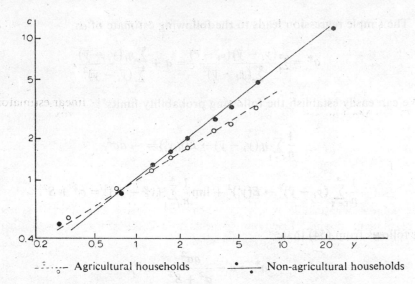

_-:-:--_ Agricultural households   _•——_ Non-agricultural households

Fig. 6. Consumption and income in families in the United States (1935–1936, in thousands of dollars).

than in other occupations. Indeed we see that the estimated marginal propensity a^* is lower. (See, for example[†], fig. 6.)

The usual statistical tests can therefore lead to wrong conclusions, since they assume a model which does not hold in this case. Thus a Student test on the data for fig. 6 would lead us to reject the hypothesis that the marginal propensity to consume was identical for farm and for non-farm families. But this test is not justified if decisions to consume depend on permanent income rather than observed income.

We need a different statistical theory from that described in ch. 3 if we are to deal with models in which the explanatory variables are not directly observed. Chapter 10 will be devoted to such '_models with errors in the variables_', which can obviously be applied in many situations other than the present one. Discussion of the most appropriate tests or methods of estimation for such models would be premature at this point.

According to Friedman, the distinction between observed and permanent income is indispensable for the interpretation of aggregate time series as well as for that of family budgets. Besides the observed income Y_t of an entire group of

---

[†] The graph in fig. 6 is taken from FRIEDMAN [1957], p. 59. It shows the regression lines between consumption and observed income. The points represent the mean income of households in the same class of _observed_ income. The bias is explained by the fact that the points furthest to the right correspond to households which have on the average a positive transitory income, and therefore an observed income higher than their permanent income. An unbiased estimate of a and b could be obtained if we could find the average consumption of households classified according to _permanent_ income, since it would be sufficient to fit a line to the corresponding representative points.

households during a period t, we should define its permanent income Y_t^p and its transistory income Y_t^t during the same period. The model (48)–(49) then applies after an obvious change in notation. A direct regression between consumption C_t and income Y_t would lead to underestimation of the true marginal propensity to consume. The bias would decrease as the variance of transitory income decrease relative to the variance of permanent income.

This analysis clearly illustrates a situation which we mentioned previously and which is revealed in the last column of the following table. The marginal propensity estimated by simple regression tends to be lower when the data cover a shorter period of time, and when income shows a smaller increase over the period. The variance of permanent income is then correspondingly reduced.

Since the income observed during the period is an imperfect measure of the true explanatory variable, would it not be possible to find a better approximation to permanent income? Friedman suggests an average of incomes in the period of observation and some preceding periods. Where global consumption is concerned, he proposes estimating permanent income by:

$$(1 - c) \sum_{\tau=0}^{\infty} c^{\tau} Y_{t-\tau}, \qquad (58)$$

where c is positive and less than 1. According to this formula, permanent income would depend on all previous developments in observed income, but the weight given to previous years would decrease exponentially with time.

The introduction of this formula for permanent income into a global regression

TABLE 1

Relations between consumption and income in the United States
in different periods[†]

Period	Average income[††]	Average propensity to consume	Marginal propensity to consume
1897–1906	420	0.89	0.72
1907–1916	495	0.89	0.65
1919–1929	591	0.88	0.60
1929–1941	607	0.94	0.45
1897–1949[†††]	558	0.90	0.82

[†] Consumption does not include expenditure on consumer durable goods, but does include an evaluation of their services. The source is FRIEDMAN [1957], p. 126.
[††] Average annual disposable income per head, in dollars at 1929 prices.
[†††] The war years 1917, 1918 and 1942–1945 are excluded.

of the type:

$$C_t = aY_t^p + b + \varepsilon_t \tag{59}$$

leads to a model with distributed lags on observed income (in fact almost exactly to eq. (15) above). Therefore we come back to a type of equation already discussed. The hypothesis of permanent income gives a new meaning to the regressions shown in section 4.

However, the difficulty is not completely resolved by substitution of an observable value for the unobservable notion of permanent income, since expression (58) does not measure it perfectly. Therefore there will still be an error in the explanatory variable when Y_t^p has been replaced in model (59) by a weighted mean of the $Y_{t-\tau}$, and we shall still have to investigate the resulting bias in the estimation of the propensity to consume.

The distinction between observed variable and true explanatory variable raises other problems when the model has to be used for prediction. Will the prediction be conditional with respect to a given value of the explanatory variable, or with respect to a value of the observed variable? What are the suitable formulae in each case, and what are then the properties of the predictions? These questions are too involved for present discussion, but will be dealt with in ch. 10 which is concerned with models with errors in the variables.

8   Conclusion

This rather brief discussion of an applied econometric problem has demonstrated the importance of specification of the model on which statistical estimation is based. Different models generally lead to different results, and the best specification is not obvious a priori.

It is really the task of theoretical analysis to determine the appropriate model for each practical problem and to specify completely its random characteristics. Unfortunately economic theory often still lacks sufficient precision to provide the econometrician with a framework on which he can rely. He must always have a highly critical attitude when choosing his model.

Can the model not be found by some rigorous inductive method? Or less ambitiously, can a choice between two models not be based on the facts? As we saw in ch. 2, every inference presupposes a set of assumptions, that is, a model. The choice between two models can be decided empirically only when both are particular cases of a more general model for which an inference procedure can be established.

We could certainly follow this principle and attempt to choose from the different models discussed in this chapter. To take a relatively simple case, suppose that we have to decide between the two specifications:

$$C_t = a_0 Y_t + a_1 Y_{t-1} + b + \varepsilon_t \tag{9}$$

and

$$C_t = a_0 Y_t + c C_{t-1} + b + \varepsilon_t. \tag{10}$$

In this case we consider the model:

$$C_t = a_0 Y_t + a_1 Y_{t-1} + c C_{t-1} + b + \varepsilon_t. \tag{60}$$

The specifications (9) and (10) are particular cases of this model subject to the additional assumptions $c = 0$ for (9) and $a_1 = 0$ for (10). A rigorous statistical method could be used for choosing between these two assumptions on the basis of an observed sample. We shall consider it at the end of ch. 8.

Unfortunately, economic data are not plentiful enough to allow fruitful application of this principle as soon as the situation is even slightly complex. In most cases the choice of model will result from an analysis in which our empirical knowledge will be less rigorously taken into account.

Subsequent parts of the book will describe the statistical methods appropriate to some of the models on which econometric studies have been based up till now, Throughout the rest of the book the specification of the selected models will be discussed only incidentally. However, the reader must never forget that in practice the choice of a good model is as important as the application of a correct statistical method.

Part 2

LINEAR ESTIMATION

CHAPTER 5

The general theory of linear estimation

Part 2 is devoted to the statistical treatment of linear models similar to that discussed in ch. 3, but containing several variables. We shall no longer be concerned with the conceptual problems arising from definition of the model, which have already been fully discussed. Obviously no new logical difficulty is raised by increasing the number of variables.

As the reader may well expect after reading ch. 3, we shall now go on to give strong justification for the methods of multiple regression. We shall make a close study not only of the general theory on which they are based, but also of the particular problems arising from their use in econometrics. At many points we shall complete the previous discussion of simple regression.

In the present chapter we shall examine a geometric model, that allows direct formulation of the general theory, which will later be applied in several different situations. Geometric intuition is often very helpful for the type of problems to be dealt with, since the essential properties can be more easily understood when they receive simple geometric interpretations[†].

In particular, the following presentation broaches in a natural way two difficulties raised by a truly general discussion of the problem: in the first place, the fact that the covariance matrix Q may be singular (see equation (2) below), and in the second place, the fact that the matrix Z of the known multipliers of the coefficients to be estimated may have rank less than the number of the coefficients (see section 6(i) below). Recent statistical literature deals with these problems by bringing in various concepts for the 'generalized inverse' of a singular matrix and using the notion of 'estimable linear function' of the coefficients[††]. But the algebraic proofs, which in any case are often very heavy, hardly reveal the true nature of the properties.

Some of the formulae resulting from these proofs do indeed suggest methods of calculation in practical applications; but the formulae in question can easily be derived from the properties themselves (see section 6).

[†] The geometric representations to be used will involve vectors, linear manifolds and sets in n-dimensional Euclidean space. The simplest results of the theory of Euclidean spaces will be used without proof, and we shall establish only the less well-known properties. The theory of vector spaces of finite dimension is fully discussed in HALMOS [1948].

[††] See, for example, SCHÖNFELD [1968] or RAO [1972] and, for the use of estimable linear functions, SCHEFFÉ [1959] and RAO [1965].

We must also point out that the formulation given in this chapter would be more elegant if it used the language of affine geometry and not the rather more restrictive language of Euclidean geometry[†]. But it would also be less accessible to many readers.

For those who wish to avoid geometric proofs, the appendix to this chapter gives an algebraic treatment of the principal properties, limited to the case in which neither of the two particular difficulties mentioned above appears.

1   The linear hypothesis

We start by defining the problem that is the subject of this chapter.

Let x be a random vector in a Euclidean space, which can have any dimension n. We assume that x has a expected value y, say:

$$y = E(x) \tag{1}$$

and a covariance matrix, which is, by definition:

$$Q = E[(x - y)(x - y)'] \tag{2}$$

and is independent of y. (As is clear from the definition, the diagonal elements of the covariance matrix are the variances of the components of x).

We know that y must necessarily belong to a linear manifold[††] or vector subspace, L, of p dimensions in the n-dimensional space considered. But *a priori* we know nothing about the position of y in L.

The general problem of linear estimation can be defined in the following terms[†††]:

Problem P.   *Given an observation on the random vector x, its covariance matrix Q and the linear subspace L which contains its mean y, estimate the position of y in L.*

[†] It has certainly long been known that linear estimation theory can be expressed in terms of affine geometry. KRUSKAL [1961] advocated its use, showed how the principal results could be stated and used it in the investigation of a particular problem. DRYGAS [1970] systematically uses the affine geometry approach in dealing with linear estimation and shows how the results in this book can be established.

PHILOCHE [1971] gives an elegant proof of the Gauss-Markov theorem by considering the dual space of the vector space to which the sample belongs. His approach has some affinities with that followed in geometric proofs.

[††] By definition, a set L in a vector space is a '*linear manifold*' or equivalently a '*vector subspace*' if, for any real number α and any vectors y^1 and y^2 of L, αy^1 and $y^1 + y^2$ belong to L.

[†††] The model specified in the statement of the problem P is often called the '*linear hypothesis*'.

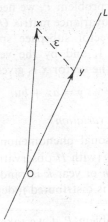

Fig. 1.

We shall often write:

$$\varepsilon = x - y; \tag{3}$$

so that ε is a vector with zero mean and covariance matrix Q.

We shall consider three simple examples which demonstrate how the problem P arises in mathematical statistics and in econometrics. There will be other examples in later chapters.

(a) *The mean of a sample of independent observations*

Given T independent observations, $x_1, x_2, \ldots, x_T$, on the same real random variable whose variance is defined, we wish to estimate its mean, a. If x is the vector of the x_t, this problem comes into the above category. The covariance matrix Q is $\sigma^2 I$, where σ denotes the standard deviation of the random variable, and I the unit matrix of order T.

The vector subspace L is defined in this case as the set of vectors whose components are all equal, since:

$$y_t = a \qquad \text{for} \qquad t = 1, 2, \ldots, T. \tag{4}$$

The subspace is one-dimensional.

(b) *Model of simple regression*

Returning to the problem of ch. 3, we suppose that, for a given value of z_t, the mean of the random variable x_t is equal to $az_t + b$, where a and b are real parameters about which nothing is known. We suppose further that the deviation from the mean:

$$\varepsilon_t = x_t - az_t - b$$

is distributed with variance σ^2, independently of z_t. Given T independent observations, $x_1, x_2, \ldots, x_T$, on x_t, corresponding to non-identical values, $z_1, z_2, \ldots, z_T$, of z_t, we wish to estimate the parameters a and b.

To reduce this case to the problem P, we need only take for x the vector of the observations on x_t. The covariance matrix Q is then $\sigma^2 I$. The linear manifold L is the two-dimensional vector subspace spanned by the vector u whose components are identically 1, and by the vector z whose components are $z_1, z_2, \ldots, z_T$. The mean y of the vector x is given by:

$$y = az + bu. \tag{5}$$

(c) *A simple case of seasonal variation*[†]

Suppose that for some seasonal phenomenon we have a series of monthly observations x_{hk} over K years (with H observations per year). Suppose that the value x_{hk} observed in month h of year k is random with mean a_h and standard deviation σ, and in addition is distributed independently of h, of k and of the other x_{hk}.

This is reduced to the problem P if we take for x the vector of the observations:

$$x_{11}, x_{21}, \ldots, x_{hk}, \ldots, x_{HK}$$

a vector in HK dimensions. The matrix Q is then $\sigma^2 I$. The linear manifold L is the H-dimensional subspace defined by the $H(K-1)$ equalities:

$$y_{11} = y_{12} = \cdots = y_{1K}$$
$$\cdots\cdots\cdots\cdots\cdots\cdots\cdots$$
$$y_{h1} = y_{h2} = \cdots = y_{hK} \tag{6}$$
$$\cdots\cdots\cdots\cdots\cdots\cdots\cdots$$
$$y_{H1} = y_{H2} = \cdots = y_{HK}.$$

2 Concentration ellipsoid of a random vector[††]

For the geometric approach to the problem P, we must give a representation of the dispersion of the random variable x, and the most suitable is the concentration ellipsoid defined by DARMOIS [1945].

Definition 1. The concentration ellipsoid of an n-dimensional random vector that has a covariance matrix Q is the set E of n-dimensional vectors ε such that:

$$|u'\varepsilon| \leqq 1 \quad \text{for every } u \text{ such that}^{[†††]} \quad u'Qu \leqq 1. \tag{7}$$

[†] In practice, the study of seasonal phenomena obviously involves more complex models, as we shall see in ch. 12.

[††] The proofs in sections 2 to 5 have been improved as a result of detailed comments by P. C. B. Phillips and L. D. Taylor on the second edition of this book.

[†††] At this stage, and during the rest of the chapter, the reader familiar with the theory of vector spaces will follow the argument more easily if he thinks of the vectors $u, v, \ldots$ as belonging to the dual space of the space containing the vectors $x, \varepsilon, \eta, \ldots$

When Q is singular there exist non-zero vectors u such that $Qu=0$ or $u'Qu=0$. For these vectors, which are considered as non-random, we therefore have, from the definition of Q,

$$E[u'(x-y)]^2 = 0;$$

that is, $u'(x-y)=0$ with probability 1.

The vector $x-y$ is therefore almost certainly contained in the linear subspace S orthogonal to all those vectors u satisfying $Qu=0$.

This linear subspace S is called the *support* of $x-y$. Its dimension is equal to the rank r of Q.

The support of $x-y$ is also the image of the n-space under the transformation which takes x into Qx. To see this, observe that (i) this image is an r-dimensional linear subspace, and (ii) it is contained in S, since if $v=Qx$ and $Qu=0$, then $v'u=x'Q'u=x'Qu=0$.

The concentration ellipsoid E of x is contained in S. For suppose there exists a vector ε of E which does not belong to S. Then there exists a vector u such that $u'\varepsilon\neq0$ and $u'Qu=0$. There also exists a number α such that $\alpha u'\varepsilon>1$. The vector $v=\alpha u$ satisfies both $v'\varepsilon>1$ and $v'Qv=0$, which is impossible because of the condition (7) on ε.

It is sometimes convenient to replace definition 1 by:

Definition 1′. The concentration ellipsoid of an n-dimensional random vector that has a covariance Q is the set of n-dimensional vectors ε such that $\varepsilon=Qv$ for some vector v for which $v'Qv\leq1$.

The equivalence with definition 1 is proved as follows.

(i) If $\varepsilon=Qv$, then Schwarz inequality implies:

$$(u'\varepsilon)^2 = (u'Qv)^2 \leq u'Qu \cdot v'Qv$$

and (7) follows from $v'Qv\leq1$.

(ii) If ε is in E according to definition 1, then $\varepsilon=Qv$ for some v since ε belongs to S. Assume $v'Qv=\beta^2>1$ and select $u=v/\beta$ so that $u'Qu=1$, then $u'\varepsilon=\beta>1$, a contradiction with inequality (7).

We can verify immediately that, if x is one-dimensional, the concentration ellipsoid is simply the interval:

$$-\sigma \leq \varepsilon \leq \sigma,$$

where σ denotes the standard deviation of x.

Figures 2 and 3 show the concentration ellipsoids of two-dimensional random vectors. The parameters σ_1 and σ_2 are the standard deviations of the two components x_1 and x_2, and ϱ is their correlation coefficient. Figure 3 corresponds to the case where $\varrho=1$, and the covariance matrix Q is singular.

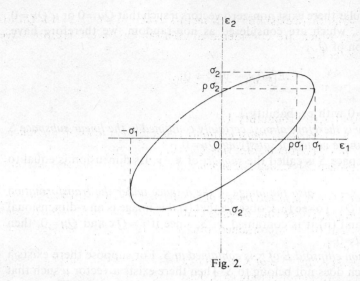

Fig. 2.

In practice, condition (7) is not very convenient to apply. This is why we shall refer instead to the results contained in the following proposition.

Proposition 1. (i) If the covariance matrix Q of x is non-singular, the concentration ellipsoid E of x is the set of vectors ε satisfying[†].

$$\varepsilon' Q^{-1} \varepsilon \leq 1. \tag{8}$$

(ii) If Q has rank r less than n and if the support of x is defined by $R'x = 0$ with a matrix R of order $n \times (n-r)$ and of rank $n-r$ such that $QR = 0$, then the concentration ellipsoid of x is the set of vectors ε satisfying $R'\varepsilon = 0$ and

$$\varepsilon' (Q + RR')^{-1} \varepsilon \leq 1. \tag{9}$$

(iii) Conversely, if the concentration ellipsoid of x is defined by the system $V\varepsilon = 0$ and $\varepsilon' U^{-1} \varepsilon \leq 1$ with a matrix V of order $[(n-r) \times n]$ and rank $n-r$, then the covariance matrix of x is

$$Q = U - UV'(VUV')^{-1} VU. \tag{10}$$

We shall prove properties (ii) and (iii). The proof of (i) is parallel to the proof of (ii), and we shall not repeat it.

We have already seen that every vector ε of the concentration ellipsoid must belong to the support S, that is, must satisfy $R'\varepsilon = 0$. To establish (9), we start

---

[†] This formula shows that, when Q is non-singular, the concentration ellipsoid is homothetic to the concentration ellipsoid introduced by H. Cramer [1946].

from the equality[†]:

$$Q = Q(Q+RR')^{-1}Q.$$

which applies in the conditions fixed for Q and R (this equation shows that $Q+RR'$ is a *generalized inverse* or 'g-inverse' of the singular matrix Q, according to the new terminology). Let W be the symmetric matrix such that $W^2 = (Q+RR')^{-1}$. The condition $u'Qu < 1$ is then equivalent to the condition that the length of WQu is at most 1, while (9) says that the length of $W\varepsilon$ is at most 1. Finally, for any vector ε such that $R'\varepsilon = 0$, the scalar product $u'\varepsilon$ is equal to the scalar product of WQu by $W\varepsilon$; for, $u'QW^2\varepsilon = u'Q(Q+RR')^{-1}\varepsilon = u'(Q+RR')^{-1}Q\varepsilon = u'\varepsilon$ (the second equality follows from the fact that $QR = R'Q = 0$ implies $Q(Q+RR') = Q^2 = (Q+RR')Q$, and the third from the fact that $R'\varepsilon = 0$ implies $Q\varepsilon = (Q+RR')\varepsilon$). Therefore:

(a) If ε satisfies (9) and $R'\varepsilon = 0$ it satisfies condition (7). For[††], the vector $W\varepsilon$ whose length is at most 1 cannot have a scalar product greater than 1 with the vector WQu whose length is at most 1.

(b) If ε satisfies condition (7) it also satisfies (9). Indeed it then satisfies $R'\varepsilon = 0$. The two vectors $W\varepsilon$ and WQu both belong to the image of S under the transformation $x \to Wx$. In fact WQu can be any vector of this image, subject to the sole condition that its length does not exceed 1. In particular, it can be the

---

[†] Consider the following lemma:

LEMMA.   If Q is a positive semi-definite matrix of order n and rank r, if R is a matrix of order $n \times (n-r)$ and rank $n-r$ such that $QR = 0$, then $Q+RR'$ is positive definite and

$$Q = Q(Q+RR')^{-1}Q,$$

For, applying the lemma in the footnote to page 36, we can define a symmetric matrix C of rank r such that $Q = C^2$. The equality $R'QR = 0$, or $R'C'CR = 0$, then implies $CR = 0$ (the vector defined by the elements of any column of CR has zero length). $R'R$ is a positive definite non-singular matrix; its inverse is positive definite; so there exists a non-singular symmetric matrix D such that $(R'R)^{-1} = D^2$ or $DR'RD = I$ (premultiply the two terms by $DR'R$ and postmultiply them by D^{-1}). The above equalities then imply

$$(C+RDR')^2 = Q+RR'$$

and

$$(C+RDR')C = Q.$$

Hence the equality to be proved follows directly if $Q+RR'$ is non-singular, as we shall establish.

For, consider a vector w such that $(Q+RR')w = 0$; the two vectors $RR'w$ and Qw have zero sum and are orthogonal since $w'RR'Qw = 0$. So each of them is zero. Since $Qw = 0$, then w is a linear combination of the columns of R. So there exists a vector s with $n-r$ components such that $w = Rs$. But then $RR'Rs = RR'w = 0$. Since the matrix $RR'R$ has rank $n-r$, the vector s is zero; consequently the vector w is zero also, and this is what we had to prove.

[††] The property according to which the scalar product of two vectors cannot exceed the product of their lengths is the well-known Schwarz inequality (cf. BASS [1956], p. 42).

vector of length 1 which is collinear with $W\varepsilon$. For the scalar product of $W\varepsilon$ and WQu never to exceed 1, it is necessary therefore that the length of $W\varepsilon$ should be at most 1, that is, that (9) should be satisfied.

We now go on to the proof of (iii). Let F be the symmetric matrix such that $U = F^2$. The two conditions $V\varepsilon = 0$ and $\varepsilon' U^{-1}\varepsilon \le 1$ imply that $F^{-1}\varepsilon$ belongs to the vector subspace H of the vectors η satisfying $VF\eta = 0$ and has length at most 1. It is equivalent to say[†] that $F^{-1}\varepsilon$ must have a scalar product which does not exceed 1 in absolute value, with any vector Fu whose orthogonal projection on H has length at most 1. Now, the orthogonal projection of Fu on H is the vector Gu defined by

$$Gu = [I - FV'(VF^2V')^{-1}VF]Fu$$

(this expression follows from (19) which will be established in section 6 (ii) of this chapter).

The two conditions $V\varepsilon = 0$ and $\varepsilon' U^{-1}\varepsilon \le 1$ are therefore equivalent to: $|u'\varepsilon| \le 1$ for any u such that $u'G'Gu \le 1$. This result shows that $G'G$ is the required covariance matrix Q. Now,

$$G = F[I - V'(VUV')^{-1}VU]$$

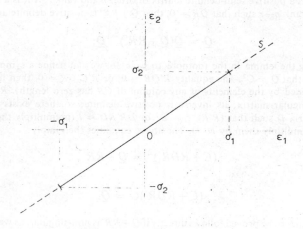

Fig. 3.

[†] For, let x be a vector of H and z the orthogonal projection on H of a vector y. The orthogonality between x and $(y-z)$ implies $y'x = z'x$. Consequently if $|x| \le 1$ and $|z| \le 1$, the Schwarz inequality implies $|y'x| \le 1$. Conversely, if $|y'x| \le 1$ for any y such that $|z| \le 1$, then $|x| \le 1$. For we can always choose y so that z is collinear with x and has length 1, so that $|y'x| = |x|$.

and so

$$Q = G'G = U - UV'(VUV')^{-1}VU,$$

which is what we had to prove[†].

3 Linear estimators

To estimate y in L from an observation on the vector x we shall study certain *estimators*, that is, certain functions $f(x)$ which associate with each vector x a vector in L, so that $f(x^*)$ is our estimate of y when x^* is the observed value.

We shall concentrate attention on linear estimators, that is, on those which satisfy the following two properties:

$$f(x^1 + x^2) = f(x^1) + f(x^2)$$
$$f(\alpha x) = \alpha f(x)$$

for any vectors x, x^1, x^2 and any number α. Any such linear function $f(x)$ can be represented by a matrix G in the sense that $f(x) = Gx$.

The following result is fundamental for the study of linear estimators.

Lemma 1. If $f(x)$ is a linear transformation from one Euclidean space into another, and if x is distributed with mean y and concentration ellipsoid E, then the mean and the concentration ellipsoid of the distribution of $f(x)$ are the images under the transformation f of y and E respectively. If x is normally distributed, so also is $f(x)$.

The matrix G of the transformation $f(x)$ is used in the proof of this property. If f is a mapping from n-dimensional space into m-dimensional space, G will have m rows and n columns, and it follows from the definition of G that $f(x) = Gx$ for every n-dimensional vector x.

(i) We can prove immediately that the expected value of $f(x)$ is equal to $f(y)$, since

$$E[Gx] = G \cdot E(x) = Gy$$

(ii) We shall show that the concentration ellipsoid of $f(x)$ is the image of E. The covariance matrix Q^* of $f(x)$ is GQG', since

$$Q^* = E[(Gx - Gy)(Gx - Gy)'] = E[G(x - y)(x - y)'G']$$
$$= G \cdot E[(x - y)(x - y)'] \cdot G' = GQG'.$$

[†] We note that if we start from a covariance matrix Q and a matrix R such that $QR = 0$ and apply successively parts (ii) and (iii) of proposition 1 with $U = Q + RR'$ and $V = R'$, then we find the same matrix Q. To verify this, we need only take account of the fact that then $UV' = (Q + RR')R = R(R'R)$ and $VUV' = (R'R)^2$.

The concentration ellipsoid E^* of $f(x)$ is therefore the set of vectors η such that:

$$|v'\eta| \leqq 1 \qquad \text{for every } v \text{ such that} \qquad v'GQG'v \leqq 1. \tag{11}$$

Now the image of E (the concentration ellipsoid of x) consists of the set of vectors η which can be written $G\varepsilon$ where ε satisfies the condition (7). We can prove that this image is identical with E^* by establishing the following properties (a) and (b).

(a) *The image of E is contained in E^*.* Let η be a vector of this image. We know that there exists a vector ε such that $\eta = G\varepsilon$ and $|u'\varepsilon| \leqq 1$ for every u such that $u'Qu \leqq 1$. Now let v be any vector such that $v'GQG'v \leqq 1$; let us consider $u = G'v$; $u'Qu \leqq 1$ and therefore $|u'\varepsilon| \leqq 1$, that is:

$$1 \geqq |u'\varepsilon| = |v'G\varepsilon| = |v'\eta|.$$

It follows that η belongs to E^*.

(b) *E^* is contained in the image of E.* Let η be a vector of E^*. Then, according to definition $1'$, $\eta = GQG'w$ for some w for which $w'GQG'w \leqq 1$. Let $v = G'w$, then $v'Qv \leqq 1$, so that $\varepsilon = Qv$ is in E. But $\eta = GQv = G\varepsilon$ is the image of ε.

(iii) Let us now establish that Gx is normally distributed if x is. The proof depends on the definition chosen for multivariate normal distributions. At the present time, the following is accepted as the best definition (see FRECHET [1951] and, for example, RAO [1965], § 8a):

The random vector x is normally distributed if any linear function $u'x$ of x has a normal distribution (u is any non-random vector).

To prove that Gx is normally distributed, we need only establish that $v'Gx$ is normal for any v. But this follows directly from the previous definition where $u = G'v$.

We might also refer to a more traditional definition according to which the random vector x with expected value y and covariance matrix Q is normally distributed if its characteristic function is

$$\varphi_x(u) = \exp\{iu'y - \tfrac{1}{2}u'Qu\}$$

(see, for example, CRAMER [1946], ch. 24).

By definition, the characteristic function of Gx is

$$\varphi_{Gx}(v) = E\{\exp iv'Gx\}.$$

This is obviously equal to $\varphi_x(G'v)$, that is, to

$$\exp\{iv'Gy - \tfrac{1}{2}v'GQG'v\}.$$

This is the characteristic function of a normal vector whose expectation is Gy and whose covariance matrix is GQG'.

This completes the proof of lemma 1.

This lemma is very important in the study of linear estimators. In particular, it explains why the whole theory can be presented in a formulation in which no coordinate system is chosen for the definition of the vectors of the sample space. It also demonstrates the usefulness of concentration ellipsoids as characteristics of second-order moments of random vectors.

In practice, when the formulation of the model gives a singular covariance matrix Q, we may consider carrying out a change of coordinates such that the support of the random vector coincides with the leading coordinate subspace and the problem can then be dealt with entirely in this subspace. But this method is often laborious, so that it is preferable to reason directly on the basis of the initial space. This is why we have not assumed in this chapter that Q is non-singular.

4   Vectors and linear manifolds conjugate with respect to a concentration ellipsoid

In what follows we shall use the notion of conjugacy with respect to an ellipsoid, and so we now recall its definition.

Definition 2.   Two vectors ε and η of the support S of a random vector x are said to be conjugate with respect to the concentration ellipsoid E of x if [†] :

$$u'Qv = 0 \tag{12}$$

for every pair of vectors u and v such that $\varepsilon = Qu$ and $\eta = Qv$.

The existence of vectors u and v satisfying $\varepsilon = Qu$, $\eta = Qv$ is guaranteed by the fact that ε and η belong the support of x and therefore to the image of n-dimensional space under the mapping $u \to Qu$.

When Q has an inverse, two vectors ε and η are conjugate if and only if they satisfy

$$\varepsilon'Q^{-1}\eta = 0. \tag{13}$$

In the case where Q has rank r less than n, we can establish a similar property. We need only use the equality [††] :

$$Q = Q(Q+RR')^{-1}Q$$

which applies with any matrix R of order $n \times (n-r)$ and rank $n-r$ such that $QR = 0$. The conjugate vectors ε and η then satisfy

$$\varepsilon'(Q+RR')^{-1}\eta = 0 \tag{14}$$

since $u'Qv = 0$ for two vectors u and v such that $\varepsilon = Qu$ and $\eta = Qv$, while

---

[†] *Translator's note.*   This is sometimes translated briefly as 'ε and η are E-conjugate'.
[††] See the lemma in the footnote to p. 163.

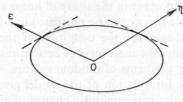

Fig. 4.

$u'Qv = u'Q(Q+RR')^{-1}Qv = \varepsilon'(Q+RR')^{-1}\eta$. Conversely, if two vectors ε and η of the support S satisfy (14), then the corresponding vectors u and v satisfy $u'Qv = 0$.

We can easily prove:

Proposition 2. *If G is a non-singular square matrix, $G\varepsilon$ and $G\eta$ are conjugate with respect to the concentration ellipsoid of Gx when ε and η are conjugate with respect to the concentration ellipsoid of x.* Consequently the relation of conjugacy is invariant under every change in the coordinate system.

From lemma 1, the support of Gx is the image of the support of x under the transformation with matrix G. Since the covariance matrix of Gx is GQG', we have to show that $u^{*'}GQG'v^* = 0$ for every pair of vectors such that $GQG'u^* = G\varepsilon$ and $GQG'v^* = G\eta$, or equivalently, since G has an inverse, $QG'u^* = \varepsilon$ and $QG'v^* = \eta$. Since ε and η are conjugate with respect to the concentration ellipsoid of x, $G'u^*$ and $G'v^*$ satisfy $(G'u^*)' \ Q(G'v^*) = 0$, which implies that $u^{*'}GQG'v^* = 0$, as was to be proved.

In particular, if Q has an inverse, there exists, by the lemma in the footnote to page 36, a non-singular matrix C such that $Q = C'C$. The conjugacy of ε and η with respect to the concentration ellipsoid of x is equivalent to the orthogonality of $C^{-1}\varepsilon$ and $C^{-1}\eta$.

When Q does not have an inverse we can still find a non-singular transformation which identifies the support of Gx with the leading coordinate subspace of appropriate dimension, and the concentration ellipsoid of Gx with a sphere in this subspace (cf. proposition 3 below). The conjugacy of ε and η is then equivalent to the orthogonality of the two vectors $G\varepsilon$ and $G\eta$ of this subspace.

All the properties of orthogonal vectors can therefore be carried over to vectors conjugate with respect to an ellipsoid E.

A vector is said to be conjugate to a linear subspace L with respect to the concentration ellipsoid of x if it is conjugate to every vector of L. Clearly this definition applies only if L belongs to the support S of $x-y$.

The set of vectors ε conjugate to the subspace L (contained in the support of $x-y$) is a linear subspace K called the *principal conjugate vector subspace of L*. If L is p-dimensional and Q has rank r, the subspace K has dimension $r-p$. The proof follows immediately from the next result.

Proposition 3. Given a p-dimensional linear manifold L contained in the support S of $x - y$, there exists a linear transformation of n-dimensional space onto itself which transform the manifold L into the leading p-dimensional coordinate subspace, and the concentration ellipsoid E of x into the unit sphere in the leading r-dimensional coordinate subspace, r being the rank of Q.

Since the support S of $x - y$ is an r-dimensional linear subspace, there obviously exists a non-singular matrix G_0 such that the transformation $x \rightarrow G_0 x$ maps S onto the leading r-dimensional coordinate subspace[†]. The covariance matrix of $G_0 x$ is then of the form:

$$G_0 Q G_0' = \begin{bmatrix} Q_1 & 0 \\ 0 & 0 \end{bmatrix},$$

where Q_1 is a positive definite square matrix of order r, and the zeros are matrices containing only zero elements. There exists a non-singular symmetric square matrix C_1 such that $Q_1 = C_1^2$. Let C be the non-singular matrix:

$$C = \begin{bmatrix} C_1 & 0 \\ 0 & I \end{bmatrix},$$

where I is the unit matrix of order $n - r$. The transformation with matrix $C^{-1} G_0$ transforms E into the unit sphere in the leading r-dimensional coordinate subspace[††]. Finally there exists a change of coordinates in this space such that L becomes its leading p-dimensional coordinate subspace, that is, there exists an orthonormal matrix P of the form:

$$P = \begin{bmatrix} P_1 & 0 \\ 0 & I \end{bmatrix}$$

such that the transformation with matrix $G = PC^{-1} G_0$ satisfies the conditions of proposition 3. Moreover the covariance matrix of Gx can be written:

$$GQG' = \begin{bmatrix} I & 0 \\ 0 & 0 \end{bmatrix}, \tag{15}$$

where I is the unit matrix of order r.

[†] To construct G_0, we need only choose a system of n orthogonal vectors, the first r of which belong to S, and then define G_0 as the matrix which transforms this system into the system of unit vectors on the coordinate axes.

[††] For, if $\eta = C^{-1} G_0 \varepsilon$, then $\varepsilon = G_0^{-1} C\eta$. The ellipsoid E is the set of vectors ε such that $R'\varepsilon = 0$ and $\varepsilon'(Q + RR')^{-1}\varepsilon \leq 1$. Its image is the set of vectors η such that $V\eta = 0$ and $\eta' U^{-1}\eta \leq 1$ where $V = R'G_0^{-1}C$ and $U = C^{-1} G_0 (Q + RR') G_0' C^{-1}$. Applying part (iii) of proposition 1 and taking account of the fact that $QR = 0$, we find that $VU = (R'R)R'G_0'C^{-1}$ and $VUV' = (R'R)^2$; therefore the concentration ellipsoid of $C^{-1}G_0 x$ corresponds to the covariance matrix $C^{-1} G_0 Q G_0' C^{-1}$, whose form is the right hand side of (15). This ellipsoid is therefore the unit sphere in the leading r-dimensional coordinate subspace.

Let L^*, S^* and E^* denote the images of L, S and E under the transformation with matrix G defined above. Two vectors ε^* and η^* will be E^*-conjugate if and only if they both belong to S^* and are mutually orthogonal. The set K^* of vectors E^*-conjugate to L^* is then the $(p+1, p+2, \ldots, r)$th-coordinate subspace. It follows from proposition 2 that the principal conjugate linear manifold of L is the $(r-p)$-dimensional subspace which is the image of K^* under the transformation with matrix G^{-1}.

It follows also that, *if K is the principal conjugate linear manifold of L, then L is the principal conjugate linear manifold of K.*

5 Generalization of the method of least squares

Let us return to the problem P and suppose from now on that the subspace L which contains the mean y is contained in the support S of $x-y$ (which is known since Q is known). If this were not so, it would be easy to reduce the problem to this case[†].

As we have said, the usual estimators are linear. More precisely, they are determined by *projections* of the n-dimensional space on the linear variety L, that is, by linear transformations which leave the vectors of L invariant and transform the whole space into L.

The projections yield unbiased estimates, as can be proved immediately by applying lemma 1 to the expected value y of x. The expected value of $f(x)$ is $f(y)$ which, in the case of a projection, is just y. Conversely, in order that a linear estimator should have an expected value equal to the expectation y of x, for every y in L, it is necessary that $f(y)$ should equal y for every y in L; so $f(x)$ must be a projection of n-dimensional space onto L. (Note that we have here used the fact that the position of y in L is completely unknown a priori.)

The absence of bias in the estimator of y provides some justification for estimators based on projections. However, we might be interested in allowing some bias if we could thereby reduce the dispersion of the errors $f(x)-y$. So we shall return in section 9 to the justification of the estimators under discussion.

If we confine ourselves to projection estimators, the concentration ellipsoid of $f(x)$ provides a picture of the dispersion of the errors $f(x)-y$. It is therefore

---

[†] For let L_1 denote the intersection of S and L, and L_2 a complementary subspace of L_1 in L, such that every vector y of L can be expressed uniquely as the sum of two vectors y_1 of L_1 and y_2 of L_2. Since the vector $x-y$ belongs almost certainly to S, x belongs almost certainly to the subspace $S+L_2$. We can therefore write x uniquely as x_1+x_2 where x_1 belongs to S and x_2 to L_2. The vector $x-y$ is then expressed as the sum of two vectors x_1-y_1 and x_2-y_2. The former clearly belongs to S, and since $x-y$ almost certainly belongs to S, x_2-y_2 is also almost certainly in S. But in addition, x_2-y_2 must belong to L_2. It follows that x_2-y_2 is almost certainly zero.

In this case x_2 will be an estimate of y_2. It will remain to determine y_1 in L_1 by means of an observation on x_1. This brings us back to the problem P.

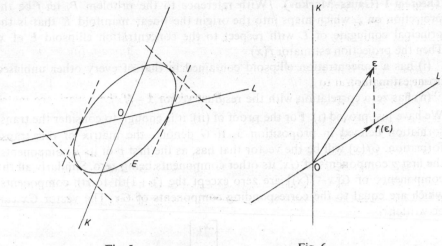

Fig. 5.   Fig. 6.

natural, when faced with a choice between two estimators to prefer the one with the smaller concentration ellipsoid. We shall now study a particular estimator which has the property that its concentration ellipsoid is contained in that of every other projection estimator, this being true for all y.

We know that the concentration ellipsoid of a projection of x on L is the image of E under this projection (cf. lemma 1). Therefore this ellipsoid contains the intersection of E and L. We shall show that it is just this intersection when the projection maps into 0 (the origin) the linear manifold K that is the principal E-conjugate of L. (We shall say that the projection is parallel to K.)

Let us suppose that this is not the case, and that there exists a vector ε of E whose projection on L parallel to K does not belong to the intersection of E and L. Let u be a vector that maximizes $u'f(\varepsilon)$ subject to the condition $u'Qu \leqq 1$. Since $f(\varepsilon)$ does not belong to E, $|u'f(\varepsilon)| > 1$. Also the derivatives of $u'f(\varepsilon) - ku'Qu$ with respect to the components of u must be zero (k being a Lagrange multiplier). It follows that $f(\varepsilon) = 2kQu$ for some number k. Now consider the vector $\varepsilon^* = \varepsilon - f(\varepsilon)$. The vector ε belonging to E is contained in the support of $x - y$, and so also is ε^* since L is contained in this support. Under the projection considered, the image of ε^* is the zero vector, and is therefore contained in K and consequently conjugate to $f(\varepsilon)$. Then let u^* be a vector such that $\varepsilon^* = Qu^*$. The fact that ε^* and $f(\varepsilon)$ are conjugate implies $2ku'Qu^* = 0$, or again $u'\varepsilon^* = 0$. It follows that:
$$|u'\varepsilon| = |u'f(\varepsilon) + u'\varepsilon^*| = |u'f(\varepsilon)| > 1,$$
which contradicts the assumption that ε belongs to E, since $u'Qu \leqq 1$.

So under a projection parallel to K of n-dimensional space onto L, the concentration ellipsoid of $f(x)$ becomes the intersection of L with the concentration ellipsoid of x.

Therefore we have:

Theorem 1 (Gauss–Markov).   With reference to the problem P, let f be the projection on L which maps into the origin the linear manifold K that is the principal conjugate of L with respect to the concentration ellipsoid E of x. Then the projection estimator $f(x)$

(i) has a concentration ellipsoid contained in that of every other unbiased linear estimator;

(ii) has zero correlation with the residual vector $x - f(x)$.

We have just proved (i). For the proof of (ii), it is enough to consider the transformation defined in proposition 3. If G denotes the matrix of this transformation, $Gf(x)$ will be the vector that has, as the first p of its n components, the first p components of Gx, its other components being zero. Similarly all the components of $G[x - f(x)]$ are zero except the $(p+1)$th to rth components, which are equal to the corresponding components of Gx. The vector Gx can be written:

$$Gx = \begin{bmatrix} x_L \\ x_K \\ 0 \end{bmatrix}, \tag{16}$$

where the vectors x_L and x_K contain the non-zero components of $Gf(x)$ and $G[x - f(x)]$ respectively.

Now from (15), the covariance matrix of Gx is such that:

$$E(x_L x_L') = I, \qquad E(x_K x_K') = I, \qquad E(x_L x_K') = 0. \tag{17}$$

The last equality obviously implies:

$$E\{Gf(x)[G(x - f(x))]'\} = 0$$

or

$$G\{E[f(x)[x - f(x)]']\}G' = 0.$$

Since G is non-singular it follows that the covariances of the components of $f(x)$ with those of $x - f(x)$ are zero.

Theorem 1 strongly justifies the estimator under discussion. It follows from this theorem and lemma 1 that the variance of every linear form of the coordinates of $f(x)$ is less than, or at most equal to, the variance of the same linear form of the coordinates of every other projection estimator[†]. The estimator $f(x)$ has therefore the smallest dispersion of all unbiased linear estimators, at least if dispersion is measured by second order moments. (Clearly this would not be true for other measures of dispersion, for example, mean deviation.)

[†] The standard deviation of a linear form $a'x$ of a random vector x is measured on the image of the concentration ellipsoid E of x under the linear transformation $x \to a'x$. If the concentration ellipsoid E_1 of the vector x_1 contains the concentration ellipsoid E_2 of the vector x_2, then var $(a'x_1) \geq$ var $(a'x_2)$.

The only restriction that this result imposes on the distribution of x is that it should have second-order moments. It is of particular interest in econometrics, since the distribution of the 'errors' is rarely known.

We must still demonstrate how to calculate this estimate in practice, which leads us to the following proposition[†].

Proposition 4. If the covariance matrix Q is regular, the Gauss-Markov estimator is that which minimizes $(x-y^*)'Q^{-1}(x-y^*)$, the vector y^* being restricted to lie in L. If Q has rank r less than n and if R is the matrix of order $n \times (n-r)$ and rank $n-r$ such that $QR = 0$, then y^* is the vector in L which minimizes the quantity[††]

$$(x-y^*)'(Q+RR')^{-1}(x-y^*).$$

The proof is the same for both parts of the proposition. We shall establish the second part. The vector $\varepsilon^* = x - y^*$ already considered in the proof of theorem 1 is conjugate with L. Then let y^0 be any vector in L; $y^0 - y^*$ and $x - y^*$ are conjugate. So (14) implies

$$(y^0 - y^*)'(Q+RR')^{-1}(x-y^*) = 0.$$

Consequently

$$(x-y^0)'(Q+RR')^{-1}(x-y^0) = (x-y^*)'(Q+RR')^{-1}(x-y^*) +$$
$$+ (y^0-y^*)'(Q+RR')^{-1}(y^0-y^*).$$

The matrix $(Q+RR')^{-1}$, is positive definite (see the lemma in the footnote to p. 163). Consequently

$$(y^0-y^*)'(Q+RR')^{-1}(y^0-y^*) > 0 \qquad \text{if} \qquad y^0 \neq y^*$$

and

$$(x-y^0)'(Q+RR')^{-1}(x-y^0) > (x-y^*)'(Q+RR')^{-1}(x-y^*).$$

Proposition 4 shows that the estimator given by theorem 1 is unique. If the support of $x-y$ is not the complete n-dimensional space, but an r-dimensional linear subspace, we can either apply the second part of proposition 4 directly or carry out a linear transformation of n-dimensional space into r-dimensional space, so that the image of the support of $x-y$ is the complete r-dimensional space; we then apply the first part of proposition 4 in this new space.

[†] This proposition corresponds to RAO's [1972] justification of one of his two methods, namely the method of 'unified least squares'. As he shows, any g-inverse of Q, as well as $(Q+RR')^{-1}$, can be used in the quadratic form to be minimised.
[††] There are various conceivable equivalent formulae for finding the Gauss-Markov estimator when Q is singular. See HOLLY [1974].

When Q is the unit matrix, the expression minimized by y^* can be written:

$$\sum_{i=1}^{n} (x_i - y_i^*)^2.$$

Thus y^* minimizes the sum of squares of the differences between the components x_i and the components y_i^* of the estimated mean. This is why the method of estimation which we have been considering is called the 'generalized method of least squares'.

6   Formulae for the Gauss-Markov estimator

We confine ourselves now to the case where Q has an inverse since we know the modification to be introduced when Q is singular. Clearly the calculations to be carried out will vary according to the analytic form of the definition of L. Two general formulae are often used.

(i) The classical case

Suppose first that L consists of the set of vectors $y = Za$ where Z is a known $(n \times p)$ matrix of rank p and a is a suitable p-vector. (The vector y is then some linear combination of p linearly independent vectors whose components are given by the columns of Z.) The estimate $y^* = Za^*$ which we are seeking minimizes:

$$(x - Za)'Q^{-1}(x - Za).$$

It is found by equating to zero the derivatives of this expression with respect to the components of a, so that[†]:

$$Z'Q^{-1}(x - Za^*) = 0$$

and

$$Z'Q^{-1}Za^* = Z'Q^{-1}x.$$

The matrix $Z'Q^{-1}Z$ obviously has an inverse[††]. Therefore a^* is given by

$$a^* = (Z'Q^{-1}Z)^{-1}Z'Q^{-1}x. \tag{18}$$

[†] One easily proves that these 'first-order conditions' are sufficient for minimisation (see for instance ch. 5, appendix 2, § (iii) in the second edition of this book).

[††] If $Z'Q^{-1}Z$ were singular there would exist a non-zero vector a such that

$$a'Z'Q^{-1}Za = 0.$$

Since Q^{-1} is positive definite, the vector $b = Za$ ought to be zero, which would contradict the fact that Z is of rank p.

(ii) Estimable functions and unidentifiability

In certain practical problems it may happen that the vector subspace L is defined by $y = Za$ with a matrix Z of order $(n \times m)$ and rank $p < m$. In this case two different vectors a^1 and a^2 of R^m correspond to the same vector y of L if and only if their difference belongs to the $(m-p)$-dimensional vector subspace H consisting of the set of vectors h such that $Zh = 0$. The vector a is not identifiable unless certain characteristics other than the first and second moments of the distribution of x depend on it.

To determine an estimate a^* of a, we could proceed as above except that $Z'Q^{-1}Z$ is singular. All the vectors a^* of a hyperplane π parallel to H satisfy the equation

$$Z'Q^{-1}Za^* = Z'Q^{-1}x. \qquad (18')$$

Given a solution a^* of this equation, all the solutions can be expressed in the form $a^* + h$, where the vector h is subject only to the condition that $Z'Q^{-1}Zh = 0$, or equivalently, $Zh = 0$.

There are two possible ways of getting round this indeterminacy; either by confining attention to linear combinations of the coefficients which are unaffected by it, or by imposing additional restrictions on the vector a. Let us examine these two possibilities in turn.

An *estimable function* is a linear combination $\varphi'a$ of the components of the vector a, which takes the same value for all solutions of $(18')$, where the vector φ is fixed and known. The linear combination $\varphi'a$ is, by definition, identifiable even though the vector a is not generally identifiable.

For the vector φ to define an estimable function, it is of course necessary that $\varphi'h = 0$ for every vector h such that $Zh = 0$, and this is sufficient. Alternatively, it is necessary and sufficient that there exist an n-vector π such that $\varphi' = \pi'Z$.

To eliminate the indeterminacy, one may alternatively impose the additional condition that a^* belongs to a p-dimensional subspace of R^m, a subspace whose intersection with π reduces to a point. So we take a matrix W of order $[(m-p) \times m]$ and rank $m-p$ and impose the condition $Wa^* = 0$. For this condition to imply complete determination of a^* it is necessary and sufficient that the system defined by $Z(a-a^*) = 0$ and $W(a-a^*) = 0$ implies $a = a^*$, that is, that the matrix $\left[\begin{smallmatrix} Z \\ W \end{smallmatrix}\right]$ with $n+m-p$ rows and m columns has rank m.

For the calculation of the estimate a^* satisfying $Wa^* = 0$, we note that $(Z'Q^{-1}Z + kW'W)a^* = Z'Q^{-1}x$ for any non-zero number k, and also that the matrix $Z'Q^{-1}Z + kW'W$ is non-singular. For,

$$h'(Z'Q^{-1}Z + kW'W)h = 0$$

can be written

$$\begin{bmatrix} Zh \\ Wh \end{bmatrix}' \begin{bmatrix} Q^{-1} & 0 \\ 0 & kI \end{bmatrix} \begin{bmatrix} Zh \\ Wh \end{bmatrix} = 0$$

and implies $[^Z_W] h = 0$. So the vector h with m components is zero since the matrix $[^Z_W]$ has rank m. Consequently the estimate a^* satisfying $Wa^* = 0$ is[†]

$$a^* = (Z'Q^{-1}Z + kW'W)^{-1}Z'Q^{-1}x.$$

Clearly this last formula also applies in finding the estimate $\varphi'a^*$ of the estimable function $\varphi'a$, the only special feature being that the result then depends neither on k nor on W.

(iii) Linear constraints

It sometimes happens in practice that the definition of L involves not only the equation $y = Za$ but also linear constraints on the vector a. The appropriate formulae here can be derived immediately from the principles just discussed. We shall not state these formulae since their general expressions are fairly complex. We restrict ourselves to the case where the constraints affect y directly.

Suppose then that L consists of the set of vectors y which satisfy $Ay = 0$, where A is a known $(n-p) \times n$ matrix of rank $n-p$. (The subspace L is then orthogonal to $n-p$ linearly independent vectors whose components are given by the rows of A.) The estimate to be found minimizes:

$$(x - y^*)'Q^{-1}(x - y^*),$$

with the condition that $Ay^* = 0$. Let $2u$ denote a vector of $n-p$ Lagrange multipliers. By equating to zero the derivatives of:

$$(x - y^*)'Q^{-1}(x - y^*) - 2u'Ay^*$$

with respect to the components of y^*, we obtain:

$$Q^{-1}(x - y^*) + A'u = 0,$$

and therefore:

$$y^* = x + QA'u.$$

Now,

$$0 = Ay^* = Ax + AQA'u.$$

The matrix AQA' clearly has an inverse[††]. Therefore:

$$u = -(AQA')^{-1}Ax.$$

Finally y^* is given by:

$$y^* = x - QA'(AQA')^{-1}Ax. \tag{19}$$

[†] Since we know that there exists a vector a^* satisfying the required conditions, we have the guarantee that $Wa^* = 0$, and this is so for any x. So we have proved

$$W(Z'Q^{-1}Z + kW'W)^{-1}Z' = 0.$$

J. C. Milleron has given a direct proof of this equality.

[††] This can be shown by applying the proof of footnote p. 163.

(iv) Finding the variances and covariances

To construct the concentration ellipsoid of the estimate, we need only determine the intersection of E, the concentration ellipsoid of x, with the linear subspace L.

Let us consider in particular case (i) above where the vectors y of L have the form $y = Za$. The n-vector ε belongs to E if $\varepsilon' Q^{-1} \varepsilon \leqq 1$, and belongs to L if there exists a p-vector α such that $\varepsilon = Z\alpha$. The concentration ellipsoid of the estimate consists therefore of the set of vectors $Z\alpha$ which satisfy:

$$\alpha'(Z'Q^{-1}Z)\alpha \leqq 1. \tag{20}$$

Since Z has rank p, there exists a linear transformation of L into p-dimensional space such that the p coordinates of the transform of every vector $y = Za$ of L are just the p components of a. The image of the concentration ellipsoid of y^* is then the concentration ellipsoid of a^*. A vector α belongs to this image if and only if it satisfies (20). The covariance matrix of a^* is therefore $(Z'Q^{-1}Z)^{-1}$.

In case (ii), where we set $Wa^* = 0$, the concentration ellipsoid of y^* again consists of the set of vectors $Z\alpha$ which satisfy (20). But we can then restrict α to satisfy $W\alpha = 0$. Moreover, there exists a linear transformation of L into R^m such that the image of a vector y is the vector a such that $Za = y$ and $Wa = 0$. Under this transformation, the image of the concentration ellipsoid of y^* is the concentration ellipsoid of a^*, which is then defined by the set of vectors α satisfying $W\alpha = 0$ and the inequality (20). It is equivalent to say that the concentration ellipsoid of a^* is defined by $W\alpha = 0$ and the inequality

$$\alpha (Z'Q^{-1}Z + kW'W)\alpha \leq 1$$

where k is any non-zero number.

By applying proposition 1 (iii), we can find the covariance matrix of a^*. We need only replace V by W and U by $(Z'Q^{-1}Z + kW'W)^{-1}$ in formula (10).

(v) Transformation of the model

To find a^*, it is sometimes convenient to make some modification to the linear model. From $x = Za + \varepsilon$ we can obviously deduce that

$$Cx = CZa + C\varepsilon$$

where C is a known matrix. The converse is also true when C is a *non-singular square matrix*, as we shall assume here. The covariance matrix of $C\varepsilon$ is $C'QC$. We can verify immediately from (18) that the estimate a^* is unchanged if we work on the transformed model, that is, if simultaneously Cx is substituted for x, CZ for Z and $C'QC$ for Q.

Such a transformation is particularly useful when it results in the covariance matrix of the errors being reduced to the unit matrix ($C'QC = I$), since then a^* can be found by classical multiple regression techniques. For this to be the case, Q need only be non-singular and C be such that $CC' = Q^{-1}$. A transformation of this type can be introduced fairly naturally in some cases, as we shall shortly see in an example[†].

(vi) Examples

We now return to the three examples of section 1, in order to show how these results can be applied. The covariance matrix Q of y is equal to $\sigma^2 I$. The quadratic form:

$$(x - y^*)'Q^{-1}(x - y^*)$$

can therefore be written:

$$\sigma^{-2}[(x - y^*)'(x - y^*)],$$

or again:

$$\sigma^{-2} \sum_{i=1}^{n} (x_i - y_i^*)^2.$$

The estimator of theorem 1 therefore minimizes the sum of squares of the differences between the observed values x_i and the 'fitted' values y_i^*. We note that it does not depend on σ^2.

In the first example (estimation of the mean of a variable from T independent observations) the estimator under discussion can be written:

$$a^* = \frac{1}{T} \sum_{t=1}^{T} x_t.$$

In the second example (the model of ch. 3), we obviously come back to the least squares estimators a^* and b^*. In the third example (seasonal variations) we obtain similarly:

$$a_h^* = \frac{1}{K} \sum_{k=1}^{K} x_{hk}.$$

The concentration ellipsoid of the estimates can also be easily obtained by applying the general procedure described above. Indeed let l denote the vector whose components are identically 1, and z the vector whose components are the z_t (second example). Let l^h denote the vector whose only non-zero components are the K components corresponding to month h, which equal 1. The

---

[†] Generally we can in principle use the following result pointed out by FULLER and BATTESE [1973]. If Q has r simple or multiple characteristic roots λ_i, we can write $Q = \Sigma_i \lambda_i R_i$ where the R_i are symmetric and mutually orthogonal projection matrices; then the condition $C'QC = I$ is satisfied by $C = \Sigma_i R_i / \sqrt{\lambda_i}$.

subspace L is defined in each case by:

First example: $y = la.$

Second example: $y = [z \quad l] \begin{bmatrix} a \\ b \end{bmatrix}.$

Third example: $y = [l^1, l^2, \ldots, l^h, \ldots, l^H] \begin{bmatrix} a_1 \\ \vdots \\ a_h \\ \vdots \\ a_H \end{bmatrix}.$

These formulae are all particular cases of the general form $y = Za$. The covariance matrix of the estimates is therefore $(Z'Q^{-1}Z)^{-1}$, which reduces in this case to $\sigma^2(Z'Z)^{-1}$. We have, therefore, in each example:

First example: $Z'Z = l'l = T$, hence the variance of a^* is:

$$\sigma_a^2 = \frac{1}{T}\sigma^2.$$

Second example:

$$Z'Z = \begin{bmatrix} z'z & z'l \\ l'z & l'l \end{bmatrix} = T \begin{bmatrix} S^2 & \bar{z} \\ \bar{z} & 1 \end{bmatrix},$$

where

$$S^2 = \frac{1}{T}\sum_{t=1}^{T} z_t^2, \qquad \bar{z} = \frac{1}{T}\sum_{t=1}^{T} z_t.$$

The covariance matrix of a^* and b^* is therefore:

$$\frac{\sigma^2}{T}\begin{bmatrix} S^2 & \bar{z} \\ \bar{z} & 1 \end{bmatrix}^{-1},$$

which is obviously identical with expression (29) in ch. 3.

Third example:

$$Z'Z = \begin{bmatrix} l^{1'}l^1 & l^{1'}l^2 & \cdots & l^{1'}l_H^H \\ l^{2'}l^1 & l^{2'}l^2 & \cdots & l^{2'}l_H^H \\ \cdots\cdots\cdots\cdots\cdots\cdots\cdots \\ l^{H'}l^1 & l_t^{H'}l^2 & \cdots & l^{H'}l^H \end{bmatrix} = \begin{bmatrix} K & 0 & \cdots & 0 \\ 0 & K & \cdots & 0 \\ \cdots\cdots\cdots\cdots \\ 0 & 0 & \cdots & K \end{bmatrix},$$

Therefore the variance of a_h^* is equal to σ^2/K.

The calculations are harder when the covariance matrix Q does not equal $\sigma^2 I$. They can often be simplified by applying a suitable linear transformation to the vector x of the observations. Indeed let C be a matrix such that $Q = CC'$. The concentration ellipsoid of the vector $u = C^{-1}x$ is the unit sphere. If y denotes the expected value of x, the vector $v = C^{-1}y$ is estimated from u by the method of least squares.

As a *fourth example* suppose that we wish to estimate the expected value of the stationary stochastic process x_t generated by the equation:

$$x_1 - a = \varepsilon_1$$
$$x_t - a = \rho(x_{t-1} - a) + \eta_t \qquad t = 2, 3, \ldots, T$$

where ρ is a given number between 0 and 1, while ε_1 and the η_t are mutually independent random terms with zero means; the variance of η_t is τ^2, and that of ε_1 is $\tau^2/(1-\rho^2)$. Given the value of the parameter ρ and T successive observations on x_t, $(t = 1, 2, \ldots, T)$, we wish to estimate the expected value a of x_t.

This problem is certainly of the type we have been considering, since the expected value y of the T-dimensional vector x must have all the components equal. The distribution of the vector $x - y$ can be determined from the above equation which defines the process. But it is simpler to replace x and y by $u = C^{-1}x$ and $v = C^{-1}y$, where:

$$C^{-1} = \begin{bmatrix} \sqrt{1-\rho^2} & 0 & 0 & \ldots & 0 & 0 \\ -\rho & 1 & 0 & \ldots & 0 & 0 \\ 0 & -\rho & 1 & \ldots & 0 & 0 \\ \multicolumn{6}{c}{\dotfill} \\ 0 & 0 & 0 & \ldots & -\rho & 1 \end{bmatrix}$$

For we can verify that

$$u_1 = \sqrt{1-\rho^2}\, x_1 = v_1 + \varepsilon_1 \sqrt{1-\rho^2} \qquad \text{where } v_1 = a\sqrt{1-\rho^2}$$

$$u_t = x_t - \rho x_{t-1} = v_t + \eta_t, \qquad v_t = (1-\rho)a \qquad \text{for } t = 2, \ldots, T.$$

If we take no account of u_1, estimation of $(1-\rho)a$ is reduced to estimation of the expected value of a sample of $T-1$ independent observations on the u_t (the first example above). The estimator of theorem 1 is then the arithmetic mean of the u_t for $t \geq 2$. If we take account of u_1, as we should for a correct application of theorem 1, we see that the covariance matrix of the u_t is still $\tau^2 I$. Final calculation gives the estimator a^* defined by

$$a^*[T(1-\rho) + 2\rho] = \sqrt{\frac{1+\rho}{1-\rho}}\, u_1 + \sum_{t=2}^{T} u_t.$$

In this case we can also establish that:

$$Q = \frac{\tau^2}{1 - \varrho^2} \begin{bmatrix} 1 & \varrho & \varrho^2 & \cdots & \varrho^T \\ \varrho & 1 & \varrho & \cdots & \varrho^{T-1} \\ \varrho^2 & \varrho & 1 & \cdots & \varrho^{T-2} \\ \cdots\cdots\cdots\cdots\cdots\cdots\cdots\cdots\cdots\cdots\cdots \\ \varrho^T & \varrho^{T-1} & \varrho^{T-2} & \cdots & 1 \end{bmatrix}$$

and hence

$$Q^{-1} = \frac{1}{\tau^2} \begin{bmatrix} 1 & -\varrho & 0 & \cdots 0 \\ -\varrho & 1+\varrho^2 & -\varrho & \cdots 0 \\ 0 & -\varrho & 1+\varrho^2 & \cdots 0 \\ \cdots\cdots\cdots\cdots\cdots\cdots\cdots\cdots\cdots \\ 0 & 0 & 0 & \cdots 1 \end{bmatrix}$$

Clearly $\tau^2 Q^{-1}$ is in fact equal to $(C^{-1})'(C^{-1})$.

7   The assumption of normality

Let us suppose now that in the problem P the random vector x is normally distributed. The above results can then be strengthened to some extent.

If Q has an inverse, x has, in n-dimensional space, a probability density of the form:

$$(2\pi)^{-\frac{1}{2}n} |Q|^{-\frac{1}{2}} \exp\{-\tfrac{1}{2}(x-y)'Q^{-1}(x-y)\}. \tag{22}$$

Proposition 3 then shows that the estimator y^* studied in the previous section becomes identical with the *maximum likelihood estimator*. For of all vectors y of L, y^* is the one which maximizes (22) for the observed value x of the random vector.

However the significance of this remark cannot easily be appreciated a priori. Maximum likelihood estimators are certainly known to have interesting asymptotic properties, but the problem P consists in estimating y from *a single* observation on x. It would therefore be rash to accept as valid in this case those properties which are meaningful only when the number of observations tends to infinity.

Fortunately we can establish the following theorem which is directly applicable to our problem.

Theorem 2.   With reference to the problem P, in the case where x is normally distributed, the Gauss-Markov estimator $y^* = f(x)$

(a) is a sufficient statistic for estimation of y in L,

(b) has a concentration ellipsoid contained in that of every other unbiased estimator α,

(c) has a p-dimensional normal distribution,

(d) is independent of the residual vector $\varepsilon^* = x - y^*$, which has an $(r-p)$-dimensional normal distribution.

For the proof of this theorem we consider the linear transformation defined by proposition 3 and expressed as (16) in the proof of theorem 1.

The vector Gx is normally distributed as is the vector x (cf. lemma 1). We know that its $n-r$ last components are necessarily zero and that the vectors x_L of its first p components and x_K of its next $r-p$ components satisfy the conditions (17). It follows that Gx has an r-dimensional normal distribution with density

$$\phi = (2\pi)^{-\frac{1}{2}r} \exp\{-\tfrac{1}{2}(x_L - y_L)'(x_L - y_L)\} \exp\{-\tfrac{1}{2}x_K'x_K\} \tag{23}$$

where y_L is the vector of the first p components of Gy which alone are not necessarily zero.

Finally, we can write:

$$Gy^* = \begin{bmatrix} x_L \\ 0 \\ 0 \end{bmatrix}, \qquad Gy = \begin{bmatrix} y_L \\ 0 \\ 0 \end{bmatrix}, \qquad G\varepsilon^* = \begin{bmatrix} 0 \\ x_K \\ 0 \end{bmatrix}. \tag{24}$$

Consequently:

(a) Gy^* is a sufficient statistic for Gy. For the probability density (23) of Gx is the product of the probability density of Gy^*, namely:

$$(2\pi)^{-\frac{1}{2}p} \exp\{-\tfrac{1}{2}(x_L - y_L)'(x_L - y_L)\}, \tag{25}$$

and a factor which does not depend on the unknown parameters, that is, the components of y_L. The conditional probability density of $G\varepsilon^*$ for given Gy^* is independent of y_L. So Gy^* is indeed a sufficient statistic (cf. CRAMER [1946], ch. 32 § 8).

(b) By examining the form of the probability density (23), we could show that Gy^* is an 'efficient' sufficient estimator and consequently its concentration ellipsoid is contained in that of every other *regular* unbiased estimator (see CRAMER [1946] ch. 32 for the definition of regular estimators). It follows from a more powerful result established by C. R. Rao [1965] that the Gauss-Markov estimator is also efficient in the class of all unbiased estimators, no regularity condition being required[†].

[†] See RAO [1965], pp. 257–8. To apply the proof to our formulation, we can give L the representation $y = Za$, where Z is a matrix of rank p and a is a p-vector varying freely in R^p. The vector Q which appears in Rao's proof is replaced in our notation by the vector $Z'Q^{-1}x$. The result obtained shows that any linear transformation of this vector, $CZ'Q^{-1}x$ say, is an efficient estimator of its expected value in the class of estimators having the same expectation identically in a. Now, the expectation of $CZ'Q^{-1}x$ is $CZ'Q^{-1}Za$. It coincides with a for all a if and only if $C = (Z'Q^{-1}Z)^{-1}$, since Z has rank p. This value of C defines precisely the Gauss-Markov estimator.

(c) Gy^* has a p-dimensional normal distribution with mean Gy.

(d) Gy^* is independent of $G\varepsilon^*$ which has a normal $(r-p)$-dimensional distribution with zero mean.

Since G is a non-singular matrix independent of the unknown parameters, the above propositions (a) to (d) imply the corresponding proposition of theorem 2. To see this we need only think of the transformation with matrix G^{-1} as a simple change of coordinates in n-dimensional space.

Theorem 2 reinforces the conclusions of theorem 1 for the particular case where x is normally distributed. Thus the proposition (b) corresponds to the proposition (i) of theorem 1, but is stronger since the concentration ellipsoid of y^* now appears minimal in the class of all regular unbiased estimators, and no longer only in the class of all unbiased linear estimators.

Theorem 2 specifies completely the distribution of y^*. We already knew from theorem 1 that the expected value of y^* was y and that its concentration ellipsoid was the intersection of E and L. This is enough to determine its distribution completely, since it is normal[†].

8   A test of an important hypothesis

Normality of the vector x plays an important part in many tests to be discussed later, all of which come under the following general scheme.

Under the assumptions of the problem P, if the observed vector x is normally distributed, does its expected value y lie in a specified q-dimensional $(q < p)$ linear subspace M contained in L?

We shall suppose for this problem that the covariance matrix Q of x has an inverse. As we saw above, we can always revert to this case by making a change of variables.

Let u and v be the projections of x on L and M according to the principal conjugate linear manifolds of L and M with respect to the concentration ellipsoid of x. It seems natural to choose a test which will lead us to reject the hypothesis that y belongs to M whenever the distance between u and v is too great. The most natural expression for this distance is:

$$\gamma = (u - v)'Q^{-1}(u - v), \tag{26}$$

---

† Actually, the distribution of y^* can always be determined completely, when the distribution of $x-y$ is known, whether or not it is normal.

For let

$$\varphi(u) = E[e^{iu'(x-y)}]$$

be the characteristic function of $x-y$, u being an n-vector. The characteristic function of Gx is:

$$\Phi(t) = \varphi(G't)$$

(see CRAMER [1946] ch. 22 § 6). If t_L denotes the first p components of t, then $\Phi(t_L, 0)$ is the characteristic function of the p components of Gy^* which are not necessarily zero.

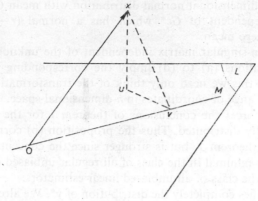

Fig. 8.

which would become the Euclidean distance after the change of variables that would transform the concentration ellipsoid into a sphere.

The hypothesis under test will therefore be rejected if the value found for γ is greater than some quantity calculated beforehand as a function of the chosen level of significance (see below).

In fact *in practical applications of the problem P we generally do not have complete knowledge of the covariance matrix Q.*

We know only that Q is of the form $\sigma^2 Q_0$, where Q_0 is a known matrix but σ is an unknown number. In particular, this is the case in the examples considered above. It does not affect the generalized least squares estimate since conjugacy with respect to the concentration ellipsoid of x is equivalent to conjugacy with respect to the ellipsoid $\varepsilon' Q_0^{-1} \varepsilon \leq 1$. But the above test no longer applies since γ clearly depends on σ^2.

Similarly the distribution of

$$\eta = (u - v)' Q_0^{-1}(u - v) \tag{27}$$

depends on σ^2 so that η cannot be used to establish a test. On the other hand, the ratio between η and

$$\xi = (x - u)' Q_0^{-1}(x - u) \tag{28}$$

is distributed independently of σ^2 as we shall see below. This ratio will naturally be small if y belongs to M and larger if the distance between y and M is considerable. A natural test would therefore lead to rejection of the hypothesis that y belongs to M when the value found for η/ξ is greater than some quantity previously calculated as a function of the chosen level of significance.

Such intuitive justifications of the above two tests can be made more rigorous. Let $\beta_\phi(y)$ be the probability that a test ϕ rejects the hypothesis that the expected value of x belongs to M when its true value is in fact the vector y. If y^0 is a vector not contained in M, then $\beta_\phi(y^0)$ is called '*the power of the test ϕ against the alternative y^0*'. Of two tests which have the same significance level, we should choose that which has the greatest power for those alternatives which we wish particularly to guard against. Of course when there are multiple alternatives the criterion is not always conclusive. However, it gives a certain kind of justification for the tests in which we are now interested.

Given some positive number γ_1, let $Y(\gamma_1)$ be the set of all the y of L whose distance from M is greater than or equal to γ_1, that is the set of all the y that are such that

$$(y - w)'Q^{-1}(y - w) \geqq \gamma_1$$

for any w of M. Let $\beta_\phi(\gamma_1)$ be the minimum power of the test ϕ for the alternatives belonging to $Y(\gamma_1)$. One can prove that, among all tests ϕ with the same significance level α, the test established as above on the basis of γ (or the ratio η/ξ) gives the greatest value for $\beta_\phi(\gamma_1)$, and this for any α and γ_1. These two tests are then said to maximize the minimum power[†], the first when Q is known and the second when Q is of the form $\sigma^2 Q_0$, where Q_0 is known and σ unknown.

We can derive the same test by a different approach which is often used, but can be justified only by asymptotic properties[††], which cannot be easily interpreted in the context of our model (since we are concerned with the expected value of a vector on which we have only one observation).

Let $\mathcal{L}_L$ denote the maximum of the probability density of x when this vector takes the observed value and when y varies in L (and more generally, when the unknown parameters take all values compatible with the model). The quantity $\mathcal{L}_L$ is sometimes called the 'maximum likelihood'. Similarly let $\mathcal{L}_M$ be the maximum when y varies in M (and more generally, when the unknown parameters take all values compatible with the hypothesis to be tested). By definition, the '*likelihood ratio test*' is that test which leads to rejection of the hypothesis that y belongs to M whenever the ratio between $\mathcal{L}_M$ and $\mathcal{L}_L$ is less than a value previously calculated as a function of the chosen level of significance.

To show that the two tests described above may be obtained as likelihood ratio tests, we consider first the case where Q is completely known. The probability density of x is given by:

$$(2\pi)^{-\frac{1}{2}n}|Q|^{-\frac{1}{2}}\exp\{-\tfrac{1}{2}(x - y)'Q^{-1}(x - y)\}.$$

Its maximum when y varies in L is:

$$\mathcal{L}_L = (2\pi)^{-\frac{1}{2}n}|Q|^{-\frac{1}{2}}\exp\{-\tfrac{1}{2}(x - u)'Q^{-1}(x - u)\}. \tag{29}$$

---

† The proof depends on the Hunt–Stein theorem and on establishing that the test considered is uniformly most powerful invariant. See LEHMANN [1959], particularly example 8, p. 338.
†† See LE CAM [1956].

Similarly:

$$\mathscr{L}_M = (2\pi)^{-\frac{1}{2}n}|Q|^{-\frac{1}{2}}\exp\{-\tfrac{1}{2}(x-v)'Q^{-1}(x-v)\}. \tag{30}$$

And, since

$$(x-v)'Q^{-1}(x-v) = (x-u)'Q^{-1}(x-u) + (u-v)'Q^{-1}(u-v):$$

$$\mathscr{L}_M/\mathscr{L}_L = \exp\{-\tfrac{1}{2}(u-v)'Q^{-1}(u-v)\} = \exp\{-\tfrac{1}{2}\gamma\}. \tag{31}$$

The likelihood ratio is thus a decreasing function of γ. It will be small when γ is large. The likelihood ratio test therefore consists of rejecting the hypothesis when γ is greater than some quantity calculated as a function of the chosen significance level.

We consider next the case where Q is of the form $\sigma^2 Q_0$, where Q_0 is known and σ unknown. The maximum likelihood is then the maximum of (29) when σ varies. In view of (28) this expression can now be written:

$$(2\pi)^{-\frac{1}{2}n}|Q_0|^{-\frac{1}{2}}\sigma^{-n}\exp\{-\xi/2\sigma^2\}. \tag{32}$$

Apart from a constant, its logarithm is equal to:

$$-n\ln\sigma - (\xi/2\sigma^2).$$

The value of σ^2 which maximizes (32) equates to zero the derivative of this logarithm and is therefore $\sigma^2 = \xi/n$. Substituting this value in (32), the maximum likelihood becomes:

$$\mathscr{L}_L = k\xi^{-\frac{1}{2}n}, \tag{33}$$

with the constant

$$k = (2\pi e/n)^{-\frac{1}{2}n}|Q_0|^{-\frac{1}{2}}.$$

Similarly:

$$\mathscr{L}_M = k(\xi + \eta)^{-\frac{1}{2}n} \tag{34}$$

$$\frac{\mathscr{L}_M}{\mathscr{L}_L} = \left[\frac{\xi+\eta}{\xi}\right]^{-\frac{1}{2}n} = [1 + \eta/\xi]^{-\frac{1}{2}n}. \tag{35}$$

The likelihood ratio is therefore a decreasing function of η/ξ. The likelihood ratio test consists of rejecting the hypothesis when η/ξ exceeds a critical value depending on the chosen significance level.

To apply these tests we must know how to calculate the critical values of γ and η/ξ. We must therefore know the distributions of these quantities when y does actually lie in M. Also it is often useful to know the power of the tests, that is, the probability that γ (or η/ξ) exceeds the critical value when y is some vector outside M. Hence we should know the distribution of γ and η/ξ as functions of the true position of y in L, whether or not it belongs to M. The following results allow us to determine these distributions.

Proposition 5. If the random n-vector x is normally distributed with mean y and non-singular covariance matrix Q, then

$$(x - y)'Q^{-1}(x - y)$$

is distributed as χ^2 with n degrees of freedom. If h is some fixed n-vector,

$$(x - h)'Q^{-1}(x - h)$$

has a non-central χ^2-distribution with n degrees of freedom. The non-centrality parameter is given by:

$$\delta^2 = (y - h)'Q^{-1}(y - h).$$

For let C be a non-singular square matrix such that $Q = CC'$. The random vector $z = C^{-1}(x - h)$ is normally distributed with covariance matrix

$$C^{-1}Q(C^{-1})' = I.$$

The sum of squares of its components has therefore a non-central χ^2-distribution with n degrees of freedom[†]. Now this sum is equal to

$$z'z = (x - h)'(C^{-1})'(C^{-1})(x - h) = (x - h)'Q^{-1}(x - h).$$

The non-centrality parameter δ is defined by

$$\delta^2 = [E(z)]' \cdot E(z).$$

Now,

$$E(z) = C^{-1}(y - h);$$

and so

$$\delta^2 = (y - h)'(C^{-1})'(C^{-1})(y - h) = (y - h)'Q^{-1}(y - h).$$

In the particular case where $h = y$, the distribution becomes an ordinary χ^2-distribution with n degrees of freedom.

Proposition 6. Let x be a normal random vector with mean y and non-singular covariance matrix Q. Let R be an r-dimensional subspace. Let x^* and y^* be

---

[†] By definition, the non-central χ^2-distribution is the distribution of the sum of squares of n independent normal variables, with variances equal to 1. This distribution depends only on n and on a 'non-centrality parameter' δ which is equal to the square root of the sum of squares of the means of these n variables. See SCHEFFÉ [1959], Appendix IV.

vectors of R which minimize respectively

$$(x - x^*)'Q^{-1}(x - x^*) \qquad \text{and} \qquad (y - y^*)'Q^{-1}(y - y^*).$$

If h is some vector of R,

$$(x^* - h)'Q^{-1}(x^* - h)$$

has a non-central χ^2-distribution with r degrees of freedom. The non-centrality parameter δ is given by

$$\delta^2 = (y^* - h)'Q^{-1}(y^* - h).$$

Indeed we can always find a linear parametric representation of the vectors of R, that is, an $(n \times r)$ matrix G such that every vector ε of R can be written $\varepsilon = G\zeta$, where ζ is a suitable r-vector. The matrix G has rank r. In particular, x^*, y^* and h can be written

$$x^* = Gu^*, \qquad y^* = Gv^*, \qquad h = Gk.$$

The mapping $x \to u^*$ is clearly linear. From lemma 1, u^* is normally distributed with mean v^* and concentration ellipsoid consisting of the set of vectors ζ such that $G\zeta$ belongs to the concentration ellipsoid E^* of x^*. In addition, proposition 4 and the proof of theorem 1 show that E^* is the intersection of R with the concentration ellipsoid E of x. A vector ζ belongs to the concentration ellipsoid of u^* if and only if $\varepsilon = G\zeta$, which necessarily belongs to R, also belongs to E, and therefore if and only if

$$\zeta'G'Q^{-1}G\zeta \leqq 1.$$

The covariance matrix of u^* is therefore $(G'Q^{-1}G)^{-1}$.

From proposition 5,

$$(u^* - k)'G'Q^{-1}G(u^* - k)$$

has a non-central χ^2-distribution with r degrees of freedom, the non-centrality parameter being defined by

$$\delta^2 = (v^* - k)'G'Q^{-1}G(v^* - k).$$

Proposition 6 follows directly since

$$(x^* - h)'Q^{-1}(x^* - h) = (u^* - k)'G'Q^{-1}G(u^* - k),$$

and similarly

$$(y^* - h)'Q^{-1}(y^* - h) = (v^* - k)'G'Q^{-1}G(v^* - k).$$

Proposition 7. Suppose that, in the problem P, the vector x is normally distributed with non-singular covariance matrix Q. Let u be the vector of L

which minimizes

$$(x - u)'Q^{-1}(x - u),$$

let v and w be the vectors which minimize

$$(x - v)'Q^{-1}(x - v) \quad \text{and} \quad (y - w)'Q^{-1}(y - w)$$

in a q-dimensional subspace M belonging to L. The quantity

$$\gamma = (u - v)'Q^{-1}(u - v)$$

has a non-central χ^2-distribution with $p - q$ degrees of freedom. The ratio

$$\frac{n - p}{p - q} \cdot \frac{\gamma}{\lambda},$$

in which

$$\lambda = (x - u)'Q^{-1}(x - u),$$

has a non-central F-distribution with $p - q$ and $n - p$ degrees of freedom. In both cases the non-centrality parameter δ is given by

$$\delta^2 = (y - w)'Q^{-1}(y - w).$$

Applying proposition 6 to the projection $x - u$ of x on the principal conjugate linear manifold K of L, we see immediately that λ has a central χ^2-distribution with $n - p$ degrees of freedom. Applying the same proposition to the projection $u - v$ of x on the linear manifold H defined as the set of vectors of L which are conjugate to M, we see similarly that γ has a non-central χ^2-distribution with $p - q$ degrees of freedom, the non-centrality parameter being defined by

$$\delta^2 = (y - w)'Q^{-1}(y - w).$$

Moreover from theorem 2, γ and λ are independent. The ratio

$$\frac{n - p}{p - q} \cdot \frac{\gamma}{\lambda}$$

has therefore the non-central F-distribution defined in the statement of the proposition[†].

[†] By definition, the non-central F-distribution with m and n degrees of freedom and non-centrality parameter δ is the distribution of the ratio

$$\frac{n}{m} \cdot \frac{U}{V}$$

when U and V are two independent random variables, the first of which has a non-central χ^2-distribution with m degrees of freedom and non-centrality parameter δ, and the second a central χ^2-distribution with n degrees of freedom. See SCHEFFÉ [1959] Appendix IV.

This last proposition specifies the random properties of the two tests defined at the start of this section. Let us consider the second test, which is most often used in practice. The same procedures would apply for the first.

The ratio η/ξ is equal to the ratio γ/λ of proposition 7. If the hypothesis that y belongs to M is correct,

$$\frac{n-p}{p-q} \cdot \frac{\eta}{\xi}$$

has a central F-distribution with $p-q$ and $n-p$ degrees of freedom. The α-level significance test will then reject the hypothesis when

$$\frac{n-p}{p-q} \cdot \frac{\eta}{\xi} > F_{p-q,n-p}(\alpha),$$

where $F_{p-q,n-p}(\alpha)$ denotes the value exceeded with probability α by a random variable distributed as F with $p-q$ and $n-p$ degrees of freedom. We need only refer to the usual statistical tables[†] to find this value.

Moreover we can calculate the power of the test with respect to an alternative according to which

$$\delta^2 = (y - w)'Q^{-1}(y - w)$$

has a given positive value. For we can find the probability β that a non-central F-variable with non-centrality parameter δ exceeds the value $F_{p-q,n-p}(\alpha)$ chosen for the test. We can use, for example, the tables[††] given in PEARSON and HARTLEY [1951].

9   Optimal properties of the method of least squares

The method of least squares, generalized as we have seen, is used universally for the statistical treatment of the problem P. To what extent does the foregoing theory justify its use? This is the question which we shall consider briefly in this section. We start with a survey of some general notions from statistical decision theory[†††].

Let $g(x)$ be some estimation procedure, that is, a function which maps n-dimensional space onto the subspace L. Let $\hat{y} = g(x)$ be the estimate obtained when the observed vector is x. The difference between the estimated and the true value of the mean of x, say $\hat{y} - y$, can be called the 'estimation error'. According to statistical decision theory (see, for example, WALD [1950a]), we

---

[†] See, for example, MORICE and CHARTIER [1954] pp. 523–24, or SCHEFFÉ [1959] pp. 424–33.
[††] These tables give the value of β for tests at significance level α, with ν_1 and ν_2 degrees of freedom (corresponding to our $p-q$ and $n-p$), and a non-centrality index $\Phi = \delta/\sqrt{\nu_1 + 1}$. Some charts have been given in appendix in SCHEFFÉ [1959], pp. 438–45.
[†††] Statistical decision theory was defined and developed by WALD [1950a]. An interesting extension was given by SAVAGE [1954].

associate with every estimation error a number which measures the 'loss' involved in this error. By definition, the loss is zero when $\hat{y} = y$, and is never negative. It may depend on the true value y and the other characteristics α on which the distribution of x depends. We denote the loss by

$$\mathscr{P}(\hat{y} - y; y, \alpha).$$

A particular estimator, g say, will yield a random estimate $\hat{y}$; therefore the error $\hat{y} - y$ and the loss will also be random. To assess this estimator we must take account of the probability distribution of the loss. We generally use as an over-all criterion the '*risk*', which is defined as the expected value of the loss. Let $\mathscr{R}(g; y, \alpha)$ denote the risk, where obviously:

$$\mathscr{R}(g; y, \alpha) = E\{\mathscr{P}[g(x) - y; y, \alpha]\}. \tag{36}$$

We should then prefer an estimator g to another estimator h if the risk $\mathscr{R}(g; y, \alpha)$ is less than the risk $\mathscr{R}(h; y, \alpha)$. However, since the true value of y and the characteristic α are not known, such a comparison will be conclusive only if

$$\mathscr{R}(g; y, a) \leqq \mathscr{R}(h; y, \alpha) \tag{37}$$

Now it often happens that, where we have two estimators g and h, the first gives the smaller risk for some values of y or of α, and the greater risk for other values.

To deal with this indeterminacy in the choice between estimators we often concentrate attention on the greatest value of $\mathscr{R}(g; y, \alpha)$ when y varies in L, or more precisely on the supremum:

$$\mathscr{S}(g) = \sup_{y, \alpha} \mathscr{R}(g; y, \alpha). \tag{38}$$

A particular estimator g is said to be 'minimax' in a certain class of estimators $\mathscr{C}$, if, for every other estimator h of $\mathscr{C}$,

$$\mathscr{S}(h) \geqq \mathscr{S}(g). \tag{39}$$

Of course there may exist several minimax estimators g which give the same value for $\mathscr{S}(g)$, but different values of $\mathscr{R}(g; y, \alpha)$ at least for certain values of y and of α.

The following is an even less selective criterion. A particular estimator g is said to be '*admissible*' in a certain class of estimators $\mathscr{C}$, if there exists no other estimator h of $\mathscr{C}$ such that

$$\mathscr{R}(h; y, \alpha) \leqq \mathscr{R}(g; y, \alpha) \tag{40}$$

for every y in L and every α, where the inequality would be strict for at least one value of y and of α.

A minimax estimator in a class $\mathscr{C}$ is not necessarily admissible in this class. But an estimator which happens to be both minimax and admissible in a certain class $\mathscr{C}$ is often considered preferable on an objective basis to every other estimator of the same class.

We now confine ourselves to the case where the loss is a positive definite quadratic form of the components of the estimation error[†] $\hat{y} - y$. Such a quadratic form is zero when the error is zero. It increases when $\hat{y} - y$ moves in a given direction away from the origin, and then it varies with the square of the length of $\hat{y} - y$. This seems a fairly natural expression for the loss, at least as a first approximation. In addition we suppose that this quadratic form depends neither on the exact position of y in L, nor on the other unknown characteristics of the distribution of x. This generally seems justified in practical cases of the problem P.

Under these conditions, the loss can be written:

$$\mathscr{P} = (\hat{y} - y)' W (\hat{y} - y), \tag{41}$$

where W is a positive definite symmetric matrix. It is convenient to express it as the square of the length of the vector $V(\hat{y} - y)$, where V is defined by $W = V'V$. We can then write:

$$\mathscr{P} = \sum_{i=1}^{n} [v_i'(\hat{y} - y)]^2, \tag{42}$$

where v_i' denotes the vector of the ith row of V.

The risk, which is the expected value of this loss, can be expressed as the sum of two terms, as follows:

$$\mathscr{R} = \sum_{i=1}^{n} E\{v_i'[\hat{y} - E(\hat{y})]\}^2 + \sum_{i=1}^{n} \{v_i'[E(\hat{y}) - y]\}^2, \tag{43}$$

since the product of

$$v_i'[\hat{y} - E(\hat{y})] \quad \text{and} \quad v_i'[E(\hat{y}) - y]$$

obviously has zero expectation. The risk can be written even more simply:

$$\mathscr{R} = \sum_{i=1}^{n} \operatorname{var}(v_i'\hat{y}) + \sum_{i=1}^{n} \{v_i'[E(\hat{y}) - y]\}^2. \tag{44}$$

The statistical theory given in this chapter leads directly to two important results.

---

† The following reasoning applies in the same way whether we consider the n components of the vector $\hat{y} - y$ in n-dimensional space, or the p linear coordinates of the same vector in the subspace L.

(i) *With respect to the problem P and the loss function (40), the generalized least squares estimator is both minimax and admissible in the class of linear estimators*[†].

We note first that, from (44), the risk associated with the generalized least squares estimator y^* is equal to the sum of the variances of the $v_i' y^*$ since $E(y^*) = y$. It is determined completely by the concentration ellipsoid of y^*, and therefore depends neither on the true value y nor on the characteristics other than Q (which by hypothesis is known) of the distribution of x.

On the other hand, the risk of a biased linear estimator $\hat{y} = g(x)$ is not bounded as y varies in L. For since g is linear, $E(\hat{y}) - y = g(y) - y$. Since $\hat{y}$ is biased, there exists at least one value y^0 in L such that $g(y^0) - y^0 \neq 0$. Since V is non-singular, at least one of the linear forms $v_i'[g(y^0) - y^0]$ differs from zero. Therefore the second term in the risk (44) is necessarily positive for $y = y^0$. Let its value be r^0. We see immediately, from the fact that g is linear, that this term is equal to $k^2 r_0$ for $y = k y^0$ for any number k. By a suitable choice of k we can therefore make this term as large as we please.

Under these conditions every biased linear estimator has a risk greater than the risk of y^* for certain values of y in L. To prove that y^* is minimax and admissible, we need only consider unbiased linear estimators. The risk (44) is then just its first term. It is a minimum for y^* whatever the values of y and the other characteristics of the distribution of x (except Q). Indeed var $(v_i' y^*) \leqq$ var $(v_i' \hat{y})$ for every v_i and every unbiased linear estimator $\hat{y}$ (cf. proposition (i) of theorem 1).

(ii) *For the problem P and with the loss function (41), the generalized least squares estimator is both minimax and admissible in the class of regular unbiased estimators, when x is normally distributed.* Indeed the expression for the risk becomes just the first term of (44) in the case of unbiased estimators. The above property follows directly from the proposition (b) of theorem 2.

The two foregoing properties establish the superiority of the generalized least squares estimator within two classes of estimators, on the one hand linear estimators, and on the other hand regular unbiased estimators. Unfortunately it seems that we cannot obtain such strong properties when we extend the class of estimators, for example to the class of all regular estimators[††].

HODGES and LEHMANN [1950] showed that, for the loss function (41), y^* is minimax in the class of all estimators, so long as we do not exclude a priori normality of x (whatever y may be in L).

But STEIN [1956] and JAMES and STEIN [1961] established that in general y^*

[†] For fuller discussion of the class of linear estimators see RAO [1976b] who shows in particular that every admissible linear estimator is a function of the generalised least squares estimator.

[††] In the same context, RADNER [1958] tried to find a minimax estimator for the case where, in the problem P, the covariance matrix Q of x is not known a priori. Unfortunately he showed that this approach does not lead to any interesting result.

is not admissible in the class of all regular estimators if L has dimension $p > 2$. They constructed a regular biased estimator which has risk smaller than that of y^* for every y in L. This estimator is a non-linear function of y^*.

However, such an estimator does not appear to be much used in applied statistics, since in practice it must be very near y^*, as is suggested by the searching investigation of a particularly important case[†] by BARANCHIK [1973]. This is why we shall subsequently conform to usual practice by taking y^* as the preferred estimator for the problem P.

10   Historical note

The properties which we have discussed, and in particular those with which theorem 1 is concerned, have a fairly long history in mathematical statistics. The interested reader may consult WHITTAKER and ROBINSON [1924], PLACKETT [1949] and HARTER [1974-1975].

The method of least squares was first proposed by LEGENDRE [1806] but appears to have been used previously by Gauss. Shortly afterwards Laplace and Gauss justified its use and distinguished certain optimal properties. LAPLACE [1812] showed that every unbiased linear estimator is asymptotically normal when the number of observations tends to infinity, and that the asymptotic variance is minimal for the least squares estimator.

GAUSS [1821-1823] established that, among all unbiased linear estimates, the least squares regression minimizes the mean square deviation between the true value and the estimated value, and that this holds for any distribution of the errors and for any sample size. The same result was given by MARKOV [1912], hence the name Markov theorem often given to theorem 1 (where $Q = \sigma^2 I$). AITKEN [1935] generalized the property to the case where Q is some positive definite matrix (see also DAVID and NEYMAN [1938]).

The geometric method which we have used originates in the work of R. A. Fisher. It was applied to a particular case of the problem P by DARMOIS [1952].

[†] For the multiple regressions discussed in ch. 6, the James-Stein estimator is proportional to a^* but slightly shrunk towards the origin. The correction is perceptible only if, simultaneously, the number T of observations is small, the number m of explanatory variables is large and the coefficient R^2 is not near 1. (See ch. 6, § 11 (v).)

CHAPTER 6

Multiple regressions

1 The basic model

When discussing the examples of chapters 2 and 4, we stated that economic models often involve several exogenous variables and sometimes, even, several endogenous variables. Therefore the econometrician must have at his disposal methods of estimation which are applicable to sets of observations on multiple variables.

In this chapter we shall use consistently a model which is a direct generalization of the model of ch. 3. Multiple regressions will be justified in the same way as was simple regression. In this chapter and the next we shall deliberately ignore various complications which often arise because of the practical necessities of econometric study. These will be dealt with in ch. 8 when we examine models which contain only one endogenous variable and only one equation, and in part 5 when we discuss models with several equations.

Suppose that there exist n endogenous variables x_i $(i=1,2,\ldots,n)$ and m exogenous variables z_j $(j=1,2,\ldots,m)$. Let x denote the vector of the endogenous variables, and z that of the exogenous variables.

The model which we shall now examine stipulates that the endogenous variables are determined simultaneously by the exogenous variables according to the equation:

$$x = Az + \varepsilon, \tag{1}$$

where A is an $n \times m$-matrix and ε an unobservable random n-vector. In other words, each endogenous variable x_i is determined by the z_j according to the equation:

$$x_i = \sum_{j=1}^{m} a_{ij}z_j + \varepsilon_i, \qquad i = 1, 2, \ldots, n. \tag{2}$$

Just as in ch. 3, the observable quantities z_j and the unobservable quantities ε_i represent the causes which determine the values of the quantities x_i. The ε_i represent the effect of all unidentifiable factors, and are considered random, since from our point of view they have all the attributes of random variables. From eqs. (1) and (2), the endogenous variables x_i are random as are the *'errors in the equations'* ε_i.

The exogenous variables z_j are considered as fixed. We do not need to inquire whether their values do in fact result from some random process, since we shall always be concerned only with the conditional distribution of the x_i for given values of the z_j. This question has been given fairly full discussion in ch. 3.

We note that the eqs. (1) and (2) have no constant terms. In fact, the model

$$x_i = \sum_{j=1}^{m} a_{ij}z_j + b_i + \varepsilon_i, \qquad (3)$$

which includes the constant terms b_i, can always be written in the form:

$$x_i = \sum_{j=1}^{m+1} a_{ij}z_j + \varepsilon_i \qquad (4)$$

provided that we set $a_{i,m+1} = b_i$ and that the exogenous variable z_{m+1} is defined as that which always has the value 1. The quantity z_{m+1} will be called a *'dummy variable'*. The use of the above convention simplifies the notation, and so we shall never introduce constant terms explicitly.

We shall often be interested in the case where there is a single endogenous variable $(n=1)$. The model will then be written:

$$x = a'z + \varepsilon, \qquad (5)$$

where a is an m-vector.

In the context of the model defined in this way, we wish to estimate the matrix A, or the vector a, from T observations on the variables x_i and z_j. *In this chapter we shall always suppose that A or a are completely unknown,* so that a priori the coefficients a_{ij} can have any real values. We shall return to this assumption in ch. 9.

We shall denote by x_{it} and z_{jt} the tth observations $(t=1,2,\ldots,T)$ on x_i and z_j, by x_t and z_t the vectors of the x_{it} and the z_{jt}. Similarly ε_{it} will denote the unobservable value of ε_i for the tth observation, and ε_t will be the vector of the ε_{it}.

We now state the assumptions which will be necessary at one stage or another during the statistical treatment of the model.

Assumption 1 (independence of the errors). The random vector ε_t is distributed independently of t, with zero mean and non-singular covariance matrix Ω which is independent of the z_θ for $\theta = 1, 2, \ldots, T$. Two vectors ε_t and ε_θ are stochastically independent[†] whenever $t \neq \theta$.

Assumption 2. The random nT-vector ε, defined by $\varepsilon' = (\varepsilon_1', \varepsilon_2', \ldots, \varepsilon_T')$, has zero mean and non-singular covariance matrix Q.

[†] For certain results to be given below, we could demand only that the errors ε_t be pairwise uncorrelated rather than mutually independent. Assumption 1 could thus be weakened for the various properties shown in sections 2–6. But in econometrics the absence of correlation is likely to seem practically just as restrictive as independence. Hence, there is not much to be gained from insisting on the distinction.

Assumption 3 (normality).   The vector ε_t is normally distributed.

Assumption 4 (absence of multicollinearity).   There exists no set of m numbers λ_j (for $j=1,2,\ldots,m$) not all zero, such that:

$$\sum_{j=1}^{m} \lambda_j z_{jt} = 0 \qquad \text{for} \qquad t = 1,2,\ldots,T. \tag{7}$$

Assumption 5.   When T tends to infinity, the matrix[†]:

$$M_{zz} = \frac{1}{T} \sum_{t=1}^{T} z_t z_t' \tag{8}$$

tends to a finite non-singular matrix M_0.

These assumptions generalize those made in ch. 3. Thus assumption 1 corresponds to the assumptions of homoscedasticity and independence of the different observations. Clearly, it implies assumption 2, which is very general since it assumes only that second-order moments of the errors exist and that the means of the errors are zero.

2   Multiple regressions and linear estimation

Estimation of A in the model (1) is based on the general theory of linear estimation and appears as a particular case of the problem P discussed in ch. 5, as can be simply shown. We set:

$$y_t = A z_t \qquad \text{for} \qquad t = 1,2,\ldots,T \tag{9}$$

and let x, y and ε denote the vectors of nT-dimensional space whose components are the x_{it}, the y_{it} and the ε_{it} (for $i=1,2,\ldots,n$ and $t=1,2,\ldots,T$). Then obviously:

$$x = y + \varepsilon.$$

In nT-dimensional space the expected value of x is y whenever the expected value of ε is zero.

Assumption 2 guarantees that this is indeed the case and that x has second-order moments. To get back to the problem P, we need only show that y is restricted to lie in a vector subspace and that the estimation of y in this subspace is equivalent to the determination of A.

Given the values of the vectors z_t $(t=1,2,\ldots,T)$, let us consider the set L of vectors y for which there exists a matrix A such that the conditions (9) are satisfied. It follows from the next two remarks that this set is a vector subspace.

[†] The reader may note that this notation differs from that used in ch. 1, since M_{zz} was then used to denote the matrix of the second-order moments *about the mean* of the z_t. It will be clear in section 5 below that this change in notation cannot cause any real confusion.

(i) If y^1 belongs to L, so also does αy^1. For if A^1 is the matrix for which y^1 satisfies the conditions (9), then αy^1 satisfies these conditions with the matrix αA^1.

(ii) If y^1 and y^2 belong to L, so also does $y^1 + y^2$. For if A^1 and A^2 are the two matrices for which y^1 and y^2 respectively satisfy (9), then $y^1 + y^2$ satisfies (9) with the matrix $A^1 + A^2$.

Obviously knowledge of A implies knowledge of y by means of the eqs. (9). Conversely, given a vector y in L, there certainly exists at least one corresponding matrix A (from the definition of L). This matrix is unique if assumption 4 is satisfied.

For if there are two non-identical matrices A^1 and A^2 corresponding to the same vector y, we have:

$$y_t = A^1 z_t = A^2 z_t \qquad \text{for} \qquad t = 1, 2, \ldots, T$$

and therefore

$$(A^1 - A^2) z_t = 0 \qquad \text{for} \qquad t = 1, 2, \ldots, T.$$

Let h be the index of a row for which at least one element $a^1_{hj} - a^2_{hj}$ of $A^1 - A^2$ is not zero. The above equality implies:

$$\sum_{j=1}^{m} (a^1_{hj} - a^2_{hj}) z_{jt} = 0 \qquad \text{for} \qquad t = 1, 2, \ldots, T.$$

The vector λ with components $\lambda_j = a^1_{hj} - a^2_{hj}$ is not zero and satisfies:

$$\sum_{j=1}^{m} \lambda_j z_{jt} = 0 \qquad \text{for} \qquad t = 1, 2, \ldots, T,$$

which is contrary to assumption 4.

Thus in the absence of multicollinearity, finding A is equivalent to finding y in L. It follows at once that the subspace L has dimension nm. We could establish its analytic equations, but as they are not very simple we can dispense with them. We need only remember that *the subspace L depends on the values of the z_t.*

What happens when assumption 4 is not satisfied? It is still true that y is contained in a subspace L, but L now has a dimension less than nm. Being given y in L is no longer sufficient to determine A. If ε is distributed independently of A, as we generally suppose, the observations on x do not allow us to determine A completely. Two values of A which give the same vector y are also equivalent from the point of view of the distribution of x. Under these conditions A is *not identifiable*.

Proposition 1. If the exogenous variables show multicollinearities and if the errors are distributed independently of A, then A is not identifiable.

To allow complete determination of the parameters, the exogenous variables must therefore satisfy assumption 4. If z_j denotes the vector with the T components z_{jt} ($t = 1, 2, \ldots, T$), the m vectors z_j (for $j = 1, 2, \ldots, m$) must be linearly independent.

When multicollinearities exist, certain linear forms of the coefficients are still identifiable, as we shall see in section 6. These identifiable linear forms are called *estimable functions* in statistical literature.

3 The method of least squares

Whenever assumption 2 is satisfied, estimation of A in the model (1) appears as a particular case of the problem P. The results of the previous chapter show that in this case there exists an estimator with interesting properties. We shall confine ourselves for the moment to finding the precise form of this estimator for the case where assumption 1, of the independence of the errors, is satisfied. In other chapters we shall find out what other form is most appropriate to each case where assumption 1 no longer holds.

From theorem 1 in ch. 5, the estimator y^* which we are seeking is such that $x - y^*$ is conjugate to L. It follows that

$$(x - y^*)'Q^{-1}y = 0 \qquad \text{for every } y \text{ in } L, \tag{10}$$

Q being the covariance matrix of x.

Assumption 1 implies that Ω is the covariance matrix of ε_t and that Q is equal to:

$$Q = \begin{bmatrix} \Omega & 0 & 0 \cdots 0 \\ 0 & \Omega & 0 \cdots 0 \\ 0 & 0 & \Omega \cdots 0 \\ \cdots\cdots\cdots\cdots\cdots\cdots \\ 0 & 0 & 0 \cdots \Omega \end{bmatrix}.$$

The condition (10) can then be written:

$$\sum_{t=1}^{T} (x_t - y_t^*)'\Omega^{-1} A z_t = 0 \qquad \text{for every } A \text{ of order } n \times m. \tag{11}$$

Since $\Omega^{-1}A$ is of order $n \times m$ and since, conversely, every A of order $n \times m$ can be written $\Omega^{-1}B$ where B is a matrix of the same order, the condition (11) is equivalent to:

$$\sum_{t=1}^{T} (x_t - y_t^*)' A z_t = 0 \qquad \text{for every } A \text{ of order } n \times m. \tag{12}$$

This last condition shows that $x - y^*$ is conjugate to L with respect to the unit sphere. Therefore the vector y^* minimizes:

$$\sum_{t=1}^{T} (x_t - y_t^*)'(x_t - y_t^*) \tag{13}$$

subject to the reservation that it is restricted to lie in L.

Since $y_t^* = A^* z_t$, we see that (13) is equal to:

$$\sum_{i=1}^{n} \left\{ \sum_{t=1}^{T} \left[x_{it} - \sum_{j=1}^{m} a_{ij}^* z_{jt} \right]^2 \right\}.$$

To minimize this expression, we must minimize each of the n sums of squares relating to a given i, that is, we must choose the a_{ij}^* so as to minimize the sum of squares of the differences between x_{it} and the expression

$$\sum_{j=1}^{m} a_{ij}^* z_{jt},$$

which appears in the equation of the model relating to x_{it}.

Thus the method of the last chapter becomes equivalent here to applying the method of least squares to each equation. This result would have been almost obvious if we had assumed independence of the errors ε_{it} and ε_{ht} relating to two different equations. (The matrix Ω of assumption 1 would then have been diagonal.) It is interesting to find that correlation between these errors gives rise to no new complication.

As is clear from the proof, this property depends on the fact that a priori, A may be any matrix of order $n \times m$. In chapter 9 and in the last part of this book we shall examine models in which A is subject to a priori restrictions. Estimation of Ω will then become an essential part of the procedure.

Theorem 1 now follows directly[†].

Theorem 1. In the models (1) which satisfy assumptions (1) and (4), least squares regression on each equation leads to an unbiased estimator A^*:

(a) whose concentration ellipsoid is contained in that of every other unbiased linear estimator,

(b) which has zero correlation with the vector of the residuals $x_t - A^* z_t$.

In this chapter we shall also find out what happens to the properties of the estimator A^* when assumption 1 is not satisfied. From the fact that A^* corresponds to a projection of n-dimensional space on L, there follows directly:

Proposition 2. In the models (1) satisfying assumptions 2 and 4, least squares regression on each equation leads to an unbiased estimator.

[†] We note that the above proof and theorem 1 still apply when Ω has rank r less than n. To see this, we need only replace Ω^{-1} by $(\Omega + RR')^{-1}$ in (11) and in the following reasoning, R being a matrix of rank $n-r$ such that $\Omega R = 0$. This substitution is justified by the theory given in the previous chapter.

4 Calculation of the estimate and its concentration ellipsoid

The least squares matrix A^* is that which minimizes expression (13), that is:

$$\sum_{t=1}^{T} (x_t - A^* z_t)'(x_t - A^* z_t).$$

By differentiation we obtain the condition

$$\sum_{t=1}^{T} (x_t - A^* z_t)z_t' = 0,$$

or again:

$$M_{xz} - A^* M_{zz} = 0, \tag{14}$$

where by definition M_{xz} is:

$$M_{xz} = \frac{1}{T} \sum_{t=1}^{T} x_t z_t'.$$

The eqs. (14) will have a unique solution if and only if M_{zz} is non-singular, that is, if there exists no non-zero vector λ such that:

$$\lambda' M_{zz} \lambda = 0$$

or again

$$\sum_{t=1}^{T} (\lambda' z_t)^2 = 0$$

or again

$$\lambda' z_t = 0 \quad \text{for} \quad t = 1, 2, \ldots, T,$$

that is, if assumption 4 is satisfied.

We shall then have:

$$A^* = M_{xz} M_{zz}^{-1}, \tag{15}$$

which generalizes the expressions for a^* and b^* in ch. 3 to the case where there may be several endogenous variables and several exogenous variables.

When the model contains a single endogenous variable (cf. formula (5)), the matrix M_{zx} reduces to a vector which we shall also denote by m_{zx}. The vector a^* of the estimates then becomes:

$$a^* = M_{zz}^{-1} m_{zx}. \tag{16}$$

The equations (14) are often called *normal equations*. Their solution may involve rather lengthy calculations because of the precision required when M_{zz} is nearly singular (approximate multicollinearity). But solution presents no difficulty for electronic computers. For methods of solution, the reader may consult, for example: MORICE and CHARTIER [1954], p. 123 and thereafter, DWYER [1951] or GOLDBERGER [1964], pp. 182–191.

We shall again resort to the concentration ellipsoid in order to measure the variances and covariances[†] of the estimates A^*. The concentration ellipsoid of x (denoted by E) is defined by:

$$\sum_{t=1}^{T} \varepsilon_t' \Omega^{-1} \varepsilon_t \leqq 1. \tag{17}$$

Theorem 1 of ch. 5 established that the concentration ellipsoid of y is the intersection of E and L. By a similar argument to that used in ch. 5 § 6, we can prove that the analytic expression for the concentration ellipsoid of A in nm-dimensional space is obtained directly from (17) by replacing ε_t by Az_t. Thus this ellipsoid consists of the set of $n \times m$ matrices A which satisfy:

$$\sum_{t=1}^{T} z_t' A' \Omega^{-1} A z_t \leqq 1. \tag{18}$$

In the particular case of the model (5), there exists a single endogenous variable, and Ω is a positive number equal to the variance of ε_t denoted by σ^2. The concentration ellipsoid (18) is then the set of all the m-vectors α which satisfy:

$$\frac{1}{\sigma^2} \sum_{t=1}^{T} z_t' \alpha \alpha' z_t \leqq 1 \tag{18'}$$

or again

$$\frac{T}{\sigma^2} \alpha' M_{zz} \alpha \leqq 1. \tag{19}$$

The covariance matrix of a^* is therefore

$$\frac{\sigma^2}{T} M_{zz}^{-1}. \tag{20}$$

In the general case, the covariance matrix of the estimates is rather more complex. For its definition, we note that the coefficient of $a_{ij}a_{hk}$ in (18) is equal to

$$T(\Omega^{-1})_{ih}(M_{zz})_{jk}.$$

Let us consider A as defining an nm-vector whose first m components correspond to the first row of A, the next m to the second row, and so on. The lefthand side of the inequality (18) then appears as a quadratic form of this vector. The square matrix of order nm of this quadratic form can be partitioned into n^2

[†] The expression for the variances and covariances can be established directly from formulae (15) and (16). Thus, we can easily find formula (20) applying to models with a single equation, and use a similar process of reasoning for models with several equations. But since we shall need the analytic expression for the concentration ellipsoid of A^* in other chapters, it is simpler to give it at this point.

square submatrices of order m. The submatrix which appears in the ith block row and the hth block column is

$$T(\Omega^{-1})_{ih}M_{zz}.$$

When the inverse matrix is expressed in the same way it will contain in its ith block row and hth block column the matrix

$$\frac{1}{T}\omega_{ih}M_{zz}^{-1},$$

ω_{ih} being obviously the element (i, h) of Ω. To verify this we need only find the product of the two following matrices[†]:

$$T\left[\begin{array}{c}(\Omega^{-1})_{ih}M_{zz}\end{array}\right],\quad \frac{1}{T}\left[\begin{array}{c}\omega_{ih}M_{zz}^{-1}\end{array}\right].$$

Thus the covariance of a_{ij}^{*} and a_{hk}^{*} is

$$\frac{\omega_{ih}}{T}[M_{zz}^{-1}]_{jk}.$$

In particular the covariance matrix of the coefficients a_{ij}^{*} corresponding to the ith equation $(j=1,2,\ldots,m)$ is equal to the expression (20) with σ^{2} replaced by $\omega_{ii}=\sigma_{i}^{2}$, the variance of ε_{it}.

It is sometimes convenient to give a different expression for the concentration ellipsoid (18). For we can write[††]:

$$\sum_{t=1}^{T}z_{t}'A'\Omega^{-1}Az_{t} = \text{tr}\left[\sum_{t=1}^{T}z_{t}'A'\Omega^{-1}Az_{t}\right]$$

$$= \text{tr}\left[\sum_{t=1}^{T}\Omega^{-1}Az_{t}z_{t}'A'\right] = T\,\text{tr}[\Omega^{-1}AM_{zz}A'].$$

[†] The second of these two matrices is the covariance matrix of the elements of A^{*}. We sometimes write:

$$\frac{1}{T}\Omega \otimes M_{zz}^{-1},$$

which is then called the *Kronecker product* of Ω/T by M_{zz}^{-1}.

[††] The sum of the diagonal elements of a square matrix U is called its *trace* and is denoted by tr U. If $U=RS$ and $V=SR$ where R is a $p \times q$ matrix and S a $q \times p$ matrix, then tr $U=$ tr V since:

$$\text{tr } U = \sum_{i}u_{ii} = \sum_{ij}r_{ij}s_{ji} = \sum_{j}v_{jj} = \text{tr } V$$

The trace is clearly a linear operator.

The concentration ellipsoid of A^* can therefore be written

$$T \operatorname{tr} \left[\Omega^{-1} A M_{zz} A' \right] \leqq 1. \tag{18''}$$

Generally Ω is not known, and must be estimated from the observations x_t themselves. We generally use for this the vector of the residuals

$$\varepsilon_t^* = x_t - A^* z_t$$

and the matrix:

$$M_{\varepsilon\varepsilon}^* = \frac{1}{T} \sum_{t=1}^{T} \varepsilon_t^* \varepsilon_t^{*\prime}. \tag{21}$$

$M_{\varepsilon\varepsilon}^*$ can be calculated directly from the residuals, or by the formula:

$$M_{\varepsilon\varepsilon}^* = M_{xx} - M_{xz} M_{zz}^{-1} M_{xz}' = M_{xx} - A^* M_{xz}', \tag{22}$$

which can be deduced from the previous formula as follows:

$$\frac{1}{T} \sum_{t=1}^{T} \varepsilon_t^* \varepsilon_t^{*\prime} = \frac{1}{T} \sum_{t=1}^{T} (x_t - A^* z_t)(x_t - A^* z_t)'$$

$$= \frac{1}{T} \sum_{t=1}^{T} (x_t - M_{xz} M_{zz}^{-1} z_t)(x_t - M_{xz} M_{zz}^{-1} z_t)'$$

$$= \frac{1}{T} \sum_{t=1}^{T} x_t x_t' - \frac{1}{T} \sum_{t=1}^{T} x_t z_t' M_{zz}^{-1} M_{xz}'$$

$$\quad - \frac{1}{T} \sum_{t=1}^{T} M_{xz} M_{zz}^{-1} z_t x_t' + \frac{1}{T} \sum_{t=1}^{T} M_{xz} M_{zz}^{-1} z_t z_t' M_{zz}^{-1} M_{xz}'$$

$$= M_{xx} - M_{xz} M_{zz}^{-1} M_{xz}'.$$

We can easily show that $(T/T-m) M_{\varepsilon\varepsilon}^*$ is an unbiased estimator of Ω. For:

$$\varepsilon_t^* = x_t - A^* z_t = \varepsilon_t + (A - A^*) z_t.$$

Moreover

$$\frac{1}{T} \sum_{t=1}^{T} \varepsilon_t z_t' = M_{xz} - A M_{zz} = (A^* - A) M_{zz}.$$

Consequently:

$$M_{\varepsilon\varepsilon}^* = \frac{1}{T} \sum_{t=1}^{T} \varepsilon_t \varepsilon_t' - (A - A^*) M_{zz} (A - A^*)'.$$

Since $E(\varepsilon_t \varepsilon_t') = \Omega$, the first term has expected value Ω. In the second term, the expected value of the element (i, h) is:

$$\sum_{jk} [M_{zz}]_{jk} \operatorname{cov} (a_{ij}^*, a_{hk}^*) = \frac{\omega_{ih}}{T} \sum_{jk} [M_{zz}]_{jk} [M_{zz}^{-1}]_{jk} = \frac{\omega_{ih}}{T} \operatorname{tr} I = \frac{m}{T} \omega_{ih}.$$

Thus:

$$E[M_{\varepsilon\varepsilon}^*] = \frac{T-m}{T}\,\Omega,$$

as we wished to prove[†].

By the same reasoning we can find the covariance matrix of a particular residual vector ε^*. It is easy to show that

$$E(\varepsilon_t^*\varepsilon_t^{*\prime}) = \left(1 - \frac{1}{T}\,z_t'M_{zz}^{-1}z_t\right)\Omega.$$

It is worth noting that this matrix varies from one observation to another, and depends on z_t as well as on M_{zz}.

5 Applications

In order to illustrate the preceding formulae we shall re-examine an example introduced in ch. 1. However, we should first of all find the form taken by these formulae when the last exogenous variable is the constant which always equals 1, that is, when the model which we set up initially has an unknown constant in each equation.

So we write in this section:

$$x_t = Az_t + b + \varepsilon_t, \tag{23}$$

where z_t is the vector of the m true exogenous variables and b is the vector of the constants. We can revert to the model (1) by writing:

$$x_t = \begin{bmatrix} A & b \end{bmatrix}\begin{bmatrix} z_t \\ 1 \end{bmatrix} + \varepsilon_t$$

and by setting

$$\hat{A} = \begin{bmatrix} A & b \end{bmatrix} \quad \text{and} \quad \hat{z}_t' = \begin{bmatrix} z_t' & 1 \end{bmatrix}.$$

It follows that:

$$x_t = \hat{A}\hat{z}_t + \varepsilon_t.$$

To apply the preceding formulae, we denote by $\hat{M}_{zz}$ the square matrix of

---

† We may ask further what is the efficiency of $(T/T-m)M_{\varepsilon\varepsilon}^*$ as an estimator of Ω. With reference to the case where there is a single endogenous variable, DRYGAS [1970], § 3e, has shown that

$$\sigma_\varepsilon^{*2} = \frac{1}{T-m}\sum_{t=1}^{T}\varepsilon_t^{*2}$$

is, of all unbiased estimators quadratic in the x_t, that which has smallest variance. For further results on this subject, see H. DRYGAS and J. SRZEDNICKA [1976].

order $m+1$ constructed from the second order moments of the $\hat{z}_i$, by M_{zz} the square matrix of order m similarly constructed from the z_t, and by $\overline{M}_{zz}$ the matrix

$$\overline{M}_{zz} = \frac{1}{T} \sum_{t=1}^{T} (z_t - \bar{z})(z_t - \bar{z})'. \tag{24}$$

We shall also use the similar notations $\hat{M}_{xz}$, $\overline{M}_{xz}$ and M_{xz}. These matrices can be deduced from each other using the formulae:

$$\hat{M}_{zz} = \begin{bmatrix} M_{zz} & \bar{z} \\ \bar{z}' & 1 \end{bmatrix}, \qquad \hat{M}_{xz} = [M_{xz} \quad \bar{x}] \tag{25}$$

and

$$\overline{M}_{zz} = M_{zz} - \bar{z}\bar{z}', \qquad \overline{M}_{xz} = M_{xz} - \bar{x}\bar{z}'. \tag{26}$$

The least squares estimates A^* and b^* of A and b must satisfy the matrix equation (14) which in this case is written:

$$\hat{M}_{xz} - \hat{A}^*\hat{M}_{zz} = 0,$$

or again:

$$[M_{xz} \quad \bar{x}] - [A^* \quad b^*] \begin{bmatrix} M_{zz} & \bar{z} \\ \bar{z}' & 1 \end{bmatrix} = 0,$$

hence:

$$M_{xz} - A^*M_{zz} - b^*\bar{z}' = 0,$$
$$\bar{x} - A^*\bar{z} - b^* = 0. \tag{27}$$

The last equality allows b^* to be calculated from A^*. It shows simply that each regression equation is satisfied by the means $\bar{x}_i$ and $\bar{z}_j$ of the endogenous and exogenous variables. It expresses the fact that, in the space of the $m+1$ variables $x_i, z_1, z_2, \ldots, z_m$, the regression hyperplane of x_i on $z_1, z_2, \ldots, z_m$ passes through the mean point of the collection of points representing the observations.

By eliminating b^* from the two eqs. (27), we obtain:

$$(M_{xz} - \bar{x}\bar{z}') - A^*(M_{zz} - \bar{z}\bar{z}') = 0,$$

or again

$$\overline{M}_{xz} - A^*\overline{M}_{zz} = 0, \tag{28}$$

which is very similar to eq. (14).

Thus in models which contain unknown constant terms, the coefficients of the true exogenous variables can be obtained either from the general formulae in §4, or from formulae which can easily be deduced from them to meet this special case. We need only substitute in them the matrices of moments about the mean for the matrices of moments about the origin.

The same principle applies to formulae for the covariances of the estimates. For (22) becomes:

$$M_{\varepsilon\varepsilon}^* = M_{xx} - [A^* \quad b^*]\begin{bmatrix} M_{zx} \\ \bar{x}' \end{bmatrix} = M_{xx} - A^* M_{zx} - b^* \bar{x}'.$$

In view of the expression for b^*, this matrix can be written:

$$M_{\varepsilon\varepsilon}^* = (M_{xx} - \bar{x}\bar{x}') - A^*(M_{zx} - \bar{z}\bar{x}') = \overline{M}_{xx} - A^* \overline{M}_{zx}.$$

An unbiased estimate of Ω will be

$$\frac{T}{T - m - 1} M_{\varepsilon\varepsilon}^*.$$

Indeed to bring the discussion back to the terms of the general model dealt with in this chapter, we must add the dummy variable $z_{t,m+1} = 1$ to the m true exogenous variables. Moreover, the covariance matrix of the coefficients of $\hat{A}^*$ involves the matrix $\hat{M}_{zz}^{-1}$ (formula (20) and other analogous formulae). Now[†]

$$\hat{M}_{zz}^{-1} = \begin{bmatrix} M_{zz} & \bar{z} \\ \bar{z}' & 1 \end{bmatrix}^{-1} = \begin{bmatrix} \overline{M}_{zz}^{-1} & -\overline{M}_{zz}^{-1}\bar{z} \\ -\bar{z}'\overline{M}_{zz}^{-1} & 1 + \bar{z}'\overline{M}_{zz}^{-1}\bar{z} \end{bmatrix}.$$

The covariance matrix of the elements of A^* therefore involves only the matrix $\overline{M}_{zz}^{-1}$.

In particular, if the model contains a single equation $x_t = a'z_t + b + \varepsilon_t$, the covariance matrix of a^* is:

$$\frac{\sigma^2}{T} \overline{M}_{zz}^{-1}.$$

The above formula also shows that in this case

$$\text{var}(b^*) = \frac{\sigma^2}{T}(1 + \bar{z}'\overline{M}_{zz}^{-1}\bar{z}). \tag{29}$$

For example, suppose we adopt the following model to represent imports of goods and services into France:

$$x_t = a_1 z_{1t} + a_2 z_{2t} + b + \varepsilon_t. \tag{30}$$

In this equation x_t denotes the volume of imports in year t, z_{1t} gross domestic production and z_{2t} stock formation during the same year. The influence of other factors is considered random and independent of the influence of z_1 and z_2. It is represented here by ε_t.

We propose to use the data in table 1 (ch. 1) to estimate the values of the numerical coefficients a_1, a_2 and b. But initial examination of the import series discloses a change in the growth rhythm about 1960 (effect of the setting-up of the Common Market). So to give an accurate representation of the phe-

---

† The reader can verify this equality directly, or establish it from the general formula given in the footnote to page 26.

nomenon, we decide to substitute for (30)

$$x_t = a_1 z_{1t} + a_2 z_{2t} + a_4 z_{4t} + b + \varepsilon_t, \tag{31}$$

the variable z_{4t} being zero for years prior to 1961 and taking the value i for the ith year subsequent to 1960 ($i = 1, 2, \ldots, 6$) (we reserve z_{3t} for consumption, introduced later).

The calculations necessary for determining the regression of x on z_1 and z_2 have already been shown in ch. 1, where we considered matrices of moments about the mean. For fitting model (31), we shall refer now to the direct formulae (16) and thereafter. Working on the data of table 1, and using the four exogenous variables z_1, z_2, z_4 and $z_5 = 1$, we find:

$$M_{zz} = 10^2 \begin{bmatrix} 10840 & 161.3 & 68.61 & 42.75 \\ 161.3 & 2.95 & 0.849 & 0.662 \\ 68.61 & 0.849 & 0.910 & 0.210 \\ 42.75 & 0.662 & 0.210 & 0.180 \end{bmatrix}$$

$$m_{zx} = 10^2 \begin{bmatrix} 1419 \\ 20.89 \\ 10.24 \\ 5.41 \end{bmatrix}$$

and so

$$M_{zz}^{-1} = 10^{-2} \begin{bmatrix} 0.0066 & -0.025 & -0.184 & -1.267 \\ -0.025 & 2.066 & 0.458 & -2.264 \\ -0.184 & 0.458 & 6.622 & 34.19 \\ -1.267 & -2.264 & 34.19 & 274.9 \end{bmatrix}$$

$$\begin{bmatrix} a_1^* \\ a_2^* \\ a_1^* \\ b^* \end{bmatrix} = M_{zz}^{-1} m_{zx} = \begin{bmatrix} 0.133 \\ 0.550 \\ 2.104 \\ -5.917 \end{bmatrix}.$$

(We note that, for the sake of accuracy, the numbers in the matrices M_{zz}, M_{zz}^{-1} and m_{zx} should be taken to many more significant digits than have been given here.)

So the least squares regression on (31) is

$$x_t = 0.133 z_{1t} + 0.550 z_{2t} + 2.10 z_{4t} - 5.92. \tag{32}$$

It is often useful to illustrate a regression by constructing a graph which shows at the same time the course of the observed endogenous variable (x_t), of the calculated endogenous variable (x_t^*) and the contributions of the different exogenous variables ($a_j^* z_{jt}$). Figure 1 shows such a graph for eq. (32) which

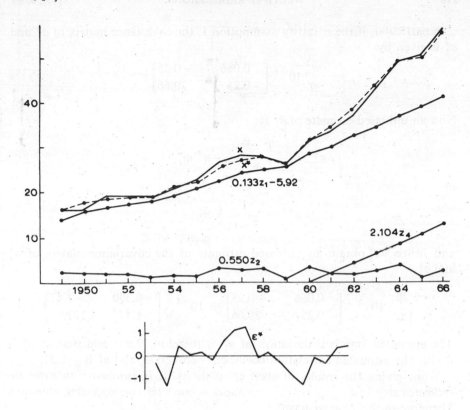

Fig. 1. Observed imports and calculated imports.

relates to imports. It allows us to appreciate the part played by variations in production ($0.133 z_{1t} - 5.92$) and by variations in stock-formation ($0.550 z_2$). The estimation residuals (ε_t^*) are shown on a scale multiplied by 4 in the lower part of the diagram. We see strong negative residuals (that is, an abnormally low real level of imports) in 1950, 1961, 1962, and strong positive residuals in 1955, 1956 and 1957.

These results, similar to those obtained in ch. 1, can now be interpreted much more precisely.

On the one hand, if we suppose that the expected value of ε is zero for any values of production (z_1) or stock formation (z_2), then we must naturally prefer the regression of x on z_1 and z_2 to the other two multiple regressions of z_1 on x and z_2, and of z_2 on x and z_1, since only the first provides unbiased estimates[†].

On the other hand, we can find out how precise are the estimates a_1^*, a_2^* and b^*, provided that we are prepared to make some additional assumption about the distribution of the ε_t.

† We have not yet proved that the regression of z_1 on x and z_2 leads to estimates of a_1 and a_2 which contain systematic errors. This will follow from the discussion in ch. 15.

In particular, if the ε_t satisfy assumption 1, the covariance matrix of a_1^* and a_2^* is given by

$$\frac{\sigma^2}{T} 10^{-3} \begin{bmatrix} 0.066 & -0.25 \\ -0.25 & 20.66 \end{bmatrix}.$$

Now an unbiased estimate of σ^2 is:

$$\sigma^{*2} = \frac{T}{T-m} (m_{xx} - a^{*'} m_{zx})$$

or

$$\sigma^{*2} = \frac{T}{T-m} 8.26,$$

and hence we obtain an unbiased estimate of the covariance matrix of a_1^* and a_2^*:

$$\frac{8.26}{14} \cdot 10^{-3} \begin{bmatrix} 0.066 & -0.25 \\ -0.25 & 20.66 \end{bmatrix} = 10^{-4} \begin{bmatrix} 0.390 & -1.47 \\ -1.47 & 121.9 \end{bmatrix}$$

The estimated standard deviation of a_1^* is therefore 0.006 and that of a_2^* is 0.110. The estimated correlation coefficient between a_1^* and a_2^* is -0.21.

When giving the results of such calculations, *it is customary to write the estimated standard deviations in parentheses beneath the corresponding estimates.* Therefore in this case we have:

$$x_t = 0.133\, z_{1t} + 0.550\, z_{2t} + 2.10\, z_{4t} - 5.92.$$
$$(0.006) \quad\ (0.110) \quad\ (0.20) \quad\ (1.27) \tag{33}$$

These results reveal that the data allow us to make a fairly exact estimate of the influence of production on imports. An interval of two standard deviations on each side of the estimated value will be:

$$0.121 \le a_1 \le 0.145. \tag{34}$$

On the other hand, we do not have a very exact measure of the influence of stock formation on production. The interval which consists of two standard deviations on each side of the estimated value is very large:

$$0.33 \le a_2 \le 0.77. \tag{35}$$

We note in passing that *this lack of precision would pass unnoticed by the reader who took account only of the goodness of fit coefficient R^2,* since in the regression (33) this coefficient has the seemingly highly satisfactory value of 0.997. In fact in the model which we have now chosen the coefficient R^2 is not of any interest and therefore its value has not been included beside the results of the regression (36).

The estimated values of the variances and covariances of a_1^*, a_2^* and b^* are unbiased when assumption 1 is satisfied. However, they could turn out to be very poor estimates, if this assumption would not hold, for example if the errors ε_t affecting the successive years were closely associated. This question will be discussed in detail in ch. 13. We need only note here that the lower part of fig. 1 suggests that there might be some association among the ε_t, but that this association is not close.

6 The effects of multicollinearity

As we saw previously, the coefficients of the model are not identifiable when there is a linear relationship among the exogenous variables z_j, that is, when these variables are multicollinear. We could then adopt the same approach as in chapter 5, § 6 (ii) and introduce supplementary linear relations among the coefficients to be estimated so as to ensure identifiability. But another line of reasoning is available.

It may happen that different exogenous quantities are connected by a number of relations, which necessarily follow from the definitions adopted. These quantities are not really independent. The model therefore becomes clearer if we give it an equivalent formulation which involves fewer, but mutually independent exogenous variables. Such a formulation will be sufficient in applications, since knowledge of the values of the discarded exogenous variables is not relevant to the determination of the endogenous variables[†].

It may also happen that the exogenous variables are linearly related in the observed sample while they are not connected by necessary relations which would hold in all circumstances. The equality

$$\sum_{j=1}^{m} \lambda_j z_{jt} = 0$$

does then apply to the $t = 1, 2, \ldots, T$ observations. But there is no reason to suppose that it will also hold for the applications which we have in mind. Such accidental linear dependence prevents identification of the coefficients of the model, and identification would be necessary to allow further use to be made of the regression. Such a situation is clearly exceptional whenever the number T of the observations is considerably greater than the number m of the exogenous variables.

[†] Suppose, for example, that there is a single linear relation among the z_j. Then there exists a matrix H of order $m \times (m-1)$ and linearly independent $(m-1)$-vectors w_t such that $z_t = Hw_t$. Equation (14) implies $M_{xw}H' - AHM_{ww}H' = 0$ so that the matrix AH is estimated without ambiguity by $M_{xw}M_{ww}^{-1}$. The matrix AH is said to be *estimable*. Similarly, every linear function of A which can be expressed as a linear function of AH is estimable on the basis of previous estimation of AH.

But it is often the case in econometrics that the exogenous variables are almost multicollinear. There approximately exist among them one or more linear relationships which may be purely accidental but which in most cases express the dependencies due to phenomena other than that described by the model.

Suppose, for example, that we propose the following model to explain the imports of goods and services into France:

$$x_t = a_1 z_{1t} + a_2 z_{2t} + a_3 z_{3t} + a_4 z_{4t} + b + \varepsilon_t. \tag{36}$$

This model includes consumption (z_3) as well as production (z_1), stock formation (z_2) and the dummy variable (z_4). This may appear to be a fairly natural choice of model, since imports respond in part directly to consumer demand. A number of imported commodities are consumed by households after a fairly slight contribution from the national production (in distribution and sometimes in some brief industrial processing).

As a rule, the data of table 1 ch. 1, allow us to estimate this model as well as the one previously considered (cf. eq. (31)). But they reveal an approximate multicollinearity between production and consumer demand. In fact,

$$z_{3t} \approx \tfrac{2}{3} z_{1t} \tag{37}$$

for all the $t = 1, 2, \ldots 18$ observations. Thus there exists an approximate linear relationship among z_1 and z_3. This is so because consumption absorbs the greatest part of production, its share having been almost constant, notably as a consequence of the economic policy followed since the end of the last war.

We shall now find out how such multicollinearity affects estimation of the model. The regression of x on z_1, z_2 and z_3 gives:

$$x_t = -0.021 \, z_{1t} + 0.559 \, z_{2t} + 0.235 \, z_{3t} + 2.10 \, z_{4t} - 8.79. \tag{38}$$

The coefficient for stock formation (z_2) does not therefore differ greatly from that obtained in the fitted eq. (32). On the other hand, the coefficient for production (z_1) has a completely different value. Must we therefore discard eq. (32) involving only z_1 and z_2 and prefer formula (38)? Not necessarily, since this last equation is not very exact.

For the estimated covariance matrix of a_1^*, a_2^*, a_3^* is:

$$10^{-4} \begin{bmatrix} 25 & -2 & -38 \\ -2 & 76 & 2 \\ -38 & 2 & 59 \end{bmatrix}. \tag{39}$$

The complete estimation of the model is therefore:

$$x_t = -0.021 \, z_{1t} + 0.559 \, z_{2t} + 0.235 \, z_{3t} + 2.10 \, z_{4t} - 8.79. \tag{40}$$
$$\quad (0.051) \qquad (0.087) \qquad (0.077) \quad (0.16) \quad (1.38)$$

We can see that the standard error of a_2^* is of the same order as that obtained in (33). But the standard error of a_1^* has increased considerably. The interval consisting of two standard errors on each side of the estimated value is now:

$$-0.123 \leq a_1 \leq 0.081 \tag{41}$$

which does not conflict with the interval (34) obtained when the exogenous variables z_3 was excluded.

Thus when the exogenous variables show approximate linear dependencies, estimation of the coefficients of the model becomes very uncertain. This uncertainty will be revealed clearly if we take the trouble to calculate the standard errors of the estimated coefficients.

For instance, we note here that the introduction of the variable z_3 into the model seems to destroy the precision with which we estimated the influence of variations in production on variations in imports, but closer examination of the results resolves this paradox.

For there is very strong negative correlation between a_1^* and a_3^*, as we can see from the expression for the covariance matrix (39). Detailed calculation reveals a correlation coefficient of -0.996 between these two estimates. Therefore there exists a linear combination of a_1 and a_3 which can be estimated from a_1^* and a_3^* with much greater precision than either a_1^* or a_3^* in isolation. In fact, the standard error of $a_1^* + \frac{2}{3}a_3^*$ is 0.005, which is the same as the standard error obtained for a_1^* when z_3 was not introduced to the model[†].

These particular features are clearly revealed if we substitute, for the intervals considered until now, regions which represent, in the space of the coefficients, domains to which the values that are sought probably belong.

Let us return for the moment to the model containing only the two exogenous variables z_1 and z_2, and consider fig. 2 with values of a_1 as abscissa and values of a_2 as ordinate. The point a^* with coordinates $(0.133, 0.550)$ represents the pair of estimated values. About this point there is drawn the ellipse obtained from the estimated concentration ellipse of a^* by displacing the latter so that its centre is no longer the origin but a^*, and then enlarging it by the factor 2. The ellipse drawn in fig. 2 therefore is the locus of the points (a_1, a_2) which satisfy:

$$10^4 [a_1 - a_1^*, \quad a_2 - a_2^*] \begin{bmatrix} 0.39 & -1.47 \\ -1.47 & 121.9 \end{bmatrix}^{-1} \begin{bmatrix} a_1 - a_1^* \\ a_2 - a_2^* \end{bmatrix} = 4.$$

The projections of this ellipse on each of the axes give the intervals consisting of two standard errors on each side of the estimated values, that is, the intervals (34) and (35) respectively. Moreover, the inclination and shape of the ellipse indicate the degree of correlation between a_1^* and a_2^*. This correlation is slight in the case of fig. 2.

† We can verify that, if z_{3t} were exactly equal to $2/3\,z_{1t}$, then the quantity $a_1 + 2/3\,a_3$ would still be 'estimable' (see footnote to page 211).

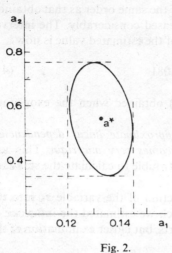

Fig. 2.   Fig. 3.

In principle we can give a similar picture for the results of the regression based on the model with the three exogenous variables z_1, z_2 and z_3. But in this case we need a three-dimensional diagram. We shall only examine here the projection of such a figure on the plane (a_1, a_3) (see fig. 3, where the scale of the abscissa is not the same as in fig. 2).

The ellipse drawn about a^* again projects on the axes the intervals consisting of two standard errors on each side of a_1^* and a_3^*. Thus, the projection on the a_1-axis once more gives the interval (41). But this time, the ellipse is very elongated because of the high correlation between a_1^* and a_3^*. The projections on the axes no longer give a correct impression of the dispersion of the estimated point a^*.

The ellipse is elongated in the direction of the vector $(-1, \frac{3}{2})$. Its projection on the perpendicular vector $(1, \frac{2}{3})$ is very much smaller, which explains why the dispersion of $a_1^* + \frac{2}{3}a_3^*$ is much smaller than that of a_1^* or a_3^*.

Similarly, if the three-dimensional figure had been projected on the plane of the two vectors whose coordinates are $(1, 0, \frac{2}{3})$ and $(0, 1, 0)$ respectively, we would have obtained a picture very similar to fig. 2.

To sum up, the paradox which was apparently revealed by comparison of (32) and (38) is now satisfactorily explained. We have still to examine the effects of multicollinearity on the significance of the results of econometric studies. For this purpose let us suppose that theoretical analysis leads us to keep consumer demand (z_3) in the model as an autonomous factor besides production (z_1). Otherwise there is no problem.

We must obviously consider the practical use which will be made of the results of statistical estimation. Let us suppose that the intention is to predict the volume of imports on the basis of the fitted relation obtained and from independent predictions of production, stock formation and consumption. Two cases must then be distinguished.

(i) The same approximate linear relationship which existed among the exogenous variables during the period of observation will still hold during the period of prediction. In our example, the predicted variations in production (δz_1) and in consumption (δz_3) will satisfy $\delta z_3 \approx \frac{2}{3}\delta z_1$, that is, eq. (37).

The predicted variation in imports (δx) will then be calculated as[†]:

$$\delta x = a_1^* \delta z_1 + a_2^* \delta z_2 + a_3^* \delta z_3 \approx (a_1^* + \tfrac{2}{3}a_3^*)\delta z_1 + a_2^* \delta z_2.$$

Although a_1^* and a_3^* are very inexact estimates of a_1 and a_3, the variation (δx) will be estimated quite precisely since $a_1^* + \frac{2}{3}a_3^*$ is a fairly exact estimate of $a_1 + \frac{2}{3}a_3$. We shall not be seriously inconvenienced by the multicollinearity between the two exogenous variables z_1 and z_3.

Also in this case we arrive at practically the same predictions whether we use the model involving z_1, z_2 and z_3 or the model with z_1 and z_2 only, since the estimated value $a_1^* + \frac{2}{3}a_3^*$ is near the coefficient of z_1 in the regression of x on z_1 and z_2. We find 0.136 in one case and 0.133 in the other, the standard errors of these estimates being 0.005 and 0.006 respectively. In spite of appearances, the regressions (33) and (40) are virtually equivalent for the purposes of the intended predictions. The introduction of consumption as an exogenous variable in the model is pointless since it causes no perceptible change in the predictions.

(ii) But clearly it may happen that the proposed variations in the exogenous variables do not obey the equation which was found to hold during the period of observation. The national development plan may provide for faster growth in capital equipment and may lay down, for example, that only half of the increase in production should be taken up by increasing consumption $(\delta z_3 = \frac{1}{2}\delta z_1)$.

The variation in imports must then be calculated as:

$$\delta x = a_1^* \delta z_1 + a_2^* \delta z_2 + a_3^* \delta z_3 = (a_1^* + \tfrac{2}{3}a_3^*)\delta z_1 + a_2^* \delta z_2 - \tfrac{1}{6}a_3^* \delta z_1.$$

The two first terms on the righthand side of this formula will have the same degree of precision as in case (i) above. But the lack of precision affecting a_3^* will be repeated in the last term $-\frac{1}{6}a_3^* \delta z_1$, which will be subject to a high coefficient of variation (0.34, as for a_3^*). The observed multicollinearity between z_1 and z_3 during the period 1949–1966 will therefore result in a great lack of precision in the predictions made on the basis of the linear model.

In this case, using the model with only the two exogenous variables z_1 and z_2 is equivalent in practice to ignoring the last term of the above formula, namely $-\frac{1}{6}a_3^* \delta z_1$. The apparent precision of the prediction is therefore illusory. In

---

[†] The use of this formula is a natural generalization of the method appropriate to linear models with a single exogenous variable (cf. ch. 3 § 9). We shall return to systematic discussion of prediction in the last section of this chapter.

fact, the estimate of the coefficient of z_1 in the model (33) is affected by an *error of specification* which exists since this model does not correctly represent the factors determining imports. This error depends on the true values of a_1 and a_3. It cannot be evaluated precisely from the data analyzed here, but it may be considerable. We saw above that it had no effect in case (i). It may be very important when the multicollinearity among the exogenous variables happens to disappear.

The conclusions of this section can clearly be generalized. S. D. Silvey [1969] has shown that the precision with which a linear form $\mu'a$ of the coefficients a_j can be estimated depends on the position of the vector μ relative to the characteristic vectors of M_{zz}. Estimation is precise if μ can be expressed approximately as a linear combination of the characteristic vectors corresponding to large roots of M_{zz}. It is imprecise if the direction of μ is near that of the characteristic vectors corresponding to small roots. When M_{zz} is singular, $\mu'a$ is 'estimable' if and only if μ can be expressed as a linear combination of characteristic vectors corresponding to non-zero roots of M_{zz}.

Since the estimates of the coefficients are individually imprecise in the case of collinearity, it may be particularly opportune to take account of additional information about the a_j. Hence we shall return to this question in our discussion of Bayesian theory in section 11.

7   *Normal distribution of the errors*

Let us suppose now that the vectors of the errors ε_t are mutually independent and have the same normal distribution (assumptions 1 and 3). We proved in section 3 above that least squares regression on each equation is then equivalent to the particular linear estimation studied in ch. 5. We can therefore make direct use here of theorem 2 of ch. 5. Moreover, since Ω is not usually known, we can see that $(A^*, M_{\varepsilon\varepsilon}^*)$ constitutes a sufficient statistic of the sample for estimation of A and Ω.

Consider the probability density of the sample. The probability density of the T vectors ε_t is

$$(2\pi)^{-nT/2} \, |\, \Omega \,|^{-T/2} \exp\left\{ -\tfrac{1}{2} \sum_{t=1}^{T} \varepsilon_t' \, \Omega^{-1} \, \varepsilon_t \right\}.$$

The Jacobian of the transformation from the ε_t into the x_t is obviously 1. So the probability density for the sample is

$$(2\pi)^{-nT/2} \, |\, \Omega \,|^{-T/2} \exp\left\{ -\tfrac{1}{2} \sum_{t=1}^{T} (x_t - Az_t)' \Omega^{-1} (x_t - Az_t) \right\}.$$

To prove that $(A^*, M_{\varepsilon\varepsilon}^*)$ constitutes a sufficient statistic we need only establish that the sum which appears in the exponential depends on the x_t only through

A^* and $M_{\varepsilon\varepsilon}^*$. Now,

$$x_t - Az_t = \varepsilon_t^* + (A^* - A)z_t,$$

and, from (14),

$$\sum_{t=1}^{T} \varepsilon_t^* z_t' = 0.$$

It follows that

$$\sum_{t=1}^{T} (x_t - Az_t)' \Omega^{-1}(x_t - Az_t) = T \operatorname{tr} \{\Omega^{-1}[M_{\varepsilon\varepsilon}^* + (A^* - A)M_{zz}(A^* - A)']\}.$$

The x_t occur only through A^* and $M_{\varepsilon\varepsilon}^*$. So we can state:

Theorem 2. In the models (1) satisfying assumptions 1, 3 and 4, least squares regression on each equation leads to an unbiased estimator A^*:

(a) which, in conjunction with $M_{\varepsilon\varepsilon}^*$, define a sufficient statistics for estimating A and Ω;

(b) whose concentration ellipsoid is contained in that of every other unbiased estimator;

(c) whose distribution is normal and independent of the vectors of the residuals $x_t - A^*z_t$, which also are normally distributed.

Combined with the results of section 4, this theorem provides a complete solution to the estimation problem in the case where the vector ε_t satisfies assumption 1 and is normally distributed with zero mean and *known* covariance matrix Ω. For the distribution of A^* is now completely defined. It is normal, with mean equal to the true value of A and concentration ellipsoid given by the eq. (18).

We have still to discuss the case where assumptions 1, 3 and 4 are satisfied but Ω is not known.

As we pointed out earlier, Ω can be estimated from the residuals $\varepsilon_t^* = x_t - A^*z_t$. In fact the following result has been established (cf. KOOPMANS [1950], pp. 110–120):

Proposition 3. In the models (1) satisfying assumptions 1, 3 and 4, the matrix $M_{\varepsilon\varepsilon}^*$ provides the maximum likelihood estimator of Ω when the latter matrix is assumed to be completely unknown.

We therefore try to find the distribution of $M_{\varepsilon\varepsilon}^*$. Let us examine, in T-dimensional space, the vectors each of which represents the set of observations on one particular variable of the model. Corresponding to the endogenous variables we have n vectors x_i (with components x_{it}, for $t = 1, 2, \ldots, T$) and we also have m vectors z_j corresponding to the exogenous variables. Applying the method of least squares to the equation i is equivalent to projecting the vector x_i on the linear subspace Z spanned by the set of the m vectors z_j. The projection y_i^* can then be expressed as a linear combination of the z_j as follows:

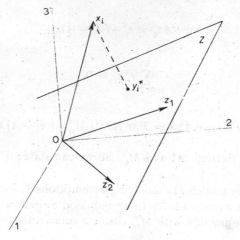

Fig. 4.

$$y_{it}^* = \sum_{j=1}^{m} a_{ij}^* z_{jt} \qquad \text{for} \qquad t = 1, 2, \dots, T.$$

The residual from the equation i is represented by the vector:

$$\varepsilon_i^* = x_i - y_i^*.$$

Clearly there exists a rotation which maps the subspace Z onto the leading m-dimensional coordinate subspace (at least if the z_j are linearly independent, that is, if assumption 4 is satisfied). Therefore there exists an orthogonal matrix P of order T such that

$$\sum_{\theta=1}^{T} p_{t\theta} z_{j\theta} = 0, \qquad \text{for any } t > m \text{ and any } j, \tag{42}$$

and

$$\sum_{t=1}^{T} p_{t\theta} p_{t\theta'} = \begin{cases} 0 & \text{if } \theta \neq \theta' \\ 1 & \text{if } \theta = \theta'. \end{cases}$$

When we have applied this rotation, the first m components of x_i are identified with the m non-zero components of y_i^*, and the other $T-m$ components of x_i with the $T-m$ non-zero components of ε_i^*. Moreover, the rotation does not affect scalar products. The matrix $M_{\varepsilon\varepsilon}^*$ then remains invariant, since each of its elements is the scalar product of two residual vectors, for example ε_i^* and ε_h^*. After this rotation, the $T-m$ non-zero components of each ε_i^* are independently normally distributed with zero means since the concentration ellipsoid of x_i is the sphere with radius σ_i. The covariance of a non-zero component of ε_i^* and the corresponding component of ε_h^* is the element ω_{ih} of Ω.

Thus,

$$\frac{T}{T-m} M_{\varepsilon\varepsilon}^*$$

is distributed as the matrix of the observed second-order moments of a sample of $T-m$ independent observations on a normal random vector with zero mean and covariance matrix Ω. This is known as the *Wishart distribution*. When $n=1$, it is identical to the well-known χ^2-distribution with $T-m$ degrees of freedom. (See ANDERSON [1958], in particular ch. 7.)

We can therefore state:

Proposition 4. In the models (1) satisfying assumptions 1, 3 and 4, the matrix

$$\frac{T}{T-m} M_{\varepsilon\varepsilon}^*$$

has a Wishart distribution of order n, with $T-m$ degrees of freedom, Ω being the covariance matrix of the corresponding normal distribution.

In particular, this proposition implies that

$$\frac{T}{T-m} M_{\varepsilon\varepsilon}^*$$

has mean Ω. It is therefore an unbiased estimator, unlike the maximum likelihood estimator $M_{\varepsilon\varepsilon}^*$.

For various applications it may be desirable to characterize the distribution of a particular residual vector ε_t^*. This distribution is known to be normal with zero mean; but its covariance matrix, given by the last equation in section 4, is not known a priori. So it is preferable to replace ε_t^* by the 'studentized residual'

$$r_t = \left(1 - \frac{1}{T} z_t' M_{zz}^{-1} z_t\right)^{-\frac{1}{2}} C^* \varepsilon_t^*$$

defined using a matrix C^* such that $C^* M_{\varepsilon\varepsilon}^* C^{*\prime} = I$. Considering the case where there is a single endogenous variable (and so $C^* = 1/\sigma_\varepsilon^*$), BECKWITH and TRUSSELL [1974] show that

$$\sqrt{\frac{T-m-1}{T-m-r_t^2}} \cdot r_t$$

has a Student distribution with $T-m-1$ degrees of freedom.

8 Asymptotic properties

We have determined completely the distribution of the coefficients estimated by the method of least squares, but at the cost of making strict assumptions about the distribution of the errors. In particular we assumed that the ε_t relating to different observations were mutually independent and that they all had the same normal distribution. Where economic data are concerned, these assumptions can rarely be justified a priori. In ch. 8 we shall examine the validity of the usual methods when the assumptions on which they depend are imperfectly satisfied. But at this point we can make some assessment of it by looking at certain asymptotic properties of regressions[†].

Asymptotic theory plays a fairly secondary part in our discussion of linear models. On the other hand, it will be our main approach from chapter 9 onwards. We recall that it is concerned with limiting properties which hold rigorously if the number of observations tends to infinity. There are two motives for establishing these properties; in the first place, to verify certain minimal demands made on statistical procedures (for example, an estimator which does not converge to the true value seems a priori to be unsatisfactory even in finite samples); in the second place, to give certain results which often will be taken as *approximately* valid in practical situations (clearly in each particular case the precision of the approximation would need to be considered).

Theorem 3. In the models (1) satisfying assumptions 1 and 5, the matrix $\sqrt{T}(A^* - A)$ has a limiting normal distribution with zero mean when the number of observations tends to infinity. Convergence is uniform[††] with respect to A.

From formula (15)

$$A^* = M_{xz}M_{zz}^{-1},$$

and so:

$$A^* = (AM_{zz} + M_{\varepsilon z})M_{zz}^{-1} = A + M_{\varepsilon z}M_{zz}^{-1},$$

or again:

$$\sqrt{T}(A^* - A) = \frac{1}{\sqrt{T}}\sum_{t=1}^{T}\varepsilon_t z_t' M_{zz}^{-1}.$$

Thus, each element of $\sqrt{T}(A^* - A)$ appears as a linear form of the T values of the corresponding component of ε_t, the coefficients of this form depending on the values of the exogenous variables. Hence, theorem 3 follows from one form

---

[†] The asymptotic properties stated here depend in particular on the fact that the ε_t all have the same distribution (cf. assumption 1). EICKER [1963] has studied the case where the ε_t are independent but not identically distributed.

[††] See RAO [1965], § 5c and particularly p. 287, for the reasons why it is important that convergence be uniform.

of the central limit theorem. The proof, which is rather technical and has been given in the second edition of this book, will not be repeated here.

It should be noted that even if M_{zz} does not satisfy the convergence condition of assumption 5 there may still be a tendency to normality.

The fact that the condition on M_{zz} may be genuinely restrictive is illustrated by the following very simple model:

$$x_t = at + \varepsilon_t$$

in which the real variable x_t corresponding to period t is taken to be proportional to the time t apart from random errors. M_{zz} is then the number

$$\frac{1}{T} \sum_{t=1}^{T} t^2 = \tfrac{1}{6}(T + 1)(2T + 1)$$

which tends to infinity with T. The variance of a^* then decreases like T^{-3} and no longer like T^{-1}. The quantity $\sqrt{T}(a^* - a)$ tends in probability to zero. However, if assumption 1 is satisfied $T^{\frac{3}{2}}(a^* - a)$ has a limiting normal distribution.

More generally, when assumption 4 is satisfied, there exists a square matrix N_T which is symmetric and regular, such that:

$$M_{zz} = N_T N_T$$

(see the lemma in the footnote to page 36). It can be shown that $\sqrt{T}(A^* - A)N_T$ has a limiting normal distribution provided that assumption 1 is satisfied and that there exists a function $\varphi(T)$, tending to infinity with T, such that the set of vectors $(\varphi(T)/\sqrt{T})z'_t N_T^{-1}$ is bounded[†].

Thus modified, the property applies to the above example, since then $(1/\sqrt{T})z'_t N_T^{-1}$ equals $(t\sqrt{6})/\sqrt{\{T(T + 1)(2T + 1)\}}$ and the condition on the z_t is satisfied with

$$\varphi(T) = \sqrt{T}.$$

Theorem 3 shows that, in large samples, the distribution of A^* is close to a completely defined normal distribution whenever the distribution of ε_t has finite second-order moments. In the next section we shall define tests and confidence regions which are exact for small samples in which the errors are normally distributed. It follows from theorem 3 that these tests apply approximately to large samples in which the errors have a distribution possessing second-order moments.

To conclude our study of asymptotic results, we note that the fact that A^*

[†] By imposing on the distribution of the ε_t a condition slightly stronger than the existence of second-order moments, we can weaken the condition on the z_t (see the second edition of this book).

tends to the true value of A can be established on the basis of even less restrictive assumptions about the exogenous variables. For we need only show that

$$\frac{1}{T} M_{zz}^{-1}$$

tends to zero when T tends to infinity. We can easily prove:

Proposition 5. In the models (1) satisfying assumption 1, the least squares estimate A^* converges in mean square to the true matrix A if and only if there is no non-zero vector u such that

$$\sum_{t=1}^{T} (u'z_t)^2$$

remains bounded for any value of T.

Now A^* converges in mean square to A if and only if each of its rows tends to the corresponding row of A, that is, if and only if the vector a_i^* of the coefficients of the ith equation converges in mean square to the true vector a_i. It is necessary and sufficient that the concentration ellipsoid E_{iT} of a_i^* shrinks to the origin.

We saw that E_{iT} consists of the set of vectors α such that

$$\sum_{t=1}^{T} (\alpha'z_t)^2 \leqq \sigma_i^2 \tag{43}$$

(see eq. (18′) above). This expression shows that E_{iT} is contained in $E_{i,T-1}$, since any vector α satisfying (43) also satisfies the equation defining $E_{i,T-1}$. It follows that E_{iT} shrinks to the origin when T tends to infinity if and only if there is no non-zero vector α satisfying (43) for any value of T. Proposition 5 can be deduced directly from this remark. For the existence of a non-zero vector u such that

$$\sum_{t=1}^{T} (u'z_t)^2$$

is always less, for any T, than a number B, implies that $\alpha = ku$ satisfies (43) for any T and any i, provided that the positive number k is taken smaller than the least of the n numbers $\sigma_i/\sqrt{B}$. Conversely, if there exists a vector α satisfying (43),

$$\sum_{t=1}^{T} (\alpha'z_t)^2$$

is clearly bounded for any T.

Roughly speaking, proposition 5 tells us that A^* is a consistent estimate of A as long as the exogenous variables do not tend to be more and more multi-collinear when the number of observations increases. Proposition 6 is still more general.

Proposition 6. In the models (1) satisfying assumption 1, the residual covariance matrix $M_{\varepsilon\varepsilon}^*$ tends in probability to the error covariance matrix Ω.

A very direct proof of this result is given by DRYGAS [1975]. We note first that $M_{\varepsilon\varepsilon}$ tends to Ω in view of the Law of Large Numbers. Then it follows from section 4 that $M_{\varepsilon\varepsilon} - M_{\varepsilon\varepsilon}^*$ is a positive semi-definite matrix whose expected value tends to zero; this implies that $M_{\varepsilon\varepsilon} - M_{\varepsilon\varepsilon}^*$ tends in probability to zero.

To conclude the discussion of asymptotic results one might consider the asymptotic efficiency of regressions in the class of all unbiased regular estimators. For this, see COX and HINCKLEY [1968].

9   Tests and confidence regions

Theorems 1 and 2 justify the usual procedures for testing the values of the elements of A or for constructing confidence regions. We shall now see how this can be done, by successive examination of several different problems with assumptions 1, 3 and 4 adopted throughout.

(i) Tests and confidence intervals for a particular coefficient

Suppose first that we are interested in a particular coefficient of the model, say a_{ij}. We know that the expected value of a_{ij}^* is the true value a_{ij}, and that its standard deviation is

$$\frac{\sigma_i}{\sqrt{T}}\sqrt{\mu_{jj}},$$

where μ_{jj} denotes the (j,j)th element of M_{zz}^{-1}. Therefore:

$$\sqrt{T}\,\frac{a_{ij}^* - a_{ij}}{\sigma_i\sqrt{\mu_{jj}}} \tag{44}$$

has a standard normal distribution.
    Moreover

$$(T - m)\sigma_i^{*2} = \sum_{t=1}^{T} \varepsilon_{it}^{*2}$$

is distributed as the sum of squares of $T - m$ independent normal variables with zero means and standard deviation σ_i. Consequently,

$$(T - m)\sigma_i^{*2}/\sigma_i^2$$

has a χ^2-distribution with $T - m$ degrees of freedom, which is independent of the distribution of a_{ij} (cf. proposition 4).

The ratio between (44) and σ_i^*/σ_i, namely

$$\sqrt{T}\frac{a_{ij}^* - a_{ij}}{\sigma_i^*\sqrt{\mu_{jj}}}$$

has a Student distribution with $T-m$ degrees of freedom. In fact,

$$\frac{\sigma_i^{*2}}{T}\mu_{jj}$$

is just the estimate of the variance of a_{ij}^*. The above ratio can therefore be written:

$$\frac{a_{ij}^* - a_{ij}}{\sigma^*(a_{ij}^*)}, \tag{45}$$

where $\sigma^*(a_{ij}^*)$ denotes the estimated standard deviation of a_{ij}^*.

Tests or confidence regions are then established by well-known methods. Thus, to test, at significance level α, whether a_{ij} is equal to a given value a_{ij}^0, against the hypothesis $a_{ij} \neq a_{ij}^0$, we choose the critical region:

$$\left|\frac{a_{ij}^* - a_{ij}^0}{\sigma^*(a_{ij}^*)}\right| > t_{T-m}(\alpha), \tag{46}$$

where $t_{T-m}(\alpha)$ denotes the two-tailed α-level value of Student's t with $T-m$ degrees of freedom. The hypothesis is rejected when (46) is satisfied.

Similarly a confidence interval for the true value a_{ij} is given by the set of values satisfying:

$$\left|\frac{a_{ij}^* - a_{ij}}{\sigma^*(a_{ij}^*)}\right| \leq t_{T-m}(\alpha). \tag{47}$$

For a practical example, we return to the linear model (36) relating to French imports and consider particularly the coefficient a_3 of consumption. At the 5% level of significance, the test (46) leads to rejection of the hypothesis $a_3 = 0$, since the ratio (45) is 3.5 and t_{13} (0.05) is 2.16. (Since the model contains a constant, there are $18 - 5 = 13$ degrees of freedom.) At the 5% significance level we have a confidence interval

$$0.069 \leq a_3 \leq 0.401.$$

We note further that the intervals consisting of two standard deviations on each side of the estimated value are confidence intervals with the significance level α defined by $t_{T-m}(\alpha) = 2$. When T is large, α is very near 5%.

If the model (31) containing the exogenous variables z_1, z_2 and z_4 is correct, and if the errors ε_t satisfy assumptions 1 and 3, the inequalities (34) and (35) define confidence intervals for the coefficients a_1 and a_2 at about the 6.5% significance level.

(ii) Tests relating to several coefficients of the same equation

Suppose now that we are interested in the set of coefficients of one equation, for example, the equation i. The methods to be described apply with obvious modifications to cases where we are concerned with some, but not all, of the coefficients of the equation i. They depend on proposition 5 of ch. 5, according to which

$$(x - y)\, Q^{-1}(x - y)$$

is distributed as χ^2 with n degrees of freedom if x is a normal random n-vector with mean y and covariance matrix Q. We know that the vector of the estimated coefficients of the ith equation has a normal distribution whose expected value is the vector of the true coefficients, and whose covariance matrix is given by:

$$\frac{\sigma_i^2}{T}\, M_{zz}^{-1}.$$

If we simplify the notation by omitting the index i, we see that

$$\frac{T}{\sigma^2}(a^* - a)' M_{zz}(a^* - a) \tag{48}$$

is distributed as χ^2 with m degrees of freedom.

Also $(T-m)\sigma^{*2}/\sigma^2$ is distributed as χ^2 with $T-m$ degrees of freedom and, from theorem 2, independently of the distribution of (48). It follows that

$$\frac{T}{m\sigma^{*2}}(a^* - a)' M_{zz}(a^* - a) \tag{49}$$

has an F-distribution with m and $T-m$ degrees of freedom.

If V^* denotes the estimate of the covariance matrix of a^*,

$$V^* = \frac{1}{T}\sigma^{*2} M_{zz}^{-1},$$

the above expression can be written:

$$\frac{1}{m}(a^* - a)' V^{*-1}(a^* - a). \tag{49'}$$

To test, at significance level α, if the vector a of the coefficients of the equation considered is equal to a given vector a^0, we reject the hypothesis if

$$\frac{T}{m\sigma^{*2}}(a^* - a^0)' M_{zz}(a^* - a^0) > F_{m,\,T-m}(\alpha), \qquad (50)$$

where $F_{m,\,T-m}(\alpha)$ denotes the upper α-level value of an F-distribution with m and $T-m$ degrees of freedom.

In the case where the test relates to only some of the coefficients of the equation i, for example to q coefficients, we must make an obvious change in the formula (50). The vectors a^* and a^0 must have only the q components tested; the divisor m on the lefthand side must be replaced by q, and the term on the righthand side by $F_{q,\,T-m}(\alpha)$. Finally, M_{zz} must be replaced by the inverse of the matrix obtained by taking the rows and columns of M_{zz}^{-1} which correspond to the coefficients tested. We can always assume that these are the first q coefficients, and write:

$$M_{zz} = \begin{bmatrix} M_{zz}^{11} & M_{zz}^{12} \\ M_{zz}^{21} & M_{zz}^{22} \end{bmatrix},$$

making a partition which isolates the first q rows and the first q columns. From the remark in the footnote to page 26, the leading square submatrix' of order q of M_{zz}^{-1} is

$$[M_{zz}^{11} - M_{zz}^{12}(M_{zz}^{22})^{-1}M_{zz}^{21}]^{-1};$$

so that in (50), M_{zz} must be replaced by

$$M_{zz}^{11} - M_{zz}^{12}(M_{zz}^{22})^{-1}M_{zz}^{21}.$$

In particular, we often wish to test the set of the m coefficients of the true exogenous variables in a model containing a constant term. If we use the notation of section 5, the term on the lefthand side of (50) has $\overline{M}_{zz}$ instead of M_{zz}, and the term on the righthand side becomes $F_{m,\,T-m-1}(\alpha)$.

In all cases, if V^* denotes the estimated covariance matrix of the q coefficients under test and if m denotes the total number of the exogenous variables including possibly the constant dummy variable, the critical region can be written

$$\frac{1}{q}(a^* - a)'V^{*-1}(a^* - a) > F_{q,\,T-m}(\alpha). \qquad (50')$$

For a practical example, suppose that in the linear model (31) relating to French imports and taken as correct, we wish to test the hypothesis that $a_1 = 0.13$, $a_2 = 0.30$, which would seem probable a priori. At the significance level $\alpha = 5\%$, the inequality (50') is in this case

$$\frac{10^4}{2}\left\{[0.003 \quad 0.250]\begin{bmatrix} 0.390 & -1.47 \\ -1.47 & 121.9 \end{bmatrix}^{-1}\begin{bmatrix} 0.003 \\ 0.250 \end{bmatrix}\right\} > F_{2,\,14}(0.05),$$

or again

$$3.05 > 3.74.$$

Since this inequality is not satisfied, the test does not reject the proposed hypothesis. This is not the case at the 10% significance level since $F_{2,14}(0.10) = 2.73$.

(iii) *Confidence regions for several coefficients of the same equation*

Using the same principles, we can establish confidence regions for the set of coefficients of an equation. Thus a confidence region at significance level α consists, in m-dimensional space, of the set of vectors a satisfying:

$$\frac{T}{m\sigma^{*2}}(a^* - a)'M_{zz}(a^* - a) \leqq F_{m,T-m}(\alpha). \tag{51}$$

Similarly, a confidence region for q coefficients of an equation consists of the set of q-vectors a which satisfy:

$$\frac{1}{q}(a^* - a)'V^{*-1}(a^* - a) \leqq F_{q,T-m}(\alpha). \tag{51'}$$

In particular, in fig. 2, the area bounded by the ellipse constitutes a confidence region for the pair (a_1, a_2), the significance level α being determined by $q \cdot F_{q,T-m}(\alpha) = 4$, or $F_{2,14}(\alpha) = 2$, or roughly $\alpha = 15\%$. A confidence region at the 5% significance level for the pair (a_1, a_2) is provided by the area bounded by an ellipse concentric with that in fig. 2, but enlarged by a factor of 1.17. For,

$$2 \cdot F_{2,14}(0.05) \approx 4 \cdot (1.17)^2.$$

Intervals consisting of 2.34 standard deviations on each side of the estimated values are defined by the projections of this new ellipse on the two axes.

It is quite clear that the projections of the ellipsoids (51') define on the axes intervals which increase with q. For the probability that an ellipsoid contains the vector of the true values is less than the probability that its projection contains the projection of this vector. If we refer to the F-tables, we can see how these intervals increase proportionately as q increases. Thus for $x=0.05$ and for high values of T, we have $[qF_{q,T-m}(\alpha)]^{\frac{1}{2}}$ equal to 1.96 when $q=1$; 2.45 when $q=2$; 2.79 when $q=3$; 3.08 when $q=4$, etc.

We shall show later that the ellipsoids (51) are particularly interesting confidence regions. However, for reasons of simplicity, we sometimes prefer to them 'rectangular' regions defined by sets of confidence intervals. Thus in our example of model (31) for French imports, a 5% confidence interval for the single coefficient a_1 is

$$0.120 \leqq a_1 \leqq 0.146$$

since $t_{14}(0.05) = 2.145$. Similarly, a 5% confidence interval for the single coefficient a_2 is

$$0.314 \leqq a_2 \leqq 0.786$$

In two-dimensional space this pair of intervals defines a rectangle which can
be taken as a confidence region for the pair (a_1, a_2). The probability that this
rectangle contains the vector of the true value is obviously less than the
probability that each interval taken by itself contains the corresponding true
value. In fact the level of significance of the rectangle is slightly less than
10%.

Two related problems arise from the use of such 'simultaneous confidence
intervals'. In the first place, how can we calculate the level of significance of a
set of intervals each of which in isolation has the significance level α? In the
second place, how can we determine a set of intervals such that they define a
confidence region with a given level of significance? On these questions the
reader may consult DURAND [1954], DUNN [1959] and BOWDEN [1970].

We shall only point out here that the relationship between the significance
level of each interval and that of the set of intervals depends on the correlations
among the estimates a_{ij}^* of the different coefficients. Thus, in the case of fig. 3,
two intervals for a_1 and a_3, which when taken separately have 5% significance
levels, define a rectangle whose significance level is very slightly higher than 5%,
while in the case of fig. 2 this last significance level is almost 10%.

The example of fig. 3 also shows that the region defined by these intervals
can be much greater than the region obtained from (51) as the interior of a
suitable ellipsoid. When the estimates of the different coefficients are strongly
correlated, there is not much interest in the simultaneous confidence intervals.

Obviously we can give a lower bound for the significance level of the rectangular region defined by such simultaneous confidence intervals. This region
contains the confidence ellipsoid defined by (51) with a value $\bar{\alpha}$ of α satisfying
$[qF_{q, T-m}(\bar{\alpha})]^{\frac{1}{2}} = t_{T-m}(\beta)$ where β is the significance level of each interval taken
individually.

(iv) *Tests and confidence regions for coefficients from several equations*

Proposition 5 in ch. 5 allows us to establish tests and confidence regions for
the matrix A of the coefficients when the covariance matrix Ω of the errors is
known. For, from theorem 2, the matrix A^* of the estimates is normally distributed with expected value equal to the true matrix A, and concentration
ellipsoid given by the formula (18). It follows that

$$\sum_{t=1}^{T} z_t'(A^* - A)'\Omega^{-1}(A^* - A)z_t \tag{52}$$

is distributed as χ^2 with nm degrees of freedom.

A confidence region is therefore defined by the set of A satisfying

$$\sum_{t=1}^{T} z_t'(A^* - A)'\Omega^{-1}(A^* - A)z_t \leqq \chi_{nm}^2(\alpha) \tag{53}$$

where α denotes the level of significance. Similarly, a test consists of rejecting the hypothesis $A = A^0$ when:

$$\sum_{t=1}^{T} z_t'(A^* - A^0)'\Omega^{-1}(A^* - A^0)z_t > \chi_{nm}^2(\alpha). \tag{54}$$

Generally Ω is not known. In that case eqs. (53) and (54) no longer provide either confidence regions or critical regions. Since $M_{\varepsilon\varepsilon}^*$ is a consistent estimate of Ω, it seems natural to establish tests in the same way as before, but using instead of (52), the expression:

$$\sum_{t=1}^{T} z_t'(A^* - A)'(M_{\varepsilon\varepsilon}^*)^{-1}(A^* - A)z_t. \tag{55}$$

When the number T of observations tends to infinity, $(M_{\varepsilon\varepsilon}^*)^{-1}$ tends in probability to Ω^{-1}. It follows that[†] the distribution of (55) tends to the distribution of (52). The asymptotic distribution of (55) is therefore a χ^2-distribution with nm degrees of freedom. The formulae obtained when $M_{\varepsilon\varepsilon}^*$ is substituted for Ω in (53) and (54) define approximate confidence regions and tests which will become more exact as the number T of observations increases.

Of course this method would lead to exact tests valid for any sample size if we took account of the exact distribution of (55) in order to calculate the second terms of inequalities similar to (53) and (54). This can now be done fairly precisely using the approximate methods of MUIRHEAD [1972] and McKEAN [1974].

To introduce other tests, we note that expression (55) in which A^0 replaces A can be written in the form $m/(1 - m/T)\text{tr}\,(NM^{-1})$ where the matrices N and M denote respectively $(T/m)(A^* - A^0)M_{zz}(A^* - A^0)'$ and $(T/T-m)M_{\varepsilon\varepsilon}^*$. If A^0 is the true value of A, the matrices N and M are independent and have Wishart distributions with the same matrix Ω and m and $T - m$ degrees of freedom. (For, it follows from theorem 2 and from the expression for the covariances of the a_{ij}^* that N has the same distribution as a matrix of the moments of a sample of m independent observations on a normal vector with zero expectation and covariance matrix Ω.)

Apart from the factor $m/(1 - m/T)$, expression (55) is equal to the sum of the characteristic roots of NM^{-1} (the trace of a matrix X is equal to the sum of its characteristic roots, as we see if we consider the coefficient of the term in λ in the expansion of $|X - \lambda I| = 0$). If the hypothesis $A^0 = A$ is true, the characteristic roots of NM^{-1} will be near 1 and their sum near n. On the other hand,

---

[†] The limit of (52) is a random variable, X say. The random variable (55) tends in probability to X. Therefore its distribution tends to the distribution of X (see LOÈVE [1955], p. 168).

if A^0 differs from the true matrix A, some of the characteristic roots will be large.

Instead of considering the trace of NM^{-1}, we can establish a test on its largest root λ^*; this approach seems in practice to give more powerful tests. Tables established by PILLAI [1967] give significance levels for $\mu^* = m\lambda^*/(T-m+m\lambda^*)$, the largest root of $| mN - \mu[mN + (T-m)M] | = 0$.

We note also that in this case the likelihood ratio test leads us to consider the product

$$\prod_{i=1}^{n} \left(1 + \frac{m\lambda_i}{T-m} \right),$$

where the λ_i denote the characteristic roots of NM^{-1}. The reader will find useful information on the three above tests and a few others in ch. 8 of AN-DERSON [1958], in MUIRHEAD [1978] and in KARIYA [1978].

However, we can discuss completely a particular case which is likely to be the most important in practice, that is, the case where *the test or the confidence region relates to the set of the coefficients of a single exogenous variable in different equations.*

We need only consider here the case where the model itself contains just one exogenous variable representing either a true economic quantity or a dummy variable. We saw earlier, when discussing tests on the coefficients of a single equation, that the proposed methods would apply in the context of models which would also contain exogenous variables whose coefficients ought not to be tested. We can use the same methods in this case.

If the model contains a single exogenous variable ($m=1$), the matrix A is a single column-vector which can be written a in this case. Similarly z_t is a number. The expression (55) then becomes

$$TS \cdot (a^* - a)'(M_{\varepsilon\varepsilon}^*)^{-1}(a^* - a), \tag{56}$$

where

$$S = \frac{1}{T} \sum_{t=1}^{T} z_t^2.$$

It is simpler to consider:

$$\tau^2 = (T - 1)S(a^* - a)'(M_{\varepsilon\varepsilon}^*)^{-1}(a^* - a), \tag{57}$$

and prove that

$$\frac{T-n}{n} \cdot \frac{\tau^2}{T-1}$$

has an F-distribution with n and $T-n$ degrees of freedom. On this topic the reader may consult ANDERSON [1958], ch. 5, particularly pages 105 and 106.

Thus to test at significance level α the hypothesis that the vector a equals a certain vector a^0, we choose the critical region:

$$(a^* - a^0)'(M_{\varepsilon\varepsilon}^*)^{-1}(a^* - a^0) > \frac{n}{(T - n)S} F_{n, T-n}(\alpha). \tag{58}$$

This is called the '*Hotelling's T^2-test*' or the generalized Student test. It is a natural generalization of the test (46).

(v) *Properties of the proposed tests*

The tests described above for the coefficients of a single equation are inspired directly by the general properties discussed in the previous chapter, particularly in section 8. These properties allowed us to obtain directly the distribution of the random quantities (45) and (49) when the hypothesis under test was true, and to deduce critical values for the different significance levels. They also allow us to obtain the valid distributions for the case where this hypothesis is false, and to deduce the *powers of* the tests. Thus by applying proposition 8 of ch. 5 we see directly that

$$\frac{T}{m\sigma^{*2}}(a^* - a^0)'M_{zz}(a^* - a^0) \tag{59}$$

has a non-central F-distribution with m and $T-m$ degrees of freedom and non-centrality parameter δ given by

$$\delta^2 = \frac{T}{\sigma^2}(a - a^0)'M_{zz}(a - a^0), \tag{60}$$

where a denotes the vector of the true values of the coefficients.

We can verify in the same way that (46) and (50) define the likelihood ratio tests, and prove that these tests maximize the minimum power (which has the same meaning as in ch. 5, § 8).

Tests on the coefficients of several equations have markedly weaker properties. It is also important in this case to distinguish Hotelling's T^2-test from similar tests on the coefficients of several exogenous variables in several equations.

The power of the T^2-test can be calculated since we can prove that

$$\frac{(T - n)}{n}S(a^* - a^0)'(M_{\varepsilon\varepsilon}^*)^{-1}(a^* - a^0) \tag{61}$$

has a non-central F-distribution with n and $T-n$ degrees of freedom and non-centrality parameter δ given by

$$\delta^2 = TS(a - a^0)'\Omega^{-1}(a - a^0), \tag{62}$$

where a denotes the vector of the true values of the coefficients. We could verify that (58) is again the likelihood ratio test. STEIN [1956] has shown that this test is admissible in the class of hypotheses attributing all possible values to the vector a. But it does not seem to have been proved that this test maximizes the minimum power of tests which apply to the hypothesis considered. (On this question, see GIRI et al. [1963].) For the general case one may refer to KARIYA [1978].

We note finally that the properties presented in this section hold good only so long as the model faithfully represents the facts to be analyzed, and the errors which appear in the model satisfy the assumptions of independence and normality which were specified at the beginning of this chapter (assumptions 1 and 3). In ch. 8 we shall discuss the validity of the methods proposed here when the errors are only approximately independent and normal.

10   Prediction of the endogenous variables

We come finally to the problems raised by prediction of the values of the endogenous variables for supposedly known values of the exogenous variables. We need only generalize the analysis of simple regression which we made in ch. 3 (cf. § 9). The exposition will be clearer if we first consider the case where the model specifies completely the distribution of x_t, that is, where the value of the matrix A and the distribution of the errors ε_t are known a priori. We shall then deal with the more interesting situation where the value of A and the distribution of the ε_t are known only from an observed sample.

The problem of prediction can be formulated as follows. For a future time θ (or for an unobserved[†] individual θ), predict the value of the vector x_θ when the vector z_θ is known to take a given value. There would be no difficulty about prediction if we were satisfied with knowing the distribution of x_θ, which can be deduced immediately from the distribution of ε_θ. But we wish to decide on a particular value of x_θ; let x_θ^P be this 'prediction'.

We now need a criterion for determining x_θ^P. If x_θ^R represents the value of x_θ which is actually realized (but is unknown), the prediction error is $x_\theta^P - x_\theta^R$. We can generally assume that the loss, or the unrealized gain, resulting from an incorrect prediction is approximately proportional to a weighted sum of squares of the prediction errors relating to the different components $x_{i\theta}$ of x_θ, or, more generally, to a positive semi-definite quadratic form:

$$(x_\theta^P - x_\theta^R)' W (x_\theta^P - x_\theta^R),$$

with an appropriate square matrix W. It then seems natural to try to *minimize the expected value of this quadratic form of the prediction errors*.

This is the criterion with which we shall proceed. It would not be suitable if the losses resulting from prediction errors of opposite signs were considerably different, for example, if too high a prediction had no seriously damaging consequences, while too low a prediction resulted in very considerable losses. Actually in such cases we should have to take account simultaneously of the form of the distribution and of the exact relation between prediction errors and losses. On the contrary, whenever the loss can be expressed by a quadratic form, we do not need to concern ourselves with the exact nature of the distribution of x_θ, but only with the values of its first- and second-order moments.

---

† Indeed nothing in this section implies that the observations are ordered in time. What we are saying applies, for example, to the prediction of the consumption of a particular household by means of a model of type (1) which holds good for the set of households.

In view of assumption 1, the expected value of the loss can be written:

$$\mathscr{P} = E(\varepsilon_\theta' W \varepsilon_\theta) + (x_\theta^P - A z_\theta)' W (x_\theta^P - A z_\theta). \tag{63}$$

This expression is valid also for the conditional expected value when the values of the x_t (and of the ε_t) are known for individuals other than θ, since we have assumed that the different errors ε_t are independent.

The value x_θ^P which minimizes the loss is given by

$$x_\theta^P = A z_\theta, \tag{64}$$

since the first term of $\mathscr{P}$ does not depend on x_θ^P and the second is never negative. So in this case we find the natural prediction which consists in using the model as if it contained no errors.

The variances and covariances of the prediction errors on the different endogenous variables $x_{i\theta}$ of the model are clearly equal to the variances and covariances of the ε_t, that is, to the elements of Ω.

Consider now the case where the parameters of the model are not known directly, but only from a sample $\mathscr{E}$ of T observations (x_t, z_t) satisfying the model. Obviously we assume that the individual θ does not belong to the sample, since otherwise the prediction problem would not arise.

By analogy with the result obtained above, it is natural to look for a formula of the type:

$$x_\theta^P = A(\mathscr{E}) z_\theta,$$

where $A(\mathscr{E})$ is an estimate of the unknown matrix A.

The expected value of the loss then becomes:

$$\mathscr{P} = E(\varepsilon_\theta' W \varepsilon_\theta) + E\{z_\theta'[A(\mathscr{E}) - A]' W [A(\mathscr{E}) - A] z_\theta\}. \tag{65}$$

The first term does not depend on $A(\mathscr{E})$. If we limit ourselves to estimate $A(\mathscr{E})$ which are unbiased and linear with respect to the sample values of the endogenous variables, the second term is minimal for $A(\mathscr{E}) = A^*$, that is, for *estimation by the method of least squares*.

For the matrix W can be written $C'C$ where C is a suitable square matrix of order n. The second term of $\mathscr{P}$ is then equal to the sum of variances of the components of a vector that is a linear function of $A(\mathscr{E}) - A$, namely:

$$C[A(\mathscr{E}) - A] z_\theta.$$

This sum of variances is minimal for A^*, since the concentration ellipsoid of A^* is contained in that of every other unbiased linear estimate $A(\mathscr{E})$.

For the reasons given at the end of the previous chapter, $A^* z_\theta$ is also minimal in the class of all predictions of the form $A(\mathscr{E}) z_\theta$, constructed from linear estimators $A(\mathscr{E})$.

Be that as it may, the prediction formula

$$x_\theta^P = A^* z_\theta \tag{66}$$

is the only one used in practice. Let us examine the precision of the estimates to which it leads.

To evaluate the variances and covariances of the prediction errors, we write:

$$x_\theta^P - x_\theta = (A^* - A)z_\theta - \varepsilon_\theta,$$

and so

$$E[(x_\theta^P - x_\theta)(x_\theta^P - x_\theta)'] = \Omega + E[(A^* - A)z_\theta z_\theta'(A^* - A)']. \tag{67}$$

The (i,h)th element in the mathematical expectation appearing in the right hand side is

$$\sum_{j,\,k} z_{j\theta} z_{k\theta} \operatorname{cor}(a_{ij}^*, a_{hk}^*). \tag{68}$$

If assumption 1 is satisfied, the formula given for the covariance of a_{ij}^* and a_{hk}^* in section 4 implies that (68) is equal to

$$\frac{\omega_{ih}}{T} z_\theta' M_{zz}^{-1} z_\theta.$$

Therefore

$$E[(x_\theta^P - x_\theta)(x_\theta^P - x_\theta)'] = \left[1 + \frac{1}{T} z_\theta' M_{zz}^{-1} z_\theta\right] \Omega, \tag{69}$$

which generalises formula (41) of ch. 3.

Thus the reader can find out for himself how the variance of the prediction error for imports in the example of section 5 varies according to the values of the three exogenous variables. He will find more detailed and lengthy discussion in a paper by BROWN [1954] on the application of formulae giving the variance of the prediction errors. Finally, for probability judgments on simultaneous predictions, the reader may profitably refer to the paper by HOOPER and ZELLNER [1961].

11　Bayesian theory

The properties of multiple regression have been obtained in this chapter by applying the principles of classical statistics. Bayesian principles lead to very similar procedures which we shall now discuss.

For simplicity, we shall limit ourselves to the one-dimensional case ($n = 1$). As has already appeared in the course of section 9, the probability distributions involved in the multivariate case are often more complex and less familiar than those relating to the situation where there exists a single endogenous variable. A few brief remarks concerning the case of n variables will be given at the end of the section.

When discussing simple regression in ch. 3 we gave a step-by-step treatment of the various concepts necessary for the application of Bayesian principles. So we can now go straight ahead without repeating that discussion.

(i)　The likelihood function

At present the Bayesian approach is practicable only for parametric models specifying the nature of the distribution of the random errors. This is why it has been applied in the case where the ε_t are normally distributed and the model satisfies assumptions 1, 3 and 4 of this chapter.

The likelihood function is then

$$l(a,\sigma) = (2\pi)^{-T/2}\sigma^{-T}\exp\left\{\frac{1}{2\sigma^2}\sum_{t=1}^{T}(x_t-a'z_t)^2\right\}. \tag{70}$$

Now, the definition of the residual ε_t^* of the multiple regression implies

$$x_t - a'z_t = \varepsilon_t^* + (a^*-a)'z_t,$$

a^* being defined as before by (16). Moreover, we know that the vector of the residuals is orthogonal to the vectors of the exogenous variables:

$$\sum_{t=1}^{T}\varepsilon_t^* z_t = 0,$$

which follows, for example, from (12). So we can write

$$\sum_{t=1}^{T}(x_t - az_t)^2 = E^* + (a^*-a)'M_{zz}(a^*-a) \tag{71}$$

where

$$E^* = \sum_{t=1}^{T}\varepsilon_t^{*2}. \tag{72}$$

In short, the likelihood function satisfies

$$l(a,\sigma) \propto \sigma^{-T}\exp\left\{\frac{-1}{2\sigma^2}[E^* + T(a^*-a)'M_{zz}(a^*-a)]\right\}, \tag{73}$$

where $\propto$ means that the two sides of the relation are proportional.

The function depends on the sample only through a^*, E^* and T which therefore constitute a sufficient statistic (this result is already known to us).

(ii) Conjugate prior distributions

The likelihood function must be combined with a prior distribution so as to give the posterior distribution of the parameters (the vector a and the number σ). Let $p(a,\sigma)$ denote the density of the prior distribution.

It can conveniently be chosen in the family of gamma-normal distributions which constitute the 'conjugate family' for the present problem:

$$p(a,\sigma) \propto \sigma^{-\mu}\exp\left\{\frac{-1}{2\sigma^2}[E + \mu(a-\alpha)'M(a-\alpha)]\right\}. \tag{74}$$

This expression involves the following parameters[†]: the vector α, the positive

---

[†] The integral of the right hand side of (74) is finite only if $\mu > m+1$. However we shall see that we may be led to choose a smaller value of μ to characterize a situation where very little is known about σ.

definite square matrix M of order m, the number $\mu \geq 1$ and the number $E \geq 0$. To find a prior distribution of the family in question is to choose precise values for all these parameters.

For a given value of a, the conditional distribution of σ belongs to the category of *inverse gamma-2 distributions*[†]. Its mean is in the neighbourhood of the value corresponding to

$$\sigma^2 = [E + \mu(a-\alpha)'M(a-\alpha)]/(\mu-1)$$

and its dispersion increases as μ decreases. Integrating (74) with respect to a, we obtain the density of the marginal distribution of σ:

$$p(\sigma) \propto \sigma^{-(\mu-m)} \exp\left\{\frac{-E}{2\sigma^2}\right\}. \tag{75}$$

This also is an inverse gamma-2 distribution, centred in the neighbourhood of the value corresponding to $\sigma^2 = E/(\mu-m-1)$. So by choosing appropriate values of E and μ we can represent situations which differ widely in respect of the prior probabilities concerning σ.

For a given value of σ, the conditional distribution of a is normal with expected value α and covariance matrix $(\sigma^2/\mu)M^{-1}$. The marginal distribution of a has density $p(a)$ obtained by integrating (74) with respect to σ:

$$p(a) \propto [E + \mu(a-\alpha)'M(a-\alpha)]^{-(\mu-1)/2}. \tag{76}$$

This is a multivariate t-distribution[††]. When $\mu > m+3$ the vector a has expected value α and covariance matrix

$$\frac{E}{\mu-m-3} \cdot \frac{M^{-1}}{\mu}.$$

If μ and E are fixed to fit the prior probabilities on σ, the vector α and the matrix M can still be chosen so as to represent the central tendency and the dispersion of the prior distribution of the vector a of the coefficients.

We note also that the marginal distribution implied by (76) for a particular component a_j is related to a classic *t*-distribution[†††] since it satisfies

$$p(a_j) \propto \left[(\mu-m-1) + \frac{(a_j-\alpha_j)^2}{\sigma_j^2}\right]^{-(\mu-m)/2} \tag{77}$$

where σ_j is the element in the jth row and jth column of the matrix

$$\frac{E}{\mu-m-1} \cdot \frac{M^{-1}}{\mu}.$$

[†] See RAIFFA and SCHLAIFER [1961], § 7.7.2 on the inverse gamma-2 distribution.
[††] See RAIFFA and SCHLAIFER [1961], § 8.3 on this distribution and its derivation.
[†††] The same applies to any linear combination of the components of the vector a.

So the ratio $(a_j - \alpha_j)/\sigma_j$ has a t-distribution with $(\mu - m - 1)$ degrees of freedom. Finally, we can also establish[†] that the quantity

$$\frac{\mu(\mu - m - 1)}{mE}(a - \alpha)'M(a - \alpha)$$

has the classic Fisher–Snedecor distribution with m and $\mu - m - 1$ degrees of freedom.

(iii)　The posterior distribution and inference procedures

Multiplication of the likelihood (73) by the prior density (74) gives an expression proportional to the density of the posterior distribution of the parameters a and σ. Here we immediately recognize a gamma-normal distribution which we can write

$$p(a, \sigma/x) \propto \sigma^{-T-\mu} \exp\left\{\frac{-1}{2\sigma^2}\left[F + (T + \mu)(a - \beta)'N(a - \beta)\right]\right\}, \qquad (78)$$

the number F, the vector β and the matrix N being determined in such a way that

$$[F + (T + \mu)(a - \beta)'N(a - \beta)]$$
$$= [E^* + T(a^* - a)'M_{zz}(a^* - a)] + [E + \mu(a - \alpha)'M(a - \alpha)]$$

which implies

$$(T + \mu)N = TM_{zz} + \mu M \qquad (79)$$

$$(T + \mu)N\beta = TM_{zz}a^* + \mu M\alpha \qquad (80)$$

$$F + (T + \mu)\beta'N\beta = E^* + E + Ta^{*\prime}M_{zz}a^* + \mu\alpha'M\alpha. \qquad (81)$$

(79) defines the matrix N; (80) defines the vector β:

$$\beta = (TM_{zz} + \mu M)^{-1}(TM_{zz}a^* + \mu M\alpha). \qquad (82)$$

Finally, F is defined by (81) which, if we take account of (79) and (80) can also be written

$$F = E^* + E + T(a^* - \beta)'M_{zz}(a^* - \beta) + \mu(\alpha - \beta)'M(\alpha - \beta). \qquad (83)$$

For investigation of the properties of the posterior gamma-normal distribution we can transpose the properties of the prior distribution. For example, the vector a of coefficients has mean β which is a linear combination of the vector a^* of the regression coefficients and the prior mean vector α. The linear combination gives increasing weight to a^* as TM_{zz} increases relative to μM, that is, as the number of observations increases (T), as the dispersion of the exogenous variables increases (M_{zz}) or as prior ideas are less precise (μM).

[†] See, for example, GEISSER and CORNFIELD [1963].

The covariance matrix of the posterior marginal distribution of a is

$$\frac{F}{T+\mu-m-3} \cdot \frac{N^{-1}}{T+\mu}.$$

Its elements decrease as the elements of the inverse of $(T+\mu)N$ decrease, and as $F/(T+\mu)$ decreases. This latter number is defined by (83) as the sum of two terms: (i) a weighted mean of E^*/T and E/μ which approximately measure the variance of the ε_t, the one arising from the regression and the other from the prior distribution; (ii) a weighted mean of $(a^*-\beta)'M_{zz}(a^*-\beta)$ and $(\alpha-\beta)'M(\alpha-\beta)$ which relate to the differences between β, the posterior expected value of a, and on the one hand the vector a^* of the regression coefficients, on the other hand the vector α of the prior expected values. So this second term will be small if a^* is near α; but it may be large in the opposite case. Here we find a property which we have already discussed when dealing with simple regression (see ch. 3, §10).

A Bayesian confidence interval can easily be constructed from the t-distribution which the posterior distribution attributes to the quantity $(a_j-\beta_j)/\sigma_j$ where σ_j^2 is the jth diagonal element of the matrix

$$\frac{F}{T+\mu-m-1} \cdot \frac{N^{-1}}{T+\mu}.$$

If $t_v(\eta)$ is the upper η-value of a t-distribution with v degrees of freedom, then

$$|a_j-\beta_j| \leq \sigma_j t_{T+\mu-m-1}(\eta) \tag{84}$$

defines an interval in which a_j will lie with posterior probability $1-\eta$.

Similarly a Bayesian confidence region for the vector a of the coefficients is defined at significance level η by the inequality

$$\frac{T+\mu}{m}(a-\beta)'N(a-\beta) \leq \frac{F}{T+\mu-m-1} \cdot F_{m, T+\mu-m-1}(\eta) \tag{85}$$

where $F_{v,\rho}(\eta)$ denotes the upper η-value of an F-distribution with v and ρ degrees of freedom.

To sum up, the vector β defined by (82) gives the Bayesian estimator of a, while (84) and (85) define corresponding confidence intervals and regions. The practical difference relative to classical inference procedures lies in the fact that elements (α, M, μ, E) of the prior distribution are taken into account. This difference disappears if we have to deal with a 'diffuse prior distribution' which is held to represent a state of complete ignorance about the values of the parameters of the model.

(iv) The case of diffuse prior distributions

A state of complete ignorance must mean that the econometrician can resort only to the sample to determine the posterior probability. Formulae (82) and (83) applying to the family (74) of conjugate distributions imply this when $\mu M = 0$, in which case $\beta = a^*$, and $E = 0$ and so $F = E^*$. The prior density is then replaced by

$$p(a, \sigma) \propto \sigma^{-\mu}. \tag{86}$$

This formula does not define a proper distribution since integration with respect to a over m-dimensional space does not give a finite result. Yet for a long time Bayesian statisticians have allowed that non-finite measures can sometimes take the place of the prior distribution, particularly when it is a question of representing a state of complete ignorance. This is to say that our initial ignorance is such that in the absence of supplementary observations it precludes true probability judgements.

Let us assume then that, in the case of complete ignorance, the prior density is replaced in Bayes' theorem by (86). We have still to choose the number μ (if μ differs from zero, then M must be the zero matrix). The measure taking the place of the prior distribution must be independent of the units chosen for x_t and the z_{jt} except possibly for multiplication by a constant. This is certainly the case for the uniform measure implied by (86) for the vector a of the coefficients since transformation of a_j into ka_j transforms the differential element da_j into kda_j and does not change the uniform character of the measure. The same is true for the measure relating to σ since replacement of σ by $k\sigma$ implies replacement of

$$\sigma^{-\mu} d\sigma \quad \text{by} \quad k^{1-\mu}\sigma^{-\mu} d\sigma.$$

This invariance condition implies nothing special.

It is customary to take $\mu = 1$, that is, to assume that complete ignorance as to σ is well represented by a uniform measure for $\log \sigma$. As we shall see, this choice has the advantage that it ensures that classical and Bayesian procedures coincide.

For, if $M = 0$, $\mu = 1$ and $E = 0$, then $\beta = a^*$. The Bayesian estimator coincides which that given by classical principles. The quantity F is equal to E^*, that is, to what was previously denoted by $(T-m)\sigma^{*2}$. The matrix $(T+\mu)N$ is equal to TM_{zz}. So the matrix

$$\frac{F}{T+\mu-m-1} \cdot \frac{N^{-1}}{T+\mu}$$

takes the form

$$\frac{\sigma^{*2}}{T} M_{zz}^{-1}.$$

Its jth diagonal element σ_j^2 then coincides with the square of the quantity denoted by $\sigma^*(a_j^*)$ in section 9. The Bayesian confidence interval (84) becomes

$$|a_j - a_j^*| \leq \sigma^*(a_j^*)t_{T-m}(\eta);\tag{87}$$

it coincides with the classical confidence interval (cf. the inequality (47) in section 9, where α denotes the significance level η). Similarly, the Bayesian confidence region (85) becomes

$$\frac{T}{m}(a-a^*)'M_{zz}(a-a^*) \leq \sigma^{*2}F_{m,T-m}(\eta):\tag{88}$$

it coincides with the classical confidence region defined by (51).

(v) Multicollinearity

It is instructive to examine the effect on Bayesian procedures of multicollinearity among the exogenous variables observed in the sample. Suppose that, contrary to assumption 4, there exist numbers λ_j, not all zero, such that $\lambda'z_t = 0$ for $t = 1, 2, \ldots, T$. For simplicity, we shall assume that all the vectors λ which have this property are collinear, that is, that M_{zz} has rank $m-1$.

We can retain expression (73) for the likelihood function unchanged with a vector a^* satisfying

$$M_{zz}a^* = m_{zx}.\tag{89}$$

Because of the assumption about the rank of M_{zz}, the difference between two vectors a^* satisfying condition (89) is collinear with λ. Consequently $(a^* - a)'z_t$ and the residuals ε_t^* keep the same values whatever solution a^* is chosen. Equality (71) therefore applies, with a number E^* defined unambiguously and relation (73) remains valid.

Relation (78), which together with (79), (82) and (83) defines the posterior probability, then applies, provided that the right hand side has a finite integral. For this to be so, it is necessary and sufficient that the matrix N is regular. This will always be the case except when $\lambda'M = 0$, since (79) shows that for every non-zero vector γ, $\gamma'N\gamma$ is positive either because of $\gamma'M_{zz}\gamma$ or of $\gamma'M\gamma$. The equality $\lambda'M = 0$ implies that the right hand side of (74) does not define a proper distribution. The corresponding measure is uniform in the direction of the line which is the support of λ; it expresses a state of prior ignorance about the component of a along this line. Observation of the sample would leave this ignorance unchanged.

If prior knowledge gives $\lambda'M \neq 0$, then (78) defines a proper posterior distribution justifying the inference procedures already discussed in section (iii). But the effect of multicollinearity among the exogenous variables is that the posterior distribution of the linear combination $\lambda'Ma$ approximately reproduces its prior distribution.

For, the posterior expected value of $\lambda'Ma$ is $\lambda'M\beta$. Now, (79) implies

$$(T+\mu)\lambda'N = \mu\lambda'M,\tag{90}$$

and (80) multiplied by λ' then becomes

$$\mu\lambda' M\beta = \mu\lambda' M\alpha.$$

The posterior expectation $\lambda' M\beta$ is equal to the prior expectation $\lambda' M\alpha$. Similarly, the posterior variance of $\lambda' Ma$ involves the number

$$\frac{1}{T+\mu}\, \lambda' MN^{-1}M\lambda$$

which is equal to $(1/\mu)\lambda' M\lambda$ in view of (90). For a given value of σ the posterior conditional distribution of $\lambda' Ma$ is identical to the prior distribution, since these two distributions have the same mean, the same variance, and are both normal. The marginal distributions are slightly different because $E/(\mu-m-1)$ which appears in the prior density is replaced by $F/(T+\mu-m-1)$ in the posterior density. But this substitution involves only a slight change if the last two terms in (83) are small and if E^*/T is near E/μ.

The above property shows how prior ideas about the values of the vector a mitigate the indeterminacy which results in classical statistics from the presence of multicollinearity.

We also note a property which can be established by similar reasoning. If the prior distribution expresses a state of complete ignorance as to the component of a along the line which is the support of a vector λ (and so if $\lambda' M = 0$) and if the exogenous variables are not multicollinear ($\lambda' M_{zz} \neq 0$), then the posterior distribution of $\lambda' M_{zz}a$ is approximately the same as in the case where the prior measure is completely diffuse.

Bayesian theory may be a particularly useful guide in the frequently encountered situation where the exogenous variables are approximately collinear. We saw in section 6 that the estimator a^* is then usually imprecise. It also often happens that some components a_j^* have implausible values with high standard errors. Common sense then suggests that a^* should be replaced by an estimator which is acceptable vis-à-vis both the observed sample and prior ideas about the phenomenon. Although the choice of prior distribution may be a delicate matter, an estimator such as β, given by (82), is preferable to a^*.

For example, for the case discussed in section 6, we may be prepared to specify a priori

$$\alpha_1 = 0.10, \qquad \alpha_2 = 0.20, \qquad \alpha_3 = 0.08, \qquad \alpha_4 = 1.0, \qquad \alpha_5 = 0.0.$$

Even if it is difficult to choose μ and M, we can choose for μM a diagonal matrix whose diagonal elements are 4000, 1000, 4000, 10 and 1 so that, with $\sigma^2 = 10$, the coefficients of variation of the conditional prior distribution of α_j will be of the order of 1/2 for α_1, α_2 and α_3, and 1 for α_4, while the standard deviation for α_5, will be of the order of 3. We then find

$$\beta_1 = 0.086, \qquad \beta_2 = 0.209, \qquad \beta_3 = 0.058, \qquad \beta_4 = 2.16, \qquad \beta_5 = -3.14.$$

and these coefficients are certainly more acceptable than the coefficients of (40). (Note that there is a curious decrease in the coefficient of z_{2t}.)

(vi) Multivariate case

We shall only indicate briefly what happens under Bayesian principles when there are several endogenous variables and we have no prior knowledge of the values of the parameters[†].

To represent this state of prior ignorance, the measure whose density is

$$p(A,\Omega) = |\,\Omega\,|^{-(n+1)/2} \tag{91}$$

is taken for A and Ω. This measure reduces to $p(a, \sigma) = \sigma^{-1}$ when $n = 1$. The likelihood function (73) is replaced by

$$l(A,\Omega) \propto |\,\Omega\,|^{-T/2} \exp\left\{ -\frac{T}{2} \operatorname{tr} \Omega^{-1} [M_{\varepsilon\varepsilon}^* + (A - A^*) M_{zz} (A - A^*)'] \right\}. \tag{92}$$

The posterior density defined by multiplying (91) and (92) implies that the conditional distribution of A given Ω is normal with expected value A^* and covariance matrix exactly that matrix obtained in section 4 when we had to determine the covariances of the sampling distribution of A^*. The density of the posterior marginal distribution of A is defined by

$$p(A/x) \propto |\,M_{\varepsilon\varepsilon}^* + (A - A^*) M_{zz} (A - A^*)'\,|^{-T/2}. \tag{93}$$

This is called the 'generalized multivariate t-distribution'.

For the marginal distribution of the vector a_i of the coefficients a_{ij} of the ith equation, it implies a multivariate t-distribution of the form discussed previously. However the exponent is no longer $-T/2$, as was the case for the prior diffuse distribution σ^{-1} in the treatment of the one-dimensional case, but is now $-(T-n+1)/2$. Apart from this change in the number of degrees of freedom, the confidence regions have the same definitions as those discussed in (iv). The change in the number of degrees of freedom results from the form (91) chosen for the density which expresses a situation of complete prior ignorance. This does not occur if the right hand side of (91) is replaced by $|\,\Omega\,|^{-n}$, which many would certainly accept as the prior density representing a state of ignorance. The exponent of (93) then becomes

$$-\tfrac{1}{2}(T+n-1) \qquad \text{instead of} \qquad -\frac{T}{2}.$$

[†] The reader will find a fuller discussion in two papers on this problem: TIAO and ZELLNER [1964] and GEISSER [1965].

When we try to establish on the basis of (93) confidence regions relating to the entire matrix A, we encounter the same multiplicity of solutions as we do under classical principles. But in practice the regions obtained are similar. Thus, in the case where $m = 1$, we again find the confidence region

$$M_{zz}(A-A^*)'(M_{\varepsilon\varepsilon}^*)^{-1}(A-A^*) \le \frac{n}{T-n} F_{n, T-n}(\eta) \tag{94}$$

which was justified in section 9 from the distribution of 'Hotelling's test'. Similarly, for any m we can define a Bayesian confidence region which coincides exactly with that associated with the likelihood ratio test in classical statistics.

12   Shrunken estimators

In cases to which the multiple regression model applies the common practice relies on least squares estimation. We just saw, however, that a 'Bayesian estimator' ought to be preferred if a well defined and widely recognized prior information was available about the values of the coefficients. On the other hand, we shall see in ch. 8, § 6, that 'robust estimators' have to be considered if the error distribution has fat tails. Finally, arguments have been given in favor of 'shrunken estimators', to which we now turn our attention.

In fact two distinct types of such estimators have been proposed. It is important to distinguish them sharply and not to be misled into thinking that shrinkage would be good *per sé*.

In the first place, faced with the multicollinearity problem, some applied statisticians have suggested *ridge regression* as an alternative to the common least squares regression. The collinearity difficulty is reflected in the fact that the near singular matrix M_{zz} has to be inverted; computations are eased and their result made more 'stable' if inversion operates instead on the matrix $M_{zz}+kI$, where k is a not too small number, chosen in advance. On this purely intuitive or practical basis, HOERL and KENNARD [1970] have defined the ridge regression estimate[†]:

$$a^R = (M_{zz} + kI)^{-1}m_{zx} \tag{95}$$

One easily sees that this is precisely the Bayesian estimator β defined by (82) if the prior distribution is such that $\alpha = 0$ and $\mu M = TkI$. It is, of course, fully justified if this prior distribution applies. Bayesian theory even shows which number k ought to be chosen. We note that k should be the smaller as the prior knowledge about a is the vaguer, and indeed we know that k should be zero in the case of a diffuse prior distribution[††].

[†] For the small sample distribution of this ridge estimator see DWIVEDI, SRIVASTAVA and HALL [1977].
[††] RAO [1976a] shows that k could be chosen as the result of an initial stage in estimation; he then uses the so-called 'empirical Bayes' method, which is not discussed in this book.

In the case of multi-collinearity the ridge regression vector a^R will usually not be proportional to the least squares regression vector a^*. If one, however, speaks of a shrunken estimator, it is because the length of a^R will in general be smaller than that of a^*.

In order to understand some problems raised by the use of ridge regression, and by shrunken estimator more generally, it is interesting to consider the particular case in which M_{zz} would be the unit matrix, so that a^R would be equal to a^* divided by $1+k$. One can then easily compare the covariance matrices of the estimation errors:

$$E(a^* - a)(a^* - a)' = \frac{\sigma^2 I}{T}$$

$$E(a^R - a)(a^R - a)' = \frac{1}{(1+k)^2}\left[\frac{\sigma^2 I}{T} + k^2 aa'\right]$$

Hence, if the loss function is quadratic, the risk of a^R will be smaller than that of a^* (with a positive k) if the true vector a is small, but will be larger in general if a is large. Indeed, whereas the risk of a^* is constant with respect to a, the risk of a^R is increasing and unbounded. This clearly shows that ridge regression cannot be said to be better than least squares regression if one does not want to introduce the Bayesian notion of some prior information on a.

Consideration of the quadratic risk associated with least squares regression reminds us, however, that Stein has proved the non-admissibility of a^* for the case in which this vector has more than two components (see ch. 5, § 9). Hence, there exist estimators whose risks are never larger and sometimes smaller than that of a^*, no matter what the true vector a is. Indeed, BARANCHIK [1973] has derived such a *James-Stein estimator* for the case of a loss function given by:

$$(a^S - a)' M_{zz}(a^S - a) \qquad (96)$$

This estimator a^S differs from a^* only when there are more than two exogenous variables ($m > 2$). It is then given by:

$$a^S = \left[1 - \frac{m-2}{T-m+2} \cdot \frac{1-R^2}{R^2}\right] a^*$$

(assuming the multiplier of a^* is not negative, in which case a^* would be taken as 0; R^2 is the ratio between the sum of squares of the fitted values x_t^* and the sum of squares of the actual values x_t).

This shrunken estimator a^S does not differ much from a^* unless the fit is poor and the number of observations small in the relation to the number of exogenous variables. The estimator a^S is very easy to compute. It has a smaller risk than a^* when the true vector a is the null vector, but it has asymptotically the same risk as the length of a increases indefinitely (which is easily understood, since R^2 then tends in probability to 1).

Some of the small sample properties of a^S are known as a result of the work of ULLAH and ULLAH [1978], who derive in particular the value of $E(a^S - a) \times (a^S - a)'$. This matrix differs from the covariance matrix of a^* by a term that is infinitely small, in relation to it, when σ^2/T is small relatively to $a'M_{zz}a$. An easily applicable formula for an approximation of this correcting term is also given, so that standard deviations of the a_j^S can be derived from the classical estimates of the standard deviations of the a_j^*.

One may wonder how the shrunken estimator a^S relates to Bayesian statistics. Roughly speaking, we can say that it appears as a kind of generalized Bayesian estimator when the prior information is represented by a non-finite measure giving an indefinitely increasing weight to values of a approaching zero and giving also more weight to very large values of a than the conjugate prior distribution (74) does[†]. Still more roughly speaking, this means that one would consider as fairly likely that a should be very near the zero vector but that, if it is not, one would consider that it could be any other vector.

One may also wonder what happens when (96) does not provide the appropriate loss function. But before answering this question, one should remember that (96) is the appropriate loss function whenever the ultimate aim is to predict the values of x_t in situations in which the behavior of the exogenous variables will not differ much from their behavior in the sample period and in which the loss will be proportional to the square of the prediction error (in this respect see formula (67) of this chapter).

Suppose then that (96) is replaced by

$$(a^S - a)'W(a^S - a) \tag{98}$$

where W is a given symmetric positive definite or semi-definite matrix. JUDGE and BOCK [1976] have shown that it is then not always possible to adapt the James-Stein estimator so as to reach, uniformly in a, a lower risk than with a^*. This depends on whether the sum of the characteristic roots of WM_{zz}^{-1} is larger than twice the largest of these roots. The condition is of course met when $W = M_{zz}$ and $m > 2$, but it is not when (98) gives weight only to one specific coefficient a_j (all elements of W are then zero except the jth diagonal term). The result of Judge and Bock shows that no modified James-Stein estimator exists that would have a lower risk than a^* not only for all values of a but also for all possible choices of the positive definite matrix W; indeed, a^* would be admissible if the definition of admissibility should make this type of reference to the whole class of quadratic loss functions.

At this stage we may pause to consider when one should recommend the use of the shrunken estimator a^S. The question does not arise of course unless the

[†] For a short presentation and access to the literature see ZELLNER and VANDAELE [1975].

number of exogenous variables is fairly large in relation to the number of observations. When this occurs, one or the other of the two following reasons may
justify the use of a^S: either prior information is of the type that was sketched
above; or one is interested not in the regression coefficients themselves but
in the global use of the model for predicting the endogenous variable x_t from
non atypical values of the exogenous variables. When these two reasons rein-
force each other, a^S is particularly advisable.

The estimator a^S is shrunken toward zero. The question may be asked why
has the null vector a particular role to play. Indeed, the argument that recommends the James-Stein estimator may be applied to justify estimators that are
shrunken toward other vectors, for instance toward a fixed vector a^0 that would
appear a priori as particularly likely.

In order to make this point clear let us first notice that a^S could be written:

$$a^S = \begin{cases} 0 & \text{if} \quad u < c \\ \left(1 - \dfrac{c}{u}\right) a^* & \text{if} \quad u \geq c \end{cases} \tag{99}$$

with

$$u = \frac{(T - m)R^2}{m(1 - R^2)} \qquad c = \frac{(m - 2)(T - m)}{m(T - m + 2)} \tag{100}$$

In this formula u is precisely the classical statistics that would be used to test
$a = 0$ (under the null hypothesis it has the Fisher distribution with m and $T - m$
degrees of freedom).

A James-Stein estimator shrunken toward a^0 is then defined by:

$$a^S = \begin{cases} a^0 & \text{if} \quad u < c \\ a^* - \dfrac{c}{u}(a^* - a^0) & \text{if} \quad u \geq c \end{cases} \tag{101}$$

in which c is given by (100) and u is the classical statistics to test the equality
between a and a^0, namely statistics (49) of this chapter, a being there replaced
by a^0. We may note that, when a is actually equal to a^0, the shrunken estimator
a^S takes the exact value a^0 with a non zero probability. For instance if $m = 5$
and T is large, this probability is equal to 0.3 (the approximate weight of the
left hand tail of the appropriate F distribution cut at $c = 0.6$).

The idea naturally comes to mind whether shrinkage could not be applied to
only a subset of the components of a, the q last ones for instance. Indeed, if
one suspects that these components may very well be zero, whereas the same
suspicion does not apply to the first $m - q$ components, the implicit non-finite
measure representing prior ideas may favor a selective shrinkage. More im-

portantly, one must remember that a^S defined by (99) or (101) dominates a^* only when the loss function is given by (96); for a particular component the mean square error of a_j^S may very well be larger than the mean square error of a_j^* (for details on this point, see RAO and SHINOZAKI [1978]). If one contemplates policy action on z_j, one may be particularly anxious to avoid a large risk of error on a_j, more anxious than the loss function (96) admits.

Such a limited shrinkage may be applied if $q > 2$ and is very easy to define. Let a^* and $\hat{a}$ be the respective least squares estimates of a without and with the restriction that the last q components be zero. Let u be the classical statistics for testing this restriction (see section 9(ii) of this chapter) then a^S may be defined as:

$$a^S = \begin{cases} \hat{a} & \text{if} \quad u < c \\ a^* - \dfrac{c}{u}(a^* - \hat{a}) & \text{if} \quad u \geq c \end{cases} \tag{102}$$

with c given by:

$$c = \frac{(q-2)(T-m)}{m(T-m+2)} \tag{103}$$

The room for such a selective shrinkage is of course wide in applications where there is a substantial number of exogenous variables. In particular it has been proposed not to apply shrinkage to the constant term, that is to the coefficient of the constant dummy variable. Selective shrinkage may also occur, and is then defined as above, when there are q linear restrictions on the coefficients of a, a case that will be considered again in ch. 8, section 8 (i).

CHAPTER 7

Analysis of variance and covariance

1 Introduction

The hypothesis considered in section 9 of the previous chapter specified the values of certain coefficients. Thus, in the model containing a single equation we were concerned with the hypothesis that the vector a of the coefficients was equal to a certain vector a^0. The expected value of the vector x of the T observations had then to be a vector y^0 whose tth component was $y_t^0 = a^{0\prime} z_t$.

We often consider also '*linear hypotheses*' which specify that the expected value y of the vector x belongs to certain linear subspaces contained in L. In organizing tests of these and the calculations involved therein, it is helpful to think in terms of the geometric lay-out of the different linear subspaces considered. It is with the practical organization of such tests that the procedure called '*analysis of variance*' is concerned. We shall now discuss its principles and some of the details of its application.

Before going any further we point out that the simplest hypotheses can often be treated by the methods given in the previous chapter as well as by the analysis of variance. Consider for instance the hypothesis that the first component a_1 of the vector of the coefficients is zero in a model with a single equation. We saw how to test a hypothesis relating to a single coefficient and therefore in particular how to test that $a_1 = 0$. This hypothesis may also be dealt with by the analysis of variance, since in T-dimensional space, according to the model, the vector y must belong to the subspace L spanned by the m vectors representing the m exogenous variables, and, according to the hypothesis under test, it must belong to the subspace M spanned by the $m-1$ vectors representing the last $m-1$ exogenous variables. As we shall see below, the two methods are equivalent when they are both applicable.

We shall confine ourselves to the study of those problems which are liable to arise most often in econometrics. We shall not attempt to make this an exhaustive study and in particular two important questions will be deliberately ignored[†].

First, the analysis of variance may be justified by models other than those defined in the course of the previous chapters. But these models are not likely to be of much use to the econometrician.

Second, important results have been obtained concerning the choice of 'experimental designs', that is, the principles which should regulate the col-

---

[†] See the description of different models leading to analysis of variance in SCHEFFÉ [1959], part II. For the basic principles of design of experiments, see DUGUÉ [1958], part II.

lection of data in order to facilitate the application of tests. But the econometrician rarely needs these results. They cannot guide his choice between the different statistical series relating to the past development of macroeconomic quantities, since in this case he must only try to give a correct description of the phenomena under analysis. As a rule he has more freedom in choosing the individuals observed in sampling surveys. But he is then concerned with many practical necessities as well as the need to facilitate statistical inference. The general remarks given in the following pages should certainly be enough to indicate how surveys may be planned in order to simplify the establishment of tests.

We shall again start by studying the general linear model. This will enable us to exhibit the principles of analysis of variance in a simple, though abstract, context. There is a twofold advantage in this. On the one hand, we shall obtain general formulae for the computation of tests, these formulae being applicable to the most widely differing linear models. On the other hand, we shall set up logical rules to be followed in the application of successive tests. Unfortunately these rules are ignored in some econometric studies.

2　Analysis of variance in the general linear model

Let us return to the problem P discussed in ch. 5, and in particular to the situation considered in section 8. Let x be a random n-vector with covariance matrix Q and expected value y. We know a priori that y belongs to a p-dimensional subspace L, and we wish to test the hypothesis that this vector belongs to a q-dimensional subspace M contained in L.

As before, let u and v denote the projections[†] of x on L and M parallel to the principal conjugate subspaces K and N of L and M with respect to the concentration ellipsoid of x. In ch. 5, § 8, we described two interesting tests of the proposed hypothesis.

(a) If Q is known completely, the hypothesis that y belongs to M will be rejected when:

$$\gamma = (u - v)'Q^{-1}(u - v) > \chi^2_{p-q}(\alpha). \tag{1}$$

(b) If Q is known to be of the form $\sigma^2 Q_0$ where Q_0 is known and σ is unknown, the hypothesis will be rejected when

$$\frac{n - p}{p - q} \cdot \frac{\eta}{\xi} > F_{p-q, n-p}(\alpha), \tag{2}$$

where

$$\eta = (u - v)'Q_0^{-1}(u - v), \tag{3}$$

[†] In the rest of this chapter, it will be understood that all projections are parallel to the appropriate conjugate subspaces with respect to the concentration ellipsoid of x, and this will no longer be stated explicitly.

$$\xi = (x - u)'Q_0^{-1}(x - u). \tag{4}$$

We recall that in these expressions α denotes the chosen level of significance and that these tests have a certain optimal character, each in its appropriate situation.

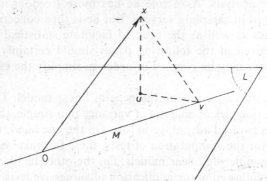

Fig. 1.

We confine ourselves for the moment to the second situation, and we see that the concepts introduced for the construction of the test (2) can conveniently be shown in the following table:

TABLE 1

Random vector	Linear subspace	Dimension	Quadratic form
$x - u$	K	$n - p$	$\xi = (x - u)'Q_0^{-1}(x - u)$
$u - v$	H	$p - q$	$\eta = (u - v)'Q_0^{-1}(u - v)$
$x - v$	N	$n - q$	$\zeta = (x - v)'Q_0^{-1}(x - v)$

This table shows that the vector $x-v$ of N has been expressed as the sum of two other vectors $x-u$ and $u-v$, the latter belonging to the subspace H, the intersection of N and L, and principal conjugate subspace of M in L. At the same time the quadratic form ζ has been expressed as a sum of ξ and η; indeed $\zeta = \xi + \eta$, since $x-u$ is conjugate to $u-v$, and consequently:

$$(x - u)'Q_0^{-1}(u - v) = 0.$$

It often happens in applications that $\xi/(n-p)$, $\eta/(p-q)$ and $\xi/(n-q)$ appear as empirical variances. So it will be convenient now to call $\xi/(n-p)$ the 'variance relative to L', $\xi/(n-q)$ the 'total variance relative to M' and $\eta/(p-q)$ the 'variance relative to M in L'. We can then say that the test depends on an analysis of the total variance with respect to M into two components, namely, the variance in L and the variance with respect to L. Hence we have the general name of '*analysis of variance*' for the type of tests proposed here.

3　Successive hypotheses

In empirical research we often have in mind a priori several particular hypotheses which are not mutually exclusive and which we intend to test. Thus when trying to determine the trend of a time series, we can choose a polynomial form without a priori knowledge of the degree of the suitable polynomial; we may then wish to test successively the hypotheses that this polynomial is not of degree greater than three, then that it is at most of degree two, and finally that it is a simple linear function. Similarly when analyzing the results of an inquiry into household budgets, we may wish to test if different ways of classifying households affect the behavior which we are studying.

Clearly such situations do not arise only in cases where the hypotheses under test are linear. We deal with them now because the analysis of variance often allows clear and efficient organization of the sequence of computation. But the few general principles which we shall state apply also to tests of successive non-linear hypotheses.

When it is a question of testing different hypotheses, it would seem logical to consider the procedure as a whole. The probabilities of first- and second-type errors should be determined for the different possible forms of the true structure and according to whether the several tests are carried out simultaneously or successively. In practice a study of the entire procedure taken as a whole would often be too laborious. But we must at least keep in mind the consequences which the carrying out of several tests may have on the properties of the final decision.

Coming back to the linear model, let us suppose therefore that there are two hypotheses, one of which stipulates that y belongs to q-dimensional M, and the other that y belongs to R, an r-dimensional subspace contained on M. Figure 2 shows the different vectors of L which must then be considered. Besides the vectors u and v already defined, we find the vector w, the projection of x on R. It is also the projection of u or of v.

We can give the calculations involved in the tests of these two hypotheses in an analysis of variance table where the vector $x - w$ is shown as the sum of $x - u$, $u - v$ and $v - w$, and the quadratic form

$$\mu = (x - w)' Q_0^{-1} (x - w)$$

as the sum of the three similar quadratic forms constructed with these vectors (cf. table 2).

We can now propose two tests of the hypothesis that y belongs to R. The two situations must be carefully distinguished.

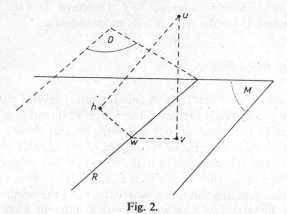

Fig. 2.

(i) *To test that y belongs to R, knowing that it belongs to L.* For this case we need only follow the computation given above, expressing $x - w$ here as the sum of $x - u$ and $u - w$. The hypothesis will be rejected when:

$$\frac{n-p}{p-r} \cdot \frac{\eta + \lambda}{\xi} > F_{p-r, n-p}(\alpha). \tag{5}$$

(ii) *To test that y belongs to R, knowing that it belongs to M.* On the same principle, we express $x - w$ as the sum of $x - v$ and $v - w$. The hypothesis will be rejected when:

$$\frac{n-q}{q-r} \cdot \frac{\lambda}{\xi + \eta} > F_{q-r, n-q}(\alpha). \tag{6}$$

TABLE 2

Random vector	Linear subspace	Dimension	Quadratic form
$x - u$	K	$n - p$	$\xi = (x - u)' Q_0^{-1} (x - u)$
$u - v$	H	$p - q$	$\eta = (u - v)' Q_0^{-1} (u - v)$
$v - w$	G	$q - r$	$\lambda = (v - w)' Q_0^{-1} (v - w)$
$x - w$	S	$n - r$	$\mu = (x - w)' Q_0^{-1} (x - w)$

We remember here that these tests are chosen because of certain optimal properties. When the frequency of errors of the first type is specified, they minimize the frequency of errors of the second type. (This property was specified precisely in ch. 5 § 8.)

If the test (5) is used in the case where y is known to belong to M, the probability of a Type 1 error is in fact α. But there is a higher probability of a Type 2 error than for the test (6).

Similarly, if the test (6) is used when we know only that y belongs to L, the probability of a Type 1 error is still α. But there would be a higher probability than there is for the test (5) of not rejecting the hypothesis that y belongs to R in the case where y actually would lie outside (and at a sufficient distance from) M.

Consequently the test (6) may still be of interest even when we are not certain that y belongs to M, provided we have tested this hypothesis previously and we have no particular a priori reason to suspect that y lies outside M and at a fairly considerable distance from it, this situation being improbable although possible.

This gives us the idea for the following procedure: Test the hypothesis that y belongs to M, using the critical region defined by the inequality (2); then, if this hypothesis is not rejected, test the hypothesis that y belongs to R, using the critical region (6).

It is quite easy to calculate the significance level associated with this procedure. For we can prove (see HOGG [1961]) that, when the hypothesis that y belongs to R is correct, the two ratios η/ξ and $\lambda/(\xi+\eta)$ are stochastically independent. If the value α_2 has been retained in the inequality (2) and the value α_6 in the inequality (6), then the probability of not rejecting the hypothesis that $y \in R$ when it is true is $(1-\alpha_2)(1-\alpha_6)$. The level of significance associated with the proposed procedure as a test of $y \in R$ is therefore $1-(1-\alpha_2)(1-\alpha_6)$, which in practice is very near $\alpha_2 + \alpha_6$. Its power has been studied by SEBER [1964].

Note that in this procedure the less restrictive hypothesis is tested first. In many studies in econometrics the opposite order is in fact adopted. For example, one considers a sequence of hypotheses $H_1 \supset H_2 \supset \ldots \supset H_{n-1} \supset H_n$ decreasing in generality. The most restrictive hypothesis H_n is first tested against the hypothesis H_{n-1} which immediately precedes it (here $y \in R$ is tested against $y \in M$). Then if H_n is rejected, H_{n-1} is tested against H_{n-2} (here $y \in M$ against $y \in L$). This process continues until one reaches the first hypothesis not to be rejected.

This frequently used procedure has the advantage of starting from the simplest situation to approach the more complex one. However, it has not been studied rigorously and we must advise against its use. In addition, according to the classical principles of mathematical statistics, it seems to have a basic fault, since it usually does not specify the most general hypothesis which is to be considered true in all events and which allows the properties of the intermediary tests to be studied. We shall come back on this procedure at the end of section 6.

4 Orthogonal hypotheses

It may also happen that, in addition to the general hypothesis that y belongs to L, we consider two subsidiary hypotheses, one of which implies that y belongs to M and the other that y belongs to a d-dimensional subspace D contained in L (but not generally in M). We then talk about 'hypothesis M' and 'hypothesis D'.

If R denotes the intersection of M and D, and if this intersection is r-dimensional, then:

(i) The test (5) applies to the hypothesis that M and D are satisfied simultaneously.

(ii) The test (6) applies to the hypothesis that D is satisfied, when we are certain that M is satisfied.

(iii) To test the hypothesis D independently of M, we must consider the projection h of x on D, and also $x-h$ expressed as the sum of $x-u$ and $u-h$ (cf. fig. 2). Generally the quadratic form corresponding to $u-h$ cannot be deduced from those given in table 2.

The situation is a little simpler in the particular case where the hypotheses D and M are conjugate. We say that *the two linear hypotheses D and M are conjugate if the subspace D contains the subspace H principal conjugate of M in L.* (M then contains the principal conjugate subspace of D in L, since no vector of L which lies outside M is conjugate to H.) When the concentration ellipsoid of x is a sphere, D and M are also said to be 'orthogonal'.

When D and M are conjugate, the subspace D can be considered as the set of linear combinations of two groups of vectors, one group being contained in H and the other in the intersection R of M and D. Since H and R have only the zero vector in common and since H has dimension $p-q$, then $d=p-q+r$. Moreover H is contained in the principal conjugate subspace of R in D, since the vectors of H are conjugate to R. The principal conjugate of R in D has dimension $d-r=p-q$, and is therefore just H.

We now consider the equality:

$$(u - h) = (u - v) + (v - w) + (w - h).$$

The vector $u-h$, conjugate to H, belongs to M (see ch. 5, the end of § 4). It is expressed as the sum of three vectors, of which one, namely $v-w$, belongs to M, and the two others belong to H ($w-h$ is conjugate to R in D, and lies in H). Now $(u-v)+(w-h)$ is contained in both H and M and is therefore the zero vector. So: $u-h=v-w$.

The quadratic form $(u-h)'Q_0^{-1}(u-h)$ is then equal to λ. In order to *test the hypothesis D independently of the conjugate hypothesis M, we choose as critical region*:

$$\frac{n-p}{q-r} \cdot \frac{\lambda}{\xi} > F_{q-r,n-p}(\alpha). \tag{7}$$

(Of course we could write $p-d$ as the denominator of the first fraction since $p-d=q-r$.)

Thus when there is conjugacy, table 2 allows us to test the hypothesis D independently of the truth of M. We note also that the test (7) is correct when M is true, but it is in this case less powerful than (6).

In order to test that y belongs to R, knowing only that it belongs to L, we might obviously think of testing separately that $y \in M$ and that $y \in D$. However, on reflection we see that such a procedure is not effective if M and D are not at least approximately orthogonal. For generally y can be near both M and D without being near their intersection. Application of the two tests separately might lead to the conclusion that y belongs to R, when a single test would lead to rejection of the hypothesis.

When the two hypotheses M and D are orthogonal, the testing procedure which involves the two separate tests seems to have a power comparable to that of the single test (see SEBER [1964]) and may be preferred for ease of computation. If the same significance level α is chosen for each of the two separate tests, then the significance level of the combination of them is near 2α in practice.

When the different hypotheses are conjugate or orthogonal, it is considerably easier to establish tests. Such a situation is systematically aimed at in the design of experiments, but it remains exceptional in econometric studies.

5   Hypotheses relating to simple regression

By way of example, we return to the simple regression of an endogenous variable x_t on an exogenous variable z_t (and on the dummy variable which always equals 1). We suppose that assumptions 1 to 4 of ch. 3 (independence, homoscedasticity and normality) are satisfied. Let us consider, in T-dimensional space, the geometric representation already introduced in ch. 3.

In the analysis of variance set-up, the general hypothesis is:

$$y_t = az_t + b, \qquad t = 1, 2, \ldots, T.$$

We can consider the two particular hypotheses

$$M : a = 0 \qquad y_t = b \qquad t = 1, 2, \ldots, T;$$

$$D : b = 0 \qquad y_t = az_t \qquad t = 1, 2, \ldots, T.$$

They define in L two one-dimensional subspaces, say M and D. Their intersection R here becomes the origin (except in the excluded case when all the z_t are equal).

The successive projections of x are then u in L $(u_t = a^* z_t + b^*)$, v in M $(v_t = \bar{x})$ and the origin in R. The matrix Q_0 is the unit matrix of order T.

In this case the quadratic form μ of table 2 is:

$$\mu = \sum_{t=1}^{T} x_t^2.$$

Its decomposition is expressed by:

$$\sum_{t=1}^{T} x_t^2 = \sum_{t=1}^{T} (x_t - a^* z_t - b^*)^2 + a^{*2} \sum_{t=1}^{T} (z_t - \bar{z})^2 + T\bar{x}^2.$$

Table 2 can be given in a form which is closer to current usage[†]:

TABLE 3

Variance	Linear subspace	Degrees of freedom	Quadratic form
Relative to the regression	K	$T - 2$	$\sum_t (x_t - a^* z_t - b^*)^2$
Explained by a^*	H	1	$a^{*2} \sum_t (z_t - \bar{z})^2$
Relative to the mean	N	$T - 1$	$\sum_t x_t^2 - T\bar{x}^2$
Explained by the mean	M	1	$T\bar{x}^2$
Total	R^T	T	$\sum_t x_t^2$

To test the hypothesis that $a=0$, we use the critical region:

$$(T - 2) \frac{a^{*2} \sum (z_t - \bar{z})^2}{\sum (x_t - a^* z_t - b^*)^2} > F_{1, T-2}(\alpha) = [t_{T-2}(\alpha)]^2, \qquad (8)$$

where $t_{T-2}(\alpha)$ denotes the two-tailed α-level value of Student's t with $T-2$ degrees of freedom.

Similarly, for a simultaneous test that $a=0$ and $b=0$, we shall examine whether:

$$\frac{T - 2}{2} \cdot \frac{a^{*2} \sum (z_t - \bar{z})^2 + T\bar{x}^2}{\sum (x_t - a^* z_t - b^*)^2} > F_{2, T-2}(\alpha). \qquad (9)$$

[†] In applications we obviously do not give the column referring to subspaces, which was introduced here for ease of exposition. On the other hand, an additional final column is often given, showing the numerical values of the sample variances, which are equal to the quadratic forms divided by the corresponding numbers of degrees of freedom.

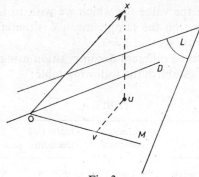

Fig. 3.

Before going further, we note that here we find the tests already defined in ch. 3, at the end of section 6. Thus the test (8) can be written:

$$\frac{|a^*|}{\sigma_a^*} > t_{T-2}(\alpha).$$

Similarly the test (9) can be found by setting $a=0$ and $b=0$ in formulae (31) and (32) of ch. 3. This is not surprising since the same procedures lead to the analysis of variance and to the tests examined in ch. 3.

To test that $b=0$, when it is known that $a=0$, we choose the critical region:

$$(T-1)\frac{T\bar{x}^2}{\sum x_t^2 - T\bar{x}^2} > F_{1,T-1}(\alpha) = [t_{T-1}(\alpha)]^2, \tag{10}$$

which can also be written:

$$\sqrt{T}\,|\bar{x}| > t_{T-1}(\alpha)\cdot\sigma_x,$$

where

$$\sigma_x^2 = \frac{1}{T-1}\sum(x_t - \bar{x})^2.$$

This is the usual test that the mean of a random variable, on which there are T independent observations, is zero.

To enable us to test with the help of table 3 that $b=0$ independently of any hypothesis about a, the variety D must be orthogonal to M, that is, we must have:

$$\sum_{t=1}^{T}(az_t\cdot b) = 0$$

for any a and b, and therefore $\bar{z}=0$. Clearly in applications it will be exceptional for the mean of the observed values of the exogenous variable to be zero (or, more generally, to take the value for which we wish to test that the expected value of x is zero). A test on the sample mean $\bar{x}$ is therefore not sufficient for testing directly the hypothesis that $b=0$.

But we can always effect a different decomposition using the projection of the vector u on D. We then establish the following table:

TABLE 4

Variance	Linear subspace	Degrees of freedom	Quadratic form
Relative to a regression with constant term	K	$T-2$	$\sum_t (x_t - a^* z_t - b^*)^2$
Explained by b	$\bar{U}$	1	$T(\bar{x} - a^*\bar{z})(\bar{x} - \tilde{a}\bar{z})$
Relative to a regression with no constant term	D^*	$T-1$	$\sum_t (x_t - \tilde{a}z_t)^2$

where D^* denotes the principal conjugate subspace of D, U the intersection of D^* and L, and $\tilde{a}$ the coefficient of the regression with no constant term.

The hypothesis that $b=0$ must be rejected if:

$$T(T-2)\frac{(\bar{x} - a^*\bar{z})(\bar{x} - \tilde{a}\bar{z})}{\sum_t (x_t - a^* z_t - b^*)^2} > F_{1,T-2}(\alpha) = [t_{T-2}(\alpha)]^2. \tag{11}$$

It can be verified that this inequality can also be written:

$$|b^*|/\sigma_b^* > t_{T-2}(\alpha).$$

We find here the tests already discussed in previous chapters, and this will also be the case for less simple problems. But we shall see that for such problems the presentation of the analysis of variance is particularly suggestive.

6 The choice of exogenous variables in multiple regressions

Let us now consider the rather more complex situation where an endogenous variable x_t is considered as a linear function of several exogenous variables $z_{1t}, z_{2t}, \ldots, z_{mt}$ and an unobservable random term ε_t:

$$x_t = a_1 z_{1t} + a_2 z_{2t} + \cdots + a_m z_{mt} + \varepsilon_t. \tag{12}$$

We keep assumptions 1 and 3 of ch. 6 (independence, homoscedasticity and normality).

As we saw previously, such models are introduced in order to determine the set of factors which explain the values taken by the quantity x. We often ask ourselves the following questions: are all the exogenous variables $z_{1t},\ldots z_{mt}$ necessary for the explanation of x_t? Would not the phenomenon be equally well represented if we choose, for example, only the first q variables? Can we not assume that the coefficients $a_{q+1}, a_{q+2}, \ldots, a_m$ of the model (12) are zero?

In other words, we wish to test the hypothesis that the T-vector x has a mathematical expectation y which is a linear combination of the vectors $z_1, z_2, \ldots z_q$ only:

$$y_t = a_1 z_{1t} + a_2 z_{2t} + \cdots + a_q z_{qt} \quad \text{for} \quad t = 1, 2, \ldots, T. \quad (13)$$

In view of the model (12), we know also that y is a linear combination of the m vectors $z_1, z_2, \ldots z_m$, and therefore that it belongs to the m-dimensional subspace L spanned by these vectors.

The test of the hypothesis that $a_{q+1} = a_{q+2} = \cdots = a_m = 0$ can be obtained directly by the method of ch. 6 (§ 9, (ii)). It can also be deduced from the general principles of analysis of variance, since we have again here the problem of section 2 with the subspace spanned by $z_1, z_2, \ldots, z_q$ for the subspace M and (in view of assumptions 1 and 3 of ch. 6) the unit matrix for the matrix Q_0.

Let $a_1^1, a_2^1, \ldots a_m^1$ denote the coefficients of the regression of x on $z_1, z_2, \ldots, z_m$, and $a_1^2, a_2^2, \ldots, a_q^2$ the coefficients of the regression of x on $z_1, z_2, \ldots, z_q$. Table 1 then takes the following form:

TABLE 5

Variance	Degrees of freedom	Quadratic form
Not explained by $z_1, z_2, \ldots, z_m$	$T - m$	$\xi = \sum_{t=1}^{T} (x_t - a_1^1 z_{1t} \ldots a_m^1 z_{mt})^2$
Explained by $z_{q+1}, \ldots, z_m$	$m - q$	$\eta = \zeta - \xi$
Not explained by $z_1, z_2, \ldots, z_q$	$T - q$	$\zeta = \sum_{t=1}^{T} (x_t - a_1^2 z_{1t} \ldots a_q^2 z_{qt})^2$

The hypothesis that $a_{q+1}, a_{q+2}, \ldots, a_m$ are zero must be rejected if:

$$\frac{T - m}{m - q} \cdot \frac{\eta}{\xi} > F_{m-q, T-m}(\alpha). \quad (14)$$

The calculations are simplified considerably if the coefficients of the first q exogenous variables are the same in both regressions, that is, if $a_j^2 = a_j^1$ for all

$j \leqq q$. We can easily prove[†] that this is the case *if the two groups of variables* $z_1, z_2, \ldots, z_q$ *and* $z_{q+1}, z_{q+2}, \ldots, z_m$ *are 'orthogonal'*, that is, if:

$$\sum_{t=1}^{T} z_{jt} z_{kt} = 0 \quad \text{for any } j \leqq q, \quad \text{and} \quad k > q. \tag{15}$$

A situation like that in section 3 above arises when we propose to test two distinct hypotheses:

(i) the hypothesis A that the variables $z_{q+1}, z_{q+2}, \ldots, z_m$ do not occur in the model (12) $(a_{q+1} = a_{q+2} = \cdots = a_m = 0)$;

(ii) the hypothesis B that the variables $z_{r+1}, z_{r+2}, \ldots, z_q$ do not occur in the model $(a_{r+1} = a_{r+2} = \cdots = a_q = 0)$.

The different tests defined in sections 3 and 4 apply directly here. As we have seen, the situation is simpler when the hypotheses A and B are orthogonal, that is, when the subspace D contains the subspace H orthogonal to M in L. In this case the subspace M consists of the linear combinations of the q vectors $z_1, z_2, \ldots, z_q$, and D consists of the linear combinations of the $r + m - q$ vectors $z_1, z_2, \ldots, z_r, z_{q+1}, \ldots, z_m$. *In particular, the two hypotheses A and B are orthogonal when the two groups of variables* $z_1, z_2, \ldots z_q$ *and* $z_{q+1}, z_{q+2}, \ldots, z_m$ *are orthogonal;* for then H is the set of linear combinations of $z_{q+1}, z_{q+2}, \ldots, z_m$ and therefore contained in D.

To sum up, orthogonality of the exogenous variables makes it easier to compute and order the various proposed tests. Unfortunately such orthogonality is exceptional in econometric studies. The exogenous variables generally represent observable quantities whose values are beyond the control of the econometrician. It would be very surprising for equalities such as (15) to be realized exactly. This is hardly likely to happen except for the dummy exogenous variables which allow the treatment of observations grouped in distinct classes. In fact real economic variables most often show pronounced multicollinearities which are in a sense the opposite of orthogonality.

The definition of precise rules for choosing variables to explain a given quantity is of increasing importance since nowadays data involving a very large number of variables are available to the econometrician. Often prior knowledge of the phenomenon is insufficient to determine which variables play a major part in explanation. So the selection of the exogenous variables results from an exploratory scrutiny of the data. In the practical field, various and often fairly unsystematic methods are used in this scrutiny.

Theorists sometimes try to assess the methods used. We shall cite two useful articles.

Faced with data involving a large number of variables, the econometrician

---

[†] This property was stated and proved in ch. 1, § 8. The regression then involved a constant term, so that orthogonality was defined slightly differently. But the proof and the definition apply directly to regressions with no constant terms.

often looks for variables which are correlated with some particular quantity. But, to consider sample correlations significant after such a selective search, one must obviously be more and more exacting as the number of available variables increases. DIEHR and HOFLIN [1974] give tables for this purpose. Given a sample of T independent observations on $m+1$ independent normal variables, they consider the multiple correlation coefficient R^2 of the regression of the first variable on those q of the other m variables which give the best R^2; they then tabulate the distribution of this maximum R^2 in order to determine the significance levels to choose. For example, if $q = 3$ explanatory variables are chosen from $m = 5$ available variables, then R^2 is significant at the 5 % level if it is greater than 0.382 when $T = 20$ and 0.097 when $T = 100$; if $q = 3$ variables are chosen from $m = 10$, the 5 % significance level rises to 0.448 when $T = 20$ and 0.132 when $T = 100$.

KENNEDY and BANCROFT [1971] are interested in comparing the method of progressive addition of variables to a regression with the method of progressive elimination of them. They assume that there are m available exogenous variables z_j of which the first q are certainly involved in the explanation of x and that the remaining $m-q$ are ordered naturally so that z_{j+1} does not appear in the explanation if z_j does not. In the method of progressive addition, the introduction of $z_{q+1}, z_{q+2}, \ldots$ is investigated successively and no more variables are introduced when the Fisher test accepts the hypothesis that the last variable introduced has no effect. The method of successive elimination, on the other hand, starts from the complete regression involving all m variables z_j, investigates the effect of eliminating $z_m, z_{m-1}, \ldots$ successively, and stops elimination when the Fisher test rejects the hypothesis that the variable to be eliminated has no effect. Comparison shows the second method to be preferable, as we could expect after the discussion at the end of section 3. However, we should note that in some cases where the relationship is weak, the first method appears slightly preferable.

The use of tests in the choice of a regression raises another type of question: since the final objective is to estimate a linear relation, what significance level should be chosen for the tests? We shall treat this question in the last section of ch. 8.

7   Analysis of variance for classified observations

The name analysis of variance is often reserved for a particular category of tests belonging to the general type defined at the beginning of this chapter but excluding tests relating to regressions[†]. A particular quantity is measured on different observed individuals. Each individual belongs to a class defined by one or more factors. The model stipulates that the value of the measured quantity is a random variable whose expected value depends only on the class

[†] On the other hand, the analysis of variance is sometimes justified on the basis of models other than those studied in this book.

to which the individual considered belongs, the other characteristics of its distribution being in no way dependent on this individual.

We shall limit ourselves here to some brief remarks concerning two simple models.

Let us suppose first that the T observed individuals are divided into p classes represented by an index α $(\alpha = 1, 2, \ldots, p)$, and assume the following relation for the observed quantity x_t:

$$x_t = a_\alpha + \varepsilon_t, \tag{16}$$

where a_α is a characteristic unknown constant of the class α to which t belongs, and ε_t an unobservable 'error' satisfying assumptions 1 and 3 of ch. 6 (independence, homoscedasticity and normality).

To fix ideas, x_t may represent the wage rate of an unskilled worker in the building industry in the district t; α may represent the category to which t belongs, for example, rural area, small town, average town, large urban area. The model stipulates that category of district is the only systematic factor influencing the wage rate under discussion.

This model can be considered as a particular case of the multiple regression model (12). For let $u_{\alpha t}$ be a dummy variable which has the value 1 when the individual t belongs to the class α, and the value 0 when it does not. The relation (16) can be written:

$$x_t = \sum_{\alpha=1}^{p} a_\alpha u_{\alpha t} + \varepsilon_t \tag{17}$$

and the a_α appear as the coefficients of the p dummy variables u_α (for $\alpha = 1, 2, \ldots, p$).

Let us then consider the hypothesis that, for any α, a_α is equal to a certain constant a independent of the class α. The wage rate considered would be the same on average in all types of district. In terms of our usual geometric representation, this hypothesis states that the expected value y of the vector x belongs to a one-dimensional subspace M contained in the subspace L of the linear combinations of p vectors u_α. We can therefore test this hypothesis by analysis of variance.

The estimates of a_α and a obtained by the method of least squares are respectively:

$$a_\alpha^* = \bar{x}_\alpha = \frac{1}{T_\alpha} \sum_t^\alpha x_t, \qquad a^* = \bar{x} = \frac{1}{T} \sum_{t=1}^{T} x_t, \tag{18}$$

where T_α denotes the number of observed individuals in the class α, and $\sum_t^a$ the sum over all the individuals t belonging to α.

Table 1 then becomes:

TABLE 6

Variance	Degrees of freedom	Quadratic form
Within classes	$T - p$	$\xi = \sum\limits_{\alpha=1}^{p} \sum\limits_{t}^{\alpha} (x_t - \bar{x}_\alpha)^2$
Between classes	$p - 1$	$\eta = \sum\limits_{\alpha=1}^{p} T_\alpha (\bar{x}_\alpha - \bar{x})^2$
Total variance	$T - 1$	$\zeta = \sum\limits_{t=1}^{T} (x_t - \bar{x})^2$

The proposed hypothesis will be rejected if:

$$\frac{T-p}{p-1} \cdot \frac{\eta}{\xi} > F_{p-1, T-p}(\omega), \qquad (19)$$

where ω denotes the chosen level of significance.

The quadratic forms which appear in table 6 are calculated from the sample variances of x_t which are computed either over the entire set of observations or over the observations belonging to the same class α. The term analysis of variance is therefore particularly appropriate to table 6, for which it was first of all introduced.

Suppose now that the individual observations are classified according to two distinct factors, the first, α, giving p classes ($\alpha = 1, 2, \ldots, p$) and the second, β, giving q classes ($\beta = 1, 2, \ldots, q$). We assume the following relation for the observed quantity x_t:

$$x_t = a_\alpha + b_\beta + \varepsilon_t, \qquad (20)$$

where the a_α and b_β are characteristic unknown constants of the classes α and β to which the individual t belongs, and ε_t is an error satisfying assumptions 1 and 3 of ch. 6.

Thus x_t may represent a wage rate in the district t; α may be the type of district, and β the region (North, East, Central, etc.). The model stipulates that the wage rate is the sum of two systematic terms, one of which is explained by type of district and the other by region, and of a purely random term.

We see immediately that in this formulation the terms a_α and b_β are not identifiable since the distribution of the x_t is not affected by the addition of the same number k to all the a_α and the subtraction of this number k from all the b_β. By making a slight change in the definition of the a_α and the b_β, we generally express the model (20) in the more convenient form:

$$x_t = a_\alpha + b_\beta + c + \varepsilon_t,\tag{21}$$

and, in order to identify the coefficients a_α and b_β, we impose the two conditions:

$$\sum_{\alpha=1}^{p} T_\alpha a_\alpha = 0, \qquad \sum_{\beta=1}^{q} T_\beta b_\beta = 0,\tag{22}$$

where T_α and T_β denote the numbers of observations in the classes α and β.

The coefficient c then represents the average value of x, while a_α measures the *effect* attributable to the class α and b_β the effect attributable to the class β. The conditions (22) show that these effects are on the average zero for the set of observations[†].

The model (21) comes into the general category of the multiple regression model. For consider $p+q$ dummy variables u_α and v_β defined by:

$$u_{\alpha t} = \begin{cases} 1 \text{ if } t \text{ belongs to } \alpha, \\ 0 \text{ otherwise;} \end{cases}$$

$$v_{\beta t} = \begin{cases} 1 \text{ if } t \text{ belongs to } \beta, \\ 0 \text{ otherwise.} \end{cases}$$

Equation (21) can be written:

$$x_t = \sum_{\alpha=1}^{p} a_\alpha u_{\alpha t} + \sum_{\beta=1}^{q} b_\beta v_{\beta t} + c + \varepsilon_t.\tag{23}$$

In fact it is more convenient to use the dummy variables $r_{\alpha t}$ and $s_{\beta t}$:

$$r_{\alpha t} = u_{\alpha t} - \frac{T_\alpha}{T}, \qquad s_{\beta t} = v_{\beta t} - \frac{T_\beta}{T},\tag{24}$$

which satisfy:

$$\sum_{t=1}^{T} r_{\alpha t} = 0, \qquad \sum_{t=1}^{T} s_{\beta t} = 0,\tag{25}$$

and, from (22):

$$\sum_{\alpha=1}^{p} a_\alpha r_{\alpha t} = \sum_{\alpha=1}^{p} a_\alpha u_{\alpha t}, \qquad \sum_{\beta=1}^{T} b_\beta s_{\beta t} = \sum_{\beta=1}^{q} b_\beta v_{\beta t}.$$

[†] According to the equality (21), the effects attributable to the two chosen factors (for example, type of area and region) are considered to be simply additive. We must often use a more complex representation, for example:

$$x_t = c + a_\alpha + b_\beta + d_{\alpha\beta} + \varepsilon_t$$

where the $d_{\alpha\beta}$ are unknown parameters called *inter-actions* which, for purpose of identification, are restricted to satisfy conditions similar to (22). The analysis of variance applies to these more complex models which belong to the category of linear models considered here.

With these variables, the model is written:

$$x_t = \sum_{a=1}^{p} a_a r_{at} + \sum_{\beta=1}^{q} b_\beta s_{\beta t} + c + \varepsilon_t. \tag{26}$$

Two important hypotheses can be tested: hypothesis A that the effects attributable to the first factor are zero ($a_\alpha = 0$ for $\alpha = 1, 2, \ldots, p$) and hypothesis B that the effects attributable to the second factor are zero ($b_\beta = 0$ for $\beta = 1, 2, \ldots, q$). In the example quoted above, hypothesis A states that type of area has no influence on the wage rate, and the hypothesis B that region has none.

These two hypotheses conform directly to the system given in section 4. The first implies that, in T-dimensional space, y, the expected value of the vector x, is contained in the subspace M spanned by the q vectors s_β and by the vector l all of whose components are equal to 1. In view of (25), the s_β are not independent. The subspace M is q-dimensional, whenever there is at least one observation in each of the classes β. Similarly the hypothesis B implies that y is contained in the p-dimensional subspace D spanned by the vectors r_α and the vector l. Therefore the tests given in sections 1 and 2 apply here.

Hypotheses A and B are orthogonal if and only if D contains the subspace H orthogonal to M in the subspace L spanned by the vectors r_α, s_β and l. In particular it is sufficient that the vectors r_α are orthogonal to the vectors s_β. Indeed the intersection of D and M is the one-dimensional subspace containing l. The subspace L has dimension $p+q-1$, and the subspace H has dimension $p-1$. It is the subspace spanned by the r_α, since this subspace has dimension $p-1$ (provided that there is an observation in each class α), and since each vector r_α is by hypothesis orthogonal to the s_β, and is orthogonal to l in view of (25).

A sufficient condition for orthogonality of the two hypotheses A and B is therefore:

$$\sum_{t=1}^{T} r_{at} s_{\beta t} = 0, \qquad \alpha = 1, 2, \ldots, p; \qquad \beta = 1, 2, \ldots, q.$$

It follows from the definitions adopted for r_{at} and $s_{\beta t}$ that this condition is equivalent to:

$$T_{\alpha\beta} = \frac{T_a T_\beta}{T}, \tag{27}$$

$T_{\alpha\beta}$ being the number of individuals belonging both to the class α of the first factor and to the class β of the second.

The equality (27) expresses the fact that the observations in a particular class α are distributed among the different classes β in the proportions $T_{\alpha\beta}/T_\alpha = T_\beta/T$ which are independent of α. In the example suggested above, the two hypotheses that type of district and region have no effect are orthogonal if the distribution of districts among the different categories is the same in all regions.

For calculating the least squares estimates a_α^*, b_β^* and c^* and establishing tests, it is clearly convenient to use the first formulation of the model, that is, the eqs. (21) and (22). Minimizing the sum of squares of the differences between x_t and $a_\alpha^* + b_\beta^* + c^*$ subject to the conditions (22) leads for c^* to the average $\bar{x}$ over the set of T observations, and for a_α^* and b_β^* to the solutions of the system:

$$\bar{x}_\alpha - \bar{x} = a_\alpha^* + \sum_{\beta=1}^{q} \frac{T_{\alpha\beta}}{T_\alpha} b_\beta^*, \qquad \alpha = 1, 2, \ldots, p,$$

$$\bar{x}_\beta - \bar{x} = \sum_{\alpha=1}^{p} \frac{T_{\alpha\beta}}{T_\beta} a_\alpha^* + b_\beta^*, \qquad \beta = 1, 2, \ldots, q,$$
(28)

where $\bar{x}_\alpha$ and $\bar{x}_\beta$ denote the means of the x_t for the observations belonging to the classes α and β respectively.

If the orthogonality condition (27) is satisfied, the system (28) is equivalent to $a_\alpha^* = \bar{x}_\alpha - \bar{x}$ and $b_\beta^* = \bar{x}_\beta - \bar{x}$, in view of the relations (22). To estimate the effect of the first factor, it is sufficient to know the averages within classes defined by this factor only, as if the model took no account of an effect due to the second factor. This is a result of orthogonality which we have already encountered in section 6.

Statistical inquiries often provide information about the values of an economic quantity in individual observations classified on the basis of several factors. These results can easily be analyzed if the individual observations are distributed among the various classes according to conditions similar to (27), and it is sometimes possible so to organize inquiries that this is the case. But in most cases the econometrician must use data which do not obey the orthogonality conditions.

Calculation of the estimates $a_\alpha^*, b_\beta^*, \ldots$ etc. then becomes a matter of serious interest, since the differences between class means $\bar{x}_\alpha$ are too often attributed to the effect of the factor α, while they may result, in part or entirely, from differences in the composition of the α classes relative to other factors. Thus a difference in wage rates in two separate regions may simply express the effect of differences between categories of district, if the distribution of districts among categories is not the same in the two regions[†].

Formulae of type 28 are fairly complicated when the factors and the classes for each factor are more than a few in number[††]. But since the equations to be

---

[†] This holds a fortiori when the model contains *interaction* terms.

[††] Thus in a detailed analysis based on the principles discussed here, HILL [1959] gives in particular the following results for regional differences in annual salaries of males in managerial and professional occupations in Great Britain in 1954. The mean differences from the over-all mean were –£ 218 for Scotland, 0 for the North of England, £ 71 for the Midlands and Wales, and £ 24 for the South of England. The terms relating to the regional effect in a linear model were estimated as –£ 62 for Scotland, –£ 30 for the North of England, £ 93 for the Midlands and Wales, and £ 2 for the South of England. Direct comparison of the means would therefore exaggerate the lag in salaries in these occupations in Scotland and would not reveal the lead in the Midlands and Wales. (As well as region, the model in question took account of age, type of dwelling and field of activity; it contains some interaction terms.)

solved are linear, modern computing methods can be applied to this type of problem.

8 Analysis of covariance

Statistical data on households or firms are an important source for the analysis of economic behavior. Thus, observation of family budgets enables us to set up consumption laws for various goods; study of the finances of firms can lead to the determination of relations between investment and the past course of profits and sales.

In such analyses the question often arises whether the same pattern applies to all the individuals considered, or whether it is necessary to distinguish several different categories of households or firms. Does the consumption of such and such a good obey the same law for all socio-professional classes? Is the relation explaining investment policy the same for all firms, both large and small?

Certain linear models are often sufficient to answer such question. These models are of a mixed character, involving genuine exogenous variables, as do regression models, and at the same time allowing the true relation for each individual to depend on the class to which the individual belongs, as do the usual analysis of variance models. They are sometimes called analysis of co-variance models. The regression model enables us to assess the effects of quantitative factors, the analysis of variance model those of qualitative factors; the analysis of covariance model covers both quantitative and qualitative factors.

The general techniques developed in the early part of this chapter obviously apply to such models. So here we shall merely give some brief remarks concerning the following simple model:

$$x_t = a_\alpha z_t + b_\alpha + \varepsilon_t, \tag{29}$$

in which x_t and z_t denote observable quantities for the individual $t = 1, 2, \ldots, T$, a_α and b_α are real parameters depending on the class α to which the tth individual belongs $(\alpha = 1, 2, \ldots, p)$ and ε_t is an unobservable error satisfying assumptions 1 and 3 of ch. 6 (independence, homoscedasticity and normality). We can regard (29) as a simple regression model in which the coefficients a and b vary from one class to the next, or alternatively as a model of classified observations in which the average value of the observed quantity depends not only on the class considered but also on the effect of an exogenous variable z_t.

To fix ideas we can suppose that x_t is the annual expenditure on footwear per consumption unit in household t, and z_t the total annual expenditure, while α denotes the socio-professional class of household t.

The coefficients a_α and b_α in this model are easily estimated by simple regression within each class or socio-professional category. However, we usually wish to test various hypotheses about the a_α and b_α, for instance the following two†:

(i) all the coefficients a_α are equal to the same unknown number a, irrespective of the class α.

(ii) all the parameters b_α are equal to the same unknown number b, irrespective of the class α.

Let us now see how the general principles of analysis of variance apply to provide a test of the first hypothesis.

Let $u_{\alpha t}$ be the dummy variable defined in the preceding section and $z_{\alpha t}$ a new variable equal to z_t if the tth individual belongs to the class α and zero otherwise. With these conventions the model may be written

$$x_t = \sum_{\alpha=1}^{p} a_\alpha z_{\alpha t} + \sum_{\alpha=1}^{p} b_\alpha u_{\alpha t} + \varepsilon_t. \tag{30}$$

In T-dimensional space the expected value y of the vector x necessarily belongs to the subspace L spanned by the $2p$ vectors z_α and u_α ($\alpha = 1, 2, \ldots, p$). These vectors are linearly independent if there exist in each class α at least two individuals t for which the values of z_t are different, and this we shall assume to be the case. The subspace L then has dimension $2p$. Under the hypothesis of equality of all the a_α, y belongs also to the subspace M of dimension $p+1$ spanned by the u_α and the vector z with components z_t. So the problem is that stated in the first section. In this case table 1 becomes:

TABLE 7

Source of variation	Degrees of freedom	Quadratic form
Within classes with unequal effects	$T - 2p$	$\xi = \sum_{\alpha=1}^{p} \sum_t^\alpha (x_t - \bar{x}_\alpha)^2$
		$- \sum_{\alpha=1}^{p} a_\alpha^* \sum_t^\alpha (x_t - \bar{x}_\alpha)(z_t - \bar{z}_\alpha)$
Differences among the a_α	$p - 1$	$\eta = \sum_{\alpha=1}^{p} (a_\alpha^* - \tilde{a}) \sum_t^\alpha (x_t - \bar{x}_\alpha)(z_t - \bar{z}_\alpha)$
Within classes with equal effects	$T - p - 1$	$\zeta = \sum_{\alpha=1}^{p} \sum_t^\alpha (x_t - \bar{x}_\alpha)^2$
		$- \tilde{a} \sum_{\alpha=1}^{p} \sum_t^\alpha (x_t - \bar{x}_\alpha)(z_t - \bar{z}_\alpha)$

† The econometric literature speaks of the Chow test to designate a test of the type considered here. It concerns the hypothesis that both coefficients a_α and b_α do not depend on α. It is applied to multiple regressions as well, but often concerns the particular case when there are only two classes ($p=2$), i.e. two regressions; see in particular CHOW [1968].

In the expressions for the quadratic forms, $\sum_t^\alpha$ denotes summation over t for all individuals in the class α, $\bar{x}_\alpha$ and $\bar{z}_\alpha$ the means of x_t and z_t in the class α, a_α^* and $\tilde{a}$ the coefficients estimated by least squares regression, namely:

$$a_\alpha^* = \frac{\sum_t^\alpha (x_t - \bar{x}_\alpha)(z_t - \bar{z}_\alpha)}{\sum_t^\alpha (z_t - \bar{z}_\alpha)^2}, \qquad \tilde{a} = \frac{\sum_{\alpha=1}^p \sum_t^\alpha (x_t - \bar{x}_\alpha)(z_t - \bar{z}_\alpha)}{\sum_{\alpha=1}^p \sum_t^\alpha (z_t - \bar{z}_\alpha)^2}.$$

The hypothesis is rejected if:

$$\frac{T - 2p}{p - 1} \frac{\eta}{\xi} > F_{p-1, T-2p}(\omega).$$

Note that, in the expressions for the quadratic forms, the sample 'within classes' covariances of x_t and z_t occur; hence the term analysis of covariance employed for tests of this kind.

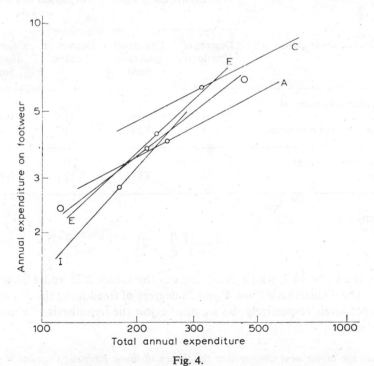

Fig. 4.

Fig. 4. Regressions between expenditure on footwear and total expenditure in households belonging to five socio-professional categories (in thousands of francs per consumption unit). C – Managerial and professional; A – Self-employed handicraft; E – Clerical; O – Manual; I – Unemployed.

As an example, fig. 4 shows certain of the results of a study by VORANGER [1957] carried out on the data of a survey of French family budgets in 1951. Each straight line represents the average relation between expenditure on footwear per consumption unit and the total expenditure per consumption unit, for households in a given socio-professional category. The small circle on each line marks the mean point for households in the corresponding category. Since logarithmic scales are used on each axis, the slope of each line corresponds to the elasticity with respect to total expenditure[†].

The figure suggests that the elasticities are not the same for the different categories. Analysis of covariance may be applied to test the hypothesis of equality of the elasticities. The five lines were fitted to an over-all number of 38 points[††]: the first three columns of the following table correspond, with these data, to the columns of table 7.

TABLE 8

Source of variation	For the five categories		For clerical and manual workers	
	Degrees of freedom	Calculated quadratic form	Degrees of freedom	Calculated quadratic form
Within classes with unequal elasticities	28	1.264	11	0.606
Differences between elasticities	4	2.548	1	0.047
Within classes with equal elasticities	32	3.812	12	0.653

The ratio

$$\frac{T-2p}{p-1}\frac{\eta}{\xi}$$

here has the value 14.7, which easily exceeds the values 2.71 and 4.07 given in tables of the F-distribution for 4 and 28 degrees of freedom at the 5% and 1% significance levels respectively. So we must reject the hypothesis of equality of the elasticities.

† We shall see in the next chapter that the theory of linear estimation applies in certain conditions to regressions between the logarithms of economic quantities.
†† In fact each point represents a mean for a set of households in the same category whose total expenditures are close to one another. We shall see in the next chapter that the techniques of regression analysis and analysis of variance still apply to grouped data of this kind, provided that the groups do not differ too much in size.

The conclusion would have been different if we had tested the equality of only two elasticities referring to the categories 'clerical staff' and 'manual workers'. The last two columns of table 8 give the necessary ingredients for the application of this test. The appropriate ratio has the value 0.85 and is much smaller than the critical value which would result in rejection of the hypothesis at any reasonable significance level.

9 Multivariate analysis

The model studied in the early part of the chapter justifies the usual procedures of analysis of variance and covariance. But it is apparently of more general import. Indeed, all the situations envisaged in the preceding sections involve only one endogenous variable. They all depend on the linear model (12) containing a single equation with a random term satisfying the assumptions of independence, homoscedasticity and normality. Thus, the covariance matrix Q of the observed random vector has the simple form $\sigma^2 I$ and depends on only one unknown parameter (σ).

Now hypotheses completely analogous to those previously examined can arise in the context of models with several endogenous variables, and they result in statistical tests analogous to analysis of variance tests. As we shall see, however, the situation is not nearly so simple.

Let us return to the general model of ch. 6:

$$x_t = Az_t + \varepsilon_t, \tag{31}$$

in which x_t denotes the vector of n endogenous variables, z_t the vector of m exogenous variables, A an $n \times m$ matrix and ε_t an unobservable random vector satisfying assumptions 1 and 3 (independence, homoscedasticity, normality). If a_j ($j=1,2,\ldots,m$) are m vectors with n components, the model may be written:

$$x_t = \sum_{j=1}^{m} a_j z_{jt} + \varepsilon_t. \tag{32}$$

Consider the hypothesis which states that the $m-q$ exogenous variables $z_{q+1}, z_{q+2}, \ldots, z_m$ play no part in the determination of the n endogenous variables; the $m-q$ vectors $a_{q+1}, a_{q+2}, \ldots, a_m$ would then be zero. This is a linear hypothesis which may be interpreted geometrically as in section 2. The vector x has now nT components, and the model implies that its expected value y belongs to the nm-dimensional linear subspace L defined by

$$y_t = \sum_{j=1}^{m} a_j z_{jt},$$

with the m vectors a_j varying. The hypothesis to be tested implies that y belongs to the nq-dimensional subspace M defined by

$$y_t = \sum_{j=1}^{q} a_j z_{jt},$$

with the q vectors a_j varying.

If u and v again denote the projections of x on L and M respectively, expression (1) becomes:

$$\gamma = \sum_{t=1}^{T} (u_t - v_t)' \Omega^{-1} (u_t - v_t), \tag{33}$$

Ω denoting the covariance matrix of the vector ε_t.

When the hypothesis to be tested is true, γ is distributed as χ^2 with $n(m-q)$ degrees of freedom. The hypothesis would then be rejected when γ exceeds $\chi^2_{n(m-q)}(\alpha)$. But to apply this test we would need to know Ω, and this is not usually the case.

The remarks made in chapter 6, § 9 (iv) apply when Ω is not known. If the number T of observations is large, we can replace Ω by the covariance matrix $M^*_{\varepsilon\varepsilon}$ of the residuals ε_t^* obtained by least squares estimation of the model (32). The quantity

$$\phi = \sum_{t=1}^{T} (u_t - v_t)' (M^*_{\varepsilon\varepsilon})^{-1} (u_t - v_t) \tag{34}$$

is distributed asymptotically as χ^2 with $n(m-q)$ degrees of freedom when y does in fact belong to M. We would then reject the hypothesis whenever ϕ exceeds $\chi^2_{n(m-q)}(\alpha)$. This and other similar tests are difficult to apply in small samples, since the exact distributions involved have been determined only in very particular cases. Nevertheless various asymptotic approximations are known which are better than the χ^2-distribution with $n(m-q)$ degrees of freedom.

In applications it is still possible to calculate ϕ according to procedures similar to those given above in connection with the analysis of variance. To demonstrate this it is sufficient to examine the simplest case of *multivariate analysis of variance*.

Suppose that n quantities $x_1, x_2, \ldots, x_n$ have been measured on each of T individuals $(t = 1, 2, \ldots, T)$, belonging to p classes $(\alpha = 1, 2, \ldots, p)$. We assume that the value taken by each quantity x_i on individual t is a random variable whose expected value $a_{i\alpha}$ depends only on the class α to which t belongs and the remaining characteristics of whose distribution do not depend at all on t. More precisely, let us set up the model:

$$x_t = a_\alpha + \varepsilon_t, \tag{35}$$

where x_t and a_α denote the vectors with components x_{it} and $a_{i\alpha}$, and ε_t the unobservable error supposed to satisfy assumptions 1 and 3 of ch. 6. Consider the hypothesis that all the $a_{i\alpha}$ are equal to the same number a_i, this being so for

$i = 1, 2, \ldots, n$. According to this hypothesis, the vector a_α of expected values has the same value a for every class.

Introducing auxiliary variables $u_{\alpha t}$ equal to 1 when t belongs to α and zero otherwise, we obtain the form (32) from the model (35), namely:

$$x_t = \sum_{\alpha=1}^{p} a_\alpha u_{\alpha t} + \varepsilon_t.$$

The least squares estimates of the a_α are then $a_\alpha^* = \bar{x}_\alpha$, $\bar{x}_\alpha$ being the vector of means $\bar{x}_{i\alpha}$ of the values of the quantities x_i for the individuals in the class α. Similarly, if the hypothesis under test is true, then a is estimated by the vector $\bar{x}$ of means taken over the entire set of the T individuals.

The matrix $M_{\varepsilon\varepsilon}^*$ is here:

$$M_{\varepsilon\varepsilon}^* = \frac{1}{T} \sum_{\alpha=1}^{p} \Sigma_i^\alpha (x_t - \bar{x}_\alpha)(x_t - \bar{x}_\alpha)'. \tag{36}$$

The vectors u_t and v_t of ϕ are:

$$u_t = \sum_{\alpha=1}^{p} a_\alpha^* u_{\alpha t} = \sum_{\alpha=1}^{p} \bar{x}_\alpha u_{\alpha t}, \qquad v_t = \sum_{\alpha=1}^{p} \bar{x} u_{\alpha t}.$$

It can easily be verified that ϕ may be written:

$$\phi = \sum_{\alpha=1}^{p} T_\alpha (\bar{x}_\alpha - \bar{x})'(M_{\varepsilon\varepsilon}^*)^{-1}(\bar{x}_\alpha - \bar{x}), \tag{37}$$

where T_α in the number of individuals in the class α. In large samples, the hypothesis of equality of the a_α is rejected if ϕ is greater than $\chi^2_{n(p-1)}(\omega)$, where ω denotes the chosen significance level.

To calculate ϕ, we can consider the two matrices:

$$U = \sum_{\alpha=1}^{p} \Sigma_i^\alpha (x_t - \bar{x}_\alpha)(x_t - \bar{x}_\alpha)', \tag{38}$$

which regroups sums of squares and cross products of deviations *within classes* and:

$$V = \sum_{\alpha=1}^{p} T_\alpha (\bar{x}_\alpha - \bar{x})(\bar{x}_\alpha - \bar{x})' \tag{39}$$

which regroups sums of squares and cross products of deviations *between classes*. Indeed, ϕ is equal to[†]:

---

† We recall that the trace of a matrix is the sum of elements of its main diagonal. In this connection, see ch. 6, section 4, in particular the transformation of (18) into (18″) and footnote †† p. 203.

$$\phi = T \operatorname{tr}[U^{-1}V]. \tag{40}$$

There is a strong analogy here with ordinary analysis of variance. Indeed the matrices U and V generalize the expressions ξ and η of table 6. Their sum is a matrix W regrouping sums of squares and cross-products of deviations relative to the over-all mean $\bar{x}$. The calculation of U and V may be shown in a table like table 6, but with as many columns for quadratic forms as there are distinct elements in U, say $n(n+1)/2$. We note also that the definition of ϕ involves the product of V and the inverse of U (just as previously we had the product of η and the inverse of ξ).

CHAPTER 8

Regressions in various contexts

The two previous chapters were devoted to the theory of regressions and corresponding tests. This theory applies and extends the theory of linear estimation discussed in ch. 5 in the context of a very general model. For practical econometric studies, it is also desirable to have some idea of the validity of inferences from regression models in situations where the assumptions of the theory are not satisfied exactly. So we should describe and discuss alternative methods which may possibly be better suited to the diverse situations encountered in applied research. This is the aim of the present chapter.

Nor shall we exhaust the subject, since many difficulties will be better understood after further progress in the theoretical study. Thus we shall not at present examine the bias in regressions when there are errors of measurement in the variables or when the estimated relations are part of a wider model. We have made an initial attack on such questions in ch. 4, and shall return to them later in chs. 10 and 15. Similarly we shall reserve for later discussion the problems arising from serial correlation of errors through time (ch. 12).

The complications to be discussed are mostly concerned with the distribution of errors in the regressions. Heteroscedasticity and correlation of the errors affecting different observations are often due to the structure of the observed sample or to particular features of the most appropriate model; so they are important in many practical situations; we shall discuss them in the first five sections. We shall go on to examine departures from normality and the robustness of different estimation methods. We shall conclude by considering some features that arise in the application of regression models.

Before embarking on our main topic, we should note that the model $x_t = Az_t + \varepsilon_t$ which was studied in the two previous chapters has greater generality than might appear at first sight. It covers very many linear models which seem a priori to be more complex. To revert to the general form we often must only choose an appropriate definition of the exogenous variables z_{jt} and introduce certain *dummy variables* as well as the variables already selected by economic analysis. This course of action raises no difficulty, since the assumptions relating to the z_{jt} are only slightly restrictive.

Thus we saw in ch. 6 § 5, that the existence of constant terms in the equations is easily taken into account by the introduction of a dummy variable equal to 1 in all observations. Similarly, when discussing the analysis of variance on grouped data, and the analysis of covariance, we defined dummy variables of the type of $u_{\alpha t}$ which equals 1 when the tth observation belongs to the class α, and zero otherwise.

By using the same procedure we can take direct account in the model of the effect of seasonal factors. Suppose, for example, that we are using monthly data in order to estimate a relation affected by seasonal variation. We often write:

$$x_t = a'z_t + b_h + \varepsilon_t,$$

where the constant b_h depends on the month h (with $h=1,2,\ldots,12$) during which the tth observation was made. Such models, which have been studied particularly by FOURGEAUD [1955], depend on the general theory given above, since they may be written:

$$x_t = a'z_t + \sum_{h=1}^{12} b_h u_{ht} + \varepsilon_t,$$

u_{ht} being a dummy variable equal to 1 if the tth observation was made in the month h, and zero otherwise.

It may also happen that the relation studied is affected by an event occurring with some but not all observations. Thus monthly data may be used in the study of a phenomenon for which the number of Saturdays in the month is of relevant importance (reduced industrial activity, increased commercial activity). To take account of this circumstance, we can again introduce a dummy variable equal to 1 in months with five Saturdays, and zero othcrwise.

1   The linear model and estimation of the covariance matrix

The general linear hypothesis on which ch. 5 is based assumes that the covariance matrix Q of the vector x of the observations is known, or at least that it is known apart from a multiplicative constant. Heteroscedasticity or correlations of the errors affecting different observations would cause no major difficulty if they were known precisely. Of course, the multiple regression model would no longer apply directly; but the general linear hypothesis, of which it is a particular case, would still hold. By applying the principles of ch. 5, we could obtain methods paralleling those of chs. 6 and 7 and enjoying similar properties.

The major difficulty stems from the fact that, in most of the cases with which we shall have to deal, only the existence of heteroscedasticity or correlations is known. A priori, the matrix Q is partly unknown and is partly to be estimated; it depends on q parameters $\omega_1, \omega_2, \ldots, \omega_q$.

Restricting ourselves, for simplicity, to the regular case, we can write

$$x = Za + \varepsilon \tag{1}$$

$$E(\varepsilon\varepsilon') = Q(\omega) \qquad E(\varepsilon) = 0 \tag{2}$$

Estimation starts from observation of the vector x and the matrix Z; it is directed towards the p-vector a and the q-vector ω. The $(n \times p)$ matrix Z will have rank p and $Q(\omega)$ will be considered as a non-singular matrix for all the values of ω which we shall have to consider.

It will be useful to bear in mind two simple examples of this general formulation; equation (1) applies unchanged in both cases.

First example (heteroscedasticity). The n observations belong to two samples containing T_1 and T_2 observations respectively; the vectors x, ε and the matrix Z can be partitioned vertically into two blocks of T_1 and T_2 rows.

$$x = \begin{bmatrix} x_1 \\ x_2 \end{bmatrix} \qquad Z = \begin{bmatrix} Z_1 \\ Z_2 \end{bmatrix} \qquad \varepsilon = \begin{bmatrix} \varepsilon_1 \\ \varepsilon_2 \end{bmatrix} \tag{3}$$

The vector x_i, for example, has components x_{it} where $t = 1, 2, \ldots, T_i$ ($i = 1$ or 2). For some reason or another we may assume that

$$E(\varepsilon_i \varepsilon_i') = \sigma_i^2 I \qquad E(\varepsilon_1 \varepsilon_2') = 0. \tag{4}$$

The vector ω then has two components σ_1^2 and σ_2^2, the respective variances of the ε_{1t} and ε_{2t}. The model may be said to separate into two sub-models $x_i = Z_i a + \varepsilon_i$ ($i = 1, 2$) involving the same vector a of coefficients.

Second example (autoregressive errors). The errors ε_t of the $T = n$ observations obey the following equality:

$$E(\varepsilon_t \varepsilon_\theta) = \sigma^2 \varrho^{t-\theta} \tag{5}$$

where σ is a positive number and $|\varrho| < 1$. In this case the two components of the vector ω are σ^2 and ϱ. The matrix Q is the same as for the last example in ch. 5, § 6; but the difference now is that ϱ is assumed to be unknown. As we saw in the previous case, it is more convenient to use the inverse of Q instead of Q:

$$Q^{-1} = \tau^{-2} \begin{bmatrix} 1 & -\varrho & 0 & \ldots 0 \\ -\varrho & 1+\varrho^2 & -\varrho & \ldots 0 \\ 0 & -\varrho & 1+\varrho^2 & \ldots 0 \\ \cdot & \cdots & \cdots & \cdots \\ 0 & 0 & 0 & \ldots 1 \end{bmatrix} \tag{6}$$

$$\tau^2 = \sigma^2(1 - \varrho^2).$$

We now go on to a general study of the problems of inference where the specification (1)–(2) holds.

(i) Ordinary least squares

It often happens that the only direct interest lies in estimating a and we are satisfied with ordinary regression methods as if the matrix Q had the form $\sigma^2 I$. In particular, the vector a is estimated by

$$a^* = (Z'Z)^{-1}Z'x. \tag{7}$$

Such an approach raises two main questions which we shall deal with in succession.

In the first place, what is the efficiency of a^* relative to

$$\hat{a} = (Z'Q^{-1}Z)^{-1}Z'Q^{-1}x \tag{8}$$

which, from formula (18) in ch. 5, is the generalised least squares (Gauss-Markov) estimator when Q is known?

(a) First, it is conceivable that ordinary least squares may lead to the Gauss-Markov estimator $(\hat{a} = a^*)$ even when Q does not have the form $\sigma^2 I$. For, we can establish

Proposition 1. For ordinary least squares to lead to the generalized least squares estimator for any vector ε of the errors, it is necessary and sufficient that the columns of QZ are linear combinations of the columns of Z.

For[†] it is obviously necessary that

$$(Z'Z)^{-1}Z' = (Z'Q^{-1}Z)^{-1}Z'Q^{-1} \tag{9}$$

and so

$$QZ = ZR \tag{10}$$

where $R = (Z'Q^{-1})^{-1}Z'Z$. Conversely, if there exists a matrix R such that (10) holds, we see immediately that (9) follows (since QZ has rank p, then R must be a non-singular matrix).

For a clear understanding of the condition in proposition 1, we need only look first at the case where $p = 1$. The matrix Z is then a column vector while R is a number. Equation (10) then implies that Z is a characteristic vector of Q. More generally, the condition signifies that *the p columns of Z are linear combinations* (different and also independent in the regular case) *of the same p characteristic vectors of Q*.

In the first example, Q has two distinct characteristic roots σ_1^2 and σ_2^2. When $\sigma_1^2 \neq \sigma_2^2$ a vector u is characteristic for Q if and only if either its first T_1

[†] The proof is given here for the regular case; but it applies with complete generality. See, for example, WATSON [1972].

components or its last T_2 components are zero. For example, when $p=2$, we can write $Z_i = [z_{i1}, z_{i2}]$ for $i = 1$, 2, where the column vectors z_{i1} and z_{i2} have T_i components; if neither Z_1 nor Z_2 is zero, then the generalised least squares estimator will lead exactly to the least squares estimator when z_{11} is proportional to z_{12} and z_{21} is proportional to z_{22}.

In the second example, it is more difficult to specify the characteristic vectors of Q; this is usually discussed in the study of time series. However, it is easy to obtain an approximation to the vectors in question. We need only consider a matrix differing from $\tau^2 Q^{-1}$ only in the two extreme terms of the principal diagonal, which are replaced by $1 + \varrho^2$, the value of the other diagonal terms in (6). The characteristic roots are then $1 - 2\varrho \cos j\pi/(n+1) + \varrho^2$ where $j = 1, 2, \ldots, n$ and the corresponding characteristic vectors are $z_t = \sin j\pi t/(n+1)$. So the components of each characteristic vector of Q constitute an approximately sinusoidal series.

(b) Considering still the efficiency of a^* relative to $\hat{a}$, but in the case where these two estimators are different, it is conceivable that its efficiency remains high if the form of Q is fairly near $\sigma^2 I$. In fact, we can see that *the loss in efficiency is of second order relative to the difference between Q and matrices of the form $\sigma^2 I$.* This results from the following more general proposition. (A small error in Q has only second order effect on the efficiency of estimation when the generalised least squares principle is applied.)

Proposition 2. The covariance matrix of the vector $a(S)$ which minimises

$$(x - Za)'S^{-1}(x - Za)$$

is a continuous differentiable function of the positive definite matrix S; the first derivatives of this function are zero for $S = Q$ when Q is non-singular.

The vector $a(S)$ can be written

$$a(S) = (Z'S^{-1}Z)^{-1}Z'S^{-1}x.$$

Its covariance matrix is

$$(Z'S^{-1}Z)^{-1}(Z'S^{-1}QS^{-1}Z)(Z'S^{-1}Z)^{-1}.$$

This expression contains some products and inverses, and these operations maintain continuity when, as in this case, the matrices to be inverted are non-singular.

To differentiate this expression, we need only apply two simple rules of matrix calculus:

$$d(XY) = dX \cdot Y + X \cdot dY \quad \text{and} \quad d(X^{-1}) = -X^{-1} \cdot dX \cdot X^{-1}$$

for any matrices X and Y. Clearly, the differential is zero when $S^{-1} = Q^{-1}$ and for any dS. The corresponding derivatives are therefore zero.

However, we must not be misled by proposition 2. When Q differs perceptibly from $\sigma^2 I$, *the efficiency of a^* may not be high.* For, its covariance matrix is

$$(Z'Z)^{-1}(Z'QZ)(Z'Z)^{-1} \tag{11}$$

while that of $\hat{a}$ is $(Z'Q^{-1}Z)^{-1}$.

In this context we can consider the particular case[†] where there is a single endogenous variable ($p=1$) and so Z is a column vector, which we can denote by z. To find the efficiency of a^* relative to $\hat{a}$, we can obviously replace z by a proportional vector normalized by the condition

$$z'z = 1 \tag{12}$$

Then the efficiency in question is the number e defined by

$$\frac{1}{e} = z'Qz \cdot z'Q^{-1}z. \tag{13}$$

We see immediately that $e=1$ if z is a characteristic vector of Q, a result known to us already following proposition 1.

When Q is diagonalised it can be written $H' \wedge H$ where $\wedge$ is a diagonal matrix whose non-zero elements are the characteristic roots of Q and H is an orthogonal matrix (hence $H' = H^{-1}$). If we set $w = Hz$, it follows from (12) and (13) that

$$\sum_i w_i^2 = 1 \tag{14}$$

and

$$\frac{1}{e} = \sum_i w_i^2 \lambda_i \cdot \sum_i \frac{w_i^2}{\lambda_i} \tag{15}$$

So the efficiency e is the ratio between a weighted harmonic mean of the characteristic roots and the corresponding weighted arithmetic mean. For a given matrix Q, this ratio is minimized when only the two extreme roots are weighted, and are weighted equally:

$$w_1^2 = w_n^2 = \tfrac{1}{2} \quad w_i = 0 \quad \text{for} \quad i = 2, 3, \ldots, n-2 \tag{16}$$

given that the roots λ_i are ranked in increasing order of magnitude. The minimum efficiency is then

$$e_m = \frac{4\lambda_1 \lambda_n}{(\lambda_1 + \lambda_n)^2} \tag{17}$$

---

† The general case is discussed by BLOOMFIELD and WATSON [1975] and by KNOTT [1975].

In the first example, $\lambda_1 = \sigma_1^2$ and $\lambda_n = \sigma_2^2$. If, for example, $\sigma_2^2 = 4\sigma_1^2$, we immediately find $e_m = 0.64$; but if $\sigma_2^2 = 9\sigma_1^2$ then $e_m = 0.36$. In the second example, given positive ϱ and large n, the two extreme roots are approximately $(1 - \varrho)^2$ and $(1 + \varrho)^2$. For example, when $\varrho = 0.5$, then e_m is about 0.36 but when $\varrho = 0.8$ then e_m is about 0.05. So the efficiency of a^* relative to $\hat{a}$ may be much less than 1.

(c) The ordinary least squares estimator is unbiased: $E(a^*) = a$, as is $\hat{a}$. We have just compared its covariance matrix with that of $\hat{a}$. We should not stop there since, in practice, *we usually associate with a* an estimate of its covariance matrix* together with certain tests; now, estimation is based on a theory which applies only when Q has the form $\sigma^2 I$. *How valid is such an estimate* when this is not so?

The usual estimate is

$$\sigma^{*2}(Z'Z)^{-1} \tag{18}$$

where σ^{*2} is the sum of squares of the residuals multiplied by $1/(n-p)$. The vector ε^* of residuals is

$$\varepsilon^* = [I - Z(Z'Z)^{-1}Z']\varepsilon; \tag{19}$$

it follows that the expected value of σ^{*2} is

$$\frac{1}{n-p}\{\operatorname{tr} Q - \operatorname{tr}[(Z'Z)^{-1}(Z'QZ)]\} \tag{20}$$

The expected value of (18), which is (20) multiplied by $(Z'Z)^{-1}$ *is generally different from the true covariance matrix* (11).

We note first that *the difference exists even when $a^* = \hat{a}$* if Q does not have the form $\sigma^2 I$. For, (10) implies that the true covariance matrix of a^* is $R(Z'Z)^{-1}$, while the expectation of the usual estimate is $(n-p)^{-1}(\operatorname{tr} Q - \operatorname{tr} R) \times (Z'Z)^{-1}$.

The bias in estimation of the variances and covariances of the regression coefficients is in fact a cause of serious potential error in the direct application of the usual techniques to the situations presently under discussion. For this reason, it is of great practical importance that this bias should always be thoroughly investigated.

SATHE and VINOD [1974] establish general formulae for finding the limits of this bias, on the basis only of knowledge of Q. Let P_j denote the ratio between the true variance of a_j^* and the expected value of the usual formula (that is, (20) multiplied by the jth diagonal term of $(Z'Z)^{-1}$). Let us assume that the n characteristic roots, distinct or otherwise, of Q are ranged in increasing order of magnitude from λ_1 to λ_n.

We write

$$\delta_1 = \frac{1}{n-p} \sum_{i=1}^{n-p} \lambda_i \qquad \delta_n = \frac{1}{n-p} \sum_{i=p+1}^{n} \lambda_i.$$

Very simple bounds obtain:

$$\frac{\lambda_1}{\delta_n} \le P_j \le \frac{\lambda_n}{\delta_1}. \tag{21}$$

Thus, in the first example, as long as $p < T_1$ and $p < T_2$, then $\delta_1 = T_1\sigma_1^2 + (T_2 - p)\sigma_2^2$ and $\delta_n = (T_1 - p)\sigma_1^2 + T_2\sigma_2^2$ if $\sigma_1^2 < \sigma_2^2$. The ratio $1/P_j$ lies between two weighted means of 1 with σ_1^2/σ_2^2 and σ_2^2/σ_1^2 respectively. Unfortunately this interval may still be very wide.

For the second example we can also show that, for large n and positive ϱ, the interval (21) is approximately

$$\frac{1-\varrho}{1+\varrho} \le P_j \le \frac{1+\varrho}{1-\varrho} \tag{22}$$

We shall return to these formulae later.

The role of the matrix Z in determining the bias may be clearly understood if we consider the case where $p = 1$ and Z reduces to a characteristic vector z of Q. We can then write $Qz = \lambda_h z$ where λ_h, the hth characteristic root of Q, replaces the matrix R of equation (10). The ratio P can then be deduced directly from (20) and (11):

$$P = \frac{(n-1)\lambda_h}{\sum_i \lambda_i - \lambda_h}.$$

The usual formula particularly underestimates the true variance of a^* if z is associated with the largest characteristic root of Q. We note also that in this case the upper bound of (21) is reached even though the least squares estimate is efficient.

In the first example, such a situation arises if the non-zero components of z relate only to the sub-sample with greater variance. To find the true variance it is then necessary to divide the expected value of the usual formula by a number less than 1, which is a weighted mean of 1 and the ratio σ_1^2/σ_2^2 (if $\sigma_1^2 < \sigma_2^2$), the weights being proportional to T_1 and $T_2 - 1$. This correction itself can obviously be estimated from the residuals ε_i^*.

(ii)   Two-stage estimation

We now leave the usual least squares estimate and go on to consider other estimators which may have greater efficiency. Such estimators explicitly involve not only a, but also Q or the vector ω of the parameters involved in this matrix.

In many particular cases we may think of estimating Q from the residuals ε_t^* of an initial usual least squares regression. The vector ε^* of these residuals can be written $x - Za^*$ and so also

$$\varepsilon^* = [I - Z(Z'Z)^{-1}Z']\varepsilon \tag{23}$$

Let Q^* be the resulting estimate of Q (deduced by a formula to be defined in each case). It then becomes natural to calculate the estimator

$$\hat{\hat{a}} = (Z'Q^{*-1}Z)^{-1}Z'Q^{*-1}x \tag{24}$$

by analogy with equation (8) defining $\hat{a}$, the generalised least squares estimator if Q is known.

So this can be described as two-stage estimation since an ordinary regression first gives a^* and then $\hat{\hat{a}}$ is calculated.

It is clear from (23) and (24) that $\hat{\hat{a}}$ is not a linear estimator of x, that is, of ε. So in most cases it will be difficult to study completely. Since Q^* differs from Q, except by extraordinary coincidence, and since $\hat{a}$ has minimum covariance matrix if ε is normal, then $\hat{\hat{a}}$ certainly has a lower efficiency. So a priori, there is no absolutely straightforward choice between a^* and $\hat{\hat{a}}$. A priori, there will be an intuitive preference for $\hat{\hat{a}}$ if it is likely that Q is very different from I and (10) does not hold, even approximately.

The distribution of $\hat{\hat{a}}$ must be determined in each particular case, given the definition of the formula for finding Q^*. However, the following principle will often be adopted.

The sample will be considered formally as belonging to a sequence of samples indexed by a 'number of observations' T, which tends to infinity. Each sample conforms to a model similar to (1)–(2) with $x_T = Z_T a$ and covariance matrix $Q_T(\omega)$; by hypothesis, the vectors a and ω to be estimated are the same for all samples. Once it is specified how ε_T and Z_T are related to ε_{T-1} and Z_{T-1}, and an assumption has been made about the limiting behavior of Z_T, it can often be shown that the estimator ω^* corresponding to Q^* tends to the true value of ω as T tends to infinity. It follows that $\hat{\hat{a}}$ is asymptotically equivalent to $\hat{a}$, which proves that it is asymptotically efficient and allows its limiting distribution to be specified completely.

However interesting, such asymptotic properties give no precise indication of the situation for the finite samples analyzed in practice. For want of a complete theory applying to small samples, the so-called Monte Carlo method[†] is often used for empirical determination of the distribution for some particular cases. This gives information about the degree of approximation with wh ·he asymptotic theory applies.

---

† A complete description of this method, applied in a different context, is given in ch. 13, § 3.

In the first example it is natural to define Q^* by estimating σ_1^{*2} and σ_2^{*2} by

$$\sigma_i^{*2} = \frac{1}{T_i - p} \varepsilon_i^{*'} \varepsilon_i^* \qquad i = 1, 2. \tag{25}$$

Applying (24), the corresponding estimator $\hat{\hat{a}}$ is

$$\hat{\hat{a}} = [\sigma_2^{*2} Z_1' Z_1 + \sigma_1^{*2} Z_2' Z_2]^{-1} \cdot [\sigma_2^{*2} Z_1' x_1 + \sigma_1^{*2} Z_2' x_2] \tag{26}$$

Similarly, in the second example we may define Q^* using estimators σ^{*2} and ϱ^* based on (5), for example:

$$\sigma^{*2} = \frac{1}{T} \sum_{t=1}^{T} \varepsilon_t^{*2} \qquad \sigma^{*2} \varrho^* = \frac{1}{T-1} \sum_{t=1}^{T-1} \varepsilon_t^* \varepsilon_{t+1}^* \tag{27}$$

The statistical theory behind such estimators $\hat{\hat{a}}$ will be given later; the first example is a particular case[†] of theorem 2 in ch. 9, while the second example is discussed in ch. 12. We shall see that, under natural assumptions about the limiting behavior of Z, $\sqrt{n}(\hat{\hat{a}} - a)$ has a limiting normal distribution and $\hat{\hat{a}}$ is asymptotically efficient.

However, we note that doubts may persist about the definition of σ_i^{*2}, σ^{*2} and ϱ^* in the context of such an approach; why use $T_i - p$ rather than, for example, T_i or $T_i - p/2$ as divisor in the formula for σ_i^{*2}? In the limit, the difference is unimportant since then T_i tends to infinity while p remains fixed; but it may be important in finite samples. To clear such doubts, reference should be made to a clearly stated estimation principle.

RAO [1970] establishes such a principle based on the approach which had proved so fruitful for estimation in the context of the linear model. This leads him to define 'Minimum Norm Quadratic Unbiased Estimators' for the unknown elements of Q (MINQUE). By definition, these are quadratic functions of x, or $x'Ax$, where the matrix A depends on Z; their expected values must be the true values of the elements to which they apply, and this must hold for any a and ω; moreover, they are so defined that the norm of A is minimized, the chosen norm in the circumstances being $\text{tr} A^2$. Rao shows how these estimators can be calculated from the vector ε^* of the residuals of a least squares regression.

We shall not prolong our discussion of these estimators since their definition is fairly complex in practice and experience has failed to show that the resulting $\hat{\hat{a}}$ which they give are more precise than those obtained from simpler formulae.

[†] In the context of our first example, TAYLOR [1977] shows that the expected value of the estimator $\hat{\hat{a}}$ defined by (25) and (26) is the true value a when the different components of ε are independent and symmetrically distributed. He also establishes an approximate formula for the covariance matrix of $\hat{\hat{a}}$ for finite samples.

From the asymptotic point of view, the essential feature is that ω^* converges to the true value ω, which eliminates the need for complex estimation formulae. Nor do applications of the Monte Carlo method for finite samples give any evidence of a clear-cut superiority of $\hat{a}$ estimators deduced from MINQUE over others which are easier to construct and calculate.

However, it is of interest at this point to consider MINQUE formulae for σ_1^{*2} and σ_2^{*2} in the first example. They will be stated for the case where $p = 1$, so that Z_1 and Z_2 become two column-vectors z_1 and z_2; but they are clearly particular cases of formulae which apply for all $p^{\dagger}$. They are the solution of:

$$\left.\begin{array}{c}(T_1 - 1 + \alpha_2^2)\sigma_1^{*2} + \alpha_1\alpha_2\sigma_2^{*2} = \varepsilon_1^{*\prime}\varepsilon_1^* \\ \alpha_1\alpha_2\sigma_1^{*2} + (T_2 - 1 + \alpha_1^2)\sigma_2^{*2} = \varepsilon_2^{*\prime}\varepsilon_2^*\end{array}\right\} \qquad (28)$$

where

$$\alpha_i = \frac{z_i'z_i}{z_1'z_1 + z_2'z_2} \qquad i = 1, 2. \qquad (29)$$

As T_1 and T_2 tend to infinity, the solutions of (28) become equivalent to (25) since $0 < \alpha_1 < 1$ and $0 < \alpha_2 < 1$; but for finite samples, a difference remains. We note that σ_1^{*2} is equal to $\varepsilon_1^{*\prime}\varepsilon_1^*/T_1$ when $\alpha_1 = 0$, and equals $\varepsilon_1^{*\prime}\varepsilon_1^*/(T_1 - 1)$ when $\alpha_1 = 1$, which appears fairly satisfactory intuitively.

Instead of trying to establish a principle for an estimator Q^* of Q, based on ε^*, we might also look for a general principle for simultaneous estimation of a and ω, and so of Q. We shall discuss this in the next section.

(iii)   Simultaneous estimation of Q and a

If the distribution of ε is known exactly, apart from the parameter ω, then there is no great difficulty in defining *the maximum likelihood estimator*.

In particular, it has been suggested that, for estimating a and ω, expressions should be chosen which coincide with this estimator in the case where ε is normally distributed. Since there is generally no guarantee that ε is normal, the estimator resulting from these expressions may be called *the quasi-maximum likelihood estimator*, which we shall now define.

If ε is normal, the logarithm of the likelihood of the sample x is

$$\log \mathfrak{L} = -\tfrac{1}{2}\log|Q| - \tfrac{1}{2}(x - Za)'Q^{-1}(x - Za). \qquad (30)$$

The rules of maximization of quadratic functions allow us to formulate the condition $\delta \log \mathfrak{L}/\delta a = 0$ and so we obtain directly the following relation between the estimators $\tilde{a}$ and $\tilde{Q}$ of a and Q:

$$\tilde{a} = (Z'\tilde{Q}^{-1}Z)^{-1}Z'\tilde{Q}\bar{x}^1 \qquad (31)$$

† See RAO [1970], p. 169.

Moreover, since $\tilde{Q}$ is positive definite, this value of a maximises $\mathfrak{L}$ for given $\tilde{Q}$. If a is replaced by $\tilde{a}$ in (28) and if

$$\tilde{\varepsilon} = x - Z\tilde{a} \tag{32}$$

then the expression to be maximised becomes

$$\log \mathfrak{L}^* = -\tfrac{1}{2}\log|Q| - \tfrac{1}{2}\operatorname{tr}(Q^{-1}\tilde{\varepsilon}\tilde{\varepsilon}'). \tag{33}$$

It is now a function only of Q, and so of ω.

The rules of differentiation imply that

$$d\log \mathfrak{L}^* = -\tfrac{1}{2}\operatorname{tr}(Q - \tilde{\varepsilon}\tilde{\varepsilon}')dQ^{-1}. \tag{34}$$

So, let Q^k be the matrix of the partial derivatives of Q^{-1} with respect to the parameter ω_k.

The required estimator of Q must satisfy

$$\operatorname{tr}[(\tilde{Q} - \tilde{\varepsilon}\tilde{\varepsilon}')\tilde{Q}^k] = 0 \qquad k = 1, 2, \ldots, q. \tag{35}$$

(The case where the maximum of $\mathfrak{L}$ occurs at the boundary of the set of possible Q can be considered as exceptional.)

Equations (31), (32) and (35) define how the estimators $\tilde{a}$ and $\tilde{Q}$ are jointly determined. In general, however, this system may have multiple solutions and that solution should be chosen which gives a global maximum of $\mathfrak{L}$.

Equations (24) and (31), defining the estimators $\hat{a}$ and $\tilde{a}$, are obviously very similar. The maximum likelihood estimator differs from two-stage estimators in two respects. In the first place, in finding $\tilde{a}$ it uses a matrix $\tilde{Q}$ which is no longer estimated from first stage residuals ε_i^* but from precisely those residuals $\tilde{\varepsilon}_i$ of the fit that we are trying to find; in the second place, it provides precise formulae, equations (35), for finding the estimator $\tilde{Q}$ from the $\tilde{\varepsilon}$. So it eliminates the arbitrary element which may persist in two-stage estimation. In the next section we shall consider an iterative method for finding $\tilde{a}$ and $\tilde{Q}$ simultaneously. Let us now look more closely at equations (35).

The matrix $\tilde{\varepsilon}\tilde{\varepsilon}'$ is, as it were, the sample covariance matrix of the residuals; the covariance $E(\varepsilon_i\varepsilon_h)$ is replaced in it by $\tilde{\varepsilon}_i\tilde{\varepsilon}_h$. From (35) we see that the $\tilde{\omega}_k$ are so defined that q linear combinations of the differences between theoretical covariances and corresponding sample covariances are equated to zero. In this sense, equations (35) appear fairly natural. Unfortunately from the computational point of view, the linear coefficients to be equated to zero generally depend on the $\tilde{\omega}_k$, which we are trying to determine.

However, everything is straightforward for our first example, where there is nothing to prevent us from defining $\omega_k = \sigma_k^{-2} (k = 1, 2)$ and where, for example, $\tilde{Q}^1$ is then the following partitioned matrix:

$$\begin{bmatrix} I & O \\ O & O \end{bmatrix}$$

which is independent of $\tilde{\omega}$. Equations (35) then become

$$\tilde{\sigma}_i^2 = \frac{1}{T_i} \sum_{t=1}^{T_i} \tilde{\varepsilon}_{it}^2 \qquad i = 1, 2. \tag{36}$$

This is just the expression to which we were led by intuition when writing (25). Here we find a case where the system (31)–(32)–(35) has a unique solution, which therefore necessarily maximises $\mathcal{L}$.

The situation is more complex in the second example, where it is convenient to set $\omega_1 = \tau^{-2}$, $\omega_2 = \varrho$ and $D = \tilde{Q} - \tilde{\varepsilon}\tilde{\varepsilon}'$. For $k=1$, equation (35) becomes

$$\sum_{t=1}^{T} d_{tt} + \varrho^2 \sum_{t=2}^{T-1} d_{tt} - 2\varrho \sum_{t=1}^{T-1} d_{t,t+1} = 0 \tag{37}$$

(for typographical brevity we omit the superscripts $\sim$). Similarly for $k=2$, (35) becomes

$$\varrho \sum_{t=2}^{T-1} d_{tt} - \sum_{t=1}^{T-1} d_{t,t+1} = 0 \tag{38}$$

Taking account of (38) in (37), we obtain

$$\sum_{t=1}^{T} d_{tt} - \varrho \sum_{t=1}^{T-1} d_{t,t+1} = 0. \tag{39}$$

Let

$$S_1 = \sum_{t=1}^{T} \varepsilon_t^2 \qquad S_2 = \sum_{t=2}^{T-1} \varepsilon_t^2 \qquad R = \sum_{t=1}^{T-1} \varepsilon_t \varepsilon_{t+1}. \tag{40}$$

Equations (5) lead to the following expressions for (38) and (39).

$$R = \varrho S_2 + \varrho \sigma^2 \tag{41}$$

$$S_1 - \varrho R = [T - (T-1)\varrho^2]\sigma^2 \tag{42}$$

and it follows that

$$\tilde{\rho} = \frac{R}{S_2 + \tilde{\sigma}^2}, \qquad \tilde{\sigma}^2 = \frac{S_1 - \tilde{\rho}^2 S_2}{T - (T-2)\tilde{\rho}^2}. \tag{43}$$

Elimination of $\tilde{\varrho}$ gives a third degree equation in $\tilde{\sigma}^2$. But clearly this equation has only one positive root which corresponds to the maximum likelihood.

Formulae (43) remain intuitively meaningful. Yet they are complex since $\tilde{\sigma}^2$ occurs in the first and $\tilde{\rho}^2$ in the second. We note that they differ from (27), to which we were led by intuition, since the latter are now written $\tilde{\rho} = TR/(T-1)$ $\times S_1$ and $\tilde{\sigma}^2 = S_1/T$. But, under weak assumptions, (27) and (43) are asymptotically equivalent since the three quantities S_1/T, $(S_2 + \tilde{\sigma}^2)/(T-1)$ and $S_2/(T-2)$ tend to the same limit σ^2 as T tends to infinity.

The properties of the quasi-maximum likelihood estimator $\tilde{a}$ are of course similar to those of $\hat{\hat{a}}$. In particular, the conditions which ensure the asymptotic equivalence of $\hat{\hat{a}}$ and $\hat{a}$ generally also ensure the asymptotic equivalence of $\tilde{a}$ and $\hat{a}$. When the errors ε are normally distributed, $\tilde{a}$ is a true maximum likelihood estimator; so it may then be considered to have rather stronger properties. In fact, although the classical proofs of the asymptotic efficiency of the maximum likelihood estimator do not apply in the present case, it most frequently happens that this efficiency is maximal not only in the class of estimators defined by a formula similar to (8) with an estimated matrix Q, but also in the class of all consistent regular estimators. But we must repeat that the proof of these properties depends on a more precise specification of the model than our present one.

The comparison of $\hat{\hat{a}}$ and $\tilde{a}$ for finite samples requires Monte Carlo simulations. Such as have been carried out so far reveal no marked superiority of $\tilde{a}$ over $\hat{\hat{a}}$.

Considering finite samples, we may also ask *what is the efficiency of $\tilde{a}$ or $\hat{\hat{a}}$ compared with the ordinary least squares estimator a^*?* They necessarily have greater efficiency for large samples apart from the exceptional case where proposition 1 holds. But investigations so far show that in the simplest situations (where, for example, ω and a each has two components) the vector x must have more than 20 components if the efficiency of $\hat{\hat{a}}$ or $\tilde{a}$ is to be clearly greater than that of a^*. The same conclusion emerges from a theoretical study by BEMENT and WILLIAMS [1969] of an approximate distribution of the estimator $\hat{\hat{a}}$ defined by (25) and (26) for our first example. Recently TAYLOR [1977] and FULLER and RAO [1978] have carried out much fuller studies of the same estimator and show that, even for small samples, a moderate degree of heteroscedasticity is sufficient to justify using $\hat{\hat{a}}$ rather than a^*.

(iv) An iterative computing procedure

The discussion of two-stage estimation gives rise to the notion of a similar procedure comprising a greater number of stages. For, having found $\hat{\hat{a}}$, which we can now call $a^{(2)}$ while a^* is $a^{(1)}$, we can then find a new vector $\varepsilon^{(2)}$ of residuals $x - Za^{(2)}$ just as ε^*, now $\varepsilon^{(1)}$, was $x - Za^{(1)}$; from $\varepsilon^{(2)}$ we can deduce a new estimate $Q^{(2)}$ of Q and use it to find a new estimator $a^{(3)}$; and so on. The successive iterations are based on the equations

$$a^{(s+1)} = (Z'Q^{(s)-1}Z)^{-1}Z'Q^{(s)-1}x \qquad (44)$$

$$\varepsilon^{(s)} = x - Za^{(s)}, \qquad s = 1, 2, \ldots \tag{45}$$

(where $Q^{(0)} = I$); they are completely defined when the formula giving $Q^{(s)}$ from $\varepsilon^{(s)}$ is specified.

The various $a^{(s)}$ (for $s = 1, 2, \ldots$) are so many different estimators of a. Given the usual assumptions under which $\hat{\hat{a}}$ is asymptotically equivalent to $\hat{a}$, we can generally show that so also are all the $a^{(s)}$ (when $s \geqslant 2$). So they all have the same asymptotic efficiency.

The above result gives no grounds for calculating $a^{(3)}$ when $a^{(2)}$ is available. The intuitive notion of a sequence of the $a^{(s)}$ is based on the idea that the convergence of the method gives the final estimator a symmetry which $\hat{\hat{a}}$ lacks.

For, let us assume that $a^{(s)}$ tends to $a^{(\infty)}$ as s increases (this applies to a given sample and has nothing to do with the stochastic convergence considered previously for each estimator $a^{(s)}$ when the size T of the sample to which it is applied tends to infinity). Then $\varepsilon^{(s)}$ also tends to a vector $\varepsilon^{(\infty)}$ and $Q^{(s)}$ to a matrix $Q^{(\infty)}$. So we can say that $a^{(\infty)}$ and $Q^{(\infty)}$ are calculated from each other and that, as a pair, they have an elegant symmetry which $\hat{\hat{a}}$ lacks. In practice, a small number of iterations may be sufficient for satisfactory convergence.

But is $a^{(\infty)}$ preferable to $\hat{\hat{a}}$? This can only rarely be proved. The most favorable situation is certainly that where formulae (35) are applied to find $Q^{(s)}$ from $\varepsilon^{(s)}$, and these then replace $\tilde{Q}$ and $\tilde{\varepsilon}$. The effect of the convergence is then that $a^{(\infty)}$ and $Q^{(\infty)}$ satisfy precisely those equations governing the quasi-maximum likelihood estimator. If these equations have a unique solution, then $a^{(\infty)}$ and $Q^{(\infty)}$ coincide with $\tilde{a}$ and $\tilde{Q}$; it is also possible that this property is more generally valid[†]. Calculation of the $a^{(s)}$ until they converge then becomes equivalent to a particular numerical method for finding $\tilde{a}$. The statistical properties of the result are those discussed earlier and we shall not repeat the discussion.

2   Heteroscedasticity of the errors

In classical multiple regression theory discussed in ch. 6, the errors ε_t relating to different observations are all assumed to have the same variance σ^2, which is what is meant when the errors are said to be 'homoscedastic'.

In practice there is often no difficulty in assuming homoscedasticity of errors in studies of macro time series, since the orders of magnitude of the variables are similar for the different observations, and there is no reason to fear that a particular type of heteroscedasticity exists. In the analysis of microeconomic data on the other hand, we often have to deal with widely varying units: large, medium and small firms, high-income and low-income households, etc. If the errors have the same relative importance for the different units, their ab-

---

[†] OBERHOFER and KMENTA [1974] give a formal study of the convergence properties of iterative methods for maximisation of a likelihood function. They then apply their results to just those estimators which we are discussing.

solute value will be higher for large firms than for small, for rich households than for poor. The results of family budget inquiries show that the variance of the residuals increases with household income (see PRAIS and HOUTHAKKER [1955], p. 55 and subsequently).

We shall now examine cases of heteroscedasticity where the variance σ_t^2 of ε_t is different for different observations, in the context of the specified multiple regression model and retaining the assumption that the errors ε_t and ε_θ relating to two different observations are uncorrelated. This is a particular case of the general model (equations (1) and (2)) where Q is a diagonal matrix (the first of our previous two examples illustrates this).

To avoid irrelevant complications, we shall restrict attention to the simple regression model which we write

$$x_t = a_1 z_t + a_2 + \varepsilon_t \qquad t = 1, 2, \ldots, T \tag{46}$$

So the matrix Z has two columns, the first consisting of the values of the z_t and the second of 1's.

We shall apply the general results of section 1 to this case and expand them in various ways.

(i) Ordinary least squares

It would be a quite exceptional circumstance if the ordinary least squares estimator (a_1^*, a_2^*) coincided with the generalised least squares estimator. When all the σ_t^2 are different, every characteristic vector of Q has $T-1$ zero components; so the second column of Z, all of whose components are 1, cannot be a linear combination of two characteristic vectors of Q (if $T > 2$).

Nevertheless, ordinary least squares and the associated methods are often used. So it is important to look at the sources of error involved in this practice.

The estimator (a_1^*, a_2^*) has no bias; but the usual formulae for estimating the variances of a_1^* and a_2^* do involve bias for whose assessment we need only apply the procedure of section 1(i)–(c). Without repeating it in its entirety, let us consider the formula for P_1, that is, the ratio between the true variance of a_1^* and the expected value of its usual estimator.

For large T, this formula is approximately

$$P_1 = \frac{\bar{z} \sum \sigma_t^2 (z_t - \bar{z}) + \sum \sigma_t^2 (z_t - \bar{z})^2}{\dfrac{1}{T} \sum \sigma_t^2 \sum (z_t - \bar{z})^2} \tag{47}$$

where the summations are over t and $\bar{z}$ is the arithmetic mean of the z_t.

There is no bias, that is, $P_1 = 1$ (and it can be verified that this also holds exactly for small samples) if

$$\sum \sigma_t^2 (z_t - \bar{z}) = 0 \tag{48}$$

$$\sum \sigma_t^2 (z_t - \bar{z})^2 = \frac{1}{T} \sum \sigma_t^2 \sum (z_t - \bar{z})^2. \tag{49}$$

(48) signifies that there is zero correlation between the variances σ_t^2 and the values of the exogenous variable z_t. Also (49) holds at least approximately if the different values of the σ_t^2 are randomly attributed to the different observations independently of the corresponding values of the $(z_t - \bar{z})^2$. We can summarize these two conditions by saying that there is no systematic relationship between the σ_t^2 and the z_t. In each particular case we have to check that such an assumption is tenable.

Generally, the value of P_1 given by (47) may be either less than or greater than 1. However, in most cases σ_t^2 tends to be greater when z_t is large than when it is small; the effect of this is that P_1 is greater than 1, and the usual estimator of the variance of a_1^* is biased downwards.

The following two formulae which obviously assume that all the z_t are positive, are easily deduced from (47):

$$P_1 = 2 + \frac{\sigma_z \beta_{1z}}{\bar{z}} \qquad \text{if} \quad \sigma_t^2 = k z_t \tag{50}$$

$$P_1 = \frac{\sigma_z \beta_{2z} + 3\bar{z}\sigma_z\beta_{1z} + 3\bar{z}^2}{\sigma_z^2 + \bar{z}^2} \quad \text{if} \quad \sigma_t = k z_t \tag{51}$$

where the three quantities σ_z, β_{1z} and β_{2z} are defined by the classical formulae from the empirical distribution of the z_t:

$$\sigma_z^2 = \frac{1}{T} \sum (z_t - \bar{z})^2 \qquad \sigma_z^3 \beta_{1z} = \frac{1}{T} \sum (z_t - \bar{z})^3$$

$$\sigma_z^4 \beta_{2z} = \frac{1}{T} \sum (z_t - \bar{z})^4 \tag{52}$$

In particular, if this distribution is nearly normal, then $P_1 = 2$ when σ_t^2 is proportional to z_t and $P_1 = 3$ when the standard deviation σ_t is proportional to z_t. As we can see, there is then considerable underestimation.

(ii) The usual tests

Heteroscedasticity also affects the tests usually associated with regressions. Various writers have investigated its influence on analysis of variance and shown that it seriously affects the significance level and the power of the tests, especially when class-sizes vary considerably. See Box [1954], SCHEFFÉ [1959] and Ito and Schull [1964]. Also Courrège and Priouret [1971] propose a general method for determining bounds for the significance levels of the usual tests.

We shall confine ourselves to the results of Schmidt and Sickles [1977] relating to the 'Chow test' described in ch. 7, § 8, which is concerned with the identity of regressions applied to two subsamples of T_1 and T_2 observations respectively.

If the errors are homoscedastic within each sample, with standard deviation σ_1 in the first and σ_2 in the second, then the significance level of the Chow test is sensitive to differences between σ_1 and σ_2. We can see this if we consider how the probability of the usual critical region varies as a function of σ_1^2/σ_2^2 when the regressions in the two subsamples have the same coefficients (the probability of a type 1 error). This probability P may be much higher than the supposed significance level if there is a clear difference between the standard deviations.

For example, in fig. 1 we see the curve which shows how P varies for the case where a theoretical significance level of 5 % is chosen and $T_1 = 20$, $T_2 = 30$, and where the regression is a pure linear trend (two exogenous variables). We see that, if $\sigma_1 = 10\sigma_2$, the actual significance level is 11 % rather than 5 %. The risk of accepting as distinct two truly identical regressions is twice as large as was wanted.

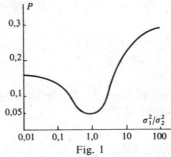

Fig. 1

(iii) Tests of homoscedasticity

If we suspect the presence of heteroscedasticity affecting the reliability of usual regression methods so that they tend to underestimate the standard errors of estimates or the significance levels of tests, we may want to test for homoscedasticity of the errors with the intention of proceeding with the usual methods if homoscedasticity is not rejected and of resorting to other methods if it is[†]. What test can we apply?

Since the errors ε_t are not directly observable, it is natural to consider the least squares residuals which, in a sense, can take the place of the errors. So we

---

[†] In the previous chapter we noted in another context that the choice of estimator on the basis of a preliminary test leads on the whole to a complex procedure whose properties are difficult to determine rigorously. We shall not re-emphasize this point.

shall see whether the size of these residuals appears to be related to some quantity which we consider critical in the circumstances. It is clearly the relationship with the exogenous variables which matters, both because it is suspected to exist and because it alone affects the validity of the usual methods.

It is then clear how tests can be constructed. Without going into the subject thoroughly we shall briefly describe the situation for the case of simple regression where (46) applies.

The most natural suggestion, by GLESJER [1969], is to test whether the coefficient k of a regression of ε_t^{*2} or $|\varepsilon_t^*|$ in z_t is zero. The only difficulty lies in the fact that it is difficult to construct the exact theory of this test because the distribution of ε_t^* obviously involves z_t, even in the case of homoscedasticity. If the Student statistic is used to test if k equals zero, then significance levels may be determined on the basis of Monte Carlo studies as described by Glesjer; but this method is still rather crude.

So other tests have been established whose theory can be worked out exactly. Such tests assume the observations to have been already ranked in increasing order of z_t, that is, $z_t \geq z_\theta$ if $t > \theta$.

GOLDFELD and QUANDT [1965] carry out two simple regressions of x_t on z_t using the first $T/2$ and the last $T/2$ observations respectively. Then let S_1 and S_2 be the two sums of squares of residuals. When the ε_t are homoscedastic and normally distributed, S_2/S_1 obviously has an F-distribution with $(T-4)/2$ and $(T-4)/2$ degrees of freedom. When there is a strong positive association between σ_t^2 and z_t, the values of this ratio are inflated.

HEDAYAT and ROBSON [1970] suggest carrying out $T-2$ regressions on the first 3, the first 4, the first 5, ..., observations. Then ε_n^* denotes the nth residual in the regression carried out on the first n observations (the ε_n^* are sometimes called the 'recursive residuals'). They prove that the ε_n^* are uncorrelated and are normally distributed if the ε_t are normal, and that $E(\varepsilon_n^{*2}) = \sigma^2 c_n^2$, where the c_n are numbers which can be calculated. Then a (parametric) test comparable to that suggested by Goldfeld and Quandt can be constructed using the ε_n^*/c_n. HARVEY and PHILLIPS [1974] show that these two tests have similar powers. They also discuss some variants which we shall not consider here.

'Non-parametric' methods like those discussed in ch. 11 have also been suggested. In particular, Hedayat and Robson propose a 'peaks test', considering the series of $T-2$ numbers $|\varepsilon_n^*|/c_n$, and from this series the number N of terms which dominate all previous terms, that is, the number of terms which are greater than all previous terms. Where there is strong positive association of σ_t^2 and z_t, this number N will tend to be large. The reader may refer to GOLDFELD and QUANDT [1965], p. 543 and HEDAYAT and ROBSON [1970] pp. 1579–1581, for a discussion of the determination of significance levels for N.

(iv) Weighted regression

Since the usual regression methods are liable to be fairly inefficient where there is considerable heteroscedasticity, it is natural to use other estimation methods, going back to what was suggested in section 1 of this chapter.

If the σ_t^2 are known, then the generalised least squares estimator is the obvious choice. This is derived by minimising

$$\sum_{t=1}^{T} \frac{1}{\sigma_t^2}(x_t - a_1 z_t - a_2)^2. \tag{54}$$

This expression is a weighted sum of squares of the residuals and hence the name 'weighted regression' is given to the estimation method.

In the absence of exact knowledge of the σ_t^2 it may often be thought reasonable to postulate a simple relation between the σ_t^2 and the z_t. If, for example, we assume that the standard deviation σ_t must be proportional to z_t as in (51), then the weighted regression consists of minimising

$$\sum_{t=1}^{T} \frac{1}{z_t^2}(x_t - a_1 z_t - a_2)^2 = \sum_{t=1}^{T} \left\{ \frac{x_t}{z_t} - a_1 - \frac{a_2}{z_t} \right\}^2. \tag{55}$$

In fact, here we revert to a simple regression between the ratio x_t/z_t and the exogenous variable $1/z_t$. We should also have arrived at this regression if, in (46), we had divided throughout by z_t and noted that the errors ε_t/z_t then become homoscedastic.

The same kind of reasoning often leads to the replacement of the initial variables by variables divided by some quantity which can be considered representative of the 'size' of the economic unit considered. Thus, in a model explaining investment by firms, the ratio between investment and turnover may be chosen as endogenous variable if the different firms vary greatly in size.

In most cases the relationship between σ_t^2 and z_t is not well known and weighted regression cannot be applied as it stands. For example, it may not be known whether it is σ_t or σ_t^2 that is proportional to z_t, so a priori it will be preferable to assume only a more general relation such as

$$\sigma_t^2 = k_0 + k_1 z_t + k_2 z_t^2. \tag{56}$$

The three coefficients k_0, k_1 and k_2 then have the same role as the components of the vector ω in the general formulation (2).

We shall not discuss[†] the application of the general methods of sections 1(ii) and 1(iii); we have already discussed them in detail in relation to example 1 in these sections. We need only consider them now in a more particular case.

3 Models with random coefficients

In ch. 4, § 6, we became aware of some problems involved in the econometric use of individual data. These data contain a great wealth of information both

---

[†] For a discussion see AMEMIYA [1978].

because they are so plentiful and because of the range of variation of the variables involved. But their analysis may require more complex models than those used for aggregate data.

In particular, the general multiple regression model may appear too rigid in that it assumes a vector a of coefficients which is the same for all the units observed. Now, when discussing individual consumption functions in ch. 4, we already introduced (21) in which the coefficients depend on the particular individual. From this point of view, there was clearly nothing special about the case.

It is, of course, impossible to estimate the coefficients for each individual from a sample of individual data. We try rather to find average values of the coefficients over the set of individuals. However the situation may require some revision of the model and of the best methods of estimating it.

For simplicity, let us return to the case of a linear relation between a single endogenous variable and a single exogenous variable. In (46), where t now denotes an observed individual, the constant $a_2 + \varepsilon_t$ does depend on t, but the slope a_1 is independent of t. For a more satisfactory model, we set

$$x_t = (a_1 + \alpha_t)z_t + a_2 + \eta_t \qquad t = 1, 2, \ldots, T. \qquad (57)$$

We then treat α_t and η_t as random variables with zero expected value

$$E(\alpha_t) = 0, \qquad E(\eta_t) = 0. \qquad (58)$$

The problem consists of estimating the mean coefficients[†] a_1 and a_2.

Clearly (46) is still legitimate provided that all the random terms are regrouped and we write

$$\varepsilon_t = \alpha_t z_t + \eta_t. \qquad (59)$$

If the pairs (α_t, η_t) relating to the different observations are uncorrelated and identically distributed we find ourselves with a particular case of the simple regression model with heteroscedastic errors.

Concentrating on the case where there is no correlation between α_t and η_t, we can write

$$\sigma_t^2 = \sigma_\alpha^2 z_t^2 + \sigma_\eta^2 \qquad (60)$$

where obviously σ_α^2 and σ_η^2 are the variances of α_t and η_t. (Zero correlation of α_t and η_t is a standard assumption in the discussion of this question. For the assumption to hold in practice, a suitable origin for the measurement of the z_t must be chosen. In most cases this origin must be such that $\bar{z}$ is near zero: zero correlation between the estimated slope of the line and its estimated level

---

[†] In ch. 4 we discussed the problems which may arise in interpreting these mean cofficients, particularly when they are used in the study of aggregate data.

for $z_t = \bar{z}$. So in what follows we shall concentrate on the case where $\bar{z}$ is zero.)

In particular, the ordinary least squares estimators a_1^* and a_2^* contain no bias; but the usual formulae for estimating their variances do. Taking account of (60) in the general formula (47), we find

$$P_{\mathsf{t}} = \frac{\sigma_\eta^2 + \sigma_\alpha^2(\sigma_z^2\beta_{2z} + 3\bar{z}\sigma_z\beta_{1z} + 3\bar{z}^2)}{\sigma_\eta^2 + \sigma_\alpha^2(\sigma_z^2 + \bar{z}^2)} \tag{61}$$

where (52) define the characteristics of the sample distribution of the z_t.

If σ_α^2 is zero, then obviously the bias is eliminated and $P_1 = 1$. If σ_η^2 is zero, then (51) applies. Generally the bias will be smaller than when σ_t is proportional to z_t; however it remains true that *almost always the true variance of a_1^* is under-estimated*[†]. We note also that, if the first term $\sigma_\alpha^2 z_t^2$ in (60) is on average equal to the second σ_η^2 and if the sample distribution of the z_t is approximately normal, then $P_1 = 2$.

In order to determine more efficient estimators of a_1 and a_2 than a_1^* and a_2^*, it is natural to think of applying the principle discussed in sections 1(ii) and 1(iii).

The attempt at simultaneous estimation of a_1, a_2, σ_α and σ_η turns out to be complex, as we can see if we try to use equations (31), (32) and (35) defining quasi-maximum likelihood estimators. Nor shall we spend time discussing the MINQUE estimators of σ_α^2 and σ_η^2, nor the corresponding estimators of a_1 and a_2.

Instead we shall concentrate on the procedure which involves estimating σ_α and σ_η from the residuals ε_t^* of an initial ordinary least squares regression, and then going on to a weighted regression in which σ_t^2 is replaced by its estimate $\sigma_t^{*2} = \sigma_\alpha^{*2} z_t^2 + \sigma_\eta^{*2}$. In particular, we shall make a closer study of the estimate σ_t^*, which we rather left hanging in section 1(ii). This will lead us to consider several estimators which, giving different results for σ_t^*, will lead to as many different estimators of a_1 and a_2.

(1) The first notion to spring to mind is that of a simple regression between the square ε_t^{*2} of the residual and the square z_t^2 of the exogenous variable, since ε_t^{*2} is near ε_t^2, whose expected value σ_t^2 is just a linear function of z_t^2, in view of (60). The estimated variance σ_t^{*2} is then the fitted value resulting from this regression of ε_t^{*2} on z_t^2.

(2) For some samples, the gradient or the constant of the above regression may be negative, which is not the case for the true values σ_α^2 and σ_η^2. To avoid such

---

[†] To see why, we need only note that the difference between the numerator and the denominator of (61) is $\sigma_\alpha^2\sigma_z^2(2w^2 + 3\beta_{1z}w + \beta_{2z} - 1)$ where $w = \bar{z}/\sigma_z$. Considered as a quadratic in w, the expression in brackets has no root and so is always positive if $9\beta_{1z}^2 < 8(\beta_{2z} - 1)$. Now $\beta_{1z}^2 \leq \beta_{2z} - 1$, as we can see if we note that the square of the correlation coefficient between $z_t - \bar{z}$ and $(z_t - \bar{z})^2$ is at most 1. So the case where the expression in brackets is negative is quite exceptional.

situations, we need only find the values u^* and v^* which are solutions of

$$\underset{u \geq 0,\, v \geq 0}{\text{Min}} \ \sum_{t=1}^{T} (\varepsilon_t^{*2} - uz_t^2 - v)^2 \tag{62}$$

and write $\sigma_t^{*2} = u^* z_t^2 + v^*$. (At the end of ch. 9 we shall briefly discuss the case of such regressions subject to sign conditions.)

(3) However, the principle on which the above two estimators are based is simplistic, since it ignores the fact that the residual ε_t^* does not have the same variance as the error ε_t. It appears preferable rigorously to determine the expressions for the $E(\varepsilon_t^{*2})$ in order to deduce estimates of the σ_t^2.

This is easily done, using general formulae. We set

$$N = I - Z(Z'Z)^{-1}Z'. \tag{63}$$

The vector ε^* of the residuals is related to the vector ε of the errors as follows:

$$\varepsilon^* = N\varepsilon \tag{64}$$

Let $\dot{\varepsilon}^*$ and $\dot{\varepsilon}$ be the vectors whose components are the squares ε_t^{*2} and ε_t^2 respectively. In view of our assumption that the errors ε_t and ε_θ relating to two distinct observations are uncorrelated, we can deduce directly from (64):

$$E(\dot{\varepsilon}^*) = \dot{N}E(\dot{\varepsilon}) \tag{65}$$

where the elements of $\dot{N}$ are the squares of the elements of N. Evaluating $E(\dot{\varepsilon})$ and defining $\dot{Z}$ in the same way, we have finally

$$E(\dot{\varepsilon}^*) = \dot{N}\dot{Z} \begin{bmatrix} \sigma_\alpha^2 \\ \sigma_\eta^2 \end{bmatrix}. \tag{66}$$

Thus the coefficients of σ_α^2 and σ_η^2 in the expression for $E(\varepsilon_t^{*2})$ are not z_t^2 and 1, but the two elements f_t and g_t of the tth row of $\dot{N}\dot{Z}$. We find

$$g_t = 1 - \frac{1}{T} - \frac{(z_t - \bar{z})^2}{T\sigma_z^2}. \tag{67}$$

This number differs from 1, but by a term which tends to zero as T tends to infinity. The explicit expression for f_t is long; we shall state it here only for the case where $\bar{z} = 0$ (which must happen in most cases if the assumption that α_t and η_t are uncorrelated is to be justified):

$$f_t = z_t^2 + \frac{\sigma_z^2}{T} + \frac{2\beta_{1z}\sigma_z}{T}z_t + \frac{\beta_{2z} - 2}{T}z_t^2 - \frac{2}{T\sigma_z^2}z_t^4. \tag{68}$$

Here again the difference from z_t^2 is of order T^{-1}.

In short, we should choose $\sigma_t^{*2} = u^* z_t^2 + v^*$, having found u^* and v^* from

$$\underset{u,\,v}{\text{Min}} \sum_{t=1}^{T} (\varepsilon_t^{*2} - u f_t - v g_t)^2. \tag{69}$$

(4) As previously, we may think it opportune to set the conditions $u \geqq 0$ and $v \geqq 0$ in minimising (69), even if this complicates things slightly.

(5) But we might also challenge simple minimisation of the sum of squares of the deviations. We write

$$\varepsilon_t^{*2} = f_t \sigma_\alpha^2 + g_t \sigma_\eta^2 + \zeta_t. \tag{70}$$

It would be wrong to consider the vector ζ as having not only zero expected value, as required by the definition of f_t and g_t, but as also having a covariance matrix of the form $\sigma_\zeta^2 I$. Now, this covariance matrix is easy to derive; since ε_t and ε_τ $(t \neq \tau)$ are independent,

$$E(\zeta\zeta') = \dot{N} \varDelta [E(\varepsilon_t^2 - \sigma_t^2)^2] \dot{N} \tag{71}$$

where $\varDelta[y_t]$ is the diagonal matrix whose diagonal elements are the y_t. In particular, if the ε_t are normal, the elements of the diagonal matrix of (71) are $2\sigma_t^4$. Replacing σ_t by an initial estimate σ_t^*, given, for example, by (1) or (2), we can then determine an estimate Q_ζ^* of $E(\zeta\zeta')$ and calculate u^* and v^* by minimising

$$(\dot{\varepsilon}^* - u f - v g)' Q_\zeta^{*-1} (\dot{\varepsilon}^* - u f - v g).$$

(6) A final estimator is obtained by imposing the constraints $u \geqq 0$, $v \geqq 0$ in the above minimisation.

Faced with this diversity of possible formulae, it is instructive to refer to the Monte Carlo studies carried out by FROEHLICH [1973]. In particular, he concludes that the precision of the estimator is systematically improved if the conditions $u \geqq 0$, $v \geqq 0$ are taken into account. On the whole, he recommends estimator (4) as offering a good compromise between the need for precision and the avoidance of heavy computation. He concludes finally that MINQUE and quasi-maximum likelihood estimators do not appear superior to estimators (3) and (5).

4   Models with composite errors

It is becoming more and more practicable for economists to use samples in which the individual units (households, firms, industrial sectors . . .) are followed up over successive periods. Thus, if there are n units $(i = 1, 2, \ldots, n)$ and T periods $(t = 1, 2, \ldots, T)$ the number of observations increases to nT. We then talk of 'time series of cross-sections'. Such basic data obviously give much fuller information than the usual time series or cross-sections. So their use in econometrics has been developing rapidly. This naturally raises some methodological problems.

(i) A specification

In this book we shall not attempt to deal systematically with all these problems; they relate to the subject-matter of different chapters and present a combination of the difficulties which we discuss separately. However, we may suggest their nature in a preliminary survey.

We adopt a linear model of the form

$$x_{it} = a'z_{it} + \varepsilon_{it} \qquad i = 1, 2, \ldots, n \qquad t = 1, 2, \ldots, T \qquad (72)$$

where the vector a of coefficients and the vector z_{it} of exogenous variables have m components. Also we shall restrict attention mainly to the case where $m = 2$ and the second component of z_{it} is 1 for all the observations (so without risk of confusion, z_{it} will also denote the first component of this vector).

There is no particular problem if the ε_{it} can be considered as homoscedastic and independent. But the nature of the sample and the ample investigation to which it can give rise generally make less simple specifications desirable. For an example, consider the case where the error would be split into two terms:

$$\varepsilon_{it} = \alpha_i + \eta_{it}, \qquad (73)$$

where both the different η_{it} and the different α_i would be homoscedastic and independent, the η_{it} being independent of the α_i.

There are three preliminary comments on this specification.

(1) It does not treat the two dimensions of the sample symmetrically. So it often appears preferable to choose a symmetric specification including a more refined decomposition of the errors:

$$\varepsilon_{it} = \alpha_i + \beta_t + \eta_{it}. \qquad (74)$$

The term α_i now represents an effect specific to the individual, and the term β_t an effect specific to the period. This is generally the case discussed under the heading of models with composite errors[†]. It leads to analytic complications which we shall avoid by keeping to the obviously simpler case of (73).

(2) We might think of introducing specific effects on the x_{it} otherwise than by purely additive terms such as α_i or β_t. In some cases the coefficients of the exogenous variables may themselves contain specific terms. The model then adds the difficulties discussed in the previous section to the new difficulties in which we are presently interested.

[†] See, in particular, MAZODIER [1971]. For other specifications, see also MAZODIER and TROGNON, 'Données en coupes répétées et modèles à double indice', I.N.S.E.E. paper.

(3) There is no need to suppose that the specific terms α_i are random. For, we can consider them purely as unknown parameters, the sample of nT observations being large enough to allow their estimation. But to approach the problem in this way is equivalent to assuming that a priori we have no idea about the set of the n terms α_i. In most cases the statistical distribution of these terms is considered comparable to that obtained by taking a sample from a stable distribution. To ignore such 'information' is to run the risk of incurring some loss of efficiency.

However, it is simple to determine the appropriate estimator for (72)–(73) if the α_i are treated as completely unknown parameters. It follows from the assumption adopted for the η_{it} that we then have to deal with a multiple regression model of the type encountered in the previous chapter for the analysis of covariance. So we need only minimise the sum of squares of the differences

$$\sum_{it} (x_{it} - a'z_{it} - \alpha_i)^2. \tag{75}$$

Minimisation with respect to α_i gives directly

$$\alpha_i = \bar{x}_i - a'\bar{z}_i \tag{76}$$

where $\bar{x}_i$ and $\bar{z}_i$ are the arithmetic means of the T observations x_{it} and z_{it} relating to the ith individual. The analytic definition of the estimate of the vector a is therefore similar to that of the ordinary least squares estimate which would have been the appropriate choice if, in the simple model (72), the ε_{it} had been assumed to be homoscedastic and independent; the only difference is that the variables x_{it} and z_{it} are replaced by their deviations $x_{it} - \bar{x}_i$ and $z_{it} - \bar{z}_i$ from the individual means. This is therefore called the 'covariance estimator'; here we shall denote it by a^c and distinguish it from the ordinary least squares estimator a^*.

(ii)   Ordinary least squares and the covariance estimator

We see that the model (72)–(73) is another particular case of the model (1)–(2). We need only write the nT observations x_{it} as a single vector, the T observations on each individual being ranged successively in a vector x_i and the n column vectors x_i being ranged successively downwards in a single column vector x. We define similarly the vector ε and the matrix Z in which each column carries the nT observations on a single exogenous variable in the above order.

The variance of ε_{it} is $\sigma_\eta^2 + \sigma_\alpha^2$, the covariance of ε_{it} and $\varepsilon_{i\tau}$ ($t \neq \tau$) is σ_α^2 and the covariance of ε_{it} and ε_{ht} ($i \neq h$) is zero. So we can write the covariance matrix Q in the form

$$Q = \sigma_\eta^2 I + \sigma_\alpha^2 K \tag{77}$$

where I is the unit matrix of order nT while K is a block-diagonal matrix in which each diagonal block is a square matrix of order T all of whose elements are 1. So Q depends on two parameters σ_η^2 and σ_α^2 (which can be considered as the components of the vector ω).

Since $K^2 = TK$, we can easily verify the following formula for the inverse of Q:

$$\sigma_\eta^2 Q^{-1} = I - (1 - \gamma)K/T \tag{78}$$

where

$$\gamma = \frac{\sigma_\eta^2}{\sigma_\eta^2 + T\sigma_\alpha^2}. \tag{79}$$

If γ is known, we can find the generalised least squares estimator, whose analytic expression can easily be determined from (78). In the case of a single genuine exogenous variable and a constant, the estimator of the slope a_1 is

$$\hat{a}_1 = \frac{\sum_{it}(z_{it} - \bar{z}_i)(x_{it} - \bar{x}_i) + \gamma T \sum_i (\bar{z}_i - \bar{z})(\bar{x}_i - \bar{x})}{\sum_{it}(z_{it} - \bar{z}_i)^2 + \gamma T \sum_i (\bar{z}_i - \bar{z})^2}, \tag{80}$$

where $\bar{x}$ and $\bar{z}$ are the overall means for the set of nT observations.

This formula leads us to consider the intraclass variance V_1 and interclass variance V_2 of the z_{it}:

$$nTV_1 = \sum_{it}(z_{it} - \bar{z}_i)^2, \qquad nV_2 = \sum_i (\bar{z}_i - \bar{z})^2. \tag{81}$$

The variance of the z_{it} is obviously $V_1 + V_2$. We can also define an indicator of the relative importance of the interclass variance:

$$w = \frac{V_2}{V_1 + V_2}. \tag{82}$$

Formula (80) for the generalised least squares estimator, and also the formulae defining the least squares estimator a_1^* and the covariance estimator a_1^c for the slope a_1, lead us to consider, for all $0 \leq \delta \leq 1$, the estimator

$$a_1(\delta) = \frac{\sum_{it}(z_{it} - \bar{z}_i)(x_{it} - \bar{x}_i) + \delta T \sum_i (\bar{z}_i - \bar{z})(\bar{x}_i - \bar{x})}{nT(V_1 + \delta V_2)} \tag{83}$$

since

$$a_1(0) = a_1^c, \quad a_1(\gamma) = \hat{a}_1, \quad a_1(1) = a_1^*. \tag{84}$$

If δ is taken as a fixed parameter chosen a priori, then $a_1(\delta)$ is unbiased. We can easily find its variance:

$$E[a_1(\delta) - a_1]^2 = \frac{\sigma_\eta^2}{nT\sigma_z^2} \cdot \frac{1 - w + \delta^2 w/\gamma}{(1 - w + \delta w)^2} . \tag{85}$$

We see that this variance is indeed minimal for $\delta = \gamma$.

Various conclusions can be drawn from this formula and the above definitions.

(1) The ordinary least squares estimator coincides with the generalised least squares estimator in three cases:
- when $\gamma = 1$, that is, when $\sigma_\alpha^2 = 0$,
- when $\bar{z}_i = \bar{z}$ for all i, in which case $a_1(\delta) = a_1^*$ for all δ,
- when $z_{it} = \bar{z}_i$ for all i and t, in which case $a_1(\delta) = a_1^*$ for all positive δ.

This result can also be deduced directly from expression (77) for Q and the condition stated in section 1(i). For, if u is any vector, then

$$(Qu)_{it} = \sigma_\eta^2 u_{it} + T\sigma_\alpha^2 \bar{u}_i.$$

It follows that Q has two characteristic roots σ_η^2 and $\sigma_\eta^2 + T\sigma_\alpha^2$. There are two types of characteristic vector: those for which $\bar{u}_i = 0$ for all i and those for which $u_{it} = \bar{u}_i$ for all i and t. The third condition for $a_1^* = \hat{a}_1$ corresponds to the case where z and l (the vector whose components are all 1) are two of the second type characteristic vectors of Q; the second condition corresponds to the case where z is a linear combination of l and a characteristic vector of the first type.

(2) The efficiency of ordinary least squares can be defined by the ratio of the variances of a_1^* and $\hat{a}_1$; now, it follows from (85) that

$$\frac{E(a_1^* - a_1)^2}{E(\hat{a}_1 - a_1)^2} = 1 + \frac{T^2 \sigma_\alpha^4 w(1 - w)}{\sigma_\eta^2 (\sigma_\eta^2 + T\sigma_\alpha^2)} . \tag{86}$$

Excluding the cases where $w = 0$ and $w = 1$, we see that the efficiency decreases as individual effects become relatively greater ($\sigma_\alpha^2/\sigma_\eta^2$ is larger) and as the number T of observations for each individual increases.

(3) For choosing between the two simplest estimators, namely the covariance estimator and the ordinary least squares estimator, we can consider the following equality deduced from (85):

$$\frac{E(a_1^* - a_1)^2}{E(a_1^c - a_1)^2} = (1 - w)\left(1 + w \frac{T\sigma_\alpha^2}{\sigma_\eta^2}\right) \tag{87}$$

(where the case $w = 1$ is obviously excluded).

It follows directly from (87) that *the variance of the covariance estimator is less than the variance of the ordinary least squares estimator* if and only if

$$T\sigma_\alpha^2 > \sigma_\eta^2 \left(1 + \frac{V_2}{V_1}\right) . \tag{88}$$

If the individual effects are liable to be relatively large, if the interclass variance of the z is not relatively very large and if the number of observations on each individual is not too small, the covariance estimator will be preferable to the ordinary least squares estimator.

Before discussing other estimators of a_1, we should note that *the usual formulae for estimating the variance of the estimated coefficient are unbiased in the case of* a_1^c, *but on the other hand they contain a bias which may be very considerable in the case of ordinary least squares.*

For, when calculating the covariance estimator a_1^c, we naturally use a ratio whose denominator contains a term which is nT times the intraclass variance $\sigma_z^2(1-w)$ while the numerator is an estimate of σ_η^2, or more precisely, the residual sum of squares divided by $nT-n-1$. We see that this formula agrees with (85).

On the other hand, for the usual formulae associated with ordinary least squares, the denominator will be nT times the total variance and the numerator will be the residual sum of squares, divided by $nT-2$. Using the method described in the first section, we find that the ratio between the true variance of a_1^* and the expected value of its estimate by the usual formula is

$$P_1 = \frac{\sigma_\eta^2 + T\sigma_\alpha^2 w}{\sigma_\eta^2 - T\sigma_\alpha^2[w - (n-1)/(Tn-2)]}. \tag{89}$$

This ratio is obviously 1 when $\sigma_\alpha^2 = 0$. It is less than 1 when $\sigma_\alpha^2 > 0$ and $\bar{z}_i = \bar{z}$ for all i ($w=0$). But in most cases it must be much greater than 1. It becomes increasingly greater as $T\sigma_\alpha^2/\sigma_\eta^2$ increases and as the part w of the interclass variance increases.

(iii) Estimation of the variances and the coefficients

As there is usually a large number of observations in cross-sectional time series, it is natural to try to estimate the two variances σ_η^2 and σ_α^2 individually. It also appears natural to use less simple methods than ordinary least squares or the covariance estimator for estimating the coefficients. Clearly the ordinary least squares estimator is best in practice in cases near to those where $a_1^* = \hat{a}_1$. Similarly, the covariance estimator is best if $T\sigma_\alpha^2$ is known a priori to be large relative to σ_η^2 and if the share of the interclass variance is not too great. But in all intermediate cases, a more elaborate estimator is likely to be preferable.

This appears to be borne out by the simulation studies due to MADDALA and MOUNT [1973], though these were admittedly limited to one case. They also suggest that there is little to be gained by using quasi-maximum likelihood or MINQUE estimators[†]. To achieve the greatest possible efficiency in practice, we need only estimate σ_η^2 and σ_α^2 from the residuals of an initial fitting, then

[†] For the quasi-maximum likelihood estimator see HARVILLE [1977].

deduce an estimate of γ which can be substituted in (80) to estimate a_1.

The first stage in such 'two-stage estimation' uses ordinary least squares or possibly, if the case is such that it appears preferable, the covariance method. In either case it concludes with determination of residuals ε_{it}^* between x_{it} and the fitted value of $a'z_{it}$.

Let us set

$$S_1^* = \sum_{it}(\varepsilon_{it}^* - \bar{\varepsilon}_i^*)^2, \qquad S_2^* = T\sum_i \bar{\varepsilon}_i^{*2}. \tag{90}$$

The residual sum of squares is $S_1^* + S_2^*$. The expected value of S_1^* is approximately $n(T-1)\sigma_\eta^2$ and that of S_2^* is approximately $(n-1)(\sigma_\eta^2 + T\sigma_\alpha^2)$. So it is natural to choose the following estimators:

$$\sigma_\eta^{*2} = \frac{S_1^*}{n(T-1)}, \quad \sigma_\alpha^{*2} = \frac{S_2^*}{T(n-1)} - \frac{\sigma_\eta^{*2}}{T} \tag{91}$$

at least if $S_1^*/n(T-1) \leqq S_2^*/(n-1)$. Where this inequality is not satisfied, we choose

$$\sigma_\eta^{*2} = \frac{S_1^* + S_2^*}{nT - 1}, \qquad \sigma_\alpha^{*2} = 0 \tag{92}$$

Just as, in the previous sections, we did not describe in detail the statistical theory of two-stage estimators, so we shall not attempt to do so in the case of composite error models. Instead, we shall consider this theory in the context of the more general model of the next section. The properties to be established can be transposed in a fairly obvious way to the case of composite error models.

5   A general linear model and the case of simultaneous regressions

(i) The model

We shall now consider a more general linear model than that discussed in chapters 6 and 7. Apart from the fact that the covariance matrix of the errors is unknown in most cases, this new model appears as a particular case of the model in chapter 5 relating to the general linear hypothesis. It is also a particular case of the non-linear regression model to be discussed in chapter 9. It is therefore very relevant to the subject-matter of this book.

It is also capable of wide application in econometric practice. In particular, we shall see that it occurs in the problem of *simultaneous estimation of seemingly unrelated regressions*.

Let us consider a linear model with n endogenous variables $x_i(i = 1, 2, \ldots, n)$ and np exogenous variables $z_{ik}(i = 1, 2, \ldots, n; k = 1, 2, \ldots, p)$. Then let x_{it}

and z_{ikt} be the values of x_i and z_{ik} respectively in the tth observation. The model is

$$x_{it} = \sum_{k=1}^{p} \alpha_k z_{ikt} + \varepsilon_{it}, \qquad i = 1, 2, \ldots, n, \tag{93}$$

where the ε_{it} are unobservable random errors with zero means and the α_k are unknown real parameters to be estimated. As in previous chapters, the z_{ikt} are assumed to be non-random.

A priori this model is very similar to that of the previous section since (93) is virtually identical to (72). But it does differ in that it incorporates much less precise ideas about the distribution of the errors. The model is conceptually such that a priori every type of stochastic relationship between ε_{it} and ε_{ht} is considered possible (although when $t \neq \tau$, then ε_{it} and ε_{ht} are assumed to be independent). So Q depends on $n(n+1)/2$ unknown variances and covariances and no longer only on two (σ_η^2 and σ_α^2) as in the previous section.

Clearly (93) covers the apparently more general case where the equations are

$$x_{it} = \sum_{k=1}^{p} \alpha_k z_{ikt} + \beta_i + \varepsilon_{it}, \tag{94}$$

the β_i being unknown real parameters to be estimated. For, we can add to the np true exogenous variables z_{ik}, n^2 dummy exogenous variables $u_{ik}(k = = p+1, \ldots, p+n)$ defined by

$$u_{ikt} = \begin{cases} 1 & \text{if} & k = p+i \\ 0 & \text{if} & k \neq p+i. \end{cases}$$

Equation (14) is then equivalent to

$$x_{it} = \sum_{k=1}^{p} \alpha_k z_{ikt} + \sum_{k=p+1}^{p+n} \beta_{k-p} u_{ikt} + \varepsilon_{it}, \tag{95}$$

which is clearly of the form (93).

We can also verify that the multiple regression model discussed in chapter 6 is a particular case of (93). It can be written in this form by taking the $p = mn$ coefficients a_{ij} for α_k, and by defining the z_{ik} as follows:

$$z_{ikt} = \begin{cases} z_{jt} & \text{if } k \text{ is the index corresponding to a pair } (i, j). \\ 0 & \text{if } k \text{ is the index corresponding to a pair } (h, j) \text{ where } h \neq i. \end{cases}$$

The essential difference between the new model (93) or (94) and the multiple regression model lies in the fact that the same coefficients α_k can appear in the equations relating to different endogenous variables, and that different exogenous variables can appear in the equations relating to different endogenous variables.

So, in the case where $p = 1$, there are n exogenous variables z_i and the model is, for example,

$$x_{it} = \alpha z_{it} + \beta_i + \varepsilon_{it},$$

with the same coefficient α for the n endogenous variables.

Suppose for example that x_{it} represents the logarithm of consumption of the ith product by the tth household, z_{it} the logarithm of income of the tth household (z_{it} is therefore the same for all products). If we assume a priori that income elasticity is the same for the n products, we arrive at the above equation. This, of course, is an extreme example. We shall encounter models in which the basic economic assumptions seem less crude.

For a different field of application, suppose that each of the n equations involves particular exogenous variables. Let $j = 1, 2, \ldots, m$ be the index of the exogenous variables, the first m_1 occurring in the first equation, the next $m_2 - m_1$ in the second, $\ldots$, the $m_i - m_{i-1}$ in the ith equation, $\ldots$ (where $m = m_n$). The model is

$$x_{it} = \sum_j a_{ij} z_{jt} + \varepsilon_{it}, \qquad i = 1, 2, \ldots, n,$$

j varying in the ith equation from $m_{i-1} + 1$ to m_i. We can revert to (13) by taking the $p = m$ coefficients a_{ij} for α_k and by defining the z_{ik} as follows:

$$z_{ikt} = \begin{cases} z_{jt} & \text{where} \quad j = k \quad \text{if} \quad m_{i-1} < k \le m_i, \\ 0 & \text{otherwise.} \end{cases}$$

A model of this type can be introduced for investigation of the same relation over different units for which observations relating to a series of periods are available. For example, investment by firm i in year t may depend on the values in that year of certain quantities characterizing the firm's activity. The model then consists of the juxtaposition of relations concerning the different firms. If the errors ε_{it} and ε_{kt} relating to two different units i and k are always independent, the different equations of the model are completely independent and must be treated singly. But there is often strong correlation between the errors ε_{it} and ε_{kt} concerning the same period. Thus, the investment behaviour of two firms is generally similarly affected by multiple unidentified factors related to the general economic situation.

In this case it is clear that *simultaneous estimation of the set of equations of the model may be more precise than simple juxtaposition of estimates established for each equation individually.* Simultaneous estimation can take account of correlation of errors, which is necessarily ignored in individual estimates. Moreover, when we wish to test equality of the true coefficients relating to different units, we must take account of correlation of errors, and avoid acting as if observations relating to two different units constitute two independent samples.

A. ZELLNER [1962] investigates exactly this type of question and puts forward the simultaneous estimation method which we are about to discuss. Considering estimation of investment laws for two American firms over the period 1935–54, he finds that the variances of the estimated coefficients are reduced by about 20% relative to the results of two independent regressions. Finally, he considers a test of equality of the true coefficients relating to the two firms.

(ii) Basic assumptions

For the formal study of the model, let x_t, ε_t and α denote the vectors with components x_{it}, ε_{it} and α_k, and Z_t the matrix with components z_{ikt}. Relation (93) can then be written more simply:

$$x_t = Z_t \alpha + \varepsilon_t. \tag{96}$$

We assume throughout this section that α is some p-vector, and is subject to *no a priori restriction*.

We also make the following two assumptions:

Assumption 1.   The vector ε_t of the errors is distributed independently of t and the Z_θ. It has zero expected value and non-singular covariance matrix Ω. The vectors ε_t, ε_θ, ..., etc. relating to different observations are stochastically independent.

Assumption 2.   For any positive definite symmetric matrix S of order n, the matrix

$$M_T(S) = \frac{1}{T} \sum_{t=1}^{T} Z_t' S Z_t$$

has rank p and tends to a non-singular matrix as T tends to infinity. The sequence of the Z_t is bounded ($t = 1, 2, \ldots$).

Assumption 1 is identical to assumption 1 in chapter 6. It implies that the errors are homoscedastic and are not related from one observation to another. Assumption 2 states that the sequence of the exogenous variables Z_t has a certain degree of stationarity. It also eliminates the possibility of multicollinearity among exogenous variables. Let us look more closely at this latter point.

Clearly $M_T(S)$ is positive definite or semi-definite and symmetric; it has order p. Suppose that its rank is less than p. Then there exists a nonzero vector d such that

$$d' \cdot M_T(S) \cdot d = 0.$$

Since S is positive definite, this is equivalent to

$$Z_t d = 0 \qquad \text{for} \qquad t = 1, 2, \ldots, T, \tag{97}$$

or again

$$\sum_{k=1}^{p} d_k z_{ikt} = 0 \qquad \text{for} \qquad \text{all } i \text{ and all } t.$$

Thus assumption 2 eliminates the case where a linear combination of the exogenous variables of an equation is simultaneously zero for all equations and all observations. In a model with several endogenous variables, multicollinearity affecting just one equation would be unimportant.

(iii) Linear estimation when Ω is known

The model as just defined is a particular case of the linear model discussed in ch. 5. In nT-dimensional space, the vector x with components x_{it} has expected value y restricted to lie in the p-dimensional linear subspace defined by the condition

$$y_t = Z_t \alpha \qquad \text{for} \qquad t = 1, 2, \ldots, T$$

where α is a suitable vector. (Assumption 2 clearly implies that this linear subspace is p-dimensional.) The vector ε of the errors has covariance matrix Q which, in view of assumption 1, can be partitioned into T^2 blocks of square matrices of order n. The matrices appearing on the main diagonal are equal to Ω, the others are zero.

So the unbiased linear estimator with minimum dispersion is defined by the vector $\hat{\alpha}$ which minimizes

$$\frac{1}{T} \sum_{t=1}^{T} (x_t - Z_t \alpha)' \Omega^{-1} (x_t - Z_t \alpha). \tag{98}$$

Differentiation of this quantity shows that $\hat{\alpha}$ is the solution of

$$\frac{1}{T} \sum_{t=1}^{T} x_t' \Omega^{-1} Z_t - \alpha' \cdot \frac{1}{T} \sum_{t=1}^{T} Z_t' \Omega^{-1} Z_t = 0$$

and so

$$\hat{\alpha} = \left[\frac{1}{T} \sum_{t=1}^{T} Z_t' \Omega^{-1} Z_t \right]^{-1} \cdot \left[\frac{1}{T} \sum_{t=1}^{T} Z_t' \Omega^{-1} x_t \right]. \tag{99}$$

This formula recalls and generalizes the expression obtained when we discussed multiple regression (note that assumption 2 guarantees the existence of the inverse which appears in the formula).

The theory of linear estimation leads directly to the first two statements in the following theorem:

Theorem 1.   Under assumptions 1 and 2, the estimator $\hat{\alpha}$ is unbiased and has a concentration ellipsoid contained in that of every other unbiased linear estimator. Its covariance matrix is

$$\frac{1}{T}[M_T(\Omega^{-1})]^{-1}.$$

When T tends to infinity, $\sqrt{T}(\hat{\alpha}-\alpha)$ has, asymptotically, a normal distribution.

To establish the last statement, consider formula (99) according to which $\sqrt{T}(\hat{\alpha}-\alpha)$ can be written

$$\sqrt{T}(\hat{\alpha}-\alpha) = \sum_{t=1}^{T} \Lambda_{tT}\varepsilon_t, \tag{100}$$

where

$$\Lambda_{tT} = \frac{1}{\sqrt{T}}[M_T(\Omega^{-1})]^{-1}Z_t'\Omega^{-1}. \tag{101}$$

The covariance matrix of $\sqrt{T}.\hat{\alpha}$ is therefore

$$\sum_{t=1}^{T} \Lambda_{tT}\Omega\Lambda_{tT}' = [M_T(\Omega^{-1})]^{-1}. \tag{102}$$

Taking account of the form of the matrices Λ_{tT} and of assumption 2, we can prove the asymptotic normality of $\sqrt{T}(\hat{\alpha}-\alpha)$ by the same kind of argument as that of theorem 3, ch. 6.

Obviously the statistical theory of model (93) could be extended. We need only carry over the various results of chapter 6. Thus, $\hat{\alpha}$ is normally distributed when the ε_t are themselves normal. We note also that the properties of $\hat{\alpha}$ in small samples do not depend on assumption 2. It is sufficient that the inverse of $M_T(\Omega^{-1})$ exists.

However from a certain point of view, $\hat{\alpha}$ is less useful than the estimator A^* obtained in ch. 6 by applying the same general theory. It depends on the value of Ω and assumes this value to be known a priori. It could not be applied in practice just as it stands, since there is never adequate knowledge of the distribution of the errors in econometric models.

(iv)   A two-stage procedure for the case where Ω is unknown

A natural solution consists of substituting for Ω an estimate which is as near to it as possible. To do this, we define the minimum S-distance estimator, $\alpha(S)$, say, as that estimator which minimizes

$$\frac{1}{T} \sum_{t=1}^{T} (x_t - Z_t\alpha)'S(x_t - Z_t\alpha), \tag{103}$$

where S is a positive definite symmetric matrix. This estimator is obtained directly:

$$\alpha(S) = [M_T(S)]^{-1} \left[\frac{1}{T} \sum_{t=1}^{T} Z_t' S x_t \right]. \tag{104}$$

If S is a given matrix, $\alpha(S)$ is an unbiased estimator which tends in probability to the true value α when T tends to infinity (according to assumption 2, its covariance matrix tends to a zero matrix).

Moreover, the theory in ch. 9 shows that, if S_T is a random matrix which tends to Ω^{-1} as T tends to infinity, then the estimator $\alpha(S_T)$ is asymptotically equivalent to the estimator $\hat{\alpha}$. This justifies the following procedure:

(i) Find a minimum distance estimator $\tilde{\alpha}$, taking for S some positive definite fixed matrix, the unit matrix for example;

(ii) Find the estimation residuals

$$\tilde{\varepsilon}_t = x_t - Z_t \tilde{\alpha} \tag{105}$$

and their empirical covariance matrix

$$\tilde{M}_{\varepsilon\varepsilon} = \frac{1}{T} \sum_{t=1}^{T} \tilde{\varepsilon}_t \tilde{\varepsilon}_t'; \tag{106}$$

(iii) Find a new minimum distance estimator $\hat{\tilde{\alpha}}$, taking for S the inverse of $\tilde{M}_{\varepsilon\varepsilon}$:

$$\hat{\tilde{\alpha}} = \left[\sum_{t=1}^{T} Z_t' \tilde{M}_{\varepsilon\varepsilon}^{-1} Z_t \right]^{-1} \sum_{t=1}^{T} \left[Z_t' \tilde{M}_{\varepsilon\varepsilon}^{-1} x_t \right]. \tag{107}$$

Theorem 2 of ch. 9 implies that, under assumptions 1 and 2 above[†], $\sqrt{T}(\hat{\tilde{\alpha}} - \alpha)$ has a limiting centred normal distribution whose covariance matrix is the limit in probability of $[M_T(\tilde{M}_{\varepsilon\varepsilon}^{-1})]^{-1}$. Moreover, when ε_t is normally distributed, $\hat{\tilde{\alpha}}$ is an asymptotically efficient estimator.

So substitution of $\tilde{M}_{\varepsilon\varepsilon}$ for Ω implies no change in the asymptotic properties of the minimum distance estimate. But it obviously affects the distribution of the estimated parameters for small samples.

By a very elegant method, A. ZELLNER [1963] succeeds in determining the distribution of $\hat{\tilde{\alpha}}$ for finite values of T in the case where the model contains two endogenous variables ($n = 2$), where the m_1 exogenous variables of the first equation are orthogonal to the m_2 exogenous variables of the second, where

---

[†] The same result is obtained by eliminating from assumption 2 the demand that the sequence of the Z_t is bounded, and by demanding in assumption 1 that the ε_t have finite fourth-order moments. The proofs for these new assumptions are given on pages 286–289 of the 1966 edition of this book.

the α_k are the $m_1 + m_2 = p$ coefficients of the exogenous variables of the two equations and where the errors are normally distributed[†]. He shows that deviations from the asymptotic distribution are not large. The $\hat{\hat{\alpha}}_k$ are unbiased estimates of the α_k; their exact distribution is very near normal; their covariance matrix is only slightly underestimated by the asymptotic formulae. So the covariance matrix is

$$\frac{k}{T} [M_T(\Omega^{-1})]^{-1},$$

the coefficient k being near 1.15 when the number of observations exceeds the number of exogenous variables by 10 ($T - p = 10$).

To the extent that these results can be generalized, they show that asymptotic theory applies as a first approximation even for small samples. However we must bear in mind that estimation of Ω by $\tilde{M}_{\varepsilon\varepsilon}$ must often be mediocre. There is the danger that the matrix

$$\frac{1}{T} [M_T(\tilde{M}_{\varepsilon\varepsilon}^{-1})]^{-1}$$

may give too favorable an impression of the real variances of the estimated parameters[††].

Obviously these considerations are not peculiar to the linear model discussed in this section. They apply with perhaps even more force to the non-linear models to be examined in subsequent chapters.

6 Robustness vis-à-vis the distribution of errors

The properties studied in chs. 6 and 7 depend on several assumptions relating to the errors ε_t which appear in the general model of multiple regression. We assumed that these errors were not correlated with the exogenous variables, that they had first- and second-order moments, were mutually independent and uniformly distributed, and finally, for certain results, that their distribution was normal.

In theory these assumptions ought to be adopted a priori when the model is being specified. They should follow from the general ideas represented by the model. In fact our a priori knowledge of the phenomena studied is often incomplete. It practically never implies the necessity for the assumptions mentioned

[†] A slight error has been found by P. C. B. Phillips and is corrected in ZELLNER [1972] p. 225.
[††] This difficulty cannot be eliminated by any 'reduction in the degrees of freedom'. Also we should note here that, even if the matrix S used in finding $\tilde{\alpha}$ is a multiple of Ω, that is, if $\Omega = \sigma^2 S$, the expected value of $\tilde{M}_{\varepsilon\varepsilon}$ is a complex expression in which not only σ^2, Ω and T, but also the Z_t occur. Even in this case, no automatic reduction in the degrees of freedom seems adequate for estimation of σ^2.

above, and at most allows us to assume that these assumptions are approximately satisfied.

It is then important to know whether the stated properties are sensitive to slight inaccuracies in the assumptions adopted for the errors. Does low (but non-zero) correlation between the errors and the exogenous variables induce slight differences from the theoretical results of the previous chapters? What happens if the distribution of the errors varies, or has no second-order moment? etc. Such questions concern us in this section and in the following one.

One describes as *robust* those statistical procedures which show little sensitivity relative to the assumptions on the stochastic variables of the model for which they were conceived. In econometrics such robust procedures are of very particular interest since stochastic assumptions are always in the nature of approximations.

However, we note from the start that the above questions and the notion of robust procedure have no precise meaning. For the same assumption may be unrealistic in many different ways and be involved in different properties of the same method (for example, the significance level and the power of a test); the type of departure from it and the property to be considered should be defined more exactly. Similarly we should define those cases in which such departures are to be described as slight. We shall confine ourselves to an examination of the inaccuracies which are likely often to affect econometric studies and shall not aim at rigor. We need only give an indication of the possible consequences of the most frequent specification errors.

When there is little a priori justification for a stochastic assumption of the model, one sometimes proposes testing it on the basis of the data which are the object of econometric analysis. If we follow this suggestion, we can exhibit certain cases in which the assumption in question is not satisfied. In addition to the fact that the appropriate tests are known for only a few simple cases, we must not exaggerate the scope of this procedure. When the test leads to rejection of the dubious assumption, we must still know what conclusion may be drawn for the estimates in other respects. And when the test does not lead to rejection, the assumption may be approximately satisfied, but it may also be the case that the available data are too few or inadequate to reveal even an important specification error.

In section 2 we discussed the consequences of heteroscedasticity of the errors. Because of its importance we shall leave the study of possible relationships among the errors corresponding to successive observations until part IV of this book. In the next section we shall discuss independence of the errors with respect to the exogenous variables. We shall now consider the distribution of errors, which are here assumed to be homoscedastic and independent. First we shall consider possible departures from the crucial assumption of the existence of second order moments. Then we shall examine the role of the much more particular assumption of normality. Finally we shall see how least squares estimators can be replaced by estimators which are more robust vis-à-vis departures from these assumptions[†].

(i)   Existence of variances of the errors

We have assumed until now that the distribution of the errors has first- and second-order moments. What can be said when this is not the case? The expected values or the variances of the estimated coefficients do not generally exist when those of the errors are not finite, since the estimates in question are linear functions of the errors. Therefore the results of chs. 5 and 6 no longer apply. In fact no theory has been developed to fit these more general cases. However, it seems fairly easy to apply the limit theorems of probability calculus and so to prove some asymptotic properties (cf. LOÈVE [1955], ch. 6).

For example, if while their variances do not exist the errors do have zero expected value, we know that the expected values of the estimates are the corresponding true values. Moreover, if the errors are independent and homoscedastic, the estimates must tend to their expected values when T tends to infinity, provided that the sequence of the z_t obeys certain conditions which are not very restrictive in practice. Similarly in most cases these estimates have limiting distributions which belong to the category of 'stable laws' studied by P. Lévy. In large samples their distribution will be very close to a distribution of this category, but will not generally be near normal as is the case for errors whose variances exist.

What is the relevance of these properties? It seems that in practice we can always assume the existence of moments of the distribution of errors. For every bounded random variable obviously has moments of every order. When dealing with a sample of T observations, we should not go seriously wrong if we set an artificial bound on the range of the errors, provided there is a very small probability that the T errors are not all contained within the bounds. Now we can choose bounds which are sufficiently wide for this condition to be satisfied. In other words, we can always 'truncate' the range in such a way that the truncated distribution is a good approximation to the true distribution.

But we cannot dispose so easily of the difficulty, as we can see by making a closer examination of two particular operations in our procedures, namely calculation of the standard error of an estimated coefficient and establishment of a test on the true value of a coefficient.

The usual estimation formulae for the variances of the coefficients can always be applied and will always give a finite result. *But this result will not generally be stable and will vary greatly from one sample to another* if its expected value is infinite, which is the case when the distribution of the errors has no variance.

[†] SCHEFFÉ [1959] devotes a chapter to the effects of inaccuracies in the specification of errors, with reference to the techniques of analysis of variance. The reader will find in his book many useful additions to the remarks of the present section.

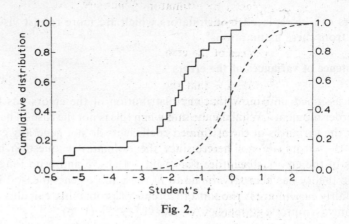

Fig. 2.

Substitution of a truncated distribution following the principle given above gives a finite expected value for the estimated variance, but does not eliminate the instability of this estimate. The usual formula therefore gives a very poor measure of the real dispersion of the estimated coefficient.

Similarly, we naturally think of a t-test for testing the value of a coefficient. But if the distribution of the errors has no variance, the limiting distribution of this statistics is different from the classical t-distribution, just as the limiting distribution of the estimated coefficient is different from the normal distribution. *Even for a large sample the classical tables are likely to give quite a wrong idea of the significance level and the power of the test.* Truncating the distribution of the errors certainly affects the limiting behavior of the test but leaves the same divergence between the true distribution and that given by the tables for the finite value of T considered.

Figure 2, showing the results of CHAMPERNOWNE [1960], reveals that the t-distribution can be quite inadequate. Several artificial samples were constructed, each containing 20 independent observations on a random variable x which had a Pareto distribution with density:

$$f(x) = 1,4x^{-2,4}, \quad \text{where} \quad x > 1. \tag{108}$$

On each sample the value of the t-statistic was calculated for the hypothesis that $E(x) = 3.5$, this hypothesis being true in this case. The unbroken curve in fig. 2 represents the cumulative frequency of the values obtained for Student's t in 20 artificial samples, while the dotted curve represents the theoretical distribution with 19 degrees of freedom. The two distributions are clearly different. In particular, the absolute value of Student's t is greater than 2 in 8 cases out of 20 whereas, according to the theoretical distribution, there is only a 5% probability of this happening. These results show that the t-test is no longer robust when the distributions of the errors differ too widely from the normal distribution.

In practice therefore it is important to find out which approximations best represent the empirical frequencies of the errors, paying particular attention to the distribution tails. If, in view of the number of observations analyzed, a distribution without variance appears most appropriate, then we should be aware that the classical procedures probably do not have the properties which are generally attributed to them.

Unfortunately the nature of the distribution of the errors affecting economic relations has not been investigated to any great extent. We must therefore be content here with some fairly general remarks. As we have seen, particular attention must be paid to the frequencies of large errors, for the shape of the tails of distributions affects the properties of our methods much more than that of their central parts.

We note first that certain economic data actually have distributions whose tails are well represented by distributions without variance[†]. The most celebrated example concerns the distribution of households in a country according to their respective incomes. We know that the Pareto distribution generally provides a very good fit for the data relating to at least the richest third of the population. The density of this distribution is:

$$f(x) = C(x - x_0)^{-\alpha - 1}, \tag{109}$$

if x denotes income and C, x_0 and α three constants. When $\alpha < 2$, which often happens in practice, the variance of the distribution is not defined. But it is interesting to note that the log-normal distribution, whose variance is defined, is more suitable for households belonging to the same socio-professional category. In this connection see ROTTIER [1958].

A Pareto distribution with $\alpha < 2$ often seems appropriate for the distribution of the micro-economic units of a broadly defined category: the distribution of households in a country according to income, wealth, etc., the distribution of firms in a region according to numbers employed or annual turnover.

In the analysis of very large collections of data relating to households or firms the errors are liable to have distributions of the same type when they reflect the influence of certain factors such as wealth of household or size of firm and when there is every chance that this influence is proportional or more than proportional. Obviously this does not apply if the factors in question are introduced explicitly as exogenous variables of the model or if the total set of individuals to be analyzed is subdivided into more homogeneous categories within which estimation is carried out.

[†] Recently MANDELBROT [1962] showed that variations in the prices of cotton can be fitted remarkably closely to a distribution whose variance is not defined. He suggests that such distributions should be involved in the representation of many economic phenomena. His ideas were again developed in MANDELBROT [1963].

(ii) Departures from normality

Even if it has finite second-order moments, the statistical distribution of the errors may be far from normal. We have just seen that this is liable to happen for samples of individual data. It also arises in the analysis of time series. Thus, considering two regressions of household consumption and G.N.P. on the money supply in the U.S.A. from 1897 to 1958, ZECKHAUSER and THOMPSON [1970] estimate the exponent θ of the distribution of the errors ε_t, whose density is assumed proportional to

$$\exp\left\{-\left|\frac{\varepsilon}{\sigma}\right|^{\theta}\right\}. \tag{110}$$

They find values of the order of 0.5 and 0.7, clearly less than 2.

Whether it is a case of individual data or of time series, we may suspect the presence of *outlying observations*, that is, of a small proportion of observations affected by exceptional factors which lead to abnormally large absolute values of the errors. It has been suggested that such a situation can be represented by taking for the error distribution a mixture of two normal distributions with zero mean; the first would apply to the great majority of the observations while the second, applying to the relatively few outliers, would have a much higher variance. The tails of the global distribution would then be much heavier than the tail of a normal distribution with the same variance, and the classical coefficient β_2 would be clearly greater[†] than 3. Thus departures from normality of the type often suspected could be explained in this way.

For small samples, the distribution of the residuals is not generally normal when that of the errors is not. The classical tests and confidence regions do not then have the properties stated in the previous two chapters. What can we say about them?

To be thorough, we should examine both the significance level and the power of the classical tests, the results then being easily transposable to confidence regions. We should determine the true probabilities of first- and second-type errors for tests established as if the distribution of the errors were normal. In fact hardly any study has been made of the effect on the power of the tests. However, PEARSON[1931] has given an example which suggests that the analysis of variance and the F-test have reduced power when β_2 takes high values.

The significance level of the tests examined in chs. 6 and 7 is not very sensitive to deviations from normality, when the tests are applied to the comparison of *means of independent samples*. The F-test and the two-tailed t-test have a significance level near that given by the tables. The probability of type 1 errors in the one-tailed t-test however is affected by the asymmetry of the true distribution.

[†] It follows immediately that if the proportion of outliers is q and their variance is k times the variance of the other observations, then the coefficient β_2 of the global distribution is $3[1+q \times (k^2-1)]/[1+q(k-1)]^2$. If $q = 1/20$ and $k = 100$, then β_2 is greater than 40.

These now well-known conclusions were established by, for example, GAYEN [1950], GEARY [1947] and RATCLIFFE [1968]. But a cautious note is given by LEE and GURLAND [1977].

BOX and WATSON [1962] studied the robustness of tests on the *regression coefficients* with respect to normality of the errors. They showed that this robustness depends on the nature of the empirical distribution of the exogenous variables and that the usual tests do have the theoretical significance levels when the empirical distribution in question is approximately normal[†].

More generally they established that we can always apply t-tests and F-tests, with no great inaccuracy in their significance levels provided that we multiply their theoretical numbers of degrees of freedom by a factor δ depending on the fourth-order moments of the distribution of the errors and of that of the exogenous variables. For example, in the case of simple regression, the t-test on the regression coefficient should be applied with $\delta(T-2)$ degrees of freedom, δ being given by:

$$\frac{1}{\delta} = 1 + \frac{(\beta_2^\varepsilon - 3)(\beta_2^z - 3)}{2T} \tag{111}$$

(where β_2^ε and β_2^z denote the coefficients β_2 defined by (28) for the distribution of ε_t on the one hand, and for that of z_t on the other). So δ is approximately 0.9 when $T = 20$, β_2^ε and β_2^z both being equal to 5. The number of degrees of freedom is 16 rather than 18.

ATIQULLAH [1962, 1964] studied robustness, in relation to normality, of tests of *analysis of variance and covariance*. He showed that it is good not only when the empirical distribution of the exogenous variables is normal, but also when these exogenous variables are such that the number:

$$z_t' M_{zz}^{-1} z_t$$

is the same for all the observations. This last condition is practically never satisfied in regression problems; but it is often satisfied in the analysis of variance of classified observations when the orthogonality condition mentioned in ch. 7, § 7 is satisfied; this is particularly the case for the tests of comparison of means to which the above mentioned results of Gayen apply[††].

Since departures from normality can affect the significance levels of the usual

---

† MARDIA [1971] generalises these results to multivariate tests.
‡†† However we must point out that, even in this case, the precision of the test would be improved by the application of the Box and Watson correction to the number of degrees of freedom. This correction becomes:

$$\frac{1}{\delta} = 1 - \frac{1}{T}(\beta_2^\varepsilon - 3)$$

since β_2^z is then 1.

tests, the question that arises is *how can we test normality of the errors appearing in the regressions*?

If there is a very large number of observations we can justifiably consider the errors as virtually identical with the residuals and apply various tests devised for the case of a sample of directly observed individual values of the same random variable. For example, we may calculate the sample coefficient corresponding to β_2, that is, the ratio b_2 between the sample moment of order 4 and the square of the sample variance; the appropriate tables have been established by D'AGOSTINO and PEARSON [1973]. (For 50 observations, the value 4 defines the 5 % significance level against the alternatives $\beta_2 > 3$.) There are various other possible tests (see MORICE [1972], SHAPIRO, WILK and CHEN [1968], and D'AGOSTINO and ROSMAN [1974]).

In the case of small samples, these tests do not apply directly to our problem since the errors are not known exactly. However, they appear to be easily transposable, since the vector of residuals has a spherical normal distribution in a linear subspace when the errors are normal. So we need only define from the residuals and using a linear transformation, $T-m$ uncorrelated quantities with the same variance, then test the normality of the corresponding random variable as if we had obtained directly a sample of $T-m$ independent observations. THEIL [1971], § 5.2 gives a complete definition of a suitable linear transformation. We can also apply the recursive method suggested by HEDAYAT and ROBSON [1970] for tests of homoscedasticity and consider the $T-m$ quantities ε_n^*/c_n (the order in which the observations are considered can then be chosen arbitrarily).

Although the idea of such a transformation of the residuals may appear intuitively fruitful, there is no guarantee that it will lead to powerful tests of the normality of the errors. In particular, if they are not normal, the transformed residuals are not generally independent even if they are uncorrelated. According to the experiments carried out by HUANG and BOLCH [1974], tests which use the residuals directly are more efficient than tests based on transformed residuals.

(iii) Robust estimation methods

When normality cannot be assumed, the estimators of the coefficients are still efficient in the class of linear estimators, but not generally efficient in the class of all estimators. Now when there is considerable departure from normality, there generally exist non-linear estimators with smaller variances than those of least squares estimators. We shall consider some of these new estimators which can be described as 'robust' vis-à-vis the distribution of the errors.

It appears natural to apply the method of maximum likelihood to a model in which the distribution of the errors is less strictly specified than when normality is assumed. Thus, for example, ZECKHAUSER and THOMPSON [1970] assume that the density of the distribution of errors of a regression is proportional to (110) and they estimate its parameter θ.

We note that, with such a distribution, the maximum likelihood method consists of estimating the regression coefficients by minimising the sum of the absolute value of the deviations raised to the power θ. If $\theta < 2$, then less weight is given to extreme deviations from the regression lines than in the method of least squares. This kind of modification appears intuitively to conform to the idea that extreme deviations (relative to the standard deviation) occur more frequently than in the case of a normal distribution.

In fact, without referring to the maximum likelihood principle or to a precise form of distribution of the errors, it has often been suggested that, instead of the least squares principle, one should use *minimisation of the sum of the absolute values of the deviations*. (When applied to estimation of the mean of a sample of independent observations of a single variable, the effect of this method is to replace the arithmetic mean by the median.) This gives estimators which are more robust relative to large deviations from normality, but which are clearly less efficient in the case of normality. In addition, the computation is much heavier.

For the model $x_t = a'z_t + \varepsilon_t$, the required estimators are defined by the vector $\hat{a}$ which minimizes

$$\sum_{t=1}^{T} |x_t - a'z_t|.$$

Determining $\hat{a}$ is equivalent to solving a linear programme involving the auxiliary unknowns e_t and f_t:

Minimize with respect to a, e_t and f_t

$$\sum_{t=1}^{T} (e_t + f_t)$$

subject to the constraints

$$\begin{cases} e_t - f_t = x_t - a'z_t \\ e_t \geq 0; \; f_t \geq 0 \end{cases} \quad t = 1, 2, \ldots, T.$$

At the required minimum, the sum $e_t + f_t$ is equal to $|x_t - a'z_t|$ since e_t is zero when $x_t - a'z_t$ is negative, while f_t is zero when $x_t - a'z_t$ is positive (if this were not so for f_t, for example, $e_t + f_t$ could be reduced by reducing e_t and f_t by the same sufficiently small positive quantity; this change would satisfy the restrictions and thus contradict the attainment of the minimum).

For ease of computation, and to avoid resorting to the general algorithm of linear programming, SCHLOSSMACHER [1973] proposes an iterative method which consists of carrying out a weighted regression at each stage s ($s = 1$, $2, \ldots$), that is, of minimising

$$\sum_{t=1}^{T} w_t^{(s)} (x_t - a'z_t)^2 \qquad (112)$$

and then determining the vector $a^{(s)}$ by a linear formula, but taking as weight $w_t^{(s)}$ the inverse of the absolute value of the corresponding residual in the previous stage: $|x_t - a^{(s-1)\prime}z_t|$ (except when this residual is near zero, in which case $w_t^{(s)} = 0$). The limit of the $a^{(s)}$ minimises the sum of the absolute values of the deviations.

Some simulations on artificial samples using the Monte Carlo method show that the estimators obtained by minimising the sum of absolute values of deviations are more efficient than least squares estimators when the tails of the distribution of errors are clearly heavier than those of a normal distribution (as for the double exponential, Cauchy or Pareto distributions, or a mixture of normal distributions). See BLATTBERG and SARGENT [1971], FORSYTHE [1972], SMITH and HALL [1972], KIOUNTOUZIS [1973].

The asymptotic normality of the coefficients estimated by least absolute deviations has been proved by BASSETT and KOENKER [1978]. The asymptotic covariance matrix is equal, except for a multiplying factor, to that applying for least squares regression; unfortunately this factor depends on the true distribution of the errors and is not easy to estimate.

There are, of course, many other available methods for reducing the influence of extreme deviations besides replacing least squares by least absolute deviations. Thus HUBER [1973] investigates minimisation of the sum of a function of the deviations; he considers in particular the method in which this function coincides with the square for small deviations and with the absolute value for large deviations. Many methods of this type are compared by RAMSAY [1977]. The least squares regression may in particular be retained after elimination of extreme deviations, or after they have been artificially reduced.

The application of these ideas leads to three-stage procedures of the following type:

(i) Calculate a multiple regression by the usual methods and find the estimation residuals ε_t^* (we assume here that there is a single equation ($n=1$), that is, that ε_t^* is a number).

(ii) Examine the T residuals and pick out those whose absolute values are exceptionally large; then reject the corresponding observations or preferably correct them so as to reduce ε_t^* to a more normal value (for example, to the value of the nearest residual among those which do not seem exceptional).

(iii) Calculate a new regression on this 'corrected' sample and then possibly apply tests.

Such a procedure which accepts the existing practice of some empirical statisticians can be systematized if a fixed rule is given for the second stage. For example, this could be that 5 % of the observations will be subject to rejection or correction. Those observations for which $|\varepsilon_t^*|$ exceeds three times the mean of the $|\varepsilon_t^*|$ might possibly be rejected. Of course, the properties of the estimators or tests given by stage three depend to some extent on the rule adopted in stage two[†].

In order to determine how to choose the proportion of observations to be rejected, or the level from which observations are to be rejected or corrected, these methods have to be investigated with some degree of generality. Some mathematical statisticians have done this, but it would be too much of a digression to describe their work here. The reader may see, for example, LEONE and MOUSSA-HAMOUDA [1973] or PRESCOTT [1978]. We do not as yet have enough perspective of the results to dwell on their practical utility.

(iv) Robust tests

Robust methods are also being elaborated for testing hypotheses on the co-efficients of a multiple regression. The simplest idea on which such methods can be built consists of using the ranks of the residuals instead of their actual values and of transforming accordingly the classical tests derived from the normal theory presented in section 9 of ch. 6. A large class of such tests is considered in ADICHIE [1978]. We shall confine ourselves here to introduce one of them.

Suppose we wish to test that q coefficients of a regression are simultaneously equal to zero. Assume that the regression contains a constant term, which is not one of these q coefficients. The normal theory would lead us to use the critical region defined by (50′) in ch. 6, where one remembers that a^* refers only to the q regression coefficients to be tested and where a now is the corresponding null vector.

It may be shown that the right hand side of the inequality can be written as a quadratic form on the vector $\tilde{\varepsilon}$ of the residuals $\tilde{\varepsilon}_t$ from a regression of x_t on the remaining $m - q$ exogenous variables (those of the coefficients not to be tested). More precisely the critical region may be written as:

$$\frac{1}{\sigma^{*2}} \tilde{\varepsilon}' U (U'U)^{-1} U' \tilde{\varepsilon} > q F_{q, T-m}(\alpha)$$

where the $(T \times q)$ matrix U has for elements u_{jt}, for each exogenous variable z_j whose coefficient is being tested, the residual of z_{jt} from its regression on the $m - q$ remaining exogenous variables. The right hand side may be seen as a quadratic form on the vector of the scalar products $\tilde{\varepsilon}' u_j$, which should clearly be small if the tested coefficients are null. In this quadratic form σ^{*-2} takes account of the dispersion of the $\tilde{\varepsilon}_t$ and $(U'U)^{-1}$ of the dispersion of the u_{jt}.

The problem with nonnormal disturbances arises from the fact that, even when the hypothesis to be tested is true, a too high proportion of the $\tilde{\varepsilon}_t$ may be exceptionally large, leading to a too frequent rejection of the hypothesis. In order to avoid this difficulty, one may think of replacing the actual residuals $\tilde{\varepsilon}_t$

[†] A fully formalized method that should have performances similar to those of regressions after rejection of outliers has been defined by KOENKER and BASSETT [1978].

by quantities that will be similarly ordered but so defined as to never be exceptionally large. We may replace $\tilde{\varepsilon}_t$ by $\psi_t = r_t/(T+1)$, where r_t is the rank of $\tilde{\varepsilon}_t$ when the T residuals are ordered from the smallest (negative) one to the largest (positive) one. The scalar product $\psi' u_j$ may then play the same role as the scalar product $\tilde{\varepsilon}' u_j$ and, for large values of T, a critical region for the hypothesis is defined as:

$$12\psi' U(U'U)^{-1}U'\psi > \chi_q^2(\alpha)$$

The substitution of a χ^2 distribution to an F distribution is explained by the fact that only the asymptotic distribution of the test has been derived. The substitution of σ^{*-2} by 12 is easily understood, since for large T the variance of the ψ_t is $1/12$. (Since the u_{jt} are residuals from a regression with a constant term, $\psi' u_j$ is also equal to the scalar product in which ψ_t is replaced by the deviation from its mean $1/2$.)

Robust tests of this type are easy to apply, but do not seem to be currently used. Their small sample properties have been worked out only for very particular cases.

7 Incorrect specification of the relations

The specification of the model may be approximate or wrong not only because of the assumptions made about the distribution of the ε_t, but also because of the form assumed for the relations. Certain exogenous variables may be left out; the true relation may not be linear; the errors may behave in a way which is not simply additive. We shall examine briefly these three points.

However we note initially that some correlation between exogenous variables and random elements or an incorrect specification of the relations cause the most serious prediction errors. The econometrician must always bear this risk in mind, even if the fit has been good over the period of observation. He must also consider the possibility of structural changes. HOLTE [1962] gives a useful methodological discussion of this problem.

(i) Independence with respect to the exogenous variables

Throughout regression theory, an essential part is played by independence of the errors with respect to the exogenous variables. More precisely, we supposed that the exogenous variables were non-random and that the expectation of the errors was zero for any values of the exogenous variables; or again that the conditional expectation of the errors was zero for given values of the exogenous variables. In the case where this assumption was not satisfied, none of the results held. In particular, the estimates generally contained bias persisting even when the number of observations tended to infinity.

We have already made a lengthy examination of the role of this assumption in the description of the simple regression model (ch. 3) and in the discussion of ch. 4. We saw in particular some of the causes which can invalidate the assumption.

If we suspect that there is some association between the errors and the exogenous variables, we should analyze the reasons for it and look for a different model which takes closer account of the particular features of the phenomenon.

However, it is interesting to find that the properties studied previously are still approximately valid when the assumption in question is approximately satisfied. We confine ourselves here to some remarks about the bias of estimates in the simple regression model.

We assume that:

$$E(\varepsilon_t) = g(z_t),   \tag{113}$$

g being a function of z_t. The formulae defining the estimates a^* and b^* of the coefficients of the simple regression lead directly to:

$$E(a^* - a) = \sum_{t=1}^{T} \lambda_{tT} g(z_t), \qquad E(b^* - b) = \frac{1}{T} \sum_{t=1}^{T} g(z_t),   \tag{114}$$

where:

$$\lambda_{tT} = \frac{(z_t - \bar{z})}{\sum_{t=1}^{T} (z_t - \bar{z})^2}.$$

If, for example:

$$g(z_t) = \gamma_1(z_t - \bar{z}) + \gamma_0,   \tag{115}$$

then

$$E(a^* - a) = \gamma_1, \qquad E(b^* - b) = \gamma_0.   \tag{116}$$

The bias in the regression coefficient is equal to the gradient of $g(z_t)$; the bias in the constant term has the value of $g(\bar{z})$. They are small if γ_1 and γ_0 are small. Similarly, if:

$$|g(z_t)| \leqq \gamma_1 |z_t - \bar{z}| + \gamma_0,$$

$$|E(a^* - a)| \leqq \gamma_1 + \gamma_0 \mu, \qquad |E(b^* - b)| \leqq \gamma_1 \nu + \gamma_0,$$

where:

$$\mu = \frac{\sum |z_t - \bar{z}|}{\sum (z_t - \bar{z})^2} \quad \text{and} \quad \nu = \frac{1}{T} \sum |x_t - \bar{z}|.$$

Here again the upper bounds of the biases decrease as $g(z_t)$ approaches zero.

It is sometimes fruitful to examine the question in a slightly different way. Suppose that z_t can be considered as a random variable distributed independently of t, and that the random pair (z_t, ε_t) has mean $(\zeta, 0)$, variances (S^2, σ^2) and correlation coefficient ϱ. The theoretical linear regression of ε on

z, that is, the linear form $\varepsilon = \beta_1 z + \beta_0$ which minimizes

$$E(\varepsilon - \beta_1 z - \beta_0)^2, \tag{117}$$

is given by

$$\varepsilon = \varrho \frac{\sigma}{S}(z - \zeta); \tag{118}$$

(cf. ch. 3 § 8). The theoretical linear regression of x on z is then

$$x = \left(a + \varrho \frac{\sigma}{S}\right) z + \left(b - \varrho \frac{\sigma}{S}\zeta\right). \tag{119}$$

The least squares estimates a^* and b^* then tend to the coefficients

$$a + \varrho \frac{\sigma}{S} \quad \text{and} \quad b - \varrho \frac{\sigma}{S}\zeta,$$

when the number T of observations tends to infinity. So *the aymptotic bias is smaller the lower the correlation ϱ between the error and the exogenous variable, and the smaller the ratio σ/S between the variances of the error and the exogenous variable.*

This result was given the name 'proximity theorem' by H. Wold, and was generalized to multiple regressions by WOLD and FAXER [1957]. It shows that even a fairly high correlation coefficient between the error and the exogenous variable entails only a small bias if the variance of the error is small. This agrees with the preceding remarks since $E(\varepsilon_t/z_t)$ is generally low when $E(\varepsilon_t)$ is zero, and $E(\varepsilon^2)$ small.

As FISHER [1961a] has shown, the same properties of continuity apply to the methods proposed for more complex models than those examined until now (cf. for example ch. 9 and part 5 of this book). Low correlation between the errors and the exogenous variables causes only a small bias, whatever the cause of this correlation.

(ii) Omission of exogenous variables

Suppose that we have adopted the model

$$x_t = A z_t + \varepsilon_t, \tag{120}$$

containing the exogenous variables z_{jt} while the endogenous variables x_{it} are really determined by the relation

$$x_t = A z_t + B u_t + \varepsilon_t, \tag{121}$$

which contains also the exogenous variables u_{kt}. A least squares fitting has led to the following estimate of A:

$$A^* = M_{xz} M_{zz}^{-1}.$$

What are the properties of this estimate?

By using (121) to expand M_{xz}, we obtain directly:

$$A^* = A + BM_{uz}M_{zz}^{-1} + M_{\varepsilon z}M_{zz}^{-1}.$$

It follows that:

$$E(A^* - A) = BC^*, \quad \text{where} \quad C^* = M_{uz}M_{zz}^{-1}, \tag{122}$$

and

$$A^* - E(A^*) = M_{\varepsilon z}M_{zz}^{-1}, \tag{123}$$

expected values being taken for fixed values of the z_t *and the* u_t, as usual.

Let us first consider formula (122) which defines the bias of the estimate A^*. This bias is the product of two matrices, the matrix B of the true coefficients of the omitted variables, and the matrix C^* defined by the regression coefficients of the u_{kt} on the z_{jt}. The bias will therefore be zero in two cases: if $B = 0$, that is, if the adopted specification (120) is correct; if $C^* = 0$, that is, if $M_{uz} = 0$, in which case each of the variables u_k is orthogonal to each of the variables z_j:

$$\sum_{t=1}^{T} u_{kt}z_{jt} = 0, \quad \text{for any } k \text{ and } j.$$

In the second case we also say sometimes that there is zero correlation between the u_k and the z_j.

Thus we can obtain an unbiased estimate of the matrix A defining the effect of the exogenous variables z_j on the endogenous variables x_i if the omitted exogenous variables u_k are uncorrelated with the z_j. This result is virtually identical with the result obtained in ch. 1 § 8. Its scope is limited because there is often great interdependence among economic quantities. However we can find situations where it applies.

Thus the consumption of certain articles by childless working-class households depends both on household income and the ages of husband and wife. However, for estimating the coefficient of income elasticity, there is no point in introducing age as an explicit exogenous variable, since working-class income is known to be only slightly correlated with age.

On the other hand, it often happens that omission of an important exogenous variable entails serious errors. It leads us wrongfully to attribute to the variables which have been included some of the influence due to the omitted variable. It is one of the most frequent sources of error in econometric studies. As formula (122) shows, the bias may be considerable. So particular attention must always be paid to the risks of making such errors.

These risks are so real that it is advisable to take into account, even approximately, the influence of exogenous quantities which are liable to interfere with the phenomenon under study. If the quantities comprising the vector u_t of (121) are not directly observable, then 'proxy' variables defining a vector v_t correlated with u_t are used. WICKENS [1972] shows that, for estimation of A, it is always preferable to introduce v_t rather than purely and simply to omit u_t.

Formula (123) shows that the distribution of $A^* - E(A^*)$ for the given values of the z_t *and the* u_t is the same as if the selected specification were strictly correct. However, the covariance matrix $M_{\varepsilon\varepsilon}^*$ of the residuals about the fitted model (120) is not a good estimate of $\Omega = E(\varepsilon_t \varepsilon_t')$. We can easily calculate:

$$E(M_{\varepsilon\varepsilon}^*) = \frac{T - m}{T}\Omega + B(M_{uu} - M_{uz}M_{zz}^{-1}M_{zu})B',$$

the term in parentheses representing the empirical covariance matrix of the residuals in the regression of the u_{kt} on the z_{jt}.

Having reached this point, we may well ask what interest lies in the distribution of A^* (and that of $M_{\varepsilon\varepsilon}^*$) for given values of u_{kt}. Why should we be interested in this distribution[†] when we do not intend to take account of the values of the exogenous variables u_k either in investigation of the observed sample or in the applications to which the model gives rise?

In fact, since the u_k were not identified as participating in the explanation of the phenomenon under consideration, we could say that, as far as we are concerned, their influence is similar to that of the errors, and we could assume that $\eta_t = Bu_t + \varepsilon_t$ constitutes the true random error in the present situation. Given our state of ignorance, we could suppose further that η_t is uniformly distributed for all the observations and has expected value zero whatever the value of z_t. The initial specification would then again be admissible, with η_t in place of ε_t. The usual procedure would be adequate.

This point of view is completely justified if we postulate that the role of the exogenous variables u_k is not, and *cannot be* identified. The preceding discussion simply shows that much would be gained if this role were recognized.

More precisely, let us consider two cases:

(a) The u_{kt} and the z_{jt} are connected by a stable linear relation, for example:

$$u_t = Cz_t + \delta_t, \tag{124}$$

with a given matrix C and a term δ_t which has a stable distribution.

Then from (121):

$$x_t = (A + BC)z_t + (\varepsilon_t + B\delta_t). \tag{125}$$

Estimation based on the initial model (33) leads to a matrix A^* which is an unbiased estimate of the matrix $A + BC$. Similarly the covariance matrix $M_{\varepsilon\varepsilon}^*$ of the residuals is a good estimate of the covariance matrix of the errors $\varepsilon_t + B\delta_t$.

As long as (124) holds, estimation based on the model (120) and the applications for which it serves are justified by the relation (125). Of course the in-

---

[†] However, we note that the distribution for given values of the z_{jt} and the u_{kt} fits perfectly when the u_{kt} are exact functions of the z_{jt} (see, for example, the next section).

fluence of the u_k is attributed partly to the z_j but this causes no serious trouble. However, explicit introduction of the u_k would lead to a gain in precision since the errors affecting the relation (125) are greater than those affecting the relation (121) so long as ε_t and δ_t are independent, as can generally be assumed.

(b) There is no stable relation between the u_k and the z_j. We can still set $\zeta_t = u_t - C^*z_t$, where C^* is defined as in (122), and write:

$$x_t = (A + BC^*)z_t + (\varepsilon_t + B\zeta_t).$$

But here ζ_t must not be considered to have a stable distribution. In applications estimation based on the model (120) will lead to incorrect results whenever ζ_t is large, that is whenever the pair (u_t, z_t) takes a value which deviates from the empirical regression observed in the sample.

This discussion is reminiscent of that arising from the examination of the effect of multicollinearity among the exogenous variables (cf. ch. 6 § 6).

(iii)   Linearity of the relations

It often happens that the analytic nature of the relations among endogenous and exogenous variables is not known a priori, and that only the regard for simplicity makes a linear form preferable to every other equally possible expression. We must therefore examine the properties of a linear regression established between data which actually are governed by non-linear relations.

To avoid misunderstanding, we point out that the econometrician is not obliged to resort to linear models. The methods discussed in this book have a much wider field of application. In the first place, ch. 9 is devoted to certain procedures appropriate to non-linear models which will allow us to solve problems encountered in other chapters. In the second place, the regression methods studied up to this point apply as long as the relations are linear with respect to the parameters to be estimated; they adjust very well to relations which are non-linear with respect to the exogenous variables.

Thus the model

$$x_t = a \log z_t + b + \varepsilon_t$$

is equivalent to the simple linear regression model

$$x_t = a w_t + b + \varepsilon_t,$$

with the new exogenous variable $w_t = \log z_t$. Similarly let

$$x_t = P_{m-1}(z_t) + \varepsilon_t,$$

where P_{m-1} denotes some polynomial of degree $m-1$ in z_t. This is really a case of a multiple linear regression model which can be written:

$$x_t = a_1 w_{1t} + a_2 w_{2t} + \cdots + a_m w_{mt} + \varepsilon_t,$$

with the exogenous variables

$$w_{1t} = 1, \qquad w_{2t} = z_t, \qquad w_{3t} = (z_t)^2, \ldots, w_{mt} = (z_t)^{m-1}.$$

Thus, many other models are particular cases of the general model of ch. 6.

Let us revert to our present topic, and suppose that a linear regression has been carried out between two variables x and z, whereas the true relation is non-linear. To fix ideas, we select a quadratic model and write:

$$x_t = a_1(z_t - \bar{z}) + a_2(z_t - \bar{z})^2 + b + \varepsilon_t. \tag{126}$$

In other words, a_1, a_2 and b are the respective coefficients of the linear term, the quadratic term and the constant in a model involving the deviations of the z_t from the sample mean.

The problem appears as a particular case of that dealt with in the preceding section. For (126) can be considered as a linear model with the two exogenous variables $(z_t - \bar{z})$ and $(z_t - \bar{z})^2$; and the situation is the same as if the second exogenous variable $(z_t - \bar{z})^2$ had been omitted from the regression. The simple regression line has gradient a^* and ordinate $b^* = \bar{x}$ (for $z_t = \bar{z}$) which are unbiased estimates of a_1 and b if a_2 is actually zero. In the general case application of (122) leads to:

$$E(a^*) = a_1 + a_2 M_3/S^2,$$

$$E(b^*) = E(\bar{x}) = b + a_2 S^2,$$

where S^2 denotes the mean of the $(z_t - \bar{z})^2$ and M_3 the quantity

$$M_3 = \frac{1}{T} \sum_{t=1}^{T} (z_t - \bar{z})^3.$$

In particular, a^* is an unbiased estimate of a_1 if the z_t are symmetrically distributed about $\bar{z}$, in the sense that $M_3 = 0$.

Figure 3 illustrates these formulae. The points represent the observed sample, and the dotted line the linear regression. The gradient of this regression line is near that of the tangent to the curve

$$x = a_1(z - \bar{z}) + a_2(z - \bar{z})^2 + b,$$

at the mean point of the sample $z = \bar{z}$.

This figure also illustrates what we said about the omission of exogenous variables. Two cases must be distinguished in applications of regression. If the

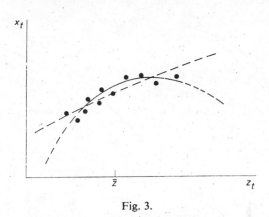

Fig. 3.

values of z under consideration are of a similar order of magnitude to the sample values, then no serious error will generally be made. If on the other hand the proposed values of z lie outside the range of the sample, there is danger of a serious mistake being made, since the linear regression is then a very bad approximation to the true relation between z and x. But, even in the first case, the eventual predictions will be less precise than they would have been if the quadratic term had not been ignored and if the model (126) had been estimated by multiple regression.

Linear relations generally suffice for the analysis of short time series. The range of variation of the variables is then too limited to allow significant deviations from linearity. Linear expressions correctly represent the relations studied within the range that the sample allows us to investigate. The addition of quadratic terms, or of terms of degree higher than two, would not generally improve our knowledge of the phenomena, since the estimated coefficients of such terms would not be significantly different from zero.

On the other hand, we must consider the possible appearance of non-linear relations whenever we are concerned with very large samples of micro-economic data. Thus in the analysis of family budgets we must generally bear in mind that the Engel curves are not linear.

It is therefore important to know how to *test the presence of deviations from linearity* for the relations under consideration. The alternative hypotheses would imply relations which would be non-linear but sufficiently regular for their oscillations to be distinguishable from the erratic movements of the ε_t. The tests which we shall describe briefly also apply more generally to detect the presence of deviations from any assumed relation whether linear, quadratic or of any other form. For ease of exposition we confine ourselves to the case where there is a single endogenous variable and a single exogenous variable. The reader may work out for himself the ways of dealing with more complex situations.

(a) As a first approach we test the linearity within a model where x_t appears

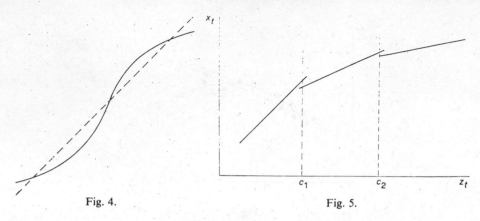

Fig. 4.   Fig. 5.

as a polynomial function of z_t. The test then aims at deciding whether the coefficients of the terms of degree more than one can be considered as zero. Thus in the context of the model (39), testing linearity is equivalent to testing the hypothesis that $a_2 = 0$. Similarly, with reference to the model

$$x_t = a_1 z_t + a_2 z_t^2 + a_3 z_t^3 + b + \varepsilon_t,$$

linearity is equivalent to the hypothesis that $a_2 = 0$ and $a_3 = 0$. The tests examined in chs. 6 and 7 apply directly to these hypotheses.

This procedure has two drawbacks. On the one hand, it may entail fairly heavy calculation. On the other hand, we must choose a priori the degree of the polynomial to be included in the model. If the degree chosen is too low, considerable deviations from linearity may not be revealed. Thus in the context of the quadratic model (126), linearity is not generally rejected if the true relation is of the form illustrated in fig. 4. In fact, however, most observed relations between economic quantities can be represented by curves which have uniform concavity throughout their length, so that a quadratic model is sufficient in most cases.

(b) A second approach consists of dividing the range of the z_t into several intervals, then splitting up the data into as many subsamples, each containing the observations for which z_t belongs to one of the intervals, then carrying out a linear estimation within each subsample, and finally testing the hypothesis that these various regressions constitute so many estimates of the same linear relation. This method is illustrated in fig. 5 where three subsamples have been introduced corresponding respectively to $z_t \leqslant c_1$; $c_1 < z_t \leqslant c_2$ and $z_t > c_2$. It leads to an analysis of covariance[†] for which calculations similar to those in table 7, ch. 7 are carried out.

[†] The test is simpler if, in each subsample, all the observations give the same value for z_t. But this case rarely arises in practice. However, when a test of linearity is proposed in many classical works, this is often the case considered.

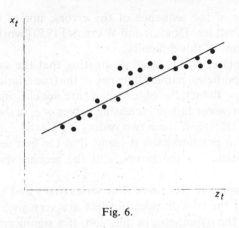

Fig. 6.

The result of this test clearly depends on the way in which the range of z is divided up. Deviations from linearity are not revealed if they are concentrated in a single interval. On the other hand too many intervals would have a bad effect on the efficiency of the test, since the regressions in the various subsamples could not be determined very precisely. It appears that in practice three or four subsamples should be enough and that division of the range of z should be the result of a compromise between the two frequently conflicting necessities of obtaining subsamples of similar size, and of choosing for z intervals of similar length.

(c) A third approach consists of examining the sequence of residuals with respect to an over-all linear regression, these residuals being arranged in the order of increasing values of the z_t. Apparently this procedure was first suggested by PRAIS and HOUTHAKKER [1955] (cf. ch. 5 § 2).

On a graph of z_t and x_t the observed points are randomly distributed on either side of the regression line if the true relation is linear. Otherwise they tend to be concentrated above the line for values of z_t belonging to some intervals, and below the line for values of z_t belonging to other intervals. In that case the sequence of the residuals does not have a purely random appearance. Positive residuals predominate in some parts, and negative residuals in others (cf. fig. 6).

We can therefore test linearity by testing if the sequence of the residuals is purely random. Description of the various possible tests would be premature at this point. They will be studied in detail in chs. 11 and 12, when we are discussing the hypothesis of independence of the successive terms of a time series. As a rule the procedure which will then be defined will also apply for tests of linearity such as we have just indicated.

However, we should point to three difficulties. In the first place, if the number of observations is fairly small, we must distinguish the residuals with respect to the regression from the errors on either side of the true relation, which is assumed to be linear by the hypothesis under test. What matters is the purely random character of the sequence of the errors, not of the sequence of the residuals. As we shall see, DURBIN and WATSON [1950] worked out a procedure which takes account of this difficulty.

In the second place, it may seem disquieting that the same formula applies for testing two hypotheses, namely linearity of the true relation and independence of successive errors. In fact, the observations are not classified in the same order in the two cases but according to increasing values of z_t in the first and increasing values of t in the second. If these two orders are clearly different, the two tests are also different in practice; then it seems that the first test is robust vis-à-vis some serial correlation of the errors, and the second vis-à-vis some lack of linearity.

But it often happens in the use of time series that t and z_t are strongly multi-collinear and that the two proposed orders are very similar. The test is then effective for both the hypotheses in question. If a significant value is found, we cannot tell which hypothesis to reject, unless one of them appears true a priori.

Finally, some of the tests devised to deal with independence of the successive terms of a time series are certainly not very efficient vis-à-vis deviations from linearity. These are those tests which can detect a clear association among two or three successive terms but not a weaker trend over a fairly large number of successive terms. The reader must bear this in mind when choosing from among the various tests of independence for a test of linearity.

For the purpose of detecting such a lack of linearity over a large range of values of the exogenous variable, HARVEY and COLLIER [1977] have devised a test based on the signs of the recursive residuals ε_n^* that were defined above in § 2 (iii) concerning tests of homoscedasticity. It is indeed easy to see that the recursive residuals tend to be systematically negative in the case of a concave curve, such as those of figs. 3, 5 and 6. For a powerful test against concavity or convexity of the relation, one need only consider the ratio being the average of these residuals and their empirical standard deviation.

(iv) Additivity of the errors

The model of linear regression

$$x_t = Az_t + \varepsilon_t$$

assumes that the errors ε_t have an additive effect on the values of the endogenous variables. This assumption is continued in the non-linear model discussed in the following chapter, namely:

$$x_t = g(z_t; \alpha) + \varepsilon_t, \tag{127}$$

where g is a function of the vector z_t of the exogenous variables and of a vector α representing certain unknown parameters. We must therefore pay some attention to this assumption of additivity.

In a certain sense the errors can be defined in such a way that they always occur additively. For let $g(z_t)$ be the conditional expected value of x_t for a given value of z_t, and ε_t the difference between x_t and its conditional expectation. We can always write

$$x_t = g(z_t) + \varepsilon_t,$$

where ε_t is an additive term with expected value zero.

Hence additivity is only restrictive in conjunction with the other assumptions of the model. We have already spoken of homoscedasticity, but have still to mention another assumption which is implicit in the definition of the model, namely *that no relation exists between the unknown parameters affecting the systematic effect $g(z_t)$ and the unknown parameters affecting the distribution of the random terms ε_t*. When the model is written in the form

$$x_t = Az_t + \varepsilon_t,$$

or in the form

$$x_t = g(z_t; \alpha) + \varepsilon_t,$$

it is implicitly assumed that the unknown characteristics of the distribution of the ε_t does not depend on the value of the matrix A or of the vector α.

For example, a priori study of the phenomenon under analysis may lead to the model:

$$x_t = g(z_t; \alpha)(1 + \eta_t), \tag{128}$$

where x_t is a real endogenous variable and η_t a random variable greater than -1, having zero mean and being distributed independently of both the value of the parameters α and of the exogenous variables z_t. (The η_t are then homoscedastic.) The conditional expectation of x_t is certainly $g(z_t; \alpha)$, but the difference ε_t between x_t and $g(z_t; \alpha)$ takes the form

$$\varepsilon_t = \eta_t \cdot g(z_t; \alpha).$$

The error ε_t is generally heteroscedastic. Its distribution may depend on α.

More precisely, suppose first that z_t denotes a unique real exogenous variable, that the systematic effect $g(z_t)$ is written simply az_t where a is unknown, and that the distribution of η_t has unknown standard deviation σ_η, and higher order moments which also are unknown. In this case $\varepsilon_t = az_t \cdot \eta_t$ presents a type of heteroscedasticity which has already been discussed. In addition, the standard deviation of ε_t can be written:

$$\sigma_t = |a| \sigma_\eta \cdot |z_t|.$$

The ratio $\sigma_t / |z_t|$ is a constant which can take any positive value a priori, whatever the value of a. Therefore there exists no necessary relationship between a and the σ_t, nor between a and the other moments of the ε_t.

Suppose now that

$$g(z_t) = az_t + b,$$

where a and b are two unknown coefficients. Then

$$\varepsilon_t = (az_t + b)\eta_t.$$

The standard deviation of ε_t is given by

$$\sigma_t = |az_t + b| \cdot \sigma_\eta.$$

The ratio

$$\sigma_t/|z_t + b/a|$$

is a constant which can take any value. But there now exists a necessary relationship between b/a and the σ_t, namely that b/a is just that number which ensures that

$$\sigma_t/|z_t + b/a|.$$

is constant.

In this case, the unknown characteristics of the distribution of the ε_t depend on the values of the coefficients a and b.

What are the consequences for the statistical methods described so far? The effects of heteroscedasticity have already been considered. We can easily discover the effects of a possible necessary relationship between the distribution of the errors and the value of the parameters of the systematic part. The existence of such an association constitutes a priori information which is ignored by the usual methods. Clearly it does not affect the distribution of the estimates, but only their efficiency.

These difficulties can often be eliminated by making an *appropriate change of variables*. Thus the model (128) can be written:

$$\ln x_t = \ln g(z_t; \alpha) + \ln(1 + \eta_t),$$

and $\ln x_t$ can be taken as endogenous variable just as well as x_t. Under the assumptions adopted\for η_t in the model (128), the random term $\ln(1+\eta_t)$ is now additive, its distribution is homoscedastic and independent of the values of the parameters α. In fact, if the expected value of η_t is zero, the expectation of $\ln(1+\eta_t)$ differs from zero. But it is a constant, so that we can take as random term the difference ε_t between $\ln(1+\eta_t)$ and its expected value. Such substitution raises no problem if, as is generally the case, the systematic term $\ln g(z_t; \alpha)$ contains an unknown additive constant.

For example, consider the fitting of Engel curves with constant elasticity on the basis of family budget data. If x_t denotes the consumption of goods of a certain category and z_t the income of a household t, we can often adopt a model of type (128) with:

$$g(z_t) = \lambda z_t^a,$$

where λ and a denote two constants to be determined. This is equivalent to a simple regression model between the logarithm of consumption and the logarithm of income, namely:

$$\ln x_t = a \ln z_t + b + \varepsilon_t.$$

On this topic the reader may consult in particular ROTTIER [1959].

8   The choice of model

It often happens that the econometrician has to choose among various models each of which appears plausible a priori. His choice will naturally tend to the model which best fits the available data. As can easily be imagined, this operation may be called for in widely different contexts and in most cases it raises questions of statistical methodology. Without attempting to cover even the most important cases, we shall briefly discuss some examples and take the opportunity to mention progressive or once and for all shifts of the model and also situations where there are switches back and forth between two regressions.

The expression 'choice of model' may give a wrong idea of the logic of the situation. As we saw in ch. 2, inference is necessarily carried out in the context of a given body of assumptions which, strictly speaking, constitute 'the model'. If a choice has to be made among several specifications, the latter must be regarded as so many particular cases of the initial model (see also ch. 4, § 8). However it may be helpful to talk of 'the choice among different models' when the specifications involved appear to be clearly distinct.

As we saw in ch. 7, § 6, we often have to consider carefully the list of exogenous variables to appear in the regression explai. .ng a given endogenous variable. For example, does z_1 alone or z_2 alone appear to influence x? Then one or other of the following two specifications is appropriate:

$$x_t = a_1 z_{1t} + b_1 + \varepsilon_t \tag{129}$$

$$x_t = a_2 z_{2t} + {}_2 + \varepsilon_t. \tag{130}$$

These two specifications are particular cases of the model in which the two causes act simultaneously:

$$x_T = a_1 z_{1t} + a_2 z_{2t} + b + \varepsilon_t. \tag{131}$$

This simple example is sufficient to exhibit the various inferential procedures of model discrimination:

(a) *Nested hypotheses*: Assuming that the model (131) is true, should we take $a_2 = 0$, that is, accept specification (129)? How must we estimate the model, that is, determine sometimes (a_1, a_2, b), sometimes (a_1, b_1)? This is the discrimination problem which was discussed mainly in ch. 7, § 3 and 6 in relation to tests, that is, for the first of the above two questions.

(b) *Alternative hypotheses*: Given that either (129) or (130) is true, which is appropriate? How to estimate sometimes (a_1, b_1), sometimes (a_2, b_2)? This second situation leads us much further away than the first from the logic of the general linear model which is the central topic of part II of this book. It arises when we have to choose between two often apparently rival theories rather than when we are looking for the simplest possible explanation.

(c) *Switching regression*: Following observations through time, sometimes (129), sometimes (130) applies without there being any knowledge a priori about which is appropriate for each observation[†]. So we must estimate each equation and determine how the observations are to be distributed between the two regimes. Situations where two or more regimes are assumed to exist are arising more and more frequently in econometrics. For example, consider a market where sometimes supply is rationed, and sometimes demand; the quantity exchanged x_t is determined by the demand law, for instance (129) in the first case and by the supply law (130) in the second. Or again, consider investment by a sample of firms, given that the way in which it is determined varies fundamentally according to the financial situation of the firm.

(d) *Structural changes*: Given the observations ordered as a time series, we want to identify the point at which a structural change occurs with (129) applying before it and (130) after it. The question may arise even if z_{2t} is the same variable as z_{1t}; the structural change then relates solely to the value of the coefficients in the two sub-periods.

Instead of undergoing an immediate change, the true structure of the model is often considered to evolve progressively and the following type of specification is chosen:

$$x_t = a_t z_t + b_t + \varepsilon_t$$
$$a_t = a_{t-1} + \alpha_t \qquad b_t = b_{t-1} + \beta_t \tag{132}$$

where the random terms α_t and β_t have characteristics which are more or less strictly specified.

It would be too much of a digression from the central theories on which this book is structured to discuss switching regressions, identification of structural changes or models with evolving coefficients. On switching regressions see QUANDT [1972] and FAIR and KELEJIAN [1974]. Models such as (132), whose

---

[†] If we know a priori which model applies for each observation t, then we are back in a simple situation, which is met by the simultaneous regression theory of section 5 albeit that we cannot treat the two regressions as mutually independent.

coefficients follow random processes, are discussed by DUNCAN and HORN [1972] and by COOLEY and PRESCOTT [1976].

(i) The preliminary test estimator

Before turning to the problem of choice between alternative hypotheses, we shall discuss a question relating to estimation in nested hypotheses models.

Consider the classical multiple regression model

$$x_t = a'z_t + \varepsilon_t \tag{133}$$

with the following additional constraint on the vector a of coefficients:

$$Ra = s \tag{134}$$

given that R, an $(r \times m)$ matrix, and s, an r-vector, are known (taking equations (131) and (129), $m=3$, $r=1$ and (134) reduces to $a_2 = 0$).

Without the constraint (134), the generalised least squares estimator is given by the multiple regression discussed in ch. 6:

$$a^* = M_{zz}^{-1} m_{zx}$$

Applying directly the principles of ch. 5, we see that, taking account of (134), the generalised least squares estimator is

$$\hat{a} = a^* - M_{zz}^{-1} R'(R M_{zz}^{-1} R')^{-1}(Ra^* - s), \tag{135}$$

This obviously approaches a^* as the difference between Ra^* and s decreases.

The problem is complicated when (134) is considered probable but not certain a priori. Here we are faced with a situation that does not belong to generalised least squares theory. It appears intuitively reasonable to estimate a by $\hat{a}$ if the hypothesis (134) is not rejected, but to choose a^* otherwise. This is done in practice (sometimes implicitly) in applied econometrics, and so the methodology should be discussed.

The estimator $\tilde{a}$, which by definition equals $\hat{a}$ in the first case and a^* in the second, is called the 'preliminary test estimator'. The classical theory given in ch. 7 prescribes the appropriate test: the hypothesis is to be rejected if

$$\frac{T(\hat{a} - a^*)' M_{zz}(\hat{a} - a^*)}{r \sigma_\varepsilon^{*2}} > \lambda \tag{136}$$

where the level λ is to be determined from an F-distribution with r and $T-m$ degrees of freedom.

What properties has this estimator $\tilde{a}$ when the ε_t are normal, homoscedastic and independent? They clearly depend on λ and on how far (134) differs from the real situation. The natural measure of this difference is the non-centrality parameter of the non-central F-distribution that applies to the left hand side of (136); this parameter is:

$$\theta = \frac{T(Ra - s)'(RM_{zz}^{-1}R')^{-1}(Ra - s)}{r\sigma^2}. \tag{137}$$

We already know that if (134) holds exactly, that is, if $\theta = 0$, then $\hat{a}$ is efficient[†] and therefore preferable to $\tilde{a}$ in so far as they differ from each other; the best value of λ is then obviously infinity. On the other hand, when θ is large, a^* is preferable to $\tilde{a}$; the best value of λ is zero. In fact $\lambda = 0$ is the best value when $\theta \geqq 1$, as is shown in a detailed study by SAWA and HIROMATSU [1973]. When θ is very large, there is a high probability that $\tilde{a}$ reduces to a^* and there is very little difference between the risks of $\tilde{a}$ and a^*.

But this is not in itself very enlightening, since obviously θ is unknown. Sawa and Hiromatsu suggest applying the principle of 'minimax regret' to choose the value of λ for the preliminary test[††]. This leads them to choose smaller values than those in the usual tests, for which the significance level is usually 5 %. Thus, where $r = 1$ the best value of λ is near 1.9 which corresponds to a 20 % significance level for the test if $T - m = 10$. In short, the unrestricted estimator a^* should be used more often than is usually done in practice.

The distribution of $\tilde{a}$ is obviously difficult to determine. The two references quoted indicate a method of calculating the covariance matrix of $\tilde{a}$. The current practice of estimating it by the covariance matrix of $\hat{a}$ when (134) is not rejected and by that of a^* when it is, obviously involves systematic underestimation.

(ii)   Principles of choice between alternative models

The choice between alternative models naturally raises the logical problems of inference reviewed in ch. 2. For a thorough grasp of the terms of this choice, we may usefully revert briefly to general principles starting from Bayesian logic as in ch. 2.

Let us consider two models involving respectively the vectors of unknown parameters ω_1 and ω_2 belonging to the sets Ω_1 and Ω_2. We can conveniently assume that the density of the vector x of the observations is $p_1(x/\omega_1)$ for the first model and $p_2(x/\omega_2)$ for the second. These elements define 'the general model' in which the space of the unknown parameters is the union $\Omega_1 \cup \Omega_2$.

In Bayesian logic we must take account of prior probabilities, the probabilities π_1 and π_2 associated respectively with the two component models ($\pi_1 + \pi_2 = 1$), and the density $p_i(\omega_i)$ of the conditional prior distribution of ω_i given that the ith model is true $(i = 1, 2)$. (Here again it is convenient to assume that

---

[†] The meaning of 'efficiency' has been discussed in chs. 5 and 6. We know from ch. 6, § 12 that $\tilde{a}$ is dominated by a James-Stein estimator a^s (see equations (102) and (103) of ch. 6, in which q must be replaced by r and u is the lefthand side of (136) above); but in practice this amounts to only a very small gain on the risk of the estimator unless the number r of restrictions is large. See JUDGE, BOCK and YANCEY [1974].

[††] An alternative solution is to choose a prior distribution for θ and then to choose λ so as to minimise the expected risk relative to this distribution. Unfortunately the result depends very much on the choice of prior distribution.

the prior distribution has a density.) Then the density of the posterior distribution on the parameter space is

$$Kp_i(x/\omega_i)p_i(\omega_i)\pi_i \qquad \omega_i \in \Omega_i \qquad i = 1, 2 \tag{138}$$

where K is the constant which makes the integral of (138) over $\Omega_1 \cup \Omega_2$ equal 1. The posterior probability Π_i associated with the ith model is then the integral of (138) over Ω_i. If he must choose between the two models, and if the loss from a mistaken choice is the same in both cases, a Bayesian statistician will choose that model with the greater posterior probability.

Aware of the arbitrary element in the choice of prior distribution, the econometrician will rarely be able to apply Bayesian principles as they stand. However he will give heed of the likelihood function defined on $\Omega_1 \cup \Omega_2$ given the observation x: this is the function $p_1(x/\omega_1)$ on Ω_1 and the function $p_2(x/\omega_2)$ on Ω_2.

He may naturally think of estimating the true model by applying the maximum likelihood principle, in which case he calculates the vectors $\hat\omega_i$ maximising $p_i(x, \omega_i)$ and chooses the first model if $p_1(x/\hat\omega_1) > p_2(x/\hat\omega_2)$.

He can also test each model by applying the likelihood ratio principle. If, for example, $p_1(x/\hat\omega_1) > p_2(x/\hat\omega_2)$, the maximum likelihood according to the general model is $p_1(x/\hat\omega_1)$, the likelihood ratio is 1 for model 1, which clearly is not rejected, and is $p_2(x/\hat\omega_2)/p_1(x/\hat\omega_1)$ for model 2, which will be rejected if this ratio lies below a certain level[†].

These principles can be applied in very varied situations, for example when we wish to find out if the errors occur additively or multiplicatively, that is, to choose between (127) and (128), or again if we have to choose between two types of error-distribution.

We should always inquire whether the appropriate model is in fact simply the union of two component models or if they are not rather particular prototypes within a continuous range of possible models. For example, if we say the choice lies between a normal and a double exponential distribution, this may be for simplicity whereas in the true model the density of the errors should be assumed proportional to (110) with a coefficient θ which is positive but may take any value a priori (and so can take values other than 1 and 2). Of course, if we have to take account of a continuous range of models we are back in a more classical situation. It may sometimes happen that the computation is simpler when such a range is considered than in the case of two separate families[††].

(iii) The choice between two regressions

In the important particular case where we have to choose between (129) and (130), the vector ω_i has three components a_i, b_i and σ_i (the standard deviation

---

† D. R. Cox has investigated the determination of approximate values for the level to be chosen. See PESARAN [1974] for an account of this work.
†† See the example given by LEECH [1975].

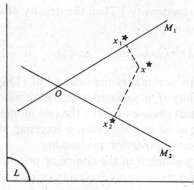

Fig. 7.

of ε_t in the ith model). The above principles can be applied fairly directly, as also in the rather more general case where we have to choose between two multiple regressions involving m_1 and m_2 exogenous variables respectively.

ZELLNER [1971] gives the Bayesian treatment of the corresponding situation for the case where the prior distributions $p_i(\omega_i)$ are 'conjugate distributions' of the type introduced in ch. 6 (see section 10.4). For example, when the prior distributions are diffuse, the ratio of the posterior probabilities is

$$\frac{\Pi_1}{\Pi_2} = \frac{\pi_1}{\pi_2}\left(\frac{S_2}{S_1}\right)^{T/2} \tag{139}$$

where S_i is the residual sum of squares of the ith regression. When the two models are equally probable a priori $(\pi_1 = \pi_2)$ or when one of the two sums S_1 and S_2 is clearly larger than the other, the number of observations being large, then by Bayesian principles *the regression giving the smallest residual sum of squares, that is, the greatest R^2 should be chosen*, at least when both mis-specification errors involve the same loss.

This is also the conclusion from the maximum likelihood principle. For we see that $p_i(x, \hat{\omega}_i)$ is proportional to S_i raised to the power $-T/2$.

To sum up, the method which defines each regression, namely minimisation of the sum of squares of residuals, is also the appropriate method for choosing between the two regressions. If the ith model is true, then on fig. 7 $E(x)$ belongs to the linear subspace M_i of T-dimensional space; L is the subspace spanned by M_1 and M_2 (in the particular case of (129) and (130), L is the range of $E(x)$ when the more general model (131) applies). If the ith model applies, the vector x_i corresponds to the least squares estimator of $E(x)$. Again the least squares method is to be recommended for estimating $E(x)$ when $E(x)$ is assumed to belong to the non-linear subset which is the union of M_1 and M_2.

This is an interesting conclusion, coming as it does when we are about to discuss in ch. 9 non-linear least squares regression in a general context.

Part 3

TWO IMPORTANT STOCHASTIC MODELS

CHAPTER 9

Non-linear models with additive errors

1 General remarks

The theory of linear estimation given in part 2 of this book was based on the following problem.

Problem P. The random vector x of N-dimensional space has a covariance matrix Q; its expected value y is contained in the linear subspace L. Given Q, L and an observation on x, to estimate y.

Many econometric models lead rather to the following problem.

Problem P'. The random vector x of N-dimensional space has covariance matrix Q; its expected value y is contained in the set Y. Given Q, Y and an observation on x, to estimate y.

P' generalizes P and differs from it only in the respect that the set to which y belongs is no longer necessarily a linear subspace. But P' does not lend itself to a general theory comparable to that given for P in ch. 5.

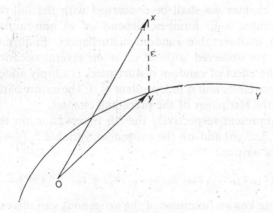

Fig. 1.

We shall, however, still define and extensively use a '*minimum distance estimator*'[†] by associating with x the vector $\hat{y}$ which minimizes $(x-y)'Q^{-1}(x-y)$

[†] The expression 'minimum distance estimator' was used by WOLFOWITZ [1954b] to denote quite a different category of estimators. But there is no risk of confusion arising from its use here.

considered as a function of y in Y. (If Q has no inverse, one must clearly work in the linear subspace which is the support of x.) This estimator exists since in practice Y is always a closed set. It is generally defined uniquely.

But no general theory of this method of estimation can be given, even for very limited classes of sets Y. The distribution of $\hat{y}$ depends both on the distribution of x and on the exact form of Y. There is no known optimal property valid for $\hat{y}$.

Only one result can be stated, and it is obvious; *if x is normally distributed, $\hat{y}$ is the maximum likelihood estimator.* But, in the first place, we are looking for a theory which does not depend entirely on normality of the errors, and in the second place, this result is of little consequence a priori since generally a maximum likelihood estimator has only asymptotic optimal properties and that within the context of very precise models, while the formulation presently given for P' makes it essentially a small sample problem.

In fact only asymptotic theory has been thoroughly investigated for models leading to the problem P' and not to the problem P. The estimate then involves a real parameter T, the number of observations on the endogenous economic variables of the model. The limiting properties of the minimum distance estimator $\hat{y}$ are determined under the assumption that T tends to infinity.

These asymptotic properties depend on the econometric model considered, for the role of T varies from one model to another, as does the correspondence between the problems P' relating to different values of T. This remark will appear more clearly after this chapter and the next, which lead to two clearly distinct asymptotic theories.

In the present chapter we shall be concerned with the following situation. Endogenous variables, n in number, depend on m non-random exogenous variables and on unobservable random disturbances. Endogenous and exogenous variables are observed without error on several occasions. Moreover we assume that the effect of random disturbances is simply added to the effect of the exogenous variables and is independent of it. The nature of this assumption was discussed in the last pages of the preceding chapter.

If x_{it} and z_{jt} represent respectively the tth observation on the endogenous variable x_i $(i=1,2,\ldots,n)$ and on the exogenous variable z_j $(j=1,2,\ldots,m)$, the model is generally written:

$$x_{it} = g_i(z_{1t}, z_{2t}, \ldots, z_{mt}; \alpha_1, \alpha_2, \ldots, \alpha_p) + \varepsilon_{it}, \qquad i = 1, 2, \ldots, n, \qquad (1)$$

where the g_i denote known functions of the exogenous variables and of the unknown parameters $\alpha_1, \alpha_2, \ldots, \alpha_p$; while the ε_{it} denote non-observable random terms independent of the z_{jt} and with zero expected values[†]. The problem then

---

[†] In this chapter we confine ourselves to the case where the z_j are truly exogenous. But the statistical methods studied could also be applied if some of the z_j represent lagged endogenous variables. The asymptotic properties certainly remain valid subject to some supplementary assumptions (see ch. 13).

consists of estimating the p parameters $\alpha_1, \alpha_2, \ldots, \alpha_p$ by means of T observations on the x_{it} and the z_{jt} $(t = 1, 2, \ldots, T)$.

The present situation generalizes the multiple regression model of ch. 6 in the respect that the effect of the exogenous variables is no longer represented by a linear term

$$a_{i1}z_{1t} + a_{i2}z_{2t} + \cdots + a_{im}z_{mt},$$

but by some function. This is indeed a case of a problem P' where $N = nT$ and y belongs to the set Y whose vectors have components that can be written:

$$y_{it} = g_i(z_{1t}, z_{2t}, \ldots, z_{mt}; \alpha_1, \alpha_2, \ldots, \alpha_p), \tag{2}$$

with appropriate values of the parameters $\alpha_1, \alpha_2, \ldots, \alpha_p$ and the observed values of the z_{jt}. (However, as we shall see later, the problem is usually rather more complex because the covariance matrix of the ε_{it} is not generally known a priori.)

A model of type (1) can be chosen when the dependence between exogenous and endogenous variables is expressed by a relation of known non-linear analytic form.

Suppose for example that the consumption of a given good by an individual depends both on his age and on the average income per head in the household to which he belongs. If x_t represents the consumption of the good in question by the household t, we may be led to set up the model:

$$x_t = (1 + ar_t) \sum_{k=1}^{m-1} b_k n_{kt} + \varepsilon_t, \tag{3}$$

where r_t is average income per head in the household, n_{kt} the number of its members who are in the age-group k, whereas a and the b_k are parameters to be estimated (b_k is the average consumption by an individual of age k in a household with zero income, and a measures the influence of household income). There are then one endogenous variable x_t, m exogenous variables r_t and the n_{kt}, and m parameters a and the b_k to be estimated.

A particularly important case arises when we adopt a linear model:

$$x_t = Az_t + \varepsilon_t, \tag{4}$$

similar to that discussed in ch. 6, x_t, z_t and ε_t then being vectors, but where A is not now allowed to be *any* matrix of order $n \times m$. This matrix depends on a number of parameters $p < nm$, or is restricted to satisfy certain constraints[†]. When we discuss econometric models with several equations we shall see that this case arises very often. The exogenous variables then do in fact occur linearly; but generally A is a non-linear function of the parameters $(\alpha_1, \alpha_2, \ldots, \alpha_p)$ of the problem.

† It may be noted that the above example (3) can be expressed in this form if the $2m-2$ new exogenous variables n_{kt} and $r_t n_{kt}$ are substituted for the m exogenous variables r_t, n_{kt}.

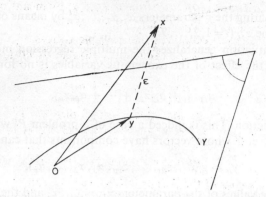

Fig. 2.

In this case the geometrical picture given by fig. 2 is often suggestive. The vector x of nT-dimensional space has expected value y belonging to a set Y, as in fig. 1. But in addition, Y is contained in the nm-dimensional linear subspace L spanned by the vectors u which satisfy $u_t = Az_t$ (for $t = 1, 2, \ldots, T$) where A is a suitable matrix of order $n \times m$, *not* restricted to satisfy the supplementary constraints which exist in the model. This is a different situation from that encountered in linear estimation since y is now to be estimated by a vector of Y and no longer by a vector of L.

In practical applications of non-linear regressions relating to model (1) above, we are often inclined to assume homoscedasticity and independence of the errors affecting different observations. But, no more than in applications of linear regressions, do we have a priori knowledge of the variances of the ε_{it} or the covariances between ε_{it} and ε_{kt}. (So the covariance matrix $\Omega = E(\varepsilon_t \varepsilon_t')$ is not known). This gives rise to a new difficulty.

When dealing with linear regression models in which assumption 1 of ch. 6 is satisfied, we saw that a priori knowledge of the covariance matrix Ω is not necessary for computing the estimators suggested by the study of the problem P. This advantage does not extend to non-linear regression models. In practice, having no knowledge of the matrix Q, we must replace the minimum distance estimator defined above by a similar estimator in which Q is replaced by a matrix calculated from the observed data. So we now find ourselves in a situation similar to that encountered in ch. 8, § 1 to 5.

To sum up, in the statistical theory with which this chapter is concerned, we have to take account of two new complications, which did not occur with multiple regressions: (i) the fact that the expected value of the vector of the endogenous variables is a non-linear function of the parameters to be estimated, (ii) the fact that, in computing the estimators of the α_k, the covariance matrix Ω must be replaced by an estimated matrix. These two complications will be dealt with simultaneously in the theoretical treatment to follow.

2   *Asymptotic theory of non-linear regression*

Let us consider model (1). To simplify notation, let α denote the vector whose components are the parameters $\alpha_1, \alpha_2, \ldots, \alpha_p$, and let α^0 be the vector of the true values of these parameters; let $g_{it}(\alpha)$ be the value of the function g_i for each possible α at the tth observation:

$$g_{it}(\alpha) = g_i(z_{1t}, \ldots, z_{mt}; \alpha_1, \ldots, \alpha_p) \quad \text{where} \quad \begin{matrix} i = 1, 2, \ldots, n \\ t = 1, 2, \ldots, T. \end{matrix} \quad (6)$$

The function g_{it} is known since g_i and the z_{jt} are known. Finally, let $g_t(\alpha)$ be the vector of the $g_{it}(\alpha)$. The model can be written in vector form:

$$x_t = g_t(\alpha) + \varepsilon_t \quad t = 1, 2, \ldots, T. \quad (7)$$

For a sufficiently general approach to minimum distance estimators, let us consider a positive definite matrix S_T that will define the distance used when dealing with the sample of size T. The matrix S_T may be random, that is, it may depend on the sample. Let $\hat{\alpha}(S_T)$, or simply $\hat{\alpha}$, denote the vector that minimizes

$$L_T(S_T, \alpha) = \sum_{t=1}^{T} [x_t - g_t(\alpha)]' S_T [x_t - g_t(\alpha)] \quad (8)$$

considered as a function of α.

(i)   Consistency of the estimators

We shall first discuss the conditions in which $\hat{\alpha}(S_T)$ tends in probability to α^0 as T tends to infinity, that is, *the conditions in which $\hat{\alpha}(S_T)$ is a consistent estimator of α*. This is not a straightforward problem, since the property in question depends in a complex way on the different elements of the model; the nature of the functions g_i, the characteristics of the sequences of the exogenous variables z_{jt}, the domain of definition of α, the distribution of the ε_t and finally, the properties of the sequence of matrices S_T. Here we shall only establish a result which is very direct but not very illuminating in itself. This result will be sufficient for the asymptotic theory of linear models subject to non-linear constraints. In econometrics, such models constitute the main field of application of non-linear regression. Some remarks will have bearing on another system of assumptions sufficient for consistency of $\hat{\alpha}(S_T)$.

For ease of notation, we first set

$$q_t(\alpha) = g_t(\alpha) - g_t(\alpha^0) \quad (9)$$

$$Q_T(\alpha) = \sum_{t=1}^{T} q_t'(\alpha) S_T q_t(\alpha) \quad (10)$$

$$\lambda_{tT}(\alpha) = \frac{q_t(\alpha)}{Q_T(\alpha)} \quad (11)$$

$$u_T(\alpha) = \sum_{t=1}^{T} \lambda_{tT}'(\alpha) S_T \varepsilon_t. \quad (12)$$

When $Q_T(\alpha) = 0$, $u_T(\alpha)$ is not defined by the above formulae. By convention, it is then taken to be zero.

We shall prove:

Lemma. If, for every closed set ω which does not contain α^0,

(i) $\mathrm{Prob} \left\{ \inf\limits_{\alpha \in \omega} Q_T(\alpha) = 0 \right\}$ tends to zero

(ii) $\mathrm{Prob} \left\{ \sup\limits_{\alpha \in \omega} u_T(\alpha) \geq \tfrac{1}{2} \right\}$ tends to zero

as T tends to infinity, then $\hat{\alpha}(S_T)$ is a consistent estimator of α^0.

For, the definitions of $\hat{\alpha}(S_T)$, $Q_T(\alpha)$ and $u_T(\alpha)$ imply

$$\sum_{t=1}^{T} \varepsilon_t' S_T \varepsilon_t \geq \sum_{t=1}^{T} [x_t - g_t(\hat{\alpha})]' S_T [x_t - g_t(\hat{\alpha})] = \sum_{t=1}^{T} \varepsilon_t' S_T \varepsilon_t + Q_T(\hat{\alpha}) [1 - 2u_T(\hat{\alpha})].$$

By comparing the left-hand side with the far right hand side, we find

$$Q_T(\hat{\alpha}) [2u_T(\hat{\alpha}) - 1] \geq 0. \tag{13}$$

Consequently either $Q_T(\hat{\alpha}) = 0$, or $u_1(\hat{\alpha}) \geq \tfrac{1}{2}$.

Let ω be any closed set which does not contain α^0. The event $\hat{\alpha} \in \omega$ implies either

$$\inf_{\alpha \in \omega} Q_T(\alpha) = 0, \qquad \text{or} \qquad \sup_{\alpha \in \omega} u_T(\alpha) \geq \tfrac{1}{2};$$

from which we have the following inequality:

$$\mathrm{Prob} \{\hat{\alpha} \in \omega\} \leq \mathrm{Prob} \{\inf_{\alpha \in \omega} Q_T(\alpha) = 0\} + \mathrm{Prob} \{\sup_{\alpha \in \omega} u_T(\alpha) \geq \tfrac{1}{2}\}. \tag{14}$$

This completes the proof of the lemma.

This lemma will be applied in section 5 to the case of linear models subject to constraints. It is also applicable to other general cases, but so to apply it would burden our discussion. The difficulty arises from the fact that conditions (i) and (ii) of the lemma involve limits in probability of upper and lower bounds of random functions, rather than the limits of these functions themselves. Here we need only discuss briefly a set of sufficient conditions given in MALINVAUD [1970].

These conditions relate to the different elements of the model. First we consider an assumption taken from linear regression theory which will be useful to us.

Assumption 1. The vectors ε_t of the errors are stochastically independent. They are identically distributed with zero mean and non-singular covariance matrix Ω.

Consider also the following conditions on S_T, on the functions g_i, on the domain of the vector α of the α_k, and on the exogenous variables z_{jt}.

(i) S_T tends in probability to a non-singular matrix S.

(ii) The functions g_i are continuous with respect to the set of their $m+p$ arguments, the z_{jt} and the α_k.

(iii) The vector α is known a priori to belong to a set Φ of p-dimensional space. Consequently α^0 belongs to Φ and $\hat{\alpha}(S_T)$ minimizes in Φ the function $L_T(S_T, \alpha)$. For the property of consistency with which we are concerned here it is sufficient that Φ is bounded, or more generally, that for all $G > 0$ the set of α's of Φ such that

$$\frac{1}{T} \sum_{t=1}^{T} [g_t(\alpha)]^2 \leq G$$

is bounded, and that this is so uniformly with respect to T, at least from some value T^0 of T. (In the case where Φ is not bounded this condition also involves the functions g_i and the exogenous variables z_{jt}.)

(iv) The conditions for the exogenous variables are fairly complex, but they spring from simple ideas. First, we assume that the vectors z_t belong to a bounded set Z of m-dimensional space. In the second place, we assume that their distribution in Z has a certain stability (see MALINVAUD [1970] for a precise formulation of this assumption), that is, that their values are distributed as if they were obtained by T independent selections from the same distribution μ. In the third place, we have to eliminate what corresponds to the multi-collinearity encountered in linear models, which prevents identification. So we assume that, for every pair of vectors α and β belonging to Φ, the set of vectors z of Z such that $g_i(z; \alpha) = g_i(z; \beta)$ for $i = 1, 2, \ldots, n$ has, according to μ, probability less than 1.

Under assumption 1 and conditions (i) to (iv), we can establish that $\hat{\alpha}(S_T')$ tends in probability to α^0.

(ii) Asymptotic normality of the estimators

Under certain regularity conditions we can characterize precisely the asymptotic distribution of $\hat{\alpha}(S_T)$ when it is consistent.

The derivatives of the $g_{it}(\alpha)$ are denoted by

$$u_{ikt}(\alpha) = \frac{\partial g_{it}(\alpha)}{\partial \alpha_k}. \tag{15}$$

By definition, the number z_{ikt} is $u_{ikt}(\alpha^0)$. The elements of the matrix Z_t of order $(n \times p)$ are the z_{ikt}. For every positive definite symmetric matrix S of order n, $M_T(S)$ represents the square matrix of order p:

$$M_T(S) = \frac{1}{T} \sum_{t=1}^{T} Z_t' S Z_t. \tag{16}$$

With this notation we adopt the following assumptions for the α_k and the g_{it}:

Assumption 2. In p-dimensional space, the domain of possible a priori values of α contains a neighborhood V^0 of the vector α^0 of the true values.

Assumption 3. In the neighborhood V^0 of α^0, the functions $g_{it}(\alpha)$ are uniformly bounded. Their derivatives of the first three orders are uniformly bounded. For any positive definite symmetric matrix S, the matrix $M_T(S)$ is regular and tends to a regular matrix $M(S)$ when T tends to infinity.

Since $M_T(S)$ must be regular, the system:

$$\sum_k d_k \frac{\partial g_{it}(\alpha^0)}{\partial \alpha_k} = 0 \qquad \text{for all } i \text{ and all } t$$

implies that all the numbers d_k are zero. At least for some observations, the functions g_{it} must not have zero derivatives at α^0 simultaneously with respect to all the α_k. This assumption implies also that the g_{it} cannot all be expressed in the neighborhood of α^0 as functions of a number of parameters that is less than p. It replaces the assumption of absence of multicollinearity, which is generally adopted for linear models. In the neighborhood of α^0, it implies the condition given at the end of (iv) in our discussion of consistency.

We shall now study the asymptotic behavior of the vector $\alpha_T(S_T)$ which minimizes $L_T(S_T, \alpha)$ for a matrix S_T which tends in probability to a regular matrix S.

We will show that this estimator is asymptotically equivalent to the pseudo-estimator constructed on the basis of the linear pseudo-model:

$$x_{it} - g_{it}(\alpha^0) = \sum_{k=1}^p z_{ikt}(\alpha_k - \alpha_k^0) + \varepsilon_{it}. \qquad (17)$$

In other words, we shall compare $\alpha_T(S_T)$ with the vector $\bar{\alpha}_T(S_T)$ which minimizes:

$$\frac{1}{T} \sum_{t=1}^T \{[x_t - g_t(\alpha^0)] - Z_t(\alpha - \alpha^0)\}' S_T \{[x_t - g_t(\alpha^0)] - Z_t(\alpha - \alpha^0)\}.$$

The vector $\bar{\alpha}_T(S_T)$ is not a true estimator since $g_{it}(\alpha^0)$ and $z_{ikt} = u_{ikt}(\alpha^0)$ are not known, so that $\bar{\alpha}_T(S_T)$ cannot be calculated from the observed data. But once the asymptotic equivalence of $\alpha_T(S_T)$ and $\bar{\alpha}_T(S_T)$ is established, we need only determine the asymptotic properties of the latter to know those of the former. Let us note incidentally that the pseudo-model (17) is virtually identical to the linear model discussed in ch. 8, § 5.

Figure 3 makes for intuitive understanding of the nature of the asymptotic equivalence between $\alpha_T(S_T)$ and $\bar{\alpha}_T(S_T)$. According to the model (21) the vector x

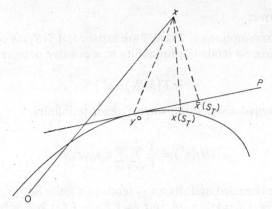

Fig. 3.

of the nT observations on the endogenous variables has expected value y which belongs to a p-dimensional variety Y. According to the pseudo-model (27), x has expected value y belonging to a p-dimensional hyperplane P. Moreover Y is very near P in the neighborhood of the true value y^0 of y. The projection $\bar{x}(S_T)$ of x on P is therefore near the projection $x(S_T)$ of x on Y, if the latter is near y^0. Now the distance between $x(S_T)$ and y^0 tends to zero when the number of observations tends to infinity. We must now make a more rigorous examination of these questions.

As the functions g_{it} are differentiable, $\alpha_T(S_T)$ must satisfy the following necessary conditions:

$$H_k(\alpha) = \frac{1}{T} \sum_{t=1}^{T} \sum_{i,h=1}^{n} [x_{it} - g_{it}(\alpha)] s_{ihT} u_{hkt}(\alpha) = 0 \qquad \text{for} \qquad k = 1, 2, \ldots, p. \qquad (18)$$

We shall examine the solutions of this system which tend to α^0 when T tends to infinity.

In the neighborhood of α^0, we shall use a limited expansion of the $H_k(\alpha)$, namely:

$$H_k(\alpha) = H_k(\alpha^0) + H_k^1(\alpha^0) \cdot (\alpha - \alpha^0) + \tfrac{1}{2}(\alpha - \alpha^0)' H_k^2(\alpha^1)(\alpha - \alpha^0) \qquad (19)$$

In this formula, α^1 is a value contained between α and α^0, and $H_k^1(\alpha)$ is the vector whose jth component is:

$$H_{kj}^1(\alpha) = \frac{\partial}{\partial \alpha_j} H_k(\alpha),$$

while $H_k^2(\alpha)$ is the matrix whose (j, l)th element is:

$$H_{kjl}^2(\alpha) = \frac{\partial^2}{\partial \alpha_j \partial \alpha_l} H_k(\alpha).$$

We can then prove:

Theorem 1.   If assumptions 1, 2 and 3 are satisfied, if $\hat{\alpha}(S_T)$ is consistent and if the random matrix S_T tends in probability to a positive definite matrix S, then

$$\sqrt{T}[\hat{\alpha}(S_T) - \alpha^0]$$

has a limiting normal distribution when T tends to infinity.
Let us consider

$$H_k(\alpha^0) = \frac{1}{T} \sum_{t=1}^{T} \sum_{ih} \varepsilon_{it} s_{ihT} z_{hkt}. \tag{20}$$

As the z_{hkt} are bounded and since s_{ihT} tends to a finite limit s_{ih}, the maximum of the $s_{ihT} z_{hkt}$ (for $i, h = 1, 2, \ldots, n$ and $t = 1, 2, \ldots, T$) is bounded by a number independent of T with a probability which tends to 1 when T tends to infinity. Therefore it follows from the central limit theorem that $T^\beta H_k(\alpha_0)$ tends in probability to zero for any $\beta < \frac{1}{2}$.

It can similarly be established that $H^1_{kj}(\alpha^0)$ tends in probability to the (k,j)th element of the matrix $-M(S)$ defined in assumption 5; and that there exists a bound which

$$|H^2_{kji}(\alpha^1)|$$

will exceed with a probability tending to zero. (The vector α^1 does in fact converge to α^0 since, by hypothesis, $\hat{\alpha}(S_T)$ does so).

Now let w'_{kT} denote the row vector

$$H^1_k(\alpha^0) + \tfrac{1}{2}[\alpha - \alpha^0]' H^2_k(\alpha^1).$$

It follows from the limits established above, and from the fact that $\hat{\alpha}$ tends to α^0 that this vector tends to the kth row of the matrix $-M(S)$. Consequently the matrix W_T formed from the p vectors w'_{kT} tends to $-M(S)$. In view of (19), system (18) can be written

$$H(\alpha^0) + W_T[\hat{\alpha} - \alpha^0] = 0 \tag{21}$$

where $H(\alpha^0)$ is the vector whose components are $H_k(\alpha^0)$.

The pseudo-estimator $\bar{\alpha}(S_T)$ defined above satisfies a similar system

$$H(\alpha^0) - M_T(S_T) \cdot [\bar{\alpha} - \alpha^0] = 0. \tag{22}$$

So the limiting distribution of $\sqrt{T}[\bar{\alpha} - \alpha^0]$ is the distribution of

$$[M_T(S_T)]^{-1} \cdot \sqrt{T} H(\alpha^0).$$

Now,

$$M_T(S_T) - M_T(S) = M_T(S_T - S)$$

tends in probability to zero since S_T tends to S and the elements of the matrices Z_t are bounded. It follows that $M_T(S_T)$ tends to the non-singular matrix $M(S)$ and $[M_T(S_T)]^{-1}$ to its inverse. The limiting distribution of

$$\sqrt{T}[\bar{\alpha}-\alpha^0]$$

is therefore that of

$$[M(S)]^{-1} \cdot \sqrt{T}H(\alpha^0),$$

that is, a normal distribution.

Moreover, (21) and (22) imply

$$[\hat{\alpha} - \alpha^0] = - W_T^{-1}M_T(S_T)[\bar{\alpha}-\alpha^0]$$

and so

$$\sqrt{T}[\hat{\alpha} - \bar{\alpha}] = [-W_T^{-1}M_T(S_T)-I][\sqrt{T}(\bar{\alpha}-\alpha^0)].$$

On the right hand side, the first term in square brackets tends to the zero matrix while the second has a limiting distribution. Consequently the whole expression tends to the zero vector.

Thus

$$\sqrt{T}[\hat{\alpha}-\alpha^0]$$

is asymptotically equivalent to

$$\sqrt{T}[\bar{\alpha}-\alpha^0]$$

and has the same limiting normal distribution. This completes the proof of theorem 1.

System (22) and equality (20) show immediately that the asymptotic covariance matrix of

$$\sqrt{T}[\hat{\alpha}-\alpha^0] \quad \text{or of} \quad \sqrt{T}[\bar{\alpha}-\alpha^0]$$

is

$$[M(S)]^{-1}M(S\Omega S)[M(S)]^{-1}. \tag{23}$$

This matrix is estimated consistently by a matrix whose expression is similar, M, S and Ω being replaced respectively by M_T, S_T and the covariance matrix of the residuals.

(iii) **Asymptotically efficient estimators**

It follows from the result just obtained that, *in the class of minimum distance estimators, those whose asymptotic efficiency is best are obtained with a matrix*

S_T *which tends in probability to* Ω^{-1}, subject to the natural reservation that theorem 1 applies. This could be established directly by studying the quadratic forms constructed from (23).

It is simpler to observe that $\bar{\alpha}(S_T)$ is an unbiased linear pseudo-estimator in the context of the linear pseudo-model (17) to which the Gauss–Markov theorem applies. When assumption 1 is satisfied by the ε_t, then in view of this theorem, $\bar{\alpha}(\Omega^{-1})$ has efficiency at least equal to that of every other $\bar{\alpha}(S_T)$. Consequently the estimator $\bar{\alpha}(\Omega^{-1})$ has asymptotic efficiency at least equal to that of every other $\hat{\alpha}(S_T)$. This property also applies if Ω^{-1} is replaced by a matrix which tends to it.

We also see that, *if* S_T *tends to* Ω^{-1}, *the asymptotic covariance matrix of* $\sqrt{T}[\hat{\alpha}-\alpha^0]$ *is the inverse of* $M(\Omega^{-1})$, since that is then the form taken by (23).

To determine in practice an estimator with this asymptotic efficiency, it is natural to proceed in the same way as for the linear model discussed in ch. 8, § 5. For example, one may consider the estimator $\hat{\hat{\alpha}}$ defined by the following three operations:

(i) Find $\tilde{\alpha} = \hat{\alpha}(S)$, taking for S any positive definite matrix, for example the unit matrix.

(ii) Find the estimation residuals

$$\tilde{\varepsilon}_{it} = x_{it} - g_{it}(\tilde{\alpha})$$

and their covariance matrix

$$\tilde{M}_{\varepsilon\varepsilon} = \frac{1}{T}\sum_{t=1}^{T}\tilde{\varepsilon}_t\tilde{\varepsilon}_t'.$$

(iii) Find the estimator

$$\hat{\hat{a}} = \hat{\alpha}(\tilde{M}_{\varepsilon\varepsilon}^{-1}).$$

We can establish

Theorem 2. Under assumptions 1, 2, 3 and the conditions required for convergence of $\hat{\hat{\alpha}}$ to α^0, the vector $\sqrt{T}(\hat{\hat{\alpha}}-\alpha^0)$ has a limiting centred normal distribution whose covariance matrix is the limit in probability of the inverse of $M_T(\tilde{M}_{\varepsilon\varepsilon}^{-1})$.

For the proof of this theorem we now need only to establish that $\tilde{M}_{\varepsilon\varepsilon}$ tends in probability to Ω. The vector $\tilde{\varepsilon}_t$ of the residuals can be written

$$\tilde{\varepsilon}_t = \varepsilon_t + [g_t(\alpha^0) - g_t(\tilde{\alpha})]$$

Now,

$$\frac{1}{T}\sum_{t=1}^{T}\varepsilon_t\varepsilon_t'$$

clearly tends to Ω. In view of proposition 14 in the appendix, the convergence of $\tilde{M}_{\varepsilon\varepsilon}$ to Ω will be proved if we establish that

$$\text{Max}_{t \leq T} \mid g_{it}(\alpha^0) - g_{it}(\tilde{\alpha}) \mid \xrightarrow{p} 0.$$

We can write

$$g_{it}(\alpha^0) - g_{it}(\tilde{\alpha}) = \sum_{k=1}^{p} (\alpha_k^0 - \tilde{\alpha}_k) u_{ikt}(\alpha^1),$$

where α^1 is a vector lying between α^0 and $\tilde{\alpha}$. Since the $\mid u_{ikt} \mid$ are bounded by a number $\bar{u}$ in a neighbourhood V^0 of α^0, we need only verify that

$$\bar{u} \sum_{k=1}^{p} \mid \alpha_k^0 - \tilde{\alpha}_k \mid \xrightarrow{p} 0,$$

which obviously follows from the convergence of $\tilde{\alpha}$ to α^0.

The estimator $\hat{\alpha}$ is clearly not the only conceivable estimator which is asymptotically efficient in the class of minimum distance estimators. We shall define another in the context of the linear model with constraints which will be discussed in section 5. For the present general model, we may think of improving the estimate of Ω by finding the estimation residuals $\hat{\hat{\varepsilon}}_{it} = x_{it} - g_{it}(\hat{\alpha})$ and their covariance matrix $\hat{M}_{\varepsilon\varepsilon}$. This naturally leads to the estimator $\hat{\alpha}(\hat{M}_{\varepsilon\varepsilon}^{-1})$.

More generally, we might consider an iterative procedure involving calculation of a sequence of estimators $\alpha^{(1)} = \tilde{\alpha}$, $\alpha^{(2)} = \hat{\alpha}$, $\alpha^{(3)}$, ..., $\alpha^{(s)}$ and a sequence of matrices $M_{\varepsilon\varepsilon}^{(1)} = \tilde{M}_{\varepsilon\varepsilon}$, $M_{\varepsilon\varepsilon}^{(2)}$, ..., $M_{\varepsilon\varepsilon}^{(s)}$ defined by the following two conditions:

(i)
$$\hat{\alpha}^{(s)} = \hat{\alpha}\{[M_{\varepsilon\varepsilon}^{(s-1)}]^{-1}\}.$$

(ii) $M_{\varepsilon\varepsilon}^{(s)}$ is the covariance matrix of the residuals obtained when $\alpha^{(s)}$ is taken as estimate of α.

The process is stopped when $\alpha^{(s)}$ no longer differ appreciably from $\alpha^{(s-1)}$.

The theory we have discussed gives no reason for preferring to $\hat{\alpha}$ those estimators involving a larger number of iterations, since they are all asymptotically equivalent. Intuition suggests that these more elaborate methods might be advantageous for small samples. But as yet evidence is lacking for a firm recommendation.

3 Normal errors and maximum likelihood estimators

In its treatment of asymptotic properties, the above theory does not involve the assumption that the errors ε_t are normally distributed. This theory may be said to be 'non-parametric', according to an expression which is sometimes used.

Granted the importance usually attributed to the assumption of normality in the definition of econometric methods, it is still interesting to see how the minimum distance estimators just discussed compare, in the case of normality, with the maximum likelihood estimators. We shall see that the latter belong to the class defined by the former, so that non-linear regression theory provides the asymptotic justification for the most commonly used estimators, and does this without using normality of the errors[†].

If the T vectors ε_t satisfy assumption 1 and are normally distributed, their probability density is

$$(2\pi)^{-nT/2} \mid \Omega \mid^{-T/2} \exp\left\{-\tfrac{1}{2} \sum_{t=1}^{T} \varepsilon_t' \Omega^{-1} \varepsilon_t\right\}.$$

Let $\mathscr{L}$ denote the probability density of the sample, that is, of the T vectors x_t. Since the Jacobian of the transformation of the ε_t into the x_t is 1, we can write

$$\log \mathscr{L} = C - \frac{T}{2} \log \mid \Omega \mid - \tfrac{1}{2} \sum_{t=1}^{T} [x_t - g_t(\alpha)]' \Omega^{-1} [x_t - g_t(\alpha)] \qquad (24)$$

where C is the constant

$$-\frac{nT}{2} \log 2\pi.$$

If Ω is known, at least apart from a multiplicative constant, then the vector α^* which maximizes the likelihood function, $\mathscr{L}$ considered as a function of α, is just $\hat{\alpha}(\Omega^{-1})$. This is also the minimum distance estimator proposed above. In particular, *when there is a single endogenous variable* ($n = 1$), *the maximum likelihood estimator coincides with the least squares estimator.*

Let us also consider the case where Ω *is subject to no a priori restriction except that it is a positive definite matrix.* This is the most frequent case in practice. However when non-linear regression theory is applied to systems with simultaneous equations, we encounter cases where there are restrictions on Ω (see, for example, ch. 18, § 4).

The maximum likelihood estimators α^* and Ω^* maximize $\mathscr{L}$ considered as a function of α and Ω. In particular, α^* maximizes $\mathscr{L}$ considered as a function of α where $\Omega = \Omega^*$. The form of (24) shows that α^* coincides with $\hat{\alpha}[(\Omega^*)^{-1}]$; so it belongs to the class of minimum distance estimators.

To be more precise, we must consider simultaneous determination of α^* and Ω^*. For convenience, we introduce the matrix

---

[†] Contrary to general belief, the asymptotic theory of maximum likelihood estimators is not sufficiently general, in its present state, to cover the model in which we are now interested. So a theory such as that of section 2 is necessary even if normality of the ε_t is assumed.

$$M = \frac{1}{T} \sum_{t=1}^{t} [x_t - g_t(\alpha)] [x_t - g_t(\alpha)]' \qquad (25)$$

which is a function of α. We can then write

$$\log \mathfrak{L} = C - \frac{T}{2} \mathfrak{M} \qquad (26)$$

where

$$\mathfrak{M} = \log |\Omega| + \text{tr}(\Omega^{-1}M). \qquad (27)$$

Maximization of $\mathfrak{L}$ is replaced by minimization of $\mathfrak{M}$ considered as a function of α and Ω.

We shall first minimize $\mathfrak{M}$ with respect to Ω for a fixed value of α, that is, for a fixed value of M. In the set of positive definite matrices (an open set of $(n(n+1)/2)$-dimensional Euclidean space), $\mathfrak{M}$ is everywhere differentiable. We shall see that its derivatives are simultaneously zero for one and only one value of Ω. Moreover, $\mathfrak{M}$ tends to infinity when Ω tends to the limits of its domain of definition. (To see this, we need only look at the behaviour of $\mathfrak{M}$ when (i) $\Omega = k\Omega^0$, where k tends to infinity and the non-singular matrix Ω^0 remains fixed, (ii) $\Omega = \Omega^0 + kI$, where k tends to zero and the singular matrix Ω^0 remains fixed). Thus $\mathfrak{M}$ is minimized with respect to Ω when its derivatives with respect to Ω are simultaneously zero. (For, let $\mathfrak{M}^0$ be the value which $\mathfrak{M}$ then takes. The set of the Ω for which $\mathfrak{M} \leq \mathfrak{M}^0 + h$, where h is a positive number, is compact and contains a matrix minimizing $\mathfrak{M}$. The latter cannot be on the boundary of the set; consequently it equates to zero all the derivatives of $\mathfrak{M}$.)

If we now refer to the rules for differentiating matrix expressions, we see that $d \log |\Omega| = \text{tr}(\Omega^{-1} d\Omega)$. Let Ω^{ih} be the cofactor of ω_{ih} in $|\Omega|$ and ω^{ih} the (i,h)th element in Ω^{-1}. By differentiating $|\Omega|$ we obtain

$$d|\Omega| = \sum_{ih} \Omega^{ih} d\omega_{ih};$$

and so

$$d \log |\Omega| = \sum_{ih} \omega^{ih} d\omega_{ih} = \text{tr}(\Omega^{-1} d\Omega).$$

Consequently the differential of $\mathfrak{M}$ is

$$d\mathfrak{M} = \text{tr}[\Omega^{-1} d\Omega(I - \Omega^{-1}M)] + \text{tr}(\Omega^{-1} dM). \qquad (28)$$

For all the derivatives with respect to Ω to be zero, it is necessary and sufficient that the first trace is zero for any $d\Omega$; therefore that $I - \Omega^{-1}M = 0$, that is, $\Omega = M$. In short, the matrix Ω^* coincides with the covariance matrix of the residual vectors $\varepsilon_t^* = x_t - g_t(\alpha^*)$, since the latter is the value of M when $\alpha = \alpha^*$.

The pair of estimators α^*, Ω^* has therefore the same property of reciprocity as the pair of estimators $\alpha^{(\infty)}$, $M_{\varepsilon\varepsilon}^{(\infty)}$ obtained as limits in the iterative procedure defined at the end of the previous section; in the first place, α^* coincides with $\hat{\alpha}[(\Omega^*)^{-1}]$, and in the second place, Ω^* is the covariance matrix of the residuals when α^* is taken to estimate α.

We can expect that a unique pair (α,Ω) has this property of reciprocity. We can also expect that the iterative procedure of section 2 converges. Under these favorable conditions, this appears a convenient procedure for finding the maximum likelihood estimators[†]. PHILLIPS [1976] proves that, given a sufficiently large number T of observations, the method of section 2 almost certainly converges to α^*, Ω^*.

If we find that several pairs (α,Ω) have the property of reciprocity, for example if the limit of the iterative procedure depends on the initial value of S, then we must find that pair which truly minimizes $\mathfrak{M}$. Since $\Omega = M$ in all cases, the pair (α^*, Ω^*) is identified by the fact that the determinant $|\Omega^*|$ is smallest (see formula (27) above). We can also say that *the maximum likelihood estimator* α^* *minimizes* $|M|$ *considered as a function of* α.

In any case, α^* is asymptotically equivalent to any minimum distance estimator for which S_T is defined so that it tends in probability to Ω^{-1}. This suggests that, *in the case where the* ε_t *are normal, such an estimator is asymptotically efficient not only in the class of minimum distance estimators but also in that of all consistent regular estimators.*

To verify this, we need only compare the asymptotic covariance matrix, $[M(\Omega^{-1})]^{-1}$ in the present case, with that obtained by inverting Fisher's 'information matrix'. The latter is defined as the negative of the expected value of the matrix of second derivatives of the log-likelihood, these derivatives being taken with respect to each of the unknown parameters[††].

To find the information matrix, the most convenient method is to consider the expected value of the second differential of $\mathfrak{M}$. From (28) we can easily deduce

$$d^2\mathfrak{M} = \operatorname{tr}\left[(\Omega^{-1}\,d\Omega)^2(2\Omega^{-1}M-I)\right] - 2\operatorname{tr}\left[\Omega^{-1}\,d\Omega\Omega^{-1}\,dM\right] + \operatorname{tr}(\Omega^{-1}\,d^2M).$$

Similarly, from (25) we can deduce expressions for dM and d^2M which we can write in the form:

$$dM = -\frac{1}{T}\sum_{k=1}^{p}\sum_{t=1}^{T}(\varepsilon_t u'_{kt} + u_{kt}\varepsilon'_t)\,d\alpha_k$$

$$d^2M = \frac{1}{T}\sum_{j,k=1}^{p}\sum_{t=1}^{T}\left\{2u_{jt}u'_{kt} + \varepsilon_t\left[\frac{\partial^2 g_t}{\partial\alpha_j\partial\alpha_k}\right]' + \left[\frac{\partial^2 g_t}{\partial\alpha_j\partial\alpha_k}\right]\varepsilon'_t\right\}d\alpha_j\,d\alpha_k.$$

[†] OBERHOFER and KMENTA [1974] make a general study of the mathematical properties of these methods.
[††] These are classical questions. See, for example, CRAMER [1946], § 32.7.

So it appears that the expected value of dM is zero and that

$$E\, d^2 M = \frac{2}{T} \sum_{j,\,k=1}^{p} \sum_{t=1}^{T} u_{jt} u'_{kt}\, d\alpha_j\, d\alpha_k;$$

hence

$$E \operatorname{tr} (\Omega^{-1}\, d^2 M) = 2 \sum_{j,\,k=1}^{p} [M_T(\Omega^{-1})]_{jk}\, d\alpha_j\, d\alpha_k.$$

Substituting in the expression for $d^2 \mathfrak{M}$, and in view of (26), we finally obtain

$$E\, d^2 \log \mathfrak{L} = -\frac{T}{2} \operatorname{tr} (\Omega^{-1}\, d\Omega)^2 - T\, d\alpha' M_T(\Omega^{-1})\, d\alpha. \tag{29}$$

This formula shows that the information matrix consists of two non-zero blocks relating to two groups of indices, one of which corresponds to the ω_{ih}, the other to the α_k. So its inverse consists of the two inverse blocks placed diagonally. In particular, the lower bound for the covariance matrices of an unbiased regular estimator of the vector α is $[T \cdot M_T(\Omega^{-1})]^{-1}$, which establishes the stated results.

4   Computation of a non-linear regression[†]

Non-linear regression involves much more complex calculations than linear regression. Although the subject of this book is the statistical theory of econometric methods rather than their application, we must devote a section to a general discussion of the different ways of minimizing $L_T(S,\alpha)$ with respect to α. Three preliminary remarks must be made.

First of all, the most convenient method for finding $\hat\alpha$ may depend on the particular model fitted to the data. In some particular case, it may be clumsy to apply general procedures. Thus, for the example of section 6, we shall give a method of solution which uses the fact that $g_t(\alpha)$ in this case is bilinear with respect to two groups of components of α. Similarly, when dealing with simultaneous equation models, we shall encounter methods adapted to them (cf. ch. 18, § 6).

In the second place, only experience can tell us which methods are most convenient and dependable in practice. A theoretical discussion can only reveal certain general properties of the techniques concerned. In many fields of applied statistics, there is growing application of non-linear regression; but as yet, there is no systematic assessment of the experience gained as to the performance of the different methods. Nor does our discussion here aim to draw any conclusions.

[†] On this question the reader may find CHAMBERS [1973] useful.

In the third place, the fact that the function $L_t(S, \alpha)$ to be minimized arises from a regression problem is perhaps not very important. If this is so, we can make more general reference to the literature on numerical techniques of minimization or maximization. Thus two of the three methods which we shall give are applicable to any problem concerning optimization of a function.

For simplicity, our formulae will refer to the one-dimensional case ($n = 1$), which does not seem unduly restrictive. It will also be useful to have a particular example in mind. So we shall choose the model

$$x_t = \alpha_1 - \alpha_2 \, e^{-\alpha_3 z_t} + \varepsilon_t \tag{30}$$

which represents the relation between an exogenous variable z_t and an endogenous variable x_t, the parameters to be estimated being α_1, α_2 and α_3. (Such a relation is sometimes suggested for phenomena in which the influence of z_t on x_t has decreasing marginal importance as z_t increases.) A regression on this model assumes minimization of

$$L(\alpha) = \sum_{t=1}^{T} \left[x_t - \alpha_1 + \alpha_2 \, e^{-\alpha_3 z_t} \right]^2 \tag{31}$$

which is a function of the three variables α_1, α_2 and α_3.

Each of the following three general methods contains a sequence of iterations ($s = 1, 2, \ldots$), the value α^{s+1} of α being obtained at the sth iteration on the basis of calculations using the value α^s determined at the previous iteration[†]. The method of selection of the initial value α^1 has no bearing on the definition of the methods.

(i) According to the *method of steepest descent* (a gradient method[††]) the vector α^s is revised progressively in the direction in which $L(\alpha)$ decreases most rapidly. If, as before, $H_k(\alpha)$ denotes the partial derivative of $-(2T)^{-1}L(\alpha)$ with respect to α_k, the revision formula is

$$\alpha_k^{s+1} = \alpha_k^s + \lambda^s H_k(\alpha^s) \qquad k = 1, 2, \ldots, p \tag{32}$$

the positive numbers λ^s being chosen a priori in some suitable way.

The justification of this method lies in the fact that, if the revisions are made in an indefinitely prolonged series of infinitesimal stages, then $L(\alpha^s)$ decreases

---

[†] In certain cases these iterative methods may be less economical than the method of systematic investigation of the domain of variation of certain parameters. Thus, for model (30), we can determine by simple regression the values $\alpha_1^*(\alpha_3)$ and $\alpha_2^*(\alpha_3)$ which correspond to each of the values assumed for α_3. The latter can be chosen a priori by some exploratory process. The values $L(\alpha_3)$ of the minimum of (31) are then calculated, the value finally chosen for α_3 being that which gives the smallest value for $L(\alpha_3)$. See WILDE [1968] for a systematic treatment of these methods.

[††] The expression 'gradient methods' is sometimes used for the class of iterative methods discussed here, in which the derivatives of the function to be minimized are calculated.

continuously with s and tends to a value for which all the derivatives of $L(\alpha)$ are zero[†].

(ii) According to what is sometimes called the *Gauss–Newton* method, the non-linear function $g_t(\alpha)$ is replaced at each stage by the linear approximation

$$g_t(\alpha^s) + \sum_{k=1}^{p} (\alpha_k - \alpha_k^s) u_{kt}(\alpha^s) \tag{33}$$

where, as before, $u_{kt}(\alpha)$ denotes the partial derivative of $g_t(\alpha)$ with respect to α_k. Minimization of $L(\alpha)$ is then replaced by minimization of

$$L^s(\alpha) = \sum_{t=1}^{T} \left[x_t - g_t(\alpha^s) - \sum_{k=1}^{p} (\alpha_k - \alpha_k^s) u_{kt}(\alpha^s) \right]^2 \tag{34}$$

The function $L^s(\alpha)$ is quadratic and positive definite.

Its minimum is found by equating to zero its p partial derivatives. So α^{s+1} is the solution of the linear system

$$\frac{\partial}{\partial \alpha_k} L^s(\alpha^{s+1}) = 0 \qquad k = 1, 2, \ldots, p. \tag{35}$$

(iii) According to *Newton's method*, which applies generally to the solution of systems of equations, the first order conditions for a minimum, $H_k(\alpha) = 0$ for $k = 1, 2, \ldots, p$, are replaced by linear equations which are equivalent to them in the neighborhood of α^s:

$$H_k(\alpha^s) + \sum_{h=1}^{p} (\alpha_h - \alpha_h^s) \frac{\partial}{\partial \alpha_h} H_k(\alpha^s) = 0 \qquad k = 1, 2, \ldots, p. \tag{36}$$

Equivalently, we can say that this method solves the system of first order conditions for a minimum of a quadratic function which approaches $L(\alpha)$ in the neighborhood of α^s; for,

$$\frac{\partial}{\partial \alpha_h} H_k(\alpha)$$

is the second derivative of $-(2T)^{-1}L(\alpha)$ with respect to α_h and α_k.

The relationship of these three methods are more clearly illustrated by fig. 4, which has been drawn for a hypothetical case in which there are only two parameters to be estimated ($p = 2$). In the (α_1, α_2) plane, the point A^s represents

[†] More precisely, this property is true for the continuous process in which the vector function $\alpha(s)$ of s is the solution of

$$\frac{d\alpha_k(s)}{ds} = H_k[\alpha(s)] \qquad k = 1, 2, \ldots, p.$$

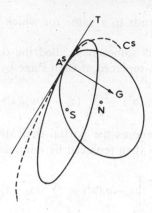

Fig. 4

the value at stage s. The curve C^s represents the contour at level $L(\alpha)$, that is, the curve on which lie the points for which $L(\alpha) = L(\alpha^s)$. The vector A^sG represents the direction of change required by the method of steepest descent (its direction is opposite to the direction of the gradient of $L(\alpha)$). The ellipse centred on N represents the contour of the function $L^s(\alpha)$ used in the Gauss–Newton method (we see immediately that $L^s(\alpha)$ and $L(\alpha)$ have the same gradient at the point A^s). The point N represents the vector α^{s+1} chosen for the next iteration by the Gauss–Newton method. Finally, the ellipse centred on S represents the contour of the quadratic approximation of $L(\alpha)$ in the neighborhood of A^s. It has the same curvature as C^s. The point S represents the vector α^{s+1} chosen by Newton's method.

Examination of these methods gives rise to several important remarks.

In the first place, none of the three necessarily yields a vector α^{s+1} giving a value smaller than $L(\alpha^s)$ for $L(\alpha)$. For example, if on fig. 4 the curve C^s coincides with the ellipse centred on S, the Gauss–Newton method gives a point N for which $L(\alpha)$ is greater than $L(\alpha^s)$. The method of steepest descent has the same effect if the length of the step defined by (32) is the length of the vector A^sG. Newton's method can also 'overshoot the mark' if $L(\alpha)$ is not a quadratic function[†]. So in each application, not only α^{s+1} but also $L(\alpha^{s+1})$ must be calculated, and it must be verified to be smaller than $L(\alpha^s)$.

It has been suggested that, at each stage, α^{s+1} should be corrected as follows (see, for example, HARTLEY [1961]). The value of $L(\alpha)$ is found not only for

---

[†] In theory it is also possible that the centre of the contour of the quadratic approximation of $L(\alpha)$ lies on the wrong side of the support plane of C^s, that is, on the side corresponding to increasing and not to decreasing $L(\alpha)$. However, such a possibility must be rare because, as we shall see later, the Newton and Gauss–Newton methods must give quite similar results in most cases. Now, with the Gauss–Newton method, the scalar product of $(\alpha^{s+1}-\alpha^s)$ and $H(\alpha^s)$ is always positive, as can be seen from system (37), where the matrix of the coefficients of the $(\alpha_h - \alpha_h^s)$ is clearly positive definite.

the vector α^{s+1} resulting from direct application of (32), (35) or (36), but also for some other vectors of the line joining α^s to α^{s+1}. Then for the $(s+1)$th stage, we choose that vector giving the smallest value for $L(\alpha)$. (In the method of steepest descent, this is equivalent to taking an appropriate value for λ_s at each stage). This suggestion must be followed if, before correction, $L(\alpha^{s+1})$ is greater than $L(\alpha^s)$. Should it be systematically incorporated in the programme? The answer may depend on the particular situation.

In the second place, when we remember that the steps are not infinitely small, we see that the direction of $\alpha^{s+1} - \alpha^s$ which results from strict application of the method of steepest descent may be very different from the direction of most rapid decrease of $L(\alpha)$. For example, on fig. 4, the direction A^sS would be greatly preferable to the direction A^sG. This situation occurs near the minimum when the contour surfaces are greatly extended in some directions rather than others. This frequently happens with economic data, since multicollinearity implies very elongated contour surfaces†. In fact experience in other fields has shown that usually the method of steepest descent gives satisfactory results during the first iterations, but becomes very mediocre in the end stages, that is, when $L(\alpha)$ is near its minimum.

To avoid this difficulty, it has been suggested that the direction used for going from α^s to α^{s+1} should not be that of the gradient of $L(\alpha)$, but another direction. But this complicates the calculations and destroys the simplicity of the method of steepest descent. In fact the algorithm is then often similar in nature to the algorithm of Newton's method. For example, GOLDFELD, QUANDT and TROTTER [1966] define α^{s+1} as the vector which, in a spherical region surrounding α^s, minimizes a quadratic function which is equivalent to $L(\alpha)$ in the neighborhood of α^s. (See also MARQUARDT [1963], and EISENPRESS and GREENSTADT [1966].)

In the third place, the difference between the Gauss–Newton and Newton's method is small if a good fit is obtained, but it may be considerable in econometrics where this rarely happens. Compare (35) and (36). In view of (34) defining $L^s(\alpha)$, system (35) can be written:

$$\sum_{h=1}^{p} \left[\frac{1}{T} \sum_{t=1}^{T} u_{ht}(\alpha^s) u_{kt}(\alpha^s) \right] (\alpha_h - \alpha_h^s) = \frac{1}{T} \sum_{t=1}^{T} [x_t - g_t(\alpha^s)] u_{kt}(\alpha^s) \qquad (37)$$

for $k = 1, 2, \ldots, p$. The right hand side coincides with $H_k(\alpha^s)$. The coefficient of $(\alpha_h - \alpha_h^s)$ in the left hand side differs from that in (36):

$$-\frac{\partial}{\partial \alpha_h} H_k(\alpha^s) = \frac{1}{T} \sum_{t=1}^{T} u_{ht}(\alpha^s) u_{kt}(\alpha^s) - \frac{1}{T} \sum_{t=1}^{T} [x_t - g_t(\alpha^s)] \frac{\partial^2 g_t(\alpha^s)}{\partial \alpha_h \partial \alpha_k}. \qquad (38)$$

---

† This feature raises difficulties in the numerical application of Newton and Gauss-Newton methods. An interesting adaptation of these methods is proposed by SMITH and SHANNO [1971].

But the difference stems only from the last term in the right hand side of (38); this term is small if x_t is near $g_t(\alpha^s)$, which happens if the fit is very good, and if α^s is near the required vector. On the other hand, when $x_t - g_t(\alpha^s)$ remains large, correction must often seem appropriate.

In the fourth place, when any one of these methods has converged to what is held to be a sufficient degree, we are not sure a priori that the true minimum has been reached. We can be, if $L(\alpha)$ is a convex function[†], a property which applies when the $g_t(\alpha)$ are linear in α but which has little chance of appearing in other cases[††]. So we may have reached only a local minimum. The only protection against this possibility is preliminary 'sounding' of the domain of α, that is, to calculate the values of $L(\alpha)$ for a certain number of vectors chosen in the different regions of the domain, and to verify that none of these values is smaller than, or even near to the value obtained.

In view of the above remarks, it seems that, for a given number of iterations, the three methods can be ranked according to performance in the order in which they were given. But the same order holds if they are ranked according to the extent of the computation necessary for each iteration. So it is conceivable that we might prefer to carry out a larger number of iterations with fewer quantities to be calculated at each iteration.

For example, consider what has to be found for estimation of the model (30), for which

$$g_t(\alpha) = \alpha_1 - \alpha_2 \, e^{-\alpha_3 z_t}$$

$$\begin{cases} u_{1t}(\alpha) = \dfrac{\partial g_t(\alpha)}{\partial \alpha_1} = 1 \\[2mm] u_{2t}(\alpha) = \dfrac{\partial g_t(\alpha)}{\partial \alpha_2} = -e^{-\alpha_3 z_t} \\[2mm] u_{3t}(\alpha) = \dfrac{\partial g_t(\alpha)}{\partial \alpha_3} = \alpha_2 z_t \, e^{-\alpha_3 z_t}. \end{cases} \qquad (39)$$

[†] The function $L(\alpha)$ is said to be convex if, given any vectors α^1 and α^2 and any number λ lying between 0 and 1,

$$L[\lambda \alpha^1 + (1-\lambda)\alpha^2] \leq \lambda L(\alpha^1) + (1-\lambda)L(\alpha^2).$$

If all the derivatives of the convex function $L(\alpha)$ are zero for a vector α^*, then α^* minimizes $L(\alpha)$. In other words, the convex function $L(\alpha)$ cannot have a local minimum which is not also an absolute minimum.
[††] The reader can verify that $L(\alpha)$ is convex if all the x_t are positive and if $g_t(\alpha)$ and $g_t^2(\alpha)$ are convex. But this situation rarely arises in practice.

The $H_k(\alpha)$ are then given by

$$
\begin{cases}
H_1(\alpha) = \dfrac{1}{T} \displaystyle\sum_{t=1}^{T} x_t - \alpha_1 + \dfrac{\alpha_2}{T} \displaystyle\sum_{t=1}^{T} e^{-\alpha_3 z_t} \\[2ex]
H_2(\alpha) = \dfrac{-1}{T} \displaystyle\sum_{t=1}^{T} x_t e^{-\alpha_3 z_t} + \dfrac{\alpha_1}{T} \displaystyle\sum_{t=1}^{T} e^{-\alpha_3 z_t} - \dfrac{\alpha_2}{T} \displaystyle\sum_{t=1}^{T} e^{-2\alpha_3 x_t} \\[2ex]
H_3(\alpha) = \dfrac{\alpha_2}{T} \displaystyle\sum_{t=1}^{T} x_t z_t\, e^{-\alpha_3 z_t} - \dfrac{\alpha_1 \alpha_2}{T} \displaystyle\sum_{t=1}^{T} z_t\, e^{-\alpha_2 z_t} + \dfrac{\alpha_2^2}{T} \displaystyle\sum_{t=1}^{T} z_t\, e^{-2\alpha_3 z_t}.
\end{cases}
\tag{40}
$$

These three quantities must be calculated at each iteration of the method of steepest descent. They are also necessary for the Gauss–Newton method, which, in addition, entails finding the matrix on the left hand side of (37):

$$
\begin{bmatrix}
1 & -\dfrac{1}{T}\displaystyle\sum_t e^{-\alpha_3 z_t} & \dfrac{\alpha_2}{T}\displaystyle\sum_t z_t\, e^{-\alpha_3 z_t} \\[2ex]
-\dfrac{1}{T}\displaystyle\sum_t e^{-\alpha_3 z_t} & \dfrac{1}{T}\displaystyle\sum_t e^{-2\alpha_3 z_t} & -\dfrac{\alpha_2}{T}\displaystyle\sum_t z_t\, e^{-2\alpha_3 z_t} \\[2ex]
\dfrac{\alpha_2}{T}\displaystyle\sum_t z_t\, e^{-\alpha_3 z_t} & -\dfrac{\alpha_2}{T}\displaystyle\sum_t z_t\, e^{-2\alpha_3 z_t} & \dfrac{\alpha_2^2}{T}\displaystyle\sum_t z_t^2\, e^{-2\alpha_3 z_t}
\end{bmatrix}
\tag{41}
$$

Finally, Newton's method involves finding a matrix which is the sum of (41) and

$$
\begin{bmatrix}
0 & 0 & 0 \\
0 & 0 & C_1 \\
0 & C_1 & C_2
\end{bmatrix}
\tag{42}
$$

where C_1 and C_2 are defined by

$$
C_1 = \dfrac{-1}{T}\sum_t x_t z_t\, e^{-\alpha_3 z_t} + \dfrac{\alpha_1}{T}\sum_t z_t\, e^{-\alpha_3 z_t} - \dfrac{\alpha_2}{T}\sum_t z_t\, e^{-2\alpha_3 z_t}
\tag{43}
$$

$$
C_2 = \dfrac{\alpha_2}{T}\sum_t x_t z_t^2\, e^{-\alpha_3 z_t} - \dfrac{\alpha_1 \alpha_2}{T}\sum_t z_t^2\, e^{-\alpha_3 z_t} + \dfrac{\alpha_2^2}{T}\sum_t z_t^2\, e^{-2\alpha_3 z_t}.
\tag{44}
$$

The heaviest part of the computation probably is caused by the different quantities expressed as sums with respect to t. We can verify that in this case the method of steepest descent involves 7 of these, the Gauss–Newton method 8 and Newton's method 10. In this case at least, the work involved in an iteration does not vary greatly from one method to another. The third seems clearly preferable because it probably involves fewer iterations for the same degree of precision.

5   Linear models with analytic constraints

Let us now consider the model

$$x_t = Az_t + \varepsilon_t$$

already introduced at the beginning of the chapter. Here A is no longer any $n \times m$ matrix as in the linear estimation model. It must belong to a subset F of nm-dimensional space. In most cases F is given by the condition that A depends only on p unknown real parameters $\alpha_k (k = 1, 2, \ldots, p)$, where p is clearly smaller than nm. We can also let α denote the vector of the α_k, and write the model in the form

$$x_t = A(\alpha)z_t + \varepsilon_t, \tag{45}$$

from which it is clear that the elements of $A(\alpha)$ are the nm known functions

$$a_{ij}(\alpha_1, \alpha_2, \ldots, \alpha_p) \qquad i = 1, 2, \ldots, n; \qquad j = 1, 2, \ldots, m.$$

The set F can then be deduced from the set Φ, the domain of α. We can write: $F = A(\Phi)$.

It may also happen sometimes that F is defined by the condition that A is restricted to satisfy certain explicit constraints. Thus, the elements a_{ij} may be related by the algebraic equations

$$\phi_h(a_{11}, a_{12}, \ldots, a_{ij}, \ldots, a_{nm}) = 0, \tag{46}$$

where the ϕ_h are q known functions $(h = 1, 2, \ldots, q)$. Obviously we can revert to (45) by solving these equations, that is, by determining the a_{ij} as explicit functions of $p = nm - q$ parameters. (These parameters can obviously be p particular elements of A). In practice, it is often simpler to estimate directly the values of the a_{ij} with the constraints (46), than to find a parametric representation and estimate the values of the parameters.

For our theoretical study, we shall first consider a model of the form (45). Then we shall consider the case where F is defined by explicit constraints of the type (46).

We shall need the following assumptions:

Assumption 4.   The sequence of the vectors z_t of the exogenous variables is bounded $(j = 1, 2, \ldots, m; t = 1, 2, \ldots)$. The matrix

$$M_{zz} = \frac{1}{T} \sum_{t=1}^{T} z_t z_t'$$

is non-singular; it tends to a non-singular limit $\overline{M}$ as T tends to infinity.

Assumption 5.   The mapping of F into Φ defined by the inverse of $A(\alpha)$ is one-to-one and continuous in the neighborhood of the true value $A^0 = A(\alpha^0)$. In other words, every sequence of vectors α^T of Φ such that $A(\alpha^T)$ tends to A^0 converges to α^0 (for $T = 1, 2, \ldots$).

In particular, assumption 5 implies that α^0 is identified as the unique solution of the equation $A(\alpha) = A^0$.

We can easily find examples where this assumption does not hold. For example, where $p = m = n = 1$, the functions $a(\alpha) = \alpha^2 - \alpha$ and $a(\alpha) = \alpha e^{-\alpha}$ do not satisfy it for $\alpha^0 = 0$, the former because $\alpha = 1$ gives $a(1) = 0 = a(\alpha^0)$, and the latter because $a(\alpha^T)$ tends to $a(\alpha^0) = 0$ as α^T tends to infinity.

Assumption 6.   The set Φ of the possible values of α contains a neighborhood V^0 of α^0 in which the functions $a_{ij}(\alpha_1, \alpha_2, \ldots, \alpha_p)$ have bounded derivatives up to the third order. The vector α^0 is not a singular point of $A(\alpha)$.

A vector α^1 is said to be a singular point of the matrix function $A(\alpha)$ if there exist p numbers λ_k, not all zero, such that

$$\sum_{k=1}^{p} \lambda_k \frac{\partial a_{ij}}{\partial \alpha_k}(\alpha^1) = 0 \qquad \text{for all} \qquad \begin{cases} i = 1, 2, \ldots, n \\ j = 1, 2, \ldots, m. \end{cases} \tag{47}$$

Since (45) is a particular case of the model (1) which we have been discussing up till now, the asymptotic theory of minimum distance estimators follows from the theory in section 2. We shall consider successively consistency, asymptotic normality and asymptotic efficiency.

(i)   Consistency of the estimators

The determination of the estimator $\hat{\alpha}(S_T)$ may in principle be split into two stages:

(a) Find the matrix $\hat{A}$ of F which minimizes

$$L_T(A, S_T) = \sum_{t=1}^{T} (x_t - Az_t)' S_T(x_t - Az_t): \tag{48}$$

(b) Find the vector $\hat{\alpha}$ of Φ such that $A(\hat{\alpha}) = \hat{A}$.

Similarly, the proof of consistency of the estimators can be taken in two stages, the first concerning the convergence of $\hat{A}$ to A^0, and the second the convergence of $\hat{\alpha}$ to α^0. This leads to the following theorem:

Theorem 3.   If assumptions 1 and 4 are satisfied and if S_T tends in probability to a non-singular matrix S, then the matrix $\hat{A}$ minimizing (48) in F is a consistent estimator of A^0. If, in addition, assumption 5 is satisfied, the corresponding vector $\hat{\alpha}(S_T)$ tends in probability to the true value α^0.

The second statement in this theorem follows directly from the first, and from the continuity of the inverse function of $A(\alpha)$.

To prove the first statement, we shall apply the lemma of section 2, but now we shall consider the unknown parameter to be A (in F) rather than α, and the estimator to be $\hat{A}$ rather than $\hat{\alpha}(S_T)$. So we replace equalities (9) to (12) by

$$Q_T(A) = T \, \text{tr} \left[M_{zz}(A - A^0)' S_T (A - A^0) \right] \tag{49}$$

$$\lambda_{tT}(A) = \frac{(A - A^0)z_t}{Q_T(A)} \tag{50}$$

$$u_T(A) = \sum_{t=1}^{T} \lambda'_{tT}(A) S_T \varepsilon_t. \tag{51}$$

If we consider $A - A^0$ as an nm-vector, then $(1/T)Q_T(A)$ appears as a quadratic form of this vector, the matrix of the coefficients being the Kronecker product $M_{zz} \otimes S_T$. If $d(A)$ denotes the usual Euclidean length of $A - A^0$,

$$d^2(A) = \sum_{ij} (a_{ij} - a_{ij}^0)^2, \tag{52}$$

then we know that[†]

$$\frac{1}{T} Q_T(A) \geq v_T d^2(A) \tag{53}$$

where v_T is the smallest characteristic root of $M_{zz} \otimes S_T$. The root v_T is positive except when S_T is singular (in which case $v_T = 0$).

In any closed set ω of F which does not contain A^0, $d^2(A)$ is bounded below by a positive number. The probability that inf $Q_T(A)$ is zero is at most equal to the probability that S_T is singular. This latter probability tends to zero in view of the fact that S_T tends to the non-singular matrix S. So condition (i) of the lemma is satisfied.

In view of the definition of $u_T(A)$ we can write

[†] For, suppose we have two symmetric matrices R and U, the latter being positive definite. The ratio $x'Rx/x'Ux$ is a differentiable continuous function, homogeneous of degree zero in x. Its values are defined by those of $x'Rx$ when $x'Ux$ is restricted to 1. The values of the vector x which maximize or minimize $x'Rx$ subject to the condition $x'Ux = 1$ are solutions of $(R - \mu U)x = 0$, where μ is a Lagrange multiplier. The condition $x'Ux = 1$ implies $x \neq 0$, and so $|R - \mu U| = 0$. Finally, for the values of x satisfying $(R - \mu U)x = 0$, we obviously have $x'Rx = \mu x'Ux$. So $x'Rx/x'Ux$ necessarily lies between the smallest and the largest root of $|R - \mu U| = 0$.

$$Q_T(A) \mid u_T(A) \mid = \left| \mathrm{tr} \left[(A - A^0)' S_T \sum_{t=1}^{T} \varepsilon_t z_t' \right] \right| \le$$

$$\le T \sum_{ijk} \left\{ \mid a_{ij} - a_{ij}^0 \mid \mid s_{ihT} \mid \left| \frac{1}{T} \sum_t \varepsilon_{ht} \cdot z_{jt} \right| \right\}. \tag{54}$$

Assumptions 1 and 4 imply that $(1/T) \sum_t \varepsilon_{ht} z_{jt}$ tends to zero in quadratic mean, and therefore also in probability.

Moreover s_{ihT} tends in probability to the finite number s_{ih}. So, to prove conditions (ii) of the lemma, we need only establish that, in any closed set ω which does not contain A^0,

$$\sup_{A \in \omega} \frac{T \mid a_{ij} - a_{ij}^0 \mid}{Q_T(A)} \tag{55}$$

is bounded above, with a probability tending to 1, by a quantity which does not depend on T. Now the fact that $\mid a_{ij} - a_{ij}^0 \mid$ cannot exceed $d(A)$, and inequality (53) imply

$$\frac{T \mid a_{ij} - a_{ij}^0 \mid}{Q_T(A)} \le \frac{1}{v_T d(A)}.$$

With a probability tending to 1, the root v_T is greater than half of the smallest characteristic root $\bar{v}$ of the positive definite matrix $\overline{M} \otimes S$ (the root v_T tends in probability to $\bar{v}$). The number $\bar{v}$ is positive. Finally, in ω the distance $d(A)$ is bounded below by a positive number. This concludes the proof of theorem 3.

(ii) Asymptotic normality

Theorem 4. If assumptions 1, 4, 5 and 6 are satisfied, and if S_T tends in probability to a non-singular matrix S, then $\sqrt{T}[\alpha(S_T) - \alpha^0]$ has a limiting normal distribution.

This property follows from theorems 1 and 3. Assumptions 4 and 6 imply the validity of assumptions 2 and 3. This is obvious for assumption 2, whose statement was included in that of assumption 6. So we need only establish the properties stated in assumption 3.

The functions $g_{it}(\alpha)$ and their derivatives with respect to the α_k are sums in which any term is the product of z_{jt} and either $a_{ij}(\alpha)$ or one of its derivatives. In V^0 the $g_{it}(\alpha)$ and their derivatives are uniformly bounded since the z_{jt} (assumption 4) and the derivatives of the $a_{ij}(\alpha)$ (assumption 6) are so bounded.

Consider then the matrix $M_T(S)$ defined before the statement of assumption 2. Clearly its (k,l)th element is the value in α^0 of a quantity which we can write

$$\frac{\partial a'}{\partial \alpha_k} R_T \frac{\partial a}{\partial \alpha_l}$$

if a denotes the nm-vector defined by the a_{ij} and R_T the positive definite matrix $M_{zz} \otimes S$. Since R_T tends to $R = \overline{M} \otimes S$, the matrix $M_T(S)$ tends to a limit $M(S)$. We need only prove that $M(S)$ and $M_T(S)$ are non-singular. The proof is the same in each case; let us consider $M(S)$.

Since R is positive definite there exists a non-singular square matrix C such that $R = C'C$. Then let μ be a vector such that $\mu' M(S) = 0$. This can also be written:

$$\sum_{k=1}^{p} \mu_k \left(C \frac{\partial a}{\partial \alpha_k} \right)' \left(C \frac{\partial a}{\partial \alpha_l} \right)_{\alpha = \alpha^0} = 0 \qquad \text{for} \qquad l = 1, 2, \ldots, p. \qquad (56)$$

In p-dimensional space, let v_k be the vector equal to $C \partial a(\alpha^0)/\partial \alpha_k$ and w be the vector

$$\sum_k \mu_k v_k.$$

Since α^0 is not a singular point of $A(\alpha)$ and C is non-singular, the p vectors v_k are non-zero and linearly independent; moreover w is not zero provided that μ is not zero. But equations (56) imply that w is orthogonal to each of the p linearly independent vectors v_k, therefore that it is zero, and therefore that μ is also zero, which is what we had to prove.

(iii)   Asymptotically efficient estimators

Since the model (45) examined here is a particular case of the non-linear model discussed in the previous section, it is natural to use for α a minimum distance estimator. Given a positive definite matrix S, by definition the vector $\alpha_T(S)$ minimizes:

$$\frac{1}{T} \sum_{t=1}^{T} [x_t - A(\alpha)z_t]' S [x_t - A(\alpha)z_t]. \qquad (57)$$

To determine the minimum of (57), it will generally pay to find the matrix A^*, that is the least squares estimator which would be appropriate to the model if A were any $n \times m$ matrix. For $\alpha_T(S)$ minimizes the following expression:

$$\frac{1}{T} \sum_{t=1}^{T} z_t' [A^* - A(\alpha)]' S [A^* - A(\alpha)] z_t, \qquad (58)$$

which again equals:

$$\text{tr} \{ [A^* - A(\alpha)]' S [A^* - A(\alpha)] M_{zz} \}. \qquad (59)$$

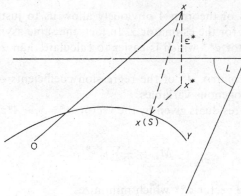

Fig. 4.

Indeed, $x_t - A(\alpha)z_t$ is the sum of the vector $\varepsilon_t^* = x_t - A^*z_t$ and the vector $u_t = [A^* - A(\alpha)]z_t$. The quantity:

$$\frac{1}{T}\sum_{t=1}^{T}[x_t - A^*z_t]'S[A^* - A(\alpha)]z_t = \frac{1}{T}\sum_{t=1}^{T}\varepsilon_t^*Su_t$$

is necessarily zero; for, in nT-dimensional space, the vector ε^* is by definition orthogonal to every vector v such that $v_t = Bz_t$ for $t = 1, 2, \ldots, T$, where B is an appropriate $n \times m$ matrix; so it is orthogonal to the vector obtained by giving B the value $S[A^* - A(\alpha)]$, this for any α. Therefore (57) is equal to the sum of (58) and the quantity:

$$\frac{1}{T}\sum_{t=1}^{T}[x_t - A^*z_t]'S[x_t - A^*z_t]$$

which does not depend on α. So any vector $\alpha_T(S)$ which minimizes (58) minimizes (57) and vice versa.

The calculation involved in finding A^* can be quickly carried out in comparison with that involved in minimizing (57). The successive approximations which are necessary for calculating $\alpha_T(S)$ can be more easily made on the basis of (59) than on (57), since the same matrices A^* and M_{zz} occur in all the iterations. Moreover we know that $E(A^*)$ is $A(\alpha^0)$ and that A^* tends in probability to $A(\alpha^0)$ when T tends to infinity. The matrix A^* will usually be neai a matrix of the family $A(\alpha)$. The minimization of (58) or (59) can therefore be carried out from an initial value of α near the required value $\alpha_T(S)$. Generally few iterations will be necessary.

Of all minimum distance estimators, the most efficient are those which correspond to matrices S_T tending to Ω^{-1}. Since Ω is not generally known, an observable matrix tending in probability to Ω is substituted for it.

The assumptions of theorem 4 obviously allow us to justify the properties stated in theorem 2 for the estimator $\hat{\hat{\alpha}}$. In fact, the same asymptotic properties apply to an estimator α^{**} which is easier to calculate than $\hat{\hat{\alpha}}$ and is defined as follows:

(i) Calculate the matrix A^* of the regression coefficients of the endogenous variables on the exogenous variables.

(ii) Calculate the residuals given by the vectors $\varepsilon_t^* = x_t - A^* z_t$ and their sample covariance matrix

$$M_{\varepsilon\varepsilon}^* = \frac{1}{T}\sum_t \varepsilon_t^* \varepsilon_t^{*\prime}.$$

(iii) Calculate the vector α^{**} which minimizes

$$\mathrm{tr}\,\{[A^* - A(\alpha)]'(M_{\varepsilon\varepsilon}^*)^{-1}[A^* - A(\alpha)]M_{zz}\}. \tag{60}$$

In view of assumptions 1 and 4, the matrix A^* tends in probability to the true matrix $A(\alpha^0)$, and $M_{\varepsilon\varepsilon}^*$ to the covariance matrix of the errors Ω (see ch. 6, propositions 5 and 6). We can therefore state:

Theorem 5.   Under assumptions 1, 4, 5 and 6, $\sqrt{T}(\alpha^{**} - \alpha^0)$ has a limiting centred normal distribution whose covariance matrix is the limit in probability of the inverse of the matrix whose (k,l)th element is

$$\mathrm{tr}\left\{\frac{\partial A'}{\partial \alpha_k}(M_{\varepsilon\varepsilon}^*)^{-1}\frac{\partial A}{\partial \alpha_l}M_{zz}\right\}_{\alpha=\alpha^*}. \tag{61}$$

The estimator α^{**} is asymptotically efficient in the class of minimum distance estimators. If the errors ε_t are normally distributed, it is also asymptotically efficient in the class of consistent regular estimators.

Of course we could obtain other asymptotically equivalent estimators by using matrices other than $M_{\varepsilon\varepsilon}^*$, provided that these matrices tend to Ω. For example, an iterative procedure might be used in which each iteration uses the matrix defined on the basis of the residuals resulting from the previous iteration. This seems to lead to some gain in precision in the estimate of Ω and probably also in that of α. In most cases, however, this gain should be small, if it exists at all. Using $M_{\varepsilon\varepsilon}^*$, estimation of Ω depends on the vector of the residuals which belongs to an $n(T-m)$-dimensional space, and has therefore $nT-nm$ degrees of freedom. Using the matrix of the residuals of a preceding iteration, estimation of Ω depends on a vector with $nT-p$ degrees of freedom. The difference is small if T is large in relation to m, or if p is not much smaller than nm. Moreover $M_{\varepsilon\varepsilon}^*$ has an advantage over other consistent estimators of Ω: it is independent of A^*, and its expected value is equal to Ω up to a scalar multiplier.

Theorem 5 involves assumption 6 according to which α^0 is not a singularity of the function $A(\alpha)$. This assumption allows us to eliminate the case where $M_T(S)$ is singular. If the matrix defined by (61) were singular, this would obviously appear in the calculation of the variances of the estimates α_k^{**}. This would be a similar situation to that arising from multicollinearity of the exogenous variables in multiple regression models. Similarly, if (61) is very nearly a singular matrix, the α_k will not be estimated with great precision, and we may even suspect that α^0 is a singularity of $A(\alpha)$.

(iv) Explicit constraints

Until now we have supposed that the matrix of the coefficients was expressed directly as an explicit function of p parameters α_k. In many cases the model may also be written in the form:

$$x_t = Az_t + \varepsilon_t,$$

the matrix A being subject to a certain number of a priori restrictions. The same estimation principles can still be applied.

Thus, an estimator $A_T(S)$ is obtained by minimizing:

$$\mathscr{L}_T(S, A) = \sum_{t=1}^{T} [x_t - Az_t]' S[x_t - Az_t],$$

subject to the restrictions imposed on A.

In the same way a three-stage procedure defines an estimator A^{**} similar to $A(\alpha^{**})$. The first two stages are the same as operations (i) and (ii) for α^{**}; the third is as follows:

(iii') Calculate the matrix A^{**} which minimizes

$$\text{tr}\,\{[A^* - A]'(M_{\varepsilon\varepsilon}^*)^{-1}[A^* - A]M_{zz}\},$$

subject to the a priori restrictions.

As we saw from theorem 3, assumptions 1 and 4 relating to the errors and to the exogenous variables are sufficient for proof of the convergence of $\hat{A}(S_T)$ to the true matrix A^0 when the random matrix S_T tends in probability to a positive definite matrix S.

To establish the asymptotic normality of

$$\sqrt{T}[\hat{A}(S_T) - A^0] \quad \text{and of} \quad \sqrt{T}(A^{**} - A^0),$$

we must clearly be able to assume some regularity in the restrictions imposed on A. Here we confine ourselves to the case where these restrictions are expressed by conditions of the following type:

$$\phi_h(a_{11}, a_{12}, \ldots, a_{ij}, \ldots, a_{nm}) = 0 \quad \text{for} \quad h = 1, 2, \ldots, q,$$

and satisfy:

Assumption 7.   There exists a neighborhood W^0 of A^0 in which the functions ϕ_h have bounded derivatives up to the third order and in which the matrix $[\partial\phi_h/\partial a_{ij}]$ of order $(q \times nm)$ has rank q.

Under this assumption, for the matrices of W^0 satisfying the restrictions, there exists a parametric representation which satisfies assumption 6 (see DIEUDONNÉ [1960], in particular theorems (10.2.2) and (10.2.3)). By using this representation we can prove the asymptotic normality of

$$\sqrt{T}[A_T(S_T) - A^0] \quad \text{and} \quad \sqrt{T}(A^{**} - A^0).$$

Theorem 6.   If assumption 1, 4 and 7 are satisfied, and if S_T tends in probability to the positive definite matrix S, then

$$\sqrt{T}[\hat{A}(S_T) - A^0]$$

has a limiting centred normal distribution. Finally, if the ε_t are normally distributed, then A^{**} is an asymptotically efficient estimator.

Formula (61) provides a consistent estimator of the covariances of the α_k^{**}; it is sufficient in practice when the a_{ij} are expressed explicitly as functions of p independent parameters α_k. But, when the a_{ij} are subject to analytic restrictions, it is generally simpler to determine the concentration ellipsoid of A^{**} directly by taking account of a geometric property which we shall now examine.

The concentration ellipsoid of $\sqrt{T}\alpha^{**}$ consists of the set of p-vectors α satisfying the condition:

$$\sum_{k,l=1}^{p} \alpha_k\alpha_l \operatorname{tr}\left[\frac{\partial A'}{\partial \alpha_k}\Omega^{-1}\frac{\partial A}{\partial \alpha_l}M_{zz}\right]_{\alpha=\alpha^0} \leqq 1$$

which can also be written:

$$\operatorname{tr}\left\{\left[\sum_{k=1}^{p}\frac{\partial A}{\partial \alpha_k}\alpha_k\right]'\Omega^{-1}\left[\sum_{l=1}^{p}\frac{\partial A}{\partial \alpha_l}\alpha_l\right]M_{zz}\right\} \leqq 1, \tag{62}$$

the derivatives of A being evaluated at $\alpha=\alpha^0$.

Consider now the $n \times m$ matrices A which can be expressed in the form:

$$A = A^0 + \sum_{k=1}^{p}\frac{\partial A}{\partial \alpha_k}(\alpha^0)\cdot(\alpha_k - \alpha_k^0), \tag{63}$$

where α is a suitable vector. In nm-dimensional space these matrices belong to the p-dimensional hyperplane which best represents, in the neighborhood of A^0, the set of matrices obeying the a priori restrictions. Although this is no

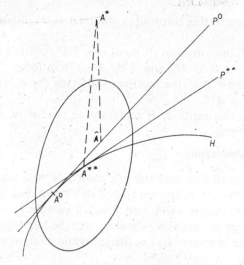

Fig. 6.

literally true, we shall say for the sake of brevity that *the matrices A of the form* (63) *satisfy the a priori restrictions in the neighborhood of A^0.*

Among all these matrices, let $\hat{A}$ be that defined by (63) with $\alpha = \alpha^{**}$. In view of the assumptions adopted, $\sqrt{T}A^{**}$ and $\sqrt{T}\hat{A}$ are asymptotically equivalent, since their difference is equal to $1/\sqrt{T}$ times a bounded quadratic form of the vector:

$$\sqrt{T}(\alpha^{**} - \alpha^0).$$

Now we can go from $\sqrt{T}(\alpha^{**} - \alpha^0)$ to $\sqrt{T}(\hat{A} - A^0)$ by means of a linear transformation. The concentration ellipsoid of $\sqrt{T}\hat{A}$ is therefore the transform of that of $\sqrt{T}\alpha^{**}$. It consists of the set of matrices that can be written:

$$A = \sum_{k=1}^{p} \frac{\partial A}{\partial \alpha_k}(\alpha^0) \cdot \alpha_k, \tag{64}$$

with a vector α satisfying the inequality (62); or again of the set of matrices that can be expressed in the form (64) with some vector α, and which satisfy:

$$\mathrm{tr}\,[A'\Omega^{-1}AM_{zz}] \leqq 1. \tag{65}$$

But this last inequality taken in isolation defines the concentration ellipsoid of $\sqrt{T}(A^* - A^0)$, as we saw in ch. 6, § 4, formula (18″).

Since (64) differs from (63) only by a change of origin, we can state the following geometric property. *When it has been centred on A^0, the concentration ellipsoid of $\sqrt{T}A^{**}$ is the intersection of the concentration ellipsoid of $\sqrt{T}A^*$ and the hyperplane of the matrices satisfying the a priori restriction in the neighborhood of A^0.*

A consistent estimate of this ellipsoid is obtained as the intersection of the two following sets:

(i) the estimated concentration ellipsoid of $\sqrt{T}A^*$, centred on A^{**}; this set is obtained by replacing Ω by $M_{\varepsilon\varepsilon}^*$ and A by $A - A^{**}$ in (65);

(ii) the hyperplane P^{**} of the matrices satisfying the a priori restrictions in the neighborhood of A^{**}.

Fig. 6 illustrates this method, H representing the set of matrices satisfying the a priori restrictions.

(v)   A test of the constraints

We have assumed until now that the true matrix A^0 did actually satisfy the a priori restrictions. We can propose a test of this hypothesis. Assuming that the linear model $x_t = Az_t + \varepsilon_t$ is valid, and given a sample of values of the x_t, z_t (for $t = 1, 2, \ldots, T$), we can ask if we should reject the hypothesis that A^0 belongs to the family of the matrices $A(\alpha)$ or obeys certain analytic constraints such as the equalities (46).

This problem recalls that which led to the techniques of analysis of variance. In fact the question which we set and the model would be identical to those of ch. 5 § 8, if the set Y were a linear manifold. However, we have just seen that, when y^0 belongs to Y, this set can be approximated by a hyperplane, provided that the number of observations tends to infinity. We can now expect that the analysis of variance tests are asymptotically justified in the non-linear model of this section, as in the linear model. We shall verify this[†].

In nT-dimensional space let M^0 be the hyperplane of the vectors x which satisfy:

$$x_t = Az_t \quad \text{for} \quad t = 1, 2, \ldots, T,$$

where A is a matrix of the form (63). This hyperplane clearly belongs to L. It is p-dimensional.

Let $\bar{A}$ be the matrix of the form (63) which minimizes

$$\text{tr}\{(A^* - A)'\Omega^{-1}(A^* - A)M_{zz}\}. \tag{66}$$

Let x^* (and $\bar{x}$) be the vectors of L (and of M^0) defined by:

$$x_t^* = A^* z_t (\text{and } \bar{x}_t = \bar{A} z_t),$$

---

† The same problem could be set in the more general context of the beginning of the chapter. Adopting the model:

$$x_{ti} = g_i(z_{1t}, \ldots, z_{mt}; \; \alpha_1, \ldots, \alpha_p) + \varepsilon_{it},$$

how do we test the hypothesis that certain of the α_k have specified values, or satisfy given analytic relations? Under assumptions 1 to 3, the techniques of analysis of variance might again be asymptotically justified, at least in cases where the regression estimators are consistent. Examination of the associated linear pseudo-model would be sufficient for this.

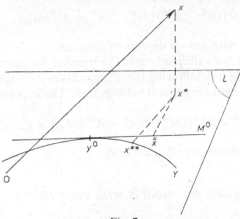

Fig. 7.

for $t = 1, 2, \ldots, T$. We can say that x^* and $\bar{x}$ are the projections of the observed vector on L and M^0 respectively. (For $\bar{x}$ minimizes in M^0 the quantity

$$\sum_{t=1}^{T} (x_t^* - x_t)' \Omega^{-1} (x_t^* - x_t)$$

which is T times (66)).

We know that x^* (and $\bar{x}$) have nm-dimensional (and p-dimensional) distributions whenever x is normally distributed. In this case

$$T \operatorname{tr} [(A^* - \bar{A})' \Omega^{-1} (A^* - \bar{A}) M_{zz}] = \sum_{t=1}^{T} (x_t^* - \bar{x}_t)' \Omega^{-1} (x_t^* - \bar{x}_t) \qquad (67)$$

is distributed as χ^2 with $nm - p$ degrees of freedom (see ch. 5, proposition 7). But in view of theorem 3, ch. 6, the asymptotic distribution of A^* (and consequently that of $\bar{A}$) depends only on Ω and not on normality of the ε_t. Therefore (67) is distributed asymptotically as χ^2, whether or not the ε_t are normally distributed. Besides,

$$T \operatorname{tr} [(A^* - A^{**})' (M_{\varepsilon\varepsilon}^*)^{-1} (A^* - A^{**}) M_{zz}]$$

is asymptotically equivalent to (67) since

$$(M_{\varepsilon\varepsilon}^*)^{-1} - \Omega^{-1} \xrightarrow{P} 0$$

and

$$\sqrt{T}(A^* - A^{**}) - \sqrt{T}(A^* - \bar{A}) \xrightarrow{P} 0.$$

This proves the following property.

Proposition 1.   If assumptions 1, 4, 5 and 6 are satisfied the limiting distribution of

$$T \operatorname{tr}\left[(A^* - A^{**})'(M_{\varepsilon\varepsilon}^*)^{-1}(A^* - A^{**})M_{zz}\right]$$

is the χ^2-distribution with $nm - p$ degrees of freedom.

If the observations are sufficiently great in number for asymptotic approximation to appear valid, the following inequality allows us to test the hypothesis that y^0 belongs to Y, assuming that it belongs to L. The hypothesis is rejected if

$$T \operatorname{tr}\left[(A^* - A^{**})'(M_{\varepsilon\varepsilon}^*)^{-1}(A^* - A^{**})M_{zz}\right] > \chi^2_{nm - p}(\lambda),$$

where λ denotes the chosen significance level.

6   Confidence regions for models with constraints

In section 4 we considered linear models with additive errors of the type:

$$x_t = Az_t + \varepsilon_t \tag{73}$$

in which the matrix A is expressed as an analytic function of p real parameters α_k, or must satisfy q analytic conditions of the form $\phi_h(A) = 0$. More generally, the matrix A of the model (73) can be restricted to lie in a sub-set H of nm-dimensional space.

In such cases, the matrix A^* resulting from the multiple regressions of the x_{it} on the z_{jt} is not an estimator of A, since it does not necessarily belong to H. Now the required estimate must lie in H for two reasons. From a purely statistical point of view, the fact that the matrix A obeys certain constraints is a priori information which must not be neglected, since it makes for greater precision in the results deduced from the sample. From an economic point of view, the equations of the model (73) are generally meaningless and can only be used correctly if the coefficients of the exogenous variables obey the conditions specified by the model. Both these remarks apply to the example considered earlier. On the one hand, substitution of the n parameters c_i for the n^2 parameters b_{ij} allows more precise estimation of the effects of variations in prices. On the other hand, each of the c_i has specific significance lacked by the b_{ij}.

However, we note that the procedures of ch. 6 may still apply in a certain way. Indeed, they allow us to determine not only an estimate of y (the projection x^*), but also a confidence region (the part of L contained in a domain C surrounding x^*). If we establish such confidence regions with probability level α, the frequency of our errors will tend to α in the long run. This result is absolutely independent of any more precise restriction on y. In the present case, we can therefore choose as confidence region the intersection of Y and C.

Suppose for example that our model contains a single endogenous variable and two exogenous variables:

$$x_t = a_1 z_{1t} + a_2 z_{2t} + \varepsilon_t$$

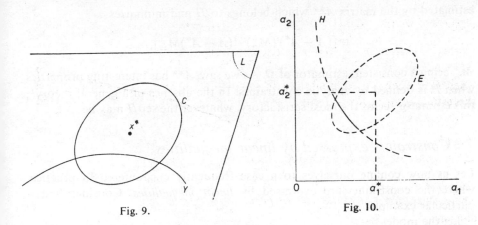

Fig. 9.   Fig. 10.

with the additional restriction:

$$a_1 a_2 = 1.$$

Without this restriction a confidence region for (a_1, a_2) is established by considering about the least squares estimate (a_1^*, a_2^*) the interior of the ellipse E:

$$\frac{T-2}{2}(a^* - a)' M_{zz}(a^* - a) = F_\alpha,$$

where F_α is the value of the F-statistic at the probability level α with 2 and $T-2$ degrees of freedom. The part of the hyperbola H (defined by $a_1 a_2 = 1$) which lies within E also constitutes a confidence region at the probability level α when it is known that $a_1 a_2 = 1$.

However, this procedure has two drawbacks:

(i) The confidence region so defined will greatly vary in size from sample to sample. If the estimate (a_1^*, a_2^*) is far from H, and this happens from time to time, it is even possible that H and E do not intersect. We then adopt for a_1 and a_2 two values chosen a priori and satisfying $a_1 a_2 = 1$; for example $a_1 = a_2 = 1$. But it is clear that the region obtained will not be the most efficient: in most cases it will be too large (when a^* is near H), whereas it will be too small when the ε_t^* take exceptional values (a^* is distant from H).

(ii) If the calculations are relatively easy when there are only two unknown parameters, they quickly become very heavy. With a single endogenous variable and m exogenous variables, we must determine the common part of H and an m-dimensional ellipsoid. When there are several equations, determination of a confidence region for the set of the parameters becomes more difficult, even independently of any a priori restriction, as we saw at the end of ch. 6.

These criticisms cannot be raised against *minimum distance estimators* and the confidence regions which can be associated with them. In fact A is then estimated by the matrix A^{**} which belongs to H and minimizes

$$tr\left[(A - A^*)'(M_{\varepsilon\varepsilon}^*)^{-1}(A - A^*)M_{zz}\right],$$

$M_{\varepsilon\varepsilon}^*$ being a consistent estimator of Ω. As we saw, A^{**} has interesting properties when H is defined by analytic constraints. In the absence of a general theory[†], this estimator seems the most satisfactory, whatever the set H may be.

7   Constraints expressed by linear inequalities[††]

Let us now confine ourselves to a case frequently encountered in practice, where the constraints are expressed by *linear inequalities*. Consider first a particular example.

Let the model be:

$$x_t = a_1 z_{1t} + a_2 z_{2t} + \varepsilon_t \tag{74}$$

containing a real endogenous variable x and two exogenous variables z_1 and z_2. Suppose that the true value of a_2 cannot be negative because of the economic meaning of this coefficient. The constraint on the vector of the coefficients is then:

$$a_2 \geqq 0. \tag{75}$$

In other words, H is the upper half-plane in two-dimensional space, with coordinates a_1 and a_2: while in T-dimensional space, Y is the half-plane defined by the set of the linear combinations of z_1 and z_2 for which the coefficient of z_2 is non-negative. This half-plane is limited by the line M, the support of z_1. It is represented by the shaded region in fig. 11.

Then let a_1^* and a_2^* be the regression coefficients of x on z_1 and z_2. If $a_2^* \geqq 0$, the restriction (75) is satisfied by (a_1^*, a_2^*) which provides the required minimum distance estimator. If on the other hand $a_2^* < 0$, we must find the vector of Y which is nearest x. This is clearly the projection of x on M. The estimate of (a_1, a_2) is then $(\hat{a}_1, 0)$, $\hat{a}_1$ denoting the simple regression coefficient of x on z_1. In practice therefore we first calculate the regression based on (74), disregarding (75). If the result does not satisfy (75), we choose the value zero for the coefficient of z_2, that is, we replace (74) by the equation:

$$x_t = a_1 z_{1t} + \varepsilon_t$$

on which a new regression is calculated.

[†] We can certainly see that, in the case where the errors are normally distributed, A^{**} is, at least asymptotically, the maximum likelihood estimator. But this has hardly any bearing; the general properties of these estimators are known only subject to fairly strong regularity assumptions (see LE CAM [1956]), which imply in the present model that the constraints on A are analytic.

[††] See ROTHENBERG [1968b] on the efficiency of the following estimators.

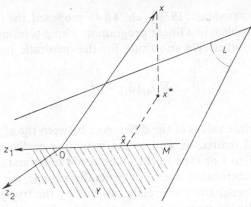

Fig. 11.

The estimator $(\hat{\hat{a}}_1, \hat{\hat{a}}_2)$ defined by this procedure has a rather particular distribution. The marginal distribution of $\hat{\hat{a}}_2$ most often has a density for the positive values, and assigns a non-zero probability to the value zero, which is obtained whenever a_2^* is negative. This distribution can clearly be deduced from that of (a_1^*, a_2^*) and we can see that it is more concentrated whenever $\{a_2^* < 0\}$ has a positive probability. In this case, $(\hat{\hat{a}}_1, \hat{\hat{a}}_2)$ contains a bias, since (a_1^*, a_2^*) has none, and $\hat{\hat{a}}_2$ is never less than, but sometimes greater than a_2^*.

The distribution of $\hat{\hat{a}}_2$ was studied by ZELLNER [1961a] for the case where z_{1t} is the auxiliary exogenous variable which always equals 1. Some of his results are given in the following table, in which $\sigma(a_2^*)$ denotes the standard error of a_2^*, and a_2^0 the true value of a_2.

$\dfrac{a_2^0}{\sigma(a_2{}^*)}$	$\dfrac{E(\hat{\hat{a}}_2) - a_2^0}{\sigma(a_2{}^*)}$	$\dfrac{\sigma^2(\hat{\hat{a}}_2)}{\sigma^2(a_2{}^*)}$
3.00	0.00	1.00
2.00	0.01	0.96
1.00	0.08	0.76
0.50	0.20	0.59
0.20	0.31	0.52
0.00	0.40	0.50

We see that the bias remains small so long as a_2^0 is not near zero.

Although based on the same principles, the calculations become more complex when there is no longer one, but several linear inequalities, and when the model contains a greater number of variables. We must then find the minimum of a quadratic form with respect to variables restricted to satisfy a set of linear inequalities, that is, we must solve a '*quadratic programme*'. There are various methods for solving these programmes. They are fairly laborious when the number of variables and constraints is large.

ARROW and HOFFENBERG [1959] (ch. 4 § 4) proposed the following method for reducing the problem to a linear programme whose solution can be obtained by the usual techniques. We substitute for the quadratic form an expression of the type:

$$\sum_{i,j} \lambda_{ij} |\hat{a}_{ij} - a_{ij}^*| \tag{76}$$

involving the absolute values of the differences between the a_{ij}^* and the elements $\hat{a}_{ij}$ of the required matrix, as well as the weighting coefficients λ_{ij} which we can take as equal to 1 or even to the inverses of the estimated standard errors of the a_{ij}^*. This substitution does not generally change the result markedly, provided that the restrictions are really satisfied by the true matrix A.

We revert to a linear programme by introducing 2 nm new variables e_{ij} and f_{ij} which are subject to the conditions:

$$e_{ij} \geq 0, \qquad f_{ij} \geq 0$$
$$e_{ij} - f_{ij} = \hat{a}_{ij} - a_{ij}^*$$

and by finding the minimum of:

$$\sum_{ij} \lambda_{ij} (e_{ij} + f_{ij}). \tag{77}$$

In the solution, at least one of the two variables e_{ij} and f_{ij} relating to a given pair (i,j) is zero, but for which we could reduce the value of the linear form by reducing both of these variables by the same amount. Consequently:

$$e_{ij} + f_{ij} = |\hat{a}_{ij} - a_{ij}^*|$$

and any minimum of (77) is also a minimum of (76).

Whether the estimate A is found by this simplified method or by the exact solution of the quadratic programme, its distribution has characteristics similar to that of the vector $(\hat{a}_1, \hat{a}_2)$ examined earlier. But it is virtually impossible to determine this distribution precisely in models containing more than a very small number of inequalities. This is why the inequalities which restrict the coefficients are rarely treated rigorously in applied econometrics. LOVELL and PRESCOTT [1970] point out the shortcomings in this area in the practical field.

CHAPTER 10

Linear models with errors in variables

1 Introduction

In the course of the previous chapters, we assumed that the variables x_{it} and z_{jt} could be observed without error. In fact this assumption is often justified. While statistical data are generally liable to be imperfect in many respects, they still have enough precision to allow us to estimate relations, which are not themselves exact. In other words, the errors affecting the equations are in most cases of much greater importance than those which may affect measurement of the variables.

However, the variables of a model are not always observed directly. Other variables which are closely, but not strictly, related to them must often be used 'in their place. For example, for the purpose of estimating the association between income and some component of consumption, the available data may be the results of an inquiry giving, in a restricted sample and in a certain period, figures for total expenditure and expenditure on the relevant category of consumption. The figures for total expenditure are then often taken as measuring incomes, although there are unknown, and sometimes considerable, differences between the two variables.

In such situations, it is essential to modify the basic assumptions of the model, to examine the properties of the method of least squares, and if necessary, to suggest different methods. This is the object of the present chapter.

We return to the regression model and suppose that a relation

$$x_t = Az_t + \varepsilon_t. \tag{1}$$

exists between the vector of exogenous variables z_t and the vector of endogenous variables x_t.

We no longer consider that the variables x_{it} and z_{jt} have been observed exactly, but that we have only the approximate measurements x_{it}^* and z_{jt}^* with:

$$x_t^* = x_t + \xi_t \qquad z_t^* = z_t + \zeta_t$$

where ξ_t and ζ_t are the vectors of the *errors in the variables*, which are supposed random like the *errors in the equations* ε_t.

The relation between the observed variables can be written:

$$x_t^* = Az_t^* + (\varepsilon_t + \xi_t - A\zeta_t), \tag{2}$$

which recalls the model (1) with errors $\varepsilon_t + \xi_t - A\zeta_t$. If these errors satisfy assumption 1 of ch. 6, it is perfectly legitimate to carry out least squares regression. This gives an estimate of A possessing all the properties discussed earlier. But what assumptions can reasonably be formulated for $\varepsilon_t + \xi_t - A\zeta_t$? It seems natural to adopt for ε_t the same assumptions as in ch. 6. As for the vectors ξ_t and ζ_t of the errors in the variables, they are generally assumed to have expected value zero and to be independent of the values taken by x_t and z_t, which implies that they are also independent of the errors in the equations ε_t. Under these conditions, the vectors $\varepsilon_t + \xi_t - A\zeta_t$ are independent of z_t but not of z_t^*, which differs from z_t by ζ_t. Now, independence of the errors with respect to z_t^* is indispensable if we wish to apply the usual theory to a regression based on the model (2). All the properties of part 2 require this assumption.

However, we note that, if the exogenous variables are measured without error, then $\zeta_t = 0$ and $\varepsilon_t + \xi_t$ is in fact independent of $z_t^* = z_t$. Therefore:

The properties investigated in chapter 6 remain true even when there are errors of measurement in the endogenous variables, provided that there are none in the exogenous variables and that the errors in the endogenous variables conform to the same assumptions as the errors in the equations.

Unfortunately, the exogenous variables are sometimes affected by considerable errors in measurement, which justifies our present study.

We shall suppose throughout that the errors in the variables, ξ_{it} and ζ_{jt}, have zero means for any values of the vectors of the true variables x_t and z_t. But it may happen in practice that the observations are affected by systematic errors. Thus, the incomes declared in the course of a family budget inquiry may be on the average lower than actual incomes (this possibility is illustrated in fig. 1). The systematic errors clearly affect the significance of the calculated regressions.

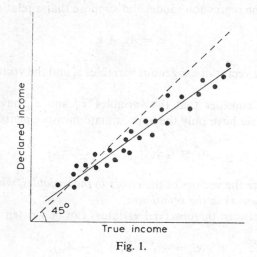

Fig. 1.

Without trying to deal completely with this difficulty, let us consider a simple regression model:

$$x_t = az_t + b + \varepsilon_t,$$

in which the errors ξ_t and ζ_t on the endogenous and exogenous variables obey:

$$E(\xi_t/z_t; \varepsilon_t) = u_1 x_t + u_0,$$

$$E(\zeta_t/z_t; \varepsilon_t) = w_1 z_t + w_0,$$

so that the systematic errors are linear functions of the variables which they affect. It is possible to define new variables $\hat{x}_t$ and $\hat{z}_t$ and new errors $\hat{\xi}_t$ and $\hat{\zeta}_t$ such that:

$$x_t^* = \hat{x}_t + \hat{\xi}_t, \qquad z_t^* = \hat{z}_t + \hat{\zeta}_t,$$

where:

$$E(\hat{\xi}_t/\hat{z}_t; \varepsilon_t) = 0, \qquad E(\hat{\zeta}_t/\hat{z}_t; \varepsilon_t) = 0.$$

We need only set:

$$\hat{x}_t = (1 + u_1)x_t + u_0, \qquad \hat{z}_t = (1 + w_1)z_t + w_0.$$

In other words, the new variables are the sum of the true variables and the systematic errors in the corresponding observations. These variables obey a simple regression model:

$$\hat{x}_t = \hat{a}\hat{z}_t + \hat{b} + \varepsilon_t,$$

where

$$\hat{a} = a\frac{1 + u_1}{1 + w_1}, \qquad \hat{b} = b(1 + u_1) + u_0 - w_0\frac{a(1 + u_1)}{1 + w_1}.$$

Thus, all that we say below about the relations between certain estimates and the parameters a and b will apply to the relations between these estimates and the quantities $\hat{a}$ and $\hat{b}$ if there are systematic errors. So the theory which follows will still be valid. It will be sufficient to replace a by $\hat{a}$ and b by $\hat{b}$ throughout. The situation is comparable to that encountered in the regression model when the expected value of the error ε_t is not zero.

2 Notation and assumptions

As we have just seen, the errors in the endogenous variables are not distinguished from the errors in the equations, at least from the standpoint of the statistical problems considered here. It is then possible to introduce for this chapter a slightly different notation from that used until now.

Without distinguishing the endogenous from the exogenous variables, we say that x_{it} represents the value of the tth observation on the ith variable where $i = 1, 2, \ldots, n$; $t = 1, 2, \ldots, T$. The vector x_t of the observed variables is the sum of two vectors, the vector y_t of the values of the *true variables* and the vector ε_t of the errors.

$$x_t = y_t + \varepsilon_t. \tag{3}$$

Among the true variables, there exists the exact linear relation:

$$Ay_t = b \qquad \text{for} \qquad t = 1, 2, \ldots, T, \tag{4}$$

in which A is some matrix of order $m \times n$ and rank m, and b some m-dimensional vector, with:

$$m < n.$$

The system (4) represents the linear equations which connect the variables. We must try to estimate it in order to know the economic laws of the phenomenon under study.

We also formulate the three following assumptions which recall assumptions 1, 3 and 5 of ch. 6.

Assumption 1.   The vector ε_t is distributed independently of t and of the y_θ for $\theta = 1, 2, \ldots, T$, with zero mean· and non-singular covariance matrix Ω. Two vectors ε_t and ε_θ are stochastically independent whenever $t \neq \theta$.

Assumption 2.   The vector ε_t is normally distributed.

Assumption 3.   The unknown vectors y_t all satisfy the same linear system (4). The matrix

$$M_{yy} = \frac{1}{T} \sum_{t=1}^{T} (y_t - \bar{y})(y_t - \bar{y})',$$

where:

$$\bar{y} = \frac{1}{T} \sum_{t=1}^{T} y_t,$$

is of rank $n - m$. When T tends to infinity, the vector $\bar{y}$ tends to a finite limit, and the matrix M_{yy} tends to a finite matrix M_0 of rank $n - m$.

We note that assumption 1 implies that all the variables are subject to errors since the covariance matrix Ω of the errors has an inverse. In practice, this restriction is troublesome only for the dummy variables which, by construction, do not contain errors. The linear model (4) was written with a vector b corresponding to the constant terms of the equations in order to take account of this fact. By proceeding in the same way as in ch. 5, we could deal directly with the general case where Ω may be singular. But the increased complexity of the reasoning and the computation would make such a discussion too involved.

The vectors y_t of the true values will be considered here as fixed. Apart from the asymptotic conditions of assymption 3, they must only all satisfy the same system of linear relations $Ay_t = b$ with a matrix A of rank m and a vector b which are completely unknown a priori[†].

We may sometimes consider a similar model in which several observations x_t are known to correspond to the same vector of the true values y_t. We shall not discuss this situation, but note only that the model can then be expressed in an interesting form. The T observations can be divided into H groups, each corresponding to a particular value of y_t. Let y_h be the value of y_t in the group h $(h = 1, 2, \ldots, H)$ and Y the matrix of order $n \times H$ consisting of the y_{ih}. Let u_{ht} be a dummy variable taking the value 1 when the tth observation belongs to the group h, and 0 otherwise. The model can then be written:

$$x_t = Yu_t + \varepsilon_t,$$

with the condition that $Ay_h = b$ for an appropriate matrix A and vector b, and for all the columns y_h of Y. Since the u_t are known, we thus obtain a model with errors in the equations in which the matrix Y to be estimated is restricted to satisfy the above condition. The general procedures given in the previous chapter can then be applied to estimate Y, A and b. The asymptotic theory applies directly if the number H of groups is fixed, and if the number of observations per group tends to infinity. The case in which the number of observations per group is fixed and H tends to infinity raises different problems of a similar kind to those examined in the course of this chapter.

Certain presentations of our model involve a supplementary assumption, namely that the vectors y_t relating to the different observations constitute independent values of the same random vector y (with a constant but unknown distribution). The expressions *structural model* and *functional model* have been proposed in order to distinguish the formulation containing this new assumption from that which does not.

We shall generally set our present discussion in the context of the functional model; for, in the economic phenomena under study, we can rarely assume that the true variables relating to the different observations have the same distribution (whether objective or subjective). However, we shall occasionally state certain results concerning the structural model, in so far as they illuminate the nature of the properties under discussion.

There is nothing in the functional model which prohibits the y_t from being random variables with distinct and unknown distributions. The random nature of the true variables is therefore not in dispute, but only the identity of the distributions relating to the different observations. If the y_t are indeed random,

---

[†] In practice there may be a priori restrictions on A and b. We shall disregard this at present, and shall say something about it in ch. 17 § 5, 3°.

we confine ourselves to the investigation of the conditional distributions of the proposed estimates, the sequence of values taken by the y_t being considered as fixed. This can be justified here in the same way as for models with errors in equations, where the exogenous variables z_t are random. The unconditional distributions of the estimates can be deduced simply from their conditional distributions when the distribution of the y_t has been specified.

The statistical study of the estimates adapted to the model with errors in the variables is much more complex than that which we carried out in previous chapters. We shall not be able to deal with all the relevant questions within the framework of the general model. In order to reveal certain particular features and to assess their approximate importance, we shall refer instead on several occasions to the following very simple model:

$$x_{1t} = v_t + \varepsilon_{1t},$$
$$x_{2t} = v_t \operatorname{tg} \theta + \varepsilon_{2t}, \tag{5}$$

in which θ is a parameter to be estimated, and v_t an unobservable real variable.

This model would be a particular case of the general model, with

$$n = 2, \qquad m = 1, \qquad A = [\operatorname{tg} \theta \quad - 1], \tag{5a}$$

if we had not supposed a priori that $b=0$. It can be shown that this simplification does not change the nature of the problem.

We also set:

$$\Omega = \begin{bmatrix} \sigma_1^2 & \varrho\sigma_1\sigma_2 \\ \varrho\sigma_1\sigma_2 & \sigma_2^2 \end{bmatrix} \tag{5b}$$

and

$$S^2 = \frac{1}{T} \sum_{t=1}^{T} v_t^2. \tag{5c}$$

We suppose further that σ_1/S and σ_2/S are small, that is, that the variance of the errors remain small with respect to the dispersion of the values of the true variables. We can then give approximate values for certain expressions by limiting ourselves to the first terms of the expansions in terms of σ_1/S and σ_2/S.

3   Errors in variables and least squares regression

We now propose to find out how the errors in exogenous variables affect the results of least squares regression. We shall suppose that the observed variables x_1 and x_2 satisfy the model (5) and that $\operatorname{tg} \theta$ has been estimated from the regression of x_2 on x_1, that is:

$$\text{tg}\,\hat\theta = \frac{\sum_{t=1}^{T} x_{1t}x_{2t}}{\sum_{t=1}^{T} x_{1t}^2}. \tag{6}$$

Using the previously defined notation, we have:

$$\frac{1}{T}\sum_{t=1}^{T} x_{1t}x_{2t} = S^2\,\text{tg}\,\theta + \frac{1}{T}\sum_{t=1}^{T}(\varepsilon_{1t}\,\text{tg}\,\theta + \varepsilon_{2t})v_t + \frac{1}{T}\sum_{t=1}^{T}\varepsilon_{1t}\varepsilon_{2t}$$

$$\frac{1}{T}\sum_{t} x_{1t}^2 = S^2 + \frac{2}{T}\sum_{t}\varepsilon_{1t}v_t + \frac{1}{T}\sum_{t}\varepsilon_{1t}^2. \tag{7}$$

In view of assumptions 1 and 3, these expressions have the same probability limits as $S^2\,\text{tg}\,\theta + \varrho\sigma_1\sigma_2$ and $S^2 + \sigma_1^2$ when the number T of observations tends to infinity[†]. So we can write:

$$\text{tg}\,\hat\theta \to \frac{S^2\,\text{tg}\,\theta + \varrho\sigma_1\sigma_2}{S^2 + \sigma_1^2}.$$

Confining ourselves to the first term of the expansion in terms of σ_1/S, we have:

$$\text{tg}\,\hat\theta \to \text{tg}\,\theta + \frac{\sigma_1}{S}\left(\varrho\frac{\sigma_2}{S} - \frac{\sigma_1}{S}\text{tg}\,\theta\right). \tag{8}$$

The errors in the exogenous variable therefore cause a *systematic bias of the order of* $(\sigma_1/S)^2$. The result of this asymptotic study is confirmed by investigation of the exact distribution of the least squares estimate in finite samples[††].

Figure 2 shows the outline of a hypothetical scatter of points and makes for intuitive understanding of the reason why the regression line Δ of x_2 on x_1 deviates from the line D on which lie the points (y_1, y_2).

The existence of this bias is important in many econometric investigations. When discussing the relation between income and consumption, we saw in ch. 4 that the direct regression between the observed values does not reveal the

---

[†] The variance of $\frac{1}{T}\sum_{t}\varepsilon_{1t}v_t$ is equal to $\frac{\sigma_1^2 S^2}{T}$. It tends to zero. So $\frac{1}{T}\sum_{t}\varepsilon_{1t}v_t$ tends in quadratic mean, and therefore also in probability, to its expected value, which is zero. Similarly $\frac{1}{T}\sum\varepsilon_{1t}\varepsilon_{2t}$ tends in probability to $\rho\sigma_1\sigma_2$ in view of the law of large numbers.

[††] See RICHARDSON and WU [1970], then HALPERIN and GURIAN [1971],

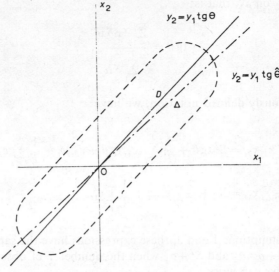

Fig. 2.

true structure if consumption depends on permanent rather than observed income. Formula (55) giving the limit of the estimated propensity to consume a^* is virtually identical to that just obtained. According to Friedman, this phenomenon would explain why propensities calculated over short periods generally lie between 0.50 and 0.70, while the true propensity would be near 0.90.

LIVIATAN [1961] argued that similar biases affect the estimation of consumption elasticities from family budget inquiries when a regression is calculated between expenditure on some commodity group and total declared expenditure. The latter differs sometimes considerably from income, which is the true explanatory variable. Liviatan assessed the importance of the bias by comparing the least squares estimate with a consistent estimate to be described later at the end of section 7. Results based on an English inquiry are given in the following table in which the second column gives the elasticity calculated according to the usual simple regression and the third gives the elasticity according to the consistent method (cf. LIVIATAN [1961], table 2, p. 345).

Total food	0.55	0.53
Clothing and footwear	1.61	1.09
Household durables	2.36	2.05
Health and culture	1.68	1.88
Sundry (incl. tobacco)	1.24	1.51

We see that the differences are particularly important for clothing and durable goods.

The possibility of errors of this type must be investigated whenever the results of regressions are to be interpreted. In particular, artificial differences may appear in the comparison of subsamples if the exogenous variables are affected by errors. The analysis of covariance and similar techniques which are justified on the assumption that there are no errors in variables, often make these differences seem 'significant'. From this standpoint the reader can compare fig. 6 of ch. 4, where a difference between two regressions is interpreted as due to errors in variables, and fig. 4 of ch. 7, where similar differences are considered to represent differences in behavior[†].

So least squares regression does not seem very suitable for models containing errors in the exogenous variables. Before discarding it completely, we must point out that BERKSON [1950] recommended it as being sometimes suitable for prediction.

For consider the two-variable model defined by system (5); let us assume that this model explains the endogenous quantity x_2 as a function of the exogenous quantity measured by x_1. Prediction consists of choosing a value x_2^p for x_2, and generally aims at minimizing $E(x_2^p - x_2)^2$. It can occur in two different ways:

(i) The model is often to be used for predicting the value of x_2 corresponding to a value of the 'true exogenous variable' v. So a family budget inquiry provides information about total expenditure per household together with consumption of a particular product. This information is used to predict the increase in national consumption of this product which will result from some supposed increase in incomes.

If $\tilde{\theta}$ denotes an estimate of θ, the prediction is $x_2^p = v \operatorname{tg} \tilde{\theta}$, and the loss is expressed by:

$$E[(x_2^p - x_2)^2/v] = v^2 E[\operatorname{tg} \tilde{\theta} - \operatorname{tg} \theta]^2 + \sigma_2^2$$

since, in view of assumption 1, the error ε_2 for the prediction is independent of the estimate $\tilde{\theta}$. To minimize the loss, we should minimize the mean square difference between the estimate $\operatorname{tg} \tilde{\theta}$ and the true value $\operatorname{tg} \theta$. At least for large samples, the least squares estimate $\hat{\theta}$ does not appear satisfactory since it converges to a value other than the true value θ.

(ii) Sometimes the model is to be used to predict the value of x_2 corresponding to a value of x_1 which is assumed to be known. For example, we may know the total expenditure of a household M which is not included in the sample,

---

[†] In the latter figure, the regression for handicraft households does seem to reveal a particular behavior in the purchase of footwear. On the other hand, the other four regressions are compatible with a single law of behaviour if total expenditure differs from 'permanent income' and if the elasticity decreases with income.

and wish to predict its consumption of the product in question. To pose the problem in its entirety, we must distinguish between the structural model and the functional model.

The structural model is appropriate if the value of v can be considered a priori to result from random selection within a population from which the v_t of the sample are T independent selections. This is the case for example if the household M and the households observed in the inquiry have been selected at random from the same group. According to this structural model, the pair (x_1, x_2) has a bivariate distribution determined by the distribution of v and by that of $(\varepsilon_1, \varepsilon_2)$. The (x_{1t}, x_{2t}) constitute T independent observations on (x_1, x_2). The least squares regression between x_2 and x_1 is then a natural predictor of x_2 as a function of x_1, since it is a consistent estimate of the theoretical linear regression of x_2 on x_1 (see ch. 3 §§ 8 and 9). The difference from the case (i) is explained by the following fact. If the known value of x_1 exceeds the average $\bar{x}_1$ of the x_{1t} of the sample, the expected value $E(\varepsilon_1/x_1)$ is positive, and the expectation $E(v/x_1)$ is smaller than x_1. It is therefore natural that, for predicting x_2 from x_1, we should use a linear relation which has a less steep gradient than that appropriate to the prediction of x_2 from v.

On the other hand, the functional model is suitable if the value of v bears no relationship a priori to the sample values of the v_t, if, for example, the household M cannot be considered to be a random selection from the same population as the sample. In this case, knowledge of x_1 provides no information about the value of ε_1. The conditional distribution of ε_1 is identical to the marginal distribution. We then take for x_2 the value $x_2^P = x_1 \operatorname{tg} \tilde{\theta}$, with the resulting error

$$x_2^P - x_2 = x_1(\operatorname{tg} \tilde{\theta} - \operatorname{tg} \theta) + (\varepsilon_1 \operatorname{tg} \theta - \varepsilon_2)$$

and the loss:

$$E[(x_2^P - x_2)^2/x_1] = x_1^2 E[\operatorname{tg} \tilde{\theta} - \operatorname{tg} \theta]^2 + E[\varepsilon_1 \operatorname{tg} \theta - \varepsilon_2]^2.$$

The estimate must aim at minimizing the mean square error

$$E[\operatorname{tg} \tilde{\theta} - \operatorname{tg} \theta]^2,$$

exactly as in the case (i).

4 Weighted regression

Let us now find how to determine the values of the matrix A and the vector b from observations on the x_t. Nothing is known about the vectors y_t of the true variables. Thus, even when the distribution of the ε_t is specified completely, that of the x_t still depends on the following parameters: the nm elements of A, the m components of b and the nT components of y_t. These parameters are not all independent. For given values of A and b, the y_t satisfy the mT relations defined by the system $Ay_t = b$ for all t. Moreover if this system is satisfied with A and b, it is also satisfied with CA and Cb, where C is some square matrix of order m. Thus the sample distribution depends on

$$m(n - m + 1) + (n - m)T$$

independent parameters.

The problem can be represented geometrically as in ch. 9. For let x be the vector of the x_t and y the vector of the y_t in nT-dimensional Euclidean space.

The vector y lies in a variety Y of

$$m(n - m + 1) + (n - m)T$$

dimensions, defined as the set of the vectors y satisfying the relations (4) for appropriate values of the matrix A and the vector b. Moreover, the distribution of $x - y$ is independent of the position of y in Y.

Clearly the variety Y is not linear. In the bivariate model (5), we see for example that the vectors y of Y satisfy:

$$y_{1t}/y_{2t} = y_{1\theta}/y_{2\theta},$$

for all t and θ, and this is obviously a non-linear condition.

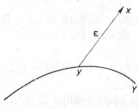

Fig. 3.

The present model is not covered by the asymptotic theory of the last chapter. Indeed, when the number T of observations increases, the number of parameters to be estimated and the dimension of Y increase also, in contrast with the situation for the model (1) of ch. 9. In fact we can distinguish between two categories of parameters:

(i) the $m(n - m + 1)$ independent parameters defining A and b occur in the distribution of all the observations x_t. For this reason, they are often called *structural parameters*[†];

(ii) the $(n - m)T$ independent parameters defining the y_t when A and b are

---

† This particular use of the term must not be confused with the sense in which the expression 'structural parameters' occurs when we wish to distinguish between the structural and the reduced form of a model (cf. ch. 17).

known. These parameters can be divided into T groups of $n-m$, each group occurring only in the distribution of the corresponding observation x_t. They are often called '*incidental parameters*'. We usually aim only at estimating the structural parameters; the incidental parameters nevertheless occur in the sample distribution.

This rather brief discussion suggests that models with errors in variables cannot be estimated by methods with such strong properties as those possessed by the methods adapted to models with errors in equations.

However, the geometric representation leads us now to consider the minimum distance estimator already defined at the beginning of the preceding chapter. In view of assumption 1, this is the estimator that minimizes

$$U = \sum_{t=1}^{T} (x_t - y_t)' \Omega^{-1} (x_t - y_t). \tag{9}$$

We shall suppose for the moment that the matrix Ω is known *a priori* and that we can therefore calculate the estimator which minimizes the expression (9) as it stands[†].

Before investigating the properties of this estimator, we must determine the formulae for calculating it, that is, the formulae giving the estimates of A, b and the y_t as functions of the observed values x_t. We could find these formulae directly, but it is simpler to deduce them from those giving the orthogonal regressions (cf. ch. 1 § 13).

For consider the non-singular square matrix D such that $\Omega^{-1} = D'D$, and define $u_t = Dx_t$ and $v_t = Dy_t$. System (4) becomes:

$$Hv_t = b, \qquad \text{for} \qquad t = 1, 2, \ldots, T \tag{10}$$

where $H = AD^{-1}$. Since D is known when Ω is, determining A, b and the y_t is equivalent to determining H, b and the v_t. Now the quantity (9) to be minimized is equal to:

$$U = \sum_{t=1}^{T} (u_t - v_t)'(u_t - v_t).$$

Thus H, b and the v_t are obtained by orthogonal regressions.

The minimum distance estimator appears in this case as corresponding to a multivariate orthogonal regression on the transformed variables. It is said to be obtained by a *weighted regression* since it results from minimization of the

---

[†] One must note that, if the covariances of the errors (Ω) are known, it is also possible to correct the regression estimates for their asymptotic bias, as suggested for instance by formula (8). A general method for such corrected regressions is given by FULLER and HIDIROGLOU [1978].

quadratic form U in which the elements of Ω^{-1} can be considered as the weighting coefficients[†].

We need now only transpose the rules for calculating orthogonal regressions in order to define a direct method for calculating the weighted regression. We adopt the usual notation of M_{xx}, M_{yy} and M_{uu} etc. for matrices of the form:

$$M_{xx} = \frac{1}{T} \sum_{t=1}^{T} (x_t - \bar{x})(x_t - \bar{x})',$$

where

$$\bar{x} = \frac{1}{T} \sum_{t=1}^{T} x_t.$$

The required calculations can be broken down as follows (cf. ch. 1 § 13).

(i) Calculate the m smallest roots of

$$|M_{uu} - \mu I| = 0.$$

Since $M_{uu} = DM_{xx}D'$ and $I = D\Omega D'$, these are also the m smallest roots of

$$|DM_{xx}D' - \mu D\Omega D'| = 0,$$

that is, also those of

$$|M_{xx} - \mu\Omega| = 0, \tag{11}$$

since D is a non-singular square matrix.

Let these m roots be μ_j $(j = 1, 2, \ldots, m)$.

(ii) Calculate the jth row h_j^* of the estimate H^* of H by solving

$$(M_{uu} - \mu_j I)h_j^* = 0,$$

where $h_j^{*\prime} h_j^* = 1$, or again

$$(DM_{xx}D' - \mu_j D\Omega D')h_j^* = 0,$$

or:

$$(M_{xx} - \mu_j\Omega)D'h_j^* = 0,$$

where

$$(D'h_j^*)'\Omega(D'h_j^*) = 1.$$

In short, the jth row $a_j^* = D'h_j^*$ of the estimate A^* of $A = HD$ is calculated by

---

[†] We have already encountered the expression 'weighted regression' when discussing models with *heteroscedastic* errors in equations (cf. ch. 8 § 2), but this should not lead to confusion. Note also that here the regression may consist of the simultaneous determination of several linear relations (the case where $m \neq 1$).

solving:

$$(M_{xx} - \mu_j \Omega)a_j^* = 0, \tag{12}$$

with the normalizing condition:

$$a_j^{*\prime} \Omega a_j^* = 1. \tag{13}$$

If there exist multiple roots of eq. (11), we proceed as for orthogonal regressions.
It is easy to verify that

$$a_j^{*\prime} \Omega a_k^* = 0$$

whenever $j \neq k$, and it follows that:

$$A^* \Omega A^{*\prime} = I. \tag{14}$$

(iii) Calculate the estimate b^* of b by $b^* = H^* \bar{u}$ or:

$$b^* = A^* \bar{x}. \tag{15}$$

(iv) Finally calculate, if so desired, the estimates v_t^* of the v_t by

$$v_t^* = u_t - H^{*\prime} H^* (u_t - \bar{u}).$$

The corresponding estimates y_t^* of the y_t are given by $y_t^* = D^{-1} v_t^*$, or

$$y_t^* = x_t - \Omega A^{*\prime} A^* (x_t - \bar{x}), \tag{16}$$

since

$$D^{-1} H^{*\prime} H^* D = D^{-1} (D\Omega D') H^{*\prime} H^* D = \Omega A^{*\prime} A^*.$$

We recall also that the minimum of U is then

$$U = T \sum_{j=1}^{m} \mu_j. \tag{17}$$

If the model contains a homogeneous linear system $Ay_t = 0$ for $t = 1, 2, \ldots, T$, that is, if we assume a priori that the vector b is zero, the same system of calculations applies to the determination of A^*, with the sole modification that M_{xx} must then be defined as:

$$M_{xx} = \frac{1}{T} \sum_{t=1}^{T} x_t x_t'.$$

5   Properties of the weighted regression

The study of the properties of weighted regression presents serious difficulties.

We can certainly state immediately the following result which derives directly from the principle adopted for defining this regression.

If assumptions 1 and 2 are satisfied (normality, homoscedasticity, etc.), the weighted regression provides the maximum likelihood estimate for A and b.

However, this remark is of no great interest. Certain general theorems do in fact state that maximum likelihood estimates are consistent and have optimal asymptotic efficiency. But these theorems assume that the sample distribution depends only on a fixed number of parameters. They do not apply when the distribution of the observations depends on certain incidental parameters besides the structural parameters to be estimated. In such cases, estimation of the structural parameters by the method of maximum likelihood may not even be consistent[†]. We shall give an example of this later (cf. § 6).

However, we can establish:

Proposition 1. If assumptions 1 and 3 are satisfied, the weighted regression provides a consistent estimate of the hyperplane $Au=b$.

For, when the number of observations tends to infinity, M_{xx} tends in probability to $M_0 + \Omega$ in view of the law of large numbers. The matrix $\Omega^{-1}M_{xx}$ tends to the matrix $\Omega^{-1}M_0 + I$. These two matrices have n real characteristic roots. The roots of $\Omega^{-1}M_{xx}$ are real continuous algebraic functions of the elements of $\Omega^{-1}M_{xx}$; they therefore tend in probability to the roots of $\Omega^{-1}M_0 + I$. (This follows from the propositions in the appendix to the previous chapter.) Now $\Omega^{-1}M_0 + I$ has m roots equal to 1 and $n-m$ roots greater than 1, since M_0 is a positive semi-definite matrix of rank $n-m$. The m smallest roots μ_j of $\Omega^{-1}M_{xx}$ therefore tend to 1.

It follows that the matrices $M_{xx} - \mu_j\Omega$ tend to M_0. Let a_j^* be the vector which is the solution of (12); $M_0 a_j^*$ tends in probability to zero. Let us consider then a vector u^0 belonging to the linear subspace $Au=0$ which contains the vectors $y_t - \bar{y}$. Since the matrix M_0 has rank $n-m$ and since $AM_0 = 0$, linear combinations of its column vectors span the linear subspace $Au=0$. So we can find v^0 such that $u^0 = M_0 v^0$ and therefore:

$$u^{0\prime}a_j^* = v^{0\prime}M_0 a_j^*$$

tends in probability to zero. The vector a_j^*, whose length is bounded below in view of the equality (13), tends to belong to the linear subspace orthogonal to $Au=0$. Moreover, the equality (14) shows that no linear combination of the a_j^* can tend to zero. So the linear subspace defined by $A^*u=0$, that of the vectors

---

[†] A general discussion of the properties of the method of maximum likelihood in models containing incidental parameters can be found in NEYMAN and SCOTT [1948], WALD [1948], WOLFOWITZ [1952], KIEFER and WOLFOWITZ [1955].

orthogonal to all the a_j^*, tends to the $(n-m)$-dimensional linear subspace $Au=0$. Since $b^*=A^*\bar{y}$, the hyperplane defined by $A^*u=b^*$ tends to the hyperplane $Au=b$ which contains the vectors y_t.

This result explains why a χ^2-distribution with mT degrees of freedom is sometimes considered to represent the distribution of

$$T \sum_{j=1}^{m} \mu_j.$$

For we saw that this quantity is equal to the minimum value of U, that is also to the expression

$$\sum_{t=1}^{T} (x_t - y_t^*)'\Omega^{-1}(x_t - y_t^*), \tag{18}$$

in which y_t^*, the estimate of y_t, is the projection of x_t on the hyperplane P^* defined by $A^*y_t=b^*$, this projection being made in the direction of the principal conjugate of P^* with respect to the concentration ellipsoid of the ε. Since the hyperplane P^* tends in probability to P, the fixed hyperplane defined by $Ay_t=b$, the vector y_t^* must be near the vector z_t, which is the projection of x_t on P. The expression (18) must then be near:

$$\sum_{t=1}^{T} (x_t - z_t)'\Omega^{-1}(x_t - z_t),$$

which is distributed as χ^2 with mT degrees of freedom, if ε_t is normally distributed (cf. ch. 5, §§ 7 and 8).

This reasoning also establishes that

$$\sqrt{T}\left[\sum_j \mu_j - m\right]$$

has a limiting normal distribution with variance $2m$, provided that assumptions 1, 2 and 3 are satisfied.

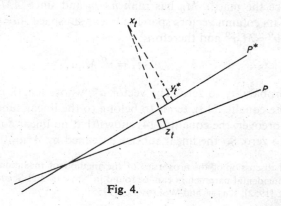

Fig. 4.

For a closer study of the asymptotic distribution of the weighted regression we now limit ourselves to the case in which the model lays down a single linear relation ($m = 1$) which can be written $a'y_t = b$ (or $a'y_t = 0$ if the right hand side is assumed a priori to be zero). The estimate a^* of a is then obtained by solving the system:

$$(M_{xx} - \mu\Omega)a^* = 0, \tag{19}$$

$$a^{*\prime}\Omega a^* = 1, \tag{20}$$

in which μ is the smallest root of

$$|M_{xx} - \mu\Omega| = 0.$$

We also set:

$$\delta a = \sqrt{T}(a^* - a),$$

$$\delta\mu = \sqrt{T}(\mu - 1),$$

$$\delta M = \sqrt{T}(M_{xx} - M_{yy} - \Omega).$$

We shall investigate the limiting distribution of δa, without worrying unduly about rigor. Thus, we shall consistently ignore those terms in the equations which tend in probability to zero when T tends to infinity. We know that $\delta\mu$ and δM have limiting normal distributions. It remains for us to show that δa also has a limiting normal distribution and to determine its covariance matrix. To calculate this matrix, we confine ourselves to the case where ε_t is normal (assumption 2). The method used is based on that adopted by LAWLEY [1953] when studying certain estimators in factor analysis.

Relations (19) and (20) imply

$$\mu = a^{*\prime}M_{xx}a^*. \tag{21}$$

These three relations lead to the following equations for δa, $\delta\mu$ and δM:

$$\delta M a + M_{yy}\delta a - \delta\mu\Omega a = 0, \tag{19'}$$

$$a'\Omega\delta a = 0, \tag{20'}$$

$$\delta\mu = a'\delta M a + 2a'M_{yy}\delta a + 2a'\Omega\delta a. \tag{21'}$$

In view of (20') and since $a'M_{yy} = 0$, the last equation can also be written

$$\delta\mu = a'\delta M a. \tag{21''}$$

Substituting this equality in (19'), we see that δa is the solution of

$$M_{yy}\delta a = -[I - \Omega aa']\delta Ma, \qquad (19'')$$

$$a'\Omega\delta a = 0. \qquad (20'')$$

This system allows δa to be determined uniquely, since M_{yy} has rank $n-1$ and $a'\Omega$ is linearly independent of the rows of M_{yy} (for there can exist no vector g such that $a'\Omega = g'M_{yy}$, since this would imply:

$$g'M_{yy}\Omega^{-1}M_{yy}g = a'M_{yy}g = 0, \qquad \text{and so} \qquad g'M_{yy} = 0;$$

and clearly $a'\Omega$ is not zero). So we calculate δa as a linear function of the elements of δM. It has a *limiting normal distribution* in the same cases as δM.

Now let V be the covariance matrix of δa:

$$V = E(\delta a \cdot \delta a').$$

The system (19''), (20'') leads to

$$M_{yy}VM_{yy} = [I - \Omega aa']C[I - aa'\Omega], \qquad (22)$$

$$a'\Omega V = 0, \qquad (23)$$

these equations defining V as a function of

$$C = E[\delta Maa'\delta M]. \qquad (24)$$

It remains to calculate this matrix. An element c_{ij} is of the form

$$c_{ij} = \sum_{hk} a_h a_k E[\delta m_{ih} \cdot \delta m_{jk}].$$

Now

$$\sqrt{T} \cdot \delta m_{ih} = \sum_t (y_{it} - \bar{y}_i)\varepsilon_{ht} + \sum_t (y_{ht} - \bar{y}_h)\varepsilon_{it} + \sum_t (\varepsilon_{it}\varepsilon_{ht} - \omega_{ih}).$$

When the ε_t are normally distributed, it is easy to calculate

$$TE[\delta m_{ih} \cdot \delta m_{jk}] = T\omega_{ij}M_{hk} + T\omega_{ik}M_{jh} + T\omega_{hj}M_{ik} + T\omega_{hk}M_{ij} \\ + T\omega_{ij}\omega_{hk} + T\omega_{ik}\omega_{jh},$$

in which M_{hk} is used to denote the (h,k)th element of M_{yy}. Since $a'M_{yy} = 0$ and $a'\Omega a = 1$, we can deduce directly

$$c_{ij} = M_{ij} + \omega_{ij} + \sum_{hk} \omega_{jh}a_h a_k \omega_{ik},$$

and so

$$C = M_{yy} + \Omega + \Omega aa'\Omega.$$

Hence:

$$[I - \Omega aa']C = M_{yy} + \Omega + \Omega aa'\Omega - \Omega aa'\Omega - \Omega aa'\Omega aa'\Omega$$

$$= M_{yy} + \Omega - \Omega aa'\Omega,$$

and similarly,

$$[I - \Omega aa']C[I - aa'\Omega] = M_{yy} + \Omega - \Omega aa'\Omega.$$

So the asymptotic covariance matrix V of $\sqrt{T}(a^* - a)$ is determined as the solution of the system

$$M_{yy}VM_{yy} = M_{yy} + \Omega - \Omega aa'\Omega,$$

$$a'\Omega V = 0.$$

(25)

By way of example, let us apply these formulae to the simplified model

$$x_{1t} = v_t + \varepsilon_{1t}$$
$$\qquad\qquad\qquad\qquad \Omega = \sigma^2 I,$$
$$x_{2t} = v_t \,\mathrm{tg}\,\theta + \varepsilon_{2t},$$

which is obtained from the general model by setting

$$a_1 = \frac{1}{\sigma}\sin\theta,$$

$$a_2 = \frac{-1}{\sigma}\cos\theta.$$

We have

$$M_{yy} = S^2 \begin{bmatrix} 1 & \mathrm{tg}\,\theta \\ \mathrm{tg}\,\theta & \mathrm{tg}^2\,\theta \end{bmatrix}, \qquad \Omega - \Omega aa'\Omega = \sigma^2 \begin{bmatrix} \cos^2\theta & \sin\theta\cos\theta \\ \sin\theta\cos\theta & \sin^2\theta \end{bmatrix}.$$

If we set $E(\theta^* - \theta)^2 = \sigma_\theta^2$, then

$$V = \frac{T\sigma_\theta^2}{\sigma^2} \begin{bmatrix} \cos^2\theta & \sin\theta\cos\theta \\ \sin\theta\cos\theta & \sin^2\theta \end{bmatrix}.$$

We need only consider the top left hand term of the matrix $M_{yy}VM_{yy}$, namely

$$\frac{TS^4\sigma_\theta^2}{\sigma^2}(1 + \mathrm{tg}^2\,\theta) = S^2 + \sigma^2\cos^2\theta,$$

and it follows that

$$\sigma_\theta^2 = \frac{\sigma^2}{TS^2} \cos^2\theta \left(1 + \frac{\sigma^2}{S^2}\cos^2\theta\right), \tag{26}$$

an asymptotic formula which can clearly be obtained directly from the expression that takes in this case the estimator θ^* corresponding to the weighted regression, namely

$$\text{tg}\, 2\theta^* = \frac{2m_{12}}{m_{11} - m_{22}}, \tag{27}$$

where tg θ^* has the sign of m_{12}, the expressions m_{11}, m_{12} and m_{22} being the elements of M_{xx}. (For the direct derivation of formulae (26) and (27), see, for example, MALINVAUD [1956].)

Formula (26) allows us to verify that, in this case and probably generally, *the weighted regression has good asymptotic efficiency at least when the dispersion of the errors is small relative to that of the true variables, and when the errors are normally distributed.*

We can compare indeed the expression found for the variance of θ^* with that of the minimum variance of unbiased estimators of θ. In this case the logarithm of the probability density can be written:

$$L = \frac{-1}{2\sigma^2}\sum_{t=1}^{T}\left[(x_{1t} - v_t)^2 + (x_{2t} - v_t \text{tg}\,\theta)^2\right] + Cte.$$

The information matrix consists of the expected values of the second derivatives of $-L$ with respect to the parameters tg θ, $v_1, v_2, \ldots, v_T$. It can be written:

$$\frac{1}{\sigma^2}\left[\begin{array}{c|c} TS^2 & v'\text{tg}\,\theta \\ \hline v\,\text{tg}\,\theta & \dfrac{1}{\cos^2\theta}I \end{array}\right],$$

v denoting the vector of the $v_1, v_2, \ldots, v_T$. Using the general formula for the inverse of partitioned matrices (cf. ch. 1 § 8, footnote, page 26), we see that the element in the first row and the first column of the inverse of the information matrix is

$$\frac{\sigma^2}{TS^2} \cdot \frac{1}{\cos^2\theta},$$

and this expression gives the minimum variance of unbiased estimators of tg θ. Now the variance of the estimator tg θ^* of tg θ is aymptotically equivalent to

$$\frac{\sigma_\theta^2}{\cos^2\theta} = \frac{\sigma^2}{TS^2} \cdot \frac{1}{\cos^2\theta}\left(1 + \frac{\sigma^2}{S^2}\cos^2\theta\right).$$

So the asymptotic efficiency of tg θ^* is

$$\left(1 + \frac{\sigma^2}{S^2}\cos^2\theta\right)^{-1},$$

which is very near 1 if σ^2/S^2 is small[†].

Formulae (25) and (26) do not give the exact asymptotic variances and covariances when the errors are not normally distributed. But they are still approximately valid if the distribution of the errors has fourth-order moments which are not too large and if the variances of the errors are small relative to those of the true variables. Thus, in the simple model, if ε_{1t} and ε_{2t} are identically distributed and mutually independent, the exact expression for the asymptotic variance of $\sqrt{T}\theta^*$ is:

$$\sigma_\theta^2 = \frac{\sigma^2}{TS^2}\cos^2\theta\left(1 + k\frac{\sigma^2}{S^2}\cos^2\theta\right),$$

the coefficient k depending on the Pearson coefficient $\beta_2 = \mu_4/\sigma^4$ of the distribution of ε_{1t} and of ε_{2t}:

$$k = 1 + (\beta_2 - 3)\sin^2 2\theta.$$

The results given in this section apply only to the asymptotic distribution of the weighted regression. Unfortunately there are few available results on the properties of this regression for finite samples. ANDERSON [1976] has recently determined the exact distribution of θ^* for the simplest model (5).

6 Weighted regression and covariance of the errors

Weighted regression has a serious drawback. It assumes that the covariance matrix Ω of the errors is known. Now, where economic data are concerned, we generally have rather vague ideas about the importance of the different errors and the correlations which may exist among them.

Unfortunately we can show that, if the regression is calculated using a matrix $\tilde{\Omega}$ other than the true matrix Ω, the estimate A^* no longer tends in general to the true value A. For example, suppose that, in the model (5), θ has been estimated by formula (27), while $\varrho \neq 0$, $\sigma_1 \neq \sigma$ and $\sigma_2 \neq \sigma$. Using the relations (7), we can easily show that tg $2\theta^*$ now tends to

$$\frac{2\,\text{tg}\,\theta + 2\varrho\sigma_1\sigma_2/S^2}{1 - \text{tg}^2\theta + \sigma_1^2/S^2 - \sigma_2^2/S^2}. \tag{28}$$

[†] Note also the following result due to WOLFOWITZ [1954c]. In functional models of the type considered here, there exists no estimator which has asymptotic efficiency equal to 1, whatever the true values of the parameters.

This expression shows also that the asymptotic bias remains small if σ_1^2/S^2 and σ_2^2/S^2 are small, that is, if the errors are not very large.

We note that the weighted regression is unchanged if Ω is replaced by $k^2\Omega$, where k is some positive number. For the characteristic roots of

$$\frac{1}{k^2}\Omega^{-1}M_{xx}$$

can be deduced from those of $\Omega^{-1}M_{xx}$ by dividing by k^2 and the homogeneous equations which allow calculation of A^* are independent of k^2. This is also apparent from formula (27) in which σ does not appear.

If k is not known (or if σ is not known in the particular model), it is possible to estimate it in view of the asymptotic properties established earlier. For let μ_j^* denote the smallest roots of (11), calculated without considering k. We know that μ_j^*/k^2 tends in probability to 1. Therefore we can estimate the coefficient k^2 by

$$\frac{1}{m}\sum_{j=1}^{m}\mu_j^*.$$

More generally, we could try to estimate Ω at the same time as A and b. This is equivalent to considering the elements of Ω as new structural parameters in the sample distribution. Since the weighted regression is obtained as the maximum likelihood estimate when the errors are normal, we might think also of finding the maximum likelihood with respect to the elements of Ω. Unfortunately this method gives no useful result. For example, we can verify that if $\Omega = k^2\Omega_0$ where Ω_0 is a known matrix and k^2 is an unknown number, the maximum likelihood estimate of k^2 is $(1/n)\sum_{j=1}^{m}\mu_{0j}$, where the μ_{0j} are the m smallest roots of (11), when Ω is replaced in it by Ω_0. This estimate tends in probability to $(m/n)k^2$ and not to k^2.

We shall return later to the general problem of simultaneous estimation of A, b and Ω. For the moment we note that the principles adopted in determining the weighted regression no longer seem to apply.

An approximate method suggested by BLOMQVIST [1972] is to determine the analytic formula for the differences between the coefficients of the multiple regression and the weighted regression as a function of the assumptions adopted for the errors. The signs and orders of magnitude of the differences can then be deduced.

7 Instrumental variables

For the model with errors in equations $x_t = Az_t + \varepsilon_t$ where z_t is random, an essential hypothesis stipulates that the errors are not correlated with the exogenous variables:

$$E(\varepsilon_t z_t') = 0,$$

or again

$$E(x_t z_t') = A E(z_t z_t').$$

The method of least squares is equivalent to replacing the expected values in this formula by the observed moments and writing

$$M_{xz} = A^* M_{zz}.$$

The asymptotic convergence of A^* to A is then explained directly by the law of large numbers, since the observed moments M_{xz} and M_{zz} tend in probability to the theoretical moments $E(x_t z_t')$ and $E(z_t z_t')$.

The method of instrumental variables is based on a similar principle. It was introduced independently by GEARY [1949] and REIERSØL [1945] and studied systematically by SARGAN [1958].

Suppose that, besides the variables x_{it} which occur in relations (3) and (4) of a model with errors in variables, we know the values of certain other variables u_{kt} called *instrumental variables*. Suppose also that it is known a priori that the errors ε_{it} in the variables x_{it} are not correlated with the variables u_{kt}. We can write

$$E[(\varepsilon_t - \bar{\varepsilon})(u_t - \bar{u})'] = 0$$

or

$$E[(x_t - \bar{x})(u_t - \bar{u})'] = E[(y_t - \bar{y})(u_t - \bar{u})'],$$

or again, since $A(y_t - \bar{y}) = 0$,

$$A E[(x_t - \bar{x})(u_t - \bar{u})'] = 0,$$

u_t being the vector with components u_{kt}. Replacing the expected value by the observed moment

$$M_{xu} = \frac{1}{T} \sum_{t=1}^{T} (x_t - \bar{x})(u_t - \bar{u})',$$

we may consider estimating A by a matrix A^* such that:

$$A^* M_{xu} = 0. \tag{29}$$

The vector b would then be estimated by $b^* = A^* \bar{x}$.

However, for these formulae to be sufficient, the system (29) must contain a non-zero solution and allow the $m(n-m)$ unknown elements of A to be determined uniquely. (Indeed, m^2 elements can be given a priori by a suitable normalization rule.) For this to be so, the matrix M_{xu} must be of rank $n-m$; this means in practice that *the instrumental variables are $n-m$ in number and that no linear combination of these variables $h'u_t$ is orthogonal to the set of variables x_{it} ($M_{xu} h = 0$).*

We shall see later how to proceed if the number of available instrumental variables is greater than $n-m$ (cf. ch. 19 § 5). In this chapter we confine ourselves to the case where there are just $n-m$ variables of this type.

The statistical properties of the estimate obtained by solving the system (29) are very similar to those of the weighted regression. The assumptions of zero correlation between the instrumental variables and the errors now plays a role analogous to the one then played by the a priori knowledge of the matrix Ω.

In order to investigate the asymptotic properties of this estimate, let us suppose that ε_t has expected value zero for every u_t and y_t, that the mean vector $\bar{u}$ tends to a finite limit, and that M_{uy} tends to a finite matrix of rank $n-m$. We confine ourselves to the case of a single linear relation among the y_{it} (that is, $m=1$). We do not specify the normalization rule adopted, but suppose only that, in the neighborhood of a, this rule is comparable to a linear condition independent of M_{uy}; we mean by this that the coefficients of this condition form a vector which is linearly independent of the vectors defined by the rows of the limit of M_{uy}. For example, the normalization rule may be $a_1 = -1$, if the linear relation $a'y_t = b$ can be solved with respect to the variable y_{1t}, since then the last $n-1$ columns of M_{uy} are linearly independent. We set

$$\delta a = \sqrt{T}(a^* - a), \qquad \delta M_{\varepsilon u} = \sqrt{T} M_{\varepsilon u}.$$

The system (29) is then asymptotically equivalent to the following:

$$M_{uy} \cdot \delta a = - \delta M_{u\varepsilon} \cdot a.$$

Since M_{uy} tends to a matrix of rank $n-1$, and since in addition δa is subject to a linear normalization condition independent of M_{uy}, $(1/\sqrt{T})\delta a$ tends in probability to zero as does $M_{u\varepsilon}$, in view of the law of large numbers. So the estimator a^* is consistent, in accordance with that was stated earlier. Similarly

$$\delta a = \sqrt{T}(a^* - a)$$

has a limiting normal distribution whenever the theorem of normal convergence applies to $\delta M_{u\varepsilon}$. To characterize this limiting distribution, we need only calculate the asymptotic covariance matrix V of $\sqrt{T}(a^* - a)$. Now

$$V = E(\delta a \cdot \delta a')$$

is the solution of

$$M_{uy} V M_{yu} = E[\delta M_{u\varepsilon} a a' \delta M_{\varepsilon u}].$$

The (h,k)th element of the right hand side can be written

$$\sum_{ij} a_i a_j \cdot \frac{1}{T} \sum_t (u_{ht} - \bar{u}_h)(u_{kt} - \bar{u}_k) E(\varepsilon_{it} \varepsilon_{jt}).$$

It is therefore equal to the (h, k)th element of $a'\Omega a \cdot M_{uu}$. Thus, the matrix V is obtained by solving

$$M_{uy} V M_{yu} = a'\Omega a \cdot M_{uu}, \tag{30}$$

along with a relation which can easily be deduced from the normalization condition. We note that this result does not depend on normality of the errors ε_t, and that the matrix V can be estimated even if Ω is not known a priori. For since the estimates a^* and b^* tend to the true values a and b, a consistent estimate of

$$a'\Omega a = E(a'\varepsilon_t)^2$$

can be calculated from the mean square distance between the observed points x_t and the hyperplane $a^{*\prime}x = b^*$ of n-dimensional space.

To consider these properties in detail, we shall refer to the simplified model (5) in which $n=2$, $m=1$. The vector u_t is then simply a real variable; (29) reduces to the equation

$$\operatorname{tg}\theta^* = \frac{\sum\limits_{t=1}^{T} x_{2t} u_t}{\sum\limits_{t=1}^{T} x_{1t} u_t}.$$

Then let ϱ_1 be the correlation coefficient between ε_{1t} and u_t, ϱ_2 that between ε_{2t} and u_t and r that between y_t and u_t. (We also make the following assumptions for the distribution of ε_{1t} and ε_{2t}: $\sigma_1 = \sigma_2 = \sigma$ and $\varrho = 0$.) A detailed study of this case leads to three conclusions, which have a more general validity[†].

(a) If $\varrho_1 = \varrho_2 = 0$, that is if the errors are actually uncorrelated with the instrumental variable, the estimate $\operatorname{tg}\theta^*$ tends in probability to the true value $\operatorname{tg}\theta$, as we established above.

(b) Always if $\varrho_1 = \varrho_2 = 0$, the asymptotic variance of the estimate is given by

$$E(\operatorname{tg}\theta - \operatorname{tg}\theta^*)^2 \sim \frac{\sigma^2}{Tr^2S^2}(1 + \operatorname{tg}^2\theta)$$

or

$$E(\theta - \theta^*)^2 \sim \frac{\sigma^2}{Tr^2S^2}\cos^2\theta,$$

these formulae being directly obtainable, or deducible from the general relation (30). *The estimate is precise only in the case of strong correlation between the instrumental variable and the systematic part of the variables of the model.* By

---

[†] The relation between the instrumental variable estimator and the maximum likelihood estimator in this simple model is considered by E. E. LEAMER [1978], who shows that the two often coincide.

comparison with formula (26), we see also that, in this case, the precision obtained is of the same order as that obtained with the weighted regression.

(c) If $\varrho_1 \neq 0$ and $\varrho_2 \neq 0$, that is if in fact the errors are correlated with the instrumental variables, an approximate expression for the asymptotic value of tg θ^* is given by

$$\operatorname{tg}\theta + \frac{\sigma}{rS}(\varrho_2 - \varrho_1 \operatorname{tg}\theta).$$

So the estimate contains an asymptotic bias. If r is near 1, this bias is of comparable size to that which results when Ω is badly specified in calculation of the weighted regression. If not, it is generally greater.

Thus, to use the method now proposed, we must find instrumental variables which are uncorrelated with the errors affecting the variables of the model, but are strictly correlated with the true values of these variables. In practice these considerations are often contradictory, and this greatly restricts the usefulness of the method.

It has been proposed that, in its application to time series, lagged values $x_{i,t-1}$ of the variables of the model should be used as instrumental variables (this necessitates a reconsideration of the statistical theory summarized above, but the conclusions are unchanged). However, the errors affecting the variables are often associated through time; consequently $x_{i,t-1}$ is not independent of ε_t. In short, this suggestion is of no great practical interest.

The use of instrumental variables does not then provide a general method of estimating models with errors in variables. Everything depends on the available data. However, the method is interesting in two respects. First, it introduces a new principle which can be applied in other types of model. Thus we shall see that it plays an important part in the estimation of certain models with errors in equations (cf. ch. 16). Secondly, it does sometimes allow effective elimination of difficulties due to the presence of errors in the exogenous variables.

For example, let us return to the problem of estimating consumption elasticities from the results of family budget inquiries. For a sample of households $t = 1, 2, \ldots, T$, total expenditure x_{1t} and consumption x_{2t} of the type of goods considered are known. The model specifies a linear relation between x_{2t} and disposable income v_t:

$$x_{2t} = a v_t + b + \varepsilon_{2t}.$$

In addition, the difference between total consumption and income is considered to be well described by a random variable with zero mean[†]:

[†] Of course this statement ignores complications which must be introduced in practical econometric studies. Thus, the model generally specifies a linear relation between the logarithms of x_{2t} and v_t rather than between their arithmetic values. A systematic difference exists between v_t and x_{1t}, due to the fact that in most cases saving tends to be positive, at least at certain levels of income. It would take too much space to discuss here the treatment of these difficulties, and the reader can find in other passages the necessary elements for achieving the solution of the problems which arise.

$$x_{1t} = v_t + \varepsilon_{1t}.$$

So we are faced with a model with errors in variables. Generally the weighted regression cannot be calculated, since we know nothing a priori about the correlation between ε_{1t} and ε_{2t} or about the ratio between the variances of these two errors.

In many cases figures for declared income are also available. This declared income, say u_t, seems to be a mediocre measure of actual income. In particular, it is affected by considerable and systematic underestimation. So, all in all, total expenditure is considered to give a better measure of true income, and a least square regression between x_{2t} and u_t would give a poor estimate of the unknown coefficients a and b.

But there is no reason why u_t should not be taken as instrumental variable. On the contrary, declared income u_t and true income v_t must be highly correlated while u_t and the difference ε_{1t} between total expenditure and income must show low correlation. The latter indeed arises from chance variations in consumption which occur in the same way at different levels of income. As LIVIATAN [1961] showed, this situation is favourable to the use of u_t as instrumental variable, that is, to estimating a by

$$a^* = \frac{\sum_{t=1}^{T} (x_{2t} - \bar{x}_2)(u_t - \bar{u})}{\sum_{t=1}^{T} (x_{1t} - \bar{x}_1)(u_t - \bar{u})}. \tag{31}$$

This avoids the bias affecting estimation of a by means of least squares regression between x_{2t} and x_{1t}.

8 Identification and specification of the model

Weighted regression and the use of instrumental variables lead to consistent estimates, if certain characteristics of the distribution of the errors are known a priori, in one case the covariance matrix, in the other the absence of correlation with the instrumental variables. It would be desirable to have methods available for simultaneous estimation of the law of the errors and the linear relations among the true variables. Unfortunately it is not certain that such methods exist.

More precisely, we must ask ourselves if the model, or any of its parameters, is identifiable when only some general assumptions are adopted a priori. No consistent method exists for estimating A and b if, when account is taken of the normalization conditions, these parameters are not identifiable; that is if the same distribution of the sequence of the observed vectors x_t may correspond to different positions of the hyperplane $Ay = b$ in n-dimensional space.

Even when A and b are identifiable in principle, there may exist no estimation method which is applicable in practice. For it may happen that the minimum variances of the estimators of A and b are so great that no useful information can be drawn from finite samples of the size available in econometrics. The situation is then virtually the same as that which arises in the absence of identifiability.

We must not lose sight of this remark in the course of this section when we are examining cases in which the structural parameters of models with errors in variables are identifiable, and giving the different estimation methods proposed for each of these cases. We should also point out that, for the present, these methods remain theoretical. They indicate certain lines of approach, but have not been tested sufficiently to be recommended for practical use.

Identification of A and b in the functional model depends on the characteristics of the unknown sequence of the vectors y_t. There has been little investigation of this[†]. So we shall refer here to the structural model, for which various results exist. These results may be thought to apply to the functional model if the empirical distribution of the values taken by the vectors y_t tends to a limiting distribution when T tends to infinity.

(i) It is not difficult to give an example in which the structural parameters are not identifiable. Suppose that in their hyperplane the y_t have a normal distribution independent of t and that two values y_t and y_θ relating to different observations t and θ are independent. The distribution of the y_t is perfectly defined by its mean y^0 and its covariance matrix Y, this matrix being positive semi-definite of rank $n-m$ and such that $AYA'=0$. Suppose also that the ε_t satisfy assumptions 1 and 2, and so in particular that they are normally distributed, but that their covariance matrix Ω is completely unknown.

[†] In fact, if identifiability is defined as in ch. 2 § 10, the functional model is identifiable under very general conditions. To show this it is enough, according to this definition, to verify that to a given distribution of the observable variables there corresponds only one 'structure', that is, a single specification of the unknown parameters. Under assumptions 1 and 2, the observed sample $(x_1, x_2, \ldots, x_T)$ is normally distributed with expected value $(y_1, y_2, \ldots, y_T)$ and covariance matrix defining Ω uniquely. If this distribution is specified, Ω and $(y_1, y_2, \ldots, y_T)$ are specified and thereby also the hyperplane to which the y_t belong (under the sole condition that the matrix M_{yy} is of rank $n-m$).

But this property is not very useful, since in this case there is no hope of determining the sample distribution exactly from a single sample. With the structural model, and with other models discussed in this book, exact determination of the distribution of an infinite sample results from the observation of a single sample, since the different observations are mutually independent and identically distributed, or have distributions corresponding to each other in some known way. But with the functional model, our lack of knowledge about the value of the incidental parameter y_θ prevents us from ever knowing the distribution of x_θ exactly, however many observations are taken on other x_t (for $t \neq \theta$).

So this discussion leads us to suggest a change in the definition of the concept of identifiability when the number of parameters to be estimated tends to infinity. By an identifiable parameter or characteristic we really mean a parameter or a characteristic for which consistent estimators can be found.

We know then that x_t and x_θ are independent if $t \neq \theta$, and that they are identically normally distributed with mean y^0 and covariance matrix

$$X = Y + \Omega.$$

It is then possible to estimate y^0 and X. But the observed values do not allow Y to be determined uniquely. For the matrix X can be expressed in many different ways as the sum of two matrices Y and Ω satisfying the assumptions of the model. For example

$$X = \begin{bmatrix} 3 & 0 \\ 0 & 2 \end{bmatrix} \quad \text{can be written} \quad \begin{bmatrix} 2 & 0 \\ 0 & 0 \end{bmatrix} + \begin{bmatrix} 1 & 0 \\ 0 & 2 \end{bmatrix},$$

or again

$$\begin{bmatrix} 1 & 1 \\ 1 & 1 \end{bmatrix} + \begin{bmatrix} 2 & -1 \\ -1 & 1 \end{bmatrix}.$$

The first decomposition leads to the linear relation $y_{1t} = 0$, the second to the relation $y_{1t} = y_{2t}$. (This example has already been introduced in ch. 2, § 10.)

In this case different distributions of the true values and of the errors, corresponding to *different positions of the hyperplane* $Ay_t = b$ lead to the *same sample distribution*. No estimation method allows exact choice among these possible positions.

(ii) REIERSØL [1950a] proved that the *hyperplane* $Ay = b$ *and the matrix* Ω *of the structural model are identifiable when* M_{yy} *has rank* $n - m$ *and the errors are normally distributed, satisfying assumption 1 with a matrix* Ω *about which nothing is known a priori, provided that the distribution of the* y_t *is not also normal*[†]. This result must be put side by side with the example given above.

What estimation methods are appropriate to this case? KIEFER and WOLFOWITZ [1956] showed that maximum likelihood estimators can be defined in this model, although nothing is known a priori about the distribution of the y_t. They proved that these estimators are consistent. WOLFOWITZ [1954a] also established the consistency of estimators defined so as to minimize a distance between the empirical and the theoretical sample distribution[††]. Unfortunately no method has been determined for calculating either of these estimators. So they remain purely theoretical for the present.

[†] The proof is given only for the case $n = 2$, $m = 1$; but it seems capable of easy generalization.
[††] The same result was established by the same author [1954b] for a functional model.

For the case where $n=2$ and $m=1$, NEYMAN [1951] defined a consistent estimator which applies to the present situation (ε_t normal) as well as to that described below (ε_{it} independent of ε_{jt}). But its calculation is long and complex. It has not been applied effectively and seems to be of no interest for small samples. (See MADANSKY [1959], pp. 197 and 200.)

(iii) REIERSØL [1950a and b] also proved various results for the case where the *errors relating to the different variables are mutually independent* (and so, in particular, Ω is diagonal). These results can be given as follows[†]:

When the errors ε_{it} are mutually independent and satisfy assumption 1 with a matrix Ω which is known to be diagonal, but apart from that may be any matrix, when M_{yy} has rank $n-m$, the hyperplane $Ay=b$ and the matrix Ω of the structural model are identifiable except in two cases:

(i) if simultaneously y_t is normally distributed and $(n-m)^2-n-m<0$;

(ii) or also if y_t is normally distributed, if $(n-m)^2-n-m\geqslant0$, but if the hyperplane $Ay_t=b$ is unfavourably situated from the point of view of identifiability.

In order to study the estimation methods, we can distinguish the two cases in which identification is possible: that in which $(n-m)^2-n-m\geqslant0$, and that in which y_t is not normally distributed.

(a) *The case where $(n-m)^2-n-m\geqslant0$*. The dimension of the hyperplane $Ay=b$ is then small relative to that of the space to which it belongs. The hyperplane $Ay=b$ and the diagonal matrix Ω are then generally determined uniquely by the expected value y^0 and the covariance matrix X of the observed vector x_t.

Consider, for example, the case where $n=3$, $m=1$. The diagonal elements of Ω are σ_1^2, σ_2^2 and σ_3^2, the variances of the three components of ε_t. The vectors y_t belong to a straight line passing through y^0. So we can write $y_t-y^0=u_t\cdot v$ where u_t is some number and v a fixed vector of unit length. If $E(u_t^2)=\tau^2$, we easily obtain

$$X=\begin{bmatrix} \sigma_1^2+\tau^2v_1^2 & \tau^2v_1v_2 & \tau^2v_1v_3 \\ \tau^2v_1v_2 & \sigma_2^2+\tau^2v_2^2 & \tau^2v_2v_3 \\ \tau^2v_1v_3 & \tau^2v_2v_3 & \sigma_3^2+\tau^2v_3^3 \end{bmatrix}.$$

Conversely, if the elements of X, the ξ_{ij} say, are known, the values of the σ_i^2,

---

[†] REIERSØL [1950b] proves that, it y_t is normal and M_{yy} of rank $n-m$, the structural parameters are identifiable only if $(n-m)^2-n-m\geq0$. Necessary and sufficient conditions are given by ANDERSON and RUBIN [1956] for the case where y_t is normal, with $m=1$ and $m=2$. REIERSØL [1950a] proves that, if $n=2$, $m=1$, the structural parameters are identifiable if and only if y_t is not normal. Generalization to the statement given in the text should present no difficulty.

the v_i and τ^2 can generally be deduced. If ξ_{12}, ξ_{13} and ξ_{23} are all non-zero, then

$$\sigma_1^2 = \xi_{11} - \frac{\xi_{21}\xi_{31}}{\xi_{23}}, \qquad \tau^2 = \frac{\xi_{21}\xi_{31}}{\xi_{23}} + \frac{\xi_{12}\xi_{23}}{\xi_{13}} + \frac{\xi_{13}\xi_{23}}{\xi_{12}}$$

and the direction of the vector v of unit length is determined by

$$\frac{v_1}{v_3} = \frac{\xi_{12}}{\xi_{23}} \quad \text{and} \quad \frac{v_1}{v_2} = \frac{\xi_{13}}{\xi_{23}}.$$

In view of the form of X and since v has unit length, the three non-diagonal terms ξ_{12}, ξ_{13} and ξ_{23} cannot simultaneously be zero, nor can only one of them be zero. So we need only examine for example the case where $\xi_{12} = \xi_{13} = 0$; $\xi_{23} \neq 0$. Clearly σ_1^2 and v_1 are then identifiable ($\sigma_1^2 = \xi_{11}$; $v_1 = 0$), but the other parameters are not. There are then only four relations among the five unknown parameters σ_2, σ_3, τ, v_2 and v_3:

$$\xi_{22} = \sigma_2^2 + \tau^2 v_2^2, \qquad \xi_{23} = \tau^2 v_2 v_3,$$

$$\xi_{33} = \sigma_3^2 + \tau^2 v_3^2, \qquad v_2^2 + v_3^2 = 1.$$

In this case, the line on which the mean vectors y_t lie is parallel to the plane defined by the last two coordinate axes. The lack of identifiability which we find here is completely analogous to that encountered earlier (cf. (i)). (Here we use the assumption that ε_t is normally distributed, since we suppose that the distribution of the x_t is defined uniquely by its first and second-order moments.)

When $(n-m)^2 - n - m \geqslant 0$, and the true hyperplane is not situated so as to make identification impossible, a consistent estimator is defined by the *weighted regression* corresponding not to the unknown true matrix Ω, but to a diagonal matrix Ω^* whose diagonal elements are equal to those of the covariance matrix $M_{\varepsilon\varepsilon}^*$ of the residuals ε_t^* with respect to this weighted regression. The residuals are then

$$\varepsilon_t^* = x_t - y_t^* = \Omega^* A^{*\prime} A^* (x_t - \bar{x}).$$

More precisely, the matrices Ω^* and A^* of this estimator must be determined simultaneously in such a way that, on the one hand, A^* could be computed by the weighted regression established as if Ω^* were the covariance matrix of the ε_t, and, on the other hand, the diagonal terms of Ω^* would be the variances of the residuals with respect to this weighted regression.

The estimator in question was first defined by LAWLEY [1940] when he was investigating maximum likelihood for the structural model in which the ε_t are normally distributed and obey assumption 1. Using the same assumptions,

ANDERSON and RUBIN [1956] proved that Ω^* and A^* have a limiting normal distribution when Ω and A are identifiable. They showed how their asymptotic variances and covariances can be determined, but the formulae are apparently too complex to be used in applications.

In practice, an iterative procedure must be used for determining Ω^* and A^*. First $A^{(1)}$ can be calculated from a weighted regression with arbitrary matrix $\Omega^{(0)}$ (for example $\Omega^{(0)} = I$); the diagonal matrix whose non-zero elements are the variances of the residuals with respect to the first weighted regression, can be taken for $\Omega^{(1)}$. Then a new weighted regression with matrix $\Omega^{(1)}$ can be calculated, and $\Omega^{(2)}$ obtained from the new residuals. This process would continue until the matrices $\Omega^{(s)}$ and $A^{(s)}$ converge sufficiently.

(b) *The case where y_t is not normal.* Consider now the case where the errors ε_{it} relating to different variables are mutually independent and, in addition, y_t is not normally distributed. GEARY [1942] showed that in this case consistent estimators of the structural parameters can be constructed by using the *cumulants* of the empirical distribution of the pairs (x_{1t}, x_{2t}).

We shall examine this method in the context of the simple model

$$x_1 = v + \varepsilon_1$$

$$x_2 = v \, \text{tg} \, \theta + \varepsilon_2. \tag{32}$$

The indices t denoting the different observations are suppressed since we need only investigate the theoretical distribution of the pair (x_1, x_2).

Let $\psi_v(t)$ denote the cumulant generating function of v, namely

$$\psi_v(t) = \ln \left[E(exp\{itv\}) \right]$$

(see CRAMER [1946], 15.9, 15.10 and 21.3). Similarly let $\psi_1(t)$ and $\psi_2(t)$ be the cumulant generating functions of ε_1 and ε_2. Also let $\psi(t_1, t_2)$ be the cumulant generating function of the pair (x_1, x_2), namely

$$\psi(t_1, t_2) = \ln \left[E(exp\{it_1 x_1 + it_2 x_2\}) \right].$$

The independence between ε_1 and ε_2 and the independences stipulated by assumption 1 imply

$$\psi(t_1, t_2) = \psi_v(t_1 + t_2 \, \text{tg} \, \theta) + \psi_1(t_1) + \psi_2(t_2). \tag{33}$$

Also let $K_v(p)$, $K_1(p)$ and $K_2(p)$ be the p-order cumulants of v, ε_1 and ε_2, and $K(p,q)$ the cumulant of order (p,q) of the pair (x_1, x_2). These cumulants are known to be defined by the following identities in t and t_1, t_2:

$$\psi(t) = \sum_{p=1}^{\infty} K(p) \frac{(it)^p}{p!}$$

for a real random variable;

$$\psi(t_1, t_2) = \sum_{p,q=0}^{\infty} K(p,q) \frac{(it_1)^p (it_2)^q}{p!q!}$$

for a random 2-vector.

Substituting these expansions in (33), and identifying the terms in $(it_1)^p(it_2)^q$ for $p > 0$ and $q > 0$, we find directly

$$\frac{K(p,q)}{p!q!} = (\text{tg}\,\theta)^q \frac{K_v(p+q)}{p+q!} \qquad \text{for} \qquad p > 0 \qquad \text{and} \qquad q > 0. \quad (34)$$

So the cross-cumulants ($p > 0$ and $q > 0$ simultaneously) of the pair (x_1, x_2) depend only on θ and the cumulants of v, but not on the distribution of ε_1 and ε_2. Equation (34) leads directly to simple relations between θ and the cumulants $K(p,q)$. In particular, if $p > 1$, $q > 1$ and $K_v(p+q-1) \neq 0$, then

$$\text{tg}\,\theta = \frac{p}{q} \cdot \frac{K(p-1,q)}{K(p,q-1)}. \quad (35)$$

Therefore the parameter θ can be determined exactly from the cumulants of the distribution of (x_1, x_2) except when all the cumulants of v of order greater than 2 are zero, that is, except when v is normally distributed. This case was excluded by hypothesis.

From this starting point, Geary proposes estimating $\text{tg}\,\theta$ by a ratio of the type

$$\text{tg}\,\hat{\theta} = \frac{p}{q} \cdot \frac{K^*(p-1,q)}{K^*(p,q-1)}, \quad (36)$$

$K^*(p,q)$ being the cumulant of order (p,q) of the empirical distribution of the (x_{1t}, x_{2t}) for $t = 1, 2, \ldots, T$. When the number T of observations tends to infinity, the empirical cumulants $K^*(p,q)$ tend in probability to the theoretical cumulants $K(p,q)$, so that $\hat{\theta}$ does provide a consistent estimator of $\text{tg}\,\theta$. In practice, the dispersion of $K^*(p,q)$ about $K(p,q)$ increases quickly with p and q. The first cross-cumulants are therefore used, namely:

$$\operatorname{tg}\hat{\theta} = \frac{K^*(1,2)}{K^*(2,1)}$$

if one can assume a priori that the distribution of v is asymmetric $(K_v(3)\neq 0)$, or

$$\operatorname{tg}\hat{\theta} = \frac{2}{3}\cdot\frac{K^*(1,3)}{K^*(2,2)}.$$

in the opposite case.

The empirical cumulants are calculated from the empirical moments about the mean according to formulae which can be deduced from the relationship between the characteristic and cumulant generating functions (see KENDALL [1948], § 3. 13). Thus

$$K(1,2) = \mu(1,2), \qquad K(2,1) = \mu(2,1),$$

$$K(1,3) = \mu(1,3) - 3\mu(1,1)\mu(0,2),$$

$$K(2,2) = \mu(2,2) - \mu(2,0)\mu(0,2) - 2[\mu(1,1)]^2,$$

$\mu(p,q)$ denoting the moment of order (p,q) about the mean.

Unfortunately, estimators obtained in this way are not very precise. MADANSKY [1959] showed how to obtain an approximate formula for the variance of tg $\hat{\theta}$. In an example he found this variance to be so large that the estimator was useless.

In short, the discussion of this section contains a rather deceptive conclusion. If in many cases structural parameters can be identified, consistent estimators appropriate to such cases are virtually useless in econometrics, since there are too few data. The most favourable situation is certainly that in which Ω can be assumed to be diagonal, and when the hyperplane $Ay_t = b$ is of small dimension relative to the space which contains it. Even then, the estimator defined in (iii) (a) must still have only fair precision for samples of less than fifty observations.

9 Grouping the data

Various other suggestions have been put forward for defining consistent estimators which do not call for a priori knowledge of the covariance matrix of the errors Ω. Each involves some particular assumption about the true variables or the errors[†]. We shall limit discussion here to a method which involves classifying the observations into groups and fitting the group means.

The principle of this method is as follows.

We assume that the observations are divided a priori into q groups ($\alpha = 1, 2, \ldots, q$), and find out what happens if, in each group α, the number of observations T_α tends to infinity. Let $\bar{x}_\alpha$ and $\bar{y}_\alpha$ be the vectors of the mean values of the x_{it} and the y_{it} in the observations of group α. If assumption 1 is satisfied, we know from the law of large numbers that $\bar{x}_\alpha - \bar{y}_\alpha$ tends in probability to zero

---

[†] In particular, when considering estimation from time series, TINTNER [1952] (cf. p. 135 and following pages) proposed that the errors ε_{it} should be separated from the true values y_{it} by calculating the successive differences of the series x_{it} according to the formulae

$$\Delta x_{it} = x_{it} - x_{i,t-1}$$

$$\ldots \Delta^{(p)} x_{it} = \Delta^{(p-1)} x_{it} - \Delta^{(p-1)} x_{i,t-1}$$

If the y_{it} are polynomials of degree $p-1$ in t,

$$\Delta^{(p)} y_{it} = 0, \quad \text{and} \quad \Delta^{(p)} x_{it} = \Delta^{(p)} \varepsilon_{it}.$$

Therefore the distribution of the $\Delta^{(p)} \varepsilon_{it}$ can be estimated from the x_{it}, and an estimate $\hat{\Omega}$ of Ω can be deduced from it. Next we need only determine the hyperplane $Ay_t = b$ by a weighted regression on the x_t with $\hat{\Omega}$ as matrix. (The reader can find an application of this method by FOURGEAUD [1951] and refer to ch. 12 § 8 for some additional remarks on the 'variate difference method'.)

There may be some reservations about the usefulness of such a method. It is most often impossible to assume that the y_{it} are polynomials of low degree in t. And, if we can assume that the y_{it} are indeed polynomials of degree $p-1$, there is another method which seems more appropriate. For we can then write

$$x_t = Dz_t + \varepsilon_t$$

where D is an unknown matrix but the vectors z_t are determined completely a priori (for example, the $z_{1t}, z_{2t}, \ldots, z_{pt}$ may be orthogonal polynomials of degree $0, 1, \ldots, p-1$ in t). The condition $Ay_t = b$ can then be written

$$AD(z_t - \bar{z}) = 0.$$

Estimation of the matrix A and the vector b can be considered as part of the estimation of the model with errors in the equations

$$x_t = Dz_t + \varepsilon_t,$$

the matrix D being restricted to have rank m so that $AD = 0$ with a matrix A of order $m \times n$. We have already given in ch. 9 the principles to be applied in estimating such a model; in ch. 20 we shall examine this type of a priori restriction.

The method given by TINTNER. [1952] might have the advantage that it does not necessitate choosing a priori the degree p of the polynomial to be used. But the properties of this method have been insufficiently investigated to allow a definite conclusion about it.

when T_α tends to infinity. *We also assume that the q vectors $\bar{y}_\alpha$ tend respectively to q different limiting vectors y_α which determine the hyperplane $Ay_\alpha = b$ uniquely* (in particular, it is necessary that $q > n - m$). Therefore the $\bar{x}_\alpha$ tend in probability to these same limits y_α and provide the elements for consistent estimators of the structural parameters A and b.

In the case where $q = n - m + 1$, the mean vectors $\bar{x}_\alpha$ are all contained in the same $(n - m)$-dimensional hyperplane and generally define it uniquely; this hyperplane is then taken as estimate of the true hyperplane $Ay_t = b$. The $m(n - m + 1)$ equations $A^* \bar{x}_\alpha = b^*$ (for $\alpha = 1, 2, \ldots, n - m + 1$), combined with the normalization conditions, define the estimates A^* and b^* of A and b. For example, if there are two variables, one linear relation between them, and two groups, the estimated straight line passes through the two mean points defined within the two groups.

In the case where $q > n - m + 1$, the mean vectors $\bar{x}_\alpha$ do not generally all belong to the same $(n - m)$-dimensional hyperplane. So such a hyperplane must be fitted to these vectors. Every fitting method leads to consistent estimates provided it is continuous with respect to the vectors $\bar{x}_\alpha$ and that it gives the hyperplane of the $\bar{x}_\alpha$ when these vectors happen to belong to the same $(n - m)$-dimensional hyperplane. For example, one may calculate the least squares regressions of m components $\bar{x}_{i\alpha}$ on the other $n - m$ components.

Thus, the group means allow calculation of consistent estimates. We have still to find the scope of this method in practice. The assumptions on which it is based make two demands which are often contradictory. For it is necessary that

(a) the observations be classified among the groups independently of the values of the errors ε_t, since otherwise the law of large numbers would not apply within the groups;

(b) the group means do not tend to the same limits, since otherwise the y_α would no longer be sufficient for determining the true hyperplane.

Systematic classification of the observations according to the order in which they appear, or classification by random selection, satisfies the first demand but not the second, since the mean vectors $\bar{y}_\alpha$ then all tend to the limiting vector y^0 of $\bar{y}$, provided that assumption 3 is satisfied. Conversely, classification of the observations according to the values of the x_t generally satisfies the second demand, but not the first, since in this case the classification is no longer independent of the errors ε_t.

Fitting the group means was first introduced by WALD [1940] who, when discussing the regression between two variables x_{1t} and x_{2t}, proposed that the observations be arranged in two groups according to the position of the value of x_{1t} with respect to the median observed value of x_1, or to some previously chosen value x_0. NEYMAN and SCOTT [1951] showed that the corresponding estimate is consistent if *and only if* the distribution of ε_{1t} is concentrated on a bounded interval, and if the true values y_{1t} are divided into two distinct groups in such a way that there is zero probability that the observation corresponding to a true value y_{1t} of the first (second) group gives a value for x_{1t} higher (lower) than x_0. Thus, the suggestion is of very limited practical interest, and the developments in theory to which it gave rise seem difficult to apply.

On the other hand, the use of group means may become advantageous when the observations are classified according to the values which they assign to variables z_{kt} other than the x_{it}. In order that the above conditions (a) and (b) should be satisfied, it is enough that the errors ε_{it} be considered as independent of the z_{kt}, and that there exist some empirical correlation between the z_{kt} and the true values y_{it}.

The following procedure was therefore adopted for determining consumption elasticities from the results of the French family budget inquiry in 1956 (cf. ROTTIER [1959]). The families were divided into groups according to their declared annual income. In each group, the means of the different categories of consumption and of total expenditure were calculated. The income-elasticity of each type of consumption was determined by fitting the group means for the relevant category of expenditure and for the total expenditure (in most cases, a least squares regression was calculated among the logarithms of the group means).

In this case, x_{1t} can represent the total expenditure of family t, x_{2t} its consumption of the particular type considered, z_t its declared income and y_t its true income. Conditions (a) and (b) are satisfied if the difference ε_{1t} between total expenditure and true income can be considered as a random variable independent of declared income and with zero mean. Therefore the method used allows the determination of good estimates of income-elasticities, and this in spite of the existence of the difference ε_{1t} between total expenditure and income[†].

Clearly the method now considered and that which consists of using the z_{kt} as instrumental variables are closely related. They depend on the same assumptions and lead to similar computation, that for fitting group means being generally slightly quicker. The results must be virtually identical whenever the number of groups is sufficiently great for the values of the z_{kt} not to vary too much within each group.

[†] In fact, if the relations among the true variables are non-linear, fitting the group means may entail bias. For example, if the particular consumption considered obeys the model

$$\ln x_{2t} = a \ln y_t + b + \varepsilon_{2t},$$

it is not strictly correct that the means $x_{2\alpha}, y_\alpha, \varepsilon_{2\alpha}$ satisfy

$$\ln x_{2\alpha} = a \ln y_\alpha + b + \varepsilon_{2\alpha}.$$

But in practice the resulting bias must remain very small.

10   Historical note

Models with errors in variables were introduced for the first time in statistics at the end of the XIXth century (see LINDLEY [1947] for complete references). In the search for stochastic formulations suitable to econometric analysis, these models seemed at first to be particularly appropriate. They were proposed by FRISCH [1934] and investigated particularly by KOOPMANS [1937] who used the weighted regression defined previously by various statisticians.

They later became less important relative to models with errors in equations which now seem generally more justifiable. Errors of measurement in economic quantities appear in most cases to be negligible compared with disturbing influences which are not represented explicitly in the relations studied. Nevertheless models with errors in variables are still very important in econometric methodology. In the first place, they provide the most suitable method of representation for certain situations. In the second place, their investigation gave rise to the definition of methods which can be applied in more complex models which we shall encounter later (notably models with distributed lags and 'overidentified' models).

Since the general statistical theory of these models is complex, most authors discuss the simplest case in which there are only two observed variables and one linear relation between them. The most important contributions were mentioned in the preceding sections. MADANSKY [1959] recently gave a complete survey of the literature.

Besides its use in econometrics, the general model with several variables and several relations has found a second field of application in quantitative psychology. For *factor analysis* one sets up the following model:

$$x_{it} = \sum_{j=1}^{T} \lambda_{ij} f_{jt} + b_i + \varepsilon_{it}, \tag{37}$$

x_{it} denoting the result obtained by the tth individual in the ith test ($t = 1, 2, \ldots, T$; $i = 1, 2, \ldots, n$), f_{jt} representing the value for the tth individual of the psychological 'factor' j. The λ_{ij} and b_i are structural parameters, the same for all individuals; and the ε_{it} denote errors or random differences with zero means, independent of the f_{jt}. The factors f_{jt} are not directly observable. They are sometimes assumed to be random, sometimes fixed but unknown. The factor analysis problem consists in the estimation of the λ_{ij}, b_i and f_{jt} from an observed sample of x_{it}.

The model is identical to that discussed in this chapter, since it can be written

$$y_t - \bar{y} = \Lambda(f_t - \bar{f}).$$

Here f_t is the vector of the f_{jt}, Λ the matrix of the λ_{ij} and y_t the vector of the expected values of the x_{it} (for given values of the f_{jt}); Λ is an $n \times p$ matrix. Since the number p of the factors is always less than the number n of the tests, Λ generally has rank p. We can then find an $(n-p) \times n$ matrix A of rank $n-p$ and such that $A\Lambda = 0$. Consequently

$$A(y_t - \bar{y}) = 0.$$

The model (37) postulates that, in n-dimensional space, the vectors x_t have expectations y_t about which nothing is known a priori except that they must all belong to the same p-dimensional hyperplane. According to whether the f_t are random or fixed, we find the structural model or the functional model of this chapter.

Thus most statistical research into factor analysis is directly transposable to models with errors in variables. Only one problem finds no application in econometrics, at least for the present, that is the problem which consists of identifying the matrix Λ when the coefficients λ_{ij} are subject to certain a priori restrictions.

ANDERSON and RUBIN [1956] have given a survey of the known properties of the different statistical methods of factor analysis.

Part 4

FITTING TIME SERIES

CHAPTER 11

Statistical analysis of time series

1 Introduction

The name time series is given to a sequence of observations which are ordered in time, say x_1, x_2, ..., x_t, ..., x_T, the interval between the dates t and $t + 1$ of two successive observations being fixed and constant throughout. Such series are often used in econometric research, where their simultaneous evolutions reveal certain characteristics of the underlying phenomena. In most cases, the econometrician refers to a model representing the phenomena in question. So the methodological discussion of the problems raised by the use of time series must be carried on with reference to general models corresponding to those used in practice. This is, in any case, the standpoint systematically adopted throughout this book.

However, just as in chapter 1 we discussed the modalities of some fitting methods independently of any model, so here we shall first look at some procedures which facilitate the examination of time series and which involve very few preconceived ideas. So in part, this chapter deals with descriptive rather than with inductive statistics.

The second object of the chapter is to study tests and estimators appropriate to the cases where the model involves only a single time series of a stochastic process and we wish to exploit the information it affords us about the properties of the process. The series is then dealt with by itself, independently of other series to which it may be related†.

The temporal analysis of economic phenomena has long distinguished different types of evolution which may possibly be combined:

– The *trend* is a slow variation in some specific direction which is maintained over a long period of years.

– The *cycle* is a movement, quasi-periodic in appearance, alternately increasing and decreasing. In most cases it is related to fluctuations in economic activity.

– *The seasonal movement* is composed of regular weekly, monthly or yearly variations. It arises from the changing seasons and the rhythm of human activity.

---

† The approach adopted in this chapter can be generalized to a set of n time series in two different ways. We can consider these series as constituting the realization of a single random process whose x_tth element is an n-vector, and deal with this process by generalizing the methods appropriate to real processes. Or we can base our reasoning on a model setting relations among these n series. The latter is the approach adopted in the following chapters.

– *The accidental fluctuations* are erratic movements with high frequencies, with a more or less stable general appearance. They are due to the influences of all kinds of events on the quantity in question.

Some statistical series show one or other of these movements in an almost pure state. But most series have a more complex appearance, for example, a general growth with some seasonal variations on which accidental fluctuations are superimposed.

When we have to explain the phenomenon described by a series, or to predict future values of the observed quantity, it is generally worth while to consider each movement in isolation. For example, we might try to find out if the growth is accelerating or slowing down, or we might wish to measure the seasonal phenomenon for correct prediction of the series over the next six months, etc.

The descriptive or inductive procedures which we are about to discuss sometimes apply directly to the observed time series which combines movements of two or more of the types defined above, and sometimes apply to some component which has previously been extracted from the series. In sections 8 and 9 we shall discuss methods of determining the components of an observed series. Rigorously, the statistical properties of the inductive procedures applied to some particular component depend on the method by which it has been determined. However, in accordance with the usual custom, we shall in most cases carry on our discussion as if the component in question had been observed directly.

2   *Principal characteristics of a series*

(i)   Time profile

When examining a time series, it is convenient first to consider its graph with the observed quantity as ordinate and time as abscissa. For example, the upper part of fig. 1 represents a quarterly index[†] of production of the French textile industry for the twenty years 1948 to 1967. It shows a general increase of an average order of 3% per annum. On this trend there is superimposed a roughly cyclical general movement with recessions or stagnations in 1949, 1952, 1955, 1958, 1961–62, 1964–65, 1967. Since the series has been corrected for it, no seasonal movement appears. On the other hand, the series shows accidental fluctuations of greater or lesser magnitude.

The study of short term fluctuations is made easier if we eliminate not only the seasonal movement, but also the trend and the greater part of the slow general

---

[†] This index is calculated from three monthly indices corrected for seasonal variations; (1) for 1956–67, the index published regularly by the I.N.S.E.E. as a component of its general index of industrial production; (2) for 1951–56, the index given by MÉRAUD and TYMEN [1960]; (3) for 1948–51, the index for the period corrected by the seasonal coefficients published in the 1951 April–June supplement to the *Bulletin Mensuel de Statistique*.

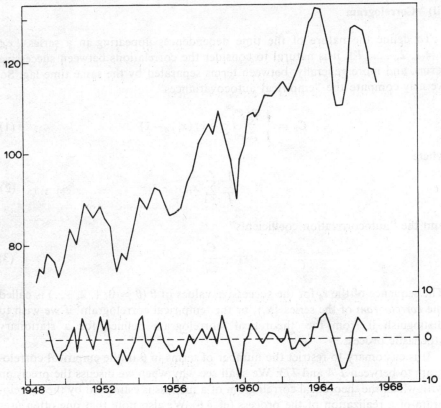

Fig. 1.

fluctuations. A graph of the residual series so obtained is often useful. There are various possible methods of elimination. We shall return to this in sections 8 and 9.

The lower part of fig. 1 shows the residual series obtained when a nine-quarter moving average of the textile production index is fitted (this is defined in section 7, formula (39)). (When the moving average is taken, the residual variations for the two extreme years 1948 and 1967 cannot be calculated.) This series has a generally stable appearance, and shows some dependence between successive terms since its variations seem less erratic than those of a purely random series.

As we shall see on several occasions, the study of residual series obtained in this way is very rewarding from various points of view. So we shall now let x_t be the series appearing in the lower part of fig. 1, and treat it as a directly observed series. We shall return later to the effects of the preliminary treatment applied to the observed index.

(ii)   Correlogram

To define the nature of the time dependences appearing in a series $\{x_t; t = 1, 2, \ldots, T\}$, it is natural to consider the correlations between successive terms, and more generally, between terms separated by the same time-lag. So we may compute the "empirical autocovariances"

$$C_\theta = \frac{1}{T} \sum_{t=1}^{T-\theta} (x_t - \bar{x})(x_{t+\theta} - \bar{x}) \tag{1}$$

where

$$\bar{x} = \frac{1}{T} \sum_{t=1}^{T} x_t, \tag{2}$$

and the "autocorrelation coefficients"

$$r_\theta = \frac{C_\theta}{C_0}. \tag{3}$$

The sequence of the r_θ for the successive values of θ ($\theta = 0, 1, 2, \ldots$) is called the *correlogram* of the series $\{x_t\}$, or the 'empirical correlogram' if we wish to distinguish it from the 'theoretical' correlogram defined for a stationary stochastic process.

It is customary to restrict the number of terms in θ in the empirical correlogram to between $T/4$ and $T/3$. We shall see why when we discuss the precision with which the theoretical correlogram of a process is estimated by the correlogram of a realization of the process (cf. § 6). We also note that one often uses somewhat different formulae from (1) when finding autocovariances. The divisor T is sometimes replaced by $T-\theta$; instead of deviations from the overall mean, one sometimes uses the mean of the first $T-\theta$ observations in the first bracket and the mean of the last $T-\theta$ observations in the second bracket. Finally, it is sometimes convenient to define C_θ and r_θ for negative values of θ according to the rule

$$C_\theta = C_{-\theta}; \qquad r_\theta = r_{-\theta}.$$

Fig. 2 represents the correlogram of the series in the lower part of fig. 1 (the index $t = 1$ corresponds to the first quarter of 1949; the index $t = 72 = T$ to the last quarter of 1966). In this series of the variations of textile production about its long term trend we detect an appreciable association between the values observed for two successive quarters ($r_1 = 0.43$), a perceptible negative association between values relating to quarters which are one year apart ($r_4 = -0.41$), or five years apart ($r_{21} = -0.30$) and considerable association between quarters abont three or six years apart ($r_{13} = 0.19$; $r_{25} = 0.49$). The last association is explained by the effect of the general cycle which appears

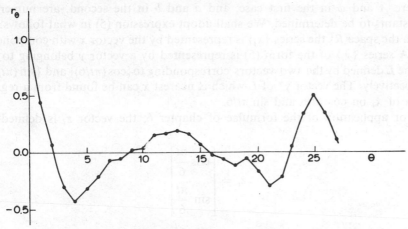

Fig. 2.

on the crude series and has been only partly eliminated by the moving average. Some statisticians might be inclined to attribute the negative correlation which characterizes the four-quarter lag to over-correction of seasonal variations.

(iii)   Determination of a sinusoidal component

In spite of the above interpretation for our example of textile production, the correlogram is not a very suitable instrument for the detection of the periodic components of a series. Thus, for a quarterly series, a three-year cycle implies a positive coefficient r_{12}; but it also implies positive r_{24} and negative r_6 and r_{18}. When cycles of differing frequencies are combined, each autocorrelation coefficient is influenced by all these cycles simultaneously.

If we wish to isolate a periodic component with a particular frequency, a natural procedure is to find the sinusoidal series y_t which has this frequency and is as near as possible to the observed series x_t. It is certainly true that few periodic movements are rigorously sinusoidal. But we know that any movement with a period P can be represented as the sum of sinusoidal series with periods P, $P/2$, $P/3$, ...; this gives us the idea of first finding the series which usually plays the major part in this representation, namely the series with period P.

So, for a three-year cycle with quarterly observations, we consider

$$y_t = A \cos \left(\frac{\pi t}{6} + \varphi \right) \tag{4}$$

or equivalently,

$$y_t = a \cos \frac{\pi t}{6} + b \sin \frac{\pi t}{6}, \tag{5}$$

where A and φ in the first case, and a and b in the second, are numerical constants to be determined. We shall adopt expression (5) in what follows.

In the space R^T the series $\{x_t\}$ is represented by the vector x with components x_t. A series $\{y_t\}$ of the form (5) is represented by a vector y belonging to the plane L defined by the two vectors corresponding to $\{\cos(\pi t/6)\}$ and $\{\sin(\pi t/6)\}$ respectively. The vector y* of L which is nearest x can be found from a regression of x_t on $\cos \pi t/6$ and $\sin \pi t/6$.

For application of the formulae of chapter 6, the vector z_t is defined by

$$z_t = \begin{bmatrix} \cos \dfrac{\pi t}{6} \\[2mm] \sin \dfrac{\pi t}{6} \end{bmatrix}.$$

We can easily verify that M_{zz} is $I/2$ when T is a multiple of 6. For example,

$$\frac{1}{T} \sum_{t=1}^{T} \cos^2 \frac{\pi t}{6} = \frac{1}{2T} \sum_{t=1}^{T} \left(\cos \frac{\pi t}{3} + 1 \right);$$

now,

$$\sum_{t=6k+1}^{6k+6} \cos \frac{\pi t}{3} = 0$$

for all k, zero or integral; therefore

$$\frac{1}{T} \sum_{t=1}^{T} \cos^2 \frac{\pi t}{6} = \tfrac{1}{2}$$

when T is a multiple of 6. Since M_{zz}^{-1} is then equal to $2I$, the regression formulae give us directly

$$a^* = \frac{2}{T} \sum_{t=1}^{T} x_t \cos \frac{\pi t}{6} \qquad b^* = \frac{2}{T} \sum_{t=1}^{T} x_t \sin \frac{\pi t}{6}. \qquad (6)$$

In our particular example on textile production, we have

$$a^* = 1.68 \qquad b^* = 0.34,$$

which allows us to deduce the expression for y_t^* in the form (4):

$$y_t^* = 1.72 \cos \frac{\pi}{6} (t - 0.4).$$

This expression shows that the component corresponding to a three-year cycle occurs with an amplitude of 1.72, which is 62% of the standard deviation of the series, and with a phase which gives the maxima near the first quarters of 1949, 1952, 1955, 1958, 1961 and 1964.

We note that the mean square of the fitted component, $m_{xz} M_{zz}^{-1} m_{zx}$ according to general regression formulae, has in this case the simple expression

$$\frac{a^{*2} + b^{*2}}{2} = \frac{A^{*2}}{2}. \tag{7}$$

The ratio between A^{*2} and the mean square of the series is twice the classical coefficient R^2, which measures the part of the dispersion explained by the fitting process. So in this example, this coefficient is 0.19.

(iv) Periodogram

What we have just done for the sinusoidal component with a period corresponding to 12 observations can be repeated for any sinusoidal component whose semi-period is a divisor of the total number of observations, that is, for any component of the form

$$A \cos \left(\frac{n\pi t}{T} + \varphi \right) \tag{8}$$

where n is an integer (the period is then $2T/n$).

Suppose that we have fitted two components of the form (8) corresponding to two different values of n, say n_1 and n_2. The mean square of each component is respectively

$$\frac{A_1^{*2}}{2} \quad \text{and} \quad \frac{A_2^{*2}}{2}.$$

The mean square of their sum is $(A_2^{*2} + A_1^{*2})/2$ if the two components are orthogonal. We can verify that this is so when n_1 and n_2 are two even numbers and neither their sum nor their difference is a multiple of $2T$. Consider for example

$$2 \sum_{t=1}^{T} \cos \frac{n_1 \pi t}{T} \cos \frac{n_2 \pi t}{T} = \sum_{t=1}^{T} \cos \frac{(n_1 + n_2)\pi t}{T} + \sum_{t=1}^{T} \cos \frac{(n_1 - n_2)\pi t}{T}.$$

The right hand side is zero under the conditions given above. In this case, the sequences

$$\left\{ \cos \frac{n_1 \pi t}{T} \right\}, \quad \left\{ \sin \frac{n_1 \pi t}{T} \right\}, \quad \left\{ \cos \frac{n_2 \pi t}{T} \right\}, \quad \left\{ \sin \frac{n_2 \pi t}{T} \right\}$$

define four orthogonal vectors in R^T. The square of the length of each vector is $T/2$.

More generally, we can define an orthonormal basis in R^T using vectors corresponding to the sequences

$$\left\{\sqrt{\frac{2}{T}}\cos\frac{2\pi kt}{T}\right\}; \qquad \left\{\sqrt{\frac{2}{T}}\sin\frac{2\pi kt}{T}\right\} \tag{9}$$

for all k which are positive integers less than $T/2$; to these we must add the constant sequence $1/\sqrt{T}$, and, if T is even, the alternating sequence $(-1)^t/\sqrt{T}$. (So in all cases we have T orthonormal vectors.)

From the series $\{x_t\}$, we can then find for each value of k a component of the form

$$y_{kt} = a_k\sqrt{\frac{2}{T}}\cos\frac{2\pi kt}{T} + b_k\sqrt{\frac{2}{T}}\sin\frac{2\pi kt}{T}, \tag{10}$$

the coefficients a_k and b_k being determined by the formulae

$$a_k = \sqrt{\frac{2}{T}}\sum_{t=1}^{T}x_t\cos\frac{2\pi kt}{T}; \qquad b_k = \sqrt{\frac{2}{T}}\sum_{t=1}^{T}x_t\sin\frac{2\pi kt}{T} \tag{11}$$

which generalise (6) when k is a posititive integer less than $T/2$. We also set

$$a_0 = \frac{1}{\sqrt{T}}\sum_{t=1}^{T}x_t, \qquad b_0 = 0 \tag{12}$$

and, if T is even,

$$a_{T/2} = \frac{1}{\sqrt{T}}\sum_{t=1}^{T}(-1)^t x_t, \qquad b_{T/2} = 0. \tag{13}$$

The space R^T referred to this new basis is sometimes called the *frequency space* as opposed to the *time space* which corresponds to R^T referred to its natural basis. In the frequency space, the coordinates of a series $\{x_t\}$ are the T quantities defined by (11), (12) and possibly (13).

The quantity

$$I_k = a_k^2 + b_k^2 \tag{14}$$

is the square of the length of the projection of x on the plane defined by the two sequences (9). It is also $T/2$ times the square of the amplitude of the component (10). The sequence of the values of I_k for $k = 0, 1, 2, \ldots, T'$ is said to be the *periodogram*; here T' denotes $T/2$ if T is even, and $(T-1)/2$ if T is odd.

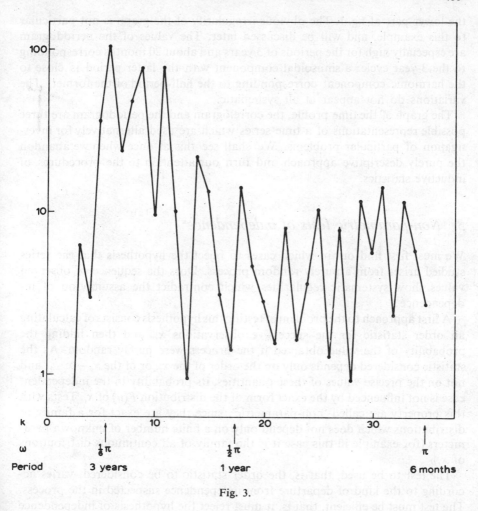

Fig. 3.

By construction, we know that

$$\sum_{k=0}^{T'} I_k = \sum_{t=1}^{T} x_t^2. \tag{15}$$

In short, *for each value of k, the periodogram defines the contribution of the sinusoidal component with period T/k to the sum of squares of the x_t.* The periodogram will tend to be high for periodicities which play an important part in the series.

Fig. 3 is a semi-logarithmic diagram of the periodogram† of the series in

---

† The observation relating to the first quarter of 1949 has been omitted so that fig. 3 gives the periodogram of the next 71 observations.

the lower part of fig. 1. The obvious irregularity of the graph is not particular to this example, and will be discussed later. The values of the periodogram are especially high for the periods of 3 years and about 20 months corresponding to the 3-year cycle; a sinusoidal component with the latter period is close to the harmonic component corresponding to the half-period of the former. The variations do not appear at all systematic.

The graph of the time profile, the correlogram and the periodogram are three possible representations of a time series which are used alternatively for investigation of particular problems. We shall see this at once when we abandon the purely descriptive approach and turn our attention to the procedures of inductive statistics.

3   Non-parametric tests of independence

We must first find out in which cases to reject the hypothesis that the series studied arises from a purely random process. Does the sequence of observed values show systematic regularities which contradict the assumption of independence?

A first approach to the problem of testing this hypothesis consists of calculating an order statistic for the successive observations x_t, and then finding the probability of the value obtained if the process were purely random. As the statistic considered depends only on the order of the x_t, or of the $x_t - x_{t-1}$, and not on the precise values of these quantities, its probability in the independent case is not influenced by the exact form of the distribution $F(u)$ of x_t. Tests with this property are called 'non-parametric', since they are exact for a family of distributions which does not depend only on a finite number of unknown parameters (for example in this case it is the family of all continuous distributions of x_t).

The test to be used, that is, the order statistic to be considered, varies according to the kind of departure from independence suspected in the process. The test must be efficient, that is, it must reject the hypothesis of independence with a high probability when the relevant departure from independence does occur. In most practical cases, we aim at testing either the existence of a general trend, or of autocorrelation between successive values. In the first case, $E(x_t)$ is a function which varies slowly with t; in the second the autocorrelation coefficients are not all zero. We are therefore interested in two types of test.

(a) *Is there a trend?*

Suppose that x_t has a continuous distribution. Let S denote the number of positive differences in the sequence $x_t - x_{t-1}$ (for $t = 2, 3, \ldots, T$). This number must be systematically large when the series has an increasing trend, and systematically small when it has a decreasing trend. It should therefore provide a basis for a fairly efficient test of the hypothesis of independence against the hypothesis of a monotone trend. In order to calculate significance levels, we need only know the distribution of S in the case where $\{x_t\}$ is purely random.

Let $a_1, a_2, \ldots, a_T$ denote the values of the x_t when they are arranged in increasing order of magnitude (and not in the order in which they were obtained). Consider the conditional distribution of S given that the values $a_1, a_2, \ldots, a_T$ occur in the sample and that the x_t are mutually independent. This distribution is obtained by consideration of the number of positive differences in each of the $T!$ permutations of the numbers $a_1, a_2, \ldots, a_T$, each permutation being equally likely. Clearly the distribution does not depend on the exact values of the $a_1, a_2, \ldots, a_T$. For example, it can be established by taking $a_1 = 1$, $a_2 = 2, \ldots, a_T = T$ (the a_θ are all different except for samples with zero probability since x_t is continuously distributed). Since the conditional distribution of S does not depend on the $a_1, a_2, \ldots, a_T$, it is also the unconditional distribution.

In this way it can be shown that the expected value of S is $\frac{1}{2}(T-1)$ and that its variance is $\frac{1}{2}(T+1)$. For all practical purposes, the distribution is normal when $T > 12$.

We can therefore test independence by calculating S for the observed series and seeing if this value differs significantly from $\frac{1}{2}(T-1)$. If the process shows an increasing trend, the value found for S will in most cases be too great, and the opposite will happen for a decreasing trend. On the other hand, this test does not allow us to detect an oscillating trend or even more simply a trend which first increases and then decreases.

Moreover, it is not very efficient for series subject to large fluctuations. Thus, we find $S = 47$ for the series in the upper part of figure 1. So the variable standardized with respect to the theoretical mean and variance is 1.17. The test does not reject the hypothesis of independence although the trend is evident on the graph.

A similar test, which takes longer to calculate, is obtained by arranging the x_t in increasing order and comparing the new order with the original one ($t = 1, 2, \ldots, T$). The two orders are independent if $\{x_t\}$ is purely random. They are correlated when there is a pronounced trend. So we can calculate Spearman's rank correlation coefficient ρ. If θ_t denotes the rank of the tth observation in the new order, Spearman's ρ is equal to

$$\varrho = 1 - \frac{6}{T(T^2 - 1)} \sum_{t=1}^{T} (\theta_t - t)^2.$$

If the process is purely random, ϱ has zero mean and variance $1/(T-1)$. The distribution of ϱ is normal for large samples. For smaller samples, it is preferable to calculate

$$\varrho \sqrt{\frac{T-2}{1 - \varrho^2}},$$

which is distributed approximately as Student's t with $T - 2$ degrees of freedom.

KENDALL [1955] established and tabulated the exact distribution of ρ for values of T less than 11.

For the textile production series we find $\rho = 0.94$, which is highly significant compared with its theoretical standard error of 0.113.

(b) Is there autocorrelation?

If there is positive autocorrelation among successive values of the x_t, we may expect that high values are often followed by high values. This suggests the following test.

Let x_v be the median of the observed sample of the x_t. Count the number N of 'runs' consisting of successive observations which are all above, or all below the median. For example, in the series given in the lower part of fig. 1, the median is 0.14 and the number N of runs is 27.

SWED and EISENHART [1943] tabulated the distribution of N under the assumption that the process is purely random. For $T \geq 50$, the normal distribution can be used directly, the mean $\frac{1}{2}(T + 2)$ and variance $\frac{1}{4}(T - 1)$ being taken for N. In our example, the value of N is significantly different from the theoretical mean 37 since the theoretical standard deviation is 4.2.

A similar test, called the Moore-Wallis test can be constructed on the basis of turning points, that is, of values of t for which

$$(x_{t+1} - x_t)(x_t - x_{t-1}) < 0.$$

Let R be the number of turning points. KENDALL [1948] established that, for a purely random process, the mean of R is $\frac{2}{3}(T - 2)$, and its variance

$$\frac{16T - 29}{90}.$$

The normal approximation is admissible for $T \geq 50$. THIONET [1966] gives various more detailed comments on this test.

In the lower series in fig. 1, the number R of turning points is 40; at the five per cent level, this is not significantly different from the theoretical mean 46.7, since the theoretical standard deviation is 3.5. This result draws attention to the fact that the Moore-Wallis test is less efficient than the Swed-Eisenhart test for detecting the existence of a periodic component.

Besides the above two tests, there are tests based on the lengths of runs of successive observations which are above or below the median, and also on the lengths of runs of successive observations which are increasing or decreasing. These tests compare the distribution of lengths obtained with the corresponding theoretical distribution for purely random processes. But this involves more lengthy calculation, without apparently increasing the power of the tests greatly.

Generally these nonparametric tests are very easy to apply since the calculations involved can be carried out quickly. For economic data there is particular advantage in the fact that the significance levels do not depend on any assumption about the true distribution of the x_t. However, these tests are less efficient than other tests which are generally based on the assumption of normality of the x_t, and which we shall now discuss[†].

4 Tests on second-order moments

Consider testing the hypothesis that the process $\{x_t\}$ is purely random, assuming that is has a normal distribution (the same for every value of t). If in fact the process is autocorrelated, certain of its coefficients ϱ_θ differ from zero. So it seems natural to base the required test on estimates of the coefficients ϱ_θ of the correlogram.

If m is the mean of $\{x_t\}$, then by definition ϱ_θ equals

$$\varrho_\theta = \frac{E[(x_t - m)(x_{t+\theta} - m)]}{E(x_t - m)^2} = \frac{E(x_t x_{t+\theta}) - m^2}{E(x_t^2) - m^2}. \tag{16}$$

The test will be established on the 'empirical autocorrelation coefficient' r_θ defined by formulae (1) to (3) which is the natural estimator of ρ_θ. However, in order to apply the test we need to know the distribution of the r_θ under the assumption that $\{x_t\}$ is normal and purely random. But the exact distribution of these coefficients is very complex, and has been determined only in particular cases. So the usual tests are established using slightly different estimates of the ρ_θ.

The whole difficulty arises from the fact that r_θ is not a symmetric function of the T observed values $x_1, x_2, \ldots, x_T$, because of the first terms and the last terms of the series. So we can substitute for r_θ a coefficient which is a symmetric function of these values. The most natural is the *circular autocorrelation coefficient*

$$r_\theta^* = \frac{\displaystyle\sum_{t=1}^{T} x_t x_{t+\theta} - \frac{1}{T}\left[\sum_{t=1}^{T} x_t\right]^2}{\displaystyle\sum_{t=1}^{T} x_t^2 - \frac{1}{T}\left[\sum_{t=1}^{T} x_t\right]^2} \tag{17}$$

for which the following convention is adopted:

$$x_{T+1} = x_1, \ldots, x_{T+\theta} = x_\theta.$$

Thus

$$\sum_{t=1}^{T} x_t x_{t+\theta} = x_1 x_{1+\theta} + x_2 x_{2+\theta} + \cdots + x_{T-\theta} x_T + x_{T-\theta+1} x_1 + \cdots + x_T x_\theta.$$

[†] See for example MOOD [1950], ch. 16, and MORICE [1958] for fuller discussion of non-parametric tests.

Since formula (17) is symmetric, there exists an orthogonal linear transformation on the T-vector x, say $u = C_\theta x$, such that

$$r_\theta^* = \frac{\sum_t \lambda_{\theta t} u_t^2}{\sum_t u_t^2},$$

where the u_t are independent variables (whenever the x_t are) and the $\lambda_{\theta t}$ are numerical coefficients. This transformation allowed ANDERSON [1942] to determine the exact distribution of the r_θ^*. When the number of observations tends to infinity, this distribution tends to a normal distribution determined independently of any assumption of normality for the x_t.

In particular, we have

$$E(r_1^*) = \frac{-1}{T-1}, \qquad \text{var}(r_1^*) = \frac{T-2}{(T-1)^2}.$$

We note in passing that *the estimate r_1^* of ρ_1 is biased*. With 72 observations, $E(r_1^*) = -0.014$ and var $(r_1^*) = 0.0139$ so that the coefficient $r_1^* = 0.43$ found for the lower series in fig. 1 leads to rejection of the hypothesis of independence.

The joint distribution of a set of several r_θ^* is also known[†] but is rarely used in practice, the tests generally being established on the basis of a single coefficient, most often r_1^*.

In fact the usual tests depend on a related quantity, *von Neumann's ratio* (see VON NEUMANN [1941]) whose distribution has been tabulated very fully by HART [1942]. The definition of this ratio arises from the following remark. If the process $\{x_t\}$ is purely random, the quantity

$$\delta^2 = \frac{1}{T-1} \sum_{t=1}^{T-1} (x_{t+1} - x_t)^2$$

is an unbiased estimate of $2\sigma^2$. Let s^2 be the usual estimate of σ^2:

$$s^2 = \frac{1}{T} \sum_{t=1}^{T} (x_t - \bar{x})^2, \qquad \text{where} \qquad \bar{x} = \frac{1}{T} \sum_{t=1}^{T} x_t.$$

The ratio δ^2/s^2 must be near 2 if the process is purely random, and smaller if there is positive autocorrelation among the x_t.

If the series is long, the initial and final terms are relatively unimportant and δ^2/s^2 is near $2(1 - r_1)$. The properties of tests based on δ^2/s^2 are therefore almost the same as those of tests based on r_1 or r_1^*.

---

† See for example the following series of three articles: WATSON [1956], DANIELS [1956] and JENKINS [1956].

What is the power of the above tests? Intuition suggests that they must constitute efficient tests of independence as against a direct time dependence. In fact in the course of ch. 13 we shall see that r_1 is the maximum likelihood estimate of ϱ_1, if $\{x_t\}$ is an autoregressive process which can be written

$$x_t = \varrho_1 x_{t-1} + \varepsilon_t \tag{18}$$

where $\{\varepsilon_t\}$ is a purely random normal process. In such a case the likelihood ratio test reduces to a test based on r_1. In short, r_1 and von Neumann's ratio δ^2/s^2 appear as particularly efficient if the process in question is well approximated by a first degree linear Markoff chain. Many processes of random disturbances are in fact represented in this way.

5 Tests of independence on the periodogram

Many works on econometrics are lead as if any possible association of the errors would take the form of an autoregressive process of the type (18). Indeed they choose a test of independence based on r_1 or a similar coefficient like the von Neumann ratio (see also the Durbin-Watson test, ch. 12 § 2). However observation shows that the process of the random disturbances rarely has such a simple form, particularly when relatively long statistical series are being considered.

The appearance of the series often suggests certain more or less marked periodicities. As we saw previously, a periodicity of this type affects all the terms of the correlogram but only a small number of terms of the periodogram, namely those corresponding to periods near the period under consideration and possibly its harmonics. So we naturally think of using the periodogram for tests of independence which should be powerful against alternative hypotheses implying harmonic processes.

A first test is based on comparison of *the maximum of the periodogram* and its average over the set of all frequencies ($k = 0, 1, 2, \ldots, T'$). The ratio of these two quantities must be high if the series under consideration has a predominant periodicity. Let $\hat{I}$ denote the maximum of the I_k and s^2 the quantity

$$s^2 = \frac{1}{T} \sum_{k=0}^{T'} I_k \tag{19}$$

and consider the ratio $\hat{I}/s^2$ (in the most usual case, where the x_t are in fact deviations from a general mean, then $I_0 = 0$ and it is preferable to replace the divisor T by $T-1$).

If the series $\{x_t\}$ is the realization of a purely random stationary normal process wich zero expected value, then the T coordinates a_k and b_k of the series in the frequency space are T independent normal variables with the same variance σ^2 and zero expectation. The I_k/σ^2 are then independent χ^2-variables with two degrees of freedom (one degree of freedom for $k = 0$ and possibly $k = T/2$).

Under these assumptions, FISHER [1929] derived the distribution of $\hat{I}/s^2$ and it was tabulated by DAVIS [1941] (table 2, pp. 601–605). At the 5% significance level, the following are the critical values of $\hat{I}/s^2$:

$$
\begin{array}{lll}
9.34 & \text{for} & T = 21 \\
11.09 & \text{for} & T = 41 \\
12.06 & \text{for} & T = 61 \\
12.76 & \text{for} & T = 81 \\
13.27 & \text{for} & T = 101.
\end{array}
$$

In the particular case of the series with the periodogram of fig. 3, the values of $\hat{I}$ and s^2 are 104.4 and 7.65 respectively. Their ratio is 13.6 At the 5% level, this shows a significant time dependence since for $T = 72$, the critical value is about 12.5.

The *Fisher test* just described is liable to fail to detect an association which manifests itself over a wide frequency band, in which case the spectral density of the process is relatively high but almost constant over a considerable fraction of the frequency domain.

A second test which seems better for the detection of such dependences, is based on consideration of the *cumulative periodogram* defined as follows, in the case where the x_t are deviations from the mean:

$$
S_k = \frac{\sum\limits_{h=1}^{k} I_h}{\sum\limits_{h=1}^{T''} } \qquad k = 1, 2, \ldots, T'' \tag{20}
$$

where T'' is $T/2 - 1$ if T is even and $(T-1)/2$ if T is odd. The cumulative periodogram can be represented by a graph in which k corresponds on the horizontal axis to the point with abscissa k/T'' (see fig. 4 relating to the series which has already appeared in figs. 2 and 3). Visual inspection of the cumulative periodogram can be as instructive as that of the periodogram itself. If components with long periodicity are predominant, the cumulative periodogram will lie clearly above the diagonal of the square in which it is drawn.

If the series $\{x_t\}$ is the realization of a purely random stationary normal process, and if T tends to infinity, then the cumulative periodogram tends to coincide with the diagonal. The ordinate corresponding to the abscissa u is in fact u times the ratio between two means of independent χ^2-variables with two degrees of freedom; the mean of uT'' variables in the numerator, and the mean of T'' variables in the denominator.

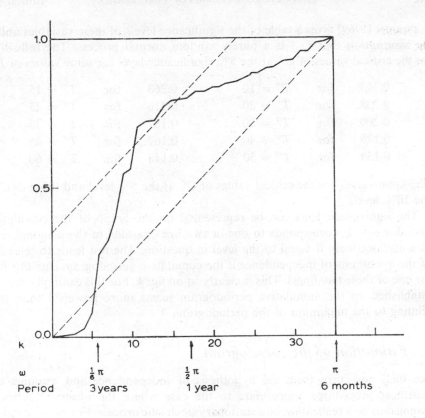

Fig. 4.

If we wish to test independence against the alternative hypothesis of large components in low frequencies, we consider for example

$$C^{+} = \operatorname*{Max}_{k} \left(S_{k} - \frac{k}{T''} \right). \tag{21}$$

If we wish to guard against an excessive number of components with small periodicity, we consider

$$C^{-} = \operatorname*{Max}_{k} \left(\frac{k}{T''} - S_{k} \right). \tag{22}$$

Finally, if we wish to guard against both these possibilities, we consider

$$C = \operatorname*{Max}_{k} \left| S_{k} - \frac{k}{T''} \right| = \operatorname{Max}(C^{+}, C^{-}). \tag{23}$$

DURBIN [1969] gives a table of the significance levels of these variables under the assumption that $\{x_t\}$ is a purely random normal process. The following are the critical values of C^+ at the 5% significance level for some values of T'':

0.313	for	$T'' = 10$	0.268	for	$T'' = 15$
0.238	for	$T'' = 20$	0.216	for	$T'' = 25$
0.200	for	$T'' = 30$	0.187	for	$T'' = 35$
0.176	for	$T'' = 40$	0.167	for	$T'' = 45$
0.159	for	$T'' = 50$	0.146	for	$T'' = 60$

The same values are the critical values of C^- at the 5% level and those of C at the 10% level.

The significance level can be represented on the graph of the cumulative periodogram. It corresponds to one or two lines parallel to the diagonal, and at a distance from it equal to the level in question. The test leads to rejection of the hypothesis of independence if the cumulative periodogram cuts this line (or one of these two lines). This is clearly so on fig. 4. For this example, the test established on the cumulative periodogram seems more powerful than that relating to the maximum of the periodogram.

6   Estimation of the correlogram

We shall now turn from the hypothesis of independence and examine the statistical procedures appropriate to the case where the observed series is assumed to be a realization of a stationary stochastic process. For our discussion of the random properties of the procedures, we shall also assume that the process is linear. This does not seem very restrictive in econometric applications[†]. The empirical correlogram and the periodogram of the series will serve for estimation of the theoretical correlogram of the process and estimation of its spectral density respectively.

Since we are dealing with a linear, and therefore ergodic process, we know that the empirical autocovariances C_θ defined by formula (1) tend in probability to the theoretical covariances as T tends to infinity. So the coefficients r_θ are consistent estimators of the autocorrelation coefficients ρ_θ (see formulae (3) and (16) in this chapter).

BARTLETT [1955] established a formula giving the limit, as T tends to infinity, of T times the covariance of r_θ and $r_{\theta+\tau}$:

$$T \cos (r_\theta, r_{\theta+\tau}) \sim \sum_{t=-\infty}^{\infty} \{\rho_t \rho_{t+\tau} + \rho_{t+\theta+\tau} \rho_{t-\theta} \\ - 2\rho_{\theta+\tau} \rho_t \rho_{t-\theta} - 2\rho_\theta \rho_t \rho_{t-\theta-\tau} + 2\rho_\theta \rho_{\theta+\tau} \rho_t^2\}. \tag{24}$$

[†] However, seasonal components with rigorously fixed periodicities cannot be held to result from a stationary linear process. For the moment we shall ignore these.

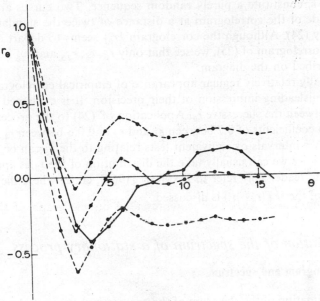

Fig. 5.

This formula, which is valid under the assumption that the fourth-order moments are finite, shows that the asymptotic covariance of r_θ and $r_{\theta+\tau}$ is a fairly complicated function of the whole theoretical correlogram. We also note that, for high values of θ, the last three terms on the right hand side of (24) are small, since they involve, as factors of finite sums, the coefficients ρ_θ or $\rho_{\theta+\tau}$ which are themselves small (since the process is linear, ρ_θ tends to zero with θ). The same is true for the second term, which is the sum of products of elements $2\theta+\tau$ positions apart in the correlogram. On the other hand, the first term is independent of θ. It is small only if τ is large.

In short, the variance of r_θ involves a term $(\sum_t \rho_t^2)$ which does not depend on θ and becomes predominant as θ increases. So the absolute precision with which r_θ estimates ρ_θ is almost constant for high values of θ. As ρ_θ tends to zero, the relative precision tends to be mediocre when we consider increasing values of θ.

This explains the practical rule that the empirical correlogram should be limited to a number of terms which is a quarter, or at most a third, of the number of observations (on figs. 2 and 5 the correlogram was extended to r_{27} so as to reveal clearly the maximum at r_{25}).

For example fig. 5 shows, besides the empirical correlogram already given in fig. 2, the theoretical correlogram of an arbitrarily chosen autoregressive process

$$x_t = \tfrac{3}{4}x_{t-1} - \tfrac{1}{2}x_{t-2} + \varepsilon_t \tag{25}$$

where the ε_t constitute a purely random sequence. Two curves are also given on each side of the correlogram at a distance of twice the standard deviation as given by (24). Although the correlogram $\{r_\theta\}$ seems to depart considerably from the correlogram of (25), we see that only r_5, r_6, r_{25} and r_{26} lie outside the band described on the diagram.

The usually relatively regular appearance of empirical correlograms is liable to give a misleading impression of their precision. It is explained by the correlation between the successive r_θ. Application of (24) to the process (25) gives correlation coefficients of 0.7 between r_1 and r_2 and 0.6 between r_4 and r_5.

Confidence intervals or equivalent tests relating to the ρ_θ can be constructed from (24), since we can usually take the distribution of the r_θ as approximately normal. The reader may refer to HANNAN [1960], ch. 2, where the asymptotic normality of the $\sqrt{T}(r_\theta - \rho_\theta)$ is discussed.

7 Estimation of the spectrum of a stationary process

(i) Periodogram and spectrum

For the estimation of the spectrum of the process $\{x_t\}$, we consider the periodogram defined by (11) and (14). We assume that the observed series of the x_t has zero mean, or that if not, the periodogram has been calculated from the series of the deviations from the empirical mean. Expanding the expressions for a_k^2 and b_k^2, we can write

$$I_k = a_k^2 + b_k^2 = \frac{1}{T} \sum_{t,\, t'=1}^{T} x_t x_{t'} \cos \frac{2\pi k}{T}(t' - t). \qquad (26)$$

We then set $t' - t = \theta$ and obtain

$$I_k = \frac{2}{T} \sum_{\theta=-T}^{T} \sum_t x_t x_{t+\theta} \cos \frac{2\pi k\theta}{T}, \qquad (27)$$

the limits of the second sum being 1 and $T-\theta$ if θ is not negative, and $-\theta+1$ and T if it is. So I_k can be written

$$I_k = 2 \sum_{\theta=-T}^{T} C_\theta \cos \frac{2\pi k\theta}{T}, \qquad (28)$$

where the C_θ are the autocovariances defined by (1). The equality (28) applies neither to I_0, which by hypothesis is zero, nor, when T is even, to $I_{T/2}$ for which the coefficient 2 before the summation sign must be suppressed.

We note that this expression for I_k is not particularly convenient for computation since it involves all the autocovariances. However the contribution of terms corresponding to high values of θ must be small. So we may think of using (28) for approximations, the values of θ being limited to a relatively small interval about zero (for example, from $-T/4$ to $T/4$). This avoids having to find the a_k and b_k of (11), which reduces the work involved in finding the I_k. However the use of electronic computers has superseded this formerly important advantage, especially in econometrics where the series to be analysed are relatively short.

As a first approximation[†] the expected values of the C_θ are equal to the theoretical covariances $\gamma_\theta = \sigma^2 \rho_\theta$. Thus, for sufficiently large values of T, the expected value of I_k is very near

$$2 \sum_{\theta=-\infty}^{\infty} \gamma_\theta \cos \frac{2\pi k \theta}{T} \tag{29}$$

which is precisely equal to 4π times the spectral density $f(\omega)$ for $\omega = 2\pi k/T$. So the periodogram provides an asymptotically unbiased estimator of $4\pi f(\omega)$.

However, it is not a consistent estimator, since the variance of I_k does not tend to zero as T tends to infinity, k/T remaining constant. More precisely, we set $\omega = 2\pi k/T$ and write $I_T(\omega)$ instead of I_k. We can prove that, if the process is linear and its fourth-order moments are finite, the covariance of $I_T(\omega_1)$ and $I_T(\omega_2)$ tends to zero with T when $\omega_1 \neq \omega_2$, while the variance of $I_T(\omega)$ tends to $16\pi^2 f^2(\omega)$. *So the coefficient of variation of $I_T(\omega)$ tends to 1 as T tends to infinity* (this formula, which is not valid for $\omega = 0$ or $\omega = +\pi$, is established for example by HANNAN [1960], ch. 3). By way of first approximation we often proceed as if $I_T(\omega)/[2\pi f(\omega)]$ were distributed as χ^2 with 2 degrees of freedom; this approximation can be justified by establishing that the distribution of the components a_k and b_k defined by the equations (11) is asymptotically normal.

Before considering the use of the periodogram in estimation of the spectral density, we note that, if ω_1 and ω_2 lie between 0 and π and are such that $\omega_1 < \omega_2$, then we can obtain a consistent estimator of $[F(\omega_2) - F(\omega_1)]$ by finding

$$\frac{1}{2T} \sum_k I_k, \tag{30}$$

the sum being taken over values of k between

[†] As we shall see in formula (22), ch. 12, the difference between $-\dfrac{T}{T-\theta} E(C_\theta)$ and γ_θ is, for linear processes, approximately equal to

$$-\frac{1}{T} \sum_{\tau=-T}^{T} \rho_\tau,$$

which tends to zero as T tends to infinity.

$$\frac{T\omega_1}{2\pi} \quad \text{and} \quad \frac{T\omega_2}{2\pi}.$$

Indeed expression (30) can also be written:

$$\sum_k \frac{2\pi}{T} \cdot \frac{I_k}{4\pi}.$$

Now, $2\pi/T$ is the difference between two values of ω corresponding to two successive integral values of k, while the expected value of $I_k/4\pi$ is the value $f(\omega)$ of the spectral density for the angle ω corresponding to k. So as T tends to infinity, the expected value of (30) tends to

$$\int_{\omega_1}^{\omega_2} f(\omega)\,d\omega = F(\omega_2) - F(\omega_1). \tag{31}$$

Also, the sum of (30) involves about

$$\frac{T}{2\pi}(\omega_2 - \omega_1)$$

terms with finite variances and with covariances of order T^{-1}.

The variance of (30) therefore decreases to zero, so that (30) tends in quadratic mean to (31). In particular, the cumulative periodogram defined by (20) is a consistent estimator of $F(\omega)/\sigma^2$ for

$$\omega = \frac{2\pi k}{T}.$$

(The equality $F(\omega) = -F(-\omega)$ completes estimation for negative values of ω.)

The cumulative periodogram is sufficient for some applications. For others, we wish to identify those intervals in which $F(\omega)$ increases most rapidly, and which would be particularly well revealed if the graph of the density $f(\omega)$ were known. Finally, for some questions we need in principle to know the value of the spectral density at specific points[†]. For one or other of these reasons, we usually look for an estimate of $f(\omega)$.

(ii) Moving average of the periodogram

Apart from a factor of 4π, the periodogram would be a good estimator if its variance were not so large. But there is very low correlation between successive terms of the periodogram. So it is natural to think of 'smoothing' it, that is, to take a moving average of a certain number of successive terms.

[†] See, for example, ch. 12, § 7.

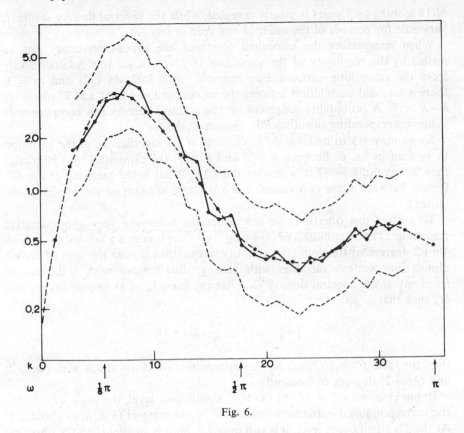

Fig. 6.

Consider in particular the estimator $f^*(\omega)$ defined by

$$4\pi f^*\left(\frac{2\pi k}{T}\right) = \frac{1}{2m+1}\sum_{h=-m}^{m} I_{k+h}, \tag{32}$$

where m is a number fixed in advance. If $f(\omega)$ is constant in the interval

$$\left[\frac{2\pi}{T}(k-m),\ \frac{2\pi}{T}(k+m)\right],$$

the estimator $f^*(\omega)$ has expected value $f(\omega)$ and a coefficient of variation near $(2m+1)^{-\frac{1}{2}}$.

For example, the unbroken line in fig. 6 represents the values of $f^*(\omega)$ obtained by applying (32) to the periodogram in fig. 3, the value of m then being 3. Comparison of figs. 3 and 6 brings out how smoothing increases the intelligibility of the periodogram. The importance of periodicities of the order of 18 months to 3 years is clearly revealed, while the spectral density seems to vary little for periods of the order of one year or less.

When interpreting the smoothed spectrum, we should obviously not be misled by the regularity of the variations in $f^*(\omega)$, since this results directly from the smoothing process. For example, with formula (32) and $m = 3$, there is artificial correlation between the values obtained for k and k' whenever $k - k' < 7$. A probability judgment on the spectral density can compare only values corresponding to sufficiently distinct angles ω.

So we may try to make some assessment of the significance of the variation to be seen in fig. 6. Between $k = 6$ and $k = 9$, the estimate $f^*(\omega)$ is greater than 3; beyond $k = 17$ it is smaller than 0.6. What is the meaning of the difference between these two values, when we take account of the precision obtained?

To answer this question, we can adopt the following very approximative reasoning[†]. The distribution of $(4m+2)f^*(\omega)/f(\omega)$ is near a χ^2-distribution with $4m + 2$ degrees of freedom (the quantity in question is near the sum of $2m + 1$ almost independent variables with near χ^2-distributions with 2 degrees of freedom). If the spectral density $f(\omega)$ has the same level at two points ω_1 and ω_2 such that

$$| \omega_2 - \omega_1 | \geq \frac{2\pi}{T}(2m+1),$$

then the ratio $f^*(\omega_1)/f^*(\omega_2)$ has an approximate F-distribution with $(4m+2)$ and $(4m+2)$ degrees of freedom.

In our case, $4m + 2 = 14$. At the 10% significance level, the value a such that the corresponding F-variable is contained in the interval $(1/a, a)$ is about 2.5. At the 2% significance level, it is still only 3.7. So it is smaller than the observed ratio 5.

The same type of reasoning shows that we could construct, on a semi-logarithmic graph and about the estimated spectral density, a band representing the confidence intervals corresponding to a given significance level (of 5%, for example). We need only refer to the χ^2-distribution to construct a confidence interval of the form

$$\left[\frac{1}{a}f^*(\omega), af^*(\omega)\right].$$

So,

$$\frac{1}{14}\chi_{14}^2$$

exceeds $a = 1.87$ with a probability of 2.5%. Fig. 6 shows a 5% confidence band

---

[†] We shall not discuss here the distribution of f^* nor that of $\hat{f}$ defined by (33) and (36). For this, see in particular BRILLINGER [1969], NEAVE [1970], [1971], GLESER and PAGANO [1973].

thus constructed by considering the intervals $[0.53f^*(\omega); 1.87f^*(\omega)]$. The precision is mediocre.

For better precision, we might be tempted to choose a higher value of m, for example $m = 8$, which gives a coefficient of variation of one quarter. But, for our available number of data, this amounts to the abandonment of the search for an estimator of the spectral *density*, since a band of $2m+1$ successive values of k would cover almost half the interval $[0,\pi]$. The mean calculated over such a wide band could hardly be considered as an estimate of the spectral density in its midpoint.

In fact every estimate of the spectral density comes up against a dilemma which is particularly acute in econometrics, where the statistical series are relatively short. *Good precision demands that the smoothing process operates over a band* (sometimes called a 'window') *containing a large number of terms of the periodogram. But the use of the moving average usually introduces a bias which increases with the size of the band.* Thus for formula (32), the expected value of $f^*(2\pi k/T)$ is approximately equal to the mean of the values of $f(2\pi h/T)$ for the $2m+1$ numbers h surrounding k. If $2\pi k/T$ corresponds to a maximum of $f(\omega)$, the expectation of $f^*(2\pi k/T)$ is smaller than $f(2\pi k/T)$, and is increasingly smaller as m increases (provided that $f(\omega)$ is monotone on either side of $2\pi k/T$ over the whole extent of the bands considered).

(iii) Estimation of the spectrum from the correlogram

Formula (32) has the advantage of simplicity: it is certainly adapted to the needs of econometrics. However, other moving average formulae are more often used. This does not arise mainly from the statistician's concern to use a smoothing process which is better related to the assumed form of the function $f(\omega)$. (We shall discuss this concern in more general terms in section 9.) It is explained chiefly by the desire for simplicity in computation; in fact, *there are other formulae which allow estimators of $f(\omega)$ to be determined directly without recourse to the periodogram*, simply from the *first* terms of the correlogram.

Given a finite sequence of numbers λ_θ (for $\theta = -n, -n+1, \ldots, n-1, n$) such that $\lambda_\theta = \lambda_{-\theta}$, let us consider the function

$$\hat{f}(\omega) = \sum_{\theta=-n}^{n} \lambda_\theta C_\theta \, e^{-i\omega\theta} = \sum_{\theta=-n}^{n} \lambda_\theta C_\theta \cos \omega\theta \tag{33}$$

where the C_θ are the first n autocovariances $C_0 r_\theta$. We shall establish that $4\pi\hat{f}(\omega)$ can be considered as resulting from a smoothing of the periodogram.

More precisely, let the angle $2\pi k/T$ be replaced by ω, and I_k by $I_T(\omega)$, in (28). We can write

$$I_T(\omega) = 2 \sum_{\theta=-T}^{T} C_\theta \cos \omega\theta = 2 \sum_{\theta=-T}^{T} C_\theta \, e^{-i\omega\theta}. \tag{34}$$

This equality now applies for every value of ω on the real line. We define the function

$$w(\psi) = \sum_{\tau=-n}^{n} \lambda_\tau e^{i\tau\psi} = \sum_{\tau=-n}^{n} \lambda_\tau \cos\tau\psi. \tag{35}$$

We shall show that

$$4\pi\hat{f}(\omega) = \int_{-\pi}^{\pi} w(\psi) I_T(\omega+\psi)\, d\psi. \tag{36}$$

The right hand side is clearly a type of moving average on the periodogram (the reader can verify that the integral of $w(\psi)$ over the interval $[-\pi,\pi]$ is $2\pi\lambda_0$ so that $\hat{f}(\omega)$ will tend to be an unbiased estimator of $f(\omega)$ only if $2\pi\lambda_0 = 1$).

Let us therefore verify (36). Substituting the values of $I_T(\omega)$ and $w(\psi)$ given by (34) and (35), we obtain

$$4\pi\hat{f}(\omega) = 2\sum_{\theta=-T}^{T} \sum_{\tau=-n}^{n} C_\theta \lambda_\tau e^{-i\omega\theta} \int_{-\pi}^{\pi} e^{i\psi(\tau-\theta)}\, d\psi.$$

Now, the integral on the extreme right is zero if $\tau \neq \theta$ and is 2π if $\tau = \theta$. So we have exactly formula (33).

Formula (33) has the advantage that it involves only the first $n+1$ auto-covariances. But it is genuinely useful only if the choice of the λ_θ involves a function $w(\psi)$ whose values are very small for values of ψ which differ greatly from zero. So definitions of the λ_θ have been sought which imply a function $w(\psi)$ satisfying this condition; $w(\psi)$ is relatively large in the neighborhood of zero and negligible in the rest of the interval $[-\pi, \pi]$; formula (36) then implies that $4\pi\hat{f}(\omega)$ is obtained from the periodogram by so to speak regarding the curve which represents it through a 'window' directed to the abscissa ω. Different formulae have been proposed for the definition of suitable windows (see HANNAN [1960], ch. 3). Here we choose the following, called *Tukey's window* or *Hanning's window*:

$$\lambda_\theta = \frac{1}{4\pi}\left(1 + \cos\frac{\pi\theta}{n}\right) \tag{37}$$

where n is a number fixed in advance. The function $w(\psi)$ then has a large lobe of sinusoidal appearance in the interval

$$\left(\frac{-2\pi}{n}, \frac{2\pi}{n}\right)$$

and takes small values outside this interval, the secondary lobes having an amplitude of less than 1% of that of the principal lobe. For the computation formula (33) is used in the form

$$2\pi \hat{f}(\omega) = C_0 + \sum_{\theta=1}^{n} C_\theta \cos \omega\theta \left(1 + \cos \frac{\pi\theta}{n}\right). \qquad (38)$$

(Also, $C_0 r_\theta$ is often used instead of C_θ.)

In practice, the choice of the width of the band, that is, the width of the window, is more important than the choice of the formula adopted for defining the window. The width is inversely proportional to n. Here we can repeat our previous remarks about the choice of m for application of (32). A high value of n gives a narrow band and less smoothing so that the variance of $\hat{f}(\omega)$ remains large (HANNAN [1960] shows in particular that with the window (37) the coefficient of variation of $\hat{f}(\omega)$ is approximately $(3n/4T)^{\frac{1}{2}}$.) A small value of n gives better smoothing and a more satisfactory variance; but it introduces considerable bias into the estimate of $\hat{f}(\omega)$. By construction, estimators of the type of $\hat{f}(\omega)$ show regular variations as a function of ω. Clearly the user should not be misled by their apparent precision.

In fact, the estimators $f^*(\omega)$ and $\hat{f}(\omega)$ generally give very similar results if the bands chosen are of comparable width[†]. For example, in fig. 6 the broken line has been obtained by applying (38) with $n = 12$ (so this involves only the first 12 terms of the correlogram in fig. 2). It follows the unbroken line very closely. In fact the principal lobe of $w(\psi)$ covers a band going from

$$\frac{-\pi}{6} \quad \text{to} \quad \frac{\pi}{6};$$

its high values lie in a band going approximately from

$$\frac{-\pi}{12} \quad \text{to} \quad \frac{\pi}{12}$$

which corresponds to 6 successive terms of the periodogram according to the correspondence $\omega = 2\pi k/T$. The unbroken curve is a simple moving average of 7 successive terms. Hannan's formula also gives a coefficient of variation of $1/\sqrt{8}$ for $\hat{f}(\omega)$ while we found $1/\sqrt{7}$ for $f^*(\omega)$. (Generally, the coefficients of variation will be the same if the band widths are defined by m in (32) and by n in (38) so that $n(m+1/2) = 2T/3$.)

(iv) Preliminary filtering

When the spectrum of a series $\{x_t\}$ is to be estimated, a frequent procedure is first to carry out a 'filtering', that is, to apply the above methods not to $\{x_t\}$

[†] In addition, (32) corresponds to an estimator of the category defined by (33) provided that n may be taken infinitely large. This is why the term *Daniell's window* is sometimes used to characterize smoothing by moving average directly on the periodogram, using formula (32).

itself, but to a series $\{y_t\}$ derived from it by applying a linear filter (cf. ch. 11, § 5). Clearly the effect of this transformation is to modify the spectrum; but it does this in a known way. In fact we saw that, if $f_x(\omega)$ and $f_y(\omega)$ denote the spectral densities of the two processes, then $f_y(\omega) = G(\omega)f_x(\omega)$, the function $G(\omega)$ being the 'gain' of the filter. So there are two stages in this method: (i) determine an estimate $f_y^*(\omega)$ of the spectrum of $\{y_t\}$ using one of the methods given above; (ii) find $f_x^*(\omega) = f_y^*(\omega)/G(\omega)$ which is taken as the estimate of the spectrum of $\{x_t\}$.

This preliminary filtering has two objectives which must be carefully distinguished: on the one hand, to eliminate the possible general trend of the series $\{x_t\}$ so that the series $\{y_t\}$ better satisfies the assumption of stationarity; on the other hand, to reduce the amplitude of the variations of the spectrum so that a priori, we can hold that the spectrum of $\{y_t\}$ must be nearer a constant than the spectrum of $\{x_t\}$.

The effect of the increased use of spectral analysis methods in applied econometrics is that more and more the attempt is made to determine the spectra of many economic series which have trends or marked long movements. Certainly these variations can be likened to the variation in a stationary process whose spectral density is high for low frequencies. But clearly in the first place we cannot pretend to estimate the required density using a series which, for these frequencies, does not even cover a cycle. In the second place, we shall see that, for good determination of the spectrum at the highest frequencies, we should first of all eliminate long movements because of the harmonics which they contain at high frequencies (cf. § 10).

Thus transformation from the quarterly series of textile production (upper part of fig. 1) to the residual series (lower part of fig. 1) was effected by means of the following fairly commonly used linear filter, which calculates the residuals with respect to a weighted mean over $2\theta+1$ successive terms:

$$y_t = x_t - \frac{1}{2\theta+2} \sum_{\tau=-\theta}^{\theta} \left(1 + \cos\frac{\pi\tau}{\theta+1}\right) x_{t+\tau}. \tag{39}$$

(Here the formula is applied for $\theta = 4$; the filtered series is denoted by y_t, as opposed to what was done in previous applications in this chapter.)

The gain of the filter is

$$G(\omega) = \left[\frac{\theta}{\theta+1} - \frac{1}{\theta+1} \sum_{\tau=1}^{\theta} \left(1 + \cos\frac{\pi\tau}{\theta+1}\right) \cos\omega\tau\right]^2. \tag{40}$$

In the present case ($\theta = 4$), the long trend is completely eliminated, the amplitude of the frequency $\pi/12$ (6-year cycle) is reduced by nine-tenths, that of the 3-year is reduced by 60%; the amplitudes of frequencies higher than $\pi/3$ are little changed.

In fact long movements can be eliminated by methods other than the application of a preliminary filtering operating over a certain number of successive terms. Thus, a polynomial of low degree can be fitted to the series, and the spectrum estimated by means of the residuals with respect to it (here estimation is meaningless for very small frequencies). This method, to which we shall return in § 10, has the advantage that it gives a transformed series containing as many terms as the original, while application of a linear filter implies a reduction in the number of terms (θ at each extremity of the series if (39) is used). At average or high frequencies the transformed series does not then rigorously have the same spectrum as the original series; but, when the number of observations is not very small, this source of error is negligible relative to the imprecision affecting the estimate of the spectrum.

Even for series without marked long movements, a preliminary filtering may seem appropriate for the reduction of the biases involved in smoothing the periodogram. The greater the variation in the spectral density, the greater these biases will be. They could be avoided by working on a series whose spectrum is almost constant. So from this standpoint, the filtering must be such that, a priori, the spectral density of the transformed series can be considered to show little variation.

This remark takes on particular force when we note that, in the first place, the spectrum of unfiltered economic series varies enormously, often from 1 to 1,000 in the frequency domain considered, and in the second place, that for the most common methods of computation which use the first terms of the correlogram, smoothing involves all the values of the periodogram for each frequency. It is true that the object of the window used is to reduce considerably the effect of values taken in frequencies which are distant from the one under study. But these effects persist to some extent because of the secondary lobes of the function $w(\psi)$ (these are said to be leakages through the edges of the window).

For example, in the particular case of our original series on textile production, the filtering carried out by (39) has as its object not only elimination of the rising trend, but also the considerable reduction of the amplitude of cycles whose periodicity is 2 years and more. Without this reduction, the results given for smaller periodicities by Tukey's window would have been considerably biased upwards.

We may also think that, in this example, the estimated spectrum for the filtered series still shows too much variation in the frequency domain for which the number of observations allows a certain precision (cf. fig. 6). The variation is only from 1 to 10, but it is rapid in the neighborhood of the maximum so that the bias may be considerable for low frequencies.

For this reason a more intensive filtering may be considered desirable. An elaborate formula is unnecessary, since the precision of the estimated spectrum remains small. So we shall only apply to the series in the lower part of fig. 1

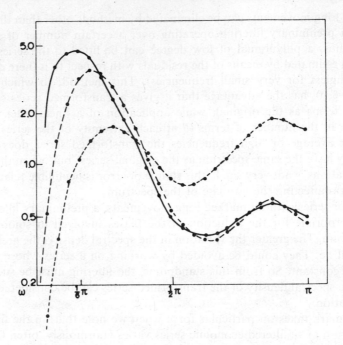

Fig. 7.

(series again denoted by $\{x_t\}$) a commonly used type of transformation

$$y_t = x_t - ax_{t-1}, \tag{41}$$

with the value 0.8 for a. According to formula (31) of chapter 11, the gain of this filter is

$$G(\omega) = 1 - 2a\cos\omega + a^2. \tag{42}$$

So the filter reduces the amplitude of the 6-year cycle ($\omega = \pi/12$) by a factor of more than 3 and that of the 2-year cycle by 30%, while it amplifies the low frequency components (by rather more than half for a 9-month cycle).

Fig. 7 shows some results obtained in this way for the spectral density. The dotted curve represents the estimate $\hat{f}_y(\omega)$ resulting from application of Tukey's window (with $n = 12$) to the filtered series $\{y_t\}$. The unbroken curve represents the corresponding estimate $\hat{f}_y(\omega)/G(\omega)$ of the spectrum of $\{x_t\}$. Finally, the broken curve represents the estimate of $f_x(\omega)$ obtained previously by applying the same window to $\{x_t\}$.

For the spectral density of $\{x_t\}$, the results are virtually identical over fre quencies corresponding to cycles of periodicity less than or equal to 2 years (the minimum is less marked because $\hat{f}_y(\omega)$ varies slightly more than $\hat{f}_x(\omega)$ at low frequencies; but the difference is negligible relative to the coefficient of variation of the estimate). On the other hand, the difference is considerable for the maximum, which now lies at the periodicity of 3 years exactly ($\omega = \pi/6$ and no longer $5\pi/24$) and which is about 20% greater. This new estimate can be considered as much less biased than the previous one, since the curvature of $\hat{f}_y(\omega)$ is much less marked than that of $\hat{f}_x(\omega)$ in the important domain $(\pi/24, \pi/3)$.

The necessities of smoothing the spectrum also explain why we usually prefer to deal with series corrected for seasonal variations rather than with crude series (unless of course it is the seasonal movement which is to be determined). The presence of maxima of the spectrum for the one-year cycle and its harmonics often gravely affects the estimate of the spectral density for many other periodicities.

8   Parametric decomposition of a time series

Up till now we have considered inference procedures applying to stationary processes. We must now discuss the treatment of non-stationary series of the type encountered in economics.

As we saw at the beginning of this chapter, it has long been customary to distinguish two or more components in most economic time series: trend, cycle, seasonal movements and random movements may have their effects combined in various ways. Now, we often find it necessary to isolate each of these components for better analysis and prediction of the phenomenon under study. Each component fits into a particular explanatory system. This analysis simplifies investigation of the phenomenon.

Methods for the decomposition of time series fall into two categories. The first derive from general regression and linear estimation theory, the second depend mainly on the application of more or less elaborate linear filters. Here we shall make only a few brief remarks about the former, since the second part of this book is devoted to them.

Suppose then that the series in question, x_t, has three components relating respectively to the trend, seasonal movement, and random disturbances, u_t, s_t and ε_t, say. Suppose also that u_t and s_t can be expressed by a small number of unknown parameters. For example, we may agree to represent the trend by a polynomial of low degree in t, and consider the seasonal movement to be stable, so that it depends only on $S-1$ parameters, where S is the number of observations per 'year' (see below). We assume also that the process of the ε_t is purely random with zero expected value and finite variance. Finally, we assume a linear composition

$$x_t = u_t + s_t + \varepsilon_t. \tag{43}$$

All the usual conditions for valid application of least squares are fulfilled[†].
More precisely, let us write

$$u_t = a_0 + a_1 t + a_2 t^2 + \ldots + a_p t^p, \tag{44}$$

$$s_t = c_1 \delta_{1t} + c_2 \delta_{2t} + \ldots + c_S \delta_{St}, \tag{45}$$

where the a_j and the c_h denote the unknown parameters while the δ_{ht} are dummy variables, δ_{ht} being 1 when the tth observation concerns the hth 'month', and being 0 in all other cases. For the reason already discussed in chapter 7, § 8, the c_h are not identifiable without a supplementary condition. This is why the equality

$$\sum_{h=1}^{s} c_h = 0 \tag{46}$$

is usually adopted.

Application of the method of least squares subject to the constraint (46) gives estimates of the $p + S + 1$ unknown coefficients $a_0, \ldots, a_p, c_1, \ldots, c_s$. So it allows us to determine the two components (44) and (45).

This formalization of the problem, which has long been familiar, was recently presented systematically by JORGENSON [1964]. The computation involved used to seem heavy before the widespread use of electronic computers, and a set of simplifying methods was developed, in particular, the use of orthogonal polynomials and the Buys-Ballot table[††]. Nowadays these methods are practically obsolete.

Before finding the parameters, or even after obtaining a first set of estimates, it is usual in practice to eliminate observations which are abnormal either for a known cause (for example, a strike) or simply because they deviate too much from the evolution of the series. We saw in chapter 8, § 5 (i) that this practice may have strong justification however arbitrary it seems.

Model (43) and its treatment by least squares depends on a certain number of assumptions. But there can obviously be many variants of the methods proposed here, each adapted to a particular set of assumptions about the nature of each component, about the random elements, or about the way the series is formed from its components.

[†] GRETHER and NERLOVE [1970] and PAGAN [1975] advocate less rigid formulae. The first two terms of (43) may be random and obey, for example,

$$u_t = \beta_1 u_{t-1} + \beta_2 u_{t-2} + \ldots + \beta_h u_{t-h} + \xi_t$$
$$s_t = \gamma s_{t-s} + \eta_t.$$

We shall not discuss here the analysis of series subject to such decomposition.

[††] See, for example, the brief remarks in ch. 12, § 3a and c of the first edition of this book.

Thus in the representation (45) of the seasonal movement, we may reserve the possibility that the component relating to a given 'month' increases or decreases in the course of time. The coefficient c_h is then replaced by $c_h + d_h t$, the d_h being restricted by the condition that their sum is zero. For decomposition of the series, $S - 1$ additional parameters must be estimated. This situation is conceivable with long series.

While keeping to the model (43), we may assume that its accidental fluctuations are strongly autocorrelated. For example, we may consider a process of the type

$$\varepsilon_t = \rho \varepsilon_{t-1} + \eta_t$$

probably to hold, where ρ is near 1 and the η_t are not autocorrelated. Here it is preferable to apply least squares to the relation written with the first differences $\Delta x_t = x_t - x_{t-1}$ rather than with the directly observed values. We can write

$$\Delta x_t = \Delta u_t + \Delta s_t + \Delta \varepsilon_t$$

and, by hypothesis, the autocorrelation among the $\Delta \varepsilon_t$ is much smaller than among the ε_t. If u_t is a polynomial of degree μ in t, then Δu_t is a polynomial of degree $\mu - 1$. If u_t is a periodic function with period u, then so also is Δu_t. If u_t is sinusoidal, so also is Δu_t. So the methods proposed in this section apply with only minor modification[†].

In place of the additive schema (43), a multiplicative schema such that

$$x_t = u_t s_t \exp(\varepsilon_t),$$

or

$$\log x_t = \log u_t + \log s_t + \varepsilon_t \tag{47}$$

is often preferred.

An exponential trend u_t corresponds to a linear increase in $\log u_t$; a periodic evolution of s_t to an evolution of the same kind of $\log s_t$. Determination of the trend and the seasonal component can be carried out as before by means of a regression on the logarithms of the x_t.

If the ε_t of (47) are strongly correlated, we can still carry out decompositions using the first differences $\log x_t - \log x_{t-1}$, that is, the logarithms of the ratios x_t / x_{t-1}.

So there are numerous methods for finding the trend and the seasonal movement of a time series. Our aim here is not to study them in detail, but to demonstrate their common logical nature. Clearly the method appropriate to each particular case depends on the best assumptions which can be made about

---

† MQRLAT [1963] has simultaneously determined the seasonal component and autocorrelation of the residual component. The principle of his method will be discussed in ch. 12, § 7.

the nature of the trend, the seasonal movement and the accidental fluctuations[†].

However all the schemas discussed up till now are subject to the same limitation, which is often troublesome in practice; they do not contain a term representing the 'cycle'. They are valid only for phenomena which, when we disregard seasonal or accidental fluctuations, show a regular development which can be expressed by a simple analytic function depending on a small number of parameters. But many economic series are affected by considerable movements related to the general state of the economy or to some particular feature of the phenomenon which they describe. These movements contain large-scale oscillations, and so are called 'cycles'. However, from our point of view, this term is inadequate to the extent that it implies a regularity which does not exist in reality.

The biggest difficulty involved in finding seasonal components of industrial production, foreign trade and many other economic series lies in the choice of methods whose results will be relatively unaffected by irregular fluctuations in the economy as a whole[††]. For this reason, preference is generally given to the filtering methods which we are about to discuss.

In this discussion we shall not repeat what has just been said about the possible variants of the formulation of the decomposition model. Our previous discussion carries over directly.

9   Linear filters for the decomposition of a time series

We return to the composition schema (43); but we shall not specify the form of the trend u_t precisely, taking it as a movement which is assumed only to have a regular evolution. We shall first concentrate on the determination or elimination of the trend. So we write the process in the form

$$x_t = u_t + \varepsilon_t. \tag{48}$$

In order to determine a regular movement with the same general evolution as x_t but relatively unaffected by random disturbances, it is natural to substitute for x_t a weighted mean of the values observed in an interval $[t-\theta,\ t+\theta]$ enclosing t. So u_t is estimated by

$$u_t^* = \sum_{\tau=-\theta}^{\theta} a_\tau x_{t+\tau} \tag{49}$$

where the sum of the coefficients a_τ is 1. This is repeated for each value of t.

[†] See MORICE and CHARTIER [1954], ch. 6, for a more detailed discussion.

[††] We do not mean by this systematic disturbances related to certain identifiable events such as public holidays. These can easily be accounted for by a priori corrections, or by the introduction of dummy variables to the model as indicated previously (ch. 8).

Thus a *moving average* of the series $\{x_t\}$ is said to be obtained. This operation corresponds to a "linear filter". The choice of a moving average formula is reduced to that of the length of the interval (and so of the number θ) and of the coefficients a_τ. We see intuitively that, the greater the regularity attributed to the trend a priori, the larger must θ be. Similarly, it seems that the coefficients a_τ must be larger towards the centre of the interval $[t-\theta, t+\theta]$ than at its extremities.

There are several possible principles on which the choice of the a_τ may be based. Here we shall examined only three.

(i) Local fitting of a polynomial for determination of the trend

The first method adopts a formula (49) equivalent to that yielded by fitting a polynomial of degree $p-1$ to the $2\theta+1$ terms of the series $\{x_{t+\tau}\}$ in the interval $[t-\theta, t+\theta]$, this fitting being carried out by a method to be defined. The number p is chosen a priori. Obviously it must be less than $2\theta+1$. It also expresses certain a priori ideas about the form of the trend.

Suppose, for example, that this method is applied with $p = 3$ and $\theta = 2$. The value of u_t^* is defined by a formula of the type

$$u_t^* = a_{-2}x_{t-2} + a_{-1}x_{t-1} + a_0 x_t + a_1 x_{t+1} + a_2 x_{t+2}, \qquad (50)$$

the numerical coefficients a_{-2}, a_{-1}, a_0, a_1 and a_2 being such that $u_t^* = x_t$ if x_t is a polynomial of second degree in t. For example, if

$$x_{t+\tau} = \alpha_0 + \alpha_1 \tau + \alpha_2 \tau^2,$$

then we must have $u_t^* = x_t = \alpha_0$ for any α_0, α_1 and α_2. Identification of the coefficients α_0, α_1 and α_2 in (50) leads directly to the three conditions:

$$\begin{cases} a_{-2} + a_{-1} + a_0 + a_1 + a_2 = 1, \\ -2a_{-2} - a_{-1} + a_1 + 2a_2 = 0, \\ 4a_{-2} + a_{-1} + a_1 + 4a_2 = 0. \end{cases} \qquad (51)$$

So two of the five coefficients can be chosen arbitrarily. There remains an arbitrary coefficient if we impose a symmetric formula in which $a_{-1} = a_1$ and $a_{-2} = a_2$, since then the second condition of (51) is automatically satisfied.

For two given values of p and θ, the arbitrary element in the formula can be eliminated by fixing a fitting rule. Thus KENDALL [1948] investigates the moving averages obtained when the polynomial is fitted by multiple least squares regression. Of all the formulae corresponding to the same values of p and θ, these moving averages allow the most precise estimation of u_t if the trend is actually a polynomial of degree p in t and if the process $\{\varepsilon_t\}$ is purely random.

Without precise indication to the contrary, they may appear the most useful[†]. Thus, when $p = 3$ and $\theta = 2$, the fitting of a polynomial

$$\alpha_0 + a_1 \tau + a_2 \tau^2$$

to the five observations $x_{t+\tau}$ (where $-2 \le \tau \le 2$) assumes the determination of estimates α_0^*, α_1^* and α_2^*. (These estimates will differ for the different values of t.) A least squares regression gives the following normal equations:

$$\begin{cases} \sum_\tau x_{t+\tau} = \alpha_0^*(2\theta+1) + \alpha_1^* \sum_\tau \tau + \alpha_2^* \sum_\tau \tau^2 = 5\alpha_0^* + 10\alpha_2^* \\ \sum_\tau \tau x_{t+\tau} = \alpha_0^* \sum_\tau \tau + \alpha_1^* \sum_\tau \tau^2 + \alpha_2^* \sum_\tau \tau^3 = 10\alpha_1^* \\ \sum_\tau \tau^2 x_{t+\tau} = \alpha_0^* \sum_\tau \tau^2 + \alpha_1^* \sum_\tau \tau^3 + \alpha_2^* \sum_\tau \tau^4 = 10\alpha_0^* + 34\alpha_2^* \end{cases}$$

which imply

$$35^*\alpha_0 = 17 \sum_\tau x_{t+\tau} - 5 \sum_\tau \tau^2 x_{t+\tau}.$$

The formula for $u_t^* = \alpha_0^*$ is then

$$u_t^* = -\frac{3}{35} x_{t-2} + \frac{12}{35} x_{t-1} + \frac{17}{35} x_t + \frac{12}{35} x_{t+1} - \frac{3}{35} x_{t+2}, \qquad (52)$$

whose coefficients clearly satisfy (51).

When θ is a fairly large number, this method gives moving average formulae which may appear fairly heavy because of the rather complicated values of the coefficients a_τ. More simple formulae have long been used in practice (see KENDALL [1948], ch. 29).

(ii) Local fitting of a harmonic function

A similar procedure rests on the use of a formula derived by fitting a harmonic function of the type

$$u_t = \alpha_0 + \sum_{j=1}^p [\beta_j \cos \varphi_j \tau + \gamma_j \sin \varphi_j \tau], \qquad (53)$$

the number p and the angles φ_j being chosen a priori, while the fitting deter-

---

[†] This principle is applied by DUVALL [1966] to estimation of the trend of a series with a seasonal component. The moving averages are calculated over a period exceeding that of the seasonal phenomenon; their weights are established as above but correspond to the fitting of the series to the sum of a polynomial and a seasonal component.

mines the coefficients α_0, β_j and γ_j. Since it is a question of representing a trend, some of the angles φ_j must be relatively small with respect to the frequency corresponding to the length of the interval, that is, with respect to $\pi/(\theta+1)$.

It is interesting to compare this method with formula (39) used in section 7 for preliminary filtering for the determination of the spectrum of the textile production series. Let us therefore consider local fitting of a trend of the type

$$u_{t+\tau} = \alpha_0 + \alpha_1\tau + \beta\cos\frac{\pi\tau}{\theta+1} + \gamma\sin\frac{\pi\tau}{\theta+1}. \tag{54}$$

This is a mixed formula involving a linear term and a sinusoidal component whose period is the length of the interval of the fitting. If we try to apply a multiple regression for the determination of α_0, α_1, β and γ, we can write two of the normal equations, namely those which correspond to equating to zero the derivatives with respect to α_0 and β of the sum of squares of the differences between the $x_{t+\tau}$ and the $u_{t+\tau}$:

$$\left[\begin{array}{l} \sum\limits_{\tau=-\theta}^{\theta} x_{t+\tau} - (2\theta+1)\alpha_0^* - \beta^* = 0 \\[2mm] \sum\limits_{\tau=-\theta}^{\theta} x_{t+\tau}\cos\frac{\pi\tau}{\theta+1} - \alpha_0^* - \theta\beta^* = 0 \end{array}\right.$$

(the coefficients of α_1^* and γ^* are zero in these two normal equations). Summing these equations, we obtain

$$\alpha_0^* + \frac{\beta^*}{2} = \frac{1}{2\theta+2}\sum\limits_{\tau=-\theta}^{\theta}\left(1+\cos\frac{\pi\tau}{\theta+1}\right)x_{t+\tau},$$

which is identical to the value implied by (39) for the trend. For $\tau = 0$, equation (54) gives $u_t^* = \alpha_0^* + \beta^*$. Thus according to (39), used for elimination of the trend, the sinusoidal component of (54) is attributed half to the trend and half to random movements. (On fig. 8, the curve represents the result of the multiple regression on (54); the point represents the value of the trend u_t given by (39).)

(iii)　Elimination of the trend by successive differences

We must give brief mention to the method of differences which was widely investigated in the inter-war period. TINTNER [1940] gives a complete review of it.

Let Δx_t be the difference $x_t - x_{t-1}$, and $\Delta^p x_t$ the difference of order p, which

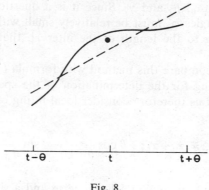

Fig. 8.

by definition is

$$\Delta^{p-1}x_t - \Delta^{p-1}x_{t-1},$$

where $\Delta^1 x_t = \Delta x_t$. To find the differences of order p of a random process $\{x_t\}$ is to define another random process $\{\Delta^p x_t\}$. The operator Δ^p is a linear filter.

If a random process $\{x_t\}$ is the sum of a trend term $\{u_t\}$ and a stationary process $\{\varepsilon_t\}$, then the process $\{\Delta^p x_t\}$ is clearly the sum of the sequence $\{\Delta^p u_t\}$ and the stationary process $\{\Delta^p \varepsilon_t\}$. If the trend u_t has a regular evolution, Δu_t will generally be small and $\Delta^2 u_t$ still smaller. On the other hand, the differences $\Delta \varepsilon_t$ and $\Delta^2 \varepsilon_t$ will generally have values of the same order of magnitude as the values of the ε_t. So the trend component will be of less importance in the processes $\{\Delta x_t\}$ and $\{\Delta^2 x_t\}$ than in the process $\{x_t\}$. From this comes the idea of substituting a process $\{\Delta^p x_t\}$ for $\{x_t\}$ in order to eliminate the trend component.

Two questions are raised by this substitution. To what extent is the trend component eliminated in $\{\Delta^p x_t\}$? It will be completely eliminated if and only if u_t is a polynomial of degree at most $p-1$ in t. But generally $\Delta^p u_t$ will not be zero. Even if the trend component disappears completely, what information does observation of $\{\Delta^p \varepsilon_t\}$ give about the properties of $\{\varepsilon_t\}$? To answer this question we must look at the correspondence established by the operator Δ^p between the characteristics of $\{\varepsilon_t\}$ and those of $\{\Delta^p \varepsilon_t\}$. The statisticians who worked on the method of differences looked closely at this problem, which we have already discussed in the general context of linear filters.

There is a fairly strict relationship between the use of moving averages and the method of differences. KENDALL [1961] showed that the calculation of moving averages is equivalent to the application of differences to a linear combination of some successive terms of the x_t. More precisely, to every moving average formula which can be expressed in terms of fitting a polynomial of degree $p-1$ to $2\theta+1$ successive terms, there correspond $2\theta - p + 1$

numbers β_τ, (for $p - \theta \leq \tau \leq \theta$) such that

$$u_t^* = x_t - \Delta^p \left[\sum_{\tau=p-\theta}^{\theta} \beta_\tau x_{t+\tau} \right]. \tag{55}$$

We can easily verify this result for the case where $p = 3$, $\theta = 2$. For,

$$\Delta^3[\beta_1 x_{t+1} + \beta_2 x_{t+2}] = \beta_2 x_{t+2} + (\beta_1 - 3\beta_2)x_{t+1} + (3\beta_2 - 3\beta_1)x_t +$$
$$+ (3\beta_1 - \beta_2)x_{t-1} - \beta_1 x_{t-2}.$$

So (55) defines a moving average whose coefficients

$$a_{-2} = \beta_1, \qquad a_{-1} = \beta_2 - 3\beta_1, \qquad a_0 = 1 + 3\beta_1 - 3\beta_2,$$
$$a_1 = 3\beta_2 - \beta_1, \qquad a_2 = -\beta_2$$

satisfy the conditions (51). In the particular case of (52), $\beta_1 = -3/35$ and $\beta_2 = 3/35$, which shows that subtraction of this estimate of the trend is equivalent to application of the operator Δ^4, apart from a factor $3/35$.

(iv) Seasonal variation

Let us again consider a series containing a seasonal component

$$x_t = u_t + s_t + \varepsilon_t. \tag{56}$$

Suppose, to fix ideas, that x_t is a monthly series, and so the period S of s_t is 12. We now concentrate our attention on estimation or elimination of the seasonal component s_t.

If the series has no trend u_t, or more precisely, if it has a constant trend, then a natural method for estimating c_h, the value of s_t in the hth month (see (45) above), is to find the arithmetic mean $\bar{x}_h$ of the observations x_t referring to this month. The estimate of c_h will then be the difference between $\bar{x}_h$ and the overall mean $\bar{x}$. But the presence of u_t means that this estimate will be biased (except in the exceptional case when u_t and s_t are orthogonal). For example, if 6 consecutive years have been observed and if the trend is increasing, then the difference $\bar{x}_1 - \bar{x}$ relating to January contains, because of u_t, a negative component approximately equal to the negative of the average increase during five and a half months. So in estimating s_t, account must be taken of the trend u_t.

A first method is to carry out preliminary elimination of the trend. But the moving averages which we have considered for this purpose generally affect s_t. If the trend is estimated by a formula of the type (49), its elimination does not affect s_t if and only if

$$\sum_{\tau=-\theta}^{\theta} a_\tau s_{t+\tau} = 0. \tag{57}$$

For this to be so for all t and for all possible values of the c_h obeying (46) it is necessary that

$$\sum_{\tau=-\theta}^{\theta} a_\tau \delta_{h,\,t+\tau} \tag{58}$$

is a constant which does not depend on h, nor on t ($\delta_{ht} = 1$ if t refers to the hth month, and zero otherwise). This is a very restrictive condition. For example, if $S = 12$ and $\theta = 6$, then (58) will equal a_k if there is a difference of k months between h and the month to which t refers (where $-5 \le k \le 5$) and will equal $a_{-6} + a_6$ if this difference is 6 months. So the only 13-month moving average which is certain to leave the seasonal component unchanged is that defined by

$$\begin{cases} a_\tau = \dfrac{1}{12} & \text{for} \quad -5 \le \tau \le 5. \\[2mm] a_{-6} = a_6 = \dfrac{1}{24} \end{cases} \tag{59}$$

But the corresponding filter is very mediocre for estimation or elimination of the trend; only linear trends are completely eliminated[†]. To an oscillating trend it gives a corresponding estimate in which the oscillations are fairly largely reduced.

Faced with this dilemma, it is usual in practice to apply iterative methods whose main line of attack can be described as follows[††]:

(i) First apply the filter corresponding to (59) for initial crude elimination of the trend. Let $\{x_t^{(1)}\}$ be the resulting residual series.

(ii) Find a first estimate $c_h^{(1)}$ of the seasonal terms from the monthly averages $\bar{x}_h^{(1)} - \bar{x}^{(1)}$ of the series $\{x_t^{(1)}\}$. Find

$$x_t^{(2)} = x_t - \sum_h c_h^{(1)} \delta_{ht},$$

the first estimate of the de-seasonalized series.

(iii) Apply to $\{x_t^{(2)}\}$ a filter which allows more complete elimination of the trend, using, for example, one of the filters defined in section 9(i). Let $\{x_t^{(5)}\}$ be the new residual series.

[†] It replaces quadratic trends by constants which are also eliminated if deviations from the mean are considered, as is usually the case.

[††] For a complete description of the varying methods used in practice, see SHISKIN and EISENPRESS [1958], MÉRAUD and TYMEN [1960] or CALOT [1965], ch. 8. The reader interested in improvement of these methods may also refer to DURBIN [1963a] who proposes some simplifications in and improvements on the usual formulae.

(iv) Find a second estimate $c_h^{(3)}$ of the seasonal terms from the monthly averages of the series $\{x_t^{(3)}\}$.

(v) Possibly carry out one or two additional iterations of the same kind.

As HANNAN [1963] points out, we may dispense with iterative methods of this type and apply to the original series a linear filter which gives good elimination of the trend, since it is possible to determine precisely the modification required in seasonal terms to correct the effect of the preliminary filtering. For each filter, it is sufficient to determine once for all a set of S coefficients v_k ($k = 0, 1, \ldots, S-1$) allowing transition from the seasonal terms $\hat{c}_h$ calculated from the filtered series to unbiased estimates c_h^* of the c_h, by means of the formula

$$c_h^* = \sum_{k=1}^{S} \hat{c}_k v_{k-h} \qquad h = 1, 2, \ldots, S, \tag{60}$$

where

$$v_{k-h} = v_{k-h+12} \quad \text{if} \quad k-h < 0.$$

HANNAN [1963] explains how the coefficients v_k can be calculated; he gives their values for the case of monthly series and for three particular filters[†]. WALLIS [1974] moreover presents linear approximations for the commonly used filters.

10   Spectral analysis of non-stationary series

We saw in section 7 how the periodogram of a realization of a stationary process allows us to estimate the spectral density of this process. We also saw that it may at times be appropriate to work on a de-seasonalized process, since otherwise the necessary smoothing of the periodogram would be affected by the presence of peaks for periods corresponding to the seasonal phenomenon (S and its harmonics). We shall now examine the case of series with a trend u_t:

$$x_t = u_t + \varepsilon_t, \tag{61}$$

where the ε_t constitute a stationary process[††].

[†] In practice it is sometimes also necessary to take account of the fact that the seasonal terms develop through time so that estimation of them requires methods other than a simple averaging of the residuals relating to the same month. The references given above define the usual methods for this. NETTHEIM [1965] investigates this difficulty for the case where Hannan's method applies.

[††] So the only deviations from stationarity to be considered here concern the expected value of the process of the x_t. In applications it is also necessary to investigate the existence of a possible trend affecting the variance of the process or certain other of its characteristics. A change of variables, for example to logarithms, will often improve the stationarity of the series.

It may seem a priori that the methods for studying stationary processes apply to such series since the trend is comparable to a movement with very long periodicity. On the periodogram of the observed series $\{x_t\}$, values corresponding to low frequencies then represent the trend.

This approach to the problem ignores the fact that what gives point to the decomposition (61) is the idea that the two components play distinct rôles. For example, for prediction of future values of the x_t, ε_t is meant to be treated as a residual process showing some characteristics of serial correlation, while u_t is taken as a function of t or is even explained on the basis of other quantities.

To fix ideas, suppose we are considering a linear trend

$$u_t = \alpha_0 + \alpha_1 t.$$

Over every finite interval ($t = 1, 2, \ldots, T$), the periodogram of this function has a very precise form. But as T increases, this periodogram does not tend to a limit, since the importance of low frequencies increases indefinitely. That is, the periodogram of a linear function is not a useful representation of it.

Similarly, the periodogram of (61) is approximately the sum of the periodogram of u_t and that of ε_t. Because of the trend u_t, it is not a useful characteristic of the phenomenon under study.

However we must bear two points in mind. In the first place, knowledge of the periodogram of the observed series $\{x_t\}$ may be useful in the investigation of the properties of certain statistical procedures. We shall find examples of this in succeeding chapters. Thus, when estimating some econometric models it is sometimes opportune to consider the cumulative periodogram of certain exogenous variables (the dotted line on fig. 4 represents that of the crude textile production series; the predominant importance of low frequencies is clear). But then the periodogram is no longer regarded as an estimator of the spectrum of a process.

In the second place, there is a certain arbitrary element in (61), since neither the nature of the trend nor the form of the spectrum of the random series ε_t for low frequencies is strictly specified. To take maximum advantage of spectral analysis, it is often preferable to give a fairly restrictive definition of the trend which is first to be eliminated.

This elimination can be carried out in two ways:

(i) The first method takes for the ε_t the residuals with respect to the fitting of a low degree polynomial. The trend u_t is then identified as being near this polynomial, while the spectrum of the ε_t is estimated by that of the residuals. Of course the residuals necessarily differ from the errors, so that this estimate of the spectrum contains a bias (we shall come across this again in ch. 13). But this bias is small at low frequencies, provided that the series is not too short[†].

[†] In principle, this bias can also be corrected because the linear operator defining the correspondence between the errors and the residuals is known. See HANNAN [1960], ch. 5.

(ii) The second method eliminates the trend by a linear filter. Of course this filter also affects the ε_t; the spectral density $f_y^*(\omega)$ estimated from the transformed series differs systematically from the density $f_\varepsilon(\omega)$ of the process $\{\varepsilon_t\}$. But, given the gain $G(\omega)$ of the filter, it is easy to correct $f_y^*(\omega)$ by substituting the estimate $f_\varepsilon^*(\omega) = f_y^*(\omega)/G(\omega)$.

We must point out that the second method has no clear consequence for estimation of the trend. Even when the latter is eliminated by a moving average filter conceived as providing a local fitting of the series, it is not considered to be estimated by the difference $u_t^* = x_t - y_t$ since the precise object of the correction is to rectify a systematic deviation between the series of the y_t and that of the ε_t. (Here there is an obvious difference in outlook from sections 9(i) and 9(ii) above.) The trend is considered to be composed both of a functional term completely eliminated by the filter (that is, a term z_t, solution of the difference equation $z_t = \sum_\tau a_\tau z_{t+\tau}$) and of components with long periodicity which are more normally attributed to the trend rather than to random movements. But neither the functional term nor these components are estimated by this method.

The margin of choice in definition of the trend is reduced in practice by application of the following rule that common-sense suggests once the principle of an extensive definition of the random process has been adopted. When $f_y^*(\omega)$ is obtained as a moving average of $2m+1$ successive terms of the periodogram, this estimate is provided only from the following value of ω:

$$\omega_0 = \frac{2\pi}{T}(m+1).$$

The density $f_\varepsilon^*(\omega)$ is then only estimated for $\omega \geq \omega_0$. It seems that a similar rule should be adopted when the estimate $f_y^*(\omega)$ is calculated from the correlogram. Then the periodic components of the trend have frequencies ω less than ω_0.

Fig. 9 shows, for example, three estimates of the spectral density of the textile production series (upper part of fig. 1). These three estimates were obtained by moving averages of 7 successive terms of the periodograms. The broken line relates to the series itself. It is influenced, even at high frequencies, by the presence of the trend. This explains why it lies entirely above the other two estimates, for which the trend has been eliminated. The unbroken line relates to the residuals with respect to a third degree polynomial fitted to the whole series by least squares. The dotted line concerns an estimate for which the trend has been eliminated by application of the filter (39); so this line is deduced from that in fig. 6 by dividing by the gain $G(\omega)$ given by (40). The two unbroken and dotted lines are not absolutely comparable since they correspond to different delimitations of the trend. However, we see that they are fairly close. The spectral density of the residuals with respect to a third degree polynomial is smallest at frequencies less than $\pi/6$, which is not surprising since this density

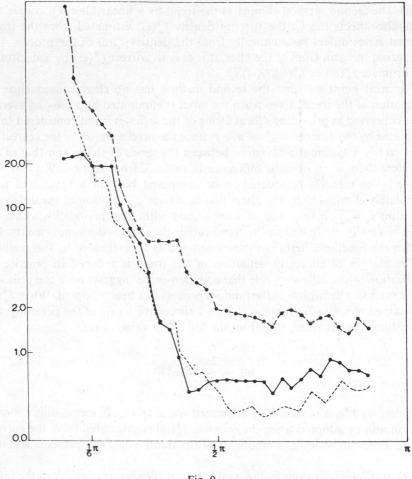

Fig. 9.

has not been corrected. It is higher at other frequencies. This may be explained by the eight additional observations contained in the series of the residuals relative to the filtered series (the extreme years 1948 and 1967). But it may also be due to the fact that the filter (39) gives better elimination of the trend.

DURBIN [1961] attacks the problem in general terms. Concentrating on the case where the filter used for elimination of the trend is a difference, he establishes the following results:

(1) The use of differences of order p and the corresponding transformation $f_y^*(\omega)/G(\omega)$ leads identically to the same estimate $f_\varepsilon^*(\omega)$ of the spectrum of $\{\varepsilon_t\}$ as a periodogram constructed from the residuals $\hat{\varepsilon}_t$ between x_t and the polynomial $\hat{u}_t$ of degree p defined, apart from a constant, by the conditions

$$\Delta^r \hat{\varepsilon}_T = \Delta^r \hat{\varepsilon}_1$$

or equivalently,   for $r = 0, 1, \ldots, p-1.$

$$\Delta^r \hat{u}_T - \Delta^r \hat{u}_1 = \Delta^r x_T - \Delta^r x_1$$

(The values $x_0, x_{-1}, \ldots, x_{-p+1}$, that are necessary for finding $\Delta^p x_1$ are assumed known.) So $\hat{u}_t$ is determined uniquely from the first and last terms of the series. The trend component u_t is completely eliminated only if the residuals $\hat{\varepsilon}_t$ do not depend on it, that is, only if u_t itself is a polynomial of degree p. (The transformation defining $\hat{\varepsilon}_t$ is in fact linear. It operates separately on u_t and on ε_t and transforms u_t into a constant if and only if it is a polynomial of degree p in t.)

(2) However, if u_t is a sufficiently regular function of t, the bias in $f_\varepsilon^*(\omega)$ resulting from the trend component is important only for low frequencies. More precisely, for the frequencies $\omega_j = 2\pi j/T$ (where $j = 1, 2, \ldots, (T-1)/2$), the bias decreases with j at least as $j^{-2(p+1)}$. For comparison, we can consider the bias of a periodogram constructed from the residuals of a polynomial of degree p fitted over the whole series by least squares. The bias due to the trend in this case decreases only as j^{-2}.

So the method of differences allows complete elimination of the trend only if the latter is polynomial in which case the method of least squares gives the same result and leads to a more precise estimate of the polynomial. But, whenever the trend is regular, the method of differences leads to better estimation of the spectral characteristics of $\{\varepsilon_t\}$ for high frequencies; now, it is exactly in the study of these frequencies that we want to eliminate the trend.

According to (55), every moving average is identical to a difference applied to a linear combination of a small number of successive terms. So it seems that smoothing by moving average must enjoy approximately the useful properties of the method of differences in the study of high frequencies of the residual random process $\{\varepsilon_t\}$.

On the three lines in fig. 9, we see that the spectral density decreases strongly in the whole frequency domain corresponding to cycles of more than a year. The variations are small for higher frequencies. GRANGER [1966] remarks that this type of evolution is present in the large majority of series used in econometrics. He even goes so far as to talk of *the typical spectrum of economic series*. For example, fig. 10 shows the spectral densities estimated respectively for production, employment and weekly hours of work in French textile industries[†]. The employment series, whose graph is fairly regular, gives the most widely varying spectrum; it is 1 000 times higher for the 6-year cycle than for high frequencies. Although the series on weekly hours of work has only a very weak trend component, its spectrum has the same decreasing form as those of the other two series, since the 6-year cycle predominates in it also.

[†] Estimates obtained from time series corrected for seasonal variations and relating to the period 1948-67. The three series have been double filtered using (39) and (41) with $\theta = 4$ and $a = 0.8$. They have then been treated by Tukey's window operating on the first twelve terms of the correlogram.

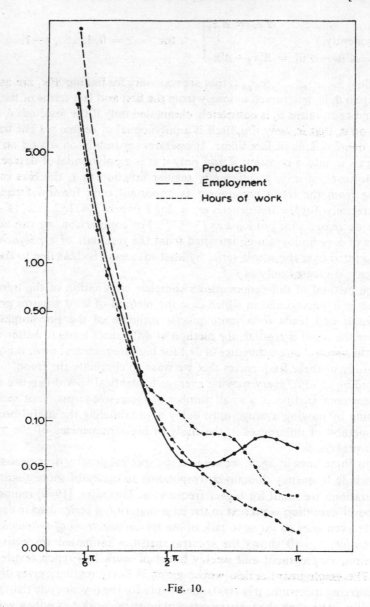

.Fig. 10.

The fact that economic series have spectra showing similarities should not be surprising; this simply reflects the importance and generality of fluctuations in the economy as a whole and of long-term movements of economic growth. Differences also exist, as can be seen in fig. 10. However, this common appearance of the spectra of economic series has implications for econometrics, as we shall see in succeeding chapters.

11 What series should we use for econometric estimation?

The two previous sections have given us the opportunity to discuss a question which is not directly related to the subject of this chapter but which is of great practical importance in econometrics.

As we have just seen, different components corresponding respectively to the trend, to cyclical fluctuations and to seasonal variations are often distinguished in a time series. Such an analysis leads to easier interpretation of current statistical data. Thus from one month to the next, variation in the index of industrial production reflects in part seasonal influences and in part more fundamental movements in economic activity. The student of the current economic outlook is interested in these last movements especially, and therefore uses a 'de-seasonalized' index which he obtains by subtracting from the calculated index an estimate of the seasonal component. Similarly, it is sometimes useful to consider series from which the trend has been extracted. For example, the consumption of electric power in France grows approximately at a constant rate, corresponding to its doubling in ten years. Its fluctuations from one year to the next can be described by an index of its ratio to the trend, which is more suggestive than the crude data.

Prior to the statistical estimation of an economic model, we may ask whether we should not make some corrections to the directly observed time series. To fix ideas, suppose we wish to establish a regression between raw material imports and industrial production on the basis of quarterly statistics. Should we first eliminate from the series seasonal variations, and perhaps even the trend?

This question must be answered only after careful examination of the meaning of the model to be estimated. Let the supposed relation be

$$x_t = az_t + b + \varepsilon_t.$$

Does it apply to the crude data for imports (x_t) and industrial production (z_t)? Or does it apply to the corrected data (after elimination of seasonal variation and perhaps also the trend)? In the former case, the regression must be carried out on the crude data, in the latter case on the corrected data.

The model constitutes a (causal) explanation of the level of imports based on the volume of industrial production. If it so happens that in some particular quarter, say the third, industrial production is generally lower, imports must also be reduced. The comparative extent of seasonal movements in the two series is an important element for estimation of the model. To eliminate these movements means that we deprive ourselves needlessly of part of the information contained in the observed series. So it is preferable to use the crude data.

This argument assumes that the model gives a complete explanation of the level of imports in each quarter. One may argue that in fact the relationship is more complex. For example, seasonal stock-formation of imported raw materials takes place. If the consumption of imported raw materials is in fact explained directly by the volume of industrial production, the crude figures of imports are also affected by this seasonal stock-formation. Previous elimination of seasonal variations from the two series allows us to ignore this.

Similarly the volume of imports may be influenced by progressive changes in international specialization. The general trend of imports is therefore not explained solely by the trend of the volume of industrial production. Once again, this difficulty is resolved if the regression between the series is established after elimination of the trend in each.

These arguments are not wholly convincing. Once we have started, we cannot very well see where to stop applying corrections to the series. And the more we change the basic data, the more cautiously must we regard the estimated relationship, and in any case the more difficult does its interpretation become. If the initial model does not provide a sufficient explanation of the phenomenon under study, we must rather try to improve it by explicit introduction of the factors which it does not take into account (stock-formation, variation in the structure of production, etc.).

However, it should be pointed out that no model is perfect. We must often work with fairly crude representations, otherwise we would achieve no result. In particular, it is very difficult to measure certain elements which may play an important part in the relationships studied (for example, exchange and tariffs policy). The only practical solution to the problem sometimes lies in taking account of these elements in the indefinite form of 'seasonal factors' or 'trend factors'.

But on this topic, we should not lose sight of two facts which appear particularly clearly when a multiple regression technique has been used for eliminating seasonal or trend factors[†].

In the first place, *every corrected series has a smaller number of degrees of freedom than that of the observations*. It is indeed a series of the residuals isolated by the elimination procedure. If the latter is a multiple regression implying the estimation of p seasonal or trend coefficients, the T values of the corrected series are restricted a priori to satisfy p linear relations. In applying the general formulae relating to estimators or tests, T must therefore be replaced by $T - p$. The situation is less simple when the elimination procedure is non-linear. But the phenomenon persists; the corrected series contains less information than an uncorrected series of the same length which is directly subject to the model studied. This reduction in the number of degrees of freedom, which may be significant, is often overlooked in econometric works.

In the second place, *in the cases where seasonal or trend factors interfere with the phenomenon under study, it is possible to construct a model which applies to the crude series* and which combines all the possible a priori ideas about their reciprocal relationships. It is sufficient to introduce the factors in question

---

† The two following remarks have recently been presented very clearly by LOVELL [1963]. See also THOMAS and WALLIS [1971].

explicitly, for example by adding, to the true explanatory variables z_{jt}, time (or a polynomial function of time) to represent the trend and particular dummy variables to represent seasonal effects (see ch. 8)[†].

Viewed with reference to this complete model, the usual procedure appears as an estimation method in which the computation falls into two successive stages: (i) elimination of the seasonal or trend factors, (ii) fitting of the model applying to the corrected data. The properties of this procedure can thus be examined in each particular case.

For example, consider the case where a real variable x is a linear function of another variable z, the additive constant depending on the season. The complete model is written:

$$x_t = az_t + c's_t + \varepsilon_t,$$

where s_t denotes the vector of the dummy variables relating to the seasons. If they are calculated by multiple regression, the deseasonalized series relating to x and z are

$$u_t = x_t - m_{xs}M_{ss}^{-1}s_t, \qquad w = z_t - m_{zs}M_{ss}^{-1}s_t$$

with the usual notation. It is easy to verify that, in this case, the regression coefficient a^* between the deseasonalized series is identical to the coefficient obtained for z by fitting the complete model by multiple regression using the crude series (see for example the formulae given in the footnote on p. 26). This result, which was first established by FRISCH and WAUGH [1933], shows that in this case fitting based on corrected series enjoys the characteristic efficiency properties of multiple regressions[††].

12 Spectral investigation of the dependences among series

When in chapter 1 we were considering the characterization of the dependences among economic quantities, we were led to introduce regressions established using empirical covariance matrices. At that time we were interested solely in the relationships among concomitant values of these quantities, for example x_t and z_t. The ordering of series in time leads to an investigation of possible dependences among values relating to different observations. It may take some time for the quantity z to act on the quantity x so that the relationship established between z_{t-1} and x_t may be stronger than that established between z_t and x_t. How can this kind of relation be revealed?

[†] The method proposed in ch. 8 assumes that the seasonal influence is purely additive. Formulations of the type chosen for analysis of covariance allow more complex situations to be treated. See for example LADD [1964].
[††] The result was generalized by WALLIS [1974] to cases in which the estimated model is not a multiple regression but a distributed lag relation (see ch. 14).

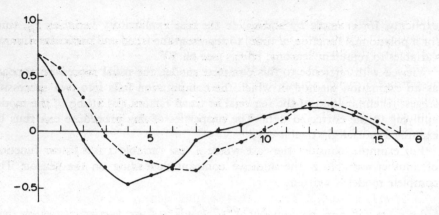

Fig. 11.

(i)   Cross-correlogram and periodogram

It seems natural to find the covariances between series which have been displaced relatively to each other, and possibly some regressions containing such displacements. For the moment we disregard regressions, to which we shall return in chapters 13 and 14 for the estimation of well-specified models. Here we shall only define

$$C_\theta(x, z) = \frac{1}{T} \sum_{t=1}^{T-\theta} (x_t - \bar{x}) (z_{t+\theta} - \bar{z}) \qquad (62)$$

and

$$r_\theta(x,z) = \frac{C_\theta(x,z)}{[C_0(x,x)C_0(z,z)]^{\frac{1}{2}}}. \qquad (63)$$

The $C_\theta(x,z)$ are the lagged covariances of x and z while the sequence of the $r_\theta(x,z)$ is the *cross-correlogram* of x and z. The terms of the empirical correlogram of x defined by formulae (1) to (3) at the beginning of this chapter are obviously the $r_\theta(x,x)$. We note that $C_\theta(x,z)$ and $r_\theta(x,z)$ generally differ from $C_\theta(z,x)$ and $r_\theta(z,x)$ respectively. It is convenient to define these quantities for negative values of θ by the conventions

$$C_\theta(x,z) = C_{-\theta}(z,x) \qquad r_\theta(x,z) = r_{-\theta}(z,x). \qquad (64)$$

For example, fig. 11 shows the cross-correlogram of two quarterly series relating to the French textile industry from 1948 to 1967, namely employment (x) and production (z).[†] The unbroken line corresponds to positive values of

---

[†] In fact x_t is employment *at the start* of the quarter and z_t is production *during* the quarter. The trend in each series was previously eliminated by applying the filter (39) with $\theta = 4$.

θ (lag in production relative to employment), and the broken line to negative values (lag in employment relative to production). As with correlograms proper to a given series, the values of θ are usually stopped at a fraction of T, in this case $|\theta| \leq 16$. We see that here the $r_\theta(x,z)$ tend to be higher for negative than for positive θ, which shows that there is a certain lag in the adjustment of employment to variations in production.

Similarly, we can define a *cross-periodogram* which generalizes the periodogram defined for each series in isolation. For each frequency

$$\omega_k = \frac{2\pi k}{T}$$

formulae (11) in section 2 associate two quantities a_k and b_k with the series of the x_t. It will now be convenient to represent these two quantities by the complex number $X_k = a_k + ib_k$, which we can call the Fourier component, and so to rewrite the equations (11) in the form

$$X_k = \sqrt{\frac{2}{T}} \sum_{t=1}^{T} x_t \, e^{i\omega_k t} \qquad k = 1, 2, \ldots, T'', \tag{65}$$

where i obviously denotes the imaginary number $\sqrt{-1}$ and T'' is $(T-1)/2$ or $(T/2) - 1$ according as T is odd or even. Formula (14) defining the periodogram of $\{x_t\}$ can then be written

$$I_{xk} = X_k \bar{X}_k. \tag{66}$$

Here, without risk of confusion with arithmetic means, $\bar{X}_k$ denotes the conjugate complex number $a_k - ib_k$ of X_k.

Similarly, we can associate with the sequence of the z_t the complex number

$$Z_k = \sqrt{\frac{2}{T}} \sum_{t=1}^{T} z_t \, e^{i\omega_k t}$$

and the periodogram $I_{zk} = Z_k \bar{Z}_k$. The cross-periodogram of x with respect to z is then defined naturally as

$$J_k(x,z) = X_k \bar{Z}_k. \tag{67}$$

This is a complex number whose interpretation we shall shortly see. The conjugate number is equal to $J_k(z,x)$, the cross-periodogram of z with respect to x.

(ii) Transfer function and coherence

X_k and Z_k can also be represented in the complex plane (cf. fig. 12). The periodograms I_{xk} and I_{zk} measure the lengths of the corresponding vectors,

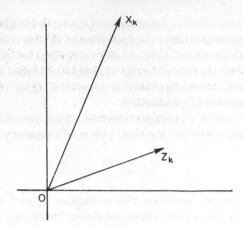

Fig. 12.

that is, the size of the frequency ω_k in the Fourier representation of the two series. (As we saw in section 2, the unit vectors of the axes of the complex plane relate to the series $\cos \omega_k t$ and $\sin \omega_k t$ each being multiplied by $\sqrt{2/T}$; except for this multiplier the vector X_k relates to the series $A_{xk} \cos (\omega_k t + \varphi_{xk})$, where A_{xk} and φ_{xk} are the length of X_k and the angle made by X_k with the real axis.)

In order to characterize the relative positions of two sinusoidal components with frequency ω_k, say $A_{xk} \cos (\omega_k t + \varphi_{xk})$ and $A_{zk} \cos (\omega_k t + \varphi_{zk})$, we can choose the complex number X_k/Z_k, also equal to $J_k(x,z)I_{zk}$. The modulus of this number is equal to the ratio between the amplitudes A_{xk}/A_{zk}, and the argument to the difference of the phases $\varphi_{xk} - \varphi_{zk}$. We can deduce that the modulus of the cross-periodogram $J_k(x,z)$ is A_{xk}/A_{zk}, and its argument $\varphi_{xk} - \varphi_{zk}$.

However, the X_k and Z_k obtained for the successive values of k vary fairly erratically. We saw why in section 7. Rather than take directly the ratio X_k/Z_k, it is more useful for us to find a characteristic which applies on average in an interval $[k-m, k+m]$ enclosing k. We can state the problem in the following terms.

Suppose that, in the interval considered, the phase displacement and the ratio between the amplitudes of the Fourier components corresponding to the same frequency ω_{k+h} tend to be constant; we then propose to estimate them. More precisely, we adopt the model

$$X_{k+h} = T_k Z_{k+h} + E_{k+h} \qquad h = -m, \ldots, m-1, m \qquad (68)$$

where T_k is a complex number independent of h and E_{k+h} is an erratic complex component[†]. The problem reduces to estimation of T_k from the $(2m+1)$ observations on the pair of variables (X_{k+h}, Z_{k+h}).

[†] For a case in which a more complex specification is considered refer to HANNAN and THOMPSON [1971, 1973].

Applied to this situation, the method of least squares amounts to choosing for T_k the number which minimizes the sum S_k of the products of the $(X_{k+h} - T_k Z_{k+h})$ by their respective conjugate values. (This sum of products can be considered as the square of a distance in the space $R^{2(2m+1)}$ that is homeomorphic to the cartesian product of the $(2m+1)$ complex planes associated with the different values of h.)

For minimization of the sum S_k, we define T_k^* as

$$T_k^* = \sum_{h=-m}^{m} X_{k+h} \bar{Z}_{k+h} \bigg/ \sum_{h=-m}^{m} Z_{k+h} \bar{Z}_{k+h} \tag{69}$$

and we write

$$X_{k+h} - T_k Z_{k+h} = [X_{k+h} - T_k^* Z_{k+h}] + [(T_k^* - T_k) Z_{k+h}]. \tag{70}$$

If S_k is expanded, using the right hand side of (70), the sum of the cross products becomes zero because of the definition of T_k^*; each of the other two sums is non-negative; so S_k is minimized for $T_k = T_k^*$.

Thus the complex number T_k^* characterizes the dependence of the series $\{x_t\}$ on the series $\{z_t\}$ in the neighborhood of the frequency ω_k. We can also write $T^*(\omega_k)$ and consider it as a function of ω_k; it is the *transfer function* of $\{x_t\}$ relative to $\{z_t\}$. Its modulus defines the quantity by which the amplitude of the components of $\{z_t\}$ whose frequency is near ω_k must be multiplied in order to obtain approximations of the corresponding components of $\{x_t\}$. Similarly, its argument defines the phase displacement to be applied.

Generally the dependence is not perfect, and this is expressed by the additive term E_{k+h} in model (68). In order to characterize it fully, its degree of precision must also be measured. The square R^2 of the classical multiple correlation coefficient used in regression theory is equal here to the ratio between the sum of the $(T_k^* Z_{k+h}) \overline{(T_k^* Z_{k+h})}$ and the sum of the $X_{k+h} \bar{X}_{k+h}$, namely

$$C^*(\omega_k) = \frac{\displaystyle\sum_{h=-m}^{m} X_{k+h} \bar{Z}_k \ _h \cdot \sum_{h=-m}^{m} \bar{X}_{k+h} Z_{k+h}}{\displaystyle\sum_{h=-m}^{m} Z_{k+} \angle_{k+h} \cdot \sum_{h=-m}^{m} X_{k+h} \bar{X}_{k+h}}. \tag{71}$$

This coefficient, called the *coherence*, is 1 if (68) applies with $E_{k+h} = 0$ for all h from $-m$ to m. In all other cases it is less than 1, as is established by the classic Schwarz inequality.

(iii)   Cospectra

The transfer function $T^*(\omega_k)$ and the coherence function $C^*(\omega_k)$ are the two characteristics which we were seeking. For their calculation and for an examination of their properties, it is useful to make some modification to (69) and (71), in which we find quantities encountered previously in the spectral investigation of one series taken in isolation. Thus,

$$\sum_{h=-m}^{m} X_{k+h}\overline{X}_{k+h} = \sum_{h=-m}^{m} I_{x,k+h} = 4\pi(2m+1)f_x^*(\omega_k),$$

where $f_x^*(\omega)$ is the estimator given by (32) for the spectrum of $\{x_t\}$.

Similarly, we can define the empirical *power cospectrum* of x with respect to z as the complex function $c^*(\omega) - iq^*(\omega)$ defined by

$$4\pi[c^*(\omega_k) - iq^*(\omega_k)] = \frac{1}{2m+1} \sum_{h=-m}^{m} J_{k+h}(x,z). \tag{72}$$

(If the variables to which the power cospectrum refers are to be specified precisely, we must write $c_{xz}^*(\omega)$ and $q_{xz}^*(\omega)$. We omit this for simplicity of notation, just as we did previously with the functions $T^*(\omega)$ and $C^*(\omega)$.) The functions $c^*(\omega)$ and $q^*(\omega)$ are said to be the *cospectrum* and the *quadrature spectrum* respectively. We must avoid the possible confusion arising from simultaneous use of the expressions 'power cospectrum' and 'cospectrum'.

Under this new definition, we can replace (69) and (71) by

$$T^*(\omega) = \frac{c^*(\omega) - iq^*(\omega)}{f_z^*(\omega)} \tag{73}$$

and

$$C^*(\omega) = \frac{[c^*(\omega)]^2 + [q^*(\omega)]^2}{f_x^*(\omega) \cdot f_z^*(\omega)}. \tag{74}$$

If $[G^*(\omega)]^{\frac{1}{2}}$ and $\varphi^*(\omega)$ denote the modulus and the argument of $T^*(\omega)$, we can also write

$$G^*(\omega) = C^*(\omega) \cdot \frac{f_x^*(\omega)}{f_z^*(\omega)} \tag{75}$$

and

$$\varphi^*(\omega) = - \operatorname{Arc\,tg}[q^*(\omega)/c^*(\omega)] + \delta\pi, \tag{76}$$

δ being zero if $c^*(\omega)$ is positive, and 1 if it is negative. If $c^*(\omega)$ happens to be zero, then $\varphi^*(\omega)$ is $\pm(\pi/2)$ according as $q^*(\omega)$ is negative or positive.

To calculate the functions $c^*(\omega)$ and $q^*(\omega)$, we must isolate the real and imaginary parts of $J_{k+h}(x,z)$. Returning to formulae (11) applied to $\{x_t\}$ and

$\{z_t\}$, which then define a_{xk}, b_{xk}, a_{zk} and b_{zk}, and taking account of the fact that

$$X_k = a_{xk} + ib_{xk} \qquad \text{and} \qquad Z_k = a_{zk} + ib_{zk},$$

we can deduce from (67) and (72):

$$4\pi c^*(\omega_k) = \frac{1}{2m+1} \sum_{h=-m}^{m} (a_{x,k+h} a_{z,k+h} + b_{x,k+h} b_{z,k+h})$$

$$4\pi q^*(\omega_k) = \frac{1}{2m+1} \sum_{h=-m}^{m} (a_{x,k+h} b_{z,k+h} - b_{x,k+h} a_{z,k+h}).$$

We have considered the different quantities introduced up till now as empirical characteristics of time series. They are also estimators of the characteristics of a two-dimensional stochastic process of which the two-component series $\{x_t, z_t\}$ is a realization. So the empirical covariance $C_\theta(x,z)$ corresponds to the theoretical covariance

$$\gamma_\theta(x,z) = E\{[x_t - E(x_t)] \, [z_{t+\theta} - E(z_t)]\}. \tag{77}$$

The empirical power cospectrum corresponds to the theoretical power cospectrum

$$c(\omega) - iq(\omega) = \frac{1}{2\pi} \lim_{T \to \infty} \sum_{\theta=-T}^{T} \gamma_\theta(x,z) e^{-i\omega\theta} \tag{78}$$

whose definition recalls that of the spectral density as given by formula (11) in chapter 11. (In this case we assume that the limit exists, as in the case where the spectral density of a one-dimensional process exists.) Similarly, the transfer function and the coherence correspond to the theoretical characteristics which are easily defined by transposition of (73) and (74).

The cospectrum $c(\omega)$ and the quadrature spectrum $q(\omega)$ are comparable to densities. We can show that[†], for the value $\omega = \omega_k$ and apart from a factor of $1/4\pi$, they are equal to the expected values of the real part and the negative of the imaginary part of the cross-periodogram $J_k(x, z)$. But the variance of the latter does not tend to zero with T any more than that of the ordinary periodogram I_{xk}. Just as $f_x^*(\omega)$ was substituted to I_{xk} for estimation of the spectral density, so $c^*(\omega)$ and $q^*(\omega)$ are substituted to $J_k(x,z)$ for estimation of $c(\omega)$ and $q(\omega)$. Formula (72), which is comparable to (32), shows that smoothing of

---

† As in section 7, we assume here and subsequently that the series x_t and z_t have zero means, or that, if they do not, the periodograms are calculated from deviations from the means.

the crossperiodogram is then carried out by a moving average of $2m+1$ successive terms, that is, by using 'Daniell's window'.

But if $f_x(\omega)$ and $f_z(\omega)$ have been estimated by a smoothing process which uses another window, then this process should also be used for estimation of $c(\omega)$ and $q(\omega)$. In particular, if the smoothing process allows direct estimation of the spectral density from the first terms of the correlogram, the estimators $\hat{c}(\omega)$ and $\hat{q}(\omega)$ will be calculated directly from the terms of the cross-correlogram corresponding to small values of $|\theta|$. Formula (33) is replaced by

$$\hat{c}(\omega) - i\hat{q}(\omega) = \sum_{\theta=-n}^{n} \lambda_\theta C_\theta(x,z) e^{-i\omega\theta} \qquad (79)$$

which for computation can be written in the form

$$\hat{c}(\omega) = \lambda_0 C_0(x,z) + \sum_{\theta=1}^{n} \lambda_\theta [C_\theta(x,z) + C_\theta(z,x)] \cos \omega\theta \qquad (80)$$

$$\hat{q}(\omega) = \sum_{\theta=1}^{n} \lambda_\theta [C_\theta(x,z) - C_\theta(z,x)] \sin \omega\theta. \qquad (81)$$

(The numbers λ_θ characterize the window; they have the property that $\lambda_\theta = \lambda_{-\theta}$.) Thus the transfer function and the coherence function which appear in fig. 13 were calculated from estimates $\hat{c}(\omega)$ and $\hat{q}(\omega)$ obtained with $n = 12$ and with Tukey's window defined by (37).

(iv) Precision of the estimated characteristics

The different empirical characteristics just defined can thus be considered as estimates of theoretical characteristics of a two-dimensional stationary process. From this point of view, the measure of precision of calculated characteristics becomes meaningful. For example, let us consider the two questions which are of prime importance in applied econometrics[†]. What is the precision of the estimate of the transfer function $T(\omega)$? Does the calculated coherence indicate a real association between the series $\{x_t\}$ and $\{z_t\}$ for the frequency ω?

To examine these questions, we shall again consider the equations (68), applying them now not only to the observed series but also to the underlying stochastic process. More precisely, we shall assume that we can define complex random variables[††] E_{k+h} which are neither mutually correlated nor correlated

---

[†] See PARZEN [1967] for a fuller discussion and for the determination of the variances of the cospectra.

[††]The distinction between the E_{k+h} thus defined and those introduced for calculation of the cross-periodogram corresponds exactly to the distinction between errors and residuals in the treatment of the usual linear models.

with the Z_{k+h} and are such that (68) applies in a small frequency band of width $(2m+1)$ about ω_k. The spectral theory of multidimensional stochastic processes offers justification of this model, which is valid to the extent that the transfer function $T(\omega)$ is constant over the band considered, which we assume as a first approximation[†].

According to this theory, the complex variable E_{k+h} can be identified with a random vector with two components, the real part RE_{k+h} and the imaginary part IE_{k+h} of E_{k+h}; the covariance matrix of this vector has the form $\Sigma_k^2 I$, where Σ_k is an appropriate number. The $2m+1$ independent values of the E_{k+h} can then be identified with a vector E of $2(2m+1)$-dimensional Euclidean space, this vector having a spherical concentration ellipsoid. Similarly the values of the X_{k+h} can be identified with a vector X of the same space.

Under the assumption that the theoretical transfer function T_k is zero, the coherence $C^*(\omega_k)$ has the same distribution as the square R^2 of the multiple correlation coefficient calculated after a regression on a sample of $2(2m+1)$ observations which are not mutually correlated. As a first approximation, we can act on the assumption that the process of the $\{x_t\}$ is normal, and use the usual statistical tables. Thus, in the case where $m = 3$, the coherence is comparable to a multiple correlation coefficient calculated from a regression on 2 exogenous variables with 14 observations. The 5% critical value F_0 of the F-distribution with 2 and 12 degrees of freedom is 3.88. Consequently the 5% critical value of $C^*(\omega_k)$ is given by

$$1 - \frac{1}{1 + \dfrac{2}{12} F_0} = 0.39.$$

More generally,

$$\frac{2m C^*(\omega_k)}{1 - C^*(\omega_k)}$$

is distributed as an F-variable with 2 and $4m$ degrees of freedom.

Let us now consider the precision with which the transfer function $T(\omega)$ is estimated.

The complex number T_k can be likened to a vector T whose two components are the real part RT_k and the imaginary part IT_k of T_k. It remains for us to find how to transform the set of the $2m+1$ complex numbers Z_{k+h} in such a way that we revert to a linear model of the classic type. In the right hand side of (68), the first term can be written

$$RT_k \cdot RZ_{k+h} - IT_k \cdot IZ_{k+h} \text{ for the real component of } X_{k+h}$$

and

$$RT_k \cdot IZ_{k+h} + IT_k \cdot RZ_{k+h} \text{ for the imaginary component.}$$

[†] See KOOPMANS [1964].

In the construction of the matrix M_{zz} of ch. 6, the observation relating to the real component of X_{k+h} corresponds to

$$\begin{bmatrix} (RZ_{k+h})^2 & -RZ_{k+h} \cdot IZ_{k+h} \\ -RZ_{k+h} \cdot IZ_{k+h} & (IZ_{k+h})^2 \end{bmatrix}$$

Similarly, the observation relating to the imaginary component of X_{k+h} corresponds to

$$\begin{bmatrix} (IZ_{k+h})^2 & -IZ_{k+h} \cdot RZ_{k+h} \\ -IZ_{k+h} \cdot RZ_{k+h} & (RZ_{k+h})^2 \end{bmatrix}.$$

Thus summation of the matrices corresponding to all the components of X leads to the following identification:

$$M_{zz} = \frac{I}{2(2m+1)} \sum_{h=-m}^{m} Z_{k+h} \bar{Z}_{k+h}, \tag{82}$$

when I denotes the unit matrix of order 2.

Similarly we can make the following identifications of the numbers m_{xx} and $a^{*\prime} M_{zz} a^*$ of chapter 6:

$$m_{xx} = \frac{1}{2(2m+1)} \sum_{h=-m}^{m} X_{k+h} \bar{X}_{k+h}$$

$$a^{*\prime} M_{zz} a^* = \frac{T_k^* \bar{T}_k^*}{2(2m+1)} \sum_{h=-m}^{m} Z_{k+h} \bar{Z}_{k+h}.$$

Taking account of (66), (69) and (71), the estimate

$$\sum_k^{*2} \quad \text{of} \quad \sum_k^2, \quad \text{or} \quad m_{xx} - a^{*\prime} M_{zz} a^* \text{ multiplied by } \frac{2m+1}{2m},$$

can be written

$$\sum_k^{*2} = \frac{1 - C^*(\omega_k)}{4m} \sum_{h=-m}^{m} I_{x, k+h}. \tag{83}$$

The covariance matrix of the real and imaginary parts of T_k^* is then estimated by the product of

$$M_{zz}^{-1} \quad \text{by} \quad \sum_k^{*2}/2(2m+1).$$

The form of M_{zz} shows that these real and imaginary parts are not mutually correlated and that they have the same variance estimated by

$$\frac{1 - C^*(\omega_k)}{4m} \cdot \frac{f_x^*(\omega_k)}{f_z^*(\omega_k)}. \tag{84}$$

To interpret the transfer function, we usually examine its modulus and its argument rather than its real and imaginary parts. So we write it in the form

$$T(\omega) = \sqrt{G(\omega)} \, e^{i\varphi(\omega)} \tag{85}$$

and find an approximate formula for the variances of the estimates $\sqrt{G_k^*}$ and φ_k^* given by $T_k^* = \sqrt{G_k^*} \, e^{i\varphi_k^*}$. Let us assume that the difference between T_k^* and $T(\omega_k)$ is small, so that it can be represented by a differential element dT. Then from (85) we can write for the real and imaginary parts of dT:

$$\begin{cases} d \, RT = \cos\varphi \, d\sqrt{G} - \sqrt{G}\sin\varphi \, d\varphi \\ d \, IT = \sin\varphi \, d\sqrt{G} + \sqrt{G}\cos\varphi \, d\varphi \end{cases}$$

and we obtain by solving these,

$$\begin{cases} d\sqrt{G} = \cos\varphi \, dRT - \sin\varphi \, dIT \\ \sqrt{G}\, d\varphi = \sin\varphi \, dRT + \cos\varphi \, dIT. \end{cases}$$

Since there is zero correlation between dRT and dIT and they have the same variance, the product $\sqrt{G} \, d\sqrt{G} \, d\varphi$ has zero expected value. *The correlation between $\sqrt{G_k^*}$ and φ_k^* is zero as a first approximation.* Moreover the approximate variances of $\sqrt{G_k^*}$ and φ_k^* are obtained from (84):

$$\mathrm{Var}\,\sqrt{G^*}(\omega_k) = \frac{1 - C^*(\omega_k)}{4m} \cdot \frac{f_x^*(\omega_k)}{f_z^*(\omega_k)}$$

$$\tag{86}$$

$$\mathrm{Var}\,\varphi^*(\omega_k) = \frac{\mathrm{Var}\sqrt{G^*}(\omega_k)}{G^*(\omega_k)}.$$

The formulae just established apply to quantities estimated directly from the periodograms. If we start from quantities $\hat{c}(\omega)$ and $\hat{q}(\omega)$ calculated from the correlograms by (80) and (81), the factor $2m$ which occurs in the definition of the distribution of $C^*(\omega)$ and in the denominator in (84) and (86) must be replaced by a factor which depends on the window used for smoothing. In particular, if Tukey's window defined by (37) has been used, we can use the correspondence already chosen in § 7 (iii), namely

$$2m = \frac{4T}{3n} - 1 \tag{87}$$

where n is the number occurring in (37) or (80), which defines the number of terms in the correlograms, or the width of the window.

(v)   Interpretation of the transfer function

The transfer function may itself be considered as the goal of the statistical analysis. However, in most cases we try to interpret it, that is, to give it an analytic expression which allows the dependence of $\{x_t\}$ on $\{z_t\}$ to be described by a simple model. The possibility of doing this is certainly the main advantage of spectral analysis for the econometrician.

In fact, the decomposition illustrated by equation (68) may appear as a suitable method for the descriptive study of the relationship between the series of the z_t and that of the x_t in each frequency band. Examination of the way in which T_k and Σ_k^2 vary from one band to the others may suggest a model with only a small number of parameters, which describes the phenomenon and may possibly allow its analysis by the parametric methods with which the next three chapters are principally concerned.

Thus we shall often be prepared to assume a priori that the dependence of the x_t on the z_t can be expressed by a model of the type[†]:

$$x_t = \sum_{\tau=0}^{\infty} a_\tau z_{t-\tau} + \varepsilon_t, \tag{88}$$

where the a_τ are fixed numerical coefficients and the ε_t constitute a non-observable stationary stochastic process (here again we adopt the case where the means of x_t and z_t are zero). With such a model, which covers widely varying forms of relationship, the components X_k and Z_k satisfy the relation

$$X_k = T(\omega_k)Z_k + E_k, \tag{89}$$

where E_k represents the Fourier component of the ε_t and $T(\omega_k)$ the theoretical transfer function

$$T(\omega) = \sum_{\tau=0}^{\infty} a_\tau e^{i\omega\tau}. \tag{90}$$

[†] The interpretation of transfer functions is simple only if the direction of the causalities can be specified a priori; here $\{z_t\}$ determines $\{x_t\}$ with no 'feed back'. When the phenomenon implies mutual interdependences, as is often the case in econometrics, it becomes essential to specify a relatively precise model.

(Equation (89) is only approximate because of the extreme terms of the series of the z_t.)

Conversely, if we have determined the empirical transfer function $T^*(\omega)$ and the function $\Sigma^*(\omega)$ which describes how the amplitude of the E_k varies from one frequency band to the others, we shall usually be in a position to specify more strictly the sequence of the coefficients a_t and the spectral characteristics of the process of the ε_t.

Consider, for example, the relationship between employment (x_t) and production (z_t) in the French textile industry. Fig. 13 shows in each of its three parts the values relating to $\hat{G}(\omega)$, $\hat{\varphi}(\omega)$ and $\hat{C}(\omega)$ respectively, these values having been obtained from the first thirteen terms of the correlograms by applying the smoothing process defined[†] by (37). On the upper two parts of the figure, two dotted lines are shown at a distance of two standard deviations on each side of $\hat{G}(\omega)$ and $\hat{\varphi}(\omega)$. This was done by applying formulae corresponding to (86) with $2m = 7$, in accordance with what (87) gives in this case. On the figure relating to the coherence, the dotted line represents the value defining the significance level at the 5% level. (We should remember that these standard deviations and significance levels are found by applying approximate formulae.)

We see that the coherence is significant for low frequencies but not generally for those corresponding to a period of a year or less. The modulus $\hat{G}(\omega)$ decreases fairly regularly with ω, while $\hat{\varphi}(\omega)$ tends to be positive, at least for low frequencies.

This suggests a model of the type (88) with

$$a_t = ab^t \tag{91}$$

where a and b are two positive constants. The corresponding function $T(\omega)$ is

$$T(\omega) = a \sum_{\tau=0}^{\infty} b^\tau e^{i\omega\tau} = \frac{a}{1 - b\,e^{i\omega}} \tag{92}$$

and so

$$G(\omega) = \frac{a^2}{1 - 2b\cos\omega + b^2} \qquad \varphi(\omega) = \text{Arc tg}\,\frac{b\sin\omega}{1 - b\cos\omega} \tag{93}$$

which correspond to the functions actually obtained. The broken lines on fig. 13

[†] In order to eliminate the biases in estimation of the spectra and cospectra, the two crude series were first filtered by successive application of the two filters (39) and (42). This operation changes proportionally the values of all the spectra and cospectra relating to the same frequency. So it does not occasion any correction for the estimation of transfer and coherence functions, as we see in (73) and (74). The crude employment series was displaced by one and a half months relative to the crude production series (employment on the first day of the quarter, production during the preceding quarter). This displacement was eliminated in the calculation of $\hat{\varphi}(\omega)$ so that a quantity appears which is convenient for interpretation.

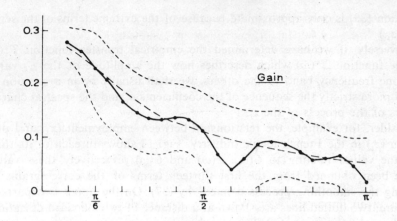

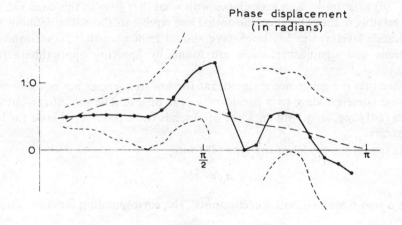

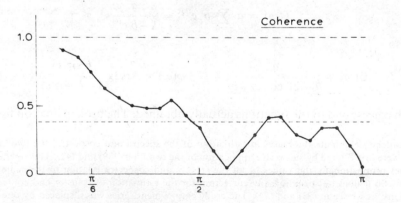

Fig. 13. Spectral relationship between
employment and textile production.

represent the evolutions of $G(\omega)$ and $\varphi(\omega)$ calculated in this way with $a = 0.121$ and $b = 0.7$. A very satisfactory agreement is obtained.

We note also that (83) can be written

$$f_\varepsilon^*(\omega_k) = \left(1 + \frac{1}{2m}\right)[1 - C^*(\omega_k)]f_x^*(\omega_k) \tag{94}$$

since we can consider $\Sigma_k^{*2}/2\pi$ as close to an unbiased estimator of $f_\varepsilon(\omega_k)$, the spectral density of ε_t. (The bias is zero if $f_\varepsilon(\omega)$ is strictly constant in the frequency band relating to ω_k.)

In our particular example, assuming that (88) applies to the deviations of the crude series from their respective trends, we see that the spectral density of ε_t varies in an important way. While the spectral density of employment is 400 times greater for $\pi/8$ than for $\pi/2$, that of the error ε_t is still 100 times greater for $\pi/8$ than for $\pi/2$ (because $1 - C^*(\omega)$ is four times smaller). This strong variation of the spectral density reveals a considerable serial correlation among the errors ε_t relating to successive quarters.

(vi) Multiple spectral regression

When a series $\{x_t\}$ seems a priori to depend on two or more series $\{z_{jt}\}$ ($j = 1$, $2, \ldots, m$), then clearly we should not confine ourselves to investigation of its dependence on each of the series $\{z_{jt}\}$ taken in isolation, but introduce them all simultaneously, as in ordinary multiple regression. This raises no difficulty in theory, but leads to much more complicated formulae.

Consider the case of two series $\{z_{1t}\}$ and $\{z_{2t}\}$. Then for (68), we substitute

$$X_{k+h} = T_{1k}Z_{1,k+h} + T_{2k}Z_{2,k+h} + E_{k+h}. \tag{95}$$

By a process of reasoning identical to that already followed in section (ii), we can establish that the minimum of the sum S_k of the products of $(X_{k+h} - T_{1k}Z_{1,k+h} - T_{2k}Z_{2,k+h})$ and their conjugate values is attained at T_{1k}^* and T_{2k}^* defined by

$$\begin{bmatrix} T_{1k}^* \\ T_{2k}^* \end{bmatrix} = \begin{bmatrix} \sum Z_{1,k+h}\bar{Z}_{1,k+h} & \sum Z_{2,k+h}\bar{Z}_{1,k+h} \\ \sum Z_{1,k+h}\bar{Z}_{2,k+h} & \sum Z_{2,k+h}\bar{Z}_{2,k+h} \end{bmatrix}^{-1} \begin{bmatrix} \sum X_{k+h}\bar{Z}_{1,k+h} \\ \sum X_{k+h}\bar{Z}_{2,k+h} \end{bmatrix} \tag{96}$$

all the sums being taken for h varying from $-m$ to m.

Let us define the complex quantities:

$$4\pi(2m + 1)f_{xj}^*(\omega_k) = \sum_{h=-m}^{m} X_{k+h}\bar{Z}_{j,k+h} \qquad j = 1,2$$

$$4\pi(2m + 1)f_{ij}^*(\omega_k) = \sum_{h=-m}^{m} Z_{i,k+h}\bar{Z}_{j,k+h} \qquad i,j = 1,2$$

We note that $f_{jj}^*(\omega)$ is the spectral density of the series $\{z_{jt}\}$, while $f_{ij}^*(\omega)$ can be written $c_{ij}^*(\omega) - iq_{ij}^*(\omega)$, where the functions $c_{ij}^*(\omega)$ and $q_{ij}^*(\omega)$ denote respectively the cospectrum and the quadrature spectrum of $\{z_{it}\}$ and $\{z_{jt}\}$. Apart from a factor of $[4\pi(2m+1)]^2$ the determinant of the square matrix of (96) is equal to $f_{11}^*(\omega_k)f_{22}^*(\omega_k)[1 - C_{12}^*(\omega)]$ where the function $C_{12}^*(\omega_k)$ denotes the coherence of $\{z_{1t}\}$ and $\{z_{2t}\}$. We can then easily calculate, for example,

$$T_{1k}^* = \frac{[f_{22}^*c_{x1}^* - c_{12}^*c_{x2}^* + q_{12}^*q_{x2}^*] - i[f_{22}^*q_{x1}^* - c_{12}^*q_{x2}^* - q_{12}^*c_{x2}^*]}{f_{11}^*f_{22}^*[1 - C_{12}^*]} \tag{97}$$

in which the arguments ω_k have been omitted for simplicity. The real and imaginary parts of T_{1k}^* appear directly.

In the same way as before, it would be possible to find the precision of the estimates so obtained.

CHAPTER 12

Serial correlation of errors
in regression models

1 Serial correlation of errors

For estimation of the coefficients of a linear model with errors in equations, we introduced in particular the assumption of independence between the errors ε_t and ε_θ relating to two different observations t and θ (assumption 1 of ch. 6). This allowed us to obtain the essential results used in various chapters. We must now investigate the validity of this assumption.

In fact when the model is estimated from time series relating to the variables x_{it} and z_{jt}, it often happens that there is stochastic dependence of greater or lesser extent among the successive errors $\varepsilon_t, \varepsilon_{t+1}, \varepsilon_{t+2}, \ldots$

Nor is this surprising, for the errors express the effect of factors of which no explicit account is taken in the model, either because they cannot be observed independently, or because individually they are of too little importance, or even because the part which they play in the phenomenon under investigation is not known. As for all economic quantities, the evolutions of these factors often show more regularity than a purely random series. If their effect ε_t is positive for the tth observation, then it has a good chance of being positive for the $(t+1)$th observation also.

It may also happen that errors of measurement in the variables introduce an artificial correlation, since they often affect two successive observations in the same way. Similarly, if the true relationship between the endogenous and exogenous variables is not exactly linear, the fitting of a linear relation will reveal additional differences which in most cases will be similar in size for two successive observations, since the exogenous variables generally change slowly.

A significant serial correlation of errors often exists, even when annual data are used. It becomes obviously pervasive when the model is fitted to quarterly or monthly statistical series. Now, improvement in statistical information actually leads to increasing use of data of this kind.

Before taking explicit account of correlation of the successive ε_t, we must point out that too strong a time dependence among the errors often indicates some flaw in the model. Some important factors have probably not been recognized. It is better to investigate them and introduce them explicitly than to keep to an incomplete model which may lead to wrong interpretations.

The theorems of ch. 6 showed that the method of least squares entails no bias in estimation of the parameters, even when the errors are correlated. But in that case the method is no longer most efficient. Also the usual formulae for calculating the standard errors are no longer valid.

In the following sections, we shall examine tests of independence of the errors, asymptotic distributions of the estimates, valid formulae for calculating standard errors in the case of serially correlated errors, efficiency of the method of least squares and finally other estimation methods.

Throughout this chapter we shall deal with linear models which can be written in the form:

$$x_t = a'z_t + \varepsilon_t. \tag{1}$$

We assume therefore that the model contains a single endogenous variable, and that *lagged values $x_{t-\theta}$ of this endogenous variable do not occur in the relation to be estimated.* It is only for simplicity in exposition that we exclude the case of models with several equations. The generalization is fairly direct, as was shown by ZELLNER [1961b] in an article which may be of interest to the reader.

On the other hand, the presence of lagged values of the endogenous variable puts all the results of this chapter back on trial. Until now we have always supposed that the z_{jt} were true exogenous variables, and so have not discussed equations in which lagged values $x_{t-\theta}$ appear. This limitation becomes particularly important here for reasons which will be given in the following chapter and which justify an explicit warning.

We assume here that the errors ε_t constitute an ergodic stationary stochastic process and that their expected value is zero, whatever the values taken by the exogenous variables z_{jt}. Stationarity and ergodicity are involved in the discussion of asymptotic properties; they are not truly restrictive when discussion is limited to small samples.

The existence of serial correlations among the ε_t is not incompatible with the assumptions of ch. 5 in which the theory of linear estimation was given. For the regression model (1) reduces to the general linear model for the vector x with components $x_1, x_2, ..., x_T$, with a non-diagonal matrix Q for the covariances of the vector of the errors $\varepsilon_1, \varepsilon_2, ..., \varepsilon_T$. So the geometric method given in ch. 5 applies to the treatment of correlated errors in small samples, as to that of heteroscedasticity. However, we shall confine ourselves here to an analytic representation, and shall also quote numerous results without proof. WATSON [1956] in particular investigated small sample theory in a paper in which the reader can find various complementary results as well as an account of the geometric nature of certain properties.

In addition, if serial correlation of errors is a problem, this is because it is never known completely. So the general model to be adopted is not the model of ch. 5, but the model of the first part of ch. 8. So we shall return in a particular context to the various questions then raised and give more detailed answers adapted to the present case.

2 Tests of independence of the errors

The first problem consists in the establishment of tests of independence which will allow us to detect serial correlation of errors when it is considerable. In conformity with the usual practice, we shall confine ourselves to the study of the significance levels of tests which on an intuitive basis appear efficient enough to reveal correlation between ε_t and some immediately preceding $\varepsilon_{t-\theta}$. So we need only examine the distribution of these tests for the cases in which the errors are mutually independent.

If the errors affecting an economic model of type (1) could be observed directly, we could apply the tests given at the start of the preceding chapter. But the errors remain unknown. Only the estimation residuals are available. For the method of least squares, these residuals are

$$\varepsilon_t^* = \varepsilon_t + (a - a^*)' z_t, \tag{2}$$

where

$$a^* - a = [M_{zz}]^{-1} m_{z\varepsilon}. \tag{3}$$

However, we know that a^* tends to a when the number T of observations tends to infinity (cf. theorem 3 and proposition 5 of ch. 6). Therefore the residuals ε_t^* tend to the errors ε_t. So the methods of ch. 11 apply for large samples.

In particular, the various non-parametric tests can be applied to the sequence of the residuals, at least if the number of observations is not too small. The significance levels given by the theoretical distributions are certainly not exact since they assume that tests have been established on the sequence of the errors. But the calculations involved can be made quickly and reveal the most obvious cases of serial correlation of errors. Thus a first useful indication is obtained by applying the Swed–Eisenhart test to the residuals given by the graph representing the results of the regression (see for example the lower part of fig. 1, ch. 6). Also R. C. Geary has suggested taking account of the number of changes of sign of the residuals[†].

But of course this method is only approximate for small samples. It is important to determine exact tests applicable to regressions based on short series. As formulae (2) and (3) remind us, the sequence of the residuals depends not only on the sequence of the errors, but also on the sequences of values taken by the exogenous variables z_{jt}. So there are no tests which can be applied rigorously to the residuals independently of the values of the z_{jt}. However, DURBIN and WATSON [1950] established tables giving the lower and upper limits of significance levels for von Neumann's test. These tables are sufficient for practical purposes. An extract from them is given in this chapter. Before showing how to use them, we examine the basic logic of the test.

[†] See HABIBAGATHI and PRATSCHKE [1972] for a comparison of this non-parametric test with the Durbin-Watson test.

The expression

$$d = \frac{\sum\limits_{t=1}^{T-1} (\varepsilon_{t+1}^* - \varepsilon_t^*)^2}{\sum\limits_{t=1}^{T} \varepsilon_t^{*2}} \tag{4}$$

represents the value of 'von Neumann's ratio' applied to the residuals. The efficiency of this test is similar to that of r_1, the first autocorrelation coefficient of the residuals. According to what was said in the previous chapter, we know that this test is especially powerful if the errors constitute a first degree auto-regressive process. So it seems well adapted to economic models. The power of the test is discussed in the Durbin-Watson paper and by TILLMAN [1975]. Its robustness against some forms of non-normality is established by KARIYA [1977].

The value of d in the sample depends both on the sequence of the z_t and the values of the ε_t (for $t = 1, 2, \ldots, T$). However, Durbin and Watson showed that, for given values of the ε_t, d is necessarily contained between two limits d_L and d_U which are independent of the values of the z_t and are functions only of the numbers T and m, so that:

$$d_L \leqq d \leqq d_U.$$

Also the limits d_U and d_L are attained for certain values of the sequence of the z_t. The interval $[d_L, d_U]$ is therefore the smallest that can be defined, if we do not wish to take the exact values of the exogenous variables into consideration.

The limits d_L and d_U are random variables whose distribution can be determined for each pair of numbers (T, m), under precise assumptions about the distribution of the ε_t. Naturally Durbin and Watson adopted assumptions 1 and 3 of ch. 6: normality, homoscedasticity and independence of successive errors. They determined the probability densities of d_L and d_U and tabulated the values d_1 and d_2 giving the confidence levels of d_L and d_U for certain significance levels α (5%, for example).

Figure 1 shows how these levels d_1 and d_2 are determined. The unbroken

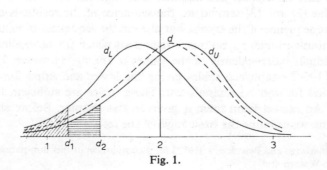

Fig. 1.

TABLE 1

Distribution of the Durbin–Watson test

T	$m' = 1$		$m' = 2$		$m' = 3$		$m' = 4$		$m' = 5$	
	d_1	d_2	d_1	d_2	d_1	d_2	d_1	d_2	d_1	d_2
15	1.08	1.36	0.95	1.54	0.82	1.75	0.69	1.97	0.56	2.21
20	1.20	1.41	1.10	1.54	1.00	1.68	0.90	1.83	0.79	1.99
30	1.35	1.49	1.28	1.57	1.21	1.65	1.14	1.74	1.07	1.83
50	1.50	1.59	1.46	1.63	1.42	1.67	1.38	1.72	1.34	1.77
100	1.65	1.69	1.63	1.72	1.61	1.74	1.59	1.76	1.57	1.78

The above table gives the values of d_1 and d_2 at the 5% significance level (for the test against the single alternative of positive autoregression) as a function of m' (the total number of exogenous variables excluding the constant dummy variable) and of T (the number of observations). It is reproduced by kind permission of the editors of Biometrika.

curves represent the probability densities of d_L and d_U, densities which are mirror images of one another in the vertical line with abscissa 2. The dotted curve represents the density of d for a hypothetical sequence of the z_t.

Suppose now that, as is usual, we wish to test independence of the errors against the hypothesis of positive autocorrelation expressed by a small value of d. We must find out if the value d^* obtained for d is exceptionally small in the case of independence, and therefore determine the confidence level as the value such that the tail of the distribution to its left has probability α. In this way we obtain d_1 and d_2 corresponding to d_L and d_U respectively. Table 1 gives the values of d_1 and d_2 for $\alpha = 5\%$ and for different values of T and of m', the number of true exogenous variables of the regression (therefore excluding the constant)[†]. Durbin and Watson give much more complete tables.

To use the tables in practice we compare the obtained value d^* with d_1 and d_2.

(a) If $d^* < d_1$, the probability of a value as small as d is certainly less than α. The hypothesis of independence is rejected[††].

(b) If $d^* > d_2$, the probability of a value as small as d is certainly greater than α. The hypothesis of independence is not rejected.

(c) If $d_1 \leqq d^* \leqq d_2$, the tables leave us in some doubt. It is possible that the hypothesis of independence should be rejected at the significance level α. But this could only be ascertained by studying the distribution of d with the sequences of values actually taken by the exogenous variables z_{jt}. In practice, we are often content in this case to state that the value of d^* lies in the indeterminate zone of the tables.

---

† If the model contains no constant term, the test must not be calculated on the residuals of the regression without constant term, but on those of an auxiliary regression on the same exogenous variables but with a constant.

†† This assumes that the ε_t are normally distributed. But work carried out on related tests suggests that the confidence levels are not very sensitive to moderate deviations from normality.

It is usual nowadays to show the value d^* beside regressions calculated on time series and to state where this value lies with respect to d_1 and d_2. Thus for the example dealt with in ch. 6, § 5, relation (33) is given in the form:

$$x_t = 0.132z_{1t} + 0.550z_{2t} + 2.10z_{4t} - 5.92, \qquad d^* = 1.20$$
$$(0.006) \quad (0.110) \quad (0.20) \quad (1.27)$$

Here d^* falls in the doubtful zone for 18 observations, 3 exogenous variables and a 5% significance level. So the test is not sufficient for rejection of the hypothesis of independence.

Although the exact value of the significance level of d is not usually computed, we may have some idea of its approximate position in the interval $[d_1, d_2]$. For the proofs given by Durbin and Watson show that d is near d_U if the sequence of the z_{jt} are approximately linear combinations of a constant and of sinusoidal sequences with long periods, more precisely with periods $2T, T, \frac{1}{3}2T, \ldots, 2T/(m-1)$. On the other hand, d is near d_L if the z_{jt} are approximately linear combinations of a constant and of sinusoidal sequences with short periods: periods $2T/(T-1), 2T/(T-2), \ldots, 2T/(T-m+1)$. In most cases, the sequences of exogenous variables have gradual evolutions so that d is near d_U. Thus in econometric studies, a value of d contained in the interval $[d_1, d_2]$ generally indicates significant correlation of errors.

DURBIN and WATSON [1971] returning to various points of their 1950 paper show how a number $a + bd_2$ can be chosen as an approximation to the exact level of d, the values a and b being calculated from the sequences of values of the exogenous variables.

Until now we have supposed that we wish to test independence of the errors, fearing positive correlation. It may also happen that the alternative hypothesis is that of negative correlation. For instance, the method of least squares is sometimes applied not to the sequences x_t and z_t themselves, but to the sequences of the first differences:

$$\Delta x_t = x_t - x_{t-1} \quad \text{and} \quad \Delta z_r.$$

The statistical procedures are then valid to the extent that the model can be written:

$$\Delta x_t = a'\Delta z_t + \eta_t,$$

where the η_t have no time dependence. But a negative correlation exists among the η_t if the ε_t of the formula

$$x_t = a'z_t + \varepsilon_t$$

are mutually independent, or nearly so.

The Durbin–Watson test is easily applied to the hypothesis of independence against the alternative of negative correlation. We must ask if the value of d^* is exceptionally large in the case of independence, that is, if the value of $4-d^*$ is exceptionally small. As is shown by the symmetry of fig. 1, the probability densities of $4-d_U$ and $4-d_L$ are respectively equal to those of d_L and d_U. Consequently the significance level for $4-d^*$ is contained between d_1 and d_2. To test independence therefore we need only look at the position of $4-d^*$ relative to d_1 and d_2.

Similarly, if it is necessary, the Durbin–Watson tables allow two-tailed tests when the alternative hypothesis stipulates positive or negative autocorrelation of errors[†].

The Durbin-Watson test is powerful for serial correlation of the errors which is expressed by a first order autoregressive process for $\{\varepsilon_t\}$. The actual serial correlation may be more complex, particularly when the analysis deals with monthly or quarterly series[††]. So we may wish to use a test with a less restricted category of alternative hypotheses.

In ch. 11, § 5, we discussed tests of independence applied to the periodogram and likely to reveal correlations corresponding to a less simple correlogram than that of a first order autoregressive process. We may think of using the same tests on the estimation residuals.

DURBIN [1969] considers in particular the cumulative periodogram of the residuals:

$$S_k^* = \frac{\sum\limits_{h=1}^{k} I_h^*}{\sum\limits_{h=1}^{T''} I_h^*} \qquad k = 1, 2, \ldots, T'' \tag{5}$$

where $T'' = T/2-1$ if T is even, and $T'' = (T-1)/2$ if T is odd, and I_h^* is the periodogram of the residuals ε_t^* for the frequency $2\pi h/T$ (see formulae (11), (14) and (20) in ch. 11). In the case of direct serial correlation of the errors this periodogram tends to describe a line situated above the diagonal of the square in which it lies, with k/T'' as abscissa and S_k^* as ordinate (cf. fig. 2).

We saw in chapter 11 that, if S_k^* is calculated from the errors ε_t themselves, a test of independence is obtained by comparing C^+, the maximum of the

---

[†] DURBIN [1957] showed how the test given here applies to autocorrelation of errors of an equation belonging to a multiple equation model of the type discussed in part 5 (see in particular chs. 18 and 19). If the model involves m exogenous variables including the constant dummy variable and if the equation in question has been fitted by the Cowles Commission method, Durbin suggests that d^* should be calculated as in formula (4) from the residuals ε_t^* of the equation and that the test should be applied by referring to the tables established for single equation models (where $m'=m-1$).

[††] There are conceivable appropriate tests for other precisely specified alternatives. Thus WALLIS [1972 b] discusses a test similar to d, but in which $\varepsilon_{t+1}^*-\varepsilon_t^*$ is replaced by $\varepsilon_{t+4}^*-\varepsilon_t^*$ in the numerator of (4): this test applies in the treatment of quarterly series when seasonal effects, evolutionary or otherwise, are suspected to disturb the estimated relation.

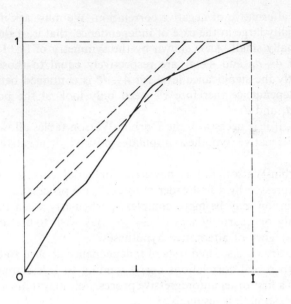

Fig. 2.

vertical distance from the diagonal to the line, with a critical number C_0 whose value was given for the 5% significance level and certain values of T''.

Although the distribution of S_k^* depends on the values of the z_{jt}, the same reasoning as was applied for the Durbin-Watson test shows that this distribution can be bounded by two others which do not depend on them. More precisely, Durbin establishes the following results:

(a) If, for at least one value of k, we observe

$$S_k^* > C_0 + \frac{2k}{T-m},$$

the probability of this situation is certainly less than 5% in the case of independence. So the hypothesis is rejected in favour of the hypothesis of direct serial correlation.

(b) If

$$S_k^* \leq C_0 + \frac{2k-m+1}{T-m}$$

for all k, the probability of this situation is certainly at least 5% in the case of independence. The hypothesis is accepted (at least provisionally).

On a graph similar to fig. 2, the right hand sides of the above inequalities can be represented by two parallel straight lines which have a slightly higher slope than the diagonal of the square. The test is inconclusive when the line traced out by S_k^* cuts the lower of these two lines but remains below the upper line.

So, like the Durbin-Watson test, this test leaves some doubt in a certain number of cases. Since in most cases, the regressions are carried out on variables with gradual evolutions, we may suspect that the doubtful cases correspond to those real situations in which independence should be rejected (it should be rejected, in fact, if the exogenous variables are linear combinations of a constant and of sinusoidal sequences with periods T, $T/2$, $T/3$, ..., $T/(m-1)$).

It is obviously troublesome that procedures in common use do not lead to a conclusion in a certain number of practical cases, cases in which we should in theory determine the exact distribution, which is very difficult to obtain even using approximations (see HENSHAW [1966] for these approximations). So a search has been made for alternative methods without this drawback. The attempt has been made to define quantities which correctly reveal serial correlation of the errors, but whose distributions are independent of the values of the exogenous variables. Two similar approaches have been suggested, both involving fairly heavy computation.

Following a suggestion made by H. Theil and developed by J. Koerts and A. P. J. Abrahamse, we should find, using a linear transformation of the observations, a vector with $T-m$ components $\hat{\varepsilon}_t$ which are not mutually correlated and have the same variance if the unobservable errors ε_t are homoscedastic and mutually independent. (The $\hat{\varepsilon}_t$, obtained by a linear transformation, will be normally distributed if the ε_t are). We can then apply to the $\hat{\varepsilon}_t$ the tests of independence given in sections 3 to 5 of ch. 11 (see, for example, THEIL [1965] and ABRAHAMSE and KOERTS [1968] for the formulae defining from M_{zz} the linear transformation from the x_t to the $\hat{\varepsilon}_t$).

DURBIN [1970 b] suggests finding a vector $\tilde{\varepsilon}$ with T components $\tilde{\varepsilon}_t$ and with the same distribution as the vector of the residuals of a regression of the ε_t on dummy exogenous variables which are convenient for the application of tests (for example, exogenous variables to which there applies one or other of the limits of the doubtful zone).

Suppose then that the z_{jt} have gradual evolutions and that z_{mt} is a constant. We propose to apply the upper bound d_2 of the Durbin-Watson test to the ε_t. We define the dummy variables w_{jt} by

$$w_{jt} = \cos \frac{(2t-1)j\pi}{2T} \qquad j = 1, 2, \ldots, m-1. \tag{6}$$

Durbin proves that we can test independence by the following process, which has exact validity if the ε_t are normally distributed.

(i) Calculate a multiple regression of x_t on the z_{jt} and the w_{jt} (if there is strict multicollinearity we reduce the number of dummy exogenous variables). Let $\hat{a}_j$ and $\hat{b}_j$ be the regression coefficients obtained for the z_{jt} and the w_{jt} respectively; let G_1 be the matrix of the covariances estimated for the first $m-1$ coefficients $\hat{a}_j$, and G_2 the covariance matrix of the $\hat{b}_j$; let $\hat{\varepsilon}_t$ be the residuals.

(ii) Find the triangular matrices P_1 and P_2 such that $P_1 P_1' = G_1$ and

$P_2 P_2' = G_2$; find $P_2^{-1} = Q_2$. We can apply the following formulae, for example, for triangulation:

$$p_{11} = \sqrt{g_{11}} \qquad\qquad p_{j1} = g_{j1}/p_{11} \qquad j = 1, 2, \ldots, m-1$$
$$p_{22} = \sqrt{g_{22} - p_{21}^2} \qquad p_{j2} = (p_{j2} - p_{21}p_{j1})/p_{22}$$
$$p_{33} = \sqrt{g_{33} - p_{31}^2 - p_{32}^2} \qquad p_{j2} = (g_{j3} - p_{31}p_{j1} - p_{32}p_{j2})/p_{33}$$

etc.

and, for the inverse of a triangular matrix,

$$q_{11} = 1/p_{11}$$
$$q_{21} = -p_{21}q_{11}/p_{22} \qquad\qquad q_{22} = 1/p_{22}$$
$$q_{31} = -(p_{31}q_{11} + p_{32}q_{21})/p_{33} \qquad q_{32} = -p_{32}q_{22}/p_{33}$$

etc.

(iii) Find N^*, the matrix of the residuals of the first $m-1$ variables z_{jt} in the regressions on the w_{jt} and on $z_{mt} = 1$.

(iv) Find

$$\tilde{\varepsilon}_t = \hat{\varepsilon}_t + N^* P_1 Q_2 \hat{b}$$

where $\hat{b}$ is the vector of the $\hat{b}_j$.

(v) Find $\tilde{d}$ by applying (4) to the $\tilde{\varepsilon}_t$ and reject the hypothesis of independence if $\tilde{d}$ is less than d_2 with $m' = m-1$.

This process was carried out, for example, on the regression relating to French imports in the period 1949–66. The value 1.71 was found for $\tilde{d}$. This is almost equal to the critical value $d_2 = 1.70$ which applies when $T = 18$, $m' = 3$, and the 5% significance level is adopted.

3   Asymptotic properties of the regressions

In most cases, models of the type

$$x_t = a'z_t + \varepsilon_t$$

are fitted by the method of least squares, even when the errors constitute a stochastic process showing some serial correlation. We must therefore investigate the properties of the current estimates and tests in cases where the assumption of independence of the errors is not satisfied. We shall always assume here that $E(\varepsilon_t) = 0$ whatever the values of the exogenous variables z_{jt} and that the process of the errors is stationary, which in particular implies homoscedasticity.

Lemma 1 of ch. 5 applies to the case where the errors are serially correlated.

It establishes that the estimate a^*, obtained by least squares estimation, has expected value a and that it is normally distributed when ε_t is. Moreover, one can generalize the results of the asymptotic study of ch. 6 § 8, dealing with the convergence of a^* to the true value a, and with the asymptotic normality of:

$$\sqrt{T}(a^* - a).$$

This generalization is certainly not straightforward. Convergence and asymptotic normality assume certain conditions on the process $\{\varepsilon_t\}$ and the sequence of the z_t to be satisfied. We shall confine ourselves to a simple case in order to reveal the nature of the properties and to show the type of conditions which they require[†].

We therefore consider the model:

$$x_t = a'z_t + \varepsilon_t \tag{1}$$

and suppose that the ε_t constitute an autoregressive process:

$$\varepsilon_t = \gamma\varepsilon_{t-1} + \eta_t, \tag{7}$$

γ being a constant less than 1 in absolute value and $\{\eta_t\}$ a purely random process with finite variance σ_η^2. Relation (7) can also be written:

$$\varepsilon_t = \sum_{\tau=0}^{\infty} \gamma^\tau \eta_{t-\tau}.$$

The jth component of the least square estimate a^* of a can be written:

$$a_j^* = a_j + \frac{1}{T} \sum_{t=1}^{T} \lambda_t^T \varepsilon_t,$$

where λ_t^T is the jth component of the vector $z_t' M_{zz}^{-1}$. We set:

$$d = \sqrt{T}(a_j^* - a_j),$$

which can also be written:

$$d = d_1 + d_2,$$

where d_1 and d_2 are independent terms given by

$$d_1 = \frac{1}{\sqrt{T}} \sum_{\tau=-\infty}^{0} \sum_{t=1}^{T} \lambda_t^T \gamma^{t-\tau} \eta_\tau, \tag{8}$$

$$d_2 = \frac{1}{\sqrt{T}} \sum_{\tau=1}^{T} \sum_{t=\tau}^{T} \lambda_t^T \gamma^{t-\tau} \eta_\tau. \tag{9}$$

First of all we consider the term d_1. Its variance can be written:

$$\mathrm{var}(d_1) = \frac{\sigma_\eta^2}{T(1-\gamma^2)} \left[\sum_{t=1}^{T} \lambda_t^T \gamma^t \right]^2. \tag{10}$$

It tends to zero as T tends to infinity, when the sum in square brackets remains bounded in absolute value. This condition is satisfied under fairly unrestrictive assumptions about the sequence of the z_t. For example, it is sufficient to assume, as we did in ch. 6, that the matrix M_{zz} tends to a limit. The term d_1 then tends in probability to zero, and the asymptotic distribution of d is identical to that of d_2, if it exists.

The term d_2 can be written:

$$d_2 = \sum_{\tau=1}^{T} a_{\tau T} \eta_\tau, \tag{11}$$

where

$$a_{\tau T} = \frac{1}{\sqrt{T}} \sum_{t=\tau}^{T} \lambda_t^T \gamma^{t-\tau}. \tag{12}$$

We can calculate directly

$$\mathrm{var}(d_2) = \sigma_\eta^2 \alpha_T^2, \tag{14}$$

where α_T^2 is defined by

$$\alpha_T^2 = \sum_{\tau=1}^{T} a_{\tau T}^2. \tag{15}$$

The limiting behavior of d_2 depends on the distribution of η_t and the properties of the sequence of the $a_{\tau T}$. To establish that $d_2/\sqrt{T}$ tends in probability to zero, and a_j^* to a_j, it would be sufficient to show that α_T^2 is bounded. In particular, *if the z_t are bounded and if M_{zz} tends to a limit* which is non-singular then $|\lambda_t^T|$ is bounded by a number $\hat{\lambda}$ which is independent of t and T. It follows that

$$\alpha_T^2 \leqq \frac{\hat{\lambda}^2}{(1-|\gamma|)^2}$$

which is easily verified. *The estimate a* therefore tends in probability to the true value a.*

Asymptotic normality requires slightly stricter conditions. To establish it, one must call on general results of central limit theorems. If $|\lambda_\tau^T|$ is bounded, so also is $\sqrt{T}|a_{\tau T}|$. One then needs only find if α_T^2 tends to a finite non-zero limit α_∞^2. For this to be true, the evolution of the sequence of the z_t must show a certain regularity. This may seem a natural condition for a theoretical study which aims at distinguishing the properties valid for samples containing a finite, though large, number of observations.

4 The process of the errors and characteristics of the residuals

The process of the errors cannot be observed directly. On the other hand, the least-square residuals are known. So it is important to understand what information is given by the characteristics of the residuals about the properties of the process of the errors. We have already said something about this with reference to tests of independence. We must now discuss it more systematically.

The residuals are connected to the errors by the equations:

$$\varepsilon_t^* = \varepsilon_t + (a - a^*)'z_t \tag{2}$$

and

$$a^* - a = [M_{zz}]^{-1}m_{z\varepsilon}. \tag{3}$$

In the conditions laid down above, the estimate a^* tends in probability to the true value; consequently the residual ε_t^* tends to the error ε_t. Therefore the estimation procedures proposed in ch. 11 apply to large samples. Unfortunately, in most cases the econometrician has only small samples at his disposal. Hence the necessity to investigate characteristics calculated from the ε_t^*.

Let the autocovariance coefficients be:

$$\gamma_\tau = E(\varepsilon_t \varepsilon_{t+\tau}) \tag{16}$$

and their empirical equivalents calculated from the residuals:

$$C_\tau = \frac{1}{T} \sum_{t=1}^{T-\tau} \varepsilon_t^* \varepsilon_{t+\tau}^*, \qquad \tau = 0, 1, 2, \ldots \tag{17}$$

We also define

$$M_{zz}^\tau = \frac{1}{T} \sum_{t=1}^{T-\tau} z_t z_{t+\tau}', \qquad \tau = 0, 1, 2, \ldots \tag{18}$$

and

$$R_\tau = [M_{zz}]^{-1} M_{zz}^\tau. \tag{19}$$

We make the convention:

$$M_{zz}^{-\tau} = M_{zz}^{\tau}, \qquad R_{-\tau} = R_{\tau}.$$

The R_{τ} appear so to speak as autocorrelation matrices relating to the T vectors of the exogenous variables z_t,[†].

Taking account of relations (2) and (3) in definition (17), we obtain directly

$$C_{\tau} = \frac{1}{T} \sum_{t=1}^{T-\tau} \varepsilon_t \varepsilon_{t+\tau} - m_{\varepsilon z}[M_{zz}]^{-1} m_{z\varepsilon}^{\tau} - m_{\varepsilon z}[M_{zz}]^{-1} m_{z\varepsilon}^{-\tau}$$
$$+ m_{\varepsilon z}[M_{zz}]^{-1} M_{zz}^{\tau}[M_{zz}]^{-1} m_{z\varepsilon}, \qquad (20)$$

with the vectors

$$m_{z\varepsilon}^{\tau} = \frac{1}{T} \sum_{t=1}^{T-\tau} z_t \varepsilon_{t+\tau} \qquad \text{and} \qquad m_{z\varepsilon}^{-\tau} = \frac{1}{T} \sum_{t=1}^{T-\tau} z_{t+\tau} \varepsilon_t.$$

In the right hand side of (20), the expected value of the first term is γ_{τ}. The expected value of the next three terms represents the bias in the estimation of γ_{τ} by C_{τ}.

The three terms can be studied in the same way. Let us consider only the first. We can write:

$$E\{m_{\varepsilon z}[M_{zz}]^{-1} m_{z\varepsilon}^{\tau}\} = E\,\mathrm{tr}\,\{[M_{zz}]^{-1}[m_{z\varepsilon}^{\tau} m_{\varepsilon z}]\} = \mathrm{tr}\,\{[M_{zz}]^{-1} E[m_{z\varepsilon}^{\tau} m_{\varepsilon z}]\} \qquad (21)$$

Now,

$$m_{z\varepsilon}^{\tau} m_{\varepsilon z} = \frac{1}{T^2} \sum_{t=1}^{T-\tau} \sum_{t'=1}^{T} z_t \varepsilon_{t+\tau} \varepsilon_{t'} z_{t'}'$$
$$= \frac{1}{T^2} \sum_{\theta=1+\tau-T}^{T-1} \sum_{t} z_t \varepsilon_{t+\tau} \varepsilon_{t+\tau+\theta} z_{t+\tau-\theta}'.$$

In the last sum, t varies:

from 1   to $T+\theta-\tau$ if $1+\tau-T \leqq \theta \leqq 0$,
from 1   to $T-\tau$ if $0 \leqq \theta \leqq \tau$,
from $1+\theta-\tau$ to $T-\tau$ if $\tau \leqq \theta \leqq T-1$,

as can be seen in fig. 3.

[†] It may be useful to give the following numerical results obtained by AMES and REITER [1961]. These two authors considered 100 annual statistical series of 25 observations referring to the period 1929–1953, and taken at random from the annual abstract of statistics of the United States. On average, the first five autocorrelation coefficients came out at 0.84, 0.71, 0.60, 0.53 and 0.45 for the crude series; and at 0.68, 0.38, 0.15, −0.03 and −0.01 for the series after elimination of the trend. Such results agree with what we saw in chap. 11, § 7, concerning the 'typical spectrum' of economic time series.

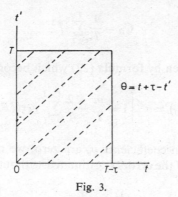

Fig. 3.

In each case, $E(\varepsilon_{t+\tau}\varepsilon_{t+\tau-\theta})$ is equal to γ_θ. The sum:

$$\sum z_t z_{t+\tau-\theta}$$

is near $T M_{zz}^{\tau-\theta}$. We can now write

$$E[m_{z\varepsilon}^\tau m_{\varepsilon z}] \approx \frac{1}{T} \sum_{\theta=1+\tau-T}^{T-1} \gamma_\theta M_{zz}^{\tau-\theta},$$

the approximation being good only if the $M_{zz}^{\tau-\theta}$ and similar matrices obtained from a smaller number of vectors z_t tend fairly rapidly to zero as $|\tau-\theta|$ increases, or if the $|\gamma_\theta|$ decrease rapidly to zero as θ increases.

Taking account of (21) and (19), we find:

$$E\{m_{\varepsilon z}[M_{zz}]^{-1}m_{z\varepsilon}^\tau\} \approx \frac{1}{T} \sum_{\theta=1+\tau-T}^{T-1} \gamma_\theta \operatorname{tr}(R_{\tau-\theta}).$$

Similar expressions can be obtained for the expected values of the last two terms of (20). Finally the expected value of C_τ obeys the relation:

$$E(C_\tau) \approx \gamma_\tau + \frac{1}{T} \sum_{\theta=1+\tau-T}^{T-1} \gamma_\theta[\operatorname{tr}(R_\tau R_\theta) - 2\operatorname{tr}(R_{\tau-\theta})]. \tag{22}$$

This formula allows us to form some idea of the bias contained in C_τ for small samples. If the R_τ have been calculated, we can correct the C_τ by subtracting from each the value that takes the second term of the right hand side of (22) after substitution of C_θ for γ_θ. We must note in any case that the bias depends both on the correlogram of the ε_t and on the type of evolution of the sequence of the vectors z_t relating to the exogenous variables (on the matrices R_τ).

Consider in particular the mean square residual

$$C_0 = \frac{1}{T} \sum_{t=1}^{T} \varepsilon_t^{*2}.$$

Its expected value is given by formula (22) which becomes

$$E(C_0) \approx \sigma^2 \left[1 - \frac{m}{T} - \frac{2}{T} \sum_{\theta=1}^{T-1} \varrho_\theta \operatorname{tr}(R_\theta) \right]. \tag{23}$$

If all the autocorrelation coefficients ϱ_θ are zero, we revert to the formula of ch. 6. The variance σ^2 *of* the errors is estimated without bias by

$$\sigma^{*2} = \frac{T}{T-m} C_0.$$

On the other hand, *when the errors are subject to some time dependence, the estimate σ^{*2} of σ^2 generally contains a bias* equal to:

$$-\frac{2\sigma^2}{T-m} \sum_{\theta=1}^{T-1} \varrho_\theta \operatorname{tr}(R_\theta).$$

The variance σ^2 is underestimated if positive terms predominate in the sequences $\{\varrho_\theta\}$ and $\{\operatorname{tr}(R_\theta)\}$, as must often happen.

For example, suppose that $\varrho_\theta = (0.8)^\theta$ (the case of a first order autoregressive process: $\varepsilon_t = 0.8\,\varepsilon_{t-1} + \eta_t$), that there are two exogenous variables, one of which is constant (the case of simple regression) and that

$$R_\theta = \begin{bmatrix} (0.8)^\theta & 0 \\ 0 & 1 \end{bmatrix} \qquad \theta \geq 0. \tag{24}$$

The bias can be calculated directly, and is near

$$-11.5 \frac{\sigma^2}{T-2}.$$

Certainly the approximation is valid only when the number of observations is about thirty. However, this example reveals a very considerable bias.

Formula (22) also gives the biases involved in estimation of the correlogram of the errors on the basis of the correlogram of the residuals. This formula only gives a good approximation for values of τ which are small relative to T. But, in any practical case, we limit attention to the first terms of the correlogram. The examination of some simple cases reveals some interesting features.

(a) If the process of the errors is purely random, all the γ_τ are zero except $\gamma_0 = \sigma^2$. In these conditions, the expected value of C_0 is $\sigma^2(1-(m/T))$, that of C_τ (for $\tau \neq 0$):

$$-\frac{\sigma^2}{T}\operatorname{tr}(R_\tau).$$

The general term of the correlogram of the residuals is $r_\tau = C_\tau/C_0$, whose expected value is therefore near

$$\frac{-1}{T-m}\operatorname{tr}(R_\tau).$$

The autocorrelation coefficients of the ε_t^* express the autocorrelation of the exogenous variables, after a considerable reduction in size and a change of sign.

(b) If the sequence of the z_t is random in appearance, in the sense that the R_τ are near the zero matrix (except obviously $R_0 = I$), formula (22) reduces to

$$E(C_0) \approx \sigma^2(1 - (m/T)), \qquad E(C_\tau) \approx \sigma^2 \varrho_\tau (1 - (2m/T)) \qquad \text{for} \qquad \tau > 0.$$

The autocorrelation coefficients r_τ still contain a bias:

$$E(r_\tau) \approx \varrho_\tau \left(1 - \frac{m}{T-m}\right). \tag{25}$$

The empirical correlogram tends to underestimate the autocorrelation of the errors.

(c) If there is a single constant exogenous variable, that is, if the model specifies that the x_t constitute a stationary process whose mean is not known, then all the R_τ are scalars and equal to 1. Formula (22) reduces to

$$E(C_\tau) \approx \gamma_\tau - \frac{1}{T}\gamma_0 - \frac{2}{T}\sum_{\theta=1}^{T-1}\gamma_\theta.$$

The same systematic error affects all the C_τ, including the empirical variance C_0; let this error be $-\sigma^2 B/T$, where

$$B = 1 + 2\sum_{\theta=1}^{T-1}\varrho_\theta.$$

As a first approximation, the expected value of the empirical correlogram is given by

$$E(r_\tau) \approx \varrho_\tau - \frac{B}{T}(1 - \varrho_\tau). \tag{26}$$

This correlogram tends to underestimate a positive correlation of the errors and to overestimate a negative correlation. For example, if $\varrho_\theta = (0.8)^\theta$, the coefficient B is near 9, the bias on ϱ_1 near $-1.8/T$, the bias on ϱ_2 near $-3.2/T$, etc.

These few cases are enough to show that the deviations between the true correlogram $\{\varrho_\theta\}$ and the correlogram calculated from the residuals $\{r_\theta\}$ may be substantial in samples of the size of those used in econometrics.

Of course we can try to correct the correlogram of the residuals in such a way that the bias is eliminated. Thus we often assume that the errors constitute a first order autoregression process:

$$\varepsilon_t = \varrho\varepsilon_{t-1} + \eta_t$$

where the η_t form a purely random process. The coefficient ϱ is then often estimated by the first coefficient r_1 of the empirical correlogram (or by the equivalent quantity $1 - \frac{1}{2}d^*$, where d^* is the value found for the Durbin–Watson test). An estimate containing no sizable bias is given by

$$\left(1 + \frac{m}{T - m}\right)r_1,$$

if the exogenous variables have very irregular evolutions ($R_\tau \approx 0$ for $\tau > 0$) and by

$$r_1 + \frac{m}{T}(1 + r_1)$$

if these variables have smooth evolutions ($R_\tau \approx I$ at least for small values of τ). It seems that, in practice, an estimate such as $r_1 + (m/T)$ must be more suitable than r_1 in most cases.

To the systematic deviations between the autocovariances of the residuals and those of the errors, there obviously correspond systematic deviations between the spectrum estimated from the residuals and the spectrum of the errors. These deviations can be determined by using the formula that defines the spectral density (see also HANNAN [1960] pp. 133–8).

5   Variances of the estimates and tests of hypotheses

When the errors do not constitute a purely random process, the usual formulae given in ch. 6 are no longer valid for calculating the covariance matrix of a^*. For:

$$a^* - a = [M_{zz}]^{-1}m_{z\varepsilon},$$

and it follows that

$$E[(a^* - a)(a^* - a)'] = [M_{zz}]^{-1} \cdot E[m_{z\varepsilon}m_{\varepsilon z}] \cdot [M_{zz}]^{-1},$$

which corresponds to formula (11) in ch. 8. Now, as we saw above,

$$E[m_{z\varepsilon}m_{\varepsilon z}] \approx \frac{1}{T}\sum_{\theta = 1 - T}^{T-1}\gamma_\theta M_{zz}^\theta,$$

which leads immediately to the formula

$$E[(a^* - a)(a^* - a)'] \approx \left[\sum_{\theta=1-T}^{T-1} \varrho_\theta R_\theta \right] \cdot \left[\frac{\sigma^2}{T}(M_{zz})^{-1} \right], \tag{27}$$

a formula first[†] given by WOLD [1952].

The second factor in this expression does not depend on the autocorrelation of the errors. Only the first is new. It is exactly equal to I in two cases: if all the ϱ_θ are zero (except $\varrho_0 = 1$), this being a case which we already know; if all the R_θ are zero (except $R_0 = I$). So the usual formulae apply if the exogenous variables show no autocorrelation, irrespective of any autocorrelation of the errors. But this case is rare in practice.

To obtain a more exact idea of the importance of the first factor in formula (27), we suppose that the correlogram of the errors satisfies

$$\varrho_\theta = \varrho^\theta, \qquad \text{where} \qquad |\varrho| < 1. \tag{28}$$

We suppose also that there are two exogenous variables, the second being the auxiliary variable which always equals 1 (the case of simple regression). Finally we assume that the matrix R_θ can be written:

$$R_\theta = \begin{bmatrix} \lambda^\theta & 0 \\ 0 & 1 \end{bmatrix}, \qquad \text{where} \qquad |\lambda| < 1. \tag{29}$$

The first factor of (27) will then be near

$$\begin{bmatrix} k_1 & 0 \\ 0 & k_2 \end{bmatrix}, \qquad \text{where} \qquad k_1 = \frac{1 + \varrho\lambda}{1 - \varrho\lambda}, \qquad k_2 = \frac{1 + \varrho}{1 - \varrho}.$$

The numbers k_1 and k_2 represent the factors by which we should multiply the formulae which, in ch. 3, gave the variances of the estimates of the slope and the intercept of the regression line. We note that, when λ varies from -1 to 1, the domain of k_1 indeed corresponds to the interval (22) of ch. 8, which applies for large T.

But for estimating variances and covariances, we must also have an estimate of σ^2. The use of σ^{*2} generally introduces a new source of errors, which may be important for small T. The bias defined by formula (23) is added to the bias which we have just investigated.

In the particular example under consideration, the usual expressions for estimating the variances of the slope and the intercept must be multiplied by

---

[†] LYTTKENS [1964] established a more general formula for models in which the exogenous variables are random and possibly correlated with the errors affecting other observations. (So this author assumes that $E(\varepsilon_t z_t) = 0$, but not necessarily $E(\varepsilon_{t-\tau} z_t) = 0$ when $\tau \neq 0$.)

the following factors if we wish to obtain unbiased estimates:

$$k_1' = \frac{\sigma^2}{E(\sigma^{*2})} k_1, \qquad k_2' = \frac{\sigma^2}{E(\sigma^{*2})} k_2.$$

The following table gives the values of k_1' and k_2' for some values of ϱ and λ and for a sample of $T = 22$ observations[†].

In short, the standard errors estimated by the usual formulae are fairly near the true standard errors if there is low autocorrelation of the errors or of the exogenous variable. On the other hand, if the errors and the exogenous variable simultaneously show high autocorrelation, the true standard errors may be twice or four times greater than their estimates based on the usual formulae.

Now most of the quantities introduced as exogenous variables have fairly smooth evolutions. They are generally highly autocorrelated. We must therefore bear in mind that *the usual formulae seriously overestimate the precision of the estimates whenever there is considerable serial correlation of the errors.*

These considerations also allow an exact assessment of the gain in precision

TABLE 2

Autocorrelation of the errors (ϱ)	Autocorrelation of the exogenous variable (λ)				
	−0.4	0	0.4	0.6	0.8
	Coefficient k_1' relating to the slope				
−0.4	1.4	1	0.7	0.6	0.5
0	1	1	1	1	1
0.4	0.8	1.1	1.5	1.8	2.1
0.6	0.8	1.2	1.9	2.6	3.6
0.8	1.2	1.7	3.4	6	11
	Coefficient k_2' relating to the intercept				
−0.4	0.4	0.4	0.4	0.4	0.5
0	1	1	1	1	1
0.4	2.5	2.5	2.5	2.5	2.6
0.6	4.6	4.7	4.8	4.9	5.0
0.8	14	15	16	18	22

[†] A general discussion and results for other cases may be found in NICHOLLS and PAGAN [1977].

to be obtained from breaking down the periods of observation, and thus multiplying the number of data available for the purpose of estimation. Until recently, hardly any but annual data were used in econometric models. But the growth of quarterly national accounts and the improvement in statistical series make it possible to use quarterly data.

For a period of fixed duration, the number of observations is thus multiplied by four. However, the standard errors of the estimates are not halved, for at least two reasons[†]: in the first place, we must generally estimate certain new parameters characterizing the seasonal fluctuations of the phenomenon; in the second place, serial correlation of the errors increases when we go from an annual to a shorter period.

To illustrate this last point, we suppose that the errors actually constitute an autoregressive process with the autocorrelation coefficients (28) and that this holds for half-yearly data. We can easily calculate the autocorrelation coefficients of the corresponding annual errors, namely

$$\hat{\varrho}_\theta = \tfrac{1}{2}\varrho^{\theta-1}(1+\varrho), \qquad \text{where} \qquad \theta = 2, 4, 6, \ldots .$$

The variance of the estimate of the constant term involves the factor

$$k_2 = \frac{1+\varrho}{1-\varrho},$$

for half-yearly data, and the factor

$$\hat{k}_2 = \frac{1}{1-\varrho}.$$

for annual data. So the effect of substituting a half-yearly series for an annual series is to multiply the variance of the constant term by $\tfrac{1}{2}(1+\varrho)$ (and not by $\tfrac{1}{2}$). If for example $\varrho=0.40$, the first autocorrelation coefficient of the series of the annual errors is $\hat{\varrho}_2=0.28$, and the variance of the constant term is multiplied by 0.7. If $\varrho=0.80$ and $\hat{\varrho}_2=0.72$, this variance is multiplied by 0.9.

There is a less marked difference between the terms k_1 and $\hat{k}_1$ relating to the coefficient of an ordinary exogenous variable; the adoption of a half-yearly or quarterly series allows us to take better advantage of the irregularities in the evolution of this variable. Such irregularities are often minor relative to the gradual trend of the phenomenon. But it may also happen that they play a large part in some of the laws studied. Thus the econometric analysis of general fluctuations in activity has made a perceptible gain in precision since quarterly data began to be used in models. In the post-war period, cyclical movements of various characteristic quantities largely disappear in annual data, but on the contrary are evident in quarterly data.

[†] In practice, we must also take account of the fact that the statistical standard of quarterly series is often still very inferior to that of the corresponding annual series.

The usual tests on the coefficients a_j of the model are clearly sensitive to auto-correlation of the errors in the same way as the formulae relating to the variances of the estimates.

Thus, in a simple regression, the usual test on the slope assumes that the quantity

$$\frac{a^* - a}{\sigma_a^*}$$

is distributed as Student's t with $T-2$ degrees of freedom, σ_a^* then being defined by

$$\sigma_a^{*2} = \frac{\sigma_\varepsilon^{*2}}{\sum (z_t - \bar{z})^2}, \quad \text{where} \quad \sigma_\varepsilon^{*2} = \frac{1}{T-2} \sum_{t=1}^{T} \varepsilon_t^{*2}.$$

If the errors are normal, homoscedastic and not autocorrelated, this property follows from the fact that $a^* - a$ has a centred normal distribution with variance:

$$\sigma_a^2 = \frac{\sigma^2}{\sum (\hat{z}_t - \bar{z})^2}$$

and that $(T-2)\sigma_\varepsilon^{*2}/\sigma^2$ has a χ^2 distribution independent of that of $a^* - a$. If the errors are autocorrelated, then $a^* - a$ is normally distributed but with a different variance from that given above. Moreover, $(T-2)\sigma_\varepsilon^{*2}/\sigma^2$ is no longer distributed as χ^2 and is no longer independent of $a^* - a$.

The level of significance and the actual power of the usual tests have been little investigated for cases in which the errors are serially correlated. COURREGE and PRIOURET [1971] have given a method for finding bounds on the level of significance. VINOD [1976] gives tables that apply to such bounds in some cases and do not depend on the values of the exogenous variables. The bias in estimation of the variance of the coefficients a_j^* seems to be the greatest source of error. We may hope that correction of this bias will make the tests approximately exact again. Thus, for a simple regression, the distribution of

$$(a^* - a)/\sqrt{k_1'}\sigma_a^*$$

is probably near the Student distribution with $T-2$ degrees of freedom.

6   Efficiency of the method of least squares

When the successive errors are not independent, the method of least squares no longer enjoys the optimal properties discussed in ch. 6. What is its efficiency in this case? This question has been studied particularly by GRENANDER [1954] and ROSENBLATT [1956].

Let us assume that the errors constitute a purely indeterministic stationary stochastic process having an autoregressive representation. We can define a sequence of numbers $\{b_\tau\}$ and a stationary process of uncorrelated variables $\{\eta_t\}$ in such a way that:

$$\varepsilon_t - b_1 \varepsilon_{t-1} - \cdots - b_\tau \varepsilon_{t-\tau} - \cdots - = \eta_t. \tag{31}$$

Then let u_t and w_t be a variable and a vector obtained from the x_t and z_t as follows:

$$\begin{aligned} x_t - b_1 x_{t-1} - \cdots - b_\tau x_{t-\tau} - \cdots - &= u_t, \\ z_t - b_1 z_{t-1} - \cdots - b_\tau z_{t-\tau} - \cdots - &= w_t. \end{aligned} \tag{32}$$

These definitions allow us to rewrite the model in the form:

$$u_t = a' w_t + \eta_t. \tag{33}$$

Since the η_t are not autocorrelated, the least squares regression of u_t on w_t provides a linear estimate of a, this estimate being unbiased and having minimal dispersion. (Actually a complete definition requires that a rule is given for defining the u_t and w_t from only the observed values of x_t and z_t, i.e. from those corresponding to $t \geq 1$. We shall see below how this is done in a particular case.)

This method can rarely be used in practice since the process of the errors is not generally known, nor are the b_τ occurring in the autoregressive representation. Even if the process is known, the method can be applied only approximately unless all the b_τ beyond a certain point are zero. For the definitions involve an unlimited number of $x_{t-\tau}$ and $z_{t-\tau}$, while the observed sample gives only a finite number of values.

Be that as it may, the linear method with minimal dispersion constitutes a basis of reference for assessment of the efficiency of estimates obtained by the usual methods. A general study of this question leads to the following conclusions:

(a) If the sequence of the errors $\{\varepsilon_t\}$ shows only low autocorrelation, the efficiency of the method of least squares differs from 1 by only infinitesimals of second order (with respect to the autocorrelation coefficients). This result is a direct application of proposition 2 of ch. 8.

(b) The efficiency of the method of least squares (applied to x_t and z_t) depends both on the autocorrelation characteristics of the ε_t and on the nature of the sequence $\{z_t\}$. For some sequences of exogenous variables (constants, sinusoidal functions or time polynomials,...), this efficiency tends to that of the optimal linear method when the number T of observations tends to infinity.

The general study of these two points would be fairly complex[†], and we shall

---

[†] For a more thorough analysis, other examples and a lower bound of the efficiency of the usual estimator see Hannan [1960], p. 108–117.

discuss only the case [†] of a first order autoregressive process, which was already considered in ch. 5, section 6 and in ch. 8, second example:

$$\varepsilon_t = \varrho\varepsilon_{t-1} + \eta_t.$$

The linear method with minimal dispersion is equivalent to the least squares regression of

$$u_1 = \sqrt{(1 - \varrho^2)}x_1 \quad \text{and} \quad u_t = x_t - \varrho x_{t-1} \quad \text{for } t > 1$$

on

$$w_1 = \sqrt{(1 - \varrho^2)}z_1 \quad \text{and} \quad w_t = z_t - \varrho z_{t-1} \quad \text{for } t > 1.$$

The covariance matrix of the estimate is then

$$\frac{\sigma_\eta^2}{T} M_{ww}^{-1}.$$

Now, for large T:

$$\sigma_\eta^2 = (1 - \varrho^2)\sigma^2 \quad \text{and} \quad M_{ww} \approx (1 + \varrho^2)M_{zz} - 2\varrho M_{zz}R_1.$$

The covariance matrix can also be written:

$$[(1 - \varrho^2)\{(1 + \varrho^2)I - 2\varrho R_1\}^{-1}] \cdot \left[\frac{\sigma^2}{T} M_{zz}^{-1}\right]. \tag{34}$$

To assess the efficiency of the method of least squares applied directly to x_t and z_t, we must compare the first terms in square brackets in expressions (27) and (34). For example, if there is a single exogenous variable with $R_\theta = \lambda^\theta$, the efficiency in question is given by:

$$\frac{1 - \varrho^2}{[(1 + \varrho^2) - 2\varrho\lambda]} \cdot \frac{1 - \varrho\lambda}{1 + \varrho\lambda}$$

whose expansion, as far as terms of second degree in ϱ, is

$$1 - 2\varrho^2(1 - \lambda^2).$$

In accordance with the general results given above, we can observe that this expression is of second degree in ϱ and takes the value 1 for $\lambda = \pm 1$ (fig. 4 shows how this efficiency varies as a function of ϱ for four values of λ). The efficiency of the ordinary least squares regression is still fairly high for values of ϱ up to 0.5. Its minimum, obtained when λ is near 0.27, is about 0.72.

[†] If the observations are annual a first order autoregressive process is probably sufficient as ugh representation of correlation errors. But on the other hand it is liable to be rather unsatisfactory for monthly or quarterly data.

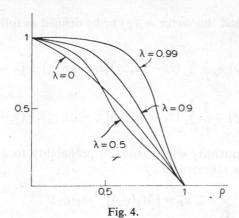

Fig. 4.

However it must be remembered that smaller values of the efficiency can be obtained using other sequences of exogenous variables. As we saw from formula (17) in ch. 8, the absolute minimum is about 0.36 when $\varrho = 0.5$.

7   Estimation in models with correlated errors

If the coefficients b_τ of the autoregressive representation of the process $\{\varepsilon_t\}$ are known, it is possible to apply the linear method with minimal dispersion to estimate a. As we saw in the preceding section, we need only calculate a least squares regression on the transformed variables u_t and w_t, or at least on approximate values of these variables obtained by limiting the expansion (32) to a few terms.

But in practice the stochastic process of the errors is not known. So here we find a particular case of the general model of ch. 8, § 1. Several of the various estimation methods which we shall discuss are based on the approach in ch. 8.

The estimates defined in (a), (b) and (c) below assume that the autoregressive representation is known except for the values of a few coefficients b_τ. They are generally asymptotically equivalent to the linear estimate with minimal dispersion. For they are determined by means of the same formulae as this estimate, the unknown coefficients b_τ being replaced by computed coefficients b_τ^*. *It is then sufficient for asymptotic equivalence of the estimates that the b_τ^* tend to the b_τ.*

We shall show this for the case where the errors constitute a first order autoregressive process:

$$\varepsilon_t = \varrho \varepsilon_{t-1} + \eta_t, \qquad \text{where} \qquad |\varrho| < 1.$$

The minimal dispersion estimate $\hat{a}$ was considered at the end of the last section. It may be written:

$$\hat{a} = [M_T(\varrho)]^{-1} m_T(\varrho),$$

the matrix $M_T(\varrho)$ and the vector $m_T(\varrho)$ being defined as follows:

$$M_T(\varrho) = \frac{1}{T} \sum_{t=2}^{T} (z_t - \varrho z_{t-1})(z_t - \varrho z_{t-1})' + (1 - \varrho^2) z_1 z_1'$$

$$m_T(\varrho) = \frac{1}{T} \sum_{t=2}^{T} (x_t - \varrho x_{t-1})(z_t - \varrho z_{t-1}) + (1 - \varrho^2) x_1 z_1$$

Then let ϱ_T be a quantity which tends in probability to ϱ when T tends to infinity, and let the estimate be

$$a_T = [M_T(\varrho_T)]^{-1} m_T(\varrho_T).$$

We must show that $\sqrt{T}(a_T - \hat{a})$ tends in probability to zero; for then $\sqrt{T}(a_T - a)$ does in fact have the same limiting distribution as $\sqrt{T}(\hat{a} - a)$.

Now, neglecting the particularities coming from the first terms, which play no role asymptotically, we can easily calculate

$$\sqrt{T}(a_T - \hat{a}) = \{ [M_T(\varrho_T)]^{-1} - [M_T(\varrho)]^{-1} \} \frac{1}{\sqrt{T}} \sum_t \eta_t z_t$$

$$- \{ \varrho_T [M_T(\varrho_T)]^{-1} - \varrho [M_T(\varrho)]^{-1} \} \frac{1}{\sqrt{T}} \sum_t \eta_t z_{t-1}$$

$$+ (\varrho - \varrho_T) [M_T(\varrho_T)]^{-1} \cdot \frac{1}{\sqrt{T}} \sum_t \varepsilon_{t-1}(z_t - \varrho z_{t-1})$$

$$+ (\varrho - \varrho_T)^2 [M_T(\varrho_T)]^{-1} \cdot \frac{1}{\sqrt{T}} \sum_t \varepsilon_{t-1} z_{t-1}.$$

Each of the four terms of this sum is the product of a matrix and a vector. To establish that $\sqrt{T}(a_T - \hat{a})$ tends to zero, we need only show that the matrices tend to the zero matrix and that the vectors have limiting distributions. Now the matrices tend to zero whenever the z_t are bounded, M_{zz} tends to a non-singular matrix and R_1 to a limit; for then $M_T(\varrho_T)$ and $M_T(\varrho)$ tend simultaneously to the same non-singular limit. (If this limit is singular, then there exists a vector u such that

$$\frac{1}{T} \sum [u'(z_t - \varrho z_{t-1})]^2$$

tends to zero. But then, in view of the Schwarz inequality, $(1/T) \sum +u'z_t)^2$ also tends to zero, and the limit of M_{zz} is singular.) Similarly the vectors have limiting normal distributions whenever the z_t are bounded and the η_t form a purely random stationary process with zero mean.

This result shows in particular that the asymptotic covariance matrix of a_T is the same as that of $\hat{a}$. A consistent estimate of this matrix is given by

$$\sigma_T^2 [M_T(\varrho_T)]^{-1},$$

where σ_T^2 denotes the mean of the squares:

$$(\varepsilon_t^T - \varrho_T \varepsilon_{t-1}^T)^2$$

constructed from the residuals ε_t^T. This formula for the asymptotic covariance matrix applies therefore to the estimates defined in (a), (b) and (c) below.

(a) A first method consists of the following operations: direct least squares fitting of the variable x_t with respect to the variables z_{jt}; estimation of the unknown coefficients b_τ of the autoregressive representation from the residuals ε_t^*; approximate calculation of the variables u_t and w_{jt}; final fitting by least squares regression of the variable u_t^* with respect to the variables w_{jt}^* so calculated.

This method is asymptotically equivalent to linear minimum variance estimation, at least if a convergent procedure is applied for calculating the b_τ. In the next chapter we shall show that the coefficients b_τ of a random process can generally be calculated by means of the autocorrelation coefficients ϱ_θ. Here the ϱ_θ are replaced in the formulae by the coefficients r_θ computed on the residuals. Convergence of the r_θ to the ϱ_θ implies that of the estimated coefficients b_τ^* to the corresponding true values.

However, the asymptotic justification of the method does not give a strong guarantee for small samples. On the one hand, the number of terms in the autoregressive expansion must be chosen a priori; in most cases we must be satisfied with the first two, that is, we must proceed as if the true representation were autoregressive of first order. On the other hand, estimation of the b_τ will involve significant bias, like that of the ϱ_θ by the r_θ (cf. section 4 above).

(b) The same principle can be applied more systematically (see in particular KLEIN [1953], pp. 85–89, for the definition of this method, and SARGAN [1964] for various interesting complements).

We can *estimate a and the coefficients b_τ simultaneously* by fixing a priori the number of terms in the linear expansion of the ε_t. Suppose for example that we keep to a first order autoregressive process. The relation (33) can then be written:

$$x_t = \varrho x_{t-1} + a'z_t - \varrho a'z_{t-1} + \eta_t, \tag{35}$$

if the relation applying to x_1 is neglected[†].

A direct estimate of this relation provides both the value of ϱ and that of a. The model (35) has two particular features. In the first place, there is an a

---

[†] Actually BEACH and MACKINNON [1978] have shown that the loss of efficiency resulting from the neglect of the relation on x_1 may be significant. But they also showed that the following method for the simultaneous estimation of a and ϱ can be adapted so as to take this relation into account.

priori restriction on its coefficients, since the coefficient of $z_{j,t-1}$ must be equal to minus the product of the coefficients of z_{jt} and x_{t-1}. We have already found how to deal with this type of difficulty. In addition, the model establishes an autoregressive relationship between x_t and x_{t-1}. In the next chapter we shall see that this does not lead to any modification of the regression methods, although it considerably affects the properties of the estimates[†].

So in practice, ϱ and a are determined in such as way as to minimize the sum S of squares of the differences between x_t and

$$\varrho x_{t-1} + a'z_t - \varrho a'z_{t-1}.$$

Differentiating S with respect to ϱ and to a, we obtain non-linear equations which are rather difficult to solve. So the following iterative method is preferable:

(i) on the basis of a value $\varrho^{(0)}$ of ϱ chosen a priori (for example $\varrho^{(0)}=0$), determine the vector $a^{(1)}$ which minimizes S for $\varrho=\varrho^{(0)}$, that is, calculate the regression of $x_t-\varrho^{(0)}x_{t-1}$ on $z_t-\varrho^{(0)}z_{t-1}$;

(ii) determine the number $\varrho^{(2)}$ which minimizes S for $a=a^{(1)}$, that is, calculate the first order autocorrelation coefficient for the residuals

$$\varepsilon_t^{(1)} = x_t - a^{(1)\prime}z_t;$$

(iii) determine the vector $a^{(3)}$ which minimizes S for $\varrho=\varrho^{(2)}$, that is, calculate the regression of $x_t-\varrho^{(2)}x_{t-1}$ on $z_t-\varrho^{(2)}z_{t-1}$; and so on[††].

Each stage implies only the solution of a system of linear equations. A few iterations ordinarily establish convergence to the required estimates of a and ϱ, so that the computation remains fairly light[†††].

[†] Model (35) can also be approached by bayesian procedures, if one prefers.   See ZELLNER and TIAO [1964].

[††] We see that the method proposed in (a) amounts to starting from $\varrho^{(0)} = 0$ and stopping at the estimate $a^{(3)}$.

[†††] SARGAN [1961] showed under which conditions the same principle can be applied for the calculation of asymptotically efficient estimates in models containing several equations $x_t = Az_t$ and affected by errors constituting a multivariate autoregressive process of the type:

$$\varepsilon_t = R\varepsilon_{t-1} + \eta_t,$$

R being a square matrix of order n which is not completely specified a priori.

Under certain conditions, this principle applies even when the matrix A is subject to certain restrictions of the type to be discussed in part 5.

In particular, we note the case of an equation in an overidentified model (equation h, for example). Let us assume that the error ε_{ht} follows an autoregressive process

$$\varepsilon_{ht} = \varrho_h\varepsilon_{h,t-1} + \eta_{ht}$$

which does not involve the errors of the other equations. Of course, ε_{ht} may be correlated with the other components of ε_t through the intermediary η_{ht}. The coefficients of equation h and the parameter ϱ_h can then be estimated by the iterative procedure described above, applying at the stage $(2p+1)$ the Cowles Commission method to the variables

$$x_t - \varrho_h^{(2p)}x_{t-1} \quad \text{and} \quad z_t - \varrho_h^{(2p)}z_{t-1},$$

and determining $\varrho^{(2p+2)}$ as the autocorrelation coefficient of the residuals with respect to the fitted equation at the stage $(2p+1)$.

The same approach is generalized by PIERCE [1971] to the case where the process of the errors is an autoregressive moving average process. The author characterizes completely the asymptotic distribution of the estimators of the different parameters.

(c) The method just proposed is still fairly laborious, and there will often be some hesitation about its use in practice. DURBIN [1960a, b] suggested a quicker procedure with the same asymptotic efficiency. The computation is just about as lengthy as for the first method described above and it seems that the efficiency for small samples must be better. Here we need only give the method for errors constituting a first order autoregressive process.

The difficulty in fitting relation (35) rests in the a priori restriction connecting the coefficients of z_{t-1} with those of x_{t-1} and z_t. But a consistent estimate of ϱ is still obtained if this a priori restriction is ignored, that is, if a linear regression is carried out on:

$$x_t = \varrho x_{t-1} + a' z_t + b' z_{t-1} + \eta_t.$$

Let $\hat{\varrho}$ be the estimate thus obtained.

Durbin proposes estimating ϱ by $\hat{\varrho}$ and determining the vector $\hat{a}$ of the estimated coefficients by a second linear regression between:

$$x_t - \hat{\varrho} x_{t-1} \quad \text{and} \quad z_t - \hat{\varrho} z_{t-1}.$$

(d) A less precise procedure, which is often as satisfactory in practice, consists of calculating *two least squares regressions, that of x_t on z_t and that of $x_t - x_{t-1}$ on $z_t - z_{t-1}$*. STONE[1954a] in particular made systematic use of this method. Let us examine its logic.

For economic data, the serial correlation of errors can often be represented satisfactorily be a first order autoregressive process, with an autocorrelation coefficient ϱ lying between 0 and 1. Markov dependence is sufficient for annual series and for certain quarterly series; the coefficient ϱ is hardly ever negative since the same factors act on two successive errors; the process being stationary, this coefficient is less than 1.

The linear method with minimal dispersion is roughly equivalent to a least squares regression of $x_t - \varrho x_{t-1}$ on $z_t - \varrho z_{t-1}$. In accordance with the theory of linear estimation, it corresponds in T-dimensional space to a projection of the vector x (representing the values of the endogenous variable) on the m-dimensional subspace L (representing the vectors y such that $y_t = a' z_t$ for an appropriate vector a). The direction in which this projection is made depends on ϱ. As ϱ varies from 0 to 1, the projection $y(\varrho)$ moves along an arc contained in L. This arc is not linear. However, we can show that in a certain sense $y(\varrho)$ is intermediary between $y(0)$ and $y(1)$.

For we can set:

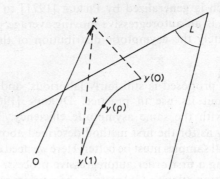

Fig. 5.

$$m_{zx}(\varrho) = \frac{1}{T-1}\sum_{t=2}^{T}(z_t - \varrho z_{t-1})(x_t - \varrho x_{t-1})$$

and

$$M_{zz}(\varrho) = \frac{1}{T-1}\sum_{t=2}^{T}(z_t - \varrho z_{t-1})(z_t - \varrho z_{t-1})'.$$

The projection $y(\varrho)$ corresponds to the vector $a^*(\varrho)$ for the estimated coefficients, where

$$M_{zz}(\varrho) \cdot a^*(\varrho) = m_{zx}(\varrho).$$

Now, we can easily establish

$$m_{zx}(\varrho) \approx (1 - \varrho)^2 m_{zx}(0) + \varrho m_{zx}(1),$$
$$M_{zz}(\varrho) \approx (1 - \varrho)^2 M_{zz}(0) + \varrho M_{zz}(1).$$

Hence we can deduce the relation:

$$(1 - \varrho)^2 M_{zz}(0)[a^*(\varrho) - a^*(0)] + \varrho M_{zz}(1)[a^*(\varrho) - a^*(1)] = 0,$$

which allows us to calculate $a^*(\varrho)$ from $a^*(0)$, $a^*(1)$ and the corresponding matrices M_{zz}.

Since the matrices M_{zz} are positive definite, this relation also shows that for every value of ϱ lying between 0 and 1:

$$[a^*(\varrho) - a^*(0)]'M_{zz}(1)[a^*(\varrho) - a^*(1)] \leqq 0,$$

$$[a^*(\varrho) - a^*(1)]'M_{zz}(0)[a^*(\varrho) - a^*(0)] \leqq 0.$$

(36)

If there is a single exogenous variable ($m=1$), one or other of these relations shows that $a^*(\varrho)-a^*(0)$ and $a^*(\varrho)-a^*(1)$ are of opposite sign, and that consequently $a^*(\varrho)$ necessarily lies between $a^*(0)$ and $a^*(1)$. In the general case, the relations (36) define the sense in which $a^*(0)$ and $a^*(1)$ encompass $a^*(\varrho)$.

In short the values $a^*(0)$ and $a^*(1)$ obtained in the two proposed regressions contain between them the value $a^*(\varrho)$ which would be found if the linear method with minimal dispersion could be applied. If $a^*(0)$ and $a^*(1)$ are near each other, they define the estimate of a with sufficient precision. If they are considerably different, then the correlation of the errors must be examined more closely, and for example one or other of the methods given above must be applied. In practice it often happens that $a^*(0)$ and $a^*(1)$ are near each other.

(e) The above methods start from simplifying assumptions as to the form of the random process of the errors. In their practical applications they do not generally go beyond the case of a first order autoregressive process. Such a specification may be fairly mediocre. Also it appears that, in those cases where the analyzed series are relatively long, more precise results would be obtained by using methods of greater generality.

In fact there is a very natural procedure applying to the spectral representations of the series in the frequency space (HANNAN [1963b] suggests this procedure; DUNCAN and JONES [1966] give a method for carrying it out).

Returning to the notation of ch. 11, § 12, we represent the series $\{x_t\}$ by the T'' complex components:

$$X_k = \sqrt{\frac{2}{T}} \sum_{t=1}^{T} x_t\, e^{i\omega_k t} \qquad k = 1, 2, \ldots, T'' \tag{37}$$

where

$$\omega_k = \frac{2\pi k}{T}$$

and T'' is $(T-1)/2$ or $T/2-1$ according as T is odd or even. Similarly let Z_{jk} and E_k be the spectral components of the series $\{z_{jt}\}$ and $\{\varepsilon_t\}$. Clearly the regression model (1) implies

$$X_k = \sum_{j=1}^{m} a_j Z_{jk} + E_k \qquad k = 1, 2, \ldots, T''. \tag{38}$$

The stationarity of the process $\{\varepsilon_t\}$ implies that there is zero correlation between E_k and E_h for $h \neq k$, and also between the real and imaginary parts of E_k. On the other hand, the variances of these real and imaginary parts generally change with k (the serial correlation of the errors affecting the model conceived in the time space becomes heteroscedasticity for the model as conceived in the frequency space).

We usually assume that the spectral density of $\{\varepsilon_t\}$ varies regularity with ω; the common variance of the two parts of E_k is then estimated on a frequency band ω_{k+h} on either side of ω_k with h varying from $-m'$ to m'. Let $\Sigma_k^{*2} = = 4\pi f_\varepsilon^*(\omega_k)$ be the chosen estimate. In most cases Σ_k^* results from the spectral analysis of the series (see, for example, formula (83) in ch. 11 applying to the case of a single exogenous variable).

For estimation of the a_j, model (38) suggests a regression of the X_k/Σ_k^* on the Z_{jk}/Σ_k^*. If the Σ_k^{*2} are precisely equal to 4π times the values of the spectral density of $\{\varepsilon_t\}$ for the different frequencies ω_k, then the linear estimator thus obtained coincides with the efficient Gauss-Markov estimator. Now, the procedure adopted for estimating the spectral density can usually be justified by the property that it tends to the true density as the number of observations tends to infinity. (Detailed discussion of this point would distract us too far from our main topic so we shall not attempt it here.). So the estimators $\hat{a}_j$ defined in this way are asymptotically efficient.

The proposed regression must consist of minimizing

$$\sum_{k=1}^{T''} \frac{1}{\Sigma_k^{*2}} \left[X_k - \sum_{j=1}^m a_j Z_{jk} \right] \left[\overline{X}_k - \sum_{j=1}^m a_j \overline{Z}_{jk} \right], \tag{39}$$

where $\overline{X}_k$ denotes the complex conjugate of X_k. It leads to normal equations which we can write in matrix form:

$$m_{XZ} - M_{ZZ}\hat{a} = 0 \tag{40}$$

where

$$[m_{XZ}]_j = \frac{1}{2T''} \sum_{k=1}^{T''} (X_k \overline{Z}_{jk} + \overline{X}_k Z_{jk})/\Sigma_k^{*2} \tag{41}$$

$$[m_{ZZ}]_{ij} = \frac{1}{2T''} \sum_{k=1}^{T''} (Z_{ik} \overline{Z}_{jk} + \overline{Z}_{ik} Z_{jk})/\Sigma_k^{*2}. \tag{42}$$

So these matrices involve the cross-periodograms of $\{x_t\}$ with the $\{z_{jt}\}$ and those of the $\{z_{jt}\}$ among themselves.

If the spectral analysis of the series has been carried out, then usually the smoothed estimate of the power cospectrum, denoted here by $c_{xj}^*(\omega_k) - i q_{xj}^*(\omega_k)$, is substituted for $X_k \overline{Z}_{jk}/4\pi$.

Finally, if we carry out the same operation for the other cross-periodograms, (41) and (42) are replaced by

$$[m_{XZ}]_j = \frac{1}{T''} \sum_{k=1}^{T''} c_{xj}^*(\omega_k)/f_\varepsilon^*(\omega_k) \tag{43}$$

$$[M_{ZZ}]_{ij} = \frac{1}{T''} \sum_{k=1}^{T''} c_{ij}^*(\omega_k)/f_\varepsilon^*(\omega_k). \tag{44}$$

Formulae (40), (43) and (44) show that $\hat{a}$ is determined from estimates of the real cospectra of the different variables.

It is simple to find the precision of the estimated vector $\hat{a}$. We can either apply the usual multiple regression formulae with (43), (44) and

$$m_{XX} = \frac{1}{T''} \sum_{k=1}^{T''} f_x^*(\omega_k)/f_\varepsilon^*(\omega_k), \tag{45}$$

or we can take the unit matrix of order 2 as the covariance matrix of the real and imaginary parts of E_k/Σ_k^* and take $M_{ZZ}^{-1}(2T'' - m)$ as estimate of the covariance matrix of the vector $\hat{a}$.

Here is an illustrative example. Suppose we wish to analyze the effect of fluctuations in textile production on hours of work in the textile industry. We have 80 de-seasonalized quarterly observations for the period 1948–67 (production is given as an index with base 100 in 1959, hours of work are given weekly). We first carry out a regression of hours of work on production and on a long trend which we take as a polynomial of degree 3 in t. The coefficient relating to production is 0.119, with a standard error of 0.014 according to the usual formulae. But the Durbin-Watson d^* is only 0.74, which indicates strong correlation of the errors and deprives the estimated standard error of any significance.

We now consider the observations as transformed by application of the filter defined by (39) in ch. 11 (with $\theta = 4$). As we have already seen, the effect of this filter is first to eliminate the trend, and also to make a very considerable reduction in the serial correlation of the errors. Spectral analysis of the transformed series relating to hours of work and to production gives a conclusion favourable to the assumption of a transfer function $T(\omega)$ which is a real constant, that is, to the assumption of the simple regression model (see ch. 11, § 12).

A simple regression on the transformed series gives a coefficient of 0.102 for production, with a standard error of 0.018 according to the usual formula. But the test S_k^* using the cumulative periodogram of the residuals all but rejects the hypothesis of independence of the errors at the 5% significance level. In fact a smoothing operation based on a moving band of 7 successive frequencies gives a spectral density for the residuals which has a maximum of 0.67 for the frequency $2\pi/9$ and is between 0.20 and 0.25 for almost all frequencies greater than $7\pi/18$.

We then apply (40), (43) and (44) on the one hand with this estimate of the spectral density of the errors, and on the other hand with the estimate given by investigation of the transfer function (formula (83) in ch. 11). In both cases we use spectra and cospectra arising from a smoothing operation based on 7 terms of the periodograms. The results are very close, giving a coefficient of 0.091 in the first case and 0.086 in the second. The standard error attributed to this coefficient is then 0.018.

(f) Each of the above methods except that in (d) is asymptotically efficient when the error process is the type of process for which the method is conceived: first order autoregressive process for the methods as discussed in (a), (b) and (c), continuous spectral density process for method (e). However two general questions arise. What is the efficiency of each method for a different error process? What is its efficiency in the treatment of finite samples such as are available to the econometrician?

With regard to the first question, ENGLE [1974a] gives a theoretical discussion which we have already touched on in general terms at the beginning of ch. 8. First, he shows how to find the asymptotic efficiency of any method based on incorrect specification of the error process. Then he considers the particular case where the process is assumed to be first order autoregressive when in fact it is second order autoregressive. In particular, he demonstrates that, under certain extreme conditions, ordinary least squares is then preferable to methods (a), (b) and (c) (if the spectrum of the exogenous variables is large at the lowest frequencies while, for these frequencies, the gradient of the spectrum of the errors is inverse to its average gradient over the set of frequencies).

In COOLEY and PRESCOTT [1973] and in PESARAN [1973] we also find conclusions based on empirical investigations. They consider the case where the error process is of the moving average type. They are interested particularly in assessing the methods when a first order autoregressive process is assumed.

With regard to the second question, GRILICHES and RAO [1969] consider the case where there is a single exogenous variable with a first order autoregressive process while the error process is also of this type. Using a large number of simulated samples each of 20 observations, they compare methods (a), (b), (c) and also ordinary least squares against each other. No method proves consistently superior. If the absolute value of the first autocorrelation coefficient of the residuals of the simple regression is less than 0.3 it appears preferable to keep to this regression (for the samples in question where $T = 20$). Otherwise Durbin's method (c) appears to give the best results; the efficiency of the most elaborate method (b) appears less than that of (a) or (c).

Using much larger artificial samples ($T = 50$, 100 or 200), ENGLE and GARDNER [1976] compare some variants of method (e) and also ordinary regression and method (b) applied on the assumption that the error process is a first order autoregressive process. The efficiency of these methods is similar so long as there is not too much variation in the spectrum of the errors. When the spectrum decreases continuously from high values for low frequencies, method (b) is clearly preferable. When it has a large maximum for an intermediate frequency, method (e) is best.

All in all there is a high degree of consistency among these various results.

8   Prediction in models with serially correlated errors

When dealing with prediction of the endogenous variables in models with independent errors, we proposed and examined the formula $x_\theta^P = a^{*\prime} z_\theta$, according to which the model is applied as if it contained no errors, and as if the vector of the true coefficients coincided with the least squares estimate a^*. When there is serial correlation among the errors, this formula can no longer be justified by the reasoning of ch. 6. For the sample gives information, although imperfectly, about the values of the errors during the period of observation. Because of the serial correlation, it also provides some indication on subsequent values of the errors. So we can do better than assume them to be zero, at least if the prediction relates to a time which is not too far ahead of the period of observation.

To investigate this idea, we shall suppose first that the vector of the coefficients and the distribution of the errors are completely known a priori; then that the vector a is estimated by means of a sample, but that the distribution of the errors is still known a priori. Only afterwards shall we say something about the only case which interests us in practice, that in which a and the characteristics of the ε_t must be estimated simultaneously by means of a sample.

(1) If the vector a of the coefficients and the process of the errors ε_t are known, the prediction of $x_{T+\theta}$ reduces to that of

$$\varepsilon_{T+\theta} = x_{T+\theta} - a'z_{T+\theta}.$$

If $\varepsilon_{T+\theta}^P$ is the prediction of $\varepsilon_{T+\theta}$, we take as the prediction of $x_{T+\theta}$:

$$x_{T+\theta}^P = a'z_{T+\theta} + \varepsilon_{T+\theta}^P. \tag{46}$$

So we need only apply the principles of prediction in random processes and determine $\varepsilon_{T+\theta}^P$ on the basis of the known values $\varepsilon_1, \varepsilon_2, \ldots, \varepsilon_T$.

More precisely, if the loss is measured by the expected value of the square of the prediction error, we must choose

$$x_{T+\theta}^P = E(x_{T+\theta}/x_T, \ldots, x_1; z_{T+\theta}; z_T, \ldots, z_1),$$

that is:

$$\varepsilon_{T+\theta}^P = E(\varepsilon_{T+\theta}/\varepsilon_T, \varepsilon_{T-1}, \ldots, \varepsilon_1).$$

Since the sequence of the errors is generally comparable to the realization of an indeterministic stationary process, $\varepsilon_{T+\theta}^P$ is calculated from the linear representation of the process, namely:

$$\varepsilon_t = b_1\varepsilon_{t-1} + b_2\varepsilon_{t-2} + \cdots + \eta_t, \tag{47}$$

where the η_t constitute a stationary process without autocorrelation.

The introduction in formula (46) defining $x_{T+\theta}^P$ of a non-zero predicted error $\varepsilon_{T+\theta}^P$ clearly arises from the fact that knowledge of the errors up till time T allows better prediction of the error of time $T+\theta$ than if the ε_t were mutually independent. However, as θ increases, $\varepsilon^P_{T+\theta}$ tends to zero. The advantage resulting from serial correlation of the errors quickly becomes negligible.

The same prediction formula can be obtained by slightly different reasoning. For consider the transformation (32) on the endogenous and exogenous variables, and the model expressed in the form (33), namely:

$$u_t = a'w_t + \eta_t.$$

A prediction of $u_{T+\theta}$ is:

$$u^P_{T+\theta} \doteq a'w_{T+\theta},$$

from which we can deduce by recurrence a prediction of $x_{T+\theta}$:

$$x^P_{T+\theta} - b_1 x^P_{T+\theta-1} - \cdots - b_{\theta-1} x^P_{T+1} - b_\theta x_T - b_{\theta+1} x_{T-1} - \cdots$$
$$= a'[z_{T+\theta} - b_1 z_{T+\theta-1} - \cdots - b_\theta z_T - \cdots].$$

Taking account of the definition of the model, we see that this equality can also be written:

$$\varepsilon^P_{T+\theta} = b_1 \varepsilon^P_{T+\theta-1} + \cdots + b_{\theta-1} \varepsilon^P_{T+\theta} + b_\theta \varepsilon_T + b_{\theta+1} \varepsilon_{T-1} + \cdots \qquad (48)$$

It coincides with the recurrence formula proposed for the prediction of $\varepsilon_{T+\theta}$.

(2) If a is estimated from a sample, and if the characteristics of the process $\{\varepsilon_t\}$ are known a priori (except perhaps its variance σ^2), we can still use the autoregressive representation of this process and come back to the model $u_t = a'w_t + \eta_t$ in which the errors are not autocorrelated.

In order to minimize the mean square error of the prediction, we choose

$$u^P_{T+\theta} = \hat{a}'w_{T+\theta},$$

where $\hat{a}$ denotes the vector of a least squares regression of u_t on w_t.

The same transformations as above allow us to show that the prediction is equivalent to that defined by

$$x^P_{T+\theta} = \hat{a}'z_{T+\theta} + \hat{\varepsilon}^P_{T+\theta}, \qquad (49)$$

in which $\hat{\varepsilon}^P_{T+\theta}$ is the 'prediction' calculated on the sequence of the estimation residuals $\hat{\varepsilon}_t$.

The variance of the errors of the prediction (49) are easily calculated. Since there is no correlation between $\hat{a}$ and the $\hat{\varepsilon}_t$, this variance is the sum of that of $\hat{a}'z_{T+\theta}$ and that of $\hat{\varepsilon}_{T+\theta}$.

(3) Generally we must estimate from a sample the characteristics of the process

of the errors as well as the vector of the coefficients a. The problem is then much more complex, as we have shown above.

Although this method is not the most efficient, in practice it is often sufficient to estimate a by applying the method of least squares directly to x_t and z_t. Let a^* be the vector obtained and ε_t^* the residuals. By analogy with formulae (46) and (49), it is natural to predict $x_{T+\theta}$ by

$$x_{T+\theta}^P = a^{*\prime} z_{T+\theta} + \varepsilon_{T+\theta}^{*P}, \tag{50}$$

where $\varepsilon_{T+\theta}^{*P}$ is calculated from $\varepsilon_T^*, \varepsilon_{T-1}^*, \ldots$, according to the recurrence formula (39). If the sample size tends to infinity, the prediction tends in probability to the prediction (37), at least under fairly general conditions.

To calculate this prediction, we must obviously estimate the characteristics of the process of the errors from the residuals ε_t^*. For example, the first terms of the correlogram of the ε_t^* are calculated and fitted to an autoregressive process of low order. The prediction probably remains fairly imprecise when the sample contains only a small number of observations. To find an order of magnitude for its precision, we can evaluate the variance of $a^{*\prime} z_{T+\theta}$ and the variance of $\varepsilon_{T+\theta}^P - \varepsilon_{T+\theta}$ separately. Rigorously, the variance of $x_{T+\theta}^P - x_{T+\theta}$ is not their sum since a^* and the ε_t^* are mutually correlated. But the differences between the ε_t^* and the ε_t, and the errors of estimation affecting the characteristics of $\{\varepsilon_t\}$, must generally be unimportant relative to the variance of ε_t.

CHAPTER 13

Autoregressive models

1 Lagged endogenous variables in economic models

The explanation of the value taken by a quantity during a certain period often takes account of the value of the same quantity in the course of preceding periods. Thus, as we saw in ch. 4, we often assume that consumption in one year varies according to the level of disposable income during that year, but also according to the level of consumption already reached in the preceding year.

This is why economic models often contain, besides current values of the endogenous variables, the values of some of these variables in previous periods. They are said to contain *lagged endogenous variables* which take part, together with the exogenous variables, in the determination of the endogenous variables proper. Alternatively, the expression 'predetermined variables' is used to denote both the exogenous variables and the lagged endogenous variables.

In ch. 4 we have already recognized the advantage which may arise from the introduction of lagged endogenous variables. But until now we have discussed only models in which they do not occur. This omission must be rectified.

In fact the treatment of models with lagged endogenous variables does not call for new estimation methods. The method of least squares and its variants can be applied without modification. But their statistical properties are much weaker[†].

For the basic assumptions used in establishing the general theorems of part 2 no longer hold. If we restrict ourselves to the case of a single linear equation, our general system was written:

$$x_t = a'z_t + \varepsilon_t, \tag{1}$$

the vector z_t of exogenous variables being considered to be non-random. We must now set a relation of the type:

$$x_t = b_1 x_{t-1} + b_2 x_{t-2} + \cdots + b_h x_{t-h} + a'z_t + \varepsilon_t. \tag{2}$$

We can no longer suppose $x_{t-1}, x_{t-2}, \ldots, x_{t-h}$ to be non-random since they are determined by the random variables $\varepsilon_{t-1}, \varepsilon_{t-2}, \ldots, \varepsilon_{t-h}$.

[†] However, the distinction between regression models and autoregressive models disappears in Bayesian theory. The posterior distributions of the unknown parameters are obtained in the same way from the prior distributions and from likelihood functions which can be given exactly the same form in both types of model. So the methods given in ch. 6, § 11, apply directly to autoregressive models whose errors are normally distributed.

Of course we did observe that, if z_t is actually random, all our results still apply to the conditional distributions, the sequence of the z_t being restricted to the values actually observed in our sample. (For example, the standard errors of the estimates a_j^* are conditional, since their formula involves the values of the z_t.) But we can no longer preserve this point of view. It would become completely sterile. If the sequence of the x_t is restricted to the values actually observed, no random element is left in our model and we can no longer talk of the statistical properties of the estimates.

We might consider solving the relations (2) with respect to x_t, so as to express this variable as a function of some initial values $(x_0, x_{-1}, \ldots, x_{1-h})$, and also as a function of the sequences of the z_t and the ε_q. But this would greatly complicate the model. Moreover, after solving, the terms ξ_t corresponding to the effect on x_t of the random errors $(\varepsilon_t, \varepsilon_{t-1}, \varepsilon_{t-2}, \ldots, \varepsilon_1)$ would have a complex distribution in which $b_1, b_2, \ldots, b_h$ would occur as parameters. If the valid assumptions for the ε_t are simple, those to be adopted for the ξ_t would be very complicated. The methods considered up till now would be difficult to apply to the resolved form; their statistical properties would not necessarily be very good[†].

Equation (2) recalls that set up for the definition of linear autogressive processes. The only difference lies in the addition of the term $a'z_t$. This is why the name *autogressive models* is given to those models in which lagged endo-genous variables appear.

The sequence $\{x_t\}$ of the endogenous variables can obviously be considered as a stochastic process which is the solution of the difference equation (2). We shall generally assume that the process $\{\varepsilon_t\}$ of the errors is stationary. The presence of the term $a'z_t$ shows that the process $\{x_t\}$ is not generally stationary. But the statistical properties of the process $\{x_t\}$ vary fundamentally according to whether the solution of (2) converges or not towards a stationary process when the sequence of the z_t is identically zero. We shall always adopt the first position. In other words, we shall assume that the h roots of the equation in u:

$$u^h - b_1 u^{h-1} - b_2 u^{h-2} - \cdots - b_h = 0 \tag{3}$$

have moduli less than 1.

What is the real importance of this *stability condition* for economic models of the type (2)? If one (or more) of the roots of eq. (3) has modulus greater than 1, the sequence $\{x_t\}$ has an explosive evolution (except for exceptional values of the z_t, the ε_t and the initial conditions). The model therefore describes an explosive phenomenon in which the oscillations of the exogenous variables z_t and the errors ε_t are repeated and amplified over the whole future sequence of the endogenous variables. Clearly this is never the case in actuality.

[†] We shall see in the next chapter that solving in this way would lead to a model with distri-buted lags. We shall then be in a better position to understand the difficulties involved in this suggestion.

However, the condition adopted in this chapter would not be accepted in all circumstances by all economists. Some do in fact think that general fluctuations in economic activity only reflect the fluctuations of certain exogenous quantities according to a process which dies away naturally. They can accept a model of the type (2) satisfying the stability condition. But others think that the economic system is essentially unstable, that every initial disturbance tends to propagate and amplify over time, that only the presence of 'obstacles', of 'ceilings' or 'floors' checks these explosive tendencies. In this case a good model should be unstable near its equilibrium position, and describe the obstacles which put an end to explosive evolutions. It would necessarily be non-linear.

If in this book we confine ourselves essentially to stable linear models it is not so much because we adopt a particular theoretical position as because we wish to keep to well-established statistical theory which can be presented systematically.

It follows from the dynamic nature of the model that x_t depends not only on the errors $\varepsilon_1, \varepsilon_2, \ldots, \varepsilon_t$ and on the exogenous variables $z_1, z_2, \ldots, z_t$, but also on the *initial values* $x_0, x_{-1}, \ldots, x_{1-h}$. In most cases we shall treat these values as unknown secondary parameters. We can also treat them as non-observed random variables; this other approach sometimes leads to different theoretical results, particularly for small samples, since the distribution of x_t is then different.

In presenting the theory we must also clearly distinguish two cases to which, as we shall see, different statistical methods apply. In sections 2 to 4 we shall restrict ourselves to *the case where errors ε_t corresponding to different observations are uncorrelated*. In sections 5 and 6 we shall discuss the problems raised by time dependence of the errors.

Even in the case of uncorrelated errors, the statistical theory is much less straightforward than it is for the regression model of ch. 5. If the least squares method is again applied, its properties are weaker and more difficult to establish. In section 3 we shall see that the results which are rigorously valid for small samples are not in themselves very conclusive. This is why theoreticians have concentrated on the limiting properties related to the potential situation where the number of observations tends to infinity (section 2).

It would overburden the text to give proofs of the various properties. So we shall only discuss some examples without too much detail and state the general properties without giving proofs.

Throughout this chapter we shall again restrict ourselves to single equation models. There is no basic difficulty in the direct discussion of multiple equation models but there is no real benefit from thus further complicating the text.

2 Asymptotic properties of the method of least squares

Let us then first consider the case *where there is no time dependence of the errors*.

Suppose that estimates a_j^* and b_t^* of the coefficients of (2) have been obtained by a multiple regression of x_t on $x_{t-1}, x_{t-2}, \ldots, x_{t-h}$ and the z_{jt}. Let us assume also that the number T of observations tends to infinity. Under certain general conditions it has been proved that in this case the estimates tend to the true values. In addition, their limiting distribution is identical to the distribution obtained if multiple regression theory could be applied with $x_{t-1}, \ldots, x_{t-h}$ considered as exogenous variables.

The conditions required for the proof of these results have been progressively elucidated by mathematicians over the past thirty years. There is no question of giving a complete description of the theory here. But it appears opportune to present proofs for a simple example in order to give an idea of the nature of the theory.

(a) Discussion of an example

Let us consider the model

$$x_t = bx_{t-1} + az_t + \varepsilon_t \tag{4}$$

where a and b are two numerical coefficients to be estimated, z_t is an observable exogenous variable and ε_t is an unobservable random variable obeying the usual assumptions; the ε_t are mutually independent and identically distributed with zero mean and finite variance σ^2.

We propose to study the properties of the estimators a^* and b^* obtained by the method of least squares, that is, by solving the system

$$\begin{cases} b^*[x_{-1}^2] + a^*[zx_{-1}] = [xx_{-1}] \\ b^*[x_{-1}z] + a^*[z^2] = [xz] \end{cases} \tag{5}$$

in which the square brackets conventionally denote the empirical moments so that

$$[x_{-1}^2] = \frac{1}{T} \sum_{t=1}^{T} x_{t-1}^2 \qquad [zx_{-1}] = \frac{1}{T} \sum_{t=1}^{T} z_t x_{t-1} \tag{6}$$

(here we assume the value x_0 of x_t for $t = 0$ to be known, this assumption clearly being unimportant in an asymptotic study).

The form of system (5) reveals immediately that a^* and b^* are non-linear functions of the random variables x_t. This is a prime difference from estimators of the same kind applying to the usual regressions with no lagged endogenous variables. The properties of a^* and b^* can no longer be derived from the general theory of linear estimation. For example, their expected values are difficult to calculate and depend on the precise form of the distribution of ε_t.

Model (4) directly implies the following relations between the empirical moments and the true values a and b:

$$\begin{cases} b[x_{-1}^2] + a[zx_{-1}] + [\varepsilon x_{-1}] = [xx_{-1}] \\ b[x_{-1}z] + a[z^2] + [\varepsilon z] = [xz] \end{cases} \tag{7}$$

(To obtain the first equation we need only multiply (4) by x_{t-1}, sum with respect to t and divide by T). By combining systems (5) and (7), we obtain

$$\begin{cases} (b^* - b)[x_{-1}^2] + (a^* - a)[zx_{-1}] = [\varepsilon x_{-1}] \\ (b^* - b)[x_{-1}z] + (a^* - a)[z^2] = [\varepsilon z] \end{cases} \tag{8}$$

The asymptotic properties of $(a^* - a)$ and $(b^* - b)$ follow from those of $[\varepsilon x_{-1}]$ and $[\varepsilon z]$ since the matrix

$$M = \begin{bmatrix} [x_{-1}^2] & [zx_{-1}] \\ [x_{-1}z] & [z^2] \end{bmatrix}$$

tends in probability to a non-singular matrix, as will be established.

Equation (4) does not reveal directly how x_t depends on the exogenous elements of the model: the variables z_t and the random errors ε_t. For the study of the random properties of a^* and b^*, we need a relation which makes this dependence explicit. Obviously we can write

$$x_{t-1} = bx_{t-2} + az_{t-1} + \varepsilon_{t-1}$$

and substitute this in (4) to obtain

$$x_t = b^2 x_{t-2} + az_t + abz_{t-1} + \varepsilon_t + b\varepsilon_{t-1}.$$

The same method can be used to eliminate x_{t-2}, and by using this iterative procedure, we obtain

$$x_t = b^t x_0 + a \sum_{\tau=0}^{t-1} b^\tau z_{t-\tau} + \sum_{\tau=0}^{t-1} b^\tau \varepsilon_{t-\tau}, \tag{9}$$

which we can write

$$x_t = b^t x_0 + ay_t + \zeta_t \tag{10}$$

where

$$y_t = \sum_{\tau=0}^{t-1} b^\tau z_{t-\tau}, \qquad \zeta_t = \sum_{\tau=0}^{t-1} b^\tau \varepsilon_{t-\tau}. \tag{11}$$

Expression (10) facilitates the study of the asymptotic behaviour of the various empirical moments which appear in (8). For this we make the following three assumptions in addition to the assumption for the errors ε_t.

(i) $|b| < 1$; this is the stability assumption mentioned previously.

(ii) The z_t are bounded by a number B $(|z_t| \leq B)$; the quantities

$$\frac{1}{T} \sum_{t=1}^{T-\tau} z_t z_{t+\tau} \tag{12}$$

tend to limits γ_z^τ as T tends to infinity, and they do this uniformly with respect to τ; the limit $\gamma_z^0 = S_z^2$ is positive.

(iii) The distribution of the ε_t has a finite fourth-order moment.

Under these assumptions it is apparent that the y_t are bounded by $B/(1-b)$. Moreover, the empirical variance

$$\frac{1}{T} \sum_{t=0}^{T-1} y_t^2$$

has a finite limit which we denote by S_y^2. We can verify that

$$\frac{1}{T} \sum_{t=0}^{T-1} y_t^2 = \sum_{\tau=0}^{T-1} b^{2\tau} \sum_{\theta=-\tau}^{T-\tau} b^\theta \cdot \frac{1}{T} \sum_{t'=t_0+1}^{T-\tau} z_{t'} z_{t'-\theta} \tag{13}$$

(where t_0 is the maximum of 0 and θ). For given values of θ and τ the limit of the last term of this expression is γ_z^θ. The convergence is uniform with respect to θ and τ. The series of terms $b^\theta \gamma_z^\theta$ is dominated by the convergent series $b^\theta \gamma_z^0$ so that (13) has a limit.

We can now establish that M tends in probability to a limit. Consider its most complex element $[x_{-1}^2]$. By combining (6) and (10) we can write this element as the sum of six terms:

– The two terms

$$\frac{x_0^2}{T} \sum_{t=0}^{T-1} b^{2t} \quad \text{and} \quad \frac{2ax_0}{T} \sum_{t=0}^{T-1} b^t y_t$$

clearly tend to zero since the sums which they contain are bounded respectively by $1/(1-b^2)$ and $B/(1-b)^2$. (If the z_t are not assumed to be bounded, then we can use the Schwarz inequality and replace the second bound by $\sqrt{T} S_y / \sqrt{1-b^2}$, which is sufficient.)

– The two terms

$$\frac{2x_0}{T} \sum_{t=0}^{T-1} b^t \zeta_t \quad \text{and} \quad \frac{2a}{T} \sum_{t=0}^{T-1} y_t \zeta_t$$

can be written

$$2x_0 \sum_{\tau=0}^{T-1} b^{2\tau} \cdot \frac{1}{T} \sum_{\theta=1}^{T-\tau} b^\theta \varepsilon_\theta \quad \text{and} \quad 2a \sum_{\tau=0}^{T-1} b^\tau \cdot \frac{1}{T} \sum_{\theta=1}^{T-\tau} y_{\theta+\tau} \varepsilon_\theta$$

respectively. The standard deviations of the second terms of each of these expressions are bounded respectively by $\sigma/T \sqrt{1-b^2}$ and $\sigma B/(1-b) \sqrt{T}$, so that the standard deviations of the whole expressions are bounded by $2x_0\sigma/T(1-b^2)^{\frac{1}{2}}$ and $2a\sigma B/(1-b)^2 \sqrt{T}$. (If the z_t are not assumed bounded, the second bound can be replaced by $2a\sigma S_y/(1-b) \sqrt{T}$). These two bounds tend to zero with T. So the two corresponding terms of $[x_{-1}^2]$ tend to zero in quadratic mean.
  – The term

$$\frac{a^2}{T} \sum_{t=0}^{T-1} y_t^2$$

tends to S_y^2 as we have already seen.
  – In the case of the term

$$\frac{1}{T} \sum_{t=0}^{T-1} \zeta_t^2 \tag{14}$$

an expression similar to (13) applies, with $z_t \cdot z_{t'-\theta}$ being replaced by $\varepsilon_t \cdot \varepsilon_{t'-\theta}$. The expectation of the last term of the product is zero if $\theta \neq 0$ and is σ^2 otherwise. It follows that the expected value of (14) is $\sigma^2/(1-b^2)$ which we shall denote by σ_ζ^2.

We shall not write the expansion of the expected value of the square of (14), which is a complex expression involving terms of the form

$$E(\varepsilon_t \cdot \varepsilon_{t'-\theta} \varepsilon_{t''} \cdot \varepsilon_{t''-\theta'}). \tag{15}$$

Now these terms are zero except in two cases:
  (i) If $\theta' = \theta \neq 0$ and $t'' = t'$, then (15) equals σ^4.
  (ii) If $\theta = 0$ and $\theta' = 0$, then (15) equals σ^4 when $t'' \neq t'$, and equals μ_4, the fourth-order moment of ε_t when $t'' = t'$.

We see that the sum of the terms in μ_4 tends to zero as T tends to infinity and the sum of the terms in σ^4 tends to $\sigma^4/(1-b^2)^2$, that is, to σ_ζ^4. Thus the expected value of the square of (14) tends to the square of the limiting expected value of (14), that is, the variance of (14) tends to zero. Thus (14) tends to its expected value σ_ζ^4.

To sum up, we have just seen that $[x_{-1}^2]$ tends to $a^2 S_y^2 + \sigma_\zeta^2$. In the same way we can establish that the limit of $[zx_{-1}]$ is aS_{yz}, which is a times the limit of

$$\frac{1}{T} \sum_t y_t z_t.$$

So the limit of M is

$$\begin{bmatrix} a^2 S_y^2 + \sigma_\zeta^2 & a S_{yz} \\ a S_{yz} & S_z^2 \end{bmatrix}. \tag{16}$$

This is a non-singular matrix, since

$$\sigma_\zeta^2 > 0 \quad \text{and} \quad S_y^2 S_z^2 \geq S_{yz}^2,$$

because of the Schwarz inequality.

Similar reasoning establishes that the second terms of (8), $[\varepsilon x_{-1}]$ and $[\varepsilon z]$, tend to zero. It therefore follows that a^* and b^* are consistent[†] estimators of a and b.

To establish that the pair $\sqrt{T}(a^* - a)$ and $\sqrt{T}(b^* - b)$ has a limiting normal distribution, we need only show that this is so for

$$\sqrt{T}[\varepsilon x_{-1}] \quad \text{and} \quad \sqrt{T}[\varepsilon z].$$

Consider, for example, $\sqrt{T}[\varepsilon x_{-1}]$, which in view of (10) can be expressed as the sum of three terms:

$$\frac{x_0}{\sqrt{T}} \sum_{t=0}^{T-1} b^t \varepsilon_{t+1} \tag{17}$$

which obviously tends to zero since the sum which appears in it has finite variance;

$$\frac{a}{\sqrt{T}} \sum_{t=0}^{T-1} y_t \varepsilon_{t+1} \tag{18}$$

which has a limiting normal distribution since the y_t are bounded and the ε_t, which are mutually independent, have a variance;

$$\frac{1}{\sqrt{T}} \sum_{t=0}^{T-1} \zeta_t \varepsilon_{t+1} \tag{19}$$

which is a linear combination of expressions such as

[†] We see that the consistency is established even if the z_t are not bounded. The stability condition ($|b| < 1$) was used in the above proof to establish that certain expressions tend to limits. In the case where this condition is not satisfied, some elements tend to infinity. This explosive tendency seems bound to be more marked in the elements of M than in the right hand sides of (8). Far from preventing the consistency of a^* and b^*, it should in fact facilitate it. This explains why theorem 1, which follows, does not involve the stability condition.

$$\frac{1}{\sqrt{T}} \sum_t \varepsilon_{t-\tau}\varepsilon_{t+1}. \tag{20}$$

It is (19) which raises difficulties. While it is true that each term (20) has a limiting normal distribution since $\varepsilon_{t-\tau}\varepsilon_{t+1}$ has a finite second order moment σ^4, (19) is a sum of such terms which are not independent, neither mutually independent nor independent of (18). So it must be shown explicitly that the sum of (18) and (19) does in fact have a limiting normal distribution. This is proved by SCHÖNFELD [1971].

Finally, it follows that the pair $\sqrt{T}(a^* - a)$ and $\sqrt{T}(b^* - b)$ has a limiting normal distribution.

For the determination of the asymptotic covariance matrix of $\sqrt{T}(a^* - a)$, $\sqrt{T}(b^* - b)$, we consider in particular the limit of $TE\{[\varepsilon x_{-1}]^2\}$. The expectation in question can be written

$$E\left[\frac{1}{T^2} \sum_{tt'} \varepsilon_t \varepsilon_{t'} x_{t-1} x_{t'-1}\right]. \tag{21}$$

All the terms for which $t \neq t'$ have zero expectation, since ε_t is then independent of $\varepsilon_{t'}$ and x_{t-1}; in order that the term in t, t' should not have zero expectation, it is necessary that ε_t be correlated with $x_{t'-1}$, which assumes that $t \leq t' - 1$. But then $t' > t - 1$ and $\varepsilon_{t'}$ is independent of ε_t, $x_{t'-1}$ and x_{t-1}. Therefore (21) involves only terms for which $t = t'$, and can be written

$$\frac{\sigma^2}{T} E\{[x_{-1}^2]\}.$$

So the limit of $TE\{[\varepsilon x_{-1}]^2\}$ is σ^2 times the limit of $[x_{-1}^2]$.

Similarly we can establish that the limit of the covariance matrix of the pair $\sqrt{T}[\varepsilon x_{-1}]$ and $\sqrt{T}[\varepsilon z]$ is σ^2 times the limit of M. Thus the asymptotic covariance matrix of $\sqrt{T}(b^* - b)$, $\sqrt{T}(a^* - a)$ is

$$\sigma^2[\lim M]^{-1}. \tag{22}$$

This formula is identical to that which applies to linear regression theory. The only difference is that it is asymptotically valid and no longer holds for small samples.

These are not results particular to the example of model (4), as is shown by a general theory whose conclusions we shall state.

(b) General theorems

We first state the various assumptions used.

Assumption 1.   The random vectors ε_t are identically distributed with zero mean and finite second-order moments. Two errors ε_t and ε_θ are stochastically independent whenever $t \neq \theta$.

Assumption 2.   The random error ε_t is normally distributed.

Assumption 3.   The h roots in u of equation (3) have moduli less than 1.

Assumption 4.   When T tends to infinity, the z_t are bounded and each of the matrices

$$M_{zz}^{\tau} = \frac{1}{T} \sum_{t=1}^{T-\tau} z_t z_{t+\tau}' \qquad (23)$$

tends to a limit M_{τ}^0 (where $\tau = 0, 1, 2, \ldots$). The convergence is uniform with respect to τ. The matrix M_0^0 is non-singular.

These assumptions recall those formulated at the start of chapters 6 and 9, apart from the stability condition and the convergence of the matrices M_{zz}^{τ}.

If the ε_t satisfy assumptions 1 and 2, the distribution of $(\varepsilon_1, \varepsilon_2, \ldots, \varepsilon_T)$ has density:

$$C \exp\left\{ -\frac{1}{2\sigma^2} \sum_{t=1}^{T} \varepsilon_t^2 \right\},$$

where C is an appropriate constant and σ^2 is the variance of ε_t. The conditional distribution of $(x_1, x_2, \ldots, x_T)$ for the given initial values $(x_{1-h}, \ldots, x_{-1}, x_0)$ (and for the given z_t, if z_t is random) has density

$$C \exp\left\{ -\frac{1}{2\sigma^2} \sum_{t=1}^{T} (x_t - b_1 x_{t-1} - b_2 {}_{t-2} - \cdots - b_h x_{t-h} - a'z_t)^2 \right\}. \qquad (24)$$

For, since the matrix of the linear transformation of $(x_1, x_2, \ldots, x_T)$ into $(\varepsilon_1, \varepsilon_2, \ldots, \varepsilon_T)$ has only 1's on its main diagonal and zeros above, the jacobian of the transformation is 1.

The form (24) of the probability density shows that the maximum likelihood estimate of the parameters $b_1, b_2, \ldots, b_h$ and a is defined by the values of these parameters which minimize the sum of squares of the differences:

$$\sum_{t=1}^{T} (x_t - b_1 x_{t-1} - b_2 x_{t-2} \cdots - b_h x_{t-h} - a'z_t)^2.$$

It is therefore the least squares estimate calculated as if the lagged endogenous variables were exogenous.

The method of maximum likelihood is justified by the fact that the estimates obtained are consistent and asymptotically most efficient. In fact the usual proofs apply only in the case of samples consisting of independent observations. Here the x_t are not mutually independent.

However, several general theorems concerning the asymptotic properties of these estimates have been established[†]. Some theorems deal with convergence to the true values and some with the asymptotic distribution. The positions relative to 1 of the roots of (3) affect the nature of the asymptotic distribution: here we shall discuss only the relevant result when the stability assumption holds. This assumption, however, is not involved in the case of the property of convergence. So the two principal results are as follows:

Theorem 1. If assumptions 1 and 4 are satisfied, the estimates $b_1^*, b_2^*, \ldots, b_h^*$, a^* tend in probability to the true values when the number T of observations tends to infinity.

Theorem 2. If assumptions 1, 3 and 4 are satisfied,

$$\sqrt{T}(b_1^* - b_1), \ldots, \sqrt{T}(b_h^* - b_h), \sqrt{T}(a^* - a)$$

are asymptotically normally distributed with covariance matrix $\sigma^2 N^{-1}$ where

$$N = \begin{bmatrix} \overline{M}_{xx} & \overline{M}_{x0} \\ \overline{M}'_{x0} & M_0^0 \end{bmatrix}. \tag{25}$$

If, in addition, assumption 2 is satisfied, the estimators $b_1^*, b_2^*, \ldots, b_h^*, a^*$ are efficient in the class of consistent regular estimators.

In (24), M_0^0 is defined by assumption 4, $\overline{M}_{xx}$ is a matrix of order h whose elements are the limits in probability of the

$$\frac{1}{T} \sum_{t=1}^{T} x_{t-\theta} x_{t-\theta'}, \qquad \theta, \theta' = 1, 2, \ldots, h.$$

$\overline{M}_{x0}$ is a matrix of order $(h \times m)$ whose elements are the limits in probability of the

$$\frac{1}{T} \sum_{t=1}^{T} x_{t-\theta} z_{jt}, \qquad \theta = 1, 2, \ldots, h; \qquad j = 1, 2, \ldots m.$$

Theorem 2 shows that, if assumptions 1, 3 and 4 are admissible, *we can apply the method of least squares as if the lagged endogenous variables were exogenous.*

[†] We shall not give the general proofs of theorems 1 and 2 since they are fairly laborious. The relevant literature is not easily accessible and there appears to be no published systematic account of the proofs of the various properties which are presently known. STIGUM [1974] is the best reference for access to this literature.

The b_θ^* and a^* are calculated from normal equations like those of ch. 6; σ^2 is estimated by means of the residuals ε_t^* (since the latter tend in probability to the errors ε_t); the covariance matrix of the b_θ^* and a^* is estimated by σ^{*2}/T multiplied by the inverse of the matrix M constructed over all the predetermined variables (since this matrix is a consistent estimate of N); tests and confidence regions are established by the usual methods for normal random variables (since the asymptotic distribution of the estimates is normal).

But this procedure is now only asymptotically justifiable. While the theory in ch. 6 did not depend on the size of the sample considered, that just given assumes that the sample is large enough for asymptotic approximation to be valid. In this sense already the properties of the method of least squares are weaker in autoregressive models than in regression models.

(c) Inference procedures on the autoregressive form of a stationary process[†]

Before continuing with the study of model (2) we can stop briefly to consider a related question concerning the statistical analysis of stationary random processes.

As we pointed out in ch. 11, the autoregressive representation of a process is particularly useful for prediction of the future evolution of any realization. Now, the problems which face the economist are essentially problems of prediction. He is always concerned to find out how the future will depend on facts observed today. Moreover, the models themselves are often autoregressive in form. So when he has to deal with a random process, the economist will generally use statistical methods devised for application to the autoregressive representation

$$x_t - b_1 x_{t-1} - b_2 x_{t-2} - \cdots - b_\tau x_{t-\tau} - \cdots = \varepsilon_t. \tag{26}$$

In fact every more particular assumption about the process reduces to either a relation on the b_τ, or an assumption about the nature of the distribution of the ε_t. In economics we are rarely interested in the properties of the distribution of the ε_t, unless indirectly for carrying out tests or predictions; in most cases we are content to estimate the variance of the ε_t. The most frequent assumptions concern the coefficients b_τ. Here we shall assume that they depend on a finite number of unknown parameters which are represented by a vector α. The essential difference from the case previously discussed lies in the fact that the b_τ are not parameters to be estimated, but functions of these parameters. This situation recalls that discussed in ch. 9.

A time series, a realization of the process $\{x_t\}$ for $t = 1, 2, \ldots, T$, must allow estimation of the value of α or tests on this value. Consider the expression

$$V = \sum_{t=\theta+1}^{T} (x_t - b_1 x_{t-1} - \cdots - b_\theta x_{t-\theta})^2 \tag{27}$$

[†] See WOLD [1938] and WHITTLE [1954, 1961] for more detailed treatment of this subject.

where θ is fixed in advance. Apart from the omission of the terms in $\tau > \theta$ in the expansion of (26), V is the sum of squares of the errors for t varying from $\theta+1$ to T. A natural estimate of α is that which minimizes V; let this estimate be α_θ^*. If θ is a fixed proportion of T (and therefore increases with T), we can show, under some general assumptions, that α_θ^* tends to the true value of α when the number of observations tends to infinity.

This principle applies in a particularly straightforward way if the process is autoregressive, since then (26) involves only a finite number of b_τ which can all be taken into account for finding V (provided that there is a sufficient number of observations).

A similar principle can be applied for tests. Let us assume that the b_τ depend on n parameters and that a hypothesis H_0 specifies that m of these parameters are zero. Then let V^* and V_0^* respectively be the values of the minimum of V with respect to the n parameters and with respect to the $n-m$ parameters which do not appear in H_0. The ratio between V_0^* and V^* can be used to test H_0. If θ is a constant fraction of T we can show that asymptotically,

$$(T-n)\left[\frac{V_0^*}{V^*} - 1\right]$$

is distributed as χ^2 with m degrees of freedom.

Before leaving this question, we note that an autoregressive process in which the b_τ are themselves the unknown parameters can be estimated very closely by identifying the first terms of the empirical correlogram with the corresponding terms of the theoretical correlogram. We can show this by considering a third-order autoregressive process:

$$x_t = b_1 x_{t-1} + b_2 x_{t-2} + b_3 x_{t-3} + \varepsilon_t.$$

Multiplying by x_{t-1} the first time, by x_{t-2} the second, and by x_{t-3} the third, and taking the expected values, we obtain directly the system:

$$b_1 + b_2 \varrho_1 + b_3 \varrho_2 = \varrho_1,$$
$$b_1 \varrho_1 + b_2 + b_3 \varrho_1 = \varrho_2, \qquad\qquad (28)$$
$$b_1 \varrho_2 + b_2 \varrho_1 + b_3 = \varrho_3,$$

where ϱ_1, ϱ_2, ϱ_3 are the first three terms of the theoretical correlogram of $\{x_t\}$.

Also, the normal equations used in fitting are:

$$b_1 \sum x_{t-1}^2 + b_2 \sum x_{t-1}x_{t-2} + b_3 \sum x_{t-1}x_{t-3} = \sum x_t x_{t-1},$$
$$b_1 \sum x_{t-1}x_{t-2} + b_2 \sum x_{t-2}^2 + b_3 \sum x_{t-2}x_{t-3} = \sum x_t x_{t-2},$$
$$b_1 \sum x_{t-1}x_{t-3} + b_2 \sum x_{t-2}x_{t-3} + b_3 \sum x_{t-3}^2 = \sum x_t x_{t-3}.$$

Apart from the end terms of the sums, this system is reduced to the previous one by substituting the empirical coefficients

$$r_1 = \frac{\sum x_t x_{t-1}}{\sum x_t^2}, \qquad r_2 = \frac{\sum x_t x_{t-2}}{\sum x_t^2}, \qquad r_3 = \frac{\sum x_t x_{t-3}}{\sum x_t^2}$$

for the theoretical coefficients ϱ_1, ϱ_2 and ϱ_3.

DURBIN [1960b] gave a simple iterative method for determining the estimates b_τ^* satisfying systems such as (28) written with the empirical coefficients r_τ.

3 Least squares fitting in small samples

Short statistical series comprising for example only twenty successive observations are often used in econometrics. It would therefore be useful to have more precise knowledge of the distributions of the estimates obtained by the method of least squares especially for small samples. Unfortunately these distributions are very complex, and have been established only in very particular cases.

We must also state precisely whether we are considering the conditional distributions for the fixed initial values $x_{1-h}, x_{2-h}, \ldots, x_{-1}, x_0$, or the unconditional distributions taking account of the fact that these values are themselves random. The two types of distribution are asymptotically equivalent; but they differ for small samples.

Consider, for example, the simplest model:

$$x_t = b x_{t-1} + \varepsilon_t. \qquad \text{where} \qquad |b| < 1. \tag{29}$$

The least squares estimate b^* of b is given by

$$b^* = \frac{\sum_{t=2}^{T} x_t x_{t-1}}{\sum_{t=2}^{T} x_{t-1}^2}, \tag{30}$$

that is, by the first coefficient of the empirical correlogram defined according to formula (3) of ch. 11. This formula is not symmetric ('circular') as we have already seen. However, HURWICZ [1950] investigated the distribution of b^*, and showed that there is a bias in small samples. When the process of the x_t is considered as stationary and the initial value x_0 as random, when b is small in absolute value and T is large, the expected value of b^* is given, to the first order of approximation in b and in $1/T$, by the formula

$$E(b^*) \sim b\left(1 - \frac{2}{T}\right).$$

Of course when T tends to infinity, the bias $-2b/T$ is infinitely small relative to the standard error of b^*. which is asymptotically equivalent to

$$\sqrt{\frac{1-b^2}{T}}.$$

However, for samples of about twenty observations, it reaches about 10% of the true value[†].

Faced with the difficulty of an analytic approach, we must confine ourselves to the examination of experimental results if we wish to assess the properties of the usual methods. Investigation of such results can be conducted systematically. We need only construct a certain number of artificial samples on the basis of a given autoregressive model and determine the estimates which would have been obtained from each sample if this sample only had actually been observed. So for each estimator we have as many values as there are samples. The empirical distribution of these values provides an approximation to the theoretical distribution which we wish to find. This method, called the 'Monte-Carlo method', has been used for the problem which now concerns us particularly by COCHRANE and ORCUTT [1949a, b], by MALINVAUD [1961b] and by ORCUTT and WINOKUR [1967].

In the second reference, the model investigated contains a lagged endogenous variable, an exogenous variable and a constant term, namely:

$$x_t = bx_{t-1} + az_t + c + \varepsilon_t. \tag{31}$$

Artificial samples each of twenty observations led to an estimate b^* of b whose distribution density is represented approximately in fig. 1. The true value of b was 0.60. We find that b^* underestimates b in three cases out of four and that the distribution is clearly skew with a considerable tail towards small values of b. The bias $E(b^*)-b$ is of the order of -0.08.

The study of artificial samples also allows us to assess the statistical procedures associated with the method of least squares. We saw that asymptotic theory justifies the use of the usual formulae for calculating the variances of the estimates and for establishing tests and confidence regions. But these formulae are rigorously valid only for large samples. It is important to know if they entail substantial errors for the samples generally studied in econometrics.

From this point of view, the artificial samples constructed using the model (30) lead to two conclusions which may have fairly general validity.

(a) The usual formula for calculating σ_b^{*2} gives on the average a fairly exact measure of the variance of the estimate b^*, but tends somewhat to under-

---

[†] COPAS [1966] uses the Monte Carlo method to investigate the distribution of the estimator b^* for a normal process of the type (29). He compares b^* with other estimators. REEVES [1972] studies this distribution more closely and shows how it can be approximated. Such approximations are given by PHILLIPS [1977]. See also PHILLIPS [1978].

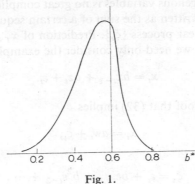

Fig. 1.

estimate the mean square error about the true value b, namely $E(b^*-b)^2$. For the samples considered, σ_b^{*2} underestimated $E(b^*-b)^2$ in about three cases out of four.

(b) The confidence interval defined by

$$|b^* - b| \leqq 2.11\,\sigma_b^*$$

should, according to the usual theory, include the true value in 95% of cases, lie to the right in 2.5% and to the left in 2.5% (this being so for 17 degrees of freedom). In the model considered, its real significance level seems to differ somewhat from 5%. More precisely, the interval lies to the left of the true value in about 7% of cases, and to the right in only one case in 300.

In short, these results confirm that the theory developed for regression models is not applicable just as it is to autoregressive models[†]. But they suggest that in practice no serious error is committed if we apply the usual methods conceived for regression models to the treatment of autoregressive models. Of course this optimistic conclusion is valid only in so far as the errors ε_t are not autocorrelated. We shall return to this point later.

4 Prediction

In order to study the problems raised by prediction using a autoregressive model, let us suppose first that the values of the coefficients b_θ and a_j of the model are known a priori.

If the model contains no exogenous variable and satisfies the stability condition (assumption 3), if the errors are not autocorrelated (assumption 1), then the stochastic process of the x_t is stationary and its linear representation is given by the model. So prediction is carried out as in every other stationary linear process.

[†] The finding that the tails of the distribution are somewhat heavy is confirmed by BASMANN, RICHARDSON and ROHR [1974].

The presence of exogenous variables is no great complication. For the process of the x_t can then be written as the sum of a certain sequence depending on the z_t and a stationary linear process $\{\xi_t\}$. Prediction of $x_{T+\theta}$ is equivalent to that of $\xi_{T+\theta}$. To show this, we need only consider the example of the model

$$x_t = bx_{t-1} + az_t + \varepsilon_t. \tag{32}$$

We assume without proof that (32) implies

$$x_t = aw_t + \xi_t, \tag{33}$$

where

$$
\begin{aligned}
\xi_t &= \varepsilon_t + b\varepsilon_{t-1} + b^2\varepsilon_{t-2} + \cdots, \\
w_t &= z_t + bz_{t-1} + b^2 z_{t-2} + \cdots.
\end{aligned}
\tag{34}
$$

(While (32) is identical to (4), the representation (33) differs from (10) in that w_t and ξ_t involve all previous values of z_t and ξ_t, including values prior to the period of observation.)

The process $\{\xi_t\}$ then satisfies:

$$\xi_t = b\xi_{t-1} + \varepsilon_t.$$

One can show that the value of $x_{T+\theta}$ which minimizes the mean square of the prediction error is:

$$x_{T+\theta}^P = aw_{T+\theta} + \xi_{T+\theta}^P,$$

where

$$\xi_{T+\theta}^P = b\xi_{T+\theta-1}^P \quad\text{and}\quad \xi_{T+1}^P = b\xi_T.$$

This prediction can also be written:

$$x_{T+\theta}^P = b^\theta x_T + a(z_{T+\theta} + bz_{T+\theta-1} + \cdots + b^{\theta-1}z_{T+1}).$$

In this example, and more generally in all autoregressive models satisfying assumptions 1 and 3, the prediction $x_{T+\theta}^P$ can be determined by recurrence from a linear formula deduced directly from the model, in this case:

$$
\begin{aligned}
x_{T+1}^P &= bx_T + az_{T+1} \\
x_{T+\theta}^P &= bx_{T+\theta-1}^P + az_{T+\theta} \quad\text{for}\quad \theta = 2,3,\ldots
\end{aligned}
\tag{35}
$$

The variance of the prediction errors can be determined. For example, in the case of the model (32) we obtain

$$E(x_{T+\theta}^P - x_{T+\theta})^2 = (1 + b + \cdots + b^{\theta-1})\sigma_\varepsilon^2. \tag{36}$$

Suppose now that the coefficients of the autoregressive model have been estimated from a sample and that the assumption of independence of successive errors still holds.

The method of least squares leads to estimates which until now have had the strongest justification. So it is natural to proceed in the same way as above after substituting the estimates for the true values of the coefficients. Thus, in the case of the model (32), we use the recurrence formulae:

$$x_{T+1}^P = b^* x_T + a^* z_{T+1}$$
$$x_{T+\theta}^P = b^* x_{T+\theta-1}^P + a^* z_{T+\theta} \qquad \text{for} \qquad \theta = 2, 3, \ldots \tag{37}$$

If the sample is sufficiently large, the estimates b^* and a^* differ by very little from the true values b and a. So the variance of the prediction error can be calculated from formula (36), ignoring the differences between b^* and b.

On the other hand, when the sample is 'small' we should take account of estimation errors. Unfortunately it is very difficult to determine an tically the characteristics of the distribution of the prediction error. To see why, we need only consider the simplest case:

$$x_t = b x_{t-1} + \varepsilon_t.$$

The prediction error on x_{T+1} is then:

$$x_{T+1}^P - x_{T+1} = (b^* - b) x_T - \varepsilon_{T+1} = \frac{x_T \sum \varepsilon_t x_{t-1}}{\sum x_{t-1}^2} - \varepsilon_{T+1}.$$

The ratio which appears on the right hand side is very complex. At most we can say that the expected value of the prediction error is zero when the distribution of ε_t is symmetric, and that this is so even if b^* is biased.

Here again the examination of artificial samples can take the place of analytic investigation to some extent. Thus samples built up from the model (31) were used to verify that the prediction error has a distribution centred in the neighborhood of zero and to assess the importance of estimation errors. In the examples considered, it appeared that, for the first predicted value ($\theta = 1$), the variance of the error was roughly 20% greater than the result of formula (36); but that, as early as the third predicted value ($\theta = 3$), the actual variance of the error was as much as twice that given by this formula. So it looks as if the imprecision of the estimates has a cumulative effect on the values of successive predictions, contrary to what would be observed in the case of a non-autoregressive model.

5 Serial correlation of errors and least squares fitting

Assumption 1 used in the preceding section stipulates that there is no stochastic dependence between the errors ε_t and ε_{t+1} relating to two successive periods. Now we have already emphasized that such dependence frequently exists in economic data. So we must find out what properties our methods have when the errors are autocorrelated.

For the non-autoregressive models studied in part 2 correlation of errors does not prevent the estimates obtained by the method of least squares from tending to the true values nor from being unbiased even for small samples. Only the formulae giving the standard errors of the estimates have to be revised, as we showed in the previous chapter.

The situation is radically different in the case of autoregressive models. The bias affecting the estimates obtained by the method of least squares may become very considerable. It does not generally tend to zero when the number of observations tends to infinity. In fact the estimates typically tend to values which are different from the true values.

In principle it is even possible that the parameters of the model are not identifiable (at least as long as we have no precise knowledge of the correlation of the errors). For example, consider the model:

$$x_t = bx_{t-1} + \varepsilon_t, \tag{38}$$

and suppose that the errors ε_t can be written:

$$\varepsilon_t = \eta_t + \alpha\eta_{t-1}, \tag{39}$$

where the variables η_t constitute a purely random stationary process. (The ε_t then constitute a 'moving average' process.) Suppose also that $\alpha = -b$. Relations (38) and (39) lead to:

$$x_t - \eta_t = b(x_{t-1} - \eta_{t-1}) = \cdots = b^t(x_0 - \eta_0).$$

Since $|b| < 1$, the process $\{x_t\}$ tends to become identical to the purely random process $\{\eta_t\}$, even if it differs from it in the initial period. So the distribution of the x_t no longer depends on b (except possibly for the very first values). If the x_t process is effectively stationary, the parameter b is not identifiable since the distribution of the x_t does not depend on it. If b is estimated by formula (30) above, we find a value which tends in probability to zero whatever b may be.

This may seem to be an artificial case. For more exact appreciation of the situation we shall consider two simple examples in which the errors constitute an autoregressive process. The second example involves an exogenous variable, but the first does not. The method of exposition follows that used by GRILICHES [1961].

First example.   Consider the system:

$$x_t = bx_{t-1} + \varepsilon_t,$$
$$\varepsilon_t = \varrho\varepsilon_{t-1} + \eta_t, \tag{40}$$

where the first equation defines the model valid for the observable variable x_t, while the second states the law which governs the unobservable errors ε_t. The η_t process is purely random.

After elimination of the ε_t, the system can be written:

$$x_t = (b + \varrho)x_{t-1} - b\varrho x_{t-2} + \eta_t. \tag{41}$$

To evaluate the asymptotic bias in b^*, we multiply (41) by x_{t-1} and sum with respect to t:

$$\sum x_t x_{t-1} = (b + \varrho)\sum x_{t-1}^2 - b\varrho \sum x_{t-1}x_{t-2} + \sum \eta_t x_{t-1}.$$

or again:

$$b^* = b + \varrho - b\varrho \frac{\sum x_{t-1}x_{t-2}}{\sum x_{t-1}^2} + \frac{\sum \eta_t x_{t-1}}{\sum x_{t-1}^2}.$$

When the number of observations tends to infinity, the first ratio has the same probability limit as b^*, and the second ratio tends in probability to zero. So the above equation can be written:

$$\lim b^* = b + \varrho - b\varrho \lim b^*,$$

which gives the formula:

$$\lim b^* = \frac{b + \varrho}{1 + b\varrho}. \tag{42}$$

So the estimate b^* contains a bias which tends to

$$\frac{\varrho(1 - b^2)}{1 + b\varrho}.$$

Figure 2 shows how $\lim b^*$ varies as a function of ϱ in the case where $b = 0.5$. We see that the error is considerable, even for small values of ϱ. Formula (42) shows also that $\lim b^*$ varies between -1 and 1, whatever b may be.

Suppose also that, with a view to estimating ϱ, we calculate the first auto-correlation coefficient of the residuals:

$$\varepsilon_t^* = x_t - b^* x_{t-1}.$$

Let this coefficient be

$$\varrho^* = \frac{\sum \varepsilon_t^* \varepsilon_{t-1}^*}{\sum \varepsilon_t^{*2}}.$$

According to the usual formulae:

$$\frac{1}{T}\sum \varepsilon_t^{*2} = \frac{1}{T}\sum x_t^2 - b^{*2} \cdot \frac{1}{T}\sum x_{t-1}^2.$$

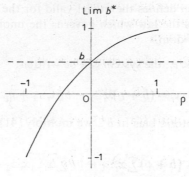

Fig. 2.

Now, $(1/T)\sum x_t^2$ tends in probability to the variance of x_t, namely σ_x^2, since the linear process defined by (22) is ergodic. Thus $(1/T)\sum \varepsilon_t^{*2}$ tends to $(1-b^{*2})\sigma_x^2$. Similarly it follows from the definitions of b^* and ε^* that

$$\frac{1}{T}\sum \varepsilon_t^* \varepsilon_{t-1}^* = -b^* \cdot \frac{1}{T}\sum x_t x_{t-2} + b^{*2} \cdot \frac{1}{T}\sum x_{t-1} x_{t-2}.$$

Multiplying the relation (41) by x_{t-2}, summing with respect to t, subtracting

$$-b^* \cdot \frac{1}{T}\sum x_{t-1} x_{t-2},$$

and taking the probability limits, we see that the limit of

$$\frac{1}{T}\sum x_t x_{t-2} - b^* \frac{1}{T}\sum x_{t-1} x_{t-2}$$

is equal to that of

$$[(b+\varrho - b^*)b^* - \varrho b]\sigma_x^2.$$

Thus ϱ^* behaves in the limit like

$$\frac{-b^*[(b+\varrho - b^*)b^* - \varrho b]}{1-b^{*2}}.$$

And so finally:

$$\lim \varrho^* = \frac{\varrho b(b+\varrho)}{1+b\varrho}. \tag{43}$$

Formulae (42) and (43) imply:

$$\lim (b^* + \varrho^*) = b + \varrho.$$

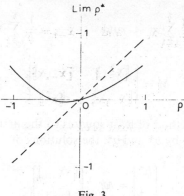

Fig. 3.

So estimation of ϱ by ϱ^* entails an asymptotic bias which is exactly opposite to that entailed in estimation of b by b^*. Figure 3 shows how ϱ^* varies as a function of ϱ, for $b=0.50$. We see that ϱ^* considerably underestimates the correlation among the errors.

The study of this example leads to two conclusions. In the first place, *correlation of the errors may greatly bias estimation of the parameters of an autoregressive model, when this estimation is carried out by the method of least squares.* There may be very considerable bias affecting the results obtained. In the second place, *it is not possible to make a correct assessment of the correlation of the errors using the autocorrelation coefficient of the residuals.* The latter is generally near zero even if the correlation is fairly considerable.

Of course this is rather an extreme example. The model (32) contains no exogenous variables. The following example will show that the situation can be much improved when they are present.

Second example. Consider the system:

$$x_t = bx_{t-1} + az_t + c + \varepsilon_t,$$
$$\varepsilon_t = \varrho\varepsilon_{t-1} + \eta_t,$$

(44)

with the same definitions as those of system (40), a real exogenous variable z_t and a constant term c. In accordance with the usual assumptions, we suppose that the η_t are independent of the z_θ.

To simplify the formulae, we introduce a new notation for sample moments; we set for example $[xx_{-1}]$ for

$$\frac{1}{T}\sum_{t=1}^{T}(x_t - \bar{x})(x_{t-1} - \bar{x}_{-1}),$$

where

$$\bar{x} = \frac{1}{T} \sum_{t=1}^{T} x_t \quad \text{and} \quad \bar{x}_{-1} = \frac{1}{T} \sum_{t=1}^{T} x_{t-1},$$

and write

$$M = \begin{bmatrix} [x^2_{-1}] & [x_{-1}x] \\ [x_{-1}x] & [x^2] \end{bmatrix}.$$

Application of the method of least squares to the first equation of (36) leads to estimation of b and a by b^* and a^*, the solutions of

$$\begin{bmatrix} b^* \\ a^* \end{bmatrix} = M^{-1} \begin{bmatrix} [xx_{-1}] \\ [xz] \end{bmatrix}.$$

Since x_t obeys the relations of (36), the above equality can also be written:

$$\begin{bmatrix} b^* \\ a^* \end{bmatrix} - \begin{bmatrix} b \\ a \end{bmatrix} = \varrho M^{-1} \begin{bmatrix} [\varepsilon_{-1}x_{-1}] \\ [\varepsilon_{-1}z] \end{bmatrix} + M^{-1} \begin{bmatrix} [\eta x_{-1}] \\ [\eta z] \end{bmatrix}.$$

When the number of observations tends to infinity, the last vector tends in probability to zero. Thus[†]

$$\begin{bmatrix} b^* \\ a^* \end{bmatrix} - \begin{bmatrix} b \\ a \end{bmatrix} \to \varrho \begin{bmatrix} \lambda_b \\ \lambda_a \end{bmatrix} \tag{45}$$

where by definition λ_b and λ_a are the coefficients of the least squares regression of ε_{-1} on x_{t-1} and z_t. So we need only examine the probability limits of λ_b and λ_a, which are the solutions of the system

$$[x^2_{-1}]\lambda_b + [x_{-1}z]\lambda_a = [\varepsilon_{-1}x_{-1}],$$
$$[x_{-1}z]\lambda_b + [z^2]\lambda_a = [\varepsilon_{-1}z]. \tag{46}$$

First of all it is simple to prove that *the effect of introducing the exogenous variable z_t is to reduce the absolute value of the asymptotic bias of b^**. For since $[\varepsilon_{-1}z]$ tends in probability to zero, elimination of λ_a in (46) leads to

$$\lambda_b \left\{ [x^2_{-1}] - \frac{[x_{-1}z]^2}{[z^2]} \right\} \to [\varepsilon_{-1}x_{-1}]. \tag{47}$$

We introduce the variables ξ_t and w_t defined by formulae (34) above, and write the model:

[†] In this and the following formulae, the sign $\to$ means that both terms tend in probability to the same limit.

$$x_t = aw_t + \frac{c}{1-b} + \xi_t.$$

In these conditions

$$[x_{-1}^2] \to a^2[w_{-1}^2] + [\xi_{-1}^2], \qquad [x_{-1}z] \to a[w_{-1}z]$$

and

$$\left\{ [x_{-1}^2] - \frac{[x_{-1}z]^2}{[z^2]} \right\} \to \left\{ [\xi_{-1}^2] + a^2 \left[[w_{-1}^2] - \frac{[w_{-1}z]^2}{[z^2]} \right] \right\}.$$

In the right hand side, the term in square brackets is equal to the residual variance of the regression of w_{t-1} on z_t. It is necessarily positive (and zero only when z_t is constant). The multiplier of λ_b in formula (47) is therefore asymptotically greater than $[\xi_{-1}^2]$, which is its value if there is no exogenous variable. As for the right hand side of formula (47), it is asymptotically equivalent to $[\varepsilon_{-1}\xi_{-1}]$; it has the same limit whether or not the model contains an exogenous variable. Thus the limit of λ_b and that of b^*-b are maximal in absolute value when there is no exogenous variable.

Similarly taking probability limits in system (46) we find that asymptotically

$$\left[\frac{1+b\varrho}{(1-b\varrho)(1-b^2)} \cdot \frac{\sigma^2}{a^2S^2} + \frac{1+2H}{1-b^2} \right] \lambda_b + \frac{H}{ba} \lambda_a \to \frac{1}{1-b\varrho} \cdot \frac{\sigma^2}{a^2S^2}$$

$$\frac{aH}{b} \lambda_b \qquad\qquad + \lambda_a \to 0.$$

(48)

where

$$\sigma^2 = E(\varepsilon_t^2); \qquad S^2 = \lim \frac{1}{T}\sum (z_t - \bar{z})^2$$

and

$$H = \sum_{\tau=1}^{\infty} b^{\tau} R_{\tau},$$

the R_τ being the autocorrelation coefficients of the z_t, defined as in the previous chapter. System (48) allows us to calculate the values of the asymptotic biases for any system of values of the coefficients and any sequence of the z_t. We see in particular that the bias is of the order of $\alpha = \sigma^2/a^2S^2$. It will therefore be small if variability of the exogenous variables greatly exceeds that of the errors and if the coefficient a is not near zero.

For example, consider the case where $b=0.60$ and $\varrho=0.50$. If there is no exogenous variable, the asymptotic bias of b^* is about 0.25. The quantity H is at most 1.5. If $H=1.2$, which corresponds to a very smooth evolution of the exogenous variable, then $\lim (b^*-b)$ is about 0.20 when $\alpha=1$ and about 0.08 when $\alpha=0.25$. If $H=0$, that is, if the exogenous variable has an irregular evolution, then $\lim (b^* - b)$ is about 0.17 when $\alpha = 1$ and about 0.08 when $\alpha = 0.25$.

In short the asymptotic bias remains significant in most cases. It would seriously affect the conclusions which we might be tempted to draw from the examination of large samples for which the variances of b^* and a^* would be small.

This analytic examination of two simple examples allows us to assess the asymptotic tendencies of the least squares estimates when the errors are auto-correlated. But it gives only imperfect information about the results of practical econometric investigations which in most cases are based on short series of ob-servations. In the paper mentioned earlier (cf. MALINVAUD [1961b]) artificial samples were constructed for the model (44), that used in the second example above. The three following conclusions were drawn from this analysis.

(i) The asymptotic bias calculated in accordance with formulae (45) and (48) seems almost equal to the difference between the expected values of the estimate in the model with serially correlated errors on the one hand and in the corre-sponding model with independent errors on the other. In other words we can obtain a fairly exact idea of $E(b^*)$ or $E(a^*)$ in the model with serially correlated errors by adding the asymptotic bias to the value of $E(b^*)$ or $E(a^*)$ in the model with independent errors. It may even happen sometimes that the asymptotic bias compensates the bias whose existence was established in section 3 (see in particular fig. 1).

(ii) The actual variances of the estimates b^* and a^* obviously differ from the values given by the usual formulae for non-autoregressive models with in-dependent errors. On the contrary, they appear on the average as near the values given by the formulae which apply to non-autoregressive models with serially correlated errors, lagged endogenous variables being then treated as exogenous variables (see ch. 12 § 5).

(iii) As was shown by the analytic study of the first example, the residuals ε_t^* are clearly less autocorrelated than the errors ε_t. In the samples considered, while the errors constituted a first order autoregressive process with a coefficient equal to 0.50, the first autocorrelation coefficient of the residuals had values which were widely dispersed about an average near 0.30.

This last statement has an important consequence for tests relating to auto-correlation of the errors. Certainly the theory of the test proposed by Durbin and Watson applies only to non-autoregressive models. But it often happens that this test is used, for want of any other, in autoregressive models, and that reference is made to the tables from which an extract is given in ch. 12 § 2. In fact, since the residuals are less autocorrelated than the errors, the *Durbin-Watson test is not very powerful in autoregressive models*. Thus in the examples considered, in which the errors constituted the process:

$$\varepsilon_t = 0.5\,\varepsilon_{t-1} + \eta_t, \tag{49}$$

d^* was less than d_L in only one case out of four (d_L being taken to correspond to a 5% significance level). So in most cases the test does not reveal a moderate degree of serial correlation of the errors.

DURBIN [1967] proves that in autoregressive models the significance level of the usual Durbin-Watson test differs also asymptotically from that given in the tables. He also suggests an asymptotically valid test for such models.

If the alternative hypothesis specifies a first-order autoregressive process of the errors, this test compares with a standardized normal variable the quantity

$$\frac{1}{k} \cdot \frac{\sum_{t=2}^{T} \varepsilon_t^* \varepsilon_{t-1}^*}{\sum_{t=2}^{T} \varepsilon_{t-1}^{*2}} \tag{50}$$

where k is the square root of

$$k^2 = \frac{1}{T} - \sigma^{*2}(b_1^*) \tag{51}$$

and $\sigma^{*2}(b_1^*)$ is the usual estimate of the variance of b_1^* (as defined in section 2 of this chapter). In the case of independence, (50) is asymptotically normally distributed with zero mean and standard deviation 1. (If (51) gives a negative value for k^2, the hypothesis of independence is rejected.)

When the errors are normally distributed this test is asymptotically equivalent to the likelihood ratio test, so that it should have good asymptotic efficiency. However, it may be that its power remains small in small samples because the correlation of the residuals is usually less marked than that of the errors. For the 100 examples in MALINVAUD [1961b], and for the process (49), the value of (50) is greater than 1.28 (the theoretical 10% critical value against the alternative of positive correlation) in 62 cases, which with one exception are precisely those cases in which the Durbin-Watson statistic is less than d_2 at the 10% significance level. Other investigations based on the Monte Carlo method were carried out by MADDALA and RAO [1973] and by KENKEL [1974], from which it appears that the test based on (50) is not clearly preferable in practice to other conceivable tests.

If we wish fully to understand the properties of the method of least squares in autoregressive models with serially correlated errors, we must also examine the formulae applied for prediction. Thus, for the model (28) of the second example, predictions are usually obtained by means of the recurrence relations:

$$x_{T+1}^P = b^* x_T + a^* z_{T+1} + c^*$$

$$x_{T+\theta}^P = b^* x_{T+\theta-1}^P + a^* z_{T+\theta} + c^* \qquad \text{for} \qquad \theta = 2, 3, \ldots .$$

These predictions are obviously affected by the asymptotic bias in b^*, a^*

and c^*; they are certainly biased, except for favourable values of the sequence of the exogenous variables $z_{T+1}, z_{T+2}, \ldots, z_{T+\theta}, \ldots$. Nevertheless it may be the case that these biases are not very large in many applications.

For suppose that in the model:

$$x_t = bx_{t-1} + az_t + c + \varepsilon_t, \qquad (44)$$

the errors constitute the process:

$$\varepsilon_t = \varrho\varepsilon_{t-1} + \eta_t,$$

where the η_t make a purely random process. The x_t then satisfy:

$$x_t = (b + \varrho)x_{t-1} - b\varrho x_{t-2} + az_t - a\varrho z_{t-1} + c(1 - \varrho) + \eta_t. \qquad (52)$$

So the application to (44) of the method of least squares, as if the ε_t were purely random, is equivalent to making in (52) the specification error which consists of taking no account of the predetermined variables x_{t-2} and z_{t-1}. When we discussed the effect of specification errors of this kind in non-autoregressive models, we saw that they do not entail bias in prediction, provided that the omitted variables are connected to the other exogenous variables by stable stochastic linear relations[†]. So we may think that the bias in prediction will remain small in the models now considered if the evolution of the exogenous variables during the prediction period follows the average evolution during the estimation period.

However, in this case as for non-autoregressive models, there is a loss in precision if we ignore the serial correlation of the errors ε_t which appear in relation (44), or the presence of the variables x_{t-2} and z_{t-1} in formula (52). At least when the observed sample is fairly large, the variance of the usual predictions is greater than that of the predictions which take better advantage of the autoregressive representation (52).

This discussion leads us naturally to the examination of estimation methods other than direct least squares.

6 Various methods for treating serial correlation of the errors

When the errors are not autocorrelated, least squares fitting is suitable for autoregressive models as for simple regression models. Similarly the methods used for dealing with autocorrelation of the errors are virtually the same in both types of model. But their properties depend to a large extent on the presence or absence of lagged endogenous variables. So we shall return to the same esti-

---

[†] Cf. ch. 8 § 7(ii). We then discussed only exogenous variables proper, and the reasoning cannot be transposed rigorously to the case in which some of the omitted variables are lagged values of the endogenous variables. Nevertheless it suggests that a more general phenomenon exists.

mation procedures as in ch. 12 § 7, but shall find different properties for them.

(a) *If the precise form of correlation of the errors is known,* a change of variables may be applied in order to transform the model in such a way as to eliminate this correlation, and we may then go on to least squares fitting. The estimates thus obtained are consistent and enjoy the asymptotic properties stated in theorems 1 and 2 above.

Suppose that in the second example of the previous section, the value of ϱ is known a priori. The model can be written:

$$(x_t - \varrho x_{t-1}) = b(x_{t-1} - \varrho x_{t-2}) + a(z_t - \varrho z_{t-1}) + \eta_t.$$

Least squares regression of $x_t - \varrho x_{t-1}$ on $x_{t-1} - \varrho x_{t-2}$ and $z_t - \varrho z_{t-1}$ yields the consistent estimates $\hat{b}$ and $\hat{a}$ of b and a. The considerations presented in ch. 12 suggest that, in small samples, the first observations x_1, x_0 (assumed to be known), z_1 must be replaced respectively by $\sqrt{1-\varrho^2}x_1$, $\sqrt{1-\varrho^2}x_0$, $\sqrt{1-\varrho^2}z_1$. However, MAESHIRO and HINH [1978] show that, in such samples, ordinary least squares may still be more efficient if ϱ is small and b is large.

Similarly prediction of the values of the $x_{T+\theta}$ may be made using the recurrence formulae:

$$x_{T+\theta}^P = \varrho x_{T+\theta-1}^P + \hat{b}(x_{T+\theta-1}^P - \varrho x_{T+\theta-2}^P) + \hat{a}(z_{T+\theta} - \varrho z_{T+\theta-1}).$$

This approach is justified as in section 4 above.

The correlation of the errors is not generally so well known, so that we must resort to methods which are less simple or less strongly justified.

(b) In order to assess the importance of the effect of this correlation on the estimates obtained, *two least squares fittings are sometimes carried out, one on the variables themselves* (x_t, x_{t-1} and z_t for example) *and the other on their first differences* ($x_t - x_{t-1}$, $x_{t-1} - x_{t-2}$ and $z_t - z_{t-1}$ for example). If the results are similar, we are entitled to think that the values of the coefficients are fairly well determined without there being any need for deeper investigation of the correlation of the errors (cf. ch. 12 § 7, (d)).

However, we should not have too many illusions about the usefulness of this method. It only allows us to see if the estimates depend on the assumptions made about the correlation of the errors, but yields no solution when the estimates actually do so depend.

Thus, for the first example of the previous section, we know that least squares fitting applied to the variables x_t and x_{t-1} yields an estimate b^* which tends in probability to

$$\frac{b + \varrho}{1 + b\varrho}.$$

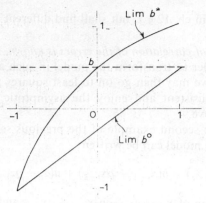

Fig. 4.

Similarly least squares fitting applied to the first differences yields the estimate:

$$b^0 = \frac{\sum(x_t - x_{t-1})(x_{t-1} - x_{t-2})}{\sum(x_{t-1} - x_{t-2})^2},$$

whose probability limit is

$$\tfrac{1}{2}[b(1 + \varrho) - (1 - \varrho)].$$

Figure 4 shows how $\lim b^*$ and $\lim b^0$ vary as functions of ϱ when $b = 0.5$. We see that there is a considerable interval between these two limits. Thus for $\varrho = 0.5$, this interval tends in probability to

$$0.125 \leqq b \leqq 0.800.$$

It is too large to allow us to obtain a useful estimate of b.

The presence of exogenous variables reduces this interval, but does not always do this sufficiently for its extent to appear negligible.

(c) The coefficients of the autoregressive model and the parameters characterizing the correlation of the errors can be *estimated simultaneously*.

For example, consider the model:

$$x_t = bx_{t-1} + az_t + c + \varepsilon_t \tag{44}$$

and suppose that we know a priori that the errors constitute a first order autoregressive process:

$$\varepsilon_t = \varrho\varepsilon_{t-1} + \eta_t.$$

The x_t then satisfy the relation

$$x_t = (b + \varrho)x_{t-1} - b\varrho x_{t-2} + az_t - a\varrho z_{t-1} + c(1 - \varrho) + \eta_t. \tag{52}$$

By applying the iterative method defined in chapter 12 § 7, (b), we can determine the estimates $\hat{b}$, $\hat{a}$, $\hat{c}$ and $\hat{\varrho}$ which minimize the sum of squares of the residuals corresponding to formula (52). Transposing Durbin's suggestion used in ch. 12 § 7, (c), we can alternatively carry out an ordinary regression on a relation of the form:

$$x_t = b_1 x_{t-1} + b_2 x_{t-2} + a_0 z_t + a_1 z_{t-1} + d + \eta_t,$$

then estimate ϱ by $\varrho^* = -a_1^*/a_0^*$, and finally estimate b, a and c by means of a second ordinary regression of $x_t - \varrho^* x_{t-1}$ on $x_{t-1} - \varrho^* x_{t-2}$ and $z_t - \varrho^* z_{t-1}$. Finally, we can find the maximum likelihood estimators, as in HENDRY and TRIVEDI [1972][†].

Simultaneous estimation of the correlation of the errors and the coefficients of the model makes it possible to use formula (52) for computing predictions of the endogenous variable. For if the model now considered is completely known a priori, the best predictions are made using the recurrence formulae:

$$x_{T+\theta}^P = (b + \varrho)x_{T+\theta-1}^P - b\varrho x_{T+\theta-2}^P + a z_{T+\theta} - a\varrho z_{T+\theta-1} + c(1 - \varrho).$$

Knowing the consistent estimates $\hat{b}$, $\hat{a}$, $\hat{c}$ and $\hat{\varrho}$ of the coefficients, we can therefore apply for the predictions the formulae:

$$x_{T+\theta}^P = (\hat{b} + \hat{\varrho})x_{T+\theta-1}^P - \hat{b}\hat{\varrho}x_{T+\theta-2}^P + \hat{a}z_{T+\theta} - \hat{a}\hat{\varrho}z_{T+\theta-1} + \hat{c}(1 - \hat{\varrho}). \tag{53}$$

So in principle, simultaneous estimation of the coefficients of the model and the correlation of the errors provides a satisfactory solution to the problem.

However, we should not delude ourselves as to the practical scope of this method in econometrics. For it is justified by theorems 1 and 2 which identify asymptotic properties enjoyed by the least squares estimate of the auto-regressive form with independent errors, form (52) in our example, or by maximum likelihood estimators[††]. But in the first place, considerable asymptotic bias may remain if the nature of the correlation of the errors is incorrectly specified; in the second place, the properties of these estimates in small samples appear much less favourable than their asymptotic properties.

[†] They consider the case of a moving average error process as well as the case of an autoregressive process, whereas ANDERSON [1977] discusses the general case of an autoregressive moving average process. HANNAN and NICHOLLS [1972] define and apply an asymptotically efficient iterative method for the case of moving average errors. ESPASA and SARGAN [1977] define the maximum likelihood estimator for the case in which the spectrum of the errors is a step function.

[††] Theorems 1 and 2 do not apply directly when, as here, the coefficients of the autoregressive form are subject to a priori restrictions. However, we can establish by means of proofs similar to those used for non-linear models (ch. 9) that least squares fitting yields consistent estimates which are also asymptotically efficient in the case where the errors are normally distributed. We can similarly determine the asymptotic covariance matrix of these estimates.

Let us consider the first point. If it is a question only of getting some indication about the effect of correlation of the errors on statistical methods which assume them to be independent, we may well take a simple autoregressive process for the errors. So we can stipulate that the errors obey a relation of the type:

$$\varepsilon_t = \varrho \varepsilon_{t-1} + \eta_t. \tag{54}$$

But, if it is a question of estimating the autocorrelation structure, the specification (54) may not describe correctly the process of the errors. With this latter application in view, it is important to investigate the sensitivity of the estimates of the coefficients in relation to the assumptions made about the nature of this process. Now, it seems that the estimates are indeed sensitive.

For example, suppose the following formulae describe the model and the process of the errors:

$$x_t = 0.5\, x_{t-1} + \varepsilon_t,$$
$$\varepsilon_t = 0.3\, \varepsilon_{t-1} + 0.1\, \varepsilon_{t-2} + \eta_t, \tag{55}$$

where the η_t constitute a purely random process. Suppose that the econometrician does not know the exact form of system (55) and chooses the specification:

$$x_t = bx_{t-1} + \varepsilon_t,$$
$$\varepsilon_t = \varrho \varepsilon_{t-1} + \eta_t, \tag{56}$$

which, we may say in passing, may appear very near the correct specification. Let $\hat{b}$ and $\hat{\varrho}$ be the estimates of b and ϱ obtained from least squares fitting to the autoregressive form deduced from (56), namely:

$$x_t = (b + \varrho)x_{t-1} - b\varrho x_{t-2} + \eta_t. \tag{57}$$

It is easy to prove that $\hat{b}$ and $\hat{\varrho}$ tend in probability to 0.67 and 0.13 respectively when the number of observations tends to infinity. So there is an asymptotic bias of 0.17 in the estimate of b, and this is so although we did not choose an extreme situation.

We note, however, in this case that the asymptotic bias of the estimates will not greatly affect the predictions. For, while system (55) implies the autoregressive form:

$$x_t = 0.80\, x_{t-1} - 0.05\, x_{t-2} - 0.05\, x_{t-3} + \eta_t,$$

least squares fitting to (49) leads asymptotically to the very similar form:

$$x_t = 0.80\, x_{t-1} - 0.09\, x_{t-2} + \eta_t.$$

This suggests therefore that *the estimates of the coefficients may be imprecise*;

but the predictions to which they lead are nevertheless fairly good. The same conclusions seem to hold for small samples, at least if the results of the previously quoted analysis of some artificial samples (cf. MALINVAUD [1961b]) can be generalized.

The following model was chosen:

$$x_t = bx_{t-1} + az_t + c + \varepsilon_t,$$

$$\varepsilon_t = \varrho\varepsilon_{t-1} + \eta_t,$$

the parameters having the following values: $b=0.60$; $a=0.40$; $c=0.00$; $\varrho=0.50$. These parameters were estimated simultaneously from successive samples of twenty observations by means of the iterative method mentioned above. The estimates $\hat{\varrho}$ were very widely dispersed with mean 0.25 and standard deviation 0.28. Similarly the estimates of the coefficients b, a and c showed greater dispersion on either side of the true values than did the direct estimates obtained by least squares fitting to:

$$x_t = bx_{t-1} + az_t + c + \varepsilon_t$$

(estimates which 'ignore' the correlation of the errors). Nevertheless, the predictions determined by the formulae (53) on the basis of simultaneous estimation of the coefficients and of ϱ were comparable in precision to those deduced from the formulae (37) which ignore the correlation of the errors. The formulae (53) even gave more precise results for the very first prediction ($\theta=1$).

The Monte Carlo studies carried out by HENDRY and TRIVEDI [1972] suggest that simultaneous estimation of the coefficients of the model and the correlation of the errors is to be recommended for fairly long series of, for example, 50 observations. According to SCHMIDT [1971], simultaneous estimation would appear to be advantageous even with series of 20 observations. But MADDALA and RAO [1973] show that direct least squares fitting remains preferable if the correlation of the errors does not exceed that of the exogenous variables and the autocorrelation coefficient b.

(d) An estimation method has been proposed specially for autoregressive models with serially correlated errors. It consists of using certain of the lagged exogenous variables as *instrumental variables.*

We consider the model already discussed:

$$x_t = bx_{t-1} + az_t + \varepsilon_t \tag{58}$$

and formulate no assumption about the errors ε_t unless that their expected value is zero whatever the values of the exogenous variables z_t.

The existence of the asymptotic bias when (58) is fitted by the method of least squares arises from the fact that x_{t-1} and ε_t are not independent when there is a stochastic dependence between ε_t and the errors in previous periods. To eliminate this difficulty, we can substitute z_{t-1} for x_{t-1} as 'instrumental variable' in the normal equations defining the estimates. The exogenous variable z_t and its lagged value z_{t-1} are then the two instrumental variables in estimation[†]; and the coefficients b and a are estimated by the solutions $\hat{b}$ and $\hat{a}$ of the system:

$$\sum x_t z_t = \hat{b} \sum z_{t-1} z_t + \hat{a} \sum z_t^2,$$

$$\sum x_t z_{t-1} = \hat{b} \sum x_{t-1} z_{t-1} + \hat{a} \sum z_t z_{t-1}. \tag{59}$$

We can easily determine probability limits:

$$\frac{1}{T} \sum x_t z_t \to a S^2 (H + 1),$$

$$\frac{1}{T} \sum x_{t-1} z_t \to \frac{a S^2}{b} H,$$

$$\frac{1}{T} \sum x_t z_{t-1} \to a S^2 (R_1 + b + bH),$$

using the same definitions as in section 5 for S^2, R_τ and H. So, at the limit, system (59) becomes

$$abH + ab = a\hat{b}H + \hat{a}b,$$

$$abH + ab + aR_1 = a\hat{b}H + a\hat{b} + \hat{a}R_1,$$

or again:

$$abH + ab = a\hat{b}H + \hat{a}b,$$

$$aR_1 = a\hat{b} + \hat{a}(R_1 - b),$$

whose solution is in fact $\hat{b} = b$ and $\hat{a} = a$.

If the errors ε_t satisfy assumption 1, then the standard deviations of $\hat{b}$ and $\hat{a}$ are greater than those of the least squares estimates b^* and a^*. This loss of precision may, however, be acceptable whenever it is uncertain that successive errors are independent and when the number of observations is sufficiently large.

The study of artificial samples confirms this loss of precision. For the models discussed in MALINVAUD [1961b], the standard deviations of $\hat{b}$ and $\hat{a}$ were about 50% greater than those of b^* and a^*. Since the asymptotic bias was small, least squares fitting gave better results than estimation with the instrumental variables

---

[†] More generally, if the model contains h lagged values of the endogenous variable and m exogenous variables, the instrumental variables are the z_{jt} themselves and h lagged values $z_{j,t-\tau}$. The choice of these values is inspired by the principles given in ch. 10.

z_t and z_{t-1}. But the samples contained only about twenty observations. Estimation using instrumental variables would seem preferable if considerably longer series have to be analyzed. This impression is confirmed by the results of another study of artificial samples, which we shall now discuss briefly in connection with a last estimation method.

(e) WALLIS [1967] proposes estimation using instrumental variables, as described above, as a first step. Since the estimates of the coefficients are consistent, the residuals ε_t can be used to estimate the correlation of the errors; we can then carry out further estimation using precisely the method adapted to this correlation of the errors. WALLIS [1972 a] shows that the asymptotic efficiency of the resulting estimate of the coefficients is little less than the efficiency of the maximum likelihood estimate.

For example, if a first-order autoregressive process of the type (54) is specified a priori for the errors, we calculate $\hat{\rho}$, the first autocorrelation coefficient of the ε_t. This estimate will have no asymptotic bias if the chosen specification is correct. So it can be used for applying linear estimation methods. Thus, to fit model (58), we find the regression of $x_t - \hat{\rho} x_{t-1}$ on

$$x_{t-1} - \hat{\rho} x_{t-2} \quad \text{and} \quad z_t - \hat{\rho} z_{t-1}.$$

Wallis, who calls this the 'generalized least squares method' investigated its properties using artificial samples each of 50 observations. In the case of considerable correlation of the errors, the estimators obtained were found to be superior both to those resulting from ordinary regressions applied directly to the model and to those arising from the methods using instrumental variables (the $\hat{a}$ and $\hat{b}$ of section (d) above).

This examination of the various possible methods for treating autoregressive models with serially correlated errors leads to rather a pessimistic conclusion. When the available series are short, none of the proposed methods guarantees precise estimation of the serial correlation of the errors. In these conditions, direct least squares fitting is often the most reasonable method of estimating the coefficients. But the distribution of the estimated coefficients cannot be determined very well. So the tests and confidence intervals are necessarily very approximate.

CHAPTER 14

Distributed lag models

1 Introduction [†]

The behavioral relations involved in our economic models describe how one or more endogenous variables are determined from the values taken by certain exogenous variables. The dependence between the exogenous and endogenous variables is rarely immediate since time is needed for economic decisions to be made. Of course the period of observation is generally fairly lengthy, so that often no explicit account has to be taken in the relations of the lag in behavior. A reaction that is completed within two or three months can be considered as immediate if the observation period is annual. But some reactions take longer. Lags must often be expressed in our models, and this must be increasingly so with the growing practice of fitting quarterly or even monthly data.

In most cases it would be wrong to assume that changes in behavior take place once and for all after some fixed delay. If the exogenous variables remained constant over a long period and then underwent a violent change at time t_0 with no subsequent variation we should see not a violent change in each endogenous variable at time $t_0 + \theta$, but rather the progression from one equilibrium value to another, with an evolution similar to that shown in fig. 1.

To fix ideas, suppose that there is a single endogenous variable x_t and a single exogenous variable z_t taking the value z^0 before t_0 and z^1 from t_0 onwards. Suppose also that the dependence between z_t and x_t is linear and exact in such

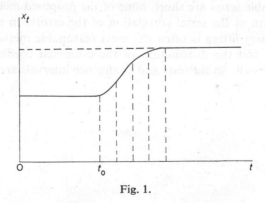

Fig. 1.

[†] On the subject of this chapter the reader is referred to the survey articles by GRILICHES [1967] and by SIMS [1974].

a way that the equilibrium value of x_t is $az^0 + b$ before t_0 and $az^1 + b$ after adjustment to the new value of z_t has been made. It is natural to assume that in the interval the value of x_t depends linearly on z^0 and z^1 with coefficients which are functions only of the difference $t - t_0$. We can then write:

$$x_{t_0 + \tau} = a d_\tau z^1 + a(1 - d_\tau) z^0 + b, \qquad \tau \geqq 0.$$

We can set:

$$c_0 = d_0 \quad \text{and} \quad c_\tau = d_\tau - d_{\tau - 1} \quad \text{for} \quad \tau > 0$$

and write:

$$x_{t_0 + \tau} = a(c_0 + c_1 + \cdots + c_\tau) z^1 + a(c_{\tau + 1} + c_{\tau + 2} + \cdots + c_h) z^0 + b,$$

having assumed that d_τ equals 1 from h onwards, and that consequently $c_\tau = 0$ for $\tau > h$. The same formulae would apply with $h = \infty$ when the d_τ increase indefinitely and tend to 1.

More generally, if the exogenous variable z_t has any kind of evolution, the value of the endogenous variable x_t can be considered as a linear function of the previous values of z_t, say:

$$x_t = a \sum_{\tau = 0}^{h} c_\tau z_{t - \tau} + b,$$

where

$$\sum_{\tau = 0}^{h} c_\tau = 1,$$

or again

$$x_t = a_0 z_t + a_1 z_{t - 1} + \cdots + a_h z_{t - h} + b$$

with no condition imposed on the coefficients a_τ. Finally, we should take account of random errors; this leads to the general form of the linear distributed lag model containing a single endogenous variable and a single exogenous variable:

$$x_t = a \sum_{\tau = 0}^{h} c_\tau z_{t - \tau} + b + \varepsilon_t, \tag{1}$$

where

$$\sum_{\tau = 0}^{h} c_\tau = 1, \tag{2}$$

or again

$$x_t = a_0 z_t + a_1 z_{t - 1} + \cdots + a_h z_{t - h} + b + \varepsilon_t. \tag{3}$$

We have already considered models of this type in our discussion of the consumption function (ch. 4, § 4). We shall discuss later some reasons for their appearance in econometric studies.

We have also seen how an equation of the type that applies to distributed lag models naturally interprets the result of a spectral analysis of the correlation between two series $\{x_t\}$ and $\{z_t\}$, provided that we can say a priori that $\{z_t\}$ is the cause of $\{x_t\}$ and not the converse (see equation (88) in chapter 11 and the example of the connection between production and employment in the textile industry). Such a spectral analysis would seem to constitute the best estimation method for distributed lag models when nothing is known a priori about the coefficients a_τ nor about the process of the errors ε_t, which however is assumed to be stationary. We should not find it surprising that in such a situation, estimation requires relatively long series.

Certainly we generally have *some a priori idea about the coefficients c_τ of the model*. For example, we may know that the c_τ are all positive, that is, that a change in one of the values z_θ will affect all the values x_t (for t varying from θ to $\theta + h$) in the same direction. We may also know that the first coefficients c_0, c_1, c_2 are the largest, and that c_τ decreases with τ at least after a certain value of τ.

If we wish to use short time series, we must adopt still more specific assumptions about the c_τ, which will make the sequence $\{c_\tau\}$ depend on a small number of parameters. So we shall now discuss some assumptions which may seem a priori to be convenient and admissible.

In certain cases an abstract economic analysis also suggests a precise functional relationship for the determination of the c_τ. In others, we may think ourselves justified in specifying the process of the errors fairly strictly.

For one or other of the above reasons, we often have to deal with a parametric model. The spectral analysis discussed in ch. 11, § 12 does not then provide the answer to the estimation problem with which we are faced. When the series are long enough, however, they may be used to verify the specific assumptions of the model which relate to the sequence of the a_τ. This verification may depend on comparing the transfer function resulting from spectral analysis with the transfer functions compatible with the model (see equation (72) of ch. 11 and equation (5) below).

We note also that there is an interesting correspondence between autoregressive models and distributed lag models. *A linear distributed lag model with only one exogenous variable* (or with exogenous variables not exceeding endogenous variables in number) *can usually be expressed in autoregressive form*. However, it may be necessary to introduce an infinite number of lagged values of the endogenous variable or variables. Similarly we can as a rule transform any stable autoregressive linear model with only one endogenous variable into a distributed lag model.

In fact relation (3) can be considered formally as a difference equation on z_t with the right hand side $x_t - b - \varepsilon_t$. It can generally be solved so that z_t appears as a linear function of the successive values of the right hand side. We shall see some very simple examples of this in section 3.

For a general approach to this question, let D denote the symbolic operator which transforms x_t into x_{t-1}, so that $Dx_t = x_{t-1}$, $D^2x_t = x_{t-2}$, etc. Relation (3) can be written

$$x_t = [a_0 + a_1D + \cdots + a_hD^h]z_t + b + \varepsilon_t,$$

the sum in the square brackets possibly being infinite.

Consider now the polynomial, or more generally, the function of the complex dummy variable z (not to be confused with z_t):

$$A(z) = \sum_{\tau=0}^{h} a_\tau z^\tau \qquad (4)$$

(the sum always converges for $|z| \le 1$ if the a_τ are positive, since they have a finite sum). We note in passing that with the function $A(z)$ we can associate

$$T(\omega) = A(e^{-i\omega}), \qquad (5)$$

the transfer function which links the sequence of the z_t to the sequence of the systematic parts of the $x_t - b$, or

$$\sum_\tau a_\tau z_{t-\tau}.$$

Taking account of (4), we can write (3) in the form

$$x_t = A(D)z_t + b + \varepsilon_t. \qquad (6)$$

We can usually associate with the function $B(z)$, which is the inverse of $A(z)$, a series expansion that can be written in the form

$$B(z) = \frac{1}{a_0} \sum_{\tau=0}^{\infty} b_\tau z^\tau \qquad \text{where} \qquad b_0 = 1. \qquad (7)$$

By definition, the product $B(z)A(z)$ is 1. Consider then the expression $a_0B(D)x_t$. In view of (5) and (7), we see that it is equal to both sides of the following equation

$$\sum_{\tau=0}^{\infty} b_\tau x_{t-\tau} = a_0 z_t + e + \xi_t \qquad (8)$$

where

$$e = b \sum_{\tau=0}^{\infty} b_\tau, \qquad \xi_t = \sum_{\tau=0}^{\infty} b_\tau \varepsilon_{t-\tau}, \qquad (9)$$

and this equation is therefore established. If the roots of $B(z) = 0$ all have modulus greater than 1 (a stability condition) and if the process $\{\varepsilon_t\}$ is stationary than so also is $\{\xi_t\}$. So model (3) takes the autoregressive form

$$x_t = -\sum_{\tau=1}^{\infty} b_\tau x_{t-\tau} + a_0 z_t + e + \xi_t. \qquad (10)$$

The inverse transformation of an autoregressive model into a distributed lag model can be carried out in a similar way. If there are several exogenous variables, this procedure generally allows us to eliminate the lags of only one of the variables. It leads to a mixed model containing lagged values both for the endogenous variable and for some of the exogenous variables.

As we shall see below, the correspondence is useful in that the β_τ take a remarkably simple form for certain general assumptions about the c_τ. Estimation based on the autoregressive form may then be easier than on the direct expression for the distributed lag model.

However, we must point out that the errors are transformed when we go from the one form to the other. So the properties of the ξ_t are not the same as those of the ε_t. If the errors ε_t are not serially correlated, the errors ξ_t generally will be. So we must examine in detail how the transformation operates on the errors, and study its consequences for the properties of fitting procedures based on the autoregressive form.

2 Distributed lag models in econometrics

Distributed lag models are likely to play a large part in econometrics. Because of technical, institutional and psychological rigidities, behavior is not adapted immediately to changes in the variables which condition it. In most cases this adaptation is progressive. This is well known in economic theory which often distinguishes between short run and long run reactions. Thus, a change in the relative prices of two raw materials which can be substituted for each other causes a speedy revision of production methods; but its full effect is felt only after the renewal of capital equipment designed to use one raw material rather than the other. Similarly, as we saw in ch. 4, reactions to an increase in disposable income take their full effect only after some time has passed. So to represent the facts properly we must often introduce distributed lags explicitly.

Moreover, the empirical determination of time-lags is very important in applied economics. The role of many economic measures can be correctly understood only if we know when they will begin to take effect and when their effects will be fully worked out. This is the case with reductions or increases in direct taxes, with changes in discount rates, with devaluation of the currency. The econometrician will naturally be consulted about the times at which these measures will have successive repercussions on behavior of various kinds.

The usefulness of distributed lag models was understood at a very early stage in econometrics by FISHER [1925, 1937], ALT [1942] and TINBERGEN [1949], to give only three examples. But gaps in statistical information made them difficult to apply. They must play an increasing part now that economic data are becoming more and more numerous and systematic.

The progressive nature of adaptations in behavior can be expressed in various ways. We can set up a distributed lag model without trying to make a precise analysis of the reasons for the many delays. This will often be the case in practice. The causes for these delays differ too widely for their formal representation to be of much use. But it also happens sometimes that the specification of the model attributes the distributed lags to a very precise cause and that the model therefore takes a particular form. We take from NERLOVE [1958] an example of fairly general relevance, since many phenomena are simply interpreted when we assume that the expectations of economic agents obey the assumption introduced below for prices.

We assume that the demand q_t for a particular product during a period t depends not only on its observed price, say p_t, but also on the price p_t^N which buyers consider to be normal for the product. The demand can be expressed as

$$q_t = ap_t + bp_t^N + c + \varepsilon_t.$$

In addition we assume that the normal price is revised upwards or downwards in each period according as it is lower or higher than the observed price. More precisely, we set:

$$p_t^N - p_{t-1}^N = \beta(p_t - p_{t-1}^N),$$

β being a numerical coefficient between 0 and 1 characterizing the way in which the notion of 'normal price' is formed. This finite difference equation is easily solved with respect to p_t^N. It gives

$$p_t^N = \beta \sum_{\tau=0}^{\infty} (1 - \beta)^\tau p_{t-\tau}.$$

The normal price is a weighted mean of prices observed in the past, the weights forming a decreasing geometric progression[†]. Thus the demand can be expressed as a function of the sequence of observed prices as follows:

$$q_t = \alpha p_t + \gamma \sum_{\tau=1}^{\infty} (1 - \beta)^\tau p_{t-\tau} + c + \varepsilon_t,$$

where $\alpha = a + b\beta$ and $\gamma = b\beta$. This is a case of a distributed lag model of the form (1), the coefficients c_τ decreasing at a constant rate from the second coefficient onwards.

We note also that taking account of progressive adaptations may lead in some cases to autoregressive models rather than to distributed lag models as such. Let us consider an example.

Suppose that the demand for a product is established as a function of a long term equilibrium level which buyers consider appropriate to the observed price.

[†] The same reasoning can be used to justify the expression given for 'permanent income' by FRIEDMAN (cf. formula (58) of ch. 4 and its insertion in the consumption function (14) in the same chapter).

Let q_t^E be this equilibrium demand for which we assume the relation:

$$q_t^E = ap_t + b + \varepsilon_t.$$

Actual demand differs from equilibrium demand because the domestic or industrial equipment in which the product must be used is not perfectly adapted, or more generally because certain costs are involved if the transition from one level of demand to another is too swift. In these conditions it seems natural to assume that the variation in demand $q_t - q_{t-1}$ depends on the difference between this demand and equilibrium demand $q_{t-1} - q_t^E$ and to set as a first approximation:

$$q_t - q_{t-1} = \delta(q_t^E - q_{t-1}) + \eta_t,$$

where δ is a coefficient between 0 and 1 and η_t a random error. From the above two equalities we can deduce immediately the autoregressive model:

$$q_t = (1 - \delta)q_{t-1} + \alpha p_t + \gamma + \xi_t,$$

where $\alpha = a\delta$, $\gamma = b\delta$ and $\xi_t = \eta_t + \delta\varepsilon_t$. Of course we can transform this model so as to eliminate q_{t-1} and include distributed lags in p_t. But this transformation has an effect on the random elements and we may hesitate to apply it for fear of losing the precise significance of the errors contained in the model.

The essential difference between the two preceding examples indeed lies in the part played by the random elements. In the first example, demand in period t depends only on the random factors occurring in this period along with observed price p_t and normal price p_t^N. In the second example, demand in period t depends indirectly on the random factors which took part in the determination of q_{t-1}, q_{t-1}^E, q_{t-2} etc. The effects of random disturbances are therefore felt over several periods instead of affecting demand only in the period in which they appear.

So we ought to be precise, so far as this is possible, in our ideas about the errors appearing in the relations from which the model is constructed. We must avoid the unfortunately current practice which consists of setting up a deterministic model, then applying to it various more or less complex transformations and only finally introducing errors with no discussion of their origin.

However, we must recognize the difficulty involved in precise specification of the properties of the random terms and try to determine the extent to which our methods are sensitive to imprecise specification. This we shall try to do.

It would be particularly helpful if distributed lag models could be strictly specified following a preliminary theoretical investigation of the behavior to be represented. And indeed, a distributed lag model can be justified as formalizing rational behavior in a rather general context, as shown by JUST [1977]. But rigorous research has also shown that the theory requires very particular and rather implausible assumptions if the model is to be simple. As NERLOVE

[1971] concludes, in this area the econometrician usually lacks a rigorous context.

3 Assumptions about the coefficients of the model

We generally have some idea about the coefficients $a_0, a_1, \ldots, a_h$. The influence of the value of an exogenous variable during period t_0 must be especially important for values of the endogenous variable in immediately succeeding periods. More precisely, the sequence $a_0, a_1, \ldots, a_h$ may be increasing in its first terms but must be continuously decreasing once the maximum has been passed. In many cases, even, the coefficient a_0 is the biggest of all and it is valid to assume that $a_\tau < a_{\tau-1}$ for every value of τ between 1 and h.

It is clearly advantageous to express this a priori knowledge in a simple analytic form, that is, to represent a_τ as a given function of τ and a small number of parameters. This is equivalent to assuming that the sequence of the a_τ belongs to some particular family. Since the data do not generally allow very precise determination of the coefficients of the model and since our a priori ideas about the sequence of the coefficients are rather summary, the choice of assumption for the a_τ is based on considerations of simplicity. This assumption must be of a kind which facilitates estimation.

Thus, FISHER [1935] proposed the assumption that, from a certain point onwards, the a's decrease in *arithmetic progression*. For example, a_0 and a_1 may have any values but succeeding coefficients obey

$$a_\tau = a_2 \left(1 - \frac{\tau - 2}{h - 1} \right) \qquad \text{for} \qquad 2 \leqq \tau \leqq h.$$

So the sequence of the coefficients depends on four parameters a_0, a_1, a_2 and h.

As KOYCK [1954] maintained, it often seems preferable to stipulate a *geometric decrease* affording an evolution of more satisfactory appearance and eliminating the problem of choosing the maximum lag h. For example, a_0 and a_1 may have any values and succeeding coefficients obey

$$a_\tau = a_2 c^{\tau-2} \qquad \text{for} \qquad \tau = 2, 3, \ldots \text{ ad infinitum.}$$

Again there are only four parameters a_0, a_1, a_2 and c. In addition, as we saw in the examples of the previous section, this type of assumption can be shown directly in the specification of the model.

Arithmetic and geometric assumptions have the drawback that they apply to the whole series only if the a_τ decrease immediately after the first term. It will sometimes be possible to assume that this is the case, but it will rarely be so if the period of observation is short (monthly or even quarterly). A formula applicable to the whole series has the advantage of reducing the total number of parameters to be estimated without necessarily prejudicing the representation of whatever a priori knowledge we may have.

ALMON [1965] made I. Fisher's proposal more flexible by adopting the assumption that the a_τ are expressed as a polynomial function of τ in an interval $[0, h]$, the degree of the polynomial being chosen in advance and considerably less than h. Many other assumptions can be used.

In the expression (1) of the model we included weighting coefficients c_τ subject to the condition:

$$\sum_\tau c_\tau = 1.$$

In addition it is generally natural to assume that all the a_τ have the same sign, and therefore that $c_\tau \geqslant 0$. Thus, the c_τ obey the same conditions as a probability distribution on the set of non-negative integers, and c_τ may be considered formally as the probability assigned to the integer τ. Our a priori ideas about the evolution of the a_τ imply that this distribution is unimodal and skew. Subject to this restraint, *the standard distributions on the non-negative integers provide as many possible assumptions for the sequence of the c_τ.*

In particular, FISHER [1937] proposed the *log-normal distribution*, according to which c_τ is the probability that a normal variable with mean μ and standard deviation σ takes a value between $\ln \tau$ and $\ln(\tau+1)$. Also THEIL and STERN [1960] fitted a distributed lag model in which the c_τ were computed from the probability density:

$$\lambda^2 \tau \exp(-\lambda\tau)$$

defined on the positive line $\tau \geqslant 0$.

The *geometric distribution:*

$$c_\tau = (1 - c)c^\tau$$

again gives us the assumption of geometric decrease already considered. When there is only one exogenous variable, this distribution has the advantage of leading to a model whose autoregressive form is particularly simple.

The model can be expressed as

$$x_t = d \sum_{\tau=0}^{\infty} c^\tau z_{t-\tau} + b + \varepsilon_t \tag{11}$$

where $d = a(1-c)$. It can also be written

$$x_t = cx_{t-1} + dz_t + e + \xi_t, \tag{12}$$

where $e = b(1-c)$ and $\xi_t = \varepsilon_t - c\varepsilon_{t-1}$. As we shall see, this is a considerable advantage for estimation.

In this case, the function $A(z)$ has the simple expression $d(1-cz)^{-1}$, so that $B(z)$ is $(1-cz)/d$. Equation (12) then corresponds to the autoregressive form (10) (see in particular equation (7) in the first section).

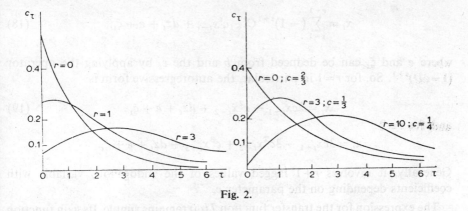

Fig. 2.

The transfer function $T(\omega)$ associated with $A(z)$ can be defined by its gain:

$$G(\omega) = \frac{d^2}{1 - 2c \cos \omega + c^2} \tag{13}$$

and its phase-displacement

$$\varphi(\omega) = \text{Arc tg} \frac{c \sin \omega}{1 - c \cos \omega}. \tag{14}$$

SOLOW [1960] suggested using the *negative binomial distribution*, also called 'Pascal distribution', which leads to a simple autoregressive form and allows an increase in the first terms of the sequence $\{a_\tau\}$.

The negative binomial distribution defines c_τ as follows:

$$c_\tau = (1 - c)^{r+1} C^r_{r+\tau} c^\tau. \tag{15}$$

It involves only two parameters c and r (to which we must add the multiplier a). It reduces to the geometric distribution when $r = 0$ and gives, for other values of r, a fairly large selection of possible evolutions (cf. fig. 2).

The function $A(z)$ is then equal to

$$A(z) = d \sum_{\tau=0}^{\infty} C^r_{r+\tau} c^\tau z^\tau = \frac{d}{(1 - cz)^{r+1}} \tag{16}$$

where $d = a(1 - c)^{r+1}$. So we can write

$$B(D) = \frac{(1 - cD)^{r+1}}{d}, \tag{17}$$

from which we can immediately deduce the expression for the autoregressive form

$$x_t = \sum_{\tau=1}^{r+1} (-1)^{\tau+1} C_{r+1}^\tau c^\tau x_{t-\tau} + dz_t + e + \xi_t, \tag{18}$$

where e and ξ_t can be deduced from b and the ε_t by applying the operator $(1-cD)^{r+1}$. So, for $r=1$ in particular, the autoregressive form is

$$x_t = 2cx_{t-1} - c^2 x_{t-2} + dz_t + e + \xi_t \tag{19}$$

and, for $r=2$:

$$x_t = 3cx_{t-1} - 3c^2 x_{t-2} + c^3 x_{t-3} + dz_t + e + \xi_t.$$

Generally, it involves $r+1$ lagged values of the endogenous variable with coefficients depending on the parameter c.

The expression for the transfer function $T(\omega)$ remains simple. Its gain function is

$$G(\omega) = \frac{d^2}{[1-2c \cos \omega + c^2]^{r+1}} \tag{20}$$

and its phase displacement

$$\varphi(\omega) = \text{Arc tg} \frac{\sum_{\tau=1}^{r+1} (-1)^{\tau+1} C_{r+1}^\tau c^\tau \sin \tau\omega}{\sum_{\tau=0}^{r+1} (-1)^\tau C_{r+1}^\tau c^\tau \cos \tau\omega}. \tag{21}$$

JORGENSON [1961] recommends using *rational distributed lag models*, by which he means that $A(z)$ is a rational function and so can be written as the ratio of two polynomials, $P(z)/Q(z)$. We can always find a rational approximation to any function. Also, the class of rational distributed lag models is very large. But Jorgenson has a more specific proposal for applications, namely that the maximum degree of the polynomials $P(z)$ and $Q(z)$ should be fixed in advance. If, for example, we restrict ourselves to second degree polynomials

$$\begin{cases} P(z) = p_0 + p_1 z + p_2 z^2 \\ Q(z) = 1 - q_1 z - q_2 z^2 \end{cases}, \tag{22}$$

the function $A(z)$ depends on five unknown parameters.

The model can then be given the following simple expression:

$$Q(D)x_t = P(D)z_t + Q(1)b + Q(D)\varepsilon_t. \tag{23}$$

For example, in the case of second degree polynomials,

$$x_t = q_1 x_{t-1} + q_2 x_{t-2} + p_0 z_t + p_1 z_{t-1} + p_2 z_{t-2} + e + \xi_t \tag{24}$$

where

$$e = (1-q_1-q_2)b \quad \text{and} \quad \xi_t = \varepsilon_t - q_1 \varepsilon_{t-1} - q_2 \varepsilon_{t-2}.$$

Equations (23) and (24) show lags both on the endogenous variable and on the exogenous variable. But for estimation, their form is simple since the parameters to be estimated occur linearly in them. So they have the same simplicity as the autoregressive form of the model (11), which is a particular case of them with P having degree 0 and Q degree 1.

4   Specification and estimation

Before discussing some estimation methods we must remind ourselves of the difficult judgments facing econometricians in the applied field. Of course the difficulty vanishes in the ideal case where reliable economic theory imposes a strict specification of the sequence of coefficients and the time dependence of the errors; but we saw at the end of section 2 that we cannot be too optimistic about such a situation arising. The difficulty also disappears if a very large number of observations allows simultaneous estimation of the a_τ and the correlations among the ε_t without introducing dubious restrictions to the model. But the time series available to econometricians are almost always too short to allow this.

So we must always bear in mind the risk of specification errors necessarily involved in practice. There will obviously be bias in estimation if too small a number h of terms is chosen for the a_τ or if the polynomials P and Q defining 'rational lags' are not taken as of high enough degree or again, if Almon's assumption is adopted when the coefficients have a Pascal distribution.

The various specifications introduced in the previous section may also leave the user dissatisfied in so far as his ideas about the coefficients are more qualitative and less precise. The choice of a particular specification may thus appear somewhat arbitrary.

An interesting alternative is to adopt a Bayesian standpoint and introduce a prior distribution to express preliminary ideas about the sequence of the a_τ. Thus SHILLER [1973] considers a law in which differences of order p have identical, independent, normal prior distributions: for example, if $p = 2$ the second differences $a_{\tau+1} - 2a_\tau + a_{\tau-1}$ have the same centred normal prior distribution $(\tau = 1, 2, \ldots, h - 1)$. Choosing a very small variance for this distribution is equivalent to demanding that the sequence of the a_τ is very near a polynomial of order $p - 1$; choosing a very large variance is equivalent to eliminating all restrictions on the a_τ (except that their number is $h + 1$). An intermediate assumption gives relative flexibility in estimation and leads to a fairly regular sequence a_τ. In spite of this additional flexibility this kind of Bayesian method still has an arbitrary element since the choice of prior distribution influences the result to some extent.

The risks of specification errors do not arise solely from the particular assumptions made about the sequence of coefficients. They may also arise from the treatment of serial correlation of the errors. In ch. 13, § 5, the second example discussed corresponds to an exponential distributed lag model written in the autoregressive form; we saw then how least squares fitting is biased by correlation of the errors. In § 6 (c) of the same chapter we saw that there is bias in simultaneous estimation of the coefficients and the correlation of the errors if the latter is incorrectly specified.

We must also mention the risk of errors stemming from the division into time periods. SIMS [1971 and 1972] shows that if the real phenomenon accommodates to a continuous representation by a continuous distributed lag model, observations at successive discrete periods are not strictly subject to a distributed lag model of the type discussed here. The same type of difficulty exists if the periodicity of the observations is longer than that of the phenomenon[t] (quarterly observations of a phenomenon involving some monthly lags).

We should like to think that specification errors do not affect estimation of the more synthetic characteristics, which are often considered to be of greatest interest; the long period effect $a = \sum a_\tau$ and the mean lag $\sum \tau a_\tau / a$. Unfortunately this is not so. When discussing model (43) in ch. 4, § 6, we saw that the regression coefficient (44) is a downwards biased estimator of the long term marginal propensity. Such a result, though obtained in a different context from our present one, is nevertheless fairly typical[tt].

So in practical applications a balance has to be struck between two opposing risks: the risk of bias arising from specification errors if too strict assumptions are adopted, and the risk of obtaining very imprecise estimates if the assumptions are not restrictive enough. The decision clearly depends on the availability of observations; the longer the series to be analysed, the less strict need the specifications be.

Such a situation must have repercussions on the statistical theory. This theory, necessarily asymptotic, should be based on limiting arguments applied to a sequence of specifications that become progressively less strict as the number of observations increases. The construction of such a theory is obviously difficult and has not yet been achieved.

The following sections have been written in the context of relatively short series, which are most frequently encountered in econometrics. So we shall concentrate on the simplest methods applying to fairly strict specifications. No further mention will be made of the risk of specification error but it should clearly be borne in mind. MERRIWETHER [1973] considers a particular case and shows that the correct choice of specification is more important than the choice of a particular estimation method from those which naturally come to mind. Also CARGILL and MEYER [1974], having carried out Monte Carlo studies for a case where a simple multiple regression gives precise results, show that the introduction of particular assumptions about the sequence of coefficients leads to damaging specification errors.

[t] GEWEKE [1978] again considers the question and brings new results.
[tt] The presence of errors in the exogenous variables z_t may also lead to bias in estimation of time-lags in reaction, as GRETHER and MADDALA [1973] show.

5 Direct estimation by linear and non-linear regressions

The distributed lag model:

$$x_t = a_0 z_t + a_1 z_{t-1} + \cdots + a_h z_{t-h} + b + \varepsilon_t \tag{3}$$

comes into the general category of regression models discussed in ch. 6, at least if no particular assumption is adopted for the coefficients $a_0, a_1, \ldots, a_h$. For we can consider $h+2$ exogenous variables z_{jt}^0 defined as follows:

$$z_{jt}^0 = z_{t+j-1} \qquad \text{for} \qquad j = 1, 2, \ldots, h+1,$$

$$z_{h+2,t}^0 = 1 \qquad\qquad \text{for every } t.$$

The model can then be written:

$$x_t = a' z_t^0 + \varepsilon_t,$$

where a denotes the vector of the $h+2$ coefficients $a_0, a_1, \ldots, a_h, b$. So it is reduced to a multiple regression model which presents no particular difficulty.

If the specification of the model imposes no restriction on the a_τ, we obtain unbiased estimates $a_0^*, a_1^*, \ldots, a_h^*, b^*$ by a least squares regression. These estimates enjoy the properties examined in ch. 6 or 13 according as the errors ε_t do or do not constitute a purely random process.

However, we can often obtain only fair precision in this way. For the sequence of the z_t is generally fairly regular, z_t being near z_{t-1} and still nearer

$$2z_{t-1} - z_{t-2} = z_{t-1} + \Delta z_{t-1}.$$

In these conditions, fairly strict multicollinearities appear among the $h+2$ exogenous variables z_j^0. The matrix M_{zz} which they define is near a singular matrix. Its inverse, which is used in computing the variances of the a_t^*, has very large elements, and these variances are too large, for small samples at least.

This is also why it would be a mistake to ignore the a priori reasons for thinking that the a_τ have a regular evolution of a more or less strictly defined type. Often it is only the specification of reasonable assumptions for the a_τ which allows us to determine with a modicum of precision the ways in which the endogenous quantity adapts itself to variations in the exogenous quantity.

However calculation of the a_τ^* is to be recommended in an exploratory stage of the fitting procedure, a stage during which a spectral analysis can also be carried out. Then systematic trends can be discerned behind irregularities in the estimated sequence of the a_τ^*. The subsequent introduction of assumptions on the a_τ which conflict with these trends will be avoided.

A particular problem also arises for the econometrician who is not prepared to adopt any assumption for the a_τ. He has to fix the maximum time lag after which the a_τ can be considered to be zero. In principle, this maximum time lag should be determined from the data. But as we shall see, the available methods do not seem to give a very satisfactory answer to the question, at least for small samples.

A first method consists of computing successive regressions on models with increasingly greater maximum time lags, for example on

$$x_t = a_0 z_t + a_1 z_{t-1} + b + \varepsilon_t,$$

$$x_t = a_0 z_t + a_1 z_{t-1} + a_2 z_{t-2} + b + \varepsilon_t,$$

$$x_t = a_0 z_t + a_1 z_{t-1} + a_2 z_{t-2} + \bar{a}_3 z_{t-3} + b + \varepsilon_t.$$

One could then choose the longest among all those regressions which determine the estimated coefficients a_τ^* with sufficient precision. Alternatively one might stop when the addition of a supplementary time lag upsets the orders of magnitude of the coefficients estimated in previous regressions. One might also adopt a slightly more rigorous procedure of the same kind by applying a sequence of analysis of variance tests; if a long time lag h is fixed a priori, one could make successive tests of the hypotheses:

$$H_1: \quad a_2 = 0, a_3 = 0, \ldots, a_h = 0,$$

$$H_2: \quad a_3 = 0, a_4 = 0, \ldots, a_h = 0,$$

$$H_3: \quad a_4 = 0, a_5 = 0, \ldots, a_h = 0.$$

(for the required computation, see ch. 7, § 6); one would then stop at the first hypothesis H_θ not to be rejected; for example, one would choose the regression with z_t, z_{t-1} and z_{t-2} if H_1 is rejected but not H_2. In practice these three methods must lead to similar results.

However, they are hardly convincing since they systematically favour models involving only the first lagged values. Very possibly only a third or a half of the effect of a variation in the exogenous variable is felt after the first period following this variation, and in spite of this the model chosen may be:

$$x_t = a_0 z_t + a_1 z_{t-1} + b + \varepsilon_t.$$

For this to happen, it is sufficient that the values $z_{t-2}, z_{t-3}, \ldots, z_{t-h}$ can be expressed approximately as fixed linear combinations of z_t and z_{t-1}. Also, extension of the period covered by the data often leads to the addition of new time lags in the chosen regression. Thus H_1 may not be rejected in a sample of 20 successive observations and be rejected in a sample of 40 observations making for greater precision.

So it may be important to take account of a priori restrictions on the a_τ. But this does not necessarily imply the abandonment of direct application of least squares fitting to the distributed lag model. In ch. 9 § 5, we gave a method which is easy to apply here and enjoys the properties laid down in theorem 4 in the same chapter.

Let us write the model in the form:

$$x_t = a_0(\alpha)z_t + a_1(\alpha)z_{t-1} + \cdots + a_h(\alpha)z_{t-h} + b + \varepsilon_t, \tag{25}$$

where α denotes the vector of the unknown parameters and $a_\tau(\alpha)$ is the function determining the value of the coefficient a_τ for every set of values of the parameters. For example under the assumption of a geometric distribution, the components of α are the two parameters d and c, and $a_\tau(\alpha) = dc^\tau$.

Suppose first that the ε_t constitute a purely random stationary process with zero mean and variance σ^2 (assumption 1 of ch. 6). As before, let a_τ^* be the coefficients obtained by linear least squares regression on formula (3), no account being then taken of the particular specification chosen for the a_τ. The covariance matrix of the a_τ^* is $(\sigma^2/T)M^{-1}$, where M denotes the square matrix of order $h+1$ whose $((\tau+1) \times (\theta+1))$th element is

$$\frac{1}{T}\sum_{t=1}^{T}(z_{t-\tau} - \bar{z}_{-\tau})(z_{t-\theta} - \bar{z}_{-\theta}),$$

where

$$\bar{z}_{-\tau} = \frac{1}{T}\sum_{t=1}^{T}z_{t-\tau}.$$

Let a^* and $a(\alpha)$ be the vectors with components a_τ^* and $a_\tau(\alpha)$. Applying to (25) the method of least squares is equivalent to choosing, as estimate of α, the vector which minimizes

$$[a^* - a(\alpha)]'M[a^* - a(\alpha)] \tag{26}$$

considered as a function of α.

Of course, this estimate is not generally easy to calculate[†]. The expression (26) is of second degree in the $a_\tau(\alpha)$; but these functions may be of high degree in the components of α. Moreover, the specification of the model may introduce an unlimited number of lags. Thus, to apply the method proposed here, we must disregard lags greater than an arbitrarily chosen number h of periods. This is no doubt a minor drawback in practice, but it has to be mentioned.

For example, consider the assumption of a geometric distribution $a_\tau(\alpha) = dc^\tau$ and suppose we choose $h=5$, which must be broadly sufficient if c is not near 1. The expression (26) is then of second degree in d, but of tenth degree in c. It is

---

[†] The method thus defined assumes that the z_t are known for dates previous to $t = 1$ ($z_0, \ldots, z_{1-h}$). This is not generally the case in practice so that, for the first values of t, the form of the model is different from (25). See KLEIN [1958] and AMEMIYA and FULLER [1967] for the treatment of this difficulty.

fairly difficult to find its minimum. We must try to locate the values of c and d which equate to zero the derivatives of (26), and find out if they correspond to minima or maxima. To determine the values of c and d precisely, we can use one of the methods of successive approximations given in ch. 9, § 4.

The computation is quicker if we assume an arithmetic decrease, say for example:

$$a_\tau = a_1 \left(1 - \frac{\tau - 1}{h}\right) \quad \text{for} \quad 1 \leq \tau \leq h,$$

a_0 taking any value and $a_\tau = 0$ for $\tau > h$. For a given value of h, the model can be written:

$$x_t = a_0 z_t + a_1 \sum_{\tau=1}^{h} \left(1 - \frac{\tau - 1}{h}\right) z_{t-\tau} + b + \varepsilon_t.$$

The coefficients a_0, a_1 and b are estimated by an ordinary multiple regression on

$$x_t = a_0 z_t + a_1 w_{ht} + b + \varepsilon_t,$$

where, by definition,

$$w_{ht} = \sum_{\tau=1}^{h} \left(1 - \frac{\tau - 1}{h}\right) z_{t-\tau}.$$

The computation can be carried out in this way for successive values $1, 2, \ldots,$ etc. of h. Finally we can choose that fitted model which gives the smallest value for the sum of squares of the residuals[†], that is, for the multiple correlation coefficient R^2.

The same principles apply if we adopt a polynomial assumption for the a_τ, say[††]

$$a_\tau = \alpha_0 + \alpha_1 \tau + \cdots + \alpha_q \tau^q \quad \text{for} \quad \tau = 0, 1, 2, \ldots, h.$$

the coefficients $\alpha_0, \alpha_1, \ldots, \alpha_q$ constituting the parameters to be estimated. The model can then be written:

$$x_t = \sum_{\theta=0}^{q} \alpha_\theta w_{\theta t} + b + \varepsilon_t$$

with the new exogenous variables

$$w_{\theta t} = \sum_{\tau=0}^{h} \tau^\theta z_{t-\tau}.$$

[†] Similarly, if we have to fit a negative binomial distribution with unknown parameter r, we can minimize (26) with respect to c and d for each value, $0, 1, 2, \ldots$ of r and choose the value of r which minimizes (26), that is also the sum of squares of the residuals.
[††] AMEMIYA and MORIMUNE [1974] show, on the basis of Monte Carlo studies, that this polynomial assumption is very appropriate for a wide variety of situations, even in most cases with a relatively small value of q.

ALMON [1965] has also shown that the number of parameters to be estimated can be reduced by two if we introduce the natural assumption that the polynomial representation takes the value 0 beyond the two extremes, that is, for $\tau = -1$ and $\tau = h + 1$. It is then sufficient to express the a_τ as linear combinations of $q - 1$ Lagrange interpolation polynomials which are zero for $\tau = -1$ and $\tau = h + 1$. However it is not advisable to impose the condition $a_\tau = 0$ for $\tau = -1$ since it is too restrictive (for a polynomial of low degree, it requires in most cases that the several initial terms a_τ be increasing, which may be incorrect).

Until now we have supposed that the errors ε_t constitute a purely random stationary process, without which assumption the covariance matrix of the a^* is no longer $(\sigma^2/T)M^{-1}$. However we can still apply the same estimation principle if the errors constitute a stationary process depending on only a small number of unknown parameters.

Suppose, for example, that the errors constitute a first order autoregressive process:

$$\varepsilon_t = \varrho \varepsilon_{t-1} + \eta_t.$$

If the a priori restrictions on the a_τ are ignored, there are various known methods allowing simultaneous determination of consistent estimates $\tilde{a}_0, \tilde{a}_1, \ldots, \tilde{a}_h, \tilde{b}$ and $\tilde{\varrho}$ of the coefficients of the model and the parameter ϱ (cf. ch. 12 § 7a, b and c). We know that the asymptotic covariance matrix of

$$\sqrt{T}\,\tilde{a}_0, \quad \sqrt{T}\,\tilde{a}_1, \ldots, \sqrt{T}\,\tilde{a}_h$$

is the limit of $\sigma^2 \cdot \tilde{M}^{-1}$, where $\tilde{M}$ denotes the square matrix of order $h + 1$ whose $((\tau + 1) \times (\theta + 1))$th element is

$$\frac{1}{T} \sum_{t=1}^{T} \left[(z_{t-\tau} - \bar{z}_{-\tau}) - \tilde{\varrho}(z_{t-\tau-1} - \bar{z}_{-\tau-1}) \right] \left[(z_{t-\theta} - \bar{z}_{-\theta}) - \tilde{\varrho}(z_{t-\theta-1} - \bar{z}_{-\theta-1}) \right].$$

Hence, we can proceed as above, determining α so as to minimize

$$[\tilde{a} - a(\alpha)]' \tilde{M} [\tilde{a} - a(\alpha)], \tag{27}$$

which replaces (26) and whose minimum is calculated in the same way[†].

At this point we can also say that, in a distributed lag model, the correlogram calculated from the residuals of a multiple regression generally gives an estimate with little bias for the correlogram of the errors. This follows from the general formulae given in ch. 12 § 4, and particularly from formula (22).

Indeed, consider a multiple regression on

---

† AMEMIYA and FULLER [1967] give the computation required for applying this estimation principle. They also show the relationship between this principle and an estimation procedure proposed by HANNAN [1965].

$$x_t = a_0 z_t + a_1 z_{t-1} + \cdots + a_h z_{t-h} + \varepsilon_t.$$

The matrix M_{zz}^{τ} defined by relation (18) in ch. 12 has a particular structure in this case, since the $((\theta+1) \times (\theta'+1))$th element is very near the $(\theta \times \theta')$th element, both being near $W_{\tau+\theta-\theta'}$, where we define

$$W_{\tau} = \frac{1}{T} \sum_{t=1}^{T-\tau} z_t z_{t+\tau'}$$

Thus the matrices M_{zz}^0, M_{zz}^1, M_{zz}^2 are respectively near

$$\begin{bmatrix} W_0 & W_1 & W_2 & \cdots & W_h \\ W_1 & W_0 & W_1 & \cdots & W_{h-1} \\ W_2 & W_1 & W_0 & \cdots & W_{h-2} \\ \cdots\cdots\cdots\cdots\cdots\cdots\cdots\cdots\cdots \\ W_h & W_{h-1} & W_{h-2} & \cdots & W_0 \end{bmatrix}, \begin{bmatrix} W_1 & W_0 & W_1 & \cdots & W_{h-1} \\ W_2 & W_1 & W_0 & \cdots & W_{h-2} \\ W_3 & W_2 & W_1 & \cdots & W_{h-3} \\ \cdots\cdots\cdots\cdots\cdots\cdots\cdots\cdots\cdots \\ W_{h+1} & W_h & W_{h-1} & \cdots & W_1 \end{bmatrix},$$

$$\begin{bmatrix} W_2 & W_1 & W_0 & \cdots & W_{h-2} \\ W_3 & W_2 & W_1 & \cdots & W_{h-3} \\ W_4 & W_3 & W_2 & \cdots & W_{h-4} \\ \cdots\cdots\cdots\cdots\cdots\cdots\cdots\cdots\cdots \\ W_{h+2} & W_{h+1} & W_h & \cdots & W_2 \end{bmatrix}.$$

Then let P be the permutation matrix:

$$P = \begin{bmatrix} 0 & 1 & 0 & \cdots & 0 & 0 \\ 0 & 0 & 1 & \cdots & 0 & 0 \\ \cdots\cdots\cdots\cdots\cdots\cdots\cdots \\ 0 & 0 & 0 & \cdots & 0 & 1 \\ 1 & 0 & 0 & \cdots & 0 & 0 \end{bmatrix}.$$

The matrix M_{zz}^1 is very like $M_{zz}^0 P$ except in its first column; similarly M_{zz}^2 is very like $M_{zz}^0 P^2$ except in its first two columns. It follows that R_1, defined by formula (19) in ch. 12 is very similar to P; that R_2 is very similar to P^2,... and that R_τ is very similar to P^τ, the approximation being acceptable only if τ is small relative to h. The multipliers

$$[\operatorname{tr}(R_\tau R_\theta) - 2\operatorname{tr}(R_{\tau-\theta})],$$

which occur in formula (22) of ch. 12, are near

$$[\operatorname{tr}(P^{\tau+\theta}) - 2\operatorname{tr}(P^{\tau-\theta})],$$

at least so long as τ and θ remain small relative to h. So they are near zero except for $\theta = -\tau$ and $\theta = \tau$.

In short, *if the γ_τ decrease sufficiently quickly to zero and if h is fairly large,* formula (22) of ch. 12 becomes

$$E(C_\tau) \approx \gamma_\tau(1 - (h/T)).$$

The bias is proportionately the same for all the C_τ; and *the bias is approximately zero for the first terms of the correlogram of the residuals* $\{r_\tau\}$.

6   Least squares fitting of the autoregressive form

Instead of using the direct form of the distributed lag model, we might consider estimating the unknown coefficients from the autoregressive form. This idea seems attractive if the autoregressive form is simple, and so if the coefficients of the model have a geometric distribution or a negative binomial distribution.

For example, the autoregressive form can be written:

$$x_t = cx_{t-1} + dz_t + e + \xi_t, \tag{28}$$

if the a_τ have a geometric distribution $a_\tau = dc^\tau$; and

$$x_t = 2cx_{t-1} - c^2 x_{t-2} + dz_t + e + \xi_t, \tag{29}$$

if the a_τ have a negative binomial distribution with parameter $r = 1$. *The least squares estimate obtained from the autoregressive form* is then much easier to calculate than the estimates proposed in the previous section. For the geometric distribution, we need only apply the usual regression formulae. For negative binomial distributions slightly more complex equations have to be solved.

For example, consider the simplest case in which $r = 1$. The autoregressive form is then given by eq. (29). The required estimates must minimize

$$\sum_t (x_t - 2cx_{t-1} + c^2 x_{t-2} - dz_t - e)^2. \tag{30}$$

Differentiating this expression with respect to $\hat{c}$, d and e, we obtain the three necessary conditions:

$$\sum_t (x_{t-1} - cx_{t-2})(x_t - 2cx_{t-1} + c^2 x_{t-2} - dz_t - e) = 0,$$

$$\sum_t z_t(x_t - 2cx_{t-1} + c^2 x_{t-2} - dz_t - e) = 0,$$

$$\sum_t (x_t - 2cx_{t-1} + c^2 x_{t-2} - dz_t - e) = 0,$$

which can also be written:

$$- c^3[x^2_{-2}] + 3c^2[x_{-1}x_{-2}] + cd[x_{-2}z]$$

$$- c([xx_{-2}] + 2[x^2_{-1}]) - d[x_{-1}z] + [xx_{-1}] = 0$$

$$c^2[x_{-2}z] - 2c[x_{-1}z] - d[z^2] + [xz] = 0 \tag{31}$$

$$c^2\bar{x}_{-2} - 2c\bar{x}_{-1} - d\bar{z} - e + \bar{x} = 0$$

where we use condensed notation of the following type:

$$\bar{x}_{-2} = \frac{1}{T}\sum_{t=1}^{T} x_{t-2}, \qquad [x_{-1}x_{-2}] = \frac{1}{T}\sum_{t=1}^{T}(x_{t-1} - \bar{x}_{-1})(x_{t-2} - \bar{x}_{-2}).$$

In system (31), the last relation gives the value of e once c and d have been determined; the second gives the value of d once c has been determined. To calculate c, we must solve the equation obtained by eliminating d from the first two relations. This is a third degree equation in c. Only roots with moduli less than 1 matter. If there are several[†], we must choose that which minimizes the sum (30). The same method can be applied whatever the value of r, and then leads to an equation of degree $2r+1$ in c.

The above discussion is based on the supposition that r is known a priori. This is not generally the case, and then c, d and r must be estimated simultaneously. The best method is probably to carry out estimation as above for different values of r, for example $r = 0, 1, 2$ and 3; then to choose for r the value which minimizes the sum of squares of the residuals *for the distributed lag model*, in its original form. SOLOW [1960] proposes choosing the value of r which minimizes the sum of squares of the residuals of the autoregressive form. A theoretical or empirical investigation of the respective properties of the two methods would be useful. It seems probable that the first gives the better results.

The properties of the estimates obtained by least squares applied to the autoregressive form derive from the general results stated in the previous chapter. Asymptotically, the estimates tend to the true values *if the errors ξ_t affecting the autoregressive form constitute a purely random process*. Otherwise the estimates are asymptotically biased.

Now a priori there is no reason to suppose the absence of serial correlation of the ξ_t, except perhaps when the specification of the model leads directly to the autoregressive form, this case having been excluded in this chapter. When we have to deal with a true distributed lag model, the ξ_t are transforms of the

---

† There is known to be a root which tends in probability to the true value c, which has modulus less than 1 (for the meaning of this convergence, see the remarks which follow proposition 15 in the appendix to ch. 9). But a priori it is not certain that, in any sample whatever, the third degree equation has a solution between 0 and 1. If this is not the case, the method fails, and a different estimation procedure must be used.

errors ε_t; they must show some serial correlation, by the very fact of the trans-formation which defines them.

To examine this difficulty, we consider a distributed lag model whose coefficients have a negative binomial distribution, and assume that the errors ε_t affecting the model constitute a first order autoregressive process:

$$\varepsilon_t = \varrho\varepsilon_{t-1} + \eta_t.$$

We know that ξ_t, ε_t and η_t are connected by the following two formulae, written with the symbolic operator D:

$$\xi_t = (1 - cD)^{r+1}\varepsilon_t, \qquad \varepsilon_t = (1 - \varrho D)^{-1}\eta_t$$

and consequently

$$\xi_t = (1 - cD)^{r+1}(1 - \varrho D)^{-1}\eta_t. \tag{32}$$

This relation defines the second order characteristics of the random process of the ξ_t.

In particular, if it is possible to assume that the ε_t constitute a purely random process ($\varrho = 0$), then the ξ_t form a moving average process whose correlogram depends on the value of c. Thus, for the geometric distribution ($r = 0$), the first coefficient of this correlogram is

$$\frac{-c}{1 + c^2},$$

the others are zero; for $r = 1$, the first two coefficients are respectively

$$\frac{-2c(1 + c^2)}{1 + 4c^2 + c^4} \quad \text{and} \quad \frac{c^2}{1 + 4c^2 + c^4},$$

the others are zero. Since c is practically always positive, the ξ_t are predominantly negatively autocorrelated.

If the ε_t are positively correlated ($\varrho > 0$), formula (32) is more complex. Nevertheless we can see that, for high positive values of c, the ξ_t are less strongly autocorrelated than when there is no correlation of the ε_t. Let us confine ourselves to the case where the distribution of the coefficients is geometric. It is easy to calculate the value of the autocorrelation coefficient of order k, namely

$$\varrho^{k-1}\frac{\varrho(1 + c^2) - c(1 + \varrho^2)}{(1 + c^2) - 2c\varrho}.$$

As formula (32) shows directly, the ξ_t constitute a purely random process when $c = \varrho$. The ξ_t are positively autocorrelated when $c < \varrho$, negatively when $c > \varrho$. In the last case, the first autocorrelation coefficient is smaller in absolute

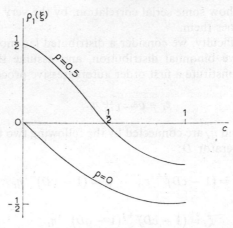

Fig. 3.

value than when $\varrho = 0$. Figure 3 shows how this coefficient varies as a function of c for $\varrho = 0$ in the first place and $\varrho = \frac{1}{2}$ in the second.

In practice, we may have some idea about the serial correlation of the errors ε_t which represent the influence on the endogenous variable x_t of all factors other than z_t. It is sometimes probable that the errors are not serially correlated. We must then know that the errors ξ_t of the autoregressive form show a negative autocorrelation which is more marked as the value of c increases. In other cases, it seems probable that there is some serial correlation of the ε_t, so that the serial correlation of the ξ_t can be considered as low.

However that may be, the extent of the asymptotic bias depends on the sequence of the exogenous variables z_t. As we saw in ch. 14, this bias is small when the fluctuations in the exogenous variable are large relative to the dispersion of the errors ξ_t. The variance of the ξ_t is itself proportional to that of the ε_t, the proportionality coefficient being a function of ϱ, of c and of r. In many applications, the asymptotic bias is therefore likely to be small.

We also saw in the last chapter that the asymptotic properties give incomplete information about the quality of the estimates for small samples. For such samples, the method of least squares generally tends to underestimate c, even independently of any serial correlation of the ξ_t. A negative autocorrelation of these errors must aggravate this underestimation slightly.

In spite of the imperfections revealed by the above discussion, least squares applied to the autoregressive form is often the best method for estimating a model whose coefficients have a geometric or a negative binomial distribution. For there are two considerable advantages in this method: the computation involved is fairly simple; it has a fairly high degree of efficiency since it leads to estimates whose variances are smaller than those of other estimates and which are not often too highly biased.

7 Other methods of estimation for the autoregressive form

As we saw in the previous chapter, other methods can be used for estimation of the autoregressive form.

(a) If the exact form of the correlation of the errors ξ_t *of the autoregressive form* is known, least squares fitting could be carried out, no longer on the variables $x_t, x_{t-1}, \ldots, x_{t-r-1}, z_t$, but *on transformed variables*. For example, in the case of a geometric distribution, if we know that, as a first approximation, the ξ_t constitute a first order autoregressive process:

$$\xi_t = \lambda \xi_{t-1} + \zeta_t,$$

where λ is a given coefficient, we can carry out a regression of $x_t - \lambda x_{t-1}$ on $x_{t-1} - \lambda x_{t-2}$ and $z_t - \lambda z_{t-1}$. In this way the asymptotic bias is eliminated, at least as a first approximation.

We are hardly likely to find such a favourable situation in practice. In the first place, we can rarely formulate precise assumptions about the correlation of the errors ε_t affecting the model. In the second place, the correlation of the ξ_t depends both on that of the ε_t and on the true value of the parameter c, which is just what we are trying to estimate.

It may then be useful to *find out if the estimates are sensitive to the assumptions adopted about the serial correlation of the ξ_t.* For this purpose, the application of least squares to the values of the variables may be compared with its application to two other sets of values; first to

$$x_t - x_{t-1}, x_{t-1} - x_{t-2}, \ldots, x_{t-r-1} - x_{t-r-2}, z_t - z_{t-1}$$

which gives prominence to the effect of a pronounced positive correlation of the ξ_t; and then to

$$x_t + x_{t-1}, x_{t-1} + x_{t-2}, \ldots, x_{t-r-1} + x_{t-r-2}, z_t + z_{t-1}$$

which gives prominence to the effect of a pronounced negative correlation. If we find that the three procedures give similar results, we have grounds for assuming that the correlation of the ξ_t is unimportant.

If this is not the case, we may in principle consider *simultaneous estimation of the parameters of the model and the correlation of the ξ_t.* But the various possible methods for doing this are certainly of only limited practical interest. In the first place, the type of process constituted by the ξ_t is fairly complex (see for example formula (32) above). In the second place, for fairly small samples the estimates which result from these methods are less precise than those resulting from direct fitting (see ch. 13, at the end of § 6c).

The first difficulty at least does not affect *estimation by means of the instru-*

mental variables z_t *and* z_{t-1}. The formulae given in ch. 13, § 6d, can be applied directly here to the case where the coefficients have a geometric distribution. Similarly, estimation of

$$x_t = 2cx_{t-1} - c^2 x_{t-2} + dz_t + e + \xi_t$$

leads to the system:

$$[xz] - 2c[x_{-1}z] + c^2[x_{-2}z] - d(z^2) = 0,$$

$$[xz_{-1}] - 2c[x_{-1}z_{-1}] + c^2[x_{-2}z_{-1}] - d[zz_{-1}] = 0,$$

$$\bar{x} - 2c\bar{x}_{-1} + c^2\bar{x}_{-2} - d\bar{z} - e = 0,$$

which implies solving an equation of second degree in c. For any negative binomial distribution, we would have to solve an equation of degree $r+1$ in c. The computation is therefore simpler than for least squares fitting, which necessitates solving an equation of degree $2r+1$. Unfortunately it seems that the estimates have only mediocre precision, even for samples of about fifty observations.

With a view to simplifying the computation involved by least squares fitting, SOLOW [1960] proposed *the use of the instrumental variables* z_t *and* x_{t-1} which also leads to an equation of degree $r + 1$ in c. The variances of the estimates obtained in this way are greater than those of the least squares estimates (except if $r = 0$ since then the two methods coincide); these variances are probably less than those of the estimates obtained by using the instrumental variables z_t and z_{t-1}. But in the case where the ξ_t are correlated, the use of z_t and x_{t-1} leads to asymptotic bias, a drawback which does not exist with z_t and z_{t-1}.

(b) It seems that, in estimating the model, we ought to take account of the fact that the correlation of the ξ_t depends on the value of the coefficient c. The preceding methods take no account of it. KOYCK [1954] and KLEIN [1958] put forward a method which is more satisfactory from this point of view. We shall confine ourselves here to the case where the distribution of the coefficients is geometric and refer to SOLOW [1960] for generalization to the case of a negative binomial distribution.

We return to the model:

$$x_t = d \sum_{\tau=0}^{\infty} c^\tau z_{t-\tau} + b + \varepsilon_t. \tag{4}$$

We can also write

$$(x_t - \varepsilon_t) = c(x_{t-1} - \varepsilon_{t-1}) + dz_t + e, \tag{33}$$

where $e = b(1-c)$. Relation (33) is just the autoregressive form with the error ξ_t expressed explicitly as a function of the errors ε_t and ε_{t-1} of the original model.

But this relation is written in such a way that ε_t and ε_{t-1} may appear as 'errors in the variables' x_t and x_{t-1}. This explains why, for estimation, we shall propose to resort to the *weighted regression* defined in ch. 10.

Suppose also that the ε_t constitute a first order autoregressive stationary process

$$\varepsilon_t = \varrho \varepsilon_{t-1} + \eta_t.$$

Relation (33) can be transformed into

$$(u_t - \eta_t) = c(u_{t-1} - \eta_{t-1}) + dw_t - f, \tag{34}$$

where

$$f = (1 - \varrho)e; \qquad u_t = x_t - \varrho x_{t-1} \quad \text{and} \quad w_t = z_t - \varrho z_{t-1}.$$

Thus u_t and w_t are variables transformed from x_t and z_t. They are known if ϱ is known; they coincide with x_t and z_t if the ε_t constitute a purely random process ($\varrho = 0$).

Consider first the case where ϱ is known. Relation (34) then appears as a model with errors in variables in which the covariance matrix of the errors in the variables u_t, u_{t-1} and w_t is

$$\Omega = \sigma_\eta^2 \begin{bmatrix} 1 & 0 & 0 \\ 0 & 1 & 0 \\ 0 & 0 & 0 \end{bmatrix}.$$

The situation is particularly advantageous since this matrix depends only on a multiplying constant. A weighted regression constructed with the matrix Ω gives consistent and probably fairly efficient estimates of c, d and f. The operations defined in (i), (ii) and (iii) of section 4 of ch. 10 are then applied to the variables u_t, u_{t-1} and w_t.

In fact there is a particular feature of model (34) which we ignore here. If it is considered as a model with errors in variables for the vector with three components (u_t, u_{t-1}, w_t), the successive observations are not independent since the first component of (u_t, u_{t-1}, w_t) is necessarily equal to the second component of (u_{t+1}, u_t, w_t). This remark applies simultaneously to the vector of the observed values (u_t, u_{t-1}, w_t), the vector of the errors $(\varepsilon_t, \varepsilon_{t-1}, 0)$ and the vector of the 'true values' $(u_t - \varepsilon_t, u_{t-1} - \varepsilon_{t-1}, w_t)$. The fact that this constraint is ignored does not affect the asymptotic convergence of the estimates but certainly reduces the efficiency of the method, as is shown by AMEMIYA and FULLER [1967].

If it is unrealistic to assume that the errors ε_t constitute a purely random process, we must still take account of the fact that the coefficient ϱ characterizing their serial correlation is not known. KOYCK [1954] suggests trying different values of ϱ and finding out if this affects the estimates of c, d and e. He shows in several practical examples that the estimated coefficients vary very little as a function of ϱ and that the correlation of the errors is therefore unimportant.

In the case where this is not so, the best estimate of ϱ and the coefficients c, d and e is probably that which minimizes the sum of squares of the residuals with respect to the distributed lag equation written with the transformed variables

$$u_t = x_t - \varrho x_{t-1} \quad \text{and} \quad w_t = z_t - \varrho z_{t-1}.$$

So, from all the values tried for ϱ, we choose that which minimizes this sum. The final estimates of the coefficients are those obtained with this value. Another estimation principle proposed for determining ϱ does not seem to give useful results (see MALINVAUD [1961a]).

8   Maximum likelihood. Estimation of the variances of the coefficients

The previous sections may leave the reader dissatisfied in so far as they lead to no clear conclusion about the choice of method among the various methods proposed. Hence two common sense remarks should be borne in mind:

– in most cases, least squares fitting on the autoregressive form leads to the simplest computation;
– but, *if there is no time dependence of the ε_t*, regression (linear or non-linear) on the direct form must generally be most efficient.

The second remark, apparently corroborated by the Monte Carlo study carried out by MORRISON [1970], is based on the results of the theories discussed in chs. 6 and 9. It may appear all the more natural since regression on the direct form is equivalent to maximum likelihood estimation when the ε_t are normally distributed.

This also suggests that *even where there is time dependence of the ε_t* it would be advantageous in most cases to proceed as if the errors were normal and calculate the estimator which then maximises the likelihood function. This leads to a method similar to that suggested in the second part of section 5, but extending to *simultaneous estimation* of the coefficients and the correlation of the errors. BOX and JENKINS [1970] apply this method systematically in their treatment of the case of rational distributed lags and errors following a linear process with a rational transfer function.

However, the maximum likelihood principle does not eliminate the difficulty of choosing the degrees of the polynomials to be included in the rational functions relating to the lags or the correlation of errors. For this, Box and Jenkins suggest a method aimed at achieving the best balance between the search for precision and the risk of specification error.

In practical applications we are often faced with another difficulty which arises with all the methods suggested in this chapter, the difficulty of correctly estimating the standard errors of the estimated coefficients. As we have seen, the specifications chosen for the coefficients of the model often involve discrete parameters: the number h of lags and the degree q of the polynomial in Almon's assumption, the integer r in the Pascal distribution, the degrees of the polynomials P and Q in the assumption of rational lags. In most cases these discrete parameters are estimated by trying different values in succession and examining the results they give. But clearly the fitting finally chosen does not have the same precision as when the values of the discrete parameters are known a priori.

Thus estimation on the direct form of a model using Almon's assumption is often equivalent in practice to carrying out a set of linear regressions for a set of integral values of h and q and then choocing the regression which appears best after considering R^2 and the variances of the fitting coefficients. But the usual formulae for these variances are valid only in the case where h and q are known a priori. Using them to measure the precision of the best regression incurs the risk of a seriously biased measure.

It appears that the only practical method of finding a correct estimator of the variances of the coefficients is to define a model with continuous parameters which embodies, at least approximately, the model actually estimated and then to find the standard errors of the resulting estimates as if this new model had been estimated. SCHMIDT[†] [1973] applies this principle to the case of a Pascal distribution.

To illustrate this method, let us consider the very simple case of a model obeying I. Fisher's assumption:

$$x_t = a \sum_{\tau=0}^{h} \left(1 - \frac{\tau}{h}\right) z_{t-\tau} + b + \varepsilon_t. \tag{36}$$

The parameters to be estimated are the coefficients a and b together with the number h of lags which is considered as integral. There is nothing to prevent this model being embodied in the following one:

$$x_t = a \sum_{\tau=0}^{[h]} \left(1 - \frac{\tau}{h}\right) z_{t-\tau} + b + \varepsilon_t \tag{37}$$

where h can take any positive value while $[h]$ denotes the integral part of h.

Suppose also that the value chosen for h is the value giving the highest R^2; so the parameters a, b and h are estimated by a non-linear regression giving the values a^*, b^* and h^*. If such a regression had been applied to (37), a consistent estimate of the covariance matrix of (a^*, b^*, h^*) would have been obtained by the method defined in ch. 9. Assuming that the true value h_0 of h is not integral, we can in fact replace (37) by its linear approximation

---

[†] SCHMIDT [1974] shows the advantages of using a Gamma distribution all of whose parameters can be considered as continuous.

$$x_t = aw_{1t} + (h - h_0)\frac{a_0}{h_0} w_{2t} + b + \varepsilon_t \tag{38}$$

where a_0 is the true value of a while w_{1t} and w_{2t} are defined by

$$w_{1t} = \sum_{\tau=0}^{[h_0]} \left(1 - \frac{\tau}{h_0}\right) z_{t-\tau}, \qquad w_{2t} = \sum_{\tau=0}^{[h_0]} \frac{\tau}{h_0} z_{t-\tau}. \tag{39}$$

If we ignore the fact that h is estimated, the estimate $\hat{v}_a$ of the variance of a^* is calculated by the usual formula applying to the simple regression of x_t on w_{1t}^*, a variable defined like w_{1t} except that h^* replaces h_0. An obviously better estimate v_a^* is given by the formula applying to the multiple regression of x_t on w_{1t}^* and w_{2t}^*. We see immediately that the ratio $\hat{v}_a/\hat{v}_a^*$ equals $1 - K^2$, where K is the correlation coefficient between w_{1t}^* and w_{2t}^*. Now these last two variables constitute two different smoothings of the same sequence of the z_t so that K is high if the z_t series evolves gradually. The estimate $\hat{v}_a$ is then strongly biased downwards.

However the bias in estimation of the variance is different if we concentrate, not on the 'short term propensity' a, the multiplier of z_t in (36), but on the 'long term propensity' $a(h+1)/2$ which applies to the case where the same variation occurs simultaneously in $z_t, z_{t-1}, \ldots, z_{t-h}$. It is easy to show that $\hat{v}_a(h^*+1)^2/4$ is often very near the value given by multiple regression theory for the variance of $a^*(h^*+1)/2$. The ratio between them is

$$(1 - K^2)(1 - 2KH + H^2)^{-1} \quad \text{where} \quad H = \frac{h^*}{h^* + 1}:$$

It has a maximum at 1 for $H = K$. Thus, in the example of model (36) choosing the formulae which hold for the case where h is known leads to considerable exaggeration of the precision in estimation of the short term propensity but not of the long term propensity. It is worth remarking that SCHMIDT [1973] reaches the same conclusion for a different example.

Having concluded our discussion of estimation in distributed lag models, we should take care not to delude ourselves about the precision with which the lag effect in economic reactions can be estimated. With the relatively short statistical series which are usually available, we may be led to adopt fairly narrow specifications whose choice is liable strongly to condition the results obtained. GRILICHES [1967] describes some experiments which may lead to useful reflection.

Part 5

SIMULTANEOUS EQUATION MODELS

CHAPTER 15

Simultaneous equation models in econometrics

In many fields, economic theory proposes models involving several endogenous quantities and several relations. These quantities are then considered as interdependent, that is, as simultaneously determined by all the relations of the model. We have already discussed the logical interpretation of this interdependence in ch. 2 § 6, and there is no point in returning to it here.

The statistical methods of parts 2, 3 and 4 were not discussed with any close reference to the case of multiple relations. We sometimes assumed that the model contained only one endogenous variable. The proposed method of treatment often applied with little modification to models with several endogenous variables, and we took advantage of this in order to discuss this case. But we did not tackle certain complications which necessarily arise when the model contains several relations; we must now fill in this gap.

Throughout this part of the book we shall assume that the model is linear with respect to the observed variables and that the errors occur additively in the relations. This means that we confine ourselves to the study of linear models with errors in equations, which are the only ones to have been discussed seriously in econometric methodology. The roles of linearity of the relations and additivity of the errors have been sufficiently discussed previously for the reader to be aware of the cases in which a model whose initial specification is different can be given this form, and of the cost involved.

Before dealing with questions of statistical methodology, it seems profitable to discuss some general notions in detail, and to assess the part played in econometrics by simultaneous equation models. This is the object of the present chapter.

1 Structural equations and reduced equations

The concepts which we shall be using can be made clear by consideration of an example, the classical study by GIRSCHIK and HAAVELMO [1947] of the demand for food products in the United States.

Apart from the variable t representing the year, their model contains the following variables:

x_{1t} food consumption per capita during year t,
x_{2t} index of retail prices of food products, divided by the general index of retail prices,

x_{3t} real disposable income per capita,

x_{4t} production of agricultural food products per capita,

x_{5t} index of prices received by farmers for agricultural food products, divided by the general index of retail prices,

z_{2t} investment per capita.

Five relations express the various laws recognized by the model. More precisely, the demand for food products is considered as a function of retail prices, disposable income in the current and the preceding period and an autonomous trend factor:

$$x_{1t} = \beta_{12}x_{2t} + \beta_{13}x_{3t} + \delta_{13}x_{3,t-1} + \gamma_1 t + \lambda_1 + \eta_{1t}, \tag{1}$$

$\beta_{12}, \beta_{13}, \delta_{13}, \gamma_1$ and λ_1 being unknown coefficients and η_{1t} an unobservable random error. The supply of food products to the retail market is a function of retail prices, the production of agricultural produces and a trend factor:

$$x_{1t} = \beta_{22}x_{2t} + \beta_{24}x_{4t} + \gamma_2 t + \lambda_2 + \eta_{2t}. \tag{2}$$

Disposable income depends on income in the preceding period and investment in the current period:

$$x_{3t} = \delta_{33}x_{3,t-1} + \gamma_{32}z_{2t} + \lambda_3 + \eta_{3t}. \tag{3}$$

The production of agricultural foodstuffs is a function of prices received by producers in the current and the preceding period and a trend factor:

$$x_{4t} = \beta_{45}x_{5t} + \delta_{45}x_{5,t-1} + \gamma_4 t + \lambda_4 + \eta_{4t}. \tag{4}$$

Prices received by producers depend on retail prices and a trend factor:

$$x_{5t} = \beta_{52}x_{2t} + \gamma_5 t + \lambda_5 + \eta_{5t}. \tag{5}$$

Finally it is assumed that net investment is determined independently of the supply and demand for foodstuffs.

Thus the model contains five endogenous variables, the x_{it}, and three exogenous variables, time t, investment z_{2t} and the dummy variable which always equals 1. Moreover lagged values of disposable income or prices received by producers occur in three of the equations. The model can be expressed in the following more compact matrix form:

$$Bx_t + Cz_t + Dx_{t-1} + \eta_t = 0, \tag{6}$$

where x_t and η_t denote the vectors with the five components x_{it} and η_{it} $(i = 1, 2, \ldots, 5)$ respectively; z_t is the vector with the three components $(t, z_{2t}, 1)$;

B, C and D are the following matrices of the coefficients of the variables in the different equations:

$$B = \begin{bmatrix} -1 & \beta_{12} & \beta_{13} & 0 & 0 \\ -1 & \beta_{22} & 0 & \beta_{24} & 0 \\ 0 & 0 & -1 & 0 & 0 \\ 0 & 0 & 0 & -1 & \beta_{45} \\ 0 & \beta_{52} & 0 & 0 & -1 \end{bmatrix}, \quad C = \begin{bmatrix} \gamma_1 & 0 & \lambda_1 \\ \gamma_2 & 0 & \lambda_2 \\ 0 & \gamma_{32} & \lambda_3 \\ \gamma_4 & 0 & \lambda_4 \\ \gamma_5 & 0 & \lambda_5 \end{bmatrix}$$

$$D = \begin{bmatrix} 0 & 0 & \delta_{13} & 0 & 0 \\ 0 & 0 & 0 & 0 & 0 \\ 0 & 0 & \delta_{33} & 0 & 0 \\ 0 & 0 & 0 & 0 & \delta_{45} \\ 0 & 0 & 0 & 0 & 0 \end{bmatrix}. \tag{7}$$

Equations (1) to (5) are considered to explain the values of the endogenous variables as a function of those of the exogenous variables and the errors. They can be solved with respect to the endogenous variables, and thus lead to a new system in which each of these variables is expressed as an explicit function of the z_{jt} and the η_{it}. The transformation is expressed simply on the matrix form (6), which is equivalent to:

$$x_t = Az_t + B_1 x_{t-1} + \varepsilon_t, \tag{8}$$

the matrices A, B_1 and the vectors ε_t being defined by

$$A = -B^{-1}C, \quad B_1 = -B^{-1}D, \quad \varepsilon_t = -B^{-1}\eta_t. \tag{9}$$

Written in this new form, the model belongs to the category which we have investigated up till now, since the endogenous vector x_t is a linear function of the exogenous vector z_t, the lagged endogenous vector x_{t-1} and an unobservable random vector ε_t. We shall effectively reduce the statistical study of simultaneous equation models to that of multiple regression models or autoregressive models. But we must distinguish between the forms (6) and (8), and stress the problems which may arise when we go from the one to the other.

More generally, linear models with errors in equations contain n endogenous variables x_{it} $(i=1,2,\ldots,n)$, m exogenous variables z_{jt} $(j=1,2,\ldots,m)$ and possibly lagged values of the endogenous variables. Each one of the n equations of the model is introduced as representing a particular category of behavior or of relationship, just as were eqs. (1) to (5) above. Hence the name *structural equations* attributed to them. The model is then given in a form similar to system (6). By solving, the structural equations can be transformed into n *reduced equations*, each expressing an endogenous variable as a function of the predetermined variables and the errors. The model has then a form similar to system (8).

In fact by linear combination of eq. (6), we can obtain many systems, all equivalent. If P is any regular square matrix of order n, the system

$$PBx_t + PCz_t + PDx_{t-1} + P\eta_t = 0$$

is equivalent to (6) as well as (8). However, these two formulations have special roles. The reduced equations are the most convenient for calculating values of the endogenous variables. The structural equations are the most informative about the fundamental laws of the system, to the extent to which we wish to identify them individually.

To estimate these models, it may seem natural to concentrate attention on the reduced equations which define directly the conditional distribution of the endogenous variables for given values of the predetermined variables. Some of the statistical methods which we shall give indeed start with the determination of the coefficients of the reduced equations. But we shall also, in all cases, look for estimates of the coefficients of the structural equations, for it is these which have precise economic meaning.

Thus, in the model considered here, we wish to estimate β_{12}, the coefficient characterizing the price-elasticity of demand for food products. Knowledge of this coefficient is necessary for the answer to many questions. The reduced equations alone will not always be sufficient. Suppose for example that we are studying the application of a tax or a subsidy to food products. Equation (5) must be abandoned and replaced by a new relation between price paid to producers and retail price. The other four structural equations of the model are still valid and give the information required provided that the values of their coefficients are known. On the other hand, the reduced equations can no longer be used since all their coefficients are affected by the change in relation (5).

Here we find, applied to the case of models with errors in equations, a discussion already given in general terms in ch. 2 § 10. Whenever we wish to use a model for situations which differ somewhat from those to which the data relate, it is important to identify the structure of the model, and we cannot generally be content with estimating the conditional distribution of the endogenous variables. (The reader may refer to MARSCHAK [1953] for a fuller discussion of this.)

We must also note that the general forms (6) and (8) are liable to make us forget an important element in the problem. B, C and D are not any matrices whatever. Only some of their elements have to be estimated, the others being specified a priori. This appears clearly in the expressions (7). The matrix B does not have 25 unknown elements, but only 6. We can still say that B is a square matrix of order 5 subject to the following *a priori restrictions*:

$$\beta_{11} = \beta_{21} = \beta_{33} = \beta_{44} = \beta_{55} = -1,$$

$$\beta_{14} = \beta_{15} = \beta_{23} = \beta_{25} = \beta_{31} = \beta_{32} = \beta_{34} = \beta_{35} = 0, \qquad (10)$$

$$\beta_{41} = \beta_{42} = \beta_{43} = \beta_{51} = \beta_{53} = \beta_{54} = 0.$$

In addition to pure normalization conditions, these restrictions express certain assumptions about the laws composing the model. Thus we know that the volume of agricultural production and prices received by farmers do not affect consumer demand, and so they must not appear in the first equation.

Similarly, the matrices C and D depend respectively on 10 and 3 unknown parameters and not on 15 and 25 as the representation (6) might lead us to think. In all, the model contains only 19 unknown parameters, at least if we omit for the moment those on which the distribution of the random terms may depend.

The a priori restrictions are easily formulated for the structural equations. But clearly they also affect the reduced equations. The 40 coefficients of the matrices A and B_1 are not unrestricted. In fact they depend only on the 19 unknown parameters of the model. The matrices of the reduced form have fewer elements than those of the structural form. So it may happen that the restrictions on the coefficients of the structural equations imply no restriction on those of the reduced equations. But this is not the case in our example.

Some of the restrictions on the matrices A and B_1 are very simple. Thus, the model contains lagged values only for the variables x_3 and x_5. So in B_1, the 15 coefficients of $x_{1,t-1}$, $x_{2,t-1}$ and $x_{4,t-1}$ are necessarily zero. Moreover, the structural equation (3) is already in reduced form; we see directly that $x_{5,t-1}$ and t do not occur in this equation; therefore a_{31} and $b_{1,35}$ are zero. So 17 of the 21 restrictions on A and B_1 are very simple. But the last four are much more complex, as the reader may verify for himself.

Estimation of the reduced form proceeds from the principles already given for multiple regressions and autoregressive models. But the existence of restrictions on the coefficients complicates the question considerably. This is why we shall distinguish between *overidentified models* and *simple models* according to whether there are or are not restrictions on the reduced equations.

Since the coefficients of the structural form are sometimes more numerous than those of the reduced form, the former cannot always be determined uniquely from the latter. In accordance with the general definition given in ch. 2, we shall say that the model is not 'identifiable' if they cannot be determined uniquely.

Before dealing with them systematically, we shall illustrate the above ideas by studying some econometric problems for which simultaneous equation models have been introduced. Already when discussing the consumption function, we saw why we should not always stop at considering one equation in isolation even when it constitutes the sole object of econometric study (cf. ch. 4 § 3). We shall not return to that example.

2   Demand and supply. Identification problems

As long ago as before the first World War, some economists attempted the empirical determination of demand laws relating the quantity demanded of a product to its price. To this end they used statistical series giving quantities

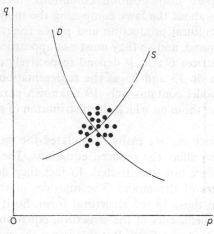

Fig. 1.

consumed and prices in the same country in different periods (H. WORKING [1925] gives a bibliography of these first studies). Some of the results obtained seemed rather surprising; MOORE [1914] found a demand for cast-iron increasing with price.

E. J. WORKING [1927] first showed clearly that the fitting methods applied did not necessarily reveal the demand laws. Indeed, according to generally accepted ideas, the price and the quantity consumed of a product are determined simultaneously from demand and supply. The situation is often represented by a diagram with price as abscissa and quantity as ordinate. A falling curve D determines the quantities demanded at the different prices, and a rising curve S the quantities supplied. Equilibrium is established at the point of intersection of these two curves.

Of course this theoretical system corresponds only approximately to the facts. Factors other than price may affect supply and demand. But, if the effect of these factors remains small, the observed point must lie near the intersection of the curves D and S. The set of data observed for a sequence of periods must define a scatter of points about this intersection and cannot give information about the shape of the demand curve (cf. fig. 1).

This situation may be represented by a stochastic linear model. For suppose there are two relations:

$$q_t = b_1 p_t + f_1 + \eta_{1t},$$
$$q_t = b_2 p_t + f_2 + \eta_{2t},$$

(11)

expressing respectively supply and demand, b_1, b_2, f_1, f_2 being fixed unknown coefficients, η_{1t} and η_{2t} random terms with zero means expressing the effect of unidentified factors. System (11) defines the model in its structural form.

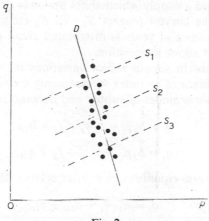

Fig. 2.

Solution with respect to p_t and q_t is possible since, by hypothesis, supply and demand have one and only one common point $(b_1 \neq b_2)$. This solution leads to the reduced equations:

$$q_t = a_{10} + \varepsilon_{1t},$$

$$p_t = a_{20} + \varepsilon_{2t}, \tag{12}$$

where

$$a_{10} = \frac{b_2 f_1 - b_1 f_2}{b_2 - b_1}, \qquad a_{20} = \frac{f_1 - f_2}{b_2 - b_1},$$

$$\varepsilon_{1t} = \frac{b_2 \eta_{1t} - b_1 \eta_{2t}}{b_2 - b_1}, \qquad \varepsilon_{2t} = \frac{\eta_{1t} - \eta_{2t}}{b_2 - b_1}.$$

These two equations show that quantity and price must take values distributed at random about a_{10} and a_{20}, which define the coordinates of the point where average supply (S) coincides with average demand (D).

A sample of observations on p_t and q_t (for $t = 1, 2, \ldots, T$) allows a_{10} and a_{20} to be determined more or less precisely, and also the distribution of the pair $(\varepsilon_{1t}, \varepsilon_{2t})$. But it is not sufficient for determination of the coefficients b_1, f_1, b_2, f_2 and the distribution of (η_{1t}, η_{2t}). In particular, the two relations defining a_{10} and a_{20} cannot be solved uniquely for b_1, f_1, b_2, f_2. Given the coefficients of the reduced equations, those of the structural equations have still two degrees of freedom. *So the structural relations, of supply and demand, are not identifiable.*

The situation is not always so unfavourable in practice. For many agricultural products, we actually observe an inverse association between price and quantity consumed. This is in fact due to the behavior of consumers, since the harvest, which varies from one year to the next, must be disposed of at a price which ensures that the market is cleared. So the market consists of a stable demand (curve D in fig. 2) and a supply which shifts upwards or downwards according to the richness of the harvest (curves S_1, S_2, S_3 etc.). The scatter of points observed over a sequence of years is distributed about the demand curve and so gives information about its position.

Since the variations in supply reflect variations in weather conditions, we can assume the existence of an index w_t measuring the state of these conditions in year t. The stochastic model of supply and demand can then be written:

$$q_t = b_1 p_t + c_1 w_t + f_1 + \eta_{1t},$$
$$q_t = b_2 p_t \qquad\quad + f_2 + \eta_{2t}, \tag{13}$$

and these two structural equations give, after solving, the reduced equations

$$q_t = a_{11} w_t + a_{10} + \varepsilon_{1t},$$
$$p_t = a_{21} w_t + a_{20} + \varepsilon_{2t}, \tag{14}$$

where

$$a_{11} = \frac{b_2 c_1}{b_2 - b_1}, \qquad a_{10} = \frac{b_2 f_1 - b_1 f_2}{b_2 - b_1}, \tag{15}$$

$$a_{21} = \frac{c_1}{b_2 - b_1}, \qquad a_{20} = \frac{f_1 - f_2}{b_2 - b_1},$$

The reduced equations show that the observed point depends both on random factors and on the more or less favourable weather conditions during the year under consideration.

Since w_t can be observed, the coefficients a_{11}, a_{10}, a_{21}, a_{20} can be estimated from the reduced equations. We need only have a sample giving the observed values of q_t, p_t and w_t during a certain number of years. The coefficients b_2 and f_2 of demand are in fact identifiable since they can be calculated from a_{11}, a_{10} a_{21} and a_{20}. For relations (15) imply

$$b_2 = a_{11}/a_{21}, \qquad f_2 = a_{10} - b_2 a_{20},$$

if $a_{21} \neq 0$, which we shall assume for the present.

On the other hand, these relations are not sufficient to allow the supply coefficients b_1, c_1 and f_1 to be determined uniquely from a_{11}, a_{10}, a_{21}, a_{20}. There is still one degree of freedom.

We assumed here that the autonomous factor w_t affecting supply had been observed. If this were not so, we should in principle come back to the previous situation, the effect of weather conditions being taken as a random disturbance. However, the shape of the scatter of points would then suggest that an important factor had a systematic effect on the phenomenon under study, and this factor would have to be investigated. Its origin would easily be found and it would be seen to affect only supply and not demand. The data could then be used in order to determine demand.

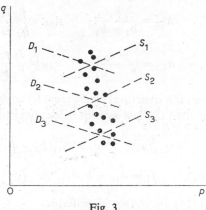

Fig. 3.

Two remarks must be made here. In the first place, the fact that the points have an elongated scatter is not in itself sufficient guarantee that the observed dependence expresses the reaction of demand to changes in price. A priori the systematic factor could affect demand as well as supply. The two curves O and S could shift simultaneously, with the scatter of points, lying along the path of their point of intersection (cf. fig. 3). If we take this path to describe the demand curve, it is because we can validly assume that demand is independent of weather conditions.

In the second place, even when demand is stable and supply variable, estimation of the curve D raises problems to which we shall return in the next section.

It is also possible that both supply and demand depend on factors other than price. On a two-dimensional graph the scatter of points no longer has a precise shape. But clearly this does not prevent identification of the relations of supply and demand. For some distinguishable factors affecting supply may leave demand unchanged, while some distinguishable factors affecting demand may not affect supply. This is sufficient for identification of the two laws.

Let us assume, for example, that demand depends on disposable income of the households R_t and that the structural equations can be written:

$$q_t = b_1 p_t + c_1 w_t \qquad\quad + f_1 + \eta_{1t},$$
$$q_t = b_2 p_t \qquad + c_2 R_t + f_2 + \eta_{2t}. \tag{16}$$

The reduced equations are then:

$$q_t = a_{11}w_t + a_{12}R_t + a_{10} + \varepsilon_{1t},$$
$$p_t = a_{21}w_t + a_{22}R_t + a_{20} + \varepsilon_{2t}, \tag{17}$$

where

$$a_{11} = \frac{b_2 c_1}{b_2 - b_1}, \qquad a_{12} = \frac{-b_1 c_2}{b_2 - b_1}, \qquad a_{10} = \frac{b_2 f_1 - b_1 f_2}{b_2 - b_1},$$

$$a_{21} = \frac{c_1}{b_2 - b_1}, \qquad a_{22} = \frac{-c_2}{b_2 - b_1}, \qquad a_{20} = \frac{f_1 - f_2}{b_2 - b_1}.$$

Knowledge of the a_{ij} allows the structural coefficients to be determined uniquely if $a_{21} \neq 0$ and $a_{22} \neq 0$; for then the last system is identical to the following:

$$b_1 = a_{12}/a_{22}, \qquad b_2 = a_{11}/a_{21}, \qquad c_1 = a_{21}(b_2 - b_1),$$

$$c_2 = -a_{22}(b_2 - b_1), \qquad f_1 = a_{10} - b_1 a_{20}, \qquad f_2 = a_{10} - b_2 a_{20}.$$

The coefficients of model (16) are in fact identifiable.

3   Estimation of demand laws[†]

Let us return to the simplest of those cases in which demand can be identified, that is, the case in which the scatter of points is distributed about a stable demand curve (cf. fig. 2). The properties of the different possible estimators clearly depend on the stochastic model which is considered adequate. This fact was little considered in the first estimates of demand laws. H. WORKING [1925] first brought it clearly into the open in economic literature. He emphasized particularly the role of errors in variables, which we have already discussed sufficiently in ch. 10. But some of his remarks take their true meaning only in a model involving demand and supply simultaneously. We shall now enlarge on these in a discussion which will be similar in many respects to that of the consumption function (cf. ch. 4 § 3).

We return to the model

$$q_t = b_1 p_t + c_1 w_t + f_1 + \eta_{1t},$$
$$q_t = b_2 p_t \qquad\quad + f_2 + \eta_{2t}. \qquad\qquad (13)$$

where the two relations represent supply and demand respectively. Let us imagine the determination of the pair (p_t, q_t) in a period for which w_t has a given value. To do this, we draw the function of average supply

$$q_t = b_1 p_t + c_1 w_t + f_1,$$

and the function of average demand

$$q_t = b_2 p_t + f_2$$

on a diagram with p as abscissa and q as ordinate (curves O and S of fig. 4).

† On this topic see SCHULTZ [1938], WOLD [1952] and ROY [1958].

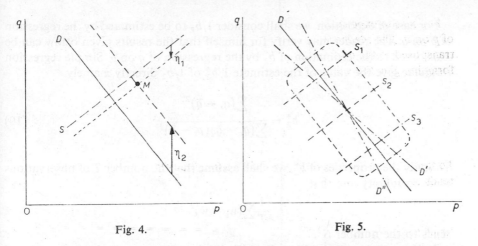

Fig. 4.   Fig. 5.

In the absence of unidentified factors, quantity q_t and price p_t take the values defined by the point of intersection of S and D. But, because of η_{1t} and η_{2t}, the observed values correspond to the point of intersection M of two curves deduced respectively from S and D by vertical displacements of length η_{1t} and η_{2t}. If w_t takes the same value for all observations, the observed points are distributed about the intersection of S and D, a positive disturbance η_2 corresponding most often to high values of p and q, and a positive disturbance η_1 to a high value of q, but to a low value of p.

The same tendency persists, though in a less clear-cut way, in a sample obtained over periods during which w_t has taken differing values.

A dotted curve has been drawn in fig. 5 to represent the contour of a hypothetical scatter of points. High values of p correspond most often to positive η_2's, low values of p to negative η_2's.

Although the points are scattered along the demand curve D, a regression of q on p gives a line D' which is more inclined to the horizontal than D. Conversely, a regression of p on q gives a line D'' which is less inclined than D. Neither regression seems suitable.

For a more detailed treatment of these general considerations, we must give a more exact definition of the random characteristics of model (13). For the same reasons as in the case of regression models, it seems natural to consider w_t as a non-random exogenous variable. We can also assume that the errors η_{1t} and η_{2t} representing the effect of unidentified factors are distributed independently of t and have zero expectation whatever the value of w_t. On the other hand, we must avoid assuming a priori independence between η_{1t} and η_{2t}, since some of the unidentified factors may affect supply and demand simultaneously. So we set:

$$E(\eta_{1t}^2) = \sigma_1^2, \qquad E(\eta_{2t}^2) = \sigma_2^2, \qquad E(\eta_{1t}\eta_{2t}) = \varrho\sigma_1\sigma_2. \qquad (18)$$

For ease of exposition, we shall consider $1/b_2$ to be estimated by the regression of p on q. The reader may verify for himself that the results given below can be transposed to the estimation of b_2 by the regression of q on p. Simple regression formulae give the value of the estimate $1/b_2^*$ of $1/b_2$ directly, namely

$$b_2^* = \frac{\sum_t (q_t - \bar{q})^2}{\sum_t (q_t - \bar{q})(p_t - \bar{p})}. \tag{19}$$

To study the properties of b_2^*, we shall assume that the number T of observations tends to infinity and that

$$\frac{1}{T}\sum_t (w_t - \bar{w})^2$$

tends to the number S^2.

In b_2^*, p_t and q_t are both random. Their expressions are given by the reduced equations

$$q_t = a_{11}w_t + a_{10} + \varepsilon_{1t},$$
$$p_t = a_{21}w_t + a_{20} + \varepsilon_{2t}, \tag{14}$$

the a_{ij}, ε_{1t} and ε_{2t} being computed from the coefficients of (13) and from η_{1t} and η_{2t} as we saw in the preceding section. The assumptions adopted for η_{1t} and η_{2t} imply that ε_{1t} and ε_{2t} have zero expectations whatever the value of w_t, and that the distribution of the pair $(\varepsilon_{1t}, \varepsilon_{2t})$ is independent of t. As a result we have the following probability limits:

$$\frac{1}{T}\sum_t (q_t - \bar{q})^2 \to a_{11}^2 S^2 + E(\varepsilon_{1t}^2),$$

$$\frac{1}{T}\sum_t (q_t - \bar{q})(p_t - \bar{p}) \to a_{11}a_{21}S^2 + E(\varepsilon_{1t}\varepsilon_{2t}).$$

Now

$$a_{11} = b_2 a_{21}$$

and

$$\varepsilon_{1t} = b_2\varepsilon_{2t} + \eta_{2t},$$

and so

$$a_{11}^2 S^2 + E(\varepsilon_{1t}^2) = b_2[a_{11}a_{21}S^2 + E(\varepsilon_{1t}\varepsilon_{2t})] + E(\varepsilon_{1t}\eta_{2t}).$$

Thus the limit of b_2^* is given by

$$b_2^* \to b_2 + \frac{E(\varepsilon_{1t}\eta_{2t})}{a_{11}a_{21}S^2 + E(\varepsilon_{1t}\varepsilon_{2t})}. \tag{20}$$

Estimation of b_2 by b_2^* generally contains an *asymptotic bias*. The latter is small if $c_1^2 S^2$ is large relative to σ_1 and σ_2, that is, if the values taken by $c_1 w_t$

(effect of the exogenous variable) show much greater dispersion than those taken by the errors η_{1t} and η_{2t}. The asymptotic bias is zero in the particular case where

$$E(\varepsilon_{1t}\eta_{2t}) = 0.$$

We must now study this case in more detail.

According to the definition of ε_{1t}, we can write

$$(b_2 - b_1)E(\varepsilon_{1t}\eta_{2t}) = b_2 E(\eta_{1t}\eta_{2t}) - b_1 E(\eta_{2t}^2).$$

This last quantity is zero in particular if $\varrho=0$ and $b_1=0$. We can now state: *the regression of price on quantity constitutes a consistent estimator of the demand law if supply is inelastic ($b_1=0$) and if the errors affecting supply and demand are mutually independent ($\varrho=0$).*

As Fox [1958] showed in a particularly clear way, this result justifies the use of the regression of price on quantity for estimation of the demand for many foodstuffs. Many of these products cannot be stocked, so supply is virtually identical to production. Now production often reacts slowly to variations in price. We can therefore assume that the elasticity of supply with respect to current price is very small. Also there seems to exist no reason for the unidentified causes affecting producers' behavior on the one hand and consumers' behavior on the other to be similar in nature. So, as a first approximation, we can also assume the absence of correlation between η_{1t} and η_{2t}.

Dealing with the market for pork in the United States, Fox found indirect verification of these assertions. For he compared two estimates of demand, the first obtained by a multiple regression of retail price on consumption and household income (y), the second by a consistent method which we shall mention below, namely the method of least squares applied to the reduced equations[†]. The following are the results for the direct regression:

$$p_t = -1.16\,q_t + 0.90\,y_t, \tag{21}$$
$$(0.07) \quad (0.06)$$

and for the consistent indirect method:

$$p_t = -1.14\,q_t + 0.90\,y_t. \tag{22}$$

We see that the two results are virtually identical.

Clearly we must not think that this is always so. In other cases the results differ much more widely. Thus, WOLD [1960b] compared different estimates of the

[†] The variables in the regressions are the first differences of the logarithms of the observed quantities over the twenty years from 1922 to 1941. For further details see Fox [1958], pp. 66–76.

demand for water-melons in the United States for the years 1930 to 1951. The direct regression of price on quantity was

$$p_t = -1.41 q_t + 1.61 y_t - 0.89 z_t - 1.69,$$

where z_t is an index of the transport cost for water-melons and the variables are the logarithms of the observed quantities. The indirect method gave

$$p_t = -1.11 q_t + 1.53 y_t - 0.68! z_t - 0.14,$$

whose coefficients differ notably from the preceding ones. In this case it does indeed seem that supply in one year must be considerably affected by the price realized on the average during that year.

These two examples show that, before proceeding to an estimate of a demand law, we should study supply conditions. In certain favourable cases, supply will appear as independent of price, and the regression of price on quantity will give a consistent estimator of demand. But this will not always be so.

As can easily be proved by the same line of reasoning as above, the regression of quantity on price constitutes a consistent estimator of the demand law if supply is perfectly elastic and if the errors affecting supply and demand are mutually independent. In this case, the supply function becomes, for example,

$$p_t = c_1 z_t + f_1 + \eta_{1t},$$

z_t being an exogenous variable depending neither on price p_t nor on quantity q_t. The supply price is then determined independently of the value which may be taken by consumption q_t.

The fitting of quantity to price is particularly well suited to the study of the demand for public services. In this case the nominal price is fixed for periods which are generally fairly long; it does not react to variations in demand. The real price, which is involved in consumer decisions, is generally measured by the ratio between the nominal price and an index of the general price-level which also does not depend perceptibly on the demand for the public service under consideration. Similarly, the random factors which take part in the determination of this real price are probably different from those affecting the demand which is being studied. Thus three French investigations into postal services, tobacco and passenger railtransport used regressions of quantity on real price (see MORICE [1938], GARNIER [1946] and BRICHLER [1946]).

What should we do when supply is neither perfectly elastic nor perfectly inelastic? A detailed answer to this question will be given in the following chapters. But we can now see a fairly simple solution for model (13).

We supposed that the errors η_{1t} and η_{2t} of the structural equations had zero expected values whatever the values taken by the exogenous variable w_t. We saw that the same property also applied to the errors ε_{1t} and ε_{2t} of the reduced equations. Similarly, if the pair (η_{1t}, η_{2t}) is distributed independently of t, the pair $(\varepsilon_{1t}, \varepsilon_{2t})$ also has the same distribution for all the observations.

Now, the basic assumptions of the method of least squares apply to the reduced equations. Consistent estimators of a_{11} and a_{21} are obtained by means of two simple regressions on the two equations of system (14), namely

$$a_{11}^* = \frac{\sum_t (q_t - \bar{q})(w_t - \bar{w})}{\sum_t (w_t - \bar{w})^2}, \qquad a_{21}^* = \frac{\sum_t (p_t - \bar{p})(w_t - \bar{w})}{\sum_t (w_t - \bar{w})^2}.$$

Since $b_2 = a_{11}/a_{21}$, a consistent estimator of this coefficient is defined by

$$\tilde{b}_2 = \frac{a_{11}^*}{a_{21}^*} = \frac{\sum_t (q_t - \bar{q})(w_t - \bar{w})}{\sum_t (p_t - \bar{p})(w_t - \bar{w})}. \tag{23}$$

We shall say that this estimator results from an *indirect regression*.

Thus, in his study of the market for pork, Fox[1958] set the following supply and demand laws:

$$q_t = b_1 p_t + c_1 z_t \qquad\qquad + \eta_{1t},$$

$$q_t = b_2 p_t \qquad\qquad + c_2 y_t + \eta_{2t}.$$

with the two exogenous variables y_t, household income, and z_t, production of pork. Two regressions on the reduced equations gave the following results:

$$q_t = 0.84 z_t - 0.06 y_t,$$

$$p_t = -0.96 z_t + 0.97 y_t.$$

The estimate quoted above for the demand law (see relation (22)) was obtained by eliminating z_t between these two equations.

4   Recursive models

Although price and quantity consumed result from a confrontation between supply and demand, we have found two cases in which a direct regression of demand provides a consistent estimator.

In the first, supply is completely inelastic and the model is written:

$$q_t = c_1 w_t + f_1 + \eta_{1t},$$
$$p_t = \frac{1}{b_2} q_t + f_2' + \eta_{2t}', \qquad \text{where} \quad E(\eta_{1t} \eta_{2t}') = 0 \tag{24}$$

(the constant f_2' and the error η_{2t}' are deduced from f_2 and η_{2t} after division by b_2). The relationships established by the model constitute a *causal chain*, since quantity is determined by the exogenous variable w_t and the error η_{1t}; while price is deduced from quantity and the error η_{2t}'. The situation is illustrated by the following arrowed diagram:

$$w_t \to q_t \to p_t$$
$$\eta_{1t}^{\nearrow} \quad \eta_{2t}'^{\nearrow} \tag{24'}$$

Similarly, in the second simple case, supply is perfectly elastic and the model is written:

$$
\begin{aligned}
p_t &= c_1' w_t + f_1' + \eta_{1t}' \\
q_t &= b_2 p_t + f_2 + \eta_{2t}
\end{aligned}
\qquad \text{where} \qquad E(\eta_{1t}'\eta_{2t}) = 0 \tag{25}
$$

(the constants c_1', f_1' and the error η_{1t}' being deduced from c_1, f_1 and η_{1t} after division by $-b_1$, the coefficient of q_t in the supply function then being zero). The dependences again constitute a causal chain illustrated by the scheme:

$$w_t \to p_t \to q_t$$
$$\eta_{1t}'^{\nearrow} \quad \eta_{2t}^{\nearrow} \tag{25'}$$

In the first case, q_t and η_{2t}' act as two independent factors determining p_t, without there being any 'feedback' of price to quantity. A regression of price on quantity is justified. In the second case, p_t and η_{2t} represents the two independent factors of consumption. A regression of quantity on price is justified.

Models of the type (24) or (25) have been called 'recursive' by Wold, who first studied them. More generally, let

$$Bx_t + Cz_t + \eta_t = 0 \tag{26}$$

be the structural form of a simultaneous equation model. *The model is said to be recursive if there exists an ordering of the endogenous variables $(i = 1, 2, \ldots, n)$ such that the matrix B is triangular and if the covariance matrix of η is diagonal*, that is, if

$$
\begin{aligned}
b_{ij} &= 0 &\text{for all} \quad & j > i, \\
E(\eta_{it}\eta_{jt}) &= 0 &\text{for all} \quad & j \neq i.
\end{aligned}
\tag{27}
$$

The ith structural equation can then be considered as representing the causal determination of the ith endogenous variable x_i by the error η_i and the other variables occurring in this equation. There is no relation of dependence of x_i on $x_1, x_2, \ldots, x_{i-1}$. *A multiple regression of x_i on the other variables occurring in the ith structural equation provides a consistent estimator of this equation.*

This definition and this property generalize to models involving lagged endogenous variables. Consider for example the 'cobweb' model, which has often been proposed for the description of the market for certain commodities of agricultural origin, in particular for pork. Supply is a function of price in the preceding year while demand depends on current price; for the decision to produce must be taken long in advance on the basis of the prices observed during the preceding season. For example, the model can be written:

$$q_t = d_1 p_{t-1} + f_1 + \eta_{1t},$$

$$p_t = \frac{1}{b} q_t + f_2' + \eta_{2t}'. \tag{28}$$

The dependences can be represented by the following system

$$
\begin{array}{c}
\cdots \rightarrow p_{t-1} \rightarrow q_t \rightarrow p_t \rightarrow q_{t+1} \cdots \\
\eta_{2,t-1}' \nearrow \quad \eta_{1t} \nearrow \quad \eta_{2t}' \nearrow \quad \eta_{1,t+1} \nearrow
\end{array}
\tag{28'}
$$

The chain is now infinite, but that scarcely affects the estimation problems which interest us here.

However, as PHILLIPS [1956] showed clearly, the model constitutes a pure causal chain only if the errors satisfy fairly restrictive conditions. For there to be no correlation between η_{2t}' and q_t, then η_{2t}' must not be correlated with η_{1t}, nor with $\eta_{2,t-1}'$, $\eta_{1,t-1}$, etc. We must add to system (28) the conditions:

$$E(\eta_{2t}' \eta_{1,t-\tau}) = 0 \qquad \text{for all} \qquad \tau \geqq 0,$$

$$E(\eta_{2t}' \eta_{2,t-\tau}') = 0 \qquad \text{for all} \qquad \tau > 0. \tag{29}$$

So the errors η_{2t} must show no serial correlation, nor must they be correlated with previous or concomitant values of the η_{1t}.

This is not a surprising condition since system (28) can be considered as an autoregressive model in the vector with two components (q_i, p_t). Now, as we have seen, absence of serial correlation of the errors must be stipulated for the least squares regression to provide a consistent estimator of an autoregressive model. Where there is serial correlation, the errors will also be correlated with the predetermined variables on which the regressions are calculated.

Let us consider more generally the model with lagged endogenous variables:

$$Bx_t + Cz_t + D_1 x_{t-1} + \cdots + D_h x_{t-h} + \eta_t = 0, \tag{30}$$

whose different equations constitute the structural relations. The model is said to be recursive if the errors are neither mutually correlated nor serially correlated, and if there exists an ordering of the endogenous variables $(i = 1, 2, \ldots, n)$ such that the matrix B is triangular, namely:

$$b_{ij} = 0 \qquad \text{for all} \qquad j > i,$$

$$E(\eta_{it} \eta_{j,t-\tau}) = 0 \qquad \text{for all} \qquad i, j \text{ and all } \tau > 0,$$

$$E(\eta_{it} \eta_{jt}) = 0 \qquad \text{for all} \qquad j \neq i. \tag{31}$$

In a recursive model, a multiple regression of x_i on the other variables occurring in the ith structural equation provides a consistent estimator of that equation.

Recursive models have a certain advantage for the econometrician, since they can be estimated by simple methods, each equation being treated independently of the others. In the analysis of phenomena which a priori bring several laws into play, we must always see if a recursive description is not a sufficient approximation of the real dependences; for the choice of too general a model implies that complex procedures will be necessary for its estimation, and, what is still more serious, that no great precision will be obtained in the results. The art of the econometrician consists in finding the set of assumptions which are both sufficiently specific and sufficiently realistic to allow him to take the best possible advantage of the data available to him.

But it seems difficult to maintain, as Wold has done for some time, that every model should be recursive. We have already discussed this point in ch. 2 § 6, and we need not return to it here. However, it should be noted that, when dealing with deterministic models, we did not introduce the assumption of independence of the errors affecting the different equations. This further restricts the field of application of recursive models; for we may often suspect that the same unidentified factors affect the different kinds of behavior represented by the structural equations[†].

5 Structural equations and theoretical regressions

To justify the simple regression model:

$$x_t = az_t + b + \varepsilon_t,$$

we often state that the expectation of x_t conditional on z_t is given by the linear expression $az_t + b$. In other words, $x = az + b$ is the theoretical regression of x on z. This way of setting the model applies to the case where z can be considered as random (cf. ch. 3 § 8). It is very suitable for the predictions for which the model must serve, since

$$x^P = az + b = E(x/z)$$

[†] Wold proved that we can find a recursive system equivalent to any simultaneous equation system (cf. WOLD [1952], § 12.7). Thus, for any system of the form (26), there exists one (or more) square matrix P such that

$$PBx_t + PCz_t + P\eta_t = 0$$

is a recursive model. The same result applies to models of the form (30). On the basis of this property, we could say that every model can be given in three special forms: the structural form, the reduced form and the recursive form (or forms). But the equations of a recursive form thus defined do not generally have the same autonomy as the structural equations; they may all be affected by a structural transformation concerning only one kind of behavior. So it is difficult to see why a recursive form should be preferred to every other form in which the model can be expressed, and particularly to the reduced form.

constitutes, in a certain sense, the best prediction of x which we can make, given the value of z (cf. ch. 2 § 11 and ch. 3 § 9).

WOLD [1960a, b] maintained that the same approach can be applied to the various structural equations of a simultaneous equation model. Each structural equation should represent a particular kind of behavior which leads to the determination of the value taken by one particular variable. According to Wold, this equation should be capable of interpretation as the theoretical regression of this variable on the others.

Thus, suppose that the behavior of consumers fixes the price at which a certain quantity is disposed of. The demand function:

$$p_t = \frac{1}{b_2} q_t + f_2' + \eta_{2t}'$$

defines the theoretical regression of p on q, namely:

$$E(p_t/q_t) = \frac{1}{b_2} q_t + f_2. \tag{32}$$

It provides the best possible prediction of p when q and the coefficients of the model are known exactly.

If this approach is accepted, each structural equation can be estimated individually by a least squares regression between the variable explained by this equation and the others. Such an estimator is consistent (cf. WOLD [1960a] and ch. 3 § 8 above).

For example, a regression of price on quantity gives a consistent estimator b_2^* of b_2 if the theoretical regression is actually that defined by (32). Indeed, formula (20) established above shows that the asymptotic bias in b_2^* becomes zero when ε_1 and η_2 are not correlated. Now relation (32) implies that η_2 is not correlated with q, nor therefore with ε_1 (the first reduced equation (14) shows that ε_1 differs from q by a non-random quantity).

So this approach leads to a conclusion which runs generally counter to that given above. We must find out where exactly it differs from the approach which was introduced in this chapter and will be maintained subsequently. We may also note that it has already been encountered and discussed when we were dealing with the elementary Keynesian model (cf. ch. 4 § 3). We shall now resume that discussion on a slightly higher level of generality.

We note first that the interpretation of structural equations as theoretical regressions raises no problem in recursive models. For example, the model:

$$q_t = c_1 w_t + f_1 + \eta_{1t}$$
$$p_t = \frac{1}{b_2} q_t + f_2' + \eta_{2t}', \qquad \text{where} \qquad E(\eta_{1t} \eta_{2t}') = 0, \tag{24}$$

implies

$$E(q_t/w_t) = c_1 w_t + f_1,$$

$$E(p_t/q_t) = E(p_t/q_t, w_t) = \frac{1}{b_2} q_t + f'_2,$$

since η_{1t} and η_{2t} have zero expectations for any value of w_t. The assumptions adopted here and those proposed by Wold are equivalent in this case. But this no longer holds in less particular models.

In the first place, it is generally arbitrary to select, in each structural equation, one variable whose value would be determined by the behavior which the equation describes. Thus, the model of supply and demand implies simultaneous determination of quantity and price. Except in particular cases like that of model (24), we cannot say without being arbitrary which of the two variables is determined by supply and which by demand. We have already discussed this point in ch. 2 § 6.

In the second place, in non-recursive models the theoretical regressions have different meanings according to whether the exogenous variables are or are not random. Suppose we consider quantity to be determined by supply and price by demand, although that seems artificial. WOLD suggests that we consider demand as defining the expectation of p_t conditional on q_t:

$$E(p_t/q_t) = \frac{1}{b_2} q_t + f'_2. \tag{32}$$

If the exogenous variable w_t is non-random, this relation constitutes an assumption that few of us are prepared to accept, namely that $E(p_t/q_t)$ does not depend on w_t, that is, that the price at which a given crop is disposed of does not depend on the average on weather conditions in that year. In fact it seems that, if these conditions are unfavourable, the crop reaches the volume considered only as a result of the favourable interplay of other factors affecting supply (η_{1t}) and demand (η'_{2t}), and that this is accompanied on the average by a price higher than if weather conditions were favourable. It would only be otherwise if $E(\eta_{2t}\varepsilon_{1t})$ were zero, therefore if η_{1t} and η'_{2t} were negatively correlated with coefficient $\varrho = b_1 \sigma_2 / b_2 \sigma_1$ (the coefficient b_2 being naturally negative).

If the exogenous variable w_t is considered as random and its values for different observations as independent, relation (32) can be considered as defining the coefficients b_2 and f'_2. It determines what is on average the value of p_t *when that of q_t is known and that of w_t is not known*. But to take this relation as the basis for prediction is equivalent to abandoning the theory expressed by the model. For this implies that the exogenous variable w_t can be predicted independently, while quantity and price must be jointly predicted by a simultaneous examination of supply and demand.

The model can certainly be expressed by theoretical regressions; but these will be regressions expressing the conditional expectation of each endogenous variable for given values of the exogenous variables. These regressions correspond to the reduced equations:

$$E(q_t/\theta_r) = a_{11}\theta_t + a_{10},$$

$$E(p_t/\theta_t) = a_{21}\theta_t + a_{20}.$$

Thus, the reduced equations define the form of the model which can be used most directly for prediction.

6 Estimation of production functions

In the preceding sections the example chosen was the fitting of demand laws. Clearly there are many other fields in which estimation of a structural relation necessitates the consideration of simultaneous equation models. Before concluding this chapter, we shall mention briefly two problems which have figured largely in econometric literature: estimation of production functions from data relating to a sample of firms, determination of price-elasticities in international trade.

The production function of a firm represents the technical constraints to which it is subject. It determines the output to be obtained from every combination of factors employed. To simplify the exposition, we restrict ourselves to the case where there is only one product whose quantity is denoted by Q, and two factors whose quantities are respectively L and K. (In many applications L represents labour and K capital.) The production function is then written:

$$Q = f(L, K).$$

In practice we generally adopt more or less restrictive assumptions about the form of this function. We shall assume that this is a case of a *Cobb–Douglas function* which can be written:

$$Q = AL^{\alpha}K^{\beta}. \tag{33}$$

A, α and β being unknown constant coefficients. This type of function is known to be appropriate as a first approximation in many cases. It is equivalent to a linear relation among the logarithms q, l and k of Q, L and K, namely:

$$q = \alpha l + \beta k + \gamma, \tag{34}$$

where $\gamma = \lg A$.

It is often assumed that firms in the same sector of industry are subject to similar technical constraints and therefore approximately to the same production function. Thus, shortly before the last war the idea spread of estimating the parameters α, β and γ occurring in the average function of a sector from data (q_i, l_i, k_i) observed for a sample of firms in the sector during a fixed period $(i = 1, 2, \ldots, T)$. More precisely, these parameters were then determined as the coefficients of a multiple regression of q on l and k. We shall now discuss some doubts which were fairly quickly expressed about the value of this approach.

(A complete list of the first studies, and the discussions to which they gave rise, appears in MARSCHAK and ANDREWS [1944]).

Since the firms do not all have exactly the same production function, it is natural to write the function for firm i in the form:

$$q_i = \alpha l_i + \beta k_i + \gamma + \eta_{1i}, \tag{35}$$

where η_{1i} can be considered as a random variable with zero expectation, because we have no knowledge of the effect of differences between the constraints applying to this firm and the constraints affecting other firms in the same sector.

A priori, relation (35) seems to justify a regression of q_i on l_i and k_i. But a closer examination shows that, in the practical situations considered, l_i and k_i cannot be considered as exogenous. Factor quantities would actually be exogenous if the data were derived from genuine experimentation, for example, if we had forced firm i to employ arbitrarily chosen quantities L_i and K_i, and then observed the resulting production[†] Q_i. But in practice it is the firm itself which has determined L_i and K_i in its own best interest, at the same time fixing the desired production Q_i. So we must examine in more detail how L_i, K_i, and Q_i have been jointly determined.

According to cases, the firms studied may find themselves in fairly different situations. The models which must describe these situations will also vary from one case to another. Clearly there is no question here of examining all the possibilities and we shall confine ourselves to two examples.

We suppose first that the sector considered consists of private enterprises and that the markets for the product as for the factors are competitive. Then there exist a price p for the product and two prices w and r for the two factors L and K. To maximize its profit, firm i should choose L_i, K_i and Q_i so that the marginal productivities of the two factors are exactly equal to w/p and r/p. For the production function (35), this implies

$$(q_i - l_i) + \lg \alpha = \lg \frac{w}{p},$$

$$(q_i - k_i) + \lg \beta = \lg \frac{r}{p}.$$

As the management of the firm is doubtless not perfect, we must expect some differences, positive or negative, between marginal productivities and relative prices. So we write

† Of course when possible, experimental determination of production functions can yield excellent estimates. Thus, numerous experiments allowed the fitting of appropriate functions for various agricultural productions. See HEADY and DILLON [1961].

$$q_t - l_i = \lg \frac{w}{\alpha p} + \eta_{2i},$$

$$q_i - k_i = \lg \frac{r}{\beta p} + \eta_{3i},$$

$$(36)$$

where η_{2i} and η_{3i} are additive terms considered as random and with zero expectation.

In this situation the three quantities q_i, l_i and k_i are in fact determined by equations (35) and (36). If all firms were perfectly managed and had exactly the same production function, these three quantities would take the same values for all firms[†]. The sample would not allow the calculation of a regression of q_i on l_i and k_i.

The existence of the additive terms η_{1i}, η_{2i} and η_{3i} explains why the observed results show some dispersion. But the regression of q_i on l_i and k_i corresponds in no way to the production function (35). For by solving the structural equations (35) and (36) we obtain the following reduced equations:

$$q_i = q_0 + \varepsilon_{1i},$$

$$l_i = l_0 + \varepsilon_{2i},$$

$$k_i = k_0 + \varepsilon_{3i},$$

$$(37)$$

the constants q_0, l_0 and k_0, or the random terms ε_{1t}, ε_{2i} and ε_{3i} being expressions in α, β and the constants γ, $\lg w/p$, $\lg r/p$, or the terms η_{1i}, η_{2i}, η_{3i}. The two coefficients of the regression of q_i on l_i and k_i depend on the correlations among the ε, which are functions both of α, β and the correlations among the η.

Thus, the calculated regression is not a satisfactory estimate of the production function. It constitutes a purely artificial relation which depends on the correlations among the differences η_{1i}, η_{2i}, η_{3i} just as much as on α and β.

There is no point in lingering over this situation, all the more since a realistic description would need to take account of imperfection of the markets. The reader who wishes to go more deeply into the subject may refer to MARSCHAK and ANDREWS [1944], to WALTERS [1963] and to NERLOVE [1965]. In particular he will find various suggestions for estimating production functions in sectors under purely private control.

Suppose now that the sector constitutes a public service and that the various concerns are obliged to satisfy the demand which appears at some imposed price. Production Q_i is a given exogenous fact. On the other hand the quantities employed of the two factors are chosen by the concern so as to minimize its cost price. We assume also that the concerns are localized in distinct communities and that the prices of the factors, say w_i and r_i, may vary from one concern to another.

[†] A complete discussion of the question should pay more attention to the possibility of multiple solutions. We can ignore this complication here.

The production function being given by relation (35), minimization of the cost price of concern i implies

$$\frac{w_i L_i}{\alpha} = \frac{r_i K_i}{\beta},$$

which can also be written:

$$l_i - k_i = \lg \frac{\alpha r_i}{\beta w_i}. \tag{38}$$

The structural relations (35) and (38) define the endogenous variables l_i and k_i as a function of the exogenous variables q_i, r_i and w_i. For the reasons already discussed in this chapter, a regression of q_i on l_i and $\cdot k_i$ does not provide a consistent estimate of the first structural relation.

NERLOVE [1963] determined an estimation method which is very appropriate to this case. Rather than use the reduced equations giving l_i and k_i as a function of q_i, r_i and w_i, he referred to the expression for the cost C_i of concern i as a function of the same exogenous variables. Starting from relations (35) and (38) and from the definition

$$C_i = w_i L_i + r_i K_i,$$

he deduced

$$\lg C_i = \frac{1}{\alpha + \beta} q_i + \frac{\alpha}{\alpha + \beta} \lg w_i + \frac{\beta}{\alpha + \beta} \lg r_i + \lambda + \varepsilon_i, \tag{39}$$

λ being a constant, a function of α, β and γ, and ε_i the random variable

$$-\frac{1}{\alpha + \beta} \eta_{1i},$$

(the transformations are elementary, though rather laborious). Relation (39) expresses the new endogenous variable $\lg C_i$ as a linear function of the exogenous variables only. It can be estimated by the method adopted in ch. 9. For we see that the coefficients of the three exogenous variables depend on only two parameters. (If the price of one of the factors, for example r_i, is the same for all concerns, it is sufficient to carry out a regression of $\lg C_i$ on q_i and $\lg w_i$).

In short, for estimating production functions from data relating to firms in the same sector, we must take account of all the relations explaining the determination of inputs and outputs. So a simultaneous equation model will most often be involved, its form varying from one situation to another[†].

7   Price-elasticities in international trade

A rise in the domestic prices of imported goods tends to cause a reduction in the volume of imports. The extent of this phenomenon can be characterized by an

---

† As HOCH [1962] has shown, a simultaneous equation model is generally no longer necessary when the data relate to a sample of firms observed during a sequence of periods.

elasticity coefficient a_1 equal to the ratio between the relative variation in imports and the relative variation in prices which gave rise to it. For the statistical determination of the value of this coefficient, the following relation has been assumed:

$$x_{1t} = a_0 + a_1 p_{1t} + a_2 z_{1t} + \eta_{1t}, \tag{40}$$

according to which the logarithm of the volume of imports during year t (namely x_{1t}) is a linear function of the logarithm of a price index for imported goods (p_{1t}), of the logarithm of the real national product (z_{1t}) and of various influences represented by a random variable with zero expectation (η_{1t}). (We see immediately that this relation would not be appropriate to a country using quantitative regulation of imports.)

Similarly, an elasticity coefficient b_1 defines the ratio between the relative variation in the volume of exports and the relative variation in the external prices of exported goods. For estimation of b_1, the following relation has been set:

$$x_{2t} = b_0 + b_1 p_{2t} + b_2 z_{2t} + \eta_{2t}, \tag{41}$$

according to which the logarithm of the volume of exports during year t (namely x_{2t}) is a linear function of the logarithm of a price index of national goods on external markets (p_{2t}), of the logarithm of the world real product (z_{2t}) and of other unidentified factors globally represented by the random variable η_{2t}. Relations (40) and (41) have been fitted by the method of least squares to data relating to different countries for the inter-war years[†]. The results were surprising, for the values obtained for a_1 and b_1 were small in absolute value, say of the order of -0.50 to fix ideas. According to these results, a decrease in export prices of 1% would be accompanied by only about a 0.5% rise in the volume of exports, and consequently by a decrease in the value of exports expressed in international currency.

Values as low as this for price-elasticities imply consequences which run counter to those expected by classical economists and by the large majority of the experts who decide the external economic policy of nations. It is generally assumed that exports are greatly stimulated by a devaluation which brings about a lasting decrease in the prices of national goods on external markets.

The values found for aggregate imports or aggregate exports also appear suspect when compared with price-elasticities estimated for more narrowly defined groups of products. Thus MACDOUGALL [1951–1952] found an elasticity of substitution of about 3 between American exports and British exports on third markets.

These considerations suggest that the method adopted for the empirical

---

[†] Various authors have attacked this question, the fitted relations varying somewhat from one to another. Here we refer more particularly to the equations chosen by CHANG [1945–1946, 1948]. The reader will find fairly complete references to other works in MALINVAUD [1950] and ORCUTT [1950].

determination of a_1 and b_1 is probably inadequate. A critical assessment should be made of the model and the estimation procedure adopted.

Fist of all we can say that the model assumes that rapid adjustments are made to variations in price and income, since exports and imports in any one year are considered to be functions only of prices and incomes in the same year. In fact the trade flows between countries result from contracts, which are not made from one day to the next, and which moreover imply a commercial organization and habits, which are slow to be established. So a precise description of the demand relations requires the introduction of distributed lag models. The estimates determined by relations (40) and (41) are liable to capture only short period reactions.

But, even if we pass over this fact, which does not relate to the present chapter, we can still ask if a multiple regression of x_1 on p_1 and z_1 is appropriate for estimating relation (40), and a multiple regression of x_2 on p_2 and z_2 for estimating relation (41). This question has great practical importance, since most of the variation in x_1 was in fact explained by z_1, and most of the variation in x_2 by z_2, so that the values found for a_1 and b_1 vary greatly with the estimation method adopted.

Consider relation (40). It is certainly admissible as a first approximation to consider the real national product as exogenously determined independently of the volume and price of imports, although even this assumption is not quite appropriate to periods of underemployment. But what can we say about the price index of imported goods? This index depends on prices in international markets, which can be considered as exogenous, provided that the country in question does not carry too much weight in these markets. But the index in question also depends on the effective exchange rate, that is, on the ratio between the exchange value with the addition of customs duties, and the general price level in the country.

Similarly in relation (41), the real world product can be considered as exogenous. But the index of external prices of national goods depends on the exchange rate and also on the volume of exports to the extent that the national supply of exported goods is not perfectly elastic with respect to internal prices.

So the two variables p_1 and p_2 depend on the real exchange rate. Now it was difficult to consider the latter as exogenous relative to the volume of imports and the volume of exports in the inter-war period. For most countries revised their exchange rates on several occasions so as to balance their foreign trade.

In short, p_1 and still more p_2 are not really determined independently of x_1 and x_2. Both depend on the exchange rate, which was altered whenever the difference between the value of imports and that of exports caused too much anxiety. Moreover the index p_2 depends on exports x_2 through the medium of the national supply, provided that the latter has not been perfectly elastic. So the multiple regressions which were used may be considerably biased. It is to be regretted that no investigation into the possible order of magnitude of this bias has been made.

CHAPTER 16

Estimation problems illustrated by some examples

Estimation of simultaneous equation models raises a fair number of problems which should be discussed successively. Before we can usefully approach a systematic treatment of the general methods, we must begin by looking at examples in which we shall encounter some of these problems in a simple context. This approach will not lead to much unnecessary repetition in this and the next two chapters, and will certainly facilitate a better understanding of the various questions to be tackled.

1 Indirect regressions

Let us consider first of all the simplest conceivable simultaneous equation model, that already introduced for the consumption function (ch. 4) as a summary representation of the Keynesian theory of under-employment equilibrium. The model is

$$x_{1t} = \alpha x_{2t} + \beta + \eta_t,$$
$$x_{2t} = x_{1t} + z_t,$$
$$\text{where} \quad E(\eta_t/z_t) = 0, \tag{1}$$

the two endogenous variables x_1 and x_2 representing consumption and income respectively, and the exogenous variable z investment. There are two structural parameters α and β, and a random error η whose expected value is zero whatever the value of z. The justification for this model was given in ch. 4 and will not be repeated here.

System (1) constitutes the structural form and we can easily determine the reduced form:

$$x_{1t} = (a - 1)z_t + b + \varepsilon_t,$$
$$x_{2t} = az_t + b + \varepsilon_t, \tag{2}$$

where

$$a = \frac{1}{1 - \alpha}, \qquad b = \frac{\beta}{1 - \alpha}, \qquad \varepsilon_t = \frac{\eta_t}{1 - \alpha}. \tag{3}$$

Like η_t, the error ε_t has zero expectation whatever the value of z_t. It follows that a and b can be estimated without bias by a simple regression of x_2 on z (cf. the second reduced equation). Let a^* and b^* denote the estimates thus obtained. Their properties are well known.

If the η_t all have the same variance and are not mutually correlated, the same holds for the ε_t. Among all linear estimators, a^* and b^* have smallest variances. And we know how to estimate these variances. Subject to a weak assumption about the sequence of the z_t, a^* and b^* tend to the true values a and b when the number of observations tends to infinity. If moreover η_t is normally distributed, so also are a^* and b^*, and they are efficient estimators.

As the model is often used in its reduced form, we could stop at this point and be content to estimate system (2). But it is also useful to have an estimate of the structural form (1). In the first place, α and β have more direct meaning in economic theory. In the second place, it is on the structural form that we shall know how to introduce the changes required for certain applications.

Since we have good estimates of a and b, it is natural to choose for α and β the estimates which correspond to them according to formulae (3), that is, to estimate the structural parameters by

$$\alpha^* = 1 - (1/a^*) \quad \text{and} \quad \beta^* = b^*/a^*, \tag{4}$$

since (3) implies

$$\alpha = 1 - (1/a) \quad \text{and} \quad \beta = b/a. \tag{5}$$

More generally, whenever there exists a one-to-one correspondence between the structural parameters and the coefficients of the reduced form, we can estimate these coefficients by multiple regressions and use the correspondence to deduce estimates of the structural parameters. This is said to be the method of *indirect regressions*.

What are the statistical properties of the estimators α^* and β^*? We shall now examine the question in the light of this example so as to reveal certain general characteristics of indirect regressions. First we consider the asymptotic properties.

In view of theorem 3, ch. 6, the pair:

$$\sqrt{T}(a^* - a), \quad \sqrt{T}(b^* - b)$$

has a limiting normal distribution when the η_t are not mutually correlated and all have the same variance, and when the quantity:

$$\frac{1}{T}\sum_t (z_t - \bar{z})^2$$

tends to a positive limit. It follows that the pair:

$$\sqrt{T}(\alpha^* - \alpha), \quad \sqrt{T}(\beta^* - \beta)$$

has, under the same conditions, a limiting normal distribution which can be completely characterized. For example, consider

$$\sqrt{T}(\alpha^* - \alpha).$$

Relation (4) implies

$$\alpha^* - \alpha = \frac{a^* - a}{a^* a}.$$

Consequently† $\sqrt{T}(\alpha^* - \alpha)$ has the same limiting distribution as

$$\frac{\sqrt{T}}{a^2}(a^* - a).$$

In particular, the asymptotic standard deviation of $\sqrt{T}(\alpha^* - \alpha)$ is equal to that of $\sqrt{T}(a^* - a)$ divided by a^2.

A simple procedure allows us to obtain the correspondence between the limiting distribution of the regression coefficients of the reduced form and the limiting distribution of the estimates of the structural parameter. Differentiation of relations (5) gives

$$d\alpha = \frac{1}{a^2}da \qquad d\beta = \frac{1}{a}db - \frac{b}{a^2}da. \qquad (6)$$

By analogy, we conclude that $\sqrt{T}(\alpha^* - \alpha)$ and $\sqrt{T}(\beta^* - \beta)$ have the same limiting distribution as

$$\frac{\sqrt{T}}{a^2}(a^* - a) \qquad \text{and} \qquad \frac{\sqrt{T}}{a}(b^* - b) - \frac{b}{a^2}\sqrt{T}(a^* - a).$$

Of course the reasoning of the previous paragraph is necessary to make this procedure rigorous.

The existence of limiting distributions for $\sqrt{T}(\alpha^* - \alpha)$ and $\sqrt{T}(\beta^* - \beta)$ implies in particular the convergence of the estimators α^* and β^* to the true values α and β. If η_t is normally distributed, these estimators are also asymptotically efficient since they are then identical to maximum likelihood estimators. Indeed, the expression for the probability density of the sample can be written either with the parameters a and b, or with the parameters α and β. The values α^* and β^* maximize this density in its second form, since the values a^* and b^* maximize it in its first form.

$\dagger$ Here we are applying the following property:

Proposition. If the random variable x_T tends in probability to a number ξ, and if the random variable u_T has a limiting distribution, then $u_T x_T$ has the same limiting distribution as $u_T \xi$.

This proposition applies here since $1/a^*$ tends in probability to $1/a$. (The specification of the model and in particular the first equality (3) imply that a is not zero.)

There also exists a correspondence between the distribution of (a^*, b^*) and that of (α^*, β^*) in small samples, since (α^*, β^*) is a well-defined function of (a^*, b^*). In the discussion of the properties of our estimates for small samples, let us confine ourselves to a^* and α^*.

If the η_t are normal, not mutually correlated and homoscedastic, a^* is normally distributed with mean a and standard deviation σ_a. Its probability density is therefore

$$f(a^*) = \frac{1}{\sqrt{2\pi}\sigma_a} \exp\left\{ -\frac{(a^* - a)^2}{2\sigma_a^2} \right\}.$$

In view of formula (4) defining α^*, the probability density of α^* is then

$$g(\alpha^*) = \frac{1}{\sqrt{2\pi}\sigma_a} \cdot \frac{1}{(1-\alpha^*)^2} \cdot \exp\left\{ \frac{-1}{2\sigma_a^2}\left[\frac{1}{(1-\alpha^*)} - \frac{1}{(1-\alpha)}\right]^2 \right\}.$$

It defines a skew distribution of an unusual type (the distribution of the inverse of a normal variable with non-zero mean). In particular, the expected value of α^* does not exist, since it is defined by a divergent integral; the estimator α^* is biased.

Of course, in order to make probability judgments about α, we could in this case make use of a^*. Thus, supposing that σ_a^* is the usual estimator of σ_a, a confidence interval for a at significance level π is given by

$$a^* - t_\pi\sigma_a^* \leqq a \leqq a^* + t_\pi\sigma_a^*,$$

t_π being the value of Student's t for the level π and $T-2$ degrees of freedom. We can easily deduce a confidence interval for α at the same probability level, namely:

$$\frac{1}{1-\alpha^*} - t_\pi\sigma_a^* \leqq \frac{1}{1-\alpha} \leqq \frac{1}{1-\alpha^*} + t_\pi\sigma_a^*.$$

But this is a particularly favourable case, where a structural parameter is a function of only one of the coefficients of the reduced form. Generally each structural parameter depends on several coefficients, just as here β depends on a and b. To make a rigorous probability jugdment on such as structural parameter, it is necessary to refer to the joint distribution of the set of coefficients of the reduced form, and the computation becomes very laborious.

So in practice one is often content with asymptotic approximation. For example one takes the distribution of α^* to be that of a normal variable with mean α and standard deviation σ_a/a^2.

Before saying a little about the effects of this approximation, we must recognize that, in econometrics, every probability judgment is necessarily ap-

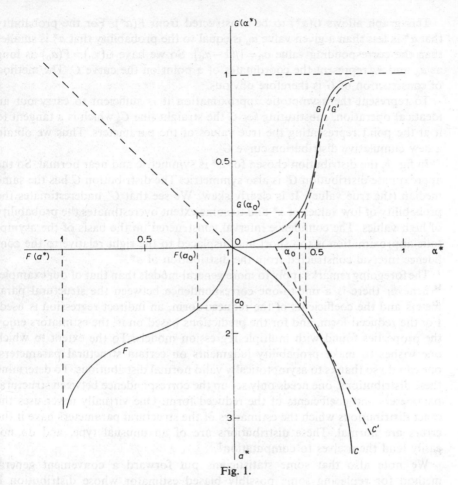

Fig. 1.

proximate, since the nature of the distribution of the errors is not known. In these conditions, the resort to a new approximation may have no serious consequences if it entails only small errors relative to the other specification errors.

Hardly any study has been made of the effects of asymptotic approximation on judgments about the structural parameters. So we shall confine ourselves here to a graphical investigation for the estimator α^*.

Figure 1 is a four part graph. The first quadrant, with coordinates α^* and $G(\alpha^*)$, shows the cumulative distribution of α^*. The second quadrant, with coordinates a^* and α^*, contains the curve C representing the correspondence between these two estimators. The third quadrant, with coordinates a^* and $F(a^*)$, contains the graph of the cumulative distribution of a^*. The bisector is drawn in the fourth quadrant.

This graph allows $G(\alpha^*)$ to be constructed from $F(a^*)$. For the probability that α^* is less than a given value α_0 is equal to the probability that a^* is smaller than the corresponding value $a_0 = 1/(1-\alpha_0)$. So we have $G(\alpha_0) = F(a_0)$ as long as a_0 and α_0 represent the coordinates of a point on the curve C. The method of construction of G is therefore obvious.

To represent the asymptotic approximation it is sufficient to carry out an identical operation, substituting for C the straight line C' which is a tangent to it at the point representing the true values of the parameters. Thus we obtain a new cumulative distribution curve G'.

In fig. 1, the distribution chosen for a^* is symmetric and near normal. So the approximate distribution G' is also symmetric. The distribution G has the same median (the true value). It is clearly skew. We see that G' underestimates the probability of low values of α^* and to some extent overestimates the probability of high values. The confidence interval constructed on the basis of the asymptotic approximation is too short and displaced to the right relative to the confidence interval constructed from the distribution of a^*.

The foregoing remarks apply to more general models than that of our example. Whenever there is a one-to-one correspondence between the structural parameters and the coefficients of the reduced form, an indirect regression is used. For the reduced form, and for the predictions based on it, the estimators enjoy the properties found with multiple regression models. To the extent to which one wishes to make probability judgments on certain structural parameters, one can do so thanks to asymptotically valid normal distributions. To determine these distributions, one needs only set up the correspondence between structural parameters and coefficients of the reduced form. One virtually never uses the exact distributions which the estimators of the structural parameters have if the errors are normal. These distributions are of an unusual type, and do not easily lend themselves to computation[†].

We note also that some statisticians put forward a convenient general method for replacing some possibly biased estimator whose distribution is difficult to determine by another which has an approximate t-distribution (see MILLER [1974], for example). This method does not appear to have been used in econometric applications.

2   Restrictions on the distribution of the errors

When dealing with supply and demand models in the preceding chapter, we considered a case where demand depends on price alone and supply depends

[†] A recent study must be brought to the reader's attention. BERGSTROM [1962] considered the model (1) given above and assumed that the errors η_t were normally distributed. He then determined the exact distributions of the estimator α^* defined in the text and the estimator $\hat{\alpha}$ defined by a direct regression of the first equation of (1). The distribution of α^* has a more elongated tail than that of $\hat{\alpha}$; but it is better centered about the true value. Even for small samples, it seems that α^* should be preferred to $\hat{\alpha}$.

on price and an exogenous variable, Let us return to this type of model, namely:

$$x_{1t} = \beta_{12}x_{2t} \qquad\qquad + \lambda_1 + \eta_{1t},$$
$$x_{2t} = \beta_{21}x_{1t} + \gamma_2 z_t + \lambda_2 + \eta_{2t}, \tag{7}$$

where x_1 and x_2 denote the two endogenous variables, z the exogenous variable, η_1 and η_2 the two errors, while β, γ and λ are unknown structural parameters.

The reduced form of the model is

$$x_{1t} = a_1 z_t + b_1 + \varepsilon_{1t},$$
$$x_{2t} = a_2 z_t + b_2 + \varepsilon_{2t}, \tag{8}$$

where the coefficients a_1, a_2, b_1, b_2 and the errors ε_1 and ε_2 obey

$$a_1 = \delta\beta_{12}\gamma_2, \qquad a_2 = \delta\gamma_2, \qquad b_1 = \delta(\lambda_1 + \beta_{12}\lambda_2),$$
$$b_2 = \delta(\lambda_2 + \beta_{21}\lambda_1), \qquad \varepsilon_{1t} = \delta(\eta_{1t} + \beta_{12}\eta_{2t}), \tag{9}$$
$$\varepsilon_{2t} = \delta(\eta_{2t} + \beta_{21}\eta_{1t}),$$

with, by definition,

$$\delta = \frac{1}{1 - \beta_{12}\beta_{21}}.$$

As we have already seen, knowledge of the reduced form of the model does not lead to unique determination of the values of the structural parameters, at least if nothing is known of the distribution of the pair (η_{1t}, η_{2t}). These parameters are not all identifiable. Of course, we can always calculate

$$\beta_{12} = a_1/a_2 \qquad \text{and} \qquad \lambda_1 = b_1 - (a_1/a_2)b_2.$$

But we can take for β_{21} any value other than a_2/a_1 and calculate $\gamma_2 = a_2 - \beta_{21}a_1$, then $\lambda_2 = b_2 - \beta_{21}b_1$. Only the first structural equation is identifiable.

In some models we sometimes assume that the errors affecting the various structural relations are mutually independent, each relation representing a kind of behavior which is assumed to obey specific factors. If this assumption is added to model (7), then identification of all the structural parameters is assured.

For we can write:

$$E(\eta_{1t}\eta_{2t}) = 0. \tag{10}$$

Relations (9) imply:

$$\eta_{1t} = \varepsilon_{1t} - \beta_{12}\varepsilon_{2t}, \qquad \eta_{2t} = \varepsilon_{2t} - \beta_{21}\varepsilon_{1t}.$$

So condition (10) entails

$$\beta_{21}E(\varepsilon_{1t}^2) - (1 + \beta_{12}\beta_{21})E(\varepsilon_{1t}\varepsilon_{2t}) + \beta_{12}E(\varepsilon_{2t}^2) = 0. \tag{11}$$

Now, the second-order moments of the ε_{1t} and ε_{2t} can be estimated under the same conditions as the coefficients of the reduced form. If the sample size tends to infinity, and the conditions of asymptotic convergence are satisfied, the second-order moments of the residuals of the regressions between endogenous and exogenous variables tend in probability to the second-order moments of the ε_{1t} and ε_{2t}. In these conditions, relation (11) allows β_{21} to be determined uniquely from the values of the second-order moments and the value of $\beta_{12}(= a_1/a_2)$.

More generally, the introduction of a priori assumptions about the errors in the structural equations can render identifiable parameters which would not be so otherwise. These assumptions occur as a priori restrictions on the structural form of the model. They have the same role as those which stipulate the absence of certain variables in certain relations.

Let us now consider estimation of the structural parameters. We confine ourselves first to the case where nothing is known a priori of the correlation between η_{1t} and η_{2t}.

As in the previous example, we may propose an indirect regression for estimating β_{12} and λ_1. The properties of the estimators β_{12}^* and λ_1^* will be similar to those of the estimators α^* and β^* defined on that occasion. The expression of these estimators reveals an analogy of which we shall later take advantage.

For let a_1^*, a_2^*, b_1^* and b_2^* be the estimators of the reduced form, whose expressions need not be repeated here. An indirect regression yields the following estimators for β_{12} and λ_1:

$$\beta_{12}^* = a_1^*/a_2^* \quad \text{and} \quad \lambda_1^* = b_1^* - \beta_{12}^* b_2^*,$$

for which we can easily obtain the expressions:

$$\beta_{12}^* = \frac{\sum\limits_t (x_{1t} - \bar{x}_1)(z_t - \bar{z})}{\sum\limits_t (x_{2t} - \bar{x}_2)(z_t - \bar{z})}, \qquad \lambda_1^* = \bar{x}_1 - \beta_{12}^* \bar{x}_2. \tag{12}$$

Exactly the same estimators would be obtained by using z_t as *instrumental variable* for fitting the first structural equation:

$$x_{1t} = \beta_{12} x_{2t} + \lambda_1 + \eta_{1t}$$

(see ch. 10 § 7).

Indeed it is easily seen that this case is favourable to the use of z_t as instrumental variable. Let y_{1t} and y_{2t} be the expected values of x_{1t} and x_{2t} (conditional expectations with respect to z_t). The reduced form implies

$$y_{1t} = a_1 z_t + b_1 \quad \text{and} \quad y_{2t} = a_2 z_t + b_2;$$

and the first structural relation can be written

$$y_{1t} = \beta_{12}y_{2t} + \lambda_1.$$

By hypothesis, the errors ε_{1t} and ε_{2t} on the variables x_{1t} and x_{2t} are independent of z_t; and this variable is strictly correlated with the 'true variables' y_{1t} and y_{2t}. It follows from the discussion in chapter 10 § 7 that the use of z_t as instrumental variable is particularly indicated in this case.

Estimation by instrumental variables was introduced as a result of a type of reasoning which has general relevance and which we now recall. For this we first assume that the exogenous variables are random, and that their values can be considered as resulting from T independent selections from the same distribution.

In order to simplify the expressions, we shall use two particular notations for the theoretical and empirical second-order moments. For example, we shall set:

$$E[x_{1t} - E(x_{1t})]^2 = [[x_1^2]], \qquad E\{[x_{1t} - E(x_{1t})][z_t - E(z_t)]\} = [[x_1 z]]$$

$$\frac{1}{T}\sum_{t=1}^{T}(x_{1t} - \bar{x}_1)^2 = [x_1^2], \qquad \frac{1}{T}\sum_{t=1}^{T}(x_{1t} - \bar{x}_1)(z_t - \bar{z}) = [x_1 z].$$

The models which we are considering imply certain relations between the structural parameters and the theoretical second-order moments of the observed variables. According to the method of instrumental variables, estimates of the parameters are obtained by solving some of these relations after substitution of the empirical moments for the theoretical moments.

Thus the first equation of model (7) implies

$$[[x_1 z]] = \beta_{12}[[x_2 z]]. \tag{13}$$

An estimate β_{12}^* of β_{12} is obtained by solution of

$$[x_1 z] = \beta_{12}^*[x_2 z]. \tag{14}$$

When the number of observations tends to infinity, the empirical moments tend in probability to the theoretical moments, at least if the law of large numbers can be applied to them, as we assume. It follows that generally the estimates obtained by the procedure described above tend to the true values of the corresponding parameters.

As is easily seen, the assumption that the exogenous variables are random is not essential here. It is sufficient that we can adopt for the limiting behavior of the sequence of these variables an assumption similar to that given in ch. 6 (assumption 5). For the observed second-order moments still tend to limits to which there apply the relations stated among the theoretical moments. It does not really matter that the latter relations can properly be said to exist only if the exogenous variables are random.

For example, consider relation (14) and suppose that $\bar{z}$ and $[z^2]$ tend to limits z^0 and S^2, where $S^2 > 0$. In view of the reduced eqs. (8), $[x_1 z]$ and $[x_2 z]$ tend in probability to $a_1 S^2$ and $a_2 S^2$ respectively. So in place of relation (13), we can write

$$\lim [x_1 z] = \beta_{12} \lim [x_2 z],$$

which allows us to establish, in the same way as above, the convergence of β_{12}^*.

To determine the relations to be used, it is simpler to act as if the exogenous variables were random. So we allow this course of action and write theoretical moments which do not strictly exist when the exogenous variables are fixed.

Let us apply the above principle to estimation of the structural parameters in the case where we know a priori that the errors η_{1t} and η_{2t} are mutually independent. We can easily obtain three relations among the theoretical second-order moments from the three assumptions:

$$[[z\eta_1]] = 0, \qquad [[z\eta_2]] = 0, \qquad [[\eta_1\eta_2]] = 0,$$

which can also be written:

$$[[x_1 z]] - \beta_{12}[[x_2 z]] = 0,$$

$$[[x_2 z]] - \beta_{21}[[x_1 z]] - \gamma_2[[z^2]] = 0,$$

$$(1 + \beta_{12}\beta_{21})[[x_1 x_2]] - \beta_{21}[[x_1^2]] - \beta_{12}[[x_2^2]] - \gamma_2[[x_1 z]] + \gamma_2\beta_{12}[[x_2 z]] = 0.$$

In view of the first relation, we can also suppress the last two terms of the third relation.

Consistent estimates of β_{12}, β_{21} and γ_2 are obtained by solution of

$$[x_1 z] - \beta_{12}^*[x_2 z] = 0,$$

$$[x_2 z] - \beta_{21}^*[x_1 z] - \gamma_2^*[z^2] = 0, \qquad (15)$$

$$(1 + \beta_{12}^*\beta_{21}^*)[x_1 x_2] - \beta_{21}^*[x_1^2] - \beta_{12}^*[x_2^2] = 0$$

We can easily add to them consistent estimates of λ_1 and λ_2, namely

$$\lambda_1^* = \bar{x}_1 - \beta_{12}^*\bar{x}_2, \qquad \lambda_2^* = \bar{x}_2 - \beta_{21}^*\bar{x}_1 - \gamma_2^*\bar{z}. \qquad (16)$$

These estimates could have been obtained in another way. As we shall see, they correspond to the *maximum likelihood* estimates when (η_{1t}, η_{2t}) is normally distributed with variances σ_1^2 and σ_2^2 independent of t and zero covariance, the errors relating to different observations being mutually independent. So, in this case, the proposed estimates have maximum asymptotic efficiency. If the distribution of the errors is nearly enough normal, and if the other conditions stated above are satisfied, the estimates must still have good asymptotic efficiency.

Let us prove that they are equivalent to the maximum likelihood estimates for the case defined above. The probability density of the T pairs (η_{1t}, η_{2t}) is then

$$(2\pi\sigma_1\sigma_2)^{-T}\exp\left\{-\frac{1}{2}\sum_{t=1}^{T}\left(\frac{\eta_{1t}^2}{\sigma_1^2}+\frac{\eta_{2t}^2}{\sigma_2^2}\right)\right\}.$$

The probability density of the T pairs (x_{1t}, x_{2t}) is therefore

$$(2\pi\sigma_1\sigma_2)^{-T}(1-\beta_{12}\beta_{21})^T\exp\left\{-\frac{1}{2}\sum_{t=1}^{T}\left[\frac{1}{\sigma_1^2}(x_{1t}-\beta_{12}x_{2t}-\lambda_1)^2\right.\right.$$
$$\left.\left.+\frac{1}{\sigma_2^2}(x_{2t}-\beta_{21}x_{1t}-\gamma_2z_t-\lambda_2)^2\right]\right\}$$

since the jacobian of the transformation of (η_{1t}, η_{2t}) into (x_{1t}, x_{2t}) is equal to $(1-\beta_{12}\beta_{21})$. Apart from a constant, the logarithm of this density is

$$-T\lg\sigma_1\sigma_2+T\lg(1-\beta_{12}\beta_{21})-\frac{1}{2\sigma_1^2}\sum_{t=1}^{T}(x_{1t}-\beta_{12}x_{2t}-\lambda_1)^2$$
$$-\frac{1}{2\sigma_2^2}\sum_t(x_{2t}-\beta_{21}x_{1t}-\gamma_2z_t-\lambda_2)^2. \quad (17)$$

For this expression to be maximal with respect to λ_1 and λ_2, it is necessary that

$$\lambda_1=\bar{x}_1-\beta_{12}\bar{x}_2, \qquad \lambda_2=\bar{x}_2-\beta_{21}\bar{x}_1-\gamma_2\bar{z}. \quad (18)$$

After dividing by T and substituting the preceding values for λ_1 and λ_2, (17) becomes

$$-\lg\sigma_1\sigma_2+\lg(1-\beta_{12}\beta_{21})$$
$$-\frac{1}{2\sigma_1^2}[(x_1-\beta_{12}x_2)^2]-\frac{1}{2\sigma_2^2}[(x_2-\beta_{21}x_1-\gamma_2z)^2], \quad (19)$$

where the square brackets conventionally denote empirical moments, as above.

To determine the maximum of this expression, we first write the conditions which result when we equate to zero the derivatives with respect to σ_1 and σ_2, namely:

$$\sigma_1^2=[(x_1-\beta_{12}x_2)^2], \qquad \sigma_2^2=[(x_2-\beta_{21}x_1-\gamma_2z)^2]. \quad (20)$$

When the derivatives with respect to the structural parameters are equated to zero we have

$$\frac{-\beta_{21}\sigma_1^2}{1 - \beta_{21}\beta_{12}} + [x_1 x_2] - \beta_{12}[x_2^2] = 0, \tag{21}$$

$$\frac{-\beta_{12}\sigma_2^2}{1 - \beta_{21}\beta_{12}} + [x_2 x_1] - \beta_{21}[x_1^2] - \gamma_2[x_1 z] = 0, \tag{22}$$

$$[x_2 z] - \beta_{21}[x_1 z] - \gamma_2[z^2] = 0. \tag{23}$$

After multiplication by $(1 - \beta_{21}\beta_{12})$ and substitution for σ_1^2 of its value (20), relation (21) becomes

$$(1 + \beta_{12}\beta_{21})[x_1 x_2] - \beta_{21}[x_1^2] - \beta_{12}[x_2^2] = 0. \tag{24}$$

By carrying out the same operation with (22), and taking account, of (24), we obtain

$$(1 + \beta_{12}\beta_{21})[x_1 z] - 2\beta_{12}[x_2 z] + \beta_{12}\gamma_2[z^2] = 0$$

which, in view of (23), reduces to

$$[x_1 z] - \beta_{12}[x_2 z] = 0. \tag{25}$$

The relations (25), (23) and (24) are identical to the relations (15); the relations (18) to the relations (16). This establishes the stated result.

In the following examples we shall have occasion to compare estimation methods using instrumental variables with those which consist of finding the maximum likelihood estimates as if the errors were normally distributed. But we shall not return to systematic discussion of estimation of the structural parameters in models containing a priori restrictions on the distribution of the errors. The foregoing remarks show how the problem may be tackled.

3   Estimation of an equation in an overidentified model

As we saw in the previous chapter, the a priori restrictions on the coefficients and on the errors in the structural relations can imply restrictions on the reduced form. The method of estimation by indirect regression is then no longer applicable. Other methods must be proposed. In accordance with the approach adopted in this chapter, we shall examine this question with the help of a simple example. Chapter 20 will be concerned with the generalization of the methods defined below.

Suppose there is a model containing two endogenous variables and two exogenous variables, whose structural equations are

$$x_{1t} = \beta_{12}x_{2t} \qquad\qquad + \eta_{1t},$$
$$x_{2t} = \beta_{21}x_{1t} + \gamma_{23}z_{3t} + \gamma_{24}z_{4t} + \eta_{2t}. \tag{26}$$

The errors η_{1t} and η_{2t} have zero expectations. But no assumption is made about their covariance matrix. The only a priori restrictions lie in the absence of z_{3t} and z_{4t} among the variables of the first structural equation. This model contains no constant terms. But subject to some complications in presentation, the following results apply to a similar model with constant terms.

The reduced form of the model is written:

$$x_{1t} = a_{13}z_{3t} + a_{14}z_{4t} + \varepsilon_{1t},$$

$$x_{2t} = a_{23}z_{3t} + a_{24}z_{4t} + \varepsilon_{2t}. \tag{27}$$

The coefficients can be deduced from those of the structural equations by means of the relations:

$$a_{13} = \delta\beta_{12}\gamma_{23}, \qquad a_{14} = \delta\beta_{12}\gamma_{24},$$

$$a_{23} = \delta\gamma_{23}, \qquad a_{24} = \delta\gamma_{24}, \tag{28}$$

where, by definition,

$$\delta = \frac{1}{1 - \beta_{12}\beta_{21}}.$$

From these relations it is easy to deduce

$$\beta_{12} = \frac{a_{13}}{a_{23}} = \frac{a_{14}}{a_{24}}. \tag{29}$$

The first structural relation is therefore identifiable. The second is not, since we can arbitrarily fix the value of β_{21}, subject to the reservation that it differs from a_{23}/a_{13}, and deduce values of γ_{23} and γ_{24}. Consequently we consider here only estimation of the first equation, that is, of the parameter β_{12}.

The model is 'overidentified' since there is a restriction on the coefficients of the reduced form. Condition (29) implies that the coefficients of z_{3t} and z_{4t} in the two equations are proportional.

Faced with a situation of this type, we can try either to fit the first structural equation, taking account of the existence of a second equation in which z_{3t} and z_{4t} appear, or to estimate the reduced form subject to the constraint (29). We shall start with the first approach, which is sufficient if we are interested only in the first structural equation. The methods which we shall later propose allow estimation of the reduced form. So they apply to the case where we intend to use the whole model for predictions.

In what follows we shall assume that η_{1t} and η_{2t} have zero expectations whatever the values of z_{3t} and z_{4t}, that these errors have the same variances σ_1^2 and σ_2^2 and the same covariance σ_{12} for all the observations, and that the errors relating to the different observations are mutually independent. We shall also suppose that the sequence of the vectors z_t, with components z_{3t} and z_{4t}, is such that the matrix

$$M_{zz} = \frac{1}{T} \sum_{t=1}^{T} z_t z_t'$$

tends to a non-singular matrix

$$\begin{bmatrix} S_3^2 & S_{34} \\ S_{34} & S_4^2 \end{bmatrix}.$$

Finally, let

$$\begin{bmatrix} V_3^2 & V_{34} \\ V_{34} & V_4^2 \end{bmatrix}$$

denote the inverse of M_{zz}.

We may first think of an *indirect regression* for estimating the first structural equation. We then calculate the coefficients a_{13}^*, a_{14}^*, a_{23}^*, a_{24}^* of the two regressions of x_{1t} and x_{2t} on z_{3t} and z_{4t}:

$$a_{13}^* = [x_1 z_3] V_3^2 + [x_1 z_4] V_{34}$$
$$a_{23}^* = [x_2 z_3] V_3^2 + [x_2 z_4] V_{34}.$$

Then we take, for example,

$$\beta_{12}^* = \frac{a_{13}^*}{a_{23}^*}$$

and thus obtain a consistent estimator, since a_{13}^* and a_{23}^* tend respectively to their true values a_{13} and a_{23}. However this procedure ignores the information contained in the values a_{14}^* and a_{24}^* which estimate two numbers a_{14} and a_{24} whose ratio is β_{12}.

We may think of using a kind of average of β_{12}^* and a_{14}^*/a_{24}^*. This, in short, is what is proposed by KHAZZOOM [1976] who 'solves' the overidentified system

$$\begin{bmatrix} a_{23}^* \\ a_{24}^* \end{bmatrix} \beta_{12} = \begin{bmatrix} a_{13}^* \\ a_{14}^* \end{bmatrix}$$

using the Moore-Penrose inverse of the left hand column matrix. This gives

$$\beta_{12}^* = \frac{a_{23}^* a_{13}^* + a_{24}^* a_{14}^*}{(a_{23}^*)^2 + (a_{24}^*)^2}$$

which obviously tends to β_{12}.

However, the general use of such an indirect regression method would lead to estimators whose asymptotic efficiency is less than that of other estimators using the same information.

Before coming to estimators which do not have this particular feature, let us consider those defined when we use either z_3 or z_4 as *instrumental variable* for estimation of the first equation. Such a method is well justified since, by hypothesis, $[[z_3\eta_1]] = 0$ and $[[z_4\eta_1]] = 0$. So the following two formulae define consistent estimators:

$$\hat{\beta}_{12} = \frac{\sum x_{1t}z_{3t}}{\sum x_{2t}z_{3t}}, \qquad \tilde{\beta}_{12} = \frac{\sum x_{1t}z_{4t}}{\sum x_{2t}z_{4t}}. \tag{30}$$

Of course these two estimators do not generally coincide. We may ask which should be chosen. Since both tend to the true value β_{12}, a simple rule consists of choosing the estimator with smaller asymptotic variance.

The asymptotic variances of $\hat{\beta}_{12}$ and $\tilde{\beta}_{12}$ can be calculated by applying the general principles given in ch. 10 § 7. For example, consider $\hat{\beta}_{12}$. The equation defining this estimator can be written:

$$\hat{\beta}_{12}[x_2z_3] = [x_1z_3]$$

or, taking account of the first structural equation,

$$(\hat{\beta}_{12} - \beta_{12})[x_2z_3] = [\eta_1z_3]$$

The expression $TE([\eta_1z_3])^2$ tends to $\sigma_1^2 S_3^2$; while $[x_2z_3]$ tends to a limit which can be written in the form $r_{23}S_2S_3$, where S_2^2 denotes the limit of $[x_2^2]$ and r_{23} the limiting correlation coefficient between x_2 and z_3. Thus the asymptotic variance of $\sqrt{T}(\hat{\beta}_{12} - \beta_{12})$ is equal to

$$\frac{\sigma_1^2}{r_{23}^2 S_2^2}. \tag{31}$$

Similarly the asymptotic variance of $\sqrt{T}(\tilde{\beta}_{12} - \beta_{12})$ is equal to

$$\frac{\sigma_1^2}{r_{24}^2 S_2^2}.$$

In short, of z_3 and z_4 we should choose, as instrumental variable for estimating the first structural equation, the variable which is most strictly correlated with x_2.

The use of the exogenous variables of the model as instrumental variables can also be conceived in a less rigid way. Let w_t be some linear combination of z_{3t} and z_{4t}:

$$w_t = v_3z_{3t} + v_4z_{4t}.$$

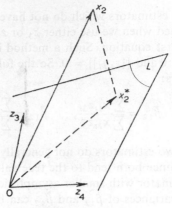

Fig. 2.

This new quantity can serve as instrumental variable[†] since

$$[[\eta_1 w]] = v_3[[\eta_1 z_3]] + v_4[[\eta_1 z_4]] = 0.$$

Now, by judicious choice of v_3 and v_4, we can generally find a variable w which is more strictly correlated with x_2 than z_3 or z_4, and thus obtain an estimate of β_{12} which is aymptotically more precise than $\hat{\beta}_{12}$ or $\tilde{\beta}_{12}$.

For consider, in T-dimensional space, the vectors z_3, z_4 and x_2 representing the two exogenous variables and the second endogenous variable. Let L be the two-dimensional linear subspace spanned by z_3 and z_4. The variable w that has the highest correlation with x_2 must be represented by a vector of L which makes the smallest possible angle with x_2[††], that is, by a vector which is collin-

[†] The reader can easily verify that we revert to the indirect regression estimate $\beta_{12}{}^*$ if we use the particular instrumental variable w_t defined with $v_3 = V_3{}^2$ and $v_4 = V_{34}$.

[††] Suppose we have some w_t. The definition of $x_{2t}{}^*$ implies

$$\sum_t w_t(x_{2t} - x_{2t}^*) = 0,$$

that is,

$$\sum_t w_t x_{2t} = \sum_t w_t x_{2t}^*.$$

The correlation coefficient of x_{2t} and w_t is certainly not greater than that of x_{2t} and $x_{2t}{}^*$, since this property can be written

$$\frac{\{\sum x_{2t} w_t\}^2}{\sum x_{2t}^2 \sum w_t^2} \le \frac{\{\sum x_{2t} x_{2t}^*\}^2}{\sum x_{2t}^2 \sum (x_{2t}^*)^2},$$

which, in view of the equality recalled above, is equivalent to

$$\frac{\{\sum x_{2t}^* w_t\}^2}{\sum w_t^2} \le \frac{\{\sum (x_{2t}^*)^2\}^2}{\sum (x_{2t}^*)^2},$$

or more simply, to the fact that the correlation coefficient between $x_{2t}{}^*$ and w_t has modulus less than 1.

ear with the projection x_2^* of x_2 on L.

Now, the components x_{2t}^* are the fitted values of x_{2t} in a least squares regression of x_2 on z_3 and z_4. The corresponding estimator is

$$\beta_{12}^0 = \frac{\sum x_{1t} x_{2t}^*}{\sum x_{2t} x_{2t}^*}$$

which can also be written:

$$\beta_{12}^0 = \frac{\sum x_{1t} x_{2t}^*}{\sum (x_{2t}^*)^2} \tag{32}$$

since x_2^* is orthogonal to $x_2 - x_2^*$.

Formula (32) shows that β_{12}^0 can be calculated by a double application of the method of least squares. The first stage is to determine the regression of x_2 on z_3 and z_4 and the fitted values x_{2t}^* of x_{2t}. In the second stage, the regression of x_1 on x_2^* gives the estimate β_{12}^0.

We shall justify this 'two-stage least squares method' in a general context, and show that in practice it often constitutes the best estimation method for overidentified models. It involves relatively light computation and its results have a fairly good degree of precision.

Moreover the advantage of this method can be understood directly. For, since the coefficients of a multiple regression are consistent estimators, x_{2t}^* tends in probability to

$$a_{23} z_{3t} + a_{24} z_{4t}$$

when the sample size tends to infinity. So in the limit the errors η and ε have zero correlation with x_{2t}^*. Now we can write

$$x_{1t} = \beta_{12} x_{2t}^* + \xi_t \tag{33}$$

where ξ_t is an error equal to

$$\eta_{1t} + \beta_{12}(x_{2t} - x_{2t}^*),$$

which tends in probability to $\eta_{1t} + \beta_{12}\varepsilon_{2t}$. Since ξ_t has limiting zero correlation with x_{2t}^*, relation (33) asymptotically satisfies the necessary conditions for the least squares regression to provide an efficient and unbiased estimator.

The principle of two-stage least square fitting can be applied in two different ways. We could first calculate the fitted values x_{1t}^* of x_{1t} in a multiple regression on z_{3t} and z_{4t}, and then establish the regression of x_{2t} on x_{1t}^*. This gives the estimator β_{12}^{00} defined by

$$\frac{1}{\beta_{12}^{00}} = \frac{\sum x_{2t} x_{1t}^*}{\sum (x_{1t}^*)^2}.$$

It is easy to verify that generally β_{12}^{00} does not equal β_{12}^0.

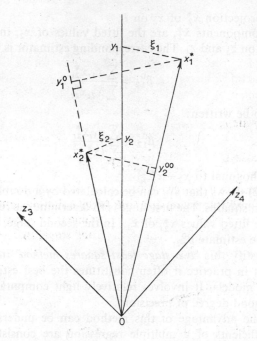

Fig. 3.

Although β_{12}^0 is obtained after determining the 'optimal' linear combination of the exogenous variables z_{3t} and z_{4t}, a different estimator β_{12}^{00} can be defined by applying the same principle. This is easily explained. To define β_{12}^0, we considered the relation

$$x_{1t} = \beta_{12}x_{2t} + \eta_{1t},$$

and chose as criterion the asymptotic variance of the estimator of β_{12}. Consequently we found the linear combination of z_3 and z_4 which is most highly correlated with x_2. We could have defined β_{12}^{00} by considering the relation

$$x_{2t} = \frac{1}{\beta_{12}}x_{1t} - \frac{\eta_{1t}}{\beta_{12}},$$

and finding the linear combination of z_3 and z_4 which is most highly correlated with x_1, with the object of minimizing the asymptotic variance of the estimator of $1/\beta_{12}$.

The relationships between the different estimators appear on a figure representing the subspace L of all linear combinations of the vectors z_3 and z_4 (cf. fig. 3). In addition to the vectors z_3, z_4, x_1^* and x_2^* already defined, the figure shows the vectors y_1 and y_2, the expectations of x_1 and x_2, namely:

$$y_1 = a_{13}z_3 + a_{14}z_4,$$
$$y_2 = a_{23}z_3 + a_{24}z_4.$$

The regression of x_1 on x_2^* is represented by the vector y_1^0, the projection of x_1 (or of x_1^*) on the line which is the support of x_2^*. Similarly the regression of x_2 on x_1^* is represented by the vector y_2^{00}, the projection of x_2^* on x_1^*.

In this figure the estimator β_{12}^0 is represented by the ratio between y_1^0 and x_2^*, the estimator β_{12}^{00} by the ratio between x_1^* and y_2^{00}. So we can say that the expectations y_1 and y_2 of x_1 and x_2 are estimated in the first case by y_1^0 and x_2^*, in the second case by x_1^* and y_2^{00}. In this sense, the two-stage least squares method allows simultaneous estimation of the structural parameter β_{12} and of the reduced form. One of the equations of the reduced form is estimated directly by an ordinary multiple regression, the other equation is obtained indirectly after estimating the structural parameter β_{12}.

The geometric representation suggests an estimation method which seems preferable a priori to β_{12}^{00} as to β_{12}^0. In the space L of linear combinations of z_3 and z_4, the numerical multipliers of these vectors can be taken as coordinates. The vectors y_1 and y_2 have then the coordinates (a_{13}, a_{14}) and (a_{23}, a_{24}), the vectors x_1^* and x_2^* the coordinates (a_{13}^*, a_{14}^*) and (a_{23}^*, a_{24}^*). We can consider x_1^* to differ from y_1 by an 'error' ξ_1 with coordinates $(a_{13}^* - a_{13}, a_{14}^* - a_{14})$, and x_2^* to differ from y_2 by an error ξ_2 with coordinates $(a_{23}^* - a_{23}, a_{24}^* - a_{24})$.

To estimate the direction common to y_1 and y_2 it seems that we can profitably use what knowledge we may have of the distribution of ξ_1 and ξ_2. Estimation of this direction by that of x_2^*, and of β_{12} by β_{12}^0, is equivalent to ignoring ξ_2. To take the direction of x_1^* and estimate β_{12} by β_{12}^{00} is equivalent to ignoring ξ_1. Now we know an estimate of the covariance matrix of the four-dimensional vector defined by the coordinates of ξ_1 and ξ_2. So we can do better than ignore either ξ_1 or ξ_2.

In a four-dimensional space we can define the vectors x^* and y with coordinates $(a_{13}^*, a_{14}^*, a_{23}^*, a_{24}^*)$ and $(a_{13}, a_{14}, a_{23}, a_{24})$, as well as the vector $\xi = x^* - y$. We know that $E(x^*) = y$, we know the three-dimensional variety to which y belongs in view of the equality (29), we have an estimate of the covariance matrix of ξ. So to estimate y from x^*, we can apply a principle similar to that given in ch. 9.

The estimator thus arrived at turns out to be that which is obtained by applying the principle of maximum likelihood, the distribution of the errors being assumed to be normal. It will not be given in more detail here, but will be examined in ch. 19 when the *Cowles Commission method* is discussed. The preceding introduction allows us to form an intuitive idea of its relationship with the two-stage least squares estimator.

4 Regressions in recursive models

In the course of the previous chapter we discussed the properties of direct regressions as estimates of structural relations. We saw in particular that the fitted values of the parameters tend to the true values if the model is recursive in form. We can now make a fuller study of this situation.

Consider the system:

$$x_{1t} = \gamma_1 z_t + \eta_{1t},$$
$$x_{2t} = \beta_{21} x_{1t} + \gamma_2 z_t + \eta_{2t}, \tag{34}$$

containing the two endogenous variables x_{1t} and x_{2t} and the exogenous variable z_t. The same assumptions as before are adopted for the errors η_{1t} and η_{2t}.

A regression without constant term of x_{1t} on z_t gives an unbiased estimate of the first structural equation since it satisfies the basic assumptions of the simple regression model. If no restriction is imposed on the covariance matrix, or on the moments of order greater than one of the pair (η_{1t}, η_{2t}), the second structural equation is not identifiable, since every linear combination of the two structural relations has the same form as the second.

Let us therefore examine the case where the model (34) is recursive. The errors η_{1t} and η_{2t} are then mutually independent, or at least not mutually correlated. In view of the first structural equation, this assumption, $E(\eta_{1t}\eta_{2t})=0$, is equivalent to $E(x_{1t}\eta_{2t})=0$. Since moreover $E(z_t\eta_{2t})=0$, the basic conditions are satisfied for the regression of x_{2t} on x_{1t} and z_t to give an unbiased estimate of the second structural equation.

This regression could be justified by a process of reasoning similar to that which appears in section 2 above for the model defined by relations (7) and (10). For the absence of correlation between η_{2t} and x_{1t} or z_t can be expressed as follows:

$$E(x_{1t}x_{2t}) = \beta_{21}E(x_{1t}^2) + \gamma_2 E(x_{1t}z_t),$$

$$E(z_t x_{2t}) = \beta_{21}E(x_{1t}z_t) + \gamma_2 E(z_t^2).$$

Substitution of the empirical moments for the theoretical moments leads directly to the normal equations of the regression of x_2 on x_1 and z.

Moreover it is easy to show that the two direct regressions define the maximum likelihood estimates if the errors are normally distributed. For the logarithm of the probability density of the set of T pairs (η_{1t}, η_{2t}) is then, apart from a constant,

$$- T \lg \sigma_1 \sigma_2 - \frac{1}{2} \sum_{t=1}^{T} \left(\frac{\eta_{1t}^2}{\sigma_1^2} + \frac{\eta_{2t}^2}{\sigma_2^2} \right).$$

The jacobian of the transformation of (η_{1t}, η_{2t}) into (x_{1t}, x_{2t}) being equal to 1, the logarithm of the probability density of the sample of the x's can be written:

$$- T \lg \sigma_1 \sigma_2 - \frac{1}{2\sigma_1^2} \sum_{t=1}^{T} (x_{1t} - \gamma_1 z_t)^2 - \frac{1}{2\sigma_2^2} \sum_{t=1}^{T} (x_{2t} - \beta_{21} x_{1t} - \gamma_2 z_t)^2.$$

To maximize this expression, we must minimize each of the two sums of squares separately, since the first contains only the parameter γ_1 which does not appear elsewhere, while the second contains only β_{21} and γ_2 which occur in it alone. So we come back to the direct least squares regressions on each of the two structural equations.

Consider now the following second recursive model:

$$x_{1t} = \gamma_1 z_t + \eta_{1t},$$
$$x_{2t} = \beta_{21} x_{1t} \qquad + \eta_{2t}, \tag{35}$$
$$E(\eta_{1t} \eta_{2t}) = 0.$$

It differs from model (34) in that z_t does not appear in the second equation.

As above, we can justify the method which consists of fitting each structural equation by a direct regression, and therefore estimating γ_1 and β_{21} by

$$\hat{\gamma}_1 = \frac{\sum_t x_{1t} z_t}{\sum_t z_t^2}, \qquad \hat{\beta}_{21} = \frac{\sum_t x_{2t} x_{1t}}{\sum_t x_{1t}^2}.$$

In particular, these are the maximum likelihood estimators if η_{1t} and η_{2t} are normally distributed. The proof is identical to that given for the previous model.

Model (35) is overidentified, since its identification is assured without the need for the last condition. For, let the reduced form be

$$x_{1t} = a_1 z_t + \varepsilon_{1t},$$
$$x_{2t} = a_2 z_t + \varepsilon_{2t}, \tag{36}$$

with the coefficients:

$$a_1 = \gamma_1, \qquad a_2 = \beta_{21} \gamma_1.$$

It is easily seen that $E(\eta_{1t} \eta_{2t}) = 0$ implies the following restriction on the reduced form:

$$a_1 E(\varepsilon_{1t} \varepsilon_{2t}) - a_2 E(\varepsilon_{1t}^2) = 0. \tag{37}$$

Clearly we can estimate the reduced form by ignoring this condition and calculating two regressions which yield unbiased and consistent estimators, a_1^* and a_2^*. We can deduce consistent estimators of β_{21} and γ_1, namely:

$$\beta_{21}^* = \frac{a_2^*}{a_1^*} = \frac{\sum x_{2t} z_t}{\sum x_{1t} z_t}, \qquad \gamma_1^* = \frac{\sum x_{1t} z_t}{\sum z_t^2}.$$

In short, β_{21}^* and γ_1^* result from an 'indirect regression'[†].

It is interesting to make a brief comparison of these two estimation methods. They lead to the same estimator of γ_1. We can confine ourselves to comparison of $\hat{\beta}_{21}$ and β_{21}^*.

(a) If in fact there is zero correlation between η_{1t} and η_{2t}, then $\hat{\beta}_{21}$ and β_{21}^* both tend to the true value β_{21}, but $\hat{\beta}_{21}$ has smaller variance. For fixed values of the x_{1t}, the conditional variance of $\hat{\beta}_{21}$ is

$$\sigma_2^2 / \sum_t x_{1t}^2.$$

That of β_{21}^* is

$$\sigma_2^2 \frac{\sum_t z_t^2}{\left[\sum_t x_{1t}z_t\right]^2}.$$

The first expression is never smaller than the second in view of the Schwarz inequality:

$$\left[\sum_t x_{1t}z_t\right]^2 \leqq \sum_t x_{1t}^2 \cdot \sum_t z_t^2.$$

They would be equal only if the x_{1t} were exactly proportional to the z_t, and we can exclude this case. Since the conditional variance of β_{21}^* is always smaller than that of $\hat{\beta}_{21}$, the same holds for the unconditional variances.

(b) If there is other than zero correlation between η_{1t} and η_{2t}, then β_{21}^* still tends to the true value β_{21}, while $\hat{\beta}_{21}$ tends to a different value, namely:

$$\beta_{21} + \frac{\varrho\sigma_1\sigma_2}{\lim \frac{1}{T}\sum x_{1t}^2},$$

where ϱ denotes the correlation coefficient between η_{1t} and η_{2t}.

To sum up, if we are sure that we have to deal with a recursive model in which the errors occurring in the two structural equations are mutually in-

---

[†] The reader can verify that exactly the same estimators are obtained by applying the method of two-stage least squares defined in section 3, that is, by first finding the fitted value $x_{1t}{}^*$ of x_{1t} in a regression on the first equation, then replacing x_{1t} by $x_{1t}{}^*$ in the second equation before applying a regression to it. For we can write

$$\beta_{21}^* = \frac{\sum x_{2t}x_{1t}^*}{\sum (x_{1t}^*)^2},$$

which can be compared with the formula for β_{21}. The fact that indirect regression and two-stage least squares give the same result stems from the fact that the model is 'just identifiable' (see chs. 17 and 19).

dependent, we shall prefer the direct regressions on the structural equations. Even apart from the ease of computation, the corresponding estimators seem to enjoy the better statistical properties.

On the other hand, if we suspect that there is a substantial correlation between the errors affecting the different relations, we may prefer the indirect regressions in spite of the triangular form of the matrix of the coefficients, in order to avoid the effects of a 'specification error'.

These conclusions apply generally. Indirect regressions, two-stage least squares and the other methods of the same kind can very well be used for estimating models in which the matrix of the coefficients is triangular. It is only when the errors affecting the various structural equations can be considered as mutually independent that the direct regressions on the different structural equations have a definite advantage.

CHAPTER 17

Identification

1 The structural form

In the two previous chapters we considered various examples of simultaneous equation models either when discussing certain practical econometric questions or when making a preliminary examination of estimation problems. The systematic treatment of these models starts with the study of identification of the structural equations[†].

We shall obtain certain properties which specify when a model is either identified or overidentified. These properties will become more and more specific as we put stricter limitation on the class of restrictions imposed on the different parameters. But first we must give a general representation of the structural and reduced forms.

The structural form will generally be written:

$$Bx_t + Cz_t = \eta_t, \tag{1}$$

where x_t denotes the vector of the n endogenous variables, z_t the vector of the m exogenous variables and η_t the vector of the n errors. Each equation of this system corresponds to one of the basic laws which define the model. The determination of these laws is the final objective of econometric research.

The aim of the complete model is to determine how the values of the endogenous variables (x_t) are determined by the values of the exogenous variables (z_t) and some random errors (η_t). Consequently system (1) must have a unique solution in x_t for every set of values of z_t and η_t, which justifies the following assumption.

Assumption 1. B is a non-singular matrix.

Sometimes the model contains not only true exogenous variables, but also lagged values of certain endogenous variables. In order to keep the notation simple, we shall most often retain expression (1) above, the components of the vector z_t then being the set of predetermined variables corresponding to the tth observation, namely the exogenous variables proper and the lagged values of the endogenous variables. For certain questions, and in particular for identification, the presence of lagged endogenous variables does not affect the reasoning and the results. It is pointless to include it in our formulation.

The specification of the model contains not only the list of the endogenous

[†] For this chapter, the reader may profitably consult KOOPMANS [1949].

and exogenous variables, but also more precise stipulations which can conveniently be grouped in three categories, the *general stochastic hypothesis*, the *a priori restrictions* and the *normalization rule*.

The general stochastic hypothesis relates to the distribution of the errors. For our present discussion of identification, we shall adopt the following

Assumption 2. The η_t are mutually independent. They are identically distributed with zero mean.

Later we shall need to strengthen the general stochastic assumption for the theory of estimation and tests. For example, we shall assume that the vector η_t has a finite covariance matrix Σ or that it has finite moments of all orders or that it is normally distributed. For the present we shall keep to a very general assumption[†] which nevertheless does not allow for serial correlation of errors. The example at the beginning of ch. 13, § 5 shows that the latter may complicate identification. We shall not discuss this point here. (See HANNAN [1971] and DEISTLER [1978].)

In fact this assumption is unnecessarily restrictive. The reader can verify that the properties established are also valid when the η_t form a stationary stochastic process with zero mean. But the proofs are more difficult. On the other hand, we shall have to strengthen the general stochastic hypothesis for the theory of estimation and tests. For example, we shall assume that the vector η_t has finite covariance matrix Σ, or has finite moments of all orders, or even is normally distributed.

The *a priori restrictions* further limit the values of the coefficients of B and C, or the distribution of the errors η_t. In particular, certain variables do not appear in certain equations; the corresponding elements of B and C must be zero. The coefficients of the same variable in different equations are sometimes assumed to be equal. It may also happen that the errors affecting the different equations are considered as mutually independent, the matrix Σ then being diagonal.

Of course the distinction between the general stochastic hypothesis and the a priori restrictions is purely conventional. Its only object is to facilitate the discussion of identification problems, and it is based on no necessary logical principle.

Each equation of the structural form expresses one of the laws of the model. Clearly this law is unmodified if both terms of the equation are multiplied by the same number. In order to avoid the resulting indeterminacy, it will be useful to adopt a *normalization rule*. Except when otherwise specified, we shall assume that in the ith structural equation the coefficient of the ith endogenous variable is equal to 1. This convention, which was adopted in most of the examples considered in the course of the preceding chapters, assumes that the ith endogenous variable occurs in the ith equation with a non-zero coefficient. We shall suppose that this assumption is justified in practice.

---

† So our present treatment says nothing about the elegant theory put forward by ROTHENBERG [1971] and BOWDEN [1973] for identification in *parametric* models.

The presence of *identities* among the equations of the model would be covered by the a priori restrictions. But it is more convenient for our theory to represent them explicitly when they exist. Let us examine briefly why they appear and how they can be represented.

For prediction of general changes in the national economy, recourse has recently been made to models with many equations. In such cases the system often contains, apart from the structural equations mentioned so far, some accounting equations or identities which connect the exogenous and endogenous variables. Consider, for example, a very simple general model in which consumption C_t during period t is a function of wages W_t and profits P_t earned during the period; investment I_t is a function of profits P_t and P_{t-1}; total wages is a function of global income Y_t, of Y_{t-1} and of a time trend. In the accounting equality where Y_t is the sum of W_t, P_t and net transfers T_t to the government, the term T_t is regarded as an exogenous datum. Similarly, the equilibrium condition on the market for goods and services expresses the equality between Y_t and the sum of C_t, I_t and government demand G_t, which is also considered as exogenous[†].

The model consists of the following five equations:

$$\left.\begin{aligned}
C_t &= \delta_1 W_t + \delta_2 P_t + \delta_3 + \eta_{1t} \\
I_t &= \delta_4 P_t + \delta_5 P_{t-1} + \delta_6 + \eta_{2t} \\
W_t &= \delta_7 Y_t + \delta_8 Y_{t-1} + \delta_9 t + \delta_{10} + \eta_{3t} \\
Y_t &= W_t + P_t + I_t \\
Y_t &= C_t + I_t + G_t
\end{aligned}\right\} \qquad (2)$$

The δ_i are numerical coefficients to be estimated and the η_{it} are random errors. The endogenous variables are C_t, I_t, W_t, Y_t, P_t; the exogenous variables are T_t, G_t and t.

The first three equations are of the nature of structural relations comparable to those appearing in the models so far discussed. The last two equations have the double feature that they contain neither random errors nor unknown coefficients. We shall call them 'identities'.

Of course, the identities could be used to eliminate some of the endogenous variables. But this has the drawback of introducing, as coefficients in the structural equations, more or less complex expressions of the parameters of the initial form. Each element of the matrices B and C would no longer be either known or entirely unrestricted, as we shall assume later on.

Thus, we could eliminate Y_t and P_t from (2). This gives the following system of three equations:

---

† This is a somewhat simplified version of a model introduced by KLEIN [1953] as a summary description of the American economy, useful for teaching purposes. Various authors refer to this model to illustrate their analyses.

$$(1-\delta_2)C_t = \delta_2 I_t + (\delta_1 - \delta_2)W_t + \delta_2 G_t - \delta_2 T_t + \delta_3 + \eta_{1t}$$

$$(1-\delta_4)I_t = \delta_4 C_t - \delta_4 W_t + \delta_5 C_{t-1} + \delta_5 I_{t-1} - \delta_5 W_{t-1}$$

$$+\delta_4 G_t - \delta_4 T_t + \delta_5 G_{t-1} - \delta_5 T_{t-1} + \delta_6 + \eta_{2t} \qquad (3)$$

$$W_t = \delta_7 C_t + \delta_7 I_t + \delta_8 C_{t-1} + \delta_8 I_{t-1} + \delta_7 G_t$$

$$+\delta_8 G_{t-1} + \delta_9 t + \delta_{10} + \eta_{3t}$$

The 25 non-zero coefficients of this system depend only on the 10 parameters δ_i, so that (3) is not a very convenient form. So we shall look for statistical procedures which can be applied directly to the model in its initial form containing the identities.

However, for the theoretical discussion, it is useful to consider system (1) as representing the structural form after elimination of the identities and to introduce a different general notation for the structural form containing the identities. More precisely, if there are n' identities in addition to the n true structural equations, we assume that the $n+n'$ endogenous variables are divided into two categories defining respectively a vector x_t with n components and a vector q_t with n' components. They will be divided out in such a way that the identities allow us to determine q_t from x_t and z_t, which is always possible, the identities in the specification of the model being of course linearly independent. We then write the model as follows:

$$B_1 x_t + B_2 q_t + C_1 z_t = \eta_t$$
$$B_3 x_t + B_4 q_t + C_2 z_t = 0. \qquad (4)$$

The true structural equations are grouped in the first part of the system and the identities in the second. By definition, the matrices B_3, B_4, C_2 consisting of the coefficients of the identities are known exactly. Moreover, B_4 is *non-singular* because of the rule adopted for allocating the endogenous variables to x_t or to q_t.

By eliminating q_t from (4) we revert to (1), the matrices B and C being defined by

$$B = B_1 - B_2 B_4^{-1} B_3$$
$$C = C_1 - B_2 B_4^{-1} C_2. \qquad (5)$$

Since B_3, B_4 and C_2 are known exactly, B and C are linear expressions of the unknown matrices B_1, B_2 and C_1.

We shall also use the notation

$$\bar{B} = \begin{bmatrix} B_1 & B_2 \\ B_3 & B_4 \end{bmatrix} \qquad \bar{C} = \begin{bmatrix} C_1 \\ C_2 \end{bmatrix} \qquad \bar{\eta}_t = \begin{bmatrix} \eta_t \\ 0 \end{bmatrix} \qquad (6)$$

where $\bar{\eta}_t$ is then a vector with $n+n'$ components. Finally, we shall interpret assumption 1 as stipulating in this case that $\bar{B}$ is non-singular, which implies non-singularity of the matrix B defined by (5) ($Bu = 0$ implies $B_1 u - B_2 B_4^{-1} B_3 u = 0$, that is, v being the vector $-B_4^{-1} B_3 u$, both $B_1 u + B_2 v = 0$ and $B_3 u + B_4 v = 0$).

2 The reduced form

In the reduced form, the value taken by each endogenous variable appears as a function of the exogenous variables (or of the predetermined variables in auto-regressive models) and of certain random errors.

We shall write:

$$x_t = A z_t + \varepsilon_t. \tag{7}$$

Assumption 1 justifies the correspondence

$$A = -B^{-1}C \qquad \varepsilon_t = B^{-1}\eta_t. \tag{8}$$

If the model contains identities, we can also express q_t as a linear function of z_t and a vector χ_t of random errors. This adds nothing new to the reduced form since q_t is a known function of x_t and z_t. So as a rule we shall keep to the reduced form (7) restricted to the vector x_t. However, in some cases it will be useful to consider the 'extended reduced form':

$$\begin{bmatrix} x_t \\ q_t \end{bmatrix} = \begin{bmatrix} A \\ H \end{bmatrix} z_t + \begin{bmatrix} \varepsilon_t \\ \chi_t \end{bmatrix} \tag{9}$$

given that

$$H = -B_4^{-1}(B_3 A + C_2) \qquad \chi_t = -B_4^{-1} B_3 \varepsilon_t. \tag{10}$$

We shall then use the notation

$$\bar{A} = \begin{bmatrix} A \\ H \end{bmatrix} \qquad \bar{\varepsilon}_t = \begin{bmatrix} \varepsilon_t \\ \chi_t \end{bmatrix} \tag{11}$$

the correspondence between the extended structural and reduced forms being

$$\bar{A} = -\bar{B}^{-1}\bar{C}, \qquad \bar{\varepsilon}_t = \bar{B}^{-1}\bar{\eta}_t. \tag{12}$$

The reduced form of the model can be used directly for prediction since the problem consists of estimating the values of the endogenous variables which will correspond to values assumed for the predetermined variables. In section 10 of ch. 6 we saw why $x_\theta^P = \hat{A} z_\theta$ is suitable for predicting x_θ when z_θ is known and $\hat{A}$ is an efficient estimator of A. Moreover, we shall refer to the reduced form when we discuss estimation of the model so as to apply the general properties of linear and non-linear regression.

Like the structural form, the reduced form is subject to a general stochastic hypothesis and possibly to a priori restrictions. The stochastic hypothesis stipulates certain properties of the errors. In this chapter, assumptions 1 and 2 imply that the ε_t are mutually independent and identically distributed with zero mean. In later discussion of estimation and tests it will be necessary to make the further assumption that the ε_t have finite covariance matrix Ω, or that they have finite moments of all orders, or that they are normally distributed.

Because of the restrictions imposed on the structural form, the reduced form may also be subject to certain a priori restrictions. The limitations imposed on B and C and on the distribution of η_t may restrict A and the distribution of ε_t. We then say that the model is *overidentified*, an expression already introduced in ch. 15, § 1 (a rigorous definition will be given later).

The reduced form derives its importance from the fact that it gives the distribution of the endogenous variables directly. The reciprocal property is also true if the z_t are not strictly multicollinear. As we saw in ch. 6 (proposition 1), two different matrices A^1 and A^2 can correspond to the same distribution of x_t if the domain of the z_t is restricted so that it contains multicollinearities. To eliminate this case, we adopt

Assumption 3.　The vectors z_t are such that there exists no set of m numbers $\lambda_j(j = 1, 2, \ldots, m)$ not all zero, for which

$$\sum_{j=1}^{m} \lambda_j z_{jt} = 0 \qquad \text{for all } t.$$

We can then prove

Proposition 1.　If assumptions 1, 2 and 3 are satisfied, the complete specification of the reduced form is equivalent to that of the distribution of the endogenous variables.

Consider first the case of non-autoregressive models. Obviously exact knowledge of A and the distribution of the ε_t defines the distribution of the x_t for any value of z_t. Conversely, given the distribution of x_t as a function of z_t, we know the reduced form completely, since ε_t has the same distribution as $x_t - E(x_t)$ and A is determined uniquely by the condition that $E(x_t)$ is equal to Az_t for all possible values of z_t. Similarly, specification of the reduced form of an autoregressive model defines uniquely the conditional distribution of x_t given $x_{t-1}, x_{t-2}, \ldots, x_{t-h}$, for every possible value of z_t. Conversely, knowledge of this conditional distribution implies, as above, knowledge of A and the distribution of ε_t.

3　Definitions

When dealing generally with identification, we distinguished in ch. 2 the notions of 'model' and 'structure'. We took the word structure to denote a complete specification of the stochastic relations between exogenous and endogenous variables. A model then consists of a set of structures all of which imply relations satisfying the same set of assumptions (general stochastic hypothesis and a priori restrictions).

With a model expressed in the structural form (1), we define a structure by giving values for the matrices B and C and specifying the distribution of η_t. Similarly, with a model expressed in the reduced form (2), a structure is defined by specification of the value of A and the distribution of ε_t. We note in passing that the adjective 'structural' and the noun 'structure' are used in two different senses. But this should not give rise to any ambiguity.

Definition 1.   In a model which satisfies assumptions 1 and 2 two structures $\mathfrak{S}$ and $\mathfrak{S}'$ are said to be *equivalent* if they imply the same probability distribution for the vector x_t of the endogenous variables, this distribution obviously being a function of the values taken by the vector z_t of the predetermined variables.

Definition 2.   A parameter δ is said to be identifiable in a structure $\mathfrak{S}^0$ for which $\delta = \delta^0$ if $\delta = \delta^0$ in all the structures $\mathfrak{S}$ equivalent to $\mathfrak{S}^0$.

Definition 3.   A structural equation is identifiable in a particular structure $\mathfrak{S}^0$ if all its coefficients are identifiable.

Proposition 1 can now be reformulated to stipulate that the reduced form is always identifiable.

Proposition 1'.   Under assumptions 2 and 3, all the parameters of any structure of the reduced form are identifiable.

Indeed proposition 1 states that two structures of the reduced form can be equivalent only if they are identical.

Since there exists a one-to-one correspondence between structures of the reduced form and distributions of the endogenous variables, a structure of the structural form will be identifiable if and only if no other structure has the same reduced form. For precise formulation of the property it is convenient to let P denote the matrix of order $(n+m)n$ which groups the elements of the matrices B and C, that is, $P = [B\ C]$, or, when the model contains identities, to let P denote the matrix of order $(n+n'+m)\ (n+n')$ of all the coefficients of the model, that is, $P = [\bar{B}\ \bar{C}]$.

We can now establish

Proposition 2.   Under assumptions 2 and 3 a structure $\mathfrak{S}$ of the structural form is equivalent to another structure $\mathfrak{S}^0$ if and only if there exists a non-singular square matrix D such that $P = DP^0$ and η_t has the same distribution as $D\eta_t^0$ (or, when there are identities, $\bar{\eta}_t$ has the same distribution as $D\bar{\eta}_t^0$).

Suppose first that, given two structures $\mathfrak{S}$ and $\mathfrak{S}^0$, such a matrix D exists. We shall prove that $\mathfrak{S}$ and $\mathfrak{S}^0$ are equivalent, that is, that they imply the same distribution for x_t. Because of proposition 1 we need only show that they have the same reduced form. If there is no identity, this follows directly from the fact that $B = DB^0$ and $C = DC^0$, since

$$A = -B^{-1}C = -(B^0)^{-1}D^{-1}DC^0 = -(B^0)^{-1}C^0 = A^0$$

and

$$\varepsilon_t = B^{-1}\eta_t = (B^0)^{-1}D^{-1}\eta_t$$

has the same distribution as

$$(B^0)^{-1}D^{-1}D\eta_t^0 = (B^0)^{-1}\eta_t^0 = \varepsilon_t^0.$$

The same reasoning applies to models containing identities. We need only replace B, C and η_t by $\bar{B}$, $\bar{C}$ and $\bar{\eta}_t$. This proves that the two structures have the same extended reduced form, and therefore the same reduced form.

Conversely, suppose that $\mathfrak{S}$ and $\mathfrak{S}^0$ have the same reduced form, that is, that $A = A^0$ and ε_t has the same distribution as ε_t^0 (when there are identities, (10) shows that $H = H^0$ and χ_t has the same distribution as χ_t^0). We set $D = B(B^0)^{-1}$, which implies $B = DB^0$. Then $A = A^0$ can also be written $B^{-1}C = (B^0)^{-1}C^0$, or $C = DC^0$. Moreover, $\varepsilon_t = B^{-1}\eta_t$ has the same distribution as $\varepsilon_t^0 = (B^0)^{-1}\eta_t^0$; consequently η_t has the same distribution as $B(B^0)^{-1}\eta_t^0 = = D\eta_t^0$. So D fulfils the conditions stated in proposition 2. (When there are identities, the same reasoning applies to the extended reduced form.)

In the following sections we shall examine identifiability of the structural form for certain types of a priori restrictions. At the same time we can discuss another question whose importance was revealed in the examples of the previous chapters, namely the existence of a priori restrictions on the reduced form.

Indeed the model is first given in its structural form. Economic assumptions are naturally expressed by restrictions affecting the various structural equations which represent the fundamental laws of the phenomenon under study. The reduced form is determined only in view of use or estimation of the model. As we have seen, the restrictions on the structural form do not always imply restrictions on the reduced form. Estimation is particularly easy when the reduced form is subject only to the general stochastic hypothesis.

We shall say that the model is 'overidentified' or 'simple' according to whether there are or are not a priori restrictions on the reduced form. Since the restrictions on the reduced form can result only from those affecting the structural form, we can state the following definition.

Definition 4.   The model is simple if, and only if, to almost every matrix A of order $(n \times m)$ and to almost every random vector ε_t satisfying the general stochastic hypothesis, there correspond a non-singular square matrix B of order n, a matrix C of order $(n \times m)$ and a random vector η_t which satisfy the a priori restrictions, the general stochastic hypothesis and the relations:

$$C = -BA, \qquad \eta_t = B\varepsilon_t. \tag{13}$$

There appears in this definition a complication whose origin is easily understood. The existence of the matrices B and C and the vector η_t is not required for all matrices A and all vectors ε_t, but only for *almost all* these matrices and almost all these vectors. Without this we would scarcely ever find a simple model.

For, consider the model:

$$
\begin{aligned}
x_{1t} &= \beta_{12}x_{2t} & + \eta_{1t}, \\
x_{2t} &= & \gamma_2 z_t + \eta_{2t},
\end{aligned}
\tag{14}
$$

and suppose that there is no a priori restriction on η_t. The reduced form of the model is

$$
\begin{aligned}
x_{1t} &= a_1 z_t + \varepsilon_{1t}, \\
x_{2t} &= a_2 z_t + \varepsilon_{2t}.
\end{aligned}
\tag{15}
$$

The first system in relations (13) can be written:

$$
\begin{aligned}
0 &= -a_1 + a_2\beta_{12}, \\
-\gamma_2 &= -a_2.
\end{aligned}
\tag{16}
$$

It is equivalent to two linear equations allowing β_{12} and γ_2 to be calculated as functions of a_1 and a_2. So we can say that the model is simple. However, if $a_2 = 0$ and $a_1 \neq 0$, the first equation can never be satisfied. To avoid attributing more than its actual importance to this exceptional case, we prefer to eliminate it by saying only that system (16) can be solved for 'almost all' values of the pair (a_1, a_2).

Similarly, consider the model:

$$
\begin{aligned}
x_{1t} &= \beta_{12}x_{2t} & + \eta_{1t}, \\
x_{2t} &= \beta_{21}x_{1t} + \gamma_2 z_t + \eta_{2t},
\end{aligned}
\tag{17}
$$

and suppose that the vector η_t is subject to a single a priori restriction, namely $E(\eta_{1t}\eta_{2t}) = 0$. As we saw in the previous chapter (§ 2), the relations between the structural and reduced forms then amount to:

$$
\begin{aligned}
0 &= -a_1 + a_2\beta_{12}, \\
-\gamma_2 &= a_1\beta_{21} - a_2, \\
\beta_{21}E(\varepsilon_{1t}^2) - (1 + \beta_{12}\beta_{21})E(\varepsilon_{1t}\varepsilon_{2t}) + \beta_{12}E(\varepsilon_{2t}^2) &= 0.
\end{aligned}
\tag{18}
$$

We can say that the model is simple, since we can solve the above system with respect to β_{12}, β_{21} and γ_2. The first equation gives β_{12}, the third then gives β_{21}

and the second γ_2. However solution is impossible if $a_2 = 0$ and $a_1 \neq 0$, or if

$$a_2 E(\varepsilon_{1t}^2) = a_1 E(\varepsilon_{1t}\varepsilon_{2t}).$$

Here again we prefer to eliminate these exceptional cases and say only that system (18) has a solution for 'almost all' values of the pair (a_1, a_2) and 'almost all' random vectors ε_t.

To be strictly rigorous, we should define what we mean by 'almost all'. We shall not attempt a general definition. Here we need only consider the case where the restrictions on the structural form relate only to B, C and Σ, the other characteristics of the distribution of η_t not being subject to any particular specification a priori. So, for the reduced form, there can exist restrictions only on A and Ω. We are content to verify that structural parameters can be determined for almost all values of the pair (A, Ω), that is, for all values except those of a set which has zero Lebesgue measure in the domain of $\frac{1}{2}n(2m+n+1)$-dimensional space to which this pair belongs.

Definition 4 also applies when the model contains identities. It may seem difficult to use because the restrictions generally relate to the matrices B_1, B_2 and C_1 rather than to B and C. However, with every matrix A and every random vector ε_t, the equations (10) associate a matrix H and a vector χ_t. Instead of finding matrices B, C and a random vector η_t satisfying conditions (13), we can find matrices B_1, B_2, C_1 and a random vector η_t satisfying the a priori restrictions together with

$$C_1 = -B_1 A - B_2 H \qquad \eta_t = B_1 \varepsilon_t + B_2 \chi_t. \qquad (19)$$

The equations (10) on H and χ_t imply that the equations (19) are equivalent to

$$C_1 - B_2 B_4^{-1} C_2 = -(B_1 - B_2 B_4^{-1} B_3)A$$

$$\eta_t = (B_1 - B_2 B_4^{-1} B_3)\varepsilon_t$$

which, in view of (5), are just the equations (13).

4 The case where the restrictions do not affect the errors

We shall now examine the most important case in practice, where there is no a priori restriction on the random errors η_t but only on the elements of B and C. In most cases, the econometrician has little basis for adopting very specific assumptions about the distribution of the random terms. However he may sometimes postulate independence of the errors affecting two different equations; this is the case where the equations describe distinct phenomena for which the random terms appear to differ completely in origin. We shall pay no special attention to this case, which is discussed in particular by FISHER

[1963] (see also WEGGE [1965] who gives a general criterion applicable to it).

When there is no restriction on the distribution of the errors η_t, the condition in proposition 2 can be expressed more simply. We can adopt

Assumption 4. The distribution of η_t is completely unknown except for its first-order moments, which are zero.

Proposition 3. Under assumptions 1, 2, 3 and 4, a structural coefficient β_{ih} or γ_{ij} is identifiable in the structure $\mathfrak{S}^0$ if and only if $\beta_{ih} = \beta_{ih}^0$ (or $\gamma_{ij} = \gamma_{ij}^0$) in all the matrices $P = DP^0$ which satisfy the a priori restrictions and the normalization rule (where D is any square matrix).

For the proof of the direct property. suppose that $\beta_{ih} = \beta_{ih}^0$ in all the matrices $P = DP^0$ satisfying the a priori restrictions and the normalization rule. Consider a structure $\mathfrak{S}$ equivalent to $\mathfrak{S}^0$. In view of proposition 2, there exists a matrix D such that $P = DP^0$. This implies $\beta_{ih} = \beta_{ih}^0$ since P, the matrix of the coefficients of $\mathfrak{S}$, necessarily satisfies the a priori restrictions and the normalization rule. Therefore the coefficient β_{ih} is identifiable in $\mathfrak{S}^0$.

Conversely, suppose that β_{ih} is identifiable in $\mathfrak{S}^0$ and that there exists a matrix D such that $P = DP^0$ satisfies the a priori restrictions and the normalization rule but has an element β_{ih} which differs from β_{ih}^0. To prove the proposition we need only find a structure $\mathfrak{S}$ equivalent to $\mathfrak{S}^0$ and containing P as matrix of the coefficients, since this contradicts the assumed identifiability of β_{ih}. Consider therefore the structure defined by P and the random vector $D\eta_t^0$. Obviously it is equivalent to $\mathfrak{S}^0$ provided that it belongs to the model. When there is no identity, this is a structure of the model since the vector $\bar{\eta}_t = \eta_t$ is subject to no restriction (assumption 4). To complete the proof, we must verify that, when there are identities, the last n' components of the random vector $D\bar{\eta}_t^0$ are identically zero. This is quite straightforward.

Let us write

$$D = \begin{bmatrix} D_1 & D_2 \\ D_3 & D_4 \end{bmatrix};$$

it follows that

$$D\bar{\eta}_t^0 = \begin{bmatrix} D_1\eta_t^0 \\ D_3\eta_t^0 \end{bmatrix}.$$

We must verify that $D_3\eta_t^0 = 0$. But $P = DP^0$ and P^0 both contain the known matrices B_3, B_4 and C_2 in the lower part of the partition (6).

$$\left. \begin{aligned} D_3 B_1^0 + D_4 B_3 &= B_3 \\ D_3 B_2^0 + D_4 B_4 &= B_4 \\ D_3 C_1^0 + D_4 C_2 &= C_2 \end{aligned} \right\} \tag{20}$$

Now, $\eta_t^0 = B_1^0 x_t + B_2^0 q_t + C_1^0 z_t$. So, taking account of (20), we can write

$$D_3 \eta_t^0 = (I - D_4)(B_3 x_t + B_4 q_t + C_2 z_t).$$

In view of the identities, the expression in the second brackets is zero, and this concludes the proof of proposition 3.

When the restrictions concern only the matrix P of the coefficients, proposition 3 characterizes the identifiability of a parameter, A parallel result deals with overidentification of the model.

Proposition 4. When assumption 4 is satisfied, the model is simple if and only if to any matrix A, except perhaps for a set of matrices whose Lebesgue measure in R^{nm} is zero, there corresponds a non-singular square matrix D of order $n + n'$ such that $D[I - \bar{A}]$ satisfies the a priori restrictions, $\bar{A}$ being defined from A by (10) and (11).

Suppose first that the model is simple. Definition 4 implies that with almost every A (and ε_t) we can associate a non-singular matrix B such that $[B - BA]$ satisfies the a priori restrictions. As indicated at the end of section 3, the definition also applies to the case where there are identities; it can then be interpreted as stating that we can associate matrices B_1 and B_2, and therefore $\bar{B}$, such that $[\bar{B} - \bar{B}\bar{A}]$ satisfies the restrictions. The condition in proposition 4 is then satisfied, D being B or $\bar{B}$.

Conversely, if this condition is satisfied, let us consider any matrix A and any random vector ε_t with zero mean. Then the existence of a matrix D such that $D[I - \bar{A}]$ satisfies the restrictions implies the existence of corresponding matrices B and C which also satisfy them and are related to A through $C + BA = 0$. The vector $B\varepsilon_t$ is an admissible vector η_t since the latter is subject to no restriction (assumption 4). The model is therefore simple.

5 Linear restrictions on the coefficients of the same equation. An identifiability criterion

Let us place a further limitation on the type of a priori restrictions to be considered, and assume that each of them implies that a homogeneous linear form of the coefficients of the same equation is equal to zero. These are by far the most frequent restrictions in practice, when the problem is presented roughly in the following terms.

To explain the values of the n endogenous variables, the econometrician introduces several structural equations each representing a definite economic law. In all, he brings in m predetermined variables. However, he knows that some of the endogenous variables and some of the predetermined variables do not have to appear in such or such a structural equation. The corresponding elements of B and C must be zero.

In a situation of this kind, each restriction stipulates that a particular co-efficient (β_{ih} or γ_{ij}) must be zero. We can therefore talk of an *exclusion restriction*. More generally, if p_i denotes the vector of the coefficients of the ith structural equation, that is, the vector consisting of the elements of the ith row of P, we shall assume that each restriction stipulates that a certain homogeneous linear form of the components of a certain p_i must be zero.

Assumption 5. Each restriction on the structural form is expressed by a homogeneous linear relation among the coefficients of the same equation. The hth restriction on the ith equation can be written:

$$\phi'_{ih} p_i = 0, \tag{21}$$

where ϕ_{ih} is an $(n+m)$-vector.

We note that assumption 5 implies assumption 4 since it states that there are no restrictions on the random terms.

In the case of an exclusion restriction, all the components of the vector ϕ_{ih} are zero except that corresponding to the coefficient to which the restriction relates. Thus model (14) above contains two restrictions, one on each structural equation. The corresponding vectors ϕ_{11} and ϕ_{21} are

$$\phi_{11} = \begin{bmatrix} 0 \\ 0 \\ 1 \end{bmatrix} \qquad \phi_{21} = \begin{bmatrix} 1 \\ 0 \\ 0 \end{bmatrix}.$$

For simultaneous representation of all restrictions affecting the ith structural equation, we need only consider the matrix Φ_i whose columns are the vectors ϕ_{ih} relating to this equation (Φ_i has $n+m$ rows and μ_i columns if there are μ_i restrictions on the ith equation). We can then set directly

$$\Phi'_i p_i = 0. \tag{22}$$

Thus, in the model

$$x_{1t} = \beta_{12} x_{2t} \qquad\qquad\qquad + \eta_{1t},$$
$$x_{2t} = \qquad\qquad \gamma_{23} z_{3t} + \gamma_{24} z_{4t} + \eta_{2t}, \tag{23}$$

the matrix of the restrictions on the first equation is

$$\Phi_1 = \begin{bmatrix} 0 & 0 \\ 0 & 0 \\ 0 & 0 \\ 1 & 0 \\ 0 & 1 \end{bmatrix}$$

When there are identities, the restrictions affecting the true structural equations can be expressed either in the first form of the model or in the form which is derived after elimination of the identities. The correspondence (5) between these two forms shows that the vectors p_i are related by a known linear transformation; the coefficients of the ith equation of the derived form are homogeneous linear functions of the vector of the coefficients of the ith equation of the first form. Consequently assumption 5 is verified for one form if it is verified for the other. But in large models, the restrictions are usually simpler for the first form than for the derived form.

A useful example is the following system, which can be considered as a very simple version of the accelerator-multiplier model:

$$\left.\begin{array}{l} C_t = aY_t + bC_{t-1} + c + \eta_{1t} \\ I_t = e(Y_t - Y_{t-1}) + f + \eta_{2t} \\ C_t + I_t = Y_t \end{array}\right\} \qquad (24)$$

with three endogenous variables (consumption C_t, investment I_t, income Y_t) and three predetermined variables (C_{t-1}, Y_{t-1} and the constant dummy variable). Elimination of I_t gives

$$\left.\begin{array}{l} C_t - aY_t = bC_{t-1} + c + \eta_{1t} \\ -C_t + (1-e)Y_t = -eY_{t-1} + f + \eta_{2t} \end{array}\right\} . \qquad (25)$$

When the variables are taken in the above order, the restrictions for the first form are given by the two matrices

$$\Phi_1 = \begin{bmatrix} 0 & 0 \\ 1 & 0 \\ 0 & 0 \\ 0 & 0 \\ 0 & 1 \\ 0 & 0 \end{bmatrix} \qquad \Phi_2 = \begin{bmatrix} 1 & 0 & 0 \\ 0 & 0 & 0 \\ 0 & 1 & 0 \\ 0 & 0 & 1 \\ 0 & 1 & 0 \\ 0 & 0 & 0 \end{bmatrix} . \qquad (26)$$

After eliminating I_t, the restrictions are given by

$$\Phi_1^* = \begin{bmatrix} 0 \\ 0 \\ 0 \\ 1 \\ 0 \end{bmatrix} \qquad \Phi_2^* = \begin{bmatrix} 1 & 0 \\ 1 & 0 \\ 0 & 1 \\ 1 & 0 \\ 0 & 0 \end{bmatrix} \qquad (27)$$

We can now prove the main result concerning identifiability in simultaneous equation models.

Theorem 1. Consider a model satisfying assumptions 1, 2, 3 and 5. In a structure with the matrix of coefficients P^0, the ith equation is identifiable if and only if the matrix $P^0\Phi_i$ has rank $n+n'-1$.

The matrix $P^0\Phi_i$ has n rows and μ_i columns. Its ith row is equal to $(p_i^0)'\Phi_i$; in view of (22), it contains only zeros. So the rank of $P^0\Phi_i$ is at most $n+n'-1$.

Suppose the matrix $P^0\Phi_i$ has rank $n+n'-1$. Let there be a structure[†] $P^1 = DP^0$ equivalent to the structure P^0. Since P^1 satisfies the a priori restrictions, we can write in particular

$$(P^0\Phi_i)'d_i = \Phi_i'p_i^1 = 0, \tag{28}$$

where d_i denotes the vector of the elements in the ith row of D. Since $P^0\Phi_i$ has rank $n+n'-1$, the vectors d_i satisfying (28) are all collinear. By hypothesis, this system is satisfied when D is the unit matrix. Therefore all the components except the ith of the vector d_i are zero. Under these conditions, $(p_i^1)' = d_i'P^0$ is proportional to $(p_i^0)'$. But since P^0 and P^1 both satisfy the normalization rule, p_i^1 is equal to p_i^0. So the ith equation is in fact identifiable.

Conversely, suppose that this equation is identifiable. The matrix $P^0\Phi_i$ necessarily has rank $n+n'-1$. For, if it is of lower rank, we can find a vector d_i, which is a solution of system (28) and not collinear with the vector e_i all of whose components are zero except the ith (which equals 1). Consequently $\lambda d_i - e_i$ is non-zero whatever the number λ. Then let D be the matrix whose ith row consists of the elements of d_i and whose other rows are the same as in the unit matrix. Then the matrix $P^1 = DP^0$ satisfies all the a priori restrictions. But its ith row is not proportional to that of P^0, since $p_i^0 = \lambda p_i^1$ would imply

$$(P^0)'(\lambda d_i - e_i) = 0,$$

which is impossible since $\bar{B}^0$ is non-singular and P^0 has rank $n+n'$. Therefore the ith equation is not identifiable.

The criterion defined by theorem 1 can be applied quickly. For example, for model (23), the two matrices $P^0\Phi_1$ and $P^0\Phi_2$ are

$$P^0\Phi_1 = \begin{bmatrix} 0 & 0 \\ -\gamma_{23}^0 & -\gamma_{24}^0 \end{bmatrix}, \qquad P^0\Phi_2 = \begin{bmatrix} 1 \\ 0 \end{bmatrix}.$$

These matrices generally have rank 1, and the two equations are identifiable. However, in the case where

$$\gamma_{23}^0 = \gamma_{24}^0 = 0,$$

the first equation is not identifiable since $P^0\Phi_1$ has zero rank. We note in passing

---

† For simplicity we now identify a structure and its matrix of coefficients. It would be pedantic to go on repeating 'a structure with the matrix of coefficients...'

that a model most of whose structures are identifiable may possess some particular unidentifiable structures.

We can verify that, when identities exist, the criterion gives the same answer whether it is applied to the original form or to the derived form. Consider, for example, the second equation of (24) and (25). The criterion focuses attention respectively on the two matrices

$$
P^0 \Phi_2 = \begin{bmatrix} -1 & a & b \\ 0 & 0 & 0 \\ 1 & -1 & 0 \end{bmatrix}, \qquad P^0 \Phi_2^* = \begin{bmatrix} a-1 & b \\ 0 & 0 \end{bmatrix}.
$$

$P^0 \Phi_2$ has rank $2 (n + n' = 3)$ and $P^0 \Phi_2^*$ has rank 1 $(n + n' = 2)$ except when simultaneously $a = 1$ and $b = 0$. The second equation is identifiable in all structures where this special case does not arise.

When all the restrictions demand that some coefficients are zero, the matrices $P \Phi_i$ can be constructed very quickly. The matrix relating to the ith equation is obtained by taking those columns of P for which the element in the ith row is restricted to zero.

Consider then a model with three endogenous variables and two exogenous variables and with the following matrix P obeying the a priori restrictions and the normalization rule:

$$
\begin{bmatrix} 1 & 0 & 0 & 0 & \gamma_{12} \\ \beta_{21} & 1 & 0 & \gamma_{21} & 0 \\ \beta_{31} & 0 & 1 & 0 & \gamma_{32} \end{bmatrix}. \tag{29}
$$

We see at once that this model is overidentified, since there are three restrictions on the first equation (see below section 6).

For the matrices P obeying the restrictions, $P\Phi_1$, $P\Phi_2$ and $P\Phi_3$ can be written

$$
P\Phi_1 = \begin{bmatrix} 0 & 0 & 0 \\ 1 & 0 & \gamma_{21} \\ 0 & 1 & 0 \end{bmatrix} \qquad P\Phi_2 = \begin{bmatrix} 0 & \gamma_{12} \\ 0 & 0 \\ 1 & \gamma_{32} \end{bmatrix} \qquad P\Phi_3 = \begin{bmatrix} 0 & 0 \\ 1 & \gamma_{21} \\ 0 & 0 \end{bmatrix}.
$$

$P\Phi_1$ has rank 2 for all structures; the first structural equation is always identifiable. $P\Phi_2$ has rank 2 except if $\gamma_{12} = 0$; the second equation is identifiable except in structures which give the value zero for γ_{12}. Finally, $P\Phi_3$ has rank 1; the third equation is never identifiable. Hence no structure of the model is identifiable.

Although the above *rank condition* is quick to apply, a still simpler *order condition* has also been considered. As we saw, the matrix Φ_i has as many columns as there are restrictions on the ith equation (say μ_i). The matrix $P^0 \Phi_i$

has the same number of columns. For its rank to be $n+n'-1$, μ_i must not be less than $n+n'-1$. The order condition states that: for an equation to be identifiable, its coefficients must be subject to at least $n+n'-1$ a priori restrictions. Clearly this condition is not sufficient.

6   An overidentification criterion

Let us now consider a criterion which allows us to say if a model is overidentified or simple. We shall need to formulate a new assumption.

Assumption 6.   For almost every matrix P satisfying the restrictions defined by assumption 5, there exists no non-zero linear combination of $n+n'-1$ rows which satisfies the restrictions imposed on the remaining row.

This assumption implies a certain form of independence among the restrictions affecting the different equations[†]. The meaning of 'almost every' is clear. In $n(n+n'+m)$ dimensional space, the matrices P satisfying the a priori restrictions constitute a linear subspace. The expression 'almost every' refers to the Lebesgue measure on this subspace.

Let us prove the following proposition:

Proposition 5.   A model satisfying assumption 5 is overidentified if there exists at least one true structural equation i $(i = 1, 2, \ldots, n)$ and matrices B_1, B_2, C_1 of orders $(n \times n)$, $(n \times n')$, $(n \times m)$ which do not necessarily obey the a priori restrictions, and if $P\Phi_i$ has rank $n+n'$ when P consists of the above

---

[†] Here is an example in which assumption 6 is not satisfied:

$$x_{1t} = \beta_{12}x_{2t} + \gamma_1 z_{3t} - \gamma_1 z_{4t} + \eta_{1t},$$

$$x_{2t} = \beta_{21}x_{1t} + \gamma_2 z_{3t} - \gamma_2 z_{4t} + \eta_{2t}.$$

In this case the restrictions require that the coefficients of z_{3t} and z_{4t} are equal numerically but of opposite sign in the first equation as in the second. The model is overidentified, since in the reduced form:

$$x_{1t} = a_{13}z_{3t} + a_{14}z_{4t} + \varepsilon_{1t},$$

$$x_{2t} = a_{23}z_{3t} + a_{24}z_{4t} + \varepsilon_{2t},$$

the coefficients of z_{3t} and z_{4t} must also be equal but of opposite sign.

This example allows us to understand why, when defining overidentified models, we must require that the matrix B is not singular. Indeed, in the present case, even if the restriction on the reduced form were ignored, we could almost always find a linear combination of its two equations such that the coefficients of z_{3t} and z_{4t} be equal but opposite in sign. This linear combination could be chosen both for the first structural equation and for the second. But B would be singular and the 'structural form' thus obtained would not represent completely the determination of the endogenous variables as a function of the exogenous variables.

three matrices and known matrices B_3, B_4, C_2. Moreover, if assumption 6 holds, the converse is also true.

We need only establish propositions (i) and (ii) below.

(i) If the model is simple, $P\Phi_i$ has rank at most $n+n'-1$ whatever the matrices B_1, B_2, C_1 (note that here they are not made subject to the a priori restrictions).

Let us write P in the form $[\bar{B}\ \bar{C}]$ and suppose first that $\bar{B}$ is non-singular. The matrix $-\bar{B}^{-1}\bar{C}$ can be considered as the matrix of an extended reduced form. To see this, we set

$$-\bar{B}^{-1}\bar{C} = \begin{bmatrix} A \\ H \end{bmatrix}. \qquad \text{The condition} \qquad \bar{B}\begin{bmatrix} A \\ H \end{bmatrix} + \bar{C} = 0$$

implies in particular $B_3 A + B_4 H + C_2 = 0$. Consequently H can be found from $\bar{B}$ by using (10). But, since the model is simple, we can find (except perhaps for matrices $-\bar{B}^{-1}\bar{C}$ forming a set of measure zero) a non-singular matrix D such that the matrix

$$D[I\ \ \bar{B}^{-1}\bar{C}] = D\bar{B}^{-1}P$$

satisfies the restrictions. Now let g_i' be the vector with $n+n'$ components which corresponds to the ith row of $D\bar{B}^{-1}$. In view of the a priori restrictions,

$$g_i'P\Phi_i = 0. \tag{30}$$

As $D\bar{B}^{-1}$ is not singular, g_i' is not identically zero. Equality (30) implies that $P\Phi_i$ has rank at most $n+n'-1$.

It remains to consider the two particular cases which we excluded earlier: that in which $\bar{B}$ is singular, and that in which $\bar{B}^{-1}\bar{C}$ belongs to the set of measure zero with which no non-singular matrix D can be associated. The corresponding matrices P constitute a set E of measure zero in $n(n+n'+m)$-dimensional space. Now the determinants obtained from the matrix $P\Phi_i$ are continuous functions of P. They are certainly zero on E if they are zero everywhere else. So the rank of $P\Phi_i$ cannot exceed $n+n'-1$ in this case either.

(ii) If $P\Phi_i$ has rank at most $n+n'-1$ for every P and every i, then the model is simple. For let A be a matrix of order nm, and let P be the corresponding matrix. Since $P\Phi_i$ has rank smaller than $n+n'$, there exists a non-zero vector d_i such that

$$d_i'P\Phi_i = 0. \tag{31}$$

Consider the matrix D whose rows are the n vectors d_i' and n' vectors e_i' with components that are all zero except for the ith taken equal to 1 ($i = n+1$, $n+2\ldots n+n'$). The matrix DP satisfies the a priori restrictions. To prove that the model is simple, we need only establish that D is non-singular except for a set of matrices A of measure zero. We use reductio ad absurdum; suppose that there exists a set of matrices A, of non-zero measure, such that all the corresponding matrices DP satisfying the restrictions are constructed from singular matrices D. The matrices DP have rank at most $n+n'-1$. At least one of their rows can be obtained as a linear combination of the other rows. They constitute a set of non-zero measure in the set of matrices P satisfying the restrictions. Their existence contradicts assumption 2.

We can give a more simple statement of proposition 5 by introducing an *order condition*. We need only make explicit the very natural convention that the μ_i restrictions on the ith equation are linearly independent. The matrix Φ_i then has rank μ_i. Since B_4 is non-singular, P has rank $n+n'$ whenever B_1 is also non-singular, which can always be assumed since its choice is free in proposition 5. The rank of $P\Phi_i$ is therefore equal to the minimum of $n+n'$ and μ_i. So we can write:

Assumption 7.   Each matrix Φ_i has rank μ_i equal to the number of restrictions on the ith equation $(i = 1, 2, \ldots, n)$.

Theorem 2.   A model satisfying assumptions 5 and 7 is overidentified if there are more than $n+n'-1$ restrictions on any one of the n true structural equations. Moreover, if assumption 6 holds, the converse is true.

Theorem 1 indicates that, for a structure to be identifiable, the restrictions must be fairly numerous. Theorem 2 shows that the model is overidentified when the restrictions are too numerous. This explains the terminology. However it is slightly misleading since there exist overidentified models, no structure of which is identifiable. The model with matrix (29) is an example of this since its third equation is not identifiable and the model is overidentified because of the restrictions on the first equation. A fortiori, we should avoid the expression 'just identified model' which is often used for the model which we have called simple.

However, when all the restrictions have the form specified in assumption 5, we can find some justification for the usual terminology if it is applied to a particular equation and if we adopt the following definition:

Definition 5.   The ith structural equation is said to be overidentified if, in the absence of restrictions affecting the other structural equations, the whole model would have been overidentified.

We can see that, if we ignore the restrictions on the equations other than the ith, assumption 6 is unnecessary in proposition 5 and theorem 2 since, in the proof of (ii), D can always be chosen as non-singular. Theorems 1 and 2 then imply:

If $\mu_i < n+n'-1$, the ith equation is neither identified nor overidentified; it is often said to be 'underidentified'.

If $\mu_i > n+n'-1$, the ith equation is overidentified. It is also identified in almost all structures since $P\Phi_i$ almost always has rank $n+n'-1$, if we ignore the restrictions on the other equations.

If $\mu_i = n+n'-1$, the ith equation is not overidentified. It is identified in almost all structures. It is often said to be 'just identified'.

7 Generalizations

Theorem 1 above was established by KOOPMANS *et al.* [1950]. In their paper the reader will find a discussion of the identification of the structural equations of a linear model for the case where there are both restrictions on the covariance matrix of the errors η_t and homogeneous linear restrictions on the coefficients of the different equations. Here we shall only say a little about the generalizations which may follow from theorem 1 in three different directions[†].

(1) Let us examine first the case of a model of type (1), in which the only existing restrictions each affect the coefficients of the same equation, but are no longer necessarily linear.

Let

$$\phi_{ih}(p_i) = 0 \qquad (32)$$

be the hth restriction on the vector p_i of the coefficients of the ith equation. Restrictions of this form generalize those examined above and represented by the conditions (21). In the absence of the normalization rule, the nature of the ith equation is not changed if we multiply all its coefficients by the same number. So the function ϕ_{ih} must be homogeneous. We assume also that it has first derivatives with respect to all its arguments.

Given an identifiable structure P^0, it seems natural to consider a limited expansion of ϕ_{ih} in the neighborhood of p_i^0. Let Φ_{ijh}^0 be the value taken for p_i^0 by the derivative of ϕ_{ih} with respect to p_{ij}:

$$\Phi_{ijh}^0 = \frac{\partial \phi_{ih}}{\partial p_{ij}}(p_i^0).$$

In the neighborhood of p_i^0, the restriction (32) can be replaced by

$$p_i' \Phi_i^0 = 0, \qquad (33)$$

where Φ_i^0 denotes the matrix whose elements are the Φ_{ijh}^0; indeed $\phi_{ih}(p_i^0)=0$ since p_i^0 satisfies the restrictions; and $(p_i^0)' \Phi_i^0 = 0$, since ϕ_{ih} is homogeneous.

Thus, for structures near P^0, it seems that we can revert to the previously examined case of homogeneous linear restrictions. This remark suggests the advantage afforded by a definition of *local identifiability*.

A structural parameter β_{ik}^0 (or γ_{ij}^0) of a structure containing the matrix P^0 is locally identifiable if there exists a number $\delta > 0$ such that:

[†] The theory of section 5 is generalized in a natural way to the case of linear restrictions on coefficients from different equations (see RICHMOND [1974] and KELLY [1975]).

$$\beta_{ik}^1 = \beta_{ik}^0 \qquad (\text{or } \gamma_{ij}^1 = \gamma_{ij}^0)$$

in all the matrices P^1 equivalent to P^0 and such that $\| P^1 - P^0 \| < \delta$. Here the distance $\| P^1 - P^0 \|$ is for example the Euclidean distance in $n(n+m)$-dimensional space.

F. M. FISHER [1959] investigated identifiability in the situations considered here. Among other results, he proved the following generalization of the sufficient condition of theorem 1.

In a structure with the matrix of coefficients P^0, the ith equation is locally identifiable if the matrix $P^0 \Phi_i^0$ has rank $n-1$.

In Fisher's article the reader will find the statement of necessary conditions for local identifiability and of sufficient conditions for unique or complete identifiability of a structure[†].

This has been generalized by WEGGE [1965] and ROTHENBERG [1970] to a much wider class of restrictions, namely all those which stipulate that certain differentiable functions of the coefficients (which may possibly be taken from different equations) and the covariances of the errors are zero. Wegge gives a general necessary rank condition for local identifiability of a structure and discusses in which cases this condition is sufficient.

(2) The model:

$$Bx_t + Cz_t = \eta_t$$

is linear with respect both to the endogenous and exogenous variables and to the parameters to be estimated. Clearly we may be led to consider non-linear structural relations and find out about their identifiability. F. M. FISHER [1961b] studied this question for models which are linear with respect to the parameters to be estimated, and for the case where there exist only homogeneous linear restrictions each affecting the coefficients of the same equation.

As before, the model concerns n endogenous variables x_{it} and m exogenous variables z_{jt}; but it involves p functions q_{kt} of the x_{it} and z_{jt} $(k=1,2,\ldots,p)$, say

$$q_{kt} = f_k(x_{1t}, \ldots, x_{nt}; z_{1t}, \ldots, z_{mt}). \tag{34}$$

The structural form of the model is

$$Pq_t = \eta_t, \tag{35}$$

where P is an $n \times p$-matrix defining the coefficients. The a priori restrictions constitute relations of the form (21) obeying assumption 1.

---

† WALD [1950b] has given a necessary and sufficient condition for local identifiability of a structural parameter when the restrictions stipulate that certain differentiable functions of the coefficients and of the covariances of the errors are zero, but apart from that can be any restrictions whatever (cf. theorem 3.3). But the corresponding criterion is difficult to apply in practice. In particular, it assumes that the restrictions are solved with respect to certain parameters of the model.

For example, consider a two-equation model containing two endogenous variables and one exogenous variable:

$$x_{1t} = \beta_{12}z_{2t} \qquad\qquad + \gamma_1 z_t + \lambda_1 + \eta_{1t},$$
$$x_{2t} = \beta_{21}x_{1t} + \beta_{23}(x_{1t})^2 + \gamma_2 z_t + \lambda_2 + \eta_{2t}. \tag{36}$$

The first equation is linear, but the second is of second degree in the variable z_{1t}. The form (35) applies here with a vector q_t and a matrix P defined by

$$q_t = \begin{bmatrix} x_{1t} \\ (x_{1t})^2 \\ x_{2t} \\ z_t \\ 1 \end{bmatrix}, \quad P = \begin{bmatrix} 1 & 0 & -\beta_{12} & -\gamma_1 & -\lambda_1 \\ -\beta_{21} & -\beta_{23} & 1 & -\gamma_2 & -\lambda_2 \end{bmatrix}.$$

Of course, models of this form which would be linear in the endogenous variables would raise no new problem, since we could always adopt a definition for the exogenous variables that would make the model completely linear. But this method does not apply when the structural equations are not linear in the endogenous variables.

In particular, Fisher succeeded in generalizing theorem 1 to models of this kind in which there exists at least one non-constant exogenous variable. Whenever the system is written so as to obey a condition which is not very restrictive in practice, the ith equation of the structure P^0 is identifiable if and only if the matrix $P^0\Phi_i$ has rank $n-1$ in the non-linear as in the linear model. (F. M. FISHER [1965] states the condition in question.)

Thus, with model (36), the first equation is identifiable for all structures in which $\beta_{23}^0 \neq 0$, since

$$P^0\Phi_1 = \begin{bmatrix} 0 \\ \beta_{23}^0 \end{bmatrix}.$$

If the two equations represent a supply law and a demand law respectively, supply is identifiable although it is affected by the same exogenous variable as demand. In a certain way, non-linearity of demand allows identification of supply.

(3) Here we have discussed only model with errors in equations. Identification problems of the same kind may arise about models with errors in variables.

When we discussed these models in ch. 10, we assumed that the coefficients A and b of the linear relations $Ay_t = b$ were not subject to any restriction, and we tried to estimate only the position of the hyperplane $Ay_t = b$, being content with one among many equivalent representations. But, in order to assume the existence of m linear relations among the 'true variables' y_{it}, we must rely on a clear analysis of the phenomena, which generally leads us to attribute particular characteristics to each of the relations. As for models with errors in equations, it will be known that such and such a variable does not occur in such and such a relation. Moreover, we try to estimate not only the position of the hyperplane $Ay_t = b$, but each of the relations which constitute the economically significant representation of this hyperplane.

We shall not try here to discuss that case in depth. Multivariate models with errors in variables are little used in econometrics. We need only note that the results of this chapter can be applied to these models.

Thus the model can be said to be 'overidentified' or 'simple' according to whether the a priori restrictions on A and b do or do not restrict the position of the m-dimensional hyperplane $Ay_t = b$ in the n-dimensional space to which y_t belongs. If almost any position of this hyperplane is admissible, the model is simple. If the restrictions satisfy assumptions 1 and 2, P denoting in this case the $m \times (n+1)$-matrix $[A \quad b]$, then theorem 2 applies, so that the model is overidentified if and only if there exist more than $m-1$ independent restrictions on the same equation.

The estimation methods discussed in ch. 10 do not suit overidentified models since they ignore the existence of a priori restrictions on the hyperplane. In theory, a minimum distance estimator can be defined for overidentified models as for simple models with errors in variables whenever the covariance matrix Ω is known. But the required computation is liable to be heavy.

In ch. 10 we discussed at some length identification of the hyperplane $Ay_t = b$. But identifiability of this hyperplane does not imply that each of the equations of its structural representation is determined uniquely. For the structure containing the matrix P^0 to be identifiable, it is necessary and sufficient that the hyperplane is identifiable and that there exists no square matrix $D \neq I$ such that DP^0 satisfies the a priori restrictions as well as the normalization rule.

When the a priori restrictions are linear and homogeneous, and each relates to the coefficients of the same equation (assumption 1), the ith equation of the structure P^0 is identifiable if and only if the hyperplane is identifiable and the matrix $P^0 \Phi_i$ has rank $m-1$.

CHAPTER 18

General estimation methods in models with several equations

1 Structural form and reduced form

For a general discussion of estimation in systems with several equations, we shall refer to the model whose structural form is

$$Bx_t + Cz_t = \eta_t, \tag{1}$$

and whose reduced form is

$$x_t = Az_t + \varepsilon_t. \tag{2}$$

This formulation does not explicitly cover the case where the model involves lagged values of the endogenous variables. We shall see in the next section how to modify the presentation of the assumptions and properties so as to deal simultaneously with models containing lagged endogenous variables. It is only for the sake of simplicity in exposition that we restrict ourselves to systems (1) and (2).

The structural form and the reduced form correspond to each other through the equalities:

$$BA + C = 0, \tag{3}$$

$$\eta_t = B\varepsilon_t. \tag{4}$$

If there are no a priori restrictions on the errors η_t the condition $BA+C=0$ by itself allows identification of the structural equations. Before discussing estimation methods proper, it is therefore important to examine the correspondence which exists between A and (B, C) because of the equality $BA+C=0$, the a priori restrictions on B and C, and the normalization rule. In particular, we should know the assumptions under which this correspondence is continuous, so that the consistency of the estimators of the reduced form implies the consistency of the corresponding estimators of the structural form.

We shall denote by A^0, B^0 and C^0 the true values of the matrices A, B and C. Clearly we shall deal with the case where the true structure is identifiable. More precisely, we shall set the following general assumptions for the a priori restrictions.

Assumption 1. In $n(n+m)$-dimensional Euclidean space, the a priori restrictions and the normalization rule require that (B, C) belongs to a compact set (that is, to a set which is bounded and closed).

Assumption 2. The matrix B^0 is non-singular. No pair (B, C) other than $(B^0,$

C^0) satisfies at the same time the a priori restrictions, the normalization rule and the equality:

$$BA^0 + C = 0.$$

Assumption 2 expresses the fact that the restrictions on B and C are sufficient for identification of the structural equations. It also requires that B^0 is regular, that is, that the model is sufficient for determination of the conditional distribution of the endogenous variables as a function of the exogenous variables.

If the a priori restrictions demand that some coefficients of B and C are zero, the normalization rule can be so chosen that assumption 1 is satisfied. For example, we need only fix the value of a positive definite quadratic form of the coefficients of each equation, and choose a priori the sign of a coefficient having non-zero value in the true structure.

Proposition 1. If assumptions 1 and 2 are satisfied, the correspondence which allows us to define the coefficients of the structural form from those of the reduced form is continuous in the neighborhood of the true structure.

The exact meaning and the proof of this property result from the following lemma.

Lemma. Let $y=f(x)$ be a function from a metric space into another metric space; let this function be defined on a compact set X, continuous at x^0 and such that the only solution of $f(x^0)=f(x)$ is x^0. Given any $\varepsilon>0$ there exists η such that $\|f(x)-f(x^0)\| < \eta$ implies $\|x-x^0\| < \varepsilon$ on X.

For, suppose that there exists an $\varepsilon>0$ for which we can find no η satisfying the above condition. With every sequence of positive numbers η^s tending to zero $(s=1,2,\ldots)$, we can associate a sequence $\{x^s\}$ of X such that

$$\|f(x^s) - f(x^0)\| < \eta^s \quad \text{and} \quad \|x^s - x^0\| \geq \varepsilon.$$

A limit point x^∞ of this sequence must satisfy both $f(x^\infty)=f(x^0)$ and $\|x^\infty - x_0\| \geq \varepsilon$, and this contradicts the assumptions of the lemma.

For the proof of proposition 1, we need only apply the lemma with $x=(B, C)$, $y=A$. The set X contains all the structures (B, C) satisfying the a priori restrictions and the normalization rule. Finally, $y=f(x)$ is the function $A = -B^{-1}C$ which is continuous at (B^0, C^0) since B^0 is non-singular.

Proposition 1 is mainly useful because of the following consequence. Let $\{A_T\}$ be a sequence of random matrices satisfying the a priori restrictions on A and tending in probability to A^0 when T tends to infinity. With every matrix A_T we can associate two matrices B_T and C_T satisfying the a priori restrictions, the normalization rule and

$$B_T A_T + C_T = 0.$$

Proposition 1 establishes that $\{B_T\}$ and $\{C_T\}$ tend in probability to B^0 and C^0 (see proposition 3 in the appendix to ch. 9). So we can associate consistent estimators of B and C with a consistent estimator of A.

In order to establish a correspondence between the asymptotic distributions of estimators of A on the one hand and of B and C on the other, we shall need more precise assumptions for the a priori restrictions. So we shall represent the normalization rule and the restrictions on B and C by the following equations:

$$\Psi_r(b_{11}, \ldots, b_{ih}, \ldots, b_{nn}; c_{11}, \ldots, c_{ij}, \ldots, c_{nm}) = 0, \tag{5}$$

r varying from 1 to q.

We then make

Assumption 3. In a neighborhood of (B^0, C^0), the ratio between the distances:

$$\| B^{-1}C - (B^0)^{-1}C^0 \| \qquad \text{and} \qquad \| (B, C) - (B^0, C^0) \|$$

is bounded below by a positive number on the set of pairs (B, C) satisfying the a priori restrictions and the normalization rule.

This assumption strengthens assumption 2. From the identifiability of (B^0, C^0) we already know that

$$\| B^{-1}C - (B^0)^{-1}C^0 \|$$

is not zero for any pair (B, C) other than (B^0, C^0). Here we demand that this distance does not tend to zero faster than

$$\| (B, C) - (B^0, C^0) \|.$$

Assumption 4. In a neighborhood of (B^0, C^0) the derivatives up to the third order of the functions Ψ_r exist and are bounded; the matrix

$$[\partial \Psi_r / \partial b_{ih}; \ \partial \Psi_r / \partial c_{ij}],$$

of order $[q \times n(n+m)]$ has rank q.

We now establish

Proposition 2. If assumptions 1, 2, 3 and 4 are satisfied, there exists in the neighborhood of (A^0, B^0, C^0) a parametric representation:

$$[A(\alpha), \qquad B(\alpha), \qquad C(\alpha)]$$

of the matrices satisfying the a priori restrictions and the normalization rule. The vector α of the parameters has $p = n(n+m) - q$ components. The derivatives up to the third order of the functions $A(\alpha)$, $B(\alpha)$ and $C(\alpha)$ are bounded. There exists no set of p numbers λ_k, not all zero, such that

$$\sum_{k=1}^{p} \lambda_k \frac{\partial A}{\partial \alpha_k}$$

is zero at α^0, or that

$$\sum_{k=1}^{p} \lambda_k \frac{\partial B}{\partial \alpha_k} \quad \text{and} \quad \sum_{k=1}^{p} \lambda_k \frac{\partial C}{\partial \alpha_k}$$

are simultaneously zero at α^0.

In view of assumption 4, we know that there exists in a neighborhood of (B^0, C^0) a parametric representation $B(\alpha)$, $C(\alpha)$ of the matrices satisfying equations (5) (see DIEUDONNÉ [1960], in particular theorems (1C.2.2) and (10.2.3)). The vector α, the components of which may be chosen among the b_{ih} and c_{ij}, then has $p = n(n+m) - q$ components. The derivatives up to the third order of the functions $B(\alpha)$ and $C(\alpha)$ are bounded. Finally, the value α^0 of α corresponding to the true structure (B^0, C^0) is not a singularity of the representation; that is, there exists no set of p numbers λ_k, not all zero, such that

$$\sum_{k} \lambda_k \frac{\partial B}{\partial \alpha_k} \quad \text{and} \quad \sum_{k} \lambda_k \frac{\partial C}{\partial \alpha_k}$$

are simultaneously zero at α^0.

According to assumption 2, the matrix B^0 is regular. So there exists a neighborhood of α^0 in which $B(\alpha)$ is non-singular, its inverse being bounded. Let $A(\alpha)$ be the matrix

$$- [B(\alpha)]^{-1} C(\alpha).$$

In a suitable neighborhood of A^0 there exists no matrix A satisfying the restrictions other than those matrices of the form $A(\alpha)$. For, to every sequence of matrices A_T tending to A^0, there corresponds, in view of proposition 1, a sequence $\{B_T, C_T\}$ tending to (B^0, C^0); and consequently, from a certain value of T onwards, a sequency $\{\alpha_T\}$ such that

$$B_T = B(\alpha_T), \qquad C_T = C(\alpha_T);$$

it necessarily follows that $A_T = A(\alpha_T)$.

Clearly the derivatives up to the third order of the function $A(\alpha)$ are bounded in a neighborhood of α^0. It remains to show that α^0 is not a singularity of the representation $A(\alpha)$. Suppose that there exist p numbers λ_k not all zero, such that

$$\sum_{k} \lambda_k \frac{\partial A}{\partial \alpha_k}$$

is zero. Let us then consider the vector sequence $\{\alpha^s\}$ defined by

$$\alpha_k^s = \alpha_k^0 + 2^{-s}\lambda_k \qquad \text{(for } s = 1, 2, \ldots).$$

The ratio between

$$\| A(\alpha^s) - A^0 \| \qquad \text{and} \qquad \| \alpha^s - \alpha^0 \|$$

tends to zero. Because of assumption 3, the ratio between

$$\| [B(\alpha^s), C(\alpha^s)] - (B^0, C^0) \| \qquad \text{and} \qquad \| \alpha^s - \alpha^0 \|$$

also tends to zero; it follows that

$$\sum_k \lambda_k \frac{\partial B}{\partial \alpha_k} \qquad \text{and} \qquad \sum_k \lambda_k \frac{\partial C}{\partial \alpha_k}$$

are zero, which is impossible since α^0 is not a singularity of the parametric representation of the pairs (B, C).

Proposition 2 is useful in two ways. First, it establishes a certain regularity of the set of matrices A satisfying the a priori restrictions. Second, it allows us to prove the asymptotic normality of certain estimators of B and C. For, let $\{A_T\}$ be a sequence of random matrices satisfying the a priori restrictions and such that $\sqrt{T}(A_T - A^0)$ has a limiting normal distribution. Let B_T and C_T be the matrices, and α_T the vector of parameters, corresponding to A_T. Clearly $\sqrt{T}(\alpha_T - \alpha^0)$, and consequently $\sqrt{T}(B_T - B^0)$ and $\sqrt{T}(C_T - C^0)$, have limiting normal distributions.

In practice the parametric representation alluded to above may be of a simple kind. If the a priori restrictions demand only that certain coefficients are zero, we can often take as parameters the non-zero coefficients with the exception of one in each equation, this latter coefficient having a non-zero value in the true structure and by convention being equal to 1. This is just the procedure which was used in the examples of ch. 16.

We note that assumptions 2 and 3 assume identifiability of all the structural coefficients forming the matrices B and C. We could also deal with the case where only some of the coefficients are identifiable.

For example, assumption 2 could be replaced by

Assumption 2. The matrix B^0 is non-singular. All the pairs (B, C) satisfying at the same time the a priori restrictions, the normalization rule and the equality $BA^0 + C = 0$, give the value b_{11}^0 for the coefficient b_{11}.

We could then prove

Proposition 1'. If assumptions 1 and 2' are satisfied, the correspondence which allows us to calculate b_{11} from the reduced form is continuous in the neighborhood of the true structure.

A simpler method consists of introducing artificial restrictions on the structure (B, C), which allow complete identification of B and C but do not introduce supplementary restrictions on the reduced form.

2 Simple models

Estimation of the coefficients of the structural form raises no complex problems when the model is both simple and identifiable.

More precisely, let us consider the case where there are no other restrictions on the errors η_t than those resulting from the general stochastic hypothesis, and where *to almost every $n \times m$-matrix A there corresponds one and only one pair of matrices (B, C) satisfying the normalization rule*, the restrictions on the coefficients of the structural form and the equations $BA + C = 0$. We adopt the following two assumptions:

Assumption 5. The vectors η_t are mutually independent. They are identically distributed with zero mean and non-singular covariance matrix Σ, which is subject to no a priori restriction.

Assumption 6. The vectors z_t are bounded. The matrix M_{zz} is non-singular. It tends to a non-singular matrix when T tends to infinity.

For estimating B and C we generally use an *indirect regression*. The coefficients of the reduced form are estimated by least squares fitting of each endogenous variable x_i with respect to the various exogenous variables $z_1, z_2, \ldots, z_m$. Let A^* be the matrix so determined. The estimates of B and C are obtained by solving $BA^* + C = 0$ jointly with the normalization rule and the a priori restrictions.

It follows from the regression theory given in ch. 6 that, if assumptions 5 and 6 are satisfied and if B^0 is regular, A^* is a consistent unbiased estimator whose covariance matrix is given by a known formula. Under the same conditions, the asymptotic distribution of $\sqrt{T}(A^* - A^0)$ is normal. Finally, if the vector η_t is normally distributed, A^* is an efficient estimator.

The convergence of the estimators B^* and C^*, obtained after an indirect regression, to the true values B^0 and C^0 follows from assumptions 1, 2, 5 and 6. If in addition assumptions 3 and 4 are satisfied, as is generally the case in simple models, the correspondence between reduced form and structural form is differentiable. Limiting normal distributions exist for

$$\sqrt{T}(B^* - B^0) \quad \text{and} \quad \sqrt{T}(C^* - C^0).$$

Finally, we can calculate estimates of the asymptotic covariances of these matrices from the estimated covariances of A^* by applying the procedure given in ch. 16 § 1 (see also RAO [1965] pp. 319–22).

Similar asymptotic properties exist for indirect regressions in models involving lagged values of the endogenous variables.

Consider a model whose structural form is

$$Bx_t + Cz_t + D_1 u_{t1} + \cdots + D_h u_{th} = \eta_t, \tag{6}$$

where $u_{t\tau}$ denotes a vector whose n_τ components are chosen from the n components of $x_{t-\tau}$ (thus, for the model given in the first section of ch. 16, u_{t1} has the two components $x_{3,t-1}$ and $x_{5,t-1}$). The matrix D_τ then has n rows and n_τ columns. The reduced form of the model is

$$x_t = Az_t + B_1 u_{t1} + \cdots + B_h u_{th} + \varepsilon_t. \tag{7}$$

For models of this type, assumption 6 should generally be supplemented by the following

Assumption 6'. When T tends to infinity, the z_t are bounded, each of the matrices

$$M_{zz}^\tau = \frac{1}{T} \sum_{t=1}^{T-\tau} z_t z_{t+\tau}'$$

tends to a limit M_0^τ uniformly with respect to τ (where $\tau = 1, 2, \ldots$).

Finally we shall need a stability condition for which we write the model in the form:

$$Bx_t + Cz_t + F_1 x_{t-1} + \cdots + F_h x_{t-h} = \eta_t, \tag{8}$$

F_τ being a square matrix of order n which has the same non-zero elements as D_τ but contains in addition $n - n_\tau$ columns of zeros. We shall denote by B^0, C^0, $F_1^0, \ldots, F_h^0$ the true values of the matrices $B, C, F_1, \ldots, F_h$.

Assumption 7.   The nh roots in μ of the equation:

$$|\mu^h B^0 + \mu^{h-1} F_1^0 + \cdots + \mu F_{h-1}^0 + F_h^0| = 0 \tag{9}$$

have moduli less than 1.

The model will be said to be simple if the η_t are subject to no restriction other than the general stochastic hypothesis, and if, to almost every set of $h+1$ matrices $A, B_1, \ldots, B_h$ of suitable orders, there corresponds one and only one set of matrices $B, C, D_1, \ldots, D_h$ satisfying the normalization rule, the a priori restrictions and

$$C + BA = 0, \qquad D_1 + BB_1 = 0, \ldots, \qquad D_h + BB_h = 0. \tag{10}$$

For a simple autoregressive model, we can still apply an indirect regression.

We then estimate the coefficients $A^*, B_1^*, \ldots, B_h^*$ of the reduced form by regressions of each endogenous variable x_{it} on the set of predetermined variables

$$z_{1t}, z_{2t}, \ldots, z_{mt}; u_{1t1}, u_{2t1}, \ldots, u_{n_h th}.$$

Next we estimate the coefficients of the structural form by solving simultaneously the normalization rule, the a priori restrictions and equations (10) in which $A, B_1, \ldots, B_h$ are replaced by $A^*, B_1^*, \ldots, B_h^*$. Let $B^*, C^*, D_1^*, \ldots, D_h^*$ be the estimates thus obtained.

In view of the theorems of ch. 13, if assumptions 5, 5′, 6, 6′ and 7 are satisfied, the estimators $A^*, B_1^*, \ldots, B_h^*$ tend to the true values $A^0, B_1^0, \ldots, B_h^0$, and the random matrices

$$\sqrt{T}(A^* - A^0), \qquad \sqrt{T}(B_1^* - B_1^0), \ldots, \sqrt{T}(B_h^* - B_h^0)$$

have limiting normal distributions whose variances and covariances can be determined. Finally, if η_t is normally distributed, these estimators are asymptotically efficient.

In the same conditions as above, we can deduce that $B^*, C^*, D_1^*, \ldots, D_h^*$ tend to the true matrices $B^0, C^0, D_1^0, \ldots, D_h^0$, and that

$$\sqrt{T}(B^* - B^0), \qquad \sqrt{T}(C^* - C^0), \qquad \sqrt{T}(D_1^* - D_1^0), \ldots, \sqrt{T}(D_h^* - D_h^0)$$

have limiting normal distributions whose variances and covariances can be calculated by the process given in ch. 16. It is sufficient to add the new assumptions 5′, 6′ and 7 to assumptions 1 to 6, and to reformulate assumptions 1 to 4, substituting $(B, C, D_1, \ldots, D_h)$ for (B, C) and eqs. (10) for $BA + C = 0$.

In the rest of this chapter we shall discuss overidentified models for which the coefficients of the reduced form are subject to restrictions. For the sake of simplicity, we shall consider explicitly only models without lagged endogenous variables. But the proposed methods apply easily to autoregressive models. It is sufficient to treat the lagged endogenous variables in the same way as exogenous variables. The asymptotic properties of the estimators are not affected by the presence of these lagged variables, at least if assumptions 5′, 6′ and 7 are satisfied. For further details, the reader may consult the fundamental article by MANN and WALD [1943].

We shall also restrict ourselves to the case where the errors satisfy assumption 5, to avoid overburdening the text. In particular HENDRY [1971 and 1974] deals with cases where the errors are time dependent.

Finally we note also that JÖRESKOG [1973] and GOLDBERGER [1973] discuss the statistical treatment of models with both errors in some variables and simultaneous equations.

3   Minimum distance estimators and quasi-maximum likelihood estimators

In overidentified models the matrix A of the reduced form:

$$x_t = Az_t + \varepsilon_t$$

is subject to restrictions. However, we can retain the principle of indirect regression, in the sense that we can estimate A, taking account of the restrictions on it, and deduce estimates of B and C.

In particular, the non-linear regression methods given in ch. 9 apply to estimation of A. Let S be a positive definite matrix of order n. We defined the estimator $A_T(S)$ as the matrix A satisfying the restrictions and minimizing the 'distance'

$$L_T(S, A) = \sum_{t=1}^{T} (x_t - Az_t)'S(x_t - Az_t). \tag{11}$$

We can find two estimators $B_T(S)$ and $C_T(S)$ corresponding to it by simultaneous solution of the a priori restrictions, the normalization rule and the equality

$$BA_T(S) + C = 0.$$

Under fairly general conditions these estimators tend to the true values B^0 and C^0. This results from the following theorem.

Theorem 1.   If assumptions 1, 2, 5 and 6 are satisfied and if the positive definite random matrix S_T tends in probability to a positive definite matrix S, then $B_T(S_T)$ and $C_T(S_T)$ tend in probability to the true matrices B^0 and C^0.

For, since the true matrix is regular and the η_t obey assumption 5, the ε_t satisfy assumption 1 of ch. 9. The z_t satisfying assumption 6, it follows from theorem 6 of ch. 9 that $A_T(S_T)$ tends in probability to A^0. Proposition 1 then implies that $B_T(S_T)$ and $C_T(S_T)$ tend to B^0 and C^0.

BROWN [1960] proposed estimators $B_T(I)$ and $C_T(I)$ corresponding to the case where S is the unit matrix. He gave this estimation procedure the name 'simultaneous least squares' and showed that, at least in an example, the results were very near those obtained by other methods which we shall discuss below. NAKAMURA [1960] proved the convergence of $B_T(I)$ and $C_T(I)$.

Since there is no restriction on Σ, there is none either on Ω. The theory developed in chap. 9 then shows that $A(S_T)$ is asymptotically efficient in the class of minimum distance estimators when S_T tends to the covariance matrix of ε_t, namely

$$\Omega = (B^0)^{-1} \Sigma (B^{0\prime})^{-1}.$$

This will be the case in particular for the estimators B^{**} and C^{**} defined as follows:

(i) Let A^* be the matrix of the regression coefficients of the endogenous variables x_i on the exogenous variables $z_1, z_2, \ldots, z_m$.

(ii) Let $M_{\varepsilon\varepsilon}^*$ be the matrix of the second order moments of the residuals

$$\varepsilon_t^* = x_t - A^* z_t.$$

(iii) Let A^{**} be the matrix which satisfies the restrictions on the reduced form and minimizes

$$L_T[(M_{\varepsilon\varepsilon}^*)^{-1}, A].$$

(iv) Let B^{**} and C^{**} be the matrices which satisfy $BA^{**} + C = 0$ jointly with the a priori restrictions and the normalization rule.

We can prove

Theorem 2. If assumptions 1 to 6 are satisfied, and if the matrix S_T tends in probability to the positive definite matrix S, then

$$\sqrt{T}[B_T(S_T) - B^0] \quad \text{and} \quad \sqrt{T}[C_T(S_T) - C^0]$$

have a limiting normal distribution. If in addition the η_t are normally distributed then B^{**} and C^{**} are asymptotically efficient estimators.

For, in view of proposition 2, there exists a parametric representation $A(\alpha)$ of the matrices satisfying the restrictions on the reduced form. It follows from theorems 4 and 5 of ch. 9 that

$$\sqrt{T}[A_T(S_T) - A^0]$$

has a limiting normal distribution and that A^{**} is asymptotically efficient when η_t is normally distributed. Still in view of proposition 2, we go from A to (B, C) by a differentiable transformation. So analogous properties apply to $B_T(S_T)$, $C_T(S_T)$ and B^{**}, C^{**}.

In the next chapter, we shall see how the estimators B^{**} and C^{**} may correspond to those proposed for the examples in ch. 17. Every other asymptotically equivalent estimator has apparently similar advantages, in the present lack of knowledge about the properties which hold for small samples.

This is particularly so for the estimator which maximizes the likelihood when the errors are normal and when Σ, and consequently Ω, are subject to no restriction. We have discussed this estimator in the general context of ch. 9 (cf. § 3) and we can easily deduce its definition for simultaneous equation models.

In this case, the matrix M defined by equation (25) in ch. 9 is

$$M = \frac{1}{T} \sum_{t=1}^{T} (x_t - Az_t)(x_t - Az_t)'. \tag{12}$$

The maximum likelihood estimator of A is the matrix $\hat{A}$ which minimizes $|M|$ while satisfying the restrictions on the reduced form. The maximum likelihood estimators of B and C are the matrices which satisfy $B\hat{A} + C = 0$ together with the a priori restrictions and the normalization rule.

The first systematic work on the estimation of multiple equation models was carried out by the 'Cowles Commission', a research group attached to the University of Chicago. The maximum likelihood principle was applied under the assumption that the distributions of the errors were normal. This led in particular to the estimator which we have just determined[†].

In addition the Cowles Commission researchers emphasized the fact that the estimators which they found had asymptotic properties which were little dependent on normality of the errors. So they proposed to apply them even when this normality was not certain, and then to give them the name *quasi-maximum likelihood estimators*.

4   Restrictions on the covariance matrix of the errors

We have assumed until now that there is no restriction on the covariance matrix Σ of the errors affecting the structural equations. We shall make a brief examination of the form of the quasi-maximum likelihood estimators when Σ is subject to certain restrictions. This will lead us back to direct fitting of the structural equations as a good estimation method for recursive systems.

Whenever there are restrictions on Σ, it is simpler to base our reasoning directly on the structural form of the model. When the η_t are mutually independent and identically normally distributed the logarithm of the probability density of the T vectors η_t is

$$-\tfrac{1}{2}nT \lg 2\pi - \frac{T}{2} \lg |\Sigma| - \tfrac{1}{2} \sum_{t=1}^{T} \eta_t' \Sigma^{-1} \eta_t.$$

We can ignore the constant $-(nT/2) \lg 2\pi$ and write the expression for the logarithm of the probability density of the T vectors x_t in the form:

$$T \lg |B| - \tfrac{1}{2}T \lg |\Sigma| - \tfrac{1}{2}T \operatorname{tr} \Sigma^{-1} N \tag{13}$$

where

$$N = \frac{1}{T} \sum_{t=1}^{T} (Bx_t + Cz_t)(Bx_t + Cz_t)' \tag{14}$$

---

† The systematic presentation of the Cowles Commission work has been given by KOOPMANS *et al.* [1950] and KOOPMANS and HOOD [1953]. Their approach is followed in most of the recent books concerned with the econometric theory of simultaneous equation models: see in particular CHRIST [1966] and FISK [1967].

(for $|B|$ is the jacobian of the transformation of η_t into x_t).

To determine the estimates of B, C and Σ, we must maximize (13) with respect to these three matrices, taking account of the restrictions on them and the normalization rule.

The most interesting case in practice is that where we can assume that *the errors affecting the different structural equations are mutually independent*. We then know a priori that Σ must be diagonal, but we have no information about the variance σ_i^2 of the errors affecting the ith structural equation. Expression (13) can then be written:

$$T \lg |B| - \frac{T}{2} \sum_{i=1}^{n} \lg \sigma_i^2 - \sum_{i=1}^{n} \frac{1}{2\sigma_i^2} \sum_{t=1}^{T} (b_i' x_t + c_i' z_t)^2 \qquad (15)$$

if b_i and c_i denote the vectors of the coefficients of the endogenous and the exogenous variables in the ith structural equation.

To maximize (15), we can first fix B and C and find suitable values of the σ_i. Maximization with respect to σ_i^2 requires

$$\hat{\sigma}_i^2 = \frac{1}{T} \sum_{t=1}^{T} (b_i' x_t + c_i' z_t)^2.$$

So the estimator of σ_i^2 is the variance of the residuals with respect to the estimated structural equation. After substituting this value of σ_i^2, dividing by T and eliminating the constant

$$- \tfrac{1}{2} n (1 + \lg T),$$

expression (15) becomes

$$\lg |B| - \tfrac{1}{2} \sum_{i=1}^{n} \lg \left\{ \sum_{t=1}^{T} (b_i' x_t + c_i' z_t)^2 \right\}. \qquad (16)$$

The estimators of B and C are obtained by maximizing (16) under the constraint of the a priori restrictions and the normalization rule (for an application, see KLEIN [1953] pp. 100–107).

5 Recursive models

This maximization is particularly simple in *recursive models* which have already been discussed in ch. 15, section 4. Let us recall the characteristics of these models in detail.

(i) There exists an ordering of the endogenous variables and an ordering of the structural equations such that the ith structural equation involves the ith endogenous variable and possibly also endogenous variables of rank less than i, but no endogenous variable of rank greater than i. (If the model is autoregressive, lagged values of all the endogenous variables may occur in each equation.) We generally consider that the ith equation explains the determination of the ith endogenous variable as a function of the endogenous variables of rank lower than i and of the predetermined variables.

When the endogenous variables and the equations are arranged in this way, $b_{ih}=0$ whenever $h>i$. *The matrix B is 'triangular'*, having only zeros above the main diagonal. We can decide as normalization rule that the coefficient b_{ii} of the ith variable in the ith equation is equal to 1. Then the determinant of B necessarily equals 1.

(ii) The errors η_{it} affecting the different structural equations are mutually independent. *The matrix Σ is diagonal.*

(iii) The restrictions on the coefficients of the structural equations each affect a single equation. So we can divide these restrictions into n groups, the ith group comprizing restrictions relating to the coefficients of the ith structural equation and to these coefficients alone.

If conditions (i) and (ii) are satisfied, the expression (16) to be maximized reduces to the sum of n terms, the ith term involving only the coefficients of the ith structural equation. If condition (iii) is also satisfied, the quasi-maximum likelihood estimators of the coefficients of the ith structural equation are obtained independently of the estimators of the coefficients of the other equations. More precisely, they are determined in such a way as to minimize

$$\sum_{t=1}^{T} (b_i' x_t + c_i' z_t)^2$$

subject to the constraints of the restrictions affecting the ith equation, and with the normalization rule $b_{ii}=1$.

We can also state that, *in a recursive model* which satisfies the above conditions (i), (ii) and (iii) and whose errors obey assumption 5, *the ith structural equation can be treated by the method of least squares exactly as if $x_{1t}, x_{2t} \cdots, x_{i-1,t}$ were exogenous variables.*

To back up this statement, we confine ourselves to the case where the a priori restrictions stipulate only that certain coefficients are zero. The estimates of the coefficients of the ith equation which are not necessarily zero are obtained by a regression of x_{it} or the other variables occurring in this equation. Let these estimates be b_{ih}^* and c_{ij}^* (h corresponding to some of the indices 1 to $i-1$; j to some of the indices 1 to m). Let η_{it}^* be the estimation residual for the tth observation.

We can consider the conditional distributions of the b_{ih}^*, c_{ij}^* and η_{it}^* relating to the ith equation for fixed values of $x_{1t}, x_{2t}, \cdots x_{i-1,t}$, or equivalently for fixed values of $\eta_{1t}, \eta_{2t}, \cdots, \eta_{i-1,t}$. These conditional distributions have properties which follow directly from multiple regression theory.

Thus the conditional expectations of b_{ih}^* and c_{ij}^* are equal to the true values b_{ih} and c_{ij}. Their conditional variances and covariances define a matrix equal to $\sigma_i^2 W_i^{-1}$, where σ_i^2 denotes the variance of η_i and W_i the matrix of the observed moments of the variables other than x_i occurring in the ith equation. Let the number of these variables be m_i. The conditional distribution of the η_{it}^* is independent of that of the b_{ih}^* and c_{ij}^*. The conditional expectation of the sum of squares of the η_{it}^* is $(T-m_i)\sigma_i^2$. Let $(T-m_i)\sigma_i^{*2}$ be this sum of squares. The matrix $\sigma_i^{*2} W_i^{-1}$ estimates without bias the conditional covariance matrix of the estimated coefficients. Finally, if η_{it} is normally distributed, the b_{ih}^* and the c_{ij}^* have a conditional normal distribution, and

$$(T - m_i)\frac{\sigma_i^{*2}}{\sigma_i^2}$$

has a conditional χ^2-distribution with $T-m_i$ degrees of freedom.

Thus the usual procedures are easily justified. For example, the unconditional expectation of b_{ih}^* is equal to the true value b_{ih}, since the conditional expectation is always equal to this value. If σ_{ih}^{*2} denotes the conditional variance of b_{ih}^* as it is estimated in $\sigma_i^{*2} W_i^{-1}$ and if η_{it} is normally distributed, the ratio

$$\frac{b_{ih}^* - b_{ih}}{\sigma_{ih}^*}$$

has a t-distribution with $T-m_i$ degrees of freedom, and this whether or not the $x_{1t}, \ldots, x_{i-1,t}$ are considered as fixed.

It is due to H. Wold that the operating advantages of recursive models are so well understood, thanks to a series of publications the most important of which are included in our bibliography[†].

6 Computation methods for models containing only exclusion restrictions

(i) General remarks

Except in the case of recursive models, the general estimation methods just given reduce to the maximization of quantities which are complicated expressions of unknown parameters. Of course, some models may have a very symmetric structure and so be easy to handle. Others may have only three or four

---

[†] Recently H. Wold, E. Lyttkens and a group of Swedish econometricians worked out estimation methods for models that are not recursive. Their work is still in progress while I am putting the last hand to this edition. I feel it is now too early for a satisfactory exposition of these methods, an exposition that should cover the stochastic hypotheses of the models, the computation algorithms and the statistical properties of the resulting estimates.

equations and a sufficiently small number of parameters so that we can work directly, without too much difficulty, on the explicit forms of the quantities to be maximized. But many economic models result from the juxtaposition of a more or less large number of laws, each of which expresses a type of behavior or a particular institutional constraint. These laws involve a greater or lesser number of exogenous variables, a greater or lesser number of endogenous variables. The resulting models are totally lacking in symmetry and often have a much more complex structure than that of the model described at the start of ch. 15[†]. The computation involved for one of the general methods given in ch. 9, § 4 is liable to be very heavy.

However, in most cases the only a priori restrictions in the model are those specifying the variables occurring in each structural equation ('exclusion restrictions'). The matrix Σ is not then subject to restriction, while in B and C, some elements are necessarily zero, and the others can have any value a priori. In this case, the computation can be organized to make it easier. As we shall see, we can also make some simplifying adjustments to the general methods.

Suppose then that we are trying to find the minimum distance estimators $B_T(S)$ and $C_T(S)$ subject to the constraint that certain of their elements are specified to be zero. We also suppose that the normalization rule specifies that the coefficient of x_{it} in the ith structural equation is 1:

$$\beta_{ii} = 1 \qquad \text{for} \qquad i = 1, 2, \ldots, n. \tag{17}$$

The expression (11), which is to be minimized, can be written

$$T \, \text{tr} \, (SM) \tag{18}$$

where M is the matrix defined by (12). The first order conditions for minimization are expressed compactly by

$$\text{tr} \, (S \, dM) = 0, \tag{19}$$

given that this equality must be satisfied identically for every value of dM which obeys the a priori restrictions and the normalization rule in the neighborhood of the solution M. We shall make this condition quite explicit by taking account of the particular form of the a priori restrictions.

We must bear in mind the fact that S can be defined in various ways. For the estimators B^{**}, C^{**}, we set $S = (M_{\varepsilon\varepsilon}^*)^{-1}$. For the maximum likelihood estimators $\hat{B}$, $\hat{C}$, we take $S = \hat{M}^{-1}$ so that S must be revised progressively as better

---

[†] The KLEIN and GOLDBERGER [1955] model of the American economy is a fairly typical example of models of moderate, though already considerable, size. It involves 18 exogenous variables and 15 structural equations. Recently models with many more variables and equations have been used for prediction of general fluctuations of the national economy.

approximations to $\hat{B}$, $\hat{C}$ and $\hat{M}$ are obtained. (The particular value chosen for S results from the analysis given in ch. 9, § 3; we also note that the first order condition for a minimum of $|M|$ is $\text{tr}(M^{-1}\, dM) = 0$, as is shown by the differentiation rules given in appendix 2 to ch. 5.)

The differential dM can be written $dH + dH'$ where

$$dH = \frac{-1}{T} \sum_{t=1}^{T} dA \cdot z_t(x_t - Az_t)'. \tag{20}$$

Since S is symmetric, condition (19) can also be written $2\text{tr}(S\, dH) = 0$. Moreover, $A = -B^{-1}C$ implies

$$dA = B^{-1}\, dBB^{-1}C - B^{-1}\, dC. \tag{21}$$

We introduce the following notation:

$$P = [B \quad C] \qquad y_t = \begin{bmatrix} x_t \\ z_t \end{bmatrix} \qquad \tilde{y}_t = \begin{bmatrix} -B^{-1}Cz_t \\ z_t \end{bmatrix}. \tag{22}$$

As in ch. 17, P is the matrix of all the coefficients, y_t is the vector of the $n+m$ variables, while $\tilde{y}_t$ is a similar vector in which the observed values of the endogenous variables (x_{it}) have been replaced by their means $(x_{it} - \varepsilon_{it})$ considered as functions of the unknown coefficients. Using these definitions, we can write

$$dA \cdot z_t = -B^{-1}\, dP \begin{bmatrix} -B^{-1}C \\ I \end{bmatrix} z_t = -B^{-1}\, dP\tilde{y}_t \tag{23}$$

and

$$x_t - Az_t = B^{-1}Py_t.$$

Consequently

$$dH = \frac{1}{T} \sum_{t=1}^{T} B^{-1}\, dP\tilde{y}_t y_t' P'(B')^{-1} \tag{24}$$

and $\text{tr}(S\, dH) = \text{tr}(J\, dP)$ where

$$J = \frac{1}{T} \sum_{t=1}^{T} \tilde{y}_t y_t' P' V^{-1} \tag{25}$$

and

$$V = BS^{-1}B'. \tag{26}$$

In particular, in the case of quasi-maximum likelihood estimators, $S^{-1} = M$ and the matrix V can also be written

$$V = \frac{1}{T} \sum_{t=1}^{T} (Bx_t + Cz_t)(Bx_t + Cz_t)'; \tag{27}$$

this is the covariance matrix of the residuals of the structural equations. In all circumstances, it is an estimate of Σ.

The condition tr $(J \, dP) = 0$ is useful because it shows explicitly the system of equations to be solved. Consider equating to zero a derivative of the expression L_T to be minimized, for example, the derivative with respect to the unknown coefficient β_{ih}. This is precisely equivalent to equating to zero the (h,i)th element of J. Thus we establish the system of equations directly from this matrix by taking those of its elements which correspond to the unknown elements of P'.

The form of J shows that this system is difficult to solve, since $\tilde{y}_t$ and V depend on the unknown coefficients of P. If we are not content with a first approximation, then we must use an iterative method, concentrating either on solution of the first-order conditions, or directly on minimization of L_T (both approaches lead in fact to similar procedures).

We also note that, in the present case, the quasi-maximum likelihood estimators do not seem notably more difficult to calculate than any other estimators of the class considered here. So we can fix attention on them and choose the form given by (27) for the matrix V in what follows.

(ii) Three-stage least squares

We first examine an approximate method which is suggested by the form of J. In every element of J, the vector $y_t'P'$ introduces terms which are linear with respect to the parameters to be estimated. So the system of first-order conditions becomes easy to solve if the elements of the $\tilde{y}_t$ and V in it are replaced by quantities which remain fixed in the computation. A priori, this substitution seems bound to lead to a good approximation if the elements of $\tilde{y}_t$ are replaced by preliminary estimates which are already near the expected values of the variables and if the elements of V are replaced by the covariances of the residuals which appear in the structural equations after preliminary estimation.

The above idea lies behind the *method of three-stage least squares* proposed in 1962 by A. Zellner and H. Theil and often applied since. We shall see in ch. 19 that a procedure called the 'method of two-stage least squares' determines consistent estimators in a relatively simple way. The first stage of this procedure consists of a classical multiple regression of each endogenous variable on all the exogenous variables: it provides preliminary estimates of the expected values of the endogenous variables (the values calculated by these particular regressions). With the addition of the observed values of the exogenous variables, this gives a vector y_t^* with the same structure as $\tilde{y}_t$. The second stage gives estimators of B and C, and hence, by application of (27), an estimator V^* of the covariance matrix V. The third stage, which is added in the method of three-stage least squares, consists of solving the system formed by equating to zero all the (h,i)th or (j,i)th elements which, in the matrix

$$J^* = \frac{1}{T} \sum_{t=1}^{T} y_t^* y_t' P'(V^*)^{-1}, \qquad (28)$$

correspond to the unknown elements β_{ih} or γ_{ij}. This defines a system of N linear equations relating to the N unknown coefficients of P. It is solved by the usual methods for linear systems.

We shall see later that the estimators so obtained are asymptotically equivalent to quasi-maximum likelihood estimators. So the approximation obtained is very satisfactory since the resort to quasi-maximum likelihood is justified only by its asymptotic properties.

We note also that, *if V^* is a diagonal matrix, the three-stage least squares estimators coincide with the two-stage least squares estimators.* Consider the equation which corresponds, for example, to the unknown coefficient β_{ih}. After elimination of a multiplicative constant, it becomes

$$\sum_{t=1}^{T} \sum_{k=1}^{n+m} y_{ht}^* y_{kt} p_{ik} = 0. \qquad (29)$$

It involves only the coefficients p_{ik} of the ith structural equation of the model. The juxtaposition of equations similar to (29) and corresponding to the unknown coefficients of only the ith structural equation defines exactly the same system as that solved in the second stage of the method of two-stage least squares applied in estimation of this structural equation (see ch. 19, § 4). So the third stage purely and simply repeats the results of the second. Thus, the resort to three-stage least squares is useful only if V^* is not diagonal, that is, if the residuals of the different structural equations are mutually correlated.

(iii) Durbin's method and Newton's method

The form of J also suggests the following method proposed by DURBIN [1963].

(i) On the basis of preliminary estimates $\beta_{ih}^{(0)}$ and $\gamma_{ij}^{(0)}$, for example the two-stage least squares estimates, find the corresponding values $\tilde{y}_t^{(0)}$ and $V^{(0)}$ of the $\tilde{y}_t$ and V, using (22) and (27). Then find new estimates $\beta_{ih}^{(1)}$ and $\gamma_{ij}^{(1)}$, and so a new matrix $P^{(1)}$, by solving the linear system obtained by equating to zero the appropriate elements of

$$J^{(0)} = \frac{1}{T} \sum_{t=1}^{T} \tilde{y}_t^{(0)} y_t' P' [V^{(0)}]^{-1}.$$

(ii) From $P^{(1)}$ calculate new values $\tilde{y}_t^{(1)}$ and $V^{(1)}$; then solve for β_{ih} and γ_{ij}

the system obtained from the new matrix

$$J^{(1)} = \frac{1}{T} \sum_{t=1}^{T} \tilde{y}_t^{(1)} y_t' P' [V^{(1)}]^{-1}.$$

Let $P^{(2)}$ be the resulting new estimate of P.

(iii) Proceed in this way until convergence occurs.

We can see that this method of Durbin's solves at each stage of the iteration a system in which some of the terms appearing in the equations of Newton's general method, discussed in ch. 9, § 4, (see particularly equations (36)), have been ignored.

To apply Newton's method to this present problem, we must calculate the expressions denoted by $(\partial/\partial \alpha_h) H_k(\alpha^s)$ in ch. 9, that is, the derivatives of the appropriate elements of J with respect to all the unknown coefficients. If $\tilde{y}_t$ and V are not functions of these coefficients, the derivatives depend only on P and the equations of Newton's method are identical with those in Durbin's. But complete differentiation of J gives additional terms arising from $\tilde{y}_t$ and V.

After differentiating (22) defining $\tilde{y}_t$, we find that the derivatives of its last m components are zero, while the derivatives of its first n components are given by

$$\frac{\partial \tilde{y}_{\lambda t}}{\partial \beta_{ih}} = -b^{\lambda i} \tilde{y}_{ht}, \qquad \frac{\partial \tilde{y}_{\lambda t}}{\partial \gamma_{ij}} = -b^{\lambda i} z_{jt}, \qquad (30)$$

where $b^{\lambda i}$ denotes the (λ, i)th element of B^{-1}.

After differentiating (27) relating to V, we see that the derivatives of $v_{\lambda \mu}$ with respect to β_{ih} and γ_{ij} are zero if λ and μ both differ from i and

$$\frac{\partial v_{i\mu}}{\partial \beta_{ih}} = \frac{1}{T} \sum_{t=1}^{T} x_{ht} \cdot p_\mu' y_t, \qquad \text{if} \qquad \mu \neq i, \qquad (31)$$

and twice this quantity if $\mu = i$. (Here p_μ is the vector of the coefficients of the μth structural equation, that is, the vector of the elements in the μth row of P). If we now consider the derivative

$$\frac{\partial v^{rs}}{\partial \beta_{ik}}$$

of the (r,s)th element of V^{-1}, and recall that $dV^{-1} = -V^{-1} \cdot dV \cdot V^{-1}$, we can write

$$\frac{\partial v^{rs}}{\partial \beta_{ih}} = -\sum_{\lambda \mu} v^{r\lambda} v^{\mu s} \frac{\partial v_{\lambda \mu}}{\partial \beta_{ih}}$$

$$= -\sum_\mu (v^{ri} v^{\mu s} + v^{r\mu} v^{is}) \cdot \frac{1}{T} \sum_{t=1}^{T} x_{ht} \cdot p_\mu' y_t. \qquad (32)$$

The same formula applies to the derivative of v^{rs} with respect to γ_{ij}, except that x_{ht} is replaced by z_{jt}.

Equations (30) and (32) have been so expressed as to reveal the form of the additional terms involved by the application of Newton's method. It would be too laborious to write out here in full the system of equations to be solved. The calculations at each stage of the iteration are more complicated than for Durbin's method, but they are of the same order of difficulty. According to a pilot study by CHOW [1968], convergence is much quicker for Newton's method than for Durbin's, so that the total time spent in computation is less.

The various adjustments to Newton's method as described in ch. 9, § 4, clearly have a part to play in calculations for simultaneous equation models. Other gradient methods can also be used (see CHERNOFF and DIVINSKY [1953], BROWN [1959] and EISENPRESS [1962]).

During recent years other iterative methods have been proposed which lead either to a quasi-maximum likelihood estimator or to an approximation to such an estimator (see, in particular, LYTTKENS [1973] and BRUNDY and JORGENSON [1971]). They are very similar in nature to those just discussed, as is clearly shown by HAUSMAN [1975].

(iv)   Covariance matrix of the estimators

Examination of the system constructed by equating to zero the appropriate elements of J reveals a simple method for estimating the asymptotic covariance matrix of the estimated coefficients.

To make this quite clear, we shall rewrite the system of first-order conditions in another form. This form will also have the advantage of making clear the calculations to be carried out for application of the different methods whose principles have just been discussed.

Let us again write the ith structural equation in the form

$$x_{it} = \delta_i' u_{it} + \eta_{it} \tag{34}$$

where δ_i denotes the vector of only the unknown coefficients of this equation (the kth component of this vector is δ_{ik}), and u_{it} the *vector* of the components of y_t which appear in the equation with unknown coefficients. Using this new notation,

$$(Py_t)_i = x_{it} - \delta_i' u_{it}.$$

The (k,i)th element of J is then

$$\frac{1}{T} \sum_{h=1}^{n} \sum_{t=1}^{T} \tilde{y}_{kt}(x_{ht} - \delta_h' u_{ht}) v^{hi},$$

where v^{hi} is the (h,i)th element of V^{-1}.

We must equate to zero this quantity for those components of $\tilde{y}_{kt}$ which appear in the ith structural equation with unknown coefficients. If $\tilde{u}_{it}$ denotes the *vector* of these components, we can write the system of the first-order conditions in the form

$$\frac{1}{T} \sum_{h=1}^{n} \sum_{t=1}^{T} \tilde{u}_{it}(x_{ht} - \delta_h' u_{ht}) v^{hi} = 0 \qquad \text{for} \qquad i = 1, 2, \ldots, n. \qquad (35)$$

The advantage of this notation lies in the fact that it reveals explicitly, and with no supplementary condition, the system of equations to be solved. For each value of i, $\tilde{u}_{it}$ has as many components as there are unknown coefficients in the corresponding structural equation. The number N of the equations (35) is equal to the number of unknowns to be calculated.

In order to distinguish clearly between estimates and true values, let $\hat{\delta}_{hj}$ be the value of δ_{hj} in the solution of (35). Similarly let $\hat{u}_{ikt}$ be the value of $\tilde{u}_{ikt}$ and $\hat{v}^{hi}$ be the value of v^{hi}. In short, we can write (35) in the form

$$\frac{1}{T} \sum_{h=1}^{n} \sum_{t=1}^{T} \hat{u}_{it}(x_{ht} - \hat{\delta}_h' u_{ht}) \hat{v}^{hi} = 0 \qquad \text{for} \qquad i = 1, 2, \ldots, n. \qquad (36)$$

Let x_{ht} be replaced in this system by its value given by the hth structural equation, $\delta_h' u_{ht} + \eta_{ht}$. We obtain

$$\frac{1}{T} \sum_{h=1}^{n} \sum_{t=1}^{T} \hat{u}_{it}(\hat{\delta}_h - \delta_h)' u_{ht} \hat{v}^{hi} = \frac{1}{T} \sum_{h=1}^{n} \sum_{t=1}^{T} \hat{u}_{it} \hat{v}^{hi} \eta_{ht} \qquad (37)$$

for $i = 1, 2, \ldots, n$.

Let δ and $\hat{\delta}$ denote the N-vectors composed respectively of the δ_h and the $\hat{\delta}_h$.

$$\delta = \begin{bmatrix} \delta_1 \\ \delta_2 \\ \cdot \\ \cdot \\ \cdot \\ \delta_n \end{bmatrix} \qquad \hat{\delta} = \begin{bmatrix} \hat{\delta}_1 \\ \hat{\delta}_2 \\ \cdot \\ \cdot \\ \cdot \\ \hat{\delta}_n \end{bmatrix}.$$

(We continue to let δ_{hj} denote the components of δ.) We set

$$g_{ik,\,hj} = \frac{1}{T} \sum_{t=1}^{T} \tilde{u}_{ikt} v^{hi} u_{hjt} \qquad (38)$$

and

$$f_{ik} = \frac{1}{T} \sum_{h=1}^{n} \sum_{t=1}^{T} \tilde{u}_{ikt} v^{hi} \eta_{ht} \qquad (39)$$

and let $\hat{g}_{ik,hj}$ anf $\hat{f}_{ik}$ denote the values of these quantities when the $\tilde{u}_{it}$ and v^{hi} are replaced in them by the $\hat{u}_{it}$ and $\hat{v}^{hi}$. Let G and $\hat{G}$ be the square matrices of order N consisting of the $g_{ik,hj}$ and the $\hat{g}_{ik,hj}$; let f and $\hat{f}$ be the N-vectors composed of the f_{ik} and the $\hat{f}_{ik}$.

With this new notation, the system of N equations (37) can be put in the more compact form

$$\hat{G}(\delta - \delta) = \hat{f} \tag{40}$$

and so

$$\hat{\delta} = \delta + \hat{G}^{-1}\hat{f}. \tag{41}$$

Consider now the asymptotic behavior of $\sqrt{T}(\hat{\delta} - \delta)$. It would be tedious to give in detail the assumptions necessary for the validity of the properties which we shall state. These assumptions are similar to those in ch. 6, § 8 and ch. 9, § 5.

Since $\hat{\delta}$ tends in probability to δ, the matrices $\hat{G}$ and G have the same limit in probability, say G_∞; the vectors $\sqrt{T}\hat{f}$ and $\sqrt{T}f$ have the same limiting distribution. Consequently $\sqrt{T}(\hat{\delta} - \delta)$ has the same limiting distribution as $G_\infty^{-1} \sqrt{T}f$. Now, $\sqrt{T}f$ has a limiting normal distribution, the (ik,hj)th element of whose covariance matrix is the limit of

$$\frac{1}{T}\sum_{t=1}^{T} \tilde{u}_{ikt}\tilde{u}_{hjt} \cdot \sum_{r,s=1}^{n} v^{ri}\sigma_{rs}v^{sh}. \tag{42}$$

With methods such as quasi-maximum likelihood or minimum distance estimators in which $S^{-1} = M_{\varepsilon\varepsilon}^*$, the matrix V tends in probability to Σ. So in the limit, expression (42) above is equivalent to

$$\frac{1}{T}\sum_{t=1}^{T} \tilde{u}_{ikt}v^{hi}\tilde{u}_{hjt}. \tag{43}$$

Now, this quantity is equivalent to $g_{ik,hj}$ since it differs from it only by a term which tends in probability to zero. Thus the asymptotic covariance matrix of $\sqrt{T}f$ is G_∞; therefore that of $\sqrt{T}(\hat{\delta} - \delta)$ is G_∞^{-1}. So we can take $1/T(\hat{G}^{-1})$ as a consistent estimate of the covariance matrix of $\hat{\delta}$.

The above asymptotic reasoning also applies to every system

$$G^*(\hat{\hat{\delta}} - \delta) = f^* \tag{44}$$

in which G^* has the same limit in probability as $\hat{G}$, and $\sqrt{T}f^*$ the same limiting distribution as $\sqrt{T}f$. More precisely, by comparing (40) and (44), we can write

$$G(\hat{\delta} - \hat{\hat{\delta}}) = (\hat{f} - f^*) + (\hat{G} - G^*)(\delta - \hat{\hat{\delta}}).$$

If $\hat{G}$ and G^* have the same limit in probability and if $\sqrt{T}(\hat{f} - f^*)$ tends in probability to zero, then $\sqrt{T}(\hat{\delta} - \hat{\hat{\delta}})$ also tends to zero, so that the estimators $\hat{\delta}$ and $\hat{\hat{\delta}}$ are asymptotically equivalent.

The above remark proves *the asymptotic equivalence of three-stage least squares estimators and quasi-maximum likelihood estimators.* For, replacement of J by J^* is expressed by the replacement of the $\tilde{y}_t$ and V by the vectors y_t^* and the matrix V^*, which have the same limits in probability. The resulting matrix G^* has the same limit as G, and the vector $\sqrt{T}f^*$ has the same limiting distribution as $\sqrt{T}f$.

(v) The treatment of identities

We have assumed up till now that the model contains no identities. Certainly, we can always eliminate them. But as we have seen, this complicates the restrictions on the coefficients. If the initial form of the model involves only exclusion restrictions, the form obtained after elimination is often subject to less simple restrictions. However we shall see that the methods given above can be applied directly to the initial form.

We return to the notation of ch. 18 and write the model with its identities:

$$\left. \begin{array}{l} B_1 x_t + B_2 q_t + C_1 z_t = \eta_t \\ B_3 x_t + B_4 q_t + C_2 z_t = 0 \end{array} \right\} . \tag{45}$$

Elimination of the identities brings us back to the usual form $Bx_t + Cz_t = \eta_t$, the matrices B and C being defined by

$$\left. \begin{array}{l} B = B_1 - B_2 B_4^{-1} B_3 \\ C = C_1 - B_2 B_4^{-1} C_2 \end{array} \right\} . \tag{46}$$

We let P still denote the matrix $[B \ C]$ of the coefficients of the form obtained after elimination of the identities and let P_* denote the matrix $[B_1 \ B_2 \ C_1]$ of the coefficients of the initial form. The unknown coefficients of (45) all belong to P_*, which is also subject to a certain number of exclusion restrictions. While keeping the notation (22) for y_t and $\tilde{y}_t$, we can also write

$$y_{t^*} = \begin{bmatrix} x_t \\ q_t \\ z_t \end{bmatrix} = \begin{bmatrix} x_t \\ -B_4^{-1}(B_3 x_t + C_2 z_t) \\ z_t \end{bmatrix} \tag{47}$$

and set

$$R = \begin{bmatrix} I & 0 \\ -B_4^{-1} B_3 & -B_4^{-1} C_2 \\ 0 & I \end{bmatrix} . \tag{48}$$

The system (46) and the definition (47) then imply

$$P = P_* R \qquad y_{t*} = R y_t. \tag{49}$$

With $\tilde{y}_t$ we can associate a vector of the same form as y_{t*}, the vectors x_t and q_t of the endogenous variables being replaced by their means:

$$\tilde{y}_{t*} = \begin{bmatrix} -B^{-1} C z_t \\ B_4^{-1}(B_3 B^{-1} C - C_2) z_t \\ z_t \end{bmatrix} = R \tilde{y}_t. \tag{50}$$

The condition $\operatorname{tr}(J\,dP) = 0$ established in section 6(i) obviously still applies in this new situation, the matrix J still being defined by (25). But the matrix dP no longer has as simple a structure when it is expressed in terms of the differentials of the unknown coefficients of the initial form. To revert to a condition which is easily interpreted, we must write dP in terms of dP_*. The first of the equalities (49) gives directly $dP = dP_* R$, since R is completely known. So for $\operatorname{tr}(J\,dP) = 0$ we can substitute the condition $\operatorname{tr}(J_*\,dP_*) = 0$ where $J_* = RJ$. The first-order conditions then imply that the elements of J_* which correspond to the unknown coefficients of P'_* are equated to zero.

Now, the equalities (49) imply $Py_t = P_* y_t^*$. Taking account of (25) and (50), the matrix J_* can be written

$$J_* = \frac{1}{T} \sum_{t=1}^{T} \tilde{y}_{t*} y'_{t*} P'_* V^{-1}, \tag{51}$$

where V can be interpreted as the covariance matrix of the residuals of the initial structural equations, (27) implying

$$V = \frac{1}{T} \sum_{t=1}^{T} (Py_t)(Py_t)' = \frac{1}{T} \sum_{t=1}^{T} (P_* y_{t*})(P_* y_{t*})'. \tag{52}$$

Thus, for the condition $\operatorname{tr}(J\,dP) = 0$ we have substituted the condition $\operatorname{tr}(J_*\,dP_*) = 0$, and for the matrix J defined by (25), the matrix J_* defined by (51) which has a strictly similar structure but is obtained directly from the initial form of the model without preliminary elimination of the identities. *So to apply Durbin's method, Newton's method or the method of three-stage least squares, we need only consider directly the model in its initial form containing identities.*

CHAPTER 19

Estimation of an equation in a simultaneous equation model

1 The principle of limited information estimates

The estimation methods described in the previous chapter remain laborious for models involving more than three or four equations. The question is often valid whether such complex computation is justified when the data have only fair precision, or when the model itself is only a fairly crude representation of the actual phenomena.

This is why there has been a search for methods which demand less heavy computation. This was particularly important immediately after the last war when the principles for treating simultaneous equation models were worked out, since modern digital computers were not then available. To simplify the computation, the usual procedure was to ignore the restrictions affecting the coefficients of other equations when each structural equation was being estimated. This led to estimators which are as a rule less efficient than those discussed in the previous chapter but which enjoy the same properties of consistency.

The model is not then estimated en bloc, but each of its n structural relations is considered in succession. To estimate the ith structural equation, we take account, in the first place, of the fact that the endogenous variables x_t depend on the exogenous variables z_t according to a relation of the type:

$$x_t = Az_t + \varepsilon_t; \tag{1}$$

and, in the second place, of the fact that the coefficients relating to certain variables are necessarily zero in this equation. Thus at each stage we bring into play the a priori restrictions affecting the equation under study, excluding every other restriction. This is why we call this the '*limited-information*' method. For estimation of the ith structural equation, we make no use of our knowledge about the coefficients of the other equations. So we obtain implicitly n different estimates of the matrix A, each one compatible with the restrictions relating to one particular structural relation[†].

Given that each of the n structural equations has been estimated in this way, there is obviously nothing to prevent our solving them in order to deduce ex-

---

[†] As we saw in the preceding chapter, limited-information estimates are not only interesting in themselves, but may also provide initial values for the iterative computation of full information estimates.

plicitly the corresponding reduced equations and an estimate $\hat{A}$ of the matrix A. However, as DHRYMES [1973] points out, this estimate will not necessarily be more precise than the estimate A^* obtained from a direct and unconstrained regression of x_t on z_t, since the method which leads to $\hat{A}$ operates in a sense as if the errors affecting the different structural equations are uncorrelated, which may be far from true.

We shall adopt the limited information estimation principle during the present chapter[†]. So we shall consider one particular equation from a model with errors in equations involving in all n endogenous variables and m exogenous variables. Moreover it may happen that we are interested in this equation alone, and that we never go on to estimate the other structural relations. For we saw in ch. 15, that models with several equations are often introduced to allow correct estimation of a single relation.

In fact it is not even necessary to describe the model in complete detail. We need only specify the structural equation to be estimated, distinguish its exogenous and endogenous variables, and indicate which other exogenous variables should be included in a model which represents completely the determination of the endogenous variables. (Obviously we must still specify the assumptions to be adopted for the random errors ε_t.) There is no advantage in knowing what other endogenous variables appear in the complete model. They introduce no limitation on the nature of the general relationship between the exogenous variables and the endogenous variables contained in the equation under consideration.

In view of this remark, and to simplify the notation, we shall proceed as if the model contains only the n endogenous variables of the structural equation to be estimated. Among the m exogenous variables z_{jt}, we shall distinguish the m_1 variables (denoted by r_{jt}) appearing in the equation from the $m_2 = m - m_1$ variables (say s_{jt}) which do not appear in it. The reduced form is then

$$x_t = A_r r_t + A_s s_t + \varepsilon_t \tag{2}$$

where obviously $A = [A_r \quad A_s]$. The structural equation to be estimated is

$$b' x_t + c' r_t = \eta_t, \tag{3}$$

where the b_i and c_j are numerical coefficients and η_t the random error[††].

The problem is then to estimate A_r, A_s, b and c with the conditions:

$$b' A_r = - c', \qquad b' A_s = 0. \tag{4}$$

[†] The estimators to be discussed derive from those studied in ch. 9, which deals with non-linear regression. ZELLNER [1968], DRÈZE [1968 and 1976] show how Bayesian estimators can be constructed on the limited information principle.
[††] Thus, we confine ourselves to the case where the equation is affected only by exclusion restrictions. In section 4(v) we shall discuss briefly the slightly more general case of homogeneous linear restrictions.

For estimation of the reduced form (2), we need only take account of the condition that the matrix A_s has rank at most $n-1$.

In view of the order condition, the structural equation (3) is identifiable only if $m_2 \geq n-1$. Now there is no difficulty in estimation if $m_2 = n-1$. Every $n \times m_2$-matrix A_s then necessarily has rank lower than n, so that there is no restriction on the reduced form. We can estimate b and c by an indirect regression.

Thus in what follows we shall suppose that

$$m_2 \gtreqless n, \tag{5}$$

so that the restriction on A_s is effective. To ensure identifiability of the structural equation considered, we adopt the following assumption:

Assumption 1. The true value A_s^0 of the matrix A_s has rank $n-1$.

We shall also assume that the normalization rule demands that the vector (b, c) has given length, and fixes the sign of an element of b which is non-zero in the true structure. (However, see below a slightly different rule in formula (14).)

Under these conditions, assumptions 1 to 4 of the previous chapter are satisfied if the pair of matrices (B, C) is everywhere replaced by the pair of vectors (b, c). In accordance with assumption 1 of ch. 18, the vector (b, c) belongs to a compact set. In accordance with assumption 2, no pair (b, c) other than the pair of true values (b^0, c^0) satisfies the normalization rule, $b'A_r^0 + c' = 0$, and $b'A_s^0 = 0$. The a priori restrictions and the normalization rule satisfy assumption 4. (The only restrictions to be taken into consideration are those which establish that the coefficients of the s_{jt} are zero in one of the structural equations.)

Verification of assumption 3 is not quite so straightforward. We must find out if the ratio between the distances

$$\| A - A^0 \| \qquad \text{and} \qquad \| (b, c) - (b^0, c^0) \|$$

is bounded below by a positive number. For this, we can choose the following distances:

$$\| A - A^0 \| = \max_{ij} | a_{ij} - a_{ij}^0 |,$$

$$\| b - b^0 \| = \max_i | b_i - b_i^0 |, \qquad \| c - c^0 \| = \max_j | c_j - c_j^0 |,$$

$$\| (b, c) - (b^0, c^0) \| = \max \{ \| b - b^0 \|, \| c - c^0 \| \}.$$

The first equality of system (4) allows us to write:

$$(c - c^0)' = b'(A_r^0 - A_r) + (b^0 - b)'A_r^0,$$

from which we can directly deduce:

$$\| c - c^0 \| \leq \lambda \| A_r - A_r^0 \| + \mu \| b - b^0 \|, \tag{6}$$

where

$$\lambda = n \| b \| > 0 \qquad \text{and} \qquad \mu = n \| A_r^0 \| \geq 0.$$

Moreover, in the neighborhood of b^0, we can write:

$$n \| b \| \cdot \| A_s - A_s^0 \| \geq \| b'(A_s - A_s^0) \| = \| (b - b^0)' A_s^0 \| \geq v \| b - b^0 \|,$$

where v is a positive number. Indeed the equality follows directly from the second equality of system (4), and the last inequality from the facts that A_s^0 has rank $n-1$ and that $b - b^0$ is orthogonal to b^0 in the neighborhood of b^0. Consequently

$$\| b - b^0 \| \leq \sigma \| A_s - A_s^0 \|, \tag{7}$$

where

$$\sigma = \frac{n}{v} \| b \| > 0.$$

Taking account of (7) in (6), we obtain directly:

$$\| c - c^0 \| \leq \tau \| A - A^0 \|, \tag{8}$$

where

$$\tau = \lambda + \mu \sigma > 0.$$

We must prove that there exists $\varepsilon > 0$ such that

$$\| A - A^0 \| \geq \varepsilon \| (b, c) - (b^0, c^0) \| \tag{9}$$

in the neighborhood of (b^0, c^0). Now,

(i) If $\| c - c^0 \| \geq \| b - b^0 \|$, this result follows directly from the inequality (8) with $\varepsilon = 1/\tau > 0$.

(ii) If $\| b - b^0 \| \geq \| c - c^0 \|$, the inequality (9) follows directly from the inequality (7) with $\varepsilon = 1/\sigma > 0$.

Finally, for the errors ε_t and for the exogenous variables we adopt the usual assumptions:

Assumption 2. The vectors ε_t are mutually independent and identically distributed with zero mean and non-singular covariance matrix Ω.

Assumption 3. The vectors z_t are bounded. The matrix M_{zz} is non-singular. It tends to a non-singular matrix when T tends to infinity.

2   The minimum distance estimator of an equation with no exogenous variable

(i)   Calculation of the estimators

Assumptions 1 and 2 above imply the validity of assumptions 1 to 6 of the preceding chapter. So certain minimum distance estimators enjoy useful properties for the estimation of b and c. We must define and study these estimators in the context of our present problem.

To facilitate discussion, we shall first consider the case where the equation to be estimated does not contain any exogenous variable ($m_1 = 0$). The model is then

$$x_t = Az_t + \varepsilon_t, \tag{10}$$

with the constraint:

$$b'A = 0. \tag{11}$$

The structural equation under study is simply

$$b'x_t = \eta_t. \tag{12}$$

For reasons given above, if suffices to deal with the case where $m \geqq n$ and the matrix A^0 has rank $n-1$.

Let us find the formulae which allow us to calculate the estimators A^{**} and b^{**} defined in the previous chapter. To this end let A^* be the matrix of the regression coefficients of the endogenous variables on the exogenous variables; let $M_{\varepsilon\varepsilon}$ be the matrix of the moments of the residuals

$$\varepsilon_t^* = x_t - A^* z_t.$$

(to simplify notation in this chapter we omit the asterisk in $M_{\varepsilon\varepsilon}$). We shall find the matrix A^{**} and the vector b^{**} which minimize

$$\operatorname{tr} \left[(A - A^*)' M_{\varepsilon\varepsilon}^{-1} (A - A^*) M_{zz} \right] \tag{13}$$

with the constraint (11).

We adopt as normalization rule:

$$b' M_{\varepsilon\varepsilon} b = 1 \tag{14}$$

and we demand that b_1 is positive, assuming that the first endogenous variable does not have a zero coefficient in the true structural equation.

This rule differs from those introduced up till now in that it depends on the values taken by the random errors $\varepsilon_1, \varepsilon_2, \ldots, \varepsilon_T$. Clearly it is asymptotically equivalent to $b'\Omega b = 1$ which does not depend on the ε_t; and the equality (14) makes the computation considerably easier.

To carry out the minimization of (13), we first fix the value of b and find the matrix A which minimizes (13) for this value of b. The minimum obtained is expressed as a function of b. Finally we determine the vector b^{**} which allows us to obtain the minimum of these minima. The computation resembles that carried out for the weighted regression in models with errors in variables.

(a) b known

We must find the minimum of (13) with the constraint (14). Introducing the Lagrange multipliers $-2\lambda_j$ and differentiating with respect to a_{ij}, we obtain the necessary condition:

$$[M_{\varepsilon\varepsilon}^{-1}(A - A^*)M_{zz}]_{ij} - \lambda_j b_i = 0$$

which is expressed in matrix form by

$$M_{\varepsilon\varepsilon}^{-1}(A - A^*)M_{zz} - b\lambda' = 0. \tag{15}$$

Premultiplying by $b'M_{\varepsilon\varepsilon}$ and taking account of (14), we obtain

$$- b'A^*M_{zz} = \lambda',$$

and hence, substituting in (15):

$$M_{\varepsilon\varepsilon}^{-1}(A - A^*) + bb'A^* = 0; \tag{16}$$

finally, A^{**} is given by

$$A^{**} = (I - M_{\varepsilon\varepsilon}bb')A^*. \tag{17}$$

Formula (16) substituted in (13) gives the minimum of the quadratic form

$$\text{tr}\,[A^{*'}bb'M_{\varepsilon\varepsilon}bb'A^*M_{zz}]$$

which is equal to

$$b'A^*M_{zz}A^{*'}b. \tag{18}$$

(b) b unknown

We must now determine b so as to minimize (18) with the normalization condition (14). If μ denotes a Lagrange multiplier, we must have

$$(A^*M_{zz}A^{*'} - \mu M_{\varepsilon\varepsilon})b = 0, \tag{19}$$

and therefore

$$|A^*M_{zz}A^{*'} - \mu M_{\varepsilon\varepsilon}| = 0. \tag{20}$$

Moreover μ must be the smallest root of this equation, since, according to (19) and (14), it is exactly equal to (18).

In short, we must carry out the following computation:

– determine A^* by the method of least squares, ignoring the a priori restrictions;

– determine the smallest root in μ of (20);

– solve for b the system consisting of (14) and the eqs. (19).

We could also apply the *quasi-maximum likelihood* estimation principle to this problem. We should arrive at *exactly the same estimator* of b, as was shown by ANDERSON and RUBIN [1949]. More precisely, with the normalization rule (14), the quasi-maximum likelihood estimators of b, A and Ω are respectively[†]:

$$b = b^{**}$$

$$\hat{A} = [I - M_{\varepsilon\varepsilon}\hat{b}\hat{b}']A^* \qquad\qquad (21)$$

$$\hat{\Omega} = M_{\varepsilon\varepsilon} + \mu M_{\varepsilon\varepsilon}\hat{b}\hat{b}'M_{\varepsilon\varepsilon},$$

μ being the smallest root of eq. (20).

(ii)   Covariance matrix of the estimators

Let $\hat{b}^0$ be the true value of the vector b normalized by the equality (14); this vector $\hat{b}^0$ is random like $M_{\varepsilon\varepsilon}$ but lies on a fixed line. We distinguish it from b^0, the vector giving the true value of b normalized by $b'\Omega b = 1$. If assumptions 1 and 2 are satisfied, we know that $\sqrt{T}(b^{**} - \hat{b}^0)$ has a limiting normal distribution, and that b^{**} is asymptotically efficient when ε_t is normally distributed. It remains to determine the asymptotic concentration ellipsoid of $\sqrt{T}(b^{**} - \hat{b}^0)$, so as to characterize the precision with which b^{**} estimates b^0, and as to provide asymptotically valid tests for b^0.

To do this, we can use the property established in ch. 9 § 5, that the asymptotic concentration ellipsoid of $\sqrt{T}(A^{**} - A^0)$ can be constructed as the intersection E of the concentration ellipsoid of $\sqrt{T}(A^* - A^0)$ with the linear subspace H_0 parallel to the hyperplane of the matrices which satisfy the a priori restrictions in the neighborhood of A^0.

The matrices of rank $n-1$ depend on $(n-1)(m+1)$ parameters: the $n-1$ independent parameters of a normalized vector b, and the $(n-1)m$ independent parameters of the matrices satisfying $b'A = 0$ for a given value of b. In particular, the matrices satisfying $b^{0'}A = 0$ define an $(n-1)m$-dimensional linear subspace K_0 belonging to H_0.

As we are interested only in the distribution of b^{**} and not in that of the other $(n-1)m$ parameters on which A^{**} depends, we must find a representation of the matrices of H_0 which allows us to consider the marginal distribution of b^{**} directly. A simple method consists of defining the linear subspace L_0 of H_0 that is conjugate to K_0 with respect to the concentration ellipsoid of $\sqrt{T}(A^* - A^0)$. Every matrix of H_0 can then be written as the sum of two matrices, A_K belonging to K_0 and A_L belonging to L_0.

[†] These results can be obtained directly by examining the application of the iterative procedure defined at the end of section 2 of ch. 9. We see that the procedure stops at the second iteration, having converged to the estimators defined by (21).

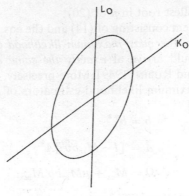

Fig. 1.

In particular, this decomposition can be applied to the matrix of H_0 which is nearest to

$$\sqrt{T}(A^{**} - A^0).$$

The concentration ellipsoid of its A_L component will define the asymptotic second order moments of

$$\sqrt{T}(b^{**} - b^0);$$

since two matrices have the same component in L_0 if and only if they correspond to the same value of the vector b. In short, the asymptotic concentration ellipsoid of $\sqrt{T}(b^{**} - b^0)$ can be deduced directly from the intersection of L_0 with the concentration ellipsoid of $\sqrt{T}(A^* - A^0)$ (see fig. 1).

It can be verified that the matrices A_L must have the form:

$$A_L = \Omega b^0 d' A^0 \tag{22}$$

where d is a vector restricted only to satisfy

$$d'\Omega b^0 = 0. \tag{23}$$

Indeed:

(i) the matrices $(A^0 + A_L)$ have rank $n-1$, since

$$(b^0 - d)'(A^0 + A_L) = (b^{0'}\Omega b^0)d'A^0 - d'A^0 - (d'\Omega b^0)d'A^0 = 0;$$

(ii) the concentration ellipsoid of $\sqrt{T}(A^* - A^0)$ consists of the set of matrices A such that

$$\mathrm{tr}\,[M_{zz}A'\Omega^{-1}A] \leqq 1;$$

then every matrix A_L is indeed conjugate to every matrix A_K such that $b^{0'}A_K = 0$, since

$$\mathrm{tr}\left[M_{zz}A_K'\Omega^{-1}A_L\right] = \mathrm{tr}\left[M_{zz}(A_K'b^0)d'A^0\right] = 0.$$

The intersection of the concentration ellipsoid of $\sqrt{T}(A^*-A^0)$ and of L_0 therefore consists of the set of matrices A_L which have the form (22) with a vector d satisfying (23) and

$$\mathrm{tr}\left[M_{zz}A^{0'}dd'A^0\right] \leqq 1,$$

which can also be written:

$$d'A^0M_{zz}A^{0'}d \leqq 1. \tag{24}$$

Since

$$(b^0 - d)'(A^0 + A_L) = 0,$$

the vector d is near the vector

$$\sqrt{T}(b^{**} - b^0)$$

when the matrix A_L is near

$$-\sqrt{T}(A^{**} - A^0).$$

Moreover the correspondence between A_L and d is linear. The asymptotic concentration ellipsoid of

$$\sqrt{T}(b^{**} - b^0)$$

therefore consists of the set of vectors d satisfying (23) and (24).

This ellipsoid depends on A^0, b^0 and Ω which are unknown. But they can be estimated by means of A^{**}, b^{**} and $M_{\varepsilon\varepsilon}$. The ellipsoid can be estimated by the set of vectors d such that:

$$d'A^{**}M_{zz}A^{**'}d \leqq 1,$$

$$d'M_{\varepsilon\varepsilon}b^{**} = 0.$$

Taking account of formula (17) and the above equality, the inequality can also be written:

$$d'A^*M_{zz}A^{*'}d \leqq 1.$$

According to the general formulae of multiple regression theory,

$$A^*M_{zz}A^{*'} = M_{xx} - M_{\varepsilon\varepsilon}.$$

Thus the asymptotic concentration ellipsoid of

$$\sqrt{T}(b^{**} - b^0)$$

can be estimated by the set of vectors d such that:

$$d'(M_{xx} - M_{\varepsilon\varepsilon})d \leqq 1,$$
$$d'M_{\varepsilon\varepsilon}b^{**} = 0. \tag{25}$$

Proposition 1 of chapt. 5 then implies the following estimate of the asymptotic covariance matrix of $\sqrt{T}(b^{**} - \hat{b}^0)$:

$$Q_b^{**} = (M_{xx} - M_{\varepsilon\varepsilon})^{-1}(I - N^{**}), \tag{26}$$

where

$$N^{**} = \frac{M_{\varepsilon\varepsilon}b^{**}b^{**\prime}M_{\varepsilon\varepsilon}(M_{xx} - M_{\varepsilon\varepsilon})^{-1}}{b^{**\prime}M_{\varepsilon\varepsilon}(M_{xx} - M_{\varepsilon\varepsilon})^{-1}M_{\varepsilon\varepsilon}b^{**}} \tag{27}$$

(iii) Confidence region and a test of overidentification

In view of the above results,

$$\sqrt{T}(b^{**} - \hat{b}^0)$$

has an asymptotic $(n-1)$-dimensional centred normal distribution whose concentration ellipsoid is known. It follows that

$$T(b^{**} - \hat{b}^0)'A^{0}M_{,,}\dot{A}^{0'}(b^{**} - \hat{b}^0)$$

has an asymptotic χ^2-distribution with $n-1$ degrees of freedom. Since

$$A^{**}M_{zz}A^{**\prime}$$

tends in probability to $A^0M_{zz}A^{0'}$,

$$T(b^{**} - \hat{b}^0)'A^{**}M_{zz}A^{**\prime}(b^{**} - \hat{b}^0) \tag{28}$$

also has an asymptotic χ^2-distribution with $n-1$ degrees of freedom. Now, expression (28) can be written:

$$T\hat{b}^{0'}A^{**}M_{zz}A^{**\prime}\hat{b}^0. \tag{29}$$

Thus, for the true value $\hat{b}^0$ normalized by $b'M_{\varepsilon\varepsilon}b=1$, we can establish directly the confidence region:

$$T\hat{b}^{0'}A^{**}M_{zz}A^{**\prime}\hat{b}^0 \leqq \chi^2_{n-1}(\alpha), \tag{30}$$

$\chi^2_{n-1}(\alpha)$ denoting the value corresponding to the probability level α for the χ^2-variable with $n-1$ degrees of freedom.

We can also carry out a simple test of the basic hypothesis of the model, namely that the matrix A^0 has rank $n-1$, that is, that there exists an identifiable structural equation in which none of the exogenous variables occurs. This is usually called a *test of overidentification*.

For, the smallest root $\bar{\mu}$ of (20) is equal to the minimum of expression (13). The asymptotic distribution of $T\bar{\mu}$ is a χ^2-distribution with $m-n+1$ degrees of freedom if the hypothesis under test is true. To see this we need only apply the principles given in ch. 9; $T\bar{\mu}$ is equal to the appropriate distance between the projection vector x^* obtained by the method of least squares and the vector x^{**} corresponding to the projection of x^* on the variety H^0 associated with matrices of rank lower than n. Asymptotically,

$$\sqrt{T}(x^* - x^{**})$$

tends to belong to a linear subspace of dimension $nm - [(n-1)(m+1)] = m-n+1$.

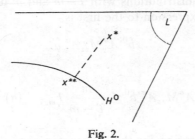

Fig. 2.

In short, the value of $T\bar{\mu}$ is considered as significantly different from zero if it exceeds $\chi^2_{m-n+1}(\alpha)$. To take account of the systematic error in estimation of Ω by $M_{\varepsilon\varepsilon}$ we may consider $(T-m)\bar{\mu}$ in preference to $T\bar{\mu}$. In fact McDonald [1972] suggests the quantity $(T-m)\bar{\mu}/(m-n+1)$ whose approximate distribution in small samples appears as an F-distribution with $m-n+1$ and $T-m$ degrees of freedom.

(iv)   Exact methods

When the errors are normally distributed we can also justify two methods which are rigorously valid even for small samples.

In the first place, consider a test of the hypothesis that the true vector b^0 is equal to a given vector β. The number $u_t = \beta' x_t$ can be expressed as the sum of $w_t = \beta' A_0 z_t$ and $\xi_t = \beta' \varepsilon_t$. Now w_t is zero if $b^0 = \beta$; when A_0 has rank $n-1$, w_t is zero in this case only, since the normalisation rule demands that two collinear vectors are equal. Let u_t^* be the residual of the regression of u_t on z_t. The two vectors $u_t - u_t^*$ and u_t^* are normal and independent. The expected value of the former is zero if and only if $b^0 = \beta$; the expected value of the latter is zero in all cases. A test of the hypothesis $b^0 = \beta$ can be based on

$$\frac{T - m}{m} \sum_t (u_t - u_t^*)^2 / \sum_t u_t^{*2}.$$

From examination of the standard errors of $u_t - u_t^*$ and u_t^* we see that the above quantity has an F-distribution with m and $T - m$ degrees of freedom. See REVANKAR and MALLELA [1972].

In the second place we know that, in the direct application of least squares, the vector of the residuals ε_t^* and the estimate A^* have independent normal distributions of $n(T - m)$ and nm dimensions respectively. Consequently the vector of the $b^{0'}\varepsilon_t^*$ and the vector $b^{0'}A^*$ have independent centered normal distributions of $T - m$ and m dimensions. If b^0 is normalized by $b'\Omega b = 1$, then

$$b^{0'}M_{\varepsilon\varepsilon}b^0 \quad \text{and} \quad b^{0'}A^*M_{zz}A^{*'}b^0$$

have independent χ^2-distributions with $T - m$ and m degrees of freedom. The ratio of the second expression to the first is

$$\hat{b}^{0'}A^*M_{zz}A^{*'}\hat{b}^0.$$

Consequently

$$\hat{b}^{0'}A^*M_{zz}A^{*'}\hat{b}^0 \leq \frac{m}{T - m} F_{m, T-m}(\alpha) \tag{31}$$

defines a confidence region for the true vector normalized by $b'M_{\varepsilon\varepsilon}b = 1$, the symbol $F_{m, T-m}(\alpha)$ denoting the value of F for m and $T - m$ degrees of freedom and significance level α.

3   The Cowles Commission method

Let us return to the general problem which consists of estimating an equation:

$$b'x_t + c'r_t = \eta_t \tag{3}$$

in a model of the form:

$$x_t = A_r r_t + A_s s_t + \varepsilon_t. \tag{2}$$

The only restriction considered is that which implies

$$b'A_s = 0. \tag{4}$$

It is effective if, as we shall suppose, the number m_2 of the exogenous variables which do not appear in eq. (3) is at least equal to the number n of the endogenous variables.

To estimate b and c we shall apply the same principles as were followed in the case where $m_1 = 0$. Thus we shall obtain the estimates b^{**} and c^{**} first defined by the researchers of the 'Cowles Commission for Research in Economics'. Between 1940 and 1950 this institute, set up at the University of Chicago, was largely concerned with the study of the problems arising in the statistical treatment of economic models. The results of these investigations have appeared in numerous articles to which we have had occasion to refer, and, in particular, in two collective works edited respectively by KOOPMANS [1950] and by HOOD and KOOPMANS [1953].

The estimators b^{**} and c^{**} were obtained by the method of maximum likelihood under the assumption that the vectors ε_t are mutually independent and identically normally distributed. They were called *limited information maximum likelihood estimators* or possibly 'limited information quasi-maximum likelihood estimators' when the validity of the assumption of normality was suspect. Here we shall call them 'Cowles Commission estimators'.

For the properties of b^{**} and c^{**}, the reader may profitably refer to two articles by ANDERSON and RUBIN [1949, 1950].

To determine b^{**} and c^{**}, we must find the matrix

$$A^{**} = [A_r^{**} \quad A_s^{**}]$$

which minimizes expression (13) subject to the constraint that A^{**} has rank at most $n-1$. The calculation of A^{**} is relatively simple if the two groups of exogenous variables, which respectively constitute r_t and s_t, are orthogonal, that is, if the matrix M_{rs} is zero. For, the expression (13) to be minimized can then be written:

$$\mathrm{tr}\left[(A_r - A_r^*)M_{rr}(A_r - A_r^*)'M_{\varepsilon\varepsilon}^{-1}\right] + \mathrm{tr}\left[(A_s - A_s^*)M_{ss}(A_s - A_s^*)'M_{\varepsilon\varepsilon}^{-1}\right].$$

Under these conditions, $A_r^{**} = A_r^*$; the matrix A_s^{**}, which minimizes the second term, is calculated by the method described in the previous section, with M_{ss} replacing M_{zz}.

We can revert to this case by substituting for the vectors s_t the vectors:

$$w_t = s_t - M_{sr}M_{rr}^{-1}r_t$$

so that M_{rw} is necessarily zero. The reduced form:

$$x_t = A_r r_t + A_s s_t + \varepsilon_t$$

must be replaced by

$$x_t = A_v r_t + A_w w_t + \varepsilon_t, \tag{32}$$

where

$$A_v = A_r + A_s M_{sr}M_{rr}^{-1} \quad \text{and} \quad A_w = A_s.$$

The conditions $b'A_r + c' = 0$ and $b'A_s = 0$ become

$$b'A_v + c' = 0 \quad \text{and} \quad b'A_w = 0.$$

Moreover because of the orthogonality between the variables r_{jt} and the variables w_{kt}, least squares fitting to the reduced form (32) is particularly simple. The matrices A_v^* and A_w^* are given by

$$A_v^* = M_{xr}M_{rr}^{-1} \quad \text{and} \quad A_w^* = M_{xw}M_{ww}^{-1}.$$

In short, the Cowles Commission estimators b^{**} and c^{**} are obtained by means of the following operations:

(i) calculate

$$M_{xx}, M_{xr}, M_{xs}, M_{rr}, M_{rs}, M_{ss};$$

(ii) calculate

$$A_v^* = M_{xr}M_{rr}^{-1};$$

(iii) calculate

$$M_{xw} = M_{xs} - M_{xr}M_{rr}^{-1}M_{rs} \quad \text{and} \quad M_{ww} = M_{ss} - M_{sr}M_{rr}^{-1}M_{rs};$$

(iv) calculate

$$A_w^* M_{ww} A_w^{*\prime} = M_{xw}M_{ww}^{-1}M_{wx};$$

(v) calculate

$$M_{\varepsilon\varepsilon} = M_{xx} - M_{xr}M_{rr}^{-1}M_{rx} - M_{xw}M_{ww}^{-1}M_{wx};$$

(vi) calculate the smallest root $\bar{\mu}$ of the equation[†]:

$$A_w^* M_{ww} A_w^{*\prime} - \mu M_{\varepsilon\varepsilon}| = 0; \tag{33}$$

(vii) calculate b^{**} by solving the system:

$$(A_w^* M_{ww} A_w^{*\prime} - \bar{\mu} M_{\varepsilon\varepsilon})b^{**} = 0,$$
$$b^{**\prime} M_{\varepsilon\varepsilon}b^{**} = 1; \tag{34}$$

(viii) calculate

$$c^{**} = - A_v^{*\prime} b^{**}. \tag{35}$$

The extent of these calculations clearly depends on the number of endogenous and exogenous variables. Inversion of the matrices M_{rr} and M_{ww} can now be done easily by means of computers. In the most commonly occurring cases

---

[†] We observe that $M_{\varepsilon\varepsilon} + A_w^* M_{ww} A_w^*$ is the covariance matrix of the residuals of the regressions of the x_{it} on the r_{jt} alone. If $M_{\rho\rho}$ denotes this matrix, then (33) can be written $| M_{\rho\rho} - (\mu+1)M_{\varepsilon\varepsilon} | = 0$. Rather than work as indicated above, we can find $M_{\rho\rho}$ from M_{xx}, M_{xr}, M_{rr} and find $M_{\varepsilon\varepsilon}$ from M_{xx}, M_{xz}, M_{zz} without having to bring in the orthogonalized variables w and the corresponding matrices. In fact $M_{\varepsilon\varepsilon}$ is the covariance matrix of the residuals of the regressions of the x_{it} on the set of all the exogenous variables z_{jt}.

where m_1 and m_2 do not exceed 3 or 4, the inversion can be done fairly quickly on desk machines. If the equation under consideration contains only two endogenous variables $\bar{\mu}$ is quickly calculated. On the other hand, it becomes the lengthiest operation whenever the number of endogenous variables reaches 4 or 5. This is why application of the Cowles Commission method is a little laborious.

To determine the asymptotic variances and covariances of b^{**} and c^{**}, we can refer again to the formulae established in the previous section.

As the two groups of exogenous variables represented by r_t and w_t respectively are orthogonal one to the other, there are zero correlations among the three matrices A_v^*, A_w^* and $M_{\varepsilon\varepsilon}$. It follows that A_v^* is not correlated with b^*. Given the matrix Q_b of the asymptotic covariances of

$$\sqrt{T}(b^{**} - b^0),$$

we can easily calculate the other asymptotic covariances of the pair

$$[\sqrt{T}(b^{**} - b^0), \quad \sqrt{T}(c^{**} - c^0)],$$

the pair (b^0, c^0) denoting the true value of (b, c) normalized by

$$b' M_{\varepsilon\varepsilon} b = 1.$$

In order to simplify the notation, we set:

$$\delta b = \sqrt{T}(b^{**} - b^0),$$

$$\delta c = \sqrt{T}(c^{**} - c^0),$$

$$\delta A_v = \sqrt{T}(A_v^* - A_v^0).$$

The vector δc has the same asymptotic distribution as

$$- A_v^{*\prime} \delta b - \delta A_v' \cdot b^{**}.$$

Consequently we can write:

$$E[\delta c \cdot \delta b'] \sim - A_v^{*\prime} E[\delta b \cdot \delta b'] = - A_v^{*\prime} Q_b,$$

$$E[\delta c \cdot \delta c'] \sim A_v^{*\prime} E[\delta b \cdot \delta b'] A_v^* + E[\delta A_v' b^{**} b^{**\prime} \delta A_v]. \tag{36}$$

The limiting value of the last expectation is easily calculated. Since b^{**} tends to b^0, the (j, g)th element of

$$E[\delta A_v' b^{**} b^{**\prime} \delta A_v]$$

is equivalent to

$$\sum_{hk} b_h^0 b_k^0 E[(\delta A_v)_{hj} (\delta A_v)_{kg}]. \tag{37}$$

From multiple regression theory, we know that the expected value appearing in this last expression is equal to $\omega_{hk}(M_{rr}^{-1})_{jg}$. In view of the normalization rule, (37) reduces to $(M_{rr}^{-1})_{jg}$.

To sum up, the asymptotic covariance matrices are given by the formulae:

$$E[\delta b \cdot \delta b'] \sim Q_b,$$
$$E[\delta c \cdot \delta b'] \sim -A_v^{0'}Q_b, \tag{38}$$
$$E[\delta c \cdot \delta c'] \sim A_v^{0'}Q_b A_v^0 + M_{rr}^{-1}.$$

The matrix Q_b is defined by the concentration ellipsoid of

$$\sqrt{T}(b^{**} - b^0),$$

which is given by formulae (23) and (24) with M_{zz} replaced by M_{ww}.

To estimate these asymptotic covariances, we can, in (38), substitute for A_v^0 the matrix A_v^* and for Q_b the matrix:

$$Q_b^{**} = (A_w^* M_{ww} A_w^{*'})^{-1}(I - N^{**}), \tag{39}$$

N^{**} being defined by formula (27).

These formulae apply in the case where b^{**} and c^{**} are normalized by $b'M_{\varepsilon\varepsilon}b = 1$. We often prefer, in the presentation of the results, to give the value 1 to the coefficient of the endogenous variable determined by the behavior that the equation is deemed to represent. We can then use the procedure described in ch. 16 § 1, to find estimates of the asymptotic variances of the calculated ratios, and for example of

$$\sqrt{T}\left(\frac{b_i^{**}}{b_1^{**}} - \frac{b_i^0}{b_1^0}\right).$$

In fact in the next section we shall give an estimation method, which is simpler for the computation of the asymptotic variances and covariances of the coefficients normalized in this way.

The *test of overidentification* is easily transposed from the preceding section to the present case. It then concerns the hypothesis that the exogenous variables s_{jt} do not occur in the structural equation. Transposition raises no difficulty either for other tests and confidence regions defined in sections 2 (iii) and (iv).

4   Two-stage least squares

(i)   Estimators of the class k

In practice, application of the Cowles Commission method is often laborious. It may be considered unduly heavy, especially when imperfections in the data make the results of fitting operations very imprecise in any case. Fortunately there exists a simpler method, which leads to estimators enjoying the same asymptotic properties. This method, called the 'two-stage least squares method', has already been introduced in ch. 16 § 3. We shall now give it more systematic discussion.

THEIL [1958] devised it in 1955 and presented it persuasively in his book. Independently, BASMANN [1957] defined the same estimators using a different approach. Here we shall follow a line of reasoning adopted by Theil, and show that the two-stage least squares estimator belongs to a class of estimators which are asymptotically equivalent to that of the Cowles Commission.

In the preceding section we kept to the normalization rule:

$$b'M_{\varepsilon\varepsilon}b = 1.$$

We shall now suppose that the value -1 is given to the coefficient of one endogenous variable in the equation under study, for example to the coefficient of the variable determined by the behavior which the equation represents. We shall suppose that this is the first variable.

For what follows we shall introduce a more convenient notation, distinguishing the first endogenous variable, to be denoted p_t, and letting q_t denote the vector of the last $n-1$ components of x_t. More precisely, we write

$$x_t = \begin{bmatrix} p_t \\ q_t \end{bmatrix} \qquad b = \begin{bmatrix} -1 \\ d \end{bmatrix} \qquad \varepsilon_t = \begin{bmatrix} \xi_t \\ \zeta_t \end{bmatrix},$$

where p_t and ξ_t are real variables, while q_t, d and ζ_t are $(n-1)$-vectors. The equation under study can then be written

$$p_t = d'q_t + c'r_t - \eta_t.$$

We must now transform eqs. (34) and (35) defining the Cowles Commission estimators b^{**} and c^{**}, so as to introduce the new normalization rule and the new notation.

We note first that

$$A_w^* M_{ww} A_w^{*\prime} = M_{xw} M_{ww}^{-1} M_{wx} = M_{xx} - M_{\varepsilon\varepsilon} - M_{xr} M_{rr}^{-1} M_{rx}. \tag{40}$$

Relations (34) and (35) can then be written:

$$[M_{xx} - M_{xr} M_{rr}^{-1} M_{rx} - (1 + \bar{\mu})M_{\varepsilon\varepsilon}]b^{**} = 0,$$

$$M_{rr}^{-1} M_{rx} b^{**} + c^{**} = 0.$$

Multiplying the second relation by M_{xr} and adding them to the first, we obtain

$$[M_{xx} - (1 + \bar{\mu})M_{\varepsilon\varepsilon}]b^{**} + M_{xr}c^{**} = 0.$$

Multiplying the second relation by M_{rr}, we obtain

$$M_{rx}b^{**} + M_{rr}c^{**} = 0,$$

and hence the system:

$$\begin{bmatrix} M_{xx} - (1 + \bar{\mu})M_{\varepsilon\varepsilon} & M_{xr} \\ M_{rx} & M_{rr} \end{bmatrix} \begin{bmatrix} b^{**} \\ c^{**} \end{bmatrix} = 0. \qquad (41)$$

These relations are homogeneous and must be completed by the normalization rule. Let $(\hat{b}, \hat{c})$ denote the pair proportional to (b^{**}, c^{**}) and normalized by $b_1 = -1$. We also write M_{xx} in the form:

$$M_{xx} = \begin{bmatrix} m_{pp} & m_{pq} \\ m_{qp} & M_{qq} \end{bmatrix}.$$

The change of variables applied to the equations of system (41), excepting the first, leads directly to

$$\begin{bmatrix} M_{qq} - (1 + \bar{\mu})M_{\zeta\zeta} & M_{qr} \\ M_{rq} & M_{rr} \end{bmatrix} \begin{bmatrix} \hat{d} \\ \hat{c} \end{bmatrix} = \begin{bmatrix} m_{qp} - (1 + \bar{\mu})m_{\zeta\xi} \\ m_{rp} \end{bmatrix}. \qquad (42)$$

In other words, we can apply the Cowles Commission method by calculating the smallest root $\bar{\mu}$ of (33) and then solving the $n + m_1 - 1$ linear equations of (42) with respect to d and c.

We now define a new class of estimators of d and c, by considering, for every number k, the solutions $d(k)$ and $c(k)$ of the system:

$$\begin{bmatrix} M_{qq} - kM_{\zeta\zeta} & M_{qr} \\ M_{rq} & M_{rr} \end{bmatrix} \begin{bmatrix} d(k) \\ c(k) \end{bmatrix} = \begin{bmatrix} m_{qp} - km_{\zeta\xi} \\ m_{rp} \end{bmatrix}. \qquad (43)$$

Clearly $d(1 + \bar{\mu})$ and $c(1 + \bar{\mu})$, obtained with $k = 1 + \bar{\mu}$, are the estimators given by the Cowles Commission method. We see also that $d(0)$ and $c(0)$, obtained with $k = 0$, are the estimators which result from application of the method of least squares to the equation:

$$p_t = d'q_t + c'r_t - \eta_t.$$

For system (43) then leads to

$$\begin{bmatrix} d(0) \\ c(0) \end{bmatrix} = \begin{bmatrix} M_{qq} & M_{qr} \\ M_{rq} & M_{rr} \end{bmatrix}^{-1} \begin{bmatrix} m_{qp} \\ m_{rp} \end{bmatrix}.$$

We ask ourselves if, in the class of the estimators $d(k)$, $c(k)$, there are any with the same asymptotic properties as

$$[d(1 + \bar{\mu}), \qquad c(1 + \bar{\mu})]$$

and which are simpler to calculate. As we have already seen, the least squares estimators $d(0)$, $c(0)$ do not answer, since they converge to values other than the true values.

Relation (43) shows that if

$$\sqrt{T}[k - (1 + \bar{\mu})]$$

tends in probability to zero, then

$$\sqrt{T}[d(k) - d(1 + \bar{\mu})] \qquad \text{and} \qquad \sqrt{T}[c(k) - c(1 + \bar{\mu})]$$

also tend in probability to zero[†]. So for $[d(k), c(k)]$ to have the same asymptotic properties as $[\hat{d}, \hat{c}]$, it is sufficient that

$$\sqrt{T}[k - (1 + \bar{\mu})]$$

tends to zero.

Now we saw that $T\bar{\mu}$ was asymptotically distributed as χ^2 with $m_2 - n + 1$ degrees of freedom. So the root $\bar{\mu}$ tends to zero as does $\sqrt{T}\bar{\mu}$. Therefore the estimators $d(k)$ and $c(k)$ have the same asymptotic properties as $d(1 + \bar{\mu})$ and $c(1 + \bar{\mu})$ whenever $\sqrt{T}(k - 1)$ tends to zero as T tends to infinity. In practice it is

---

[†] To establish this, we need only apply the following proposition:

Proposition. Let $f_T(k)$ be a random function of a real variable k.

(i) If there exists a positive number h such that the probability of

$$\| f_T(k_1) - f_T(k_2) \| > h \, | k_1 - k_2 |$$

tends to zero whatever the values k_1 and k_2 belonging to a closed interval I;

(ii) and if u_T is a random variable such that $T^{\alpha}(u_T - k_T)$ tends in probability to zero for a number $\alpha \geqslant 0$ and a sequence of numbers k_T in the interior of I, then

$$T^{\alpha}[f_T(u_T) - f_T(k_T)]$$

tends in probability to zero.

Here we taken $\alpha = \frac{1}{2}$, $u_T = 1 + \bar{\mu}$; the function f_T is that which determines $[d(k), c(k)]$ through the medium of the equality (43). We can verify condition (i) above with an interval I containing the value $k = 1$. We must take account of the fact that $b_1^0 \neq 0$ and of assumptions 1, 2 and 3.

sufficient to take $k=1$ to have estimators equivalent to those proposed by the Cowles Commission[†].

(ii) Two-stage least squares estimators

The great advantage of the estimators $d(k)$ and $c(k)$ relative to $d(1+\bar{\mu})$ and $c(1+\bar{\mu})$ rests in the fact that they do not require solution of eq. (33), and thus allow us to avoid the heaviest part of the computation. We can now show that $d(1)$ and $c(1)$ are just the two-stage least squares estimators.

For simplicity, we set $d(1)=\hat{d}$ and $c(1)=\hat{c}$ and rewrite system (43) with $k=1$, giving

$$\begin{bmatrix} M_{qq} - M_{\zeta\zeta} & M_{qr} \\ M_{rq} & M_{rr} \end{bmatrix} \begin{bmatrix} \hat{d} \\ \hat{c} \end{bmatrix} = \begin{bmatrix} m_{qp} - m_{\zeta\xi} \\ m_{rp} \end{bmatrix}. \tag{44}$$

Now let q_t^* denote the calculated values of q_t following a (least squares) regression of the endogenous variables q_t on the exogenous variables r_t and s_t. We have

$$q_t^* = M_{qr}M_{rr}^{-1}r_t + M_{qw}M_{ww}^{-1}w_t.$$

Let M_{qq}^*, M_{qr}^*, m_{qp}^* be the matrices and the vector obtained by replacing q_t by q_t^* in the expression for M_{qq}, M_{qr}, m_{qp}. We can easily calculate

$$M_{qq}^* = M_{qr}M_{rr}^{-1}M_{rq} + M_{qw}M_{ww}^{-1}M_{wq} = M_{qq} - M_{\zeta\zeta}$$

$$M_{qr}^* = M_{qr} \quad \text{since} \quad M_{wr} = 0 \quad \text{by definition of } w_t. \tag{45}$$

$$m_{qp}^* = M_{qr}M_{rr}^{-1}m_{rp} + M_{qw}M_{ww}^{-1}m_{wp} = m_{qp} - m_{\zeta\zeta}.$$

Consequently system (44) can be written:

$$\begin{bmatrix} \hat{d} \\ \hat{c} \end{bmatrix} = \begin{bmatrix} M_{qq}^* & M_{qr}^* \\ M_{rq}^* & M_{rr} \end{bmatrix}^{-1} \begin{bmatrix} m_{qp}^* \\ m_{rp} \end{bmatrix} \tag{46}$$

that is, $\hat{d}$ and $\hat{c}$ are obtained by a regression of p_t on the q_t^* and the r_t.

[†] We can also take for k the value

$$1 + \frac{m_2 - n + 1}{T}.$$

As ARROW and HOFFENBERG [1959] pointed out, it is for this value of k that

$$\sqrt{T}[(1 + \bar{\mu}) - k]$$

has zero mean; for $T\bar{\mu}$ is distributed as χ^2 with m_2-n+1 degrees of freedom. NAGAR [1959] proved that, with this value of k, the bias in the estimation of d^0 and c^0 by $d(k)$ and $c(k)$ is very small, being of order less then $1/T$.

To sum up, the computation reduces to the regressions of the $n-1$ endogenous variables q_{it} on the m exogenous variables r_{jt} and s_{jt}, then to the regression of the endogenous variable p_t on the q_{it}^* and r_{jt}. Of course, in practice we do no determine the values of the q_{it}^*. We use the first equalities in relations (45) t ι obtain M_{qq}^*, M_{qr}^* and m_{qp}^*.

(iii) Covariance matrix

Adopting assumptions 1, 2 and 3, we could refer to the formulae given in the previous section to calculate the asymptotic covariances of

$$\sqrt{T}(\hat{d} - d^0) \qquad \text{and} \qquad \sqrt{T}(\hat{c} - c^0).$$

It is simpler to find this result directly. Thus we shall obtain a formula valid for the normalization rule $b_1 = -1$, whether the estimates are obtained by two-stage least squares or by the Cowles Commission method.

For simplicity, we consider only the case where the equation to be estimated contains no exogenous variable. The estimate of d is calculated by

$$\hat{d} = M_{qq}^{*-1} m_{qp}^*. \tag{47}$$

We can also write:

$$M_{qq}^* d^0 = m_{qp}^* + \frac{1}{T} \sum_{t=1}^{T} q_t^*(\eta_t - d^{0\prime} \zeta_t^*),$$

for,

$$p_t = d^{0\prime} q_t - \eta_t = d^{0\prime} q_t^* + d^{0\prime} \zeta_t^* - \eta_t.$$

Since q_t^* results from least squares fitting, clearly we have

$$\frac{1}{T} \sum_{t=1}^{T} q_t^* \zeta_t^{*\prime} = 0.$$

We then set

$$\lambda = \frac{1}{\sqrt{T}} \sum_{t=1}^{T} q_t^* \eta_t.$$

The above equations imply

$$\sqrt{T}(d^0 - \hat{d}) = M_{qq}^{*-1} \lambda. \tag{48}$$

When the number of observations tends to infinity, the matrix M_{qq}^* tends to a finite limit, say $\overline{M}_{qq}^*$. The asymptotic distribution of $\sqrt{T}(d^0 - \hat{d})$ is then the same as that of $\overline{M}_{qq}^{*-1} \lambda$.

Moreover q_t^*, the fitted value of q_t, tends to $A_q^0 z_t$, if A_q^0 is the matrix of the true coefficients in the reduced equations giving q_t. So the random variable λ has the same asymptotic distribution as

$$\frac{1}{\sqrt{T}} A_q^0 \sum_{t=1}^{T} z_t \eta_t. \tag{49}$$

We calculate directly its asymptotic covariance matrix

$$\sigma_\eta^2 \cdot A_q^0 \overline{M}_{zz} A_q^{0\prime},$$

where $\overline{M}_{zz}$ denotes the limit of M_{zz}. It is easy to see that

$$A_q^0 \overline{M}_{zz} A_q^{0\prime} = \overline{M}_{qq}^*,$$

since

$$M_{qq}^* = M_{qz} M_{zz}^{-1} M_{zq} = (M_{qz} M_{zz}^{-1}) M_{zz} (M_{qz} M_{zz}^{-1})'.$$

So the asymptotic covariance matrix of $\sqrt{T}(\hat{d} - d^0)$ is

$$\sigma_\eta^2 \cdot \overline{M}_{qq}^{*-1}.$$

It can be estimated by $\hat{\sigma}_\eta^2 \cdot M_{qq}^{*-1}$ with a value $\hat{\sigma}_\eta^2$ obtained either directly from the residuals of the fitted equation, or from the residuals relating to the reduced equations by means of

$$\hat{\sigma}_\xi^2 - 2\hat{d}' m_{\zeta\xi} + \hat{d}' M_{\zeta\zeta} \hat{d}.$$

In the general case where there are exogenous variables in the equation under consideration, the asymptotic covariance matrix of

$$\sqrt{T}(\hat{d} - d^0) \qquad \text{and} \qquad \sqrt{T}(\hat{c} - c^0)$$

is estimated by

$$\hat{\sigma}_\eta^2 \begin{bmatrix} M_{qq}^* & M_{qr} \\ M_{rq} & M_{rr} \end{bmatrix}^{-1}. \tag{50}$$

(iv)   A test of overidentification

Two-stage least squares estimators are asymptotically equivalent to those of the Cowles Commission. So they lend themselves directly to a test of the hypothesis that the structural equation considered does not involve the exogenous variables s_{jt}. This test is based on consideration of a quantity which is asymptotically equivalent to $T\bar{\mu}$ and is defined directly by the two-stage least squares estimators.

In section 2, where the r_{jt} were not involved, we saw that $\bar{\mu}$ was equal to $b^{**\prime} A^* M_{zz} A^{*\prime} b^{**}$, the vector b^{**} being normalized by $b^{**\prime} M_{\varepsilon\varepsilon} b^{**} = 1$. When exogenous variables r_{jt} are present, $\bar{\mu}$ is equal to $b^{**\prime} A_w^* M_{ww} A_w^{*\prime} b^{**}$, the same normalization rule being maintained. The following equality then applies and no longer depends on the normalization rule:

$$T\bar{\mu} = \frac{Tb^{**\prime}A_w^*M_{ww}A_w^{*\prime}b^{**}}{b^{**\prime}M_{\varepsilon\varepsilon}b^{**}} .$$ (51)

The quantity $T\bar{\mu}$ is asymptotically equivalent to

$$\frac{T\hat{b}A_w^*M_{ww}A_w^{*\prime}\hat{b}}{\hat{b}'M_{\varepsilon\varepsilon}\hat{b}} .$$ (52)

For[†], reduced to the same normalization, $\hat{b}$ and b^{**} both tend to the same limit so that the denominators of (51) and (52) tend to the same positive limit; the numerator of (51) has a limiting distribution and the difference between the numerators of (51) and (52) tends in probability to zero (to establish this last point, we need only note that, as $\sqrt{T}(b^{**}-\hat{b})$ tends in probability to zero, $\sqrt{T}A_w^{*\prime}b^{**}$ and $\sqrt{T}A_w^{*\prime}\hat{b}$ are asymptotically equivalent while $\sqrt{T}A_w^{*\prime}b^{**}$ has a limiting distribution[††]).

In view of (40), we can write

$$\hat{b}'A_w^*M_{ww}A_w^{*\prime}\hat{b} = \hat{b}'M_{xx}\hat{b} - \hat{c}'M_{rr}\hat{c} - \hat{b}'M_{\varepsilon\varepsilon}\hat{b}.$$

Moreover, if $\hat{\eta}_t = \hat{b}x_t + \hat{c}r_t$, then

$$\hat{\sigma}_\eta^2 = \frac{1}{T}\sum_{t=1}^T \hat{\eta}_t^2 = \hat{b}'M_{xx}\hat{b} - \hat{c}'M_{rr}\hat{c},$$

since (44) implies $M_{rx}\hat{b} = -M_{rr}\hat{c}$. So we can find an expression for (52) and for the overidentification test which will be convenient for applications:

$$T\left[\frac{\hat{\sigma}_\eta^2}{\hat{b}'M_{\varepsilon\varepsilon}\hat{b}} - 1\right] \geq \chi^2_{m_2-n+1}(\alpha)$$ (53)

where α is the chosen significance level for the test[†††].

(v) Homogeneous linear restrictions on the coefficients of the same equation

Up till now we have considered limited information estimation methods as applying only to the case of exclusion restrictions. We see that they can easily

---

[†] Consider in general four sequences of random variables $x_T, y_T, u_T, v_T, (T = 1, 2, \ldots)$ such that $x_T - y_T$ tends in probability to zero, u_T and v_T tend to the same positive limit a, and x_T (and so also y_T) has a limiting distribution. We can easily prove that $x_T/u_T - y_T/v_T$ tends in probability to zero.

[††]Suppose we have matrices Q_T tending to a non-singular matrix and random vectors x_T, y_T with a limiting distribution and such that $x_T - y_T$ tends in probability to zero. Then $x'_T Q_T x_T - y'_T Q_T y_T$, which can be written $(x_T - y_T)'Q_T x_T - y'_T Q_T(x_T - y_T)$ tends in probability to zero.

[†††] As indicated at the end of section 2(iii), it is advisable to replace T in the left hand member by $(T-m)/(m_2-n+1)$ and to write $F_{m_2-n+1, T-m}(\alpha)$ as right hand member.

be generalized to the case of homogeneous linear restrictions on the coefficients of the same equation (as in ch. 17, § 5). This generalization is of obvious practical interest since it allows the treatment of structural equations encountered in applied econometrics (see, for example, the second equation of (24) in ch. 17).

Suppose then that we wish to estimate a structural equation

$$b'x_t + c'z_t = \eta_t \tag{54}$$

subject to the restrictions expressed by

$$b'\Phi_b + c'\Phi_c = 0 \tag{55}$$

where Φ_b and Φ_c are known matrices having m_2 columns and such that $[\Phi'_b \ \Phi'_c]$ has rank m_2. Equation (55) is the form now taken by the condition expressed by (22) in ch. 17.

It can be shown that, if we ignore the restrictions on the other structural equations, the quasi-maximum likelihood estimators b^{**} and c^{**} are solutions of the normalization rule $b^{**\prime}M_{\varepsilon\varepsilon}b^{**} = 1$ and of

$$\begin{bmatrix} M_{xx}-(1+\bar{\mu})M_{\varepsilon\varepsilon} & M_{xz} & \Phi_b \\ M_{zx} & M_{zz} & \Phi_c \\ \Phi'_b & \Phi'_c & 0 \end{bmatrix} \begin{bmatrix} b^{**} \\ c^{**} \\ v \end{bmatrix} = 0, \tag{56}$$

which takes the place of (41) and in which v denotes a vector of Lagrange multipliers to be calculated simultaneously with b^{**} and c^{**}, while $\bar{\mu}$ is the smallest number such that the large matrix is singular.

It can also be shown that $T\bar{\mu} \geq \chi^2_{m_2-n+1}(\alpha)$ defines asymptotically a critical region at the significance level α for the hypothesis that the restrictions (55) are satisfied.

Finally, one can establish the asymptotic equivalence of (b^{**}, c^{**}) and a two-stage least squares estimator $(\hat{b}, \hat{c})$. If, for example, the a priori restrictions do not concern the first endogenous variable (Φ_b has only zeros in its first row), then we can write the structural equation:

$$p_t = d'q_t + c'z_t - \eta_t \tag{57}$$

and the restrictions

$$d'\Phi_d + c'\Phi_c = 0. \tag{58}$$

We then determine the two-stage least squares estimators $\hat{d}$ and $\hat{c}$ by minimizing

$$\sum_{t=1}^{T} (p_t - d'q_t^* - c'z_t)^2$$

subject to the constraints (58), q_t^* denoting the calculated values of the endogenous variables other than the first, these values being given by the usual multiple regressions on the z_t. Formula (53) again applies for a test of over-identification.

5   Instrumental variables

In ch. 10 we introduced the method of instrumental variables for estimation of models with errors in variables. In ch. 16 § 3, we showed that consistent estimators of the coefficients of a structural equation are obtained if the exogenous variables are considered as instrumental for the fitting of this equation. It remains for us briefly to generalize the results obtained in an example. For this section we use the article by SARGAN [1958].

For simplicity we confine ourselves to the case where the equation to be estimated contains no exogenous variable and is written:

$$p_t = d'q_t - \eta_t.$$

As is usual in models with errors in equations, we assume that the errors are not correlated with the exogenous variables, and it follows that

$$E(\eta_t z_t') = 0,$$

or again

$$E(p_t z_t') = d'E(q_t z_t'). \tag{59}$$

The method of intrumental variables consists of replacing in eqs. (59) the expectations by the observed moments, and of estimating d by the solution d^* of the system:

$$m_{pz} = d^{*\prime}M_{qz}. \tag{60}$$

This system contains $n-1$ unknowns, the components d_i^* of d^*, and m equations. Three cases can be distinguished.

(i) If $m < n-1$, system (60) is indeterminate. There are several possible sets of values for the d_i^*. This is not a surprizing situation since in this case the equation under consideration is not identifiable.

(ii) If $m = n-1$, system (60) generally has a unique solution which tends to the true value d^0 if assumptions 1 to 3 apply. In this case the model is simple, at least if we take no account of the restrictions on the other equations. We could estimate d by indirect least squares fitting. Clearly this would lead to the same result as that obtained by solving (60).

For, the matrices a_p and A_q of the reduced equations are estimated by

$$a_p^{*\prime} = m_{pz}M_{zz}^{-1}, \qquad A_q^* = M_{qz}M_{zz}^{-1};$$

hence, the fitted reduced equations:

$$p_t = m_{pz} M_{zz}^{-1} z_t,$$

$$q_t = M_{qz} M_{zz}^{-1} z_t,$$

which, by elimination of the z_t, give

$$p_t = m_{pz} M_{qz}^{-1} q_t = d^{*\prime} q_t.$$

Moreover in this case the method of two-stage least squares and the Cowles Commission method also lead to the same result. For, in view of (45), formula (47) can be written:

$$\hat{d} = (M_{qz} M_{zz}^{-1} M_{zq})^{-1} M_{qz} M_{zz}^{-1} m_{zp} = M_{zq}^{-1} m_{zp} = d^*.$$

In addition, the matrix $A^* M_{zz} A^{*\prime}$ has rank at most $n-1$, so that the smallest root of the determinant (33) of order n is necessarily zero. Thus the Cowles Commission method coincides with the method of two-stage least squares.

(iii) If $m > n - 1$, then system (60) is generally impossible. Thus we cannot choose as instrumental variables the m exogenous variables. But we can still apply the method with $n - 1$ properly chosen exogenous variables. Let u_t denote the vector of these variables. We estimate d by

$$d^* = M_{uq}^{-1} m_{up}. \tag{61}$$

Since the observed moments tend in probability to their expected values, d^* tends in probability to d, whatever the set of exogenous variables taken as instrumental (provided that they are not multicollinear, which is excluded by assumption 3). But clearly all these sets are not equivalent from the point of view of the precision in estimation of d by d^*. To be in a better position to choose, we must be able to calculate the covariance matrices of the d^*.

For this purpose, we see that

$$M_{uq} d = m_{up} - m_{u\eta}.$$

Consequently

$$\sqrt{T}(d^* - d) = M_{uq}^{-1}(\sqrt{T} m_{u\eta}).$$

When the number of observations tends to infinity, the matrix M_{uq} tends to a finite limit $\overline{M}_{uq}$ (at least if assumptions 2 and 3 are satisfied). The asymptotic covariance matrix of $\sqrt{T}(d^* - d)$ is therefore calculated by means of that of $\sqrt{T} m_{u\eta}$, which is equal to $\sigma^2 \overline{M}_{uu}$, if $\overline{M}_{uu}$ is the limit of M_{uu}. So the covariance matrix of $(d^* - d)$ can be estimated by

$$\frac{\sigma_\eta^{*2}}{T} M_{uq}^{-1} M_{uu} M_{qu}^{-1}. \tag{62}$$

Now $M_{qu} M_{uu}^{-1} M_{qu}$ is equal to the difference between the matrix M_{qq} relating to the endogenous variables and the covariance matrix relating to the residuals of the regression of the q_t on the u_t. So the variances of the estimates d_i^* will be smaller as the regression of the q_t on the u_t is stricter. Hence, we must choose the exogenous variables which play the greatest part in the determination of the endogenous variables.

Rather than choose $n-1$ instrumental variables from the m exogenous variables, we can find $n-1$ independent *linear combinations* of the exogenous variables so as to obtain the greatest possible precision in the estimate of d. This is equivalent to defining the instrumental variables u_t by

$$u_t = Cz_t,$$

where C is an $(n-1) \times m$-matrix.

To obtain the best precision, at least asymptotically, we can choose the q_t^* since these are just the linear combinations of the exogenous variables which are best correlated[†] with the endogenous variables q_t. This choice corresponds to the following value of the matrix C:

$$C = M_{qz} M_{zz}^{-1}. \tag{63}$$

However, we note that the assumption of independence between the instrumental variables q_t^* and the errors η_t is only asymptotically satisfied. For small samples, M_{qz} clearly depends on the ζ_t, as does η_t.

In view of (61) and (63), an asymptotically efficient estimate is

$$\hat{d} = (M_{qz} M_{zz}^{-1} M_{zq})^{-1} M_{qz} M_{zz}^{-1} m_{zp}.$$

[†] This result can be established in more detail. For, the inverse of the matrix appearing in expression (62) is equal to

$$M_{qu} M_{uu}^{-1} M_{uq} = M_{qz} C' (C M_{zz} C')^{-1} C M_{zq}.$$

Now, whatever the vector h, the quadratic form

$$h' M_{qz} C' (C M_{zz} C')^{-1} C M_{zq} h$$

is maximized if C is determined by (63). To show this, we need only establish that

$$h' M_{qz} C' (C M_{zz} C')^{-1} C M_{zq} h - h' M_{qz} M_{zz}^{-1} M_{zq} h \leqq 0,$$

for any h and C of rank $n-1$. Let N be the symmetric square matrix defined by $NN' = M_{zz}$. We set $g = N^{-1} M_{zq} h$ and $D = CN$. To establish the above inequality we need only show that

$$g' [D'(DD')^{-1} D - I] g \leqq 0$$

for any g and D of rank $n-1$. Now the maximum of the ratio between $g' D'(DD')^{-1} Dg$ and $g'g$ is equal to the largest characteristic root of $D'(DD')^{-1}D$. This is a (square) idempotent matrix of order m and rank $n-1$. It has $n-1$ characteristic roots equal to 1, the others being zero. Thus $g' D'(DD')^{-1} Dg$ is never greater than $g'g$.

Again we find the two-stage least squares estimate defined by relation (46). This result can easily be generalized to the case where the equation under study contains exogenous variables. It is not surprizing, in view of our existing knowledge about the asymptotic efficiency of the method in question.

In view of ch. 20 in which we shall generalize this method of using an optimal set of instrumental variables, we note that the estimator we have obtained can be defined as that maximising

$$m_{\eta z} M_{zz}^{-1} m_{z\eta} \tag{64}$$

where η_t occurs as a function of the vector to be determined, here d in $\eta_t = d'q_t - p_t$.

The study which we have just undertaken leads us back to the procedures already envisaged. However, it shows that in practice it may be sufficient to carry out fitting operations using only some of the exogenous variables. Indeed the m exogenous variables frequently show fairly strong multicollinearities. The simple omission of some exogenous variables which do not appear in the equation has little effect on the two-stage least squares estimate d, and appreciably lightens the computation.

In practice it becomes opportune to take account of only some of the exogenous variables when there is a small number of observations and a large number of exogenous variables. In fact we shall see in § 7 that two-stage least squares and Cowles Commission estimators contain, in small samples, a bias which increases as m increases and T decreases. In particular, if $T < m$, the vectors q_t^* to be calculated in the first stage of two-stage least squares coincide with the vectors q_t and so estimation reverts to ordinary least squares and we know that considerable bias may result.

6 Principal components of the exogenous variables

For the various methods which we have examined, estimation of a particular equation involves exogenous variables which do not appear in that equation. It is easy to verify that the estimators are unchanged if we substitute, for some number l of variables of this type, l new variables constituting as many linear combinations of the former ones, with the sole reservation that these combinations are linearly independent.

We also saw the advantage which may arise from the use of linear combinations of the exogenous variables as instrumental variables.

With the aim of simplifying the estimation methods while maintaining their precision as far as possible, KLOEK and MENNES [1960] proposed replacing the exogenous variables by their first principal components. This suggestion may have some practical interest and we shall discuss it briefly. The reader who wishes to examine the question in more detail may refer to the original article.

In ch. 1, section 10, we defined the principal components of a set of variables. For the m exogenous variables z_{jt}, the principal components are linear combinations of the form:

$$v_{1t} = f_1'(z_t - \bar{z}), \qquad v_{2t} = f_2'(z_t - \bar{z}), \ldots, \qquad v_{ht} = f_h'(z_t - \bar{z}),$$

the vectors of the coefficients being pairwise orthogonal, having unit length and being successively determined, f_1 in such a way that $\sum_{t=1}^{T} v_{1t}^2$ is maximized, and f_k in such a way that $\sum_{t=1}^{T} v_{kt}^2$ is maximized given $f_1, f_2, \ldots, f_{k-1}$. There are h principal components if the matrix M_{zz} has rank h.

In short, the first k principal components are the k linear combinations which, taken as a whole, have the greatest possible variability for the observed sample. The substitution of k principal components for the m exogenous variables can greatly simplify the computation if k is clearly smaller than m, and may not greatly affect the precision of the results if the other principal components have only small variability.

Suppose for example that the coefficients are estimated by two-stage least squares, but that, in the first stage of the computation, we have determined the regression of the q_{it} not on the exogenous variables z_{jt} but on their first k principal components $f_1, f_2, \ldots, f_k$. Let $\hat{q}_{it}$ denote the fitted values calculated in this way, q_{it}^* representing as previously the values fitted to the set of the exogenous variables. In the second stage of computation, we therefore calculate the regression of p_t on the $\hat{q}_{it}$ rather than on the q_{it}^*.

The formulae for calculating the vectors $\hat{q}_t$ and q_t^* show that the differences $\hat{q}_t - q_t^*$ are probably small on the average, and still have considerable variances, if the unselected principal components have little variability. In other words, there is certainly little gain in precision in fitting the q_{it} if these latter principal components are introduced. It follows that there is certainly little gain in precision either in estimating the vector d of the coefficients.

Similar considerations apply to the substitution for the exogenous variables of their first principal components in the first stage of the Cowles Commission method.

In fact the procedure suggested by Kloek and Mennes has advantage only for large models with a large number of exogenous variables. Before making any estimate, it is always useful in this case to determine the principal components of the set of observed values of these variables. Thus we discover their degree of multicollinearity. If, for example, only four principal components have appreciable variances, M_{zz} is very near a matrix of rank four. We could then aim at estimating relations involving more than five variables only if the sample were large.

7   Distributions in small samples

In this and the previous chapter, various estimation methods were justified by their asymptotic properties. For a closer appreciation of these methods and the estimators to which they lead, we need better knowledge of their properties in finite samples.

There are two aspects in which this is useful. In the first place, the statistical procedures associated with each estimation method are better defined. The validity of the tests and confidence regions is known better than by asymptotic approximation. In the second place, our ideas about the comparative advantages of the various methods may change if we know the distributions for finite samples. Some procedure which seems asymptotically inadequate may be advantageous for dealing with small samples of the size of those used in econometrics. Thus it has sometimes been suggested that direct least squares fitting of the structural equations might well constitute the best estimation method in practice. It certainly implies biases. But if the dispersions are small, the estimation errors may be smaller than with other methods.

Moreover we should distinguish carefully between two categories of distribution, one relating to the coefficients of the structural form, the other to those of the reduced form.

Distributions of the first type are important when the econometrician intends to estimate one or two structural parameters. A simultaneous equation model may be necessary for correct interpretation of the data considered. But it is not intended to make further reference to it when the values found for the structural parameters are used.

On the other hand, when the model has been devised both for econometric analysis of the data and for subsequent prediction, we are interested particularly in the distributions of the estimated coefficients of the reduced form. It is the reduced form which is used in the prediction of the values taken by the endogenous variables for values of the exogenous variables which are assumed to be known. The distribution of the predicted values is directly connected with that of the estimates of this form.

There are two conceivable approaches for the study of the distributions valid for small samples. We can find the exact analytic form of the distributions of the estimators, those of the errors ε_{it} or η_{it} being specified. We can also apply the 'Monte Carlo method', that is, we can determine the distributions of the estimators empirically by means of a sufficient number of artificial samples[†].

The first method is more powerful. It leads to exact knowledge of the distributions. It gives direct information on the changes in the distributions when the parameters of the model vary. Unfortunately it remains inapplicable in many cases, since the estimators have complex expressions, which do not easily lend themselves to computation. So we must often be content with the results obtained from artificial samples, although the generality of these results is always suspect.

(i) Theoretical results

Some recent studies in mathematical statistics have greatly improved our knowledge of the properties of estimators of the structural form. They relate mainly to the case where the equation to be estimated involves two endogenous variables and some number of exogenous variables. Here we shall consider the main results only for the case where there is no exogenous variable in the equation to be estimated. Our discussion is based mainly on ANDERSON and SAWA [1973].

Let the structural equation to be estimated be

$$x_{1t} = \beta x_{2t} + \eta_t \tag{65}$$

and the two reduced equations be

$$x_{1t} = a_1' z_t + \varepsilon_{1t}, \qquad x_{2t} = a_2' z_t + \varepsilon_{2t} \tag{66}$$

with the conditions

$$\eta_t = \varepsilon_{1t} - \beta \varepsilon_{2t}, \qquad \beta a_2 = a_1.$$

The errors $(\varepsilon_{1t}, \varepsilon_{2t})$ are assumed to be *normally distributed* and the different observations are assumed to be mutually independent.

Clearly the distribution of the various estimators of β depends on the correlation between x_{2t} and η_t, that is, between ε_{2t} and η_t. For example, when the latter correlation is zero; that is, when $\beta = \omega_{12}/\omega_{22}$, all the estimators of the class k have symmetric distributions centered on β. More generally, β occurs in the distributions only through

$$\sqrt{\frac{\omega_{22}}{\omega_{11} - \omega_{12}^2/\omega_{22}}} \left[\beta - \frac{\omega_{12}}{\omega_{22}} \right].$$

Given this situation, we shall consider only the case where $\omega_{12} = 0$ and $\omega_{11} = \omega_{22}$.

The distributions also depend directly on the 'non-centrality parameter', which is T times

$$\psi = \frac{a_2' M_{zz} a_2}{\omega_{22}}, \tag{67}$$

the latter being the ratio between the variance explained by z and the residual variance in the reduced equation relating to x_{2t} (the ratio $\psi/(\psi + 1)$ equals the multiple correlation coefficient R^2 of this equation).

Let $b(k)$ be the k class estimator of β for a given value of k in the interval $[0, 1]$. Under the usual assumptions, we can establish that $b(k)$ tends to the limit

$$\bar{b}(k) = \frac{\beta \psi}{\psi + 1 - k} \tag{68}$$

when the number T of observations tends to infinity (for simplicity we shall not distinguish here between ψ and its limiting value). Also $\sqrt{T}[b(k)-\bar{b}(k)]$ has a limiting normal distribution whose variance $\sigma^2(k)$ depends on k.

This variance is $(1+\beta^2)\psi$ for two-stage least squares $(k=1)$; but its value is systematically smaller for ordinary least squares[†] $(k=0)$ (but the difference is negligible when ψ is large). Thus, the asymptotic distribution reveals that *the choice between two-stage and simple least squares is not an obvious one*; the absence of bias supports two-stage least squares but the smaller variance of simple least squares may make this method preferable if the bias is small, that is, if β is near zero. Examination of the asymptotic distribution suggests that two-stage least squares gives the estimator with smallest mean square error precisely when

$$T > \frac{2}{\beta^2} + \tfrac{5}{2} \qquad \text{if } \psi = 1$$

$$T > \frac{5}{4\beta^2} + 1 \qquad \text{if } \psi = 4 \qquad\qquad (69)$$

$$T > \frac{1}{\beta^2} \qquad \text{if } \psi \text{ is large.}$$

Thus when $|\beta|$ is small, two-stage least squares has an advantage over simple least squares only for large samples.

However, for a finite value of T, the distribution of $\sqrt{T}[b(k)-\bar{b}(k)]/\sigma(k)$ is rather different from the standardized normal distribution; its mode has the opposite sign to the sign of β and its tail is heavier than that of the normal distribution in the direction of the sign of β. It does not have finite moments of every order. The moments are finite up to order $T-2$ for ordinary least squares but only up to order $m-2$ for two-stage least squares.

We should not find this surprising. When dealing with a very simple model in ch. 16, § 1, we determined an estimator α^* corresponding to indirect least squares fitting, equivalent in this case to two-stage least squares. When the errors are normal, this estimator is distributed like the inverse of a normal variable. So it has no finite moment (yet the limiting distribution of $\sqrt{T}(\alpha^*-\alpha^0)$ is normal and has finite moments of every order).

Approximations to the true distributions have been determined. Thus for two-stage least squares, the cumulative distribution function, that is, the probability that $\sqrt{T}[b(1)-\beta]/\sigma(1)$ is at most u is approximately

---

[†] On several occasions this property was stated on the basis of incorrect reasoning using the variance given for simple least squares by the usual regression theory, which obviously does not apply here.

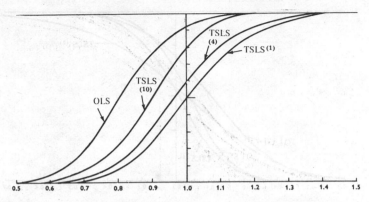

Fig. 3. Distribution function for ordinary least squares (OLS) and two-stage least squares (TSLS) for $\beta = 1$, $\Psi = 4$, $T = 20$ and values of m shown in brackets.

$$\Phi(u) - \frac{\beta(u^2 - m + 1)}{\sqrt{T\psi(1 + \beta)^2}}\,\varphi(u) \qquad (70)$$

where $\Phi(u)$ is the cumulative distribution of the standardized normal distribution and $\varphi(u)$ is its density[†].

The correction term increases as T and ψ decrease, which is not surprising. It also increases as β and m increase. The dependence on m and the comparison of two-stage least squares and ordinary least squares estimators are illustrated in fig. 3 for the case where $T = 20$, $\beta = 1$ and $\psi = 4$. We see that as m increases, the difference between the two estimators decreases. This is not surprising since, in a finite sample and for a fixed value of ψ, the explained value x_{2t}^* of the first stage of two-stage least squares approaches x_{2t} as the number of explanatory variables in the regression increases.

RICHARDSON and WU [1971] consider first and second order moments of the two-stage and simple least squares estimators; they find that in small samples the biases in the two estimators have the same sign and the ratio of the biases is less than 1 but increases as T and ψ decrease and m increases. They also calculate the ratio between the mean square errors for different values of T, ψ, m and β. Their numerical results suggest that the asymptotic distributions give good approximations for evaluating this ratio. Thus for $T = 20$ and $\psi = 1$, the ratio is about 1 for $\beta = 0.37$ when $m = 3$ and for $\beta = 0.33$ when $m = 5$, which agrees with rule (69) deduced from the investigation of asymptotic distributions[††].

We can therefore confirm our previous conclusion: *when $|\beta|$ and T are both*

[†] The approximation holds for large values of $T\psi$. ANDERSON and SAWA [1973] give an expansion up to the third order in $[T\psi]^{-\frac{1}{2}}$.

[††] Other numerical results are given by SAWA [1973].

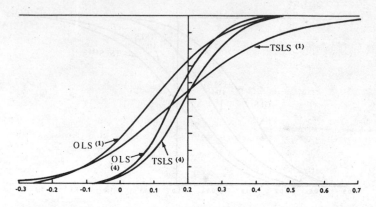

Fig. 4. Distribution function for ordinary least squares (OLS) and two-stage least squares (TSLS) for $\beta = 0.2$, $T = 20$, $m = 4$ and values of ψ shown in brackets.

small, ordinary least squares gives a more precise estimator of β than two-stage least squares. This result is illustrated by fig. 4 which, like fig. 3, is taken from ANDERSON and SAWA [1973] and concerns the case where $\beta = 1/5$ and $T = 20$ with $m = 4$ and two values of ψ (1 and 4).

However, we must not be misled concerning the significance of this result. It implies that the ordinary least squares *estimator* may be better than the two-stage least squares estimator. But it does not justify the *tests and confidence intervals* which multiple regression theory associates with the least squares estimator. If a regression of x_{1t} on x_{2t} has been carried out giving the estimator β^* of β, it is quite wrong to estimate the variance of β^* using the formulae of ch. 6. This has been clearly established by, for example, the simulations carried out by NEISWANGER and YANCEY [1959] who show that there is considerable underestimation if the variances are calculated using multiple regression formulae.

On the other hand, when $T\psi$ is not too small the asymptotic theory discussed in § 4 (iii) provides a good approximation for the variances of coefficients estimated by two-stage least squares. For, the distributions on small samples contain correction terms which can generally be ignored (see below).

ANDERSON [1974] also discusses the Cowles Commission estimator b^{**}, that is, *the limited information maximum likelihood estimator* (the errors are assumed to be normal). The chosen normalization rule is clearly the same as that used for equation (24); so it is different from the rule used in sections 2 and 3. The cumulative distribution function of $\sqrt{T}[(b^{**} - \beta)]/\sigma(1)$ is approximately, up to the first order in $[T\psi]^{-1/2}$

$$\Phi(u) - \frac{\beta u^2}{\sqrt{T\psi(1 + \beta^2)}} \varphi(u). \tag{71}$$

This approximate distribution has zero median (the cumulative distribution has value 1/2 for $u=0$), as opposed to that of formula (70) corresponding to two-stage least squares; but its tail is slightly heavier in the direction of the sign of β.

A closer examination allows us to compare the respective advantages of these two estimators. Let us fix attention on the mean square error which is $\sigma^2(1)/T$ multiplied by a term which is approximately $1+v[T\psi(1+\beta^2)]^{-1}$, where v is $m+2+9\beta^2$ for the Cowles Commission estimator and $(m-4)[(m-4)\beta^2-1]$ for the two-stage least squares estimator. When $T\psi$ is large, the mean square errors are virtually the same. On the basis of these approximations, the former estimator is preferable if

$$m > 7 + \frac{2}{\beta^2}.$$

So in small systems, the two-stage least squares estimator is preferable to the Cowles Commission estimator. KADANE [1971] obtained this result earlier using a limit approach for the case where ψ tends to infinity.

A general conclusion seems to emerge from this study of small sample properties of various simultaneous equation estimators, namely that the asymptotically efficient estimators considered thus far have distributions with rather heavy tails, so that they may not be as interesting as asymptotic theory suggests. Hence it may be worth looking for other estimators which would have good asymptotic efficiency and a rather concentrated distribution in small samples.

Considering in this spirit the estimation of the reduced form, MAASOUMI [1978] suggests replacing the three-stage least squares estimator $\hat{A}$ of the reduced form coefficient matrix by

$$\tilde{A} = \mu\hat{A} + (1 - \mu)A^*.$$

where A^* is the unconstrained ordinary least squares estimator whereas μ is the minimum of 1 and d/d_0, d being the statistics for an overidentification test of the type proposed in ch. 9, § 5, proposition 1:

$$d = T \operatorname{tr}[(A^* - \hat{A})'(M_{\varepsilon\varepsilon}^*)^{-1}(A^* - \hat{A})M_{zz}]$$

and d_0 being the critical value for d at a preassigned significance level. Theoretical exploration and Monte Carlo experiments show that this estimator is likely to outperform in practice three-stage least squares. Indeed, this estimator belongs to the general class of James-Stein estimators that were discussed in ch. 6, § 12; its use in some applications may be justified by the kind of arguments that were discussed there.

(ii) The results of simulations[†]

Until recently only SUMMERS [1965] appeared to have studied estimators of the reduced form and conditional prediction of the values of the endogenous variables. He applies the Monte Carlo method to an overidentified model containing two equations and six variables. Most of his samples are of 20 observations. Summers uses the mean absolute error to compare the results of the different methods.

Five estimation methods are adopted: the regression of each endogenous variable on the exogenous variables (this method ignores a priori restrictions on the reduced form), quasi-maximum likelihood (cf. ch. 18, § 4), the Cowles Commission method, two-stage least squares and finally direct least squares fitting of the structural equations. The last three methods lead first to estimates of the structural form, which must be solved to find estimates of the reduced form.

The results are as may be expected, as much on the grounds of the definition of the estimators as on the grounds of asymptotic theory. Least squares fitting to the structural form gives the worst results, which is quite natural since the corresponding estimators do not tend to the true values. Of the other four methods, quasi-maximum likelihood is generally best and regression on the exogenous variables worst. This is to be expected since only the former introduces all the a priori restrictions directly while the latter ignores them completely[††].

Summers' investigation also shows that when one of the a priori restrictions is wrong, then methods which take account of this restriction give worse results than methods which ignore it.

Finally, the results are similar for the structural parameters. Quasi-maximum likelihood estimators generally have the smallest mean square error and direct least squares fitting of the structural equations leads to the largest.

Summers' results relate to models which do not involve lagged values of the endogenous variables. WAGNER [1958] and NAGAR [1960] studied various estimates obtained from artificial samples for an overidentified model with two equations in which the lagged value of one of the endogenous variables appears. Their results are more difficult to interpret than the previous ones, since the effects of the presence of several simultaneous equations are combined with the autoregressive character of the model. The biases observed in small samples may be due to one or other of these causes. However, the previous

---

[†] JOHNSTON [1963], ch. 10, gives a detailed account of the results of Monte Carlo studies of this present problem.

[††] However as DHRYMES [1973] shows, and as was pointed out at the beginning of the chapter, the simple regression A^* of the endogenous variables on the exogenous variables may be preferable to the reduced equations deduced by limited information methods if the errors affecting the various structural equations are highly correlated.

conclusions seem to be confirmed by the calculations of Wagner and Nagar. Direct fitting of the structural equations leads to estimates which may be affected by considerable biases. Although the variance of these estimates is small, the mean square error is often appreciably greater than that of estimates obtained by the consistent methods defined in this and the previous chapters.

Finally, we should refer to a fairly complete investigation by J. G. CRAGG [1968] into the effects of specification errors. Applying the Monte Carlo method, Cragg came to the following conclusions. Small specification errors have no perceptible effects on the results obtained. The other errors may restrict the model unduly, for example by taking as zero coefficients whose values are considerable. Such errors generally affect the estimates obtained by full information methods while in limited information methods they have no repercussions on the estimates of equations unaffected by the erroneous restriction. Since the gain in precision from the first methods relative to the second is in most cases small even when the fitted model is correct, it is to our advantage not to use full information methods when the specification of some of the equations of the model is suspect. It is also clumsy to keep to an insufficiently precise model in which possible knowledge of the phenomenon has failed to be integrated, for example, by keeping in a structural equation a variable which is known to have little effect on the behavior represented[†]. Such an error also has very noticeable consequences on the precision of the results, especially when the omitted restriction would have allowed identification of coefficients which are unidentifiable in its absence. 'The successful construction of econometric models,' says Cragg, 'is a very difficult task. We must navigate between the Scylla of specification error and the Charybdis of under-specification'.

To sum up, our knowledge of the valid distributions for small samples is still fragmentary. However, what we know so far in no way contradicts the conclusions of asymptotic theory. The latter is still the most important source of ideas about the different estimation methods and their properties.

---

† See ROTHENBERG [1968a] for a systematic study of this question.

CHAPTER 20

Systems non-linear in the endogenous variables

The large models in practice consist of a set of structural equations each of which represents some particular behavior or constraint. It often happens that these equations are non-linear in the endogenous quantities whose determination is represented by the system. As we saw when discussing identification in ch. 17, § 7, the simultaneous involvement of prices, volumes and values is a very frequent cause of such departures from linearity. But obviously this is not the sole cause; thus a Cobb-Douglas production function is non-linear with respect to capital, a Phillips relation is non-linear with respect to the unemployment rate, etc.

We shall study estimation of such non-linear models in the context of a structure consisting of n equations in which the errors appear additively, as before:

$$f_i(x_t, z_t, \alpha) = \eta_{it} \qquad \begin{aligned} i &= 1, 2, \ldots, n \\ t &= 1, 2, \ldots, T \end{aligned} \tag{1}$$

where x_t is the vector of the n endogenous variables x_{it} and z_t is the vector of the m exogenous variables z_{jt} while α is the vector of the p 'coefficients' α_k to be estimated together with the covariance matrix Σ of the vector η_t (η_t has zero expected value and two different vectors η_t and η_θ are assumed to be independent).

In this short chapter we shall introduce the theory and shall not attempt a comprehensive treatment of the subject. The methodology of estimation in such models is still relatively undeveloped. Also the asymptotic properties, which are the only known properties, will be stated without proof since the proofs are often tedious; nor shall we state all the necessary assumptions for the validity of the proofs.

For a good grasp of the particular problems of estimation in the new context of model (1) it will be helpful first to consider the case of a single equation ($n = 1$). Estimation of Σ is not then essentially involved and the other estimation problems can be isolated. We shall then treat the general case of a system of n equations and go on to discuss limited information estimation of a non-linear equation involving several endogenous variables. This is the plan of the three sections of this chapter.

1　A non-linear equation in x_t

Let us consider the vector α that is to be estimated from T observations on the variables x_t and z_{jt} $(j=1, 2 \ldots, m)$, these quantities being related by the equation

$$f(x_t, z_t, \alpha) = \eta_t. \tag{2}$$

Of course f is a known function. But we shall also assume that *equation* (2) *implies a one-to-one correspondence between* x_t *and* η_t; in other words, this equation could be solved for x_t given any values of z_t and of α in their respective domains of definition (the vector z_t is non-random as in previous chapters).

It will be helpful in this section to refer to an example and so we consider the following particular model:

$$x_t - ax_tz_t - bz_t = \eta_t. \tag{3}$$

It contains a single exogenous variable $(m=1)$ and two coefficients a and b; thus $\alpha' = (a, b)$ and $p=2$. It can be solved for x_t:

$$x_t = \frac{bz_t + \eta_t}{1 - az_t} \tag{4}$$

provided that no z_t equals $1/a$, as we shall assume.

Of course, (4) can be written in the form:

$$x_t = \frac{bz_t}{1 - az_t} + \varepsilon_t \quad \text{where } \varepsilon_t = \frac{\eta_t}{1 - az_t}.$$

This form recalls models which are non-linear in the coefficients and which we discussed in ch. 9. But an important difference remains which essentially distinguishes our present situation from that in ch. 9: not the heteroscedasticity of the errors in itself, but the fact that it depends on the coefficients to be estimated.

Be that as it may, analytic solution of (2) for x_t is often impracticable and is not considered as the first stage of an estimation method.

Essentially two methods have been investigated; the first uses instrumental variables while the second estimates by maximum likelihood under the assumption that η_t is normally distributed.

(i)　Instrumental variables

Suppose we have observed a vector w_t of instrumental variables, that is, of quantities uncorrelated with the errors η_t. This leads naturally to an estimation method.

If w_t is a p-vector, we can determine the estimator $\hat{\alpha}$ of α as a solution of the system of p equations defined by

$$m_{fw} = \frac{1}{T} \sum_{t=1}^{T} f(x_t, z_t, \alpha) \cdot w_t = 0 \tag{5}$$

As we shall see below this gives a useful estimator provided that *the instrumental variables defining w_t are correlated with the partial derivatives of f with respect to the p coefficients α_k.*

More generally, if w_t has more than p components we can apply the method defined in ch. 19, § 5, that is, find the p linear combinations of the components of w_t which are most highly correlated with f. Then $\hat{\alpha}$ is determined as the estimator which minimises

$$m_{fw} M_{ww}^{-1} m_{wf}. \tag{6}$$

For equation (3) we may, for example, think of choosing a vector w_t with two components z_t and 1. The two equations (5) are

$$\left. \begin{array}{l} [xz] - a[xz^2] - b[z^2] = 0 \\ \bar{x} - a[xz] - b[\bar{z}] = 0 \end{array} \right\} \tag{7}$$

where, as in ch. 16, for example, $[uv]$ denotes the sample moment corresponding to the product of the two variables u_t and v_t. System (1) can be solved immediately:

$$\hat{a} = \frac{\bar{z}[xz] - [z^2]\bar{x}}{\bar{z}[xz^2] - [z^2][xz]}, \qquad \hat{b} = \frac{[xz]^2 - [xz^2]\bar{x}}{[z^2][xz] - \bar{z}[xz^2]}. \tag{8}$$

To determine the asymptotic distribution of $\hat{\alpha}$, which satisfies (5) or minimises (6), consider the following approximate equation:

$$f(x_t, z_t, \alpha) = f(x_t, z_t, \alpha^0) + (\alpha - \alpha^0)'g_t \tag{9}$$

in which α^0 is the true value of α and g_t is the p-vector defined by

$$g_{kt} = \frac{\delta}{\partial \alpha_k} f(x_t, z_t, \alpha^0) \qquad k = 1, 2, \ldots, p. \tag{10}$$

Equation (9) can also be written

$$f(x_t, z_t, \alpha) = \eta_t + (\alpha - \alpha^0)'g_t. \tag{11}$$

The solution of (5) can then be expressed as

$$\sqrt{T}(\hat{\alpha} - \alpha^0) = \sqrt{T} M_{wg}^{-1} m_{w\eta}. \tag{12}$$

We can easily think of possible conditions[†] to imply first that M_{wg} tends to a non-singular matrix (this is the precise form of the condition stated after (5)) and secondly that the vector $\sqrt{T}m_{w\eta}$ has a limiting normal distribution with zero mean and covariance matrix equal to the limit of $\sigma^2 M_{ww}$ where σ^2 is the variance of η_t. Under these conditions $\hat{\alpha}$ *tends to the true value* α^0. Moreover $\sqrt{T}(\hat{\alpha}-\alpha^0)$ has a limiting normal distribution with zero mean and covariance matrix

$$\sigma^2 M_{gw}^{-1} M_{ww} M_{wg}^{-1}. \tag{13}$$

(It would be pedantic to distinguish matrices such as M_{gw} or M_{ww} from their limits.)

Similarly the estimator that minimises (6) is the solution of the following system of equations in α:

$$m_{f(\alpha)w} M_{ww}^{-1} M_{wg(\alpha)} = 0 \tag{14}$$

where the dependence on α is made explicit and where $g_t(\alpha)$ is defined by a formula similar to (10), with α replacing α^0.

Approximately,

$$g_t(\alpha) = g_t + H_t \cdot (\alpha - \alpha^0)$$

where

$$H_{hkt} = \frac{\delta^2}{\delta\alpha_h\delta\alpha_k} f(x_t, z_t, \alpha^0).$$

Equation (14) can then be written approximately

$$m_{\eta w} M_{ww}^{-1} M_{wg} + (\alpha - \alpha^0)' M_{gw} M_{ww}^{-1} M_{wg} + m_{\eta w} M_{ww}^{-1} M_{wH(\alpha - z^0)} = 0. \tag{15}$$

We can easily think of conditions which ensure that $M_{gw} M_{ww}^{-1} M_{wg}$ tends to a non-singular matrix and that $\sqrt{T}m_{w\eta}$ has a limiting normal distribution with zero mean. Under these conditions $\hat{\alpha}$ tends in probability to α^0 and the last term of (15) is negligible. It follows that $\sqrt{T}(\hat{\alpha}-\alpha^0)$ *has a limiting normal distribution with zero mean and covariance matrix*

$$\sigma^2 [M_{gw} M_{ww}^{-1} M_{wg}]^{-1}. \tag{16}$$

This last formula indicates the best choice of instrumental variables. For, the matrix

$$M_{gg} - M_{gw} M_{ww}^{-1} M_{wg}$$

† Relevant references will be given in the next section.

is the covariance matrix of the residuals of the regression of g_t on w_t; it is necessarily at least positive semi-definite. Since M_{gg} does not depend on the choice of instrumental variables, *the precision of $\hat{\alpha}$ will increase as the instrumental variables better 'explain' the partial derivatives g_{kt}.*

Generally the g_{kt} are not known since α^0 is not. Also they are random quantities since they depend on the x_t. So strictly speaking they cannot serve as instrumental variables. However the choice of instrumental variables may be based on the form of the g_{kt}. We can also think of iterative methods which lead, asymptotically at least, to instrumental variables which are as highly correlated as possible with the g_{kt}. This high correlation will be obtained if the instrumental variables perfectly explain the expectations Eg_{kt}. For this reason it will be useful to consider the ideal case where the instrumental variables are just the Eg_{kt}.

In example (3), the vector g_t is

$$g_t' = (-x_t z_t \quad - z_t). \tag{17}$$

Obviously z_t should be chosen as one of the instrumental variables. Together with z_t, the other instrumental variable should give the best possible fitting of $x_t z_t$, that is, in view of (5), the best possible fitting of $z_t^2/(1-az_t)$. If in most cases the az_t are large then the constant 1 will be a good instrumental variable since $z^2/(1-az_t)$ is then approximately equal to $-(az_t+1)/a^2$; but if in most cases the az_t are small then z_t^2 is preferable to 1 as the second instrumental variable.

We can also consider the following two-stage method:

– calculate $\hat{a}$ and $\hat{b}$ from (8), that is, using the instrumental variables z_t and 1;
– define $w_{1t} = z_t$ and $w_{2t} = z_t^2/1 - \hat{a}z_t$ and apply these two 'instrumental variables' to obtain new estimates $\hat{\hat{a}}$ and $\hat{\hat{b}}$.

The quantity w_{2t} thus defined is not altogether an instrumental variable since it depends on the random quantity $\hat{a}$; its correlation with η_t is not strictly zero. However when T is large $\hat{a}$ is near the fixed number a^0; there is negligible correlation between w_{2t} and η_t.

The above asymptotic reasoning[†] suggests that the largest possible number of instrumental variables should be chosen since this can only improve the explanation of g_t by w_t. However in small samples a loss of precision would certainly result from unduly increasing the number of instrumental variables.

Before leaving the use of instrumental variables for estimation of a single equation let us consider a generalisation which will be helpful in the next section. Suppose that in (2) the errors are no longer necessarily homoscedastic and mutually independent. Let us assume that the T-vector η satisfies

---

[†] The conditions for validity of this reasoning have not been clearly stated. Note that, in particular, they involve convergence of $1/T \sum_t (1-az_t)^{-1}$, which implies that not too many of the az_t should be too close to 1.

$$E(\eta) = 0 \qquad E(\eta\eta') = \Omega \tag{18}$$

where Ω is a positive definite matrix.

Also let f be the T-vector with tth component $f(x_t, z_t, \alpha)$ and let W be the matrix of the observations on the instrumental variables. Then (6) can be written

$$f'W(W'W)^{-1}W'f$$

apart from the coefficient $1/T$.

Instead of minimising this expression we may prefer to minimise

$$f'QW(W'QW)^{-1}W'Qf \tag{19}$$

where Q is a suitably chosen positive definite symmetric matrix.

The approximate formulae for the estimator $\hat{\alpha}$ minimising (19) are no longer given by (15) with the last term ignored, but by

$$\eta'QW(W'QW)^{-1}W'QG + (\alpha - \alpha^0)'G'QW(W'QW)^{-1}W'QG = 0 \tag{20}$$

where G is the $(T \times p)$ matrix whose elements are the g_{kt}.

Looking at this equation we might ask what is the best choice of Q given Ω, G and W? But the answer is not very illuminating; it suggests taking for Q a matrix which depends in a complex way on Ω, G and W.

However if W coincides with the expectation of G, which we shall write $\bar{G}$ (and we saw earlier why we should try to approximate to such a situation), then (20) reduces approximately to

$$\eta'Q\bar{G} + (\alpha - \alpha^0)'\bar{G}'Q\bar{G} = 0 \tag{21}$$

since $\bar{G}'QG$ approximately equals $\bar{G}'Q\bar{G}$. So the covariance matrix of $\sqrt{T}(\hat{\alpha} - \alpha^0)$ is approximately

$$T(\bar{G}'Q\bar{G})^{-1}\bar{G}'Q\Omega Q\bar{G}(\bar{G}'Q\bar{G})^{-1}. \tag{22}$$

This expression is minimal and equals

$$T(\bar{G}'\Omega^{-1}\bar{G})^{-1} \tag{23}$$

precisely[†] when $Q = \Omega^{-1}$.

More generally we could prove that the simultaneous choice of $W = \bar{G}$ and $Q = \Omega^{-1}$ minimises the approximate covariance matrix which can be deduced from (20).

[†] This property was proved earlier. See ch. 8, § 1, proposition 2.

In practical applications neither $\bar{G}$ nor Ω is known a priori. However the above property may often suggest a method consisting of successive stages as follows:

– find a (consistent) estimate $\hat{\Omega}$ of Ω,
– choose instrumental variables $\hat{W}$ which provide a good explanation of the expected values of the partial derivatives $\bar{G}$,
– determine $\hat{\hat{\alpha}}$ by minimising

$$f'\hat{\Omega}^{-1}\hat{W}(\hat{W}'\hat{\Omega}^{-1}\hat{W})^{-1}\hat{W}'\hat{\Omega}^{-1}f. \tag{24}$$

This method gives an asymptotically normal consistent estimator which probably has good asymptotic efficiency.

(ii)   Normal errors and maximum likelihood

Let us return to the case where $\Omega = \sigma^2 I$ and assume in addition that η is normal. It is then very easy to define the maximum likelihood estimator $\tilde{\alpha}$.

For, apart from a constant, the logarithm of the probability density of η is

$$L = - T \log \sigma - \frac{1}{2\sigma^2} \sum_{t=1}^{T} \eta_t^2.$$

The logarithm of the probability density of the vector x of observations on the endogenous variable is then

$$L = \sum_{t=1}^{T} \log \left| \frac{\delta f_t}{\delta x_t} \right| - T \log \sigma - \frac{1}{2\sigma^2} \sum_{t=1}^{T} [f(x_t, z_t, \alpha)]^2 \tag{25}$$

where the first term is the logarithm of the Jacobian of the transformation from η to x.

Maximisation of L with respect to σ implies, as usual, that σ^2 is estimated by

$$\tilde{\sigma}^2 = \frac{1}{T} \sum_{t=1}^{T} f_t^2 ; \tag{26}$$

$\tilde{\alpha}$ is then the vector which minimises

$$L^* = \sum_{t=1}^{T} \log \left| \frac{\delta f_t}{\delta x_t} \right| - \frac{T}{2} \log \sum_{t=1}^{T} f_t^2 . \tag{27}$$

We may note that, without the first term in this sum, $\tilde{\alpha}$ would be very near the estimators obtained in our discussion of instrumental variables; minimisation of the sum of squares of the f_t leads to an equation similar to (5) with w_t replaced by $g_t(\alpha)$. But the presence of the first term alters matters.

For example, for model (3) L^* is:

$$L^* = \sum_{t=1}^{T} \log|1 - az_t| - \frac{T}{2} \log \sum_{t=1}^{T} (x_t - ax_t z_t - bz_t)^2. \qquad (28)$$

Equating to zero the derivative with respect to b gives the first of equations (7) which therefore remains unchanged (there are two reasons for this: first, the Jacobian of the transformation does not depend on b and secondly, the derivative of f_t with respect to b is equal to $-z_t$, that is, to the instrumental variable which was chosen to obtain the first of equations (7)).

On the other hand, if the derivative with respect to a is equated to zero we have

$$[x^2 z] - a[x^2 z^2] - b[xz^2] - \frac{\tilde{\sigma}^2}{T} \sum_{t=1}^{T} \frac{z_t}{1 - az_t} = 0 \qquad (29)$$

This equation differs from that obtained if any instrumental variable w_t is used. Note that the last term to some extent corrects the bias which appears if the 'pseudo-instrumental variable' $x_t z_t$, the partial derivative of f_t with respect to $-a$, is used, that is, the bias resulting from correlation between $x_t z_t$ and η_t; formulae (5) show precisely that the covariance of $x_t z_t$ and η_t is $\sigma^2 z_t/(1 - az_t)$.

In short, the system consisting of the first of equations (7) and equations (26) and (29) defines the estimators $\tilde{a}$, $\tilde{b}$ and $\tilde{\sigma}$. These estimators maximise the likelihood of the sample when the errors are normal.

More generally, (27) shows that the condition $\delta L^*/\delta \alpha_k = 0$ can be expressed as

$$\frac{1}{T} \sum_{t=1}^{T} f_t g_{kt} - \frac{\tilde{\sigma}^2}{T} \sum_{t=1}^{T} \cdot \frac{\delta g_{kt}}{\delta \eta_t} = 0 \qquad (30)$$

since

$$\frac{\delta}{\delta \alpha_k} \log \left| \frac{\delta f_t}{\delta x_t} \right| = \frac{\delta g_{kt}}{\delta x_t} \Big/ \frac{\delta f_t}{\delta x_t} = \frac{\delta g_{kt}}{\delta \eta_t}.$$

Equation (30) can be interpreted as resulting from the use of the pseudo-instrumental variable g_{kt}, with the second term correcting the bias of the first term.

To justify this interpretation and to establish that $\hat{a}$ tends to α^0, we need the property

$$E(\eta_t g_{kt}) = \sigma^2 E \left[\frac{\delta g_{kt}}{\delta \eta_t} \right]. \qquad (31)$$

Now, this property holds in two cases:

– either when g_{kt} happens to be linear in η_t, as we see in the particular example of model (3),

– or when η_t is normally distributed[†].

Thus the *estimator $\hat{\alpha}$ defined by the solution of* (26) *and* (30) *is consistent and asymptotically normal in either of these two cases*[††] *but is not generally so.* On the other hand, the 'quasi-maximum likelihood' estimators which we have introduced up till now by proceeding as if the errors were normal (in chs. 6, 9 and 18, for example) were consistent and asymptotically normal whatever the true distribution of the errors. Here is the first difference from the results of previous chapters.

In the case where η_t is normal it is not surprising to find that the asymptotic covariance matrix of $\sqrt{T}(\tilde{\alpha} - \alpha^0)$ is the inverse of the limit of the matrix whose elements are

$$-\frac{1}{T} \cdot \frac{\delta^2 L^*}{\delta\alpha_k \delta\alpha_h} \qquad h, k = 1, 2, \ldots, p. \tag{32}$$

In the particular case of model (3), this limit is the limit of

$$\frac{1}{T\sigma^2}\left[\begin{matrix} \sum_t \dfrac{b^2 z_t^4 + 2\sigma^2 z_t^2}{(1 - az_t)^2} & \sum_t \dfrac{bz_t^3}{1 - az_t} \\[2ex] \sum_t \dfrac{bz_t^3}{1 - az_t} & \sum_t z_t^2 \end{matrix}\right] \tag{33}$$

We can then verify that when η_t is normal, *the estimator $\tilde{\alpha}$ obtained by using even optimal instrumental variables is not fully efficient asymptotically.* (Here is the second difference from our earlier results.) To verify this we need only compare the asymptotic covariance matrix of $\sqrt{T}(\hat{\alpha} - \alpha^0)$ with that of $\sqrt{T}(\tilde{\alpha} - \alpha^0)$ and see that the latter is sytematically smaller. Now when the optimal instrumental variables $Eg_{kt} = \bar{g}_{kt}$ have been used, the asymptotic covariance matrix of $\sqrt{T}(\hat{\alpha} - \alpha^0)$ can be obtained by applying (16), which then reduces to

$$\sigma^2 M_{\bar{g}\bar{g}}^{-1} \tag{34}$$

For example, in the particular case of model (3) the inverse of this matrix is obviously

---

[†] The expected value of $\delta g_{kt}/\delta\eta_t$ is in fact the integral of the product of this function of η_t and the probability density of η_t. Integration by parts shows that it is also the negative of the integral of the product of g_{kt} and the derivative of the density.

[††] See AMEMIYA [1977] for the proofs.

$$\frac{1}{T\sigma^2}\begin{bmatrix} \sum_t \dfrac{b^2 z_t^4}{(1-az_t)^2} & \sum_t \dfrac{bz_t^3}{1-az_t} \\ \sum_t \dfrac{bz_t^3}{1-az_t} & \sum_t z_t^2 \end{bmatrix} \tag{35}$$

We see that (35) is systematically smaller than (33). However the difference is small when σ^2 is markedly smaller than $b^2[z^2]$, that is, when the errors are not large.

2 Non-linear three-stage least squares

Our discussion of the case of a single endogenous variable has clarified the main problems involved in estimating a system of equations non-linear in the endogenous variables. We are now in a position to study system (1) for general n.

It is convenient to consider directly the vector η whose nT components are arranged in order of their indices: $(1, 1), (2, 1), \ldots, (n, 1); (1, 2), \ldots, (n, 2); \ldots; (1, T), \ldots, (n, T)$. The assumptions on the errors of model (1) imply

$$E(\eta) = 0 \qquad E(\eta\eta') = \Sigma \otimes I \tag{36}$$

where $\otimes$ denotes the Kronecker product defined in ch. 6, § 4. These equalities show that model (1) is basically a particular case of the model discussed when we set up equations (18).

To estimate this model it is then natural to think of the method of instrumental variables defined in the previous section.

More precisely, we shall assume that we have a previous estimate $\hat\Sigma$ of Σ and that this estimate is consistent as the number T of observations tends to infinity. We shall see in the next section that $\hat\Sigma$ can be obtained by a non-linear two-stage least squares fitting. So we shall define a 'three-stage least squares estimate' as a vector $\hat{\hat\alpha}$ which minimises

$$f'(\alpha)(\hat\Sigma \otimes I)^{-1} W[W'(\hat\Sigma \otimes I)^{-1} W]^{-1} W'(\hat\Sigma \otimes I)^{-1} f(\alpha) \tag{37}$$

where $f(\alpha)$ is obviously the vector with the nT components $f_i(x_t, z_t, \alpha)$ while W is a fixed matrix with nT rows and r columns representing the 'instrumental variables' (the uniqueness of α then requires that $r \geq p$). Rigorously W can also be random when its correlation with η is zero, at least asymptotically.

The choice of instrumental variables can be approached in different ways. JORGENSON and LAFFONT [1974], the first to investigate three-stage least squares, and also GALLANT [1977], assume that r independent functions $w_h(z_t)$ of the z_{jt} have been defined $(h = 1, 2, \ldots, r)$; they then set

$$w_{it, h} = w_h(z_t) \tag{38}$$

(thus the same values are chosen for all the equations ($i = 1, 2, \ldots, n$) relating to the same observation t).

We saw at the end of § 1 (i) that it appears preferable to define instrumental variables which can be considered as approximations to the expected values of the partial derivatives of f. So we choose $r = p$ and

$$\hat{w}_{it,k} \sim E \, \frac{\delta}{\delta \alpha_k} f_i(x_t, z_t, \alpha), \qquad k = 1, 2, \ldots, p. \tag{39}$$

This is suggested by AMEMIYA [1977]. Generally different components of α will occur in the different equations; the columns of $\hat{W}$ then consist of zeros except for the index i relating to the equation in which the corresponding component α_k appears. When the instrumental variables are chosen in this way, estimation of the covariance matrix of $\hat{\hat{\alpha}}$ is particularly straightforward since, by applying (23), we need only calculate

$$[\hat{W}'(\hat{\Sigma} \otimes I)^{-1} \hat{W}]^{-1} \tag{40}$$

In the above references the reader will find *proofs of the consistency and asymptotic normality of non-linear three-stage least squares estimators*; he will also find the list of conditions adopted for the proofs.

It is not surprising that *non-linear three-stage least squares estimators do not generally have maximum asymptotic efficiency* since we have seen that this property does not apply even in the case of a single equation.

We may obviously think of trying to estimate Σ and α jointly by the general method of maximum likelihood. Thus, if η is known to be normal, we can determine the formulae to be satisfied by the estimators $\tilde{\Sigma}$ and $\tilde{\alpha}$. For this we need only appeal to the reasoning which led to (26) and (30), and this raises no difficulty.

If the errors are in fact normal, $\tilde{\alpha}$ will be consistent, asymptotically normal and asymptotically efficient. Unfortunately none of these properties will generally hold if the formulae defining the maximum likelihood estimator in the case of normality are applied in a situation where η is not normally distributed.

See AMEMIYA [1977] for more details on the complete information maximum likelihood estimator.

3 Limited information estimators

We have just seen that the effective use of instrumental variables for estimating a complete non-linear model assumes the existence of a previous estimate of the covariance matrix Σ. It is natural to construct this estimate $\hat{\Sigma}$ from the residuals $\hat{\eta}_{it}$ of an initial fitting of the equations and to calculate

$$\hat{\sigma}_{ih} = \frac{1}{T} \sum_t \hat{\eta}_{it} \hat{\eta}_{ht}.$$ (41)

Also it is natural to determine this first fitting by estimating the n equations in succession, each equation being treated independently of its predecessors and successors. In other words, it is natural that the first fitting should be a 'limited information' fitting.

Let us see how limited information estimators can be regarded in the context of models non-linear in the endogenous variables.

We are not concerned here only with the first stage in complete information estimation of the model. As we have seen for linear models, a limited information fitting is often adequate in itself. This is especially true if we are interested only in one particular structural equation, in which case it may even happen that there is difficulty in specifying a complete system for the set of endogenous variables.

Before producing a model, let us see clearly why this situation does not revert simply to the situation discussed in § 1.

It is true that we shall focus attention on a single structural equation such as (2). It is true that in the expression for this equation or in the definition of estimators using instrumental variables, the fact that x_t is a single endogenous variable rather than a vector of endogenous variables has no effect. But of course we must start from a complete random specification if we are to investigate the statistical properties of the estimators; now, the specification is incomplete if it is limited to a single equation, such as (2), involving a vector x_t of n endogenous variables and if it does not define the other $n-1$ equations which are necessary to determine x_t.

As is customary in practical applications, we shall consider that the chosen structural equation is mainly concerned with one of the endogenous variables which it contains. For ease of notation we shall call this variable x_{0t}. But the equation also contains other endogenous variables whose number we shall assume, for convenience, to be n and we shall define a vector with components x_{it} ($i = 1, 2, \ldots, n$). In short, the structural equation to be considered is

$$f(x_{0t}, x_t, \alpha) = \eta_t.$$ (42)

The vector α of the coefficients which occur in this equation has p unknown components α_k.

The variables x_{it} are considered as determined by the observable exogenous variables z_{jt} according to a classic linear system:

$$x_t = Az_t + \varepsilon_t$$ (43)

where the vector of the random errors ε_t is such that

$$E(\varepsilon_t) = 0 \qquad E(\varepsilon_t \varepsilon_t') = \Omega$$
$$E(\varepsilon_t \varepsilon_\theta') = 0 \qquad \text{if } t \neq \theta \tag{44}$$

This way of setting up the problem calls for some comment.

In the first place, equation (42) does not involve as argument the exogenous variables proper. This is a simplification for our subsequent discussion, comparable to that in sections 2 and 5 of ch. 19. It is not essential; for example, if there is one exogenous variable in the equation we can consider it as the first component x_{1t} of x_t, also attribute to it the first component z_{1t} of z_t. In system (43) we then know the first row of the matrix A (1 followed by zeros) and we know that $\varepsilon_{1t} = 0$. The first row and the first column of Ω are then zero. However it will be appropriate later to consider the case where there are no such constraints on the reduced equations (43).

In the second place these reduced equations are linear, which may seem surprising in the discussion of non-linear models. It would obviously be wrong to pretend that this is unimportant. However, it may be justified either on the grounds that it is adequate to represent a situation where the econometrician has little knowledge of how the endogenous variables other than x_{0t} are determined, or in order to allow the use of rigorous statistical theory applying to the simplest case (since rigorous treatment of the case where (43) is replaced by a non-linear system would be very difficult).

In the third place, we assume that there is no restriction on the matrices A and Ω. No particular information about them is included (except in the case, not discussed here, where some of the components of the x_{it} are exogenous). As compared with the reduced equations of ch. 19, § 2, equations (43) are subject to no constraint. This is a particular feature resulting from the explicitly recursive structure which we have chosen for the determination of the endogenous variables: the x_{it} $(i = 1, 2, \ldots, n)$ are determined from the z_{jt}, then x_{0t} is determined from the x_{it}. This again is a convenient simplification like that introduced in linear two-stage least squares theory (since one particular endogenous variable is there also singled out).

Finally, as it is our special intention to explore the use of adequate instrumental variables it will be convenient and not very restrictive to assume that the structural equation (42) has been solved for x_{0t}:

$$x_{0t} = f(x_t, \alpha) + \eta_t \tag{45}$$

This will be convenient because the partial derivatives of f with respect to the α_k will not depend on x_{0t} and this will make it easier to calculate their expected values. This is not very restrictive since, by hypothesis, (42) must be solvable for x_{0t}. The only restriction stems from the fact that we shall assume the errors η_t of equation (45) to be homoscedastic, but this property does not play an essential part when we are discussing estimation using instrumental variables (in contrast with the situation with, for example, a maximum likelihood estimator).

To estimate α it is obviously possible to work on equation (45) as we did in § 1 on equation (2), We need only use a vector w_t of instrumental variables such that $\sqrt{T}m_{w\eta}$ has a limiting normal distribution and $M_{gw}M_{ww}^{-1}M_{wg}$ tends to a non-singular matrix, g_{kt} being the value in the tth observation of the partial derivative of f with respect to α_k. It follows that $\sqrt{T}(\hat{\alpha} - \alpha^0)$ has a limiting normal distribution with zero mean and covariance matrix which is the probability limit of

$$\sigma^2[M_{gw}M_{ww}^{-1}M_{wg}]^{-1}. \tag{46}$$

The best choice of vector w_t of instrumental variables seems bound to be the p-vector defined by

$$w_{kt} = E\left[\frac{\delta}{\delta\alpha_k} f(Az_t + \varepsilon_t, \alpha)\right]. \tag{47}$$

But in the first place, the values of these expectations are not known and their expressions are complex[†] in A, α and Ω except obviously in the case where f is linear with respect to x_t. In the second place, we cannot exclude the possibility that the estimator obtained by using the instrumental variables (47) is less efficient than another estimator taking advantage of possible correlation between η_t and the errors ε_{it} of the reduced equations[††]. So we resort to other methods.

The method of two-stage least squares established for linear models suggests the choice of $w_t = A^*z_t$ where A^* is the matrix of regression coefficients of the x_{it} on the z_{jt} (see ch. 19 § 5). Given that A^* tends in probability to the true matrix A^0, w_t is asymptotically equivalent to a vector of linear combinations of the exogenous variables and the condition on $m_{w\eta}$ is clearly satisfied. But first this is not a suitable choice if $n < p$ or $m < p$ which can obviously happen (the matrix in brackets in (46) is then necessarily singular); secondly, the reasons for choosing linear combinations A^*z_t were related to the form of the

---

[†] To see this, we need only consider the case where $n = 1$ and the function f is

$$\frac{bx_t}{1 - ax_t}$$

(an expression similar to that deduced from the example in § 1). The derivative with respect to a is $bx_t^2/(1 - ax_t)^2$ whose expected value is obviously a complex function of the coefficient a, the row vector A and the variance Ω.

[††] In fact we can show that when f is non-linear there exist estimators which are asymptotically preferable to the estimator obtained by using the instrumental variables (47).

structural equation to be estimated and they are nullified when this equation is non-linear.

However if $p \leq m$ we can still use the same principle and choose for w_t the vector z_t of the set of exogenous variables themselves. α is then said to be estimated by *the method of non-linear two-stage least squares*.

If the number p of parameters to be estimated is relatively large and the number m of exogenous variables is relatively small, it may be helpful to step up the number of instrumental variables; it will even be necessary to do this if $p > m$. It is essential here to find variables which are not linear combinations of the z_{jt} and are not correlated with η_t. For example, successive powers of the z_{jt} can be introduced.

In the absence of a theory for small samples, it is difficult to decide how far to go in increasing the number of instrumental variables. Common sense together with the study of the distributions for small samples in the linear case (cf. ch. 19 § 7) suggest that the process should be extended as the number T of observations increases.

On the other hand a precise asymptotic theory presented by AMEMIYA [1975] shows that *in the case where the equation to be estimated is non-linear, where η_t is correlated with some of the ε_{it} and where the random vector (η_t, ε_t) is normal*, it is advantageous to use a very large number of pseudo-instrumental variables. More precisely, this leads to an estimator with smaller asymptotic variance than the non-linear two-stage least squares estimator. It is sufficient to minimise (6) where the vector w_t consists of $T - n$ variables w_{kt} chosen in such a way that, in T-dimensional space, the subspace spanned by the $T - n$ vectors w_k with components w_{kt} is orthogonal to that spanned by the n vectors ε_t^* whose components are the residuals ε_{it}^* of the regressions of the x_{it} on the z_{jt} (where $i = 1, 2, \ldots, n$). The first m variables w_{kt} may then obviously coincide with the m exogenous variables z_{jt}; but the next $T - n - m$ variables are random (like the vectors ε_i^* of the residuals).

At the present stage it is difficult to assess the real benefits of this result for applied econometrics. However, it does indicate that new developments in the treatment of non-linear systems of equations are both possible and probable.

CONCLUSION

In the course of this work, the properties of various statistical procedures have been discussed systematically. Although many gaps remain, substantial theoretical results have now been obtained. Once he has chosen his model, the econometrician will generally be in a position to judge which test or which estimation method is appropriate to the particular case in which he is interested.

However, the choice of the model conditions every econometric investigation and in fact always raises a delicate problem. The model condenses all the a priori information, which, together with the analyzed data, makes statistical inference possible. This information is generally vague and badly formulated. It often appears fairly subjective.

The art of the econometrician consists as much in defining a good model as in finding an efficient statistical procedure. Indeed this is why he cannot be purely a statistician, but must have a solid grounding in economics. Only if this is so, he will be aware of the mass of accumulated knowledge which relates to the particular question under study and must find expression in the model.

Finally, we must never forget that our progress in understanding economic laws depends strictly on the quality and abundance of statistical data. Nothing can take the place of the painstaking work of objective observation of the facts. All improvements in methodology would be in vain if they had to be applied to mediocre data.

References

ABRAHAMSE, A. P. J. and J. KOERTS (1969), "A Comparison between the Power of the Durbin-Watson Test and the Power of the BLUS Test", *Journal of the American Statistical Association*, Sept. 1969.

ADICHIE, J. W. (1978), "Rank Tests of Sub-Hypotheses in the General Linear Regression", *Annals of Statistics*, Sept. 1978.

AGOSTINO, D', R. B. and E. S. PEARSON (1973), "Test for Departure from Normality. Empirical Results for the Distributions of b_2 and b_1", *Biometrica*, Dec. 1973.

AGOSTINO, D', R. B. and B. ROSMAN (1974), "The Power of Geary's Test of Normality", *Biometrica*, April 1974.

AITKEN, A. C. (1935), "On Least Square and Linear Combination of Observations", *Proceedings of the Royal Society of Edinburgh*, vol. 55, p. 42.

AITKEN, A. C. (1939), *Determinants and Matrices*, Edinburgh, 1939.

ALMON, S. (1965), "The Distributed Lag Between Capital Appropriations and Expenditures", *Econometrica*, Jan. 1965.

ALT, F. (1942), "Distributed Lags", *Econometrica*.

AMEMIYA, T. (1975), "The Non Linear Limited-Information Maximum-Likelihood Estimator and the Modified Nonlinear Two-Stage Least-Squares Estimator", *Journal of Econometrics*, 1975, p. 375–386.

AMEMIYA, T. (1977), "The Maximum Likelihood and the Nonlinear Three-Stage Least-Squares Estimator in the General Nonlinear Simultaneous Equation Model", *Econometrica*, May 1977.

AMEMIYA, T. (1977), "A Note on a Heteroscedastic Model", *Journal of Econometrics*, Nov. 1977.

AMEMIYA, T. (1978), "L'estimation des Modèles à Equations Simultanées Non Linéaires", *Cahier du Séminaire d'Econométrie*, no. 19, 1978.

AMEMIYA, T. and W. A. FULLER (1967), "A Comparative Study of Alternative Estimators in a Distributed Lag Model", *Econometrica*, July-Oct. 1967.

AMEMIYA, T. and K. MORIMUNE (1974), "Selecting the Optimal Order of Polynomial in the Almon Distributed Lag", *Review of Economics and Statistics*, Aug. 1974.

AMES, E. and S. REITER (1961), "Distributions of Correlation Coefficients in Economic Time Series", *Journal of the American Statistical Association*, Sept. 1961.

ANDERSON, R. L. (1942), "Distribution of the Serial Correlation Coefficient", *Annals of Mathematical Statistics*, vol. 13, 1942, p. 1–13.

ANDERSON, T. W. (1948), "The Asymptotic Distributions of the Roots of Certain Determinantal Equations", *Journal of the Royal Statistical Society*, Series B, vol. 10, no. 1.

ANDERSON, T. W. (1951), "Estimating Linear Restrictions on Regression Coefficients for Multivariate Normal Distributions", *Annals of Mathematical Statistics*, Sept. 1951.

ANDERSON, T. W. (1958), *Multivariate Statistical Analysis*, John Wiley, New York, 1958.

ANDERSON, T. W. (1959), "On Asymptotic Distributions of Estimates of Parameters of Stochastic Difference Equations", *Annals of Mathematical Statistics*, vol. 30.

ANDERSON, T. W. (1974), "An Asymptotic Expansion of the Distribution of Limited Information Maximum Likelihood Estimate of a Coefficient in a Simultaneous Equation System", *Journal of the American Statistical Association*, June 1974.

ANDERSON, T. W. (1976), "Estimation of Linear Functional Relationships: Approximate Distributions and Connections with Simultaneous Equations in Econometrics", *Journal of the Royal Statistical Society*, serie B, vol. 38, no. 1, 1976, p. 1–36.

ANDERSON, T. W. (1977), "Estimation for Autoregressive Moving Average Models in the Time and Frequency Domains", *Annals of Statistics*, Sept. 1977.

ANDERSON, T. W. and H. RUBIN (1949), "Estimation of the Parameters of a Single Equation in a Complete System of Stochastic Equations", *Annals of Mathematical Statistics*, vol. 20. no. 1, March 1949.

ANDERSON, T. W. and H. RUBIN (1950), "The Asymptotic Properties of Estimates of the Parameters of a Single Equation in a Complete System of Stochastic Equations", *Annals of Mathematical Statistics*, vol. 21, no. 4, Dec. 1950.

ANDERSON, T. W. and H. RUBIN (1956), "Statistical Inference in Factor Analysis", *Proceedings of the Third Berkeley Symposium on Mathematical Statistics and Probability*, vol. V, Berkeley, 1956.

ANDERSON, T. W. and T. SAWA (1973), "Distributions of Estimates of Coefficients of a Single Equation in a Simultaneous System and their Asymptotic Expansions", *Econometrica*, July 1973.

ARROW, K. (1960), "Decision Theory and the Choice of a Level of Significance for the t-Test", in I. Olkin et al. (1960).

ARROW, K. J. and M. HOFFENBERG (1959), *A Time Series Analysis of Interindustry Demands* (cf. ch. 4 § 4), North-Holland Publishing Company, Amsterdam, 1959.

ATIQULLAH, M. (1962), "The Estimation of Residual Variance in Quadratically Balanced Least-Square Problems and the Robustness of the F-Test", *Biometrika*, Jan. 1962.

ATIQULLAH, M. (1964), "The Robustness of the Covariance Analysis of a One-Way Classification", *Biometrika*, Dec. 1964.

BARANCHIK, A. J. (1973), "Inadmissibility of Maximum Likelihood Estimators in Some Multiple Regression Problems with Three or More Independent Variables", *Annals of Statistics*, March 1973.

BARTLETT, M. S. (1955), *Stochastic Processes*, Cambridge University Press.

BASMANN, R. L. (1957), "A Generalized Classical Method of Linear Estimation of Coefficients in a Structural Equation", *Econometrica*, 1957.

BASMANN, R. L. (1961), "A Note on the Exact Finite Sample Frequency Functions of Generalized Classical Linear Estimators in Two Leading Over-Identified Cases", *Journal of the American Statistical Association*, Sept. 1961.

BASMANN, R. L. (1963 a), "A Note on the Exact Finite Sample Frequency Functions of Generalized Classical Linear Estimators in a Leading Three-Equation Case", *Journal of the American Statistical Association*, vol. 58, p. 161–171.

BASMANN, R. L. (1963 b), "Remarks Concerning the Application of Exact Finite Sample Distribution Functions of GCL Estimators in Econometric Statistical Inference", *Journal of the American Statistical Association*, Dec. 1963.

BASMANN, R. L., D. H. RICHARDSON and R. J. ROHR (1974), "Finite Sample Distributions Associated with Stochastic Difference Equations: Some Experimental Evidence", *Econometrica*, Sept. 1974.

BASS, J. (1956), *Cours de Mathématiques*, Masson et Cie, 1956.

BASSETT, Jr., G. and R. KOENKER (1978), "Asymptotic Theory of Least Absolute Error Regression", *Journal of the American Statistical Association*, Sept. 1978.

BEACH, C. M. and J. G. MACKINNON (1978), "A Maximum Likelihood Procedure for Regression with Autocorrelated Errors", *Econometrica*, Jan. 1978.

BECKMAN, R. J. and H. J. TRUSSELL (1974), "The Distribution of an Arbitrary Studentized Residual and the Effects of Updating in Multiple Regression", *Journal of the American Statistical Association*, March 1974.

BEMENT, T. R. and J. S. WILLIAMS (1969), "Variance of Weighted Regression Estimators when Sampling Errors are Independent and Heteroscedastic", *Journal of the American Statistical Association*, Dec. 1969.

BENNION, E. G. (1952), "The Cowles Commission's 'Simultaneous Equation Approach'. A Simplified Explanation", *Review of Economics and Statistics*, Feb. 1952.

BENTZEL, R. and B. HANSEN (1954), "On Recursiveness and Interdependency in Economic Models", *Review of Economic Studies*, 22, p. 153–168.

BENZECRI, J. P. et al. (1973), *L'analyse des Données*, Dunod, Paris 1973.

BERGSTROM, A. R. (1962), "The Exact Sampling Distributions of Least Squares and Maximum Likelihood Estimators of the Marginal Propensity to Consume", *Econometrica*.

BERKSON, J. (1950), "Are there two regressions?", *Journal of the American Statistical Association*, vol. 45.

BLATTBERG, R. and T. SARGENT (1971), "Regression with Non-Gaussian Stable Disturbances: Some Sampling Results", *Econometrica*, May 1971.

BLOMQVIST, A. G. (1972), "Approximating the Least-Squares Bias in Multiple Regression with Errors in Variables", *Review of Economics and Statistics*, May 1972.

BLOOMFIELD, P. and G. S. WATSON (1975), "The Inefficiency of Least Squares", *Biometrika*, April 1975.

BOITEUX, M. (1956), "L'amortissement – Dépréciation des automobiles", *Revue de Statistique appliquée*, vol. 4, no. 4, Dec. 1956.

BOWDEN, D. C. (1970) "Simultaneous Confidence Bands for Linear Regression Models", *Journal of the American Statistical Association*, March 1970.

BOWDEN, R. (1973), "The Theory of Parametric Identification", *Econometrica*, Nov. 1977.

BOX, G. E. P. (1953), "Non Normality and Tests on Variances", *Biometrika*, vol. 40, 1953.

BOX, G. E. P. (1954), "Some theorems on Quadratic Forms Applied in the Study of Analysis of Variance I", *Annals of Mathematical Statistics*.

BOX, G. E. P. and G. M. JENKINS (1970), *Time Series Analysis: Forecasting and Control*, Holden-Day, San Francisco.

BOX, G. E. P. and G. S. WATSON (1962), "Robustness to Non-Normality of Regression Tests", *Biometrika*, June 1962.

BRICHLER, M. (1946), "Le transport des voyageurs par chemin de fer", I.N.S.E.E., Études théoriques, no. 2.

BRILLINGER, D. R. (1969), "Asymptotic Properties of Spectral Estimates of Second Order", *Biometrika*, Aug. 1969.

BROWN, T. M. (1952), "Habit Persistence and Lags in Consumer Behaviour", *Econometrica*, vol. 20, July 1952.

BROWN, T. M. (1954), "Standard Error of Forecast of a Complete Econometric Model", *Econometrica*, April 1954.

BROWN, T. M. (1959), "Simplified Full Maximum Likelihood and Comparative Structural Estimates", *Econometrica*, Oct. 1959.

BROWN, T. M. (1960), "Simultaneous Least Squares: A Distribution Free Method of Equation System Structure Estimation", *International Economic Review*, Sept. 1960.

BRUNDY, J. and D. W. JORGENSON (1971), "Efficient Estimation of Simultaneous Equations by Instrumental Variables", *Review of Economics and Statistics*, Aug. 1971.

CALOT, G. (1965), *Cours de Statistique descriptive*, Dunod, Paris.

CALOT, G. (1967 a), *Cours de Calcul des Probabilités*, 2e édition, Dunod, Paris.

CALOT, G. (1967 *b*). "Significatif ou non significatif? Réflexions à propos de la théorie et de la pratique des tests statistiques", *Revue de Statistique Appliquée*, 1967, no. 1.

CARGILL, T. F. and R. A. MEYER (1974), "Some Time and Frequency Domain Distributed Lag Estimators: A Comparative Monte Carlo Study", *Econometrica*, Nov. 1974.

CHAMBERS, J. M. (1973), "Fitting Non Linear Models Numerical Techniques", *Biometrika*, April 1973.

CHAMPERNOWNE, D. G. (1960), "An experimental investigation of the robustness of certain procedures for estimating means and regression coefficients", *Journal of the Royal Statistical Society*, Series A, vol. 123, part 4.

CHANG, T. C. (1945–46), "International Comparison of Demand for Import", *The Review of Economic Studies*, vol. 34.

CHANG, T. C. (1948), "A Statistical Note on World Demand for Export", *Review of Economics and Statistics*, May 1948.

CHERNOFF, H. and N. DIVINSKY (1953), "The Computation of Maximum-Likelihood Estimates of Linear Structural Equations", in HOOD, W. C. and T. KOOPMANS (1953).

CHOW, G. (1968), "Two Methods of Computing Full-Information Maximum Likelihood Estimates in Simultaneous Stochastic Equations", *International Economic Review*, Feb. 1968.

CHRIST, C. (1966), *Econometric Models and Methods*, John Wiley, New York.

COCHRANE, D. and G. H. ORCUTT (1949 *a*), "Application of Least Squares Regression to Relationships Containing Auto-Correlated Error Terms", *Journal of the American Statistical Association*, vol. 44, p. 32–61.

COCHRANE, D. and G. H. ORCUTT (1949 *b*), "A Sampling Study of the Merits of Autoregressive and Reduced Form Transformations in Regression Analysis", *Journal of the American Statistical Association*, vol. 44, p. 356–372.

COOLEY, T. and E. PRESCOTT (1973), "Tests of an Adaptative Regression Model", *Review of Economics and Statistics*, May 1973.

COOLEY, T. and E. PRESCOTT (1976), "Estimation in the Presence of Stochastic Parameter Variation", *Econometrica*, Jan. 1976.

COPAS, J. B. (1966), "Monte Carlo Results for Estimation in a Stable Markov Time Series", *Journal of the Royal Statistical Society*, Series A, vol. 129, Part. 1.

COUREGE, P. et P. PRIOURET (1971), "Sur l'Evaluation des Intégrales Multiples Exprimant le Niveau des Tests *F* en Statistique Mathématique", *Bulletin des Sciences Mathématiques*, no. 95, 1971, p. 93–150.

COX, D. R. and D. V. HINKLEY (1968), "A Note on the Efficiency of Least-Squares Estimates", *Journal of the Royal Statistical Society*, series B, no. 2, 1968.

CRAGG, J. G. (1966), "On the Sensivity of Simultaneous-Equations Estimators to the Stochastic Assumptions of the Models", *Journal of the American Statistical Association*, March 1966.

CRAGG, J. G.\(1968), "Some Effects of Incorrect Specification on the Small Sample Properties of Several Simultaneous Equation Estimators", *International Economic Review*, Feb. 1968.

CRAMER, H. (1946), *Mathematical Methods of Statistics*, Princeton University Press.

DANIELS, H. E. (1956), "The Approximate Distribution of Serial Correlation Coefficients", *Biometrika*, vol. 43.

DARMOIS, G. (1936), *Méthodes d'estimation*, Hermann, Paris.

DARMOIS, G. (1937), "Résumés exhaustifs d'un ensemble d'observations", *Bulletin de l'Institut International de Statistique*, p. 288–293.

DARMOIS, G. (1945), "Sur les limites de dispersion de certaines lois", *Revue de l'Institut International de Statistique*, 13th year, p. 9–15.

DARMOIS, G. (1952), "Sur l'estimation des grandeurs par leurs mesures", *Annuaire du Bureau des Longitudes*.

DAVID, F. N. (1947), "A Power Function for Tests of Randomness in a Sequence of Alternatives", *Biometrika*, p. 335–339.

DAVID, F.N. and J. NEYMAN (1938), "Extension of the Markoff Theorem on Least Squares", *Statistical Research Memoirs*, vol. II, Dec. 1938, London.

DAVIS, H. (1941), *The Analysis of Economic Time Series*, The Principia Press, Bloomington.

DEBREU, G. and I. N. HERSTEIN (1953), "Non-negative Square Matrices", *Econometrica*, Oct. 1953.

DEISTLER, M. (1978), "The Structural Identifiability of Linear Models with Autocorrelated Errors in the Case of Cross-Equation Restrictions", *Journal of Econometrics*, Aug. 1978.

DHRYMES, P. J. (1973), "Restricted and Unrestricted Reduced Forms: Asymptotic Distribution and Relative Efficiency", *Econometrica*, Jan. 1973.

DIEHR, G. and D. R. HOFLIN (1974), "Approximating the Distribution of the Sample R in Best Subset Regressions", *Technometrics*, May 1974.

DIEUDONNE, J. (1960), *Foundations of Modern Analysis*, Academic Press, New York, 1960.

DOOB, J. L. (1953), *Stochastic Processes*, John Wiley, New York.

DREZE, J. (1968), "Limited Information Estimation From a Bayesian Viewpoint", Mimeographed, CORE, Louvain.

DREZE, J. (1976), "Bayesian Limited Information Analysis of the Simultaneous Equation Model", *Econometrica*, Sept. 1976.

DRYGAS, H. (1970), *The Coordinate-Free Approach to Gauss-Markov Estimate*, Springer Verlag, Heidelberg, 1970.

DRYGAS, H. (1975), "A Note on a Paper by T. Klock Concerning the Consistency of Variance Estimation in the Linear Model", *Econometrica*, Jan. 1975.

DRYGAS, H. and J. SRZEDNICKA (1976), "A New Result on Hsu's Model of Regression Analysis", *Bulletin de l'Académie Polonaise des Sciences*, vol. 24, no. 12.

DUESENBERRY, J. S. (1952), "Income, Saving, and the Theory of Consumer Behavior", Harvard University Press, Cambridge, Massachusetts.

DUGUÉ, D. (1958), *Traité de Statistique théorique et appliquée*, Masson et Cie.

DUGUÉ, D. et M. GIRAULT (1959), *Analyse de variance et plans d'experience*, Probabilités, Statistique, Recherche opérationnelle, Dunod, Paris.

DUNCAN, D. B. and S. D. HORN (1972), "Linear Dynamic Recursive Estimation from the Viewpoint of Regression Analysis", *Journal of the Statistical Association*, Dec. 1972.

DUNCAN, D. B. and R. H. JONES (1966), "Multiple Regression With Stationary Errors", *Journal of the American Statistical Association*, Dec. 1966.

DUNN, O. J. (1959), "Confidence Intervals for the Means of Dependent Normally Distributed Variables", *Journal of the American Statistical Association*, Sept. 1959, vol. 54.

DURAND, D. (1954), "Joint Confidence Regions for Multiple Regression Coefficients", *Journal of the American Statistical Association*, March 1954, vol. 49.

DURBIN, J. (1953), "A Note on Regression when there is Extraneous Information about one of the Coefficients", *Journal of the American Statistical Association*.

DURBIN, J. (1957), "Testing for Serial Correlation in Systems of Simultaneous Regression Equations", *Biometrika*, Dec. 1957.

DURBIN, J. (1960 a), "Estimation of Parameters in Time-Series Regression Models", *Journal of the Royal Statistical Society*, Series B, vol. 22, no. 1, 1960, p. 139–153.

DURBIN, J. (1960 b), "The Fitting of Time-Series Models", *Revue de l'Institut International de Statistique*, vol. 28, no. 3, p. 233–244.

DURBIN, J. (1961), "Trend Elimination by Moving-Average and Variate-Difference Filters", *Bulletin de l'Institut International de Statistique*, 33rd session, Paris, 1963.

DURBIN, J. (1963 a), "Trend Elimination for the Purpose of Estimating Seasonal and Periodic Components of Time Series", in M. Rosenblatt (1963).

DURBIN, J. (1963 b), "Maximum-Likelihood Estimation of the Parameters of a System of Simultaneous Regression Equations", Communication at the Copenhagen Meeting.

DURBIN, J. (1967), "Testing for Serial Correlation in Least-Squares Regression when some of the Regressors are Lagged Dependent Variables", Mimeographed.

DURBIN, J. (1968), "An Exact Test for Serial Correlation in Least-Squares Regression when the Bounds Test is Inconclusive", Mimeographed.

DURBIN, J. (1969), "Tests for Serial Correlation in Regression Analysis Based on the Periodogram of Least-Squares Residuals", Biometrika, March 1969.

DURBIN, J. (1970 a), "Testing for Serial Correlation in Least-Squares Regression when Some of the Regressors are Lagged Dependent Variables", Econometrica, May 1970.

DURBIN, J. (1970 b), "An Alternative to the Bounds Tests for Testing Serial Correlation in Least-Squares Regression", Econometrica, May 1970.

DURBIN, J. and G. S. WATSON (1950 and 1951), "Testing for Serial Correlation in Least Squares Regression", Biometrika, Dec. 1950 and June 1951.

DURBIN, J. and G. S. WATSON (1971), "Testing for Serial Correlation in Least-Squares Regression-III", Biometrika, April 1971.

DUVALL, R. M. (1966), "Time Series Analysis by Modified Least-Squares Techniques", Journal of the American Statistical Association, May 1966.

DWIVEDI, T. D., V. K. SRIVASTAVA and R. L. HALL (1977), "Finite Sample Properties of Ridge Estimators in Linear Regression Models", International Institute of Statistics, New Delhi.

DWYER, P. S. (1951), Linear Computations, John Wiley & Sons, New York.

EICKER, F. (1963), "Asymptotic Normality and Consistency of the Least Squares Estimators for Families of Linear Regressions", Annals of Mathematical Statistics, June 1963.

EISENPRESS, H. (1962), "Note on the Computation of Full-Information Maximum-Likelihood Estimates of Coefficients of a Simultaneous System", Econometrica, April 1962.

EISENPRESS, H. and J. GREENSTADT (1966), "The Estimation of Nonlinear Econometric Systems", Econometrica, October 1966.

ENGLE, R. (1974 a), "Specification of the Disturbance for Efficient Estimation", Econometrica, Jan. 1974.

ENGLE, R. (1974 b), "Band Spectrum Regression", International Economic Review, Feb. 1974.

ENGLE, R. and R. GARDNER (1976), "Some Finite Sample Properties of Special Estimators of a Linear Regression", Econometrica, Jan. 1976.

ESPASA, A. and J. SARGAN (1977), "The Spectral Estimation of Simultaneous Equation Systems with Lagged Endogenous Variables", International Economic Review, Oct. 1977.

FAIR, R. C. and H. H. KELEJIAN (1974), "Methods of Estimation for Markets in Desequilibrium: A Further Study", Econometrica, Jan. 1974.

FÉRON, R. (1956), "Information, Régression, Corrélation", Publications de l'Institut de Statistique de l'Université de Paris, vol. 5, no. 3–4.

FISHER, F. M. (1959), "Generalization of the Rank and Order Conditions for Identifiability", Econometrica, July 1959.

FISHER, F. M. (1961 a), "On the Cost of Approximate Specification in Simultaneous Equation Estimation", Econometrica, April 1961.

FISHER, F. M. (1961 b), "Identifiability Criteria in Nonlinear Systems", Econometrica, Oct. 1961.

FISHER, F. M. (1963), "Uncorrelated Disturbances and Identifiability Criteria", International Economic Review, May 1963.

FISHER, F. M. (1965), "Identifiability Criteria in Non-linear Systems: A Further Note", Econometrica, Jan. 1965.

FISHER, I. (1925), "Our Unstable Dollar and the so-called Business Cycle", Journal of the American Statistical Association, vol. 20.

FISHER, I. (1937), "Note on a Short-cut Method for Calculating Distributed Lags", *Bulletin de l'Institut International de Statistique*, vol. 29.

FISHER, R. A. (1929), "Test of Significance in Harmonic Analysis", *Proceedings of the Royal Society*, A.

FISHER, W. (1962), "Estimation in the Linear Decision Model", *International Economic Review*, Jan. 1962.

FISK, P. R. (1967), *Stochastically Dependent Equations*, C. Griffin and Co, London.

FORSYTHE, A. B. (1972), "Robust Estimation of Straight Line Regression Coefficients by Minimizing *p*th Power Deviations", *Technometrics*, Feb. 1972.

FOURGEAUD, C. (1951), "Recherche de relations à forme linéaire dans un système économique", *Cahiers du séminaire d'économétrie*, no. 1.

FOURGEAUD, C. (1955), "L'estimation dans les modèles à composante saisonnière", *Thèse*, Faculté des Sciences, Paris.

FOX, K. A. (1954), "Structural Analysis and the Measurement of Demand for Farm Products", *Review of Economics and Statistics*, Feb. 1954.

FOX, K. A. (1958), *Econometric Analysis for Public Policy*, Iowa State College Press, Ames, Iowa.

FRÉCHET, M (1943), "Sur l'extension de certaines évaluations statistiques au cas de petits échantillons", *Revue de l'Institut International de Statistique*.

FRIEDMAN, M. (1957), *A Theory of the Consumption Function*, National Bureau of Economic Research, New York.

FRISCH, R. (1928), "Correlation and Scatter in Statistical Variables", *Nordisk Statistisk Tidskrift*, Band 8.

FRISCH, R. (1934), *Statistical Confluence Analysis by Means of Complete Regression Systems*, University Institute of Economics, Oslo.

FRISCH, R. and F. V. WAUGH (1933), "Partial Time Regression as Compared with Individual Trends", *Econometrica*, vol. 1, p. 221–223.

FROEHLICH, B. R. (1973), "Some Estimators for a Random Coefficient Regression Model", *Journal of the American Statistical Association*, June 1973.

FULLER, W. A. and G. E. BATTESE (1973), "Transformations for Estimation of Linear Models with Nested-Error Structure", *Journal of the American Statistical Association*, Sept. 1973.

FULLER, W. A. and M. A. HIDIROGLOU (1978), "Regression Estimation after Correcting for Attenuation", *Journal of the American Statistical Association*, March 1978.

FULLER, W. A. and J. N. K. RAO (1978), "Estimation for a Linear Regression Model with Unknown Diagonal Covariance Matrix", *Annals of Statistics*, Sept. 1978.

GALLANT, A R. (1977), "Three-Stage Least-Squares Estimation for a System of Simultaneous, Nonlinear, Implicit Equations", *Journal of Econometrics*, Jan. 1977.

GARNIER, J. (46), *La consommation de tabac en France de 1921 à 1938*, I.N.S.E.E., Études théoriques, no. 2.

GAUSS, K. F. (1821–1823), *Theoria Combinationis Observationem erroribus minimis obnoxiale*, French translation by J. Bertrand, Paris, 1855.

GAYEN, A. K. (1950), "The Distribution of the Variance Ratio in Random Samples of any Size Drawn from Non-Normal Universes", *Biometrika*.

GEARY, R. C. (1942), "Inherent relations between random variables", *Proc. Roy. Irish Acad.*, vol. 47, Sect. A, no. 6.

GEARY, R. C. (1947), "Testing for Normality", *Biometrika*.

GEARY, R. C. (1949), "Determination of Linear Relations between Systematic Parts of Variables with Errors of Observation the Variances of which are Unknown", *Econometrica*, vol. 17.

GEISSER, S. (1965), "Bayesian Estimation in Multivariate Analysis", *The Annals of Mathematical Statistics*, Feb. 1965, vol. 36.

GEISSER, S. and J. CORNFIELD (1963), "Posterior Distributions for Multivariate Normal Parameters", *Journal of the Royal Statistical Society*, Series B, vol. 25.

GEWEKE, J. (1978), "Temporal Aggregation in the Multiple Regression Model", *Econometrica*, May 1978.

GIRI, N., J. KIEFER and C. STEIN (1963), "Minimax Character of Hotelling's T^2 Test in Simplest Case", *Annals of Mathematical Statistics*, Dec. 1963, p. 1524–1535.

GIRSHICK, M. A. and T. HAAVELMO (1947), "Statistical Analysis of the Demand for Food", *Econometrica*, April 1947; partially reprinted in HOOD, W. C. and T. C. KOOPMANS ed. (1953).

GLEJSER, H. (1969), "A New Test for Heteroscedasticity", *Journal of the American Statistical Association*, March 1969.

GLESER, L. J. and M. PAGANO (1973), "Approximating Circulant Quadratic Forms in Jointly Stationary Gaussian Time Series", *Annals of Statistics*, March 1973.

GOLDBERGER, A. S. (1961), "Stepwise Least Squares, Residual Analysis and Specification Errors", *Journal of the American Statistical Association*, p. 998–1000.

GOLDBERGER, A. S. (1964), *Econometric Theory*, John Wiley, New York.

GOLDBERGER, A. S. (1973), "Structural Equation Methods in the Social Sciences", *Econometrica*, Nov. 1973.

GOLDBERGER, A.S. and O. D. DUNCAN, eds. (1973), *Stuctural Equation Models in the Social Sciences*, Seminar Press, New York.

GOLDFELD, S., R. E. QUANDT and H. F. TROTTER (1966), "Maximization by Quadratic Hill-Climbing", *Econometrica*, July 1966.

GOLDFIELD, S. M. and R. E. QUANDT (1965), "Some Tests for Homoscedasticity", *Journal of the American Statistical Association*, June 1965.

GOLDSMITH, R. W. (1955), *A Study of Saving in the United States*, vols. 1, 2, 3, Princeton University Press.

GRANGER, C. W. J. (1966), "The typical Spectral Shape of an Economic Variable", *Econometrica*, Jan. 1966.

GRENANDER, U. (1954), "On the Estimation of Regression Coefficients in the Case of an Autocorrelated Disturbance", *Annals of Mathematical Statistics*, June 1954.

GRENANDER, U. and M. ROSENBLATT (1956), "Statistical Analysis of Stationary Time Series", Stockholm.

GRETHER, D. M. and G. S. MADDALA (1973), "Errors in Variables and Serially Correlated Disturbances in Distributed Lag Models", *Econometrica*, March 1973.

GRETHER, D. M. and M. NERLOVE (1970), "Some Properties of Optimal Seasonal Adjustment", *Econometrica*, Sept. 1970.

GRILICHES, Z. (1961), "A Note on Serial Correlation Bias in Estimates of Distributed Lags", *Econometrica*.

GRILICHES, Z. (1967), "Distributed Lags: A Survey", *Econometrica*, Jan. 1967.

GRILICHES, Z. and POTLURI RAO (1969), "Small-Sample Properties of Several Two-Stage Regression Methods in the Context of Autocorrelated Errors", *Journal of the American Statistical Association*, March 1969.

GRUNFELD, Y. (1961), "The Interpretation of Cross Section Estimates in a Dynamic Model", *Econometrica*, July 1961.

GRUNFELD, Y. (1963), *Measurement in Economics: Studies in Mathematical Economics and Econometrics in Memory of Yehuda Grunfeld*, Stanford University Press.

GUILBAUD, G. TH. (1951), "L'étude statistique des oscillations économiques", *Cahiers du Séminaire d'Econométrie*, no. 1, Librairie de Médicis, Paris.

GUILBAUD, G. TH. (1968), *Statistique des Chroniques*, Dunod, Paris, 1968.

HAAVELMO, T. (1943), "The Structural Implication of a System of Simultaneous Equations", *Econometrica*, vol. 11.

HAAVELMO, T. (1944), "The Probability Approach in Econometrics", *Econometrica*, vol. 12 Supplement.

HABIBAGAHI, H. and J. PRATSCHKE (1972), "A Comparison of the Power of the von Neumann Ratio, Durbin-Watson and Geary Tests", *Review of Economics and Statistics*, May 1972.

HALMOS, P. R. (1948), *Finite Dimensional Vector Spaces*, Princeton University Press. A second edition was published in 1958 by Van Nostrand, Princeton.

HALPERIN, M. and J. GURIAN (1971), "Estimation in Straight Line Regression when both Variables are Subject to Errors", *Journal of the American Statistical Association*, Sept. 1971.

HANNAN, E. J. (1960), *Time Series Analysis*, Methuen and Co., London.

HANNAN, E. J. (1963 *a*), "The Estimation of Seasonal Variation in Economic Time Series", *Journal of the American Statistical Association*, March 1963.

HANNAN, E. J. (1963 *b*), "Regression for Time Series", in M. Rosenblatt (1963).

HANNAN, E. J. (1965), "The Estimation of Distributed Lags", *Econometrica*.

HANNAN, E. J. (1971), "The Identification Problem for Multiple Equation Systems with Moving Average Errors", *Econometrica*, Sept. 1971.

HANNAN, E. J. and D. F. NICHOLLS (1972), "The Estimation of Mixed Regression, Autoregression, Moving Average and Distributed Lag Models", *Econometrica*, May 1972.

HANNAN, E. J. and P. J. THOMPSON (1971), "The Estimation of Coherence and Group Delay", *Biometrika*, Dec. 1971.

HANNAN, E. J. and P. J. THOMPSON (1973), "Estimating Group Delay", *Biometrika*, Aug. 1973.

HART, B. I. (1942), "Tabulation of the Probabilities of the Ratio of the Mean Square Difference to the Variance and Significance Levels for the Ratio of the Mean Square Difference to the Variance", *Annals of Mathematical Statistics*, vol. 13, p. 207–214 and 445–447.

HARTER, H. L. (1974–5), "The Method of Least Squares and Some Alternatives", *International Statistical Review*.

HARTLEY, H. O. (1961), "The Modified Gauss-Newton Method for the Fitting of Non-Linear Regression Functions by Least Squares", *Technometrics*, May 1961.

HARVEY, A. C. and P. COLLIER (1977), "Testing for Functional Misspecification in Regression Analysis", *Journal of Econometrics*, July 1977.

HARVEY, A. C. and G. D. A. PHILLIPS (1974), "A Comparison of the Power of Some Tests for Heteroscedasticity in the General Linear Model", *Journal of Econometrics*, Dec. 1974.

HARVILLE, D. A. (1977), "Maximum Likelihood Approach to Variance Component Estimation and Related Problems", *Journal of the American Statistical Association*, June 1977.

HAUSSMAN, J. A. (1975), "An Instrumental Variable Approach to Full Information Estimators for Linear and Certain Nonlinear Econometric Models", *Econometrica*, July 1975.

HEADY, E. O. and J. L. DILLON (1961), *Agricultural Production Functions*, Iowa State University Press, Ames.

HEDAYAI, A. and D. S. ROBSON (1970), "Independent Stepwise Residual for Testing Homoscedasticity", *Journal of the American Statistical Association*, Dec. 1970.

HENDRY, D. F. (1974), "Stochastic Specification in an Aggregate Demand Model of the United Kingdom", *Econometrica*, May 1974.

HENDRY, D. F. and P. K. TRIVEDI (1972), "Maximum Likelihood Estimation of Difference Equations with Moving Average Errors: A Simulation Study", *Review of Economic Studies*, April 1972.

HENSHAW, R. C. (1965), "Testing Single Equation Least-Squares Regression Models for Autocorrelated Disturbances", *Econometrica*, vol. 34.

HILL, T. P. (1959), "An Analysis of the Distribution of Wages and Salaries in Great Britain", *Econometrica*, vol. 27, no. 3, July 1959.

HOCH, I. (1962), "Estimation of Production Function Parameters Combining Time-Series and Cross-Section Data", *Econometrica*, Jan. 1962.

HODGES Jr, J. L. and E. L. LEHMANN (1950) "Some Problems in Minimax Point Estimation", *The Annals of Mathematical Statistics*, vol. 21, no. 2, June 1950.

HOERL, A. E. and R. W. KENNARD (1970), "Ridge Regression: Biased Estimation for Non-Orthogonal Problems", *Technometrics*, vol. 12, 1970, p. 55–67 and 69–82.

HOGG, R. V. (1961), "On the Resolution of Statistical Hypotheses", *Journal of the American Statistical Association*, Dec. 1961.

HOLLY, A. (1974), "Sur l'Estimation des Paramètres d'un Modèle Linéaire lorsque la Matrice des Variances-Covariances des Résidus est Singulière", *Revue de Statistique Appliquée*, no. 2, 1974.

HOLTE, F. C. (1962), *Economic Shock-Models*, Norwegian Universities Press, Oslo.

HOOD, W. C. and T. C. KOOPMANS, eds. (1953), "Studies in Econometric Method", *Cowles Commission Monograph*, no. 14, John Wiley, New York.

HOOPER, J. W. and A. ZELLNER (1961), "The Error of Forecast for Multivariate Regression Models", *Econometrica*, Oct. 1961.

HOTELLING, H. (1951), "A Generalized T Test and Measure of Multivariate Dispersion", *Proceedings of the Second Berkeley Symposium on Mathematical Statistics and Probability*, University of California Press.

HUANG, C. and B. BOLCH (1974), "On the Testing of Regression Disturbance for Normality", *Journal of the American Statistical Association*, June 1974.

HUBER, P. J. (1964), "Robust Estimation of a Location Parameter", *Annals of Mathematical Statistics*, vol. 35, no. 1, March 1964.

HUBER, P. J. (1973), "Robust Regression: Asymptotics, Conjectures and Monte Carlo", *The Annals of Statistics*, Sept. 1977.

HURWICZ, L. (1950), "Least Squares Bias in Time Series", in KOOPMANS, T. C., ed. (1950).

ITO, K. (1960), "On Multivariate Analysis of Variance Tests", *Bulletin de l'Institut International de Statistique*, 32nd session, vol. 4 (Tokyo).

ITO, K. and W. J. SCHULL (1964), "On the Robustness of the T_0^2 Test in Multivariate Analysis of Variance when Variance-Covariance Matrices are not Equal", *Biometrika*, vol. 51, June 1964.

JAMES, W. and C. STEIN (1961), "Estimation with Quadratic Loss", *Proceedings of the Fourth Berkeley Symposium on Mathematical Statistics and Probability*, Berkeley.

JENKINS, G. M. (1956), "Tests of Hypotheses in the Linear Autoregressive Model II', *Biometrika*, vol. 43.

JOHNSTON, J. (1963), *Econometric Methods*, McGraw-Hill, New York.

JÖRESKOG, K. G. (1973), "A General Method for Estimating a Linear Structural Equation System", in A. S. GOLDBERGER and O. D. DUNCAN (1973).

JORGENSON, D. (1964), "Minimum Variance, Linear, Unbiased Seasonal Adjustment of Economic Time Series", *Journal of the American Statistical Association*, Sept. 1964.

JORGENSON, D. (1966), "Rational Distributed Lag Functions", *Econometrica*, Jan. 1966.

JORGENSON, D. W. and J. J. LAFFONT (1974), "Efficient Estimation of Nonlinear Simultaneous Equations with Additive Disturbances", *Annals of Economic and Social Measurement*, 1974, p. 615–640.

JUDGE, G. G., M. E. BOCK and T. A. YANCEY (1974), "Post Data Model Evaluation", *Review of Economics and Statistics*, May 1974.

JUDGE, G. G. and M. E. BOCK (1976), "A Comparison of Traditional and Stein-Rule Estimators under Weighted Squared Error Loss", *International Economic Review*, Feb. 1976.

JUST, R. E. (1977), "Existence of Stable Distributed Lags", *Econometrica*, Sept. 1977.

KADANE, J. B. (1971), "Comparison of *k*-class Estimators when Disturbances are small", *Econometrica*, Sept. 1971.

KARIYA, T. (1977), "A Robustness Property of the Tests for Serial Correlation", *Annals of Statistics*, Nov. 1977.

KARIYA, T. (1978), "The General MANOVA Problem", *Annals of Statistics*, Jan. 1978.

KELLY, J. S. (1975), "Linear Cross-Equation Constraints and the Identification Problem", *Econometrica*, Jan. 1975.

KENDALL, M. G. (1948), *The Advanced Theory of Statistics*, vol. 2, Charles Griffin, London, 1948.

KENDALL, M. G. (1955), *Rank Correlation Methods*, Griffin, London, 2nd edition.

KENDALL, M. G. (1961), "A Theorem in Trend Analysis", *Biometrika*, vol. 48.

KENKEL, J. L. (1974), "Some Small Sample Properties of Durbin's tests for Serial Correlation in Regression Models Containing Lagged Dependant Variables", *Econometrica*, July 1974.

KENNEDY, W. J. and T. A. BANCROFT (1971), "Model Building for Prediction in Regression Based upon Repeated Significance Tests", *Annals of Mathematical Statistics*, Aug. 1971.

KEYNES, J. M. (1936), *The General Theory of Employment, Interest and Money*, Harcourt Bruce, New York.

KHAZZOUM, J. D. (1976), "An Indirect Least Squares Estimator for Overidentified Equations", *Econometrica*, July 1976.

KIEFER, J. and J. WOLFOWITZ (1956), "Consistency of the Maximum Likelihood Estimator in the Presence of Infinitely Many Incidental Parameters", *Annals of Mathematical Statistics*, vol. 27.

KIOUNTOUZIS, E. A. (1973), "Linear Programming Techniques in Regression Analysis", *Applied Statistics*, no. 1, 1973.

KLEIN, L. (1951), "Estimation Patterns of Savings Behavior from Sample Survey Data", *Econometrica*, vol. 19, no. 4, Oct. 1951.

KLEIN, L. (1953), *A Textbook of Econometrics*, Row, Peterson and Company, Evanston, Illinois, 1953.

KLEIN, L. (1955), "The Empirical Foundations of Keynesian Economics", in KURIHARA, K. K., ed., *Post-Keynesian Economics*, George Allen and Unwin Ltd, London.

KLEIN, L. (1958), "The Estimation of Distributed Lags", *Econometrica*, Oct. 1958.

KLEIN, L. (1960), "The Efficiency of Estimation in Econometric Models", in *Essays in Economics and Econometrics*, University of North Carolina, 1960.

KLEIN, L. and A. S. GOLDBERGER (1955), *An Econometric Model of the United-States, 1929–52*, North-Holland Publishing Company, Amsterdam.

KLOEK, T. and L. B. M. MENNES (1960), "Simultaneous Equations Estimation Based on Principal Components of Predetermined Variables", *Econometrica*, Jan. 1960.

KNOTT, M. (1975), "On the Minimum Efficiency of Least Squares", *Biometrika*, April 1975.

KOENKER, R. and G. BASSETT, Jr. (1978), "Regression Quantiles", *Econometrica*, January 1978.

KOOPMANS, L. H. (1964), "On the Multivariate Analysis of Weakly Stationary Stochastic Processes", *Annals of Mathematical Statistics*, Dec. 1964.

KOOPMANS, T. C. (1937), *Linear Regression Analysis of Economic Time Series*, Haarlem.

KOOPMANS, T. C. (1949), "Identification Problems in Economic Model Construction", *Econometrica*, April 1949.

KOOPMANS, T. C., ed. (1950), "Statistical Inference in Dynamic Economic Models", *Cowles Commission Monograph*, no. 10, Wiley, New York.

KOOPMANS, T. K. and W. C. HOOD (1953), "The Estimation of Simultaneous Linear Economic Relationships", in HOOD, W. C. and T. C. KOOPMANS, eds. (1953).

KOOPMANS, T. C. and O. REIERSØL (1950), "The Identification of Structural Characteristics", *The Annals of Mathematical Statistics*, June 1950.

KOOPMANS, T. C., H. RUBIN and R. B. LEIPNIK (1950), "Measuring the Equation Systems of Dynamic Economics", in KOOPMANS, T. C., ed. (1950).

KOYCK, L. M. (1954), *Distributed Lags and Investment Analysis*, North-Holland Publishing Company, Amsterdam.

KRUSKAL, W. (1961), "The Coordinate-Free Approach to Gauss-Markov Estimation and its Application to Missing and Extra Observations", in J. Neyman ed., *Proceedings of the Fourth Berkeley Symposium on Mathematical Statistics and Probability*, vol. 1, University of California Press.

LADD, G. W. (1964), "Regression Analysis of Seasonal Data", *Journal of the American Statistical Association*, June 1964.

LAPLACE, P. S. (1812), *Théorie analytique des probabilités*, Paris.

LAWLEY, D. N. (1940), "The Estimation of Factor Loadings by the Method of Maximum Likelihood", *Proceedings of the Royal Society of Edinburgh*, vol. 60.

LAWLEY. D. N. (1953), "A Modified Method of Estimation in Factor Analysis and Some Large Sample Results", *Factor Analysis; Selected Publications from the Uppsala Institute of Statistics*, vol. 9.

LEAMER, E. E. (1978), *Specification Searches*, John Wiley, New York.

LEAMER, E. E. (1978), "Least-Squares versus Instrumental Variable Estimation in a Simple Errors in Variables Model", *Econometrica*, July 1978.

LE CAM, L. (1956), "On the Asymptotic Theory of Estimation and Testing Hypotheses", *Proceedings of the Third Berkeley Symposium on Mathematical Statistics and Probability*, University of California Press.

LEE, A. F. S. and J. GURLAND (1977), "One-Sample *t*-Test when Sampling from a Mixture of Normal Distributions", *Annals of Statistics*, July 1977.

LEECH, D. (1975), "Testing the Error Specification in Nonlinear Regression", *Econometrica*, July 1975.

LEGENDRE, A. L. (1806), *Nouvelles méthodes pour la détermination des orbites des comètes*, Paris.

LEHMANN, E. L. (1959), *Testing Statistical Hypotheses*, John Wiley and Sons, Inc., New York, Chapman and Hall Limited, London.

LEHMANN, E. L. (1964), "Asymptotically Nonparametric Inference in Some Linear Models With One Observation per Cell", *Annals of Mathematical Statistics*, vol. 35, no. 2, June 1964.

LENTIN, A. and J. RIVAUD (1958), *Eléments d'algèbre moderne*, Vuibert, Paris.

LEONE, F. C. and E. MOUSSA-HAMOUDA (1973), "Relative Efficiencies of O-Blue Estimators in Simple Linear Regression", *Journal of the American Statistical Association*, Dec. 1973.

L'HARDY, Ph. (1966), "Application des méthodes bayésiennes à l'estimation d'élasticités de consommation", *Revue de Statistique Appliquée*, 1966. vol. 14, no. 4.

LINDLEY, D. V. (1947), "Regression Lines and the Linear Functional Relationship", *Journal of the Royal Statistical Society*, vol. 9, Supplement, nos. 1 and 2, p. 218.

LIVIATAN, N. (1961), "Errors in Variables and Engel Curve Analysis", *Econometrica*, July 1961.

LIVIATAN, N. (1963), "Tests of the Permanent Income Hypothesis Based on a Reinterview Savings Survey", in GRUNFELD, Y., (1963).

LOEVE, M. (1955), *Probability Theory*, Van Nostrand Company, Inc., New York.

LOVELL, M. C. (1963), "Seasonal Adjustment of Economic Time Series and Multiple Regression Analysis", *Journal of the American Statistical Association*, Dec. 1963.

LOVELL, M. C. and E. PRESCOTT (1970), "Multiple Regression with Inequality Constraints", *Journal of the American Statistical Association*, June 1970.

LYTTKENS, E. (1964), "Standard Errors of Regression Coefficients by Autocorrelated Residuals", in WOLD, H. (1964).

LYTTKENS, E. (1973), "The Fix-point Method for Estimating Interdependent Systems with the Underlying Models Specifications", *Journal of the Royal Statistical Society*, series A, part 3, 1973.

MAASOUMI, E. (1978), "A Simplified Stein-like Estimator for the Reduced Form Coefficients of Simultaneous Equations", *Econometrica*, May 1978.

MACDOUGALL, D. (1951–1952), "British and American Exports: A Study suggested by the Theory of Comparative Costs", *Economic Journal*, Dec. 1951 and Sept. 1952.

MADANSKY, A. (1959), "The Fitting of Straight Lines when Both Variables are Subject to Errors", *Journal of the American Statistical Association*, vol. 54.

MADDALA, G.S. and T.D. MOUNT (1973), "A Comparative Study of Alternative Estimators for Variance Component Models Used in Econometric Applications", *Journal of the American Statistical Association*, June 1973.

MADDALA, G.S. and A.S. RAO (1973), "Tests for Serial Correlation in Regression Models with Lagged Dependent Variables and Serially Correlated Errors", *Econometrica*, July 1973.

MALINVAUD, E. (1950), "Les élasticités par rapport aux prix dans les échanges internationaux", *Journal de la Société de Statistique de Paris*, May–June 1950.

MALINVAUD, E. (1956), "Réflexions sur l'emploi des modèles à erreurs sur les variables", *Les modèles dynamiques en économétrie*, C.N.R.S., Paris.

MALINVAUD, E. (1957), "L'agrégation dans les modèles économiques", *Cahiers du Séminaire d'Econométrie*, no. 4, Paris.

MALINVAUD, E. (1961 a), "The Estimation of Distributed Lags: A Comment", *Econometrica*, July 1961.

MALINVAUD, E. (1961 b), "Estimation et prévision dans les modèles économiques autorégressifs", *Revue de l'Institut International de Statistique*, vol. 29, no. 2.

MALINVAUD, E. (1969), "The Consistency of Non-Linear Regressions", *Annals of Mathematical Statistics*.

MANDELBROT, B. (1962), "Sur certains prix spéculatifs: faits empiriques et modèle basé sur les processus stables additifs non gaussiens de Paul Lévy", *Comptes rendus de l'Académie des Sciences*, 21 May 1962.

MANDELBROT, B. (1963), "New Methods in Statistical Economics", *Journal of Political Economy*, Oct. 1963.

MANDELBROT, B. (1963), "The Variation of Certain Speculative Prices", *The Journal of Business of the University of Chicago*, vol. 36, no. 4, Oct. 1963.

MANN, H. B. and A. WALD (1943), "On the Statistical Treatment of Linear Stochastic Difference Equations", *Econometrica*, July 1943.

MARKOFF, A. A. (1912), *Wahrscheinlichkeitrechnung*, chap. 7, translated by H. Liebmann, second edition, Leipzig and Berlin.

MARQUARDT, D. W. (1963), "An Algorithm for Least Squares Estimation of Non-Linear Parameters", *Journal of the Society of Industrial Applied Mathematics*, vol. 11, no. 2, June 1963.

MARSCHAK, J. (1953), *Economic Measurement for Policy and Prediction*, in HOOD, W. C. and T. C. KOOPMANS, eds. (1953).

MARSCHAK, J. et W. H. ANDREWS (1944), "Random Simultaneous Equations and the Theory of Production", *Econometrica*, July 1944.

MAESHIRO, A. and D. HINH (1978), "A Total Reappraisal of the Small-Sample Econometrics of AR(1) Disturbances", University of Pittsburg.

MARDIA, K. V. (1971), "The Effect of Nonnormality on Some Multivariate Tests and Robustness to Nonnormality in the Linear Model", *Biometrika*, April 1971.

MAZODIER, P. (1971), "L'estimation des Modèles à Erreurs Composées", *Annales de L' I.N. S.E.E.*, May–Aug. 1971.

MCDONALD, J. B. (1972), "The Exact Finite Sample Distribution Function of the Limited, Information Maximum Likelihood Identifiability Test Statistics", *Econometrica*, Nov. 1972.

MCKEON, J. J. (1974), "F-approximations to the Distribution of Hotelling's T_0^2", *Biometrika*, Aug. 1974.

MÉRAUD, J. and A. TYMEN (1960), "Les variations saisonnières de l'activité économique", *Études et Conjoncture*, April 1960.

MERRIWETHER, J. (1973), "Small Sample Properties of Distributed Lag Estimation with Misspecified Lag Stuctures", *Journal of the American Statistical Association*, Sept. 1973.

MEYER, J. R. and H. L. MILLER Jr. (1954), "Some Comments on the 'Simultaneous Equation Aproach'", *Review of Economics and Statistics*, Feb. 1954.

MILLER, R. (1974), "The Jacknife-Review", *Biometrika*, April 1974.

MISRA, P. N. (1972), "Distribution of OLS Estimates of Coefficients and Disturbance Term in a General Regression Model", *Sankhya*, Dec. 1972.

MODIGLIANI, F. and R. BRUMBERG (1955), "Utility Analysis and the Consumption Function; An Interpretation of Cross-Section Data" in KURIHARA, K. K., ed., *Post-Keynesian Economics*, George Allen and Unwin, London.

MOOD, A. (1950), *Introduction to the Theory of Statistics*, McGraw-Hill Book Company, Inc., New York, 1950.

MOORE, H. L. (1914), *Economic Cycles: Their Law and Cause*, Macmillan Co., New York.

MORICE, E. (1938), "Loi de la demande d'un service monopolise", *Econometrica*, vol. 6.

MORICE, E. (1958), "Quelques tests non paramétriques", *Journal de la Société de Statistique de Paris*, Oct.–Dec. 1958.

MORICE, E. (1972), "Tests de Normalité d'une Distribution Observée", *Revue de Statistique appliquée*, no. 2, 1972.

MORICE, E. et F. CHARTIER (1954), *Analyse statistique*, Imprimerie nationale, Paris.

MORLAT, G. (1963), "Modèle pour les chroniques économiques mensuelles", *Revue de Statistique appliquée*, vol. XI, no. 2.

MORRISON, J. L. (1970), "Small Sample Properties of Selected Distributed Lag Estimato", *International Economic Review*, Feb. 1970.

MOSBAECK, E. and H. WOLD (1970), *Interdependent Systems-Structure and Estimation*, North-Holland Publishing Company, 1970.

MUIRHEAD, R. J. (1972), "The Asymptotic Non-Central Distribution of Hotelling's Generalized T_0^2", *Annals of Mathematical Statistics*, Oct. 1972.

MUIRHEAD, R. J. (1978), "Latent Roots and Matrix Variates: A Review of Some Asymptotic Results", *Annals of Statistics*, Jan. 1978.

NAGAR, A. L. (1959), "The Bias and Moment Matrix of the General K-Class Estimators of the Parameters in Simultaneous Equations", *Econometrica*, Oct. 1959.

NAGAR, A. L. (1960), "A Monte Carlo Study of Alternative Simultaneous Equations Estimators", *Econometrica*, July 1960.

NAKAMURA, M. (1960), "A Note on the Consistency of Simultaneous Least Squares Estimation", *International Economic Review*, Sept. 1960.

NASSE, P. (1970), "Estimation de Fonction de Consommation Trimestrielles", *Annales de L' I.N.S.E.E.*, Jan.–April 1970.

NEAVE, H. R. (1970), "An Improved Formula for the Asymptotic Variance of Spectrum Estimates", *Annals of Mathematical Statistics*, Feb. 1970.

NEAVE, H. R. (1971), "The Exact Error in Spectrum Estimates", *Annals of Mathematical Statistics*, June 1971.

NEISWANGER, W. A. and T. A. YANCEY (1959), "Parameter Estimates and Autonomous Growth", *Journal of the American Statistical Association*, June 1959.

NERLOVE, M. (1958), "Distributed Lags and Demand Analysis for Agricultural and other Commodities", *Agricultural Handbook* no. 141, U.S. Department of Agriculture.

NERLOVE, M. (1963), "Returns to Scale in Electricity Supply", in GRUNFELD, Y. (1963).

NERLOVE, M. (1964), "Spectral Analysis of Seasonal Adjustment Procedures", *Econometrica*, July 1964.

NERLOVE, M. (1965), *On the Estimation and Identification of Cobb-Douglas functions*, North-Holland Publishing Company, Amsterdam.

NERLOVE, M. (1972), "Lags in Economic Behavior", *Econometrica*, March 1972.

NETTHEIM, N. F. (1965), "Fourier Methods for Evolving Seasonal Patterns", *Journal of the American Statistical Association*, June 1965.

NEUMANN, J. VON (1941), "Distribution of the Ratio of the Mean-Square Successive Difference to the Variance", *Annals of Mathematical Statistics*, vol. 12.

NEYMAN, J. (1951), "Existence of Consistent Estimates of the Directional Parameter in a Linear Structural Relation between two Variables", *Annals of Mathematical Statistics*, vol. 22.

NEYMAN, J. and E. SCOTT (1948), "Consistent Estimates Based on Partially Consistent Observations", *Econometrica*, vol. 16, 1948.

NEYMAN, J. and E. SCOTT (1951), "On Certain Methods of Estimating the Linear Structural Relation", *Annals of Mathematical Statistics*, vol 22, p. 352 and vol. 23, p. 115.

NICHOLLS, D. F. and A. R. POGAN (1977), "Specification of the Disturbance for Efficient Estimation – An Extended Analysis", *Econometrica*, Jan. 1977.

OBERHOFER, W. and J. KMENTA (1974), "A General Procedure for Obtaining Maximum Likelihood Estimates in Generalized Regression Models", *Econometrica*, May 1974.

OLKIN, I. et al. (1960), *Contributions to Probability and Statistics. Essays in Honor of Harold Hotelling*, Stanford University Press, Stanford.

ORCUTT, G. H. (1950), "Measurement of Price Elasticities in International Trade", *Review of Economics and Statistics*, vol. 32.

ORCUTT, G. H. and H. S. WINOKUR (1969), "First Order Autoregression: Inference, Estimation and Prediction", *Econometrica*, July 1969.

PAGAN, A. (1973), "A Note on the Extraction of Components from Time Series", *Econometrica*, Jan. 1973.

PARZEN, E. (1967), "On Empirical Multiple Time Series", in L. Le Cam and J. Neyman, ed., *Proceedings of the Fifth Berkeley Symposium on Mathematical Statistics and Probability*.

PEARSON, E. S. (1931), "The Analysis of Variance in Case of Non-Normal Variation", *Biometrika*.

PEARSON, E. S. and H. O. HARTLEY (1951), "Charts of the power functions of the analysis of variance tests, derived from the non-central F-distribution", *Biometrika*, vol. 38, p. 112–130.

PESARAN, M. H. (1973), "Exact Maximum Likelihood Estimation of a Regression Equation with a First-Order Moving-Average Error", *Review of Economic Studies*, Oct. 1973.

PESARAN, M. H. (1974), "On the General Problem of Model Selection", *Review of Economic Studies*, April 1974.

PHILLIPS, A. W. (1956), "Some notes on the estimation of time-forms of reactions in interdependent systems", *Economica*.

PHILLIPS, P. C. B. (1976), "The Iterated Minimum-Distance Estimator and the Quasi-Maximum Likelihood Estimator", *Econometrica*, May 1976.

PHILLIPS, P. C. B. (1978), "Edgeworth and Saddlepoint Approximations in the First-Order Non-Circular Autoregression", *Biometrika*, April 1978.

PHILOCHE, J. L. (1971), "A propos du Théorème de GAUS-MARKOV", *Annales de l'Institut Henri Poincaré*, vol. VII, no. 4, 1971, p. 271–281.

PIERCE, D. A. (1971), "Least Squares Estimation in the Regression Model with Autoregressive-Moving Average Errors", *Biometrika*, Aug. 1971.

PIGOU, A. C. (1943), "The Classical Stationary State", *The Economic Journal*, Dec. 1943.

PILLAI, K. C. S. (1967), "Upper Percentage Points of the Largest Characteristics Root of a Matrix in Multivariate Analysis", *Biometrika*, vol. 54, p. 189–194.

PILLAI, K. C. S. and P. SAMSON, JR. (1959), "On Hotelling's Generalization of T^2", *Biometrika*, 46, 160.

PLACKETT, R. L. (1949), "A Historical Note on the Method of Least Squares", *Biometrika*, vol. 36, part 3 and 4, p. 458.

PLACKETT, R. L. (1972), "Studies in the History of Probability and Statistics: XXIX–The Discovery of the Method of Least Squares", *Biometrika*, Aug. 1972.

PRAIS, S. J. and J. AITCHISON (1954), "The Grouping of Observations in Regression Analysis", *Revue de l'Institut International de Statistique*, p. 1–22.

PRAIS, S. J. and H. S. HOUTHAKKER (1955), *The Analysis of Family Budgets*, The University Press, Cambridge.

PRESCOTT, P. (1978), "Selection of Trimming Proportions for Robust Adaptive Trimmed Means", *Journal of the American Statistical Association*, March 1978.

QUANDT, R. E. (1972), "A New Approach to Estimating Switching Regression", *Journal of the American Statistical Association*, June 1972.

RADNER, R. (1958), "Minimax Estimation for Linear Regressions", *Annals of Mathematical Statistics*, Dec. 1958.

RAIFFA, H. and R. SCHLAIFER (1961), *Applied Statistical Decision Theory*, Harvard University Press, Boston.

RAMSAY, J. O. (1977), "A Comparative Study of Several Robust Estimates of Slope, Intercept and Scale in Linear Regressions", *Journal of the American Statistical Association*, Sept. 1977.

RAO, C. R. (1965), *Linear Statistical Inference and its Applications*, John Wiley, New York.

RAO, C. R. (1970), "Estimation of Heteroscedastic Variances in Linear Models", *Journal of the American Statistical Association*, March 1970.

RAO, C. R. (1972), "Some Recent Results in Linear Estimation", *Sankhya*, Dec. 1972.

RAO, C. R. (1976 a), "Characterization of Prior Distributions and Solutions to a Compound Decision Problem", *The Annals of Statistics*, Sept. 1976.

RAO, C. R. (1976 b), "Estimation of Parameters in a Linear Model", *The Annals of Statistics*, Nov. 1976.

RAO, C. R. and N. SHINOZAKI (1978), "Precision of Individual Estimators in Simultaneous Estimation of Parameters", *Biometrika*, April 1978.

RATCLIFFE, J. F. (1968), "The Effect on the t-Distribution of Non-Normality in the Sampled Population", *Applied Statistics*, no. 1, 1968.

REEVES, J. E. (1972), "The Distribution of the Maximum Likelihood Estimator of the Parameter in the First-Order Autoregressive Series", *Biometrika*, Aug. 1972.

REIERSØL, O. (1945), "Confluence Analysis by Means of Instrumental Sets of Variables", *Arkiv for Mathematik, Astronomi och Fysik*, vol. 32.

REIERSØL, O. (1950 a), "Identifiability of a Linear Relation between Variables which are Subject to Error", *Econometrica*, vol. 18.

REIERSØL, O. (1950 b), "On the Identifiability of Parameters in Thurstone's Multiple Factor Analysis", *Psychometrika*, vol. 15.

REVANKAR, N. and P. MALLELA (1972), "The Power of an F-Test in the Context of a Structural Equation", *Econometrica*, Sept. 1972.

RICHARDSON, D. H. and DE-MIN-WU (1970), "Alternative Estimators in the Errors in Variables Model", *Journal of the American Statistical Association*, June 1970.

RICHARDSON, D.H. and DE-MIN-WU (1971), "A Note on the Comparison of Ordinary and Two-Stage Least-Squares Estimators", *Econometrica*, Nov. 1971.

RICHMOND, J. (1974), "Identifiability in Linear Models", *Econometrica*, July 1974.

ROBINSON, P. M. (1978), "On Consistency in Time Series Analysis", *Annals of Statistics*, Jan. 1978.

ROSENBLATT, M. (1956), "Some Regression Problems in Time Series Analysis", *Proceedings of the Third Berkeley Symposium on Mathematical Statistics and Probability*, vol. 1.

ROSENBLATT, M. ed. (1963), *Time Series Analysis*, John Wiley, New York.

ROTHENBERG, T. (1968 *a*), "The Value of Structural Information: a Bayesian Approach", Mimeographed CORE, Louvain.

ROTHENBERG, T. (1968 *b*), "Estimation with Inequality Restrictions", Mimeographed, CORE Louvain.

ROTHENBERG, T. (1971), "Identification in Parametric Models", *Econometrica*, May 1971.

ROTHENBERG, T., F. M. FISHER and C. B. TILANUS (1964), "A Note on Estimation from a Cauchy Sample", *Journal of the American Statistical Association*, June 1964.

ROTTIER, G. (1958), "La distribution des revenus non agricoles", *Consommation*, Jan. 1958.

ROTTIER, G. (1959), "Niveau de vie et consommation de la population non agricole", *Consommation*, no. 3, 1959.

ROY, R. (1958), *Éléments d'économétrie*, lecture notes of the École d'Application de l'INSEE, INSEE, Paris.

RUBIN, H. (1950), "Consistency of Maximum-Likelihood Estimates in the Explosive Case", in KOOPMANS, T. C., ed. (1950).

SAMUELSON, P. A. (1948), *Economics*, McGraw-Hill Book Company, Inc., New York.

SARGAN, J. D. (1958), "The Estimation of Economic Relationships using Instrumental Variables", *Econometrica*, July 1958.

SARGAN, J. D. (1961), "The Maximum Likelihood Estimation of Economic Relationships with Autoregressive Residuals", *Econometrica*, July 1961.

SARGAN, J. D. (1964), "Wages and Prices in the United Kingdom: A Study in Econometric Methodology", *Proceedings of the 16th Symposium of the Colston Research Society*, Butterworths Scientific Publications, London.

SATHE, S. T. and H. D. VINOD (1974), "Bounds on the Variance of Regression Coefficients Due to Heteroscedastic or Autoregressive Errors", *Econometrica*, March 1974.

SAVAGE, L. J. (1954), *The Foundations of Statistics*, John Wiley, New York.

SAWA, T. (1969), "The Exact Sampling Distribution of Ordinary Least Squares and Two-Stage Least Squares Estimators", *Journal of the American Statistical Association*, Sept. 1969.

SAWA, T. (1973), "The Mean Square Error of a Combined Estimator and Numerical Comparison with the TSLS Estimator", *Journal of Econometrics*, vol. 1, 1973, p. 115–132.

SAWA, T. and T. HIROMATSU (1973), "Minimax Regret Significance Points for a Preliminary Test in Regression Analysis", *Econometrica*, Nov. 1973.

SCHEFFÉ, H. (1959), *The Analysis of Variance*, John Wiley, New York.

SCHLOSSMACHER, E. J. (1973), "An Iterative Technique for Absolute Deviation Curve Fitting", *Journal of the American Statistical Association*, Dec. 1973.

SCHMIDT, P. (1971), "Estimation of a Distributed Lag Model with Second Order Autoregressive Disturbances: A Monte Carlo Experiment", *International Economic Review*, Oct. 1971.

SCHMIDT, P. and R. SICKLES (1977), "Some Further Evidence on the Use of Chow Test Under Heteroscedasticity", *Econometrica*, July 1977.

SCHMIDT, P. (1973), "On the Difference between Conditional and Unconditional Asymptotic Distributions of Estimates in Distributed Lag Models with Integer-Value Parameters", *Econometrica*, Jan. 1973.

SCHMIDT, P. (1974), "An Argument for the Usefulness of the Gamma Distributed Lag Model", *International Economic Review*, Feb. 1974.

SCHÖNFELD, P. (1967), "Generalized Best Linear Unbiased Estimation", CORE discussion papers, Louvain.

SCHÖNFELD, P. (1971), "A Useful Central Limit Theorem for m-Dependent Variables", *Metrika*, April 1971.

SCHULTZ, H. (1938), *The Theory and Measurement of Demand*, Chicago University Press.

SEBER, G. A. F. (1964), "Linear Hypotheses and Induced Tests", *Biometrika*, vol. 51, June.

SHAPIRO, S. S., M. B. WILK and Mrs H. J. CHEN (1968), "A Comparative Study of Various Tests for Normality", *Journal of the American Statistical Association*, Dec. 1968.

SHILLER, R. J. (1973), "A Distributed Lag Estimator Derived from Smoothness Priors", *Econometrica*, July 1973.

SHISKIN, J. and H. EISENPRESS (1958), "Seasonal Adjustments by Electronic Computer Methods", National Bureau of Economic Research, *Technical Paper* 12.

SILVEY, S. D. (1968), "Multicollinearity and Imprecise Estimation", Mimeographed, University of Glasgow.

SILVEY, S. D. (1969), "Multicollinearity and Imprecise Estimation", *Journal of the Royal Statistical Society*, B, no. 3, 1969.

SIMS, C. A. (1971), "Discrete Approximations to Continuous Time Distributed Lags in Econometrics", *Econometrica*, May 1971.

SIMS, C. A. (1972), "The Role of Approximate Prior Restrictions in Distributed Lag Estimation", *Journal of the American Statistical Association*, March 1972.

SIMS, C. A. (1974), "Distributed Lags", in M. D. Intriligator and D. A. Kendrick, *Frontiers of Quantitative Economics*, vol II, North-Holland Publishing Co., Amsterdam 1974.

SMITH, F. B. and D. F. SHANNO (1971), "An Improved Marquardt Procedure for Nonlinear Regressions", *Technometrics*, Feb. 1971.

SMITH, V. K. and T. W. HALL (1972), "A Comparison of Maximum Likelihood Versus BLUE Estimators", *Review of Economics and Statistics*, May 1972.

SOLOW, R. (1960), "On a Family of Lag Distributions", *Econometrica*, April 1960.

STEIN, C. (1956 a), "Inadmissibility of the Usual Estimator for the Mean of a Multivariate Normal Distribution", *Proceedings of the Third Berkeley Symposium on Mathematical Statistics and Probability*, vol. 1, 1956.

STEIN, C. (1956 b), "The Admissibility of Hotelling's T^2-Test", *Annals of Mathematical Statistics*, Sept. 1956.

STIGUM, B. P. (1974), "Asymptotic Properties of Dynamic Stochastic Parameter Estimates – III", *Journal of Multivariate Analysis*, vol. IV, no. 4, Dec. 1974, p. 351–381.

STONE, R. (1954 a), *The Measurement of Consumer's Expenditure and Behavior in the United Kingdom 1920–38*, Cambridge University Press.

STONE, R. (1954 b), "Linear Expenditure Systems and Demand Analysis, an Application to the Pattern of British Demand", *Economic Journal*, Sept. 1954, vol. 64.

STONE, R. and D. A. ROWE (1956), "Aggregate Consumption and Investment Functions for the Household Sector Considered in the Light of British Experience", *Nationalokonomisk Tidsskrift*, vol. 94, p. 1–32.

SUMMERS, R. (1965), "A Capital Intensive Approach to the Small Sample Properties of Various Simultaneous Equation Estimators", *Econometrica*, Jan. 1965.

SWED, F. S. and C. EISENHART (1943), "Tables for Testing Randomness of Grouping in a Sequence of Alternatives", *Annals of Mathematical Statistics*, vol. 14.

TAYLOR, W. E. (1977), "Small Sample Properties of a Class of Two Stage Aitken Estimators", *Econometrica*, March 1977.

THEIL, H. (1951), "Estimates and their Sampling Variance of Parameters of certain Heteroscedastic Distributions", *Revue de l'Institut International de Statistique*, vol. 19, no. 2 p. 141.

THEIL, H. (1954), *Linear Aggregation of Economic Relations*, North-Holland Publishing Company, Amsterdam.

THEIL, H. (1958), *Economic Forecasts and Policy* (cf. in particular chapter 6), North-Holland Publishing Company, Amsterdam.

THEIL, H. (1965), "The Analysis of Disturbances in Regression Analysis", *Journal of the American Statistical Association*, vol. 60.

THEIL, H. (1971), *Principles of Econometrics*, John Wiley and Sons, 1971.

THEIL, H. and A. S. GOLDBERGER (1960), "On Pure and Mixed Statistical Estimation in Economics", *International Economic Review*, vol. 2.

THEIL, H. and R. M. STERN (1960), "A Simple Unimodal Lag Distribution", *Metroeconomica*, vol. 12.

THIONET, P. (1966), "Sur certains tests non paramétriques bien connus", *Revue de l'Institut International de Statistique*, vol. 34, no. 1.

THOMAS, J. J. and K. F. WALLIS (1971), "Seasonal Variation in Regression", *Journal of the Royal Statistical Society*, series A, part 1, 1971.

TIAO, G. C. and A. ZELLNER (1964), "On the Bayesian Estimation of Multivariate Regression", *Journal of the Royal Statistical Society*, Series B, no. 26, p. 277-85.

TILLMAN, J. A. (1975), "The Power of the Durbin-Watson Test", *Econometrica*, Sept.-Nov. 1975.

TINBERGEN, J. (1949), "Long-Term Foreign Trade Elasticities", *Metroeconomica*.

TINTNER, G. (1940), *The Variate-Difference Method*, Bloomington Press, Indiana.

TINTNER, G. (1946), "Multiple Regression for Systems of Equations", *Econometrica*, vol. 14.

TINTNER, G. (1952), *Econometrics*, John Wiley, New York.

TOYADA, T. (1974), "Use of the Chow Test under Heteroscedasticity", *Econometrica*, May 1974.

ULLAH, A. and S. ULLAH (1978), "Double k-Class Estimators of Coefficients in Linear Regression", *Econometrica*, May 1978.

VALAVANIS, S. (1959), *Econometrics – An Introduction to Maximum Likelihood Methods*, McGraw-Hill Book Company, Inc., New York, 1959.

VANGREVELINGHE, G. (1966), "L'évolution à court terme de la consommation des ménages", *Études et Conjonctures*, Sept. 1966.

VINOD, H. D. (1976), "Effect of ARMA Errors on the Significance Tests for Regression Coefficients", *Journal of the American Statistical Association*, Dec. 1976.

VORANGER, J. (1957), "Analyse de l'influence de la dépense totale et de la catégorie socioprofessionnelle sur la dépense de chaussures", *Annales de Recherches et de Documentation sur la Consommation*, 3rd year, no. 4, Oct.-Dec. 1957.

WAGNER, H. (1958), "A Monte Carlo Study of Estimates of Simultaneous Linear Structural Equations", *Econometrica*, Jan. 1958.

WALD, A. (1940), "The Fitting of Straight Lines if both Variables are Subject to Errors", *Annals of Mathematical Statistics*, vol. 11, p. 284-300.

WALD, A. (1948), "Estimation of a Parameter when the Number of Unknown Parameters Increases Indefinitely with the Number of Observations", *Annals of Mathematical Statistics*, June 1948.

WALD, A. (1950 *a*), *Statistical Decision Functions*, John Wiley, New York, 1950.

WALD, A. (1950 *b*), "Note on the Identification of Economic Relations", in KOOPMANS, T. C., ed. (1950).

WALLIS, K. F. (1967), "Lagged Dependent Variables and Serially Correlated Errors: A Reappraisal of Three-Pass Least Squares", *The Review of Economics and Statistics*, Nov. 1967.

WALLIS, K. F. (1972 *a*), "The Efficiency of the Two-Step Estimator", *Econometrica*, July 1972.

WALLIS, K. F. (1972 *b*), "Testing for Fourth Order Autocorrelation in Quarterly Regression Equation", *Econometrica*, July 1972.

WALLIS, K. F. (1974), "Seasonal Adjustment and Relation Between Variables", *Journal of the American Statistical Association*, March 1974.

WALRAS, L. (1874), *Éléments d'économie politique pure*, ed. F. Rouge, Lausanne.

WALTERS, A. A. (1963), "Production and Cost Functions: An Econometric Survey", *Econometrica*, Jan.–April 1963.

WATSON, G. S. (1955), "Serial Correlation in Regression Analysis", *Biometrika*, vol. 42, p. 327.

WATSON, G. S. (1956), "On the Joint Distribution of the Circular Serial Correlation Coefficients", *Biometrika*, vol. 43.

WATSON, G. S. (1967), "Linear Least Squares Regression", *Annals of Mathematical Statistics*, Dec. 1967.

WATSON, G. S. (1972), "Prediction and the Efficiency of Least Squares", *Biometrika*, vol. 59, no. 1, April 1972.

WEGGE, L. (1965), "Identifiability Criteria for a System of Equations as a Whole", *The Australian Journal of Statistics*, Nov. 1965.

WEGGE, L. (1971), "The Finite Sampling Distribution of Least Squares Estimators with Stochastic Regressors", *Econometrica*, March 1971.

WHITTAKER, E. and G. ROBINSON (1924), *The Calculus of Observations*, Blackie and Son Limited, London and Glasgow.

WHITTLE, P. (1954), "Some Recent Contributions to the Theory of Stationary Processes", Appendix 2 in WOLD, H., *A Study in the Analysis of Stationary Time Series*, 2nd edition, Stockholm, 1954.

WHITTLE, P. (1961), "Gaussian Estimation in Stationary Time Series", *Bulletin de l'Institut International de Statistique*, 33rd session, Paris.

WICKENS, M. R. (1972), "A Note on the Use of Prony Variables", *Econometrica*, July 1972.

WILDE, D. J. (1964), *Optimum Seeking Methods*, Prentice Hall.

WOLD, H. (1938), *A Study in the Analysis of Stationary Time Series*, 2nd edition, Almquist and Wiksell, Stockholm, 1954.

WOLD, H. (1952), *Demand Analysis—A Study in Econometrics*, Uppsala and New York.

WOLD, H. (1954), "Causality and Econometrics", *Econometrica*, April 1954.

WOLD, H. (1955), "Possibilités et limitations des systèmes à chaîne causale", *Cahiers de Séminaire d'Econométrie*, no. 3, C.N.R.S., Paris.

WOLD, H. (1960 *a*), "A Generalization of Causal Chain Models", *Econometrica*, vol. 28, no. 2, April 1960.

WOLD, H. (1960 *b*), "Ends and Means of Econometric Model Building", in GRENANDER, U., ed., *Probability and Statistics*. The Harald Cramer volume. Almquist and Wiksell, Stockholm.

WOLD, H. (1964) ed., *Econometric Model Building; Essays on the Causal Chain Approach*, North-Holland Publishing Company, Amsterdam.

WOLD, H. and P. FAXER (1957), "On the Specification Error in Regression Analysis", *The Annals of Mathematical Statistics*, vol. 28, no. 1, March 1957.

WOLFOWITZ, J. (1952), "Consistent Estimators of the Parameters of a Linear Structural Relation", *Skandinavisk Actuarietidskrift*.

WOLFOWITZ, J. (1954 *a*), "Estimation of the Components of Stochastic Structures", *Proceedings of the National Academy of Sciences*, vol. 40.

WOLFOWITZ, J. (1954 *b*), "Estimation by the Minimum Distance Method in Nonparametric Difference Equations", *Annals of Mathematical Statistics*, vol. 25.

WOLFOWITZ, J. (1954 *c*), "Estimation of Structural Parameters when the Number of Incidental Parameters is Unbounded". Abstract. *Annals of Mathematical Statistics*, vol. 25.

WORKING, E. J. (1927), "What do 'Statistical Demand Curves' Show?", *Quarterly Journal of Economics*, Feb. 1927.

WORKING, H. (1925), "The Statistical Determination of Demand Curves", *Quarterly Journal of Economics*, August 1925.

DE-MIN-WU (1973), "Alternative Tests of Independence Between Stochastic Regressors and Disturbances", *Econometrica*, July 1973.

WU, R. (1973), "On Some Aspects of Linearly Aggregated Macro Models", *International Economic Review*, Oct. 1973.

ZEUKHAUSER, R. and M. THOMPSON (1970), "Linear Regression with Non-Normal Error Term", *Review of Economics and Statistics*, Aug. 1970.

ZELLNER, A. (1957), "The Short-Run Consumption Function", *Econometrica*, vol. 25, Oct. 1957.

ZELLNER, A. (1961 *a*), "Linear Regression with Inequalities Constraints on the Coefficients: An Application of Quadratic Programming and Linear Decision Rules", International Center for Management Science, Rotterdam, 1961.

ZELLNER, A. (1961 *b*), "Econometric Estimation with Temporally Dependent Disturbance Terms", *International Economic Review*, May 1961.

ZELLNER, A. (1962), "An Efficient Method of Estimating Seemingly Unrelated Regressions and Tests for Aggregation Bias", *Journal of the American Statistical Association*, June 1962.

ZELLNER, A. (1963), "Estimators of Seemingly Unrelated Regression Equations: Some Exact Finite Sample Results", *Journal of the American Statistical Association*, Dec. 1963.

ZELLNER, A. (1968), "Bayesian Inference in Econometrics", Mimeographed, University of Rome.

ZELLNER, A. (1971), *An Introduction to Bayesian Inference in Econometrics*, Wiley, New York, 1971.

ZELLNER, A. and M. S. GEISEL (1970), "Analysis of Distributed Lag Models with Applications to Consumption Function Estimation", *Econometrica*, Nov. 1970.

ZELLNER, A. and H. THEIL (1962), "Three-Stage Least Squares: Simultaneous Estimation of Simultaneous Equations", *Econometrica*, Jan. 1962.

ZELLNER, A. and G. C. TIAO (1964), "Bayesian Analysis of the Regression Model with Auto-correlated Errors", *Journal of the American Statistical Association*, vol. 59, p. 763–778.

ZELLNER, A. and W. VANDAELE (1975), "Bayes-Stein Estimators for k-Means, Regression and Simultaneous Equation Models", in S. E. Fienberg and A. Zellner, eds., *Studies in Bayesian Econometrics and Statistics*, North-Holland Publishing Company, Amsterdam, 1975.

Subject Index

Author Index